A History of the Fens of South Lincolnshire ... Second edition, greatly enlarged.

William Henry Wheeler, E A. Hayward Leonard Charles Batty

A History of the Fens of South Lincolnshire ... Second edition, greatly enlarged.
Wheeler, William Henry
British Library, Historical Print Editions
British Library
Batty, E A. Hayward Leonard Charles
1897
489 p. ; 8°.
10353.c.7.

The BiblioLife Network

This project was made possible in part by the BiblioLife Network (BLN), a project aimed at addressing some of the huge challenges facing book preservationists around the world. The BLN includes libraries, library networks, archives, subject matter experts, online communities and library service providers. We believe every book ever published should be available as a high-quality print reproduction; printed on- demand anywhere in the world. This insures the ongoing accessibility of the content and helps generate sustainable revenue for the libraries and organizations that work to preserve these important materials.

The following book is in the "public domain" and represents an authentic reproduction of the text as printed by the original publisher. While we have attempted to accurately maintain the integrity of the original work, there are sometimes problems with the original book or micro-film from which the books were digitized. This can result in minor errors in reproduction. Possible imperfections include missing and blurred pages, poor pictures, markings and other reproduction issues beyond our control. Because this work is culturally important, we have made it available as part of our commitment to protecting, preserving, and promoting the world's literature.

GUIDE TO FOLD-OUTS, MAPS and OVERSIZED IMAGES

In an online database, page images do not need to conform to the size restrictions found in a printed book. When converting these images back into a printed bound book, the page sizes are standardized in ways that maintain the detail of the original. For large images, such as fold-out maps, the original page image is split into two or more pages.

Guidelines used to determine the split of oversize pages:

- Some images are split vertically; large images require vertical and horizontal splits.
- For horizontal splits, the content is split left to right.
- For vertical splits, the content is split from top to bottom.
- For both vertical and horizontal splits, the image is processed from top left to bottom right.

A HISTORY OF THE FENS
—OF—
SOUTH LINCOLNSHIRE,

BEING A DESCRIPTION OF THE RIVERS WITHAM AND WELLAND AND THEIR ESTUARY, AND AN ACCOUNT OF THE RECLAMATION, DRAINAGE, AND ENCLOSURE OF THE FENS ADJACENT THERETO.

BY

W. H. WHEELER, M.Inst.C.E.,

AUTHOR OF

"*Tidal Rivers, their Hydraulics, Improvement and Navigation,*" and "*The Drainage of Fens and Low Lands by gravitation and steam power.*"

SECOND EDITION.   GREATLY ENLARGED.

BOSTON:
J. M. Newcomb.
LONDON:
Simpkin, Marshall & Co.

PREFACE.

THE first edition of the "History of the Fens of South Lincolnshire" was published in 1868. The fact that this has long been out of print, and that the publisher is frequently applied to for copies, appears to warrant the issue of a second edition.

In the preface to the first edition it was stated, as a reason for its publication, that the author, having had occasion to examine documents relating to the outfall of the drainage of the Fens, had been induced by the interest of the subject to extend his researches into the various reports and papers which relate to the general history of the reclamation and drainage of this district, and had collected together sufficient facts and statistics to enable him to complete a short History of the Fens of this part of the County of Lincoln.

During the six and twenty years that have elapsed since this was written, the author has had further opportunities of making himself acquainted with a large number of Acts of Parliament, Reports and other documents which have come into his possession or which are to be found in charge of the officers of the several drainage districts; at the British Museum, the Record Office, the Library of the Gentlemen's Society at Spalding, and the Stock Library at Lincoln. These documents, scattered about in different places, are practically inaccessible to persons requiring information on the subjects to which they relate. Upwards of one hundred and sixty Acts have been passed relating to the drainage, reclamation and enclosure of this part of the Fenland. The greater part of these Acts are now out of print and difficult to procure.

With the information obtained from these sources, it has been possible to give a much more complete history of the early condition and reclamation of the Fenland than was contained in the first edition. In fact, the book has been entirely re-written, and now contains a record of events and statistics which, it is hoped, will render it useful as a work of reference to the officers and commissioners having control over the drainage works, and also to the inhabitants who find the funds for maintaining the same, and, as a source of information, to those interested in the Fenland.

PREFACE.

The first part of the book is devoted to the early history of the Fenland from the time of the Britons up to the reclamation carried out in the middle of the last, and the beginning of the present, century. In the subsequent chapters a history of each district is given separately, including an abstract of the Acts of Parliament under which the works have been carried out, the constitution of the Trusts, the rate of taxation and the cost of management. These chapters include matter relative to the Court of Sewers, with a description of its history and functions; the enclosures and drainage system of the parishes in North and South Holland, including the South Holland Drainage and Embankment Districts; to the river Witham and the six districts into which the level is divided; to the Black Sluice and Holland Fen; to the rivers Welland and Glen, with an account of Bicker Haven and Crowland Washes; to Deeping Fen and Crowland; to the Estuary and the proposed schemes of reclamation; to Boston Harbour and the Witham Outfall.

The Drainage system of the Fenland is described in a separate chapter and an account is given of the several kinds of pumping machinery in use, and the cost of construction and working.

In the chapter on Agriculture the history of this industry is traced from the time of the Saxons; the rent and value of land at different periods, both before and since the reclamation, the rate of wages and the price of produce at different times, the crops grown, and the tenures under which the land is held, are all fully dealt with.

Roads, waterways, bridges, railways and means of transit are described, as also the various changes made in the management of the highways, turnpike roads and main roads, with the cost of their management.

The concluding chapters deal with geology, water supply, natural products, climate and health.

In the Appendix will be found a list of the names of places, rivers, and principal drains, with the different ways of spelling the same and their derivation. The spelling of many of the names in old records varies frequently from that used in the present day, and in some cases the old names have become obsolete and difficult to trace. The author has endeavoured, as far as he was able, to give a guide to these. The area and rateable value of each parish is also given and the changes that have been made in the Fen Allotments under the Divided Parishes Act.

A glossary of words used in the Fenland; the titles and dates of all the Acts of Parliament relating to the drainage, reclamation, navagation and roads; a list of the books and reports relating to the Fenland; an abstract of the verdict giving the names and situation of the public sewers in North Holland are also given. In South Holland it has not been the practice of the Court to

PREFACE.

have similar verdicts made, so that the position of these sewers is not given. The rainfall, and statistics as to floods, temperature, wind and tides, the levels of all the principal sills of the sluices and sea banks above *Ordnance datum*, and borings taken at various places, showing the strata, are also included.

The illustrations comprise a general map of the Fenland; and separate maps of each district, showing their past and present Drainage Systems. These maps have been prepared from those found in old reports and from the Ordnance Map, and, as far as practicable, are all reduced to the same scale.

The author takes this occasion of thanking the many friends from whom he has derived assistance and who have allowed him the use of reports and other documents in their possession. He begs especially to acknowledge the valuable information as to the river Witham and the East and West Fens which he was enabled to obtain from several volumes of pamphlets, reports and papers, collected by Sir Joseph Banks and now in the library at Revesby Abbey, which were kindly placed at his disposal by the late Right Honorable Edward Stanhope.

The author hopes that the time and trouble which he has devoted to collecting and recording the information contained in this book will be accepted by the reader as a set-off against its literary defects.

CONTENTS.

Preface.

Chapter
1. Early history of the Fens.
2. The Court of Sewers.
3. The North Holland parishes.
4. South Holland, including the South Holland Drainage District and the South Holland Embankment Trust.
5. The River Witham.
6. The Witham Drainage Districts.
7. The Black Sluice.
8. The Black Sluice Districts.
9. The Welland and the Glen, Bicker Haven and Crowland Washes.
10. Deeping Fen, Bourne South Fen and Thurlby Fen.
11. The Estuary and proposed schemes of reclamation.
12. Boston Harbour and the Witham Outfall.
13. The Drainage system of the Fenland, with a description of the pumping machinery.
14. Agriculture of the Fenland. Rent and value of land. Rate of wages. Value of produce.
15. Waterways, roads, bridges, and railways.
16. Geology and water supply.
17. Natural history and products, climatology and health.

APPENDIX.

1. Names of places, with the area and rateable value of the parishes.
2. Books and reports relating to the Fenland.
3. Titles and dates of Acts of Parliament relating to the Fenland.
4. Glossary of words used in the Fenland.
5. Rainfall, floods, temperature, wind and tides.

CONTENTS.

6. Levels of the sills and sluices, sea banks, &c., &c., reduced to Ordnance datum.
7. Borings, showing strata.

ILLUSTRATIONS.

1. Sketch map of the ancient Fenland.
2. General map of the South Lincolnshire Fenland at the present time.
3. Brands used for marking cattle in the Fens.
4. South Holland.
5. South Holland before the enclosure of the marshes.
6. The Witham from Lincoln to Boston in 1762, before improvement.
7. The First, Third and Sixth Districts of the river Witham.
8. The East Fen in 1661, before the construction of the Adventurers' Drains.
9. The Fourth District of the Witham and Skirbeck Hundred, including the East Holland towns and Boston Deeps.
10. The Black Sluice Level and parishes in Kirton Hundred.
11. Bicker Haven.
12. Deeping Fen and Crowland Washes at the present time.
13. Deeping Fen in 1645.
14. Deeping Fen in 1763.
15. Diagram, showing the geological strata and relative level of surface of land and sea level.
16. Diagram, showing annual rainfall.

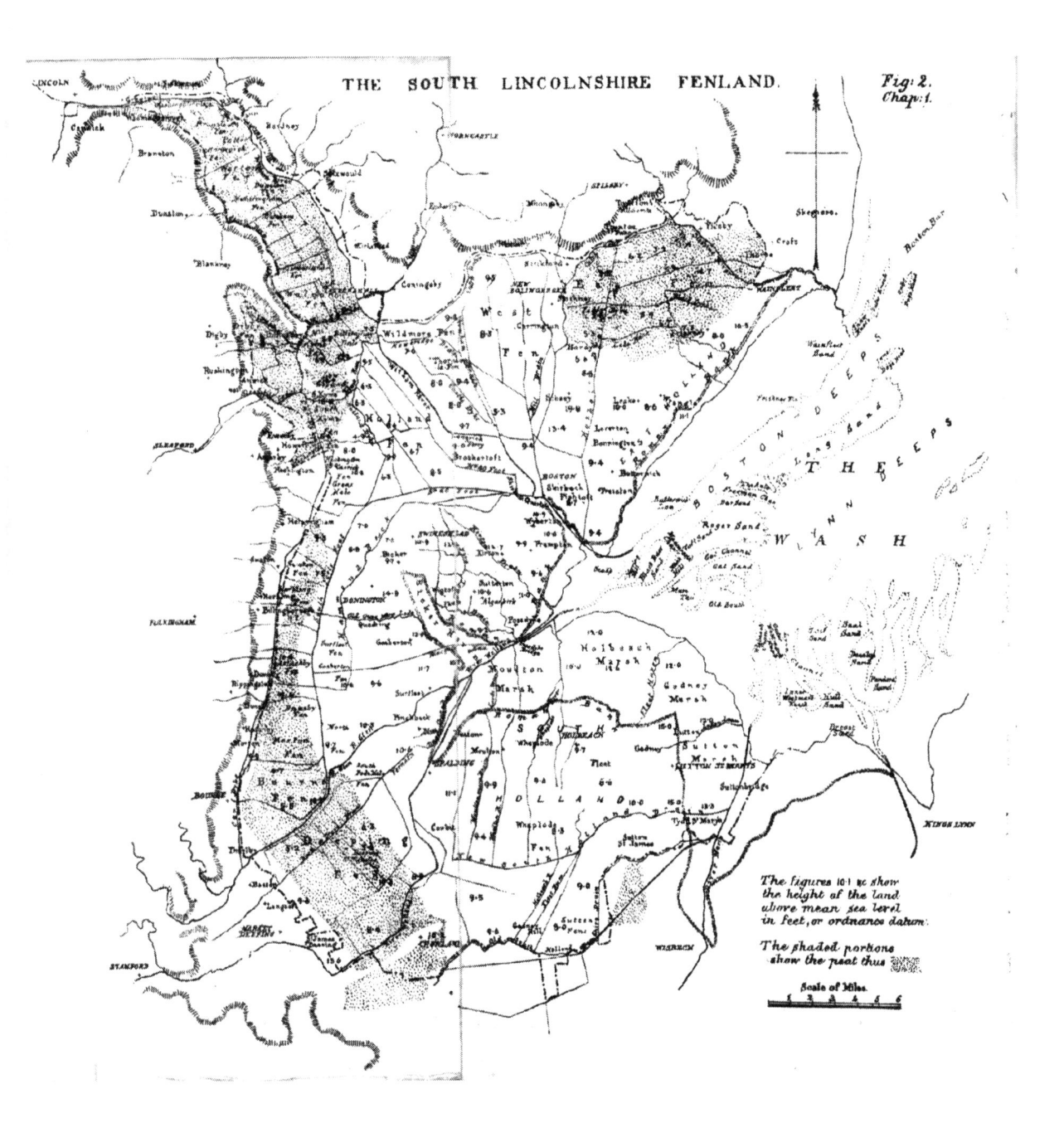

THE SOUTH LINCOLNSHIRE FENLAND.

Fig: 2.
Chap: 1.

The figures 10.1 &c show
the height of the land
above mean sea level
in feet, or ordnance datum.

The shaded portions
show the peat thus

Scale of Miles

CHAPTER I.

Early History of the Fens.

THE Great Level of the Fens comprises a tract of land on the East Coast, extending southwards from the highlands in Lincolnshire, for a distance of about 60 miles, and occupying portions of six counties. It is only the history of the part in South Lincolnshire that is dealt with in this book, or the area that is bounded approximately on the north by the Steeping river and the catch water drains, and by Revesby, Tattershall, Kirkstead, Bardney and Lincoln; on the west by the Car dyke, and on the south by Bourne, Market Deeping, Crowland and the old South Holland or Shire drain, to the Nene, and on the east and north by the river Nene and the coast of the Wash to Wainfleet. *(BOUNDARY OF THE LINCOLNSHIRE FENLAND.)*

This tract comprises the lands adjacent to the Witham, known as the *Six Witham Districts*, including the East, West and Wildmore Fens; the East Holland towns, or the parishes from Wainfleet to Boston, lying along the east coast of the Wash; the parishes lying between the Witham and the Glen; the Black Sluice Level, with Holland Fen; Deeping Fen and the lands on the north of the Welland; the South Holland District; and the land along the coast from Fosdyke to the Nene. The Witham District, the Black Sluice Level, Deeping Fen, the South Holland Drainage District and some smaller districts are managed under special Acts of Parliament. The rest of the area remains under the jurisdiction of the Court of Sewers.

The whole of the Holland division of Lincolnshire is in the Fenland, which also extends on the north of Sibsey, by an irregular line into the Lindsey division, and on the west of Swineshead into Kesteven.

The area of the South Lincolnshire Fenland is about 363,043 acres, of which 118,726 acres is in Lindsey and Kesteven. The greater part of the land, amounting to 277,795 acres, consists of rich alluvial deposit, the surface of which averages from $1\frac{1}{2}$ to $5\frac{1}{2}$ feet below the level of high water in spring tides, and the remaining 85,248 acres of fen or peat, the surface of which is from $6\frac{1}{2}$ to $12\frac{1}{2}$ feet below high-water level, the average being about $7\frac{1}{2}$ feet below. The area of lowland drained by steam power is 124,600 acres. The *(ACREAGE. LEVEL OF THE LAND.)*

towns and villages are situated entirely on the alluvial land, the level of the ground on which they are situated being the highest in the neighbourhood and varying from 1½ to 3 feet below high water. The ground on which the churches stand is generally about the level of ordinary spring tides. Scattered about are plots of ground, formerly called islands, which are more elevated than the rest of the district, of which Stickney, Sibsey and Gedney are examples. The high ground in these places is above even the highest tides, as is also that in Boston, Spalding, Donington, Kirton, Holbeach, Fleet, Pinchbeck and Gosberton.

PHYSICAL CONDITION.
The Fens have obtained a world-wide notoriety; and a general, though very erroneous, impression prevails among those who do not know the county, that this part of Lincolnshire is a dull and dreary land, to be avoided by all except those whom necessity or the calls of business compel to visit its unattractive scenery. But it will be found, on closer investigation, that the Fenland has many attractive features, while the rich grazing and corn lands stand unrivalled for their productiveness, and are cultivated by inhabitants, whose condition, general intelligence, physique and health will bear very favourable comparison with those of any other part of Great Britain. An inspection of the tombstones in the village churchyards, or of the parish registers, will show that life is frequently prolonged to an unusual age, while a visit to one of the Fenland towns on a market day, or at a fair, will convince the visitor that more robust or healthier working men, or comelier damsels, are not to be met under similar circumstances in any other part of Great Britain.

If the country lacks the interest that is derived from a variation of hill and dale, it is recompensed by other features. The air generally is clear and transparent; a day's fog is very rare and the inhabitants enjoy "as sunny skies, as beautiful starlit nights and as magnificent cloudscapes as any people in England." The sunsets frequently are of surpassing grandeur and beauty. The heavy snowdrifts and storms of other parts are mitigated in the Fenland and when many parts of England lying along the river valleys are frequently suffering from floods and inundations the Fenland is free from such disasters, its drainage being thoroughly under control.

ATTRACTIVE FEATURES OF THE FENLAND.
A journey through the Fenland provides a constant source of interest. In the northern part, the county-city of Lincoln stands out pre-eminently for the varied relics which it contains of past ages, and for the beautiful cathedral, which, towering high above the Fens, is visible for many miles. Along the Witham, besides ruins of Kirkstead Abbey, will be found near Tattershall a most perfect specimen of brickwork in the castle built by Cromwell, treasurer to Henry VII; and scarcely is this lost sight of, when the magnificent tower of Boston Church rises high above the level plain, with its beacon lantern standing like a guardian over the Fenland.

Passing along through the villages will be found churches which, either from their size, the beauty of their design, or their historical associations, stand out as monuments of the piety of the ancient Fenmen, and will well repay a visit of inspection. As the southern extremity of the Fen is reached the ruins of Crowland Abbey and the unique triangular bridge recall all that we owe of religion and learning to St. Guthlac and his pious successors. As the Cathedral of Lincoln is conspicuous on the north, so Peterborough attracts attention in the south. The general characteristics of the district are not without their interest. In the late summer or early autumn the Fenland roads and the wide drains are flanked on each side either by the golden waves of the ripening corn, moving gently in the breeze, and extending far away on the horizon, or by rich pasture fields, in which are grazing cattle and sheep of a quality and size indicative of the richness of the land on which they are reared. The whole, a picture of luxuriant nature, which justifies the remark of Cobbet, when he made his excursion through the Fenland, that "everything taken together, here are more good things than man could have the conscience to ask of God."

PREVIOUS TO THE ROMAN INVASION.

No trustworthy record of the state of the Fens previous to the invasion of the Romans, shortly before the Christian era, exists. The condition of the Fenland and the history of its inhabitants can therefore, only to be gathered from scattered remarks in Tacitus and other Roman writers. Generally it may be assumed that originally the whole of that part of the east of England extending from the Trent to Huntingdon, except the high land about Lincoln, was one vast morass, into which the waters of the Trent, the Witham, the Welland, the Nene and the Ouse discharged themselves, and which, being below the level of high tides, was subject to constant inundation by the sea. Gradually the land rose by the deposition of alluvial matter and the constant growth of vegetation, leaving, however, large creeks, or arms of the sea, which afterwards became pools of stagnant water. On the accreted land, interspersed amongst the pools and meres, were spots of high ground, on which the few and scattered inhabitants lived, their only means of communication with the mainland, in winter, being by coracles, or wicker boats covered with skins. These islands, although no longer standing out prominently amidst a vast area of submerged territory, may, as already mentioned, still be traced by their higher elevation and by the terminations of their names.

Motley's Dutch Republic.

"The original inhabitants of the Fens most probably migrated from the opposite coasts of Holland and Belgium, from the delta formed by the mouths of the Rhine, the Scheldt and the Meuse, a district resembling the Fenland, inasmuch as it consisted of wide morasses, in which oozy islands were interspersed among lagoons and shallows, a district partly below the level of the tides and subject to constant overflow from the rivers, and to frequent inundations from the sea." In Cæsar's account of Britain it is stated that the Fen coast was peopled by Belgæ, drawn thither by the love of war and plunder. Strabo says that the latest emigration of Gauls and Belgæ took place only a few years before Cæsar's invasion.

<small>SELECTION OF LOW LANDS FOR SETTLEMENTS.</small>

It is a singular fact in the early history of civilization that, while land was plentiful and people few, selection should have been made for purposes of settlement of low and swampy tracts of land, which could only be inhabited by maintaining a constant struggle with the rivers and the sea. The ancient Egyptians carried out most extensive works of reclamation. The Romans, not content with appropriating land all over the world, added to their territory at home by draining lakes and reclaiming marshes. Holland is a wonderful example of land gained from the sea, and held by the enterprise and skill of man. In more recent times our own colonists, with all the vast territory of America to choose from, yet selected the low swampy plains bordering on the Mississippi as one of their principal settlements, which could only be made profitable after an enormous cost had been incurred in embanking and confining the river. The Fenland affords another example of this singular peculiarity and we can only wonder why the Britons, Romans, Saxons and Danes should all successively have made settlements amongst the meres and swamps of the Fens.

<small>THE COR-ICENI.</small>

The tribe of Britons who occupied Lincolnshire were known as the Iceni, from the word *Ychen*, oxen. They were closely connected with the Coritani, who occupied the east coast up to Cambridge and Huntingdon, and whose name was derived from *Cor*, a sheep.

<small>Henry's *Great Britain*.</small>

The joint tribe being known as the *Cor-Iceni*. Their principal occupation and chief means of subsistence was pasturage, the rich

<small>Kemble's *Saxons in England*.</small>

marshes and higher land in the Fens affording excellent feeding ground for their herds. They lived almost entirely on flesh, milk and birds, and grew little or no corn, until taught by the Romans. Lindcoit (Lincoln) was the principal town of the Cor-Iceni and is referred to by Ptolemy as a place of importance. Bardney is supposed to have been their chief Druidical station, its name

<small>Oliver's *Religious Houses on the Witham*.</small>

"Bard's Island," denoting its origin. The remains of two British encampments have been discovered, one on the moor near Tattershall and the other at Revesby, where the contour of the land at the present day shows traces of what are supposed to have been British settlements.

<small>THE ROMAN PERIOD. 60 B.C.</small>

The Romans first came to Britain about sixty years before the Christian era. Soon afterwards they found their way into the Fen district. In A.D. 61 Suetonius Paulinus subdued the Coritani and Iceni, and Roman military colonists began to settle in this county. At the end of the first century, a Roman colony was founded at

Lincoln. The soldiers are said to have cruelly oppressed the inhabitants and, not content with turning them out of their houses and depriving them of their lands, insulted them with the name of slaves. Prasutagus, the king of the Iceni, a prince renowned for his opulence and grandeur, was killed, all his possessions were seized and plundered by the Roman soldiers, his Queen was beaten with stripes for remonstrating, his daughter violated and his relations taken as slaves. The chiefs of the Iceni were deprived of their possessions and the inhabitants who were left complained that the Roman governor lorded it over their persons, and the Procurator over their fortunes. At last the Iceni, inflamed with resentment, flew to arms and, being joined by the Trinobantes, poured in a torrent on the Roman colony at Camalodunum, put to the sword all who fell in their hands and laid all the buildings in ashes. Afterwards Boadicea, who was queen of the Iceni, headed a further revolt against the Romans, but was subdued by Suetonius Paulinus. *Henry's History* A.D. 64.

After this the Romans made great changes in the country of the Cor-Iceni, by introducing the cultivation of corn and by building forts and stations. Lindum Colonia (Lincoln) was one of the nine colonies held by the veteran soldiers of the legions on condition of rendering military service. The place was strongly fortified, the eastern wall running nearly in a line with the transepts of the present minster, which stands partly within the site of the fortress. In time it became one of the most considerable towns which the Romans occupied in Britain, and is mentioned several times by Ptolemy and Antoninus. Lincoln, in fact, became a minature Rome, governed by similar laws and adorned with temples, courts, theatres and statues. LINDUM COLONIA.

The rich lands bordering on the Fens, under the tillage of the Roman colonists, proved very productive, and this county was one of the most plentiful provinces of the empire, and a market for export to other conquered countries. A fleet of 800 vessels, which had been built on the Rhine, for transporting food for the use of the armies, was sent to Britain to fetch corn; and the colonies on the upper Rhine were preserved from famine chiefly by corn sent from Britain. A.D. 359.

The principal port used by the Romans in their traffic with the continent was Wainfleet (*Vainona*) and this place was connected with Lincoln by a road passing through the Fens to Horncastle (*Banovallum*). Another road went to Burgh, which was also a Roman station. Boston then had no existence either as a town or port. The whole country between Washingborough and Boston was at the time of the Roman invasion a vast swamp and it is extremely improbable that any defined channel existed of sufficient size to be navigable. Wainfleet, on the other hand, was the first sheltered land their vessels would make after leaving the open ocean and, being protected by Gibraltar Point, the boats would lie in a VAINONA.

Fig: 1.

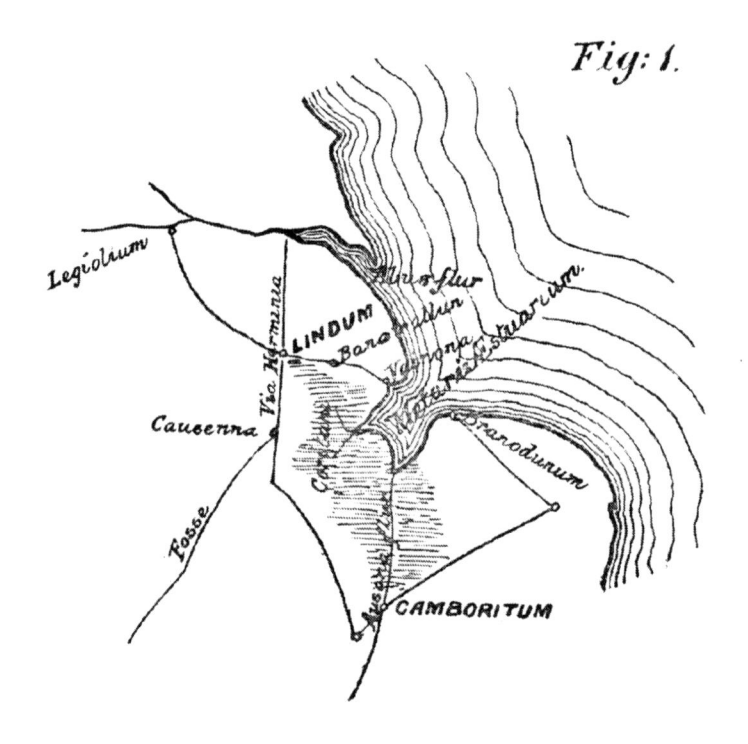

safe haven. After the cut or canal had been made between Lincoln and Dogdyke the vessels would, no doubt, pass up the Deeps and reach Lincoln through Boston.

ROMAN TREATMENT OF THE INHABITANTS. After having subdued the country, the policy of the Romans appears to have been to try to make the inhabitants forget their nationality and become Roman citizens. For this purpose, Tacitus tells us in his life of Agricola that in order to reclaim the natives from the rude and unsettled state which prompted them to war and to make them reconciled to quiet and tranquility, they were incited by private instigation and public encouragement to erect temples, courts of justice and dwelling houses. Liberal education was provided for the sons of the chieftains, so that they became ambitious and acquired a taste for those luxuries which stimulate vice. The captives taken in war, and the more menial of the natives were made slaves, and were occupied in carrying out works of improvement. Galgacus, a British chieftain, in a harangue to the Britons on the eve of one of the battles between the natives and the Romans, thus addressed his followers:—" Our children are torn away by levies to serve in foreign lands, our estates and possessions are consumed in tributes, our grain in contributions, our bodies are worn down amidst stripes in clearing woods and draining marshes."

They were also employed in the formation of roads for the purpose of connecting together the chief military stations and ports. A description of those made in the Fenland will be found in the chapter on roads.

Tradition has always given credit to the Romans for the construction of the sea banks running along the coast, which protect the Fens from inundation from the tides, and are known at the present day as "the Roman Banks." Dr. Stukeley considered that these banks were made in the time of Severus, which seems not obscurely hinted at by Herodian III, who observed in speaking of this general, "But he had it in his particular care to make passes over the Fens, that the soldiers might stand firm and fight upon hard ground; for many places in Britain are marshy through the frequent overflowing of the ocean, over which the inhabitants will swim and walk, though up to their middle in water." *[THE ROMAN BANKS.]*

While there is no trustworthy evidence to prove that such is the case, every fact seems to point out the Romans as the only people who could possibly have carried out such a large undertaking. The length of these banks on the Lincolnshire coast, extending from Wainfleet to the outfall of the Witham, and on the coast between the Witham and the Welland, and also between the Welland and the Nene is not less than 50 miles. The average height may be taken at ten feet. The construction of a work of such magnitude would require a vast army of men, and an organization which could only be supplied by the Roman government. These banks are not works of a character that could be carried out in portions and spread over a great number of years. The enclosure of a large tract of marsh covered by the spring tides is a work that requires great vigour and must be carried on continuously, or the earth put into the bank during one set of tides will be washed away again. Even with the experience of the present day, there have been attempts at enclosure which have utterly failed: the banks have been carried a certain distance, but the final closing in has been found so difficult and costly that the attempt has been abandoned.

It is known from history that the Romans, either previous to the time when the Lincolnshire banks were constructed, or soon afterwards, carried out very large works of a similar character, a detailed account of which is given by Dugdale. From Pliny we learn that in the year 593, B.C., when C. Anicius Gallus and M. Cornelius Cethegus were consuls, the senate being in counsel concerning the provinces, there was a motion made concerning the improvement of a great level of waste land lying under water, about 40 miles from Rome, in Latium . . . . *[Dugdale's Embanking and Draining.]*
The senate thought they should deserve the praise of good

husbands for the commonwealth, if, in this opportunity of leisure, they should gain such a quantity of rich land to Italy. Neither was this employment thought too mean for the legions, though consisting of free-men; for the Roman and Italian infantry, as well accustomed to the spade and basket as to the sword and buckler, worked for the common good in time of security. The consuls, *(anno 566,)* had given a precedent, who, lest their soldiers should be idle, employed them in making of highways. Hereupon it was decreed that one consul should attend the enemy and the other undertake the draining of the Pompeian marshes. By order of the senate the Pompeian Fens were laid dry by Cornelius Cethegus the consul, and were made good ground. The Fens about Placentia were secured by banks from the inundations of the Po. The country in Gallia Cisalpina lying flat and towards the sea, which was a fenny marsh was, by the help of banks and trenches, drained and made useful for tillage. The Emperor Claudius employed 30,000 men for the space of eleven years in draining the Fucine lake in Italy.

It is also recorded that Probus prevented the irregularities of the soldiers by employing the legions in constant and useful labours. When he commanded in Egypt, he executed many considerable works for the splendour of that rich country. The navigation of the Nile was improved, and temples, bridges, porticoes and palaces were constructed by the hands of the soldiers, who acted by turns as architects, as engineers, and as husbandmen. It was reported of Hannibal that, in order to preserve his troops from the dangerous temptations of idleness, he had obliged them to form large plantations of olive trees along the coast of Africa. . . . . He thus converted into tillage a large and unhealthy tract of marsh ground near Sirmium.

Gibbon's Decline and Fall of the Roman Empire.

Another powerful motive that would lead to the embanking of the Fens doubtless arose from the security they afforded to the natives, who, as related by Marcellinus, "not dwelling in the towns but in cottages within fenny places, compassed with thick woods, having hidden whatsoever they had most estimation of, did more annoyance to the wearied Romans than they received from them." In fact the Fens formed a sort of camp of refuge for the Britons, as later they did for the Saxons, where it would be impossible for any military force to follow and dislodge them; and it is evident the Romans could neither pasture their cattle on the marshes nor enjoy any security for their property until the natives were hunted out of their retreats.

That the native inhabitants were also employed in these embankments may be gathered from the expression used in the speech of the British Chief, Galgacus, already quoted, in which he complained that their bodies were worn down in clearing woods and draining marshes.

There is every probability that the Britons resisted the raising of the sea banks and the presence of the Romans in the Fens, as much as their successors did when these were finally reclaimed; and attempts would be made to frustrate the enclosure by cutting through and destroying the newly-made banks for several years after their construction. To prevent this, it would be necessary to have watchmen stationed along the banks, and probably for this purpose the raised mounds, which exist up to the present time along the course of the banks, were constructed. Various theories have been assigned for the origin of these mounds, but it is more reasonable to suppose that they were used for this purpose than, as has been suggested, for places of sepulture or of worship. It is hardly likely that sites would be chosen for either of these purposes on land constantly flooded with water and away from all habitations. No bones or traces of sepulture have ever been discovered when these mounds have been cut into, or removed. If these mounds were constructed at the same time as the banks, they would afford forts or places for the encampments of the guards on watch, and a refuge for any men who might be overtaken at high tides, during the construction. The position of these mounds is almost invariably near a fen or river bank. Several of them have been levelled, but mounds are yet to be found, at Friskney Row, two miles from the bank, at Wrangle, on the high land within a mile of the Outer Fen Bank, but close to the bank known as Wrangle Sea Dyke. Another, known as King's Hill, is close to the bank on the south side of Wrangle Common and on the site of an ancient circular camp: both these banks were probably made as part of the general scheme, or previous to the construction of the outer banks. At Freiston 1¼ miles from the Sea Bank. In Skirbeck an elevation is still known as Toot or Look Out Hill. Near Rochford Tower in Fishtoft; and at Sandholme in Frampton. On the Witham, the Mill Hill, opposite the Hammond Beck Outfall; and on each side of the river at Fishtoft and Wyberton. The latter has within the last few years been removed: no antiquities or remains of any kind were discovered during its removal. At Kirton Skeldyke; and between Kirton and Fosdyke; in Sutterton, Swineshead, Drayton, Wigtoft, and Donington Eaudyke, all about 1 mile from the banks of Bicker Haven; two near Holbeach Clough; one each at Fleet, and Gedney; and seven others near the banks between the Nene and the Ouse.

Fen Mounds.

The only other probable solution of the origin of these mounds is that they were erected by the Saxon settlers, after the Roman banks had been built, for the purpose of lighting beacon fires in order to give notice all along the coast when the Danish marauders were dis-covered approaching. It is on record that a tax of twelve pence was levied on every hide of land, for guarding the coast against the Scandinavian invaders. Fires lighted on these mounds might have formed a part of this system of warning and defence.

ROMAN DRAINAGE WORKS. At the time when the Romans settled in Lincolnshire, the land on which the lower part of the city of Lincoln now stands, and also a very considerable area on its west side, was low swampy ground, frequently covered by water. The deepest part of this swamp is still a pool, and is known as Brayford Mere. The city derives its name from this pool, the ancient British word for a deep pool being *Lynn*. The meaning of the word Lincoln is, therefore, "the settlement by the deep pool." The Witham and the Till discharged their water into the Lynn, and the swampy and low ground was frequently flooded by the overflowing of the Trent, which was then unembanked. The overflow from Brayford Mere would be either by a natural water course along the line of the Fosdyke, or through the gap in the high land below the high part of the city, into the meres on the south, where was another great mere, extending from Washingborough to Chapel Hill, into which the Langworthy, the Bane and the Slea discharged their waters. The outlet for this mere was a winding tidal creek, extending through the marshes below Chapel Hill to the Scalp at Fishtoft, which has since become the channel of the Witham. In order to drain these meres and swampy grounds, the Romans either enlarged an old waterway, or cut the channel to the Trent, now known as the Fosdyke, the prefix of this name being the Roman word for an embanked cutting or ditch, the affix being Saxon and having the same meaning. For the drainage of the mere below Lincoln, the Cardyke, (*Car* being the British word for Fen) was cut, skirting the higher ground on the west side and preventing the highland brooks from pouring their contents into the mere. The Cardyke was continued along the west side of the Black Sluice level, which was a continuation of the same mere and ran southwards to Thurlby and thence to the Welland and the Nene. It was made navigable and afforded communication between Peterborough and Lincoln and thence by the Fossdyke to the Trent. The course of this canal can be clearly traced at the present day, many parts being still in use for drainage purposes. Remains of forts, placed for its protection, have been discovered at Billingborough, Garwick, Walcot, Linwood, and Washingborough.

THE FOSDYKE.

THE CARDYKE.

THE LOWER WITHAM. For the drainage of Brayford Mere and of the swampy ground round Lincoln and to afford a better outlet for the Witham water, a straight cut was made by the Romans through the gap in the cliff below the city to Shortferry and thence, skirting the high land, to the tidal creek at Chapel Hill. This cut now constitutes the channel of the river Witham. This catchwater drain intercepted the water of the Langworthy and all the other brooks and water courses which formerly passed their water into the mere. The absence of all winding in the course of the channel between Lincoln and Chapel Hill, and the fact that portions of the fen lie on the east side, between it and the high land, indicate that this river was never a natural stream.

The watercourse now known as the Hammond Beck was either cut for the purpose of diverting the water from the mere of the Lindsey Level or was a natural stream, straightened and improved.

The course of another artificial cut or drain may be traced in the Westlode, which drained the low lands towards Deeping Fen and emptied into the Welland.

Ample testimony to the wisdom that designed this system of catchwater drains is provided by the various projects that have been brought forward by modern engineers, for utilising such parts of the Cardyke as passed through the fens then immediately under their consideration; and the system of catchwater drainage was adopted by Mr. Rennie for the East and West Fens.

Other works, supposed to have been carried out by the Romans, are the Roman bank, extending from the Welland, near Cowbit, in an easterly direction to the Delph bank, which joins the sea wall. At Whaplode Drove, Gedney Hill and Sutton St. Edmunds, traces of Roman Camps have been discovered.

Numerous remains of buildings, which from time to time have been discovered buried beneath the surface of the present city of Lincoln, testify to the fact that it must have been an important place during the Roman occupation. These discoveries tend to show that the old Roman city lies about 9 to 12 feet below the surface of the present town. Amongst other ruins, the bases of large pillars of sandstone were discovered in 1878. A Roman hypocaust was also found below the foundation of the present castle prison; a tesselated pavement was uncovered below the minster cloisters; and, in 1879, another pavement was partially bared, below the Exchequer gate, and also part of the frescoed wall, on the stucco of which the pattern was still visible. A Roman milestone stood near the Bailgate, at the point where the eastern and western streets of the military town crossed Ermine street. On it is an inscription, which states that it was placed there, in the time of the Emperor Gallienus, by Victorinus, who ruled in Britain 265-7, A.D. The most interesting remnant of the occupation of the Romans is the Newport gate, which was built by them and through which passed one of their main roads. A shield, supposed to be of Roman and British origin, and swords and spears of the same period were discovered in the Witham when it was deepened in 1788. At Wainfleet, a coin of the Emperor Claudian was discovered about 40

LINCOLN.

ROMAN ANTIQUITIES.

Anderson's *Lincoln Guide.*

years ago, and, at an earlier period, when cellars for the Angel Hotel were being dug, a pitcher of Roman make was found. Roman coins have also been found at Boston, Spalding, Gedney, Sutton St. Edmunds, and at Fleet, a large number of them being of the reign of the Emperor Gallienus; also a Roman sword, near Fleet mill; at Horncastle, Roman urns, coins of the reigns of Vespasian, Trajan, Caligula and Nero. A quantity of pottery and coins have also been found at Whaplode Drove and Fleet.

<small>END OF ROMAN OCCUPATION 420 A.D.</small>

After an occupation of upwards of 400 years, the Romans, about the year 420 A.D., withdrew their legions from Britain, to assist in the defence of their territories nearer home, and the country then became an easy prey to the Saxons, who had, for some time previously, been making invasions of this part of the coast. The colonists and Latinised natives, demoralised by the social refinements and luxurious habits acquired from the Romans, and degenerated from their original standard of manliness and virtue, soon gave place to the hardy and adventurous Saxons, and, within an apparently short time, all trace of the forms of Roman government and subjection disappeared. The great Roman city of Lincoln, being taken possession of by Cerdic the Saxon, became one of the principal settlements of the Angles and was made the capital of Mercia and the residence of the Saxon king.

The colonists who now took possession of the Fenland were offshoots from that vast, restless body of Saxons which gradually spread north-west and across Central Europe, and extended to the coast, along the course of the Elbe. The tribe who settled near the coast were known as the *Angles*, and these men, crossing the North Sea in pursuit of plunder, and finding the Fenland not unlike the land from whence they came, finally settled here.

<small>THE SAXONS.</small>

The new settlers, who were known as the *Gyrwas*, or Fen-men, appear to have thoroughly appropriated the land and all that belonged to it, as their successors have since done in America and the other colonies. All traces of the Britons have disappeared, and hardly a single name is to be found in the fen district to show that they, or the Romans, once occupied it. The only places whose names bear any indication of British origin are Lincoln, Bardney and Kirton. Even the names of the rivers, which in other parts of the country have retained their ancient British designations, in the Fens, afford, with perhaps the exception of the Glen and the Bane, no link with the past. The Romans left their enduring stamp on the country in the magnificent works which they carried out, in the remains of their forts and dwellings, and in the coins and other relics which, even to this day, are occasionally discovered; but so completely did the Saxons take and retain possession of the Fenland and absorb or dispossess the previous occupants, that only two names, Lincoln and Fossdyke, remain bearing Roman traces and, even in these two cases, only one half the name is Roman, the other half of the latter being Saxon.

The Anglo-Saxons, having once taken possession of the Fens, held their own against all comers, and, to this day, the Fenland, in its names and manners, is more purely Saxon than any other part of England. The Danes gained some foothold, but so far as names of villages, places and people indicate they were unable to dispossess the Saxons. The names of most of the villages skirting the Fenland are of Danish origin, but only a few within the Fenland, and these near the rivers and the coast, can be traced to the Danes. Of the villages in the Fenland 29 have a Saxon origin, eight appear to be more Danish than Saxon, and five are doubtful. Of the former, fourteen have the termination *Ton*, four that of *Ey*, and three of *Fleet*; and, of the latter, two have *Beck* for a termination, three *Toft*, and one *Wick* and *Beck*.

_{SAXON NAMES OF PLACES.}

The Saxons, having settled down and colonised the land, not only adapted themselves to the use of the products peculiar to the district, by learning to eat fish, but brought with them from their Teutonic homes the arts of agriculture and raised considerable quantities of wheat for bread, and of barley for making beer, of which they consumed very large quantities. From the numerous grants of salt pans contained in old Saxon documents, it is evident also that they had acquired the art of evaporating salt from the sea water of the estuary.

Many of the Saxon chiefs, who came over in the first instance for plunder, returned with their families and settled down as colonists. These settlers constructed wattled huts on the highest ground they could find, and for protection from sudden incursions, whether of the water or their enemies, fenced the homestead round with a bank.

These first settlements were called *Tons* by the Saxons, each being known by the name of the head of the community, and were, no doubt, connected together by a causeway, raised above the level of the floods in winter, which enabled the inhabitants to communicate with each other. In some cases, these *Tons* had been the homes of dispossessed Britons, as probably in the case of Bardney and Kirton. Each settlement devoted space for worship and burial, the Druidical grove or altar giving way to the early churches of the Saxons and their successors. The present site of the village churches may, therefore, be regarded as the spot where the first settlement of the families of the early colonists took place, and the present main roads, as running along the site of the early causeways. As the family increased, the banks of the *Ton* were extended and the number of dwellings increased, and thus was commenced the foundation of those scattered collections of houses and cottages to which the Normans gave the name of villages.

_{SAXON TONS.}

These *Tons* were subsequently joined into the Hundreds or Wapentakes of Skirbeck, Kirton and Elloe by King Alfred.

<small>INTRODUCTION OF CHRISTIANITY INTO THE FENLAND.</small>

During the seventh century, when Christianity was replacing Paganism, four priests were sent from the monastery at Lindisfarne in Northumberland, into Mercia, and their chief, Paulinus, after having been made instrumental in the conversion of Edwin, King of Northumberland, accompanied that monarch in his conquest of Lindsey, the event being thus chronicled by Holinshed, who gathered his account from Matthew of Westminster. "Moreover, Pauline, after that he had converted the Northumbers, preached the word of God unto them of Lindsey, which is a part of Lincolnshire; and first he persuaded one Blecca, the Governor of Lincoln, to turn unto Christ, together with all his family. In that city he also builded a church of stone work." This movement had a material effect on the prosperity of the Fenland. Many of the early monks, for pious purposes, settled in the district, and round their settlements gradually sprang up monasteries, where the Abbots reclaimed the fen around their dwellings and became the prime movers in all works of improvement. The places where these settlements took place were on the islands or high places in the Fens. An old writer, describing these, says: "For by the inundations and overflowing of the rivers, the water standing upon the level ground maketh a deep lake and so rendereth it uninhabitable, except in some high places which God of purpose raised (as may be thought) to which there is no access but by navigable vessels."

<small>Hollinshed.</small>

<small>ST. GUTHLAC.</small>

One of the earliest of these settlers was St. Guthlac, a youth of the royal race of Mercia, who sought a refuge in the very heart of the fens, at Crowland. His youth had been spent in accordance with the wild barbarism of the times, in constant feuds with his neighbours, in robbing them of their cattle, in sacking and burning towns and homesteads. Suddenly, we are told, as he lay one night sleepless in the forest, amongst his sleeping war band, there rose before him the thought of his crimes and of the doom that waited on him. At the abbey of Repton, the burying place of the royal line of Mercia, he shore off the long hair which marked the noble, and, moved by the life of the hermit saints, of which he had heard, took himself to the heart of the Fens. Its birds became his friends, they perched unhindered on his shoulder and rested in the thatch that covered the little cell he had built, until his solitude was broken by the crowds of devotees, by Abbot, and by Monk, by Thegn and by Ceorl, as they flocked over the fen to the solitary cell, and so great was the reverence that he won, that two years after his death the Abbey of Crowland was raised over his tomb.

<small>Ingulph.</small>

The Biographer of St. Guthlac gives us, in the following description, some idea of the fens at the beginning of the eighth century:—" There is in the middle part of Britain a hideous fen of a huge bigness, which, beginning at the banks of the river Grante, extends itself from the south to the north in a very long tract, even to the sea: oft-times clouded with moist and dark vapours, having within it divers islands and woods, as also crooked and winding rivers. When, therefore, that man of blessed memory, Guthlac, had found out the desert places of this vast wilderness, and by God's assistance had passed through them, he enquired of the borderers what they knew thereof, who relating several things of its dreadfulness and solitude, there stood up one among them, called Tatwine, who affirmed that he knew a certain island, in the more remote and secret parts thereof, which many had attempted to inhabit, but could not for the strange and uncouth monsters and several terrors wherewith they were affrighted: whereupon, St. Guthlac earnestly entreated that he would show him that place. Tatwine, therefore, yielding to the request of this holy man, taking a fisher's boat (Christ being his guide through the intricacies of this darksome fen) passed thereunto, it being called Croyland, and situate in the midst of the lake, but in respect of its desertness formerly known to very few; for no countrymen, before that devout servant of Christ, S. Guthlac, could endure to dwell in it, by reason that such apparitions of devils were so frequently seen there."

"Not long after, S. Guthlac, being awoke in the night time, betwixt his hours of prayer, as he was accustomed, of a sudden he discerned his cell to be full of black troops of unclean spirits, which crept in under the door, as also at chinks and holes, and coming in, both out of the sky and from the earth, filled the air as it were with dark clouds. In their looks they were cruel, and of form terrible, having great heads, long necks, lean faces, pale countenances, ill-favoured beards, rough ears, wrinkled foreheads, fierce eyes, stinking mouths, teeth like horses, spitting fire out of their throats, crooked jaws, broad lips, loud voices, burnt hair, great cheeks, high breasts, rugged thighs, bunched knees, bended legs, swollen ancles, preposterous feet, open mouths and hoarse cries; who with such mighty shrieks were heard to roar that they filled almost the whole distance from heaven with their bellowing noises; and, by and by, rushing into the house, first bound the holy man; then drew him out of his cell, and cast him over head and ears into the dirty fen; and having so done, carried him through the most rough and troublesome parts thereof, drawing him amongst brambles and briers for the tearing of his limbs."

A modern writer of more practical turn of mind suggests that the ague which this pious saint suffered from was the cause of many of the pains which he ascribed to the malice of the evil spirits; or, as Kingsley suggests in *The Hermits*, "The whistle of the wind through the dreary night; the wild cries of the water fowl, were translated into the howls of witches and demons; and the delirious fancies of marsh fever made those fiends take hideous shapes before the inner eye, and act fantastic horrors round the Fenman's bed of sedge."

The reputation for piety acquired by St. Guthlac soon made Crowland famous, and, after his death, Ethelbald, King of Mercia, whose Confessor he had been, determined to erect a monastery to his memory, and endowed it with the whole Isle of Crowland, together with the adjacent fens lying on both sides of the river Welland. The ground on which the monastery was built, being so moist and fenny as not of itself to bear a building of stone, a great number of piles were driven deep into the ground, and a quantity of firm, hard earth, brought from a distance of nine miles, was thrown amongst them, and upon this foundation the building was erected.

Turner's Anglo-Saxons

The historian is in error as to the building being placed on piles. The peat here being underlaid by a hard bed of gravel, piles would be unnecessary. From the report recently made on the present ruins of Crowland Abbey by Mr. Pearson, it appears that the peat on which the tower rests is less than two feet thick, and that the bottom of it is 7ft. 9in. below the ground line.

The foundations rested on the peat which, owing to the improved drainage, has shrunk, and caused the destruction of the building.

The bounty of the King was thus celebrated in poetry :—

"The Royal bounty here itself displays,
And bids with mighty pains a temple raise.
The soft, the slippery, the unsettled soil
Had long disdained the busy workman's toil.
No stone foundations suit this marshy land,
But piles of oak in goodly order stand;
And boats, for nine long leagues, fetch filling land:
The fickle soil cements to solid ground.
The sacred pile on the firm base they found,
And art and labour grace the work around."

It will be unnecessary further to pursue the history of the Abbey of Crowland; suffice it to say that, though the Monks " had ample possessions in the fens yet they yielded not much profit, in regard that so great a quantity of them lay for the most part under water." The Fens, however, served other purposes than that of profit, for, in the many incursions of the Danes, they became the chiefest refuge of the Monks, their lives being secured by means of these spacious fens, in the reeds and thickets whereof they hid themselves to avoid the cruelties of this barbarous people, whilst the rest of their convent was murdered and their abbey burnt. Saint Guthlac became the patron saint of the Fens, and the numerous churches that are dedicated to his memory attest the esteem and popularity of the first Christian reclaimer of this part of England. In a niche in the wall of the parish church of Fishtoft is a statue of St. Guthlac, its patron saint; and there is a tradition

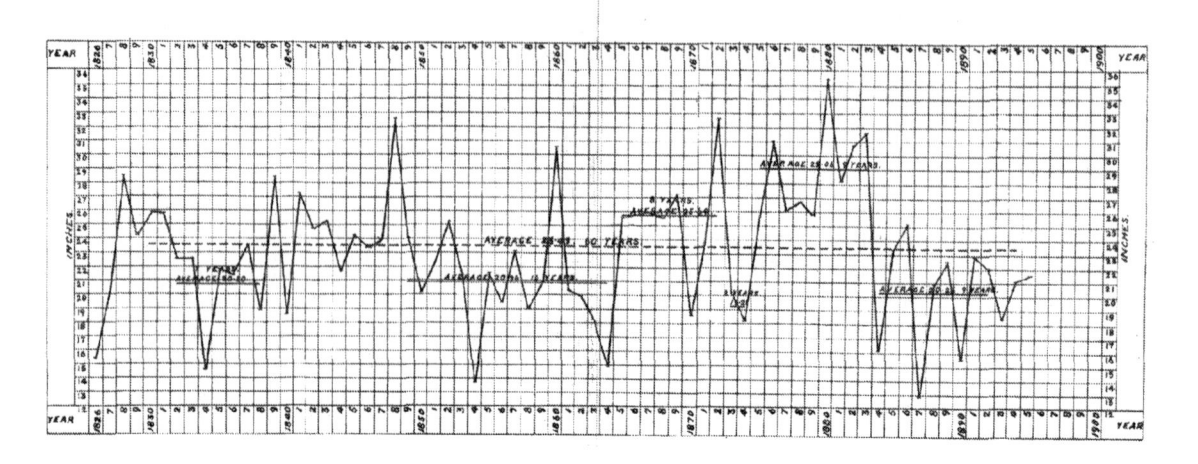

DIAGRAM SHOWING THE ANNUAL RAINFALL AT BOSTON.

Fig. 16.

connected with this statue that so long as the whip, the usual insignia of the saint, remained in his hand, the parish of Fishtoft should not be infested with rats and mice.

Thompson's Boston.

Another pious settler in the Fens was St. Botolf. He had been sent to Belgium, as a youth, to be educated, and, having acquired a great reputation for holiness and learning, returned to England with high testimonials and a letter of recommendation to the Saxon earl, Ethelmund, King of Mercia. Being desirous of retiring to a lonely place, away from the wickedness of the world, he asked from the King a gift of land in the Fens, which being granted, he choose a desolate spot on one of the holmes or islands which rose a little above the level of the surrounding fen, which he could occupy without dispossessing any previous owner. In this spot, described as an untilled place, a wilderness where no man dwelt, he founded a monastery in 654, and was held in high esteem by the Mercian Prince, whose confessor he was. St. Botolf, who is described as having locks as white as wool, and with a heart like the down of the thistle, lived long enough to see a monastery spring up on the land which he had chosen for its isolation, and over which he ruled in an exemplary manner, till his death, in 680. The monastery was destroyed by the Danes in 870. The buildings were, however, restored, and the place where it was situated was called after St. Botolf, its pious founder. Round this nucleus gradually sprang up other dwellings, till *Botolf's ton* became an important place and developed into a town, the name being shortened into Boston about two centuries ago.

ST. BOTOLF. 654.

In 678 Egfried of Northumbria founded the Bishopric of Lindissee. In 767, Ceowulf was consecrated Bishop of Lincoln.

678.

Several monasteries were established along the Witham and in South Holland, and, around these, works of reclamation and improvement were carried out by the abbots, and the land made to produce corn and cattle.

In the year 870, the Marshes, as the Fens were then termed, are described by Hugo Candidus as furnishing wood and turf for fire, hay for cattle, reeds for thatching, and fish and water fowl for subsistence. This growing prosperity, however, was much checked by the incursions of the Danes. In 866, a Danish armament, under Hubba and Hingva, invaded East Anglia.

The following account of the invasion of the Fens by a body of Danes, in the year 870, is given by Sharon Turner:—"They embarked on the Humber, and, sailing to Lincolnshire, landed at Humberston, in Lindsey. After destroying the monastery and slaying all the monks of Bardney, they employed the summer in desolating the country around with sword and fire. About Michaelmas they passed the Witham, and entered the district of Kesteven. The Earl Algar drew out the youth of

INVASION OF THE DANES. 866. Sharon Turner.

Holland: his two seneschals, Wibert and Leofric, assembled, from Deeping, Langtoft and Baston, 300 valiant and well-appointed men; 200 more joined him from Croyland monastry: they were composed of fugitives, and led by Tolius, who had assumed the cowl, but who previous to entering the sacred profession, had been celebrated for his military character. Morcar, lord of Brunne (Bourne), added his family, who were undaunted and numerous. Osgot, the sheriff of Lincoln, collected 500 more from the inhabitants of the country. These patriots, not 3,000 in number, united in Kesteven, with the daring hope of checking, by their valour, the progress of the ferocious invaders. On the feast of St. Maurice, they attacked the advanced bands of the Northmen with such conspicuous bravery, that they slew three of their kings and many of their soldiers: they chased the rest to the gates of their entrenchments, and, notwithstanding a fierce resistance, they assailed these till the advance of night compelled the valiant Earl to call off his noble army. The English ultimately beaten, the Danes burned and destroyed all the towns and villages and ravaged and destroyed Croyland Abbey. The venerable Abbot was hewed down at the altar, and the Prior and the rest of the monks murdered; all the tombs and monuments were broken, and the 'superb edifice' devoured by fire; having accomplished which, they set out for Peterborough, then called Medehampstead. The Danes were finally defeated in 878, and Alfred the Great re-ascended the throne of England. The monks returned to their ruined homes, which they soon set about rebuilding, and although, during the intervening period of the Norman Conquest, several incursions were made by the Danes, in which the Fenmen were engaged, no special fact is recorded by history which throws any light on the state and condition of the Fens during this period."

In the churchyard of Algarkirk Church, whither it has been removed from the church, is the effigy of a man, which is reputed to be that of the Earl Algar here mentioned, from whom the Parish takes its name, but its identity is doubtful.

Later on, there was another invasion under Guthrum, who, having murdered the Saxon King, Edmund, took his throne and ruled over Mercia and East Anglia. During the latter half of the ninth century, the Danes had so completely got possession of the North and West of Lincolnshire that it became almost a Danish province, and, in common with the adjoining district of East Anglia, this part of the country was governed by Danish lords. After continual struggles between the Danes and the dispossessed Saxons, a final arrangement was come to with King Alfred, by which this part of the East Coast was given up to the Danes, and the country governed by them became known as the *Danelagh*, *i.e.*, the district under Danish laws. The part most exclusively Danish stretches from the coast, in the neighbourhood of Alford, over the Wolds to Horncastle. The smooth, sandy shore between Theddlethorpe and Skegness was a favourite landing place for the Danish boats, and the families whom they brought over settled along the edge of the Fen, from Firsby round by Coningsby, Digby, Asgarby, Haconby, to Stamford. Over this district they have left their mark in the numerous villages and places, the names of which are of Danish origin, and in the Danish derivation of numerous words common only to East Lincolnshire.

Streatfield's Lincolnshire under the Danes.

East of the boundary line above given, names of Danish origin are as conspicuous by their absence, as on the higher land skirting the fen they are plentiful.

A final attempt to subdue the Fenmen was made by Sweyn, the Dane, in 1013. He ravaged Kesteven, and burnt and pillaged Boston. In 1016, Canute, or Knut, the Dane, ruled over all Mercia. It is stated on the authority of Camden, that King Canute first allotted the Common Rights on the Fens, and "ordered the Fen to be parcelled out among the several towns upon it, by Turkill the Dane, who divided it in such manner that each town had such a proportion of Fen for its own, as each town had firm land abutting on the opposite Fen. He ordained that no township should dig or mow without leave in the Fen belonging to another, and that they should all have a common right of pasturage, *i.e.*, horn under horn, in order to maintain peace and harmony among them."

1013.

CANUTE'S ALLOTMENT OF THE FENS. 1016.

Following the Danes, came the Normans, under William the Conqueror. Not only did the Fenmen long and successfully resist these Norman invaders, but the Fens became the refuge of the discontented Saxons from all the country round; or, as Dugdale puts it, "This land environed with fens and reed plecks was unpassable; so that they feared not the invasion of an enemy, and in consequence of the strength of this place, by reason of the said water encompassing it, divers of the principal nobility of the English nation had recourse unto it as their greatest refuge against the strength and power of the Norman Conqueror." The fenny districts of the kingdom of Mercia became the 'camps of refuge' of the scattered and discomfited Saxons. When William the Conqueror had subdued all the rest of England, a brave body of men in the Fens still refused him allegiance; their remote situation and solitary habits made them conservative of their ancient rights and privileges, and zealous in their allegiance to their liege lords and masters. "It is men of this kind, whose position gives them more natural security than their neighbours, and consequently more independence, who have been found the last to be conquered in every country where their subjugation has been attempted. What the rock and defile were to the mountaineer, the reed field

THE NORMANS.

and mere were to the Fenman—his home, the source of his subsistence, and his defence in seasons of oppression or misfortune." Under Hereward, son of Leofric, Lord of Bourne, many a bold fight was made for liberty against the usurpers, Ivo of Taillebois, Guy de Croun and other Normans, to whom King William had given the land of the Saxons. Driven by the conquerors from place to place, they at last made the Isle of Ely their final camp of refuge, where were collected many of the principal Saxon nobility and ecclesiastics.

<small>S. H. Miller's *Camp of Refuge.*</small> The struggles between the Fenmen and the Normans at Ely, and in the adjacent Fens, are well described in the "Camp of Refuge," which, being written by an author living in and thoroughly knowing the Fenland, conveys to the mind a most interesting and true picture of the Fens at that time.

<small>Kingsley's *Hereward.*</small> Long and nobly did Hereward, by his sagacity, bravery, and self-devotedness baffle all the attempts of the Normans to obtain possession of the stronghold. The deeds of Hereward long lived in the traditions of the people, and have come down to our day in the narratives of the ancient chronicles, and have lately been revived by a modern writer in the graphic and touching romance of *Hereward, the last of the English,* in which the writer shows a knowledge of the fen country in Saxon times, such as only one who had studied the chronicles could give. One short quotation from this interesting work may here be given, as descriptive of the fen country between Bourne and Crowland.

Hereward had just returned from Flanders to his native country, and arriving at Bourne, the home of his ancestors, he finds the place beseiged, and, on enquiring what has happened, is answered, "What has happened makes free Englishmen's blood boil to tell of. Here, Sir Knight, three days ago, came in this Frenchman, with some twenty ruffians of his own, and more of one Taillebois, too, to see him safe; says that this new King, this base-born Frenchman, has given away all Earl Morcar's lands, and that Bourne is his; kills a man or two; upsets the women; gets drunk, raffles and roysters; breaks into my lady's bower, calling her to give up her keys, and when she gives them will have all her jewels too. She faces them like a brave princess, and two of the hounds lay hold of her, and say that she shall ride through Bourne as she rode through Coventry. The boy Godwin—he that was the great Earl's godson, our last hope—draws sword on them, and he, a boy of 16 summers, kills them both out of hand; the rest set on him, cut his head off, and there it sticks on the gable spike to this hour." Hereward, enraged beyond endurance by this and other accounts of the evils that had fallen on his country, his family, and his friends, rushed down to the hall, where were assembled the Frenchmen, engaged in drunken revelry, and with his own hand slays the whole of the guard left in charge of Bourne, fourteen in number. The next day he set out for Crowland Abbey, with his mother, the Princess Godiva, "and they went down to the water and took barge, and laid the corpse of young Godwin therein; and they rowed away for Crowland by many a mere and many an ea; through narrow reaches of clear, brown glassy water; between the dark green alders, between the pale green reeds, where the coot clanked and the bittern boomed, and the sedge bird, not content with its own sweet song, mocked the song of all the birds around: and then out into the broad lagoons, where hung motionless, high over head, hawk beyond hawk, buzzard beyond buzzard, kite beyond kite, as far as the eye could see. Into the air, as they rowed on, whirred up the great skeins of wild fowl innumerable, with a cry as of all the bells of Crowland, or all the hounds of Bruneswald; and clear above all the noise sounded the wild whistle of the curlews, and the trumpet note of the great white swan; out of the reeds, like an arrow, shot the peregrine, singled one luckless mallard from the flock, caught him up, struck him stone dead with one blow of his terrible heel, and swept his prey with him into the reeds again."

The King having at last subdued Ely, the Fenmen, in common with the rest of England, had to submit to the conquering arm of William of Normandy, and numerous grants were made to his followers, the land in this district being chiefly shared by Allan Rufus, Earl of Brittany and Richmond, Walter D'Eyncourt, Guy de Creon or Croun, and Gilbert de Gand. The Earl of Brittany had his chief residence at Kirton, and there is reason to suppose that the Earl of Richmond had a seat in the parish of Boston, prior to the thirteenth century. Walter D'Eyncourt also had a residence at Kirton, although the head of his barony was at Blankney; Guy de Croun resided at Freiston.

But although, to a great extent, the Fenland had been parcelled out in grants to the followers of the Conqueror, the Normans were never able to subdue the Fenmen to the same state of vassalage as the inhabitants of other parts of the country. Instead of the Fenmen becoming Normans in manner and language, the Normans gradually became converted into Fenmen.

The real spirit of Norman feudalism obtained but little hold in this district. The Fenman still retained his sturdy independance and, at the time when the Domesday book was compiled, no shire in England could vie with that of Lincoln in the number of its freeholders. While the language of the rest of England was being corrupted by the Norman French introduced by the Conqueror, the Fens yielded neither to their language nor their manners, and in the ordinary conversation of a Lincolnshire Fenman of the present day is to be found purer Saxon English than in any other

Oliphant's Standard English.

LANGUAGE OF THE FENLAND.

part of the country. It was from the fen town of Bourne that 'the poet and the patriarch of true English' Robert Manning, or Robert of Brunne, as he was generally called, went (A.D. 1300) to Cambridge, where he became 'the first great writer in modern classic English.'

In fact, the Normans left as little impression on the Fenland, so far as the names of the people and the places are concerned, as either the Britons or the Romans.

The retention of the expression *Ton*, in place of village, is one among many proofs of this. The parishes on the east coast from Friskney to Boston are still described as the "Holland towns" and those on the south as 'the Eleven towns' the 'town' being a corruption of the Saxon *Ton*.

<small>ORIGIN OF NAMES AND PLACES.</small>

The names which had been given to the villages by the Saxons afford a clue to the physical condition of the place at the time it was named. Thus Friskney, Stickney, Sibsey, Bardney, Fulney, Gedney, were, more or less, islands surrounded by water. Stickford was the place on the main road for crossing the swamp between the East and West Fens. Butterwick and Wigtoft were havens, or places where boats landed their goods, the latter being then on the margin of Bicker Haven. Swineshead is derived from *Swin*, a narrow channel or creek. Benington, Leverton, Freiston, Boston, Wyberton, Frampton, Algarkirk, Donington, Gutheram-Cote, Hubbert's Bridge, Hammond Beck, derive their names from earls or chiefs, or other great men of the time, most of these places having been settlements of the Saxon families of the Benings, or the Dunnas, or of the Earls Leofric, Wibert, Algar, Hubba, Guthrum, etc. Waynflete, Surfleet, and Hoffleet show their position near tidal creeks. Skirbeck and Pinchbeck, their position near fresh water streams; Cowbit was a cow pasture; Kirton was the site of a temple or church, and was probably a British settlement, the prefix meaning a circle, from which followed the words kirk and church; Langrick means simply the *Long Reach* which the river has in this neighbourhood; Dogdyke, formerly spelt Docdyke, means a dock, or place where boats may lie surrounded by a bank; Fishtoft a place of fishermen, a tidal creek running up to the village. The whole of the Saxon names of the parishes in the Fenland are mentioned in Domesday book, except Benington, Brothertoft, Boston, Cowbit, Sutterton and Swineshead.

<small>Domesday Book: Smith's Translation.</small>

The omission of Boston is supposed to be due to its being included in the Parish of Skirbeck, the place at that time consisting only of the monastery founded by St. Botolf, and the habitations which had grown up around it.

<small>FEN CHURCHES IN THE NORMAN TIMES.</small>

The churches mentioned in Domesday Book, as existing in or near the Fenland at that time, were those at Bourne, Bicker,

Butterwick, Blankney, Bolingbroke, Dunston, Frampton, Fishtoft, Heckington, Helpringham, Kirton, North and South Kyme, Leverton, Metheringham, Nocton, Skirbeck, Stickney, Steeping, Stickford, Sibsey, Thorpe, Tydd St. Mary, Toynton St. Peter's and Wyberton.

There were monasteries at the time of the Conquest at Bardney, Boston, Crowland and Spalding. *MONASTERIES.*

After the Norman conquest, the Fens became a favourite place with the monks. On the banks of the Witham, twelve houses were erected, within the space of twenty miles. On the east, were Monk's House, Barlings, Bardney, Tupholme, Stixwould, Kirkstead and Tattershall; and on the west, Kyme, Haverholme, Catley, Mere and Nocton.

In fact, the fen country was described by William of Malmesbury, as being full of monasteries, and as having large bodies of monks settled on the islands of these waters, to whom were made grants of land and rights of fishing, fowling and *turbary* (digging turf for fuel). *Oliver's Religious Houses on the Witham.*

Reference has already been made to the attempts of the Abbots to improve and reclaim the fen land around their monasteries; and, as these increased in size and importance, they attracted numerous tenants, retainers and servants, and the Abbots became the principal landowners in the Fens.

Mr. Morton, in his History of Lincolnshire Churches, remarks that, "on their first introduction the members of these monasteries were laborious men, who drained marshes, cleared woods, cultivated wastes, and protected the country from the wolves, then numerous. A colony of monks, in small numbers at first, transported themselves into some uncultivated place, and there, as missionaries and labourers at once, in the midst of a people as yet pagan, they accomplished their double task with as much of danger as of toil." Mr. Oliver also says, "The monks were expert agriculturists and by persevering industry converted the ground adjoining their houses into a rich and prolific tract, which distinguished them from the estates of the neighbouring proprietors. Thus, Temple Bruer was built on the barren heath; Catley, Haverholme, and Kyme in a flooded fen; Epworth Priory in a wood; Swineshead Abbey amongst the willows in a marsh." *Morton's Lincolnshire Churches.*

The character born by these different monasteries is thus given in an old rhyme.

> Ramsay, the rich of gold and fee,
> Thorney, the flower of many a fair tree,
> Croyland, the courteous of their meat and drink,
> Spalding, the gluttons, as all men do think,
> Peterborough the proud.
> Sautrey, by the way,
> That old abbey,
> Gave more alms in one day than all they.

In the eleventh century, Abbot Egelric so improved a portion of the marshes round Crowland, as to be able to plough and sow them, and was able to supply the whole country round with corn.

Dugdale.

In the same century, also, Richard de Rulos, the king's chamberlain, being much given to good husbandry, such as tillage and the breeding of cattle, took in a great part of the common of Deeping Fen and converted it into meadow and pasture. He also enclosed the river Welland by a mighty bank, and, erecting on that bank divers tenements and cottages, did, in a short time, make it a large town."

The example thus set was followed by other owners.

1085.

In 1085, "The people of Hoyland, at Multon, Weston and Spalding, in imitation of those at Depynge, by a common enactment agreed to among them, divided among themselves, man by man, their marshes which were situate above the river Asendyk; on which some put their portions in tillage, others preserved them for hay, while some again allowed theirs, as before, to be for pasture for their own cattle apart from the others, and found the earth to be rich and fruitful."

Ingulph.

The impression which the fens made on those who visited them at this time may be gathered from the remarks made by Henry of Huntingdon, who, writing in the thirteenth century, says, "This fenny country is very pleasant and agreeable to the eye, watered by many rivers which run through it, diversified with many large and small lakes and adorned with many roads and islands." William of Malmesbury also describes the Fens as "a very paradise and a heaven for the beauty and delight thereof, the very marshes bearing goodly trees......there is such abundance of fish as to cause astonishment to strangers, while natives laugh at their surprise. Water-fowl are so plentiful that persons may not only assuage their hunger with both sorts of food, but can eat to satisfy for a penny."

STATE OF THE FENLAND, 1287.

The land, owing to its fruitfulness and the variety of fruit which was grown, was described as affording "a mutual strife between nature and husbandry, that what the one forgetteth the other might supply and produce."

The Fens were not always the paradise described by Henry of Huntingdon, for frequent floods and inundations caused great misery and loss to the inhabitants. Thus, on New Year's day in 1287, according to Stowe's Chronicle, "as well through the vehemency of the wind as the violence of the sea, the monasteries of Spalding and many churches were overthrown and destroyed. The whole of Holland, in Lincolnshire, was, for the most part, turned into a standing pool; so that an intolerable multitude of men, women and children were overwhelmed with the water, especially the town of Boston, or Buttolph's town, a great part whereof was destroyed."

The duty of repairing the banks and sluices which protected the land from the inundations of the sea, and also of maintaining the channels of the watercourses in good order, devolved upon the several owners of the lands adjacent to the same, according to "antient and approved customs," but no special authority existed for superintending such works, and insuring their maintenance in proper condition. There were, consequently, frequent floods and damage, caused by the neglect of the owners to maintain the banks and drains. Dugdale, in his history of embanking and draining, gives numerous extracts from the records of petitions to the King, by inhabitants of the Fens, who had thus suffered, praying for his interference.

Such drainage as the Fens had at this time was by means of the natural streams, and the remains of the works carried out by the Romans. The Car Dyke on the west partially intercepted and carried off the water from the numerous highland brooks and streams, that extended from Lincoln to Bourne, and the Witham fulfilled the same function on the east side of the Fens, down to Boston; below Chapel Hill, it had an exceedingly tortuous course, and its channel, from neglect, had become nearly filled up with weeds and deposit. The East and West Fens were flooded all the winter, the outlet for the drainage of the former being by Good Dyke into Wainfleet Haven, and, for the latter into the Witham, at a gote, about two miles above Boston. The Sibsey river and Hilldyke drain discharged into the Witham, above Boston. Skirbeck was drained by the Scire beck, which had an outlet into the Haven, below the town, and which also took one of the principal drains from Boston, the other, the Bar ditch, emptying into the Witham. Fishtoft was drained by the Graft drain, which emptied into Boston Haven, about three miles below Boston. The other parishes between Boston and Wainfleet were drained by sewers, which discharged by sluices through the Roman bank. Such drainage as the Lindsey, or Black Sluice, Level had, was by the Ouse Mere Lode into Bicker Haven, on the south, and by the Hammond Beck into Boston Haven, on the north. Holland Fen and the lands adjacent drained into Kyme Eau and the Skirth, which discharged into the Hammond beck, near Swineshead. Frampton Town drain, Kirton drain, The Five Towns drain, Risegate Eau, the river of Byker, Coln drain, Lafen lode, and the Old Bech drain, are all watercourses which were in existence previous to any attempt at reclamation being carried out.

Deeping Fen, which was little better than a lake all the winter, found an outlet into the Welland. Spalding was drained by the Westlode; Crowland, by drains made by the monks, which discharged into the Welland, and into a branch of the

Nene, now known as the Old Shire drain, which formed the principal outlet for the drainage of the district, south of the Raven bank. The land north of this drained by the Moulton, Holbeach and Whaplode rivers, and by Lutton Leam and Fleet Haven, all of which had sluices in the Roman bank, which was the only sea bank at that date.

The general condition of the Fens, as here sketched out, remained with little alteration, for a period of about five hundred years. With the exception of small enclosures, made by the religious houses which were established on the borders of the Fens, no substantial reclamation was attempted.

The only works of which there is any record are those of John of Gaunt, Duke of Lancaster, who resided at Bolingbroke Castle, upon the border of the Fens, and who held considerable rights in the Level, and of Margaret, Countess of Richmond, who, with a view to the better drainage of the district, " procured an admeasurement and division of all the surrounded grounds on the north of Spalding, which, beforetime, lay promiscuously, a great work of excellent use, not for those times only, but the fruit of it hath continued ever since."

THE GREAT SLUICE AT BOSTON, 1142.

In King Stephen's reign, Alan de Croun and Margaret, Countess of Richmond, " caused to be made, a great sluice, below the town of St. Botolph, where the Hundreds of Kirton and Skirbeck divide and separate, in order to increase the rush and force of the waters, by which the harbour is made clear; which harbour is almost obstructed, and has perished, by reason of the quantity of mud and sand brought up and deposited from day to day by the flow of the sea; and in order also that the channel, by this means, might become deeper, so that the waters from all the marshes of Lindsey, Holland and Kesteven, and from the lands of the whole country, might come down and flow into the sea more easily." This structure is referred to subsequently, as the Great Sluice (*Magna Slusa*) in the channel of the water of the Witham, below the town of Boston. In 1316, an inquisition was held at Boston, concerning the "Great Sluice in the Witham, at Boston," when the Jury made a presentment that the sluice was ruinous and in great decay, "because many doors are wanting, and also 500 piles from the number with which it was constructed, and new fastenings have to be brought, and also beams, planks, piles, and binders of every kind suitable for use in water, to the great danger of all the district in Holland and Kesteven and the marshes of Lindsey and Kesteven." This sluice was again mentioned in Henry the Seventh's reign (1543) when an ordnance of sewers was made at Donington, by which it was enacted that the floodgate, or sluice, under

Boston Bridge, shall be made of new, because it was in decay, and it was to be builded again in sort and order, as the most noble Margaret, Countess of Richmond, first made it, and this was to be done at the cost and charges of the Parts of Holland, that is, the Wapentake of Kirton and Skirbeck Hundred equally, to the half of the whole, the Wapentake of Elloe, one quarter, and Town of Boston, one quarter.

It is not known where this strucure was situated. Probably it was superseded by the sluice erected by May Hake.

Records exist of occasional grants of marsh or fen lands made about this time. Thus a grant of marsh was made early in the 13th century by King John to Thomas de Muleton, the land being described as lying between the waters of Tydd. *1205.*

In the reign of Henry III, some attempt was made to remedy the condition of the Fens, as it is related that the King, taking notice that not only the landowners in those parts, but himself, had suffered considerable damage by the overflowing of the sea, and also of the fresh water, through default in repair of the banks, sewers and ditches, directed the Shirereeve to distrain the goods of all landowners who ought to have repaired the banks and scoured out the drains. *1216.*

The King's intervention did not take much effect, as subsequent floodings and inundations are frequently recorded, some being due to causes beyond human control, but most of them to carelessness, and even, in some cases, to wilful injury to the banks.

In 1287, through the vehemence of the wind and the violence of the sea, the monastery of Spalding and many churches were overthrown and destroyed. "All the whole country in the parts of Holland was for the most part turned into a standing pool, so that an intolerable multitude of men, women and children where overwhelmed with the water, especially in the town of Boston, a great part whereof was destroyed." *Stow's Chronicle, 1287.*

In 1335, one Roger Pedwardine was accused of having cut the sea and river banks and thereby inundated the low country. *1335.*

In Richard the Second's reign, an inquisition taken at Bolingbroke and subsequently a presentment made in the court of King's Bench, held at Lincoln, by the jurors of divers Wapentakes, showed "that the marshes of East Fenne and West Fenne, as also divers lands, meadows, and pastures lying in the towns of Leek, Wrangle, Friskeneye, and Waynflete, betwixt the waters of Wytham and Waynflete, were drowned by a great inundation of water, so that all the inhabitants of those towns and of the Soke and Wapentake of Bolingbroke did wholly lose the benefit of their lands and marshes there, through the defects of a certain floodgate at Waynflete, which was so narrow that the course of the waters passing that way could not get to the sea; and that the *1394.*

town of Waynflete ought to repair that floodgate, as anciently they had wont to do......and that it would be necessary to have another floodgate new erected, near unto the same, xxii ft. in breadth and that the towns of Leek, Wrangle, Friskeney, and Waynflete, together with the Soke and Wapentake of Bolingbroke, as also all those which had common of pasture in the said marshes, ought to contribute to the making thereof."

Ingulph, 1439.

In 1439, there was such an excessive quantity of water in the rivers and streams, in consequence of the extraordinary rains, that the embankments around Croyland were unable to hold out against the force of the impetuous torrent. The consequence was that the waters, having swollen and beaten with all their force against the embankments, broke through and inundated the entire surface of the adjacent commons.

1467.

In 1467, there was "so great an inundation of the waters, by reason of the snows and continuous rains, that no man then living could recall to mind the like. Throughout the whole of South Holland there was scarcely a house or building but what the waters made their way and flowed through it; and this remained continuously during a whole month, the waters either standing there without flowing off, or else, being agitated by strong gusts of wind,

Ingulph.

swelled and increased still more and more, day after day. Nor, on this occasion, did the embankments offer any effectual resistance, but on the contrary, though materials had been brought from other quarters for the purpose of strengthening them, they proved of very little service for that purpose. However diligently the work might have been attended to in the day time, as the water swelled and rose, the spot under repair was completely laid bare during the night."

A century later, in the reign of Queen Elizabeth, another serious flood occured, when, owing to a violent tempest of wind and rain, the whole country was flooded. An immense number of ships were wrecked on the coast, churches and

Hollinshed, 1571.

buildings were swept away, and many lives lost. At Mumby Chapel the whole town was lost, except three houses; and the church was wholly otherthrown, except the steeple. A ship was driven upon a house, the sailors saving themselves by clinging to the roof; and the narrative adds to the romance by telling us that "the sailors thought they had bin upon a rocke and committed themselves to God; and three of the mariners lept out from the shippe and chaunced to take hold of the house toppe, and so saved themselves; and the wife of the same, lying in childbed, did climb up into the top of the house, and was also saved by the mariners, her husband and child being both drowned." Holland, Leverington, Long Sutton, and Holbeach were all overflowed, and many sheep, oxen, and horses were drowned.

Bourne was overflowed to the midway of the height of the church. This calamity extended over many counties, and did an enormous amount of harm.

The continual complaints made to the Crown, as to the loss arising from the constant flooding of the land, led to the issuing of numerous Commissions, which had power to order such works to be done as they considered necessary for the security of the Fenland, and to direct by whom the works were to be carried out, and to assess the mode of payment. These Commissions were renewed by succeeding sovereigns, till the time of Henry VIII, when an Act was passed, investing the Chancellor with perpetual authority to grant Commissions whenever they should be required. The ordinance recites, that " whereas formerly the marshes and low grounds had been, by politic wisdom, won and made profitable for the good of the commonwealth, and though divers provisions had formerly been made, yet none of them were sufficient remedy for the reformation thereof."

<small>SEWERS' COMMISSIONS.</small>

This Act, with others subsequently passed, constitutes the origin of the Court of Sewers, which now has control over the banks and sewers in all that part of the Fenland which has not been removed from its jurisdiction by special Acts of Parliament. The more detailed history of this Commission is given in a subsequent chapter.

After the establishment of the Court of Sewers, several efforts were made to improve the Fens, but, owing to the difficulty of arriving at a basis for the distribution of the payment of the cost of carrying out the works proposed, and the inability of the Court of Sewers to compel the payment of the taxes for the new works, no effectual scheme was carried out.

In the reign of Henry VII, a council was held to settle what means could be devised for the improvement of the navigation and drainage of the Witham, and it was determined to erect a sluice across the river at Boston, to stop the tide from flowing up the channel; and an acre rate was levied on all the parishes in Holland, to provide the money to pay for it. This sluice proved of no advantage to the drainage, but the wooden bridge, which was built over it, provided a means of communication between the east and west side of the town of Boston, which could only previously be accomplished by means of a ferry. Further particulars as to the erection of this sluice will be found in the chapter on the Witham.

<small>MAY HAKE'S SLUICE ON THE WITHAM, 1500.</small>

Some improvement was made in the condition of the Fens lying north of Boston, in the reign of Queen Elizabeth, by the cutting of Maud Foster drain, and the erection of the original outfall sluice, under the direction of the Court of Sewers.

<small>MAUD FOSTER DRAIN, 1568.</small>

FIRST ATTEMPT AT RECLAMATION.

In the same reign, also, prominent attention was given to the question of reclamation of the East and West Fens, by the attempt which was then being made by the Earl of Bedford and others to reclaim the great Bedford Level, which, at that time, included South Holland. The preamble of an Act, authorising a scheme for the reclamation of this Level, recites that it was passed for the "recovering of many thousands of acres of marshes and other grounds, commonly subject to surrounding, within the Isle of Ely and the counties of Cambridge, Huntingdon, Northampton, Lincoln, Norfolk, Suffolk, Sussex, Essex, Kent and Durham;" that "it is apparent to such as have travelled in the execution of Commissions of Sewers, that the washes, commons, marshes and fenny grounds, there subject to surrounding, may be recovered by skilful and able undertakers, whereby great and inestimable benefit would arise;" that the draining of these lands was chiefly hindered owing to the great part of them being commons, the holders of rights having, therefore, no power to make bargains for the work to be done, or, on account of their poverty, to pay the charges. This Act enabled the majority of the Commoners and owners to contract with any persons who were willing to undertake the drainage, and to grant to them part of the commons for so doing.

Bedford Level Act, 43 Eliz.

The advantages expected to be gained by the enclosure of the Fens are thus set forth in a subsequent Act, relating to the Bedford Level; "that, if drained, the great Level may be made profitable and of great advantage to the commonwealth, and to the particular owners, commoners and inhabitants, and be fit to bear cole seed and rape seed in great abundance, which is of singular use to make soap and oils within the nation, to the advancement of the trade of clothing and spinning of wool; and much of it will be improved into good pasture for feeding and breeding of cattle, and of tillage to be sown with corn and grain, and for hemp and flax in great quantity, for making all sorts of linen, cloth and cordage for shipping within the nation, which will increase manufactures, commerce and trading at home and abroad; will relieve the poor by setting them to work, and will, in many other ways, redound to the great advantage and strengthening of the nation."

Bedford Level Act, 1649.

1603.

Shortly after James the First's accession to the throne, a series of destructive floods burst the embankments of the Fens on the East Coast, and swept over farms, homesteads, and villages, drowning large numbers of people and cattle. The King, on being informed of the great calamity which had befallen the inhabitants of the Fens, principally through the decay of the old works of drainage and embankment, declared that, for the honour of his kingdom, he would not any longer suffer these countries to be abandoned to the will of the waters, nor let them lie waste and unprofitable; and that, if no one else would undertake their drainage, he himself would become the "undertaker." However, a measure of taxation for the recovery of these lands, which was accordingly proposed to the Commons, was rejected.

In 1625, a very high tide occured, described as being the highest ever known in the Thames, and the sea walls in Kent, Essex and Lincolnshire were overthrown, and great desolation caused to the lands near the sea.

During this reign, a large tract of marsh land in South Holland, lying between the Roman bank and the South Holland embankment, was enclosed by a bank, extending from the Welland to the Nene at Tydd. In 1615, a grant was made to certain adventurers, on behalf of the Duke of Argyle, of the marsh lands left by the sea, in Wigtoft, Moulton, Holbeach, and Tydd St. Mary. These were to be reclaimed at the expense of the Earl, with a reservation of a fifth portion, and a rent of £76 5s. 0d. to the King. The grant included also certain common lands. In 1640, a grant was made to the Duke of Lennox, by Charles I, of Sutton marshes, with power to embank and enclose them.

Vermuiden, in a report to the King on the draining of the great fens, the particulars of which are fully set out in his *Discourse on Draining*, published in 1642, advised that the rivers Glen and Welland should be diverted to the Nene, and the waters of the three rivers carried in one common outfall to the sea. This scheme was opposed by Andrew Burrell, in a pamphlet, published in 1642. In the same reign, several Courts of Sewers were held, and Commissioners appointed by the King, and orders made for works to be carried out for the reclamation of the Fens, and rates to be levied for payment of the same, and, in default of the owners to pay these, the Fens were to be handed over to certain "adventurers," who, in consideration of grants of a portion of the reclaimed land, undertook to carry out the necessary banks, drains and sluices for the "exsiccation" of the Fens. Sir Anthony Thomas was the "undertaker" for the Fens between the Witham and the coast. He commenced operations in 1631, and completed the work three years after. For seven years, the Adventurers enjoyed the fruit of their labours, building houses, sowing corn, and feeding cattle therein; at the end of that time, the dispossessed Fenmen, finding that done of which they themselves despaired, in a riotous manner, fell upon the Adventurers, broke the sluices, laid waste their lands, threw down the fences, spoiled the corn, demolished the houses, and forcibly regained possession of the land.

The condition of Holland fen attracted a great deal of attention in the reign of Charles the first, and the King, at one time, intended himself to undertake its reclamation, but subsequently parted with his interest in it to Sir William Killigrew, who, with the Earl of Lindsey, then Lord High Chamberlain, joined the Adventurers, and undertook the drainage of the fens lying between Kyme Eau and the Glen, called after the principal adventurer, the Lyndsey Level, and subsequently the Black Sluice District. On the completion of the drainage work in 1636, the Earl and his fellow Adventurers inclosed the fens, built houses and farmsteads, and, having brought the land into cultivation, continued in peaceable possession for about three years. At the end of this time, the Commoners and Fenmen, after a vain attempt to dispossess the Adventurers by petitions to parliament, broke down the sluices, filled in the drains, destroyed the crops, and, having driven the Adventurers away, "held possession, to the great decay and ruin of those costly works and exceeding discommodity to all that part of the country."

Dugdale, 1635.

Subsequently, a grant was made to the same Adventurers, giving leave to drain 72,000 acres of the Fens, extending from the River Glen to Lincoln, and thence to the Trent, and the Adventurers were put in possession of 14,000 acres, as a recompense for the outlay they had incurred.

State Papers, 1667.

There is no record as to what was done under this grant.

In Queen Elizabeth's reign, an Act was passed, giving power to make the Welland navigable from Stamford to the sea. The work was carried out, under the superintendence of the Court of Sewers, at the expense of the Corporation of Stamford and their friends. A Court of Sewers, held at Bourne, in the reign of Charles I, granted to Thomas Lovell a concession of the right to drain Deeping Fen, on receiving, as compensation, a third of the reclaimed lands. Sir Thomas Lovell made an attempt, and partially drained the Fen, but failed to carry out the works in accordance with his contract. King Charles the First " being desirous that the work should be prosecuted for the country's good and his own service, in a manner that would most conduce to the public and general advantage of the whole Fens, was pleased to declare himself the sole Adventurer for the drainage of Deeping Fen." The King, however, was unable to carry out his intentions, and a fresh contract was made, in 1638, with Sir Anthony Thomas and Sir William Ayloff. By the works executed by these Undertakers, the land was so well drained, that in summer the whole Fen yielded great quantities of grass and hay, and would have been made winter ground, but the Fenmen, taking advantage of the confusion throughout the whole kingdom, which prevailed at that time, took possession of the land, and, the banks and sewers being neglected, it became again overflowed.

STAMFORD CANAL.

DEEPING FEN, 1638.

The more detailed account of the various schemes and works carried out at this period, and subsequently, will be found in the chapters giving the history of the different districts in which they were situated.

The Crown and the Adventurers, having failed in their attempts to reclaim the Fen, principally from the lawlessness of the Fenmen, the land reverted back very much to its original condition, and so remained for upwards of a century.

In Cox's *Magna Britannia*, published in 1728, it is remarked, regarding the Fens of Lincolnshire, that "several attempts have been made to drain this level, and some gentlemen, who have estates under water, have endeavoured to get an Act of Parliament, but have met with such opposition from the gentlemen in the higher parts of the country, who fear that, if these Fens be drained, it will sink the value of their estates, that they have not been able to effect it." *Cox. Magna Britannia, 1728.*

Previous to the final reclamation of the Fenland, in the middle of the last and the beginning of the present century, this district was thus described by Dugdale, "and if we weigh the great inconvenience which these overflowings have produced, certainly the advantage by the general draining ought the more to be prized; for in the winter-time, when the ice is strong enough to hinder the passage of boats, and yet not able to bear a man, the inhabitants upon the hards and the banks within the Fens can have no help for food, nor comfort for body or soul; no woman aid in her travail, no means to baptize a child, or partake of the Communion, nor supply of any necessity, saving what those poor desolate places do afford; and what expectation of health can there be to the bodies of men, where there is no element good? The air being for the most part cloudy, gross and full of rotten harrs; the water putrid and muddy, yea, full of loathsome vermin; the earth, spongy and boggy, and the fire, noisome by the stink of smoaky hassocks." *CONDITION OF THE FENLAND PREVIOUS TO THE RECLAMATION. Dugdale's Embanking and Draining.*

Macaulay also describes the inhabitants as a half-savage people, leading an amphibious life, sometimes rowing, sometimes wading from one firm mound to another, and known as *Breedlings*. *Macaulay's History of England.*

Both these pictures are overdrawn. The Fenland, before the reclamation, was made up of two parts, the larger area consisting of a level tract of alluvial, or marsh land, which, although imperfectly drained, was seldom actually flooded. Interspersed amongst this were the Fens, large tracts of low, peaty land, always more or less flooded in winter, and a large part of which consisted of meres, and pools of water. These marshes and fens afforded valuable summer grazing for horses, cattle and sheep. On the higher patches of ground lived the Fenmen, who attended to the cattle, and gained their subsistence by fishing and fowling and rearing large flocks of geese. On the higher land, adjacent to the Fens, were the villages and churches, which, with the exception of Frithville, Midville, Eastville, and Langrick-ville, which were newly created at the enclosure, were the same then as now. The condition of the inhabitants of these villages, and their means of communication with the rest of the world, was neither better nor worse than that of many other parts of England.

<small>THE FENS.</small>

<small>Elstob's History of the Bedford Level.</small>

Elstob says, "The Fens were formerly in the nature of meadow land, fruitful, healthful and profitable to the people in the high country in time of drought, hence we find Leland and other writers very lavish in their praises of this once fruitful country." In wet seasons, however, their condition differed very much from this description. A writer, who lived near Kyme Fen in the early part of the last century, describing Holland Fen, says that, previous to the improvement of the Witham and the making of the Grand Sluice, he had, "times out of number, seen cows loosed out of their hovels and swim across the water with nothing but their faces and horns above the surface, and then take footing at mid-rib-deep, but not one spot of dry land, and then forage till weary and return to their hovels by swimming. No place was more famous for this than Chapel Hill, inaccessible, but by boat or riding horse belly-deep, and more in water than mud. I have also known in the whole parish of Dogdyke, not two houses communicable for whole winters round, and sometimes scarcely in summer. Sheep used to be carried to pasture in flat bottomed boats. Clip them in the boat and afterwards fetch them away in the same conveyance."

The road which ran from the high country to Boston, through the West Fen, and known as the Nordyke and Hilldyke Causeway, was only distinguished from the surrounding marshes by rows of willows and was frequently covered over a great part of its length by water. In places there were swamps, which being quite impassable by strangers, guides, who moved about on stilts, were employed to take persons across.

<small>Clarke's Fen Sketches.</small>

Mr. Clarke in his *Fen Sketches* quotes from a pamphlet called the *Anti-Projector*, written about 1606, in the time of James I, "The Undertakers have always vilified the Fens and misinformed many parliamentary men that all the fen is a mere quagmire, and that it is a level hurtfully surrounded and of little or no value. But those who live in the Fens, and are neighbours to it know the contrary; for first, the Fens breed infinite numbers of serviceable horses, mares and colts, which till our land and furnish our neighbours. Secondly, we breed and feed great store of young cattle and we keep great dairies, which afford great store of butter and cheese to victual the navy. Multitudes of heifers and Scots and Irish cattle have been fatted on the Fens, which afford hides and tallow. Thirdly, we mow off our Fen fodder, which feeds our cows in winter, which being housed, we gather such quantities of compost and dung that it enriches our pastures and corn ground, half in half, whereby we have the richest and certainest corn land in England, especially for wheat and barley, wherewith by sea we do and can abundantly provide London and the northern parts in these necessities. Fourth, we keep great flocks of sheep upon the fens. Fifth, our fens are a great relief not only to our neighbours, the uplanders, but remote countries in which otherwise some years thousands of cattle would want food. Sixth, we have great store of osier, reed and sedge, which are such necessaries as the countries cannot name them for many uses, and sets many poor on work. Lastly, we have many thousand cottagers which live in our fens, which otherwise must go a begging."

The arguments for and against reclamation were thus expressed in a pamphlet published at the time. It was said that the Fens were "nurseries and seminaries" of fish and fowl, which would be destroyed by the drainage; that the sedge, turf and reed would likewise be destroyed, and that many thousands of people then gained their livelihood by fishing and fowling in the fens, while the turf furnished fuel for the poor. The answer to this was that a tame sheep was better than a wild duck; and a good fat ox than a well grown eel; that the sedge would be replaced by good grass and grain, and that a man would not have any cause to complain who had a suit of buckram taken from him and one of velvet given instead.

In addition to the opposition of the natives, other agencies were brought to bear against the fen Drainers. Satirical poems and ballads were composed and sung with great applause in the fen towns, and their cause was even advocated by men of learning and social standing. Amongst others, Fuller, in his history, speaks of the attempted enclosure of the fens as a trespass on the divine prerogative for man to presume to give other bounds to the water than that which God had appointed; and he intimates that Providence had specially left this district for the production of fish and fowl, and of sedge, turf and reeds.

In isolated spots, scattered over the low, flooded fen part, lived the Fen Slodgers, the half amphibious beings described by Macaulay, who got their living by fishing and fowling. These men lived in huts, erected on the mounds scattered amongst the chain of lakes, which were bordered with a thick crop of reeds, their only way of access to one another, and of communication with the towns or villages near, being by means of small boats or canoes, which they paddled along with a pole, and also used in their fishing and fowling expeditions. These men were violently opposed to any attempts to alter the state of the Fens, believing they had a kind of vested interest in the fishing and fowling, by which they gained their scanty subsistence. Although their condition was very miserable, they nevertheless enjoyed a sort of wild liberty amidst the watery wastes, which they were not disposed to give up. Though they might alternately burn and shiver with ague, and become prematurely bowed and twisted

THE FEN SLODGERS.

Smiles' *Lives of the Engineers.*

with rheumatism, still the fen was their native land, such as it was, and their only source of subsistence, precarious though it might be. The fens were their commons, on which their geese grazed. They furnished them with food, though the finding thereof was full of adventure and hazard. What cared the Fenmen for the drowning of the land? Did not the water bring them fish, and the fish attract wild fowl, which they could snare and shoot? Thus the proposal to drain the fens and convert them into wholesome and fruitful lands, however important in a national point of view, as enlarging the resources and increasing the wealth of the country, had no attraction whatever in the eyes of the Slodgers. They muttered their discontent, and everywhere met the reclaimers with opposition, and frequently assembled to fill up the cuts which the labourers had dug, and to pull down the banks which they had constructed; and to such an extent was this carried that in some places the men had frequently to work under the protection of an armed guard. But their numbers were too few, and they were too widely scattered to make any combined effort at resistance.

THE FEN CODE, 1549.

In the general management of the Fens, so early as the reign of Edward VI, a code of fen laws had been enacted for defining the rights and privileges of the commoners, and for the prevention of disputes and robbery. The code, drawn up by the Council of the Duchy of Lancaster at the Great Inquest of the Soke of Bolingbroke, held in 1548, was confirmed in Queen Elizabeth's reign, (1573), and remained in force until the enclosure of the Fens at the beginning of the present century. The code consisted of seventy-two articles, a short summary of which may be interesting, as affording an insight into a state of society now passed away for ever.

Thompson's Boston, and old MS.

One of the first rules related to the brands or marks which each person who stocked the fens was required to place upon his cattle. Each parish had a separate mark and no man was allowed to turn cattle out to common until they were marked with the town brand. The illustration on the next page shows the character of some of these brands.

No foreigner, or person not having common right, was allowed to put cattle on the fens, under a penalty of forty shillings; fish or fowl at any time; or gather any turbary or fodder in the East Fen, without a licence from the approver, under a penalty......for each offence. Penalties were also attached to the following offences: putting diseased cattle on the fens; disturbing the cattle by baiting with savage dogs; for leaving any dead animal unburied for more than three days; for putting swine on the fen, unrung, or geese which were not pinioned and foot-marked; for taking or leaving dogs there after sunset; for bringing up crane birds out of the East Fen. Rams were not allowed to be kept in the Fen between St. Luke's day and Lammas. No person was allowed to gather wool who was above twelve years of age, except impotent persons; no cattle were to be driven out of the fens, except between sunrise and sunset; and no cattle were to be driven out of the fens during divine service upon the sabbath, or holy days; all cattle were to be 'roided' or 'voided' out of the East Fen before St. Barnaby's day, yearly; no reed thatch, reed star, or bolt was to be mown before it was of two years' growth; each sheaf of hatch gathered or bound up was to be a yard in compass; wythes were only to be cut between Michaelmas and May-day; no man was allowed to 'rate' any hemp or flax in the common sewers or drains.

Fig. 3 Chap. 1.
The forms or Fashion of the severall marks or Brands belonging to each Towne in the Soake of Bullingbrooke & East Holland.

Town	Mark	Town	Mark
Boston		Steeping	
Skirbeck		Thorpe	
Fishtoft		Spilsby	
Frieston		Raithby	
Butterwick		Hundleby	
Bennington		Bullingbrooke	
Leverton		Lusby	
Leake		Enderby	
Sibsey		Asgarby	
Stickney		Hairby	
Stickford		Miningsby	
West Keale		Revesby	
East Keale		East Kirkby	
Toyntons		Hagnaby	
Halton			

By an order, passed in Queen Elizabeth's reign, every township in the parts of Holland, claiming common in the West Fen, was ordered to show to the Queen's steward, at the next court-day, its charter or title to such common right. No swans', cranes', or bitterns' eggs, or any eggs excepting those of ducks and geese, were allowed to be brought out of the fens. No fodder was to be mown in the East or West Fen before Midsummer-day annually. No person was allowed to use any sort of net or other engine to take or kill any fowl, commonly called moulted ducks, in any of the fens, before Midsummer-day, yearly. A code of seventeen articles was also devised by the fishermen's jury, relative to the fish and fishing in the fens. The principal fish referred to were pike, eels, roach and perch. The laws related chiefly to the kind of nets allowed and to the manner of using them.

Before being sent into the common fen, the live stock were collected at certain defined places and marked, and again, on being taken off in the autumn, they were brought to the same place to be claimed by their owners. Thus in Pinchbeck the stock were collected at the Market Cross and a due called *Hoven* was paid. Bailiffs were appointed to look after the stock. On the marshes in South Holland a *Marsh Reeve* was also annually appointed, and a *Marsh Shepherd*, their wages being paid by a rate of 1s. 6d. for each horse and neat beast, and 3d. for each sheep, grazed on the commons.

WITHAM ACT, 1762.

The Fens remained in the condition described until the year 1762, when an Act was obtained for the improvement of the low lands on the Witham. The Witham was straightened and deepened, the Grand Sluice at Boston erected and the fens drained and reclaimed. The Witham Act was followed by one for the better drainage and reclamation of Holland Fen, and of the Black Sluice District, in 1765. The Act for the enclosure of the East and West Fens was passed in 1801, and for Deeping Fen about the same time. The works carried out under these Acts will be described in the following chapters.

HIGH TIDES AND STORMS.

Even after these works had been carried out the country was still subjected to severe losses from floods and high tides. At the end of the last and the beginning of the present century, several very high tides occurred which did much damage. On January 1st, 1779, a heavy gale of wind caused the tide to flow unusually high, to the damage of Boston and the neighbourhood. On October 19th, 1801, and on November 30th, 1807, high tides occurred, which flowed so high as to deluge the streets of Boston and to inundate the houses. Indeed the latter tide caused the water to rise so high as to enter the church and flow as far as the pulpit. The extraordinary high tide of November 10th, 1810, was attended by the most calamitous results, caused by breaches of the sea banks in several places along the coast. Particulars as to the damage caused by this tide will be found in the chapter on North Holland. In 1815, a very high tide again flowed over the banks in some places and did a great deal of injury. In March, 1820, there was a high tide, which rose 4 inches higher than the tide of 1810. This tide is the highest on record. It proved disastrous to the private banks enclosing the out-marshes from Butterwick to Wainfleet. The highest tide in recent years was in 1883. It rose at Boston to within four inches of that of 1810.

TIDE OF 1883.

The wind had been previously blowing strongly from the North-West, and this, occuring during equinoctial spring tides, caused the water to rise four feet three inches above the ordinary height of a spring tide. The low parts of Boston were flooded. The river banks in Boston Haven, and on the river Welland, had breaches made in them in several places, but as these only protected modern enclosures, the flooding of the land and damage was confined to a comparatively small area.

By so precarious a tenure is the fen land held, and so great is the necessity for constant and unremitting vigilance and care, that with the least neglect, only, perhaps, an unseen rat hole, the waving corn fields may be turned into a sea of water. So important has everything that is conducive to the preservation of these banks been deemed by the Legislature of the country, that, in an Act passed *for the preservation of Fish in Ponds and Conies in Warrens*, in 1765, it was enacted that the provisions as to rabbits should not extend to the fen banks, the exempting clause reciting that " Whereas great mischief has been, and still may be, occasioned by the increase of conies upon the sea and river banks in the County of Lincoln, or upon the land or ground within a certain distance from the said banks; for remedy thereof be it enacted that nothing in this Act contained shall extend to prevent any person from killing and destroying, or from taking or carrying away in the day time any conies that shall be found on any sea or river banks, erected, or to be erected, for the preservation of the adjoining lands from being overflowed by the sea or river waters, so far as the flux and reflux of the tide does extend, or upon any land within one furlong distance of such banks, but that it shall be lawful for any person to enter upon any such banks, land or ground, as aforesaid, within the County of Lincoln, and to kill, destroy, and carry away in the day time, to his or their own use, any conies so found upon any such, doing as little damage as may be to the owner or tenant."

<small>PRESERVATION OF SEA BANKS.</small>

<small>5 Geo. III, c. 14, 1765.</small>

<small>RABBITS.</small>

This Act was repealed by the 7 & 8, Geo. II, c 27, but a similar clause was re-enacted in the 24 & 25 Vict., c. 96, sec. 17, which runs as follows:—" Provided that nothing in this section contained shall affect any person taking or killing in the day time any rabbits on any sea bank or river bank in the County of Lincoln so far as the tide shall extend or within one furlong of such bank."

<small>24 & 25 Vict., c. 27.</small>

It is also forbidden under the laws of the Court of Sewers to keep rabbits anywhere near the banks. Thus, by an order of the Court, sitting at Boston, made in 1750, two occupiers of land at Freiston were presented, as keeping rabbits so near the sea bank as to do damage thereto, and were ordered to destroy the rabbits and restore the damage done to the bank, under a penalty of £10.

<small>Minutes. Court of Sewers. 5th July, 1750.</small>

In the Deeping Fen Act of 1856, a penalty of 40/- is provided for any person who shall be convicted of knowingly permitting any rabbits or geese to be upon any of the banks or forelands belonging to Deeping Fen. It is also forbidden that horses or cattle should be allowed to go on to the banks, and orders have been made to this effect, from time to time, A presentment having been made that cer-

<small>19 Vict., c. 65. 1856.</small>

<small>HORSES ON THE BANKS.</small>

<small>Minutes. Court of Sewers. Jan., 1813</small>

tain banks had been damaged by horses and carts using the same, the dykereeves were ordered to put up stop gates, to prevent this. The laws, even in olden times, were very stringent as to the preservation of the banks. Swine were not allowed to go upon them, unless they were ringed, under a penalty of one penny—equal to a shilling of our money. In case of a breach, the Sheriff was authorised to impress diggers and labourers for repairing the embankments. A terrible penalty for neglect is mentioned by Harrison, in his preface to *Hollinshed's Chronicle*, who says, that " such as having walls or banks near unto the sea, and do suffer the same to decay, after convenient admonition, whereby the water entereth and drowneth up the country, are by a certain ancient custom apprehended, condemned, and *staked in the breach*, where they remain for ever a parcel of the new wall that is to be made upon them, as I have heard reported."

Yet important as the preservation of these ramparts is to the security of the country, perhaps little thought is given by the occupier of the land as he pursues his daily calling, as to how much he owes to these works of the ancient Romans. Custom makes all things common ; and yet when the danger comes the sturdy independence and self-help, so characteristic of the Fenmen, is called forth to the fullest extent.

" No one has ever seen a fen bank break without honouring the stern quiet temper which there is in the fen men, when the north-easter is blowing above, the spring tide roaring outside, the brimming tide-way lapping up to the dyke top, or flying over in sheets of spray ; when round the one fatal thread which is trickling over the dyke, or worse, through some forgotten rat hole in its side, hundreds of men are clustered, without tumult, without complaint, marshalled under their employers, fighting the brute powers of nature, not for their employer's sake alone, but for the sake of their own year's labour, and their own year's bread. The sheep have been driven off the land below : the cattle stand, ranged shivering on high dykes inland : they will be saved in punts, if the worst befall, but a hundred spades, wielded by practised hands, cannot stop that tiny rat hole. The trickle becomes a rush, the rush a roaring waterfall. The dyke top trembles—gives. The men make efforts, desperate, dangerous, as of sailors in a wreck, with faggots, hurdles, sedge, turf; but the bank will break, and slowly they draw off, sullen, but uncomplaining ; beaten but not conquered. A new cry rises among them. Up, to save yonder sluice; that will save yonder lode; that again yonder farm; that again some other lode, some other farm, far back inland, but guessed at instantly by men who have studied from their youth, as the necessity of their existence, the labyrinthine drainage of lands which are all below the water level, and where the inner lands in many cases are lower still than those outside.

"So they hurry away to the nearest farms; the teams are harnessed, the waggons filled, and drawn down and emptied; the beer cans go round cheerily, and the men work with a sort of savage joy at being able to do something, if not all, and stop the sluice on which so much depends. As for the outer land, it is gone past hope; through the breach pours a roaring salt cataract, digging out a hole on the inside of the bank, which remains as a deep sullen pond for years to come. Hundreds, thousands of pounds are lost already, past all hope. Be it so, then. At the next neap tide perhaps they will be able to mend the dyke, and pump the water out; and begin again, beaten but not conquered, the same everlasting fight with wind and wave which their forefathers have waged for now 1800 years."

Another telling description of the breaking of a bank in the Fens will be found in George Manville Fen's *Dick o' the Fens*, in which the fen scenery and surroundings are very vividly and truthfully described.

The principle on which the drainage of the Fens was originally designed was that of gravitation, but, as in process of time the peat subsided, it became necessary to supplement this by steam power. Further details of the works of drainage, and of the constitution of the various Commissions which have the control over them, will be given in connection with the history of each Level. The reclamation of the Fens, and their present wonderfully fertile condition, is due to the ingenuity and perseverance of their inhabitants, aided by the skill of the most talented engineers who have lived during the last hundred years. During this period nearly every engineer of eminence has left his mark on some part of this great level, but prominently above all stands the name of John Rennie. Smeaton, the engineer of the Eddystone Lighthouse; Telford, the great road maker and bridge builder; Labelye, the designer of the old Westminster Bridge; Mylne, the builder of old Blackfriars Bridge; Cubitt, Brunel, Walker, Robert Stephenson, Hawkesley, Hawkshaw and Coode, have all been called in at various times; and even now it is only by the constant and vigilant attention of skilled men that the Fens are preserved. The ruin and devastation, the long and costly litigation, and the ultimate heavy tax on the land, caused by the Middle Level inundation in Norfolk, is a sad instance of the serious consequences arising from neglect, and shows how dependent is the preservation of the land on the skill and attention of the engineer.

FEN DRAINAGE.

CHAPTER 13.

ENGINEERS ENGAGED IN THE FENS.

The change that has come over the Fenland is thus vividly described by a modern writer. "The Fens, upon which our Danish fore-elders looked from their upland homes, and into which perhaps they sometimes descended for purposes of plunder, are no more. The vast mere, studded with the island homes of English Colonists

THE FENLAND BEFORE AND AFTER RECLAMATION.

Streatfeild's *Lincolnshire and the Danes*.

which stretched from Horncastle and Spilsby to Ramsey and Huntingdon has disappeared, and given place to one of the richest agricultural districts in England. As we contemplate the never ending fields of corn, and mustard, and potato in our railway journey from Huntingdon to Firsby, we can scarcely repress a sigh after the beds of osier and sedge, which were so much more natural, if far less profitable. We, perhaps, confess that things are better as they are; yet we cannot dissemble our regret at the change. Gladly would we recall the water fowl that have taken their flight from these regions, never to return, save in the form of a rare and occasional visitant, coming, we may fancy, as the representative of an exiled race, to weep over the progress of the plough, and then too often to be ruthlessly butchered by the gun: an abomination of desolation unknown to the swans and ruffs and oyster-catchers of happier days, when bird-stuffers and museums were as yet unknown. Again, as we picture to ourselves the lovely insects, which, after swarming for ages amid the willows and water plants of Lincolnshire, have become lost, not only to the county but to England, within the memory of living man; or when in some rich herbarium we examine the faded specimens of aquatic plants, whose place in the British Isles knows them now no more, how can we help longing to look out upon the scene that met the eye of Asgeir, Askr, and Hundolf, as they gazed from their new abodes over Stickenai, and Sibolsey to Botulfston and Swinesheafod beyond? But while much, very much, has gone and much more is going, it is a thought full of interest that so many natural objects remain to connect the present with the past. As we gather the wayside flowers there is pleasure in recollecting that they are sprung from those which Britons, Romans, Saxons, and Danes have plucked before us. As we wander through the woods that still remain, is there no interest in the thought that where the Englishman now shoots the rabbit and the pheasant, our rude forefathers hunted the wild boar and waged hereditary warfare on the wolf? It may be mere sentiment, but as we hear the shrill whistle of the curlew, or watch the marshalled ranks of wild geese, as they fly from the salt marsh to the Wolds we find pleasure in the remembrance that Geirmund and Ulfric saw the same sights a thousand years ago. It may be mere sentiment, yet it is sentiment springing from the loving sympathy that knits one generation to another, and that forms a bond between man and the world of nature that ministers to his wants."

CHAPTER II.

THE ORIGIN AND CONSTITUTION OF THE COURT OF SEWERS.

UNTIL the reign of Henry the VIII, the watercourses and sea banks of the country may be said to have been without any special protection, and great loss was frequently incurred by the eruption of the tides through neglected banks, and by the flooding of the country, owing to obstructions in the rivers caused either by accumulation of deposit, or by weirs and mill dams placed across them by persons for their own profit and advantage. The difficulty and uncertainty of obtaining redress by proceedings at common law led generally to an appeal to the King, for "our ancient monarchs were much interested in preserving their dominions from the ravages of the sea, and their subjects were as careful to second their designs by keeping up a system of drainage. Accordingly, on the one hand, it is to be found in our legal history, that it was not only the custom of the Kings of England, but their duty also, to save and defend the realm against the sea, as well as against enemies, so that it should neither be drowned nor wasted; and, on the other, that to stop the water channels which were made from time to time, for public or private convenience, was a grievous offence punishable by action or indictment, according to the nature of the wrong; that it was held that the King's subjects ought by the common law to have their passage through the realm by bridges and highways in safety; so that if the sea walls were broken, or the sewers and gutters not secured, that the fresh waters might have their direct course, the King was empowered to grant a commission to enquire into and hear and determine the defaults." Again, Fitzherbert says, that "Royal Commissions were granted when the sea walls were broken, or when the sewers and gutters were in need of repairs so that the fresh waters could not have their courses; and that the Commissions in question issued, because the King was bound of right so to keep his kingdom against the sea, as that it were not drowned, or wasted, and also to provide that his subjects should pass through the kingdom with safety."

By Magna Charta it was provided that no town, nor freeman, should be distrained to make bridges or banks, but such as of old time and of right had been accustomed to do so. By which it

<small>DUTIES OF THE CROWN WITH REGARD TO RIVERS AND DRAINS.</small>

<small>Callis.</small>

<small>Woolrych's *Law of Sewers*.</small>

appears that the maintaining of the sea defences had been considered a special grievance by those who had been distrained for their repairs.

<small>EARLY COMMISSIONERS OF SEWERS.</small>

The Commissions, issued by the King, consisted of two or more persons holding either a judicial position in the kingdom, or of considerable standing, who were directed to visit the locality and to hear all complaints, and had power to levy fines and make orders for the necessary works to be done for repairing and maintaining the sea banks, and cleansing and keeping open the sewers. They were issued by virtue of the King's prerogative at common law, until the reign of Henry VI, when it was enacted by Parliament that, considering the great damage and losses which had happened by the great inundation of waters in divers parts of the realm—Lincolnshire being particularly mentioned—and that much greater damage would be likely to ensue if remedy were not speedily provided, that during the ten years next ensuing several Commissions of Sewers should be made to divers persons by the Chancellor of England for the time being, who were to enquire as to the defaulters to repair the sea banks, and make such orders as they deemed necessary, with power to fine and distrain those who refused to obey them.

<small>6 Henry VI, C 5. 1428.</small>

<small>THE BILL OF SEWERS. 23 Henry VIII, C 5. 1531.</small>

These Commissions were renewed by succeeding Parliaments until the sixth year of Henry the VIII, when they were declared to endure for ever, and the Chancellor was invested with perpetual authority to grant such Commissions wherever need should require. This Act was incorporated with another, passed in the 23rd year of the same reign, called *The Bill of Sewers*, in which all the former enactments were contained; and although some alterations and additions were made in the reigns of Edward VI and Queen Elizabeth, yet the Act passed in the reign of Henry VIII still continues as the chief structure on which the powers and duties of Commissions of Sewers have been reared. In the reign of William IV several alterations were made in the original enactment, to adapt its working to modern times; but the principle of its original constitution remained unaltered.

<small>3 & 4 William IV, C 22. 1833.</small>

The purpose for which the Court was created was the preservation of marsh and low lands, the maintenance of the sea banks and other defences, and the removal of impediments and obstructions made in the streams or sewers by the erection of mills, mill-dams, weirs, gates, &c. It was invested with jurisdiction over "all walls, fences, ditches, banks, gutters, gates, sewers, callies, ponds, bridges, rivers, streams, water courses, &c."

<small>SEWER.</small>

The word *Sewer* in modern times has a much more restricted, if not different, meaning attached to it than that originally intended. The word is now invariably associated with the disposal of the refuse water from dwelling houses and towns; whereas formerly, it was applied to water courses and streams in general. Authorities differ as to the derivation of the word, the opinion of Sergeant Callis, the great authority on the Law of Sewers, being that it was the diminutive of a river. Others tracing it to a corruption of the word *issue*; or *seoir*, to sit, and *eau*, water; or to the words *sea* and *mere*.

The word *Gowt, Gote, Goyt,* or *Goat*, which is of frequent occurence and may also be considered as peculiar to fens and marshes, is used to express a construction in connection with drainage, as for instance, Anton's Gowt, Slippery Gowt. The word is derived from the Saxon, and is defined by Callis to be " an engine erected and built with percullesses and doors of timber, stone, or brick." Its use is said by the same authority to be two-fold: the first to cause fresh water which has descended on low grounds to be let out through them into some creek of the sea; and the second, to return back salt water direct, which during some great floods of the sea may have flowed in upon the land. These structures are now generally known as *Sluices*, and consist of a culvert passing through a bank, and provided with doors which allow the inland water to flow out and prevent the river or sea water from flowing in and flooding the land inside the bank.

GOTES.

Romney Marsh, a tract of land in the county of Kent, possesses the distinction of having first drawn up any definite rules for the guidance of Commissions of Sewers, which formed a precedent for the custom of all other fens and marshes. Nearly all the Commissions, and even the statute of Henry VIII, direct that the laws and customs of the Commissioners are to be made after the " laws and customs of Romney Marsh." Thus also, at the building of the Grand Sluice at Boston, by May Hake, in the reign of Henry VII, assessment was made to raise the money, and the same was ordered to be levied " according to the laws of Romney Marsh," whence also were derived the offices of *Bailiff, Jurats,* and *Levellers*. These laws were drawn up by Sir Henry de Bathe, a judge in the reign of Henry III; and Lord Coke observed, " that not only those parts of Kent, but all England receive light and direction from those laws."

THE LAWS OF ROMNEY MARSH.

The banks and sewers of Romney Marsh were originally placed under the care of 24 Jurats or Marshmen, chosen by the commoners, and sworn to do their duty. Their origin and powers were derived from a charter which had been granted by the King. These powers not being well defined, and opposition having arisen as to the order made, Sir Henry de Bathe and two other Commissioners were empowered by King Henry III to enquire into the matter. At the request of the *Council of the Commonalty of the Marsh*, these Commissioners made and constituted six ordinances for the future good management of the Marsh, of which the following is a summary:—

1. Twelve men were to be chosen, who, after being sworn, were to measure the sea banks, the measure being the perch of 20 feet. By the same measure all the land and tenements subject to danger in the level were also to be measured. This being done, the 24 existing Jurats were to set off the several portions along the bank, and to appoint to every owner his share, which he should be bound to repair according to the proportion of acres subject to danger.
2. On danger of a breach of the banks, the Jurats were to meet together and view the banks, and determine to whom the defence of the same should be assigned.
3. The Bailiff of the Marsh was then to give notice to the persons liable to do the work within the time assigned by the Jurats; and on default of their doing as ordered, the Bailiff was to make good the repairs, and the defaulter to be called upon to pay double the charge incurred; the sum to be recoverable by a distress on lands situate within the marsh.
4. When land was held in partnership, the Jurats were to determine the portion to be repaired by each partner, and in default of any one partner to do the work assigned to him, the work was to be done by the other partner, who would hold the land of the defaulter till double the cost incurred was repaid.
5. In case of all the partners being negligent, then the Bailiff was to do the work, and recover double the cost, by distraint if necessary.
6. That all the lands in the level should be kept and maintained against the violence of the sea, and the floods of the fresh waters, with banks and sewers, by the oath and consideration of 24 Jurats, at the least, for their preservation, as anciently had been the custom.

At a subsequent Commission, issued by King Edward I, it was ordered that the Bailiff of the Level should be elected "by the lords of the towns lying therein or their attornies," and that the Bailiff so chosen should be a person residing and having lands in the level.

In spite of these ordinances the maintenance of the banks was continually neglected, and floods occurred; those who were most disposed to do the work knowing that, by the carelessness and neglect of their neighbours, their own lands were still liable to be drowned.

THE COURT OF SEWERS.

Notices of several of the Commissions issued by the Crown from time to time, for the purpose of preserving the sea banks in Lincolnshire, and for keeping open the various sewers and watercourses and maintaining the gates and sea defences, have been already given in the introductory chapter. It is therefore unnecessary to refer to them again.

The Court of Sewers, as now constituted, consists of persons holding freehold property in any part of the county to which the Commission belongs, and who have qualified themselves by taking the necessary oaths.

Persons qualified must, by the Act of William IV, be in possession of property in the county in which they shall act as Commissioners, in their own right or that of their wives, of the yearly value of £100; or of lands held for a term of years of the clear yearly value of £200; or be heirs apparent to a person possessed of freehold property of the clear value of £200; or a leaseholder of an estate for 21 years, of which 10 years are unexpired, of the yearly value of £200; or the agent of qualified persons or bodies corporate holding freehold property of the yearly value of £300. Every Commissioner before he can act must take an oath in the form set out in the statute of Henry VIII, to perform his duties faithfully, and also as to his proper qualification. The Mayor, Aldermen and Burgesses of a Corporate town within the Level to which the Commission relates are *ex-officio* members of the Court.

It will be observed that the word *Court* is used. The proceedings are not purely ministerial, but are judicial, and, as Callis observes, "their Court is one of record, and an eminent Court of record," and so Lord Coke, when writing of courts, enumerates among them "The Court of Commissioners of Sewers."

In former times the Commissions only lasted for ten years, or until the demise of the reigning sovereign. The commission is now, by the provisions of 24 & 25 Vict. c. 133, a perpetual body, fresh members being added when necessary by an application made by the Court to the Lord Chancellor.

The Court may meet at such times as its members think fit, but ten days notice of the intended meeting must be given by advertisement in a newspaper of the county. Emergency meetings may be held on the requisition of the Clerk and two members of the Court. Three members form a Court, except when the construction of new works is under consideration, when six are required, and at each meeting those present elect their chairman. A payment of 4s. is allowed to each member who attends the Court, to cover his expenses.

The Court has power to direct the sheriff to summon a jury "to enquire of or concerning any of the matters and things authorised and directed to be enquired into, under any of the Acts and Laws of Sewers of old time accustomed, and to administer oaths to such jury."

The first duty of a new Commission was to summon a jury, who were to make a presentment as to the persons liable to maintain and repair, or to contribute towards the repair and maintenance of all defences, banks, and other works under their jurisdiction ; and the verdict of such jury, once made, held good during the whole time of the existence of the Commission.

The Commissioners have power to levy rates, as occasion may require, for every distinct level, valley, or district ; and to appoint any surveyors, collectors, treasurers, and other officers for such district. This is the wording of the Act, but the ordinary course of proceeding in this district is for each parish to appoint two officers, called *Dykereeves*, to lay and collect the necessary rates and maintain the banks and sewers,—and these appointments, and all that relates to them, are subject to the approval of the Court. The Dykereeves present their accounts to the vestry of the parish, at Easter. For the general expenses of the Court a call is made on the dykereeves of the several parishes, in proportion to the amount at which the parish is assessed to the rate. Surveyors are appointed by the Court itself, who have the general supervision of the works, and, when defects exist, their duty is to make a presentment to the Court, which then orders the Dykereeves of the parishes, in which the work is situated, at once to amend and repair the same and to levy rates for payment of the cost.

RIDING JURIES.

Court of Sewers Minutes, 24 June, 1816 to July, 1818.

In the Kirton and Skirbeck Wapentakes, a *Riding Jury* used annually to make an inspection of the sea banks and works of drainage, and report to the Court as to any defects. They were allowed 10s. per day for horse hire and expenses in their own wapentake, and 14s., if they attended out of it. By an order of Court made in 1818, Dykereeves and Jurors were allowed sums varying from 4s.6d. to 6s., for their expenses at the Court, according to the distance of their parish therefrom.

PROPERTY LIABLE TO RATES

It has been held that the persons liable to be rated to the Sewers' rates are those whose property, situate within the Commission derives benefit or avoids danger from the execution of the works, and that this principle was affirmed by the Act of Henry VIII, and has been preserved in all subsequent statutes ; and therefore the rate is leviable according to the value of the property, and not according to its superficial extent, houses and similar property being therefore rateable.

Court of Sewers, 23 April, 1884.

The practice has, however, always been in this district, up to recent times, to make the rate an acre rate. In 1883, when some considerable repairs were required to the bank in Skirbeck Quarter, Counsel's opinion was taken as to whether the rate ought to be levied on the assessment of the several parishes over which the charge was spread, instead of making it an acre rate, and on this opinion the Dykereeves were ordered to have the rate made on the assessment.

In carrying out works, the Commissioners are bound to have the same executed in a skilful manner and to take all reasonable precautions to prevent damage being done to other persons. It has been held that even where Commissioners are a public body, bound to discharge a public duty without reward and without funds, they are liable for the negligence of those whom they employ. This was decided in the celebrated case of the failure of the Middle Level Sluice and consequent inundation, (*Coe v. Wise*). The employment of a competent contractor will not free the Commissioners from liability, but they must be able to show that the work was skilfully designed and carried out under the direction of a qualified superintendent, and that there was no negligence.

[margin: LIABILITIES OF THE COMMISSIONERS.]

The obligation to maintain the sea banks was originally on those whose lands adjoin the sea, and this was called the *Custom of Frontagers*. This duty can only be put off by showing that some other persons are bound by prescription, or otherwise. This obligation attaches to some lands by the nature of their tenure, although such lands may not be near the sea. The difficulty, however, of dealing with individual liabilities, when the safety of a whole Level depends on immediate action, has in some cases thrown the obligation of repairs, by custom, on the whole township. A few instances still remain in this county in which individual proprietors are liable; and in case such persons do not maintain the particular banks, sluices, or sewers for which they are liable, after seven days' notice from the surveyor or dikereeve, the court may order the same to be done, and the expenses can then be recovered by distress.

[margin: OWNERSHIP AND MAINTENANCE OF THE SEA BANKS.]

At the time of the great tide of 1810, when the whole level was inundated, the Court of Sewers, sitting at Boston, submitted a case to Sergeant Lea and Mr. Dampier, two of the most eminent Counsel of that day, "as to whether the expense of repairing the breaches in the sea bank, and also of heightening and strengthening the banks is not chargeable upon the whole level, they being found insufficient in height for the defence of the country; whether that expense must be borne by the parties only who are liable to the ordinary repairs thereof, and in particular how far the level can in the present instance be made to extend." The case was afterwards amended by an enquiry as to whether the Court had the power to charge the lands in the East Fen and the lowlands adjacent thereto, on extraordinary occasions, although those lands are in the Lindsey Division and on ordinary occasions under the jurisdiction of the Spilsby Court.

[margin: Boston Court of Sewers.Minutes 13 Nov., 1810.]

Acting on the advice given by Counsel, the Court spread the charge over the whole level of the Wapentakes of Skirbeck and Kirton, the extent of land liable and the proportion in which the money required should be paid being settled by a jury for each Wapentake, summoned by the Sheriff, at the request of the Court, for that purpose.

In 1883 on some extensive repairs being done to the bank in Skirbeck Quarter, which were deemed by the Court to be extraor-

[margin: Boston Court of Sewers.Minutes 18 Aug., 1883.]

dinary, and not such as persons by prescription could fairly be liable to, an order was made that the cost of the work of reparation be paid by the entire district which would be liable to be damaged by a breach.

<small>ORDERS MAKING BANKS REPAIRABLE BY PARISH.</small>

Orders have also been made by the Court setting aside the individual liability of owners in certain parishes, and making the maintenance of the banks a charge on the whole parish. Thus, a petition having been presented to the Court as to the method of repairing the sea banks in Algarkirk and Fosdyke, a Commission was appointed to view the banks and report. They made a presentment to the following effect. That these banks were known as 'best' and 'worst' banks and had been maintained on all ordinary occasions at the cost of the owners of land, in the proportion of 7 feet of the best banks, and 1 foot of the worst, to every acre of land, and to every cottage having less than an acre attached thereto; that by a verdict made in 1800 the proportion had been set out by boundary posts, but that these had all been displaced, owing to the works rendered necessary by the great tide of 1810; that by this system it was found very inconvenient and difficult to get repairs executed, and to enforce payment by the parties charged with the same; and that it was desirable that the whole system should be changed, and that, for the future, on all ordinary occasions, the banks should be repaired by the landowners chargeable with the dykereeve rate, by an equal rate in proportion to their holdings, to which course also the Vestries of the parishes had offered no objection. The Court accordingly ordered that this presentment should be adopted and made a law of Sewers.

<small>Court of Sewers. Minutes. March 19, 1818.</small>

<small>OWNERSHIP OF THE SEA BANKS.</small>

As regards the ownership of of the banks, Callis says, that "the ownership of a bank of the sea belongs to him whose grounds are next adjoining, according to the principle adopted concerning highways." This ownership, of course, is only a limited one. The freehold belongs to the frontager or other person entitled thereto, and all advantages and privileges, as the herbage of the bank, &c., are his; but the Court of Sewers has complete control over the bank, and the owner cannot do any act to injure the safety or stability of the same. The custom with respect to the herbage of the banks is various. There can be no doubt that originally, where the frontager was liable to repair, this herbage naturally belonged to him; but when this obligation of repair was shifted to the township or parish, the privileges attaching, in most cases, went with it, as a means, partly, of defraying the expense of the maintenance of the banks. In many parishes the grass on the banks is regularly let, and the proceeds carried to the credit of the parish fund; in others the banks have been treated as common or waste land and sold under *Inclosure Awards*; while again, in other parishes the frontagers still continue to exercise this right. Custom has operated so long in each case as to have created a right.

A frontager liable for the repair of a sea bank, which is under the jurisdiction of the Court, can only be made to carry out reasonable repairs, and is only liable for damage due to negligence on the part of himself or his predecessors. He cannot be held answerable for damage caused by extraordinary high tides, tempests, or floods. During an extraordinary storm and high tide which occurred in January, 1881, considerable damage was done to a sea wall in the Fobbing Level in Essex. The owner of the land repaired the sea bank, under an order of the Court of Sewers, and then sued the Court for the expenses incurred in so doing. Evidence was given to show that the owners of this land had, from time to time, repaired this bank; and that, about seven years previously, on an order of the Court, in common with other frontagers, they had raised the height of the bank. It was held that the evidence of these repairs did not make the owner of the land liable to a large and indefinite liability, such as that caused by extraordinary tides and floods, but only to damage due to ordinary causes and negligence.

DAMAGE CAUSED BY STORMS AND HIGH TIDES.

Regina v. Commissioners of Sewers for Fobbing Level.

The Court of Sewers has not a general jurisdiction over all sea banks, simply because they are a means of defending the land from the invasion of the sea, but only over banks which have been placed specially under their control. A case bearing on this was tried at the Norfolk Summer Assizes of 1885, where an action was brought against an owner of land to recover damages for loss sustained from the flowing of the tide through a gap in the bank, and, a nonsuit being entered, this was appealed against in the Queen's Bench Division, in December 1885, and confirmed ; and, on being carried to the Court of Appeal, in the following March, it was again upheld. The facts of the case were as follows. The defendant in the case was the owner of land near Lynn, abutting on the river Nar, at its junction with the Ouse. On this land was an old river bank, which was situated some distance back from the river, an outer bank having been erected at the same time nearer the river. The defendant, or his tenant, had for the purpose of his business, cut through this inner bank, and made a considerable opening in it. In March, 1883, there occurred an extraordinary high tide in the river Ouse, which was higher than any tide known within the memory of living man. The water poured through the opening and flooded the premises of the plaintiffs, doing very considerable damage. The plaintiffs contended (1) That the inner bank was an ancient bank, erected for the protection of the adjacent lands, which the owner of the land was bound to maintain for the benefit of the adjoining owners ; or at least to leave in an undamaged condition. (2) That the bank was vested in the Court of Sewers, and that, therefore, the act of the defendant, on the authority of the case, *Attorney General v. Tomline*, in cutting through it was actionable. At the trial the Judge ruled that no sufficient evidence was given to connect the

West Norfolk Manure Company v. Archdale.

defendant with the act complained of. The only evidence as to the liability to re pair was that the tenant had previously done repairs, which was held to be insufficient. Upon the question of this bank's being under the control of the Court of Sewers, the evidence was also held to be insufficient, no presentment of this bank having been produced. The only evidence given was that a Commission had issued, vesting the sea defences of Norfolk in the Commissioners. There was, however, in this case an outside bank, the date of which was unknown, and which might have been the ancient bank. He, therefore, withdrew the case from the jury, and entered a nonsuit. On the appeal, the Judge held that the plaintiff's case rested on two alternatives, either that the bank was an ancient bank, which the defendant was bound to maintain *ratione tenuræ*, or that the bank was under the jurisdiction of the Commissioners of Sewers. Upon the first point the evidence was not sufficient; and on the second it was held that the mere fact that the bank was an old one was not sufficient to bring it within the jurisdiction of the Commissioners, there being no evidence of any exercise of jurisdiction over it. The 47th section of the Act of 4 William IV only showed what banks the Commissioners might, if the proper steps were taken, bring within their jurisdiction: so that a protecting bank does not *ipso facto* vest in the Commissioners.

Throughout the greater part of South Lincolnshire sea banks have been erected outside the old Roman bank, either by private owners or by special Acts obtained by the parishes. The repair of these banks does not come under the jurisdiction of the Court. When the obligation to maintain these banks is not defined under the powers by which they were erected, disputes have arisen as to *Hudson v. Tabor* the liability of one frontager to another for damage caused by neglect. Formerly the liability to repair sea banks and defences against the sea was regarded as a public duty, but a case was decided otherwise in 1876. The land of a proprietor in Essex, abutting on a tidal creek, was flooded during an extraordinary high tide, and he brought an action against an adjoining frontager, for having neglected to maintain his portion of the bank. At the trial there were no evidence to show that the defendant was bound by prescription to repair the bank, and the Court held that the mere fact of each owner having for his own protection kept up the wall did not establish a liability to do so for the protection of an adjoining owner, and that the length of time during which such repairs had continued added nothing to the argument. The plaintiff also contended that as it was the duty of the Crown to protect lands adjoining the sea from being flooded, that therefore the liability must be capable of enforcement: but the Court held that there was no obligation at common law to repair, and that as this bank was not under the jurisdiction of the Court of Sewers, the Crown, through the Court, could not be called on to order the bank to be maintained. While this case settles that a frontager is not bound, at common law, to maintain his portion of a sea bank, and that he is not necessarily responsible for injury caused to the adjoining lands by a breach, it has, on the other hand, been decided that if injury arises from interference with any natural barrier, such as a bank of shingle, by which interference damage is caused by the tide or waves, the person causing such damage will be liable, and that it is the duty of the Crown to afford protection to the land of the subject. A clear distinction in this case is drawn between *artificial* and *natural* barriers. *Attorney General v. Tomline.*

Where the obligation is imposed, either by any special enactment of the legislature or by prescription, on Commissioners, or others, to maintain sea or river banks against floods, if the damage is caused by extraordinary floods, and no negligence can be shown, and if all reasonable precautions have been taken, there will be no liability as to damage caused by such floods. During a flood in the river Glen, in 1872, a breach of the bank occurred, and a large area of land was inundated. An action was brought to recover damages against the Black Sluice Commissioners, the parties liable for the maintenance of the bank. The case was tried at the Lincoln Spring Assizes in 1873. The question left to the jury was, whether the bank in question was in a fit and proper condition to protect the lands from such floods as might reasonably be contemplated. The jury finding in the affirmative, the verdict was recorded for the defendants, and was afterwards held good on appeal. On the other hand, in the case of a breach which occurred in the banks of the South Delph, during an unusual flood in the river Witham, the Great Northern Railway Company were found liable for the damage caused, the evidence satisfying the jury, at the Lincoln Assizes, where the case was tried, that the liability to repair the bank rested on them; that repairs which had been executed by the Company had not been done in a skilful manner; and that the breach was not due to the backing up of water owing to the default of the river Commissioners. On appeal, this verdict was sustained. *Hardwick v. Wyles.* *Cawdron v. Great Northern Railway Company.*

In connection with the ownership of the sea banks it will not be out of place to refer to the great dispute which took place in the reign of Edward III, between the Abbots of Peterborough and Swineshead, as to the proprietorship of the marsh land on the exterior of the banks of Bicker Haven, which accreted by the deposition of the alluvium washed up by the tides, a process which was evidently going on rapidly in those days. The various commissions, arbitrations and trials concerning this suit were spread over a period of 25 years, and it was only finally settled by an appeal to Parliament. The contention appears to have been as to the ownership of certain marshes in Gosberton (part of Bicker Haven) which had accreted, and which lay in front of the manor of the Abbot

OWNERSHIP OF LANDS COVERED BY THE TIDE.

of Swineshead, on which ground he claimed it. The Abbot of Peterborough, on the other hand, set up a claim, because, although the land lay in front of the Abbot of Swineshead's Manor, it was separated from it by a creek, the accretion having gradually extended from the Manor of Peterborough in a lateral direction, so as to overlap the land of the adjoining proprietor. The following is an account of the commencement of the proceedings:—"*Memorandum.* That in the year of our Lord MCCCXLII, 16 Edward III, the Abbot of Swinesheved and Sir Nicholas de Ry, Knight, did implead the Abbot of Peterborough for CCCXL acres of marsh, with the appurtenances, in Gosberchirche, *viz.*, the Abbot of Swinesheved for CC and Sir Nicholas for CXL, by two writs. And the first day of the Assizes at Lincolne was on Wednesday, being the morrow after the feast of St. Peter *ad Vincula*; at which time there came thither Gilbert de Stanford, then Celerer to the convent, John de Achirche, bailiff of the said Abbot's Mannors; together with Sir John de Wilughby, Lord of Eresby; Sir John de Kirketon, and Sir Saier de Rochford, knights; John de Multon, parson of Skirbek, as also divers others of the said Abbot's Counsel. And because the defence of this suit seemed difficult and costly to the Abbot, in regard that his adversaries had privately and subtilly made the whole country against him, especially the Wapentake of Kirketon, he submitted to an amicable treaty of peace, on the day preceding the assize, the place of their meeting being in the chapter house of Lincolne: at which treaty, in the presence of Sir Nicholas de Cantilupe (who was the principal mediator betwixt them, as a friend to both sides) and other knights and friends, above specified, the said Abbot of Swynesheved and Sir Nicholas de Ry did set forth their claim in that marsh; affirming that it did belong to them by right, by the custom of the country; because that it was increased and grown to their own ancient marshes by addition of sand which the sea had by its flowings cast up; insomuch as by that means coming to be firm land, they said that they ought to enjoy it, as far as Salten Ee; and in regard that the said Abbot of Peterborough had possessed himself thereof, contrary to right, and against the said custom, they had brought the assize of *novel disseizin* in form aforesaid. Whereunto the Counsel for the Abbot of Peterborough answered that the custom of this province of Holand, so stated by the plaintiffs, ought thus to be understood and qualified, *viz.*, that when, by such addition of any silt or sand, there should happen an increase of land, and, by the sea's leaving thereof, become firm ground, it ought to belong unto him to whose firm and solid ground it first joined itself, without any respect whether it grew directly to it, or at one side. And they further said that the before specified marsh did originally join itself to the ancient marsh of the said Abbot of Peterborough, whereof that monastery had been seized

Dugdale's Embanking and Draining.

time beyond memory, as it appeared by Domesday Book, where it is recorded that the Abbot of Peterborough had XVI salt pans in Donington; moreover, in the Charter of King Richard I, there were confirmed to the said Abbot three carucates of land, with the salt pans and pastures, and all their appurtenances, in Holland; so that the said soil, increasing little by little, ought not to belong to the Abbot of Swinesheved and Sir Nicholas, according to the custom of the country; because that a certain part of Salten Ee, which was not then dry land, did lye betwixt the old marsh belonging to the said Abbot of Swinesheved and Sir Nicholas, and the marsh whereof they pretended to be disseized; which part of Salten Ee could not at all be drained; because that the fresh waters used to run through that place from the parts of Kesteven to the sea."

It will be unnecessary to follow the case through all its various stages. The final settlement was made by six arbitrators who awarded that the Abbot of Peterborough was to pay a certain sum of money to the others, and they in return were to give up all their right to the marsh. "And as to the future increase of ground, which might happen to either party, that it should be enjoyed by him to whose land it did lie most contiguous." And this was confirmed by the Parliament which sat in the seventeenth year of the reign of King Edward III. The question was again raised and was not finally settled till the 41st year of King Edward's reign, " when was that memorable verdict touching the customs of the country, that the lords of manors adjoining to the sea should enjoy the land which is raised by silt and sand, which the tides do cast up."

It is now held that the title to the fore-shore, between high and low water mark, is in the Crown, the department charged with its care being the Board of Trade. By ancient grant, charter, or prescription, it may have become vested in the subject, and purchases from the Crown are now frequently made.

Land gradually and imperceptibly formed by alluvium, until its surface reaches above the level of ordinary high water, becomes the property of the owner of the land to which it is attached.

The Court of Sewers has power, besides the maintenance of old and existing defences, to improve existing works, when it is necessary for the more effectually defending and securing any lands within the jurisdiction of the Court, against the irruption or overflowing of the sea, or the draining and carrying off of the superfluous waters. When the cost of such works exceeds £1000, plans and estimates must be prepared and notice given by advertisement for two months previous to the order being made; notices, also, must be affixed to the church doors of the parishes, for three successive Sundays. If the proprietors of half the rateable area dissent, the Commissioners cannot proceed with the work. If there is no such dissent, the Court can borrow money for the execution

POWER OF COURT OF SEWERS TO EXECUTE WORKS.

of such works, to be repaid within a period not exceeding fourteen years.

With regard to the soil thrown out of a sewer when it is being cleaned out, widened or deepened, this may be removed by the frontager for his own use (3 and 4 William IV, c. 22, clauses 22 and 23.) But if he does not remove it within six months the Commissioners can order the owner or occupier to remove it, or they can themselves remove or dispose of it.

FORMATION OF NEW COURTS OF SEWERS.

Under the Land Drainage Act of 1861, Commissions of Sewers may, with the approval of the Inclosure Commissioners, be issued for districts where they have not formerly existed, if it can be shown that the state of the drainage is such as to require some controlling body to superintend the outfalls; but as the Act also gives the option between a Commission of Sewers or an Elective Drainage District, the latter method has been generally adopted in these places where the provisions of the Act have been applied.

LINCOLNSHIRE COURTS.

Thus it will be seen that the Court of Sewers is not only an ancient but a very important body of Commissioners, with responsible duties and extensive powers. They can summon juries, administer oaths, lay rates, levy fines, and issue distresses. Many of their acts are judicial, and can only be set aside by appeals to the higher courts. Before the existence of the Witham, Black Sluice, Deeping Fen, South Holland, and other Drainage Commissions, the whole of the sewers and banks in this neighbourhood were under the control and management of the Court of Sewers, and even now there are few parishes which do not, to some extent, depend on the sewers, gotes, and sluices of the Court of Sewers for their drainage.

Although there are several Courts in Lincolnshire, the Commission extends to the whole county, and the members have the right of attending and voting at any of the Courts, a privilege which is sometimes taken advantage of on important occasions, or when the appointment of a clerk or other officer is made. As a rule, however, the members confine their attendances to the Court which has jurisdiction over the neighbourhood in which they reside.

The two Courts in the division of Holland are that for the Wapentake of Skirbeck and Kirton, in the north; and of Elloe, in the south.

A full exposition of the law relating to Courts of Sewers and copies of the various Sewers Acts will be found in a work published in 1884, by Messrs. G. G. Kenedy, Recorder of Grantham, and J. S. Sanders, of the Midland Circuit.

CHAPTER III.

NORTH HOLLAND PARISHES.

NORTH HOLLAND contains the Hundreds of Skirbeck and Kirton. The Skirbeck Hundred includes all the parishes lying on the east coast, between the Witham and the Lindsey Division, known as the East Holland Towns, namely, Boston, Skirbeck, Fishtoft, Freiston, Butterwick, Leverton, Benington, Leake and Wrangle. The Kirton Hundred includes the following parishes, lying south of the Witham, and between this river and the Hammond Beck on the west, *viz.*, Algarkirk, Bicker, Brothertoft, Donington, Fosdyke, Frampton, Gosberton, Kirton, Quadring, Skirbeck Quarter, Sutterton, Swineshead, Surfleet, Wigtoft and Wyberton; also the following places, formerly extra-parochial, *viz.*, Hart's Grounds, North Forty Foot Bank, Amber Hill, Great and Little Beats, Copping Syke, Drainage Marsh, Ferry Corner Plot, The Friths, Hall Hills, Pelham's Lands, Pepper Gowt Plot, Seven Acres, Shuff Fen, Simon Weir and South of Witham. Skirbeck Hundred contains, exclusive of the Borough of Boston, 29,064 acres; Kirton Hundred 63,513 acres; and the new parochialised places 6,929 acres.

<small>SKIRBECK HUNDRED.
Map. Fig. 9.

KIRTON HUNDRED.
Map. Fig. 10.</small>

The sewers and ancient sea banks in North Holland are under the jurisdiction of the Court of Sewers for the Wapentakes, or Hundreds, of Skirbeck and Kirton, which meets at Boston. The former includes the parishes on the coast, north of the river Witham, known as the East Holland Towns, and also Friskney and Sibsey, which, although in the Lindsey Division of the County, are under the jurisdiction of the Boston Court. The fen portion of these hundreds has been withdrawn from the jurisdiction of the Court, the East and West Fens being in the *Fourth District* of the Witham Commission; and the fens in the Kirton Hundred, in the Black Sluice District.

<small>DRAINAGE AND SEA BANKS.</small>

Owing to enclosures which have been made during the present century, the ancient sea banks are now nearly all inland, the exceptions in North Holland being a short length in the parishes of Skirbeck and Skirbeck Quarter, both on the river, and part of the bank in Freiston and Wrangle.

The principal parish sewers in North Holland empty themselves either into the Hobhole, or the Maud Foster, Drain, but a few discharge their contents by sluices through the sea bank.

The drains in the Kirton Wapentake are larger and of more importance than those in the Skirbeck Hundred, and most of them have two outfalls, one into Boston Haven, or the river Welland, on the east side, and the other into the Hammond Beck on the west side, the sewers running continuously from one outfall to the other.

HAMMOND BECK.

The principal watercourse is the Hammond Beck which is probably a natural stream straightened and improved by the Romans. It is eighteen miles long. It commences at a short distance north of the Glen, in the parish of Pinchbeck, and formerly discharged direct into Boston Haven, but now falls into the Black Sluice. It forms the boundary between the fen and the high land. Its outfall into the Haven was at the point where the Parish of Boston and the Hamlet of Skirbeck Quarter join. It was formerly navigable for small boats, and a bridge was built to carry the road from Boston to Kirton over it. The remains of the old sluice and bridge were uncovered in 1835, and the arch was found to be 6ft. wide and 6ft. high. There were two pointing doors each 5ft. 6in. high and 3ft. wide. This Sluice was probably erected in 1597.

Thompson's
Boston.

The channel and banks of this stream were formerly under the jurisdiction of the Court of Sewers, and were maintained by the parishes through which it passed. Frequent references are made to its condition in the old Inquisitions of the Court of Sewers, and in 1713 the Court ordered it to be made 24 feet wide and 4 feet deep, as decreed by the *Redstone Gowt Law*. By the Act of 1765, it was transferred to the Black Sluice Commissioners, who now maintain it.

The other ancient sewers, frequently referred to, are the Risegate Eau, the Ouse Mer Lode, which formerly emptied into Bicker Haven, but now into the Risegate Eau; the 'River of Byker,' which commences at Bicker Gauntlet, and, running through the village, forms the eastern boundary of the parish of Donington, and also formerly discharged into Bicker Haven; and the old Beche drain, which forms the boundary, for part of the way, between Pinchbeck and Surfleet, and discharges into the Glen.

The Glen, (called the 'River of Surfleet,' where it passed through that parish), before it was placed under the charge of the present Commission, was under the jurisdiction of the Court of Sewers, and its banks and channel were maintained by the parishes through which it passed. It was a constant source of trouble, and frequent references were made in the old Inquisitions, to the flooding caused by neglect to maintain it in proper order.

DUGDALE.

A rather singular dispute as to the drainage of this district occurred in the reign of Edward I (1283). The Abbot of Peterborough brought an action against Ranulph de Rye and others for putting him out of possession of his freehold, consisting of 40 acres of marsh at Gosberton. The defendants pleaded in defence that eighteen years previously the sea had made a hollow in the land of the Abbot; which continuing for a long time, they afterwards drained it, and that they were justified in so doing because "the custom of that country was such that whensoever the sea did by its raging overflow any man's lands, and, meeting with any resistance, or upon its going back, waste away any of the said land, and make a hollow place, no man ought to fill up that place, but to cleanse and drain it for the common benefit of the country, and so to let it remain in the same condition that the sea first left it." The jurors, however, found that the land was "the several ground of the Abbot, in which no person without his leave had anything to do"; that a great flood had happened which broke the Abbot's bank, which breach the Abbot had repaired as was lawful for him to do, and that the said defendants had afterwards made a ditch upon the soil of the Abbot, against his leave, and excluded him from coming to the marsh. The Abbot had judgment to recover his seizin and twenty shillings damages.

COMMISSIONS OF SEWERS 1293.

In the twenty-third year of Edward I, at an Inquisition held at Gosberton, it was found that the water from the sewers in Donington ought to have a free passage into the river of Byker, which runneth to the sea (Bicker Haven), and to be opened at all times, except when there should happen an abundance of water that the sewers could not suffice, but that the province of Holand would be drowned; in such case it was to be lawful for them to stop the said sewers. It was also found that the channel of Byker ought to be repaired by the town of Byker; that the sewer of Quadring Ee ought to be repaired on one side by the town of Quadring, and on the other by the town of Gosberchirche, and thence to the sea by the town of Surflet, and that the river of Surflet (the Glen) into which the Beche did descend, ought to be 16ft. wide, and that it was then so straightened by the men of Surflet, and raised to such a height, that the water of Beche could not have its current to sea as formerly. That the Hachelode was a common sewer, and ought to be 1ft. wide at its entrance from the marsh, and, lower down, 6ft. as far as the sea, and be repaired by the town of Pinchebec till it came to the sea.

1316.

In the ninth year of the reign of Edward II, at an Inquisition held at Boston, orders were made relating to the same sewers; and, with reference to the river of Byker, that it would be proper that the town of Byker, for its own benefit and commodity of the whole country, should make a certain clow with two doors, each of them 4ft. in breadth; which clow should be always open, unless a great inundation of the sea should happen.

At the same Inquisition it was also found that the sewer called the Hammond Beck, at the South End of Boston, was obstructed by the inhabitants of that town, on the west part of the bridge, and also by the inhabitants of Skirbeck; and that it ought to be repaired by the said men of Boston.

1362.

In the thirty-fifth year of Edward III, a Commission, having made enquiry, found that "Wigtoft Gote ought to be repaired by the towns of Wygtoft and Swinesheved, that the town of Swinesheved ought to repair Swineshed Ee from the north side of Swinesheved unto Bicker Ee, that the towns of Bicker, Donington, Quadring and Gosberkirk ought to repair Bicker Ee from the beginning of Bicker to the sea, and to make it 24ft. in breadth and 6ft. in depth ; *viz.*, the town of Bicker to Bonstake, and from thence the town of Donington to Quadring, and from thence Quadring and the Commoners thereof to Gosberkirke, and Gosberkirke to the sea, and that it ought to run all the year. It was also presented that the gutter of Quadring called Augot was broken; and that it was necessary that it should be removed nearer to the sea by a hundred perches ; as also that the ditches wherein the salt water came should be stopped ; moreover, that the Gote called Sangote in Gosberkirke was ruinous and that it ought to be repaired by the owners of certain lands in Surflete and Gosberton; and that the Newgote of Surfleet ought to be repaired and made 2ft. deep, by the town of Surfleet unto Totisbrige ; and that the town of Gosberkirke ought to maintain the gutter called the Thurgote, because at that time the said town and Surflete were almost drowned by an arm of the sea, which grew by reason of the said gutter and Salten Ee." The Jurors also "presented that the sea banks and others belonging to Surflete, Gosberkirke and Quadring were too weak and low"; and the town's representatives having acknowledged before the Shire-reeve that they ought of right to repair them, "they were amerced and distrained thereto; and the town of Sotterton with all the rest were likewise amerced, because they came in by great distress."

1376.

In the forty-ninth year of Edward III, a Jury found that the towns of Wiberton, Frampton, Kirton and the West of Boston ought to repair and maintain the Edykes from the Schust to Deynboth; as also the towns of Swynesheved and Wyktofte ought to scour the sewer called Swineshed Ee from Candleby Hill to Bicker Ee. In the following year the inhabitants of Surflete acknowledged that they ought to repair a bridge in Surflete and cleanse the river of Burne (the Glen), every fourth year, from Newsende in Pinchbec Marsh, which ought to be repaired by the town of Pinchebec unto Surflet, and and from Surflet to the sea, according to a decree made by the Justices of Sewers for those parts.

From this time up to the reign of Elizabeth there is no record in *Dugdale* of any order of importance as to the banks and sewers of this part of the county. In the fifteenth year of Elizabeth's reign

1571.

an Inquisition sitting at Boston found that the Mer Lode could not convey away the water falling thereinto, and decreed that it should be scoured and made 16ft. wide and 6ft. deep, from the infall out of the Fen, unto a certain place called Elwood Elmes, by the townships of Quadring and Donington; and that from here it should be turned and made of the like breadth and depth by the inhabitants of the said town of Quadring to Gosberton Ee, and at the falling thereof into the said Ee there should be a substantial stone bridge made and erected for the public roadway, at the charges of Quadring and Donyngton, and likewise a dam at Partye Bridge; and moreover that the inhabitants of Quadring and Donington should for ever after enjoy, for the commodity of their said watercourse of Merlode, the same drain called Gosberton Ee, under the sea dyke, from the infall of Merlode thereinto. In consideration whereof it was decreed that Quadring and Donington should make another drain in Gosberkirk Ee, to stop and turn the watercourse of Rysegate from the old course towards the sea dyke at a place near Challan Bridge, where it was decreed that a bridge should be made at the charge of Quadring and Donington, and that these townships should scour a new drain to be called the Newe Ee of Surflet and Gosberkirk, which would be beneficial for the speedy conveyance of the water of Kesteven and Holand from the said old course in Rysegate Ee by the same New Ee. By a decree of Sewers, made at Helpringham three years later, it was reported that the "New Gote, set in the sea dyke of Surflet, did of a sudden, after three weeks settling thereof, sink into a quicksand, and it was ordered that the same should be made again, more substantially, and set upon a better and firmer foundation;" also that two new bridges should be erected upon the Newdike sewer at Rysgate Ee-mouth by the inhabitants of Gosberkirke and Surflete, one in Quadring up-Fen for the road coming from Westrop, and the other within the limits of Byker in Hekendale Wathe, of such height as boats might well pass under; also that one bridge over the sewer at Kyrton Fen, another at Frampton Fen, and another at Lichfield End, should be repaired by the townships and persons who of right ought to do the same, and that they should be of 12ft. in breadth and of height sufficient for boats to pass under.

The history of the Risegate Eau will be found further on, and other orders of the Court of Sewers, in the chapter on the Black Sluice.

The sewers in North Holland are divided into two classes, the first being public sewers maintained by the Dykereeves of the respective parishes out of the rates, and the other private or petty sewers, which are maintained by the frontagers.

SEWERS.

The last Inquisition, Presentment and Verdict for the wapentakes of Skirbeck and Kirton, was made in 1862. The jury, for both wapentakes, consisted of Joseph Pocklington, Algarkirk; John Ward, Boston; John H. Farr, Boston West; James Lancaster, Boston; Thomas L. Clayton, Boston West; Samuel Belton, Boston West; Joseph Perry, Boston; John Hurl, Boston; Jonathan Fox, Brothertoft; John Roberts, Wyberton; Charles Benton,

VERDICT OF 1862

Frampton; George Ward, Frampton; Robert Ownsworth, Kirton Fen; George W. Hides, Sutterton Fen; Richardson Dring, Sutterton Fen; James Sharp, Sutterton Fen; George Wadsley, Sutterton Fen; Richard Sellers, Sutterton Fen; William Wadsley, Algarkirk Fen; Jonathan Ward, Algarkirk Fen; Edward Woods Ullyatt, Algarkirk Fen; William Plant Harrison, Frithville; John Bland, Frith Bank; David Lawrence, Frith Bank; John Fountain, Kirton Fen; Frederick Cooke being then clerk of the Court, and Frederick Lyon Hopkins, chairman.

A list of the banks and sewers presented at this Inquisition will be found in the appendix. The total area of land, as determined thereat, was 20,214 acres in Skirbeck Hundred, and 30,483 acres in Kirton Wapentake.

SEA BANKS.

The sea and river banks protecting North Holland from the tides have been a constant source of trouble, and the minutes of the Court of Sewers contain numerous records of breaches, and orders made on the persons liable for repairs. Thus, in 1713, it is recorded that by the rage and violence of the spring tides, the haven banks, west of Shuff Fen, had been overflowed, and the Sheriff was asked to summon a Jury to examine the same; and again, in 1715, it was presented that the banks protecting Wildmore Fen were in a defective condition, and full of 'gooles.'

The most disastrous results to the country from breaches and overflowings of the banks were from the great tide of 1810. This occurrence was thus described at the time.

GREAT GALE OF 1810.

Boston Gazette, Nov. 13, 1810.

"On Saturday morning, about seven o'clock, it began to rain at Boston, and continued to do so throughout the day. The wind accompanied the rain impetuously from E.S.E., and gradually increased in roughness. From eleven o'clock in the day till six in the evening, it blew extremely hard; and from that hour till nine, a perfect hurricane. The consequence of this continued gale for so many hours in one point was, that the tide in the evening came in with great rapidity, and rose, half an hour before the expected time of full flood, to a height exceeding by *four inches* what it is recorded to have attained on any occasion preceding. The consternation produced by the rise of water *several feet* above its usual level, may well be imagined to be excessive. Houses, which on no occasion whatever before had been invaded by the tide, were now, by its over-pouring all probable bounds, filled to a great depth with the water, which rushed into kitchens and cellars, and inundated every apartment until it found its level. Whole streets were thus circumstanced; and some were for two or three hours inacessible but to those who had resolution enough to wade up to the knees. The performance of divine service on Sunday in the parish church, Boston, was prevented by the tide on the preceding evening having completely flooded the area appropriated to public worship. The height of the water against the western end of the steeple, was two feet eight inches and a half—four inches higher than in the year 1807. Friskney new sea bank was broken by the tide in two or three places; Leverton new sea bank the same; of Freiston new bank scarcely a vestige was left; the old bank, also, in that parish was broken in many places, as was Boston East old bank, and the banks at Skirbeck Quarter, Wyberton, Frampton, and Fosdyke.—It may be well here to observe, that the *new* banks are those lately made on the enclosure of the marshes from the sea, but are not relied upon for the defence of the country at large. The old sea banks, unhappily for the country, have proved insufficient in height, as the surge passed over them almost along *the whole line*: and this was the cause of the breaches,—the overflow having first scoured away the banks, from the summit to the base, on *the land side*. The situation of the country, in consequence, from Wainfleet almost to Spalding, a distance of 30 miles, is such as exceeds our powers of description. The hotel (Plummer's) at Freiston Shore was for some hours in danger of being quite washed down; the great bow window of the dining-room, although a considerable height from the ground, was forced from the building by the water, and carried to the distance of several fields. Dead sheep are seen lying in numbers from every road that is passable. The roads from Boston towards the sea at Fosdyke Wash are nearly impassable, being horse-belly deep in water, and the communications along the sea banks are cut off by the breaches in them; but the Court of Sewers is sitting daily at Boston, issuing orders for the security of the country. What was an extraordinary thing was, that the tide, when it had flowed to its highest, did not perceptibly subside for more than an hour."

For several days the water remained on the land, and was so deep that the Commissioners appointed by the Court of Sewers to view the banks at Fosdyke were unable to do this, as the roads leading from Boston to Wyberton, Frampton, Kirton, and Algarkirk, were so completely inundated as to be impassable on horseback. This tide rose 4ft. 7½in. above an ordinary spring tide, or 17·93ft. above *ordnance datum*, and from 6ft. to 10ft. above the surface of the land. There is a mark cut on the west side of the tower of Boston Church, showing the height to which the churchyard was flooded.

The Court of Sewers met at Boston on the following day, Sunday, when it was reported that the whole line of sea bank within the two wapentakes, extending from Friskney to Fosdyke, was overflowed in places, and several large breaches made, particularly in the parishes of Boston East, Skirbeck, Fishtoft, Freiston, Boston West, Skirbeck Quarter, Frampton, Kirton, Algarkirk, Fosdyke and Surfleet. The Court appointed John Farnsworth, for the Kirton

Court of Sewers. Minutes Nov. 11, 1810.

wapentake, and Francis Pinkerton, for the Skirbeck wapentake as 'particular surveyors,' with unlimited powers to employ men and obtain materials for repairing the breaches. At a subsequent Court, Mr. John Rennie of London was appointed engineer, to examine the banks, and report as to the works to be done to make the same secure for the future; and Anthony Bower, of Lincoln, was appointed to take the levels of the banks from Friskney to Fosdyke, with cross sections of the same. They were also directed to ascertain the extent of the country liable to be flooded, which would be benefited by raising and strengthening the banks.

<small>Court of Sewers. Minutes 10 Dec. 1810.</small>

At a Court of Sewers held at the Guildhall, Boston, on the 11th Feb. 1812, the report of Mr. Rennie was read, in which he stated that he had examined the sea banks from Wainfleet to the Grand Sluice at Boston, and thence, on the north-east side of the river, to the river Glen; and that by his direction Mr. A. Bower had taken levels of the banks. These levels showed that the lowest part of the bank, from Wainfleet to Boston, was only one foot above ordinary spring tides, and that from Boston to the Five Towns Sluice, on the river Welland, the banks were above the level of ordinary spring tides. The ancient bank, over which the Court had jurisdiction, was round Bicker Haven, but owing to the enclosure of this estuary, the interior banks were much neglected, and in many paces were under the level of spring tides; and in their then condition they were not generally calculated to resist much more than the ordinary spring tides. He advised that all the banks should be raised and strengthened, the sea-slope being brought to a batter of 5 to 1 and the land-slope of 2 to 1. The estimated cost from Friskney to Boston was £21,511; and from Boston to the south-west side of Bicker Haven, including a new bank on the Glen, £11,467, both estimates being exclusive of land required for getting materials.

<small>J. Rennie, Feb. 4, 1812.</small>

As regards the land that would continue to be inundated if the breaches made by the tide of 1810 had not been repaired, Mr. Rennie stated, in a subsequent report, that, as far as he could form an opinion, the tidal water would be stopped on the west side of the Witham, by the banks of the Black Sluice Drain, Hammond Beck, Pinchbeck township, the river Glen, and the Vernatts; on the east, by the banks of Frith Bank Drain, Newdike to Freiston Common, Hobhole Drain to Benington Bridge, Lade Bank Drain, and on to the Steeping river bank and the high lands in Wainfleet.

<small>J. Rennie, March 16, 1812.</small>

The Court, having considered the report, resolved "that the plan recommended by Mr. Rennie for strengthening and heightening the sea banks in the Wapentakes of Skirbeck and Kirton, for the more effectual defence and preservation of the country against the sea, is of too serious a magnitude to be adopted at the present, and that therefore this Court will confine its deliberations to the

<small>Court of Sewers. Minutes Feb. 11, 1812.</small>

business of repairing the breaches and defects in the sea banks, and placing the country in the same state of security that it was deemed to be in immediately previous to the 10th of November, 1810."

The Court after duly considering the cost of making a survey and obtaining levels of the land, came to the conclusion that all the lands within the Wapentakes of Skirbeck and Kirton were, with some small exceptions, considerably below the high water mark of the 1810 tide, and that the whole level should be subjected to charge accordingly.

Special Juries were summoned by the Sheriff of the County to view the lands in the Skirbeck and Kirton Wapentakes, and determine which of those lands ought to be brought into charge upon the level.

At a subsequent Court, George Meeds, the foreman of the Skirbeck Jury, presented the verdict, by which it was found that the parishes were liable in the following proportions :— *(Court of Sewers. Minutes, Jan. 19, 1813.)*

KIRTON WAPENTAKE.

Parish	a.	r.	p.	Assessment Per Acre. s. d.
Skirbeck Quarter	439	0	0	10 0
Wyberton	1522	2	0	10 0
Frampton	1987	3	21	7 0
Kirton	3150	2	0	6 0
Swineshead	1264	0	0	2 6
Wigtoft	1477	3	0	4 0
Sutterton	1791	3	0	5 0
Algarkirk	1617	3	0	7 0
Fosdyke	815	2	0	9 0
Quadring	1208	2	0	2 0
Quadring Hundred	519	2	0	2 6
Gosberton	2614	2	0	3 0
Surfleet	2025	1	0	5 0
	20,434	1	21	

Special Collectors were appointed for each parish, to gather in the rate.

The verdict of the Skirbeck Jury was presented at another Court by Mr. Joshua Aspland, the foreman, and the lands held liable were assessed, as follows :— *(Court of Sewers Minutes, March 18, 1813.)*

SKIRBECK WAPENTAKE.

Parish	a.	r.	p.	Assessment. Per Acre. s. d.
Boston East	468	3	13	6 8
Skirbeck	2394	2	17	6 8
Fishtoft	2087	0	38	5 0
Fishtoft Hundred	369	0	2	4 0
Freiston	3135	0	37	6 8
Butterwick	1251	2	32	4 0
Benington	1886	0	5	3 4
Leverton	2236	0	31	2 8
Leake	4123	2	26	2 0
Wrangle	4727	0	35	1 6
Friskney	4220	3	19	1 2
	26,900	2	15	

The verdict of the Jury in each case was ordered to be made 'A Law and Ordinance of the Sewers.' The amount required for repairing the breaches and the other expenses relating thereto was ordered to be raised by an acre-tax upon the lands set out in the verdict. From the above verdict it would appear that the cost of making good the damage and strengthening the banks amounted to £5,662 in Kirton Hundred and £4,794 in Skirbeck.

Thompson's Boston.

One account states that the loss sustained throughout Holland was very large, great numbers of sheep and cattle being drowned and corn and hay stacks swept away. The damage done was estimated at £16,840 for individual losses, injury to the public sea banks at £3,500, and to private sea banks at £8,000, or £28,340 in all. A subscription was set on foot to relieve in some degree the distress of those who had been injured by this great calamity. It is evident that the damage to the sea banks is much under-estimated in the above account.

HIGH TIDE OF 1816.

In February, 1816, a very high tide occurred, which covered the top of the sea banks in several places, by as much as from six to nine inches. A Jury was summoned by the Sheriff to view the condition of the sea banks, and, on their report, Mr. Farnsworth was appointed by the Court 'Particular Surveyor' of the sea banks which were presented as defective, and he was directed to furnish the dykereeves with a specification of the manner in which the said defective work should be made good.

SEA BANKS RAISED.

Court of Sewers. Minutes, 27 Nov., 1817.

Under this and other orders, the banks, particularly in Skirbeck Quarter, Wyberton, Frampton, Kirton, Algarkirk, Fosdyke, Boston, Skirbeck, Fishtoft and Freiston, were raised and strengthened in the defective places, and land was purchased for the purpose.

LEVEL STONES.

Court of Sewers. Minutes, 21 Oct., 1820 25 Nov., 1820 15 Dec., 1820

The Riding Jury who viewed the sea banks in 1820 made a presentment that, owing to the difficulty of ascertaining the proper heights to which the banks should be maintained, it was desirable that level stones should be affixed, in each parish, with figures cut in them giving the height at which the top of the bank should be above these stones. Mr. J. Cole was accordingly appointed by the Court to take the necessary levels, and these stones were fixed according to his directions.

HEIGHT OF SEA BANKS.

The top of the sea bank was ordered to be two feet above the great tide of 1810. This makes the bank 6ft. 7in. above ordinary spring tides, or 19·93ft. above *Ordnance datum*. The heights given on the stones will be found in the Abstract of the Jury of 1862. (*Appendix viii.*)

The Sewers' rates, laid in the several parishes in recent years, amount to about the following sums. In addition to these, special rates have been laid to pay the interest and instalments of loans raised for the works done to the Five Towns and Risegate Eau Drains.

SKIRBECK HUNDRED.			KIRTON HUNDRED.		
Boston East	2d.	in the £	Boston West	2d.	in the £
Sibsey	4d.	per acre	Skirbeck Quarter	6d.	per acre.
Fishtoft	3d.	,,	Wyberton	4d.	,,
Fishtoft Hundred	2d.	,,	Frampton	3d.	,,
Leake	3d.	,,	Algarkirk	5d.	,,
Wrangle	3d.	,,	Sutterton	6d.	,,
Butterwick	3d.	,,	Fosdyke	6d.	,,
Friskney	3d.	,,	Kirton	3d.	,,
Skirbeck	6d.	,,	Wigtoft	1s.	,,
Leverton	4d.	,,	Quadring	4d.	,,
Freiston	6d.	,,	Gosberton	4d.	,,
Benington	5d.	,,	Swineshead North	6d.	,,
			,, South	6d.	,,
			Surfleet	6d.	,,

RATES.

PARISH SEWERS. In the following pages, the system of drainage of each separate parish is described, so far as it is under the jurisdiction of the Court of Sewers, and abstracts are given of the Acts which have been passed for the enclosure of the common lands in these parishes, and for the embankment of the marshes.

BOSTON. BOSTON.—The drainage of the lands in this Parish is by several sewers. On the east side of the town the principal sewer discharges at a sluice, formerly known as Dipple Gowt, into the River Witham, immediately below the Grand Sluice. It is now entirely covered over. It passes through the town in a circular course, under the Red Lion Hotel, the Corn Exchange, and at the back of the Grammar School, to another sluice at the Ferry at the end of St. John's lane, where tidal water is taken in for flushing it. Other smaller sewers run down Main Ridge and Chapel street, and, also another, under Bargate Green, discharge into Maud Foster Drain. A sewer, commencing at Frith Bank and running along the Frith Bank road, Robin Hood's walk, Norfolk street (formerly Sluice Lane) and then across the end of North street, empties into Bargate drain near Bargate Bridge (formerly Pedder's Bridge). This sewer is also covered over where it passes through the town. On the West side the main outlet was formerly into Hammond Beck in Skirbeck Quarter. This sewer continued as an open drain at the back of King street and Liquorpond street, and also extended to West street and Fydell marsh. The outfall of this sewer is into the Haven in Skirbeck Quarter. The lower part now consists of a large brick culvert. The remainder of this open sewer has been filled in and superseded by brick sewers under the streets. That portion of the Parish known as Boston West, formerly part of Holland Fen, is dealt with in the account of the *Second District*.

BOSTON EAST ENCLOSURE. Early in the present century, an Act was obtained for enclosing the common lands, containing 1,388 acres, lying between Hilldyke, and Long Hedges and Willoughby Hills, commonly known as Boston East, and also the lands allotted to the Parish of Boston in

50 Geo. iii, c. 50, 1810.

the East and West Fens under the Enclosure Act of 1801. John Burcham of Coningsby, Charles Wedge of Westley Bottom, and Anthony Bower of Lincoln, were appointed Commissioners for dividing and allotting these lands. For the purpose of estimating the value of the land, Robert Millington of Gedney, William Thacker of *Langrett* Ferry, and Thomas Rockliffe of Fulletby were appointed 'quality men, valuers and appraisers.' The Commissioners were allowed three guineas a day, including their expenses, and the *Quality Men* two guineas, for their services. The Commissioners were empowered to make roads and drains, and to allot three acres of land to the Surveyor of Highways for the repair of the roads. The Mayor and Burgesses of Boston, as Lords of the Manor, were to have one thirtieth part of the commonable lands in Boston East, and in lieu of the tithes, of which they were the owners, one ninth part of the common and a plot, equal in value to one fifth of the arable land there under cultivation, and two seventieths of the other land, in lieu of great and small tithes, whilst the remainder was to be allotted amongst the owners of houses and toftsteads. The award when made was to be enrolled with the Town Clerk and he was bound to supply copies of any part thereof at the rate of four pence per sheet of 72 words, and to allow any person interested in the award to inspect the same for a fee of one shilling.

TRANSFER OF LAND TO OTHER PARISHES, 1881.

The land dealt with by this Act was transferred from Boston parish, under the divided Parishes Act, in 1881 and 1882; that in the East Fen, containing 397 acres, to Leake; the allotment in the West Fen at Carrington, containing 25 acres, to that parish; the allotments in the West Fen at Mount Pleasant, containing 880 acres, to Frithville and that at Boston East, about 770 acres, to Fishtoft.

BOSTON WEST.

Boston West is in the Kirton Wapentake, and runs by the side of the river Witham, from Boston nearly to Langrick Ferry, being bounded on the south by the North Forty Foot drain, and on the west by the parish of Brothertoft. It contains 1,502a. 2r. 5p., and forms part of the Municipal Borough of Boston. It elects one member on the Black Sluice Commission. It was allotted to the parish of Boston by the award made under the Holland Fen Enclosure Act, and was divided and allotted under the powers of an Act, obtained in 1771, for dividing and enclosing the common fen belonging to Boston West. The quantity allotted was 1,513a. 3r. 14p., the difference between the rateable area and this quantity being due to roads and drains.

INCLOSURE ACT.

7 Geo. iii, 1767.
10 Geo. iii, c 40, 1770.
2 Geo. iii, c 110, 1771.

Thomas Staveley of Kirton, Peter Packharness of Benington, and William Elstobb of London were appointed Commissioners to allot the land, and to set out the roads (which were to be sixty feet wide and to become highways), bridges and drains. They were to be paid £84 each for their time and expenses. The award was to be enrolled with the Clerk of the Peace for the division of Holland, and be open to inspection on payment of a fee of one shilling and two pence for every hundred words copied. This award was printed and issued by C. Preston of Boston. Sixty acres of land abutting on Hall Hills road were sold by auction by the Commissioners to pay the expenses, in lots of ten acres, at an average price of £42 an acre.

The principal drain of the district commences at the north west part, near Brothertoft, and discharges into the North Forty Foot Drain, near where the New Cut commences. The drainage is under the jurisdiction of the *Second Witham District Commissioners*. DRAINAGE.

This district is subject to the sixpenny and eightpenny Witham Second District Tax; the sixpenny Black Sluice rate; the Witham Outfall rate; and the Second District Interior Rate. DRAINAGE RATES.

SKIRBECK.—The principal drain for this parish, before the works were carried out for draining the Fens, was the Scire Beck, which commences near High Hills, at the north-west extremity of the parish, whence it runs along Robin Hood's Walk, crossing Norfolk-street, and running towards the present Bargate Bridge. At the point where it crossed Bargate near Mill Hill, it was spanned by Pedder's Bridge, whence it ran nearly in the same direction as the present Maud Foster Drain, its course, however, being very tortuous. Near Mount Bridge it diverged to the west, passing near the *Muster Roll Houses*, and, after crossing the Skirbeck-road, joined Boston Haven by an outlet a little below the site of the old Gallows Mills, which were situated where the south end of Boston dock now is. The upper part of the drain is still open, and in use. The middle part may be traced by the boundary line between the parishes of Boston and Skirbeck. The lower part has been converted into a brick sewer, and discharges into Maud Foster Drain near the Muster Roll Houses. The oak framing and planking of the old culvert and sluice in the river bank, which had been abandoned since the cutting of Maud Foster drain in the 17th century, was laid bare when the river bank was removed during the construction of the dock. SCIRE BECK.

The whole of the drainage of this parish discharges into Maud Foster drain, except a small area, which drains into the Graft Drain in Fishtoft. The outlet into Maud Foster is on the east side, near Bargate Bridge, and on the west side by two sluices near the Boston Cemetery. DRAINAGE.

By an arrangement, made in 1881 and confirmed by the Court of Sewers, the land which drains into the Graft pays the parish of Fishtoft at the rate of threepence an acre. GRAFT DRAIN.
Court of Sewers.
Minutes,
6 Aug. 1881.

The liability to repair the sea bank, until recently, devolved on the owners of a large number of plots of land, but is now undertaken by the Dykereeves, on behalf of the parish. A great part of the bank was either removed or superseded when the Boston Dock was built. SEA BANK.

By the award made under the West Fen Enclosure Act 446a. 1r. 29p. of land were allotted to this parish in the West Fen. There were also in the parish other commonable salt marshes and commonable lands, and an act was obtained in 1818 for enclosing and allotting these. John Bircham of Coningsby was appointed Commissioner for the purpose. The act directed that two acres should be set out for the repair of the roads and that the herbage of this should be let by the Surveyor, and the rents applied to the repair of the roads; the Lord of the Manor was to be allotted one thirty-fifth in value of the marsh and other commonable lands, in lieu of his rights, and the rector and vicar 193a. 3r. in the West Fen, in lieu of both great and small tithes. A public road, called Watson's Hurn, was set out, 30ft. wide. The Award is dated 19th November, 1833, and is deposited at the Sessions House, Boston, and the charge for copying, as fixed by the Act, was fourpence per sheet of 72 words.

marginalia: ENCLOSURES. 7 Geo. iii, 1767. 58 Geo. iii, 1818.

The allotment belonging to this parish in the West Fen was transferred by order of the Local Government Board, in 1880, confirmed by the Act 44 Vict. c. 17, to Sibsey.

marginalia: TRANSFER OF LAND TO SIBSEY.

FISHTOFT.—The principal sewer is the Graft Drain, which commences at the northern extremity of the parish, near Willoughby Hills, and running nearly through its centre terminates at the river Witham, a little above the outfall of Hobhole Drain. It was formerly "a creek of considerable magnitude, which flowed from near Fishtoft Church to the neighbourhood of the present Hobhole Sluice, and it is stated that persons still living remember fishermen drying their nets on the Churchyard wall."

marginalia: GRAFT DRAIN. Thompson's Boston.

In 1711, a Law of Sewers was enacted for erecting a new Gote where the old Fishtoft Gote formerly stood, which had blown up and become dilapidated. The new Gote was made of good and substantial wood and timber, 40ft. long, 3ft. 8in. wide and 4ft. deep, with two doors, hung on hinges. Robert Clarke and Thomas Lote of Fishtoft, were appointed *Surveyors General* of the work; and an order was made on the owners of land in the parish for the cost, which amounted to £243 8s. 8d.

marginalia: FISHTOFT GOTE, 1711.

The portion of the creek between the Sluice and the river was known as 'Scotia Creek.' This name was taken from a steam boat, named the *Scotia*, which traded between London and Boston, before the river was straightened and improved, and was docked in this creek.

Within the last few years, owing to a defect in the Gote, it has been abandoned, and the drainage diverted into Hobhole Drain.

The lands allotted to this Parish in the East and West Fen, containing 2,794 acres, and other commonable and waste lands, were enclosed under an Act obtained in 1810. The preamble recites that there were in this parish several open fields and ings, containing together 2,795 acres, and marshes containing 95 acres; and that

marginalia: INCLOSURE. 50 Geo. iii, c. 53. 1810.

this common land was intermixed and dispersed, and, therefore, incapable of improvement, and it was desirable that it should be divided and inclosed. This commonable land consisted principally of allotments in the East, West and Wildmore Fens. There were also some small pieces of waste land within the boundary of the parish, and some salt marshes, which had accreted on the coast. The Commissioners appointed by the Act to divide this land were John Burcham of Coningsby, William Whitelocke of Brotherton, and Charles Wedge of Westley Bottom ; but the award was subsequently made by William Simonds, William Porter and Samuel Vessey. Their remuneration was fixed at three guineas a day, while engaged, and was to include travelling and other personal expenses. They were empowered to alter the roads, to make drains where required ; to allot a plot, not exceeding two acres, for the repair of the highways, (the herbage from the same to be let by the Highway Surveyor) ; to allot to the Rector, in lieu of all tithes, a plot of land in the West or Wildmore Fen, equal in value to one-fifth part of all the arable land in the parish, which was in cultivation at the time, and one-tenth of the open fields and ings, and one-ninth of the marshes and other commonable lands. The cost of the enclosure was to be met by the sale of sufficient land.

ROADS.

The public roads set out under the award were, the Hurn Road, 30ft. wide ; Gay's Field Road, 30ft. ; Bailey's Acre Road, 30ft. ; Church Green Road, 40ft. ; Burton Croft Road, 30ft. ; Clamp Gate Road, 30ft. ; Penhill Field Lane, 30ft. ; Wythes Road, 30ft. ; Freiston Low Road, 30ft. ; Freiston High Road, 60ft. ; Ings Road, 15ft. ; Medlam Drain Bank, 50ft. ; Whistley Bridge Road, part 15ft., and the remainder 30ft. ; Mere Booth Road, part 20ft., and part 40ft. ; and Leeds Gate Road, 25ft.

The award is deposited at the Sessions House, Boston.

ALTERATION OF PARISH.

The outlying portion of Fishtoft, then inclosed, was taken from the Parish in 1881 and added to other Parishes under the *Divided Parishes Act*, that in Wildmore Fen being transferred to Langrick-ville, and that in the West Fen, known as Fishtoft Fen, to Frithville. At the same time, land at Willoughby Hills and Long Hedges, taken from the parish of Boston, was added to the Parish of Fishtoft.

ENCLOSURE OF SALT MARSH.

About a hundred years ago the area of the parish was increased by the enclosure of 176 acres of salt marsh from the estuary, now known as the Milk House Farm ; and by another enclosure of 50 acres, being part of the bed of the old river and known as the Blue Anchor Bight. When the new cut was made for the river Witham through Burton's Marsh, in 1833, a small part of the parish was severed and is now divided by the channel of the river. In 1872, another small enclosure was made and added to the Milk House Farm, but the greater part of this enclosure was taken for the new bed of the

Outfall. In the Court of Sewers' verdict the Parish is divided into two parts, namely Fishtoft and Fishtoft Hundred.

DRAINAGE.

FREISTON AND BUTTERWICK.—These Parishes are drained by a number of small sewers, discharging by culverts emptying into Hobhole Drain. The lands lying outside the Roman Bank in Butterwick drain by a sluice in the sea bank, about half a mile below the Coastguard station.

In 1733, a Petition was presented to the Court of Sewers, by the parishes of Freiston, Butterwick and Fishtoft Hundred stating that there was a great want of fresh water for the cattle, and that this could be supplied by means of a water engine placed near the Howdyke Drain in Freiston, and that this engine would also be useful in better draining the parish. The Court accordingly made an order sanctioning the erection of the engine.

ENCLOSURE OF MARSHES. 48 Geo. iii, 1808.

In the beginning of the present century, an Act was obtained for embanking the salt marshes in the parishes of Freiston and Butterwick, and for enclosing the same and also other common lands. The area of land embanked from the sea, lying outside the Roman Bank, was 300 acres. The open fields and ings enclosed were 1,500 acres and also about 100 acres of waste ground. A Committee, consisting of John Linton, Samuel Barnard, John Coupland, Richard Hanson, William Plummer, Richard Bazlinton and Henry Cook, was appointed to superintend the works relating to the embanking and draining of the marsh, which were to be carried out under the direction of an engineer. The Enclosure Commissioners were John Burcham of Coningsby, William Whitelock of Brotherton, and John Bonner of Langton, their remuneration being fixed at three guineas a day, including expenses. They were directed to enclose and allot the commonable lands, alter roads and make drains and sluices, where necessary; to allot 2 acres to the Surveyors of Highways for the purpose of getting materials for the repair of the roads; to sell sufficient land to pay expenses, and to allot the remainder in the proportion of one half to the owners of houses having common rights and the other to owners of land and of the tithes. On completion of the Enclosure Works a Surveyor was to be appointed to take charge of the same by the majority of the owners of the marshes present, at a meeting to be held on the Thursday in Easter week. The Surveyor was empowered to levy rates for the maintenance of the bank. A special rate, not to exceed £10 an acre, can be laid at a meeting of not less than three proprietors.

ALTERATION OF PARISHES.

The Allotments in the West Fen belonging to Freiston were transferred to the new Parish of West Fen, and those in the East Fen belonging to Butterwick, to Leake, under an order of the Local Government Board of Dec. 1881, which was confirmed by the Act 44 Vict. C. xvii.

SEA BANKS.

The ancient sea bank in this parish is nearly three miles in length. It suffered very severely during the great tide of 1810, after which it was heightened and strengthened. The duty of keeping it in repair devolved on a great number of the owners of land in the parish, whose respective lengths were set out by boundary posts. There are no less than 900 portions of bank so set out, the proportion being calculated at the rate of 5½ft. of bank to one acre of land. By an order of the Court of Sewers the bank is now repaired by the Dykereeves, the cost being paid out of the dykereeve rate.

In 1891 a petition was presented to the Court of Sewers, praying that the whole of the Sewers' work in the parish might be done by the Dykereeves, but it was held by the Court that the petition could not be legally granted. *Boston Court of Sewers. Minutes. 9 July, 1881.*

BENINGTON.—That part of this parish which is inside the Roman bank, is drained by sewers, discharging into Hobhole drain. The land outside the Roman bank discharges its drainage at Benington Gowt in the sea bank, and by another smaller sluice about three-quarters of a mile more to the north. *DRAINAGE.*

In 1815 an Act was obtained for embanking and enclosing the common lands in this parish, consisting of 527 acres, allotted to the parish in the East Fen by the award made under the Act of 1801. A plot, containing 400 acres, was allotted to the Rector, in lieu of all tithes. In 1880 this outlying portion of the parish in the East Fen was transferred to Leake. *EMBANKMENT AND ENCLOSURE 55 Geo. iii, c. 86, 1815.*

The marsh enclosed outside the Roman Bank is about one mile in length, and half a mile wide.

LEAKE.—This parish is drained by sewers, which discharge into Hobhole drain, the principal outlets being at Benington and Simon House bridges. The land outside the Roman bank discharges its drainage by a sluice in the sea bank, which was probably built in 1749, as an order was made by the Court of Sewers at that time for a new outfall sluice to be erected for Leake and Leverton parishes. *DRAINAGE.*

In 1810 an Act was obtained for enclosing and dividing the common lands, and for making provision for the maintenance of the new sea bank. The Act provides for a meeting of the owners of lands, to be held yearly on the Thursday in Easter week, when a surveyor is to be appointed, and a rate laid for the maintenance of the new sea bank, and also of the ancient sewers bank, and all other works connected therewith. *INCLOSURE ACT. 50 Geo. iii, c. 127, 1810.*

The allotments to this parish, under the Fen Enclosure Acts, in the East Fen, amounted to 1,523 acres.

The outlying lands, consisting of allotments in the East Fen in the Parishes of Benington, Boston, Butterwick, Leverton and Revesby, were transferred to this parish in 1881. *ALTERATION OF PARISH.*

LEVERTON.—This parish is drained by sewers which discharge into Hobhole drain, the principal outlet being at the Ings Bridge. The land outside the Roman bank discharges its drainage by two *DRAINAGE.*

sluices in the sea bank, the principal of which is 4ft. in diameter. In 1735 this parish complained that the Benington land, being higher than theirs, caused injury by overflowing the land from Scott's dyke; and an order was made by the Court of Sewers that Benington should embank Scott's dyke and should pay dykereeve rate to Leverton for the Ings land which drains to Leverton drain.

INCLOSURE ACT. 50 Geo. iii, c. 126, 1810. In 1810 an Act was obtained for inclosing the common lands and providing for the repairs of the new sea bank.

SEA BANKS. A tract of marsh land containing 395 acres had been embanked in 1801, at a cost of £5,000. The bank in this parish is 1½ miles long and about half a mile nearer the sea than the old bank. No sufficient provision was made for the maintenance of the banks. It was therefore provided by the Act of 1810 that an annual meeting should be held on Thursday in Easter week, when a Surveyor was to be appointed and rates laid. The Surveyor was empowered to maintain and repair the new bank and the ancient sewer's bank, and the drains, sluices and other works belonging to the enclosed land. The Commissioners appointed to allot and divide the common lands were Samuel Vessey, William Simonds and William Porter.

ALTERATION OF PARISH. The outlying portions of this parish in the West Fen were transferred by the Act 24 Vict. c. 17, in 1881, to the new parish of West Fen, and those in the East Fen to Leake.

EXPENDITURE. The amount raised by special taxation for the sea banks, according to the return of 1892-3, was £20, of which £16 was spent on works and £2 on management. In the previous year, work cost £31.

DRAINAGE. WRANGLE. The newly enclosed land in this parish is drained by sewers which discharge by sluices in the sea bank. The remainder of the parish discharges its waters into sewers which communicate with those of the *Fourth Witham District*, and through them into Hobhole Drain, the principal outlet being at Lade Bank.

INCLOSURE ACT. 47 Geo. iii, 1807. In 1807 an Act was obtained for enclosing and dividing Wrangle Common, containing 1,250 acres, and also other common lands amounting to 150 acres. The Commissioners for carrying out the Act were John Burcham of Coningsby and William Whitelock of Brotherton. The Commissioners were empowered to make such drains and roads as they considered necessary, to allot two acres of land to the Surveyors of Highways for the repair of the roads; 35 acres were to be allotted in satisfaction of the manorial rights; one-ninth part of the common was to be allotted to the Impropriator of the tithes, and a plot equal in area to one-fifth of the arable lands within the parish, and two-sevenths of all the other lands. One moiety of the remainder was to be divided amongst the owners of houses in Wrangle, having right of common, and the other half amongst the owners of land having right of common.

MARSH ENCLOSURE. A tract of marsh land outside the Roman bank about half a mile in width was enclosed, in this and the adjoining parish of Friskney, in the year 1808.

DRAINAGE. FRISKNEY. This parish is in the Lindsey Division, but is within the jurisdiction of the Boston Court of Sewers. The sewers in this parish discharge into the Fodderdyke and other drains belonging to the *Fourth Witham District* and thence into Hobhole. The marsh enclosure, outside the Roman bank, drains through a sluice in the new bank.

THE FENS. Oldfield's Wainfleet. A large area of low land in this parish was, previous to its enclosure, generally flooded for six months in the year, the water seldom entirely subsiding until the month of May, or later. The fen land was known as the Moss-berry or Cranberry Fen, from the quantities of cranberries which grew in it. In some favourable seasons, as many as 4,000 pecks were collected, the average being 2,000. The price paid to those who picked them was 5/- a peck.

Friskney was also noted for its decoys and the immense quantity of wild fowl caught in them. In one season, prior to the enclosure of the fens, ten decoys, five of which were in Friskney, furnished 31,200 duck, widgeon and teal for the London markets.

INCLOSURE AND EMBANKMENT ACT. 49 Geo. iii, 1809. In 1809, an Act was obtained for embanking and enclosing the salt marsh outside the Roman bank, and also for enclosing and dividing 'the moss or moor ground, open fields and commonable lands.' A Committee was appointed under the Act for superintending the embankment and the draining of the marshes, consisting of Sir James Winter Lake, Edward Greathead, Thomas Booth, Edward Shaw, the Rev. Joseph Walls, Joseph Hunt and Thomas Hunt Oliver, each being allowed five shillings a day for his expenses. The works were to be done under the direction of an Engineer appointed by the Committee, who were authorised to lay a tax on the owners of the marsh land for defraying the cost of embanking. After the work was completed, it was to be placed under the charge of a Surveyor, appointed annually, at a meeting of the proprietors to be held on the Thursday in Easter week, who was to be paid such yearly salary as should be thought reasonable at the time of his appointment. The Surveyor is authorized to lay an acre rate, such being approved by a majority present at a meeting of the proprietors. In default of payment, an application may be made to a Justice of the Peace for the parts of Lindsey to order a distress.

The Act also directs that the owners and occupiers of the newly embanked marshes and also of the old embanked marshes shall keep the boundary ditches 4ft. wide, at the top, and 3ft. deep, and cause the same, from time to time, to be *roaded* and scoured, and bridges and tunnels to be laid where necessary. In default, after 14 days notice, the work is to be done and the defaulter charged with the cost.

For enclosing and dividing the common land, Anthony Bower was appointed Commissioner. The usual powers were given to make roads and drains; two acres were to be allotted to the Surveyor of Highways for the maintenance of the roads; one thirtieth part of the commonable lands to the Duchy of Lancaster as owner of the manorial rights; one half of the remainder amongst the owners of houses having right of common, and the rest amongst the owners of land having right of common.

The Award, when enrolled with the Clerk of the Peace for the Parts of Lindsey, was to be deposited in the Church at Friskney.

The area of the Fen Land was 813 acres, and there were also 137 acres of other common land. The area of the marsh enclosed from the sea was 620 acres.

BANK RATES.

The amount raised by taxation for the sea embankments in 1892-3 was £24, the expenditure on works was £21 (in the previous year £22) and on management, £5.

THE HAVEN.

WAINFLEET. This parish is in the Lindsey division and under the jurisdiction of the Spilsby Court of Sewers, but its general drainage system is intimately mixed up with that of the East Fen and the Fourth District. Wainfleet was a town in the time of the Romans, being then called *Vainona*. Dr. Stukeley says that the haven was then near where St. Thomas' Church stands, now called Northolme. It seems to have been 30ft. wide, a mile above the church, as appears by an old clough which existed there. The Haven was the only place on the coast where the vessels of the Romans could ride safely and find protection, and Wainfleet was the principal landing place for their station at Lincoln. A road was made from Wainfleet, across the Fens to Horncastle, and thence to Lincoln and Doncaster, and Salter's Gate is supposed to be the remains of it, as this communicates with Friskney, where are the remains of salt works. Traces of a road are also visible from Wainfleet to Burgh, which was also a Roman station.

DRAINAGE.

Previous to the enclosure of the East Fen the drainage of this parish was under the control of the Spilsby Court of Sewers, and numerous records exist as to Commissions held to enquire as to the condition of Wainfleet Haven, and the drainage of the East Fen.

Oldfield.

From the earliest period of which there is any record it appears that the waters of the East Fen, and even part of those of the West Fen, drained into Wainfleet Haven. About the year 1532, a considerable part of the fen water was diverted to the Witham. The Adventurers who undertook to drain the East Fen in the middle of the 16th century, " by the advice of experienced artists in draining, finding that Wainfleet Haven was not a proper and fitting sewer for the Fens to drain by to the sea, enlarged the ancient sewers which led to the river Witham and Boston Haven." The further history of the drainage of this parish is dealt with in that of the East Fen.

In 1813 an Act was obtained for embanking, enclosing and draining the Salt Marshes in this parish, containing 500 acres, and also for enclosing and dividing about 60 acres of other common lands. Anthony Bower of Lincoln, and John Burcham of Coningsby, were appointed Commissioners for carrying out the provisions of the Act. The former died before the enclosure was finished, and Samuel Bower was appointed in his place. The sum of three guineas a day, including expenses, was allowed for their remuneration. The usual powers for making drains and roads were given. Such portion of the common lands was to be allotted to the Bethlehem Hospital and the Duchy of Lancaster, as Lords of the Manor, as the Commissioners should deem equal in value to their manorial rights, and the remainder amongst the Commoners according to their respective rights. The Commissioners were also to embank the open salt marshes, and provide for their drainage and carry it through any ancient enclosures in the parish, if necessary. The owners and occupiers of the marshes to be embanked, and also of the then embanked marshes, were directed by the Act to keep their boundary ditches 4ft. wide and 3ft. deep, and to cause the same from time to time to be *roaded* and scoured.

INCLOSURE AND EMBANKMENT ACT.
53 Geo. iii, c. 201, 1813.

After the embankment should be completed, the works were to be maintained by a Surveyor, appointed annually by the proprietors, at a meeting to be held on Thursday in Easter-week. The Surveyor was empowered to levy an equal acre rate, and also to levy the same on such of the old embanked lands as were improved by the drainage to be effected under this Act ; the rate to be approved at a meeting of proprietors. In default of payment a distress warrant can be issued by a Justice of the Peace for the parts of Lindsey.

By an amended Act, James Bradley of Boston was appointed as an additional Commissioner. By the first Act, the Commissioners were empowered to levy a rate on the owners of the marshes, for the purpose of the work, not exceeding £20 an acre : by the second Act it was enacted that every proprietor, having a frontage of land towards the sea, should keep in repair so much of the said sea bank as might adjoin his frontage, and in case of neglect, the surveyor, afters three days' notice, was authorised to do the work, and charge the owner with the expenses.

6 Geo. iv, 1825.

SIBSEY.—This parish is in the Lindsey Division, but its drainage is under the jurisdiction of the Boston Court of Sewers. Before the enclosure of the Fens, the principal watercourse for the drainage was the Sibsey river, which ran from Cherry Corner to Cow Bridge, and thence along Frith Bank to the Witham at Anton's Gowt. This water course was straightened and improved and the part between Cherry Corner and Cow Bridge, known as Stone Bridge Drain, forms one the catch-water drains of the *Fourth District* System. Part of the drainage went to Hilldyke,

DRAINAGE

which at one time was a watercourse of considerable importance, connected with the Witham, which boats were able to navigate. In 1568 a scheme was promoted for supplying the town of Boston with water from this stream. Boston must have had some right to this water, as, in 1376, in a pleading in the King's Bench, it was found that Boston and Skirbeck ought to cleanse the sewer from Hilldyke to the Witham, in consideration of which they had commons in the marsh of Bolingbroke.

NORDYKE CAUSEWAY. A large part of the water from the East Fen was formerly discharged by a drain which crossed the road at Nordyke Bridge, and went thence to the Witham. Owing to the bad condition of the Outfall, this part of the parish was frequently flooded, and it is recorded that in the 13th century, two men, carrying a corpse from Stickney to 'Cibecy,' to be buried in the churchyard, were drowned when passing along Nordyke Causeway, and, at an enquiry, it was found that 'divers persons were every year drowned,' in consequence of which the Sheriff was commissioned to seize the land of the Abbot of Revesby, until security was given for the repair of the causeway, it being his duty to keep it in order, in consideration of lands which had been given him for the purpose.

DRAINAGE BY MAUD FOSTER SLUICE, In 1735 a new sluice, called Maud Foster, was built under an order of the Court of Sewers, in Boston Haven, and the drainage of Sibsey, in common with that of other lands to the east of it, was diverted from Anton's and New Gote, in the Witham above Boston, to the new outfall. The area of land in Sibsey taxed towards the new works was 2,400 acres. Subsequently, attempts were made to bring the water of the West Fen and also of the northern part of the East Fen into the new system, the Sibsey Cut being made from the south west corner of the East Fen, to Hilldyke, and an opening being made from the West Fen, by means of Medlam Drain, to Cherry Corner; and, a sluice which existed there being removed, the West Fen water was allowed to escape into Mill Drain. The controversy over this matter led to serious rioting, of which Sibsey was the centre.

INCLOSURE ACT 50 Geo. iii. In 1810 an Act was obtained for enclosing and allotting the common land awarded to this parish in the East and West Fens. Under this Act, 1a. 3r. 25p. in Chapel field was allotted for the repairing of the Church.

ALTERATION OF THE PARISH. In 1881 an order was made under the *Divided Parishes Act*, for transferring the outlying portion of the parish in the West Fen and adding it to Frithville, whilst fen land in Frithville and Skirbeck was added to this parish.

KIRTON WAPENTAKE.

BOSTON WEST. The description of the enclosure of this parish will be found with Boston East, in the Skirbeck Hundred.

SKIRBECK QUARTER. The main outfall for the drainage of this parish is into the South Forty Foot Drain. A tract of land in the

Hamlet, called **Loate's Plot**, containing 45 acres, drains into Wyberton Town Drain and consequently pays dykereeve rate to that parish, in accordance with a Law of Sewers.

<small>DRAINAGE. Court of Sewers. Minutes, Oct. 22, 1754.</small>

The sea or river bank in this hamlet has been a constant source of trouble and expense, and the records of the Court of Sewers contain numerous entries ordering repairs to be done. In 1734 a petition was presented that the bank, from *the Shotlles* to Marsh corner, was very much out of repair and gone to decay, whereby the country was in great danger of being overflowed with salt water; and asking that the bank should be repaired at the cost of the landowners, and an order was made accordingly. The hamlet suffered very much from the great tide of 1810, and again from that of 1815.

<small>SEA BANK.</small>

A great part of the old sea bank is now inland, owing to several enclosures of marsh which have been made, but there still remains the length from the outfall of the Old Hammond Beck to the corner opposite Boston Dock.

By the verdict of 1862 it was found that the repair of this bank devolved on the owners of seventeen different plots of land in the hamlet.

In 1883 the condition of the bank below the Black Sluice had become dangerous, and the top had subsided below its proper height, owing to the settling of the foot of the bank into the river, caused by the deepening of the Haven and the scour of the tides and freshets, and an order was made by the Court for its repair. The bank was accordingly strengthened at the back, and raised. The cost of this work was £270.

It being held by the Court that these repairs were extraordinary, being occasioned by the alteration in the bed of the river, and not such as persons, liable by prescription, could fairly be answerable for, the costs were ordered to be paid by an acreage rate over the entire district that would be liable to be damaged by a breach. By a subsequent order, the rate was laid on the assessable value, and not by the acre. The following are the parishes on which the levy was made and the proportion allotted to each.

<small>Court of Sewers Minutes, 10 Nov. 1883.</small>

<small>23 April, 1884</small>

	a.	r.	p.	s.	d.	£	s.	d.
Skirbeck Quarter	557	0	26	2	6	69	12	6
Wyberton	2040	0	0	0	9	76	10	0
Frampton	3040	3	11	0	4	50	13	0
Kirton	4834	3	7	0	3	60	8	6
Swineshead North	1043	0	0	0	3	13	1	0

(Assessment.)

The rate for Skirbeck Quarter amounted to 1s. 8d. in the pound.

The fen portion of this hamlet lies about three-quarters of a mile west of Boston, between the North and South Forty Foot drains. It contains 276a. 2r. 20p. It forms part of Holland Fen, and was awarded under the *Holland Fen Enclosure Act*.

<small>THE FEN</small>

<small>7 Geo. iii, 1767.</small>

Skirbeck Quarter elects one member of the Black Sluice Commission, and the owners of land in the fen portion one member of the Second Witham District Commission.

INCLOSURE ACT.
29 Geo. iii, c. 3, 1789.

The fen was enclosed under an Act obtained for *Dividing and Inclosing the Common Fen belonging to Skirbeck Quarter in the Parish of Skirbeck*. William Gee of Swineshead, Thomas Staveley of Kirton, and Edward Hare of Castor, were appointed Commissioners for dividing and alloting the land, and they were to be paid twenty guineas each for their services.

The award, when executed, was to be enrolled with the Clerk of the Peace for the Division of Holland, and to be open to inspection on payment of a fee of one shilling and two-pence for every 72 words copied. The award is deposited at the Boston Sessions' House.

DRAINAGE RATES.

The old portion of the parish is subject to the dykereeve rate of the Court of Sewers. The fen is subject the sixpenny Black Sluice rate and to the sixpenny and eightpenny Witham District rates. The whole parish is subject to the Witham Outfall tax.

DRAINAGE.

WYBERTON. This parish is drained by a sewer called the *Town Drain*, which runs from the Hammond Beck through the centre of the parish, to the sluice in the old sea bank at Slippery Gowt, whence it has since been continued through a newly enclosed marsh to the channel of the Witham.

In 1733 an order of the Court of Sewers was made that the then existing Sluice should be wholly taken down, and rebuilt with brick and timber, 38ft. long, 4ft. high and 3½ft. wide. The cost of this new sluice was £297 11s.

Previous to the straightening of the river, the channel came close to this sluice. After the fascine work had been put in and the marsh grew up, this outfall silted up and became disused, the drainage finding its way into the Hammond Beck. In the year 1864 the Boston Harbour Commissioners embanked the marsh. On this being done, the Vestry of Wyberton required that an outfall for the drainage should be provided in the new bank, and further contended that, as the outfall of the sewers had become blocked up owing to the works of the Commissioners, they were bound to open up the drain across the marsh. After some litigation, the Commissioners agreed to do this. A sluice was built in the new bank and the drain cleaned out and deepened. The outer sluice is kept in repair by the Boston Harbour Commissioners, the Dykereeves of the parish having the management of the doors.

There are 45 acres of land in Skirbeck Quarter and 562 acres in Frampton which drain by the Wyberton Town Drain and pay dykereeve rates to this parish.

THE FEN.

The allotment in Holland Fen awarded to this parish is situated about three miles north-west of the village, and is not divided from the rest of the parish. Access is given to that part of the fen lying on the north side of the South Forty-Foot Drain, by the Wyberton

Chain Bridge, across the Hammond Beck, and by the bridge over the Forty-Foot, on the main road; and to Shuff Fen, by a brick bridge across the North Forty-Foot, known as Benton's Bridge.

The allotments made to Wyberton, under the *Holland Fen Award* were, the Bridge Piece, containing 87a. 0r. 22p., on the south side of the main road from Boston to Swineshead; part of the Middle Fen lying on both sides of the New Hammond Beck, 169a. 3r. 14p.; the Great Fen lying on the north side of the South Forty Foot drain, containing 473a. 0r. 20p., and Shuff Fen on the north side of the North Forty-Foot, containing 261a. 1r. 15p., making a total of 991a. 2r. 0p.

In addition to the land in Holland Fen, there was also other common land, known as *the Reaches Marsh*, containing 25 acres. This land is described 'as formerly left by the sea,' and is part of the old bed of the river Witham, lying about half-a-mile north-west of Langrick Ferry. It was originally let by the parish in aid of the rates, the inhabitants, before it was inclosed, having exercised common rights over it. There was also another small piece of common land, containing four acres.

INCLOSURE ACT. 29 Geo. iii, 1789.

In 1789 an Act was obtained for dividing, allotting, and enclosing the above described lands. Stanley Marshall of Freiston, Joseph Newman of Boston, and John Parkinson of Asgarby, were appointed Commissioners, their remuneration being fixed at £63, and £1 11s. 6d. a day each, for every day engaged in viewing, valuing, exchanging, and allotting the ancient inclosures and other lands exchanged under the powers of the Act.

The Commissioners were directed to set out, form, and put in good repair, a public road, 40ft. wide, across the Great Fen, from Wyberton Great Bridge to the bridge over the North Forty-Foot Drain, and from thence over Shuff Fen to the Turnpike-road leading from Langrick Ferry to Swineshead, and such other roads as they might deem necessary. The owners of the land were not to be allowed to plant trees within fifty yards of the roads.

Reaches Marsh was directed to be sold, and the proceeds applied to defraying the expenses of enclosure; and one-ninth in value of the whole fen, and a plot, equal in value to $188\frac{3}{4}$ acres of the average value, to be awarded to the Rector in respect of the tithes.

The Award, after being enrolled by the Clerk of the Peace for the Division of Holland, was to be deposited in the parish chest in the church, and be open to any person interested, on payment of one shilling; and for copies of any part, at the rate of two-pence for 72 words.

DRAINAGE RATES.

The old part of this parish is liable to the dykereeve rate of the Court of Sewers. The fen land is in the Sixpenny District of the Black Sluice, it also pays the tax of the *Second Witham District*, and sends one representative to each Trust. The whole parish is liable to the Witham Outfall Tax.

ENCLOSURE OF MARSH. About 300 acres of marsh land were embanked and brought under cultivation, about 1864-6, by the Boston Harbour Commissioners, Mr. Edward Black, and the Crown.

DRAINAGE. FRAMPTON. This parish is drained by a sewer which extends from the Hammond Beck to the Witham Outfall, where it discharges a small part of the drainage through a sluice in the bank.

THE FEN. A portion of the parish, containing 562 acres, drains into the Wyberton Town Drain, and, in accordance with a law of Sewers made in 1754, pays dykereeve rate to that parish.

The Allotment awarded under the Holland Fen Award is adjacent to the old enclosed land in the parish, lying about 3½ miles north-west of the village. The Fen is divided by the New Hammond Beck and the South Forty Foot Drain, access being obtained over these by means of Baker's Bridge and Hubbert's Bridge.

Holland Fen Award, 1767. The Allotment consists of a part of the *Bridge Piece*, lying between the Old and New Hammond Becks, containing 262a. 3r. 16p.; part of the Middle Fen, lying between the New Hammond Beck and the South Forty Foot Drain, containing 468a. 3r. 1p.; and part of the Great Fen on the north side of the South Forty Foot, containing 526a. 1r. 33p.; together, 1,258a. 0r. 10p. There were also 10 acres of other commonable land in the parish; the Holmes, containing 22 acres let by the parish in aid of the rates, and part of the Reaches Marsh, containing 100 acres and 'formerly left by the sea,' and part of the bed of the old river Witham lying about three quarters of a mile north-west of Langrick Ferry; also the common land known as the Mill Field, Spot Field, Whorley Dale Field, &c.

ENCLOSURE ACT. 24 Geo. iii, 1784. An Act was obtained for dividing and enclosing these fens and other common land in the year 1784. John Parkinson of Asgarby, Edward Hare of Castor, and Joseph Newman of Boston were the Commissioners appointed to carry out the work. They were to have £63 as their remuneration, out of which they were to pay their expenses. They were directed to make such public roads, not less than 40ft. wide, as they deemed necessary, and to allot the herbage of both the ancient highways, as well as of the roads set out under this Act, which should be made open, and not fenced on both sides, to the owners of the lands through which such roads passed. One-ninth part of the fen was to be allotted in lieu of tithes, and other land to the value of £10 a year, and also 223a. 1r. 25p. in lieu of tithes on the old land, and 22a. 2r. 16p. in lieu of tithes of *Wykes Demesnes*. The Rector and the tenants of these allotments were given right of footway over the banks of the North and South Forty Foot Drains to the same. The Commissioners were also to set out to the Vicar and Churchwardens and to the Lords of the Manors of Earl Hall and Stone Hall a piece of the fen of the annual value of £20, for the benefit 'of indigent and industrious persons' belonging to the parish, who receive no weekly or monthly contribution therefrom; which land was never to be let for a longer term than 4 years at one time, one moiety of the rent to be distributed in coal and the other at the discretion of the trustees. It was provided by the Act that the sum of £20, clear of all deductions, should be paid annually to the Vicar of Frampton by the owner of the great tithes, rectory and glebe lands, and that the Commissioners should allot 6 acres of fen of average value for augmenting the vicarage. Power was given to put up fences and gates at the ends of any roads or highways, except turnpike roads, to prevent cattle from trespassing about the parish, which gates were to be maintained by the Surveyor of Highways.

The Award, after being enrolled, was to be deposited in the parish chest in the Church and to be open to inspection on payment of one shilling; a copy to be supplied of the whole or any part at the rate of two-pence for 72 words. The Commissioners were empowered to ascertain the value of the tithe on certain salt marshes which were likely to be enclosed, such value not to exceed one-seventh, or be less than one-tenth, of the value of the land embanked. Tenants for life, or trustees holding part of the marsh, were empowered to borrow £3 per acre, on the security of the land enclosed, towards the cost of the work. The trustees of the Donnington turnpike road were empowered to let Amber Hill, subject to the right of the Surveyor of Highways to get materials for the repair of the roads in Frampton, but no building was to be erected thereon.

REACHES MARSH. The Reaches Marsh is part of the old river Witham, lying between the North Forty-Foot Drain and the river, about three-quarters of a mile north-west of Langrick Ferry, and between 6 and 7 miles distant from the village of Frampton. It was proposed to add this land to the parish of Coningsby, under the Divided Parishes Act, but, this being opposed by the inhabitants, it still remains a portion of the parish.

DRAINAGE RATES. The old portion of this parish is subject to the dykereeve rate of the Court of Sewers, the fen portion to the Black Sluice Sixpenny District rate and the *Second Witham District* rate, and the whole of the parish to the Witham Outfall tax. The owners of land in the parish are entitled to elect one member of the Black Sluice Trust and those in the fen portion one member of the *Second District Trust*.

KIRTON. The main sewer in this parish, called 'Kirton Town's Drain,' extends from the Hammond Beck at Kirton Holme in a south-easterly direction to the sea bank at Kirton Skeldyke, where there is a sluice, and thence along an open drain 15 chains in length, across the marshes to the Welland. The length of the drain from one sluice to the other is over 8 miles. The sluice

DRAINAGE.

in the bank at the Welland end has 4ft. 6in. of waterway, and that at the Hammond Beck 5ft. 9in. The level of the sill of the former, or sea sluice, is 4·8ft. above *Ordnance datum*, and that in the Hammond Beck 6·89ft. above. The bottom of the drain at Kirton Bridge is 1·4ft. above the sill of the sea sluice. Considerable difficulty has been found in keeping open the drain across the marshes to the Welland, from its tendency to fill up with alluvial matter. The sluice has frequently been closed and the whole of the drainage has at such times found its way to the Hammond Beck.

THE WELLAND OUTFALL. In 1715 the outfall sluice into the Welland was reported by a Jury of the Court of Sewers as defective, owing to the sandy foundation, and it was advised that a new sluice should be erected between Kirton and Fosdyke, and that the old one should be blocked up. A Law of Sewers was made ordering this work to be done. In 1881 £470 10s. was expended in repairs and improvements of Kirton drain. In 1894 a proposal was made to erect a new sluice at the end of the creek running between the newly enclosed marshes in Kirton and Fosdyke and to connect the two banks, the estimated cost being £3,400, but this scheme did not receive the sanction of the Court of Sewers.

WELLAND TAXATION, 1867.
30 and 31 Vict., c. 195.
In the session of 1867 the Welland Commissioners obtained an Act of Parliament empowering them to raise further money. The area of taxation was extended, and included land in the parish of Kirton which is rated at fourpence per acre. The inhabitants petitioned against the Bill, contending that they derived no benefit from the works in the Welland, the sill of the Outfall Sluice being from 4ft. to 5ft. above low water in that river. (By the Welland Act of 1794 it was proposed to bring the outfall of the river Welland to Wyberton roads, and lands in Kirton and the adjoining parishes were to be made subject to a tax of twopence per acre. This scheme was not carried out, and, by the Welland Act of 1824 the lands in Kirton were exempted from this taxation.) The Petitioners further contended that Kirton was sufficiently drained by means of the Outfall into the Hammond Beck, and only partially by the Welland, and that if better drainage were required, the Black Sluice Commissioners had power, by mutual agreement, to give a more complete drainage. A clause in the Act gave the right to claim exemption in case the parish were able to prove that Kirton was not drained by the Outfall of the Welland. If the Trustees after hearing the parishioners would not entertain their claim to exemption, there was to be an appeal to the Quarter Sessions at Spilsby. As the Trustees declined to give any relief, the parishioners appealed, and the case was heard at the Quarter Sessions at Spilsby, in 1869, with the result that the parish remained liable to the tax.

THE FEN. The land in Holland Fen allotted to this parish lies on the north side of the South Forty-Foot Drain, in the centre of Holland

Fen, and is about six miles long by three-quarters of a mile wide. Access from the older part of the parish is obtained by Hubbert's Bridge. There is also a portion of the fen on the south side of the drain, extending up to Kirton Holme, and along the north side of the old Hammond Beck.

The area of land allotted to Kirton under the Holland Fen Award was 3,448a. 0r. 23p. There were also in the parish other common lands, known as the Meers, the Russian Ings, Little Hurn, Kirton Ings, Little Ings, Maumsgate—otherwise Mornsgate—Middle Field, Grave's Field, Broad Field, Ax Head, Handtoft, Eau Bridge Field, Great and Little Mantle, Cerncroft, Hurn Field, Skeldike Field, Bendike Field, Hallstock, and Bucklegate Field, containing altogether 600 acres. *Holland Fen Award, 1707.*

This land was enclosed and allotted under an Act passed in 1772. The Commissioners appointed were Peter Packharnis of Benington, Thomas Hogard of Spalding, and John Hudson, of Louth. Their remuneration was fixed at £84 each. The expenses to be incurred in carrying out the Act were to be paid by an equal pound rate, or acre tax, levied according to the value of land allotted. *ENCLOSURE ACT 12 Geo. iii, 1772*

Sixty acres in the High Fen, abutting, on the east, on the road leading to Langrick Ferry, were allotted to the Vicar in lieu of the vicarial tithes ; 310 acres and also 25 acres in the High Fen were allotted to the owners of the great tithes ; and, in addition to this, one-ninth part of the commons, in lieu of both great and small tithes and all ecclesiastical dues and payments, except Easter offerings, mortuaries and surplice fees ; and 101 acres to the Earl of Exeter, the Lord of the Soke of Kirton, in lieu of his rights of *brovage*, and as 'Lord Paramount' or 'Lord and Owner of the Soil.' The remainder of the land was to be allotted in the proportion of eight acres to every house, four acres to every toftstead, and the rest amongst the owners of the enclosed lands, in proportion to the rates paid to the dykereeve assessments. The Commissioners were empowered to make such roads, ditches and fences as they deemed necessary.

The award was to be engrossed, and, after being enrolled with the Clerk of the Peace for the Parts of Holland, was to be deposited in the common chest of the Parish Church, a fee of one shilling being charged for inspection, and twopence for every 100 words for a copy of the whole, or of any part.

The right of the parish to obtain materials for the repair of the roads from Amber Hill was confirmed, subject to the Trustees having power to let the same.

The old lands in this parish are liable to the dykereeve rate of the Court of Sewers, but they are not liable to the Black Sluice tax, as the drainage by the Hammond Beck is an ancient right. The fen portion is in the Sixpenny District of the Black Sluice, and pays the *DRAINAGE RATES.*

rates of the *Second Witham District*. The whole parish pays the Witham Outfall Tax.

WIGTOFT, SUTTERTON, ALGARKIRK, FOSDYKE AND SWINESHEAD.

<small>DRAINAGE.</small> The drainage of the five parishes or 'towns' of Wigtoft, Sutterton, Algarkirk, Fosdyke, and part of Swineshead is effected by what is known respectively in the different parts as the *Five Towns, Four Towns, Three Towns* and *Two Towns* Drain. This system of drainage is connected both with the Hammond Beck and the Welland. The dividing line of the watershed is at Acre Land Clough, at Fishmere End, on the northern boundary of Wigtoft. Northwest of this, the main drain is known as the Simon Weir Drain, and passes through Swineshead to the Hammond Beck, which it joins a little above the Kirton Outfall. About mid-way on the Simon Weir Drain are doors across the drain, pointing towards the Hammond Beck. Wigtoft is drained by two sewers running on the east and west side of the parish. The East Drain runs from Cawdron's Sluice to Fishmere End, and discharges into the Simon Weir Drain to the west of Acre-land Clough. The water of the West Drain runs partly north and partly south, the division being about mid-way between the turnpike road from Fosdyke to Swineshead, and that from Boston to Spalding. The northern portion joins the Cross Drain, and empties into the East Drain. The southern portion runs along the west side of the parish, and through Sutterton to the outfall at Fosdyke Bridge. From near Acre-land Clough one drain passes through the east side of Algarkirk parish and Fosdyke, to the Outfall near Fosdyke Bridge, a second, starting from the same point, crosses the main road from Boston to Spalding, and passes about mid-way between Sutterton and Algarkirk churches, crossing the main road to Fosdyke, to the same outfall. The length of the Simon Weir Drain from Acre-land Clough to the Hammond Beck is 3 miles 35 chains. The Five Towns Drain, from Acre-land Clough to the Welland, is 6 miles 20 chains in length. The highest part of the drainage system is at Acre-land Clough, from which point the drains fall both ways, the fall in the bottom being 2ft. 11in. to the Hammond Beck, and 5ft. to the sill of the sluice in the Welland. There is no sluice at the Hammond Beck, but only an archway, having 5ft. 6in. water-way. The old sluice near Fosdyke Bridge, had 6ft. 6in. water-way. The area drained by the Five Towns Drain is 9,000 acres. In 1883 a new Outfall Sluice was <small>FIVE TOWNS SLUICE.</small> built at the Welland, having 8ft. of opening, the sill being placed 0·62ft. below *Ordnance datum*, or about 4ft. below the old sill. The drain was widened and deepened to adapt it to the new sluice, the bottom being made 8ft. wide. In floods, the water runs about 3ft. deep on the sill. In summer, the water is held up to 6ft. 6in. above the sill. The estimated cost of this cleaning and deepening of the drain was £888. The new sluice was

erected by Messrs. Pattinson & Co., in 1881, under the direction of Mr. John Kingston, the cost being £2,394. The deepening of the drain was let to Mr. Barwell. To cover the cost of these works a sum of £3,500 was borrowed in 1883, repayable within 20 years.

For rating purposes the *Five Towns* Drain includes the lands in Swineshead, which pay dykereeve rate and lie to the south of Black Jack Road, from Coney Hill to Pippin Hall Bridge, known as Swineshead South, and land in Wigtoft, Sutterton, Algarkirk and Fosdyke; the *Four Towns*, the land in Wigtoft, Sutterton, Algarkirk and Fosdyke; the *Three Towns*, Swineshead South, Wigtoft, and Sutterton; the *Two Towns*, Wigtoft and Sutterton. In each case the fen land is excluded, and only such parts of the parishes as are liable to dykereeve rates are taxed to the sewers rate. {RATING AREA.}

Under the *River Welland Act* of 1794 the lands in these parishes drained by the Welland were made liable to a tax of twopence per acre as a contribution towards the cost of the intended new Outfall; as this Act was not carried out, it was repealed by the Act of 1824. By the Act of 1867 the lands in the Five Towns District, except those in Swineshead, were made liable to a rate not exceeding 4d. per acre. The parishioners appealed against the rate, in the manner provided in the Act, but were not able to obtain any relief. {WELLAND TAX. 30 and 31 Vict., c 195.}

A considerable area of land in these parishes was removed from the jurisdiction of the Court of Sewers by the *Black Sluice Act*. The particulars of this, and of the enclosure of the common lands in these parishes, will be found described in the chapter on the Black Sluice.

The land in the old part of the parish is subject to dykereeve rate, and to the *Witham Outfall Tax*, to which also the fen portion is liable. {DRAINAGE RATES.}

The allotments in Holland Fen made to the Parishes of Algarkirk and Fosdyke are situated about nine miles distant from the villages of the parishes to which they were originally allotted and from which they are now separated under the Divided Parishes Act. {ALGARKIRK AND FOSDYKE FENS. Holland Fen Award, 1767.}

Algarkirk Fen is a narrow tract of land in Holland Fen, being about five and a half miles long and three-quarters of a mile wide, extending from the South Forty-Foot Drain to Kyme Eau and bounded on the west by the Skirth and Holland Dyke. It is described in the Act as comprising Clay Hills, Little Sand Hills, Great Sand Hills, Fleet Wood and part of the Common Rakes, and containing 2,380a. 1r. 22p. Fosdyke Fen lies adjacent to the river Witham, the eastern boundary being the course of the old river, and the western a narrow strip of land adjacent to the North Forty-Foot Drain. It is described in the Act as comprising part of the Gowt Plot and part of Langrett Plot and as containing 879a. 2r. 30p. These fens are in the Sixpenny District of the Black Sluice and *Second Witham District*. The taxable area of Algarkirk Fen is 2,337a. 1r. 19p. and of Fosdyke Fen 887a. 1r. 23p. Each of these allotments elects one member of the Black Sluice and of the Second District Commissions.

ALGARKIRK IN-CLOSURE ACT.
2 Geo. iii, c. 69, 1767.

The Fen allotments were divided and allotted under an Act obtained in 1767. The Commissioners were Daniel Douglas of Falkingham, Thomas Hogard of Spalding, and Thomas Stavely of Kirton, each of whom was to be paid £63 for his services and expenses. They were empowered to divide and allot the land, and to set out roads and drains.

The Award, when executed and enrolled with the Clerk of the Peace for the division of Holland, was to be deposited in the Common Chest in the Parish Church of Algarkirke *cum* Fosdyke, and to be open to inspection on payment of a fee of one shilling, and twopence for every hundred words copied.

ALTERATION OF THE PARISHES.

The fen portion of the parish of Fosdyke was transferred to Brothertoft Parish in 1881. Algarkirk Fen was transferred to the new Parish of Amber Hill in 1880.

MARSH ENCLOSURE.

In 1864 an embankment was constructed, enclosing the marsh land in Fosdyke bordering on the Welland Outfall, Mr. W. Bett being the Contractor; and in 1870 a second enclosure, extending up to Kirton Outfall, was made.

SUTTERTON ENCLOSURE ACT.
2 Geo. iii, 1772.

The Act for enclosing the land awarded to Sutterton under the *Holland Fen Enclosure Award*, containing 2,488a. 2r. 22p., and the other commonable lands was obtained in 1772. Thomas Hogard of Spalding, William Elstob of London, and William Jepson of Lincoln were appointed Commissioners under the Act. Edward Hare of Castor was appointed Surveyor. By direction of the Act, 137a. 1r. 30p. of marsh land and 140a. in *Rose Platts* were awarded to the Vicar in lieu of the tithes in the parish; to the Impropriator of the great tithes, land to the value of £20 a year; also to the Vicar and owner of the great tithes, one-ninth in value of of the common fen and marsh lands, of which the former was to have three-fifths and the latter two-fifths. The Lord of the Manor was awarded 86 acres in lieu of his rights of *brovage*. A number of public roads are set out in the award, varying in width from 60ft. to 30ft. The Award is dated 25th March, 1774, and is desposited at the Sessions House, Boston. The fee for inspection, as directed by the Act, is one shilling for complete copies, or twopence for 100 words. It was also directed that a copy should be deposited in the Parish Chest.

SWINESHEAD. THE FEN.
Holland Fen Award, 1767.

The land awarded to Swineshead under the Holland Fen Award comprised the following places: Chapel Hill Hurn, adjoining the Witham five miles above Langrick Ferry; part of Great Smeeth Hall, adjoining the North Forty-Foot at the North End of Kirton Fen; part of the Common Rakes, on the north side of, and adjoining the South Forty-Foot Drain, on the west of Algarkirk Fen; part of Far Cattle Holme, on the south side of the South Forty-Foot, between the Hammond Beck and the main road to Sleaford; part of Brand End, on the west side of the East Plot; part of the Rushes; Creasy Plot, near Sykemouth, the whole of First Cattle Holme; part of Fore Fen, near Kirton Holme, on the west side of the Five Towns Drain. There was also other common land in the parish, called Sidecroft Common, the whole containing 2,095 acres. The owners of lands and toftsteads in Swineshead, together with those in Wigtoft, also had common rights over Wigtoft Marsh in Bicker Haven, containing 450 acres.

This land was divided and allotted under an Act passed in 1773. The Commissioners for carrying out the Enclosure, were Peter Packharniss of Benington, Thomas Hogard of Spalding, and William Fillingham of Flawborough. Each Commissioner was entitled to receive £84 for his services and expenses. The award, after being enrolled, was to be deposited in the parish churches of Swineshead and Wigtoft, and to be open to inspection on payment of a fee of one shilling, and twopence for every 100 words extracted.

INCLOSURE ACT. 13 Geo. iii, 1773.

The Commissioners were authorised to make roads over such public and private lands as they deemed necessary, and to do all necessary ditching and fencing. The herbage of the roads was vested in the Surveyor of Highways, and was to be let by him for the benefit of the parish. The right of the parish to obtain materials for the repair of the road from Amber Hill was reserved.

The expenses attending the carrying out of the Act were paid by an equal *pound rate* or *acre tax*. The Earl of Exeter, as Lord of the Soke of Kirton and as Lord Paramount of the Soil, was to be allotted 15 acres in Wigtoft Marsh. Two-thirds of the remainder were allotted to Swineshead, and one-third to Wigtoft. One-tenth of the Wigtoft allotment was set apart for the Impropriator and Vicar, in lieu of the great and small tithes. One acre was allotted to the owners of houses, and half-an-acre to owners of toftsteads, and the remainder amongst the owners of land in the parish in proportion to the dykereeve rates paid.

In Swineshead the allotment to Trinity College, as Impropriator, was 320 acres in Brand End Plot; 20 acres near the Black Sluice Drain and the turnpike road; to the Vicar a plot of the value of £5 a year; and also to the Impropriator and Vicar one-ninth part in value of the common land; to the Lord Paramount, as owner of one-third part of the soil and of the *brovage*, 72 acres; and to the owners of the Manor of Swineshead, Swineshead Abbey or 'Swineshead de-la-Mere' and 'East Evening,' such quantity as the Commissioners should consider sufficient recompense; five acres to each owner of a house; two and a half acres to each owner of a toftstead; and the remainder amongst the owners of the enclosed lands, in proportion to the amount they were assessed at to the dykereeve rate.

In order to increase the value of the living of Swineshead, land to the value of £30 a year, out of the quantity allotted to the Impropriator, was to be set aside; and the Governors of Queen

Anne's Bounty were authorised to contribute out of their funds a sum of £100.

DRAINAGE RATES.

The fen land is in the *Sixpenny District* of the Black Sluice, the area of land paying rates being 2,117a. 1r. 0p. It is also in the *Second Witham District*. The parish elects one member of each of these Commissions. The old lands in the parish are subject to the dykereeve rate of the Court of Sewers, and the whole parish pays the Witham Outfall Tax.

ALTERATION OF THE PARISHES.

Under the Divided Parishes Act, the fen land at Chapel Hill belonging to Swineshead was transferred in 1880 to a new parish, called *Pelham's Lands*.

By an Order of Council (23 April, 1890), the following places, at one time extra parochial, but afterwards made into separate parishes, were added to Swineshead, viz., Gibbet Hills, Royalty Farm, Mown Rakes, Little Brand End Plot, and Great Brand End Plot.

HIGHWAY RATE OF NEW PART OF PARISH.

After the amalgamation, these places were rated to the Highway rate of the parish. This liability was contested, on the ground that when this land, part of Holland Fen, was enclosed, it was, with other lands, sold under the Act of 1767, to pay the cost of the enclosure, and that under the Local Enclosure Act, it was exempted from taxation during the first lease. The case, *Shaw v.*

Shaw v. Thorpe 1893.

Thorpe, was tried before Mr. Justice Wills and Mr. Justice Charles, in 1893, who held that, as the purpose for which the exemption was originally made no longer existed, the land was not exempt from the parochial rates.

FORMATION OF TWO LEVELS.

In 1881 a petition was presented to the Court of Sewers, praying that the land on the north of Black Jack Road in Swineshead, with the Fen Houses, should be made into a separate level for rating to the Court of Sewers, on the ground that this land did not drain to the river Welland, and an order was accordingly made that the parish should be divided into two levels, one on the north and the other on the south of the Black Jack Road, and separate dykereeve rates laid on each.

Court of Sewers. Minutes, 6 Aug., 1881. 13 May, 1882.

WIGTOFT. THE FEN.

The area of fen land in Wigtoft parish allotted under the Holland Fen Award, of 1767, was 994a. 1r. 34p. There were also in the parish other common lands, known as Green Row Common, Asperton Common, Easthorp Common and Burtoft Common, and other waste land, containing altogether 30 acres.

INCLOSURE ACT 12 Geo. iii, c. 112, 1772.

This land was divided and allotted under an Act passed in 1772.

13 Geo. iii, 1773.

The tract of land known as Wigtoft Marsh, over which the parishioners, in common with those in Swineshead, had rights, was divided and allotted under the Swineshead Enclosure Act of 1773.

The Enclosure Commissioners apppointed under the Act were, William Jepson of Lincoln, Thomas Hogard of Spalding and William Elstobb of London. They were to be paid £63 for their remuneration. The expenses of carrying out the Act were to be defrayed by '*an equal pound rate or acre tax*,' according to the value of the land allotted. The allotment to the Vicar was to consist of 60 acres at the east end of Sykemouth, and to the Vicar and Impropriator land of the annual value of £120, and also one-tenth of the whole fen in lieu of tithes, one-third of which was to belong to the Vicar. To the Lord of the Soke, for his rights as Lord Paramount, or owner of one-third part of the soil and of the *brovage*, 33 acres; to every owner of a house in the parish five acres; to every owner of a toftstead two-and-a-half acres; and the remainder amongst the owners of land, according to their assessment to the dykereeve rate.

The Commissioners were empowered to set out such public or private roads and to make such ditches and fences as they should deem necessary.

The award, when engrossed and enrolled, was to be open to inspection on payment of one shilling, and a copy supplied at the rate of twopence for every 100 words. A copy was to be deposited in the common chest in the parish church.

The right of the Surveyor of Highways to obtain materials from Amber Hill, for the repair of the roads, was continued, and no building was to be erected thereon.

The old portion of this parish is subject to dikereeve rate. The fen portion is in the *Sixpenny District* of the Black Sluice, the rateable area being 981 acres, and in the *Second Witham District*. The whole parish is liable to the Witham Outfall Tax.

GOSBERTON, QUADRING AND SURFLEET.—The Main Drain for such parts of these Parishes as are not in the Black Sluice district is the Risegate Eau, which extends from the Hammond Beck in Gosberton Risegate, to the Welland, about a mile above Fosdyke Bridge. The length between the two points is seven miles. The drain has an outfall at both ends, the natural division for the flow of the water being about midway at Belney Bridge, the lands on the west side of the bridge draining to the Hammond beck, and those on the east side to the Welland.

RISEGATE EAU.

There is frequent mention made of this Sewer in the records of the Court of Sewers. In the reign of Edward III, upon an inquisition taken at Gosberchirche, it was found that "the Sewer of Risegate had gutters which ought to be repaired and maintained by the towns of Gosberchirche and Rysgate and that it was obstructed by Ranulph de Rye towards the marsh, and likewise that it ought to be of the same breadth and depth, and that there ought to be a Sluice betwixt the marsh and it, of sixteen feet wide; and that the course of that Sewer, which towards the sea was called Newe Eegate had wont anciently to run directly through the midst of the marsh in Gosberchirche belonging to the Abbot of Peterborough, until 36 years before, and that, by the flowing of the sea and of the

Dugdale.
1295.

fresh water, it became obstructed, and thereupon by force made itself another current, which it then held."

571.
In Queen Elizabeth's reign the Commissioners of Sewers sitting at Boston found that " the sewer called the Merlode (*Ouse Mer Lode*) could not, without an excessive charge, carry away the water falling thereinto, nor have any fit place at the outfall thereof, whereon to erect a sufficient gote, and decreed that it should be secured and made 16ft. wide and 6ft. deep, from the infall out of the fen unto a certain place called *Elwood Elmes*, by the townships of Quadring and Donington; and that thence it should be turned and made of the like breadth and depth, at all times henceforth, by the inhabitants of Quadring to Gosberton Ee, and that at the falling thereof into the said Ee there should be a substantial stone bridge made and erected for the public roadway there at the charges of Quadring and Donyngton, and likewise a dam at Partye bridge; and that the inhabitants of Quadring and Donington should for ever after enjoy for the commodity of their said watercourse of Merlode the same drain called Gosberkirk Ee, under the sea dyke, from the infall of Merlode thereinto; and from the said dam to be made towards the sea unto the gote which thenceforth should be appointed to be made for them and their said drain of Merlode by all the limits thereof, unto the outfall of that their drain into the sea at their private drain. In consideration whereof they decreed that the townships of Quadring and Donington should make another sufficient drain in Gosberkirke Ee to stop and turn the watercourse of Rysegate out of and from the old course thereof, towards the sea dyke aforesaid, at a place in Gosberkirke, near unto Challan bridge, where they decreed that a bridge should be made and set up at the charge of the townships of Quadring and Donington; and that there the townships should scour a new drain from thence, of the like breadth and depth, which should be called the New Ee of Surflet and Gosberkirk; the accomplishing of these directions being most beneficial to the receipt and speedy conveyance of the waters both of Kesteven and Holland from the said old course in Rysegate Ee by the same New-Ee in form before

1574.
recited." By a subsequent decree, made at Helpringham in Queen Elizabeth's reign, " it appearing that the New Gote, set in the sea dyke at Surfleet at the charge of the inhabitants of Donyngton and Quadring, did of a sudden, after three weeks settling thereof, sink into a quicksand, it was ordered that the same should be made again more substantially, and set upon a better and firmer foundation." By the same commission it was also ordered " that upon the sewer called Newdike two new bridges should be erected at Rysgate Ee mouth, by the inhabitants of Gosberkirke and Surflete in their limits, and in Quadring Up Fen against the common way running from Westrop; and the other within the limits of Byker, in Hekendale Wathe, over to Hekendale Hills, of such height as boats might well pass under."

At the time when these orders were made, Bicker Haven had not been enclosed, and was an open salt water estuary or creek, and Risegate Eau discharged into it at the upper end, the gote referred to above being that now known as Lampson's Clough. When Bicker Haven was enclosed Risegate Eau was carried across it by a new cut to an Outfall in the Welland, where a sluice was built. An illustration, showing Bicker Haven before Enclosure, will be found in Chapter IX, *On the Welland*.

In 1710 a new Outfall Sluice was ordered to be built, and an assessment made, for payment of the cost, on the landowners in Gosberton, Surfleet, Quadring, Quadring Hundred and Donington, according to the Law of Sewers formerly made. In 1884 an order was obtained under the *Land Drainage Act* of 1861, authorising the following works, and the borrowing of £7,630 to pay for the same, viz., (1) the making of a new sluice in the river Welland and diverting the course of the drain to the new sluice, 10 chains to the west of the old Outfall, the estimated cost of this work being £3,500; (2) the widening and deepening the drains from the existing inner sluice to Lampson's Clough and Five Bells Bridge, and the removal of the inner sluice and Lampson's Clough, and the erection of a bridge in its place, the estimated cost being £4,175; (3) the deepening of the Merlode drain at a cost of £340. The first work was to be charged on lands paying dykereeve rate in Gosberton, Quadring, Quadring Hundred and Surfleet, also lands in Gosberton, Surfleet, Quadring, Algarkirk and Sutterton, lying south of the Roman Bank, and west of the old Sea Bank; the second work, on lands in Gosberton, Quadring, Quadring Hundred and Surfleet, subject to sewer rate; and the third work by lands in Quadring, subject to sewer rate.

1710.

NEW SLUICE.

Boston Court of Sewers.Minutes, 24 May, 1884.

The old sluice in the Welland, erected in 1803, was superseded, and the new sluice erected in its place. The old sluice had an opening of 5ft. and its sill was 5·83ft. above *Ordnance datum*. This sill was subsequently lowered to 3ft. above, and in 1873 to 2·69ft. above, *Ordnance datum*. The new sluice has an opening of 8ft., and its sill is about 9in. below *Ordnance datum*, or 3ft. below the sill of the old sluice. It was built under the direction of Mr. John Kingston, by Mr. J. Barwell, at a cost of £2,800. In heavy floods the water runs 2ft. 9in. above the sill, the summer level being 7ft. 3in. above. The deepening of the Risegate Eau and the Merlode Drain was done by Messrs. Cooke and Bennett.

The taxable area covers 9,000 acres, but about 11,000 acres discharge their water by this drain, one part going to the Welland, and the other to the Hammond Beck. The marsh lands, which hitherto had not paid dykereeve rate, were brought into taxation for the new works.

The sluice in the Hammond Beck has 7ft. 4in. of opening, and is 6ft. 3in. above *Ordnance datum*.

From the Hammond Beck to Lampson's Clough, Risegate Eau has to be maintained by Gosberton and Surfleet; thence to the sea by these parishes in conjunction with Quadring and Quadring Hundred.

DRAINAGE RATES.

The old lands in these parishes are subject to the dykereeve rate of the Court of Sewers. The fen portion is in the *Eighteenpenny District* of the Black Sluice, and each parish sends one representative to the Trust. The fen land is also subject to the Witham Outfall Tax. The lands draining by the Risegate Eau, east of Quadring Bank, and the road in continuation of this bank, leading to Pinchbeck, in the parishes of Quadring, Surfleet and Gosberton, are subject to the Welland Tax of fourpence an acre, levied under the Act of 1867. These lands are free from the Witham Outfall Tax.

GOSBERTON DRAINAGE.

In addition to the Risegate Eau, Gosberton and Surfleet drain by Lathom's or Lafen Lode, and the old Beche Drain.

There are several cloughs and sewers, also connected with the Glen, for obtaining a supply of fresh water.

GOSBERTON FEN.

There are 305 acres of land in Gosberton Parish which drain by the Merlode and pay dykereeve rates to Quadring. The fen land in this parish is in the Black Sluice District and is bounded by Surfleet Fen on the north, *the Beche* separates it from Pinchbeck Fen on the south, the South Forty-Foot Drain is on the west, and the Hammond Beck Drain on the east. The district contains 1,170a. 2r. 13p. and elects one member of the Black Sluice Trust.

INCLOSURE ACT. Geo. iii, 1799.

In 1799 an Act was obtained for dividing, allotting and inclosing the common fen *droves* and waste lands in Gosberton. The Act recites that this land in its then condition was of very little value, but was capable of improvement, and that it contained 1400 acres. William Ashton of Brandon, John Renshaw of Owthorpe, and William Golding of Donington were appointed Commissioners, with power to enclose, divide and allot the land, and were to be paid two guineas a day for their services. They were to set out such public roads as were necessary, forty feet wide. These roads were to be formed by a Surveyor appointed for the purpose, at the expense of the proprietors, and after being certified as completed to become public highways. The bank between Gosberton and Pinchbeck Fens, by the side of the higher land drain, was to be raised and strengthened to prevent the water flowing out of Pinchbeck Fen.

SURFLEET FEN.

The fen land in Surfleet lies between Gosberton and Quadring Fens, and between the Hammond Beck on the east, and the South Forty-Foot on the west. It is in the *Eighteenpenny District* of the Black Sluice, its rateable area containing 760a. 0r. 31p. It elects one member of the Black Sluice Trust.

INCLOSURE ACT. 17 Geo. iii, c.140, 1777.

The Fen was enclosed under an Act obtained in 1777 for dividing and enclosing the common fen, common marsh, common fields and waste grounds in the Parish of Surfleet. The total area dealt with by the Act includes, in addition to the fen which is in the Black Sluice District, the marsh lying near the Welland, formerly part of Bicker Haven, containing about 400 acres.

Thomas Pilgrim of Heckington, John Hudson of Louth, and Benjamin Rippin of Kirton were appointed Commissioners for dividing and enclosing the fen, and they were to be paid sixty guineas each for their services and expenses. They were to set out the public roads necessary, 40ft. wide, which were to become, when constructed, public highways. The Commissioners were directed to erect two new engines for draining the Fen and also such banks, drains, sluices and bridges as they found necessary. The Award, when executed, was to be enrolled and deposited with the Clerk of the Peace for Holland and to be open for inspection on payment of a fee of one shilling, and two pence for every 100 words copied.

DRAINAGE RATES.

The old lands in Surfleet are subject to the dykereeve rate of the Court of Sewers and the *Fourpenny* Welland tax; and the fen lands, to the Black Sluice and Witham Outfall taxes.

QUADRING.

The principal drain in Quadring and Quadring Hundred is the *Mer* or *Ouse Mer Lode*, which runs from Stong's Tunnel to Risegate Eau at Lampson's Clough and so to the Welland, and a branch called the *Coln Drain*. There are 305 acres in Gosberton which drain by the Merlode and pay dykereeve rates to Quadring. Quadring and Quadring Hundred have jointly with Gosberton and Surfleet to maintain the Risegate Eau from Lambson's Clough to the Welland.

QUADRING FEN

The fen land in Quadring in the Black Sluice District lies between the Ouse Mer Lode on the north and Surfleet Fen on the south, being bounded by the South Forty-Foot on the west and the high lands in Quadring and Gosberton on the east. It includes Quadring High Fen, Quadring Hundred Fen and the Shoff, Quadring containing 65a. 3r. 29p., Quadring Fen Shoff 1,859a. 2r. 3p., and Quadring Hundred Fen 400a. 1r. 7p., together 2,325a. 3r. 4p. Each of these fens returns one member of the Black Sluice Trust. The whole are situated in the *Eighteenpenny District*, and are liable to the Witham Outfall tax.

INCLOSURE ACT, 15 Geo. iii, c. 1775.

In 1775 an Act was obtained for dividing and inclosing the common fens, common meadows, common fields and waste grounds in the Parishes of Quadring and in Quadring Hundred. The High Fen is described as containing, with the Shoff, 1,300a, and the Low Fen in Quadring Hundred, 1,100a.

The Commissioners appointed were Daniel Douglas of Folkingham, John Hudson of Louth, and William Jepson of Lincoln, who were to be paid seventy guineas for their services.

The Commissioners were authorised to set out any roads required, and to give directions for the erection of banks, sluices, bridges, drains and engines, as they might think convenient. The public roads were to be sixty feet wide, and to be deemed highways.

A copy of the Award, when executed and enrolled with the Clerk of the Peace, was to be deposited in the parish church of Quadring, so far as it related to that parish, and the other part in the parish church in Gosberton, and be open open to inspection on payment of a fee of one shilling, and twopence for every 100 words copied.

DRAINAGE.
Dugdale.

1293.

DONINGTON.—The ancient sewers in this parish have received notice from very early times. In the reign of Edward I., at an Inquisition held at Gosberton it was found that "the sewers of Scathergast, Swyneman Dam, and Swane Lode, in Donington, ought, and had used to be 16 ft. in breadth, and so deep as that the water might have a free passage; and that they ought to be repaired by the town of Donington, unto the river of Byker, which runneth to the sea; and to be opened at all times, except when such an abundance of water the sewers could not suffice, but that the province of Holand would be drowned." In such case it was to be lawful for them to stop the said sewers. It was also found that the channel of Byker ought to be repaired by Byker. At a subsequent Session it was found that the portion belonging to Byker extended to Bondistac; the town of Donington having to maintain it from Bondistac to Quadring, to the breadth of 24ft.; the town of Quadring to repair it to Gosberton; and the town of Gosberton thence to the sea (Bicker Haven.) The sewer here referred is that which runs through the village of Bicker, and along the northern boundary of Donington, and formerly emptied into Bicker Haven, but now discharges into the Hammond Beck.

A large portion of this parish consists of fen and ing land. This tract, called *the New Enclosures*, lies to the east of the South Forty-Foot Drain, and is intersected by the old Hammond Beck. It is bounded on the north by Bicker Fen and Ings, on the east by the high lands in Donington, and on the south by Quadring Fen. It includes the parts known as the North Ings, the North Fen, West Dales, Gibbet Fen, Mallard Hurn, Up Fen, Shoff Fen, and the South Ings. It comprises 3,100 acres, or about half the land in the parish.

The land lying on the west of the Hammond Beck drains into the South Forty-Foot, and that on the East into the Hammond Beck, except a small area lying in the North Fen, which finds its way into the Forty-Foot by a tunnel under the Hammond Beck. The surface of the land varies from 15 feet in the lowest part to 21 feet in the highest, above the sill of the Black Sluice, 12 miles distant.

The Bridge End, or Holland, Causeway passes through this Fen. This was a road originally made by the Romans and its surface is raised considerably above the level of the adjacent land,

and before the Enclosure of the Fens formed a barrier to the water which was poured into the fen lying south of it from the numerous becks which came from the high lands. The maintenance of the west end of this bank devolved on the Abbot of St. Saviour's Priory, which stood at the west end of the road, where the hamlet of Bridge End now is, certain lands having been given to the Priory to provide the funds for this purpose. The eastern part of the bank had to be kept in repair by the inhabitants of Donington. A bridge over the Hammond Beck, then known as *Peecebrigge* had been built by the Abbot of Spalding, who took toll of persons passing over it, and a Jury found that he ought to maintain it.

In 1767 an Act was obtained for dividing and enclosing the open fields, meadows, common fens and other commonable places within the parish of Donington, and for draining and improving the same. Under this Act Commissioners were appointed to allot the common lands, and to make such roads, drains, bridges and engines as they thought necessary. The public roads were to be set out sixty feet wide. Bicker parish was to be entitled to get earth for repairing Bicker Ing or the North Fen Bank. The Commissioners were to meet once a year, on the Monday in Easter week, to appoint an officer to manage the works and to collect the rates. On the death or resignation of a Commissioner, a new Commissioner was to be appointed by the majority of the proprietors. By this Act persons proved guilty of maliciously injuring the works were to be deemed guilty of felony. Under the powers of this Act the fen was drained by three wind engines with scoop wheels, two of which were erected for lifting the water off the low land into the Forty-Foot and one for lifting the water into Hammond Beck. One of these wooden wind engines remains in existence at the present time; the others have been rebuilt. The length of the drain made under the powers of the Act was about seven and three-quarter miles. Arthur Young gives the cost of enclosure as £1,100 on 1,728 acres of land, the original value of which was £380 and the improved value in 1799 £681.

INCLOSURE ACT
7 Geo. iii, c. 62
1767.

The wind engines were only capable of lowering the water 2ft. below the average surface of the low lands and 3ft. 6in. below the average level of the whole district. In times of heavy floods the water in the South Forty-Foot, before the improvement of the Outfall, used to rise at Donington Bridge three feet above the lowest land, the ordinary wet weather and winter flow in the drain being 2ft. 5in. below the average surface of the low lands. The lower lands were consequently frequently flooded and the drainage was generally in an unsatisfactory state.

Report, W. H. Wheeler.
1883.

The powers of the existing Commissioners, as laid down by the Act of 1767, were too limited to admit of their carrying out the required improvements. In 1884 this Fen was therefore con-

DRAINAGE DISTRICT.

tituted a Drainage District under the provisions of the Land Drainage Act, 1861, the provisional order to that effect being confirmed by Parliament. The Drainage Board consists of twelve members, who are qualified by being proprietors, or heirs apparent, or agents to proprietors of not less than twenty acres, or by the tenancy of not less than forty acres. All persons paying drainage rates are entitled to vote at the election of members.

47 and 48 Vict.,c. 41, 1884.

RATES.

The amount raised by rate in 1892-3 was £69. The expenditure in maintenance was £56, and in management £39, total £95. There was no outstanding loan.

The fen land is subject to the Black Sluice Drainage Rate of eighteenpence an acre, the rateable area being 4,470a. 1r. 21p. Donington sends one representative to the Black Sluice Trust. The parish is also subject to the Witham Outfall Tax.

DRAINAGE.

BICKER.—The principal Sewer in this Parish runs through the village, and was formerly known as the *River of Byker*. It has been referred to in the account of the parish of Donington. The fen land in the Black Sluice District lies to the west of the village, between the Hammond Beck and the South Forty-Foot Drain, and between Donington Fen on the south, and Swineshead Low Ground on the north.

INCLOSURE ACT. 6 Geo. iii, c. 82, 1766.

The fen and other common lands were enclosed under an Act passed in 1766, in which it is stated that the fen and open fields contained 2,300 acres, and included Priest field, Meeking Hill field, Wilson Dyke field, and Graft Bull Hurn, containing together about 100 acres, and the Church lands.

John Landon of Milton, Joseph Robertson of Sibsey, and Samuel Elsdale of Surfleet, were appointed Commissioners to divide and allot the common land. They were directed to sell the outlying pieces named above, in lots of 10 acres, towards paying the expenses; to allot the Vicar a plot equal to an annual value of £200 and the Lay Impropriator of £40 in lieu of tithes; the Lord Paramount and Owner of the Soil, 18 acres; and the Lords of the Manor of Bicker Beaumont, Helpringham-cum-Bicker, Whaplode Hall, and Huntingfield Hall, two acres each. Three-fifths of the remainder were to be allotted to the owners of houses and toft-steads in Bicker having right of common of the yearly value of six shillings; and two-fifths to the commoners.

The Ing or North Fen Bank, which had from time immemorial been repaired with earth taken from Donington North Fen, was, in future, to be repaired in the same manner. Four and a half acres were set aside for providing materials for repairing the roads, the herbage of the same to vest in the Surveyor of highways. The Commissioners were to set out the necessary roads, which, if public, were to be 60ft. wide and to be deemed highways; they were also to see to the necessary drains, engines and other works.

After the enrolment of the award with the Clerk of the Peace, the Commissioners were to hold a meeting annually, on the first Friday in October, at the Bull Inn, Donington, notice of the meeting being given at the parish church. At this meeting a Superintendent of the Drainage Works and a Collector of Taxes were to be appointed. On the death of any Commissioner, or on his vacating his office, the surviving Commissioners were directed to call the proprietors of the land together, to appoint a new Commissioner. Two Commissioners are empowered to act, and they have power to lay the necessary tax to maintain the works.

Bicker Fen is in the *Eighteenpenny District* of the Black Sluice, the area contributing being 2,560A. 2R. 18P., and is liable to the Witham Outfall Tax. The drainage of the other portion of the parish is under the control of the Court of Sewers, and pays dykereeve rates.

CHAPTER IV.

South Holland.

BOUNDARY.

Plate 4.

ROMAN BANKS.

SOUTH HOLLAND consists almost entirely of alluvial land, and is bounded by the river Welland on the west, the coast of the Wash on the north and east, the river Nene on the east, and the South Holland or Shire Drain on the south, which separates it from the Bedford Level.

The central portion, about 5 miles in width, lying on the north and south sides of the main road leading from Spalding to Sutton St. Mary, was enclosed by banks constructed during the Roman occupation, the northern bank still being known as the *Roman Bank* and the southern bank as the *Raven Bank*. The outlets or the drainage through the Roman Bank may still be traced in the names 'Moulton Sea End,' 'Holbeach Clough,' 'Fleet Hurn,' 'Gedney Dyke' and 'Lutton Gate.'

On the south of the Raven Bank was a tract of low fen land subject to inundation from the overflowing of the Welland and the Nene, and north of the Roman Bank was the coast of the Wash. The general features and characteristics of the central portions show that it was inhabited in early times and there are also remains of Roman *Castella* at Whaplode Drove and Gedney Hill. The villages are all situated in this central portion, and, from the names which they now bear, show that they owe their original settlement to the Saxons, the termination *ton* in Weston, Moulton, Lutton and Sutton,

NAMES OF VILLAGES.

denoting that these were originally settlements of Saxon Chiefs; the termination *lode* of Whaplode refers to the stream which runs through it; Fleet takes it name from the salt water creek now known as Fleet Haven; *Bech* in Holbech means a boundary stream; and the termination of Gedney, an island, or tract of land surrounded by water, inhabited by a Saxon family of the name of *Geden* or *Gedden*, hence Geden's Ey, shortened into Gedney.

SALT MARSH RECLAIMED.

The coast gradually accreted outside the Roman Bank until the salt marshes extended northwards from the ancient bank, for a width varying from 2 to 5 miles, the surface of this land being about 3 feet higher than that inside the bank, the level of the land between the South Holland Embankment and the Roman Bank, being from 13 to 14 feet above the mean level of the sea, and that between

Plate 5.

the Roman Bank and the Raven Bank from 9 to 11 feet.

Fig: 4.
Chap: 4.

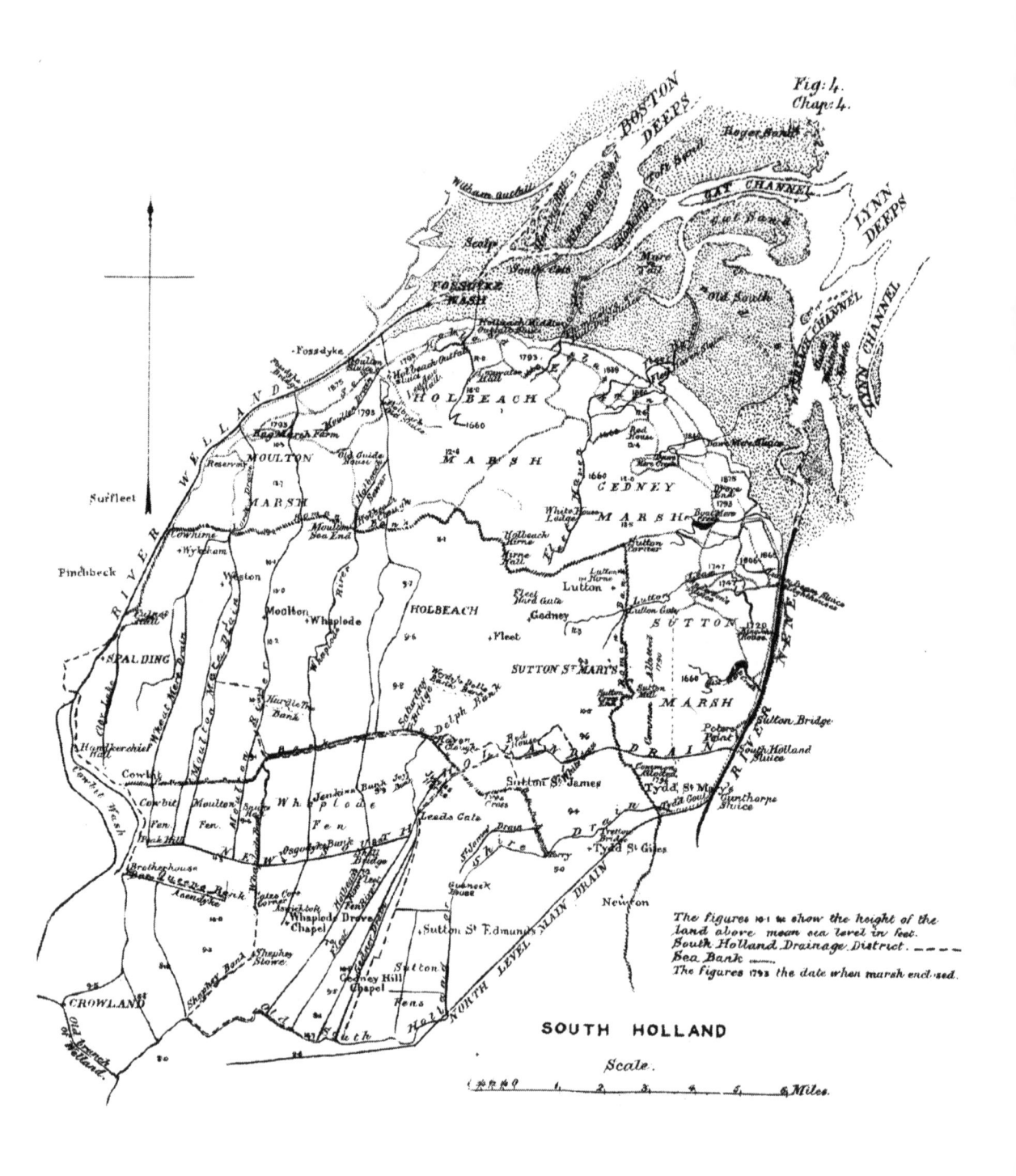

SOUTH HOLLAND

The figures 10.1 &c show the height of the land above mean sea level in feet.
South Holland Drainage District. -----
Sea Bank ———
The figures 1793 the date when marsh enclosed.

Scale.
0 1 2 3 4 5 6 Miles.

Fig: 5.
Chap: 4.

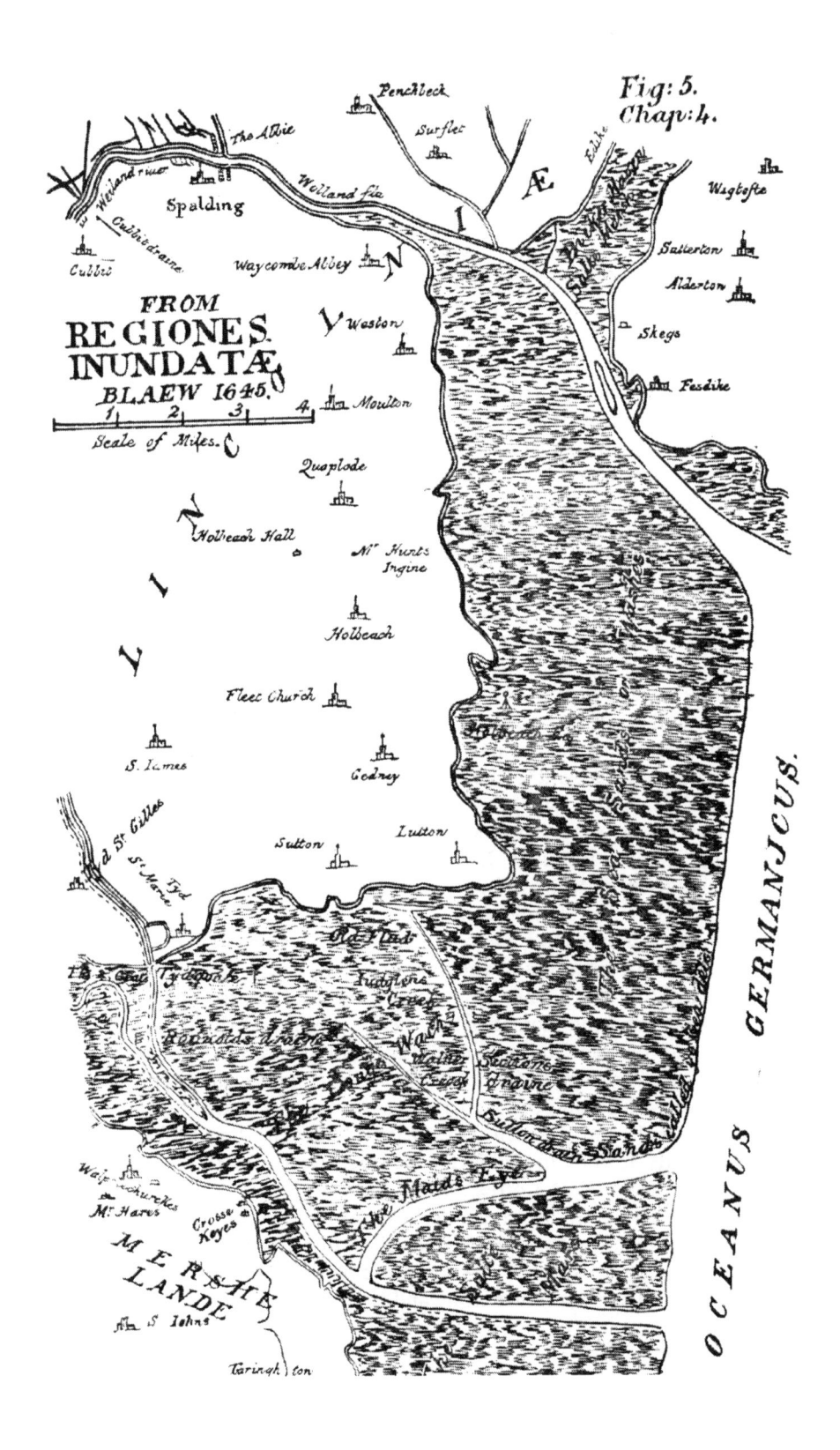

FROM
REGIONES
INUNDATÆ
BLAEW 1645.
Scale of Miles.

The area of land which has been reclaimed from the sea in South Holland, between the Nene and the Welland, since the enclosure made by the Romans, is about 35,162 acres.

Inclosures from the sea.

The first notice that occurs as to these enclosures is that of a grant made by King James I to C. Glemmond and John Walcot of London, as nominees of the Earl of Argyle, of a certain marsh (*mariscus salus*) left by the sea in Wigtoft, Moulton, Whaplode, Holbeach, and Tydd St. Mary, which was to be drained at the expense of the Earl; one fifth being reserved to the king, and also certain common lands to the neighbouring townships. In a subsequent document it is stated that the king, having granted to James, Earl of Carlisle, all salt or fresh water marsh grounds to be inned and banked" from the sea which belong to the king by his royal prerogative, the Earl of Lindsey and others named are directed to compose any difference which may happen between Sir Peregrine Bertie and Sir Philip Lunden (to whom the Earl had granted all the salt marshes within the counties of Lincoln and Cambridge, except Long Sutton) and the adjacent lords, freeholders and others who pretend to right of common in the marshes.

State Papers, Domestic, 1615.

State Papers, 1634.

An enclosure of marsh was made in the parish of Tydd St. Mary in 1632 containing 1121 acres, and lying between the old Shire Drain on the south and Dereham Drain (now the *New South Holland Drain*) on the north.

Sutton and Lutton marshes, containing 6,760 acres, were enclosed in 1660. This enclosure comprises the land lying between Dereham Drain on the south, the bank running by Sutton Bridge, West Mere Creek and King John's House to Anderson's Sluice in Lutton Leam on the east; then westwards, along the parish boundary to the Roman Bank at Lutton Corner, the west boundary being formed by the Roman bank, which ran due south through Sutton St. Mary to Dereham Drain.

In 1660 a very extensive enclosure containing 17,374 acres was made by certain Adventurers in the parishes of Gedney, Whaplode, Holbeach and Moulton. This enclosure comprised nearly all the marsh lying between the Roman Bank on the south and that afterwards enclosed by the South Holland Embankment on the north. The bank commenced near the Boat Mere Creek and went northward, past Drove End and the Red House, thence westward, north of Lapwater Hall and Leaden Hall, past Holbeach Old Outfall, then southwards to the old Guide House, then westward to Wrag Marsh and the Welland at Lord's Drain Outfall.

In 1720 an enclosure of 1,332 acres was made near the Nene, the bank starting three quarters of a mile N.E. of Sutton Wash and running on the other side of the present channel of the Nene, to where the lighthouse towers are now, and then westward to Anderson's Sluice.

In 1747 the Govenors of Guy's Hospital made an enclosure of 528 acres adjoining the last, the bank running from near where the lighthouse towers are, northwards by Baxter's Sluice to Boat Mere Creek. Other enclosures, outside this, were subsequently made, one in 1806 and the other in 1865, containing together 944 acres.

In 1793 the South Holland Embankment, or Sixteen Mile Bank was made, enclosing 4,595 acres; this will be more fully described later on. Outside this, enclosures of 533 acres were made by Johnson and Sturt in 1838, of 597 acres by T. Steer in 1840 and 1850; the Gedney enclosure of 360 acres in 1875; and the Moulton enclosure of 400 acres in the same year. These several enclosures will be found marked on the plan of South Holland.

Plate 4.

THE FEN.

Partial attempts at the reclamation of the fen or southern part of South Holland had been made from time to time by the different owners. The Abbots of Crowland had constructed banks, enclosing the land round the Abbey, and made drains for carrying away the water. They also made a bank from Crowland to Spalding, in order to obtain a road between the two places, which assisted in keeping the flood water of the Welland out of this part of South Holland. The attempts made by other proprietors are shown by the names now existing, as 'Jiggin's or Jenkin's Bank' in Holbeach Fen, 'Jay's Bank' in Fleet Fen, 'Osgodyke Bank,' 'Weydyke' 'Dales Bank,' 'Mill Bank' and the 'Delph Bank.' Ingulph states that a large tract of land was reclaimed in the 9th century in 'Holbeche and Capelode.' Several orders have been made by the Commissioners of Sewers respecting this district. In a Commission issued in the reign of Henry II (1178), it was recited that through the inundation of the sea inestimable damage had happened.

SEWERS COMMISSIONS.

Dugdale.

1294.

1307.

In 1294 an order was made for repairing the banks of Sutton Marsh, betwixt Scoft and Gedney. And it was also found that the towns of Tydd and Sutton "could not be preserved except the fresh water of Scoft near Trokenhou were restrained unto the breadth of four feet." In the reign of Edward II, Commissioners were appointed to inspect the banks and sewers upon the sea coast (betwixt Tid Brigge and Surflete Brigge), "which had been broken by tempestuous waves" and they were directed to be made higher and thicker. Numerous orders were also issued as to the size the principal water courses and sewers were to be made. It was also ordered "that Fishermen should not prejudice the common sewers by lepes, weels, or other obstructions whereby the passage of the waters of Spalding or Pinchbeck towards the sea might be hindered"; and it was ordained "that all persons, as well rich as poor, should be obedient to all *mene works* to be made as well in the sewers as in the marsh; and that every man having one messuage and ten acres of land should find towards that work one tumbrel; and he who had less, one able man of eighteen years of age at the least; and if the tumbrel should make default, to pay for every day fourpence, and a man twopence; which hire to be allowed by the said Wardens for the behoof of those towns (Spalding and Pinchbeck); and that once in the year an account should be given thereof, upon notice given in the churches of the said towns by the Common Cryer."

The same Commission presented that "for the preservation of the town of Spalding, the Sewer of Peseholme Gote, unto the old Fen dyke, ought to be scoured and repaired to Capel Brigge, 20ft. in breadth; and from that old Current unto Hergate 18ft.; and from Hergate unto the Old Fen Dyke 16ft.; and that the sewer was in decay through the default of the tenants of the Abbot of Croyland, and the freeholders of the Prior of Spalding and the tenants of the Abbot of Angiers." Also that the roadway leading from Ratun Row unto the house of John Fitz Simon unto Westlode Outfall and thence to Peccebrigge ought to be so broad that two carts might meet thereon, and that the fen bank from the Abbot of Croyland's Mill unto Pichale should be raised 2ft.; "and that the great bridge called Spalding-brigge was then broken and ought to be repaired at the charge of the whole town" of Spalding, and also "Batemanne brigg from Westlode," and likewise that "Halmergate, Newgate, Fulnedrove, Spalding Drove and the old Fen Dike ought to be repaired and that Hevidings betwixt Spalding and Weston, abutting on Weston Mere, should be made 12ft. thick, so that the water of Weston should not enter into the fields of Spalding." They further found that the common roadway betwixt Pichale and Brotherhouse was cut in sunder by the Prior of Spalding and ordered that bridges should be made thereon, so that carts might pass, and also from Brotherhouse to Clote, and that the Common way from Clote to Croyland was then in decay, and that no more trenches be made to the hindrance of the King's highway. Again, in the tenth year of Edward II, Commissioners were appointed to view and repair the banks and sewers in the marshes of Gedney, Holbech, Sutton and Flete, and in the following year a Commission was appointed to inspect the banks and sewers upon the sea coast betwixt Tid Brigge and Surflete Brigge; and four years afterwards the banks, sewers and bridges between Holand and Tyd.

1317.

In 1571 a Dykereeve's inquest was held at Tydd and a verdict, known as Murray's verdict, given (Roger Murray being the foreman of the Jury,) setting out the various sewers and banks maintainable by the parishes, and this Jury also found that the sea bank from the Gote northward to Cross Gate ought to be amended by the land holders by 'acre silver' and that the inhabitants for their passage thereon should make common *mene work* upon the sea bank yearly if need required, upon pain of every inhabitant in default of so doing paying twelve pence. The verdict also found that other work of repair to the drainage and banks, including Tydd Gote should be done by the inhabitants by *mene work*, and that six bridges of stone

Murray's Verdict 1571.

over the common sewer ought to be repaired by 'acre silver'; that the South Ea Bank should be repaired by the land holders, and that there ought to be a stone bridge over the Ea, between the sluices at Tydd bridge, and a cart bridge over the said Ea at Low Gates End, and that the Shire Gote ought to be maintained by the township of Sutton.

Dugdale.
1553

In the reign of Edward VI a Commission was directed to Thomas Holland the Elder, Richard Ogle and others, authorising them to raise money by an assessment of one penny per acre for freehold, and one half-penny for copyhold land in the township of Sutton, for the purpose of repairing the bridges, sewers and banks which had fallen into decay, and for making a new drain from a place in Sutton called Sutton Gote to a place called *the Black Arke* upon the sea.

1617.

At a Session of Sewers held at Huntingdon in the reign of James I, the rivers called High Fen Dyke and South Ea (a branch of the Nene) were ordered to be secured from Clowes Cross to Holgate by the land owners of Sutton and Tydd St. Mary's on the north part, and from Holgate to Goldyke by the inhabitants of Gedney and Sutton, and from Goldyke to Dowesdale on the north side by the inhabitants of Whaplode, Holbech, Flete and Gedney; from Dowesdale to Crowland at the Prince's charge for his lands in Crowland.

1629.

In 1629 the *Adventurers of the Bedford Level* cut the new South Ea from Crowland to Clowes Cross and the Shire Drain from Clowes Cross to Tyd, and so to the sea, and a sluice was made at Tydd upon the Shire Drain to keep out the tides.

Very considerable difficulty appears to have arisen in constructing the sluices for the drainage of the marshes, for it is stated that "the old drains were new scoured out, the outfall being as before by the Shire drain and the sluice at Tydd, for the sluices set in the marshes are all lost, which cost £25,000."

Burrell, 1642.

In 1642 a scheme was brought forward by A. Burrell for improving the drainage of South Holland by widening and deepening the South Ea and the Catwater, and opening out the Shire Drain and continuing it one and a quarter miles, from Hills Sluice to the south-east corner of Sutton Marsh and making a sluice there with a 20ft. opening.

Numerous Commissions, besides those already referred to, were issued for the protection of the banks and drainage of the district, up to the time when the Court of Sewers was permanently established.

DRAINAGE DISTRICTS.

A large part of the drainage of South Holland has been excluded from the jurisdiction of the Court of Sewers by Acts of Parliament creating the special districts of Deeping Fen, Spalding and Pinchbeck Blue Gowt District, and the South Holland Drainage District. The remaining land, not provided for by these Acts, still remains under the jurisdiction of the Court.

The Court for this district is known as the *Hundred of Elloe* and its sittings are held at Spalding. The parishes under the jurisdiction of this Court are Cowbit, Crowland, Deeping St. Nicholas, Fleet, Gedney, Holbeach, Sutton, Moulton, Pinchbeck, Spalding, Sutton St. Mary, Tydd St. Mary, Weston and Whaplode. The outer sea banks are maintained by the South Holland Embankment Commissioners and private owners. {COURT OF SEWERS. SEA BANKS.}

The general sewers' rates vary from about 2d. to 5d. per acre, and rates for special purposes levied during recent years have been, in Tydd St. Mary 4d. to 8d.; Sutton St. James 4d. to 1/-; Sutton St. Edmund 4d. to 7d.; Sutton St. Mary, 4d. to 1/4; Lutton, 10d. to 1/2; Gedney 7d. to 1/6; Fleet, 10d. to 1/6; Holbeach, 9d. to 2/1; Whaplode, 4d.; Pinchbeck, 3d. to 4d.; Crowland, 1d. to 2½d. {SEWERS RATES.}

The principal drains under the control of the Court of Sewers are described in the parishes in which they lie, where are also to be found the particulars of the Acts which have been obtained for enclosing the marshes and common land. The account of the enclosure of Deeping Fen will be found in a separate chapter.

SOUTH HOLLAND DRAINAGE DISTRICT.—This level, which was formerly very imperfectly drained and frequently flooded, lies on the east side of the river Welland, between Spalding and Brotherhouse, extending eastwards to the Nene. It consists of the fens lying south of the Raven Bank in the parishes of Spalding, Weston, Cowbit, Moulton, Whaplode, Holbeach, Fleet, Gedney and Sutton. The boundary is set out in the original Act as extending on the north from Spalding High Bridge to the high road leading to Holbeach, nearly as far as Weston; then following the boundary between Weston and Moulton in a southerly direction to the Moulton river, down to the Roman Bank; thence along this and Hurdle Tree lane to Sutton St. Mary; thence southerly to the old South Eau; and along this in a westerly direction to the Postland Estate, the boundary of which it follows to Brotherhouse Bar; and thence along the Brotherhouse Bank to Spalding, where it crosses the river, and running round Hawthorn bank, again crosses the river at the High Bridge. Additional lands have since been admitted into the district by agreement. The boundary is marked by the dotted line shown on the plan of South Holland. {BOUNDARY. 23 Geo. iii, c. 104. Plate 4.}

The principal drain was formerly the Old Shire drain, the boundary of the county of Lincoln, and at one time the course of the river Nene, into which also the Welland at Crowland discharged a part of its waters. This watercourse has been variously known as the South Eau, the Shire Drain, and the Old South Holland Drain. The outlet sluice is into the Nene near Tydd Gote. {SHIRE DRAIN.}

The area of land included in the first Act was 19,400 acres, but this was subsequently increased, the area now being 36,400 acres. {AREA.}

SOUTH HOLLAND DRAINAGE ACT OF 1793.
23 Geo. iii, c. 109, 1793.

The Preamble of the Act of 1793 described these lands as being much annoyed in the winter season with water, for want of a proper drainage and outfall to the sea, and that they were thereby rendered in a great degree unprofitable to the owners thereof, and that they were capable of being effectually drained and preserved.

The Commissioners appointed for the purpose of draining, preserving and improving these low lands were George Maxwell of Fletton, Edward Hare of Castor, and John Walker of Sutton St. Mary. Their rate of remuneration was fixed by the Act at two guineas a day, and they were empowered to carry out the necessary works for the drainage of the district, to prevent water from Deeping Fen passing by a subterraneous tunnel under the Welland into the Lord's Drain, the Adventurers of Deeping Fen being paid £1,500 as compensation for their rights in the Lord's Drain. The Lord's Drain, the South Eau Bank and the Queen's bank, so far as they formed a barrier bank to the district, were in future to be placed under the control of the Commissioners and Trustees appointed by the Act.

WORKS CARRIED OUT BY THE COMMISSIONERS.

The following were the principal works carried out by the Commissioners: a new main drain 14 miles long, extending from the Nene at Peter's Point, about half a mile above Sutton Bridge, to Wheat Meer Drain, 24ft. wide at the lower end, with a batter of 2 to 1, and a foreland of 15ft. on the Tydd side, the bottom diminishing to 10ft. at the upper end, with a batter of $1\frac{1}{4}$ to 1, and forelands of 10ft.; the highland drain, 5 miles long, and a lowland drain 4 miles long; the erection at the outfall of the drain of a sluice of three arches of a total clear waterway of 26ft.; a bridge over Dereham Drain for the Wisbech turnpike road, with 24ft., opening and another for the road from Long Sutton to Tydd St. Mary with a waterway of 22ft.; and one at Gedney Drove, with a 22ft. waterway.

For raising the money for defraying the expenses incurred under the Act, the Commissioners were empowered to levy an *acre tax* apportioned according to the benefit accruing to the lands taxed, not exceeding forty shillings an acre, the payment to be spread over three years.

The owners of certain lands lying on the west side of the Welland between Hawthorn bank and the Westlode, were to have the right to drain by the Lord's drain and by the new cut, on their paying compensation for such drainage.

The Commissioners were empowered and directed to erect a drainage engine in either the parish of Sutton St. Mary or Tydd, to lift the water out of the main drain, which lay to the south of the Roman Bank, and to put pointing doors in the drain, to prevent the water so pumped from backing up the other part of the drain; also an engine for lifting the water out of the Lord's drain on the south side of the Roman Bank. The wheels in either case were not to lift against a greater head than 8 feet.

The Award made by the Commissioners, after being enrolled with the Clerk of the Peace, was to be deposited in the Town Chest in the parish of Holbeach, and be open for inspection or copying on payment of the usual fees.

After the execution of the Award and the completion of the works ordered by the Commissioners, a Trust was to be appointed, on which every Lord of the Manor, the Rectors or Vicars of the several parishes through which the drain was made, the Senior Bursar of of St. John's College, Cambridge, and every Proprietor of 100 acres, or every lessee under the Crown of 100 acres, or their agents duly appointed, were eligible to act. This qualification was altered by the Act of 1817. A Superintendent of the drains and works was to be appointed at the Annual Meeting to be held at the Chequers Inn at Holbeach, on the second Monday following the 4th of May, or, in default of a fresh appointment, the Superintendent retained his office. *[FORMATION OF TRUST]*

The Trustees were empowered to levy an equal acre rate, not exceeding one shilling in any one year, on the occupiers of land within the district, the rates paid by tenants to be deducted from any rent due.

Persons found maliciously injuring the drainage works, or letting in salt water through the sluices, were to be liable to be transported for seven years as felons.

Under the *Fleet Enclosure Act* of 1794 some slight amendments were made in this Act, as to the sale of lands in Fleet and Holbeach, and the position of the outfall of the new drain was more clearly defined, a clause in the Act directing "Peter's Point to be that point of land which projects into the bay of the sea at a certain salt marsh in Tydd St. Mary in the County of Lincoln, belonging to the Governors or Trustees of Guy's Hospital." The new drain was to commence at the salt marsh and continue in a straight line across the sea bank, and thence by the side of an ancient gote and across a part of the embanked marsh belonging to Guy's Hospital. *[34 Geo. iii, c. 94, 1794. SOUTH HOLLAND DRAIN.]*

The drain as set out above was made between 1793 and 1796, the date on the sluice being 1795, and it, with the other works, was carried out under the superintendence of Mr. Thomas Pear of Spalding, and of his son, who succeeded him.

In the year 1795 an Act was passed dealing with the Barrier Bank and the road running along it. By an Act granted to the Adventurers of Deeping Fen in 1665 (16 and 17 Chas. II), they were required to make and maintain the bank on the east side of the Welland, from Brotherhouse to Spalding High Bridge. Subsequently, in the reign of George III, an Act (12 Geo. III), was obtained 'for the better preservation of the great bank of the river Welland...and for making and keeping in repair a road thereon, and *[BARRIER BANK. 35 Geo. iii, 1795.]*

also from thence to the village of Glinton in Northamptonshire.' On the expiration of the term granted by the Turnpike Act there was owing to the persons who advanced the money £8,925, in addition to 13 years interest. No application being made for a continuance of the term, the securities become void. It was therefore arranged amongst the Trusts interested in the preservation of the Barrier Bank, that this should be taken out of the jurisdiction of of the Deeping Fen Trust and vested in the South Holland Drainage Trust, the former paying, as compensation for getting rid of their liability for its maintenance, £1500; the Corporation of Bedford Level were also to pay £500 out of the North Level Funds, as compensation for the improvement made in the bank by the Turnpike Trust; and the South Holland Drainage Trust, £1,000, in consideration of the tolls, which after the passing of the Act they would be entitled to take. This £3,000 was to be paid to the creditors of the old Turnpike Trust, making a dividend of 40 per cent. of the principal sum due to them.

The maintenance and repair of the Barrier Bank from Spalding to Brotherhouse was, after the passing of the Act, to vest in the South Holland Drainage Trust, which was also to maintain a road on the top, and to have the right to levy tolls on all horses, cattle, or vehicles using the road, a provision being made that no toll gate was to be erected nearer to Spalding than Handkerchief Hall. The provision relating to the repair of the road was only to remain in force for 21 years. This term was subsequently extended.

The right of road over the portion of the bank leading from the south-west end of Crowland to the end of the bank at Peakirk belonging to the Corporation of the Bedford Level, was continued; the toll house called 'Gilbert's Bar,' erected by the Turnpike Trustees, was vested in the Corporation of Bedford Level; and they were authorised to collect the same tolls at this gate as were collected at the gate near Cowbit. Their power to raise, maintain and support the bank was not interfered with; and they were authorised to prevent 'during the continuance of high water the passage of any carriage in such part of the bank belonging to the Corporation.'

The South Holland Commissioners were to enlarge and raise the Barrier Bank to such height as they should deem sufficient 'to resist the water of the river Welland, and to protect the lands in South Holland from inundation,' and 'to top the bank with a sufficient quantity of gravel for making a good and permanent road thereon;' and the Trustees were afterwards to maintain the bank and road, and if at any time 'any goole or breach or overflowing of the waters' should happen through the bank between Spalding and Brotherhouse, to the annoyance of the lands in Sutton St. Edmunds, Sutton St. James, or Tydd St. Mary, or in any part of Holland

Elloe, and the same were not amended by the Trustees within ten days, then the Dykereeves of the parts affected were empowered to repair the same and recover the cost from the Trustees.

By an Act passed in 1838 this road was declared to be a turnpike road, the Committeemen of the South Holland Drainage being placed in the same position as other Turnpike Trustees. The time during which the Trustees were authorised to collect tolls was extended for 31 years after the passing of the Act. On the expiration of this term the road became a highway, and was maintained by the highway surveyors of Spalding and Cowbit respectively, the toll bar at Cowbit being removed. This, being a disturnpiked road, became a main road, under the Highway Act of 1878, and received grants towards its maintenance from the County Fund. In 1889 the maintenance of the road on the Barrier Bank passed into the hands of the Holland County Council. The toll-bar at Brotherhouse was removed in 1892. Lord Normanton, who is the owner of the Postland Estate, and had hitherto maintained the portion of the road between Brotherhouse and Crowland, having given up all rights over the road, it also became a main road under the management of the County Council. 1 and 2 Vict., c. 78, 1838.

In 1812 the South Holland Commissioners promoted a Bill for amending and rendering more effectual their previous Act. Considerable opposition was raised to the powers sought by the Commissioners by several of the Proprietors, and meetings were held at Spalding and Holbeach, in March, 1812, of which Sir Joseph Banks was chairman; and a series of resolutions was drawn up and printed. The failure of the works carried out to effect the expected improvament of the drainage was attributed by the Proprietors present at these meetings to the fact that Kinderley's Cut, in the Nene, had not been extended, and that as this extension was the main inducement for obtaining the previous Act, "the Commissioners had expended the great sums entrusted to them in the execution of a plan which they knew would prove ineffectual, unless works should be executed by parties over whom neither they nor their employers have, or ever had, any kind of control; that the Wisbech waters, when they passed near to the Sea Sluice, over-rode the South Holland waters, so as to prevent their discharge until the waters of the Nene had passed off; and that when the South Holland waters and those of the Nene were on a level, there was a depth of 5ft. 8in. on the apron of the sluice; that owing to the way in which the scheme had been designed, the works carried out, and the unfair manner in which the taxes had been levied, the proprietors present considered the Commissioners had forfeited their confidence, and had proved themselves utterly unfit for their office; that they were prepared to approve of the promotion of a new Act to authorise the execution of an effectual plan of drainage, but that, if the Commissioners pro- CONDITION OF THE DISTRICT IN 1812 ceeded with their present Bill, they were determined to oppose it when it came before Parliament."

The carrying out of the works had imposed taxes on the Proprietors of sums varying from 20/- to 40/- an acre, in return for which they received very little benefit, owing principally to the defective discharge at the outfall into the Nene, the water having to push its way to the river through beds of shifting sands.

RENNIE'S RE-PORT, 1813.

From a report made by Mr. John Rennie in 1813 'for completely draining South Holland,' it appears that, notwithstanding the works executed under the powers of these Acts, "the drainage was still found to be incomplete and many thousands of acres of valuable land were during the winter and spring so flooded that their produce was of little comparative value, and therefore little had been effected towards the great object of a complete drainage." The great defect in the drainage arose from the want of a proper outfall, the main drain terminating at Peter's Point, which was too far up the Nene, so that even in the lowest tides the water in the river did not subside sufficiently to admit of a free discharge of the water from the lands. At neap tides in summer low water stood 3ft. 9in. on the sill of the sluice at Peter's Point. The fall of the water in the river Nene at that time was so great that the water discharging by the Lutton Leam sluice, 2 miles lower down the Nene, was 18 inches below that of the South Holland Drain. Mr. Rennie therefore proposed the erection of a new sluice near the then existing sluice at the outfall of the Lutton Leam, having its sill 4ft. lower than the present sluice, and that a new cut, five furlongs long, should be made from the sluice to Crab Hole. The sluice was to have three sets of pointing doors of 12ft. opening each, or 5ft. more waterway than the then existing sluice. The total area to be drained by the new sluice would be 35,000 acres, viz., 26,000 of South Holland and 9,000 drained by Lutton Leam. From the sluice to a little above Barlieu Bridge the Lutton Leam was to be enlarged and deepened, thence to Almond's Farm Bridge a new drain was to be made to join the Bender Slough Drain, which was to be deepened and enlarged, to its junction with the South Holland Drain. The estimated cost of this scheme was £83,531.

Mr. Rennie drew attention in his report to a scheme which he thought would be of great benefit to the whole of this part of the Fens by extending the North Level Drain from Gunthorpe Sluice to the Lutton Leam, and making this extended outfall the common drain of the two districts, the great advantage being the concentration of a large body of water into one common outfall and its effect in maintaining and keeping the outfall open.

AMENDING ACT. 27 Geo. iii, c. 60, 1817.

No action was taken to carry this scheme out, and several difficulties having arisen in carrying out the provisions of the two previous Acts and in obtaining payment of the sums assessed on the lands for the work done, an amending Act was obtained in 1817. The qualification of the Trustees was altered, every person being qualified to be a Trustee who owned, or rented under the Crown, 80 acres of land, also the Bursar of St. John's College, Cambridge and the Master of Sidney Sussex College. The Trustees were to have votes for every 200 acres beyond the first 80 acres, but no one to have more than four votes, unless he owned 1,180 acres, and then to have votes for every 500 acres beyond 680, not exceeding 8 votes in all. Power was given to the Trustees to act by Agents. The Trustees were directed to meet once a year on the second Monday in May, at Spalding, instead of at Holbeach, as in the previous Act. At every third Annual Meeting the Trustees were to appoint five of their number to act as a Committee. All powers formerly vested in the Trustees were transferred to the Committee, who have full control and management of all the works, the laying and collecting of rates, the appointment of the Treasurer, Clerk, Collector, Superintendent and other officers. They are allowed all reasonable expenses attending their meetings, not exceeding £5 for each meeting. Three members form a quorum. Accounts of receipts and expenditure by the Committee are to be presented at the Annual Meeting of the Trustees. *[TRUSTEES.]*

In order to meet the outstanding debts incurred by the Commissioners, the Committee were authorised to levy for one year an extra tax of five shillings an acre, or, if this should prove insufficient, a further additional tax of two shillings. The power to levy the ordinary annual tax of one shilling an acre was continued and such further annual tax as might be deemed necessary, not exceeding sixpence an acre. The lands draining by the Lord's Drain, not included in the boundaries set out in the first Act, were to be charged sixpence an acre, to be used in discharging the expenses of maintaining the Lord's Drain. *[TAXES.]*

The Committee were authorized to borrow a sum not exceeding £3,000. This was increased by a subsequent Act to £15,000. *[BORROWING POWER. 1 and 2 Vict., c. 78.]*

The herbage of the Barrier and other banks was to be let by the Committee, to be grazed with sheep only, the rents being applied to the same purposes as the tax. Any cattle or swine found on the banks were to be impounded, under a penalty of ten shillings for swine and twenty shillings for horses or other cattle. Any person convicted of keeping rabbits on the banks was made liable to a penalty of forty shillings. *[HERBAGE OF BANKS.]*

The Committee were further empowered to admit adjacent lands into their drainage system, on proper compensation being paid, and provided that no lands not having a right of drainage into the Nene should be admitted without the consent of the Commissioners of the Nene Outfall. *[ADMISSION OF ADJACENT LANDS.]*

EFFECT OF IMPROVEMENT OF THE NENE OUTFALL.

In 1832 a new channel was made for the Nene, by a cut through Cross Keys Wash, from Gunthorpe Sluice to Crab's Hole, a distance of 5 miles, and continued for a further 1¼ miles through the sands by training banks. This new outfall lowered the level of low water in the channel of the river about 10 feet.

Prior to this improvement the water stood on the sill of the sluice to a depth of 5ft. in summer, when a shoal of sand frequently formed on the outside, and was seldom lower than 2ft. 6in. in winter. After the improvent the sill of the middle arch was lowered a foot, and the water then fell out 2ft. 9in. below the sill, making a difference of upwards of 5ft. in the level af the water in the drain.

MILLINGTON'S REPORT. 1848.

In 1848 Mr. Edward Millington made a report to the Committee of the Trustees. This report shows that the sill of the Outfall Sluice was 7ft. above low water, as then existing, below Sutton Bridge, and 8ft. 8in. above low water in Wisbech Eye. There was a fall in floods with the water running 2ft. over the sill of from 4ft. to 5ft. to the surface of low water in the Nene near the Outfall; and it was anticipated that when the improvement works in the Nene were completed there would be a fall of from 6ft. to 7ft. from the sluice in floods and from 8ft. to 9ft. in ordinary seasons. The bottom of the main drain was 3ft. below the sill of the sluice, gradually rising until it became level with it at Red House Bridge, five-and-a-quarter miles up the drain. Above this the bed rose with an inclination of from 3in. to 4in. in a mile, and in the whole length of the drain, fourteen and a quarter miles, the bottom rose 5ft. 9in. The low lands at the extremity of the drain near Peakhill were only from 6⅓ft. to 7ft. above the sill of the sluice, and were consequently frequently flooded. The land in the parish of Gedney Hill and in Fleet was from 6ft. to 6½ft. above the sill, the distance from the sluice varying from 9 to 12 miles; the land in Holbeach, between the main drain and Holbeach Drove, was from 6in. to 9in. higher than that in Fleet. The low lands in Holbeach and Whaplode Drove Common, distant from the sluice fourteen and a half miles, were from 6ft. to 7ft. above the sill.

NEW OUTFALL SLUICE.

14 and 15 Vict., 1851.

In an Act passed in 1857, it is recited that the Outfall Sluice (erected in 1795) had become dilapidated and could not be effectually repaired, and that the construction of a new Sea Sluice was immediately required. This damage was partly caused by the breaking of a dam when the sluice was under repair in 1831. At the time when the tide broke through the dam the apron was up and also the boarding in the body of the sluice, and the sluice doors had been removed. The scour of the tidal water through the sluice forced several of the sheet piles out of their places, and otherwise damaged the foundation. The damage was made good as far as possible, but the sluice was never afterwards in a satisfactory condition, and was consequently subject to leakage, especially after very high tides and was regarded by those who had charge of it as insecure. The Committeemen were authorised to levy for five years a further tax of two shillings an acre, for the purpose of raising the necessary funds for rebuilding the sluice. They were also authorised to borrow a further sum of £10,000.

<small>14 and 15 Vict., 1851.</small>

The new sluice was erected in 1852 by Messrs. Grissell & Co., under the direction of Mr. William Lewin, and had two openings of 8ft. each and one of 15ft., making a total waterway of 31ft. The sill was placed 5ft. lower than that of the old sluice and is now 5·5ft. below *Ordnance datum*, or about 4½ft. above low water of spring tides in the estuary. The cost of the sluice (and of other attendant works and expenses, £2,000) was £10,500. The water, in very high floods, rises, when the doors are closed by the tides, to over 10ft. on the sill. In ordinary floods the depth when running is from 3ft. to 5ft. The area of land draining by this sluice is about 34,000 acres. One of the first practical applications of the Centrifugal Pump to drainage works was made at the works carried out for the construction of this sluice.

In 1842, at an annual meeting of the Trustees, the following Bye Laws were passed for the management of the district, which were to take effect on notice being given to the owner or occupier; the defaulter being liable to a penalty of £5.

<small>BYE LAWS.</small>

1.—Trees or hedges growing near drains, so far as the branches overhang the drain, to be lopped and pruned.
2.—Ditches along which water from other lands has course to any public drain to be deepened and cleansed.
3.—Tunnels of adequate size and dimensions for gateways across any public drains or ditches to be provided.
4.—Headings or other works for preventing the issue of water from or into the public drains to be kept in order.
5.—No injury to be done to any drain, sluice, or other work; no obstruction to be placed in any drain; no bank or heading to be cut, or tunnel or other work opened for the purpose of directing the course of the water.

The area of land now under the jurisdiction of the Trustees, including that which has been added by petition of the owners since the passing of the original Acts, is 36,285a. or. 31p., of which 4,428¼ acres drains by Lord's Drain.

<small>TAXES AND EXPENDITURE.</small>

The taxes annually levied and other receipts are as follows:—

	£	s.	d.
One Shilling on 31,856½ acres	1,563	15	10
Sixpence on 4,428½ acres draining by Lord's Drain	110	15	10
Two Shillings on 187a. or. 37p. in Lord's Drain district now draining by Main Drain	18	14	8
	1,693	6	4

		£	s.	d.
Bank and other rents	... ...	226	9	0
Interest, &c.	... ...	80	14	9
		£2,000	10	1

The expenses as taken from the accounts for 1892-3, include:—

	£	s.	d.
Maintenance of Main Drains and Sluice	414	11	4
Parish Works	688	3	5
Lord's Drain district	90	10	8
Barrier Bank	4	1	3
Rents, Rates and Taxes	79	8	2
Management	366	9	0
	£1,643	3	10

There is a surplus income of about £400 a year, which is invested to meet heavy renewals of works, and emergencies. A large amount was paid for rebuilding one of the bridges, a few years ago, out of this fund. The balance invested at the end of 1892 was £3,100. There is no outstanding loan. The tax levied in 1894 was 1/- in the South Holland District and 6d. in the Lord's Drain District.

SOUTH HOLLAND EMBANKMENT.—A Trust was created in the year 1793, under an Act of Parliament passed in the reign of George III, (amended by a second Act obtained in 1812) for enclosing the large tract of salt marsh lying between the Welland and the Nene, north of the Roman Bank. The area of land enclosed was stated to be as follows :—

33 Geo. iii, c. 16, 1793.
52 Geo. iii, c. 175, 1812.

ACREAGE AND PARISHES.

			a.	r.	p.
Private Salt Marsh in the Parish of Spalding	35	2	3
,,	,,	Moulton	249	2	23
,,	,,	Whaplode	166	2	6
,,	,,	Holbeach	2059	2	18
,,	,,	Gedney	612	3	37
Commonable in Moulton	... ...	861	2	28
,, Gedney	... ...	609	0	29
			4,595	0	24

The Common land in Moulton was assessed by the Commissioners in their Award at £8,371 3s. 4d.; and that in Gedney at £5,968 10s. 8d.

At the time of Inclosure there were ten owners of private lands, of whom the principal were N. Garland, W. Drake, M. Dayrell, — Coates, Lord Boston and the Earl of Buckingham.

EMBANKMENT ACT. 1793.

This land is described in the Preamble of the Act as being overflowed by the sea at every spring tide, and as being of little value; and it is stated that the embanking and draining would be of great advantage to all persons interested therein. For the purpose of carrying out the work, T. G. Ewen of Norwich, Edward Hare of Castor and George Maxwell of Fletton were appointed Commissioners, their remuneration being fixed at two guineas a day. The Commissioners took the oath in July, 1793, and the bank was completed and the Award made in April, 1811, the work having thus occupied nearly eight years.

SEA BANK.

The embankment commences at the north-west corner of Wrag Marsh Farm, which is about a mile and a half above Fosdyke Bridge, and continues nearly parallel with the Welland for three miles, to Moulton Outfall, whence it continues along the coast in a broken line to Boat Mere Creek, where it terminates by a junction with the existing sea bank. The total length of the outer bank is about 15 miles. The course of the bank is shown on the plan of South Holland in this Chapter. The depth of the marsh enclosed varied from 20 or 30 chains to a mile. The size of the bank is given in the Act as being in the lowest part of the marsh 11ft. high, and 63½ft. wide at the base, with slopes of four to one on the outer slope and one and a half to one on the inner slope. On the highest part of the marsh the bank was not to be less than 8ft. high, with 47ft. base, and the same slopes. (At the present time the top of the bank is about 20ft. above *Ordnance datum*.) Cross banks were to be made with slopes of one and a half to one on both sides in the narrowest part of the marsh, wherever the Commissioners should think necessary, to prevent a general inundation in case of a breach in any part of the outer bank. The slopes were to be flagged with sods two and a half inches thick, and the banks sown with rye grass.

Plate 4.

All necessary drains and private roads were to be made by the Commissioners. The boundaries between the different owners were to be straightened, the divisions, where they abutted on the new bank, to be made in straight lines for a length of one hundred yards, and as nearly parallel as practicable. All claims to accretion after the bank was made were to be regulated by a continuation of these straight lines across the sea bank, and into the marsh for ever after acquired from the sea.

ACCRETION OUTSIDE THE BANK.

Provision was to be made for the drainage discharging by the two existing sluices, erected for the purpose of draining the lands in the parishes of Moulton, Whaplode and Holbeach, and by several private sluices for draining the lands adjoining the new enclosure, by the erection of the following new sluices, viz., one near the mouth of Holbeach Creek, 16ft. wide, with the floor 2ft. lower than the then existing Sea Sluice; one at the mouth of Holbeach Creek, for the drainage of lands in Moulton, 10ft. wide, with the floor 18in. lower than the existing sluice; one, near the mouth of the Old Fleet Haven, for draining the marshes adjoining the same, 8ft. wide, with the floor 18in. lower than any of the then

SLUICES.

existing sluices in the sea bank; one near the mouth of Dawsmere Creek, 5ft. wide, with the floor 18in. lower than the existing sluice; and another near Boatmere Creek, 4ft. wide, with the floor 12in. lower than the existing sluice, called Baker's Sluice. Drains were also to be made connecting the old and new sluices.

The new sluices and drains were to be considered as part of the works, and to be from time to time repaired, cleansed and scoured, the cost being paid out of the rates levied by the Superintendent. In default the Surveyor of Sewers was to have the necessary work done, and the cost to be recoverable from the Superintendent. Provision was also made in the case of neglect to have the sluices opened, when required, by an application to a Justice of the Peace, who was authorised to order the sluices to be opened.

TRUSTEES AND OFFICERS. Twelve Trustees were nominated in the Act, who, together with four delegates chosen by the Commoners in Moulton and Gedney, were to have the management of the banks, sluices and other works after completion. The future Trust was to consist of the heirs or assigns of the then owners, interested in the enclosed marsh to the yearly value of fifty pounds or upwards, or in any allotments made of the commonable part of the marsh of the yearly value of twenty pounds. The banks with the cess or foreland on the land side and the drains, sluices, bridges and other works were vested in the Trustees, as a Corporation in perpetual succession. The Trustees were directed by the Act to meet annually, on the Thursday in Easter week, at the Chequers Inn, Holbeach, or such other place as they might think fit. At this Annual Meeting they were to appoint a Superintendent, who was to have charge of the banks, sluices, &c.,

RATE. and to have power to levy a rate not exceeding one shilling an acre in one year, for the repair of the new bank and works, and payment of the expenses of management. He was also directed to call upon the persons who had previously repaired the old banks and sluices to keep these in order at their own cost. The rate was to be paid by the occupier of the land, and deducted from his rent, if a tenant. The Superintendent was to be appointed in writing, to find surety to the amount of £500, and be removable by the Trustees at pleasure for neglect or misconduct. The Trustees were also directed by the Act to appoint at the Annual Meeting five persons, not necessarily Trustees, to act as a Committee and to meet in any case of emergency, three of whom were to be a quorum, and they were empowered to levy such further rates as they might deem necessary for the safety of the bank, sluices and other works. Provision was made to prevent the stocking of the bank, for the first seven years after completion, with any other cattle except sheep, under a penalty of £50; and, after the expiration of this period, any swine, horses or cattle found on the banks might be impounded in the common pound until a fine of ten shillings a head for swine and twenty shillings for horses and cattle, and expenses were paid. If any owner knowingly keeps rabbits upon the marsh or banks he is liable to a penalty of forty shillings; also any person mooring any vessel to the sluices or laying the same within eighty yards is liable to a penalty of £50.

The Act of 1812 amended some of the clauses in the first Act, and provided that certain irregularities in carrying out the provisions of the same by the Commissioners should not affect the validity of, or vitiate the proceedings under the Act, and that the works done should be deemed to have satisfied the requirements thereof. This Act also repealed so much of the *Welland Act* of 34 Geo. iii, as related to the unembanked lands adjoining the sea bank. It also recited that great damage was done to the new sea bank by an exceedingly high tide, accompanied by a violent tempest, which happened in November, 1810, and gave further powers to the Commissioners to repair the damage then done, and to repay the outlay which was made by the owners at the time for the preservation of the banks. In repairing the banks it was found necessary to abandon a considerable quantity of land within the line of the original embankment, and at this part to make a fresh bank within the line of the old one. For these repairs a rate of thirty shilling an acre was laid. The Act further provided that notice of any rate made by the Committee should be given for three weeks in a newspaper circulating in the County, and by writing fixed on the principal doors of the churches of Spalding, Moulton, Whaplode, Holbeach, and Gedney, twenty days previous to the time appointed for payment. Provision was made in this Act for the appointment of a Clerk and Treasurer, for borrowing money, and the payment of the expenses of the Committee at their meetings, not exceeding five pounds for each meeting.

<small>AMENDING ACT. 52 Geo iii, c. 175, 1812.</small>

The total cost of carrying out the works, and of the Award, was £45,227, or about £10 an acre.

<small>COST OF WORKS.</small>

The rate for the maintenance of the South Holland Embankment is about one shilling an acre, the maximum amount which the Superintendent is authorised to lay without the authority of the Committee, and produces £221.

<small>RATES AND EXPENDITURE.</small>

The expenses of maintenance, according to the last annual taxation return (1892), amount to £73, and of management to £78, total £151. There is no outstanding loan.

BLUE GOWT OR SPALDING AND PINCHBECK DISTRICT.—This district, which is shown on the plan of Deeping Fen, lies to the south and east of the river Glen, and is bounded by it on the north; on the west by the Dozens Bank, on which runs the main road between Podehole and Dovehirne; on the south by the site of the Old Westlode Drain, up to Spalding; and thence on the south east,

<small>BOUNDARY</small>

up to the junction of the Welland and the Glen, by the Roman Bank. It contains about 4,500 acres. The drainage is by the Blue Gowt Drain, from which the water is lifted by an engine into the Glen, a little above its junction with the Welland.

41 Geo. iii, 1801.

DRAINAGE.

Under an Act passed in the reign of George III, for inclosing the Common lands in Spalding, Pinchbeck and the other parishes adjoining the Welland and the Glen, the drainage of this district was provided for by the deepening and widening of the Blue Gowt Drain, from its outfall to its then termination near the turnpike road leading from Spalding to Donington, and continuing it thence by a new cut to Dozens Bank. The bottom of the drain was made 10ft. at the lower end, gradually diminishing to 6ft. at the termination, with slopes of 2 to 1, and forelands of 10ft., up to Stickwith Gowt, and above that 1½ to 1, and 6ft. forelands. A sluice was erected at its junction with the Glen, having 14ft. waterway. Another drain was also directed to be made, branching from the Blue Gowt Drain near the turnpike road and extending thence to the Vernatts Drain, and so much further on the south side as might be found expedient, with a culvert under the Vernatts of 3ft. diameter, for the purpose of draining such of the lands lying between the Westlode and the Glen as are so situated as to discharge their water through the Blue Gowt Drain and Sluice into the river. The Proprietors of this part of the district were also authorized by the Act to erect a drainage engine for lifting the water off the land lying between the Vernatts and the Westlode, and west of Two Plank Bridge, for discharging the water into the Vernatts, subject to certain restrictions. The Proprietors of the whole district were also authorized to erect an engine for lifting the water out of the Blue Gowt Drain into the Glen, but this power was not exercised and that part of the Act was repealed by the Act of 1832, when fresh powers were obtained.

DRAINAGE ACT.
2 Will. iv, 1832.

The drainage being found very defective, on account of the height of the water at the outfall of the Blue Gowt Drain, it became necessary to lift the water by steam power. The powers for this purpose contained in the Act of 1801 being found insufficient, a separate Act was obtained by the Proprietors. Under this Act Leonard Browne of Pinchbeck, William Peppercorn of St. Neots, Thomas Brabins Measure of Pinchbeck, William Wiles of Pinchbeck and George Brown of Gosberton were appointed Trustees for the better effecting the drainage, and for supporting and keeping in repair the Blue Gowt Drain and other sewers and banks. The first Trustees were appointed for 3 years, when the Proprietors of the land were to have the opportunity of electing fresh Trustees if they wished, otherwise the existing Trustees were to continue in office until death or resignation, and so on, every three years. Every Owner of ten acres has one vote at the election, and an additional vote for every 50 acres up to 10 votes. If he have over 500 acres he has an additional vote for every 200 acres beyond the 500, up to 12 votes. Owners may delegate their power to their Agents by a written authority. The Trustees are to call a meeting of the Proprietors of lands once a year, on the first Monday in October, for the purpose of presenting their accounts, notice of such meeting being first advertised.

The Trustees are empowered by the Act to appoint a Clerk, Collector, Superintendent and Treasurer, and are allowed their reasonable expenses in attending meetings.

They were empowered to erect on the Blue Gowt Drain at Stickwith Gowt a good and substantial engine, to be worked by steam, with all proper machinery, houses and sluices, and also to deepen and widen the Blue Gowt Drain and to support and maintain all the works belonging to the said drain; but no part of the water of the Blue Gowt Drain was to be discharged into the Vernatts Drain, and the engines erected were not to be used when the Glen could not discharge its water owing to the height of the water in the Welland.

The Act directs that the Owners and Occupiers of land in the district shall maintain in order the droveway, outring, or partition and division dikes, to a width not exceeding 8ft. at the top, or in default, after notice given, the Superintendent is empowered to do the work at the cost of the owners or occupiers, who are further subject to a fine of three shillings a rood.

The land is divided into four districts for the purpose of rating, the lowest rated paying one-fourth of that paid by the highest, and the other two one-half and three-quarters respectively. The land lying between the Roman Bank and the Vernatts Drain, called Marsh Lands, and Monks' House Farm were exempted from taxation.

The taxes are levied on the Owners, the Occupiers being liable for payment, but being allowed to deduct the rate from the rent. Persons neglecting to pay the taxes for 14 days after the time appointed for payment are liable to have their their effects distrained upon and are subject to a penalty of 5/- in the £.

The Trustees were authorized to borrrow £5,000 for the purpose of carrying out the work.

PUMPING MACHINERY. The engine erected by the Trustees in 1833 is a low pressure condensing beam engine, 20 N.H.P., and works a scoop wheel of 24ft. diameter and 2ft. 2in. width, the scoops being 5ft. long. The wheel makes 7 revolutions to 28 of the engine. The average head is from 5 to 6ft., rising in floods to 8ft. The boiler pressure was originally 4lbs. and the coal consumption 1½ tons in twelve hours. A new boiler has recently been laid in place of the old one and the pressure increased to 20lbs. Some improvements have also been made in the engine and the coal consumption reduced to one-third of what it used to be. The area drained by the engine is 6,000 acres.

DRAINAGE RATE.

The rate generally levied by the Trustees is 3/- an acre on the district paying the maximum, and in proportion on the other districts. The amount raised by rates, according to the Government taxation return of 1892-3, was £467, and from other sources £4, total £471. The expenditure, in maintenance £542, management £134, interest £15, total £691. The outstanding loan amounted to £300. In the previous year maintenance cost £273.

PINCHBECK SOUTH FEN, OR THE FOURTH DISTRICT.—Pinchbeck South Fen, which is shown on the plan of Deeping Fen, includes part of Pinchbeck Common. It lies between the Glen on the north and west, and the Counter Drain on the south, extending np to the Dozens Bank, on the main road between Podehole and Dovehirne on the east, and the Cradge Bank on the west; it contains 1,425a. 2r. 16p.

41 Geo. iii, c. 128, 1801.

This was one of the districts set out under the *Deeping Fen Enclosure Act* of 1801, and is the only one now remaining as a separate district, the others having been done away with under the Deeping Fen Act of 1856.

Under the Enclosure Act the Owners of land in the Fourth District were directed to elect Trustees, who were empowered to erect and maintain engines, and carry out such works as they deemed necessary for the drainage, and to levy taxes not exceeding 2/- an acre in any one year, to pay for the same. By the Act of 1823 the powers of the Trustees were extended and, with the consent of three-fifths of the Owners, the annual tax can be raised to 5/-.

4 Geo. iv, 1823.

DRAINAGE ENGINE.

The main drain for this district runs parallel with the Counter Drain and crosses the main road, north of Podehole. The engine was erected in 1829 at a cost of £3,000. It is situated a quarter of a mile on the east side of the main road at Podehole, and discharges the water into the Vernatts Drain. The water is lifted by a scoop wheel, 20ft. in diameter, having 42 scoops 5ft. 6in. long and 1ft. 3in. wide. The average lift is 5ft. The wheel is driven by a beam engine of 35 N.H.P., the pressure in the boiler being from 6lbs. to 7lbs. The engine makes 30 revolutions, and the wheel 7½, in a minute. The maximum rate of 5/- is generally levied by the Trustees.

DEEPING FEN WASHES DRAINAGE DISTRICT.—This is a narrow tract of land lying between the river Glen and the Counter Drain, containing 400 acres, and was originally left to receive the overflow water from the Glen. The Counter Drain was constructed to carry off this overflow water and to relieve the Glen. The south bank is made sufficiently high to prevent the water from flowing on to Deeping Fen from the washes. The Counter Drain receives the water from Bourne South Fen and the Bourne and Thurlby pastures lying to the south of Bourne Eau, and containing about 2,000 acres. Formerly this wash was almost always flooded in winter.

Since the improvement of the drainage of Deeping Fen, the construction of a new outfall sluice for the Glen, and the strengthening of the banks, these lands are less liable to flooding than formerly.

In 1873 this area was formed into a District by a provisional order under the Land Drainage Act, subsequently confirmed by Parliament. *36 and 37 Vict, c. 24, 1873.*

The amount raised by rates, as given in the return for 1892-3, was £23; maintenance cost £5 and management £7. *DRAINAGE RATES.*

SPALDING AND PINCHBECK.—The greater part of these parishes is included in special Drainage Districts, the south-west part of Spalding, known as Spalding Common is part of the Deeping Fen District, the south-east part of the parish is in the South Holland Drainage District, the part west of the town is, with part of Pinchbeck, formed into a separate level, known as the Blue Gowt District. Pinchbeck North Fen is in the Black Sluice District and the South Fen in Deeping Fen. The drainage of the remainder of the parish is under the jurisdiction of the Court of Sewers.

WESTON.—The southern portion of this parish forms part of the South Holland Drainage District. The northern part is under the jurisdiction of the Court of Sewers and is drained by the Lord's Drain, which discharges into the river Welland about a mile below the reservoir.

MOULTON.—A large tract of land, containing 2,237 acres in this parish, in common with the marshes in Holbeach and Gedney lying outside the Roman Bank, was enclosed from the sea by a bank running westward from the Old Guide House to Wrag Marsh, constructed in 1660. A further addition of 1,081 acres was made to the parish in 1793 by the South Holland Embankment, when the part known as the Red Cow District was enclosed. Of this addition 861 acres were common marsh. In 1875, 400 acres of marsh were enclosed and added to the parish. *INCLOSURE OF MARSHES*

The parish consists of three divisions. The old part, lying between the Roman Bank and Garner's Dyke, also called the Raven Bank, and known as the 'Town Lands'; the fen, lying south of Garner's Dyke and extending up to the Queen's Bank; and the enclosed marsh land, lying north of the Roman Bank and extending up to the river Welland. The land lying south of the Roman Bank is in the South Holland Drainage District. The sea bank and Outfall Drain are maintained by the South Holland Embankment Commissioners. *DIVISION OF THE PARISH.*

The principal sewers in the parish are the Moulton Meer Drain, running along the western boundary of the fen, and discharging into Lord's Drain, north of the village of Weston; and the Moulton river, which extends from the south end of the fen to the outfall into the Welland on the north, a distance of 11 miles. The portion south of the Roman Bank discharges into the South Holland *DRAINAGE.*

Drain. The northern outfall was diverted to its present outfall into the Welland by the South Holland Embankment Commissioners.

The fen was formerly drained by a wind engine and scoop wheel, situated at Dawsdyke near Engine Bank. In 1705 this engine was repaired by Nathaniel Kinderley, at a cost of £200.

A second drainage engine was erected in 1698 on the north side of the Roman Bank at Sea's End, the work being done under the advice of, and by, Mr. Hodgkin of Little Bytham.

The Sluice in the Sea Bank, constructed in 1660, appears to have given the Dykereeves considerable trouble; as in 1693 Robert Adams was paid £26 for laying down a new sluice, to replace the old one, and Joshua Bernard £120 for its erection. This sluice also proved a failure, and in 1739 John Scribo and John Parkinson were called in to advise about it, and in the following year a new sluice was built, at a cost of £270, by W. Sands, who built the Glen Sluice about the same time.

In 1733 Mr. Grundy, Surveyor, then of Leicester and afterwards of Spalding, whose name appears prominently in various schemes for the improvement of the Witham, was employed to make a map of the parish, and to take the levels thereof; and prepare a scheme, with plan, for its better drainage. A copy of this plan is now in the possession of the Rev. T. Russell Jackson, the Vicar of Moulton. Mr. Grundy was also employed in 1739, at a fee of 20 guineas, to make a map and take the levels of the Common Salt Marsh.

BREACH OF SEA BANKS.

In 1765 the sea bank in this parish was broken by a sudden and unexpected tide, which inundated the marsh land, drowning over 2,000 sheep, 7 beasts and 13 horses. During the gale and high tide of 1810, a breach was made in the South Holland Embankment in this parish, and considerable damage was done. This bank had been constructed about 1793, and at the same time the Moulton river was diverted by a new cut at the outfall, having 12ft. waterway at the bottom; and a new sluice erected, having 10ft. opening.

THE COMMONS.

Up to nearly the end of the 18th century there was a large area of Common Marsh Land in this parish, known as the Bean Marsh, the First Marsh, the New Marsh and the Salt Marsh. A Marsh Reeve was appointed by the parish to look after this Common and was paid a salary of £4 a year. A Marsh Shepherd was also appointed at a salary of £20 a year. These expenses, together with those incurred for mowing thistles, catching moles, repairing gates and fences, &c., amounting to about £45 a year, were met by a marsh rate of 1s. 6d. for each horse and neat beast, and 3d. for each sheep grazed on the common.

ENCLOSURE ACT. 33 Geo. iii, c. 1793.

An Act was obtained in 1793 for dividing and enclosing these commonable salt marshes, droves, commons and waste lands, containing, with other waste lands, about 2,000 acres. The area of the marshes was 861a. 2r. 29p. the value of which was assessed by the Embankment Commissioners at £8,371 3s. 4d.

The Commissioners appointed under the Act were George Maxwell of Fletton, Thomas Glover Ewen of Norwich, and Joseph Newman of Boston, their remuneration being fixed at £2 2s. 0d. a day, including their expenses. They were directed to divide and allot the land; to set out and make the necessary public and private roads and such drains as they deemed necessary, the public roads to be 50ft. wide. Two acres of land were to be set out for the purpose of getting material for the repair of the roads. Provision was also made by the Act for raising the money for the share of the cost of the South Holland Embankment.

In 1873 an Act was obtained for enclosing a further tract of salt marsh, containing about 400 acres, extending up to the Welland, which had accreted outside the South Holland Embankment. The persons interested in this marsh were Lord Boston, Richard Jackson, Edgar Walter Garland; the Rev. J. Russell Jackson, as owner of the tithes; the Frontagers; and the Owners of the common rights. Edward Millington of Fleet was appointed Commissioner for the purposes of the Act, with power to make the embankments, roads and sewers necessary. Also to determine the rights of, and to make allotments to, the several claimants. The Award, when made, was to be deposited with the Clerk of the Peace. So much of the marsh was to be sold as would be sufficient to pay the expenses of embanking and carrying out the Act; and a further portion for maintaining the works. Lord Boston and the other Owners were to pay their share of the cost. After the deposit of the award and completion of the works, three Trustees were to be appointed for the management of the marsh. Every owner of an allotment is entitled to one vote and an additional vote for every acre. Every person qualified to be an Elector is qualified to be a Trustee. The Trustees remain in office for three years, or until their successors are appointed. Two Trustees are a quorum; the office is to be at Spalding; and a meeting is to be held annually, and at such other times as necessary. The Trustees have power to levy rates for the maintenance of the works, no limit being fixed as to the amount; the rate is to be paid by the Occupier and to be repaid by the Owner. Failing payment, the Trustees may distrain. The roads made were to be deemed public highways to be maintained by the Trustees, the cost being repaid by the highway Surveyors. The length of the enclosure bank was two and a quarter miles. The contract for making the bank, including the sluice, was £5,574, equal to about £13 10s. 0d. an acre.

MOULTON SALT MARSHES ACT. 36 and 37 Vict., c. 170, 1873.

HOLBEACH AND WHAPLODE.—The large tract of land, known as Holbeach Marsh, lying north of the Roman Bank, was, in common with the marshes in Moulton and Gedney, enclosed from the sea by an embankment made about 1660, and by a subsequent embank-

INCLOSURE OF MARSHES.

INCLOSURE OF MARSHES.

ment made under the *South Holland Embankment Act* of 1793. The former enclosure was made by 'the Adventurers' under a grant by James I, in 1615, to Charles Glenmand and John Walcott of London, on behalf of the Duke of Argyll, of marsh land left by the sea in Wigtoft, Moulton, Holbeach and Tydd St. Mary. This grant included a reservation of a fifth portion, and a rent of £50 to the King, and Common Lands to the neighbouring townships. This marsh is referred to in a grant made by King John to Thomas de Muleton, of 'the marsh lying between the water of Spaldyinge and the water of Tyd.'

The area of land added to the parish of Holbeach under the first enclosure was 9,798 acres, and to Whaplode 1,057 acres; and under the second, 2,059 acres in Holbeach and 166 acres in Whaplode. In 1833 an attempt was made to enclose about 900 acres in this parish, and Gedney, by Thimbleby, Woods and Sers, the contract for the work being let to Smith Simpson for £13,480; but in February, 1835, the bank was damaged by a heavy gale, and the contractor ruined. In 1838 a second attempt to enclose 533 acres of this marsh was made by Messrs. Johnson and Sturton, who had purchased the property, under the direction of Mr. Lewin of Boston, the cost of enclosure amounting to £37 an acre. This enclosure bank derived its name, 'Bull Dog Bank,' from the fact that the navvies who were engaged in its construction seized a bull dog, which a bailiff had brought with him to assist in the arrest of one of the men, and, having killed it, buried it in the bank. In 1840 the remaining portion of the marsh was enclosed under the direction of Mr. Millington.

The addition to the original area of the parish of Holbeach by these enclosures from the sea was 12,390 acres, and of Whaplode 1,223 acres.

THE FEN.

The fen, or that portion of these parishes south of the Raven Bank, is in the South Holland Drainage District, and is drained by the South Holland Drain into the Nene. The part north of the Raven Bank is under the jurisdiction of the Court of Sewers, and drains into the Welland.

DRAINAGE.

The principal drains are the Holbeach and Whaplode rivers, which run northwards through these parishes from the Raven Bank, the boundary of the South Holland Drainage District, to a common outfall in the South Holland Bank, and thence by a cut, one mile in length, to the new channel of the Welland. The Holbeach river at its upper end has two branches, called respectively 'the new river' and 'the old river,' which, after running through the fen nearly parallel, unite at Cockle Bridge, whence they flow on together for about 1½ miles, through Holbeach Clough, (the outfall before the construction of the bank of 1630), where the Holbeach and Whaplode rivers unite and discharge at the common outfall in the sea bank. The area drained by this sluice is about 10,000 acres.

The sluice is a brick structure with three openings, the centre being 10ft. wide, and the two side openings 3ft. each. As, however, the doors do not open to their full width, the clear waterway is only 12ft. The sill is 2ft. 9in. above *Ordnance datum*. The outfall drain has 21ft. bottom up to Fisher's Bridge and 15ft. up to the junction with the Whaplode river. The sluice and drain up to the inner bank were constructed under the powers of the *South Holland Embankment Act*, and are now maintained by the Trustees.

The level of the low lands in Holbeach Fen, at the upper end of the drain, is about 5ft. 9in. above the sill of the drain, and, as the water in heavy floods stands at low water to a depth of 2ft. on the sill, these lands are imperfectly drained in wet seasons. The sill of the sluice is 5ft. 3in. above ordinary low water in the Welland, and 3ft. 9in. above ordinary floods. *Report*, W. H. Wheeler, Aug 1883.

Formerly the channel of the Welland took its course in a large bend to the south, passing very near this sluice. After the river was straightened and the channel diverted, the discharge from the sluice became very obstructed, owing to its distance from low water. The water seldom ebbed out lower than 4ft. on the sill of the sluice, when its level in the channel of the river, a mile distant, was 4ft. below the sill, making a fall of 8ft. in one mile. Mr. Millington, the Surveyor to the Court, had advised the opening out of a channel through the marsh, to be made permanent with fascine work, the estimated cost being from £2,500 to £3,000, and this plan, being approved by Mr. Cubitt, was carried out. In summer and in dry seasons, this channel is still subject to be obstructed by accretion, but it has rendered the outfall very much more efficient than it was before its construction. *Report*, W. Cubitt, Dec., 1843.

This parish, in conjunction with Whaplode, obtained an Act in 1812 for inclosing its common lands, and in 1835, in conjunction with Gedney, for embanking, draining and improving lands and salt marshes in these parishes. INCLOSURE ACT. 52 Geo. iii, 1812 4 and 5 Will. v c. 64, 1835.

The Act of 1812 states that at that time there was in the parishes of Holbeach and Whaplode, a tract of land called Holbeach and Whaplode Common, containing 1,800 acres, and also waste lands and droves, and that these in their then condition were incapable of improvement, and that it would be a great advantage if the whole of these common lands were divided and inclosed.

The Commissioners appointed to carry out the Act were Samuel Dickinson of Thurganby, Robert Millington of Gedney, and Thomas Keeton of Market Deeping. They were to allot the land, to sell unnecessary droveways, to widen and repair the existing drains and make any new ones they deemed necessary; to set out 10 acres of land in each of the parishes for the purpose of obtaining material for the repair of the roads; also to set out ponds, pits and watering places on the commons for the use of the cattle of the occupiers; to sell sufficient land to defray the expenses of the Commission and to pay off the sum of £3,550, owing on mortgage of 250 acres of land inclosed under the authority of the *South Holland Drainage Act*. The Award, after being enrolled with the Clerk of the Peace of Holland, was to be deposited in the Parish Church of Holbeach; copies to be supplied at the rate of four pence per sheet of 72 words.

An account of the early history of Holbeach will be found in the *Historical Notices*, by Rev. G. W. Macdonald, vicar of Holbeach St. Marks (published by *Foster, King's Lynn*, 1890); also in the *Holbeach Parish Register* (published by *James Williamson, Lincoln*, 1892). In this book will be found information as to the bounds of the parish, &c.

INCLOSURE OF MARSHES.

GEDNEY.—The large tract of land, containing 4,027 acres, in this parish, known as Gedney marsh, lying north of the Roman Bank, was inclosed from the sea in common with the marshes in Holbeach and Moulton by an embankment made about 1660; and a subsequent addition of 1,222 acres, about half of which was common land, was made by the South Holland Embankment, in 1793. In 1840 and 1850 two further inclosures, containing 597 acres, were made by Miss Steer, and in 1875 a further inclosure of 360 acres of common marsh was inclosed under an Act obtained in 1873, making a total addition to this parish, from land reclaimed from the sea, of 6,206 acres.

State Papers, 1635.

In a petition presented to the King by R. Colville and other owners of the Manor of Gedney, it is stated that the Lords of the Manor had for time out of mind been possessed of the salt marsh called Gedney Marsh, containing 3,000 acres, which the Copyholders had in common, and had deposited 3,000 sheep on the same. Sir H. Wooton, under a grant from James I, had obtained a patent of this marsh, as land gained from the sea, at a rent of £246 a year, and his interest had passed to the petitioners. These marshes were probably included in the grant made to the Duke of Argyle in 1615, on condition that the Adventurers should '*in and embank*' them, and were inclosed by the bank made in 1660.

THE FEN.

The fen, or that part of the parish lying south of the Raven Bank, is in the South Holland Drainage District and drains to the Nene. The part north of the Raven Bank is under the jurisdiction of the Court of Sewers. North of the Roman Bank there are several public drains originally made by the South Holland Embankment Commissioners and now maintained by them. The outfalls are at Dawsmeer Sluice, with 5ft. waterway, and Boatmeer Sluice with 4ft. waterway. Two additional sluices, 'Garland's' and 'Baker's,' were constructed in the new sea bank. Owing to the inclosures which have been made since the South Holland bank was constructed, additional sluices have had to be made in the outer bank. The water originally discharging at Baker's Sluice now goes to Boatmeer.

Part of this parish drains by Lutton Leam and is taxed to pay for the new sluice erected in 1888.

This parish obtained an Act, when the South Holland Embankment was made, for *Inclosing and Dividing the Common Salt Marshes and Waste Lands in Gedney and in Gedney Fen*. A further Act was obtained, in conjunction with Holbeach in 1835, for inclosing land in these parishes. A third Act was obtained in 1873, for embanking and inclosing a further tract of about 360 acres of marsh, which had accreted outside the South Holland Embankment, since its construction about 1793. The length of the bank was 2 miles 4 chains and the contract for its construction was £7,000, equal to about £23 per acre inclosed. Considerable difficulty was experienced in the construction of this bank, the work being much damaged by a high tide and storms before it was finally completed.

<small>INCLOSURE ACT, 31 Geo. iii.</small>
<small>4 and 5 Will. iv., c. 64, 1835.</small>
<small>36 and 37 Vict., c. 213, 1873.</small>

Under the Act of 1873 a meeting of the Commoners interested in the Commonable Salt Marshes and in the Allotments, is held annually on Easter Monday, in the parish church of Gedney, to elect delegates and pass the accounts.

<small>MEETINGS OF COMMONERS.</small>

The rate laid in 1893 was 5/- an acre, which produced £91 10s. 4d. The herbage makes £5 a year. The disbursements consisted of payment to the delegates £10 10s., officer's salary £10, expenditure on the sea banks, &c., £52 7s. 3d., showing for that year an excess of receipts over expenditure of £23 13s. 1d.

<small>BANK RATES.</small>

FLEET.—The fen part of the parish, known as Fleet Fen, lying south of the Raven Bank, is in the South Holland Drainage district.

<small>DIVISION OF PARISH.</small>

The centre part of the parish, lying between the Raven Bank and the Roman Bank, and that between the Roman Bank and the South Holland Embankment, drain by Fleet Haven. The portion of this drain north of the Roman Bank, and the outer sluice, were constructed and are now maintained by the South Holland Embankment Commissioners. Fleet Haven Sluice was made with an opening of 8ft.

<small>DRAINAGE.</small>

A further enclosure of salt marsh, which had accreted outside the South Holland Bank, was made between 1834-40, and the Fleet Haven Drain was continued across this enclosure, a sluice being constructed in the new bank. 'Part of this parish drains by Lutton Leam and is taxed to pay for the cost of the new sluice erected in 1888. A small piece of marsh land, containing about 255 acres, was added to this parish by the enclosure made in 1660.

The common waste lands and droves in this parish, containing 500 acres, were enclosed under an act passed in 1794, the commissioners being George Maxwell of Fletton, Edward Hare of Castor, and John Walker of Sutton St. Mary, the remuneration for their services being fixed at £2 2s. a day. These Commissioners were to allot the common lands and also certain droves which were

<small>INCLOSURE ACT, 34 Geo. iii, 1794.</small>

considered wider than necessary ; to sell part of the land to pay the expenses ; to set out such public or private roads as they deemed necessary, the latter being not less than 40ft. wide ; and to set out two acres of the common land for the purpose of getting material for these roads. This act also amended the clauses in the *South Holland Drainage Act* of 1793, as to the sale of land in this parish and Holbeach. The Award was directed to be enrolled with the Clerk of the Peace of Holland and a copy was to be deposited in the parish church of Fleet.

LONG SUTTON.—This parish includes the hamlets of Sutton St. Mary, Sutton St. Nicholas, (otherwise, Lutton,) Sutton St. James and Sutton St. Edmund's. Each of these hamlets is separately rated to the poor and maintains its own highways.

There is a tradition, for which however there does not appear to be much foundation, that anciently there was a village called *Dalproon*, on a site near the South Holland Sluice and that it was washed away in the great flood of 1236. The tradition is preserved in the following lines :—

> When Dalproon stood,
> Long Sutton was a wood :
> When Dalproon was washed down,
> Long Sutton became a town.

INCLOSURE OF SUTTON MARSH.

State Papers, 1640.

The large tract known as Sutton Marsh, containing 6,760 acres, was enclosed from the sea in the middle of the 17th century. In 1640, King Charles I, by letters patent, granted these marshes to the Duke of Lenox under a rent of £300 a year, with power to embank and inclose them. The inclosure bank commenced at the sluice in Dereham Drain (now incorporated in the South Holland Drain) at the north-east corner of Tydd St. Mary's Marsh, and ran by Sutton Wash, West Mere Creek and King John's House, to a sluice, afterwards known as Anderson's Sluice, in Lutton Leam, about 1½ miles east of the Roman Bank. It then turned west for about 2 miles, to the point where the Roman Bank bends south, known as Sutton Corner. The Roman Bank, which runs south through Sutton St. Mary, formed the west boundary.

In 1717, Lord Lenox's interest was sold by order of the Court of Chancery, and was purchased by a Mr. Wollaston for £31,800, the unembanked lands being estimated by the purchaser as being as valuable as those which had been inclosed. Opposition was raised against the inclosure of the open marshes; and a petition was presented to the King (against a Bill which had been introduced), 'for preventing the inning and embanking' of these salt marshes. The overflowing of the tide on these marshes was stated 'as scarce ten times a year two feet deep.' The bill was withdrawn and in 1720 Mr. Newland, who had then become the owner, made an inclosure of 1,332 acres, the bank starting about three quarters of a

NEWLAND'S INCLOSURE, 1720.

mile north-east of Sutton Wash and running, in an irregular line along the east side of the present channel of the Nene, to the point where the west light tower stands, then turning west to the bank near Anderson's Sluice and Lutton Leam. Part of this inclosure now lies on the east side of the new outfall of the Nene. In 1733 these lands became the property of Guy's Hospital.

In 1747 a further inclosure of 762 acres was made, 528 acres of which lie between Lutton Leam and Gedney parish, and 234 acres south of the Leam. A new sluice was put in the Leam about 1¾ miles east of Anderson's Sluice, which was known as Bothamley's or Baxter's Sluice, now removed. GUY'S HOSPITAL INCLOSURES, 1747.

A further inclosure of 313 acres, called Shearcroft's Inclosure, was made by Guy's Hospital in 1805, and the present inner Leam Sluice was constructed. The bank of this inclosure extends from Skate's Corner, near the Lighthouse Towers, to Boatmeer Creek. 1805.

The last inclosure of 400 acres was made in 1865, and the sluice erected close to the river Nene outfall, under the direction of Mr. Millington. 1865.

Up to nearly the end of the last century there was a large tract of Common Land in this parish, containing between 3,000 and 4,000 acres. The whole of this common and the marshes from Tydd Gote to Lutton were without trees or hedges. They grew a rough grass and nettles, and were grazed by horses, cattle, sheep and pigs, often sent by owners of stock from considerable distances, on agistment. The road from Lincolnshire to Norfolk traversed this common and marsh, to the Cross Keys Wash, which was only fordable at low water. Drovers with their cattle for Lynn and Norwich markets, horses, vehicles and foot passengers were piloted over the two miles of the Wash by guides on horseback, the foot passengers being mounted on pillions behind the guides. Accidents frequently occurred, owing to the shifting nature of the sands. THE COMMONS.

In 1831 the Nene embankment and roadway towards Lynn, two miles in length, was made by a company of Proprietors, under an Act obtained in 1825. An oak bridge was constructed across the new cut of the Nene, the centre portion of which was made to open upwards to allow vessels to pass. This was replaced by a swing bridge in 1851, which in 1866 was transferred to the railway company. SUTTON BRIDGE.

Between 1788 and 1790 the common marshes and fens in this parish were divided and inclosed under an Inclosure Act. The commons dealt with were Long Sutton Common, containing 2,500 acres; a fen, called Sutton St. Edmund's Common, containing 700 acres; and several common waste grounds. INCLOSURE ACT. 28 Geo. iii, 1788.

The Commissioners appointed to carry out the Act were Edward Hare of Castor, Edward Stone of Leverington, and John Oldham of Tydd St. Mary. Their remuneration was fixed at £2 2s.

a day, including their expenses. They were to allot the lands, and sell a portion of the commons to pay the expenses; to set out such roads as they deemed necessary—one of a width of 66ft., running across the common from Dereham's Drain to the Old Leam and thence by Steward's Marsh to the turnpike, and adjoining the west side of the Guy's Hospital estate, (now known as Hospital Drove); to set out 10 acres of land, for the purpose of getting materials for the repair of the turnpike road which passed through the parish, which land was to vest in the Turnpike Trustees. The Award, when enrolled, was to be deposited in the parish church of Sutton St. Mary.

In 1827, when the New Cut for the Nene was made, a portion of this parish was severed and left on the east side of the river and about 200 acres were taken for the cut and banks.

DRAINAGE. A small part of the south-west portion of Sutton St. Mary is in the South Holland Drainage District, the remaining portion of Sutton St. Mary and Sutton St. Nicholas drain by the Lutton Leam Sluice into the Nene.

LUTTON LEAM.

Dugdale.

Lutton Leam is a very ancient outfall. In the Records of a Court of Sewers held at King's Lynn in 1613 it is described as 'the deep called Lutton Leame.' It was at that time proposed to bring the water from Wisbech and Elm, which then drained by the *Four Gotes*, across Tydd marsh and Sutton marshes to *King's Creeke*, and thence to fall into 'the deep called Lutton Leame,' which was stated to be a shorter course to the river by six miles, and as having a much better outfall.

The outfall of the Leam was originally at Lutton Gote in the Roman Bank, but when the inclosure bank of 1660 was made, a new sluice, called Anderson's Sluice, was built 1½ miles east of the Roman Bank. In 1774, a third sluice, known as Bothamley's or Baxter's Sluice, was erected, about one mile further east. This has since been removed. In 1806, when a further inclosure was made, the sluice was placed three quarters of a mile further east, where the inner sluice now stands, and about one mile from the Nene outfall. When the last, or Shearcroft's inclosure, was made in 1865, a new sluice was erected in the inclosure bank close to the channel of the Nene, and a sluice-keeper's house built near to the sluice. The first sluice for Shearcroft's inclosure was erected under the direction of Mr. Cressy, a Civil Engineer, of London. It however blew up on the night following its completion. The present inner sluice was built in 1806, under the direction of Mr. Thomas Pear, of Spalding, and has an opening of 10½ft. The outer sluice, erected in 1865 by the Governors of Guy's Hospital, under the direction of Mr. Millington, had an opening of 8ft; the decrease in the waterway, as compared with the inner sluice, being compensated for by the greater depth at which the sill was placed. In 1881, the sill of the 1806 sluice was lowered by the

Court of Sewers, the work being done by Messrs. Cooke and Bennett, Contractors.

On March 11th, 1883, the outer sluice was damaged by a high tide which made a breach through the bank of the Nene adjoining the sluice, and carried away the sluice-keeper's house. The cause of the breach was supposed to be due to a rat, or rabbit hole, in the bank. The sluice was taken down and rebuilt at some distance back from the Nene in 1888, under the direction of Mr. John Kingston, by Mr. James, the Contractor. The cost was £4,326, which, with engineering, legal and other expenses, made the total cost £5,677; of which £3,677 was paid by Guy's Hospital, and £2,000 by the Court of Sewers; the rate for the payment being levied on the parishes of Lutton, Gedney, Fleet, and Sutton St. Mary.

The total area of land draining by the Lutton Leam is 13,000 acres. Part of Gedney and Fleet is drained by this outfall.

SUTTON ST. EDMUND'S.

Sutton St. Edmund's Great and Little Commons, which lie to the south of the Old South Holland Drain and, together with Inkerson Fen, extend southward to the Old Wryde Drain, contain about 1,200 acres. This land is the only part of Lincolnshire on the south of the Old South Holland or Shire Drain. It is drained by the New South Eau in the North Level System. The Great and Little Commons are exempted from taxation to the North Level.

27 Geo. ii, 1754.

The drainage was improved under the powers of an Act obtained in 1809, for *Improving the Lands lying in the late Great Common and in the Little Common of Sutton St. Edmunds, in the Parish of Sutton St. Mary, otherwise Long Sutton.*

49 Geo. iii, c. 119, 1809.

The land was formerly drained by two windmills, driving scoop-wheels, the one, known as Woolmer's, about 50 yards north of Windmill corner; the other about 1¾ miles more to the north, called Hockerson's, which threw the water into the Old South Eau, under Murrow Bank above the Clows, and thence into the Shire Drain. The tax, at that time, was 5/- an acre.

The drainage is under the power of the Commissioners appointed by the Act of 1754.

St. Edmund's paid £1,700 to the North Level Drainage in 1828, for sending its water down the North Level Drain, to a sluice erected under the direction of Mr. Millington.

The mill and wheel were done away with when the New North Level Drain was made. Woolmer's mill was pulled down in 1843, and Hockerson's mill, after being superseded by a steam engine, was pulled down in 1838.

The amount raised by rates in the Sutton St. Edmund's Great Common District, according to the return 1892-3, was £27. The Expenditure on Works, £11; Management, £17; Interest, £4; Total £32. There was an outstanding loan of £90.

Sutton St. James.

This part of the parish was formerly drained by Lutton Leam through a branch of the old South Eau, which went east of Sutton church. About 1756 it was drained by a windmill and scoop-wheel into the Shire Drain by means of the Dunton Drain. In 1786 the Court of Sewers directed the discontinuance of the payment to the Leam drainage. In 1816 a right to drain direct into the Shire Drain by Denham's Drain, as an experiment for 20 years, was purchased from the proprietors of the Estate. In 1836 the right was made perpetual. Sutton Saint James paid £850 towards the cost of the Nene Outfall, made in 1830. It was attempted to make this land also contribute towards the cost of the North Level Drain, but, after the matter had been before a Parliamentary Committee, it was discharged from any payment. The Drainage Mill was taken down and sold in 1836.

Inclosure of Marsh, 1632.

TYDD ST. MARY.—Tydd St. Mary's Marsh, lying between the Shire Drain on the south and the New South Holland Drain (which replaced Dereham's Drain) on the north. containing about 1,121 acres, was inclosed by Vermuyden, under an agreement with King Charles, dated 1631, about which time the Bedford Level Commissioners straightened and improved the Shire Drain. Hill's Sluice at the Tydd Gote is dated 1632, and was then probably the outfall to the Shire Drain, its water subsequently being directed to the Foul Anchor, when the first Gunthorpe Sluice was erected near the Foul Anchor Inn.

The Commons.

When the marsh was inclosed about 600 acres near the village were left for the householders to use in common, no limit as to the number of stock to be put on by each inhabitant being reserved. The commons were consequently stocked so heavily that hardly a blade of grass was left. Thistles and nettles grew luxuriantly, as it was nobody's special duty to keep them down. Sheep and lambs were frequently lost amongst them and were worried to death by maggots.

Inclosure Act. 32 Geo. iii, c. 25, 1792.

In 1792 an Act was obtained for the inclosure of this common land; each householder who had stocked the common during the previous 20 years, however small his holding, being admitted as having an equal right.

Drainage Acts. 13 Geo. lii, c. 60, 1773. 48 Geo. iii, c. 23, 1808. 7 and 8 Geo. iv, c. 85, 1827.

In 1773 an Act was obtained for draining the lands in Tydd St. Mary, with those in Tydd St. Giles and Newton, these latter being in the Isle of Ely. In 1808 an amending Act was obtained, and a further amending Act in 1827. These Acts principally relate to the drainage of Tydd St. Giles, which is in the North Level.

This parish paid £300 to the *North Level District* in 1528 for the right to drain some of its outer lands, known as Rippingale, Chapel and Tilney. The tunnel into the Shire Drain at Eau, or High Bank, near Marwold Lane was constructed in 1849, and Wanton's tunnel into the South Holland Drain was lowered in 1853.

The roads in this parish, and in Long Sutton, are known as *gates*; thus, there is Bad Gate, Chapel Gate, Gilbert Gate, Acres Gate,

Broad Gate, Elder's Gate, Hunt's Gate, Low Gate, Roe Gate and Cross Gate. Some of the roads are also distinguished as *dykes*, as Master Dyke, Bully Dyke, Draw Dyke and Green Dyke.

The Hamlet of Tydd Gote is named from the fact of the outfall gote or sluice being built there. The earliest recorded sluice is mentioned in 1293, the second in 1551, the third and present—called Hill's Sluice, or Tydd Gote Bridge—in 1632. This was erected by the Bedford Level Adventurers, when they turned their North Level water from Guyhirne.

CHAPTER V.

THE RIVER WITHAM.

<small>COURSE OF THE RIVER.</small>

THE river Witham takes its rise near Thistleton and South Witham, about ten miles north of Stamford, at an elevation of 339ft. above the level of the sea, and, after a circuitous course of about 68 miles, empties itself into Boston Deeps. The shape of the river may be compared to a horse shoe, the upper part of the shoe being at Lincoln, and the two ends respectively at South Witham and Fishtoft, the distance between the two points being about 28 miles.

The Witham, on leaving Thistleton and South Witham, flows almost due north, past Colsterworth, Great and Little Ponton, to Grantham, where it is 170ft. above the sea. It then continues its northerly course past Belton and Syston, whence it takes a westerly direction to Long Bennington, receiving on its way the Honington Brook, and a stream, one head of which rises in the Vale of Belvoir and the other at Denton, and both united join the Witham at Hougham. It then again turns north, and passes Claypole, Barnaby, Beckingham, Stapleford, Thurlby, and Hykeham. At the latter place another tributary joins it, having its rise near Caythorpe and Fulbeck, and then continues through a wide valley to Lincoln, where it is only 16ft. above sea level. The principal tributaries received in this part of its course are the Brant, 15 miles long, which rises near Brandon, and the Till, 14 miles long, which passes through Saxelby, Willingham and Upton.

<small>*Water Supply of England*, De Rance.</small>

The geological formation is principally oolitic, and extends over 797 square miles, part of which is covered by alluvial deposit; 6 square miles consist of trias; 240 of lias; and 36 of greensands and gault.

The river then passes through a deep depression in the cliff which runs through this part of the country, and, after leaving Lincoln, takes an easterly direction for about 8 miles; then, bending south for about 22 miles, reaches Boston, where it becomes tidal and navigable for large vessels; and, finally, after a further course of 8 miles through a trained channel, discharges into the estuary at Clayhole. Between Lincoln and Boston it is canalised and navigable for barges.

THE LANGWORTH. The Langworth, which rises in the chalk hills between Market Rasen and Louth, after a course of 18 miles, joins the river a short distance below Lincoln.

THE BANE. The Bane, which rises in the same range of chalk hills near Ludford, is 25 miles long, and passes through Horncastle and Scrivelsby, joining the Witham near Tattershall. From Horncastle to the Witham this tributary is canalised.

THE SLEA. The Slea, which rises in the oolite near Ancaster and is fed by some strong oolite springs at Sleaford, is also canalised, and joins the Witham near Dogdyke, the length from the source being 22 miles.

LENGTH. The total length of the main stream is 89 miles, and of the principal tributaries, 98 miles.

DRAINAGE AREA. The area of the drainage basin may be divided as follows :—

	High Land. Acres.	Low Land. Acres.	Total Acres.
River Witham, above the Grand Sluice	414,998	33,897	448,895
Draining by the Black Sluice	57,490	76,861	134,351
Draining by Maud Foster and Hobhole Sluices	21,330	62,576	83,906
Draining by Outfalls under control of the Court of Sewers			13,600
			680,752

In the report of the Parliamentary Committee on River Conservancy the area of the drainage basin is given as 1,050 square miles, or 672,000 acres.

Sir John Hawkshaw makes the area draining by the Grand Sluice greater than the above, and thus divides it :—

	High Level. Acres.
Draining into the River Witham above Lincoln	152,000
Draining into the Fossdyke	53,000
Draining into north-east side of the Witham below Lincoln	167,000
Draining into the Cardyke	40,000
Draining into Billinghay Skirth	19,000
Draining into the Sleaford Navigation	34,000
	465,000
Low lands drained by pumping	39,000
Total	504,000

of which 205,000 acres lie above Lincoln, and 299,000 below.

NAME OF THE RIVER. The river has been called by three different names. Dr. Oliver states that the ancient British name was *Grant Avon*, or the divine stream. The name of the principal town on the river, Grant-ham, is evidence in favour of this. Leland is the authority for its being subsequently known as the *Lindis*. Camden also says, 'the course of Lindis river from Lincoln to Boston is 50 miles by water, as the creeks go'; but there is evidence that the river was known as the Witham long antecedent to the time when Camden wrote.

There is no record of the name by which it was known during the Roman period. Since the Saxon times it has been known as the Witham. The word Witham is probably derived from *Wye-om*, or *river plain*.

<small>ANCIENT COURSE OF THE RIVER.</small>

There is every reason to suppose that the river now known as the Witham, extending from its source above Grantham to the sea below Boston, is the result of the union of the two streams, the Witham and the Langworth. The Witham proper originally discharged its contents into the large mere above Lincoln, and so drained to the Trent. The Langworth emptied into the large mere lying between Washingborough and Chapel Hill, the outlet for its water being by the tidal creek which extended from the lower part of this mere, through the marshes where Boston now stands, to the sea. Another outlet probably ran through the East and West Fens to Wainfleet Haven. The two large lakes, one above and one below Lincoln, which existed previous to the drainage works carried out by the Romans, were separated by comparatively high ground, extending from the edge of the peat, near Greetwell, to Lincoln.

<small>Padley's Fens and Floods.</small>

The land lying west of Lincoln towards the Trent is all very low, and beneath the level of the flood water in that river. A practical proof of this was given in 1795 when the bank of the Trent at Spalford broke, and the whole area of land between the Trent and Lincoln was under water, in some parts to a depth of ten feet, the course of the water being stopped by the High-street, which is raised from 12ft. to 15ft. above the surrounding land. During the flood about 20,000 acres of land to the west of the city were submerged. In 1770 the Fossdyke embankment at Torksey gave way, the water flowing up to Lincoln.

<small>ALTERATION OF THE RIVER BY THE ROMANS.</small>

There is every reason to assume that the Romans, for the purpose of draining the low swampy ground to the north and west of the city, and for the purpose of allowing boats to get there from the Trent, either deepened and improved an existing watercourse, or cut a new channel along the line of the present Fossdyke Canal. At the same time they banked out the Trent and drained all the low ground, except the deep part of Brayford Mere. For the purpose of draining the Mere below Lincoln and also for making a canal, along which boats could get from the sea, past Boston and up to Lincoln, a cutting was made through the high land east of Brayford Mere, to Short Ferry, about two miles below Fiskerton, and thence along the edge of the high ground, until it joined the tidal creek near Chapel Hill. Down to Lincoln, the Witham, like all other rivers, has innumerable bends, while from Lincoln to Short Ferry, the course is almost a straight line, and below Short Ferry to Chapel Hill, the channel is only curved sufficiently to follow the high land, and is too direct ever to have been the course of a natural stream. There are also several small tracts of fen on the east side which have been cut off by the channel. Below Chapel Hill, before the New Cut was made in 1761, the tidal creek or river was very tortuous, there being no less than thirty bends in a length of 12 miles.

There is no record of any works having been carried out for straightening the river or making a new cut above Chapel Hill, except across the bend at Branston, since the Roman occupation.

It has been stated that the tide formerly reached Lincoln, and that vessels came up on the tide to Lincoln past Boston. There is no doubt that after the works carried out by the Romans there was communication with the sea by this course, but neither then, nor indeed, at any time, either before or since, would it have been possible for the tide to reach Lincoln under the present geological conditions of the district. Before the flow of the tide up the river was stopped by the erection of the Grand Sluice, it seldom or never went beyond Dogdyke or Chapel Hill. The bed of the river at that time was higher than it is now, and the soil excavated for the deepening of the old channel was hard clay, the surface of which at Kirkstead was 3½ft. above the sill of the Grand Sluice. Before the improvements were made the fall in the surface of the water from Lincoln to Boston was 16ft. An average spring tide rises about 13ft. at Boston, the surface of high water at spring tides being about 13.34ft. above *Ordnance datum* (mean level of the sea.) The surface of the land at Lincoln, between Brayford Mere and Stamp End Lock, varies from 18 to 20 feet above *Ordnance datum*, the surface of the Mere being considerably above the level of a high tide. By a survey of the Witham made in 1743, as nearly as the levels from the 'primary point' can be traced, and reduced to *Ordnance datum*, the bed of the river at the High Bridge at Lincoln, previous to the improvements, was 15·59ft. above *Ordnance datum*, and at Washingborough it was 11·03ft. above. The outfall below Chapel Hill, up which the tide flowed, being only a shallow winding creek, it is evident that it would not have been possible for the tide to flow up to Lincoln.

LIMIT OF THE TIDE.

Grundy.

The whole of the water coming down the upper Witham does not pass along the channel which goes through the city. A considerable portion is diverted in floods by the Syncil dyke, which, leaving the Witham about half-a-mile above the city, joins the river again near the Great Northern Railway Station. There is no record of when this drain was cut, but there can be no doubt that its original purpose was to relieve the city from flooding. Stukely says, "after the Norman Conquest the great part of the City of Lincoln was turned into a Castle. I apprehend they added the last intake southward in the angle of the Witham and made a new cut called the Sincil dyke, on the south and east side, for its security." He gives, however, no authority for this statement, and it is more probable that it was the work of the Romans, and formed part of the system of

SYNCIL DYKE.

drainage which they they carried out. Smeaton's and Grundy's report, of 1762, states that the water of Brayford Mere, into which the Witham falls, is prevented from running off below a certain height by a shoal or natural stanch in the river, between the Mere and Lincoln High Bridge, called Brayford Head; that as the bottoms of Sincil Dyke and the Gowt Bridge Drain are several inches higher than the top of the shoal at Brayford Mere, those two drains serve only as *Slaker Drains*, to ease off the passage of the water in time of flood.

Stukeley's Richard of Cirencester.

OUTFALL OF THE RIVER.

As regards the outfall of the river below Lincoln, Stukeley says, that there was an outfall for the Witham "across that natural declivity full east into the sea, as in the map of Richard of Cirencester. This channel might pass out of the present river a little below Coningsby, where the River Bane falls into it at Dock Dyke and Youledale, by the waters of Howbridge north of Hundlehouse. So running below Middelhouse to Black Sike, it took the present division between the two wapentakes all along the south side of the deeps of the East Fen, and so by Blackgote to Wainfleet, the *Vainona* of the Romans."

The Fenland. Miller & Skertchley.

Mr. Skertchley of the Government Geological Survey traced the old course across the gravel lands to the silt land of the West Fen, where, the deposits being identical, its course is indistinguishable, and he gives a diagram showing the deposit along the supposed ancient channel.

There is a free communication between the Witham and the Fossdyke and some of the Witham water finds its way to the Trent by this course. The water for locking is entirely supplied from the Witham.

THE FOSSDYKE.

Dugdale's Embanking and Draining.

Dugdale describes the Fossdyke as extending "from the great marsh below the City of Lincoln into the Trent at Torksey seven miles, made by King Henry I, in the year 1121, for bringing up of navigable vessels from the river into the city......and did no less benefit to the parts adjacent by draining that fenny level from the standing water then much annoying it." Dugdale is in error in ascribing the making of this watercourse to Henry I. There can be no doubt that Stukeley is correct in ascribing it to the Romans, and that it was originally a continuation of the Car Dyke. Lincoln at one end, and Torksey at the other, were both Roman stations. The work referred to by Dugdale was the opening out of the old canal.

In the reign of Edward III, the Fossdyke had become so grown up with grass and trodden in by cattle that boats could no longer pass along it, and a presentment as to its condition was made to the King in Parliament, by the citizens of Lincoln and the tradesmen of York, Nottingham and Hull, "representing the damage from ships and boats not being able to pass therein with merchandise and victuals from these towns to Lincoln and thence to Boston. Whereupon Commissioners were appointed to enquire into the matter, and it was found that the landowners abutting on the channel ought to repair the same." Very little more is heard of the Fossdyke till the reign of Charles II, when an Act was passed empowering any person to open up the communication through the Fossdyke to Torksey and through the Witham to Boston, and under the powers of this Act the Fossdyke was again opened out. *[margin: Dugdale. 22 and 23 Chas ii.]*

Stukeley says that "about eighty years ago (1755) when the navigation was restored to Lincoln they made a new crooked course for the Foss into the Trent. It went originally straight forwards through the riverine into the marshes....The water at the sluice is generally a yard and a half higher in the Foss than in the Trent." The fall from the Fossdyke to the Trent is given in Mr. J. Rennie's report of Dec. 1802 as 6ft. In high floods the water in the Trent rises above that in the Fossdyke, and the lock is provided with a double set of gates, one pair for the purpose of holding up the water in the Fossdyke and the other for preventing high floods in the Trent from backing up into the Fossdyke.

During the Roman occupation and after the works already referred to for connecting Lincoln and Boston, the Witham no doubt became the chief means of communication for vessels engaged in exporting corn, and for bringing wine and goods from other countries. The larger vessels which crossed the sea would probably lie in the haven below Boston or perhaps at Dogdyke and discharge into smaller boats, better adapted for the navigation of the upper reach. By this means the long transport of the merchandise by land from Wainfleet, which previously had been the sea port for Lincoln, was saved. *[margin: ANCIENT NAVIGATION TO LINCOLN.]*

There are no records of the condition of the river for a long period after the Roman occupation. In William the Conqueror's time Lincoln was one of the most important cities in England, and Leland says that men flocked there by land and water. In the time of Henry IV Lincoln possessed a very large share of the import and export trade of the kingdom. The trade between Lincoln and the Continent, especially in wool, became very considerable and this city paid in *Quinzine* duties in one year £656 12s. 2d., and Boston £780 15s. 3d., as against £830 12s. 10d. by London. In the Hundred Rolls are to be found many instances of cargoes of wool sent down the Witham. The trade was of sufficient importance to lead to the construction of a dock and warehouses at a place called Calscroft, near Sheepwash Grange, where the ships belonging to the Lincoln merchants loaded and discharged their cargoes, and where the city and king's officers attended to collect the tolls. *[margin: Oliver's Religious Houses on the Witham.]*

'There was also a dock, or place where vessels could lie and discharge their cargoes into smaller boats, at Dogdyke, formerly spelt *Docdyke*, this being the extent to which the vessels could take advantage of the tide. In the Hundred Rolls mention is made of tolls taken in 1265 for vessels going to Lincoln.

<small>EARLY CONDITION OF THE RIVER.</small>

<small>1342.</small>

The river not being under any jurisdiction capable of keeping it in order, or of compelling the removal of obstructions, the Channel deteriorated so much that navigation became difficult. In 1342, a petition was sent to the King, in which it was stated that the river was so obstructed by mud that ships laden with wine, wool and other merchandise, could no longer pass as they used to do. It was probably owing to the defective condition of the navigation that the trade fell off at Lincoln; and in 1369 the staple for wool was transferred to Boston.

<small>1393.</small>

In the reign of Edward III, mention is made of a Commission sent by the King to view the river between Boston and Lincoln, "it having been turned out of its course in sundry places, and so obstructed with mud, sand, and plantation of trees, as also by flood gates and sluices, mills, causeys and ditches, that the course of the same being hindered, caused frequent inundations of the land adjacent." Again, in the same reign, parliament was petitioned by the merchants of Lincoln and other towns, complaining of the total insufficiency of the river for navigation. A few years later a presentment was made to the court of King's Bench, showing that the channel of the Witham in Wildmore was bending and defective.

<small>Dugdale.</small>

In the fifteenth century several complaints were made as to the neglect of the Abbots of the monasteries along the river to repair the banks and channel. In the reign of Richard II a Commission was appointed for the view and repair of those banks and sewers betwixt Hildike and Bolingbroke, and betwixt the river Witham and the sea, and to do all things therein according to the law and custom of this realm, and according to the custom of Romney Marsh; and also to take so many diggers and labourers, upon competent salaries, in regard of the then urgent necessity, as should be sufficient to accomplish that work.

<small>1427.</small>

At a Court held at Stickford in 1427, complaint was made that Kirkstead Abbey had neglected to repair the banks of the Wytham from Swythut Hurne as far as Mere Dyke, by which neglect the marshes of the East and West Fens suffered. At a Court, held at Sibsey Hall in 1430, Kirkstead Abbey was again charged with neglecting to repair the banks near the grange of Langwathe, so that the waters flowed into the West Fen. At a King's Court held at Bolingbroke in 1444, it was shown that the Fossat, called Yoledale Dyke, taking the water thro' Witham Sewer and thence into Boston Haven, was out of repair, so that the water overflowed the King's Pasture and the West Fen, by neglect of the inhabitants of Coningsby. At a King's Court held in 1453 the Radyke (a bank with a road on it), called Witham Bank in the Parish of Coningsby, from Anthon's Gowt to Danebooth, was out of repair by neglect of the Abbot of Kirkstead.

It is unnecessary to give instances of the numerous complaints that were made to the Courts as to the condition of the river. The above are sufficient to shew that the duty devolving on the riparian owners of maintaining the banks and channel was carried out very indifferently, and that the river was allowed to get into a very neglected condition.

In the reign of Henry VII, a Commission was held, and an enquiry made as to the best means of improving the river, both for drainage and navigation. At this time " at a full spring tide in winter, when the flood and fresh water did meet together at Dockdyke the salt and fresh water strove so together that the water so ran over the banks and both sides of the haven that it drowned all the common fen; so that men might come with boats from Garwick to Boston town: and likewise from Boston to Kirkby land side."

The Commission appears to have come to the conclusion that this state of things would be remedied if the sea water were prevented from flowing up the river. Accordingly it was determined to erect a sluice with flood gates at Boston. For this purpose a warrant was made out and given to the dykereeves of every township in Holland, or to the 'Jurats,' to bring in the book of the number of acres in their respective parishes, and proclamation was made in the market of Boston that the Dykereeves had made certificate of the correctness of the acre books, at the Hallgarth Inn at Boston, before the Commissioners there assembled for the purpose; order was also made to levy statute duty and contributions. In order to hasten the work, a sum of £1,000 was borrowed until such time as it could be levied according to the law of Romney Marsh. The following Officers were also appointed, viz. a Receiver of the levy, or Prest; two Bailiffs of Sewers; four Collectors and two Expenditors. The work of erecting the sluice was entrusted to May Hake, probably a Dutchman, and an indenture was made with him to make and finish a sluice and dam in the Witham, in the town of Boston, on such ground as he might select. He and his man were to be paid at the rate of four shillings a day, with a gratuity of £50 on the successful completion of the work. Fourteen Stone-masons and Stone-hewers, brought from Calais, were to have five shillings a week 'broken or whole.' Ships were sent to Calais to fetch materials and 'the stuff and stone' were to be conveyed to the churchyard at Boston.

The sluice was built in the middle of the river, a little to the north of the present iron bridge. It was connected with the land on each side and formed a bridge, and with alterations and numerous repairs remained the only bridge across the river until the erection of the present iron bridge in 1807. A stone pier 13ft. wide and 43¾ft long was built in the centre of the river. On this by means of large iron hooks the doors for excluding the tide were hung, and recesses were left in the masonry for the doors when open. There were two openings, the large one 44ft. wide, and the small one 21½ft., or a total waterway of 65½ft. In a reference to this bridge in a pamphlet published in 1642, it is stated that the doors were then no longer in existence and that the tide flowed several miles above Boston. In the year 1700, spring tides are stated to have risen ten feet at a distance of five miles above Boston, and it is stated in a paper by one, Dr. Browne, written about the year 1560, "that the sluice was not according to the first meaning and determination, but should have been made with a pair of fludd gates, that the fludd should have no further course than the bridge, but so to have returned back again; and the fresh water following the salt, which should continue fresh above the bridge, to have had at all times fresh water for the commodity of the town during the time of the fludd. And also to have scoured the haven daily, both above the sluice and to the seaward."

Grundy's Report, 1757.

About the year 1601, in the reign of Elizabeth, a further attempt to improve the drainage was made by erecting a new gote of four brick tuns or openings, at Langrick, with doors pointing towards the river, for the purpose of discharging the water from the Gill Syke Drain which conveyed the water from Holland Fen, and which previously had discharged into the Welland.

LANGRICK GOTE, 1601.

Chapman's Facts and Remarks.

From this time the river continued to decay, owing partly to the decline of trade and commerce at Boston, and also to the suppression of the Religious houses by Henry VIII; the owners of which had always been assiduous in attending to the work of drainage, and had given employment to the vessels navigating the river by importing large quantities of wine and other merchandise from the Low Countries. With reference to this, Dugdale says, "It hath been a long received opinion, as well by the borderers on the Fens as others, that the total drowning of this great level hath for the most part been occasioned by the neglect of putting the laws of sewers in due execution in these latter times; and that before the dissolution of the monasteries by Henry VIII, the passages for the waters were kept with cleansing, and the banks with better repair, chiefly through the care and cost of those religious houses."

DECAY OF THE RIVER.

Dugdale's Embanking and Draining.

In 1633, when the Adventurers were attempting to drain the East and West Fens, in a communication from the King to the Court of Sewers it is stated that it was found impossible to keep the fens drained unless the banks of the Witham from the Bane to Anthon's Gote were kept in repair, and directing that a sufficient tax be laid on Wildmore or Armetree Fen and such other grounds as lie under the said bank, and to make a bargain with the undertakers for their present and perpetual maintenance. The fens along the Witham were included in a grant made to the Earl of Lindsey,

State Papers, 1633.

Sir W. Killigrew, Sir Edward Heron, and others, in the reign of Charles II. The area granted covered 72,000 acres on the north side of the Witham, extending from the river Glen to Lincoln, and from Lincoln to the Trent. The Adventurers were to drain the lands and make them winter grounds and to have as their recompense 24,000 acres. The adventure was divided into 20 shares; each shareholder finding a proportionate amount of the capital required and receiving in return his proportion of the land awarded. The Earl, within two years after the contract was made with the Court of Sewers, in accordance with the terms of the grant, began the draining and performed it according to his contract, making all the level 'winter ground,' except 7,000 acres, left 'for receptacles for water,' and he and his co-adventurers were put in possession of 14,000 acres, part of the lands contracted for. A tax of 13s. 4d. per acre had, before the contract was made, been ordered by the Court to be paid by the owners, and those who paid this, the Earl of Lincoln being one, kept their lands, although the works of drainage greatly exceeded this amount.

RECLAMATION BY THE ADVENTURERS, 1667.

State Papers, Domestic.

The works carried out by these Adventurers became ultimately abortive, owing to the opposition and lawlessness of the Fenmen.

In the reign of Charles II, an Act was passed with the object of improving the navigation between Boston and the Trent through Lincoln. The preamble of this act recites that "whereas there hath been for some hundreds of years a good navigation betwixt the Borough of Boston and the river of Trent by and through the City of Lincoln, and thereby a great trade managed to the benefit of those parts of Lincolnshire, and some parts of Nottinghamshire and Yorkshire, which afforded an honest employment and livelyhood to great numbers of people. But at the present time the said navigation is much obstructed and in great decay, by reason that the river or antient channels of Witham and Fossdyke which run betwixt Boston and Trent are much silted and landed up, and thereby not passable with boats and lighters as formerly, to the great decay of the trade and commerce of the said city and all market towns neare any of the said rivers; which hath produced in them much poverty and depopulation." By this Act power was given to the Mayor and Corporation of Lincoln to receive tolls upon the Witham and Fossdyke for the purpose of improving the river.

ACT FOR THE IMPROVEMENT OF THE NAVIGATION, 1671.

22 and 23 Chas. ii.

No improvement appears to have been effected on the Witham under this act, the works being confined to the Fossdyke.

In a report on the condition of the river made by Mr. James Scribo in 1733, he found as the result of 'an exact' survey of the river between Lincoln and Boston made by John Pitchford, that the fall of the water from Lincoln to Boston was 16ft.; that the haven or river, for above 20 miles, was very crooked and winding and in several places not above 18ft. or 20ft. in breadth and very shallow;

CONDITION OF THE RIVER IN THE 18TH CENTURY.

Scribo's Report, 1733.

and that there were several large rivers and brooks which brought down the water from the uplands, five of which were any of them larger than the aforesaid winding haven, so that after the great downfall of rains and snows, which frequently happens in the winter season, and the river below Chapel Hill not being of sufficient capacity to carry down the floods, the banks were generally overflowed and several thousand acres of rich pasture land were laid under water to the depth of three feet, to the great prejudice of the landowners, as well as the navigation; and that these waters remained on the land and stagnated for 3 or 4 months; he found the navigation between Lincoln and Boston was so bad that only vessels of very small burden could pass from one place to the other; that several proprietors had endeavoured, at great expense, to remedy the inconvenience to their drainage by cutting drains, erecting engines, and embanking their separate estates, but without success; he expressed the opinion, that if this state of things continued it would not be many years before the navigation would be entirely lost, and draining thereby rendered impracticable. To remedy this he proposed a scheme of improvement, including a new straight cut from Tattershall through Holland Fen to Lodowick's Gowt at Boston, reducing the distance from over 20 miles, which it was along the existing winding course, to $11\frac{1}{4}$ miles; or, as an alternative, a cut from Tattershall through Wildmore Fen to Anton's Gowt. Three locks were to be placed in the river, one between Lincoln and Creampoke Sluice, the second at Hare Booth, the third at the upper end of the new cut, "this to have strong sea gates to stem the salt water from flowing up the river in dry seasons." The estimate for the Holland Fen Cut was £9,706, and for the one through Wildmore Fen £6,363. Nothing, however, was done towards carrying out this scheme.

SCRIBO'S SCHEME OF IMPROVEMENT

NORTH FORTY FOOT DRAIN.

Chapman's Facts and Remarks.

Fig. 6.

About the year 1720 Earl Fitzwilliam, having made repeated application, without success, to the Court of Sewers to drain his lands lying in Billinghay Dales and Hart's Grounds, on the west side of the river near Kyme Eau, determined to undertake the work himself. For this purpose he constructed a drain, commencing above Chapel Hill, passing under Kyme Eau and running nearly parallel with the present course of the Witham, to Brothertoft, whence it turned at a sharp angle, in an easterly direction and joined the Witham near where the footpath leaves the Carlton road for Boston West. A sluice was built at its junction with the river, called *Lodowick's Gowt*, having a waterway of 15ft. This drain, known as the North Forty Foot, was subsequently diverted into the Black Sluice Drain by a cut to Cook's lock.

Great objection was raised to the cutting of this drain at the time, on the ground that it diverted water from the river, which used to find its way into Langrick Gowt and assisted in keeping the

Fig: 6
Chap 3

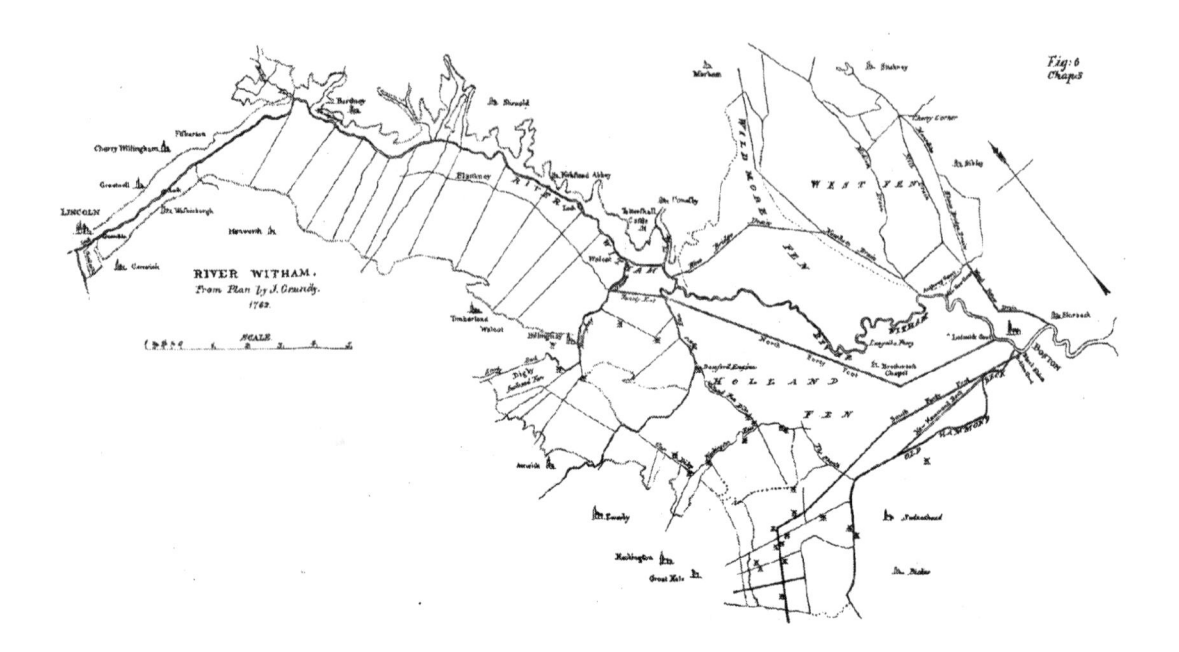

RIVER WITHAM.
From Plan by J. Grundy.
1762.

SCALE

portion of the river between there and Boston open. It does not appear to have afforded much relief to the land it was intended to benefit, for it is said that the tenants cut the banks to rid themselves of the water and let it flow into Holland Fen. It must, however, have been of some use, as, owing to the wretched condition of the Witham, it is stated that at that time the principal part of the water forced its way out of the main channel at Chapel Hill into Lord Fitzwilliam's Drain and, flowing down that, reached the Haven through Lodowick's Gowt. And to such an extent did the river continue to decay and its bed to silt up, that it was reported that "the Lady of the Manor's tenant inclosed and took to himself a great part of the old bed of the river, where it passed through Wildmore Fen, and called his new acquisition, *marshes*." N. Kinderley, who inspected the river in 1736, reported that there were "no banks from Dogdyke to Lincoln on the west side to keep the upland water from flooding the lands, and also on each side to near Tattershall, and so, by spreading, the water loseth its velocity and quantity, which, if kept in a body, would scour the river, which is now daily rising. Where it meets the sea tides every spring at Dogdyke, the land on each side, where no banks are, is constantly drowned on every land flood. The tides did not flow much above Anthony's Gowt, and the bed of the river was silted up within two feet of the top of the banks."

N. Kinderley. 1736.

The width of the river at this time was 83ft. at high water, and 65ft. at low water, near Boston Church; 63ft. through Boston Bridge, and 103ft. at high water and 66ft. at low water, at Doughty's Quay. The greatest rise of the tide at the Bridge was 13ft. and the low water stood 4ft. on the sill of Lodowick's Gowt.

The course of the river, as it then existed, is shown on the plan, *Fig. 6*, taken from Mr. Grundy's map of 1762. At this time a considerable portion of the West and Wildmore Fens, and part of the East Fen and the East Holland parishes, used to get rid of their water by drains entering the Witham at Anthony's Gowt, and by a sluice known as New Gote. In 1735 a Jury of the Court of Sewers, summoned to consider a petition of the Owners of land in this district complaining of the great losses they had sustained, owing to the defective condition of these outfalls, found that "the river Witham was nearly lost by reason of the alteration and destruction of the course of the Channel and especially through great quantities of sand thrown into the same by the force of the sea." A report, published some years later, described "this once flourishing river" as having for many years "been falling into decay by the banks being suffered to become ruinous and incapable of sustaining and containing the water in times of high water floods, so that those floods which were necessary and useful heretofore, by their velocity and weight, to cleanse out the sand and sediment

Fig. 6.

1735.

Grundy and Langley Edwards. 1761.

brought up by the tides, have been, and now are suffered to run out of their ancient and natural course, and expand over the adjoining fens and low grounds, whereby those sands, for want of a reflowing power of adequate force to carry them back, have now so much choked up the Haven from Boston to the sea, that for several years past the navigation thereof has been lost to shipping, and it is now become even difficult for barges of about 30 tons burden to get up to the town in neap tides; and for several miles above the town of Boston the said river is totally lost, in so much that its bottom is in many places some feet higher than the adjoining low grounds, and the site thereof, converted into grazing and farming purposes . . . and the flood waters lie so long stagnant on the land as to destroy the herbage thereof, and render them not only useless and unprofitable, but also extremely noxious and unwholesome to the adjacent inhabitants."

GRUNDY'S SCHEME, 1744.

In the year 1744, Mr. John Grundy of Spalding, in conjunction with his son, prepared a scheme for restoring and making perfect the navigation of the river Witham from Boston to Lincoln, and for draining the low lands contiguous.

Messrs. Grundy proposed by their first and second schemes to merely widen and deepen the existing channel between Chapel Hill and Anton's Gowt and to cut off some of the worst curves. By the third scheme they proposed to make an entirely new cut from Chapel Hill to Anthony's Gowt along the lowest part of Wildmore Fen, a distance of seven miles. The bottom of the cut to be 20ft. wide, and 5ft. deeper than the existing bed of the river. Above Chapel Hill the channel, for three miles, was to be widened and deepened; and from there to Lincoln to be scoured out and the shallow places removed. Three stanches were to be erected, between Lincoln and Tattershall, to hold up the water for navigation. The estimated cost was £4,695. If the lower part of the channel should be made with a 70ft. bottom, so as to make the river better for the navigation, and further improve the river between Tattershall and Lincoln, the estimate was increased to £7,056. For the improvement of the fens on the west side of the river, they proposed to make a new drain from near Fiskerton, through the centre of the fens, under Billinghay Skirth and joining Kyme Eau, to enter the New Cut at Chapel Hill. Sluices were to be put at the end of this new Drain, and at the outfalls of the Bane, Billinghay Skirth and Newdale dyke, to keep out the tides The cost of this, with cleaning and scouring out all the main drains on the east side, and making good the banks, was estimated at £8,257. The earth-work was estimated at three shillings a floor for barrow work, and at two shillings for part barrow and part casting, or 2½d. and 1½d. per cubic yard respectively.

In 1745, Mr. Daniel Coppin also made " proposals for the more effectual draining all the levels contiguous to the river Witham from the city of Lincoln to Chapple Hill and likewise all the fens and low grounds which empty themselves into Lodowick's Goat; and at the same time to restore the almost lost navigation upon the said river to a better state than ever it was." He proposed making a new cut from Tattershall Ferry House through Billinghay Dales, continuing along the course of the North Forty-foot, which was to be widened to 60ft., and made 8ft. deep. At Lodowick's Gowt a *Grand Sluice* was to be built, which, " when open, was to be of sufficient capacity to discharge as much water as the full run of the river can produce, and when shut to stop the sea from getting into the new made river.' The sluice was to be 65ft. wide, with 16 openings of 3ft. each, the gates to work in oak standards, one foot wide. By this plan about 20 miles of the winding parts of the river Witham were to be cut off, and the water caused to run, in almost a direct line, through a deep channel and about twelve miles nearer. In order to restore the navigation, a separate cut was to be made near the *Grand Sluice*, from the Haven into the new river, and a double lock built, having a pen 40 yards long for boats to pass through. In order to hold up the water for the navigation, stanches were to be fixed, which " in a wet season were to be taken off by means of a crane and laid by, till wanted in a dry season, and that nothing of them would remain in the river but the upright posts to which they are fixed." One stanch was to be fixed at Tattershall Ferry, and the other at Monk's Ground, near Lincoln. The cost of this scheme, as estimated by William Jackson, was, for the sluice, £2,680; for cutting the new channel, £4,601; for bridges, £500; and for supervision of work, £389; making a total of £8,270. This was to be paid for by a rate of three shillings on 56,652 acres benefitted. The cost of the navigation works was put at £2,562, which was to be paid for by the Corporation.

In November, 1752, and January, 1753, meetings of Landowners interested in the drainage were held at the *Reindeer* Inn at Lincoln, to consider the state of the river. The scheme of Messrs. Grundy, and that of Mr. Coppin, were taken into consideration, and it was determined that an application should be made to Parliament to appoint Commissioners to consider the best means of effectually draining the fens and low grounds. In order to defray the cost of carrying out the scheme, and of preserving the drainage, it was agreed to levy a yearly tax, not exceeding one shilling per acre, on all lands benefitted; of ninepence, afterwards altered to eightpence, on half-year or Lammas lands; and of sixpence, afterwards altered to fourpence, on the Commons. The sunk tunnels under Kyme Eau and Billinghay Skirth were to be taken up and the water restored to the river. Kyme Eau was to be connected with the new channel through Wildmore by a short cut and all the river and main drains emptying into the Witham were to be cleaned out, deepened and embanked. The tunnel in the bank of Kyme Eau, near Damford Sluice, was to be restricted to the purpose of letting water into Holland Fen for watering cattle in dry seasons, and similar tunnels, not exceeding 9in. square, were to be allowed through the banks for the same purpose, where judged necessary. In order to restore the navigation the Commissioners for the City of Lincoln and the town of Boston were to order and direct whatever works they considered necessary.

1753.

Subsequent meetings were held at Horncastle and Boston, in October 1753, when it was finally determined that Messrs. Grundy's plan for improving the old river by cutting off the curves should be adopted, as this was thought most practicable, in order to reconcile the interests of the several parties concerned, and they were instructed to make a further report, and "propose a method of executing the work in such a manner as may be adequate to the general drainage of all those tracts of low lands interested therein." Accordingly Messrs. Grundy prepared a report, which was submitted to a subsequent meeting held at Lincoln, from which it appears that the floor of Anthony's Gowt was 4ft. 8in. higher than the level of low water in the Haven at Fishtoft and that the surface of the land in Wildmore Fen and Billinghay Dales was 11ft. higher. They therefore advised that the bed of the new river should be as deep as the floor of Anthony's Gowt, so that when there was 4ft. of water in the river there would be 2ft. 4in. fall from the lowest land sinto it. They advised that the 'proposed *Grand Sluice*' should be erected a little above Anthony's Gowt, because at that place it would be above all the outfalls of the Wildmore, West and Holland Fens, and of Frith Bank, and also because the ground there would be more solid than in the old channel near Lodowick's Gote; that the course of the new river should be by a straight cut commencing a little above Lodowick's Gote to Anthony's Gote, and from thence in a nearly straight line across Wildmore Fen, to a place in the old river, called Midsands; there crossing the channel into Holland Fen and joining the old river again at Langrick Ferry; thence, after crossing the old channel again, proceeding in a straight direction to Coppin Sike, and thence to Chapel Hill. This line was selected as cutting off all the worst bends in the old river, equalising the land divided, as nearly as practicable, between Wildmore and Holland Fen, and as interfering very little with private property, the whole length of 10 miles, with the exception of about four furlongs, being through Common land. The first length was to be 56ft. wide at the bottom and 70ft. at the top and 7ft. deep, with forelands 40ft. wide. The estimated cost was as follows:—

GRUNDY'S REPORT, 1753

	£	s.	d.
For the new Cut	11,605	16	0
Improving the river above Chapel Hill ...	2,200	0	0

	£	s.	d.
Private land taken, estimated at from £10 to £20 an acre	236	5	0
The Grand Sluice	2,100	0	0
Supervising the works and unforseen accidents	600	0	0
	16,742	1	0
Scouring out Kyme Eau, Billinghay Skirth, Dunsdyke, &c., and putting sluices at the end of the first two	4,045	0	0
Navigation Locks and two Stanches ...	1,975	0	0
	£22,762	1	0

MEETING AT LINCOLN, 1753. At a meeting held at Lincoln in November, 1753, which lasted three days, it was resolved that an application be made to Parliament for an Act giving power to carry out a scheme on the lines laid down at the previous meetings; that the 'Grand Sluice' for stemming the tide, should be placed between Lodowick's Gote and Anthony's Gote, but as near the former as practicable; and that in order to secure the drainage no stanches, or other works for navigation, should be placed in the river between Lincoln and Boston, that would pen up the water within two feet of the surface of the land. A subscription was started towards the expense of obtaining the Act. A full report of the proceedings and copy of Mr. Grundy's report will be found in Padley's *Fens and Floods*. The Act, however, was not applied for at this time.

GRUNDY'S AMENDED SCHEME, 1757. Five years later a fresh proposition was made by Messrs. Grundy, that in place of erecting a new sluice near Anthony's Gowt, as originally proposed, the structure erected by Make Hake in 1500, and used as a bridge, should be converted into a sluice by erecting a middle pier of wood in the centre of the large tun, by altering the buttresses on each side to adapt them to receive circular doors pointing seawards, and by erecting a new stone pier on the west side, with a lock 14ft. wide, for the navigation. There would thus be four pairs of pointing doors, giving a total waterway of 65½ft. The estimated cost of this was £3,827.

Langley Edwards. This scheme was submitted to the Corporation of Boston, and on their behalf Mr. Fydell, who was one of the most active promoters of the river improvement schemes, wrote to Mr. Banks of Revesby, stating that, while the Corporation were desirous of assisting in every way in improving the drainage, they were apprehensive that Mr. Grundy's plan would not give sufficient accommodation for the navigation, and that they had taken the opinion of Mr. Langley Edwards, an Engineer living at King's Lynn, who advised that he did not consider that sufficient water-way for the drainage and navigation could be obtained at the bridge, and therefore it would be better to erect an entirely new sluice further up the river.

MEETING AT SLEAFORD, 1760.

In 1760 a further meeting of Landowners, was held at Sleaford, and Mr. Fydell was requested to employ Mr. Langley Edwards to examine the schemes of Messrs. Grundy for improving the river.

LANGLEY EDWARDS REPORT AND SCHEME. 1760.

The report of Mr. Edwards is prefaced by saying that this work " will be a lasting honour to those who are the promoters of it ; a great addition of fortune to those who have the property in the lands to be regained ; a great and extensive benefit to trade and commerce, by opening a certain inland navigation from Boston to Lincoln, and through those towns from the utmost extent of the navigation of all those inland rivers which empty themselves into the great bay, called the *Metaris Estuarium*, to the utmost extent of the navigation of all the inland rivers which empty themselves into the Humber ; a great addition to the health of all the inhabitants of the circumjacent city, towns and villages, by removing the cause of those noxious vapours which must arise from stagnant waters, and which by the various action of the winds, are wafted into the nostrils of those who are seated within the reach thereof." Mr. Edwards reported generally in favour of Messrs. Grundy's scheme, but advised that the river should be made deeper than they proposed ; and also that the Grand Sluice instead of being placed near Anthony's Gowt, should be erected " near the brick kilns above Bardyke Sluice and the river be cut to it, from where the proposed new river falls into the old one above Lodowick's Gowt, in such direction that it may discharge the water just opposite to, and about two furlongs above, Boston Bridge." The floor was to be laid level with low water at the Outfall of the river at Fishtoft, or 3ft. 1in. below the floor of Lodowick's Gowt. The bottom of the river from Langrick to Anthony's Gowt was to be 40ft. wide, and thence to Boston 50ft. bottom and 90ft. top. Instead of scouring and embanking Dunsdyke and Hareshead drains, he proposed to take out the shallow places in the Car Dyke from Hareshead Drain to Billinghay Skirth, and raise the low places in the banks, and by this means to intercept the water from the high land in the district, and convey it to the Witham. He also considered that by making the river deeper the stop doors at the ends of Kyme Eau, the Bane and Billinghay Skirth would not be required.

The estimate was £31,221, the amount being greater than that of Messrs. Grundy, owing to the increased width and depth given to the Channel, and to an increase in the rate of wages since their report was made.

Grundy, Edwards, Smeaton. 1761.

In the following year the whole matter was referred to a joint Commission of Engineers, consisting of Mr. John Grundy, Mr. Langley Edwards and Mr. J. Smeaton, who were directed jointly to report as to the best scheme to be carried out. In this report, after stating the general condition of the river and the principles on which any scheme of improvement should be based, they advised that the new sluice for stemming the tides should be erected between Lodowick's Gowt and Boston Bridge on a piece of land known as Harrison's Four Acres, the floor to be level with low water at Wyberton Roads; its clear water-way to be 50ft.; to have three pairs of pointing sea doors with draw doors on the land side. A new cut was to be made from this sluice to Anthony's Gowt, 80ft. wide at the top and 50ft. at the bottom and 10ft. deep; and another cut thence, through Wildmore Fen to Chapel Hill, having 50ft. bottom and 8ft. in depth. The banks, formed with the material excavated, to be set back 40ft. from the channel.

From Chapel Hill the river was to be continued in its then course, but to be deepened and widened, where necessary, so as to give a 40ft. bottom up to three miles above Chapel Hill; thence up to Branston Dyke the bottom to be 30ft. wide, and from thence to Stamp End in Lincoln, 24ft.; one wagon bridge and two horse bridges were to be built over the river; Kyme Eau was to be scoured out and embanked from Dampford Sluice to the river; Tattershall Bane from the mouth to Dickinson's Engine; Billinghay Skirth from the Witham to Kyme Causeway Bridge; Barling's Eau to be scoured out up to Barling's Abbey; the Dunsdyke to the Car Dyke to be deepened and embanked, or the Car Dyke to be re-instated and the water of Dunsdyke to be turned into it; also Nocton Dyke, Hareshead Drain, Washingborough Beck, up to Carr Dike, Tupham Dike, Bardney or Tile House Beck, Southery Eau, and Stixwold Beck were to be scoured out; and a new sluice was to be erected at Anthony's Gowt, for the more certain drainage of Wildmore and West Fens. The effect of these works, they considered, would be to lower the water in the river 4ft. in ordinary seasons. For the navigation, a lock was to be erected at the Grand Sluice, having two pair of doors landward, and one pair seaward, and, in place of stanches as previously proposed, three locks were to be constructed between Boston and Lincoln.

The estimated cost of this scheme was—

	£	s.	d.
The Grand Sluice	4,000	0	0
The New Cut and improvement of the river	23,465	14	5
New Sluice at Anthony's Gowt	600	0	0
Bridges and other works	1,000	0	0
Land	2,088	15	0
Scouring out and embanking the side drains	3,695	0	0
The Locks and navigation works	7,370	0	0
General superintendence and unforseen contingencies	3,000	0	0
	£45,219	9	5

The inclosed land required to be taken for the work was estimated at £30 an acre; the commons at £10 an acre; the earth-work at five shillings a floor, or fourpence a cubic yard, where it had to be moved 40ft., and for less distances, four shillings. This was exclusive of barrows and planks.

MEETING AT SLEAFORD, 1761.

At a meeting of landowners, held at Sleaford, in November, 1761, this report was approved, and the general proposals, or heads, of a Bill for carrying out the scheme were agreed to, and a subscription raised to meet the preliminary expenses. The chairman at this, and the other meetings which were held, was Lord Vere Bertie; and the others who seem to have taken the most active part in promoting the improvement of the river and drainage were Mr. John Chaplin, Mr. Richard Fydell, the Rev. Charles Beridge, Mr., afterwards Sir Joseph, Banks and Lord Manners. Mr. Robert Banks of Sleaford, was appointed Solicitor to the Bill.

A SCHEME ADOPTED.

The principal subscribers to the fund for preliminary expenses were, the Merchants and Inhabitants of Boston, by R. Fydell, £128; The Corporation of Boston, £100; Lord Vere Bertie, £36; Lord Fitzwilliam, £40; The Mayor of Boston, £30; Lady Dashwood, £21; Mr. J. Chaplin, £56/10; Mr. Jos. Banks, £23; Lord Fortescue, £21:10; Rev. John King, £26; Mr. Amcotts, £21:10; Mr. Hume, £31:10; Rev. C. Beridge, £10:10.

OPPOSITION TO THE SCHEME.

The obtaining of this Act was opposed by the Owners in Holland Fen, by the City of Lincoln and by the towns of Gainsborough, Rotherham, and Rochdale, on the ground that it would be injurious to the navigation by the Fossdyke. Nottingham and Derby petitioned in favour of the Bill.

WITHAM DRAINAGE ACT. 2 Geo. iii, c. 32, 1761.

At last, in the second year of George III, "an Act for draining and preserving certain low lands, lying on both sides of the river Witham, in the county of Lincoln, and for restoring and maintaining the navigation of the said river from the High-bridge, in the city of Lincoln, through the borough of Boston to the sea," was passed. The preamble to this Act recites, that the river Witham, in the county of Lincoln, was formally navigable for lighters, barges, boats, and other vessels from the sea through Boston to the High-bridge, in the city of Lincoln; but by the sand and silt brought in by the tide the outfall thereof into the sea had, for many years last past, been greatly hindered and obstructed, and was then in a great measure stopped up, lost, and destroyed, and thereby great part of the low lands and fens, lying on both sides of the said river (and which contain together about one hundred thousand acres), were frequently overflowed and rendered useless and unprofitable, to the great loss of the respective owners thereof, the decay of trade and commerce, and the depopulation of the country; and that in the judgment and opinion of experienced Engineers and persons of known skill and ability, the navigation of the said river Witham, and the outfall thereof into the sea, were capable of being restored and maintained, and the said low lands and fens of being drained, culti-

Fig: 7.
Chap: 5.

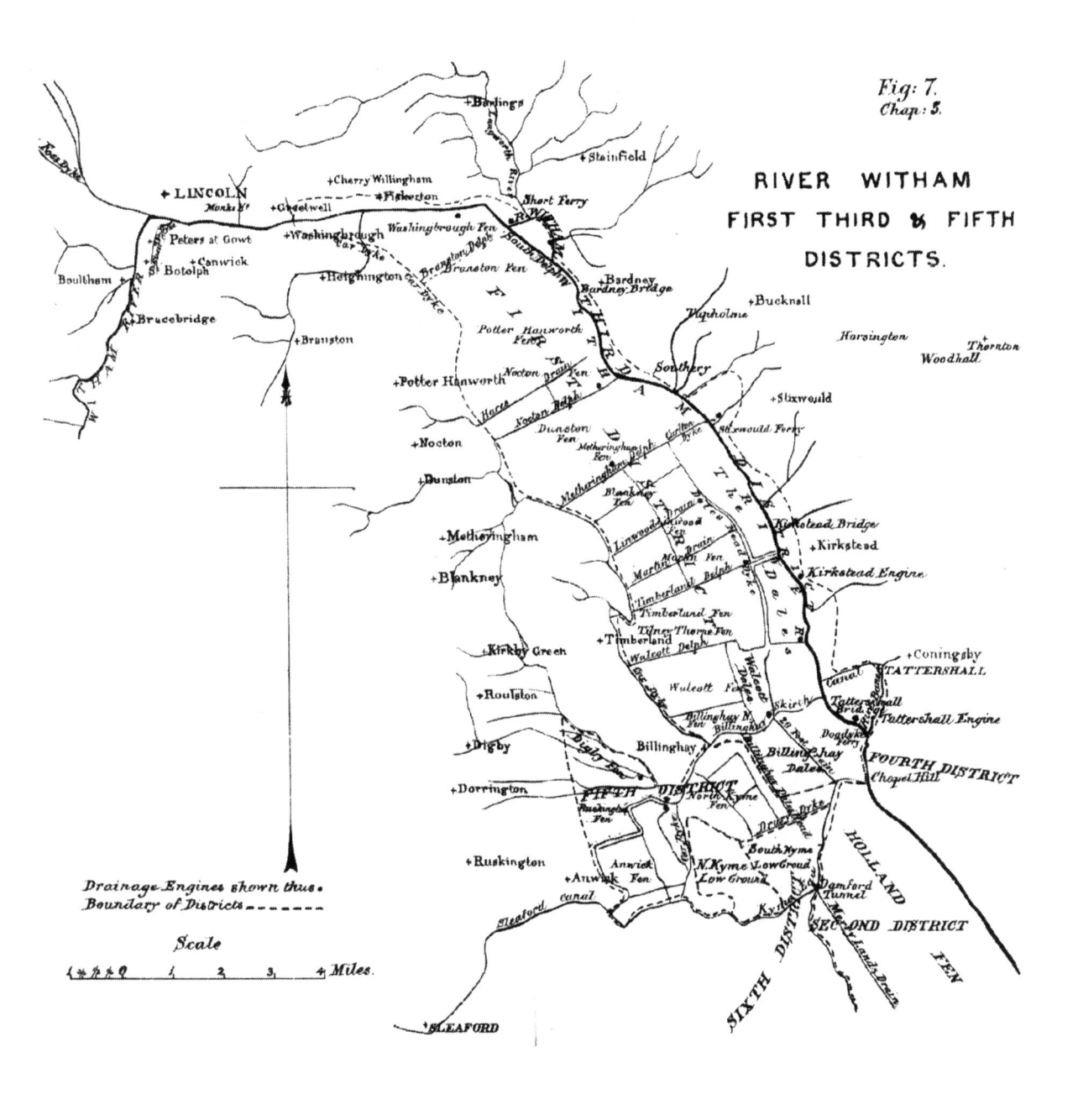

RIVER WITHAM
FIRST THIRD & FIFTH
DISTRICTS.

vated, and improved, but that the same could not be done without the authority of Parliament.

The district now included in the Witham Commission is that tract of land lying on either side of the river, extending from Lincoln on the north to the town of Boston on the south, stretching eastward as far as the higher grounds in Freiston, Butterwick, Benington, Leake, Wrangle, and Friskney, and bounded on the west by the Car Dyke, the old catchwater drain of the Romans, which separated the high lands from the fens. The East Fen was not included in the first Act, but was added in the year 1801.

For the purposes of the Act the level was divided into six Districts. The First, comprising the fens on the south-west side of the Witham, extending from Lincoln to Kyme Eau; the Second, Holland Fen and the adjoining lands, bounded by Kyme Eau on the north, the Witham on the east, and south and west by Swineshead and Heckington; the Third, comprising the fens on the north-east side of the Witham, stretching from Lincoln to the River Bane at Tattershall; the Fourth, the Wildmore and West and East Fens; the Fifth, fens in Anwick, North Kyme, Ruskington, Dorrington, and Digby; the Sixth, fens in South Kyme, Great Hale, Little Hale, Heckington, Ewerby, Howell, and Swineshead.

Fig. 7.

By this Act, the General Commission consists of 37 Members, 31 of whom are elected by the several Districts, in the following proportions. The First is entitled to send 7 Representatives, the Second 6, the Third 5, the Fourth 8, the Fifth 2, and the Sixth 3. Each Member elected must qualify for the office by taking a prescribed oath, and must be in possession of land of the value of £100 per annum, or of personal property to the value of £2,000, or be heir apparent to landed property of the value of £200 per annum. The remaining six members consist of the Mayors of Boston and Lincoln for the time being, and two Commissioners elected by the city of Lincoln, and two by the borough of Boston. The Commissioners are elected every three years, but, in default of such election taking place, the old Commissioners remain in office. An annual meeting is held every year on the first Tuesday in July, and may be called at either Lincoln, Boston, or Sleaford.

The several Districts are managed by Commissioners elected by the several parishes or places in the district, each sending one member. The General Commissioners are elected by the District Commissioners.

For the purpose of raising the funds for carrying out the works, the Commissioners were authorised to levy a rate on all lands in the First, Second, Third and Fourth Districts, not exceeding one shilling an acre on private property; eightpence for half-year lands; and fourpence on Common land, so long as it remained common, but when inclosed, the rate could be raised to a shilling. For the Fifth and

Sixth Districts the rates were not to exceed sixpence, fourpence, and twopence respectively. Power was given to inclose part of Holland, West and Wildmore Fens, and also in other places, and to let the land for 21 years—the rents to be applied towards paying the taxes. The rates levied were to be paid by the Landlords.

WORKS CARRIED OUT.

The works for the improvement of the drainage sanctioned by this Act, and subsequently carried out, consisted of straightening the course of the river Witham by making a new cut from Boston to Chapel Hill, and cleaning, widening and deepening the river from that place to Stamp End, near Lincoln. The fishing weirs and other obstructions which had hitherto hindered the full course of the waters were removed; the sides of the river were embanked and the water prevented from flowing on the adjacent lands, while its discharge was effected by the cleansing and deepening of the Kyme Eau, Billinghay Skirth, the Bane, and other tributaries and side drains. The new cut from Boston to Anthony's Gowt was made 8oft. wide at the top, 5oft. at the bottom, and 1oft. deep. The banks on each side were set back 4oft. and averaged 1oft. high. The cut from Anthony's Gowt to Langrick was to be 68ft. at the top, 5oft. at the bottom and 9ft. deep. The cut from Boston to Chapel Hill according to the Act was to be made in as straight a direction as the nature of the ground would admit. The cause of the existing bend in the channel is thus explained by Mr. Chapman, "It was intended by the Engineer to go in a direct line between those two places; but to oblige one large Proprietor the channel was turned from its proper direction so as to run by Anthony's Gowt; and to accommodate another, it was made to go off thence, at a sharp angle, towards Langrick."

Chapman's Facts and Remarks.

THE GRAND SLUICE.

At the lower end of the cut the Grand Sluice was erected for 'stemming the tide,' on a piece of ground called Harrison's Four Acres, between Lodowick's Gowt and Boston Bridge; the floor was laid 3ft. lower than the floor of the gowt, and its capacity, or clear water-way was to be 5oft., and there were to be three pairs of pointing doors to the sea-ward, to shut with the flow of the tides (a fourth opening being built by the Navigation Commissioners), and also frames, provided with drop, or draw-doors, on the land side, to be shut occasionally in order to retain fresh water in dry seasons for the use of cattle and the navigation, the top of the draw-doors being guaged to such a height as to retain the water of the river not higher, at ordinary seasons, than 2ft. below the medium surface of the lowest lands that drain therein.

ANTHONY'S GOWT

A new sluice, of 14ft. water-way, was also made at Anthony's Gowt for the discharge of the water from the West and Wildmore Fens, having a pair of pointing doors towards the Witham to prevent the floods of that river backing on to the Fens. The sluice was connected with the former system of drainage by a new Cut to the place where the old Gowt stood. The Commissioners were further empowered to build a bridge across the new Cut, or river, at a point about half-way between Anthony's Gowt and Boston, for the purpose of preserving the communication with the several lands of Boston West and Holland Fen. This part of the Act was never carried out.

The new course of the river is shown in *Figs. 7 and 9*. Figs. 7 and 9.

As it was considered necessary for the effectual scouring out of OTHER WORKS, the outfall to preserve the living water, and to confine the flood water, and also for the effectual drainage of the land, the Commissioners were empowered to carry out the necessary works in Kyme Eau to a place called the Clapps at Ewerby Corner; Tattershall Bane to Dickinson's engine; Billinghay Skirth to Billinghay Town and to Kyme Causeway Bridge and the junction of Scopwick Beck with North Kyme Fen Dyke; Dun's Dyke to the Car Dyke; Barlings Eau to the Abbey; Washingborough Beck to the Car Dyke; Stickswould Beck, Southery Eau, Tupholm Dyke, Bardney Beck, Stainfield Beck and Bullington Beck to the adjoining high grounds. A cut was to be made from Langrick Gowt to the new river; and the drains leading from Heckington Eau and the drain from the Skirth across Holland Fen were to be scoured out. Lodowick's Gowt was to be connected with the river by a new cut. All *out ring*, or division dykes, were to be maintained by the Owners or Occupiers of the land at a breadth of 9ft. and 5ft. deep. The tunnels sunk under Kyme Eau and Billinghay Skirth were to be removed, the Owners of the land in North Kyme and Billinghay Dales were to be permitted, if they found it necessary for the drainage of their lands, to lay a tunnel 2ft. square under Kyme Eau and convey their water to the Witham through Langrick Gowt. Dampford tunnel under Kyme Eau was to continue. The tunnels, not exceeding 9in. square, through the south bank of Kyme Eau, in South Kyme near Damford Sluice, and also that in Dogdyke, and at How Bridge, for conveying the water into Holland and Wildmore Fens respectively, and Heckington tunnel were to be continued. The road leading from Tattershall Ferry to Billinghay was to pass along the bank on the north-west side of the Skirth and to be a public highway, the bank being enlarged to a width of 40ft. for that purpose.

A Navigation Commission was also appointed, separate from THE NAVIGATION. the Drainage Trust, consisting of the Mayor of Lincoln and four other Members elected by the Burgesses, the Mayor of Boston, four Members elected by the Corporation, and ten Members elected by the General Drainage Commissioners. The function of this body was to take steps for the restoration of the navigation; and for this purpose they had the power to erect locks, make cuts, and clean out the river as far as the High Bridge in the City of Lincoln, and from below the Sincyl Dyke, and to build such bridges, locks, stanches, and other works, as they should think necessary, provided that the water should not be penned up higher than 2ft. below the natural surface of the land. A lock was also to be erected at Boston. To enable them to execute these works they were authorised to take tolls (not exceeding 1s. 6d. per ton) on all boats navigating the Witham, and to raise money on the security of the tolls. In pursuance of the powers so granted, the Commissioners expended £6,800 in deepening the river and building the new locks and other works, and once more made it navigable for vessels. The first navigation lock was erected at Kirkstead, where there was a rise of 1ft. 9in. into the next reach, which extended to Barlings, where there was a second lock with a rise of 2ft. 3in.; the last lock was at Stamp End, having a rise of 3ft. 8in., making the total rise 7ft. 8in. The top of the river at Stamp End was 17ft. above the sill of the Grand Sluice.

OPENING OF THE GRAND SLUICE, 1766.

The foundation-stone of the Grand Sluice was laid by Mr. Charles Amcotts, on the 26th March, 1764; and it was opened by the Engineer, Mr. Langley Edwards, on the 15th October, 1766, in the presence of a very large concourse of spectators, estimated as numbering ten thousand persons, 'amongst whom were many of the nobility and gentry from remote parts of the kingdom.' The Sluice disappointed the expectation of many who had come to witness the opening ceremony, and one of the visitors relieved himself by composing the following verse:—

Chapman's Facts and Remarks.

"Boston, Boston, Boston!
Thou hast naught to boast on,
But a Grand Sluice, and a high steeple;
A proud, conceited, ignorant people,
And a coast where souls are lost on."

The Sluice had three openings of 17ft. 2in. each, and a lock 15ft. 3in. wide, making the total water-way available in floods 66ft. 9in. The pen height of the water for navigation purposes was 9ft. on the sill. The General Commissioners expended in the erection of the sluice and other drainage works the sum of £53,650, which was raised on mortgage.

These works, having been successfully carried out as designed by the promoters, proved of immediate advantage to the drainage of the fens bordering on the Witham, between Lincoln and Chapelhill; but the East and West Fens still remained in a drowned state. The history of their reclamation will be found in the next chapter. The waters of Holland Fen and of the districts adjoining were subsequently provided for by the drainage carried out by the Black Sluice Commissioners.

The erection of a sluice across the river for 'stemming the tides' was not generally approved at the time, and the Commissioners were warned that it would probably have an injurious effect on the channel below it.

The views of those who were opposed to the erection of the sluice were thus expressed by Mr. Elstob, an Engineer employed on the Bedford Level, "And as to the great Sluice lately erected at Boston, at the mouth of a fine, and what might otherwise be, a very beneficial new river, a little above the Town, for keeping out the tide; I am so far from expecting any advantage from the said Sluice, that I am fully of opinion, if it is kept constantly in use, and under the same regulations for damming up the water above as at the first, that in the course of a few years, the channel instead of being improved, will be greatly injured, and the outfall prejudiced thereby. And had that expense been saved, and the tides had free admission into the said new river, there is great reason to believe that the Channel and Outfall would, in a short time, have been improved by the weight and force of the returning ebbs; and the outfall scoured out so deep, that vessels of twelve or thirteen feet water, or more, might, upon any ordinary tide, come up to the quays and wharfs of the Town, much better than they used to do before the late decay of the river."

Within a very few years it became apparent that this warning was well founded, and that by obstructing the free passage of the tides, a very serious error had been committed. For a short time the collecting the waters together and speedily discharging them through the remodelled drains into the Witham, and through the new cut into the haven, had a beneficial effect, by scouring out its bed and lowering the level of the water throughout the fens; but very soon the effect which invariably follows the stoppage of the tidal flow by the erection of weirs or dams of any description across a tidal river showed itself. The tidal stream, arrested in its progress by the sluice, became quiescent, and the silt and mud brought up and held in suspension, so long as the water was in motion, sunk by its own gravity directly stagnation took place, and gradually formed a deposit on the bed of the haven. Owing to the doors having become silted up in the summer of 1799, the water could not get away when the floods came, and many thousands of acres were covered with water, and the damage done was of very great magnitude.

Previous to the year 1800, in average winter seasons, the water never fell below 9ft. 6in. on the sill, and in floods rose considerably higher; while in summer time, there not being back-water sufficient to remove the deposit, it accumulated to such a degree as completely to close the doors. A few years after the erection of the sluice, it appears to have risen to a height of 10ft. on the sill, completely stopping all communication between the barges navigating the Witham and the vessels employed in exporting and importing coal and other commodities. The drainage also became defective.

Rennie's Report, 1800.

Mr. Rennie, in a report made to the Corporation of Boston on the condition of the river, speaking of the quantity of silt deposited in the Channel, says, "Had this river with its subsidiary streams been completely embanked through the fens and low lands, so as to have confined it to a Channel of dimensions sufficient to contain the water in times of flood and no more, it would then have been constrained to pass off more rapidly to seaward, and, of course, would have ground its Channel deeper, and prevented the great deposition of silt which now takes place. . . . If the Grand Sluice were entirely taken away and the tide suffered to flow up the river, it is evident it must move with a greater velocity through the Harbour of Boston to fill up the space above; and providing there is a sufficient quantity of fresh water and fall to drive back the tide water, etc. during the ebb, it is equally evident the constant action of this great body of water passing through the Harbour would grind the Channel deeper."

Telford's Report, 1823.

Mr. Telford, reporting in 1823, says, "The defective state of the Haven being so apparent, it is superfluous to enter upon any detailed description of it. . . . I am of opinion that the existing defects may be traced chiefly to the obstruction created by the Grand Sluice in preventing tidal water from flowing up further than the Town of Boston."

Chapman's Report, 1808.

Mr. Chapman, an Engineer employed by the Proprietors of lands draining into the river in the First District, to report as to the condition of the river in 1808, after calling attention to the fact that the Haven, in dry summers, was sometimes 'barred up with silt and sand to the height of ten or twelve feet above the sill of the Grand Sluice,' attributes this to the stoppage of the flow of the tides, and quotes the instance of Denver Sluice, which by stopping the flow of the tide up the Ouse, damaged Lynn Harbour; also of the Sluice erected on the Rother, which ruined Rye Harbour; and shows by the instance of the River Hull, where the tide flows freely for 20 miles, carrying the muddy water of the Humber without silting or deterioration, that the apprehensions as to the permanent silting of the Witham, if the tides were allowed a free course, were groundless. Sir John Rennie subsequently reported that he considered that great injury was done to the river 'by the obstruction occasioned by the Grand Sluice in preventing the free flow and reflow of the tides.'

Sir J. Hawkshaw's Report, 1864.

In more recent times, Sir John Hawkshaw, in reporting to the Corporation of Boston on the state of the Haven, said that one of the most effective means of improving the Channel in Boston Harbour would be to remove the Grand Sluice and allow the tide to ebb and flow in the upper Witham.

Wheeler, On the Witham, Min. Pro. Instit. C.E. Vol. 28.

The effect of the construction of sluices across tidal rivers was fully discussed at a meeting of the Institution of Civil Engineers in 1868, after the reading of a paper on the River Witham by the Author.

In 1776 a joint report was made by John Smith and James Creassy to the Commissioners on the state of the Witham, and as to how far a complete drainage is, or can be, performed by the powers given in the existing Act. They reported that between Chapel Hill and Lincoln, in winter, the water in the river was seldom below the surface of the adjoining lands. The plan proposed to remedy this, was to cut two drains, 10ft. wide at bottom, parallel to the river, from Chapel Hill to Lincoln, on each side of the river; to scour out the Car Dyke to Billinghay Skirth, under which a sunken tunnel was to be placed. The high and low land waters were thus to be kept separate above Chapel Hill, and below this the river was to be widened in the Clay Reach, so as to be of the same width as the parts which had scoured out to a greater width than left when originally made. The estimated cost of carrying out this scheme was £28,022, exclusive of the land required. SMITH'S AND CREASSY'S REPORT. 1776.

The low lands lying west of Lincoln, being the general reservoir of the waters that in floods are brought down by the Witham from the upland country, being constantly flooded and the owners finding great difficulty in obtaining an efficient drainage, Mr. J. Smeaton was instructed by a meeting of Landowners held at the *Reindeer* Inn, Lincoln, in September, 1782, to report as to the best way of improving the navigation of the Fossdyke and the drainage of these low lands. A report had previously been made by Mr. Grundy and Mr. Smeaton to Mr. Ellison on this matter, but "the contrariety of opinion among the parties interested prevented the execution of the scheme then proposed." At that time there was a fall of 14in. from Brayford Mere, the ultimate drainage of all the lands in question, through Lincoln to the Witham, at the point where the Sincyl Dyke fell into it, and a further fall of 5½in. to Stamp End. The stanch at Lincoln Lock below Stamp End had been put higher than the natural stanch at Brayford Head and consequently held up the water in Brayford Mere higher than it ought to be. To improve the drainage they considered that it would therefore be necessary to reduce the height of the stanch at Lincoln Lock to the Parliamentary height, or provide a new outfall for the Sincyl Dyke below the stanch, or else to move Lincoln Lock to a point above the present outfall of the Sincyl Dyke. This latter plan was the one recommended by Mr. Smeaton. He also proposed to deepen the Witham up to the new lock; to scour out and widen the Sincyl Dyke; to dyke and scour out Great Gowts Drain and carry it under the Witham by a tunnel 4ft. square, with doors pointing to the Sincyl Dyke; to scour out Sincyl Dyke, from the tail of the Great Gowts Drain to its upper mouth at the Witham, and construct a weir, 60ft. long, along the bank of the Witham, at the junction, the crest being one inch above ordinary summer level in the Witham, so that the Sincyl Dyke should only take the flood water; to scour out the Lesser Gowt Drain and fix a weir, 45ft. long, at its junction, the crest being 1½in. lower than the other weir; a drain to be carried from

Marginal notes: DRAINAGE AT LINCOLN. 1782. — Grundy and Smeaton. 1762. — Smeaton. 1782.

the tunnel at the head of the Great Gowts Drain to Swan Pool and be connected with the lands in Burton and Carlton by an iron pipe, 2ft. 6in. in diameter, under the Fossdyke; a navigation lock to be fixed at Brayford Mere, with gates pointing towards the Fossdyke and a weir for overfall water beyond that required for the navigation; a stanch to be fixed at Brayford Head, the top being the same height as the existing natural weir; a side weir, 100ft. long, to be fixed at Torksey, so that the top waters should run into the Trent when its level would admit of this being done, the crest being 6in. below the gauge bar of Torksey Lock. To prevent the Trent waters over-riding those of the Fossdyke, the weir was to be on a separate cut, having doors 8ft. wide at the end pointing to the Trent.

W. Jessop. 1792.

No action appears to have been taken on this report, as, ten years afterwards, Mr. W. Jessop was consulted as to the navigation of the Fossdyke and reported on this, and its effect on the drainage, to the effect that, from the obstructions at Brayford Head and the narrowness of the passage through the bridges and between the walls of the river, the flood waters of the Witham were confined to a very low discharge to the detriment of the lands west of Lincoln; but that it was an advantage to the lands below in checking the quantity of water which went down the river in floods. He advised lowering Brayford Head 2ft. and replacing it with a moveable weir, and extending the Syncil Dyke to a point below Stamp End Lock.

HORNCASTLE AND SLEAFORD CANALS. 1792.

About this time (1792-4) Acts were obtained for making navigable communication between the town of Horncastle and the Witham, by canalising the river Bane and making a new Cut as far as Tattershall; and also between the Witham and Sleaford, by canalising the river Slea.

CONDITION OF THE DRAINAGE IN 1800.

Chapman. 1800.

At the beginning of the present century Mr. Chapman thus described the condition of the Fens in a pamphlet entitled *Observations on the Improvement of Boston Haven*, " Of the last six seasons, four have been so wet that most of the new enclosed fens bordering on the Witham were inundated and the crops either lost or materially injured. Many hundred acres of the harvest of 1799 were reaped by men in boats. Of the oats fished up in this way some sold in Boston market at 25/- per last, when good oats were selling at ten pounds." In another pamphlet, written by 'A Holland Watchman,' the reaping is described as having been done by men standing up to their middle in water and clipping off the ears wherever they peeped above the surface.

J. Rennie's Report, 1802.

In October, 1802, in accordance with instructions of the Witham Commissioners, Mr. J. Rennie made an inspection of the river, and reported that he found the Grand Sluice completely silted up, there being 10ft. depth of silt on the sill, or 2ft. 6in. higher than the water in the river above the sluice. With 8ft. 6in. of water on the sill of the sluice, the depth in the Channel varied from 7ft. up to Chapel Hill to 3ft. 6in. at Tattershall, 2ft. 4in. at Kirkstead, and 1ft. 4in. on the Shoals at Bardney. The surface of the water at Lincoln High Bridge was 9ft. 5½in. above that at the Grand Sluice, equal to an inclination of 3½in. per mile. The clear waterway through Lincoln Bridge was only 15ft. 6in. The Witham was stated to be deprived of a considerable quantity of its water in summer by the working of the lock in the Fossdyke at Torksey, the fall into the Trent being generally about 6 feet. In floods, the waterway of the Witham, through Lincoln and by the Sincyl dyke, being insufficient to carry off the water, a great quantity passed away through Torksey Lock, and thus the river was deprived of the benefit of floods in winter and of a great part of the water in summer. He recommended that the Witham should be embanked, deepened and straightened where necessary, and the locks and stanches at Kirkstead and Barlings replaced with others of better construction, and in better situations; and a capacious cut should be made, from the Witham above Lincoln to the river at Washingborough, to carry off the floods; that the Till should be embanked; the Foss deepened, widened and scoured out; and reservoirs constructed for supplying the Foss navigation with water, or in preference, a steam engine erected for pumping the water from the Trent. He considered it a matter for regret, that when the works were originally designed, the Navigation Channel was not made at one level from Boston to the Trent. For the purpose of avoiding the difficulty of getting through the Grand Sluice in summer, he proposed to make either a sluice at Anton's Gowt, so that barges could navigate the Frith Bank Drain to Maud Foster; or else that a new Cut should be made from above the Grand Sluice to Skirbeck Quarter.

A further report was made by Mr. Rennie in the following year and, as objections had been raised to a proposal for making a new Cut below the Grand Sluice to Skirbeck Quarter, partly on account of the expense, he proposed that this should terminate at Boston Bridge, nearly opposite the church, though owing to the silting up of the river this would only give a navigation at spring tides. In addition to the recommendations previously made he proposed that a straight cut should be made from Dogdyke Ferry to Tattershall Bridge; also a new cut across the bend of the river above Timberland Dyke, a new lock being placed on this bend in place of the one at Kirkstead, which was then in a dangerous condition; also a straight cut from Horsley Deeps, across the bend to a little above Grub Hill, with a new lock at the lower end in place of that at Barlings Eau; that the lock at Stamp End should be rebuilt, with its sill 3ft. lower; and generally to deepen the river where required; also that the principal works recommended in Mr. Smeaton's report on the lands bordering on the Foss should be carried out. The

Rennie. 1803.

quantity of water coming down the Witham in summer he found to be 593,280 cubic feet, of which about half was used for lockage at Torksey; and that the remainder passed through Stamp End Lock. He again recommended supplying Torksey Lock with a six H.P. engine to pump the water out of the Trent, the annual cost of which, including 10 per cent. interest on outlay (£160), he estimated at £381. The estimate for the whole work was as follows:

	£
The Cut at Boston and Lock	3,500
Works in the Witham and above Lincoln	54,900
	£58,400

At a meeting of the General Commissioners, held at the *Peacock* Inn, at Boston, Mr. John Linton in the chair, it was resolved "That it appears to this meeting that it is desirable to take effectual means for completing the drainage and navigation on a dead level with the sill of the Grand Sluice"; and in 1806 Mr. Anthony Bower was directed to make an estimate of the cost of carrying out this work. This estimate amounted to £92,736, and included the new cut at Dogdyke and Horsley Deeps, and three new locks, but was exclusive of land. Mr. Bower pointed out in his report that if this were done it would "reflect the highest honour and credit on the country by effectually draining the land which, for ages, had been subject to be flooded, and totally take away the use of the engines."

Bower. 1806.

In April, 1807, at a meeting of the General Commissioners, held at Sleaford, the Earl of Buckinghamshire in the chair, a series of resolutions was passed, stating that, whereas, by the enclosure of the West and Wildmore Fens their funds had been considerably increased, they proposed to improve the navigation of the Witham by making the river on a level from the Grand Sluice to Lincoln, and removing the locks at Kirkstead and Barlings; and that it was desirable that its management should be handed over to a Company, if one could be formed for this purpose; and Mr. J. Rennie was directed to examine Mr. Bower's estimate for this work. In his report, while generally confirming the estimate, he made additions increasing it to £106,720, exclusive of the cost of any land required. He, however, pointed out that, as the lands above Washingborough Ferry are at a higher level than those below, there was no very material advantage in extending the level to Stamp End Lock, but that if a lock were constructed a little below Washingborough Church, a saving of £16,000 could be effected. He advised that the drainage of the low lands west of Lincoln could be accomplished by extending a proposed Cut from the Great Gowts Drain to Stamp End Lock down to Washingborough Ferry.

PROPOSED IMPROVEMENT OF THE RIVER.

Rennie. 1807.

Opposition arising to this scheme by some of the landowners along the river, Mr. Rennie was requested to give his opinion on the best means of supplying the lands adjoining the river with water in summer-time, for cattle and fences, so as to be able to 'satisfy the doubts of those persons who are not yet fully acquainted with the different benefits that will be derived from the execution of the proposed plan.' In his report he points out that by the removal of Kirkstead Lock, the water would be lowered in that reach 1ft. 9in.; and by the removal of Barlings Lock, the water would be reduced 2ft. 3in., or a total of 4ft.; and that when this was done the land along the former reach would be only 3ft. 6in. above the surface of the water in the river, a height not more than necessary for drainage, and sufficient to supply the ditches with water if they were properly scoured out and deepened. As the land above Barling's lock would be about 6ft. above the reduced surface of the water, he proposed that the springs at Washingborough should be conducted in a delph behind the banks, at a proper height for the supply of those lands with water. He further advised that the main river and side drains should be properly embanked, so as to contain the floods, and anticipated that if the river were deepened as proposed, many of the wind engines then in use could be dispensed with. With reference to the inconvenience suffered from the silting up of the channel, and the consequent stoppage of the flood waters at the Grand Sluice, he advised that if ever Boston Haven were to be improved it should be done by means of a straight channel to the Deeps, or by straightening and deepening the existing channel, which, he deemed, would be an essential advantage, both to the drainage and navigation.

<small>Rennie. 1807.</small>

Acting on this and the previous report, the Commissioners, in the following year, obtained an Act for carrying out these works of improvement, which recited that the powers granted by the Act of 1791 were not sufficient to enable the Commissioners to execute all the works therein contemplated, and that several of them were then uncompleted; that in consequence much land was liable to injury from floods, and the commerce of the country greatly interrupted. It will be unnecessary to refer further to this, as the money authorised (£70,000) was never raised, and the Act was repealed by a subsequent one.

<small>48 Geo. iii, c. 108, 1808.</small>

Previous to this Act being obtained Mr. Chapman was directed by the Proprietors of lands in the First District to report to them on the probable effect of carrying out Mr. Rennie's scheme for the drainage and the water-supply of their lands. He reported that at that time it was with difficulty that the water in times of flood was prevented from overflowing the banks protecting the lands in Blankney, Martin, Timberland and Billinghay Dales; that, if the water from the lands west of Lincoln were to have free admission to the Witham, no harm would accrue to the district, if the works proposed by Mr. Rennie were carried out, but that in addition the

<small>CHAPMAN'S REPORT, 1809.</small>

water-way of the Grand Sluice should be enlarged from 66ft. 9in. to 90ft. He advised that it was necessary for the purposes of Agriculture that the water in the ditches should be kept at a level of not less than 1ft. 9in., or more than 2ft. 6in., below the surface of the peat lands, and to insure this and also for providing water for cattle, he proposed that the Car Dyke should be scoured out, and that the water not required for the locks at Lincoln and Torksey should be diverted into it. Considering that it was a great error ever to have stopped the free flow of the tides by the erection of the Grand Sluice, he proposed that in enlarging it the doors should be so arranged that all ordinary tides should be allowed to have a free course through it, excluding only high spring tides in times of land floods. He further recommended that in order to obtain really efficient drainage the outfall from Boston to the sea should be improved.

RENNIE'S AMENDED SCHEME, 1811.

It being found impracticable to raise the money necessary for carrying out Mr. Rennie's scheme, he was called upon to suggest an amended plan and made a further report to the Commissioners in which the works enumerated in an Act obtained in 1812 were recommended.

WITHAM NAVIGATION ACT. 52 Geo. iii, c. 108, 1812.

By this Act the powers vested in the Commissioners of Navigation were transferred to a Company of Proprietors, who were to undertake the whole management of the navigation and the works pertaining thereto. The tolls were fixed at three shillings per ton on all goods conveyed between Lincoln and Boston, or, for shorter distances, three halfpence per ton per mile. The duties of the Proprietors of the navigation, and of the Drainage Commissioners, as to maintenance of the different portions of the river and its embankments were set out, and the following new works, as recommended by Mr. Rennie, authorized, *viz.*, the scouring out, widening, deepening, and embanking of the Witham, from the Grand Sluice to the High Bridge in Lincoln. The lower end was to be finished to a fifty feet bottom, diminishing to 36ft. at Horsley Deeps, to 24ft. at Stamp End, and 20ft. between there and the High Bridge. From Horsley Deeps a new cut was to be made to the Woadhouses in Fiskerton, with a 30ft. bottom. A new lock, 80ft. long by 16½ft. wide, was to be made at the entrance of the new cut at Horsley Deeps, with a rise of 3ft., and another at Stamp End in Lincoln, of the same dimensions, with a rise of 4ft., and a stone weir of the same level as the gauge mark at the High Bridge. The sill of the lower lock was to be level with the bed of the river, which was then 6ft. under the gauge mark at the Grand Sluice. A weir was to be built above Barlings Eau, the crest of which was to be 12ft 9in. higher than the sill of the Grand Sluice. The old locks across the river at Barlings, Kirkstead and Stamp End were to be removed; and, if found necessary, the lock at the Grand Sluice was to be enlarged to the same size as the other locks. The banks were to have slopes of 3 to

1 on the river side, and 2 to 1 on the land side. On the south side, the bank was to have a 10ft. top and to be puddled in the middle. The top was to be gravelled, and bridges put over on the side cuts so as to make an efficient towing path. Stop doors were to be fixed at the ends of Billinghay Skirth and the Bane.

In order to provide for the flood waters from the west side of Lincoln, a weir twenty-eight feet in width was to be made in the east bank of the Witham, at the head of Bargate Drain, the top level with that of the weir at Stamp End, with one or more sluices in it; the *slacker* never to be drawn when the surface of the water in the Witham was below the top of the weir, without the consent of the Mayor of Lincoln or the Lessee of the Fossdyke Navigation; the Sincyl dyke and Bargate Drain were to be scoured out and deepened, and a new cut made from the junction of the latter with the Witham, along the back of its south bank to Horsley Deeps, to join the river below the new lock at Branston; and a delph or soak dyke cut parallel with the north bank of the river from Barling's Eau, as far upwards as should be found necessary to take the water lying on the north side of the navigation.

The following works were to be maintained by the Proprietors of the navigation, *viz.*, the lock at the Grand Sluice, and the locks at Horsley Deeps and Stamp End; the weirs at Barlings Eau and at Stamp End Lock; the towing paths, bridges, fences and other works pertaining to the navigation; also the Great Gowt Drain and tunnel, and the Little Gowt Drain Weir. The Grand Sluice, the channel and banks of the river from the Grand Sluice to Stamp End Lock; the stop doors across the drains, the Sincyl Dyke and Bargate Drain, with the weir and sluices at the head of Bargate Drain, were to be maintained by the Commissioners of Drainage. The wall on the south side of the river, between Stamp End and the High Bridge, was to be maintained by the Frontagers. The Navigation Company was to scour out the old course of the river from Barlings Eau, so as to make it 20ft. wide at the bottom, and 6ft. deep, and to embank it with banks of sufficient strength for the passage of the waters of Barlings Eau and the side drains.

To carry out these works, the Company of Proprietors were authorized to raise among themselves a sum of £120,000 in shares of £100, and to borrow, on the mortgage of the tolls and dues, the sum of £60,000. In consideration of the benefit to the drainage by the improvement to the river, and an agreement on the part of the Navigation Proprietors to advance and apply the sum of £30,000 towards the execution of drainage works, the Commissioners were to contribute the sum of £1,400 per annum out of their general fund; and a like sum of £1,400 out of the funds specially provided by this Act, to the Company of Proprietors. To enable them to do this, they were authorised to collect additional taxes from the First and

Third Districts, the lands in which were divided into four districts, and rated at eighteen, twelve, six and three pence respectively.

The Company were authorised to take tolls for goods carried from any place within one mile of Lincoln High Bridge, or of the Grand Sluice at Boston. The rate was fixed at 1½d. per ton per mile, with a minimum of eighteenpence and a maximum of three shillings. Market boats were to be reckoned as carrying two tons. Skiffs or boats carrying less than two tons, and passing through the locks, were to pay one shilling, in addition to the toll due on the goods carried, or sixpence each if two boats passed through the lock at the same time. Boats navigating the Horncastle or Sleaford Canals were to remain liable to the toll of ninepence per ton, and to a further toll of one-half the amount then paid upon the Witham. The navigation tolls were exempted from parochial rates.

Rennie 1813.

Fears being entertained by the owners that the low lands lying between Kirkstead Lock and Chapel Hill would be injured by the mode in which the work was being executed, Mr. Rennie was directed to report on the matter, and replied to the effect that until the passage from the west of Lincoln was opened out no harm could accrue from carrying on the works above Kirkstead simultaneously with those below, that the 'mud-barge' was intended to work upwards and that he expected her progress would keep pace with the works above.

Rennie. 1816.

In carrying out the works it was found that the amount allowed in the original estimate was insufficient. In reporting on the works in 1816, Mr. Rennie attributes this to the construction of a new lock at Anthony's Gowt; the fall of Tattershall bridge, which had to be rebuilt; the difficulty in excavating the new channel, part of which, below Kirkstead, turned out to be a running sand and part a very hard marl. In order to obtain additional funds for carrying on the work, application was made to Parliament for power to raise a further sum of £60,000 on the security of the tolls. This also proving insufficient and further money being required, a third Act was obtained empowering the raising of a further sum of £70,000, making the total amount raised under the powers of the three Acts £310,000. By this Act the Navigation Company undertook the maintenance of all works above the junction of the South Drain with the old course of the river at Horsley Deeps. A provision was also inserted in the Act for regulating the passage of steam boats.

7 Geo. iv, c. 2, 1826.
10 Geo. iv, 1829.

REPORT ON THE ENLARGEMENT OF THE GRAND SLUICE.
Rennie. 1818.

Power was taken in the Act of 1812 to enlarge the lock of the Grand Sluice to the same dimensions as those of the locks at Horsley Deeps and Stamp End. In 1818 Mr. Rennie was directed to report as to the best means of obtaining more water-way at the Sluice. In his report he states that this could be done by decreasing the width of the pier between the lock and the adjoining drainage tun, this being thicker than the others; but this, while increasing the navigation lock, would only give a partial relief to the drainage. A more effective plan would be to convert the navigation arch into a drainage tun, enlarging it to the same size as the others and constructing a new lock for navigation on the east side, but he considered that there would be difficulty in keeping the Cut from this open, as the river then curved to the west. A more effectual scheme he therefore considered would be to make a new Cut on the west side from a short distance above the Grand Sluice to the river below the bridge, with a lock on it, near its junction with the river, turning the present lock into a drainage tun. None of these recommendations were carried out.

The works authorised under the Acts for improving the navigation were not completed until 1829. In making the excavation for the Horsley Deeps Lock a canoe was found, 8ft. under the surface. It had been hollowed out of an oak tree, was 30ft. 8in. long, and measured 3ft. in the widest part. Other canoes were also dug up, one of which is deposited amongst the collection of antiquities in the British Museum.

The condition of the river when the works were completed was as follows. The Grand Sluice had a total water-way, including the navigation lock, of 66¾ft., its sill being 5ft. 6in. above mean low water of spring tides in the estuary, or 3·20ft. below *Ordnance datum*. The Grand Sluice was situated eight miles from the outfall into the estuary, the last two miles being through shifting sands, amongst which the channel was constantly altering its position. In dry seasons, owing to the absence of back water from the stoppage of the tides, the doors were frequently blocked up with silt, which occasionally accumulated to the depth of 10ft. This accumulation had to be moved by the winter floods before a clear passage down the Haven could be secured.

From Boston to Chapel Hill the bottom of the river was 50ft wide, at Tattershall Bridge 45ft., at Bardney Lock 36ft. From Bardney Lock (Horsley Deeps) to Boston, a distance of twenty three and a half miles, the drainage and navigation channels were the same; thence to Lincoln, nine miles, there were two channels, the water in the Witham being held up at Bardney Lock and at Stamp End Lock for navigation, and communicating with the Fossdyke navigation to the Trent. The sill of Bardney Lock was 3ft. 10in. above that of the Grand Sluice and to maintain 5ft. of water on Bardney Lock sill, 9ft. had to be held up at the Grand Sluice. On the south side of the navigation, for the purpose of drainage, a new cut, called the South Delph, extended from Horsley Deeps to the junction of the Sincyl Dyke at Lincoln. At the head of the Sincyl Dyke was fixed a weir and draw-doors, over and through which are discharged flood waters from the Witham. The Sincyl Dyke also took the water from the sunken tunnel under the

CONDITION OF THE RIVER IN 1830.

Witham to the Great Gowt Drain and from the weir on the Little Gowt Drain. The water from the upper Witham, except that passing down the Sincyl Dyke, flowed into Brayford Mere and passed thence through the High Bridge at Lincoln, to Stamp End Lock, the discharge being regulated by the draw-doors and weirs at Stamp End. The quantity of water passing into the Sincyl Dyke was regulated by gauges.

CONDITION OF THE OUTFALL.

The area taxable for the purposes of the General Commissioners of Drainage was about 127,800 acres. With some alterations the arrangement of the drainage continues the same at the present time. Notwithstanding the large amount spent on the upper part of the river, owing to the defective condition of the outfall, the drainage remained in an imperfect condition. In 1821, a general meeting of all parties interested in the drainage and navigation was held, and Sir John Rennie, who had succeeded his father as Consulting Engineer to the Commissioners, was directed to make a report as to the best means of improving the river from the Grand Sluice to the sea.

SIR J. RENNIE'S REPORT, 1822.

The report was addressed to the Corporation of Boston, the Commissioners of the River Witham, the Commissioners of the Black Sluice Drainage, and all parties interested in the improvement of the River Witham. He pointed out that owing to the works which had been carried out, there was little obstruction to the drainage or navigation above Boston, but that "immediately on leaving it the channel became so circuitous and disproportionate in width, that the effect of the scour by the waters acting in one compact and undivided body, was lost, and the river, particularly during the time of ebb, not being able to maintain so great a channel clear, became dispersed into a variety of minor and insignificant channels, which, meandering through the extensive and shifting sands by which they were surrounded, with difficulty forced their way at last to the sea." As this report, and a subsequent one, and that of Mr. Telford, made in 1823, deal principally with the river below the Grand Sluice, the recommendations contained in it will be dealt with in the Chapter on the Harbour. One of the recommendations which affected the river immediately below the Grand Sluice, namely, the straightening of that part of the river lying between the bridge and the sluice, was carried out by the Harbour Commissioners in 1825.

PUMPING ENGINES.

To protect their lands from flooding, the Owners had, from time to time, embanked them, and erected windmills for lifting the water out of the drains into the river, there being no less than 14 wind engines in use between Lincoln and Dogdyke. Subsequently steam power was used. In order, if possible, to prevent this expenditure, Sir John Rennie was again instructed, by the General Commissioners, to report as to the best means of improving the outfall and lowering the water in the Witham, sufficiently to allow of the drainage of the lowest lands by gravitation; and, further, as to the effect on the general interests of the Trusts of the proposed pumping scheme.

In two reports, made in the year 1830, dated respectively the 9th of August and the 17th September, he stated that the state of drainage in the first district, was very imperfect, and that the chief impediments to the discharge of the waters arose from two causes; the first, the obstructed state of the outfall of Boston Haven, between the Grand Sluice and Hobhole; and the second, the existence of the Grand Sluice and the inadequacy of the interior drains to convey the downfall waters into the Witham. With respect to the first, he referred to the improvements already carried out by the Corporation of Boston, by straightening the river and making the new cut through Burton's Marsh, and by the removal of the old wooden bridge with its piers, and the erection, in its place, of the present iron structure; but, he thought that the outfall was capable of very considerable further improvement, and proposed a scheme, the particulars of which will be treated of more fully in a succeeding chapter; and he also recommended the making of a new cut through the Marshes, from the Black Sluice to Bell's Reach, at a cost of £89,313. For a removal of the second cause of impediment, from the confined state of the outlet of the river and the constant holding up of the water for the purpose of navigation, he proposed that a new sluice should be erected between the Grand Sluice and the Iron Bridge; that from this a new cut should be made, in a direct line, to join the North Forty-Foot above Toft Bridge, which was to be deepened and cleaned out to the Sleaford navigation, and that from there the present line of the Dales Head Dyke should be enlarged and deepened as far as Washingborough, the estimated cost being £52,873.

Sir J. Rennie.
1830.

These recommendations were not carried out, but the Commissioners, at a meeting held in 1832, passed several resolutions stating that it was their opinion that the steam engines proposed to be erected by the First and Third Districts would prove injurious to the banks of the river, and the drainage of the other Districts, and therefore they determined to oppose the powers sought to be obtained from Parliament by those Districts. The system of drainage by pumping was not, however, stopped. The total of the several engines now in use, above the Grand Sluice, is over 350 horse power.

In 1846, the loop-line of the Great Northern was constructed, the line between Boston and Lincoln running for the greater part of the distance along the east bank of the river, leaving it at Horsley Deeps, and thence to Lincoln, running on the north bank of the South Delph. At the same time the rights of the navigation were leased to the Great Northern Railway Company for 999 years, at a rent charge of £10,545 a year, equal to five per cent. on the amount

TRANSFER OF
THE NAVIGATION
TO THE G. N.
RAILWAY
9 and 10 Vict., c
71, 1846.

of the capital, which then stood at £208,900 in shares, and £2,000 in debentures, the rest of the money originally raised and expended, having been paid off. From the parliamentary return of 1870, £24,000 had then been paid off since the Railway Company took the navigation.

The Railway Company, in taking over the navigation, assumed the liabilities of the original owners with regard to the banks, and these have since proved a source of litigation.

<small>LIABILITY FOR MAINTENANCE OF RIVER BANKS.</small>

From Boston to Bardney Lock, the east bank,—and above that, both banks—of the river, and the banks of the old course of the river by Barlings Eau, have to be maintained by the Railway Company, except those in Washingborough and Heighington, their liability for these having been released by a payment of £2,000, made in 1857, to the Washingborough Trustees, who, in consideration of this sum, released the Railway Company from all past and future liability in respect of defective banks in this part of the river.

In the spring of 1862, owing to an unusually heavy rainfall, the river Witham became flooded above its ordinary height, and on the 28th March the bank of the South Delph gave way, the water pouring through the breach, which was 156ft. long, and inundating 1,800 acres of land in Branston Fen. An action was brought against the Great Northern Railway Company for compensation.

<small>Cawdron v. G.N. Railway Company.</small>

The case was tried at the following Lincoln Summer Assizes. The Company contended that the act of 1812 authorised the making of a delph, but that no mention was made of a bank, and that therefore they were not liable for its maintenance. They further contended that the flooding was due to the bad condition of the channel of the river, which was filled with weeds, and in places silted up, and which ought to have been maintained in order by the Drainage Commissioners. The Plaintiffs contended on the other hand that a delph could not be made without a bank; that the bank was made with the material excavated in making the delph, and that it was subsequently put in proper order by the Navigation Company. This bank had been raised and repaired by the Railway Company in 1858, and an arrangement made with the Branston Drainage Trustees, that the expenses should be borne jointly. It was further contended by the Plaintiffs that this work was not properly done, and several local experts were called, to prove that wet clay puddle was put in the bank instead of its being 'punned' with dry clay. The Jury gave their verdict for the plaintiffs, the damages being agreed to at £475.

A rule *nisi* was obtained to set aside this verdict, on the ground that the judge at the trial had not allowed the question to go to the Jury as to whether the mischief had not been caused by default of the Witham Drainage Commissioners in not providing a proper outlet for the waters in the river below Horsley Deeps, which had consequently backed up into the South Delph, and so caused the flooding. The rule was subsequently discharged by the Court of Exchequer, July 6th, 1863, Baron Bramwell remarking, "I desire not to have it supposed that I discharge the rule because I am of opinion that the Great Northern Railway Company would have been liable if the banks were broken through the water being pent back upon them improperly by persons below; but the rule is discharged upon the ground that we cannot collect from the summing up of the learned judge that he took a different view on the trial."

Law Times Reports.

In March, 1889, a breach occurred in the bank of the old channel of the Witham, and flooded 'Branston Island' as that portion severed from the rest of the fen by the making of the new cut for the river is called, and the land was flooded from 4 to 5ft. deep. An action was brought at the Lincoln Summer Assizes in 1889, against the Railway Company to recover damages, but the matter was settled by agreement before coming into Court, a verdict being recorded for the Plaintiffs and the Company paying £900 damages besides the costs incurred.

Ward v. G. N. Railway Company.

Continual complaints being made as to the state of the banks and of the inefficient condition of the river for carrying off the floods, Mr. William Lewin, who had been the resident Engineer to the Commissioners for a long period, was directed to make a report as to the best means of improving the drainage. In his report he first deals with the question as affecting the whole of the Fen district, and points out that no effectual remedy can be provided unless the outfall to the sea be improved, and advises that the new cut to Clay Hole, which had been recommended 120 years previously, should be carried out without delay. With regard to the river above the Grand Sluice he states that it is not in the state it ought to be in, the bed of the river being from 2ft. to 5ft. above the sill of the Sluice. He recommended that the bottom of the river should be made one foot below the sill of the Sluice from Boston to Bardney, the sill of the Sluice lowered 4ft. and that of Bardney Lock 5ft.; the Sincyl Dyke widened and deepened. The estimated cost of these works was £40,003.

INEFFICIENT CONDITION OF THE DRAINAGE. 1860.

LEWIN'S REPORT, 1860.

On the 19th of March, 1861, a deputation from the Commission waited on Sir John (then Mr.) Hawkshaw, C.E., in London, to consult him with reference to the state of the drainage, the immediate object being the improvement of the condition of the East and West Fens, but Mr. Hawkshaw was directed to turn his attention to a scheme for the general improvement of all the fens under the jurisdiction of the Witham Trust.

For the general plan of improvement Mr. Hawkshaw recommended the adoption of the old project for forming a new Cut to Clay Hole, as he considered that this would improve the outfall of all the great drains which empty themselves into the Witham.

<small>HAWKSHAW'S REPORT, 1861.</small>

Failing to obtain the consent of the other Trusts interested in the promotion of a general scheme for improving the Outfall, the Commissioners had to fall back on such measures as they could carry out themselves without the assistance of other Trusts. Sir John Hawkshaw was therefore directed ' to examine and report on the state of the drainage of the river Witham above the Grand Sluice, embracing the 1st, 3rd, and 5th Districts, with a view to any improvement that could be effected.' Accordingly, in the autumn of 1862, he caused a survey to be made of the river from the Grand Sluice to Lincoln. With the data thus obtained, and from facts gathered from other sources, he drew up his report, and laid before the Commissioners the works that he considered necessary for putting the upper part of the river in as efficient a state as possible under its present condition in connection with the navigation, the existence of the Grand Sluice, and the state of Boston Haven; which, when completed, would enable the Commissioners to lower the height of the water in the channel, and so improve the drainage of the lands, without hindering the navigation; and by strengthening the banks, remove all cause of apprehension as to their safety. The estimated cost of the works was £53,000, and the advantage to be gained by the drainage, was the lowering of the level of the water in the Witham by two feet on an average. He estimated that a very considerable saving would be effected in the cost of working the pumping engines when the works were completed. If, however, the works for improving the Outfall, as recommended in his previous report, were carried out, he considered that then the Grand Sluice sill could be lowered, and the whole of the engine-power dispensed with.

<small>DITTO. 1862.</small>

The works were on the same lines as those laid down by Mr. Lewin in his report of 1860, except that he advised the postponement of the lowering of the sill of the Grand Sluice until the Outfall below was improved. In concluding his report he drew attention to the fact that the highest flood level, which up to that time had been 14½ft. above the sill of the Grand Sluice, reached in some places along the river to the top of the banks.

<small>IMPROVEMENT ACT. 28 and 29 Vict., c. 124, 1865.</small>

The Commissioners hesitated some time before adopting this scheme of interior improvement, but at last, finding that no general plan was likely to be successfully carried out, three years afterwards they obtained an Act "*for the further Improvement of the Drainage and Navigation by the River Witham,*" which received the Royal Assent on the 19th of June, 1865. Under the powers of this Act the Commissioners were authorised to execute the following works: viz., to widen, deepen and scour out the river Witham, from a point about six miles above Boston to Horsley Deeps, so that the bottom should throughout this length be on a dead level; also to raise and strengthen the banks; to deepen, scour out and strengthen the banks of the Old Witham, Barlings Eau, Billinghay Skirth, and the several tributaries in connection with them; to alter and lower the sills of the several sluices of the above streams, and also those of the Sleaford and Horncastle navigation, and the sills of the following delphs, *viz.*, Timberland, Metheringham, Nocton and Branston.

The Great Northern Railway Company, as the owners of the navigation, were authorised to widen, scour out and deepen the channel and strengthen the banks of the South Delph, to lower the sill of Anton's Gowt and Horsley Deeps Locks, and re-build the latter, if necessary; and for this purpose they were empowered to raise the sum of £10,000 by the creation of new capital. The General Commissioners were authorised to borrow a sum not exceeding £55,000 on mortgage of new taxes, to be levied for the purpose of this Act, the extinction of the debt being provided for by the repayment of thirty-five annual instalments. The lands in the First, Third, and Fifth Districts were taxed for these special works in four classes, as arranged by the Act of 1812, with an additional annual payment of three shillings, two shillings and sixpence, two shillings, and one shilling per acre respectively. Power was also given to the Commissioners to make bye-laws for the regulation of the fishery, and other incidental rights and privileges attaching to the river and the drainage.

The works authorised under this Act, so far as they related to the drainage, were carried out under the direction of Mr. Edward Welsh, C.E., who became the resident Engineer of the Commissioners after the death of Mr. Lewin; and those connected with the navigation, by the Great Northern Railway Company.

EFFECT OF THE DEFECTIVE OUTFALL.

These improvements, when completed, only demonstrated more forcibly than ever that works carried out in the upper portion of the channel were practically useless, unless provision were made for the discharge at the Outfall to the sea.

FLOODS, 1869.

In 1869, the water rose so high in the river, after a heavy rain, that a bank was broken near Stixwould, and 1,500 acres of land were inundated. This was one of the worst floods ever known in the Witham, the water rising, at tide time, to a height of 15ft. 11in. on the sill of the Grand Sluice, and about 40 square miles of low land being inundated to a depth varying from one to five feet. The loss due to this flood was estimated at £100,000. All the lower part of the City of Lincoln was inundated. The banks of the Fossdyke, and also of the South Delph near Heighington, and those at Bardney and Branston, gave way. The bank of Billinghay Skirth was also broken, and about 3,000 acres flooded, driving the inhabitants from their homes.

The highest previous flood on record was in 1852, when the

water rose in the Witham at Nocton to 17ft., and at Boston to 14½ft. above the Grand Sluice sill, with a rainfall of 4·32 inches in the previous month, and 15·32 inches in the previous four months. A flood in November, 1875, which occurred after the improvements, rose as high at Bardney, and at Boston one foot higher, with a rainfall of 4.90 inches for the month, and 12·30 inches for the previous four months; and the flood in January, 1877, rose nine inches higher at Bardney, and seventeen inches higher at Boston, with the same rainfall for the previous month, and two inches less in the previous four months. In September, 1880, very heavy floods again occurred. The streets of Lincoln were inundated, and a large area of fen land was placed under water, which rose, in some fields in the fen, as high as the heads of the sheaves of corn which, owing to the wet season, were still standing in the fields. In 1882, there were also heavy floods; Barlings Eau bank gave way, and a very large area of land in the neighbourhood of Lincoln was under water. In 1883, the Witham overflowed its banks above Lincoln and flooded several thousand acres, and the bank gave way near Southrey.

The deposit of silt outside the Grand Sluice, at times when there were not sufficient freshets to carry it away, still continued, and the doors of the sluice were frequently blocked up. This deposit accumulated to the height of 10ft. 9in. in 1864; 9ft. 8in. in 1865; 11ft. 1in. in 1868; 10ft. 3in. in 1870; and 11ft. 4in. in December, 1874.

Owing to the serious amount of damage done by the constant flooding of the land, and to the banks, and no action being taken by the General Commissioners, the principal Landowners met together and consulted as to the best course to be pursued, and at a meeting held in London, in February, 1877, the following instructions were given to Sir John Hawkshaw, C.E.

1. That Sir John Hawkshaw be requested to examine and consider fully the whole drainage system of the valley of the Witham both above and below Lincoln, and including the water drainage of that city, and to report to this Committee upon the most efficient and most economical method of carrying off the waters of those districts to the sea without flooding.
2. That it is desirable that in making this inquiry Sir. J. Hawkshaw should examine into the causes of the late severe floods in the different districts in which they occurred.
3. That Sir J. Hawkshaw should embrace in his consideration the internal drainage of the fen lands as well as the drainage of the river Witham itself.
4. That in any proposal for letting the water from above Lincoln into the Witham below the city more freely than at present, it is essential that the low lands below Lincoln should be secured against increased danger of flooding.

5   That Sir J. Hawkshaw be requested to consider whether it would, or would not, be desirable to provide for carrying off the water above Lincoln, and the high land water below, to the Witham outfall by a separate channel or channels.

6   That considering the very heavy taxation of some of the lands below Lincoln, it would be a great advantage if a system of drainage by gravitation could be adopted, so as to avoid the expense of local engines, and the necessity of keeping up delph banks capable of resisting the pressure of a large body of water.

7   That Sir J. Hawkshaw be requested to direct his attention to the state of the bed of the river.

8   That Sir J. Hawkshaw be requested to report whether, in his opinion, the navigation of the Witham interferes with the efficient drainage of the county, or renders it more costly, and, if so, to what extent;

9   And whether it is desirable to make any change or improvement in the Grand Sluice, at Boston;

10 And also to report fully upon the outfall of the river.

11 And generally it is the wish of the Committee that Sir J. Hawkshaw's report should be as wide and comprehensive as possible, and that he should deal, in it, with the whole question referred to him, in all its bearings.

HAWKSHAW'S SCHEME. 187

In his report Sir John Hawkshaw assumed that the maximum quantity of water to be provided for, as passing down the Witham and through the Grand Sluice, off the whole drainage area of 504,000 acres was that equivalent to a continuous rainfall, of one quarter of an inch, in 24 hours, amounting to 318,000 cubic feet per minute. A quarter of an inch of rainfall in 24 hours is the quantity which has always been taken by Engineers who have been engaged in these fens, as the quantity to be provided for in the low districts; but, as the area draining by the Witham contains a large proportion of high land, the strata of which, such as the chalk and oolites, is of an absorbent character, this estimate would appear to be too high. The free flow of the water from above Lincoln he found restricted by the regulations as to Bargate Weir and at Stamp End, also by the contracted water-way under the High Bridge and through the City; the water from the western drainage district throttled by having to pass through a small culvert under the Witham; and the North and South Catchwater Drains of the West District obstructed by the height to which the waters rose during flood time in the Fossdyke and the Witham, into which they discharge.

Hawkshaw. May, 1877.

The works recommended and the estimated cost of the same were as follows:—

    1. Cutting a new Channel from the Witham near Bargate Weir to the South Delph, at a point just below the City, the channel having a bottom width of

20ft., and erecting a new Weir and Sluice near Bargate Weir. Widening the bridge under the High Street, and the Railway Bridge ... ... £ 34,000

2. Widening and deepening the channel of the South Delph, and raising and strengthening the banks to a bottom width of 20ft. 19,000

3. Widening and deepening the Witham from Horsley Deeps to the Grand Sluice and strengthening the banks. The bottom to be lowered 7ft. at the Grand Sluice, and rising at the rate of four inches a mile, the bottom width to be 108ft. from Boston to Chapel Hill and 52ft. at Horsley Deeps, with slopes of 2 to 1 197,000

4. Replacing the Grand Sluice with a new one having a width of 110ft., and its sill 7ft. lower than the present sill 80,000

5. Constructing a reservoir of about four acres near the new sluice for the purpose of taking water in at spring tides, and allowing it to flow out again in dry weather at low water for the purpose of scouring away the sand which accumulated in the Haven 4,000

6. Enlarging the water-way of the Witham below the Grand Sluice as far as Maud Foster Sluice ... 33,000

7. Widening and deepening the Witham above Lincoln from the head of the new channel to Welbourn Mill 26,000

8. Widening and deepening the river Brant to near Welbourn Ford 5,400

9. Making a short drain from the end of the main drain of the West District Drainage, and a culvert under the Witham near Bargate Weir, and erecting a 30 H.P. pumping station for the West District Drainage 4,100

10. Widening and deepening the Car Dyke from Washingborough to Billinghay Skirth, for the purpose of keeping the upland waters out of the Nocton, Metheringham and Timberland Delphs 32,500

11. Widening and deepening Billinghay Skirth and raising and strengthening the banks 7,000

12. Widening and deepening the existing low level drains between Washingborough pumping station and Chapel Hill and erecting a 300 H.P. pumping station there and doing away with the present pumping stations between Chapel Hill and Washingborough 72,200

13. Enlarging Kyme Eau from the proposed pumping station to the Witham 2,000

The total cost with contingencies (but exclusive of parliamentary or engineering expenses) being ... £567,820

The advantage to be gained were stated to be the reduction of the flood level 3ft. in the Witham at Bargate Weir; 15in. in the South Delph; 2ft. at Horsley Deeps; and 1ft. at Chapel Hill.

For the further improvement of the outfall Sir John Hawkshaw considered the most effectual way would be to carry out the new cut from Hobhole to Clay Hole, but that its cost would be too large for merely drainage purposes. The more economical plan which had been proposed by Mr. Wheeler, the Engineer to the Boston Harbour Commissioners, and approved by them, of dredging the existing channel through the Clays and turning the river to Clay Hole, although less effectual, would, he considered, be of some advantage.

The prospect of obtaining a reduction of only one foot in the flood level in the lower part of the river, after an expenditure of upwards of half a million of money, and without securing any improvement in the outfall to the sea, did not commend itself to the Landowners, and no action was taken on the recommendation contained in this report.

In the following year Mr. J. Evelyn Williams, who had succeeded Mr. Welsh as resident Engineer to the Witham Drainage Commissioners, was directed to report to them on the means of improving the drainage. Mr. Williams, in his report, stated his opinion that in the removal of obstructions to the natural flow of water, it is advisable to commence at the lowest point possible, and to work upwards. He agreed with the opinion of all the Engineers who had previously reported, that the most effectual and permanent remedy for the defective condition of the outfall for the drainage water was the scheme for making a new Cut through the Clays; but that, if the cost of this work should preclude the possibility of its being carried out, then much relief might be obtained by carrying out the scheme proposed by the Harbour Commisisoners, for training and dredging the Channel to Clay Hole. By this plan he considered " that the beneficial effect of the scour of the flood and tidal waters which was distributed and absorbed in struggling seaward through shifting sands, and in opening out fresh and minor channels, would be concentrated and utilised in maintaining one deep and fixed outlet for the flood waters. Further, the fixing and deepening of the outer channel would tend to counteract the deposition of sand in the river, in front of the sluices during dry summers, and which is now caused by the tidal water flowing over the shifting sands in the Estuary." He estimated the cost of this work at £28,500. Between Hobhole and Maud Foster Drains, he proposed that the channel should be deepened; that a straight Cut should be made for the river, from Maud Foster to St. John's Road Ferry, and suggested that the loop cut off up to the Black Sluice might be converted into a wet dock; or, if that were not found practicable, the deepening and

J. E. WILLIAMS' REPORT, 1878.

improving the channel along this length and up to the Grand Sluice; the construction of an additional drainage tun at the Grand Sluice, on the east side; and taking off the forelands, and enlarging the Witham between Tattershall Bridge and the Grand Sluice. The estimated cost, exclusive of the Cut across the bend above Maud Foster Sluice, but including the training of the river from Hobhole to Clay Hole, he put at £89,347.

If these improvements were carried out Mr. Williams estimated that they would effect a depression in the low water flood line to the extent of three feet at Hobhole Sluice, two feet at the Black Sluice, and two feet six inches at the Grand Sluice. He further suggested that if the Grand Sluice were removed from its present site to Chapel Hill, an additional sea outlet would be obtained from Kyme Eau, with five feet more fall, as it would then discharge below the point where the water would require to be held up for navigation purposes; also that the Car Dyke should be converted into a catch-water drain, and be connected with Bargate Weir, and thus the upland water, both above and below Lincoln, could be discharged at a sea sluice across the end of Kyme Eau, and below the new Grand Sluice to be erected at Chapel Hill. The estimated cost of this scheme, including the enlargement of the river and strengthening and heightening the banks below Chapel Hill and other incidental works, he estimated at £300,000. And if to this were added the improvement of the Outfall by the new Cut through the Clays, and above Maud Foster, and deepening and improving the river, £200,000 more, or together about £500,000, exclusive of land and parliamentary and engineering expenses.

WITHAM OUTFALL SCHEME, 1879.

In 1879 Mr. Thomas Garfit, who was then Member for the borough, took active steps to bring together the chief representatives of the different Trusts interested in the improvement of the drainage and navigation, and it was chiefly owing to his exertions that in August, 1879, a meeting of representatives from the Witham Drainage, the Black Sluice Drainage, and the Boston Harbour Commissioners took place at Boston, Mr. Banks Stanhope of Revesby being in the chair, to consider the improvement of the outfall of the River Witham below the Grand Sluice. At this meeting the two schemes for effecting this improvement were submitted for consideration and it was resolved to carry out the larger plan for cutting through the Clays, which had been recommended about 80 years previously. The basis of payment, which had been the cause of the failure of all previous attempts to improve the outfall, was settled on the principle that the lands paying drainage taxes, whether to the Drainage Trusts or to the Court of Sewers, should pay a uniform acre tax, the contribution of the Harbour Trust being a fixed sum. It was also agreed that the work should be carried out by an Outfall Board, consisting of representatives from the contributing Trusts.

With as little delay as possible an Act was obtained giving power to carry out the works, and the new cut was opened in 1884. Further details as to this work will be found in Chapter XIV, on Boston Harbour.

<small>WITHAM OUTFALL ACT.
43 and 44 Vict., c. 153, 1880.</small>

No continuous heavy downfalls of rain, such as occurred previous to this work being done, have happened since, to prove the efficiency of the scheme, but the predictions of the Engineers have been more than realised and the water lowered at least four feet in floods. The low water in the haven has ebbed out to 3ft. below the sill of the Grand Sluice when the freshets were not running. Another great advantage has accrued in the absence of the blocking up of the water-way by the deposit of silt below the Grand Sluice, and in this respect the exceedingly dry seasons which have occurred since the Cut has been made give a sufficient indication that such deposits are not likely to occur again.

Concurrently with the works carried on for the improvement of the Outfall, the Witham Commissioners, under the powers of an Act obtained in 1881, enlarged the Grand Sluice and improved the channel from the Sluice to Tattershall; for which purpose they were authorised to raise £40,000 and to levy additional taxes on the First, Third and Fifth Districts, to the amount of eighteenpence an acre for payment of the interest on the money borrowed for the works, and sixpence an acre for their maintenance. The money borrowed has to be paid off by 35 equal instalments. By clause 36 of the Act every Commissioner is to be allowed ten shillings and sixpence for each attendance at a meeting of the General Commissioners, and one guinea for attendance at a Committee Meeting.

<small>WITHAM IMPROVEMENT ACT.
44 and 45 Vict., c. 90, 1881.</small>

The work of altering the Grand Sluice was carried out by Mr. W. Rigby, from the plans of Mr. Williams, C.E., and consisted of replacing the old lock, which had an opening of 15ft., with a new one, 30ft. wide, thus giving 15ft. additional water-way. The sill of the new lock was laid 3ft. lower than the old sill. The contract amount for the work was £10,000. At the same time a portion of the forelands of the river was removed and the channel improved up to Tattershall.

<small>ENLARGEMENT OF THE GRAND SLUICE.</small>

At the present time the General Commission for Drainage by the River Witham is composed as follows, viz.,

<small>WITHAM DRAINAGE COMMISSION.</small>

		Acres.	Representatives.
First District,	Lincoln to Kyme Eau	24,916	7
Second ,,	Kyme Eau to Boston	19,101	6
Third ,,	Lincoln to the Bane...	4,621	5
Fourth ,,	East, West and Wildmore Fens and the 5,000 acres ...	62,395	8

			Acres.	Representatives.
Fifth	,,	adjoining Kyme Eau	5,176	2
Sixth	,,	West of Holland Fen	11,584	3
The Mayors of Lincoln and Boston			...	2
				33

The Second and Sixth Districts drain through the Black Sluice. They pay taxes for the maintenance of the west bank of the Witham. The Fourth District drains into the Haven below the Grand Sluice through Maud Foster and Hobhole sluices.

TAXES.

The taxes leviable under the different Acts obtained for the improvement of the river are as follows:

	Under the Act of 1762 & 1812	1865	1881	Total per acre.
	s. d.	s. d.	s. d.	s. d.
FIRST DISTRICT.				
Three parishes and seven dales	2 6	3 0	2 0	7 6
Eight parishes	2 0	2 6	2 0	6 6
Three parishes and two dales	1 6	2 0	2 0	5 6
FIFTH DISTRICT.				
Six parishes	0 9	1 0	2 0	3 9
THIRD DISTRICT.				
Fifteen parishes	2 6	3 0	2 0	7 6
One parish	2 0	2 6	2 0	6 6
Two parishes	1 6	2 0	2 0	5 6
SECOND DISTRICT	1 0	1 0		2 0
SIXTH DISTRICT	0 6	0 6		1 0

(Except Ewerby, which varies from 6d. to 2d.)

The terminable taxes of 1865 expire in 1900, and those of 1881 in 1917.

Besides the taxes here given, the several districts are liable to the taxes levied by the Interior Commissioners.

The Second and Sixth Districts are also liable to the Black Sluice taxes.

The lands in the First, Third and Fifth Districts are liable to the Outfall tax levied under the Act of 1880, which is not to exceed two shillings per acre, including maintenance, and is to cease in 35 years (1916), by which time the whole of the borrowed money is to be paid off. After that time the maintenance tax mentioned above continues, but is not to exceed sixpence per acre. The land in the Second and Sixth Districts contribute to the Outfall through the Black Sluice.

RECEIPTS AND DISBURSEMENTS.

The amount raised by taxes on the *General Account* of the Witham Commission is about £5,758 a year, and for foreland rents £112, making an income of £5,870. The payments are, Interest on debt at 4½ per cent., £2,400; payment to the Great Northern Railway, £2,800; maintenance of works,

£500; management, £600; a total of £6,300, leaving a yearly deficiency of about £430. This deficiency appears to be met out of a large balance in the Treasurer's hands, which has been steadily diminishing for some years past, and in 1895 was at £3,472. In addition to the above, the interest on the loans and the instalments of repayment of principal, incurred for works carried out under the Act of 1865, amounting to £2,870, and under the Act of 1881, amounting to £2,257, are met by special rates, as also that for the interest on the loan for the Witham contribution to the Outfall works, £1,446, and towards the maintenance of the same about £400 a year, making a total amount to be provided for of about £13,278.

CHAPTER VI.

THE WITHAM DISTRICTS.

<small>Fig. 7.
WITHAM FENS.</small>

BEFORE the works carried out for the improvement of the river, in the middle of the last century, the land lying along the Witham was an open common on which the inhabitants of the several parishes which adjoined it had grazing rights. In summer, this common fen afforded grazing for cattle and sheep, but was subject to be frequently flooded, and in winter, was more or less under water, as it was only partially embanked from the river. The improvement effected in the drainage by the deepening and straightening of the channel, and the erection of the Grand Sluice, was not sufficient to render these lands fit for cultivation, and for this purpose it was necessary that they should be embanked, and the water raised from them by mechanical means. It was also necessary that the Common rights should be extinguished and that the lands should be divided and allotted. For this purpose special Acts of Parliament were obtained, and, in course of time, the whole of the land was brought under cultivation.

Under the Act of 1762, the management of these Districts was provided for by separate Commissions, consisting of members elected by the several parishes. These Commissions have charge of all the interior works, and the management of the pumping engines and drains, and have power to lay rates for their maintenance. The number of Members elected, and the qualification of the Voters will be given under each District.

<small>IMPROVED VALUE OF THE LAND AFTER INCLOSURE.</small>

Arthur Young, when describing the lands along the Witham, stated that " the produce before enclosure was little, the land letting for not more than one shilling and sixpence per acre; now (1799) from eleven to seventeen shillings . . . This vast work is effected by a moderate embankment and the erection of Windmills for throwing out the superfluous water." Mr. Parkinson, one of the Commissioners, largely employed under the Enclosure Acts, gave the old rental value of 43,407 acres of this land at £5,982, and the improved value at £42,375. When the land was enclosed, part of it was sold by auction by the Commissioners to pay the expenses, the price fetched being about £14 an acre. In 1847 Mr. Clarke put the average rental of this land as varying from about 25s. to 40s., the greater part letting at 35s.

<small>*Agriculture of Lincolnshire,* 1847.

Royal Agricultural Society Journal, 1847.</small>

THE FIRST DISTRICT.—This district is situated on the South and West side of the Witham, and extends from near Lincoln to Kyme Eau. It contains 24,916 acres. It is described in the Act of 1762 as containing the Fens and Lowlands in Lincoln, Lincoln Common, Canwick, Washingborough, Heighington, Branston, Potterhanworth, Walton, Dunston, Metheringham, Blankney, Linwood, Martin, Timberland, Timberland Thorpe, Walcot, Billinghay Dales and Dogdyke. The boundaries are set out as follows, *viz.*, from twenty yards below the north end of Sincil Dyke in Lincoln to Kyme Eau by the River Witham on the north ; from the Little Bargate Bridge in Lincoln to Kyme Eau, by the high ground of Lincoln, Canwick and Washingborough, the Car Dyke, Thorpe Tilney and North Kyme Fen on the south ; and from the Witham to the high grounds of Lincoln Common by a line drawn at all places parallel within twenty yards from the east side of Sincil Dyke on the west ; and from the River Witham to North Kyme Fen by Kyme Eau and South Kyme on the east.

Fig. 7.

BOUNDARY.
2 Geo. iii, c. 32, 1762.

Eighteen Commissioners are elected, one by each of the several parishes and places named. The qualification of an Elector is the ownership of land of the yearly value of £5, and farmers at rack rents of £50, paying drainage rates, are also qualified. The election is directed to be held at the parish church, or other usual place where public business is transacted, on the first Tuesday in April, once every three years. The District Commissioners so elected are to meet on the third Tuesday in April, and elect seven Commissioners to represent them on the Witham General Drainage Commission. If no election of District or General Commissioners is held, the old Commissioners remain in office.

DRAINAGE COMMISSIONERS.

Three parishes and seven dales in this district pay 2/6 an acre, permanent tax to the Witham Drainage ; 3/- under the Act of 1865, terminable in 1900, and 2/- under the Act of 1881, terminable in 1917 ; Eight parishes 2/- permanent tax, and 2/6 and 2/- terminable ; Three parishes and two dales 1/6 permanent, and 2/- and 2/- terminable.

TAXES.

THE DALES.—When the first Enclosure Acts were applied for, owing to a fear that if the embankments were placed near the channel of the river the liability to floods would be increased, the space lying between the Dales Head Dyke and the river, about a mile in width, was left to form a 'wash,' and this screed called 'the Dales' was overflowed about nine months in the year. Several windmills from the newly enclosed lands threw their water into this Wash. In the year 1797 an Act was obtained, and this screed, containing 2,800 acres, was embanked. John Hudson of West Ashby was appointed Commissioner. By this Act the embankment was directed to be commenced at the north-east side of Billinghay Skirth, and to run parallel to the Witham to the north-east side of Blankney parish bank, and was to be 6ft. wide at the top with 40ft.

THE DALES INCLOSURE ACT. 1797.
37 Geo. iii, c. 77.
Fig. 7.

base; thence it was to continue along the north-west side of Blankney Fen to the then existing bank at the north-east corner of Blankney Fen. The side banks of Martin, Timberland Thorpe, and Walcot Fens were to be extended to join the bank near the Witham. The Blankney engine was to be removed, and be placed in Martin Fen. Power was given in the Act to appoint officers, to cleanse out the ditches and maintain and repair the banks, and to fence, in default of the Owners doing the same. The award was to be deposited in the chest in Timberland Church, and to be open for inspection on payment of a fee of one shilling. The Trustees were to meet every year on the second Tuesday in May, to lay acre rates for expenses and salary of officers. Persons convicted of destroying works were to be deemed guilty of felony.

BOUNDARY. WASHINGBOROUGH AND HEIGHINGTON FENS.—These Fens have an area of 1,800 acres, and are bounded on the north-east by the South Delph, on the south-west by the Car Dyke, and on the south-east by Branston Delph.

INCLOSURE ACT. 7 and 8 Geo. iv, c. 49, 1826. 10 Geo. iv, c. 49, 1828. In 1826 an Act was obtained for enclosing, embanking and draining the fens and low lands in the parish of Washingborough and the township of Heighington; an amending Act being obtained two years later.

The Commission, as appointed by the Act, consists of the Lord of the Manor, the Rector and two Members elected by proprietors of 30 acres, or tenants of 100 acres, in Washingborough, and two by those in Heighington. Their duties are to maintain the banks, drains and works. No new work can be undertaken without the special consent of the Proprietors. No maximum rate of taxation is fixed by the Act.

RATES AND EXPENDITURE. The average rate levied is about 1/11 per acre. According to the last Government Return of Taxation (1892-93) the rates produce £200 a year, rents, &c., £124, making a total income of £325. The cost of maintaining works is £266, of management, &c. £68; total £344. For the previous year the receipts and expenditure were rather less. There is no outstanding loan.

Local Taxation Returns, 1892-3.

PUMPING ENGINE. The engine for draining the fen is of 18 H.P., and situated about a mile below the Five-Mile House Station. It discharges into the South Delph.

BANKS. The Banks next the Witham are composed principally of peat, and are very leaky. During a flood in October, 1880, Heighington Bank was broken, and the fen flooded.

INCLOSURE ACT. 5 Geo. iii, c. 74, 1765. NOCTON, POTTERHANWORTH AND BRANSTON.—The common fen in the parish of Branston was enclosed under an Act obtained in 1765.

14 Geo. iii, 1774. In 1774 an Act was obtained for enclosing the waste land and fens in the parish of Potterhanworth, and giving power to erect banks, engines and sluices,

In 1789 an Act was obtained for embanking the enclosed fen land in the parishes of Nocton, Potterhanworth and Branston, containing 5,850 acres. This Act was subsequently amended.

29 Geo. iii, c. 32, 1789.
2 and 3 Will. iv, c. 96.

The preamble of the Act states that the fens and lowlands in these parishes " were frequently overflowed and annoyed with water, but if embanked and drained would be considerably improved, to the great advantage of all parties interested therein, and to the benefit of the public." John Hudson of Kenwick Thorpe, and John Parkinson of Asgarby, were appointed Commissioners for carrying out the works, and they were authorised to construct a bank from the lower bank of the Car Dyke, near the south-west corner of Nocton Fen, along the south-east side to the Witham, and then running parallel with the Witham, but at a distance of two furlongs from it, through the the fens of Nocton, Potterhanworth and Branston, and along the north-west of Branston Fen to the Car Dyke; the top of these banks was to be 6ft., and the base 40ft. for the side banks, and of those near the Witham 50ft. The Car Dyke was to be enlarged and the east bank raised. Delphs were to be cut on the outer sides of the banks near Branston and Washingborough, having 20ft. top, 10ft. bottom, and 5ft. in depth. The Commissioners were empowered to erect and maintain engines and other works necessary for the drainage. A stanch was to be put in the lower banks of the Car Dyke for the purpose of preserving the water issuing from the beck near Nocton Road for taking the same into the fens by means of a tunnel. The Commissioners were also authorised to put in tunnels, not exceeding 12in. in width and 7in. in depth, under the bank from the Witham. For paying for the works, power was given to raise £10,000, or by special consent of the Proprietors a further sum. To meet the charges, a tax of 50/- an acre was to be levied on the Owners of the land, and by special consent a further tax of 10/-.

INCLOSURE ACT, 1789.

When the works were completed, the duties of the Commissioners were to cease, and three Trustees were to be appointed to take charge of the works, and levy the rates, at a meeting of Proprietors of not less than 50 acres, to be held at the *Rein Deer* Inn, Lincoln, after notice given on the church doors. The Commissioners so selected were to remain in office till death or resignation. The annual taxes were not to exceed one shilling an acre, with sixpence additional by consent of the Owners. Persons convicted of maliciously or wilfully destroying the works were to be guilty of felony. The award is dated 11th January, 1793.

Under the powers of the Witham Act of 1812 the South Delph was cut through this fen, severing a portion, which is now called Branston Island. A bank was made on the sides of the south Delph with the material excavated from it. These banks were maintained by the Navigation Proprietors, and subsequently by the Great

BRANSTON ISLAND.
SOUTH DELPH BANKS.

Northern Railway. In 1858 the bank on the west side was repaired jointly by the Railway Company and the Branston Trustees, being puddled in the centre and raised from one to three feet.

In the spring of 1862 the bank of the South Delph gave way, causing a breach 156 feet long, and the fen was flooded. An action was brought against the Great Northern Railway Company, as Owners of the navigation, and a verdict obtained by the plaintiff. It is unncessary to refer further to this as the subject has already been dealt with in the Chapter on 'The Witham.'

PUMPING MACHINERY.

Up to about the year 1832, when the amending Act was obtained, giving the Commissioners further powers of taxation, a wind engine had been employed to work the scoop wheel for lifting the water off the fen. This being found inadequate it was determined that the wind engine should be replaced by a steam engine. The Witham Commissioners applied for an injunction to restrain the use of steam, on the ground that a greater quantity of water would be thrown into the river, and with greater velocity, to the injury of the banks. The application, however, was not granted.

The pumping engine is 40 H.P.; the wheel is 3ft. wide, with scoops 6ft. long. The area drained by the engine is 5,600 acres.

In March, 1889, a breach occurred in the bank of the river Witham, on the east side of Branston Island, and this part of the fen was flooded to a depth of from 4ft. to 5ft. The breach was repaired by the Great Northern Railway Company. An action was brought against them for the damage done, but they consented to a verdict before the case came to trial, and the amount of damage was settled by arbitration. The banks next the river are composed almost entirely of peat.

In 1883 a new engine was erected for the drainage of Branston Island, at a cost of about £600, by Messrs. Tuxford and Sons. This engine is of 16H.P., and drives a centrifugal pump, 20in. in diameter. The lift is 10ft. The area drained is about 230 acres.

The average rate laid has been 2s. an acre.

RATES AND EXPENDITURE.
Local Taxation Returns, 1892-3.

The income from taxation is about £420, and from rents and sundries £53; total £473. The cost of maintenance of works is about £360, management, &c., £114; total £474. In the previous year works cost £231 more, and the other items were about the same. There is not any outstanding loan.

DUNSTON AND METHERINGHAM FEN.—Contains about 3,400 acres.

INCLOSURE ACT.
29 Geo. iii, c. 69, 1789.

In 1789 an Act was obtained for draining and inclosing the inclosed commons, fens and ings in these parishes. Three Commissioners were appointed for carrying out the work; and it was directed that the private roads set out were to be repaired by the Owners of the enclosed lands; three acres were to be set apart for obtaining materials for the repairs of the roads; the herbage of the

Fig. 9.
Chap. 6.

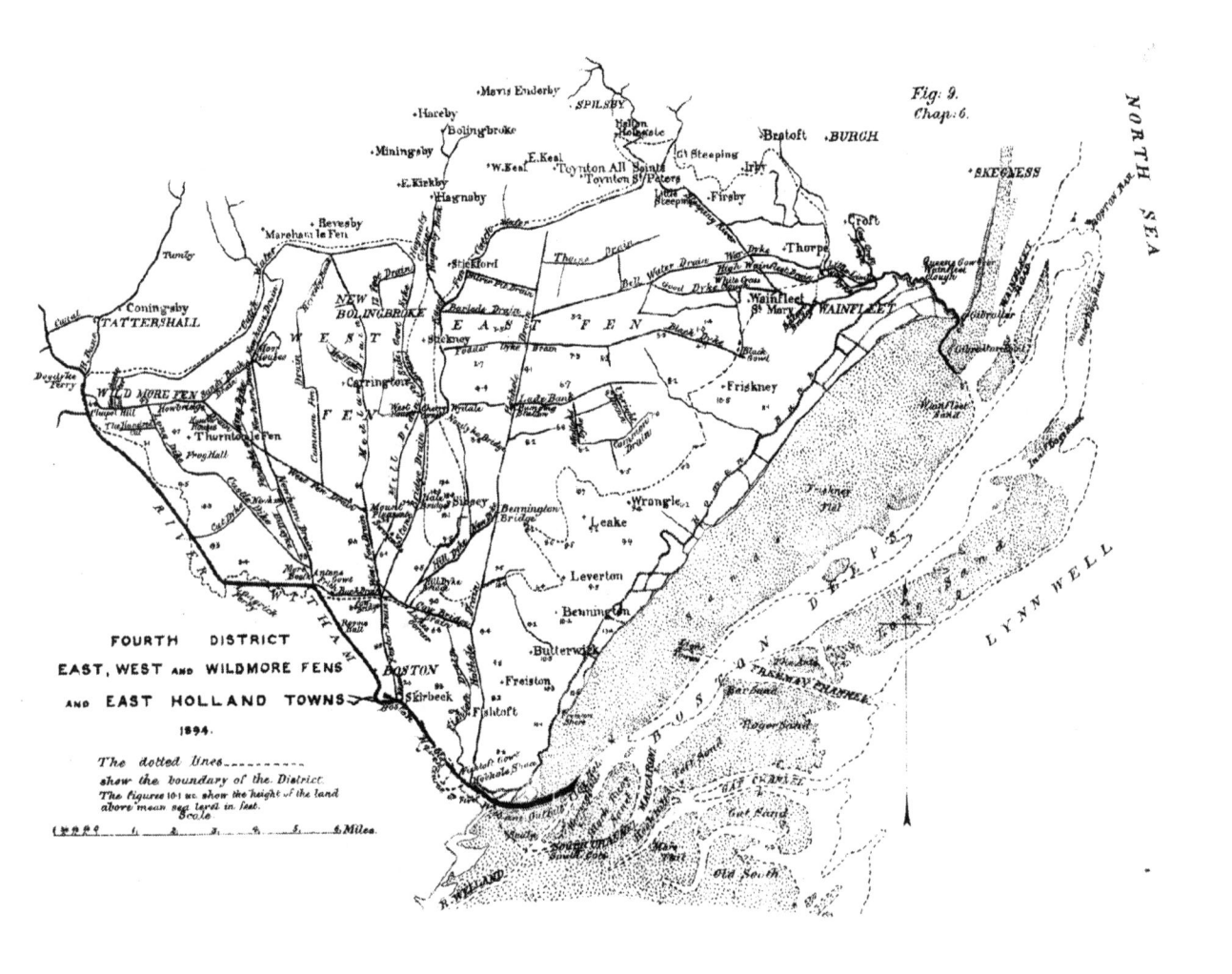

FOURTH DISTRICT
EAST, WEST AND WILDMORE FENS
AND EAST HOLLAND TOWNS
1894.

The dotted lines ---------
show the boundary of the District.
The figures 10·1 &c. show the height of the land
above mean sea level in feet.

Scale
|****| 1 | 2 | 3 | 4 | 5 | 6 Miles.

banks was to be let; and the officers of the Trust were given power to cleanse out ditches in case of the owners neglecting to do so. The Commissioners were empowered to borrow £7,000 for embanking. Three Trustees were to be chosen at the end of three years by the votes of Proprietors of 50 acres, for supporting the works. The Trustees were authorised to lay a rate of 1s. an acre, and a further shilling an acre may be raised by consent of the Owners; and 10s. more in case of accident.

The engine for draining this fen is situated about two miles from the Witham, by the side of Metheringham Delph, into which the water is discharged. It is of 20H.-P. and drives a scoop wheel. The highest lift is ten feet. The area drained by the engine is 3,400 acres. The average annual cost of maintenance, including coal and wages, is £350. *[DRAINAGE ENGINE.]*

The bank next the river is composed of peat and sand, which allows of a considerable amount of percolation of water in floods. *[BANKS.]*

The amount raised by taxation in 1892-3 was £285. Other sources produced £126, total £411. The maintenance of works cost £367, management, &c., £172, total £539. The items in the previous year were about the same. There is not any outstanding loan. *[RATES AND EXPENDITURE. Local Taxation Returns, 1892-3.]*

BLANKNEY, LINWOOD AND MARTIN.—Arthur Young, in his Survey of Lincolnshire, made in 1799, speaking of Blankney Fen, says, "Mr. Chaplin had 300 acres of fen by the side of the River Witham, which were never let for more than £10 a year. Now he could let it at 11/- or 12/- an acre, probably more. This has been effected by a moderate embankment and the erection of a windmill for throwing out the superfluous water. This drainage engine cost £1,000 erecting. The sails go seventy rounds, and it raises 60 tons of water every minute, when in full work. It raises water 4ft. Two men are necessary in winter, working night and day, at 10/6 each a week, with coals for a fire; add the expense of repairs, grease, and all together will amount to 2 per cent on the £1,000 first cost. It drains 1,900 acres. Two years ago the floods over-topped the banks, and it cleared the water out so quickly that not a single year was lost.' *[CONDITION OF THE FEN IN 1799. Young's Agriculture of Lincolnshire. WIND ENGINE.]*

A thousand acres of land in this district were let by auction at Horncastle, at the end of the last century before the Inclosure, for £10 an acre.

In 1787 an Act was passed for inclosing the lowlands and common fens in the Hamlet of Martin, and in the Parish of Blankney, and for draining these lands. *[INCLOSURE ACT. 27 Geo. iii, c. 66. 1787.]*

In 1832 a second Act was obtained for more effectually draining the lands in Blankney Fen, Blankney Dales, Linwood Fen, Linwood Dales and Martin Fen. *[2 and 3 Will. iv, c. 94, 1832.]*

The district is under the charge of three Commissioners elected by the Proprietors, whose duties are to maintain the works, consisting of the Timberland Delph, North Bank, Metheringham Delph, South Bank, Engine Drains, and the Engine.

DRAINAGE ENGINE.

The engine is situated on Martin Delph, about half-a-mile from the Witham, and is of 30H.P.

RATES AND EXPENDITURE.
Local Taxation Returns, 1892-3.

There is no limit to the amount of taxation. The rate averages about 2s. an acre. The amount raised by taxation (1892-3) was £393, special rates paid by owners £386, from other sources £143; total £921. The expenses of maintaining the works £435, interest on loan and re-payment of capital, £395, management, &c., £156, total; £984. The amount of loan then outstanding was £2,100, which is being gradually paid off at the rate of £300 a year.

INCLOSURE ACTS.
25 Geo. iii, c: 14. 1785.
2 and 3 Vict, c, 10, 1839.

TIMBERLAND AND TIMBERLAND THORPE FENS.—The Act for Inclosure of these fens was obtained in 1785, and a further Act for the more effectual drainage of the fen and dales of Timberland and Timberland Thorpe was obtained in 1839. The district is stated in the Act to contain 2,500 acres, being bounded by Martin Fen on the north, by the Car Dyke on the West, Walcot Fen on the south, and the Dales Head Dyke on the east. The Commissioners appointed to carry out the embanking and draining were John Hudson of Kenwick Thorpe, and John Dyson of Bawtry. They were authorised to enclose the low lands with a bank commencing at the north-east corner of the Walcot and Billinghay Bank, continuing along the east side of the Dales Head Dyke, and thence along the north side of the fen to the Car Dyke. The bank was to be 50ft. broad at the base, 6ft. at the top and 10ft. high. Power was given to construct the necessary drains, engines, bridges, sluices and other works. The Commissioners were authorised to let the herbage on the banks publicly, for periods not exceeding three years; the officers to have power to cleanse out all ditches, in default of the owners doing so when requested. The award when made was to be enrolled with the Clerk of the Peace, and to be deposited in a chest kept in the parish church at Timberland. A sum not exceeding £4,000 was to be borrowed for carrying out the works on the security of the rates. Special rates were authorised to be levied for paying interest, and for providing for accidents or contingencies. Persons destroying works were to be deemed guilty of felony.

When the work was completed three Trustees were to be chosen at a meeting held in the vestry of the church, on a Friday, after three weeks notice placed on the church doors, every Owner of ten acres of land or more to have a vote. Such Trustees to remain in office for three years, and to have charge of all the works, and power to levy taxes. The taxes were to be laid annually at a meeting to be held on the first Friday in April, at the *Blacksmith's Arms*, or other convenient house. The tax is not to exceed eighteenpence an acre, unless a larger tax, not exceeding two shillings, be consented to by the Owners. The Trustees have power to appoint and pay a Collector, Clerk, and other Officers.

This Act contemplated the raising of the water by wind mills, as there is a clause forbidding the erection of any buildings near the engines. The wind engine was superseded in 1839 by a 30 N.H.P. low pressure beam engine, working a scoop wheel 26ft. 6in. in diameter. This was replaced in 1881 by a 50 N.H.P. high pressure, condensing beam engine, working a centrifugal pump, having a vertical fan placed under water, 4ft. in diameter, erected by Messrs. Tuxford and Sons. The discharge pipe was 14in. in diameter. The engine has a 36in. cylinder, with 6ft. stroke, and is capable of working up to 150 I.H.P. The pump makes about 10 revolutions to one of the engine. The fly wheel is 24ft. in diameter and weighs 13 tons. The chimney is 106ft. high. The maximum lift of the water, previous to the improvement at the Grand Sluice and the Outfall was 14ft. 10in. and the average lift 11ft. 6in. ; recently the average has been reduced to 8ft. 6in. The outlet sill is about 6ft. below the level of the lowest land. The engine drains about 2,850 acres under ordinary circumstances, but in high floods the drainage extends over about 7,000 acres. The pump is calculated to lift 120 tons of water 11ft. high per minute, when running at 180 revolutions.

<small>PUMPING MACHINERY.</small>

The banks are composed of a mixture of peat and clay, and permit of a considerable amount of leakage in floods.

<small>BANKS.</small>

The average annual cost of working the engine and keeping the drains clean, &c., taking the year 1881-3, was

<small>RATES AND EXPENDITURE.</small>

	£
For coal	372
For wages, cleansing drains, and all other expenses...	262
Interest on loan	170
	£804

The annual rate laid has averaged about 4s. 6d. an acre. The amount raised by rates in 1893 was £597 and from other sources £65. For the year 1892-3, the expenses amounted to £684. The amount of the outstanding loan at that date was £1,571, which is being paid off by annual instalments of £253.

BILLINGHAY SOUTH DISTRICT.—The Act for enclosing and draining this fen was obtained in 1777. The area of the fen was set out in the Act as 4,526 acres. It is bounded by Timberland Fen on the north west; the Car Dyke and North Kyme Fen on the west; Drury Dyke and Kyme Eau on the south and the Witham and Dales Head Dyke on the east. The Commissioners for enclosing were Daniel Douglas of Falkingham, William Jepson of Lincoln, and John Hudson of Louth. They were directed to set out public roads 40ft. wide, which were to be deemed highways.

<small>INCLOSURE ACT. 17 Geo. iii, c. 70, 1777.</small>

Six acres of land were to be allotted for getting materials for making and repairing the roads. The herbage on the roads and on the land set apart for the roads was directed to be let by the Surveyor of Highways. The Commissioners were directed to embank the fen on the side next to Timberland Fen, North Kyme Fen and the Dales Head Dyke. They were empowered to divert the drain which conveyed the water from 'Tomkins' Engine,' belonging to Earl Fitzwilliam, across Billinghay Dales to the Twenty-Foot Drain and to carry it to Drury Dyke by a new drain having 6ft. bottom and 12ft. top, placing stop doors at the end. Power was given to the Officers of the Trust to scour out the dykes if the owners should neglect to do so. The Award was to be enrolled and lodged in the chest at the parish church at Billinghay. The works were to be paid for by an equal acre tax not exceeding forty shillings an acre, or ten shillings additional by consent. Power was also given to borrow £6,000 to enable the works to be carried on pending the allotting of the land. Persons found destroying works wilfully were to be deemed guilty of felony.

After the Commissioners had completed the works and made their award, three Trustees were to be appointed for maintaining the works and collecting the rates, such Trustees to continue in office for three years. The Trustees were to be elected every three years, at the vestry of the parish church, on Friday, after three weeks' notice given in the parish church, every owner of 50 acres having a vote. The Trustees were to meet on the first Tuesday in April in every year at the *Cross Keys*, Billinghay, or at some other public house in the parish, to lay a rate not exceeding one shilling an acre, or, by consent of the Owners, eighteen pence. The Trustees were authorised to appoint a Collector, a Clerk and an Officer for the management of the engine, banks and drains.

and 4 Vict, c. 90, 1840.

In 1840 a second Act was obtained for the more effectual drainage of Billinghay Fen, Billinghay Dales and Walcot Fen, Walcot Dales and North Kyme East Fen and Ings.

BILLINGHAY DALES PUMPING MACHINERY.

After the enclosure, Billinghay Dales was drained by a wind engine. This was replaced in 1841 by a 30 H.P. beam engine erected at Chapel Hill. The scoop wheel is 28ft. in diameter and 2ft. 3in. wide. The engine has a 2ft. 4in. cylinder and 6ft. 6in. stroke, steam being supplied at a boiler pressure of 25 lbs. The highest lift is 11ft. The cost of the engine and wheel was £3,600. The area drained by the engine is about 4,500 acres.

RATES AND EXPENDITURE.

According to the Government Taxation Return for 1892-3, the amount produced by taxation was £519 and from other sources £75, making a total of £597. Maintenance of works cost £205, interest and repayment of loan £196, management £91, total £488.

The amount of loan then outstanding was £843 which was being paid off at the rate of £150 a year. The rate varies from 2/6 to 4/- in the £.

BILLINGHAY NORTH FEN AND WALCOT DALES, containing 3,150 acres, are drained by a 25 N.H.P. engine erected in 1864, driving a scoop wheel 31ft. in diameter and 2ft. wide, the bottom of the wheel being 6ft. below the surface of the ground. The highest lift is 13ft. and the average, previous to the outfall improvement, was 9ft. The chimney is 90ft high. The cost of the engine and wheel was about £2,500.

The average expenses for the three years, 1881-3, were as follows;—

	£	s.	d.
Coal	270	0	0
Wages, cleansing drain and all other expenses	246	0	0
Interest	350	0	0
	£866	0	0

In January, 1877, during a high flood in the Witham, the bank near to the Skirth gave way and inundated 2,390 acres of land. The loss was estimated at £20,000.

The rate laid annually on Billinghay Fen, Walcot Fen, and Walcot Dales, amounts to about 4/6 an acre. From the Government Taxation Return for 1892-3, the rate is given as producing £475, other receipts £166; total £641. The expenses of maintenance were £220, interest and instalment of loan repaid £193, management £85, other charges £39; total £537. The amount of loan outstanding was then £844, which was being paid off at the rate of £148 a year.

THE SECOND DISTRICT.—This district extends on the south of the river Witham, from Kyme Eau to Boston, and contains 19,101 acres. It returns six Commissioners to the Witham Drainage Board. It pays taxes amounting to 1/- per acre to the Witham Trust, in return for the benefit received from the embanking and improvement of the river. This district, known as Holland Fen, forms part of the Black Sluice level, it drains into the South Forty Foot, and will therefore be described more fully in Chapter VII.

THE THIRD DISTRICT.—This district lies on the north side of the River Witham, and comprises the low lands bordering on the river, from near Lincoln to the Bane, and contains 4,621 acres. It is described in the Act of 1762 as comprising the low lands in Monks, Greetwell, Willingham, Fiskerton, Barlings, Stainfield, Bardney, Southrey, Tupholm, Bucknall, Horsington, Stixwould, Swinesike, Woodhall, Thornton, Kirkstead, Tattershall Thorpe, and Tattershall, and as being bounded as follows, *viz.*, by the high lands of the several places named on the north, the River Witham on the south, the River Bane on the east, and Lincoln on the west. Each of the parishes or places in the district elects one Commissioner, and the District Commissioners elect five General Commissioners. The qualification and means of election in each case are the same as in the First District.

DRAINAGE LEVELS. The district is divided into the following Drainage Levels, each of which has obtained separate Acts of Parliament; Greetwell; Stainfield, Barlings and Fiskerton; Bardney, Southrey and Stixwould; and Tattershall.

25 Vict. c. 149, 1861. GREETWELL DRAINAGE DISTRICT.—The Act constituting this District was obtained in 1861. It includes the low lands or fens in Cherry Willingham, Barlings and Fiskerton.

COMMISSIONERS. The district is managed by five Commissioners, each of whom to be qualified must be Owner, either in his own right or in that of his wife, of not less that 20 acres of land rated for the purposes of the Act; or be Occupier of 40 acres so rated.

An annual meeting is directed by the Act to be held at the *Saracen's Head*, Lincoln, or other convenient place in the city, on the 5th of July, except when this occurs on Sunday, and then on the following day.

The Commissioners are elected for three years, but are eligible for re-election, and continue in office until their successors are appointed. Every Owner of land has one vote in the election of Commissioners for every 20 acres of land, and each Occupier one vote for every 40 acres.

WORKS. The Commissioners may purchase land in the District, not exceeding 20 acres, and execute and maintain works, including pumping engines and machinery. They have to pay to the Great Northern Railway Company £5 a year for the extra expense incurred in maintaining the bank of the Witham, due to the larger volume of water which the pumping operations caused to flow into the river. The maintenance of the North Delph, extending from near Lincoln to Horsley Deeps, a distance of 9 miles, was transferred from the Company to the Commissioners.

DITCHES. The Act provides that all Owners and Occupiers of land in the district shall maintain and scour out the ditches adjoining or belonging to their land; or if they neglect to do so, the work is to be done by the Commissioners at the expense of the owners or occupiers in default. The Commissioners have power to go over any land in the district to destroy moles or other vermin.

TAXATION LEVELS. As soon as the drainage works were completed, the Act directed that a Valuer should be appointed to estimate the probable improvement in annual value from the works executed, and, if he thought it desirable, to divide the District into Levels, and the rates levied were to bear such proportion to one another as the Valuer should determine.

RATES. The maximum rate which the Commissioners may lay must not exceed 7/- an acre. There is a penalty of ten per cent on the amount of the rate if it be not paid at the proper time. The Commissioners have power to borrow £10,000.

The land was formerly drained by a wind engine. In 1862 a pumping station was erected at the junction of the old river with the South Delph, near Grubb Hill, consisting of a scoop wheel 31ft. in diameter and 2ft. 4in. wide, the scoop having a depth of 5ft. This wheel is driven by a horizontal engine of 30 H.P., having a 22in. cylinder with 3ft. 6in. stroke, the steam being supplied from the boiler at a pressure of 60lbs. The engine makes 30 revolutions a minute, and the wheel 6⅓ revolutions. The lift in times of flood is 12ft. and averages 9½ft. The coal consumption is about 150 tons a year. <small>PUMPING MACHINERY.</small>

The cost of erecting the wheel and engine was £949.

In 1893 an auxiliary plant was put down by Messrs. Robey & Co., consisting of two 21in. centrifugal pumps driven by a horizontal engine of 50 E.H.P., and capable of delivering 90 tons a minute in floods, or 40 tons from a level about 3ft. lower than that reached by the scoop wheel. The cost of this was £644.

The area of land drained is about 1,500 acres, and there is also a great deal of high land water which finds its way into the district drains, there being no catchwater drain. There is also a great deal of soakage through the banks of the Witham.

The rates formerly were 7/- an acre for general purposes, and 5/- for repayment of money borrowed and interest. This is terminable in 1902. The rates now are 5/- and 3/6 respectively. <small>RATES AND EXPENDITURE.</small>

The rate produces £315, and the expenses of maintenance of works £141 9s. 6d., engine and scoop wheel £58 19s. 5d., management £80; total £280 12s.

There is also an engine at Stainfield of 16 H.P. which is situated near Barlings' Lock, and pumps into the old river near Short's Ferry. This engine belongs to and is maintained by the Proprietors of the land.

BARDNEY DISTRICT.—In 1843 an Act was obtained for draining and embanking the low fen land lying in the parishes of Bardney, Southrey, Tupholme, Bucknall, Horsington, Stixwould, Edlington and Thimbleby, which, it was stated in the preamble of the Act, had been for many years past liable to inundation and thereby injured and rendered to a great degree unprofitable to the Owners and Occupiers. <small>DRAINAGE ACT. 6 and 7 Vict., c 76, 1843.</small>

The area of land in the different parishes is thus set out in the Act.

	Acres.
Bardney	640
Southrey	290

		Acres.
Tupholme	... ...	210
Bucknall	... ...	460
Horsington	... ...	320
Stixwould	... ...	600
Edlington	... ...	70
Thimbleby	... ...	130
		2,720

The Commissioners for draining the land and afterwards maintaining the works were to consist of the Lords and Ladies of the several manors of Bardney, Tupholme and Stixwould, or their agents appointed in writing. Each Commissioner before acting has to make a declaration in the form given in the Act, subject to a penalty of £50 for acting without having done so. It is directed that an annual meeting shall be held, at Lincoln, on the first Tuesday in July,—altered by the Act of 1856 to June—between the hours of 10 and 12 at noon. Two Commissioners form a quorum. The Chairman has a casting vote at all meetings. No order given is to be revoked, except at a special meeting, of which 14 days' notice must be given, stating the business to be done. John Wignall Leather of Leeds, was appointed, by the Act, the Engineer to carry out the works authorized by the Act. A Treasurer, Clerk, and Collector of Taxes were to be appointed, the two former offices being separate. Any officer taking any fee or reward on account of any thing done by virtue of his office, or in relation to the functions of the Commissioners, other than the remuneration allowed by the Commissioners, is liable to a penalty of £50. All owners of land subject to taxation are entitled to attend the annual meeting, when a statement of accounts, made up to the previous April is to be laid before them, and such information and explanation respecting the proceedings of the Commissioners in the execution of the Act as shall be required. The Statement of Account after being certified and signed, is to remain with the Clerk, and be open to inspection, and a copy forwarded to the Clerk of the Peace for the parts of Lindsey, and thereafter be open to inspection on payment of one shilling. The Commissioners were authorised to borrow £25,000, and to lay the taxes necessary to pay the interest on the same and for maintaining the works; also to make bye-laws for regulating the carrying out of their business and for the government of their officers.

The works, which by the Act the Commissioners were authorised to carry out, were the construction of one or more mills or engines, with all proper steam apparatus, machinery, houses and erections; to enlarge, or divert the existing sluices, banks, bridges or drains, and make such new works as may be necessary, and to support and maintain the same, and to have full power and control over them.

It was directed that the occupiers of lands should maintain all droveways and division dykes and tunnels adjoining their lands, and put down, when required, new tunnels under their gateways; subject to a penalty of one shilling for every rod neglected to be roaded, cleansed or repaired, after 21 days' notice given in writing; and be liable to have the work done by the Commissioners at the expense of the defaulter. Any person interfering with the tunnels and sluices next the river or outfalls, except the authorised officer, is liable to a penalty of £10.

In the event of large floods, or any accident happening to the sea doors of the River Witham, or the bursting of any of the banks of the river or tributary streams under the control of the General Commissioners, after notice in writing served on the officer in charge, the engine is to cease working for a period not exceeding 72 hours, or for a longer period by order of a Committee consisting of two General Commissioners and one Commissioner acting under this Act, subject to a penalty of £20 if the officer continue working the engine after notice given. It was also provided that a gauge should be fixed near where the engine throws the water into the Witham, and that on it should be marked the height of the water in the river at which the engine should cease working. The height was fixed by Mr. Cubitt, by an award dated 28th June, 1844, at 14ft. 6in.

The taxes levied under the Act are to be paid by the Occupiers and deducted from their rents. In case of default of payment after notice given, the occupier is liable to a penalty of 3/4 in the £, and to have the same recovered by distress. The herbage on the banks and forelands may be let for 3 years to the best bidder. The Commissioners are authorised to destroy moles and other vermin found about the lands, and to cut thistles and weeds on the banks, droves, or waste lands. Persons are subject to a penalty of £20 for injuring the works; of £50 for placing tunnels under any of the banks; of £10 for placing nets, grigs or other instrument for catching fish or for other purposes across the drains, or in any way obstructing the flow of the water. It is also forbidden to make any ditch above 2ft. in width or depth, within 40ft. from the centre of any of the banks; or to plant any tree, or place any stack, or erect any building within 300 yards from any mill or engine used for the drainage; or to make any watering place for cattle in the drains.

In 1856 an amended Act was obtained which related chiefly to the borrowing powers, it being enacted that these should not remain in force longer than 25 years after the passing of the Act, within which period money raised on loan was to be repaid. Power was also given to receive money on terminable annuities for a period not exceeding 15 years. By the previous Act the amount of rate was unlimited, but by this Act the rate to defray the working

19 Vict., 1856.

expenses of the drainage and embankment is not in any one year to exceed the amount of 10/- an acre.

RATES AND EXPENDITURE.
The rates levied have varied from 5/- to 10/- an acre. In recent years the lower sum has been found sufficient.

A rate of 5/- produces £652. The payments for the year ending April, 1893, were as follows: Labour, &c., on drains and banks and sluices £319, engine driver £63, coal £235, repairs to engine £22, management £125; total £764. There is no outstanding loan.

BREACH OF BANK.
In January, 1869, during a very high flood in the Witham, the bank of this district broke and inundated 1,500 acres of land, 5ft. deep. In February, 1883, there was again a breach in the bank at Southrey.

DRAINAGE ENGINE.
The drainage engine was erected in 1846, at cost of £3,545. It is a low pressure condensing beam engine of 30 N.H.P., having a 32in. cylinder and 6ft. stroke. The water is lifted by a scoop wheel 28ft. in diameter, 2ft. 4in. wide, having 40 scoops, 5ft. 6in. long, making 6 revolutions a minute to 18 of the engine. The average lift of the water is 4ft. The boiler consumes about $3\frac{1}{2}$ tons of coal in 24 hours, the average annual consumption being about 200 tons. The number of acres of low land paying drainage rates is 2,610, but the quantity drained is about double this, as a large area of high land outside the district drains down to the engine.

KIRKSTEAD.—About 700 acres of land in this parish are drained by steam-power. The engine, when not used for driving the scoop wheel, is employed in driving the machinery of a flour mill, which is placed between the engine and the wheel.

DRAINAGE ACT. 36 Geo. iii, 1796.
TATTERSHALL.—This district was inclosed and drained under the power of an Act passed in 1796, in which the land reclaimed is described as marsh, meadow and low grounds in Tattershall and Tattershall Thorpe, abutting on the river Witham, and as being capable of improvement by embanking and draining.

The Award is dated 9th November, 1798.

John Hudson of Ashby Thorpe, George Bourne of Hough and Samuel Turner of Busslingthorpe, were appointed Commissioners, and were empowered to maintain, heighten and improve any existing banks and drains, or make and maintain new ones, and any culverts, bridges, engines, &c., and to set out roads, 40ft. wide. Gotes were not to be put across the roads, nor any trees to be planted within 50 yards. Four acres were to be allotted for the repair of the roads. The Award after enrolment was to be kept by some person appointed by the Lord of the Manor of Tattershall, and be open to inspection by any person interested, on payment of one shilling, and copies to be supplied at the rate of twopence for every 72 words. The Commissioners were to be allowed £2 2s. per day for their services, including expenses.

In case of any of the Commissioners dying, or refusing to act, the Lord of the Manor had power to appoint a successor to one of the Commissioners, the majority of the Landowners to one, and the Rector of the parish to one; or, failing such appointment by them, the surviving Commissioners were given power to appoint to the vacancy. Part of the moor, being of a 'lingy,' and very bad quality, and not worth the expense of dividing and inclosing, was to remain a common pasture, and the Commissioners were to specify the number of beasts, horses, sheep, &c., each person should put on, and at what seasons of the year.

The low land was formerly drained by a wind engine and scoop wheel. The wind engine has been replaced by a steam engine, situated between Kirkstead and Tattershall. It was erected in 1855 and raises the water from 2,000 to 3,000 acres, besides some high land water. It is a low pressure beam engine. The scoop wheel is 24ft. in diameter, 1ft. 3½in. wide, and has 36 floats. The estimated weight of the wheel, shaft and gearing is 7 tons. DRAINAGE ENGINE.

There is no limit to the amount of the rate which can be laid. The annual average is about 4s. an acre.

The amount given in the Government Taxation Returns, as raised by rate in 1892-3 is £129, cost of maintenance of works £73, and of management £50; total £123. There is no outstanding loan. RATES AND EXPENDITURE.

FOURTH DISTRICT. Under the Act of 1762, the Fourth District is described as comprising the low lands in Coningsby, Mareham, Hundlehouse, Revesby, Middleham, Moorhouse, Hermitage, Newholme, Westhouse, Langrike, Langworth, Swinecote, Hagnaby, Stickney, Wildmore Fen and the West Fen; and as bounded by the old River Witham and Tattershall Bane on the west; by the high grounds of Coningsby, the grounds of Tumby, the high grounds of Mareham and Revesby, the grounds of East Kirkby, and the high grounds of Hagnaby on the north; by the high grounds of Stickney and grounds of Sibsey on the east; by grounds in the parish of Skirbeck and Boston East, and the site of the ancient River Witham on the south. Each parish or place named was entitled to elect a District Commissioner, and these to elect eight Representatives on the Witham General Trust. The mode of election and the qualification were the same as for the First District. The District Commissioners were to be elected on the first Tuesday in April, every third year, and to meet at the *White Hart* in Spilsby, to elect the General Commissioners, on the third Tuesday in April, every third year. The place of meeting was altered, by the Act of 1887, to the *Witham Office*, Boston. DESCRIPTION OF THE DISTRICT. 2 Geo. iii, c. 32, 1762.

Fig 9.

ELECTION OF COMMISSIONERS.

50 and 51 Vict., c. 104, 1887.

The East Fen and the low lands in Wrangle were added to the district by the Act of 1801. In 1818 the low lands in Steeping, Thorpe, Irby, Firsby, Bratoft, Croft and Wainfleet, known as ADDITION OF THE EAST FEN AND 5000 ACRES. 41 Geo. iii, c. 134 1801.

58 Geo. iii, 1818. 'the 5,000 Acres,' were added. The number of Commissioners remains the same as originally fixed.

BOUNDARIES.
Fig. 9.
The northern boundary of the district extends in an eastward direction from Dogdyke Ferry on the River Witham, along the Catchwater Drain, past Revesby, to Hagnaby Corner, where the West Fen is divided from the East Fen by a narrow strip of high land, about half a mile wide and seven miles long, in which are situated the villages of Stickford, Stickney and Sibsey. Passing round this high land, the boundary continues along the Eastern Catchwater, past Toynton and Halton Fen, to Halton Holgate, and along the edge of the higher ground, past Great Steeping, Firsby and Bratoft. The eastern boundary extends past Croft and the west side of Wainfleet, Friskney, Wrangle Low Grounds and Leake village, including Leake Common Side, and thence going in an easterly direction, nearly up to Leverton village. On the south the line runs westerly past the Ings Bridge, over Hobhole Drain to Hilldyke, and along the Cowbridge and Frith Bank Drains to Anton's Gowt on the Witham and thence to Langrick Ferry. The west boundary runs in an irregular line on the east of the Witham, up to Dogdyke Ferry.

AREA.
Min. Pro. Inst. C.E., 1865.
The area of this District is given in a report of the Committee on the Fourth District, made in July, 1861, as 57,200 acres. In Mr. Welsh's paper on the Lade Bank engines, the total watershed is given as 82,226 acres, of which 62,226 acres are taxable and 35,000 acres are drained by the pumping engines at Lade Bank.

The total area is divided as follows:

		Acres.	
Wildmoor Fen, high land	... ...	2,947	
low land	... ...	7,714	
			10,661
West Fen, high land	... ...	5,473	
low land	... ...	11,451	
			16,924
East Fen	...	29,833	
Five Thousand Acres	...	5,000	
			62,418

VILLAGES.
The only villages situated within the boundary line are those of Little Steeping, Firsby and Thorpe, and these are in the area known as 'the 5,000 Acres,' which did not form part of the district till 1818. With the exception of this newly added part of the district nearly the whole of the land was extra-parochial and consisted of a vast common, over which the inhabitants of the following surround-

COMMON RIGHTS.
ing parishes had rights of pasturage, &c., *viz.*, on the East and West Fens in the Soke of Bolingbroke:—Sibsey, Stickney, Stickford, West Keal, East Keal, High and Low Toynton, Halton, Steeping, Thorpe, Spilsby, Hundleby, Raithby, Enderby, Lusby, Hareby, Asgarby, Miningsby, East Kirkby, Revesby, Hagnaby and Bolingbroke; the Holland Towns, Boston, Skirbeck,

Fishtoft, Freiston, Butterwick, Benington, Leverton and Leake; on Wildmore Fen, Haltham, Roughton, Thimbleby, Horncastle, Ashby, Low Toynton, High Toynton, Mareham-on-the Hill, Wood-Enderby, Moorby, Wilksby, Mareham-le-Fen, Coningsby, Scrivelsby-cum-Dalderby, Tumby, Revesby, Kirkstead, Fishtoft and Frith Bank.

CONDITION OF THE FENS BEFORE RECLAMATION.

In summer these fens provided valuable pasturage for the stock of the farmers who had rights of common in them. In winter, being lower than all the surrounding ground, and no means of drainage being provided, they became covered with water over the greater part.

There were a few scattered inhabitants who lived in huts built on the patches of high ground, and who gained a living by attending to the cattle sent on in the summer; by rearing geese; and by fishing and fowling, the fens affording vast supplies of both fish and wild fowl.

ANCIENT DRAINAGE.

From an old parchment plan in the library of Revesby Abbey, not dated, but probably made during the early part of the 17th century, it appears that previous to the construction of the Adventurers' drains, the drainage of these fens was effected by the Goodyke Drain, which received Toynton Beck and Silver Pit Drain, on the north; by the Old South Lode and Valentine's Drain on the south; all of which emptied into Wainfleet Haven. Hilldyke drain received the water from Hagnaby Beck and from the Sibsey river, (now Stone Bridge Drain), also from the Barlode Drain and from the Old Mill Drain, which had the same course as the present Mill Drain. It emptied into the Witham at New Gote, about a mile above Boston. The West and Wildmore Fens were drained by the Langworth, now part of the West Fen Catchwater, which joined the Witham at Dogdyke Ferry; by the Langdyke Drain, which also emptied into the Witham through Armtree Gote, about $2\frac{1}{2}$ miles below Dogdyke; by Nunham drain and Old Drain, which emptied at Anton's Gowt.

STEEPING RIVER.

Steeping River is shown as running about $1\frac{1}{4}$ miles north of Wainfleet, and to have entered the Wash by a separate outfall from Wainfleet Haven. From Firsby Clough to White Cross Bridge this river was called 'Fendyke' and 'Lusdyke'; thence to the sea, (8 miles), 'the Haven.'

Steeping River rises amongst the Hills at Salmonby, and brings the water from Aswarby, Harrington and Partney. Before the embankment of the river and the drainage of the fens, seven-eights of the water is said to have gone on to the low lands in Steeping, Firsby, Thorpe and Croft, and thence into the East Fen. These low lands were constantly flooded.

The system of drainage as above described remained in operation till the middle of the 17th century.

COMMISSIONS OF SEWERS. 1272

The earliest known records respecting the drainage of these fens are found in the proceedings in a suit in the reign of Edward I, concerning the ditches and drains in the neighbourhood of Wainfleet, when the Jurors found that the custom was such that these should be cleansed every year, and that every inhabitant of the towns draining ought to be taxed and assessed according to the quantity of his land.

Dugdale. 1394.

From an Inquisition, taken at Bolingbroke in the reign of Richard II, it appears that the Goodike Sewer, which extended through the East Fen into the Eas end, ought then to be sixteen feet in breadth, betwixt the banks, and in depth eight feet, but that it was stopped by a weir, and was not four feet deep. The South Lode Sewer, extending from the Eas end, ought to be sixteen feet broad, and eight feet deep. Both these sewers were to be cleaned out by the Farmers of the fishing. The Sewer called the Lyme, beginning at Steeping Mill and extending to the Clow betwixt Steeping and Thorpe, was to be repaired by the township of Thorpe; and thence to the Eas end, (called the Lusdyke,) the banks to be repaired by the towns of All Hallows and St. Mary's, so that the water running into the sewers might no way enter the fen. The sewers, from the Clows of Thorpe to the Eas End, "ought to be sixteen feet broad and eight feet deep, being obstructed by a wear which the farmers of the fishing had set up; and Henry, Earl of Northumberland, of right ought to repair the same sewer from the Clowes to Southdyke-hirne, by reason that he had the fishing there, as belonging to his manor at Thorpe"; and "the Lords of Bullingbroke and Dalby, or their farmers, ought to cleanse the said sewer from Southdyke-hirne unto the Eas end, because they had the fishing there." A fourth sewer called Theviscrick, beginning in the mosses of Friskney and extending to the Eas end, where the four streams meet, was also obstructed by a weir for fishing, and ought to be repaired by the town of Friskney; and the sewer called Eas end should be 40ft. wide by 14ft. deep to the sea, and be repaired by the Soke of Bolingbroke. It was also ordered "that a new pair of flood gates should be made at the damm, twelve feet wide, according to the direction of skilful persons; and that all the towns within the Wapentake of Bolingbroke and Wrangle, Leake, Leverton, Benington, Butterwick, Freston and Tofte ought, of right, to repair, maintain, open and shut those flood gates on proper times, on their own costs and charges for ever, excepting in timber, iron work and also wages of carpenters." To prevent further disputes as to the repair and management of these flood gates, a certain sum was to be levied yearly, and placed in the hands of two men, chosen by the towns in Bolingbroke, and two by those in Skirbeck, who were to meet at Wainfleet twice a year, to oversee the flood gates and sewers.

Shortly afterwards a presentment was made in a Court of King's Bench held at Lincoln, to the effect that the marshes in the East and West Fens, and land in Leake, Wrangle, Friskney and Wainfleet were drowned by a great inundation through defects in this flood gate at Wainfleet " which also was too narrow, so that the water passing that way could not get to sea ; and that the town of Wainfleet ought to repair the flood gates, as anciently they had wont to do." It was also decreed that another flood gate was to be added near the old one, 18ft. wide, and that this should be paid for by the same places as in the former order. Subsequently a further presentment was made that the channels of Lusdyke and the Ea unto Normandeepe (Boston Deeps) should be repaired by the farmers of the fishing.

In the reign of Henry IV, and subsequently, Commissioners were appointed to view and repair the banks and sewers between Boston and Friskney, and "in respect of the great and instant necessity, were directed to take as many diggers and labourers upon competent wages, to be employed as they should think requisite." In the reign of Edward IV, a Commission of Sewers, held at Wrangle, ordained that the inhabitants of the Soke of Bolingbroke and the Lord of Dalby, and the King's farmer of fishing at Wainfleet and all others draining thereby should scour and dyke the Haven of Wainfleet from the the Ea's End unto the sea, in breadth 22ft. top and 13ft. bottom, and 3ft. deep ; and that a sufficient gote or clow should be set up at the outer end of the Haven, for stopping the salt water from the north part thereof; and also that an old gote and drain, called Symond's Gote, extending in length from the deeps of the East Fen unto the Fen Bank, and from there to the sea, should be scoured out, and also that one gote should be made at Fen Bank, and the other at the out end of the Ea.

At a Court held at Sibsey Hall, in 1430, it was presented that the Abbot of Kirkstead had neglected to repair the banks of the Witham near the Grange of Langwarthe, so that the river water flowed into the West Fen. At a King's Court, held at Bolingbroke in 1483, the inhabitants of Boston and Skirbeck were fined a mark for neglecting to repair New Gote Sewer in Sibsey.

In Queen Elizabeth's reign an order was made as to the cleaning out of Goodyke, which is described as leading from the Ea's End to the fen, and as to a new gote to be set in Wainfleet Haven within ' ten falls ' of Thorpe and Wainfleet Sea Gote, and a bank to be made on the south side of the Haven, from the New Gote, and it was, at the same time, decreed that the inhabitants of the seven towns of Holland should be at the charge of the same.

A new gote, likewise, was to be set at the Fendyke Bank to take in fresh water, and another gote, called Dale's Gote, and a new creek, 30ft. wide, were to be made from the New Gote unto the Old Gote.

<small>1571.</small>

In 1571 an order was made that the Fendyke Bank—extending from Wainfleet St. Mary to Deacon's Gap, near Friskney, from thence to the Fen Clough, and from thence to Strange-place, a distance of three miles—should, together with Simon Gote, be repaired by the Commoners, because 'they got reeds and fish from the fens and had bite for their cattle.'

<small>ATTEMPT TO DRAIN THE FENS. 1532.
Oldfield's *Wainfleet*.</small>

From records of the Duchy of Lancaster, it appears that about 1532 an attempt was made to drain the fens. "The Undertakers, by the advice of experienced artists in draining, finding that Wainfleet Haven was not a proper and fitting sewer for the fens to drain by to the sea, enlarged the ancient sewers which led to the river Witham and Boston Haven, which drained the same effectually."

<small>Maud Foster, 1568.</small>

One of these drains was a cut from 'Cow Brygge' to Boston Haven, since called Maud Foster, which was made in 1568. There is no record as to the origin of the name, Maud Foster. There was an owner of property in Boston, called Maud Foster, who is frequently mentioned in the old records. She died in November, 1581, and probably the drain, passing through some land belonging to her, took its name from the owner.

<small>NEW CUT TO COW BRIDGE. 1568.
Thompson's *Boston*.</small>

In the records of the Corporation of Boston for 1568 it is stated that the new cut to Cow Bridge was made, and it was ordered that " the dykinge of the new dreyne to Cow Brygge shall be doon with such spede as may be convenientlie ; and for the charge thereof it is agrede that the Mayor shalle dispose of the towne's money the sum of twentie marks till further orders be taken." In 1569 the ' Surveyors of the Highwaies ' were ordered to attend to the completion of the ' new dreyne.'

<small>THE LEVEL TOWNS AND WAINFLEET HAVEN. 1588.</small>

It appears that a new 'Clowe' was made at this time at Hilldyke. As in 1592 and 1597, the Surveyors of Highways of the Parish of Boston were allowed materials out of the town's store towards repairing the new Clow, and Hilldyke Drain was cleansed and scoured by Boston. About 1588, a decree was obtained in the Duchy Court for again improving the outfall by Wainfleet Haven, and an arrangement was made with the ' level towns ' of Croft, Bratoft, Irby, &c., for carrying out and maintaining the works.

Although there is no record of the fact, Black Dyke was probably made at this period for carrying off the overflow from the south-east corner of the pits in the East Fen. It passed through Friskney and emptied by Black Gote in the Roman Bank, into a creek on the foreshore. This gote is first shown on the map of 1661.

<small>1592.</small>

The arrangement made with the parishes lying on the north of the East Fen did not answer the expectations of the promoters of the scheme, as, four years later, in 1592, a bill was exhibited by certain petitioners in the Court of Exchequer, praying to be released from their coalition with the ' level towns,' the reasons assigned being as follows. " It was soon found by experience, after building the said

Gowt or Clow in Wainfleet Haven and dyking the said eau or haven, and the said drains called Goodyke, Southdyke *alias* South Stream, the said run into the sea was not beneficial for the townships in the said soke, as was at first thought the same would have been, nor was the piscary any way bettered thereby. Therefore it was about two years after making the aforesaid decree by a view of the Commissioners of Sewers for the said county, together with experienced engineers and workmen, as also by Inquisition of Sewers, found and declared, and a Decree of Sewers thereupon made, declaring that the said eau or haven was not the most proper drain of the said Fens, nor of the towns of the Soke of Bolingbroke, saving only for divers grounds lying in Little Steeping and part of Thorpe, and of the Wold towns descending by Lusdyke, and of grounds drained by Thieves' Creek, which perhaps may have some, although but very little, advantage thereby; and that by trying the bottom of the said fens it was found that the same was four feet deep in water, when the water in the said haven or at the outfall was but two feet deep; and also that the revenues of the said piscary are and were much impaired and the towns of Bolingbroke Soke not a whit bettered, so that the farmers in the said Soke had other ancient drains, sewers and outfalls to run and issue their East Fen waters into the sea, namely into the river Witham, to which the said fen waters have a natural run and descent, and a clear contrary course to Wainfleet Haven."

Oldfield's Wainfleet.

In Queen Elizabeth's reign some idea was entertained of making an attempt for the recovery of the East Fen, and a survey was made by order of the Queen, from which it was estimated to contain 5,000 acres, or thereabouts; and it was considered that half of this, being the skirts, hills and outrings, could conveniently be drained; but the other half, consisting of deep holes and pits, could not be recovered. Beyond the survey nothing further seems to have been attempted. Camden, who wrote his history in 1602, thus describes the condition of the fens. "The fen called the West Fen is the place where the ruffs and reeves resort in greatest numbers, and many other sorts of water fowl, which do not require the shelter of reeds and rushes, migrate hither to breed, for this fen is bare, having been imperfectly drained by narrow canals which intersect it for many miles. Twenty parishes in the Soke of Bolingbroke have right of common on it, but an enclosure is now in agitation. The East Fen is quite in a state of nature, and exhibits a specimen of what the country was before the introduction of draining. It is a vast tract of morass, intermixed with numbers of lakes, from half a mile to two or three miles in circuit, communicating with each other by narrow reedy straits. They are very shallow, none above four or five feet deep, but abound with pike, perch, ruffs, bream, tench, dace, eels, &c. The reeds which cover the fens are cut annually

Condition of the Fen in 1602.

Camden.

for thatching not only cottages, but many very good houses. The multitudes of stares that roost in these weeds in winter break down many by perching on them. A stock of reeds well harvested and stacked is worth two or three hundred pounds. The birds which inhabit the different fens are very numerous. Besides the common wild duck; wild geese, garganies, pochards, shovellers, and teals breed here, pewit, gulls, and black terns abound : a few of the great terns or tickets are seen among them. The great crested grebes, called gaunts, are found in the East Fen. The lesser crested, the black and dusky, and the little grebe, cootes, water hens and spotted water-hens, water-rails, ruffs, red-shanks, lapwings or wypes, red-breasted godwits and whimbrels are inhabitants of these fens. The godwits breed near Washingborough, three miles east of Lincoln; the whimbrels only appear for a fortnight in May and then quit the country."

Dugdale's Embanking and Draining.

ADVENTURERS' ATTEMPTS TO RECLAIM. 1603.

The positions of these lakes or pools is shown on the map. (*Fig 8.*)

In the next reign, in 1603, shortly after the accession of James I to the throne, a series of destructive floods burst the embankments of the fens on the East coast, and swept over farms, homesteads, and villages, drowning large numbers of people and cattle. The King, on being informed of the great calamity which had befallen the inhabitants of the fens, principally through the decay of the old works of drainage and embankment, declared that, for the honour of his kingdom, he would not any longer suffer these countries to be abandoned to the will of the waters, nor to let them lie waste and unprofitable; and that if no one else would undertake their drainage, he himself would become the 'Undertaker.' A measure of taxation for the recovery of these lands, which was accordingly proposed to the Commons, was, however, rejected, and the King, restricted in his means, confined his attention to works on the Great Level in the counties of Cambridge and Norfolk.

1631.

In the reign of Charles I, (1631), a Court of Sewers was held at Boston, the Commissioners being Robert, Earl of Lindsey, Lord Great Chamberlain of England; Edward, Earl of Dorset, Lord Chamberlain to the Queen; John Shorey, Mayor of Boston; Sir Robert Killigrew, Vice-Chamberlain to the Queen; Robert Callice, Serjeant-at-Law; and others; to make enquiry into the state of this district. After hearing evidence, "they found that the following lands were overflowed with fresh water, *viz.*, Dockdike hurne, from Armitage Causey, and Howbriggs, east, to the river of Witham, west; and from the said river of Witham, south, to Hawthorne, north, from the east end of Hundell House grounds, and so along by Raydyke, to the north side of Moorhouse grounds; from thence by Mareham, Revesby, East Kirkby and Hagnaby, to Hagnaby gate; and thence along by Barloade bank, and the west end of Stickney Severals, to Stickney Graunge; from thence on the north side of West-house grounds, along to Black-syke; from thence on the north side of Medlam to Gamock Stake; from thence directly to the east end of Hundel House grounds from Stickney Graunge, southwards, on the west side of the Severals of Stickney and Nordyke Gate, east, to Nordyke stream, south, and the West Fenne, west; wherein is included Westhouse grounds, the low grounds belonging to Stickney Grange and Thornedales, from Norlands lane, along between Sibsey Severals and the new drain to Hale Causey; from thence along to the Shottells:" and also the "East Fenne, extending in length from the Severals of Wainfleet on the east, to the Severals of Stickney on the west: and in breadth from the Severals of Waynflet, Friskney, Wrangle, Leake, and Stickney on the south: and the Severals of Stickford, Keales, Toynton, Halton, Steping, and Thorpe on the north, were for the most part surrounded grounds; and likewise that certain Severals and Commons of divers Lords and Owners, belonging to Waynflet and Friskney, lying between a bank called Fendyke Bank on the east, and East Fen on the west, and abutting on the old drain called Symon Gote towards the south, and upon Thorpe Dales towards the north, and certain severals of divers Lords and Owners belonging to Wrangle, lying between the said old drain called Symon Gote on the east, and Leake Severals on the west; and abutting upon Lade Bank towards the north, and upon the old Fendyke bank towards the south, were surrounded grounds most part of the year; and moreover that the several grounds and commons of divers Lords and Owners belonging to Leake, lying betwixt the East Fen on the north, and the Outweare bank on the south, and abutting upon Wrangle Severals towards the east, and upon Sibsey Weare bank and Stickney Wydalls towards the west; and the Severals of divers Lords and Owners of grounds belonging to Stickney Wydalls lying betwixt the East Fen on the east and north, and abutting upon Valentine Dyke towards the west, and upon a drain leading to Nordyke Brigge towards the south, were surrounded grounds in the winter time. And lastly that the Severals of certain Lords and Owners of grounds belonging to Toynton next Spillesby, called the Demesns, lying between the East Fen on the south, and a certain meadow called the East Fen on the north, and abutting upon a drain called Toynton Beck towards the east, and upon Hare Hills towards the west, were surrounded grounds also for the winter season," and that these lands were capable of recovery. They therefore deemed that a tax of ten shillings an acre should be levied for the repairs of the natural outfalls at Waynflete Haven, Black Gote, Symon Gote, Maud Foster Gote, New Gote and Anton Gote, as also any other cuts or drains that should be found necessary to be made or enlarged.

In default of payment a concession was granted to Sir Anthony Thomas, John Warsopp and others, who became the undertakers of

THE ADVENTURERS.

the drainage on being granted a certain quantity of the drained land. Commissioners were appointed to divide and set out the lands decreed to Sir Anthony Thomas and John Warsopp, out of the fens to be drained by them on the north east side of the river Witham. The Commissioners were directed to take care that 1,500 acres of the drained land and fourpence reserved on every acre be tied for the perpetual maintenance of the works; and that 1,600 acres of the lands decreed to the Undertakers in the East Fen and 400 acres in the West Fen should be conveyed to the use of the poor cottagers and inhabitants.

<small>State Papers Domestic, 1631.</small>

The Adventures commenced operations in 1631, and enlarged the drain which had been previously made, or as described in Dugdale, "made a great and navigable stream, three miles in length, from Cowbridge to the Haven, near Boston, and at the end of it the old Maud Foster Gowt was replaced by 'a very large gowt of stone and timber.'" This sluice had a water way of 13ft., and the bottom of the drain was made 30ft. wide. In 1807 a stone was found near Mount Bridge, bearing the following inscription, 'Anthony Thomas Knight buylded this sluice, 1635.' They also made 'many other petty sewers, gutters and streams, having their courses to the said main river, and over them were erected many bridges and other works, done with so much diligence' that three years after the commencement, a decree was made by the Court of Sewers "that, on a view of the late surrounded grounds, viz., East and West Fen, Earle's Fen, Armetre Fen, and Wildmore Fen, and other the drowned commons and adjacent surrounded grounds, lying on the north and north east of the river Witham, within the extent of the said Commission, they adjudged the same to be so drained as that hey were fit for arable, meadow, and pasture. And that out of 3,000 acres of pits, deeps and holes which formerly existed, there now only remained 1673 acres." And they confirmed to Sir Anthony Thomas a grant of one-half of the commons land in the East Fen, and a third of the Severals adjacent thereto; and also one-fourth of the West Fen and the surrounded grounds adjoining; 2,500 acres of the lands so granted were made liable to the maintenance of the works, and the rents were to be paid into the hands of the Mayor of Boston, to be employed for and about the repairs of the bridges, gotes and drains, until they amounted to the sum of £2,000, to the extent of which amount they were always answerable. The total quantity acquired by the Adventurers, as recompense for their undertaking, was altogether 16,300 acres, which brought them a rental of £8,000 a year. The amount expended in the drainage and reclamation was £30,000, and they subsequently spent £20,000 in improving their lands and in constructing buildings.

<small>Dugdale. 1635.</small>

The drainage of the fens, as carried out by Adventurers, is shown on the Map of the Fens, Fig. 8.

<small>Fig. 8. The Fens, 17th Century.</small>

A Map of the EAST and WEST FENNE 1661 (Dugdale)

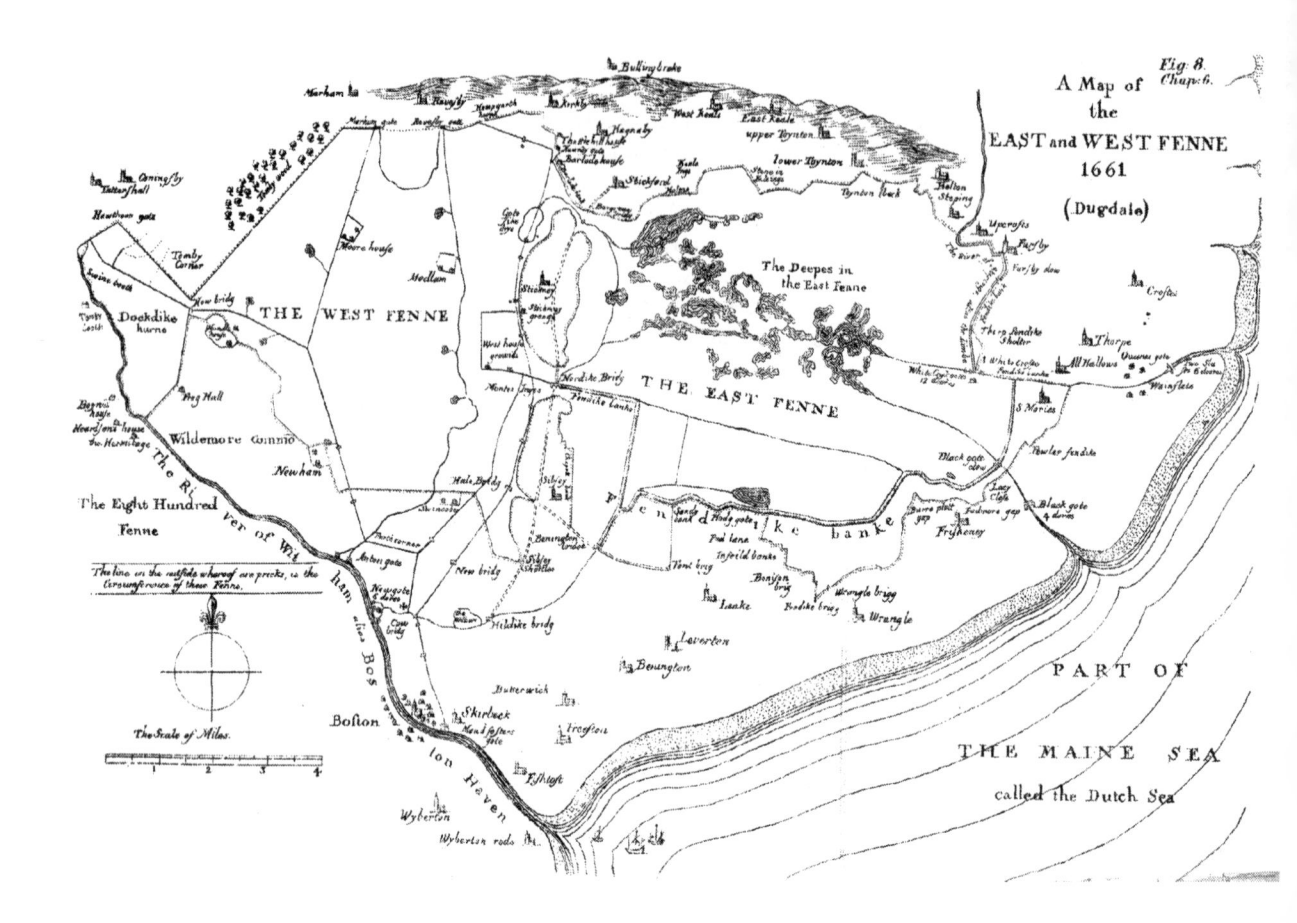

The works carried out by the Adventurers appear to have consisted in diverting the water from the West Fen and the South of the East Fen, from the Witham at Anton's Gowt to the new Maud Foster Gowt, and by constructing drains on the north to prevent the high land water from flooding the fens, and by opening out and improving the outfall to Wainfleet Haven. In the West and Wildmoor Fens, the old Nunham Drain, which discharged at Anton's Gowt, was improved, and a new drain extended from it in a westerly direction to Dogdyke.

For seven years the Adventurers' tenants enjoyed their occupations, building houses, sowing corn, and feeding cattle thereon; at the end of that time, the Commoners, "finding that done, of which they themselves despaired, made several clamours, but finding no relief in time of peace, they resolved to try if force and violence would compass that which neither justice nor reason could give; and to that end, a little before Edgehill fight, in 1642, they, being incensed by some then in faction, took arms, and in a riotous manner they fell upon the Adventurers, broke the sluices, laid waste their lands, threw down their fences, spoiled their corn, demolished their houses, and forcibly retained possession of the land." The new sluice, erected at Maud Foster, was probably destroyed at this time, as 80 years later reference is made in an order of the Court of Sewers to the erection of a new sluice at a place 'where a gote formerly existed.'

The Adventurers, finding that the Sheriff and other local authorities could not afford them protection, petitioned the Houses of Lords and Commons. With the former they were successful, the Lords passing the Bill for the relief and security of the drainers, because of the advantage accruing to the King by the improvement of his lands, from fourpence to ten and twelve shillings per acre yearly; and for repaying £50,000 expended by the Undertakers. Being opposed by the Commoners they failed to obtain an Act from the Commons. The Commoners stated in their petition that Sir A. Thomas had not fairly obtained the decree from the Court of Sewers in the first instance; that he had not fulfilled his bargain, as the lands—particularly in the West and Wildmore Fens—were not improved by his works, but were then worth from 10s. to 15s. per acre yearly; further that the quantity of land granted to him was excessive: and that he was already well paid for what he had done by his seven years' possession; that the profits the drainers had enjoyed for seven years were £57,000, which was more than they had laid out on the works. Having heard both parties, the House of Commons ordered that the Sheriff and Justices of the Peace should prevent and suppress riots, if any should happen, but expressly declared that they did not intend thereby to prejudice the parties interested in point of title to the lands, or to hinder the Com-

Fig. 8.

1642.

moners in the legal pursuit of their interest. Upon this the parties commenced proceedings at common law against the Adventurers, in which they were successful.

State Papers Domestic, 1667.

In the case of the Adventurers in the East and West Fens as presented to the court it is stated that the level contained 45,000 acres, that Sir Anthony Thomas in his lifetime by the general approbation of that part of the country undertook the draining according to a Law of Sewers made on the 15th of April, in the seventh year of Charles I, and that he was to have for his recompense 16,000 acres. That, before draining, the land was not worth fourpence per acre; but he had rendered them so fertile that they had abundant crops of all sorts of corn and grain and seed for *oyl*, and His Majesty's customs had increased thereby and the country people became much enriched who before were very poor. That the Adventurers, with the children of him (Sir Anthony Thomas), that had added so great a patrimony to the king, were by the meaner and ruder sort of people expulsed their possession, and their houses, works, crops and inclosures barbarously demolished and destroyed, which had cost £50,000.

In the proceedings it was stated that at that time 52 towns or villages, and 40,000 families had right of common in these Fens.

CONTROL RESUMED BY COURT OF SEWERS.

The Court of Sewers again resumed charge of the district, taking over such of the drains and sluices as remained after the destruction caused by the Fenmen. The drainage for a long time after this remained in a very unsatisfactory state.

At a Court of Sewers held in 1722, it was presented that a new gote ought to be erected nigh where a gote formerly existed, called Maud Foster Gote, at the cost and charges of the Soke of Bolingbroke and the towns of East Holland, the estimated expense being £1,200. At the same Court, Wainfleet Clough was presented as not being sufficient to carry off the water, as twice as much water then ran through the East Fen through Nordyke Bridge as went down Goodyke and White Cross drains; and an order was made for the erection of a new sluice. Neither of these orders was carried out.

1734.

At a general Court of Sewers held at Boston in 1734, a petition of the Landowners and Tenants in Wrangle, Leake, Leverton, Benington, Butterwick, Freiston, Fishtoft, Boston East, Skirbeck and Sibsey was presented, showing that the 'New Gote' in the Witham near Frith Bank was in great danger of being lost and asking that a Jury might be called to inspect this, and also an old gote, called 'Maud Foster's Gowt,' as owing to the bad state of the drainage the lands were constantly flooded. The Jury found that the 'New

MAUD FOSTER DRAIN & SLUICE CONSTRUCTED.

Gote' had become ineffective owing to the condition of the River Witham, which was silted up, and the Court, having viewed the fen and the gotes, found the land to be in a grievous and deplorable condition, by reason of the violent and excessive inundations of fresh waters, which in the late extraordinary wet season had descended upon them from the high country, which had overflooded and 'drownded' the same to the very great damage of the Owners, and tending to the impoverishing and utter ruin of the King's liege subjects, to the great diminution of his revenue and absolute destruction and loss of the lands of the Petitioners and others. It was ordered that " Maud Foster Gote should be cleaned, opened, repaired and mended in her tunns, dams, aprons and wings, with good and proper materials for the same, both with respect to her stone, brick, timber, iron and clay works, to be done by *acre silver* and proportioned rateably, according to the advantage and benefit of the several Landowners, and quantity of acres on their benefit in the respective towns, parishes and hamlets running and passing their waters to the said gote." Further it was found that as the gote was 'too strait and narrow and cannot carry the waters off the lands,' a new gote should be built at some convenient distance from the said Maud Foster's Gowt, of brick and stone and timber, with one tun 12ft. wide, and they estimated that the said gote and drain would cost £1,000. The drain leading from the gote to Colling's Bridge was to be ditched and cleansed and the old decayed bridges taken up and new ones erected in their stead, and the drain, from the gote to Pedder's Cross, made 30ft. wide at the bottom and 7ft. deep, at a cost of 18/- a rood; from Pedder's Cross to Colling's Bridge, 30ft. wide and 5ft. deep. Mount Bridge, Hobson's Bridge, Main Ridge Bridge, Hospital Bridge and Colling's Bridge were to be repaired or replaced. By " reason of the arduousness and multiplicity of the said works, and great numbers of artificers and workmen employed about the same, the Court appointed Maister William Stennet and Maister John Millington, persons well skilled and versed in accounts, the nature and price of materials, and mechanicks, and the rate and value of workmanship, to be Surveyors and Expenditors, and to inspect, survey, measure and direct the works and materials used thereon, and supervise and pay the workmen," and they were to be allowed and paid the sum of 3/4 each day.

This sluice was subsequently described in Grundy's report as having one arch of 15ft. and a draw door of 15ft., to retain the fresh water, and which was drawn up by two large wooden screws, and a pair of pointing doors.

At a subsequent Court it was shown on the ' modest representation' of Samuel Preston, the Treasurer " that through the general poverty of the kingdom and universal want of trade no reasonable profit for the sale of any commodities produced in these parts could be obtained, and that by reason of the particular distress of all the said parishes in East Holland very little of the money due from the rates which had been levied could be raised." The Court therefore gave time for payment and authorised their treasurer to borrow money for the purpose of defraying the more immediate expenses of the said works.

The following table gives the acreage of the lands which were taxed for the maintenance of Maud Foster Gowt and Drain.

	Acres.
Boston	370
Skirbeck	1,880
Freiston	1,980
Butterwick	779
Benington	1,560
Leverton	1,300
Leake	3,692
Wrangle	2,040
Sibsey	2,400
Frith Bank	642
Fishtoft	740
	17,383

ATTEMPT TO DRAIN THE WEST FEN BY MAUD FOSTER DRAIN.

The new sluice at Maud Foster and the cleaning out and deepening the drains leading thereto appear to have considerably improved the condition of the drainage of those lands which obtained relief for their water that way. In fact, so much so, that the occupiers of lands in the other part of the fens and in the Soke of Bolingbroke were anxious to discharge their water that way also, instead of through Anton's Gowt into the Witham, the drainage by which, owing to the silting up of the channel of the Witham, had become very imperfect. The Proprietors in the East Fen and others endeavoured to set up a right to drain by the new sluice, losing sight of the fact that, when the sluice was about to be built and the drains made, the Owners of the lands in the Soke of Bolingbroke were invited to join in the undertaking, and on account of their refusing to do so the sluice and drains were made of less dimensions than they would otherwise have been.

1754.

In 1754 at a Court of Sewers held at Spilsby, on the representation of certain owners of land, an order was obtained for deepening and widening Medlam Drain to Cherry Corner and removing the existing sluice, whereby the West Fen water found its way through Mill Drain to Maud Foster.

1754.

In 1754 the Occupiers in the other parts of the fen attemped to open up a communication between the waters of the west side of the West Fen and the new outfall by Cherry Corner. This, however, was opposed by the town of Boston on the ground that the waters coming from the land in question ought by right to drain to the Witham, and that to deprive that river of this supply would be detrimental to the navigation. They therefore petitioned the Court of Sewers to have the communication, which had been opened out, stopped again, by means of a door placed across the drain at Cherry Corner, for the purpose of preventing the waters of the East Fen and the east side of the West Fen from flowing to Maud Foster. The Boston Court made the order as requested and directed the Surveyor of the Soke of Bolingbroke to restore the drainage to its former condition, under a penalty of £200 in default.

The controversy between the contending parties was carried on for some time, and on one occasion led to some severe rioting in the neighbourhood of Sibsey. It was not finally ended until the new scheme for the improvement of the Witham was promoted. Boston, however, succeeded in obtaining the construction of Anton's Gowt in the new channel of the Witham, for taking the water from the East and West Fens, the owners of land in those fens insisting on a clause being inserted in the Act enabling them to drain by Maud Foster, in case the drainage by Anton's Gowt proved ineffectual.

In 1784, Mill Drain was deepened and enlarged by Mr. Pacey of Boston, acting under the direction of certain Proprietors of land, and the drain, leading from Nordyke Bridge to Cherry Corner, was lowered. This produced a partial drainage of the East Fen, and lowered the water in the 'deeps,' but the effect was also to destroy the herbage in the fen and hinder the navigation of the pools and dykes. The Fenmen thereupon erected a dam across the new cut. In a petition sent by the Fenmen relating to this drain, they say, "It is well known that the temperate and industrious part of the poor inhabitants of the Soke of Bolingbroke, has, for a long time, supported themselves and their families comfortably with the produce of the East Fen, by fishing and getting coarse and fine thatch. Many of us, by the blessing of God and our own industry, has procured a cow or two, which we used to graze in the said fen in the summer, and get fodder for their support in winter, but, alas, of these privileges we are in a great measure deprived by a set of men called Commissioners, who hath imbibed such a rage for drainage, that exceeds both utility and justice. Utility, because it destroys the grass and herbage, and is hurtful both to farmers and poor men; justice, because it deprives the poor of their privileges—for the fishery is ruined, the thatch is destroyed, the fodder very scarce. And to make our grievance the more intolerable, and to complete our ruin, and show how unfeeling they are, they even now are depriving us of the benefit we expected from the late rains, that is, of getting our fodder and fuel to land, by running the water away out of both fens. We, your petitioners, humbly pray you to take up our cause, and, if possible, procure redress for us, by causing a temporary dam to be made in Sibsey Cut for our present relief, and a permanent stanch for our future supply; and, if practicable, we beg leave to recommend to your consideration two Cuts, one on the north side and the other on the south side of the fen, to set bounds to the cattle

1784.

OBJECTIONS TO THE DRAINAGE OF THE EAST FEN.

and supply them with water, and secure a portion of land to bring fodder and thatch. And your humble petitioners will be effectually relieved from that state of distress and poverty which must be the inevitable effect of the measures now pursued. And your humble petitioners will ever hold themselves in gratitude and duty bound to pray for your person and family." This was signed by 105 Fenmen, of whom only 19 were unable to write their names, and made a mark.

1788.

As a result of this petition, a sluice was built across Valentine's Drain and the water in the East Fen retained at an agreed height.

Grundy's Report. 1744.

In reports made by Messrs. Grundy on the Witham in 1743 and in 1744, they stated that New New Gote which used to discharge the water of the West and part of the East Fen into the Witham, when the river ran by its mouth, had by diversion of the course become filled up and was then close dammed and neglected, and that since the building of Maud Foster Sluice the water from the fens had a better tendency that way, and that from this cause Anton's Gowt was also 'quite landed up.'

About this time several reports had been obtained on the best way of improving the River Witham and the adjacent fens, which would, to a certain extent, affect the drainage of the West and Wildmore Fens by Anton's Gote and New New Gote. In 1757 Lord Monson brought forward a scheme for conveying the water of the West and Wildmore Fens to the Witham by a new cut from the south west corner of Frith Bank, or from Anton's Gote to New New Gote, and thence by a cut to a new sluice of two arches, of 10ft. waterway each, to be erected near the lime kilns in Boston, a short distance below the present Grand Sluice, at an estimated cost of £2,836. Medlam, Newham and Howbridge Drains, and those bringing the water from the East Fen this way, were to be scoured out, and the banks of Steeping river raised, at an estimated cost for the whole of £8,200. Medlam drain was to be made the main drain for the East and West Fens, and the East Fen waters were to be brought to the new main drain by Sibsey New Cut and the old stream under North Dyke Bridge.

LORD MONSON'S SCHEME, 1757.

1761.

In 1761, in a joint report made by Messrs. Grundy and Son, Mr. Langley Edwards and Mr. John Smeaton, on the improvement of the river Withams, they advised that a new sluice should be erected in place of the old Anton's Gote, and a new cut made for the drainage of Wildmore and West Fens, the effect of which and the new channel of the Witham would be to lower the water by 4ft.

CONDITION OF THE FEN IN 1773.

In 1773 several meetings were held at Spilsby, and Messrs. Stephenson, Elmhirst, Hogard, Robertson and Lovell were appointed a Committee to view the fens and report on the best method of draining them. The report states that, on viewing the East Fen in August, the Committee found that on an average there was about 18in. of water on the surface, and in the Deeps from 5ft. to 7ft.; that Good Dyke Drain was foul with mud, and White Cross Clough in a ruinous condition, and that there was 5ft. of water on the sill; that the drain from the sluice to Salem Bridge was deficient both in depth and breadth; that the course of Wainfleet Haven from the Salem Bridge to the new sluice was very crooked, and ran through high land; that the 'meals,' or banks, along the course of the Haven from the new sluice to Gibraltar Point were increasing and running southward, and that the channel would in a short time be lost; that from Gibraltar House towards Skegness was a bold shore, where the sea set in hard against the 'meals,' and that this was a proper place for erecting a new sluice. The 'meals' consisted of a light blowing sand, but at the bottom of the channel was a strong clay. This Committee advised that an Outfall Sluice, with two tuns of 15ft. water way, with pointing and draw doors, should be erected, and a new Cut made through the marshes to Wainfleet Haven, where the living waters from Steeping River and the 'Levy' towns should join the waters from the East Fen; that a new Cut be made on the north-west side of Lord Pawlett's bank to White Cross Drain, and that the Good Dyke and South Stream into the East Fen should be enlarged. The Limb was to be made 30ft. wide, and the banks from Steeping Mill to the north-east side of White Cross were to be strengthened. The estimated cost of these works was £12,398. This report was approved, and the whole question referred to a further meeting of the Proprietors, to be held in London.

In 1774 meetings of the Landowners were held at the St. Albans Tavern, London, and in the following year at Spilsby. At the former Mr. Grundy was instructed to make a report on the drainage of lands in the East Fen and the East Holland towns draining by Wainfleet Haven and Maud Foster Sluice, and on the best means of improving the same. Mr. Grundy, in his report, thus describes the condition of the drainage. Steeping River, after passing through a bridge at Halton, 13ft. 6in. wide, fell into Wainfleet Haven at White Cross Bridge. Below this bridge it was joined by the Steeping Beck. The waters from the East Fen were brought to the Haven at White Cross Clough by 'Goodyke.' Pointing doors, which formerly had been placed in Goodyke to stop the water from going into the fen, had been demolished and disused for many years. Firsby Clough was 15ft. 3in. wide, and had a draw door. The 'Lymn,' from Firsby Clough to its outfall in Wainfleet Haven at Stone Gowt, was 5ft. 4in. wide; Bethlehem Bank formed the eastern boundary of the low lands which drained into that stream. The outfall clough, or sluice, in Wainfleet Haven was of brick, having two arches, one of 5ft. 10in., and the other of 12ft. 6in., two arches of the sluice as originally built having recently been thrown into one. The Haven, from the Outfall Sluice to Stone Gowt, was very crooked, as it was also to Queen's Gote, an old deserted sluice. The width of Stone Gote was 15ft. 2in. At a quarter of a mile above Wainfleet All Saints there was an engine with a wheel, 13ft. in diameter, for draining the low grounds in Wainfleet St. Mary. There were also engines and wheels for draining 800 acres belonging to Bethlehem Hospital and lands in Thorpe and Croft. The medium width of Wainfleet Haven, at the water line from the Sea Sluice to White Cross Clow, was 18ft. 11in., and the depth of water 3ft. 6in. The distance from Gibraltar House to the Sea Clow was 1 mile 3 furlongs, and the total distance to White Cross Clough 8 miles. Black Dyke is described as running from the East Fen through the high tofts to the sea, having a bridge at Friskney, with one arch of 10ft. 7in. Friskney was drained by an engine and wheel, 14ft. 6in. in diameter, which discharged into the sea through Friskney Clow. Hilldyke Bridge had an opening of 11ft. 7in., and Maud Foster an outlet of 15ft., which was then a good outfall, as the Haven was close under it. Hale Bridge was 14ft. wide and Stone Bridge 20ft. The low grounds in Wrangle, Leake, Leverton, Benington, Butterwick, Freiston and the Ings, Boston Long Hedges, Skirbeck and Sibsey, all drained by Maud Foster. Fishtoft Parish drained by Fishtoft Creek. There was a sea gowt at Freiston Shore, having a pair of pointing doors of 4ft. 6in., which drained the higher part of the parish; at Leverton was a gowt 4ft. wide, to drain the marshes and high land; at Wrangle was the New Marsh Clow 2ft. 4in. wide; and under Friskney Sea Bank were five outfall clows, two of 2ft., the Engine Drain 4ft. and the others 2ft. 7in. and 2ft. 8in. The level of the water in the drain at Salem Bridge was 10ft. 2in. above low water at Gibraltar House; in Black Dyke 5ft. 4in. higher. The average level of the surface of the low land lying between Wainfleet and Boston varied from 6ft. to 8ft. above low water; the water in Wainfleet Haven at Gibraltar House was then 1ft. 4½in. lower than that in Boston Haven at Maud Foster Sluice. About 24,500 acres of the level drained by Wainfleet Haven.

GRUNDY'S SCHEME. Grundy proposed to divide the District into two Levels: the low lands lying east of Stickney, and as far south as Wrangle, to drain by Wainfleet Haven; and the remainder by Maud Foster. At Wainfleet Haven a new sluice was to be built, about 1½ miles below the existing sluice near Gibraltar House, having five arches, with 68ft. of water way. This sluice was to be connected with the old one, which would inclose 63 acres of salt marsh. The Haven was to be widened to a bottom of 66ft., for a length of one mile four chains. The worst of the bends being removed. The 'Lyman' was to be enlarged and strengthened from Stone Gowt to Firsby Clough, and a new sluice erected at the end, with an opening of 13ft. Steeping River was to be deepened and enlarged for two miles, so as to have a 16ft. bottom.

A main drain was to be made for the drainage of the East Holland Towns of Wainfleet St. Mary, Friskney and Wrangle from the main river, about half-a-mile above Salem Bridge, having 14ft. bottom. Black Dyke was to be enlarged to a 12ft. bottom. Good Dyke and South Stream were to be also enlarged. The estimated cost of these works was £37,314.

As affecting this proposal to drain by Wainfleet Haven, it appears that at that time the tide flowed 2½ hours in Boston Deeps before it began to flow in the Haven opposite Gibraltar House.

In the following year schemes were brought forward by Mr. John Hudson and Mr. Joseph Robertson of Sibsey.

Mr. Hudson's proposal, as laid before the Court of Sewers at Spilsby, in July, was to widen Wainfleet Haven from the Sea Clough to Croft Outfall, so as to make the bottom 25ft. wide, decreasing it to 16ft. at Good Dyke Sluice; and to construct a pen lock, 56ft. long and 10ft. wide, instead of the sluice at Good Dyke. The estimated cost, including the widening of Steeping river and Good Dyke South Stream, was £4,143. *HUDSON'S SCHEME, 1775.*

Mr. Robertson's scheme was to add two arches of 13ft. each to Maud Foster Sluice; to enlarge the drain from 30ft. to 70ft. at the bottom, for one and a quarter miles; to enlarge Stone Bridge drain, from Collins' Bridge (Cowbridge) to Hall Bridge, to a 40ft. bottom; the drain from the East Holland towns to join Maud Foster at Collins' Bridge; a new drain from Hale Bridge to Cherry Corner to be made to a 20ft. bottom; the drains running from Cherry Corner to the west side of the East Fen and connecting the East and West Fen water, called Deepdale, to be enlarged to Valentine's Drain; Mill Drain to be enlarged from Collins' Bridge to Cherry Corner. The estimated cost of enlarging these drains, with the bridges and other works, was £18,615. *ROBERTSON'S SCHEME.*

For the improvement of the drainage of the 'Levy' towns, with Friskney and part of Wrangle, a new sluice was to be built in Wainfleet Haven, having 26ft. of opening, or else another tun to be added to the old one; the Haven to be enlarged to Stone Gowt to a 40ft. and to White Cross to a 30ft. bottom. The bank of Steeping River on the east side, from Firsby Clough to White Cross, was to be raised, and a new drain made from Wrangle, through Friskney and Wainfleet St. Mary, to the Haven. The total number of acres chargeable for this portion of the drainage was put at 11,993.

No action was taken on these reports, and the fens remained in a most unsatisfactory state, owing to their lost and flooded condition, and also from the disorder in stocking, and from those having common rights sending in much larger quantities of stock than they were entitled to. Cattle stealing and disease also detracted from the value derived from the summer feeding, so that what was gained in one year was lost in another. In fact it was stated that some of *CONDITION OF THE FENS, 1775.*

the largest common right owners had ceased for several years to send any stock to the fens.

The East Fen, being the lowest, was in the worst condition, and there were there 2,000 acres always under water. The West and Wildmore Fens are described as having 'whole acres covered with thistles and nettles, four feet high and more.' Numerous attempts were made to bring about the inclosure and drainage, but the matter was protracted, owing to the difficulty in settling the basis on which the land should be divided amongst those who claimed to have rights in the different fens.

Sir J. Banks. Sir Joseph Banks, of Revesby, took a very active part in endeavouring to reconcile the various interests for one common object. *Young, 1799.* Arthur Young says that he had much "conversation with Sir Joseph Banks, who, I was glad, but not surprised, to find had the most liberal ideas upon the subject of reclaiming the Fens. No man sees clearer the vast advantages which would result from the measure to the country in general. No man can be more desirous that it should be effected. He has collected, with the utmost assiduity, every document necessary for the measure, and is prepared for it in every respect. He makes no conditions for himself personally but will trust all to the Commissioners. . . . The waste and disgraceful state in which so many acres remain rests not, therefore, at his door. When I told him that upon enquiring why these horrid fens were not drained and divided, it was said that 'Sir Joseph Banks was like a great bull at Revesby, ready with his horns to butt at any one that meddled,' he replied, 'very true, Sir Joseph is that bull to repulse those who would pretend to carry the measure upon wild and ill concerted plans in spite of him, but let them come forward in the right way, and with any prospect of success, and they shall find that Revesby bull a lamb.'"

A. Bower, 1799. From a statement made by Mr. Anthony Bower, the resident Engineer employed in carrying out the works, in his report made to the Governors of the Bedford Level, it appears that the area of the Fens in 1799 was as follows:

	Acres.
East Fen	12,664
Lower part of West Fen	12,303
,, ,, Wildmore Fen	7,770
	32,737

This land every Winter under water.

East Fen Deeps	2,500
No Man's Friend	1,500
	4,000

Under water in Summer.

High land draining through the Fen	25,000
East Holland towns and old enclosures	25,000

This high land water overflowed the fens. "The whole of the water off this area of 61,737 acres had to find its way to sea through three small gowts or sluices; *viz.*, Anton's Gowt, which had an opening of 14ft.; Maud Foster, an opening of 13ft.; and Fishtoft, an opening of 4ft. The first was of little use, being so high up the river Witham as to be over-rode by the most trifling flood; the whole drainage therefore of the fens and low lands had to depend upon the small sluice at Maud Foster." This statement is not quite correct, as part of the East Fen water found an escape through Wainfleet Haven. There were also some small sluices in the sea bank, under the control of the Court of Sewers, and part of the water of Friskney was raised by an engine and wheel and sent to sea through a small gowt.

The general surface of the East Fen and of Wrangle Common was about 8ft. above the sill of old Maud Foster Sluice.

At a meeting of the Proprietors of Wildmore Fen, held at Horncastle in 1799, Mr. Rennie was desired "to cause the necessary levels and surveys to be taken and to report his opinion of the best mode of effectually draining Wildmore Fen separately; and also the best mode of draining the East, West and Wildmore Fens in one scheme." The surveys were made by Mr. A. Bower of Lincoln and Mr. Jas. Murray. The report is dated London, April 7, 1800. A subsequent report was made, dated Sep. 1, 1800. Mr. Rennie reported as the result of his examination that the fens were the receptacle not only of the waters which fell on their own surface but of all that which flowed rapidly down from the high lands above, and that owing to the smallness of the sluices, and their doors being over-ridden by the water in the rivers, and the badness of the drains, the greater part of the spring was gone before the water which had accumulated in the fen could be carried off. To remedy this the first object which required consideration was the outfall; the second, the discharging the water falling on the fens; and the third, the intercepting the high land water and preventing its entering the fens.

The drainage of the Wildmore and part of the West Fen was made through Anton's Gowt, by means of the sluice erected by the Witham Commissioners at the time the river was straightened, as detailed in the preceding chapter, the sill of which was 2ft. above the sill of the Grand Sluice. Through this sluice also were discharged the waters from the high country, lying in the lordships of Kirkby, Revesby, Mareham, Tumby, and Coningsby; but in times of flood the Witham over-rode the waters from these parts, and they were driven back through Medlam Drain and West House Syke to Cherry Corner, whence they found their way by Mill Drain, or Stone Bridge Drain, to Maud Foster's Gowt, which consisted of a single opening, 13ft. wide, its sill being 3in. lower than the sill of the

MEETING OF LANDOWNERS, 1799.

RENNIE'S REPORTS. 1800.

Grand Sluice. Low water of spring tides at that time stood about 4ft. 9in. on the sill, and the general surface of the lands in the West and Wildmore Fens was 9ft. above the sill, allowing a fall of 4ft. 3in. from the surface to low water mark. The lowest land in the Fen, called 'No Man's Friend,' was one foot below the rest, and was frequently covered with water to that depth. The East Fen Deeps were covered, on an average, about 2ft. in dry summers.

<small>OBJECTIONS TO RENNIE'S SCHEME.</small> The scheme recommended by Mr. Rennie, and adopted by the Commissioners, will be more fully detailed hereafter. Opinions were much divided as to the best means of dealing with the drainage. The Proprietors of Wildmore Fen were anxious, if possible, to keep this separate and to discharge the water into the Witham at Anton's Gowt. A strong feeling also prevailed that the drainage of the East Fen should be discharged into the river at the old oulet at Maud Foster, on the principle that for the preservation of an outfall the tributary stream should be conducted to its channel at the highest point possible. Others more intimately connected with the district contended that the main object to be sought was the efficient drainage of the Fens, irrespective of other considerations, and therefore advocated a new cut to Wainfleet Haven; while a third plan was that which was finally adopted, being a compromise between the two, by which the water was to be conveyed by a new cut through the centre of the East Fen, discharging into the river near Fishtoft Gowt.

Owing to the obstruction in the Witham, caused by the silt accumulating below the Grand Sluice from the want of scour, Mr. Rennie was of opinion that the surface of the water in Anton's Gowt could never be greatly lowered, even if a new cut were made from it and the water carried to the Witham below the Grand Sluice. He therefore advised against the scheme for draining Wildmore Fen in this way. As regards the drainage of the East Fen by Wainfleet Haven he says, " Were the Wainfleet Gowt to be taken away and a new one established at the angle of the sea bank just above Gibraltar House and about a mile and a quarter further to seaward than the present gowt, the sill of which might be laid lower than Maud Foster, so that nearly 4ft. of additional fall in the surface of the water more than is at present might be obtained; but before the water could be brought from the East Fen to this gowt a very expensive cut through land, generally from 12ft. to 13ft. deep, must be made for the distance of eight miles. A new and expensive cut would also be wanted for the Steeping, or Limb, River, and when all was done the quantity of water which passes through Wainfleet Haven being but small, the outfall could not be easily maintained in an efficient state." He advised therefore, after duly considering the whole of these reasons, that the only effectual place through which the East Fen, and the low grounds in the East Holland towns could be drained, was at Fishtoft, or rather lower than where the present gote is situated. He points out that the expense of this Cut would be considerable, as five and a half miles of it would require to be excavated in ground from 15ft. to 18ft. high, and the other four miles in ground from 10ft. to 12ft. high, but in his opinion the excellent drainage which would be obtained by this means would more than compensate for the expense. If, "however, Boston Haven were to be improved so as to lower the surface of the water at Maud Foster's Goat, the East Fen might also be drained through this Outfall, which would not only save the expense of the proposed catchwater drain from Sibsey Willows to Maud Foster, but also the new Cut from Hilldyke Bridge to near Fishtoft, with the goat and bridges. If this should take place (effecting a saving of £27,956)" he considered "that these fens could afford to contribute liberally to the improvement of Boston Haven; and that the money would be better bestowed in this way than in making the Cut in question." In the second report he adds, " If the Haven was to be properly improved I have no hesitation in saying the East Fen, with the low lands in Friskney, &c., may be completely drained at or near Maud Foster's Goat, but unless the gentlemen of Boston and others interested in the navigation of, and drainage by, the River Witham were to unite and bring about a proper improvement of the same, I cannot advise the drainage to be conducted to any place higher than Hobhole."

Mr. Rennie urged very strongly on the Corporation of Boston the scheme for straightening and improving the river from Maud Foster downwards.

The estimated cost of the scheme for the West and Wildmore Fens was £103,262, and for the East Fen with the Cut to Fishtoft Gowt and the sluice, £85,290; together, £188,552.

When these reports were brought before the Corporation of Boston, they expressed their willingness to contribute one-half of the expense of straightening the river from Maud Foster to Hobhole, as recommended by Mr. Rennie. This was not deemed sufficient by the Drainage Commissioners, and finally, after a great deal of consideration of the several schemes, it was determined that the water from the uplands and the West and Wildmore Fens should be conducted to Maud Foster, but that the outfall of the drainage from the sock and downfall of the East Fen should be near Fishtoft Gowt. This decision failed to give general satisfaction, and one pamphleteer, in a letter addressed to the Commissioners, asks how many *pails* of water they expect will pass down Maud Foster Drain, and observes, " If this drain is executed upon the proposed dimensions, from the sluice to Cowbridge, there will not be a supply of water to cover that drain above one inch deep."

Mr. Thomas Stone strongly advocated the claims of Wainfleet Haven as an outfall, and expressed the opinion that the proposed

T. Stone, 1800.

drain through a gowt below Fishtoft would not completely drain the pits in the East Fen, and that the Proprietors must be prepared to endure many very expensive calls upon their pockets.

POCKLINGTON'S REPORT, 1800.

Some of the Proprietors, also, who disagreed with Mr. Rennie's scheme, obtained a report from Mr. William Pocklington of Sibsey, who considered that the fens could be effectually drained at less cost and with less waste of land than by the scheme proposed by Mr. Rennie. He was of opinion that it was practicable to drain the East, West and Wildmore Fens through Maud Foster; that by bringing all the water to one outfall there would be greater certainty of preserving and keeping open the outfall. He proposed leaving the deeps in the East Fen as they were, on the ground that this would save a large amount of expense, and that they would be much more useful left, as affording a basin for the reception of water in violent floods, and as a reservoir for water for the use of the country in dry seasons; and also as a nursery for fish and fowl, and for the production of reeds for thatching and 'bumbles,' (rushes used for chair bottoms). His scheme for intercepting the high land water was practically the same as that which Mr. Rennie afterwards carried out. A new sluice with three openings was to be built in place of the old Maud Foster Sluice. For the West and Wildmore Fens the Mill Drain was to be enlarged, from Cowbridge to within half a mile of Swinecotes, and a new drain cut thence to Medlam Drain. For the East Fen Newdyke Drain was to be enlarged from Cowbridge to Jenkinson's Lane, and a new cut made through the centre of the East Fen near the Catchwater Drain by Toynton Enclosure; another Cut was to be made from the said Lane, through Leake Mere, along the sewer by Wrangle Common, and another to Toad Lane engine, and thence by Dickin Hills through the Mossberry ground, along the boundary of the fen, to the Catchwater Drain near Steeping. The estimated cost of the whole of the scheme was £56,102. This estimate was based on the drains having a capacity of six cubic feet for low fen land, and twelve cubic feet for high land, to every 1,000 acres. The cost of excavation, at that time, was from 7/- to 8/- a floor, or about sixpence per cubic yard.

FURTHER OBJECTIONS: Holland Watchman, 1800.

With reference to this proposed drainage of the East Fen by Maud Foster, a pamhlet by 'A Holland Watchman' was written to show that the scheme was not practicable, the author resting his evidence on the figures and levels given in Mr. Rennie's report, and remarking, "If the East Fen and the county adjacent, amounting to 30,000 acres, can be drained by Maud Foster, all the levels that have been taken lose their credit, and the Levellers must look to theirs as they are able....The game of Anton's Gowt is about to be repeated at Maud Foster, and as Wildmore and West Fens are now drained at the former, just so will your fen and your present low lands be drained at Maud Foster....But for your comfort give up only the

East Fen Deeps (that is 3,000 acres) to wild fowl for the London market; to fish for the Boston market; to reeds for your houses, which will be covered with tiles or slate; and to bumbles for your chairs which (like those of other good farmers) will be made of horsehair and mahogany; and then you may be drained tolerably... The question is not whether a few acres of the deepest pits (to which I see no objection) but whether three thousand acres shall be left under water just at your door."

On the other hand Mr. William Chapman, in two pamphlets, strongly advocated the scheme for making Maud Foster the main outfall, and expressed his doubt as to the wisdom of the resolution passed at Boston, by which the waters of the East Fen and East Holland towns were to be diverted to Hobhole, and also his disapproval of the plan of bringing the Anton's Gowt waters down to Maud Foster, thus depriving the channel through Boston of its aid without substituting any equivalent. He considered that it was "much to be regretted that those who are interested in the present drainages should not see the advantages of an improved haven; advantages of no little importance to the town of Boston, but of immense magnitude to the fens in general, and to the country adjacent...By an improvement of Boston Haven the town would reap some advantages, the country many.....Fully convinced of the wisdom of the proposed improvement and the lasting benefits which would result from it, I trust that the country, the town and corporation will be prepared for union, and that to accomplish an improvement of such magnitude it will not be found difficult to raise the trifling sum of £41,270."

Chapman. 1800 and 1801.

In April 1800 a meeting of the Proprietors of estates having right of common and other interests in the fens, was held at the Town Hall, Boston, Sir Joseph Banks being in the chair. At this meeting after considering Mr. Rennie's and Mr. Pocklington's reports, it was resolved that a subscription should be entered into to defray the preliminary expenses of obtaining an Act, the amount contributed to be in proportion to the number of acres owned in the fens. That three bills should be promoted in Parliament, one for draining the East, West and Wildmore Fens; one for dividing and inclosing Wildmore Fen; and the third for dividing and inclosing the East and West Fens. A subsequent meeting was held at the *Bull Inn*, Horncastle, of the Proprietors of rights in Wildmore Fen when similar resolutions were passed.

MEETING OF COMMONERS. 1800.

In December of the same year a meeting of merchants and ship owners was held at Boston to urge on the promoters of the drainage the advantages to be derived from bringing all the drainage water to Maud Foster, and recommending that a charge of fourpence per ton should be levied on all vessels entering the port, which, it was estimated, would produce sufficient to pay the interest on half the cost of improving the river from Maud Foster downwards.

At a meeting of the Proprietors held subsequently it was resolved "that the proposal of the merchants, ship owners and traders of Boston to cleanse and deepen the middle portion of the River Witham at the joint expense of themselves and the Proprietors of the fens, without deepening the outfall of the said river to the sea, is not likely in any degree to amend the actual outfall of the land waters to sea, and cannot therefore materially contribute to the improvement of the drainage."

Some difference of opinion also arose as to the manner in which the fens should be allotted, and as to the amount claimed by the Duchy of Lancaster. A meeting of the Proprietors was held at Stickney to protest against the allowance of one twentieth, proposed to be given to the Duchy, in lieu of manorial rights, after deducting the land required for defraying the costs of inclosure; it was also agreed that the land left after that taken to pay the expenses of enclosure, ought to be allotted to the owners of common rights, houses and toftsteads only, without any reference to the quantity of the land.

T. Stone, 1800.
J. Cope, 1801.

It was stated in a pamphlet by Thomas Stone, Land Surveyor, published in London in 1800, that the lands thus to be given to the Duchy of Lancaster, when drained and improved, would be worth £80,000. Mr. J. Cope, in a printed letter dated London, 1801, protested against this allotment to the Duchy, pointing out that in Deeping Fen the proportion claimed for the same rights, had only been one fortieth.

At a subsequent meeting of those who were promoting the Bill for the Inclosure, held at Boston, it was resolved that in making the allotment of land, after providing for inclosure, roads, drains and manorial rights, one moiety ought to go to common right owners and toftsteads, and that the other should be divided among the proprietors of lands who had a house and who were entitled to stock the fen, on the 27th July, 1800; in proportion to their lands lying in common-right parishes and places, quantity, quality and situation considered; and it was further determined that those who dissented from this should be left to their remedy in the Courts of law.

DRAINAGE ACT.
41 Geo. iii, c. 35.
1801.

At last in 1801 an Act was obtained entitled "An Act for the better and more effectually draining certain tracts of land, called Wildmore Fen and the West and East Fens, in the county of Lincoln, and also the low lands and grounds in the several parishes, townships, and places, having right of common in the said fens, and other lowlands and grounds lying contiguous or adjoining thereto."

43 Geo. iii, c. 118.

In 1803 an amending Act was obtained authorising alterations in some of the works set out in the first Act. By the first Act the boundaries of the Fourth District of the Witham Commissioners, as originally settled by the Witham Act of 1762, were extended and the East Fen was made to include the low grounds adjacent, being bounded as follows, "by the Parish of Skirbeck and the high lands of Fishtoft, Freiston, Butterwick, Benington, Leverton, Leake and Wrangle, by the Parishes of Friskney and Wainfleet St. Mary's and by Steeping River on or towards the east and north-east; by the Parish of Skirbeck and the high lands of Fishtoft, Sibsey Willows, the high lands of Sibsey, Stickney, Stickford and West Keal, on or towards the west; and by the high lands of East Keal, Toynton All Saints, Toynton St. Peter's and Halton Holgate, and by Steeping River on or towards the north."

Mr. John Renshaw of Owthorpe, Mr. William Whitelock of Brotherton, and Mr. Joseph Outram of Alfreton were appointed Commissioners for carrying into execution the works authorised by the Act, under the control of the Witham General Commissioners, their remuneration being fixed at £3 3s. per day. On the completion of the works they were to be vested in and remain under the control of the Commissioners. The owners of certain low lands in Friskney, Wainfleet St. Mary's and Wainfleet All Saints, and on the west side of Steeping River, which were not within the boundary of the Fourth District, had the option of being included, and of obtaining the advantages of the provisions in the Act, if four-fifths of the Proprietors (in value) signified their desire to that effect. This they did and these lands were incorporated in the Fourth District.

It was enacted that the outring and division ditches should be maintained by the Owners of the land adjacent, the dimensions being given as 9ft. broad and 5ft. deep. By a subsequent Act power was given to the Commissioners to require all Owners and Occupiers in the Fourth District, to make and keep their division ditches and tunnels sufficiently cleansed and scoured out, to such dimensions as were directed upon the inclosure, or, where not defined, to such reasonable dimensions as the Commissioners should think fit. Persons convicted of wilfully damaging any of the banks or works were to be deemed guilty of felony, or be fined at the discretion of the Court.

58 Geo. iii, c. 60, 1818.

Under the powers of these Acts the following works were executed for the drainage of the fens by Mr. Rennie.

For the drainage of the West and Wildmore Fens a catchwater drain was made, skirting the adjacent high lands. It commenced near the junction of the river Bane with the Witham, in the parish of Coningsby, and passes through Tumby, Mareham, and Revesby, to Hagnaby, running on the north side of the existing catchwater drain. At Hagnaby Corner it joined the old Gote Sike Drain, and continued along that, the Fen Side Drain and Stonebridge Drain, to Cowbridge, these drains being enlarged and deepened. This catchwater drain is about eighteen miles in length, and the bottom

DRAINAGE WORKS, 1803.

was made to an inclined plane, rising six inches in the mile. The width of the bottom, at the lower end, is thirty feet, diminishing to sixteen feet from Hagnaby Corner, and to eight feet at its commencement near Coningsby.

By the first Act it was intended that this drain should continue, by a distinct Cut, parallel with Maud Foster, to the Haven; and discharge at a new sluice to be built at the side of Maud Foster, so that the high and low land waters should have separate outlets; but by the amended Act obtained in 1803, the Commissioners were authorised to omit the making of the new Cut from Cowbridge to the Haven and the erection of the additional sluice, and, instead, to make the existing arrangement by which the upland waters flow to sea by means of Maud Foster Drain, and provision is made, as hereafter described, for the West Fen waters to flow into Hobhole when over-ridden by them.

A new sluice was built in Boston Haven, about three chains to to the east of the sluice erected in 1734. The old sluice was pulled down. The new sluice has three openings, of thirteen feet four inches each; the sill being one foot nine inches below that of the Grand Sluice. The drain was deepened and widened to Cowbridge, the bottom being made thirty feet wide, and rising six inches per mile. Across this drain, at Cowbridge, a sluice was erected, with pointing doors, to prevent the water from the high lands, which discharges below this point, from backing up into the fens. Above the doors a communication was made to admit the West and Wildmore Fen waters into Hobhole Drain when they are above the gauge weir, and in danger of flooding the low lands. This drain, which passes under Stonebridge drain, the waters of which are conveyed over it by a stone aqueduct, having three openings of 12ft. each, joins the New Dyke Drain, which was enlarged and continued from Luke's Corner to Hobhole Drain, at Freiston Common. A stop was placed above the aqueduct, for the purpose of sending all the water that was possible through Maud Foster Gowt at ordinary times; but as soon as the water rose within two feet of the surface of the low lands it ran over the weir. In times of flood, when the water was within one foot of the medium surface of the lowest lands, the doors were opened and the water allowed to flow freely to Hobhole. There is also a side cut near this place, in which is a lock to allow of the passage of boats from the West Fen to Hobhole Drain.

30 and 31 Vict., 1867.

This restriction as to the passage of the waters out of the West Fen through New Dyke into Hobhole Drain was withdrawn in the Act obtained in the session of 1867, and the Commissioners have now power to allow the stop doors to remain open for the six winter months, so that the West Fen waters are discharged at Hobhole, instead of at Maud Foster as formerly.

From Cowbridge the drainage is provided for by the West Fen Drain, which is a straight Cut, with a 30ft. bottom, as far as the junction with Medlam Drain, at Swinecotes near Mount Pleasant, where it turns to the west and joins Newham Drain; whence it continues along the old Howbridge Drain to Little Wildmore, near Dogdyke, where the bottom was made only 8ft. wide. It has an average inclination, throughout its whole length of about nine and a half miles, of five inches per mile. Newham and Sandbank drains were enlarged, so as to have 12ft. of bottom at their junction with the other drain, diminishing to 8ft. at their termination.

The old Medlam Drain, which is the principal outlet for the West Fen, was connected with the new drain at Swinecotes. It was enlarged to 18ft. at its junction with the main West Fen Drain, diminishing to 12ft. at its termination at Revesby Gap. The length is about 6 miles, and the bottom has a rise of 6in. in a mile. There is another Cut for the purpose of draining the south part of Wildmore Fen, commencing at the West Fen Drain, at Cowbridge, and extending on the south side of Frith Bank Enclosure to Anton's Gote into Newham Drain, and thence along Castle Dyke and Long Dyke Drains, which were enlarged and deepened. This drain was made 16ft. in width of the bottom, at its junction with the West Fen Drain, diminishing to 8ft. at the upper end. The length is about 8 miles, and the rate of inclination was laid out at 4½in. per mile.

For the drainage of the East Fen the highland water was prevented from flowing into it by a catchwater drain, commencing by a junction with the Old Fen Side Drain, now part of the West Fen Catchwater, about a quarter of a mile below Cherry Corner, and passing through Northdyke Bridge, across Barlode Drain, to Stickford, and thence along the skirts of the East Fen to Little Steeping. This drain was made 16ft. wide at the bottom at its commencement, diminishing to 6ft. at the termination. A new cut was made from Hagnaby Beck to Barlode Drain to divert the waters from their old course into this drain.

HOBHOLE DRAIN.

A new sluice was built in Boston Haven at Hobhole, in the Parish of Fishtoft, about 4 miles below Boston. The sluice was made with three openings of 15ft. each, the sill being laid 5ft. below that of the Grand Sluice, or about 1ft. 9in. above low water of spring tides in Boston Deeps. At the time of construction, the sill was 2ft. below low water in the river. From this sluice a new cut was made, running in a straight line in a northerly direction through the Parishes of Fishtoft, Freiston, Butterwick, Benington, Leverton and Leake, to the junction of the old New Dyke Drain with the Leake and Wrangle Drain, near Benington Bridge. From there it followed the course of the Leake and

Wrangle Drain, which was enlarged and deepened to Simon House Bridge, about 70 chains south of Lade Bank, whence a new drain was cut through Lade Bank to Toynton St. Peter's. The lower part was made with a bottom, 40ft. wide, diminishing to 12ft. at its termination at the upper end. The length is 14 miles, and it was laid out with a fall of 5in. in a mile. The lower end of this drain, for about 5½ miles, passes through high land, the depth of the cutting being from 15ft. to 18ft. Barlode Drain was enlarged and deepened to a 16ft. bottom and extended eastward to the new Hobhole Drain. On the other side Good Dyke Drain was extended westward to Hobhole Drain, which it entered opposite the junction with Barlode Drain. Lade Bank Drain was extended from Cherry Corner to Hobhole Drain, being carried under the Catchwater Drain at Nordyke Bridge, and from the east side of Hobhole Drain, along the Fen Dyke Bank to Friskney, having a 10ft. bottom. Steeping River was deepened and embanked, so as to prevent its flooding the low lands, as also the Great Steeping Beck.

These works were all carried out under the direction of Mr. Rennie, Mr. Anthony Bower being resident Engineer, and the contract for the largest works being executed by Mr. John Pinkerton.

The general surface of the lowlands in the West Fen was, at the time of the completion of the drainage, about eleven feet above the sill of Maud Foster Sluice; but a portion of the surface of Wildmore Fen was a foot lower than this. The surface of the highest part of the East Fen was about the same level, but a great deal of it was a foot lower, and the lowest parts, formerly the Deeps, were only nine feet above Hobhole sill.

To meet the expenses of carrying out and maintaining these works the General Commissioners were authorised to levy additional rates on the Wildmore and West Fens, to the extent of fourpence per acre, so long as they remained common lands; but, on their enclosure, the rate might be raised to one shilling per acre. On the East Fen a tax of one shilling per acre was imposed on the lands held in severalty—eightpence per acre on half-year lands, and fourpence on common lands—to be raised to one shilling on their enclosure. They were also authorised to enclose and sell six hundred acres of the common land, the proceeds to be applied towards the cost of the drainage.

The first stone of Hobhole Sluice was laid on March 7th, 1805, and it was opened on September 3rd, 1806. The first stone of the new Maud Foster Sluice was laid on the 21st of May, 1806, and the sluice was opened the following year.

Mr. Bower, reporting to the Bedford Level Commissioners in 1814, on the result of these works, says, " It is satisfactory to state that every wished-for object in the drainage of the whole of the fens and of the low lands adjoining is effectually obtained, and the lowest land brought into a state of cultivation. The East Fen Deeps are so perfectly drained, and so confident are the proprietors of this, that part of them now forms a considerable farm-yard; but stronger proofs of this than mere assertion have now been had. There have been within the last five years several extraordinary floods and high tides, which have not in the smallest degree affected the works or low lands; and at this moment of time, when the low lands in every part of the kingdom are overflowed by an ice flood, the East, West, and Wildmore Fens and low lands adjoining are perfectly free, and as ready for all agricultural purposes as the high country lands."

Separate Acts were obtained for the enclosure of the East and West Fens, and for Wildmore Fen.

In the Preamble of these Acts the area of the East Fen is given as 12,424 acres, West Fen, 16,924 acres, and Wildmore Fen, 29,348; total, 59,196 acres.

<small>EAST AND WEST FEN ALLOTMENT.</small>

The Commissioners appointed by the Act to allot the East and West Fens were John Renshaw of Owthorpe, William Whitelocke of Brotherton, and John Outram of Alfreton; with Anthony Bower of Lincoln, as surveyor. Robert Millington of Gedney, William Thacker of Langret Ferry, and Thomas Rockliffe of Fulletby, were appointed as 'Quality men' for valuing the land, and Samuel Tunnard of Boston, and Joseph Brackenbury of Spilsby were named as Clerks in the Act.

<small>41 Geo. iii, c. 142, 1801.
50 Geo. iii. c. 129, 1810.</small>

The Commissioners were allowed by the Act £3 3s. 0d., and the 'Quality men' £2 2s. 0d. a day, including their expenses.

The Commissioners were to set out such lands as they deemed necessary, the public carriage roads to be 40ft. wide; and it was forbidden to plant trees within 50ft. of the roads; the roads to be properly formed and completed by Surveyors appointed by the Commissioners, and the cost made part of the cost of enclosing; and two years after the making of the Award these allotted roads were to be kept in repair by the parishes in which they were situated. The costs of carrying out the Act were to be covered by the sale by public auction of sufficient land. One-twentieth of the fens was to be allotted to the Crown in right of the Duchy of Lancaster, as Lord of the Manor, for all rights of brovage and agistment; land to the value of one-ninth part of the parochial and general allotments was to be allotted to the Tithe Owners in lieu of all tithes; half of the remainder to the Owners of houses, toftsteads and lands having right of Common; and the other half to the parishes of Bolingbroke, Hareby, Asgarby, Lusby, Raithby, Hundleby, Mavis Enderby, Spilsby, Halton Holgate, Little Steeping, Thorpe, Toynton All Saints, Toynton St. Peter's, East Keal, West Keal, Miningsby, Revesby, East Kirkby, Hagnaby, Stickford, Stickney, Sibsey, Frith Bank, Boston East, Skirbeck, Fishtoft, Freiston, Butterwick, Benington, Leverton, and Leake.

The award, after enrolment with plans, was to be deposited 'in the Treasury of the Mayor and Burgesses of the Borough of Boston, with the Records and Muniments belonging to the said Borough,' and another copy at the office of Clerk of the Council of the Duchy of Lancaster; but in the subsequent Act the Award was directed to be deposited with the Clerk of the Peace for the parts of Lindsey. The Awards were to be open for inspection, on payment of a fee of one shilling, and copies supplied at the rate of fourpence per sheet of 72 words.

WILDMORE FEN.
41 Geo. iii, c. 141.
42 Geo. iii, c. 108.

Wildmore Fen was allotted under Acts passed in 1801 and 1802. The same Commissioners and Surveyor were appointed. The 'Quality men,' or Valuers, appointed were William Porter of Freiston, John Bonner of Langton, and Stephen Morris of Dunham; the Clerks appointed were Richard Clitherow of Horncastle, and Francis Thirkill of Boston. The same regulations as to roads and trees, and the sale of land for payment of expenses were enacted. The manorial rights of the Earl of Stamford and others were to be compensated by an allotment of one-twentieth of the fen; and the remainder of the land to the Owners of houses and toftsteads and to the parishes of Horncastle, West Ashby, Thimbleby, High Toynton, Low Toynton, Mareham-on-the-Hill, Moorby, Wilksby, Mareham-le-Fen, Wood Enderby, Roughton, Haltham-upon-Bane, Coningsby, Dalderby, Kirkstead, Scrivelsby, Tumby, Bolingbroke, Revesby, Toynton All Saints, Toynton Saints Peter's, Frith Bank and Fishtoft. The Award was to be deposited in the parish church of Horncastle, and copies supplied at the rate of fourpence per sheet. One-ninth of the fens, after the deductions for the Fen Chapels, was to be allotted to the Tithe Owners in lieu of all tithes.

FEN CHAPELS.
50 Geo. iii, c. 129, 1810.
42 Geo. iii, c. 108.

Under the Enclosure Acts a fund was created for the erection and maintenance of 'Chapels' and the payment of the Ministers. For this purpose, one-ninth part of the land alloted to the Crown for manorial rights in the East and West Fens, and 175 acres from the lands to be allotted to the Tithe Owners, and 156 acres out of the land to be alloted for parochial and general purposes; and in Wildmore Fen one-ninth of the manorial allotment and 50 acres from the land awarded to the Tithe Owners, and 50 acres from that awarded to the General Commissioners, were to be vested in the Chancellor of the Duchy of Lancaster, the Bishop of Lincoln, the Lord of the Manor of Armtree and Wildmore, the Bishop of Carlisle, the Archdeacon of Lincoln, and their successors, to be held in fee for the benefit of the said Chapels and their Ministers. The Chapels erected under the powers given in these acts are at Midville, Mount Pleasant, Carrington, Langrick Ville, and New Bolingbroke.

FEN TOWNSHIPS.
52 Geo. iii, c. 3, 1812.

Land, amounting to about 13,920 acres, was sold for the purpose of the above Acts. This, with the land allotted to the Lords of the Manor and for the fen Chapels, was not annexed to any parish. To remedy this, an Act was obtained in 1812, in the preamble of which it is stated, that the population of these fens was rapidly increasing, and that it would be for the public convenience if this extra-parochial land were divided and constituted into seven townships. The townships formed by this Act are East Ville, containing 2,657a. 1r. 12p.; Midville, 2501a. 1r. 6p.; Frithville, 2,716a. 3r. 37p.; Carrington, 2,416 or. 13p.; West Ville, 1,950a. 2r. 2p.; Thornton-le-Fen, 1,425a. 1r. 29p.; Langrick Ville, 1,911a. 2r. 32p. Maps showing the boundries of these townships were to be deposited with the Clerks of the Peace of Kesteven and Holland. These townships were declared to be subject to the general laws of England relating to constables and the relief of the poor.

The works carried out under these Acts left the drainage of the low lands by Wainfleet Haven untouched, and they remained very insufficiently drained. THE 6,000 ACRES.

In 1814 a report was issued by Mr. Walker addressed to the Proprietors and Occupiers of low grounds in Wainfleet All Saints, Thorpe, Croft, Irby and Firsby, draining through Wainfleet Haven, in which he advised the deepening of Wainfleet Haven, the raising and strengthening of the banks, removing the sluice and allowing the tide to have free flow up the Haven, the estimated cost being £3,360; or, as an alternative scheme, the erection of a steam engine where Thorpe engine then stood, the estimated cost of which he put at £950, and the annual expense at £200. W. Walker, 1814.

Subsequently a report was obtained from Mr. Rennie, in which he described the works he considered necessary to drain the district, and to carry off the high land water to Wainfleet Haven. The area of the district to be dealt with was 6,740 acres. J. Rennie, 1818.

An Act was obtained in 1818, by which the lowlands in Great Steeping, Thorpe, Irby, Firsby, Bratoft, Croft and Wainfleet All Saints, known as 'the Five Thousand Acres,' were incorporated with the Fourth District. For the better protection of the East Fen and of these low lands, the Witham General Commissioners were authorised by this Act to widen and enlarge the mill race of Little Steeping Mill, so that it should have 18ft. water-way; and to straighten and enlarge the Steeping River, through Little Steeping, Great Steeping and Firsby, to Firsby Clough, and thence to make a new Cut through Firsby, Thorpe and Wainfleet All Saints, to a point about one mile from Salem Bridge, the bottom width being made 21ft. Beyond this the river was to be enlarged to a 21ft. bottom; the banks were to be raised 3ft., and be 2ft. wide at an average height of nine feet above the land; a new Cut or back delph was to be made on the north-east side of the river to Wainfleet Sewer and continued thence through Wainfleet All Saints, Thorpe, Firsby, Great Steeping and Little Steeping to near Little Steeping water mill, with a 3ft. bottom to Wardike Drain, and 10ft. beyond Wardike, diminishing 58 Geo. iii, c. 69, 1818.
6,000 ACRES JOINED TO EAST FEN.
DRAINAGE WORKS AUTHORISED.

to 6ft. at Firsby Clough, and beyond that to 3ft. Great Steeping Beck was to be enlarged, from near Little Steeping Church, to a 10ft. bottom at the river, diminishing to 2ft. at the upper end. Five brick bridges, having 24ft. water way, were to be erected. Firsby Little Clough was to be rebuilt, near the junction of the new Cut with the Little River Limb, and Firsby Great Clough to be rebuilt across the Steeping River with a waterway of 24ft; Salem Bridge was also to be rebuilt with the same water way. The following drains and sewers were to be straightened, deepened and improved, and to have a bottom width, respectively, as follows : Steeping Sewer to 2ft.; Marshes Drain, Firsby Sewer and Mold Drain, 3ft., diminishing to 2ft.; Irby Beck, 3ft. to 1ft., Bratoft Beck, or Cowcroft Drain, 12ft. to 4ft.; Little River Limb to the bend in Bratoft; a new drain to be cut on the south side of the Limb from Irby Beck end in a westerly direction to the junction of the river with the new Cut; a new drain on the north side of the Little River Limb from Irby Beck in an easterly direction to its bend in Bratoft ; a new drain on the west side of Lever Gate Road from Irby Beck end through Thorpe to where Wardyke Drain crosses the new Cut with a 4ft. bottom; Wardyke Drain to be enlarged and deepened from Fen Bank Corner to the new Cut, and to have a 20ft. bottom, diminishing to 10ft. The remainder of the Wardike Drain to be straightened and enlarged to 6ft. diminishing to 2ft.; also Wainfleet Sewer from the high lands in Wainfleet All Saints to Fen Bank Corner ; thence to the New Cut, with 3ft. bottom, diminishing to 1ft. A new Cut was to be made from the West End of Wardike through the Dales to the White Cross Clough Drain, having 20ft. bottom ; also a drain across the Steeping River, between the church of Wainfleet All Saints' and White Cross Clough ; and sunken tunnels under the Little River Limb at Irby Beck End, with two arches, 7ft. wide by 5ft. high; one under the same river near Firsby Clough, 6ft. by 4ft.; and one under the New Cut, where the Wardike Drain crosses, with three arches, each 7ft. by 5ft., and a brick carriage bridge over the New Drain from the west end of Wardike Drain to White Cross Clough Drain, with a water way of 24ft.

The Steeping River and the works from Steeping Mill to Salem Bridge, and the Wardyke Drain, from the south-west bank of the new Cut to White Cross Clough Drain, were to be maintained and supported by the General Commissioners, and all other works were to be considered private, or interior, works of drainage, to be maintained by Commissioners, appointed by the parishes as their Representatives on the Board of the Fourth District, except as to Salem Bridge, which was to be maintained by the same parishes as were then liable to repair it.

By the 13th clause it was enacted that if the Owners and Occupiers of land in the Fourth District did not keep open their division ditches and tunnels, the Commissioners could cause the same to be done at the charge of the offender.

The total estimate for the works was £28,914. The Commissioners undertook to execute the whole of the works on payment to them of the sum of £18,627 by the owners of land in the several parishes liable to be flooded by the Steeping River, or otherwise benefited. Mr. John Burcham of Coningsby, was appointed Commissioner to carry out the works.

By the same Act the method of electing the District Commissioners as set out in the Witham Act of 1762, was amended as follows :— 2 Geo. iii, c. 32.

The number of Commissioners was fixed at 26 ; five to be elected by Wildmore Fen ; eight by the West Fen ; eight by the East Fen and low lands in Wrangle, Friskney and Wainfleet ; five by the low lands in Great Steeping, Thorpe, Irby, Firsby, Bratoft, Croft, and Wainfleet All Saints. The latter were divided as follows, viz., Great Steeping and Thorpe, 2; Irby and Firsby, 1; Bratoft and Croft, 1 ; Wainfleet All Saints, 1. Every Owner of ten acres and Occupier of 50 acres, chargable with taxes to the Fourth District, to have one vote ; the qualification for a Commissioner being the ownership of 20 acres or the occupation of 100 acres. Owners were to be allowed to appoint deputies to vote for them. ELECTION OF COMMISSIONERS.

The satisfactory condition of the drainage, as described by Mr. Bower in 1814, did not remain permanent. Two causes conduced to the alteration. By the complete drainage of the spongy soil of the East Fen, and its consolidation by working, the surface gradually subsided from one to two feet. Also the channel of the Outfall from Hobhole to Clayhole became raised from its former level by the deposit of silt, owing to the neglect of proper training works. To such an extent did this occur that the low water level of spring tides, which, at the time of the erection of Hobhole Sluice, stood only 2ft. on the sill, became raised to six and seven feet, and in times of flood as much as eight and even ten feet ; so that, owing to the subsidence of the land on the one hand and the deterioration of the Outfall on the other, the good effects originally felt by this drainage were in a great measure neutralised, and in wet seasons the low lands were liable to be flooded and the crops destroyed. DEFECTIVE CONDITION OF THE FEN DRAINAGE, 1866.

In the winter of 1866 a long continued and heavy downfall of rain clearly demonstrated the system of drainage to be inadequate to the discharge of the water. A very large area of land in the East Fen was for many weeks completely under water. Viewed from Keal Hill, the level was described as having the appearance of one extensive lake, the course of the drains being indistinguishable from the submerged lands. Occupiers, in some cases, had even to use boats to pass from one part of their farms to another, and the roots stored in the fields were rendered quite inaccessible.

STEAM PUMPING IN THE EAST FEN.
Hawkshaw, 1861

In 1861 Sir John Hawshaw was applied to by the General Commissioners to advise them on the drainage of this district, and requested to devise a plan for improving the drainage of the Fourth District, as well as an alternative scheme, which, while improving this particular tract of land, would also be more general in its application. In 1865 Mr. Welsh, the Surveyor to the Commissioners, was also directed to report to them on the drainage of the Fourth District. In these reports it is stated that the Fourth District, including the East, West, and Wildmore Fens, and the Five Thousand Acres, has a taxable area of 57,200 acres; and the lands north of Steeping River, of 5,000 acres; but the area drained is about 9,000 acres; that the Northern portion of the East Fen lies at a lower level, by about 3ft., than the West and Wildmore Fens; that about 25,000 acres of land in the East Fen, and 15,000 in the West and Wildmore Fens, are below the ordinary flood level; and that while the larger portion of the West and Wildmore Fens, and the land draining into Hobhole Drain below Lade Bank, are comparatively uninjured by the water in the drains rising to eleven feet above the sill of Hobhole Sluice, a considerable portion of the East Fen lying to the north of Lade Bank, when the water rose that height, was incapable of being drained by gravitation to Hobhole; that the portion of the East Fen, including lands draining into it, which extends north of Lade Bank, amounts to about 30,000 acres, one-half of which lies at so low a level as to require for its effectual drainage that the water at Hobhole should not rise higher than about seven feet above the sill, whereas that level was one foot below low water of the Witham outside of Hobhole Sluice in times of flood, which then rose to eight feet above the sill, and for this reason these low lands could not on those occasions drain naturally by Hobhole.

The general scheme for improving the Outfall, recommended by Sir John Hawkshaw, is dealt with fully in another chapter; it is not necessary, therefore, to make further allusion to it here. The local plan he advised was the placing of draw doors across Hobhole Drain, near Lade Bank Bridge, and the erection of pumping engines of 180 horse-power at that spot, to lift the flood waters from the northern to the southern side of the doors; the maximum of the lift being assumed at 5ft., and the extreme effect on the drain below the doors—the raising of the water during the time the sea doors were shut by the tides—18in. The estimated cost was £15,000 for engines, pumps, draw-doors, land and works, and £3,000 for parliamentary expenses, &c. The annual outlay for interest and repayment of principal money borrowed, spread over 35 years, was taken at £1,350, and for working expenses and maintenance £1,250;

together, £2,600, equal to a tax of about elevenpence per acre over the whole district for the first 35 years, and of fivepence afterwards.

This scheme was considered at a meeting of the Commissioners held in July, 1861, and it was then resolved:—1. That a *general* plan improving all drainage is preferable to a local one; and also that a natural drainage is preferable to an artificial one. 2. That the Fourth District ought not to pay towards the general plan a sum larger than it would have to expend for its own local drainage. 3. That if the benefit is, as anticipated, distributed to all the lands in the Fourth District, all the lands should pay according to the actual benefit received (the rate to be left to arbitration, the maximum being fixed at three shillings, and the minimum at fourpence, per acre). . . . 10. That it would be desirable first to attempt to carry out the general plan. 11. That in the event of the other parties interested not being able or willing to carry out their share of the expenses of the general plan, then it would be expedient to have recourse to the local plan of draining the district by steam power.

Mr. Welsh, in his report, recommended as an amendment on Sir John Hawkshaw's plan, that the waters from the lands north of Steeping River which, in his opinion, possessed ample elevation for drainage by gravitation, should be prevented from flowing to the proposed pumps at Lade Bank by stopping the Bellwater Drain where the railway crosses it, and conveying the water by a new cut to Fountain's Sewer, and thence to Hobhole Drain; Fountain's Sewer being enlarged. The high land sewer to run along Wrangle Bank and Wrangle Common and discharge through the Upright and Holland Sewers into Lade Bank Drain, which was also to be diverted into Fountain's Sewer. This would have reduced the area to be pumped to 25,000 acres. *Welsh's Report, 1865.*

Mr. David Martin, also, in a pamphlet addressed to the Commissioners, pointed out that the fen was pretty well drained before the Steeping District was added, since when, the East Fen had been subject to being flooded by the water from this district, which, coming from land at a greater elevation, over-rode all the water in the drains, so that the fen had became a pool for the reception of this high land water. He therefore recommended that Bellwater Drain should be made a catchwater for conveying these high land waters to the sea, and that a new drain should be cut on the west side of Hobhole Drain, from Fodder Dyke Drain to Bardolph Drain, with other alterations in the arrangement of the several sewers, so that the waters from the lower part of the East Fen might be conveyed to an engine to be erected on the west bank of Hobhole, about half way between Fodder Dyke and Bardolph. *D. Martin. 1867.*

By carrying out the scheme suggested by Mr. Martin, the engines might have been of much less power, and, having less work to do, an annual saving in working expenses might have been effected; but then, on the other hand, it was deemed that the increased outlay in the purchase of land, and the annual interest, would make the result in the end nearly the same. Sir John Hawkshaw's plan was therefore carried out as originally devised.

1866.

In 1866, the Commissioners, despairing of any general scheme being carried out, decided on applying to Parliament for the necessary powers to enable them to erect a pumping engine at Lade Bank, for the relief of the East Fen north of that point; and for the better drainage of the West and Wildmore Fens, the removal of the restriction placed on the stop-doors at Cowbridge, so that the water should be allowed to run freely out of the West Fen Drain, by Newdyke or Junction Drain to Hobhole. They also decided to apply for power to raise the sum of £20,000 on mortgage to pay for the works, and to levy a tax, not exceeding sixpence per acre, on the land, in addition to the two shillings on the West and Wildmore Fens, and one shilling on the East Fen, already sanctioned by former Acts (except on the *Five Thousand Acres* District).

OPPOSITION TO STEAM DRAINAGE.

This course did not meet with general approval. At a public meeting held at the Guild Hall, in Boston, the following resolution was passed, *viz.*, " That this Meeting views with considerable alarm the introduction into Parliament of a Bill to provide additional means for draining the Fourth District of the Witham Drainage and determines to oppose it, as being inequitable and inefficient. Inequitable, inasmuch as it proposes to lay an equal and uniform tax upon lands that must be benefitted, upon lands that do not require, and cannot receive benefit, and upon lands that may possibly be seriously injured; and inefficient, because it brings into immediate conflict the waters of the East and West Fens; does not provide for the permanent working of the steam engines to be erected; and does nothing to improve the great Outfall of the district."

The Boston Harbour Commissioners, having had before them the plan prepared by their Engineer, Mr. Wheeler, for training and improving the outfall from Hobhole to Clayhole, at an estimated cost of £20,000, endeavoured to get the Drainage Commissioners to join with them in carrying out this scheme and to try its effect before erecting the pumping engines; and, being supported by Mr. Abernethy, who had been called in to report on the feasability of the scheme, opposed the Bill of the Fourth District in Parliament; but in this they were not successful, it being alleged by the Promoters that no definite offer to carry out this or any other Outfall scheme had been made by the Harbour Authorities to the Drainage Commissioners. To remove this objection, before the Bill went into the Upper House, resolutions to the following effect were passed, and sent to the Witham Commissioners:—(1) That the Scheme propounded by Mr. Wheeler, as laid before the Committee of the House of Lords and supported by Mr. Abernethy, can be successfully carried out for £20,000. (2) That the Drainage Commissioners be asked to confer with the Corporation as to the means for carrying out this scheme, which will be efficient for the double purpose of Drainage and Navigation; that the cost of carrying out such scheme be borne by the lands beneficially affected and by the navigation; that the necessary powers be applied for in the following Session, and that in the meantime the pumping scheme be suspended. The Drainage Commissioners would not consent to this, but the Bill was not further opposed.

The Act known as the *Witham Drainage (Fourth District) Act*, received the Royal Assent on the 15th July, 1867. The Act gives the powers necessary for carring out the works above described and for borrowing £20,000, which was to be repaid within 35 years after the passing of the Act. STEAM DRAINAGE ACT. 30 and 31 Vict., 1867.

Under the Act of 1818 there are 26 District Commissioners, elected in four separate portions, by the four sub-divisions of the District and, under the original Witham Act of 1762, the District Commissioners elected eight of these to be General Commissioners. By that Act these were not obliged to be Fourth District Commissioners, but as the lands in the East Fen were lower than those in the West and Wildmore Fen and as it was desirable that the engines to be erected should be under the care of the East Fen General Commissioners, and also that the stop-gates at Cowbridge should be under the care of West and Wildmore Fen General Commissioners, it was provided that four of the eight Commissioners should be elected for the East Fen, two for the West Fen, and two for Wildmore Fen. This clause was, however, repealed in the Act obtained in 1885, by which the Hobhole Drain, steam engines, and works mentioned in that section, and the working thereof, were, by this Act, vested in the General Commissioners, and placed under the care of a Committee of five General Commissioners, of whom two are to be East Fen, one West Fen, and one Wildmore Fen General Commissioners, and one a General Commissioner, not elected for the Fourth District. 43 Geo. iii, c. 118.

2 Geo. iii, c. 32.

48 and 49 Vict., c. 158, 1885.

The new Pumping Station is situated on the west side of Hobhole Drain, at Lade Bank, on lands formerly belonging to Hunston's Charity, and was erected under the direction of Sir John Hawkshaw, by Messrs. Easton and Amos of London, Mr. H. C. Anderson acting as their resident Engineer.

A full description of the pumps will be found in the Chapter on the Drainage System. The amount borrowed for this work was £18,000, bearing interest at five per cent.

The benefit to the occupiers of land in the East Fen from these works was very considerable; the payment of the small additional tax of sixpence per acre required towards the expenses of working EFFECT OF PUMPING.

the engines, and the repayment of the money borrowed, bore no comparison to the annual loss sustained by the destruction of crops from the constant flooding to which this fen had been subject, especially during the succession of wet seasons which followed a few years after the engines were erected. The passing of the West Fen waters, also, by way of Hobhole Drain, greatly facilitates the discharge of the drainage from the West Fen.

While, however, the pumps afforded a very large amount of relief and placed the drainage of this district in comparative safety, it continued still liable to flooding from the defective condition of the Outfall, below Hobhole Sluice, the contracted area of the sluice, and the condition of the banks of the Steeping River. Hobhole Drain became incapable of discharging efficiently the large quantity of water thrown by the pumps off the low land into it, below the stop-doors at Lade Bank, and also that coming from the West and Wildmore Fens. On several occasions, especially in December, 1868, April, 1872, November, 1875, November, 1878 and September, 1880, the pumps had to cease working, owing to the water being as high as the top of the stop-doors, and some of the lowest land was flooded.

It was impossible that this condition could be remedied until the Outfall of the river was placed in an efficient condition.

WITHAM OUTFALL.
43 and 44 Vict., c. 153, 1880.

In 1880, the *River Witham Outfall Improvement Act* was passed, under the powers of which the Fourth District was to contribute towards the construction and maintenance of the new Outfall in proportion to the number of acres in the district, as compared to the whole contributing area. The Fourth District Commissioners were not to be liable for any works above Hobhole Sluice. They were authorised to borrow £49,000, to be repaid by instalments, extending over 35 years from the 6th April, 1881. And they were authorised to raise an annual tax, not exceeding one shilling per acre, for repayment of the money borrowed, and of fourpence for maintenance of the works. Certain lands in Boston, Skirbeck, Fishtoft, Freiston and Sibsey were added to the Fourth District for the purposes of this Act, and rendered liable to the Outfall Taxes.

The New Cut was opened in 1884, the bed of the Channel being made 3ft. below the sill of Hobhole Sluice. A full description of this work will be found in Chapter XII, on the Harbour, and Outfall of the river.

The advantage to the drainage of the East Fen was greater than had been anticipated. Previous to the opening of the Cut, the water never ebbed out lower than 4ft. on the sill of Hobhole Sluice, and in times of flood it did not ebb out below 7ft. or 8ft. on the sill. Sir John Hawkshaw put the gain at 2ft., but it has been found to be as much as 5ft. 6in., and the water has at times ebbed out 1ft. 6in. below the sill of the sluice.

Report on Outfall Works. J. E. Williams, 1887.

The amount contributed by the Fourth District to the Outfall works was £41,119, which was met by two loans of £28,000 and of £21,000, bearing interest at the rate of 4½ and 4¼ per cent.

In 1887 a further Act was obtained,—*Witham Drainage (Hobhole Sluice) Act, 1887*,—authorising the widening and improving of Hobhole Sluice, and the construction of a new opening, 15ft. in width, making four openings, equal to a waterway of 60ft., the sill being three feet below the old sill. The new opening was constructed on the west side of the existing sluice. The cost of the work was £5,905, of which £1,122 was for the cost of obtaining the Act, £4,486 for works, and £296 for Engineer's and other charges. The amount was paid for out of the £49,000 loan raised for this and the Outfall purposes.

ENLARGEMENT OF HOBHOLE SLUICE.
50 and 51 Vict., c. 104, 1887.

Provision was made in this Act for facilitating the collection of the taxes and making the payment of them due on certain fixed days, at Spilsby, Horncastle, Wainfleet or Boston, after notice given by advertisement. The place of meeting for the Commissioners of the Fourth District for the purpose of electing General Commissioners, named in the Act of 1762 as Spilsby, was changed to Boston.

The defective condition of the Steeping River and its Outfall at Wainfleet remained a constant source of anxiety. The water coming down very rapidly from the high land, and being unable to get away with sufficient velocity, owing to the defective condition of the channel and of the outfall at Wainfleet, rose to the level of the top of the banks in times of heavy rain. On no less than three occasions after the erection of the Lade Bank engines, the water overflowed the banks and inundated the low land in the fen. Steeping River had been much improved by the works executed under the Act of 1818, as already described, but the altered conditions of drainage rendered further works necessary. A statement was issued by the Commissioners to the Ratepayers, showing that further works were necessary for the purpose of diminishing the risk of breakage and injury to the banks on both sides of the river, for the maintenance of which the Commissioners were liable, and the consequent flooding of the East Fen and Five Thousand Acre District; for diminishing the quantity of flood water going to the Lade Bank engines and for diverting the same to an improved outfall for Steeping River; also for improving the fresh water supply to the fens.

STEEPING RIVER.

A report was made to the Commissioners by Mr. Williams, stating that the outfall channel from Salem Bridge was very circuitous, its length, at average low water at Gibraltar point, being nearly 7 miles, whereas the distance in a direct line is only 4 miles. The water was prevented from getting freely away owing to the restricted condition of Wainfleet stanch, which was only 16ft. wide. The sea sluice, which was about 4¼ miles below Salem Bridge, had two openings, 12ft. 2in. and 5ft. 9in. wide. The fall from Salem Bridge to the sea sluice was at the rate of 12in. a mile. He advised the cutting off of the worst bends of the river, and shortening the course 1 mile 12 chains, and enlarging it, so as to give 15ft. at the bottom; the erection of a new stanch with 50ft. opening; the construction of an additional opening of 15ft. to the existing sluice; and the improvement of the channel below the sluice, for a distance of 1¼ miles. The estimated cost of these works was £19,425. It was anticipated that these works would affect a depression of 2ft. in the flood level above Salem Bridge.

STEEPING RIVER ACT.
48 and 49 Vict. c. 158, 1885.

The Commissioners applied to Parliament for further powers to enable them to carry out this work, and in 1885 the *Steeping River Act* was obtained, authorising the straightening and widening of Steeping River and Wainfleet Haven, from Salem Bridge to low water in the Outfall channel, seaward of the Burgh Sluice recently erected; and the construction of a new stanch and a new Outfall sluice with a 12ft. opening to the south of the old sluice, which remained available as a flood channel. The old stanch was removed, and a new one built, near Croft Station, a mile east of the old one, with two draw doors, each of 12ft. 6in. opening. The sluice and stanch were built by Mr. S. Sherwin of Boston, at a cost of about £3,300. The total cost of the works was—

	£	s.	d.
Parliamentary, Legal and Engineering costs in obtaining the Act	3,450	12	6
Land and Legal costs	1,947	17	1
Works	9,830	10	7
	£15,449	0	2

To meet this, £15,000 was borrowed, bearing interest at 4¼ per cent., and repayable by annual instalments in 35 years, from the 6th April, 1885. To meet the interest on this sum, a tax, not exceeding sixpence per acre on the Fourth District and *the Five Thousand Acres*, was authorised; and lands in the parishes of Great Steeping, Irby, Firsby, Bratoft, Croft, Wainfleet All Saints, Wainfleet St. Mary, Stickford and Sibsey were added to the Fourth District for the purposes of this Act only. The Commissioners of Sewers were authorised to contribute yearly one-fourth of the expense of maintaining the channel in the tideway below Burgh Sluice.

RECEIPTS AND EXPENDITURE.

The amounts annually raised and expended for Fourth District purposes are, on an average, as follows:—

Receipts.

	£
General Tax, at 1/6 per acre	4,631
Foreland Rents	757
Fines and Sundries	10
	£5,398

	Payments.	£
Interest and Repayment by instalments of Loan for Lade Bank engines	... ...	1,224
Management	... ...	642
Sluicekeeper's Wages	... ...	64
Roding drains and repairs	... ...	1,635
Lade Bank Engine	... ...	674
		£4,239

Showing a surplus of income of £1,159. This annual surplus has since increased, the interest on the loan decreasing as the instalments are paid off. The cost of the Lade Bank engines has also been less during the late dry seasons, and also from the improvement of the Outfall. On the other hand, the Foreland rents have fallen off. The surplus income was for some time applied to paying off a debt due to the Treasurer, which had increased yearly from 1880, till it amounted to £5,031, since when it diminished until 1888, when it was cleared off. The balance in the Treasurer's hands on the 30th June, 1894, stood at £7,404. 53 half-yearly instalments had been paid off the loan for Lade Bank engine in June, 1894, and the whole will be paid off in 1902.

The instalments of repayment of the loans of £28,000 and £29,000, borrowed in 1881 and 1883, to pay the contributions of the Fourth District towards the Outfall, and for the enlargement of Hobhole sluice, will terminate in 1916. The interest on the first loan is $4\frac{1}{2}$ per cent. and on the second $4\frac{1}{4}$ per cent. The Precepts paid to the Outfall Board amounted to £41,118 19s. 4d., and there was spent on the Hobhole Improvement £5,919 14s. 0d. Parliamentary Expenses absorbed £1,515 1s. 10d., leaving a balance in hand of £1,446 4s. 10d. The interest and repayment of principal take £2,764 yearly which in 1892 required a rate of about tenpence an acre, which was reduced to sixpence in 1893. The ordinary contributions towards maintenance are covered by a rate of about twopence an acre, which raises £593, but there appears to have been some extraordinary charges which have required a rate of fourpence an acre. No rate was laid in 1894 and there was then a balance of £710 in the Treasurer's hands.

The Steeping River Improvement Loan of £15,000 requires about £815 a year for interest and repayment of principal, which, however, decreases annually. This is covered by a rate of sixpence an acre, producing £810. The repayments on this loan will expire in 1920.

The main drains in the district are under the charge of the General Commissioners. The engines at Lade Bank and Hobhole Drain are under the charge of a special Committee, elected by the General Commissioners.

SYSTEM OF MANAGEMENT.

INTERIOR DISTRICT.

The interior drains are under the management of the 26 Fourth District Interior Commissioners, elected in the manner set out in the Act of 1818. The tax levied for interior purposes is about fivepence per acre for the East Fen, and fourpence for the West and Wildmore Fens. A forfeit for non-payment of the taxes at the time named in the annual advertisement is imposed, amounting to one shilling for ten shillings and under, two shillings above ten shillings and so on in proportion for any greater or less sum than twenty shillings. The amount raised by taxation for the Interior District, in 1892-3, was £1,124; maintenance of works cost £742; management £366. Total £1,108.

DESCRIPTION OF THE DISTRICT.
Fig. 7.
2 Geo. iii, c. 32.

THE FIFTH DISTRICT.—This district lies on the south side of the Witham, to the north of Kyme Eau, and contains 5,176 acres. It comprises the low lands in Anwick, North Kyme, Ruskington, Dorrington and Digby, and is described in the act of 1762 as being bounded by Digby Old Skirth Dyke and the dyke which is the eastern boundary of the adjoining close, and that part of Digby Engine Drain which extends from the said dyke to the engine, Billinghay Skirth, and Billinghay Dales, on the north and east; Kyme Eau on the south; the high lands of Anwick, Ruskington, Dorrington and Digby and the Car Dyke on the west. It elects one District Commissioner for each of the parishes and places named, and these elect two Representatives on the Witham General Drainage Trust. The mode of Election and the qualification of Voters is the same as described in the First District. It is divided into four Levels, each having a separate Act of Parliament, viz., North Kyme Fen; Ruskington, Dorrington and North Kyme; Anwick and North Kyme Praie Grounds; and the Digby Drainage District. The land is low, and depends almost entirely on pumping for its drainage.

South Kyme Low Grounds, which lies within this district, drains by Damford Tunnel, which passes under Kyme Eau into the Merry Lands, in the Second District, and thence by Gill Syke to the North Forty-Foot. It does not pay drainage rates to the Second District.

INCLOSURE ACT.
31 Geo. iii, c. 93, 1791.

ANWICK FEN.—This Fen was enclosed under an Act obtained in 1791, *for dividing and enclosing the open common fields, meadow ground, half-year land, common fens, and waste lands in the parish of Anwick, and for embanking and draining the fens and enclosed lands called 'the Praie Grounds' in the township of North Kyme.*

The District is managed by three Commissioners, elected every three years by the Proprietors of not less that 50 acres. Their duties are to maintain the works, consisting of the banks surrounding the district, the engine drains and the engine. The ordinary rate is not to exceed 1/- an acre, but, with the consent of the Proprietors, the amount is unlimited,

Mr. Clarke, in his history of the Agriculture of Lincolnshire, says, that there were formerly in this district many windmills of Dutch construction; the Fens having been drained by the Flemings, more than a century before the drainage of Anwick Fen. Part of the north of the fen drained into Billinghay Dales, and the rest by windmills into Billinghay Skirth. He states that before the inclosure the whole rental of Anwick Fen was £54; after the enclosure it rose to £703. Clarke, *Roy. Agr. Soc. Journal*, 1847.

RUSKINGTON, DORRINGTON AND NORTH KYME.—This District was formed under the powers of an Act obtained in 1832, entitled, *an Act for inclosing, draining and embanking lands within the parishes of Ruskington and Dorrington, and the Hamlet of North Kyme.* The lands enclosed were described in the Act as being subject to be overflowed with water, for want of proper banks, drains, and outfalls; and as including the Common Fen, the North Fen, the Pringle and Kyme Pits, containing 462 acres; and inclosed low lands, containing 819 acres. The North Fen and Pringle had been excluded from the Inclosure Act for the parish of Dorrington, passed in 1787. The 'low lands' had been inclosed under the powers of an Inclosure Act for the parish of Ruskington, passed in 1778. INCLOSURE AND DRAINAGE ACT. 2 and 3 Will. iv. c. 70.

The District is bounded on the south by Digby and Billinghay and the Sleaford and Tattershall roads; on the west, by the high lands in Anwick, Ruskington and Dorrington; on the north, by Digby Drainage District, Billinghay and North Kyme Praie Grounds; and on the east, by Billinghay Dales. Under the Act Thomas Greetham of Fiskerton was appointed sole Commissioner and his remuneration was fixed at £3 3s. 0d. a day, and £2 2s. 0d. at the end of three years. The Surveyor was to be allowed eighteenpence an acre for surveying and mapping, and £2 2s. 0d. per day, consisting of eight hours between March and October, and six hours for the remainder of the year. The Commissioner was empowered to stop up and divert old, and to make new, roads; to scour out, enlarge, improve and embank any ancient drains; to make the drain adjoining Digby township 35ft. wide and 5ft. deep; to make new bridges, cloughs, windmills and engines as he should think needful. If Proprietors neglect to clean out drains or repair banks, bridges, &c., as directed in the Award, the Trustees are given power to do the same, after 14 days notice, and charge the defaulter with costs. Power was given to borrow £4,000. The herbage of the banks, roads, and waste lands was to be let by the Trustees for grazing sheep for three years, to the best bidder, and the proceeds applied to the drainage and repair of roads. The Award was to be deposited in a chest in the parish church of Ruskington.

After the Commissioner had completed his work, five Trustees were to be appointed; two elected by Ruskington, by Proprietors holding 15 acres; two for Dorrrington; and one for North Kyme, by

Proprietors holding 10 acres. They remain in office for three years. Meetings for election were directed to be held in the respective vestries of the churches of Ruskington, Dorrington and South Kyme, after public notice fixed on the church doors, and also by advertisement in a newspaper circulating in the County of Lincoln, three to form a quorum, and agents to have power to vote; meetings for laying rates to be held within eight miles of the parishes. If rates be not paid, power to distrain after 21 days' notice was given. A penalty of £10 was imposed on persons found guilty of opening the cloughs and letting off water, and persons proved to have destroyed any of the works were to be deemed guilty of felony. By the Act of 1778 an Engineer was to be annually appointed to take care of the engine and drains, at a vestry to be held on Easter Tuesday.

PUMPING MACHINERY.

This fen is drained by a steam engine of 16 N.H.P., working a centrifugal pump, situated about a quarter of a mile west of North Kyme Causeway, the water being discharged into Billinghay Skirth. The area drained by the engine is about 1,300 acres. This engine was erected in 1854, at a cost of £1,440.

BREACH OF BANK.

In 1880 the bank which protects the fen was broken during a high flood and the land inundated.

RATES AND EXPENDITURE.

The amount of taxation is not to exceed £350 annually, without the consent of the Owners. The amount laid used to average 5/6 an acre, but has recently been 4/-.

According to the Government taxation return for 1892-3, the amount raised by taxation was £304, and from other sources £88, making £392. The cost of maintaining the works was £239, management, &c. £66; total £305. There is no outstanding loan.

BOUNDARY.

DIGBY DRAINAGE DISTRICT.—This comprises Digby Fen, the Pry Closes, Walcot Common and other low fenland in the parishes of Billinghay, Walcot and Timberland Thorpe, and contains about 1,440 acres. Digby Fen had been previously embanked and was drained by an engine and scoop wheel. The other part of the District, being low and unembanked, was constantly flooded.

FORMATION OF DRAINAGE DISTRICT.

In 1871 this level was formed into a separate Drainage District, under *the Land Drainage Act* of 1861, the engine and wheel being purchased from the owner.

A scheme for improving the drainage was prepared by the Author, and under his direction the Scopwick Beck was deepened and straightened, and the water carried to the existing scoop wheel. The Grange Drain, skirting the high land on the north side, was improved and converted into a catchwater drain, and continued eastward to the end of the District, so as to discharge its water clear of the fen. The engine is of 14 N.H.P., and the scoop wheel 24ft. in diameter and 1ft. wide. The wheel makes $6\frac{1}{2}$ revolutions per minute, and the engine 40. The lift in floods is from 5ft. to 6ft.

From the Government Taxation Returns for 1892-3, the amount raised by rate was £221, and by special rate payable by Owners, £376; making, with £13 from other sources, £610. Maintenance of the engine and works cost £135, Interest on loan £151, Instalment of principal repaid £228, Management £77; Total £591. The amount of loan then outstanding was £2,966.

THE SIXTH DISTRICT.—This District is on the south side of the Witham, and lies to the west of Holland Fen. It contains 11,584 acres, sends three Commissioners to the Witham General Drainage Trust, and pays a tax of 6d. per acre to the Witham Commissioners.

The Outfall of the drainage of this District is the South Forty-Foot, and the land was included in the Black Sluice Level under the Act of 1765, and will therefore be described in the Chapter on the Black Sluice.

CHAPTER VII.

THE BLACK SLUICE DISTRICT.

BOUNDARY.

Fig. 10.

THE district included in the above heading is all that area of land which pays taxes to the Black Sluice Commissioners; consisting of the Sixth and Second Witham Districts, including Holland Fen, and what Dugdale calls *the Lindsey Level*. It is bounded on the north by Kyme Eau; on the east by the River Witham and the town of Boston; on the south and east by the old Hammond Beck, the Glen, and Bourne Eau; and on the west by the Car Dyke, which passes near to Bourne, Rippingale, Billingborough, Horbling, Helpringham, and Heckington. The taxable area is 64,854 acres, but the total quantity of land which discharges its water into the Witham, through the Black Sluice, is about 134,351 acres.

The outlet for the drainage of this District is at the Black Sluice, in Skirbeck Quarter. The main drain is the South Forty Foot, which runs through the centre of the fen, and is 21 miles in length, receiving throughout its course the contents of about 30 other drains, the principal of which are the North Forty Foot, the Clay Dyke and the Old and New Hammond Becks.

SECOND AND SIXTH WITHAM DISTRICT.

Fig. 6.

The principal part of the northern portion of this District, consisting of Holland Fen and the lands in the Sixth District, originally drained to the Witham by means of Kyme Eau and Gill Syke, which discharged at a sluice at Langrick. Subsequently, after the North Forty Foot Drain was cut, a portion of the drainage was discharged by it at Lodowick's Gowt, which was situated about a third of a mile to the west of the present Grand Sluice, the old course of the River Witham passing in that direction.

Owing to the defective condition of the channel and banks of the Witham, this District was continually flooded from the river.

When the Witham was straightened and improved in the last century, and the flood water banked out from Holland Fen, the Second and the Sixth Districts were included in the area of taxation liable for payment of taxes levied to meet the cost of improvement, and consequently these two Districts send representatives to the Witham Commission. The drainage was subsequently diverted and is now all discharged into the Black Sluice System by means of

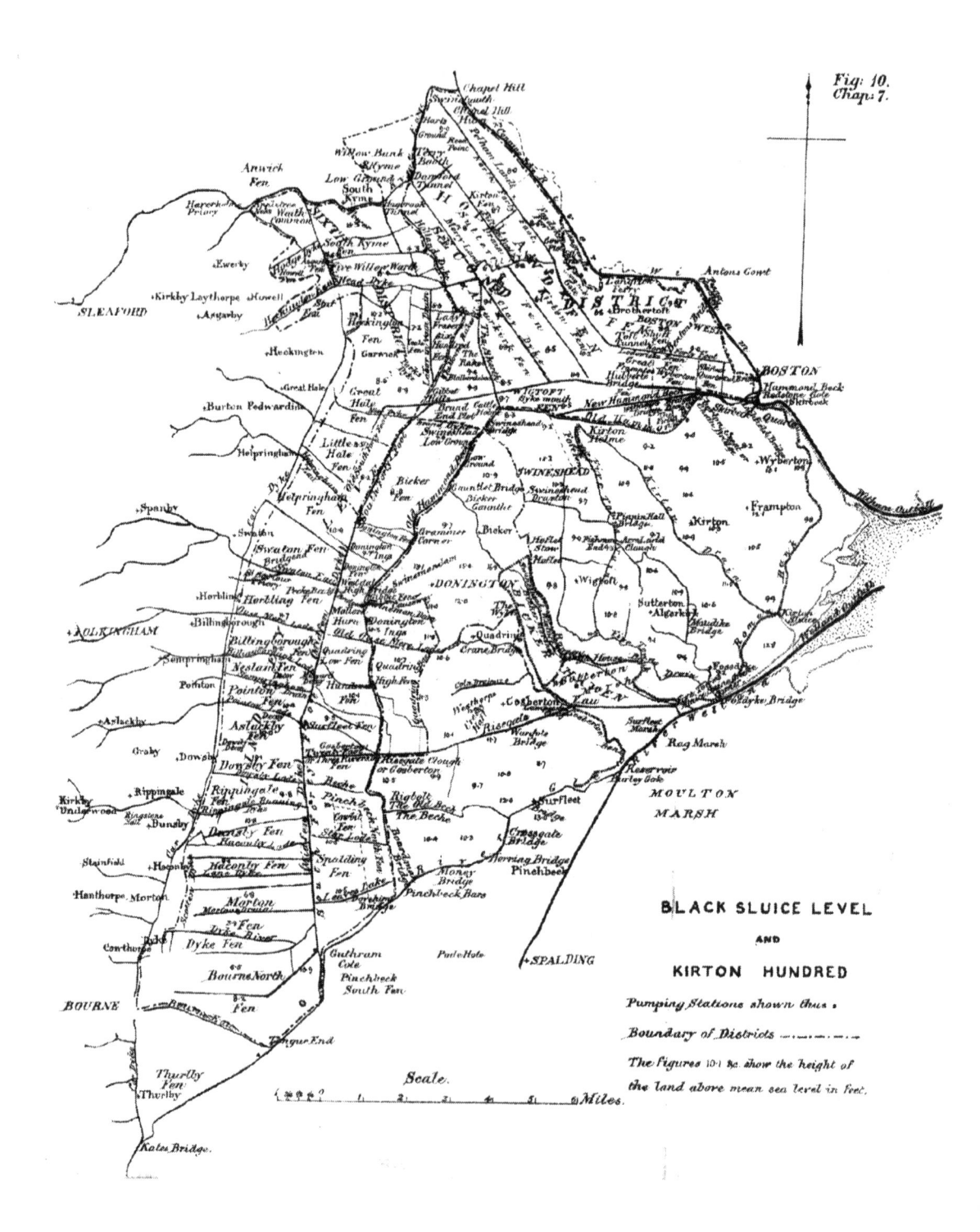

BLACK SLUICE LEVEL AND KIRTON HUNDRED

Fig: 10.
Chap: 7.

Pumping Stations shown thus.
Boundary of Districts ———
The figures 10·1 &c. show the height of the land above mean sea level in feet.

Scale. Miles.

the South Forty Foot; and these two Witham Districts now form part of the Black Sluice System, and pay taxes to it, as well as to the Witham.

The southern portion of the District, formerly known as the Lindsey Level, consists of a long narrow tract of land, lying between the Cardyke and the high land on the west, and the Hammond Beck on the east, and extends up to Bourne. This was originally the site of a mere into which a number of high land streams poured their contents. The overflow from this mere drained away to the Glen by means of the old watercourse, called the Beche; or to the Witham by the Hammond Beck. *LINDSEY LEVEL.*

The early history of the District will be found in the Chapter on North Holland.

Besides the ancient sewers, several new drains have been cut from time to time, the largest of which, the 'Mid Fen Dyke,' formed the boundary between Holland and Kesteven, and followed the course of the present South Forty-foot Drain from Gutherham Cote as far as the bend at Swineshead; it then continued along 'Barkesmere' and Holland Dyke to Kyme Eau.

In the thirteenth century, Richard I made an order freeing the inhabitants of this part of Lincolnshire from all duties relating to forest customs and the preservation of wild animals, with leave to make banks and ditches, and to enclose the lands and marshes; and also to build houses and exercise tillage as they should think fit. *DISAFFORESTATION. 1207.*

The disafforestation order related to lands, marshes, and turbaries. The only trees which grew in this fen district were sallows, willows and alders, which in places formed low thickets. The land generally was covered with rushes, reeds and clumps of sedge. To this solitary waste, deer and game and abundance of wild fowl resorted. The boundary, as described in the King's order, was " in length on the one side, from Swaston to East Deping as Kars did extend itself ... and in length on the other side towards Holand from the bridge at Byker to the great bridge at Spalding. In breadth on the one part from that great bridge to East Deping, and on the other side from the land of Swastune unto the bridge at Byker."

In the reign of Henry III a precept was directed to the Shirereeve of the county, touching the partition of Haut Huntre Fen (Holland Fen), or *Mariscus Octo Hundredorus*, as it is called in some of the old records, by the consent of those who had right therein, whereby the King gave command that each town might have its due proportion assigned to it. A perambulation was made of the boundaries by twelve lawful Knights and these were properly fixed. Subsequently, in the 44th year of his reign, the King " directing his precept to the Shirereeve of the county, whereby taking notice that not only the landowners in those parts, but himself, had suffered inestimable damage by the overflowing of the *HOLLAND FEN. 1216.*

Dugdale.

sea, and likewise of the fresh waters, through the default in the repairs of the banks, ditches, gutters, bridges, and sewers in the lands which lately belonged to William Longespe, in the Parts of Kesteven and Holland, he commanded the said Shirereeve forthwith to distrain all such Landholders who had safeguard by those banks and ditches, and ought to repair them according to the proportion of their lands, to the end that they might be speedily repaired in such sort as they ought and had used."

1279. In 1279 a Commission was sent by the King to investigate complaints as to neglect to repair the banks, sewers, ditches and gutters, and to maintain the bridges, whereby the inhabitants of the Wapentake of Kirton had sustained much loss by the overflowing of the Haute Huntre Fen, and in the year following the Prior of Spalding was summoned and ordered to repair the Peccebrigge. Again, seven years later, there was a great inundation in those parts, at which time most of Boston was drowned, and the King being informed that excessive damage had befallen the province by the want of repair of this Holand Causey, and by the decay of the banks, ditches and sewers in those parts, gave special command to the Justices itinerant to search the records and report to him as to the persons liable for such repairs; and this being done, and because it was thought that it would be too much trouble and inconvenience for so great a number of people to appear before the King wheresoever he might then be in his realm, and therefore it might be better to have the same discussed in these parts, the King appointed two

SEWERS COMMIS- SIONS. Commissioners, to enquire who ought to repair those banks and sewers and to distrain them thereto.

1293. In the 23rd year of the reign of Edward I, at an Inquisition held at Gosberton, the Jury found that "Brunne Ee, Tolhan and Blake Kyrk ought to be repaired, raised and scoured by the town of Brunne from Brunne to Goderamscote on the north side; and on the south to Merehirne, beyond which the town of Pyncebek ought to repair it unto Surflete; and the town of Surflete from thence to the sea. Also that the sewer of Briggefleeter ought to be repaired by the town of Hekytone to the river of Swynesheved, whence the river was sufficient thereof to Kyme mouth. That the sewer of Enclusc, near Boston, was stopped by the inhabitants of Boston on the west part of the bridge there, and that it ought to be 3ft. in breadth."

1307. In the reign of Edward II, the King's Justices sat at Boston to make enquiry into the state of the drainage and other matters relating to the Fens of Holland, when it was presented that, through the neglect of the Prior of Haverholme, the whole marsh of Kesteven and Holland was overflowed and drowned. It was found that the sewer called Hammond Beck, on the south end of Boston, was obstructed and ought to be repaired by the men of Boston inhabiting the west side of the bridge, and by the men of Skirbeck; and for that reason all the said Inhabitants residing on the west side of the bridge ought to common in the Eight Hundred Fen; also that the inhabitants of the 'Eight Hundreds' ought to cleanse the river of Swynesheved from Balberdebothe unto the north end of Swynesheved town; and the town of Swynesheved to do the like from the said place unto the River of Byker. The other sewers then in existence, and the places liable to their repair, were as follows, viz., the Swyneman Dam and Swane-lade, 16ft. to 20ft. wide, passing near Donington, Quadring and Gosberton, to Bicker Haven, and repaired by those parishes; Risegate Ees (Risegate Eau), extending from Gosberton to the sea, belonging to the parish of Gosberton; the sewer of the Beche, running from Pinchbeck North Fen to the sea, belonging to the parishes of Pinchbeck and Surfleet; Burne Alde Ee, running from Bourne through Surfleet to the sea; the first portion from Bourne to Gutheram Cote, belonging to the town and the Abbot of Bourne jointly; and thence to Surfleet, belonging to the town of Pinchbeck, and after that to Surfleet. Dunsby was drained by a sewer called the Soud; Hacconby, by one called Fenbrigg.

After this several Commissions were issued to view the state of the fens and fix the boundaries, the particulars of which are only a recapitulation of the above. One Inquisition, held at Thetford, found "that the banks of the Glen from Kate's Bridge to the sea were broken on both sides and they ought to be repaired, raised 2ft. and made 12ft. thicker. That this ought to be done on the north side by the towns of Thurlby, Obthorpe and Eyethorpe unto the cross near Abbote's Cote; thence by the town of Brunne to Godram Cote; thence by Pincebec and Surflete to the sea. Also that the banks of the river of Brunne ought to be enlarged from Leve Brigg in Brunne unto Tollum, and be made 2ft. higher and 12ft. thick, and that the town of Brunne ought to cleanse the Narwhee from Brunne to Godram's Cote."

In 1376, it was found by a Sewer's Jury that "the said water wathmouth at its junction with Kyme Eau, was the common passage from Kesteven unto the River Witham, and that the ditch which is called the Old Hee, lying betwixt Holland Fen and Heckington Fen, ought to be cleansed and repaired by the inhabitants of the Eight Hundreds of Holland on the east part, and by Henry de Beaumont, Lord of Heckington, and the Commoners of Heckington, and Philip de Kyme on the west part, and from Balberdebothe to the river of Kyme; and that the town of Hekington and Gerdwike ought to repair and cleanse the stream of Gerdwike unto the water of Swineshed, viz., unto Balberdebothe, but the half of the said stream, unto the park on the south side, the Parson of Hale ought to cleanse and repair." It was further presented " that at the head of Caresdik was a certain stream which is called the South Ee, and ought to be repaired and cleansed by the town of Little Hale and the Commoners thereof on the one part, and by the towns of Helpringham and Biker unto Gobion Bothe on the other part ; and that Hatchlode was a common sewer, and ought to run at the same time that the sewer of Scathegraft did ; and that it ought, at the entrance of the water from the fen, to be 1ft. in breadth, and as much in depth, and within, by the town, to be 6ft. in breadth to the sea ; and to be repaired by the town of Pincebec to the sea ; also, that Brunne Old Ee ought to be repaired, raised and cleansed and maintained by the town of Brunne ; by the Abbot of Brunne from Brunne unto Goderamscote ; and the town of Pincebec ought to repair the same to Surflet ; and the town of Surflet to the sea. For the default whereof, all the fen of Holland and Kesteven was overflown and drowned."

1362.
In the 25th year of Edward III, a petition was presented to the King and his Council in Parliament, by the inhabitants of the fens in Kesteven and Holland, showing that the ancient boundary between the two divisions of the county, the Mid-fen Dyke, and the other metes which went through the said fens from the Welland to the Witham, were at that time, by reason of floods and other impediments, so obscured as to be no longer visible, and hence frequent quarrels occured between the inhabitants : in consequence a Commission was appointed, and the boundaries properly set out and defined by stone crosses.

About this time also, a presentment was exhibited against the town of Bourne, with the hamlet of Dyke and Calthorp, and the town of Morton and Hermethorpe, for turning the fresh water towards the north, through the fens to Boston, instead of allowing it to run eastwards towards the sea.

1365.
Three years afterwards, a Commission was issued to view and repair the banks and ditches on the south side of the Witham, from the town of Skirbeck to a place called the Shuff, and two years after for those betwixt the towns of St. Saviour (Bridge End), near Gibbet Hills, and Donington.

1376.
In the same reign, "the towns of Hekyngton and Gerwick were found to be liable to repair and cleanse the one-half of Gerwick Ee, on the north side, unto the cow stalls of the Abbot of Swinesheved called Herevik ; and, by another Jury, that the inhabitants of the Eight Hundreds of Holand ought to cleanse and repair the ditch called the Old Ee, betwixt the Marsh of Holand and the Marsh of Hekington, on the west side of Balberboth and Haggeboth of West Crofte ; and the ditch from Balberboth in Hekington unto the Distrithe in Swinesheved Marsh."

After this there appears to have been a long cessation of these Commissions, until the reign of Queen Elizabeth, as Dugdale says he could not find the record of any more for this province, except in the 6th year of the reign of Henry V, when a Commission was appointed to view and take order for the repair of the banks and ditches, and to proceed according to the law and custom of the realm.

In the time of Henry VIII, the first systematic attempt at drainage was made. A Commission of Sewers was appointed and sat at Donington, and, having made survey of the fen, decreed that two great sewers, 20ft. wide and 5ft. deep, running parallel, at a distance of 36ft. from each other, should be cut from Gutheram's Cote to a point called Wragmere Stake, where they were to unite and continue in one channel, 30ft. wide, to Gill Syke, and then to the river Witham at Langrick, where was a sluice. "And the said waters from the rivers of Glen to Witham, so intended from the south to the north, should fall into, enter, and go through all the lodes and drains in the fens aforesaid which came out of the parts of Kesteven to Hammond Beck, to the end that all the water going together might the better run within its own brinks and channels, and the sooner come to the sluice at Skirbeck Gote, and the new gotes at Langrick." At Langrick a new sluice was to be built of freestone, with four doors, each 8ft. wide. The sewers were to be paid for by the several parishes through which the drains passed, and the sluice by the fen towns in Kesteven, Heckington, Kyme and Ewerby.

This order of the Court of Sewers was disobeyed by the parishes, who, instead of performing the works severally required of them, disputed the power of the Commission to make order for the execution of new works of drainage, contending that their functions only extended to the maintenance of the old and existing works. And so matters remained in abeyance till Queen Elizabeth's time, in the 8th year of whose reign a Court of Sewers was held at Sempringham, and a general tax was again laid for carrying out the works ordered by the former Court; but nothing was done until nine years afterwards. At another Court, held at Swineshead, the Countrymen complained that they were drowned more than formerly; and upon this an order was again made that those drains which the Duke of Suffolk and others had ordained to be begun about the latter end of the time of King Henry VIII, as also some others, should forthwith be set upon, and a tax was laid to pay for the same. The towns again refused to pay, and nothing was done for twenty-seven years, when the case was brought before the Court of Queen's Bench. Dugdale gives the following account of the trial:—

"In 43 and 44 Elizabeth a great controversy did arise in the county of Lincoln about the erecting of two new gotes at Skirbeck and Langare, for draining the waters of South Holland and the fens into Boston Haven, which work Sir Edward Dimock, Knight, did

1419.

1564.

1602.
Dugdale's *Embanking and Draining.*

by himself and his friends further what he could, but it was opposed by the county of Kesteven; and the exception taken thereto was that the Commissioners of Sewers could not, by the power of their Commission, make a law for the erecting of those new gotes where never any stood before; whereupon, the decision of this point coming at length before the then two Justices, *viz.*, Popham and Anderson, they delivered their opinions, that the said new gotes, if they were found to be good and profitable for the safety and advantage of the country, they might be erected by the power of this statute."

Notwithstanding this judgment the inhabitants could not be made to pay, and the works were never carried out.

In this reign, also, orders were made, at a Court held at Helpringham, " that the sewer called Ripingale South Dyke should be dyked from Berham Pooles to Irelode, and thence to the Beche, 12ft. in breadth, by the township of Pincebec; also that Irelode drain should be dyked and banked by Dowsby and Ripingale for their limits; and thence to the Beche by other townships through which it passed; that a bridge should be built by the inhabitants of Quadring and Byker within the limits of Byker in Hekendale Wathe, over to Hekendale Hills, of such height as boats might well pass under and that bridges should also be built over the sewer at Kyrton Fen; another at Frampton Fen, and another at Lichfield End, by the townships and persons who of right ought to do the same: these bridges to be 12ft. in breadth and of height sufficient for boats to pass under. Also that the Waredyke, beginning at Colehouse Stile and so extending along the river of Burne Ee to Goodram's Cote, should be continued from the said cote to Dovehirne and distant from the river 100ft., and in breadth 12ft., and depth 3ft., at the cost of the parishioners of Pincebec; and that the sewer called Newe Dyke in Dyke Fen should be perfected from Ee Dyke Bridge unto Holand Fen Dyke; also that the sewer extending against the east to Northgraft should be dyked and banked by Hakanby, Dunsby and Pincebec, and that the sewer of Northgraft, from the first fall of the water of the fen to the sea, ought to be made 12ft. broad and 6ft. deep, by Pincebec; and that the the sewer called the Beche, from Wrightbolt Clowe to the sea should be dyked and roded by the townships of Pinchbeck, Gosberkirk and Surflet; the sewer called the Marisbeck to be scoured by the landholders; the sewer from Colehouse Stile to Frere Barre Hurne, thence to Burne Barre and thence to Ee Dyke, to be dyked by the Landholders."

REDSTONE GOWT. 1601.

Under an order of the Court of Sewers, held at Boston, on March 16th, 1601, Redstone Gote was constructed for the purpose of affording a new outfall for the Hammond Beck. A new Cut, about three quarters of a mile long, was also made, from it, to join the Old Hammond Beck at Litchfield Bridge, and continued thence to Kirton Holme. This new sewer was formerly known as the Redstone Gote or Adventurers' Drain, and now as the New Hammond Beck.

NEW HAMMOND BECK.

In 1673, Redstone Gote was presented to be rebuilt and enlarged on the south side. Again in 1674, it was represented to be 'in a lost ruined condition' and that it would cost £1,000 to rebuild it. The inhabitants of Kesteven objecting to the expense, the work was deferred till 1695, when the Gote was rebuilt at a cost of £1,200, which was paid in equal portions by Kesteven and Holland.

The cost of the erection of Redstone Gote and of other works for improving the drainage, was apportioned over the District by the verdict of a Sewers' Jury and made a law of Sewers, known afterwards as 'the Redstone Gowt Law,' which was adopted as the basis for all future taxation.

REDSTONE GOWT LAW.

In the reign of Charles I, three of the Commissioners of Sewers, one of whom was Sergeant Callis, the author of the standard work on the Law of Sewers, made a representation to the King that all this fen was surrounded with water, and had no cattle on it, and praying him to take some steps for its reclamation; whereupon special courts were held at Sleaford and Boston, in the year 1633, and an order was made for the draining of the fens, a tax of 13s. 4d. per acre being laid upon the land to pay for the same. The Landowners still refusing to pay, three years afterwards, upon the direction of the King, the Commissioners, at Courts held at Sleaford, Swineshead, Boston and Bourne, on the recommendation of the King, made a contract with the Earl of Lindsey, Lord High Chamberlain of England, to drain the fens lying between Kyme Eau and the Glen, computed to contain 36,000 acres; for doing which he was to receive 24,000 acres of the reclaimed land, taken proportionately out of the several fens. Whereupon the Earl of Lindsey set vigorously to work, and completed the drainage so effectually that three years afterwards, at a Court of Sewers held at Sleaford, after survey made of the sluices, banks and sewers, decree was made that the Earl had made full performance of his contract, and the grant of land he was to receive as payment was ratified to him. The cost of this work was £45,000. On its completion the Earl and his fellow Adventurers inclosed the fens, built houses and farmsteads, brought the land into cultivation, and continued in peaceful possession about three years.

THE EARL OF LINDSEY'S RECLAMATION.

1633.

About the same time, King Charles appointed Sir Robert Killigrew and William Lackton to be the Undertakers for the drainage of the Eight Hundred, or Haut Huntre Fen, being that portion of the Level lying east of Earl Lindsey's Fen, or between Langrick and Boston, computed to contain 22,000 acres; and a tax of twenty shillings per acre was levied upon 16,000 acres, to be paid by the inhabitants of Brothertoft, Swineshead, Wigtoft, Sutterton, Algarkirk, Fosdyke, Kirton, Frampton, Wyberton, Hale, Dogdyke,

HAUTE HUNTRE FEN.

State Papers Domestic. 1633

and Boston, who claimed common therein. On this tax not being paid, the Commissioners of Sewers, at a Court held at Boston, declared the King to be the sole Undertaker for the draining thereof, and as recompense for the cost of the same, granted to him 8,000 acres of the reclaimed land. The King parted with his interest to Sir William Killigrew, who was also a fellow Adventurer with the Earl of Lindsey in his drainage of the rest of the Level; and under his direction this fen was drained and reclaimed.

ADVENTURERS' DRAINS.

The principal drains which appear to have been made by the Adventurers were a new Cut, called the South Forty-Foot, from Swineshead to Boston, for the purpose of diverting the drainage from Kyme Eau to Boston Haven; and a Gote on the north of and adjoining the present Black Sluice, about 55ft. in width, with four pairs of pointing doors. From Swineshead the main drain was continued to Bridge End Causeway, by improving the existing drain and also making a new one parallel to it, to the west of the present drain and thence to Gutheram Cote, the drains being known as the Double Twelves Drain. This work was described as 'a navigable river from Bourne to Boston, a distance of 24 miles.'

A new drain, called Clay Dyke, was cut through the centre of Holland Fen, joining the new main drain a little above Hubbert's Bridge, and a new Cut, called Brand Dyke, was also made from the Car Dyke through Hale Fen, passing under the new South Forty-Foot and discharging the high land water into the Hammond Beck. A new Cut was made to bring the water from Heckington Eau to Gill Syke, which discharged into the Witham by a sluice at Langrick.

DESTRUCTION OF THE ADVENTURERS' WORKS.
Dugdale, 1662.

The Earl and his partner, Sir W. Killigrew, were successful with the drainage, and the country began to assume a habitable appearance, but several disputes as to the rights of the Adventurers to their share of the reclaimed land having arisen, petitions were presented to Parliament by the Fenmen. After an enquiry, orders were granted by both Houses confirming the Earl in the possession of his property. "The malcontents, thus failing to obtain their way, in contempt of all law and order, destroyed the drains and buildings, and also the crops—then ready to be reaped—to a very great value"; and up to Dugdale's time had "held possession, to the great decay and ruin of those costly works and exceeding discommodity to all that part of the country." They also attempted to pull down the new sluice at Boston, which had cost £6,000. Sir W. Killigrew appealed to the Mayor of Boston, and prayed that an order might be given "to enquire out those that are now pulling that great sluice to pieces, which if it should, by this breaking up, be suncke by the water getting under it, the sea will break in all that side of the country, where no sea ever came. By the ruin of this our main sluice I conseave a hundred thousand pound damage may be done to the country, which those rogues doe not consider that doe steale and breake up the iron and the plankes of that great Sluse." The 'rogues,' however, succeeded and the sluice was completely destroyed, the water from the fen, for the next hundred years, finding its way to Boston Haven by the outfall at Redstone Gote, which was described in 1765 as 'the course of the water from the fens,' and by Lodowick's Gote and by the gote at Langrick.

It does not appear that the Adventurers could procure any relief, as the unsettled state of public affairs, party spirit, and other causes growing out of the circumstances of the period, seem to have impeded the course of justice, and Sir William died, forty years after his petition to Parliament, a poor man, ruined by his Adventure.

Thompson's Boston.

For nearly a hundred years the fen remained unreclaimed Some idea may be gained of its condition from the following description given by Mr. Thompson:—"The whole of the land between Brothertoft and Boston was frequently overflowed during the winter season. The turnpike road from Boston to Swineshead, and the intersecting roads, leading to the adjacent villages were covered with a considerable depth of water; of course they were dangerous to travel upon, and the country people brought their produce to Boston market in boats, being enabled very frequently to come in them as far as Rosegarth corner in West Street, the water often reaching to the *White Horse* Inn in that street."

NORTH FORTY-FOOT.

Fig 6.

About the middle of the 18th century Earl Fitzwilliam, for the purpose of draining his lands in Billinghay Dales, cut the North Forty-Foot through Holland Fen and diverted the water which went by Gill Syke to the Sluice at Langrick to a new outfall called Lodowick's Gote, situated on the old course of the Witham, about a third of a mile to the west of Boston Church.

GREAT FLOOD, 1763.

In the winter of 1763 and following spring, the greatest flood that was ever remembered occurred. Over the whole 22,000 acres of Holland Fen not one single acre was dry. The Parish of Brothertoft was entirely surrounded by water, which flowed into the houses. The flood extended from the high land near Heckington into the town of Boston. The banks of the Bourne Eau and the Glen being broken, it was expected that the water would make its way over the banks of the Hammond Beck, but by a great deal of labour in cradging, and a fortunate change taking place in the wind, the rest of the country was saved. This flood was caused by continued rain and the imperfection of the drainage.

MEETING OF PROPRIETORS.

On the 28th April, 1764, a meeting of Proprietors of lands in the fen was held at the *White Hart* in Boston. At this and subsequent meetings, it was determined to take steps to improve the drainage, and to open out the Old Black Sluice, which had been allowed to remain in ruins since its destruction by the Fenmen, a hundred years previously. Mr. Langley Edwards, who carried out

*LANGLEY ED-
WARDS REPORT.
1764.*

the works for the improvement of the Witham, was appointed Engineer, and presented a plan and report, by which it was proposed to bring the whole of the drainage of the level from Gutheram Cote to the Black Sluice at Boston. An objection was raised to part of this scheme by the Owners of land at the south end of the district, and they were supported in their opinion by Mr. Grundy of Spalding, who proposed that the drainage of Spalding, Pinchbeck and the other fens at the south end should discharge by the Old Beche into the Glen. Mr. Edward's plan, however, obtained the support of the majority, and was adopted, and it was determined to obtain an Act of Parliament giving the necessary powers. Mr. Edwards proposed opening out and repairing the Old Black Sluice; cleaning out the Black Sluice Drain to Swineshead; thence making a new drain along the course of the Old Double Twelves Drain, which ran in the same direction as the Mid-Fen Dyke to Gutherham; and also other drains, which are described more fully later on.

*BLACK SLUICE
ACT.
5 Geo. iii, c. 85.
1765*

A fund was raised by the principal Landowners for defraying the cost of obtaining an Act of Parliament, towards which the Corporation of Boston subscribed £40, and the *Act for draining and improving certain low marsh and fen lands lying between Boston Haven and Bourn, in the parts of Kesteven and Holland, in the County of Lincoln* was obtained.

The preamble of the Act states that "the lands to which it relates were frequently overflowed with water, through the insufficiency and decay of their Outfalls to the sea, whereby they were become of far less value and use to the Owners thereof, though they were very capable of being drained and improved."

Under the powers of this Act, the management was taken out of the hands of the Court of Sewers, to whom it had reverted after the failure of the Adventurers, and was placed in charge of a Commission, consisting of one Representative from each of the following parishes, Bourne, Dike, Cawthorp, Morton, Harmsthorp, Hackonby, Stainfield, Dunsby, Rippingale, Ringstone, Kirkby, Dowsby, Aslackby, Graby, Milthorpe, Poynton, Sempringham, Billingborough, Horbling, Swayton, Helpringham, Little Hale, Great Hale, Heckington, Asgarby, Howel, Ewerby, South Kyme, Bicker, Donington, Quadring, Quadring Hundred, Gosberton, Surfleet, Pinchbeck, Spalding and Cowbit, Boston West, Skirbeck, Quarter, Wyberton, Frampton, Kirton, Algarkirk, Fosdyke, Sutterton, Wigtoft, Swineshead and Brothertoft. All Proprietors of lands of any estate of freehold, copyhold of inheritance, or leasehold, wherein no more than half the yearly value thereof is reserved as a rent, being of the yearly value of five pounds and upwards, and lying within the parish or township; and all Farmers at rack rent of lands, being of the yearly value of thirty pounds, were authorised to have voices. It was also enacted that every person qualified to act as

Commissioner must be in possession, by his own or his wife's right, of rents of the yearly value of £100; or be entitled to a personal estate of the clear yearly value of £2,000.

The Commissioners are elected for three years, but continue in office after this period if the parishioners fail to hold an election at the end of the three years. In case of vacancy from death or refusal to act, another Commissioner to be elected within three months, or failing such election by the parishioners, the Lord of the Manor to have power to fill the vacancy. The elections are directed to take place at the vestry or the usual place of meeting in the parish, on the first Tuesday in May. Commissioners have power to appoint a Deputy for three months, provided such Deputy possesses half the qualification, or occupies £100 a year within the parish. The Commissioners or their Deputies were directed by this Act to take a prescribed oath before acting, but, by the Act of 1846, this oath was repealed and in its place a declaration has to be made, to the effect that the Commissioner is possessed of the necessary qualification and will without favour or affection, hatred or malice, truly and impartially perform the duties of the office. Each Commissioner was to be allowed five shillings a day for his expenses when attending the execution of the Act, which has to be paid by the parish represented. The limit of the tax by this Act was sixpence per acre on lands in Bourne, Dyke, Cawthorpe, Morton, Harmsthorp, Haconby, Stainfield, Dunsby, Rippingale, Ringstone, Kirkby, Dowsby, Aslackby, Graby, Milthorpe, Poynton, Sempringham, Billingborough, Horbling, Bridge End, Swaton, Helpringham, Donington, Quadring, Quadring Hundred, Gosberton, Surfleet, Pinchbeck North Fen, Bicker Common, Bicker and Swineshead Low Lands on the east side of Hammond Beck, and also the Common Marsh lying in Wigtoft and Swineshead; and threepence per acre on Swineshead Low Grounds on the west side of Hammond Beck, Little Hale, Great Hale, Heckington, Howell, Asgarby, Ewerby, and South Kyme, on the south side of Kyme Eau; and twopence per acre on such part of the Common called Holland Fen, wherein the following parishes had rights of Common, *viz.*, Boston West, Skirbeck Quarter, Wyberton, Frampton, Kirton, Algarkirk, Fosdyke, Sutterton, Wigtoft, Swineshead, and Brothertoft. The Commissioners of the Second Witham District were to pay to the Black Sluice Trust, the yearly rates of twopence and one penny per acre out of the monies raised on land in Holland Fen, for the purpose of interior drainage. If the above taxes were insufficient, the Commissioners were empowered to levy additional taxes to the extent of half the above amounts. Harts Grounds, the Great and Little Beats and the inclosed lands in Brothertoft were exempted from taxation.

The District is defined in the Act as bounded "on the north-east side by the south-west banks of the old and new River Witham, **BOUNDARY OF DISTRICT.**

excluding the said banks and the Haven of Boston from Chappell Hill Hurn, to the north side of Lodowick Gowt, excluding the said Gowt and banks thereof, and from the south side of the south bank thereof to the south side of the south bank of the South Forty-Foot at the Black Sluice by the Haven of Boston aforesaid; and on the south by the outside of the said south bank of the said Forty-Foot from the said Town to the junction of the old and new Hammond Becks with the said Forty-Foot a little below Wyberton Chain Bridge, and from thence by the north bank of the said old Hammond Beck to the east end of the Firth Lands, and thence by the east, north and west banks of the said Firth Lands, and from thence by the north bank of the old Hammond Beck to Kirton Holme, excluding the said bank; and from thence to Swineshead High Bridge, by the lands of Kirton Holme and the high grounds of Wigtoft and Swineshead, and from thence by the turnpike road through Swineshead to the Guide Post near Swineshead Drayton, and from thence by the division between Swineshead and Bicker to Hoflet Stowe, and thence by the east bank of the Wigtoft marsh to Lingerhouse, and from thence by the south end of the said marsh to Quadring Eau Dike, and to the division between the lands of Donington and Quadring, and thence by the said boundary to Crane Bridge, on the turnpike road from Donington to Quadring, and from the said bridge along the north bank of Mer Lode to the east bank of Hammond Beck, excluding the said Lode; and from thence along the west side of the said east bank, excluding the said bank, to the south side of the north bank of the River Glen, belonging to the Adventurers of Deeping Fen, and from thence westward along the south side of the said north bank to Gutheram Cote, and from thence on the south side of the north bank of the said River Glen, belonging to Bourne, as far as Tongue End, and from thence on the same side of the north bank of Bourne Eau as far as Bourne, and from Bourne on the west by the high grounds of Bourne Dike, Cawthorpe, Morton, Harmsthorp, Hackonby, Stainfield, Dunsby, Rippingale, Ringston, Kirkby, Dowsby, Aslackby, Graby, Milthorp, Poynton, Sempringham, Billingborough, Horbling, Bridge End, Swayton, Helpringham, Little Hale, Great Hale, Heckington, Asgarby, Howell and Ewerby, to the south bank of Kyme Eau, and by the said south bank, and the east bank of the said Eau to the said River Witham, near Chappell Hill aforesaid."

WORKS CARRIED OUT UNDER THE ACT. The following works were authorised to be carried out under the powers of this Act, *viz.*, the erection of a new sluice at the lower end of the South Forty-Foot Drain, on the spot where the Old Black Sluice formerly stood, the new floor lying on the old floor, and its water way being 56ft., or the same dimensions as the old floor, when found, would admit of, with 4 pairs of pointing doors; also a stanch for retaining fresh water in dry seasons for the use of cattle; the

South Forty-Foot was to be scoured and cleansed from the Black Sluice to the east side of Hale Fen, having 60ft. top and 46ft. bottom, to Clay Dyke, and from 3ft. to 5ft. deeper; thence to Hale Fen, 40ft. top and 30ft. bottom; thence a new drain to be cut to Gutherham Cote, having 40ft. top and 26ft. bottom, as far as Helpringham Eau; thence to Bridge End Causeway, 35ft. wide at top and 21ft. at bottom; thence in the same direction as the 'Double Twelves' to Gutherham Cote, gradually decreasing to 20ft. top and 10ft. bottom. The Hammond Beck from Redstone Gote to its junction with the Forty-Foot, and the Old Hammond Beck from its junction with the Forty-Foot, a little below Wyberton Chain Bridge until it met the New Hammond Beck, and thence to its junction with the Old Hammond Beck, above Hardwick Warth, 36ft. top and 20ft. bottom, decreasing to 30ft. top and 16ft. bottom; the Old Hammond Beck to be scoured out to Pinchbeck Bars, with 26ft. top and 16ft. bottom, gradually diminishing to the upper end; one of the drains from Gosberton Clough to the New Cut to be enlarged and made of the same dimensions as the New Cut at the junction; the side drain to be scoured out along the course of the new drain as the work went on.

The Deeping Fen Proprietors were to be exonerated from keeping in repair the North Bank of the Glen, from Dove Hurn to Gutheram Cote, and the Black Sluice Commissioners to maintain the same; the Deeping Fen Proprietors paying £18 per annum. They were also to keep in repair the bank from this point to the high lands in Bourne, this parish and Cawthorpe, the other Proprietors of the bank paying at the rate of 20s. a furlong for the maintenance of the same between Gutheram Cote and Tongue End, and 10s. a furlong from there to the high land in Bourne. No soil was to be taken to repair the south banks of the Glen or Bourne Eau within 20ft. of the north bank. Tunnels, not exceeding 9in. square, were to be laid through the banks on both sides, for the purpose of letting fresh water into the common lands for the use of cattle in dry seasons; and all the tunnels then existing through the banks of the Old and New Hammond Beck were to remain. Pointing doors were to be put down at the east end of Clay Dyke and on both sides of the Forty-Foot where the Skirth crosses, and at Hale East or Brand Dyke.

Bridges were to be built and maintained by the Commissioners wherever the new main drain crossed any public highway; all ancient bridges, where the drains were widened, were to be enlarged, and private bridges, where necessary, were to be erected, to preserve to the inhabitants of any place a passage to such parts of their lands as should be cut off by the new drain. By a subsequent Act a waggon bridge was to be built over Heckington Eau at Five Willow Warth, and a horse bridge across the New Cut, between Little

Hale and Bicker Fens, to be afterwards maintained by Bicker and Hale jointly.

The Eleven Towns of Holland having a right of Common in Holland Fen were authorised to erect at the expense of the Inhabitants, a bridge over the South Forty-Foot between Syke Marsh and Clay Hills, and also a waggon bridge over the drain at any place that the Commissioners might think proper. The navigation hitherto in use was not to be obstructed and the bridges were to be so constructed as not to hinder it.

The communication between Risegate Eau and the Hammond Beck was not to be stopped or interfered with, and the Proprietors of lands draining by it were to have the same rights of shutting down or keeping open the doors of Gosberton Clough.

The Commissioners were to scour out and afterwards maintain the following drains or becks, which convey the living and downfall waters from the high land into the maindrain, *viz.*, New Dyke in Bourne, Scotten Dyke, Haconby Lode, Rippingale Running Dyke, Dowsby Lode, Pointon Lode, Billingborough Lode, the Ouze Mer, between Billingborough and Horbling, Horbling New Drain, Swaton Eau, Helpringham Eau and the new Cut, leading from the Forty-Foot Drain eastward to Brand Dyke; the drain from the Clough at Hodge Dyke End in the Parish of Ewerby-by-Asgarby, and Howell Midfodder to Heckington Head Drain, and thence to Clay Dyke into the South Forty-Foot.

DRAINAGE WHEELS.

The diameters of any water wheels of the engines used for the interior drainage were not to exceed 15ft. between Bourne Eau and Rippingale Running Dyke; 14½ft. from there to Poynton Lode; 14ft. to Bridge End Causeway; and 13ft. below this.

ACCOMMODATION WORKS.

The Commissioners were to make a drain from the Swineshead and Wigtoft Marshes to the Hammond Beck, the cost to be defrayed out of the surplus money arising from the inclosure of the marsh. Redstone Gote and the drain leading thereto were, after the passing of the Act, to be repaired by the Commissioners.

Owners of land on the west side of the New Cut were to be authorised to put down clows at their own expense, at the lower end of the several drains next the Cut, for holding up water in dry seasons, the doors to be shut down only on four days in a week. For making or repairing banks the Commissioners were empowered to take soil within 300ft. of any bank on making satisfaction for the same. The Earl of Exeter was not to be hindered from taking water out of the River Glen for his two decoys near Bourne; nor the Earl of Warwick from having fresh water for the use of his lands in Algarkirk and Fossdyke from Kyme Eau, by tunnels under the South Forty-Foot, Hammond Beck and other drains.

OFFICERS.

The Commissioners were authorised to appoint a Receiver of Taxes and a Treasurer, both officers to give security; also a Clerk and Surveyor, and such other Officers as they should think fit.

For the collection of the rates each parish or township was once a year to nominate at a vestry two persons living within the parish, to collect the rates due from persons in such parish, and to pay the amount received half-yearly to the Receiver, for which they were to be paid twopence in the pound. The penalty for refusing to act after appointment was fixed at £5. By the subsequent Act it was provided that these Collectors were to be appointed within one month from the 7th of June in each year, and, if the parishes neglected to return two names in writing before that date, the Commissioners were empowered to make the necessary appointments. The nominations by the parish were to be reported to the Commissioners and confirmed. {COLLECTION OF RATES.}

In order to prevent the new works from being rendered abortive, as all previous attempts had been, by the lawlessness of the Fenmen, it was enacted that any persons proved guilty of wilfully or maliciously damaging any banks or works were to be deemed guilty of felony, and the Court before which they were tried was to have power to transport such felons for seven years. This clause was repealed in the Act obtained in the 12th year of the present reign, and in lieu thereof persons found guilty of injuring the works were to become liable to a penalty of £5. {PENALTY FOR INJURING WORKS.}

The amount authorised to be raised not proving sufficient, an amended Act was obtained, five years later, authorising the Commissioners to double the former taxes, which consequently became on the respective districts eighteenpence, ninepence, and sixpence per acre. They also obtained powers to carry out additional works, and to contribute £3,000 towards cleansing, deepening and widening the Glen from the sluice at the Reservoir to Tongue End, on the Commissioners of Deeping Fen spending a similar amount. {10 Geo. iii, c. 41}

They were further authorised to cause the Car Dyke to be scoured out and maintained from Bourne Eau to the north side of Haconby Lordship, and from there to cut a dike between Haconby and Dunsby to the old Scotten Dike, and Rippingale Running Dike to the New Cut; also that part of Heckington Head Drain from Howell Engine to the north-west corner of Truss Fen, and the Hodge Dike Drain from Howell Midfodder, between Ewerby Fen and Howell and Asgarby Fens, to the extent of the taxable lands, and the drain called Labour-in-vain Drain from the Division Drain of the fens of Heckington and Great Hale into the East Dike, and thence by the Twenty-Foot Drain into the New Cut; also the Northland Dike, the Old Forty-Foot, the New Dike to the Twenty-Foot, and thence to the New Cut; also the drains between Neslam Inclosed Grounds and Pointon Fen, and the drain between the Fens of Aslackby and Dowsby, and the drain between the Fens of Hacconby and Morton, and the drain between Bourne {DRAINS TO BE MAINTAINED BY THE TRUST.}

and Morton, from the new dike near Cooper's Engine to the east bank of the old Scotten Dike, were also to be scoured out and cleansed.

The Commissioners were empowered to cleanse and repair the Fifteen-Foot Drain, from the New Cut to Dampford Engine, and to charge the expense to the Commissioners of the Second District, in case they neglected to do this; also to scour out Wyberton Drain, Frampton Town Drain, and Kirton Town Drain, for the purpose of discharging the water from the New Cut and the Hammond Becks during the time that any work should be going on which would stop the water flowing to the Black Sluice.

A pair of pointing doors was to be erected near Gosberton Clough in Hammond Beck to prevent the flood waters flowing up the beck, south of the doors.

Certain Owners of lands north of the Glen were to be allowed to drain into their system upon payment of such rates as should be agreed on, and such lands were to be exempted from the authority of the Court of Sewers.

NAVIGATION. Power was given to erect a pen sluice, or lock, for navigation at the Black Sluice; and one at the east end of the drove-way in Little Hale Fen, and on the Hammond Beck; the top of the pen sluice at the Black Sluice, or Little Hale Fen, not to hold the water higher than within 2ft. below the mean level of the surface of the land within two miles of the New Cut and Clay Dike; and any pen stocks above this, to within 18in. below the surface, within two miles of the west side of the New Cut. Power was also given to carry out such works as were necessary for making the New Cut and the Hammond Beck navigable, and to exact tolls from boats, provided that such works did not prejudice the drainage. The pen locks or stanches were at any time to be opened, if necessary, for the drainage, on an order signed by three Commissioners.

The last attempt to drain the level was thoroughly successful. The works were efficiently carried out, and, being well-designed, entirely answered the expectation of the promoters. The fen, which, before the drainage, was little better than a morass, growing a coarse herbage and affording a scanty pasturage during the summer months, became rich arable and grass land, and the annual value increased tenfold.

INCLOSURE OF HOLLAND FEN. Two years after the Drainage Act had been obtained another was passed for enclosing and dividing Holland Fen. This Act will be referred to afterwards. The Enclosure and Drainage were not carried out without difficulty.

Several serious riots were caused by the Fenmen, the successors of those who had so effectually destroyed the works carried out by Earl Lindsey and the former Adventurers. The enclosure was regarded by these men as an infringement of rights and privileges which they had long enjoyed. Very lawless excesses were committed in opposition to, and to the destruction of, the public works; and fences which were erected in the day-time, were frequently pulled down during the night. So difficult was it found to maintain the fences put up, marking the divisions of the allotted lands, that a subsequent Act had to be obtained, authorising the removal and sale of the fencing and the substitution of ditches.

In the summer of 1768 a number of Fenmen and others assembled at Hubbert's Bridge, whence they proceeded to Boston and to the offices of Mr. Draper, the solicitor to the Commissioners, demanding all the papers relating to the Inclosure. Having seized the box which contained them, they tore the contents to pieces. They then went to the houses of those who were known to be promoters of the Inclosure, and threatened to pull their houses down if they did not promise to desist from proceeding. From Boston they went to Frampton, and in like manner threatened Mr. Tunnard and others. Finally the troops had to be called in and 'Gentleman Smith,' of Swineshead, the ringleader, was seized, and the riot quelled.

<small>RIOT OF 1768.</small>

The state of Bourne Eau and the River Glen has been a constant cause of anxiety to the Managers of the Black Sluice District. The bed of the latter river has gradually risen so high, by accumulated deposits, as to be above the level of the fen, and thus the drainage by it is very imperfect, and the banks are liable to breaches from heavy floods. These banks have given way no less than fourteen times since 1821, eight of the breaches being on the south, and six on the north side. When these breaches occurred, several thousand acres of land were inundated, to the very serious loss of the occupiers. It has been stated that the cost, during the above period, of maintaining the banks and repairing the breaches, amounted to upwards of £10,000.

<small>THE GLEN AND BOURNE EAU.</small>

The banks of Bourne Eau are even in a worse condition than those of the Glen, being low and made of light and porous earth. Doors are placed at Tongue End, pointing to the Glen, which prevent the water in floods from reverting up the Bourne Eau; an overfall of about 20ft. in length is fixed in the north bank, over which the water runs when it rises so high as to threaten a breach of the banks. This overflow is connected with the South Forty-Foot Drain near Gutherham Cote.

One of the most serious floods which has occurred since the new works were completed was in April 1872, when, on an unusually rapid flow coming down the Glen, the water rose 2ft. higher than ever known before; and a breach occurred between the lock and Bourne Eau Sluice, at Tongue End, and Bourne Fen was flooded. An action was brought by the Proprietors of the flooded land against the Black Sluice Commissioners, to recover damages for the loss sustained by negligence in permitting the water to flow over the bank. The action was tried at the following Lincoln Spring

<small>FLOOD OF 1872.</small>

Hardwick v. Wiles.

Assizes. The question left to the Jury was, "Whether the Commissioners took reasonable care that the bank in question should be in a reasonably fit and proper condition to protect the adjacent lands from water and floods reasonably to be contemplated." The Jury found for the defendants. On a second proposition, as to whether the Commissioners " had heightened and strengthened," according to the provisions of the Act, *9th and 10th Vict.*, the Jury also found in favour of the Commissioners. In 1862 the Glen had been cleaned out, from its junction with the Welland to about 1½ miles above where the breach occurred. About 3ft. was taken from the bed of the river, and half the material was put on the banks on this side. All the material, however, taken out at the immediate spot where the breach occurred, had been placed on this bank, heightening and strengthening it. In 1877 a large breach occurred in the North Glen Bank, and Bourne Fen was again inundated. This breach was supposed to have been caused by some persons cutting away the bank, and a reward of £100 was offered for the discovery of the offenders, but without effect.

INEFFICIENT CONDITION OF THE DRAINAGE.

The common effect produced on all fen lands by improved drainage is a general subsidence of the soil. The abstraction of the water from the land into the drains causes the spongy soil gradually to consolidate, and this process is still further assisted by the ploughing and working of the land. The organic matter also, accumulated during many centuries, by being exposed to the atmosphere, decomposes, and the general result is a lowering of the level of the surface of the ground. Owing to this cause and the demand for improved drainage, complaints became general as to the imperfect condition of the drainage of the Level; and the Proprietors of the land urged on the Commissioners the necessity for taking steps to obtain further powers for remedying this.

Report on the Glen by J. Kingston and A. Harrison, 1883.

The taxes levied on the district at this time amounted to £3,520, about one-fifth of which was derived from the tolls on the Navigation. This was absorbed in scouring out the drains, repairing the sluices and strengthening the banks, so that there was no surplus which could be devoted to new works.

RENNIE'S REPORT, 1815.

In 1815 the Commissioners consulted Mr. John Rennie and directed him to report generally as to the most effectual mode of improving the drainage of the District. In a preliminary report, made at a meeting held at Donington, Mr. Rennie advised the Commissioners that, in his opinion, to render the drainage perfect, it would be advantageous that Boston Haven should be improved, or that a new Cut should be made from the Black Sluice to Wyberton Roads. Acting on this advice, the Commissioners applied to the Corporation of Boston, and to the Witham Commissioners, asking if they would concur in such a scheme as Mr. Rennie advised, for the improvement of the river. These Trusts, however, declined to join in any such scheme.

With reference to the drainage above the Black Sluice, Mr. Rennie, after referring to the inadequacy of the then means of drainage, by which cause a great deal of the land was frequently flooded and seriously injured, traced the cause to the great quantity of water which came into the fen from the high lands; and he considered that no effectual drainage could be obtained, unless the water which came from a higher level could be prevented from mixing with the fen water and over-riding it. For this purpose he recommended that the Old Car Dyke should be scoured out and converted into a catch-water drain, so as to intercept all the flood water which comes down from the high lands lying between Bourne and Ewerby, and that this water should be carried by Heckington Cut and Gill Syke into the North Forty-Foot, and so by this drain to Redstone Gote, or to a new sluice, to be built a little below the Grand Sluice. By this means the Level would be relieved of the high land waters, which were the principal cause of the drowned state of the Fens. He also recommended the deepening and cleansing of several other drains, and the strengthening of the north bank of Bourne Eau, the total cost of the works being estimated at £66,160, viz.:—

	£	s.	d.
The catchwater drain from Bourne to the Witham, near to the Grand Sluice	35,832	0	0
A new Sluice for the same, of 30ft. water way, and a tunnel under the North Forty-foot	12,220	0	0
Scouring out the South Forty-Foot, Hammond Beck, and Sundries	12,406	0	0
Barrier Bank at Bourne Eau	5,702	0	0
	£66,160	0	0

These recomendations of Mr. Rennie were not carried into effect, and the condition of the drainage became so bad, that the lower lands were continually flooded and the crops destroyed, or greatly injured. The loss throughout the level was stated, in some seasons, to be £40,000, and the annual loss £20,000.

On a map of the Fens, dated 1830, there are shown no less than 46 windmills in this Level which were used for lifting the water off the low lands into the main drains.

The Proprietors of Bourne Fen, failing to obtain drainage by natural means, after considerable litigation with the Black Sluice Commissioners, obtained an Act enabling them to employ steam power, and an engine was erected near Gutheram Cote. Other parishes followed this example, and thus obtained an individual benefit at a very much greater aggregate cost than the expense of one general measure.

The work of improvement was hindered for some time by a division of opinion which existed as to be the best method of effecting the natural drainage of the Level. One party, headed by the Rev. Kingsman Foster, a Commissioner, contended that the proper outlet of the waters of the south part of the fen was the River Welland. His plan was to deepen and widen the River Glen and the Risegate Eau, and to divert a portion of the waters of the Level, by means of these two streams, into the Welland. He further complained of what he considered a great injustice inflicted on the taxpayers of the Black Sluice Level, owing to the fact of 30,000 acres of land, lying on the east of the Hammond Beck, and under the jurisdiction of the Court of Sewers, obtaining 'surreptitious drainage' by discharging their waters into the drains of the Black Sluice Level without being taxed towards the expenses of that Trust. He attributed the cause of this to the silting up of the outlets belonging to the Court of Sewers, which ought to have conveyed these waters to the Welland.

Further Reports. W. Lewin, 1843. J. Rennie, 1845.

In 1843, the Commissioners directed Mr. W. Lewin to make a report as to the best means of improving the drainage. In the following year they called in Sir John Rennie, who had succeeded his father; and, having adopted his report, dated Jan. 31st, 1845, determined to go to Parliament for fresh powers to raise money and carry out works. Both Sir John Rennie and Mr. Lewin, and also Mr. Thomas Pears, strongly advocated the plan proposed to the Commissioners by Mr. Rennie in 1815, for the conversion of the Car Dyke into a catchwater or receiving drain for the water flowing on to the Level from the high lands between Bourne and Ewerby; but against this there appears to have been so strong a prejudice that Sir John was obliged to abandon it, and he therefore prepared an amended scheme, with which the Commissioners went to Parliament, but considerable opposition being raised by the upper districts, and owing to other causes, the Bill was not carried.

Cubitt's Report, 1846.

After the loss of the Bill in the Session of 1845, the Commissioners consulted Mr. W. Cubitt, who made first a verbal report, the substance of which was printed in a memorandum, bearing date *Donington, Nov.* 14, 1845, and subsequently a written report, with a plan of the district, dated *Jan.* 1, 1846. Mr. Cubitt expressed the opinion that the main drains of the Black Sluice were in suitable positions, and that no material alteration in the position of the sluice was necessary; that the main drains, generally, wanted enlarging and deepening, and the level of the Navigation water lowering 4ft. If this were done and the drains and sluices maintained in good order, he considered that a perfect natural drainage at all times would be provided, and that the fens would be as well drained in times of flood as they were in fine weather; and that the steam engines at Bourne and Morton, and all the wind engines would become unnecessary. The effect of the works would be to provide for the discharge into Boston Haven of more than three times the quantity of water the present drains were capable of discharging within the same time. With regard to the Catchwater system which had been recommended by Mr. Rennie and Mr. Lewin, the necessary works would, in his opinion, cost £100,000, and, if this system were carried out thoroughly, and the drainage improved in all respects, the cost would amount to £300,000. With regard to the proposed Outfall into the Welland by Risegate Eau, he reported that this drain could be widened and deepened, so as to afford a drainage to the upper part of the Black Sluice Level, but the Outfall would not answer the purpose as well as that at Boston at a commensurate expense, as, for a great part of its length, the cutting for the drain would have to be 20ft. deep, owing to the height of the land; and that it would cost £50,000 to make it a fit drain. As to the diversion of the water from Boston Haven, Mr. Cubitt was of opinion that, were the respective Outfalls of the Witham and the Welland as well managed as they were susceptible of being, there would be plenty of water for both Spalding and Boston Ports.

Mr. Cubitt having been also consulted as to the principle of taxation adopted in the Level, stated that it was clear that, upon the whole, it was fair; that the Eighteenpenny District, consisting of lands which formerly were swamps and the lowest land in the level, as well as being situated the furthest from the sea, required the most works for its relief, and therefore ought to pay the highest rate; and that he did not see how any case could be made against the Owners of the untaxed lands, as they did not require artificial drainage and had to maintain the sea banks, for the support of which the Black Sluice Level was not charged, although those banks were the barriers against its being drowned by the sea.

SYSTEM OF TAXATION.

The estimated cost of the works recommended was £50,000 for enlarging the drains; £10,000 for altering bridges and sluices; £30,000 for the new sluice at Boston; making a total, with contingencies, of £100,000.

Acting on this report the Commissioners promoted a Bill in the Session of 1846, and succeeded in obtaining an Act "for better draining and improving certain low marsh and fen lands lying between Boston and Bourn, in the County of Lincoln, and for further improving the navigation through such lands." This Act recites that the general means of draining the lands had become very defective, in consequence whereof considerable losses in agricultural produce were frequently sustained, the recurrence of which might be prevented by improvements made in the drainage; and also that, no provision having been made in the former Acts for the discharge of the debt incurred in

ACT OF 1846.
9 and 10 Vict., c. 297.

carrying out the existing works of drainage, it had for many years operated as an obstacle to the application of sufficient means for maintaining them in an efficient state, and that it was desirable to make arrangements for the gradual extinction of the existing and any future debts. The debt at this time was £55,000.

The works recommended by Mr. W. Cubitt and sanctioned by the Act were as follows :—

1—The lowering of the South Forty-Foot River from end to end, to a depth of from 4ft. to 5ft. on an average, so as to bring the bottom of the river at Gutheram Cote on a level with the existing sill of the Black Sluice, and to give a gradual inclination, or fall, at the rate of 3in. per mile throughout its length.

2—The erection of a new sluice on the south side of the then existing Black Sluice, with three openings of the width of 20ft. clear (one being constructed for use as a navigation lock). The sills to be 6ft. below the sill of the existing sluice.

3—The scouring out, enlarging and deepening of the Twenty-Foot Drain, and also the old Skirth.

4—The Hammond Beck from its junction with the Forty-Foot to Dove Hirne to be deepened 3ft. on an average, so that its bottom at the junction should be 6in. below the sill of the existing Black Sluice; and to have an inclination at the rate of 3in. per mile as far as the Twenty-Foot Drain in Gosberton Fen, and above that point at the rate of 14in. per mile.

5—Clay Dyke, New Cut, Heckington Head Drain, Midfodder Drain, and Hodge Dyke were to be scoured out and deepened, so as to correspond with the improved condition of the Forty-Foot River.

6—To scour out the following and any other drains in the level which the Commissioners are liable to keep in repair; the Car Dyke from New Dyke to the north of Haconby Lordship; the Scotten Dyke, Haconby Lode, Rippingale Running Dyke; Dowsby Lode; the Ouze Mer between Billingborough and Horbling; Horbling New Drain; Swaton Eau; Helpringham Eau.

In consideration that the maintenance of the north bank of the River Glen (which bank from Pinchbeck Bars to Tongue End forms the southern boundary of the Level) is essential for securing the Level from partial inundation from the waters of that river, and that it would tend to the safety of this bank if the waters had a freer passage to the sea by means of its channel being scoured out and deepened and the sill of the Outlet Sluice lowered, the Commissioners were authorised to subscribe a sum, not exceeding £2,000, towards the carrying out of such work; but if the persons having the management of the Glen did not undertake the improvement of the river, the Commissioners were at once to raise and strengthen the north bank of the river Glen and also that of Bourne Eau.

Power was also given to the Trust to subscribe towards any works that might be carried out by the Boston Harbour Trustees, or others, for the improvement of the Haven; and also towards any works for scouring out or deeping Risegate Eau, or any other rivers or drains, provided such works would tend to accelerate the passage of the waters from the Black Sluice Level. Power was given to make bye-laws; provision was made for the exemption of the personal liability of the Commissioners; for the appointment of an Auditor by the Proprietors of lands annually, on the first Monday in June; and for compelling Owners of division dikes to keep the same scoured out, or in default for the Commissioners to do the work and recover the cost; new regulations were laid down for the management of the Navigation and collection of tolls, and several other matters relating to the internal administration of the Trust were provided for. Additional taxing powers were granted to meet the expenses of carrying the Act into execution. The extra rate for building the sluice was 2s. 6d. per acre on all lands in the Level, for a period not exceeding four years, and not raising a greater sum than £30,300. Bourne and Dyke were liable to pay only 1s. 3d. per acre, in addition to the 1s. 6d. to which they were already liable. In addition to the 2s. 6d., extra taxes for five years, for the cost of the improvement of the Forty-Foot and other drains, were imposed on the Level, in the following proportions, *viz.*, the several rates of 1s. 6d., 9d., and 6d. respectively, were doubled for a period of five years; at the expiration of this period the first-named District was to pay 2s., the second 1s., and the third 8d. per acre extra. Power was granted to raise money on mortgage, not exceeding, in the whole, a sum of £80,000, in addition to the existing debt; but after the expiration of five years, an arrangement was to be made for the extinction of the whole of the debt due by the Trust by the annual repayment of a sum of £1,200.

The Occupiers of lands in the several parishes in the Black Sluice Level were empowered to lay a rate, not exceeding half-a-crown an acre, for any one year, for defraying the expenses of interior drainage.

The Commissioners had become the Owners of a farm of 218 acres, in Bourne North Fen, the proceeds from which had to be applied to the payment of £34 5s. 5¾d. towards upholding and maintaining the north bank of the Glen and Bourne Eau, any balance being applied to the payment of the drainage taxes charged on the lands in Bourne North Fen and Dyke Fen. Subject to the redemption of the payments for the Glen, the Commissioners were empowered to sell the farm, and pay the proceeds to the Proprietors of Bourne North Fen, to be applied to the repayment of the money expended in erecting a steam engine and wheel. Power was also given to sell an estate in Wigtoft Marsh, and to apply the proceeds to the purchasing off of the drainage taxes.

The Commissioners had become possessed of this land in Bourne Fen under the following circumstances. Under the Bourne Inclosure Act of 1766 (6 Geo. iii), the Commissioners were directed to set out 340 acres, part of Bourne Fen, for roads and drove-ways, and the remainder, after that occupied by the roads, was to vest in the Black Sluice Commissioners, in trust, to let the same on lease, for periods not exceeding 21 years, the rents to be applied towards satisfying the tax laid upon the North Bank and the North Fen, the deficiency, if any, to be made up from the tax levied on the Fen. The quantity remaining was 218 acres, the rent from which was not sufficient to pay the Black Sluice Taxes until about 1811, from which time till 1816, there was a surplus of over £83 a year. From that period until 1839 the rent about covered the taxes. The farm, at this time, lets for £370 a year. In 1845 the surplus amounted to £137 and in 1895 to £284 19s. 10d.

12 and 13 Vict. c. 59. 1849.

The time granted by this Act for the execution of the works, and the funds provided, not being sufficient, an amended Act was obtained, by which the District liable to the rate of eighteenpence was charged, until October, 1852, with a capital tax of 2s. 3d.; the Ninepenny District with 1s. 1½d., and the Sixpenny, with 9d.

After the cessation of the capital tax in 1852, the general taxes were to be increased respectively to fourpence half-penny, twopence farthing, and three half-pence, making the total general taxes payable 1s. 10½d., 11¼d. and 7½d. The taxes were to be paid by the Occupiers, half-yearly, and in default, after 21 days arrears, their goods and chattels to be liable to distraint, and a penalty of twopence in the shilling added to the taxes due. Power was also taken to borrow an additional sum of £10,000.

Under the powers of these two Acts the works enumerated were carried out.

BLACK SLUICE.

The new sluice was made with three openings of 20ft. each, one being adapted for a navigation lock. The sill was laid 6ft. below the sill of the old sluice, being 8·70ft. below *Ordnance datum*, or about level with mean low water of spring tides in the estuary.

MONEY BORROWED.

The amount borrowed for these and previous works was £152,000

SLEAFORD RAILWAY. 16 and 17 Vict., 1853.

In 1853, the Boston and Sleaford railway was constructed, running along the north bank of the Forty-Foot Drain, from Boston to Swineshead Bridge. By the Company's Act it was provided that they should pay an annual rent of £50 for every mile in length of bank over which the railway ran ; that the centre line of the railway should leave a clear space of 25 feet between it and the slope of the bank, and that the Company should maintain the bank. The right of a hauling way was also reserved.

Although the works carried out effected a great improvement in the drainage of the Level, they were not as effectual as was anticipated, and as they would have been, if the recommendation of the Engineers who advised the Commission as to the conversion of the Car dyke into a catchwater drain, and the improvement of the river below the Black Sluice, had been carried out. The large area of high land water which is discharged into the main, or South Forty Foot Drain, over-rides the fen water and, owing to the obstructed condition of the outfall at the Black Sluice, was the source of constant flooding of the low lands. The hope expressed in Mr. Cubitt's report that all mechanical appliances for raising the water would be dispensed with was not realised. All the lower districts had still to resort to pumping, and in several cases engines have been erected since these works were carried out. At the present time there are six pumping stations in the Level. In winter the water never ebbed out below 7ft. on the sill of the Black Sluice, and after heavy rains below 10ft., rising in times of flood to 12 or 13ft.; in exceptional cases to 14ft.; and during tide time to 15ft.; and in 1880 to 17ft. In dry summers the silt accumulated to such an extent as completely to block up the Outfall, rising to 10ft. and 12ft. above the sill. In the dry season of 1868, the accumulation rose to 15ft. against the sea side of the sluice doors, causing a serious block to the outfall of the water when the rain came, and involving considerable labour in moving the sand away from the doors.

EFFECT OF THE IMPROVEMENTS.

In 1880 the Black Sluice Commissioners joined with the Witham Commissioners and the Boston Harbour Commissioners in promoting a Bill in Parliament for the improvement of the Outfall of the Witham. The Commissioners also promoted a separate Act, giving them power to raise the additional tax required. *The Black Sluice Drainage Act, 1880,* recited in the Preamble, that by reason of the defective state of the Channel of the River Witham and of the Outfall, the discharge of water from the said river was impeded and in time of heavy rain and flood, the lands in the Black Sluice Level were subject to inundation and great injury was caused thereby to such lands and the crops thereon. The Act empowered the Commissioners to contribute £65,000 towards the proposed Outfall works, and to levy a tax of one shilling per acre over the whole Level, which is to be applied ; (1) to paying the interest on the borrowed money ; (2) in payment of the Black Sluice share of maintenance and management of the Outfall works; (3) in providing a sinking fund for repayment of the borrowed money, the balance, after paying items *one* and *two*, being applied to this purpose. The

WITHAM OUTFALL, 1880.

43 and 44 Vict.

lands which pay the fourpenny tax to the Welland are to be allowed a drawback to this extent from the Outfall tax.

The tax is paid by the Occupiers, but may be deducted from the rent. The high land in the following parishes, which adjoins the Black Sluice and drains by means of the works in this Level, but which is not liable to the Black Sluice taxes, is made liable for the Outfall tax, *viz.*, Boston West, Skirbeck, Skirbeck Quarter, Wyberton, Frampton, Kirton, Wigtoft, Brothertoft, Swineshead, Gibbet Hills, Hart's Grounds, Quadring, Donington, Bicker, Gosberton, Surfleet, Pinchbeck, South Kyme and Dogdyke.

The works executed under the Outfall Act have proved of very great benefit to the whole of the Level. The water, which previous to these works had never been known to ebb out below 4ft. 9in. on the sill of the Black Sluice, and generally stood at about 7ft. in winter, has since the works were completed fallen as low as 9in. on the sill and seldom exceeds 2ft. at spring tides, except during floods. In the exceptionally dry summers which have since ensued there has not been the same accumulation of silt as there had been in previous years.

DEEPENING THE DRAINS, 1886.

In order to take full advantage of the improved outfall, the South Forty-Foot was cleaned out in 1886 and about 3ft. of deposit, which had accumulated in the drain since the works of 1846, was removed, the quantity at the lower end near the sluice being upwards of 6ft. The Hammond Beck, the Skirth and other drains were also cleaned out and deepened.

RATES AND EXPENDITURE.

The special taxes levied under the Act of 1846 ceased in 1888. The taxes levied now are therefore eighteenpence on the Black Sluice Level, ninepence on the Sixth District Level, and sixpence on Holland Fen, and the Outfall tax of one shilling over the whole area, except the land liable to the Welland tax, which pays eightpence.

The average income and expenditure during the two years, 1888-9 and 1889-90, since the special taxes ceased, were as follows:

Income.

	£	s.	d.
Taxes	8581	11	0
Outfall Tax	4369	14	7
Rents and Rent Charges	117	0	1
Great Northern Railway, Rent of Bank	341	5	0
Navigation Tolls	97	5	4
Licenses for Fishing and Boating	47	0	3
	£13553	16	3

Expenditure.

	£	s.	d.
Interest and Sinking Fund	6493	2	1
Interest for Witham Outfall Loan	2475	14	6
Contribution towards maintenance of Outfall	1455	5	2
Works in Black Sluice District	755	19	2
Management	982	19	0
	£12162	19	11

The amount of loans outstanding in 1892 was £112,500, against which was a sum of £5,719 invested in consols.

The following is a schedule of the parishes, the fen portions of which are comprised in the Black Sluice District, and the area of the same.

EIGHTEENPENNY DISTRICT.

PARISHES IN THE BLACK SLUICE LEVEL.

	A.	R.	P.
Aslackby	997	0	13
Bicker	2560	2	18
Billingborough	1121	2	37
Bourne Fen	3780	2	29
Bourne	893	0	29
Donington	4470	1	21
Dowsby	867	3	7
Dunsby	1329	1	6
Gosberton	1170	0	12
Haconby	1283	3	15
Helpringham	1362	0	25
Horbling	1344	2	39
Morton	2613	1	22
Pinchbeck	1864	3	13
Spalding	1307	0	3
Cowbit	282	3	35
Pointon	785	2	0
Quadring Old Enclosure	65	3	39
Quadring Fen	1859	2	31
Quadring Hundred	400	1	7
Rippingale	1173	2	34
Sempringham	879	2	9
Surfleet	760	0	32
Swaton	1394	1	6
Swineshead East	620	2	13
Wigtoft Marsh	127	1	36
Swineshead Marsh	300	3	7
	35617	3	18

NINEPENNY DISTRICT.
(*Sixth Witham District*).

	A.	R.	P.
Asgarby	76	1	0
Ewerby	736	0	0
Great Hale	1926	2	0
Heckington	2572	2	32
Howell	290	0	0
Little Hale	1332	1	3
South Kyme	2874	0	27
Swineshead West	907	2	37
	10715	2	19

Sixpenny District.
(Holland Fen: Second Witham District.)

	A.	R.	P.
Algarkirk	2334	0	38
Boston	1502	1	15
Brand End Plot	120	0	0
Brothertoft	756	3	37
Dogdyke	277	1	38
Fossdyke	888	0	5
Frampton	1301	3	10
Kirton	3390	3	19
Mown Rakes	100	3	30
Skirbeck Quarter	277	3	10
Sutterton	2482	0	7
Swineshead Fen	2131	3	36
Wigtoft	980	3	31
Wyberton	981	3	8
Pelham's Lands	717	0	0
Coningsby	36	0	15
Langriville	240	1	2
	18520	2	21

Each of the above places is entitled to elect one Representative to act on the Black Sluice Drainage Commission.

CHAPTER VIII.

The Black Sluice Districts.

The Eighteenpenny District, or Lindsey Level.

THIS district, formerly known as the Lindsey Level, includes a low tract of fen land lying between Bourne Eau and Helpringham Eau, and between the Hammond Beck, on the East and the Car Dyke on the West. This fen was common to the adjacent parishes, both in Kesteven, on the west, and in Holland, on the east; the main drain, called the 'Midfodder Dyke' being the boundary between the two divisions of the County. The fens in the parishes in Kesteven only will be referred to in this Chapter, those in Holland having been dealt with in Chapter 3, *On North Holland.* Separate Acts have been obtained for the Inclosure of the fen and commonable lands in each of the parishes. [BOUNDARY.]

HELPRINGHAM FEN.—This fen is bounded on the north by Helpringham Eau, on the east by the South Forty-Foot Drain, on the south by Swaton Fen, and on the west by the Car Dyke. It contains 1,363 acres. The surface of the land is about 6·80ft. above *Ordnance datum*, or 14½ft. above the sill of the Black Sluice. [BOUNDARY.]

The fen, with other commonable lands, amounting together to 3,000 acres, was inclosed under the powers of an Act, obtained in 1773, 'for Dividing and Inclosing the open Common Fields, Meadow Grounds, Common Fen, Cow Pasture and other Commonable Lands in the parish of Helpringham.' The Commissioners appointed to carry out the inclosure were Daniel Douglas of Falkingham, Thomas Oldknow of Nottingham ; and Richard Metheringham of Freiston. Each Commissioner was to be paid one hundred guineas for his services. The Commissioners were authorised to set out roads, the public roads being 60ft. wide; and a plot of half an acre adjoining the Sheep Dike, to be used as a pen or fold for sheep-washing by the inhabitants of the parish ; and also to cause to be erected any banks, sluices, bridges, drains and engines that they should think convenient. Land was to be set out, 12ft. in width, for widening Heckington Eau, one half of the cost of the widening to be paid by Little Hale. The Award, when executed, was to be [INCLOSURE ACT 19 Geo. iii, c. 1773.]

enrolled with the Clerk of the Peace, and be open to inspection on payment of one shilling, and two pence for every 100 words copied.

BOUNDARY.

HORBLING FEN.—This fen contains about 1,353 acres and lies between the Ouse Mer Lode and Swaton Eau, or the Old Holland Causeway; extending from the Car Dyke on the west to the South Forty-Foot on the east. The surface is about 7·30ft. above *Ordnance datum*, or 15ft. above the sill of the Black Sluice.

INCLOSURE ACT.
4 Geo. iii, c. 2.
1764.

In 1764 an Act was obtained 'for Dividing and Inclosing the open and Common Fields, Meadows and Common Fen in the Parish of Horbling, and for Draining and Improving the Fens.'

The Commissioners appointed were S. Forster of Grantham, Daniel Douglas of Falkingham, John Ward of Donington, Robert Graves of Aslackby, William Jepson of Lincoln, Thomas Hoggard of Deeping Gate and John Landen of Milton.

COMMISSIONERS.

They were authorised to divide and allot the land, to set out the public roads, 40ft. wide; and make such banks, drains, ditches, &c., as they thought necessary. When the Commissioners nominated were reduced to five by death or resignation, public notice was to be given in the parish church for a meeting of the Proprietors, to elect two new Commissioners. The Commissioners are to meet on the first Monday in October in every year, ten days' notice being previously given, to appoint an officer for managing the drainage engine and other works of drainage, and to collect the rates.

BOUNDARY.

BILLINGBOROUGH FEN.—This Fen contains about 1,122 acres, is situated between the Ouse Mer and Billingborough Lodes, and extends from the Car Dyke to the South Forty-Foot Drain. The surface is about 8ft. above *Ordnance datum*, or from 15ft. to 16ft above the sill of the Black Sluice.

INCLOSURE ACT.
8 Geo. iii, c. 15.
1768.

In 1768 an Act was obtained ' for Dividing and Inclosing the Open and Common Fields, Meadows and Common Fen, within the Parishes of Billingborough and Birthorpe; and for Draining and Improving the Fen.' In the Act it is stated that the fen was frequently overflowed with water, and yielded but little profit, and that if it were embanked and drained it would be of great advantage to all concerned.

John Thistlewood of Tupholm, Thomas Oldknow of Nottingham, and Thomas Hoggard, of Spalding, were appointed Commissioners for dividing and alloting the land, and for making such roads, banks, sluices, bridges, drains and engines as they should think convenient for draining the land. Any public roads to be set out 60ft. wide. The Award, when executed, was to be enrolled with the Clerk of the Peace of Kesteven, and be open to inspection at a fee of one shilling, and twopence per sheet for any copy taken. After execution of the Award all the works were to be vested in the Black Sluice Commissioners, who were to maintain them.

POINTON FEN.—This fen contains 785 acres, and lies between Neslam and Aslackby Fens, running from the Car Dyke on the west to the South Forty-Foot on the east. Its surface is about 8.30ft. above *Ordnance datum*, or 16ft. above the sill of the Black Sluice. *BOUNDARY.*

In 1790 an Act was passed 'for Dividing and Inclosing the Common Cow Pasture, and Common Fen in the parish of Pointon, the former being stated to contain 160 acres, and the latter 460 acres. The Commissioners were John Parkinson of Asgarby, Edward Hare of Castor, and Joseph Newman of Boston, who were to be paid at the rate of a guinea and a half a day for their services. The Award, when executed, was to be kept in the parish church of Sempringham, and be open to inspection at a fee of one shilling, and twopence for every seventy words copied. The Commissioners were authorised to divide and allot the Common Land and to give directions for making such roads, bridges, drains and engines as they might think convenient. *INCLOSURE ACT. 30 Geo. iii. c. 1790.*

This fen is drained into the Black Sluice, through Pointon Lode, which is directed, by the *Black Sluice Act of* 1765, to be maintained by the Commissioners.

ASLACKBY AND DOWSBY.—These fens, containing about 1,883 acres, lie between Pointon and Rippingale Fens, and extend from the Car Dyke on the west to the South Forty-Foot on the east. *BOUNDARY.*

They were divided and inclosed under an Act 'for Dividing and Inclosing a certain Common Fen in the Parishes of Aslackby and Dowsby, and for draining and improving the said Fen; and also certain Inclosed Low Lands adjoining to the said Fen.' The whole tract, including the low ground between the fen and the Car Dyke, is stated by the Act to contain 2,700 acres. The preamble also says that the fen was frequently overflowed, and yielded very little profit to those who had right of common, and that it would be a great improvement if the same were embanked and drained. John Grundy of Spalding, Thomas Measures of Pinchbeck and John Landen of Milton were appointed Commissioners and empowered to divide and allot the land; to set out roads and make banks, sluices, bridges, drains and engines, as they might think necessary for improving the fen. The Award was to be made in two parts, to be deposited in the parish chests kept in the churches at Aslackby and Dowsby, and to be open to the inspection of any person interested, on payment of one shilling, and a fee of threepence per sheet for any extract made therefrom. *INCLOSURE ACT. 5 Geo. iii, c. 173. 1765.*

On the death or resignation of a Commissioner, the surviving Commissioners are directed to give notice in the Parish Churches, on some Sunday after Divine Service, of a meeting to be held on the Friday following for the purpose of electing a new Commissioner; *COMMISSIONERS.*

all Owners of five acres of land, or Tenants of fifty acres, to have votes.

The Commissioners are empowered to appoint, on the first Thursday in October every year, one or more Officers for the management of the engine and drains, and for collecting the rates.

The surface of this fen is about 8·05ft. above *Ordnance datum*, or 15·75ft. above the sill of the Black Sluice.

BOUNDARY.

RIPPINGALE FEN.—This fen contains about 1,174 acres, and lies between Dowsby Lode on the north, and Rippingale Running Dyke on the south, and extends from the Car Dyke on the west, to the South Forty Foot Drain on the east. The surface is about 15ft. above the sill of the Black Sluice. The drainage was very imperfect previous to the improvement of the Outfall of the Witham, the land being liable to be covered with water in high floods.

RIPPINGALE RUNNING DYKE.

Rippingale Running Dyke, which takes the water from the high land to the South Forty Foot, is frequently referred to in the old Inquisitions of Sewers, and orders made for it to be scoured out and repaired. It is specially referred to in the *Black Sluice Act of 1765* as one of the drains that were to be scoured out and maintained by the Commissioners.

INCLOSURE ACT, 43 Geo. iii, 1803.

The fen was enclosed under an Act passed in 1803 with several other commonable lands, and is described in the Act as containing 1032 acres.

Thomas Syson of Empingham, John Burcham of Coningsby, and Leonard Bell of Stamford were the Commissioners appointed to carry out the Act, their fees being fixed at two guineas a day each. The Award was to be enrolled with the Clerk of the Peace of Kesteven and deposited at the parish church.

DUNSBY FEN.—This fen contains 1,329 acres, and lies between Rippingale Running Dyke on the north, and Haconby Lode on the south and extends from the Scotten and Car Dyke on the west, to the South Forty Foot on the east.

DRAINAGE.

The drainage of this Fen had become very imperfect, and the land subject to frequent inundation. When the water rose on the sill of the Black Sluice to 16ft., nearly all the whole of the fen land was under water. In 1876 the tenants of the land erected a centrifugal pump for lifting the water off the fen into the South Forty-Foot Drain, at a cost of £689. The pump was worked by a hired portable engine, and was calculated to discharge 900 cubic feet per minute, with a head of 17ft.

In 1883 a further sum of £1,710 was expended in a new fixed 16 h.p. semi-portable engine and centrifugal pump and in altering and adapting the drains.

The amount expended by the Tenants was subsequently repaid by the Owners of the land.

The working expenses, since the erection of the fixed engine, have been eighteenpence an acre, in wet seasons.

HACONBY.—This district consists of a tract of fen land, containing about 1,283 acres, lying between Haconby Lode on the north and Morton Fen on the south, and bounded on the west by the Scotten Dyke, and running up to the South Forty-Foot on the east. [BOUNDARY. 13 Geo iii, 1773.]

It was inclosed under an Act, passed in 1773. Daniel Douglas of Falkingham, Thomas Hoggard of Spalding, and Thomas Mewburn of Stanground were appointed Commissioners to allot and divide the land. They were to set out such land as they deemed necessary for roads, the public roads being 60ft. wide, and to become highways; and to give directions for making drains, sluices and engines. On the execution of the Award, the Black Sluice Commissioners, appointed under the Act of 1765, were to put the Act in execution, for the purpose of embanking and draining the fen, and afterwards maintaining the works. The Award was to be enrolled with the Clerk of the Peace of Kesteven, and copies furnished, at the rate of twopence for 90 words. A copy was to be deposited in the parish church. Haconby Lode is one of the drains which are specially mentioned in the Act of 1765, as liable to be scoured out and maintained by the Black Sluice Trust.

MORTON FEN.—This district consists of a tract of fen land in the parish of Morton, lying to the north of Dyke Fen, extending up to the Scotten Dyke on the west, and the South Forty-Foot Drain on the east, and containing 2,613 acres. [BOUNDARY.]

This fen, together with other commonable lands, amounting to 4,400 acres, was enclosed under the powers of an Act obtained in 1768, 'for Dividing and Inclosing the Open Common Fields, Meadow Grounds and Common Fen in the parish of Morton, and for Draining and Improving the said Fen.' The Act recites that the fen was frequently overflowed with water and yielded but little profit, and that if it were embanked, drained, divided and inclosed it might be improved, to the great advantage of all parties interested therein. [INCLOSURE ACT. 8 Geo. iii, c. 41. 1768.]

Thomas Hoggard of Spalding, John Yerburgh of Frampton, and John Dove of Bourne, were appointed Commissioners for carrying out the work. The Commissioners were authorised to make all necessary roads and drains, banks, bridges, and engines as they deemed convenient. Public roads to be set out 60ft. wide. The Award was to be enrolled with the Clerk of the Peace for the Division of Kesteven, and be open for inspection to any person interested therein, on payment of one shilling, and a fee of twopence per sheet for copying any part. After the execution of the Award the works were to vest in the Black Sluice Commissioners, appointed under the Act of 1765.

A 16 H.P. steam engine, driving a scoop wheel, has been erected by the Owners of the land, for lifting the water off the fen, and a new Engine Drain cut, and these works are maintained by them. [DRAINAGE ENGINE.]

In 1892 the fen was formed into a Drainage District, under the provisions of the *Land Drainage Act* of 1861.

BOURNE NORTH FEN.—This fen was inclosed under an Act passed in 1776, and includes, in addition to Bourne Fen, the commonable fen lands in the Hamlets of Dyke and Cawthorpe. The area of commonable land dealt with in the Inclosure Act was 2,450 acres; and of fen land in the North Fen, the South Fen and Dyke Fen, 4,440 acres. Of this, the South Fen contains 870 acres, and, with additional land found on the survey, the North and Dyke Fens contain 3,780a. 1r. 29p.

The Commissioners appointed were John Grundy of Spalding, Francis Lane of Somerby, John Landen of Milton, Daniel Douglas of Falkingham and John Parker of Edenham.

By the terms of the Act the Lords of the Manor were to have allotted to them 20 acres of the fens, in lieu of *Brovage*, and rights to the waste and soil; 340 acres of the fens were to be vested in the Commissioners appointed under the Act, to let the same on lease, for terms not exceeding 21 years, the rents to be applied to paying the tax laid upon the North Bank and the North Fen, under the Black Sluice Act of 1765. One-twelfth of the remainder of the fens, in value, was to be allotted to the Vicar, in lieu of tithes.

The Commissioners were also to set out so much of the fens as would provide a cow pasture for the Owners of the commonable houses and toftsteads in Bourne, Dyke and Cawthorpe, as should be equal to two cows for each house and toftstead, but not exceeding three acres for each, to be used as a cow pasture from May day to Martinmas yearly; the same to be depastured with sheep, at the rate of three sheep to a house, for the rest of the year. If the majority of owners in Dyke Fen wished to have their fen allotted as a cow pasture, they were to be allowed to do so.

The Commissioners were empowered to set out such public and private roads over the fens as they deemed necessary, the former to be 60ft. in width and be deemed highways.

Special provision was made for the protection of the spring known as 'the Well Head' which was to be allowed to continue its course into Bourne Eau.

The expenses of obtaining this Act and of a previous application to Parliament, and of carrying out its provisions were to be paid by the persons to whom the lands were allotted, in proportion to their value.

The Commissioners were empowered to make such banks and drains and to remove or alter any works or engines thereon as they might deem necessary for draining and preserving the fens.

The land appropriated for the repairs of the South Fen Banks had become so cut up and exhausted that materials could not be got therefrom for the repair of the same, whereby they were in great danger of being frequently overflowed. A clause was therefore inserted in the Act, giving Sir Gilbert Heathcote power to take soil from the South Fen for their repair. The cutting was not to extend more than 60ft. distant from the bank over and above the six score feet appropriated for the purpose under the Act.

After the Award was made all the works were to vest in the Black Sluice Commissioners, appointed under the Act of 1765, who were thenceforth to be the Commissioners for embanking and preserving the fens. The Award was to be enrolled with the Clerk of the Peace of Kesteven, copies being furnished at the rate of twopence for 72 words.

Power was given to tax the lands for the amount required for maintenance of the works beyond that received from the rent of the land appropriated, not exceeding a shilling an acre in any one year.

Persons found maliciously injuring the works were to be guilty of felony and liable to transportation.

By a subsequent Act the land in Bourne South Fen which had been allotted as a cow pasture to the inhabitants of Dyke and Cawthorpe, as provided by the previous Act, was allotted and divided amongst the Commoners, by Commissioners appointed for the purpose, and this became a separate District. It is dealt with in the chapter on the parishes in South Holland. *AMENDED ACT. 12 Geo. iii. 1772.*

The land in Bourne North Fen being very imperfectly drained, the Owners were desirous of improving it by pumping the water out of the Fen, into the South Forty-Foot Drain, by steam power, instead of allowing it to flow there by gravitation. To this the Black Sluice Commissioners strongly objected, on the ground that the water, thus sent into the main drain by steam power, would have a tendency to over-ride the drains from the other fens. After a protracted struggle the Proprietors succeeded in obtaining an Act, transferring the works of the interior drainage from the Black Sluice Trust, to Trustees elected by the Owners of land in the fen, and giving authority for the erection of steam pumping machinery. *FORMATION OF SEPARATE DISTRICT. PUMPING MACHINERY. 24 and 25 Vict., c. 113. 1841.*

The preamble of the Act states that "divers Engines and Works of Drainage were made under the Powers and Provisions of the Act of 1776, but such Engines afterwards became dilapidated and decayed and are entirely removed, and the land is liable to be greatly inundated and oppressed by water, and the means of Drainage are very imperfect and insufficient; and that the lands might be more effectually drained, if power were granted for erecting and building in the Fens, one or more Engines to be worked by the power of steam, and facilitating the waters from out of the Fen into the Forty-Foot Drain."

The Trustees for carrying out the provisions of the Act and for managing the drainage of the fen in the future, were to be the *FORMATION OF TRUST.*

Owners of 50 acres in Bourne North Fen and Dyke Fen. Such owners have power to nominate Agents to represent them.

An Annual Meeting of the Trustees is directed to be held at Bourne, on the second Wednesday in June, every year, between the hours of ten and two o'clock; five being a quorum. A notice of the Annual, or any Special Meetings, to be advertised in a newspaper circulating in Bourne, 7 days previous to the meeting. The Trustees have to defray their own expenses, the expense of the hire of the room being the only charge allowed on the rates. At the Annual Meeting the account of receipts and disbursements is to be presented, the same to be open for inspection at the office of the Clerk, and an abstract of the accounts to be deposited annually with the Clerk of the Peace. A penalty of £20 is provided in case of default in making such deposit. The ratepayers may, if they think fit, appoint an Auditor at the Annual Meeting to examine the accounts.

The Trustees were authorised to borrow money to carry out the works to an amount not exceeding £6,000.

WORKS. The works authorised were the erection of one or two engines with machinery and water wheels, not exceeding in the whole the power of 60 horses, and the diameter of the wheels not being more than 15ft.; and to make new, or enlarge the old, drains and to maintain the same, with all the works relating thereto, in good order.

RESTRICTIONS AS TO PUMPING. The Trustees are debarred by the Act from discharging water into the Forty-Foot Drain, when the water therein exceeds the height of a gauge, fixed by the Award of Engineers appointed specially for the purpose, power being reserved to alter the height of the gauge by agreement or by arbitration. The engine is also to suspend working for a period not exceeding 72 hours in cases of emergency; a Committee of three Black Sluice Commissioners are appointed annually, to determine such cases of emergency and give the necessary notices to the Trustees, in case they should have a reasonable apprehension of the main drain being so surcharged with water as to endanger the inundation of the country below Bourne, and from any breach of the banks or other cause. If the man in charge of the Engines neglects to cease working after notice given, he is liable to a penalty of £10.

DITCHES. By this Act it is enacted that the Occupiers of the fen shall, when necessary, cleanse, deepen, widen and repair the roadway, and the outring and division dykes adjoining their lands, and if they neglect to carry out the orders of the Trustees, after 21 days notice, the work is to be done by the Superintendent of the Trustees at the cost of the Defaulter, who shall also be liable to a penalty of three shillings for every rod of the dyke neglected.

RATES. The Trustees were empowered to levy rates for the execution of the new works, and also for their maintenance and the other expenses of the Trust, of 20s. per acre the first year; 10s. the two following years; and 2s. 6d. afterwards. The rates, if paid by the Occupier, to be repaid to him by the Owner, except in case of any agreement to the contrary. In default of payment, after 14 days public notice given, a penalty of 5s. in the £ is to be paid in addition. Rates may be recovered by action or distress.

In 1843 an Amending Act was obtained, by which the Black Sluice Commissioners were discharged from any authority over the works of the interior drainage, and the drains and works which existed previous to the formation of the Bourne Fen Trust, and which were vested in the Black Sluice Commissioners were transferred to the Trustees; who were also empowered to enlarge the Mill Drain, and to make a new drain from it to the Forty-Foot Drain. Facilities were also provided for the purchase of the land required for improving the drainage. *[AMENDING ACT. 6 Vict., c. 1843.]*

The machinery for lifting the water off the fen is situated on the side of the Forty-Foot Drain at Gutheram Cote, and was erected by the Butterly Iron Company. It consists of a condensing beam engine of 30 N.H.P., the boiler pressure being originally 6lbs., but now increased to 9lbs. The cylinder is 45 inches in diameter, and the stroke 6ft. The engine works an iron scoop wheel, 15ft. in diameter, and 4ft. 3in. wide, having 30 scoops, their length being 3ft. 10in. The dip is regulated by a vertical shuttle placed near the wheel, the dip allowed being about 2ft. The maximum lift is 4ft., the head and dip being 6ft. The engines are stopped when this lift is attained, as the water is then level with the gauge fixed under the clause in the Act. The wheel makes $4\frac{1}{2}$ revolutions a minute, and the engine 19. With a full head, $2\frac{1}{2}$ tons of coal are consumed in 24 hours. This gives a coal consumption of 20·37 lbs. per horse power, per hour, of water actually lifted, which is very extravagant, modern engines and centrifugal pumps running with a consumption of $4\frac{1}{4}$lbs. per hour; whilst the maximum allowed by the Dutch authorities is 6.60lbs.* *[PUMPING MACHINERY.]*

The area of land drained is about 4,000 acres, but only 3,500 acres are liable to taxation.

The level of the Fen varies from 4ft. to 6ft. above *Ordnance datum*, or from 12ft. to 13ft. above the sill of the Black Sluice, which is 20 miles distant.

In 1881 a report was obtained from Messrs. Easton and Anderson, as to this machinery. They advised that it should be replaced with a 40 H.P. horizontal condensing engine, driving at 60lbs. boiler pressure, a centrifugal pump of the turbine form, with a fan, 7ft. 4in. in diameter; the estimated cost being £2,700. It was also advised that the drains should be improved and enlarged, especially the Engine Drain, considerable difficulty being found, *[REPORT ON ENGINES, 1881.]*

The Drainage of Fens and Low Lands by Gravitation and Steam Power, (chap. iv.) by W. H. Wheeler, *Spon, London*, 1888.

even with the existing machinery, in getting the water to the wheel and feeding it fast enough.

WIDENING DRAINS.

The recommendation with regard to the machinery was not carried out, but a tender was subsequently accepted by the Trustees from Mr. Barwell for widening and cleansing the main drains for £1,350.

BREACH OF BANKS.

In addition to the disadvantage that this fen has suffered from, owing to the imperfect character of the drainage arrangements, it has been always liable to inundation from the overflowing and breach of the banks of the River Glen, which consist almost entirely of peat. The most serious recent flood was in 1872, when the water in the Glen rose 2ft. higher than it had ever been known to do before and a breach occurred between the lock and the Bourne Eau Sluice at Tongue End, and about 2,000 acres of the fen were flooded. This breach was about 30ft. wide, and from 7ft. to 8ft. deep. An action was subsequently brought by the Trustees, to recover damages from the Black Sluice Commissioners, on whom the repair and maintenance of the Glen bank devolves under the Act of 1765. The action (*Hardwick v. Wyles*) was tried at the Lincoln Spring Assizes of 1873. The question put before the Jury was "whether the Commissioners took reasonable care that the bank in question should be in a reasonably fit and proper condition to protect the adjacent lands from water and floods reasonably to be contemplated." The jury found that they had done so; and on a second question that was left to them, as to whether the Commissioners "had heightened and strengthened" according to the provisions of the Act, *9th and 10th Vict.*, the Jury also found in favour of the Black Sluice Commissioners.

Hardwick v. Wyles. 1873.

In 1877 a large breach occurred lower down the Glen, near the Decoy. This breach was supposed to have been caused by some person cutting through the bank, and a reward of £100 was offered for the discovery of the offender, but without effect.

RATES AND EXPENDITURE.

The maximum rate of 2s. 6d. was collected for several years, and until recently, to cover the expenses of the interior works. The rate laid in 1893 was 1s. 6d., and in 1894 was 1s. 3d. per acre. In addition to this, the Fen is subject to the Eighteenpenny rate, payable to the Black Sluice Commissioners, and to the Witham Outfall Tax.

From the annual return of taxation for 1892-3 the rate is given as producing £285, other sources, £194; total, £479. Maintenance of the engine and works cost £156, (in the previous year £190), salaries and management £100, interest on loan £36, and repayment of principal £151; total, £437. The loans then outstanding amounted to £585.

OTHER PARISHES.—The parishes already described are in the Kesteven Division of Lincolnshire; the remaining parishes in the

Eighteenpenny District, namely Bicker, Donington, Gosberton, Quadring and Quadring Hundred, Surfleet, Swineshead and Wigtoft are in North Holland, and are dealt with in Chapter 3; Bourne South Fen in Chapter 10, on Deeping Fen; and Pinchbeck, Spalding and Cowbit, in Chapter 4, on South Holland.

The Ninepenny Black Sluice, or Sixth Witham District.

This Level lies to the west of Holland Fen and contains 11,584 acres, or, according to the Black Sluice Schedule, 10,715 acres. It constitutes the Sixth District of the Witham Commission, formed under the Act of 1762, pays a rate of sixpence an acre to that Trust, and sends three Representatives to the Witham General Commission. *2 Geo. iii, c. 32.*

It comprises the low lands in South Kyme, Great Hale, Little Hale, Heckington, Lady Frazer's Six Hundred Acres, Ewerby, Howell, Asgarby, and some low lands in Swineshead West, and is described in the Act as being bounded by Holland Fen and Dogdyke on the north; Helpringham and Donington Fens on the south; Bicker Fen, Hammond Beck and part of Holland Fen on the east; and the high lands of Great Hale, Little Hale, Heckington, Howell and Ewerby on the west. *BOUNDARY.*

Each parish or place named elects one District Commissioner, on the first Tuesday in April, every third year, the election being held at the vestry room of the parish. The District Commissioners are directed by the Act to meet on the third Tuesday in April, every third year, at the *George Inn*, Sleaford, to elect three Representatives on the Witham General Trust. The qualification of a Voter is that he shall be a Taxpayer, being Owner of land of the value of £5 yearly, or a Farmer at a rack rent of £50 a year. South Kyme was deemed to be a parish for the purposes of the Act, and entitled to elect one Commissioner. If no election takes place, the District and General Commissioners remain in office. *ELECTION OF COMMISSIONERS.*

By the *Black Sluice Act of 1765* this district was made part of the Black Sluice Trust. The drainage of the land has its Outfall in the South Forty-Foot, the principal drain being the Holland Dyke. It pays the ninepenny Black Sluice tax in addition to that paid to the Witham, and is liable to the Witham Outfall Tax.

According to the Government return the rate raised in 1892-3 produced £487, the expenditure in maintenance was £281, and in management £103; total £384. There was no outstanding loan. *RATES AND EXPENDITURE.*

South Kyme Fen.—This fen contains 2,360a. 0r. 37p., or 2,874a. 0r. 27p. according to the Black Sluice Schedule. It belongs to a single Proprietor, who has embanked and drained it at his own expense. *AREA.*

It was formerly drained by a scoop wheel, 24ft. in diameter, driven by a 20 H.P. horizontal engine. The wheel was replaced *PUMPING MACHINERY.*

in 1874 by Messrs. Tuxford and Co., under the Author's direction, by a centrifugal pump, having the blades placed horizontally, and driven by a vertical shaft, geared to the existing engine. The pump has a disc 36in. in diameter, and is calculated to discharge 2,000 cubic feet of water (56 tons) five feet high per minute. The pump drains 3,000 acres. The engine costs about £220 a year for coal and other expenses of working.

TAXES.

This fen pays ninepence per acre to the Black Sluice, the Outfall tax, and sixpence to the Witham, and elects one Member of the Black Sluice Trust.

BOUNDARY.

HECKINGTON FEN.—This fen lies on the east side of the Car Dyke, and on the north side of the main road from Heckington to Swineshead, and runs up to South Kyme Fen on the north. It includes Star Fen and Truss Fen and contains a taxable area of 2,572a. 2r. 32p. It elects one Member of the Black Sluice Commission.

INCLOSURE ACT.
4 Geo. iii, c. 5.
1764.

It was inclosed under an Act obtained in 1764. The total area of commonable land inclosed under the Act was 4,000 acres. The 'Six Hundreds,' originally part of this fen, was not included in the Inclosure Award. The Commissioners were Edward Smith of Sleaford, Thomas Oldknow of Nottingham, John Landen of Walton, William Gee of Swineshead, Peter Clarke of Howell, William Vessey of Gosberton, and Stephen Bee of Aswarby. They were to allot and divide the lands, to set out roads, and to take care that communication was preserved from the turnpike road to the 'Six Hundreds' and Five Willow Warth; they were to make provision that no trees should be planted near the two ancient windmills, and that no building should be erected any further than 20ft. eastward of the Engine Drain. The Act directs that an Engineer, to take charge of the engines, banks and drains, and to collect the rates, shall be appointed annually on Easter Tuesday.

TAXES.

In addition to the Interior taxes, this fen is subject to the Ninepenny Black Sluice, the Witham Outfall and the One Shilling Sixth Witham District taxes.

BLACK SLUICE SIXPENNY AND WITHAM SECOND DISTRICT.

HOLLAND FEN.

HOLLAND FEN.
2 Geo. iii, c. 32.

ANCIENT DRAINAGE.

The tract of land known as Holland Fen forms the Second District of the Witham Drainage under the Witham Act of 1762. Originally this fen found such drainage as it had by a sluice at Langrick, and by Kyme Eau. Subsequently a large portion of the drainage was diverted by the North Forty-Foot Drain to Lodowick's Gowt at Boston. The fen was constantly drowned by the overflowing of the water from the Witham. When the improvements of this river were carried out under the Act of 1762, Holland Fen was formed into the Second District, and made liable to a tax of one shilling per acre, in return for the protection it received from flooding by the construction of the banks of the Witham.

The Boundaries of the District are described in the *Witham Act* as Kyme Eau, the River Witham, Boston West, and Kirton Holme on the east and north; South Kyme, Heckington and Great Hale on the west; and the south bank of Old Hammond Beck and Swineshead on the south. <small>BOUNDARY.</small>

Each parish, town and hamlet, the inhabitants whereof had right of pasture within the fens, was entitled by the Act to elect one Commissioner. The Commissioner was to be elected at the Vestry of the parish on the second Tuesday in July, every third year, by all Owners of ten acres, or Farmers at rack rents of £50 a year, all the Householders of Brothertoft being entitled to vote. The Commissioners so elected were to have the care, management and direction of the private works necessary to be done in the District; and they were directed to meet on the third Tuesday in April, at Boston, every three years, to elect six representatives on the *Witham General Drainage Trust*. If new Commissioners are not elected the old Commissioners are to continue in office. <small>ELECTION OF COMMISSIONERS.</small>

Owing to the rights of common in Holland Fen having become extinct by the Allotment Award and, generally, to the alteration in the tenure of the land, very few persons remained who were legally qualified to vote under the provisions of the Act of 1761. Accordingly, in 1853, the *Witham Drainage Second District Act* was obtained, which placed the election in Owners of land of ten acres or Farmers at rack rents of £50, and all Householders in Brothertoft. This District still continues to pay the Witham tax and sends six Representatives to the Witham Drainage Commission. <small>16 and 17 Vict., c. 1853.</small>

Under the *Black Sluice Act* of 1765 Holland Fen was included in the lands dealt with by that Act, and the whole of the drainage made to flow to the South Forty-Foot Drain. Each parish in the Fen was entitled to send one Representative to the Black Sluice Trust, to be elected by Owners of land of the yearly value of £5 and Farmers at rack rents of lands of the yearly value of £30. All householders in Brothertoft have one vote. <small>5 Geo. iii, c. 86.</small>

In 1767, an Act was obtained for enclosing and allotting the Fen, in which it is described as "a certain Fen called the Haute Hautre, Eight Hundred or Holland Fen." This Act was amended three years later. The Award, made in pursuance of the Act, bears date May 19th, 1769. <small>INCLOSURE ACT. 7 Geo. iii, c. 1767. 10 Geo. iii, c. 40. 1770.</small>

The Commissioners, appointed to enclose the fen and allot the land, were William Bury of Linwood, Daniel Douglas of Falkingham, Thomas Hogard of Spalding, Thomas Oldknow of Nottingham and William Elmhurst of Stainsby.

The area of land dealt with was reputed to contain 22,000 acres.

SALE OF LAND. By the Act the Commissioners were empowered to sell lands to defray expenses; the first lands to be sold being those separated from the fen by the new cut of the River Witham; namely, Coppin Syke Plot, Ferry Corner Plot and Pepper Gowt Plot, also Brand End Plot, separated by the new cut of the South Forty-Foot; and **ALLOTMENTS.** after these, Gibbet Hills. Charles Anderson Pelham was directed by the Act to have allotted to him 120 acres of land adjoining Great Beats, in satisfaction of his rights, as Lord of the Manor of Earl's Hall, and to the Brovage or Agistment of 480 head of cattle; and to Zachary Chambers, for his rights as Lord of the Manor of Swineshead, 120 acres in Brand End. The remainder of the fen was to be allotted to the several parishes of Boston West, Skirbeck Quarter, Wyberton, Frampton, Kirton, Algarkirk, Fossdyke, Sutterton, Wigtoft, Swineshead, Brothertoft, and Dogdyke, all having right of common in the fen. The land allotted was deemed to be in the parish to which it was awarded.

ROADS. The Commissioners were to set out such roads, drains and bridges as they deemed necessary, the public roads to be 60ft. wide. They were also to set out a plot of land in Amber Hill, not exceeding 30 acres, for the purpose of obtaining materials for the repair of the Boston and Donington turnpike road which passed through part of the fen and 'was very beneficial to the country,' and also for the other public roads set out under this Act.

DIVISION DITCHES. The land awarded to each parish was to be divided by an outring ditch, not less than 8ft. wide at the top and 4ft. deep, with quick planted at the side; this hedge and ditch to be afterwards maintained by the parish, as set out in the Award.

THE AWARD. The Award was to be enrolled with the Clerk of the Peace for Holland, and a copy deposited in the church or chapel of each respective parish or township, to be open for inspection on payment of a fee of one shilling, and twopence for every 100 words extracted.

The land sold by the Commissioners was as follows, realising the amounts given. The average is £23 10s. an acre.

	a.	r.	p.	£
VALUE OF LAND SOLD. Coppin Syke Plot	214	2	23	3630
Ferry Corner Plot	18	2	24	375
Pepper Gowt Plot	13	0	20	380
Brand End Plot	25	1	32	520
,, ,, ,,	2	3	14	56
Gibbett Hills	174	0	0	4400
Hall Hills	23	2	10	1050
Gowt Plot	80	0	0	1970
Land near the old Witham Marshes	45	0	0	1300
Shuff Fen	45	1	0	1440
	642	2	3	15121

The land allotted was as follows :—

	a.	r.	p.	a.	r.	p.
Sir Charles Frederick (Brothertoft)						
Great Shuff Fen				756	3	27
Earl Fitzwilliam (Dogdyke) Terry						
Booth				277	0	7
Zachary Chambers (Smeeth Hall)						
Brand End Plot				120	0	0
C. A. Pelham						
Pelham's Lands	120	0	0			
" "	571	0	18			
				691	0	18

Skirbeck Quarter.

Douran's Piece	3	3	33			
Great Fen	77	3	16			
" "	183	3	34			
				265	3	3

Wyberton.

Bridge Piece	87	0	22			
Bridge Piece and Middle Fen	169	3	14			
Great Fen	473	0	29			
Shuff Fen	261	1	15			
				991	2	0

Frampton.

Bridge Piece	262	3	16			
Middle Fen	468	3	1			
Great Fen	526	1	33			
				1258	0	10

Kirton.

Bridge Piece	197	2	20			
Syke Mouth	308	1	17			
High Fen, High Fen Bottom,						
Great & Little Smeeth Hall	2942	0	26			
				3448	0	23

Algarkirk.

Clay Hills, Little Sand Hills, Fleet						
Bank, Common Rakes				2380	1	22

Fossdyke.

Gowt Plot, Langret Plot				879	2	30

Sutterton.

High Fen Bottom, Amber Hill,						
Amber Bottoms, Brayforth Rose						
Plot, Terry Booth				2488	2	23

Wigtoft.

Fore Fen	293	2	38			
Syke Mouth, Bridge Piece,						
Creasy Plot	700	2	36			
				994	1	34

Swineshead.

Chapel Hill Hurn	88	0	30			
Great Smeeth Hall	215	2	4			
Common Rakes, Far Cattle						
Holme	705	2	4			

		a.	r.	p.	a.	r.	p.
Brand End Rushes	...	330	3	6			
Fore Fen Rushes ...	...	537	2	25			
Creasy Plot, First Cattle Holme, Fore Fen	...	197	2	25			
					2075	1	14
Boston West.							
Drowned Piece	... ...	65	0	24			
" "	... ...	30	1	7			
Shuff Fen ...	... ...	1418	1	23			
					1513	3	14
					18140	2	35

The above places, with the addition of Brothertoft containing 756a. 3r. 37p., Dogdyke 277a. 1r. 38p., Mown Rakes 101a., Coningsby 36a. 0r. 15p., Langriville 240a. 1r. 2p., are each entitled to elect one Commissioner to the Black Sluice Trust.

CONDITION PREVIOUS TO DRAINAGE. The condition of this fen previous to its drainage and inclosure has already been described. Mr. Parkinson, who was largely employed as an Inclosure Commissioner, estimated the rental value of the land, previous to the improvement works, at £3,600, or an average of about three shillings and threepence per acre; and after the works were completed and the land allotted and fenced, at £21,700, or an average of nineteen shillings and ninepence per acre. Taking the improved value at £18,100 and computing this at 25 years' purchase the increased value would represent a capital amount equal to £452,500, which was gained at an expenditure of £50,600.

FENCING. 7 Geo. iii, c. 40. 1770. Three years after the first Inclosure Act it was found necessary to obtain further powers, and an amending Act was obtained. In the preamble it recited that the post and rail division fences, which had been erected by the Commissioners, had been pulled down for many miles and destroyed, and that, therefore, it was desirable to remove the remainder and make division ditches instead, and power was given by the Act to do this, and also for repaying to Edward Draper, Clerk to the Commissioners, the expenses he had incurred in prosecuting the offenders. The ditches between the plots allotted to the several parishes and townships were not to exceed 10ft. in width, and 4ft. deep; and the Second District Commissioners were directed to scour and repair the ditches assigned to Boston West, Skirbeck Quarter, Wyberton, Frampton, Kirton, Algarkirk, Fossdyke, Sutterton, Wigtoft and Swineshead; and to lay the rates necessary for raising the money for executing the work.

THE PARISH ALLOTMENTS. The plots of land in Holland Fen not specially allotted to any parish, including those sold and awarded to the Lord of the Manor and other Proprietors, remained extra-parochial places. The allotment to the parishes also being several miles from the village and church, caused very considerable inconvenience to the inhabitants, not only for ordinary parochial purposes, but also especially with reference to the carrying out of the requirements of the Sanitary and Education Acts. To remedy this, under the *Divided Parishes Act*, these places were either parochialised and formed into new, or added to adjacent, parishes. The parish of Amber Hill was formed in 1880, and consists of the extra-parochial place, known as Amber Hill, containing 30 acres, Algarkirk Fen and Sutterton Fen, and the portion of Dogdyke in Holland Fen, making altogether 5,261 acres. The outlying portion of Swineshead at Chapel Hill Hurn was added to the tract of land near the Witham, known as Pelham's Lands, which, with the Beats Plot, was originally awarded to Mr. C. A. Pelham, as Lord of the Manor, and was in 1883 formed into a parish, called Pelham's Lands, containing 803 acres. Fossdyke Fen was added to the parish of Brothertoft, for civil purposes, in 1881, and forms part of the ecclesiastical parish of Holland Fen. The Mown Rakes, containing 100 acres, and Hall Hills, containing 20 acres, were each made into parishes and added to Boston Union in 1886.

<small>NEW PARISHES FORMED. 20 Vict., c. 19.</small>

Kirton Fen remains a portion of Kirton parish for Poor Law, School Board, and other civil purposes, but for ecclesiastical purposes it is in the parish of Holland Fen. The ecclesiastical wants of the fen had been partly provided for under the Act obtained in 1812, giving powers to constitute a Chapel-of-Ease to Fossdyke in Holland Fen. In 1867 a church was erected for this parish, in Algarkirk Fen, by the Rev. B. Beridge, at a cost of £4,500.

The ecclesiastical parish of Holland Fen was formed by order of the Queen in Council, in 1885, and contains 10,250 acres, and comprises the Fen Allotments of Algarkirk, Sutterton, Kirton and Fossdyke.

It will thus be seen that some portions of Holland Fen are in one parish for civil purposes and in another for ecclesiastical purposes.

For educational purposes two School Boards have been formed, *viz.*, the South West Holland Fen Board, formed in 1880, which takes the civil parish of Amber Hill and Dogdyke (detached); and the North East Holland Fen Board, formed 1879, taking Brothertoft, Fossdyke and the civil parish of Pelham's Lands, and Ferry Corner Plot, Hart's Grounds and North Forty-Foot Bank. Kirton Fen is provided for by the Kirton Parish School Board.

The roads in Holland Fen were formerly in a very unsatisfactory state, but after 1878 were managed by a Highway Board. The particulars relating to this will be found in the chapter on Roads. In 1895 the Highway Board ceased to exist, its powers passing to the District Council.

<small>HIGHWAYS.</small>

DRAINAGE.

The particulars of the allotment and inclosure of the fen portion of the several parishes in Holland Fen will be found in Chapter 3, on North Holland.

The drainage of the fen is effected principally by the North Forty-Foot Drain, the Fifteen-Foot and Clay Dyke, these three drains running parallel with each other through the fen, and discharging into the South Forty-Foot.

South Kyme Low Grounds, although north of Kyme Eau, drains through this district by means of Damford Tunnel, which passes under the Eau, and is connected with the Merry Lands Drain, the water passing along this drain and Gill Syke to the South Forty-Foot.

RATE.

The annual rate is sixpence an acre, in addition to which there is the Witham rate of 1s. an acre, the Black Sluice rate of sixpence and the Witham Outfall Rate.

CHAPTER IX.

THE RIVERS WELLAND AND GLEN.

BICKER HAVEN AND CROWLAND WASHES.

THE River Welland borders upon the County of Northampton on the one side, and the Counties of Leicester, Rutland, and Lincoln on the other. It springs at Sibbertoft fields, in the county of Northampton, not far from the head of the Nene and the Avon, and flows thence by Harborough and Collyweston through Stamford, Market Deeping, Crowland, Spalding and Fossdyke, to Boston Deeps in the Wash. *THE WELLAND.*

At Great Easton it is joined by the Eyebrook, a small stream about 10 miles in length; about half a mile above Stamford the Chater, another tributary, about 12 miles in length, enters the river, and at about the same distance below Stamford, the Gwash or Wash, a stream about 20 miles in length, joins it.

The Welland enters the Fen Country a little below Peakirk, and from this place it has from time to time been embanked, deepened and improved. Between Crowland and Spalding the banks are set a considerable distance apart, leaving a large area of land subject to flooding, called 'the Washes.' Below Spalding the banks are close to the channel, which is narrow and confined. *Fig. 12. Chap. 10.*

At the Reservoir, about five miles below Spalding, the Welland is joined by the Glen. Below Fossdyke the channel passes through the open marshes and lands, for seven miles, to the Wash, and unites with the Witham in Clay Hole, at the head of Boston Deeps. Part of the water is sometimes diverted to the east and finds its way through the South Cots Channel to the Gat, and so to Lynn Well. For three miles below Fossdyke the channel has been trained with fascine work. Below this the course is through shifting sands and the channel is very tortuous.

The Welland is 72 miles long and drains 707 square miles, of which 120 miles (76,854 acres) are fen land. It has a tidal course of 20 miles, spring tides flowing some distance above Spalding, and occasionally reaching as far as Crowland. Spring tides rise from 4ft. to 8ft. at Spalding, according to the condition of the *Fig. 4. Chap. 4.*

channel. The mean inclination of the surface of the water between Spalding and low water of spring tides in the estuary, a distance of 15 miles, is 14in. per mile. In floods this is increased to 21 inches per mile. The inclination is not regular. Between Spalding and Fossdyke the fall is at the rate of 2ft. per mile, in the trained portion of the channel below Fossdyke, 9in. per mile, and in the untrained part, 18in. per mile.

DRAINAGE AREA.

The average waterway of the river at Spalding is about 40ft., and the area in floods 400 square feet. The drainage area discharging there is 30,000 acres, giving 750 acres to one square foot. Below Fossdyke the capacity of the channel, allowing for the increased area draining there, is about double this.

Dugdale.

Fig. 4.

1216-72.

Formerly, and up to about the 17th century, when the works for the drainage of the Bedford Level were carried out, the Welland divided at Crowland, one branch flowing through Spalding, the other joining a branch of the Nene at No Man's Land Hirne, and discharging at Cross Keys Wash. In the reign of Henry III, a presentment was made, "setting forth that there were two courses of water in the common river of Crowland; the one nearer (by Spalding) and the other more remote, and that the nearer current was the right channel, and of sufficient depth, wherein they that did go by barges and boats might well pass to and fro, but that the Abbot of Crowland had, by planting willows thereon, so obstructed and straightened (narrowed) the said course of that stream, that boats and barges could not pass as formerly they had."

THE GLEN.

The Glen rises near Boothby Pagnel and passes near Corby, Little Bytham and Greatford. Entering the fen country at Kate's Bridge near Thurlby, it flows between Deeping and Bourne Fens, and thence passing through Pinchbeck, joins the Welland, after a course of 15½ miles from Kate's Bridge, at the Reservoir.

DRAINAGE AREA.

The area of high land drained by the Glen above Kater Bridge is 109½ square miles. Below this point the channel is confined within banks to the Outfall. Where it passes through the fen the bottom is above the surface of the land.

1324.
Dugdale's
Embanking and
Draining.

The Glen was frequently described in the old Commissions of Sewers as 'Brunne Ee.' Thus in the reign of Edward III the Commissioners found that "the water called Brunne Ee (*in the margin*, 'now the Glene') which had its course through the midst of the town of Pincebec, had its banks broken."

BICKER HAVEN.

Fig. 10. Chap. 7.

Below the junction of the Glen with the Welland, where the river used to enter the open estuary, a small bay or arm of the sea extended inland, on the west side, as far as Bicker. This bay was embanked by the Romans, and the course of the banks may be traced at the present day. The south-west bank, known as the Gosberton Bank, commences a little below the reservoir and continues in a north-westerly direction past Lampson's Clough, where the old

BICKER HAVEN.
From Blaeu's Map 1645.

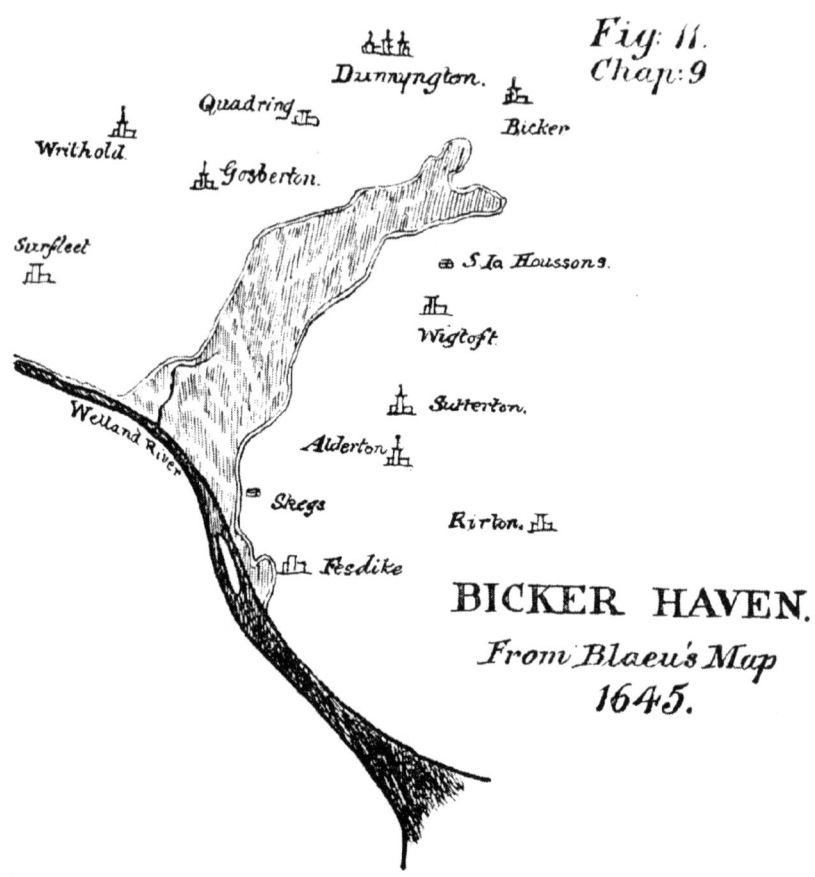

Fig. 11. Chap: 9

Risegate Ea emptied into the Haven, this drain being now continued across the site of the Haven; thence by the Wykes to Hofleet, thence back by Linga House and round Sutterton marsh to Fossdyke. The length was 5½ miles, the width at the lower end, across the mouth, 2 miles, and the upper end near Hofleet about one mile, the total length of the banks being about 12 miles. The area between the banks is 6,000 acres.

That it was of some importance in the time of the Romans, may be inferred from the fact that it was deemed necessary to carry the river bank round the Haven, instead of across the mouth.

The earliest reference to Bicker Haven is in the charter of Crowland, in the ninth century, in which mention is made of four salt pans in the parish of Sutterton. These salt pans are frequently referred to subsequently and are mentioned in Domesday book. Traces of these salt pans on the margin of the Haven are still visible.

The Haven appears to have gradually warped up and become marshland. Between the XIth and XIVth centuries about 340 acres in the parish of Gosberton had become sufficiently high to be enclosed. In the reign of Edward III, a great dispute occurred between the Abbots of Swineshead and Peterborough as to whose the accreted land should be, the decision being given in favour of the ancient custom, "that all and singular Lords possessing any manors or lands upon the sea coast had usually the silt and sand cast up to their lands by the tides."

A considerable area of land lying between Bicker and Gosberton drained into the Haven.

In 1415 an order was made that the River of Bicker, which flowed into this haven at its upper end, should be kept open to a breadth of 24ft.

THE INCLOSURE OF THE HAVEN.
Fig. 11.
State Papers. Domestic. 1615.

The time when Bicker Haven was enclosed is uncertain. It was not embanked in 1654, as Blaeu's map of that date shows it then open. It was probably included in a grant of 'salt marshes left by the sea,' in Wigtoft, Moulton, Whaplode and Holbeach, made to the Earl of Argyle by King James in 1615, which marshes were to be 'inned and embanked' from the sea. It was most likely embanked in about 1660, when the marshes in South Holland were taken in.

COMMISSIONS OF SEWERS.
1323.
Dugdale.

1324.
Dugdale.

The Welland and the Glen are frequently mentioned in the old Commissions of Sewers. In the reign of Edward II, an order was made that "fishermen should not prejudice the common sewer by lepes, weels, or other obstructions, whereby the passage of the waters of Spalding and Pinchbeck towards the sea might be hindered," and, in another Commission in the following reign, an order was made, finding that the banks of the Glen were broken and "that they ought to be made higher, and that the water should thenceforth be stopped below the Weltres, and, because that could not possibly be done by reason of the water coming from far, upon great falls of rain against which the said town could not provide, except there were a reasonable outlet made to the sea by the River of Surflet, which was too narrow by 20ft., and that unless it were widened to that proportion the town of Pinchbec would be overflowed every year; and that at every bridge it ought to be made 12ft. in breadth, at least, up to Dove Hirne and Goderam's Cote; also that the Galwe Gote ought to be repaired anew by the town of Pincebec and all the Landholders in Spalding on the north side of Westlode; and that the sewers thereof ought to be 16ft. in breadth; also that neither flax nor hemp should be watered in that sewer upon pain of forfeiture thereof."

1323.

In 1323 a Commission reported that the sea banks of Pinchbeck and the marshes were broken by tempestuous waves, and should be repaired and made higher and thicker; also that the River Glen was too narrow in Surfleet, being only 20ft. wide, and that unless it was widened by the town of Pinchbeck it would be overflowed every year.

At another Commission, held at Thetford, it was presented that "all the ditches and banks, from Kate Brigg in Kesteven unto the sea in Holand, were broken on each side, and did then stand in need of repair; that is to say—to be raised higher by 2ft. and thicker by 12ft.; and that the towns of Thurlby, Obthorpe, and Eyethorpe, lying to the north side of Kate Brigge, ought at their own proper charges, to repair, dig and cleanse the same; and from the said Cross to Abbottescot, on that side the town of Brunne." A little later, another Commission decreed that the Glen was not sufficiently wide "to admit of the proper discharge of the waters which it brought down from the higher part of the country, so that the fens on either side were drowned, and that it ought to be widened from Gutheram's Gote to the sea, so that at Surfleet it should be 20ft. wide; and that the work ought to be done by the persons who owned the land abutting on the river." The same Commission also presented that the great bridge, called 'Spalding Brigge,' was then broken, and ought to be repaired at the charges of the whole town; and also that the marsh banks, being then broken in divers places, should be repaired. The Commission further ordained that all persons, as well rich as poor, should be liable to all 'mene works,' as well for the repairs of the sewers as the banks; and that every man, having a messuage and 10 acres of land, should find one tumbril or cart, and those who had less, one able man of not less than 18 years of age; or, instead of the cart and horse, a money payment of fourpence, and instead of the man, of twopence per day.

The widening and deepening of the Glen formed part of Lovell's scheme for the reclamation of Deeping Fen, his undertaking being 'to make it at the least 6ft. deep and 40ft. wide, from the beginning of Surfleet, which had always been accounted from Newbury.' The locality of Newbury is not known.

In the 14th century, Spalding was presented by the Jurors before the Justices, because the town had neglected to scour out and repair the river Welland, where it passed through its jurisdiction, by reason of which neglect, great damage had accrued to the King's liege people. The inhabitants of Spalding, being summoned by the 'Shiereeve' to answer the charge, pleaded that the river then was, and long had been, an arm of the sea, wherein the tides did ebb and flow twice in 24 hours, and that therefore there was no obligation on them to repair it.

In 1616 a Commission of Sewers ordered that the Welland should be sufficiently "roded, hooked, haffed, scoured and cleansed" from side to side to the old breadth and bottom, thrice every year; and that no person should make any "drains, wayes, gravells, wares, stamps, stakes, flakes, herdells, cradgings, or other annoyances over the river,"

SIR C. EDMONDS'
REPORT. 1618.

Wells.

In a report made to the Privy Council in the reign of James I, by Sir Clement Edmonds 'on the state of the Fens upon a general view, taken in August, 1618,' the following account of the Welland is given. "The River Welande, running by Stamford, Deeping and Spalding to the sea, was likewise viewed by the Commissioners and found to be a very fair, open, and clean river down as far as Croyland, but from thence to Spalding very defective, for want of dykeing and cleansing; and from Spalding to the meeting of this water with the river of Glen, near unto the sea, almost silted up for want of dykeing, and a current of fresh water to scour the channel; insomuch as they were forced below Spalding, at the time of this view, and in sight of all the company, to carry their boats by cart the space of 3 or 4 miles, to a place called Fosdyke (where great ships lay at anchor) for want of a current at a low water, to carry them down the Channel; and the inhabitants of Spalding did complain that they had no water in the river to serve the necessary use of the town, but such as was unwholesome by reason of the shallowness thereof, which was less than half-a-foot deep, two miles below the towne, where the Committee now in the view did ride over."

After this, the Adventurers of Deeping Fen deepened the Welland from Waldram Hall (near St. James' Deeping) to Spalding, and thence to the Outfall.

CONDITION OF THE WELLAND IN 1634.

Brayley's *Historical Illustrations.*

In 1634 a traveller crossing the washes from Lynn to Spalding gave the following account of the condition of the river. "We feared somewhat as we entered the town, seeing the bridge pulled down, that we could not have passed the river, but when we came to it we found not so much water in it as would drown a mouse. At this the town and country thereabout much murmured; but let them content themselves, since the fen drainers have undertaken to make their river navigable, 40ft. broad and 6ft. deep, from Fossdyke Slough to Deeping, which they need not be long about, having 600 men daily at work at it. Early the next morning we heard the drum-beat, which caused us to enquire the reason thereof and roused us from our castle; and it was told us it was for a second army of water ingeniers." This refers to the works carried out by Lovell.

VERMUIDEN'S SCHEME. 1642.

Sir Cornelius Vermuiden, in his scheme for draining the Great Level of the Fens contained in 'the discourse' which he presented to the King, described the fens as being often flooded, owing to the overflowing of the rivers, especially the Glen, which frequently drowned Deeping Fen by the breaking of the banks, which in his opinion were set too close together; and from two slakers or inlets, whereby the waters, when the banks could not contain them, were let into the fen. These slakers he describes as 'an issue in a corrupt body where there is a neglect to take away the occassion by a known remedy.' He advised that the Glen and the Welland should be diverted to the

Nene at Guyhirne, and so to have one Outfall for the three rivers, which he considered would be less costly than making two Outfalls and would form a more perfect Outfall. A 'Sasse,' or sluice was to be put in the Welland at Waldram Hall, for navigation and to provide water for the country in summer. By doing this, he estimated that 'Elow' (South Holland) would be worth more by £50,000 to £60,000 than if drained the other way. He contended that the lands in South Holland descend from Spalding towards the Shire Drain, and therefore must have their best issue towards the Nene by the Shire Drain; also, that the Welland ran on a higher bottom than the Nene, and that the latter had 3ft. better Outfall than the Welland; that two rivers brought into one would make a better Outfall and serve the county better; that if the two Outfalls were maintained, it would cost £2,000 more to drain the fens. To this, a reply was made in a pamphlet written by Andrewes Burrell, Gent., in which he refers to Sir C. Vermuiden's discourse as being 'contrived in a mystical way with many impertinent objections and answers in it of purpose to dazzle the King's apprehension of the worke.' He considered that the diversion of the Welland and the Glen to the Nene would cause the Outfalls of those rivers to be silted and choaked up, and 'consequently that conceit would occasion the drowning of the lands that lie on either side of the Welland from Waldram Hall to Spalding'; that of late years, during winter floods, a great part of the Welland floods had forsaken their proper channel and passed through Crowland and then into Borough and Thorney Fens, and so stole to the sea by the Wisbech Outfall, because the Welland was filled up with silt or sand, and was not half so deep as it was made by the late Undertakers of Deeping Fen.

A. Burrell. 1642.

In 1650 a bank running from Peakirk to Brotherhouse along the Washes was constructed by the Adventurers of the Bedford Level to protect the North Level from the flood water of the Welland. This bank was made 70ft. broad at the bottom and 8ft. high, and the high road was made to run on the top, between Brotherhouse and Spalding. It was probably an enlargement of the one formerly made by the Abbot of Crowland, by order of a decree made in the reign of King Henry III, directing him to make a road from his abbey towards Spalding, as far as a place called Brotherhouse, when he pleaded that it would be a very difficult and expensive work, "because it was a fenny soil, and by reason of the lowness of the ground, in a moorish earth, it would be a difficult matter to make a causey fit and durable for passengers; because it could not be made otherwise than upon the brink of the river Welland, where there was so much water in winter time that it covered the ground an ell and a half in depth, and in a tempestuous wind two ells, at which time the ground on the side of that river

BROTHERHOUSE BANK. 1650.

was often broken by bargemen and mariners, and by the force of the wind so torn away; so that in case a causey should be made there, it would in a short time be consumed and wasted away by the power of those winds, except it were raised very high and broad, and defended by some means against such dangers." The plea of the Abbot was admitted, but the men of Kesteven and Holland again urging on the King the necessity there was for a road, the Abbot at last undertook the construction, on condition that he might levy for seven years tolls sufficient to reimburse the cost and afterwards to maintain the road in good order.

Ingulph.

In 1439, owing to excessive rains, the banks of the Welland being again overflowed and the country inundated, a Commission of Sewers held at Wainfleet ordered the Abbot of Crowland to repair the embankment of the Welland, extending from Brotherhouse to Crowland. This bank is now maintained by the South Holland Drainage Commissioners, and further particulars relating to it will be found in Chapter XI.

THE WELLAND, 1774.
2 Geo. iii, c. 23.

In the Act obtained by the Adventurers of Deeping Fen, in 1774, powers were obtained to remove all wharves, buildings or other obstructions made on the sides of the Welland within the town of Spalding, between Hawthorne Bank and the outfall at sea; and it was enacted that the channel should be maintained at a width of 65ft.

The river was widened about this time from the locks to the High Bridge. These locks were constructed to run the water from the Welland into the Westlode, to ease the Washes. They were removed in 1815.

WELLAND ACT.
34 Geo. iii, c. 102. 1794.

In the year 1794 an Act was obtained for improving the Outfall of the River Welland, and for the better Drainage of the lands discharging their water by this river; and also for making a New Cut from the Reservoir to Wyberton Roads.

The Preamble of this Act states that the Outfall of the water of the river was very defective, and the navigation much impeded; also that there were large tracts of fens and low grounds, including Deeping Fen and the Commons, and land lying between Spalding and Wyberton, which were subject to be overflowed and injured by the downfall of rain thereon, and that this could be improved by cleaning the present channel of the river and making a new cut for the lower part.

To carry out the works, John Hudson of Kenwick Thorpe; George Maxwell of Fletton, and Edward Hare of Castor, were appointed Commissioners, their remuneration being fixed at £2/2/0 a day. They were empowered to appoint such Officers as they deemed necessary.

Figs. 12 and 14.

The works set out in the Act are as follows, *viz.*, to cleanse and scour out the channel of the Welland from the Reservoir to Shepherd's Hole, and thence to make a new navigable river across the open salt marshes in the parishes of Surfleet, Algarkirk, and the inclosed land in Fossdyke, Kirton, Frampton and Wyberton, to Wyberton Roads, where at that time the Witham had its course, the termination being near 'the public Alehouse, known by the sign of the Ship.' This new cut was to be 50ft. wide at the bottom, and was to have at its lower end "a new sea sluice of stone and bricks, supported by dovetailed or grooved piling, or by inverted stone arches, with pointing doors to sea and land; the threshold thereof being laid one foot below low water mark." The waterway was to be 50ft. wide with a navigable lock 60ft. long and 18ft. wide. The old channel of the river was to have a dam made across it at the Reservoir, sufficient ' to stem the tides and to turn the land floods into the new river.' For the purpose of preserving the navigation of the river above the New Cut, another navigable lock was to be placed across the river, having eleven openings, the middle opening being not less than 18ft. wide; a navigable lock was also to be made across the Glen, with three openings, the centre one being not less than 12ft., if the Commissioners found that this became necessary to preserve the navigation of the Glen.

To meet the cost of carrying out this work the Commissioners were empowered to lay the following yearly taxes, *viz.*, in Deeping inclosed Fen, and all the fen lands and on the Commons, one shilling per acre; the inclosed lands in Spalding and Pinchbeck between the Glen and the Westlode, sixpence; lands in Pinchbeck, except the North Fen, twopence; lands in Surfleet, Gosberton, Sutterton and Quadring, Algarkirk, and Fossdyke, draining by the Risegate Eau or the Five Towns Drain, twopence. The taxes were to be levied by the Officers of the Court of Sewers, and the proceeds paid to the Trustees.

A new bridge, 16ft. wide, was to be built over the New Cut in the direction of the road from Boston to Fossdyke Inn, and the road across the marsh was to be made good from Fossdyke to Moulton. The Commissioners were authorised to collect tolls from persons using the bridge. They were also to set out the boundaries of the lands adjoining the old channel, and to define the line where the rights of the Frontagers terminated. These lands were to vest in the Trustees and be embanked when sufficient accretion had taken place to make them fit for the purpose.

Upon the completion of the works the Commissioners were to vacate office, and a permanent Trust be created, composed of the Lords of the Manors; the Rectors and Vicars of the several parishes; the principal Landowners; the Mayor of Boston and two members appointed by the Town Council; the Mayor and senior Alderman of Stamford; the Owners of the navigation of the Welland; there persons chosen by merchants resident in Spalding; two by the

Owners of the salt marshes on the south side of the channel; two each by Holbeach, Whaplode, Moulton, Frampton and Wyberton; nine by the Adventurers of Deeping Fen; three by the Landowners in Holland and Kesteven, having rights on the commons; the Owners of the Postland Estate and every Owner of 100 acres paying the taxes.

Jessop and others' Report. 1800.

In a report made by Messrs. Jessop, Rennie, Maxwell and Hare, dated August 11, 1800, on the Drainage of Deeping Fen, they advised that "as a temporary improvement of the Outfall and until means may be found to effect the whole, that part of the New Cut provided for by the Welland Act be executed, namely, from Shepherd's Hole, through the Salt Marshes of Surfleet and Algarkirk, to near Fossdyke Inn"; that the bed of the Welland be deepened and the soil taken out be applied to strengthening the banks; and that all projections from Spalding Locks downwards be removed; but that the locks be kept, as they would be necessary for stemming the tides until the whole of the works, as provided for by the Act, were carried out.

The works authorised by this Act were only partially carried out. The river was improved from the Reservoir to Fossdyke Bridge, a distance of about $2\frac{3}{4}$ miles, but the remainder of the Cut and the erection of the two sluices was not proceeded with. The powers relating to this part of the scheme were repealed by an Act passed in 1824.

Bevan's Report. 1812.

In a report made by Mr. B. Bevan in 1812 on the improvement of the navigation and drainage of the River Welland, it is stated that in Cowbit Wash the tides had deposited a shoal which penned up the water in the Welland, which shoal would be likely gradually to increase, if the tides continued to flow through Spalding Locks as at that time; that from Spalding Locks to the Vernatt's Sluice the Channel had been much improved by the flux and reflux of the tides into Cowbit Wash; that the channel had been lowered by the scour 3ft; and that, whereas at similar periods of the tides, when in the former condition of the river there would have been barely 18in. of water, there were then about 6ft.; that owing to the widening of the channel towards the lower end, a depth equal to that at the upper end could not be maintained. The average sectional area of the river at the upper end was given as 630 and of the lower end 1,215 square feet. Below Fossdyke the bottom of the channel in the open Wash was from 3ft. to 4ft. higher than that between the new banks; this channel was variable both as to position and depth, and had a circuitous course to its junction with the Witham of $7\frac{1}{2}$ miles, while the direct distance was not more than $5\frac{1}{2}$ miles, and in this distance the difference of level was 9ft.

He advised for the improvement of the navigation, that a lock should be made near the outlet of Cowbit Wash; that the channel between Spalding Locks and the Vernatt's Sluice should be lowered 2ft.; that a new channel should be excavated below Fossdyke, through the marshes, communicating with deep water by a sea sluice at Wyberton, opposite Hobhole Sluice.

In 1815 Mr. Thomas Pear, made a report to the effect that the drainage was in a very unsatisfactory condition, the water often standing 6ft. on the sill of the old Vernatt's Sluice, which was the outlet for the drainage of Deeping Fen, including an area of 30,000 acres, which was drained by 50 wind engines. This outlet was over-ridden by the waters of the Welland and the Glen. The cause of this was the defective state of the Outfall below Fossdyke bridge; neap tides, which rose 15ft. at the junction of the rivers, never reaching Spalding, a distance of 15 miles. He proposed as a remedy a new cut two miles in length, commencing at a point near the Holbeach and Whaplode Sluice, and about two miles below Fossdyke Inn, to be made through the embanked lands and open salt marshes, and ending with an outfall near Holbeach Middle Sluice; the channel to be 50ft. wide, and 5ft. above the low-water mark in the south channel, with a rise of 1ft. per mile. He also proposed the erection of a lock or new sluice, a little above the Reservoir, for the purpose of keeping up a navigable head of water in dry seasons, and to be so contrived as to admit the free influx of the tides, and at the same time to be clear for the outflowing of land water; and a similar pen sluice for the river Glen; the estimated cost of the improvements being put at £50,000. Subsequently, in a report on the drainage of Deeping Fen, this scheme for making a new cut from Fossdyke to the Witham was approved by Mr. Rennie.

T. Pear's Report. 1815.

In a pamphlet, dated October 31st, 1814, Mr. William Chapman made a strong protest against the proposal for carrying the Welland to Hobhole and erecting a sluice there. He argued that as the erection of the Grand Sluice at Boston had proved injurious to the river Witham, and as the doors were sometimes in dry seasons blocked up by deposit to a height of eight or ten feet, so the same result would, in all probability, take place at the proposed sluice at the end of the new cut for the Welland, and also that, by the withdrawal of the water from Fossdyke Reach, it would silt up, and so deprive the seaward channels of the benefit of the scour from a tidal reservoir of nearly 20 square miles.

Chapman. 1814.

This project was ultimately abandoned.

In 1824 an amended Act for the Welland was obtained and the Welland Commission reconstituted. The Trust by this Act was made to consist of thirteen Trustees, one of whom was to be elected by the Corporation of Stamford, and one by the Owners of the old enclosed lands in Spalding and Pinchbeck. The Trustees were to be elected every three years, and their special duty was 'the maintenance, support and improvement of the New Cut from the Reser-

THE WELLAND TRUST.
5 Geo. iv, c. 96
1824.

voir to Fossdyke, and the drainage and navigation thereby.' They were relieved from the liability entailed on them by the former Act of extending the new channel lower down than Fossdyke Bridge, and were authorised to carry out works for the removal of shoals in the Welland from and below the staunch fixed across the river above Spalding, and through the town, and for training the waters through Fossdyke Marsh. They were also authorised, for navigation purposes, to place draw doors across the mouth of the River Glen at the request of the Deeping Fen Adventurers and the Dyke-reeves of Gosberton, Surfleet and Pinchbeck. To assist in paying for these improvements, the tax of one shilling for Deeping Fen and such parts of the late commons as had been sold by the Inclosure Commissisoners, and sixpence per acre on the lands between the Glen and the Westlode, was continued; the allotments of the commons, the lands north of the Glen, and those draining by Risegate Eau and the Five Towns Sluice, being exonerated from further payment. The Trustees were further empowered to demand tonnage on all vessels using the new channel of the Welland, the tolls being fixed at a maximum of 2d. per ton on coal, 4d. per last on oats, 4d. for the half last of wheat, and 4d. per ton on general goods, and other rates in proportion. This Act was again amended by another obtained in 1837.

CONDITION OF THE RIVER. 1835.

J. Walker's Report. 1835.

No steps having been taken to carry out the recommendations for the improvement of the Outfall, it gradually became worse and worse, till in the year 1835 it was reported that at low water, in dry seasons, there were only a few inches of water at Fossdyke. Vessels drawing 3ft. could not float, except at the top of spring tides, and vessels drawing 6ft. could not depend on floating at springs, and no vessels, except barges, could reach Spalding at all. In fact, the state of the river had become so bad, that the Commissioners were compelled to take active measures, or see the whole drainage of the district ruined. Mr. Jas. Walker, C.E., was therefore consulted, and in a report, bearing date November 7th, 1835, he set out the works he considered desirable for the improvement of the Outfall. He found that, owing to the defective condition of the Channel, there was a fall in the surface of low water of 5ft. 2in., in the 2¼ miles of open channel between the point of confluence of the Witham and Welland; of 16ft. 9in. between Clayhole and Fossdyke; and of 21ft. 4in. between Clayhole and Spalding, a distance of 14½ miles, or at the rate of 18in. per mile.

A spring tide, which then flowed 5 hours at Clayhole, flowed only 3½ hours at the junction of the two rivers, 1½ hours at Fossdyke Bridge, and 1¼ at the Reservoir. In dry seasons, there were only a few inches of water in the channel. Vessels were frequently detained for several weeks, waiting for a high spring tide to float them. Vessels drawing more than 3ft. could not venture up to Spalding.

The works recommended by Mr. Walker, for improving the condition of the river, were the training the channel, in the first instance, as far as Holbeach Middle Sluice, a distance of nearly 3 miles, and ultimately to Clayhole. The area of the uninclosed space, or estuary, below Fossdyke Bridge, he found to be 5,000 acres, 4,000 of which were available for reclamation. The estimated cost of the fascine training for the 2 miles 74 chains was £13,000, and the advantage to be gained, a very considerable lowering of the bed of the river, and the more rapid discharge of the water. Mr. Walker also proposed the inclosing of the marsh lands between Fossdyke Bridge and Holbeach Outfall on the south side of the river, and from Fossdyke Bridge to Western Point, nearly opposite Hobhole, on the other. The length of bank required on the south side was 2½ miles, and the estimated cost £13,000; and on the north side, 5 miles, and the cost £28,000. The quantity of land to be inclosed was 700 acres and 1,800 acres respectively. The total estimate for the whole of the proposed works was £70,000. [PROPOSED IMPROVEMENTS]

He pointed out that the width of the channel, between Spalding and the Reservoir, was from 60 to 70ft., and from the Reservoir to Fossdyke Bridge, 120ft. The former, he considered, too narrow for the quantity of water, and the latter, too large for a regular channel. He advised that attention should first be paid to the works below Fossdyke. When the works he advised were completed, they would enable a vessel, drawing 10ft., to get to Fossdyke Bridge, and one drawing 6ft., to Spalding.

Mr. Walker's report having been approved, an Act was obtained, giving the necessary power for carrying out the work, and for raising the money required. This Act after reciting that the river had become deteriorated, and the dues sanctioned by former Acts were not sufficient, gave power to raise them according to a schedule. The principal dues authorised were 3d. per ton on all vessels, 3d. per quarter on wheat, on other corn 1½d., and on coal 6d. per ton. Power was given to erect quays and wharves, to embank the channel through Fossdyke Wash for the purpose of confining the water within a determinate channel to Clayhole, to take sods for the training work from any part of the unenclosed wash, except lands above high water mark, and to retain permanently a space 100 yards wide from the outer base of the bank, for the purpose of affording a supply of material for the future repair of the banks, without paying any compensation for the same; the embanking of the channel was to be done 'as occasion may require and progressively.' Provision was made for the regulation of vessels and power given to make bye-laws. [1 Vict. c. 113. 1837.]

It was also provided that no person should conduct or pilot any vessel into or out of the river and wash, or seaward thereof, without being licensed by the Hull Trinity House, under a penalty of £5. [PILOTS.]

Power was given to hire and maintain a pilot sloop, for the use of the pilots of the port, out of the pilot dues. Five of the Trustees were appointed a Sub-Commission of Pilotage by the Hull Trinity House, to manage the Pilots.

LOAN. The money required for the work was borrowed from the Exchequer Loan Commissioners.

TONNAGE DUES. In 1837 the tonnage dues had only amounted to £452. In the following year they had increased to £2,298, partly due to the increased rate allowed under the new Act and also to an increase in the shipping.

FASCINE TRAINING WALLS. The plan adopted by Mr. Walker for training the river was first proposed to him by Mr. Beasley, and was found to be so simple and inexpensive, as compared with other methods, and at the same time so effective, that it has since been used in all similar works in the estuary. It consists of training walls, or banks made of thorn faggots about 6ft. long and 3ft. in girth, which are laid in the water, in courses, varying in width in proportion to the depth, and as each course, which is weighted with clay or sods, sinks, others are laid on till the bank is raised to about half-tide level. The branches of the thorns interlace one with another, and the silt brought up by the tides rapidly deposits amongst and at the back of this fascine work, and thus a solid embankment is formed, of sufficient strength and tenacity to withstand the strongest tidal current.*

W. Cubitt. 1837 In a report made to the Commissioners of Newboro' Fen on the River Welland, by Mr. W. Cubitt, who had been called in to advise as to the effect of certain tunnels connected with the Welland, the Folly River and Newboro' Fen, respecting which litigation was going on, he gave a description of the condition of the channel through the Washes, between Deeping and Spalding, and advised a scheme for improving the navigation. This consisted of making a side Cut to the southward of Spalding for the purpose of taking the superfluous land and flood water off the Washes, at the upper end of which cut a weir was to be made, to prevent the accession of common tides, and a sluice for the purpose of effectually draining the Washes; also the erection of a navigation lock for the passage of sea-borne vessels just below Spalding, and above the point where the new Cut would enter the main channel of the river; so converting the river at Spalding into a floating dock, with from 8ft. to 10ft. of water at all times; and to pen up to a level from 2½ft. to 3ft. of water on the sill of Deeping Lock. No action was taken to carry out these recommendations.

From a report of Mr. Walker's, to the Exchequer Loan Commissioners, as to their advancing money for the work, it appears

---

*For a full description of Fascine Training, see the Chapter *On Training* in *Tidal Rivers*, by W. H. Wheeler, Longmans & Co., and the paper on *Fascine Work at the Outfall of Fen Rivers*, in the Min: Pro: Instit. C.E. Vol. 46, 1875.

that in October, 1838, the new channel had been successfully formed with fascine work for one and a half miles below Fossdyke bridge, the cost of this portion being £7,026. The result had been most satisfactory, for vessels drawing eight feet of water could get along the new channel to Fossdyke with greater certainty than those of three feet could before, the water consequently being lowered nine feet. Mr. Walker concluded this report by saying that his original design extended to carrying the channel four miles below the bridge, but that this ought not to be the limit of the work, and adds, "where nature is at hand to do so much, the direction should be extended quite to the Witham."

The fascine work was extended about another mile after this, with still further advantage, for in 1845 it is reported that the effect of the training had been to lower the river about seven feet from Fossdyke Bridge downwards.

Spalding is part of the Port of Boston, and up to the year 1842 all vessels navigating the Welland had paid tonnage and lastage dues to the Trustees of that port; but by an Act obtained in 1842, in consideration of the Welland Trustees paying to the Boston Harbour Trustees the sum of £5,000, being part of a debt then due to the Exchequer Loan Commissioners on the security of the tolls and dues, and also paying one-third of the annual expense to be incurred by the Boston Harbour Commissioners in maintaining the buoys, beacons, and sea marks of the port, the Trust was to give up all claim to dues on vessels navigating the Welland, and the Welland Trustees were authorised to collect a tonnage rate of sixpence, and a lastage rate of one penny on wheat, and one halfpenny on other corn. Under the same Act, and also another passed in the same year, the Boston Harbour Trust and the Welland Trust were empowered severally to execute any works for the improvement of the navigation of their rivers up to the point of confluence; and below that, jointly to execute any works for the improvement of the Outfall of the said waters into Clayhole.

The recommendation of Mr. Walker for the continuance of the training of the river was not carried out, and the work which had been completed, owing to a scarcity of money, was neglected, in consequence of which the tides gradually worked behind the fascine work, and the whole training wall was in danger of being swept away. After a considerable loss had been incurred, the Trustees, and some of the Proprietors interested, met at Spalding on the 27th of August, 1866, and, convinced of the urgency of the case by the report of their Superintendent, Mr. J. Kingston, determined to borrow money, on their own personal liability, to put the fascine work in sufficient repair to prevent further damage, until they could apply to Parliament for increased powers of taxation. And at a further meeting held in September, when Sir John Trollope presided, it was resolved that application be made to Parliament for an Act to authorise the taxation of lands not then charged to the Welland taxes, extending to 63,213 acres ; to obtain power to borrow money; to raise additional taxes and to effect a reconstitution of the Trust. The *River Welland Outfall Act*, 1867, was obtained in the following year.

<small>WELLAND OUT-
FALL ACT.
30 and 31 Vict.
c. 195. 1867.</small>

This Act gave power to the Trustees to bring into taxation again the lands, which, from 1794 until the Act of 1824, had been taxed ; and also other lands which had hitherto used the river as the Outfall for their waters, without contributing to the expense of its maintenance. The Preamble states that out of 85,000 acres of land draining by the Welland, only 24,000 paid taxes, producing £535 per annum; and that the dues from vessels, which in 1846 had exceeded £6,000, had gradually diminished to £998 in 1865. At this time there were charges on the Trust, to the amount of £6,000 due on mortgage, and the sum of £1,000 in addition had been borrowed of the Treasurer, on the personal security of the Commissioners, to carry out works of emergency. The revenues at the disposal of the Commissioners had become most seriously diminished, owing to the decline of the navigation, arising from the alteration in the method of transit for all articles of produce and consumption, and chiefly of corn and coal, by the formation of the Great Northern Railway. The only communication the interior of the Fens had with other parts of the country, previous to railways, was by means of boats, navigating the arterial drains and the great fen rivers; but the greater certainty and convenience of the railway system has to a great extent superseded the canals, and Spalding, with all towns similarly situated, has suffered accordingly.

<small>WELLAND OUT-
FALL TRUST.
1867.</small>

By this Act the Trust was again reconstituted, the new Board being termed 'The Welland Outfall Trustees,' and consisting of 28 members ; 4 elected by the Owners of the Adventurers' lands, and 3 by Owners of fen lands in Deeping St. Nicholas ; 2 by Owners of lands late the Commons ; 2 by Owners of lands in Pinchbeck ; 2 by those in Holbeach ; 1 by the Trustees of the Crowland and Cowbit Washes ; 2 by a vestry of the Parishioners of Spalding ; 1 by Owners of land in each of the parishes of Spalding, Surfleet, Gosberton, Quadring, Algarkirk, Fossdyke, Sutterton, Wigtoft, Kirton, Weston, Moulton, and Whaplode. In each case, except those elected by the vestry of Spalding, it is a necessary qualification that the lands of the members elected shall be subject to taxation under the powers of the Welland Outfall Acts, and that the Members be Proprietors of not less than 50 acres, or Heirs-apparent to such Proprietors, or Occupiers of not less than 100 acres. In the case of those elected by the Spalding Vestry, they must be rated to the poor rates of the parish to the amount of £40. Every Owner of taxable land has one vote in the election of

Trustees, and an additional vote for every 20 acres, or part thereof, beyond the first 20 acres. Every tenant has the same right of voting as the Owner, if the latter be absent from the meeting. Electors may appoint in writing another person to act as their Proxy. Trustees remain in office for three years, or if no successor be appointed, until they die or resign, or become disqualified. An annual meeting is to be held at Spalding, in the month of April. It is directed by the Act that a drainage map, colored to show the different rating areas, be deposited with the Clerk of the Peace for Holland, at the office of the Trust, and in the chest of each parish affected.

Lands in the first class, which includes Deeping Fen and the Commons not subject at the passing of the Act to taxation by the Welland Trustees, are subject (except the 7th District) to a tax of eightpence per acre; land in the second class, including Deeping Fen and the Commons then subject to taxation by the Welland Trustees, to sixpence per acre; land in the third class, including all other lands draining by the river Welland, shown by the blue colour on the deposited plan, to fourpence per acre. These taxes are in addition to those leviable under the previous Outfall Acts, and become payable on the 24th of June in each year. The tax is payable by the Occupiers, but recoverable from the Owners, and may be recovered by distress.

TAXES.

The Trustees were authorised to borrow £4,000, in addition to the amount then due on mortgage, to be applied in repaying the £1,000 borrowed of the Treasurer; and in repairing and renewing the existing channel of the Welland and the piers and embankments connected therewith, between the Reservoir and the termination below Fossdyke Bridge, and in repairing and renewing the Outfall Sluices which the Trustees are liable to repair under the Act 5 Geo. IV, c. 96.

BORROWING POWERS.

The powers given by the 10th section of the Act of 1837, to inclose lands outside the embankments below Fossdyke Bridge, are repealed.

The area of land, thus brought into taxation, was as follows:—

	Acres.
Lands paying Welland taxes at the time of the Act	23,900
Lands on the Commons, Pinchbeck 4th district, Bourne Fen, Thurlby Fen, Cowbit Wash, Crowland, Peakirk, Borough Fen, Northborough, Monk's House Farm, South Holland District	16393
Lands in Deeping Fen, not now charged	1207
Holbeach Parish	6178
Whaplode	4868
Moulton Marsh	2232
Weston	800

Surfleet	2475
Gosberton	3743
Quadring	3088
Fossdyke	1547
Algarkirk	2646
Sutterton	2792
Wigtoft	2391
Swineshead	2383
Lord's Drain District	4103
	80746

RECONSTRUCTION OF GLEN SLUICE. 1879. By the Act of 1824, the Welland Trustees were authorised, for navigation purposes, to place draw doors across the mouth of the River Glen, at the request of the Deeping Fen Adventurers and the Dykereeves of Gosberton, Surfleet and Pinchbeck. A sluice had been erected at the end of the Glen, about 100 years before this, It was removed in 1879, and had the following inscription : " This Sluice was erected and built by order of the Honourable Adventurers of Deeping Fen, according to the model and direction of Messrs. Smith and Grundy.—W. Sands, Bricklayer, Samuel Rowel, Carpenter, 1739." This sluice had three openings, together making 24ft. waterway.

The present sluice bears the following inscription : " This sluice was erected by the Trustees of the Deeping Fen Drainage Act, 1856, assisted by contributions from other interested districts. The first stone was laid by Lord Kesteven, on the 17th February, 1879. The sluice was opened November, 1879." Then follow the names of the Trustees and other Officials. The total cost of this sluice was £15,000, of which £10,000 was provided by the Deeping Fen Trust, £2,000 by the Black Sluice Drainage Commissioners, and £3,000 by other contributors. The new sluice has two openings of 15ft. each, and the sill is 5ft. lower than the old one, being 3in. below *Ordnance datum*.

J. KINGSTON'S REPORT ON THE WITHAM OUTFALL. 1879. In 1879 Mr. J. Kingston was directed by the Welland Outfall Trustees to report as to the proposed new channel for the Witham and its effect on the Welland. The conclusion he arrived at after a full consideration of the matter is given in his Report dated Sep. 12, 1879, as follows : " That the projected scheme of cutting a new channel for the River Witham through the Clays from Hobhole to Clayhole will have but little better effect on the depression of low water flood line in the Witham than the less costly scheme of training the channel from Hobhole to the junction of the Welland, which latter scheme would not interfere with the Welland prejudicially; that any divergence of the Outfall of the River Witham to a greater distance from the Outfall of the River Welland will have a prejudicial effect upon the Outfalls of both rivers ; that the proposed New Cut for the Witham would cost £70,000 more than the training scheme." On the strength of this Report the Welland Commissioners opposed the Witham Outfall Bill in Parliament, but only succeeded in obtaining a clause that if, within 20 years after the completion of the New Cut, they found it necessary, for the Outfall of the Welland, to make a New Cut or improved channel from the then confluence of the two rivers, near the place where Elbow Buoy was laid to the mouth of the New Cut near the Ballast Beacon, the Outfall Board shoul bear half the cost of the work. *WITHAM OUTFALL ACT. 44 and 45 Vict., c. 155. 1880.*

In 1882 Mr. John Kingston, Superintendent of the Welland, and Mr. Alfred Harrison the Superintendent of Deeping Fen, were jointly instructed by the Deeping Fen Drainage Trustees to report "upon the present state of the River Glen, and as to the best means of avoiding breaches of banks in future." The report is dated March 13, 1883, and states that the river below Kate's Bridge has, from time immemorial, been a source of danger and annoyance to the fen lands through which it passes. The water in floods, they found, had an inclination, immediately below Kate's Bridge, of four feet in the mile, diminishing to 7¾ inches at Tongue End, and along the 7 miles above the Outfall of 21¾ inches per mile. The discharge at the sluice they calculated at 60,000 cubic feet per minute, and at Kate's Bridge 117,500 cubic feet, so that the continuance of the floods over any prolonged period rapidly filled up any reservoir space and caused the water to rise above the top of the banks. With regard to the proposal for putting an overflow weir so as to allow the water to flow from the Glen into the Counter Drain Wash, calculations showed that if this were done the Wash would be flooded to a depth of 3ft. 6½in., and over-ride the head-water at the pumping station at Podehole. To raise the banks in the lower part on the Deeping Fen side would cost £17,500. The effect of the new sluice, which was erected in 1879, was to remove the low water level from the Outfall to Surfleet Bridge. They advised that the area of the river should be increased by lowering the bottom 6ft. for the first seven miles above the Outfall. From this point, the bottom to rise 18in. per mile, so as to lower the bed 2ft. 1in. at Tongue End. This would involve the reconstruction of six bridges. The estimated cost of this work was put at £40,000. *KINGSTON'S AND HARRISON'S REPORT ON THE GLEN. 1882.*

From an appendix attached to the report it appears that between 1821 and 1822, eight breaches had occurred in the south bank, and six in the north bank, some of which had caused very serious inundations and loss of property. *BREACHES IN THE GLEN BANK.*

The following are the taxes levied under the several Welland Acts:— *WELLAND TAXES AND EXPENDITURE.*

	Welland Act, 1794.	1824.	1867.	TOTAL.
	s. d.	s. d.	s. d.	s. d.
Deeping Fen ...	1 6	1 0	0 8	3 2

	Welland Act, 1794.	1824.	1867.	TOTAL.
Crowland and Cowbit Washes	0 6		0 6	1 0
Spalding and Pinchbeck Old Inclosures	0 6	0 6		1 0
Pinchbeck, North of the Glen, Surfleet, Gosberton, Quadring, Algarkirk, and lands draining by Risegate Eau and Five Towns Drain, and Kirton Outfall	0 2	Exonerated from further payment.	0 4	0 4

From the Return of Taxation for 1892-3, the amount raised by taxation was £2,137, from tonnage and port dues, £398, from other sources, £79; total, £2,614. In the previous year the dues amounted to £356. Maintenance of works cost £1,348; (and in the previous year £1,508;) salaries and management, £416, payment to Boston Harbour Trust, £190, interest on loan, £385; total, £2,339. The amount of loan outstanding was £9,000, and no provision was made for paying this off.

GLEN TAXES AND EXPENDITURE.

The banks of the Glen, not repaired by the Deeping Fen and Black Sluice Trusts, are maintained by Trustees appointed under the Act of 1801. These Trustees make a call for the amount required annually, on the persons liable thereto. The amount raised according to the Taxation Returns for 1892-93 from taxes, was £343; rents and other sources, £266; making £609. Maintenance of the banks cost £591; salaries and management, £142; a total of £733. In the previous year maintenance cost £392. There was then no outstanding loan.

THE WASHES.

CROWLAND AND COWBIT WASHES.—The right bank of the Welland, between Crowland and Spalding, is placed at a distance from the channel of the river varying from a quarter to half-a-mile, leaving an area of about 2,500 acres, which is covered with water whenever the Welland is in flood. The depth of water on this land in high floods is as much as 5ft. Originally, no doubt, the land by the side of the Welland was little better than a morass, and the banks were placed on the nearest firm ground. The land has since warped up very considerably, being now about 2ft. higher than the fen. It affords very good pasturage, and yields heavy crops of hay. Winter floods are of benefit to the land, but summer floods, which occasionly occur, are very disastrous.

These 'Washes' are considered as being, to a certain extent, of value to the drainage, by affording a reservoir, or 'boezem' as it is termed in Holland, in which the excess of flood water, which the channel below is not capable of carrying off, can spread itself.

Supposing the whole Wash be taken at 2,500 acres, and that this were covered 5ft. deep, it would be equal to half an inch of rainfall over an area of 300,000 acres, which is about the watershed of the Glen above the Washes.

Cowbit Wash, which forms part of this area, when covered with ice, affords the best skating ground in the country, and has long been celebrated for the matches which have taken place there.

SKATING.

In 1846, a meeting of the Proprietors of lands in the Washes was held at Crowland, when it was stated that these lands would be rendered much more productive and valuable if protected from the frequent and long inundations to which they were subject, by an adequate system of drainage, a result which was likely to be successful, owing to the contemplated improvements in the Welland. Mr. J. W. Hastings was accordingly directed to prepare a scheme and estimate for carrying out the proposed drainage, and this was presented at a subsequent meeting, in a report 'on the means of draining Crowland and Cowbit Washes, and adjacent lands.' Mr. Hastings proposed making a new sluice at Lock's Mill, having a waterway of 14ft., with the sill 2ft. 6in. lower than the then existing sill, and enlarging the old and making new drains where required. The estimated cost of the work was £2,948.

DRAINAGE OF THE WASHES. 1846.

J. W. Hasting's Report. 1846.

The report was approved, and an Act of Parliament obtained, 'for better draining of lands called Crowland Washes, and Fodder Lots, Cowbit Wash, and Deeping Fen Wash, in the several parishes of Crowland, Spalding and Pinchbeck, and the hamlets of Cowbit and Peakhill, and the extra-parochial places or lands called Deeping Fen, or Deeping Fen Welland Washes, all in the County of Lincoln.' This Act gave power to carry out the works recommended, and to raise money for the purpose. The works only provided for the better draining of the Washes, and the land is still subject to flooding in wet seasons, and is generally covered with water during a great part of the winter.

10 and 11 Vict., c. 267. 1848

The rates now paid for the maintenance of the works amount to about five shillings an acre. From the Government Return for 1892-3, the amount raised by taxation on the Washes was £525; and from other sources, £26; making the total receipts, £551; maintenance of works cost £381, salaries and management, £81, interest on loan, £242; total, £704. The previous years expenses were £586. The amount of loan outstanding was £4,800.

RATES AND EXPENDITURE.

Taxation Returns, 1892-3.

CHAPTER X.

DEEPING FEN, BOURNE SOUTH FEN AND THURLBY FEN.

<small>BOUNDARY.

Fig. 12.</small>

THE district dealt with in this chapter is a tract of fen and low land, lying between the Welland and the Glen, and bounded on the north and west by the River Glen, on the south and east by the River Welland, and on the south and west by the high lands in Deeping, Langtoft and Baston; it also includes a small tract of fen land, lying between the Car Dyke and Bourne Eau, on the north side of the Glen.

At one time the central part of this district, or that known as Deeping Fen, was nothing more than a large mere, or lake, at the bottom of which grew and accumulated the aquatic plants which afterwards formed the peat of which the surface of the land is composed. Round this mere, on the north and south sides, was a tract of low land, which was common to the several parishes adjoining.

<small>CROWLAND</small>

Although the boundaries given above do not include Crowland or its Abbey, their history is so mixed up with that of Deeping Fen that the chapter would not be complete without a short account of the monastery, especially as the first works of reclamation were undertaken by the Abbots of Crowland.

<small>SAINT GUTHLAC.

Sanderson's Crowland.

697.</small>

St. Guthlac, the founder of Crowland, was a descendant of the Iclings, a noble family of Mercia. He was born in 673. The early part of his life was spent as a military chief, but at the age of 24 he surrended his home and paternal wealth and entered a monastery. After a course of study at Repton, he resolved to become an anchorite. Seeking for a desolate and unknown place, he met with a Fenman called Tatwine, who conducted him in a boat to Crowland, where he landed on St. Bartholomew's Day in 697. With only two attendants, he took up his permanent residence and built for himself a house and chapel on a spot about a quarter of a mile north-east of the present abbey, which is now known as Anchor Church Hill. St. Guthlac and the island of Crowland were consecrated by Bishop Hadda, five days before the feast of St. Bartholomew, at harvest time; and in commemoration of this event Crowland fair is held annually,

Fig: 12.
Chap: 10.

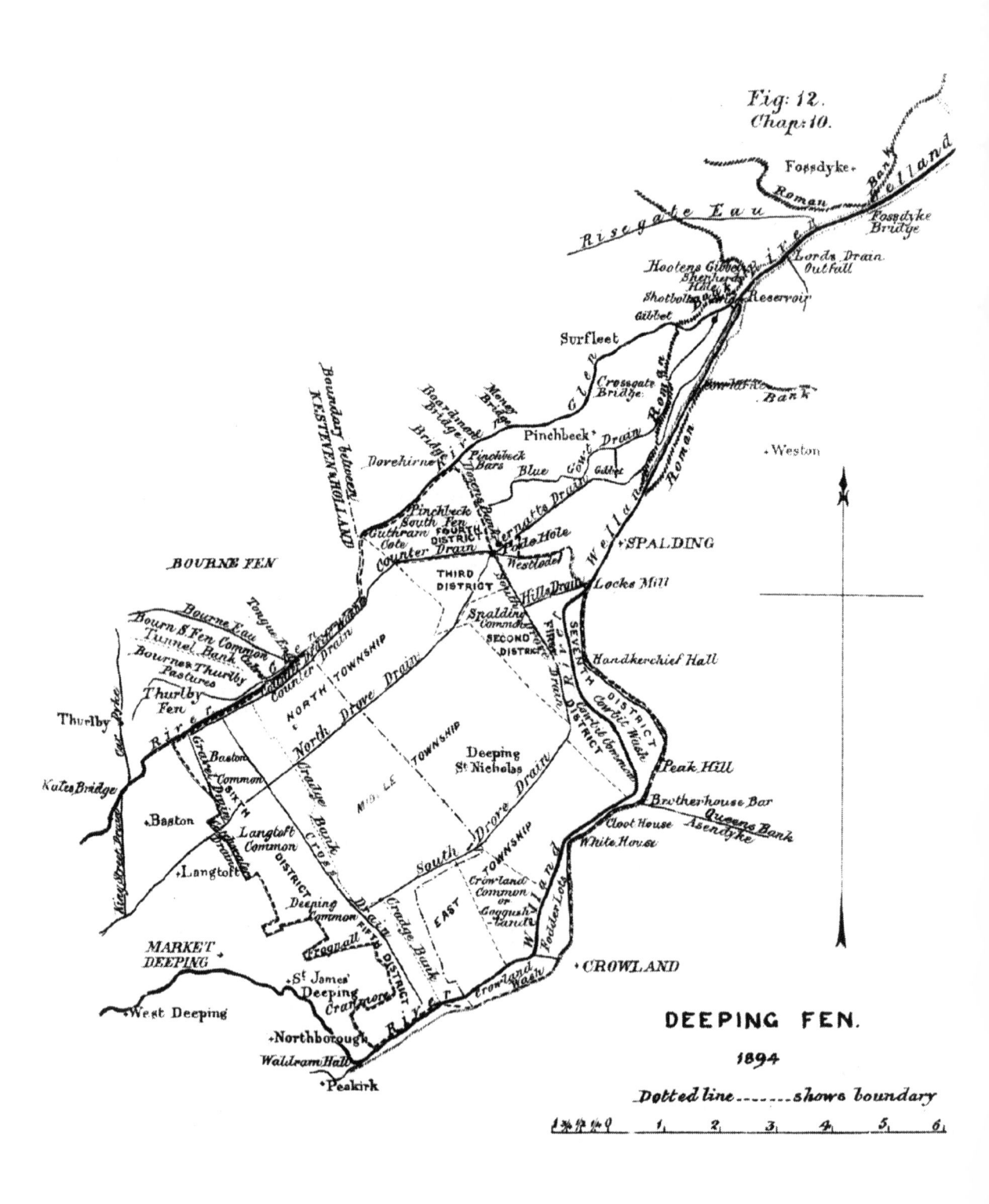

DEEPING FEN.
1894
Dotted line .... shows boundary

by Royal Charter, six days before and six days after the feast of St Bartholomew.

After St. Guthlac's death, Ethelbald, King of Mercia, whose Confessor he had been, in 716 erected a monastery to his memory and endowed it with the island of Crowland, together with the adjacent fens lying on both sides of the River Welland.

The foundations of the present abbey were laid in the beginning of the twelfth century, and the importance which this monastery had obtained may be gathered from the fact that two Abbots, two Earls, 100 Knights and upwards of 5,000 people were present at the laying of the first stone.

Crowland is also celebrated for its triangular bridge. Formerly the Welland divided into two streams, one branch leading to the Nene and the other continuing to Spalding. A stream of water was diverted from the river through the abbey grounds past the slaughter house and offices. Three roads crossed over these streams, one from Peterborough, one from Peakirk and Stamford, and one from Spalding and the Abbey. These three roads, each by a separate arch, met on the centre of the bridge. The channel of the Nene branch of the Welland has long been filled in and the stream which passed to the Abbey ground is enclosed by a culvert. The bridge is 8ft. wide and therefore only adapted for horse or foot passengers. Mention of a 'triangular bridge' is made in the Charter of Eadred, in 943, but the present structure was probably built in the fourteenth century.

The fen land adjoining the Abbey was called *Goggushland* and was regarded as a sanctuary of the church. This fen the monks, having license from the King, inclosed for their own use, 'making the ditches about it bigger than ordinary for the avoiding of discord.

The monks endeavoured to reclaim the fen by banks and drains but "though they had ample possessions in the fens, yet they yielded not much profit, in regard that so great a quantity of them lay for the most part under water." Ingulphus relates that Abbot Egelric so improved a portion of the marshes as to be able to plough and sow them with corn. In dry years he tilled the fens in four places, and for three or four years had the increase of an hundred fold of what seed soever he sowed, the monastery being so enriched by these plentiful crops that the whole country thereabout was supplied therewith. In William the Conqueror's time, the occupants of the adjacent fens consisted of the Tenants and their families, to whom the Abbot had let a great portion of the marshes and meadows, "no man delighting to inhabit here any longer than he was necessitated so to do; insomuch as those who in time of war betook themselves hither for security (as great numbers of rich and poor from the neighbouring countries did) afterwards returned back to their particular homes, for without boats there was not then any access thereto, there being no path except up to the gate of the monastery." Abbot Egelric also constructed a road from Crowland to Spalding, the foundation of which was made of wood covered with gravel, 'a most costly work, but of extraordinary necessity.'

1066.

Dugdale.

In William the Conqueror's reign, Richard de Rulos who was then Lord and Owner of part of Deeping Fen, " and was much addicted to good husbandry, such as tillage and breeding of cattle, took in a great part of the common fen adjacent and converted it into several, for meadows and pastures. He also made an Inclosure from the Chapel of St. Guthlac of all his lands up to the Cardyke, excluding the River Welland with a mighty bank; because almost every year his meadows lying near that stream were overflowed. Upon this bank he erected tenements and cottages and in a short time made it a large town, whereunto he assigned gardens and arable fields. By thus embanking the river he reduced the low grounds, which before that time were deep lakes and impassable fens, (hence the name Deep-ing or *Deep Meadow*), into most fruitful fields and pastures; and the most humid and moorish parts to a garden of pleasure. Having by this good husbandry brought the soil to that fertile condition, he converted the chapel of St. Guthlac into a church, the place being now called Market Deeping. By the like means of banking and draining he also made a village dedicated to St. James in the very pan of Pudlington, and by much labour and charge reduced it into fields, meadows and pasture, which is now called Deeping St. James."

1154.

Dugdale.

In the reign of Henry II the inhabitants of Holland, bordering on Crowland, having drained their own marshes and converted them into good and fertile arable land, whereof each town had its proper proportion, wanting pasturage for their cattle, seized the land of the Abbot of Crowland, carried away his hay, and pastured their cattle on his marshes.

Dugdale.

1381.

The following is the description given of Deeping Fen in the reign of Richard II. "The marsh called Deping Fen did extend itself from East Deping to the middle of the bridge of Crouland, and the middle of the river of Weland, and thence to the messuage of Wm. Atte Tounesend, of Spalding, and thence to a certain place called Dowe Hirne, thence to Goderham's Kote, thence to Estcote, and thence to Baston Barre, thence to Langtoft-outgonge, and thence to East Deping in length and breadth. And that the agistments of all cattle in the said marsh did then belong to the lord, and were worth annually £20; and moreover that there was a certain profit of turfs, yearly digged therein, worth £20; and likewise a profit of poundage, to be yearly twice taken of all cattle within the said marsh, *viz.*, one time of horses and afterwards of cattle; whereupon all cattle which have right of common there are delivered with payment of Greshyre, but of other cattle the lord hath Greshyre, which was worth £20 per annum. Also that there was within the said marsh a certain profit of fishing, newly taken by reason of the overflowing of the water on the north part towards Spalding, which was yearly worth £7, and that the other profits of fishing and fowling throughout the whole fen were worth 100s., and lastly that the fishing to the midst of the river of Welland to Crouland and thence to Spalding, was yearly worth 50s."

In the same reign a dispute occurred with the men residing in Kesteven, as to the boundaries of the fens, and a Commission was issued by the King. A perambulation having been made, ten crosses were erected to show the division. But within two years these were all thrown down and carried away by the Kesteven men, for which act sundry of them were hanged, some banished, and some fined in great sums, and command given for erecting new crosses of stone at the charge of these men of Kesteven.

[1391.]

In several succeeding reigns Commissions were issued by the Crown to view the banks, ditches, and water courses, and also the floodgates and sluices, and to see that all necessary repairs were executed for maintaining the same in proper order.

In the beginning of the 16th century this part of the country is thus described by Camden, in his History of England.

"Allow me, however, to stop awhile to describe the extraordinary situation and nature of this spot, so different from all others in England, and this so famous monastery (Crowland) lying among the deepest fens and waters stagnating off muddy lands, so shut in and environed as to be inaccessible on all sides except the north and east, and that only by narrow causeys. Its situation, if we may compare small things with great, is not unlike that of Venice, consisting of three streets, divided by canals of water, planted with willows, and built on piles driven into the bottom of the fen, and joined by a triangular bridge of admirable workmanship, under which, the inhabitants report, is a pit of immense depth, dug to receive the confluence of waters. Beyond this bridge, where, as the poet says, 'the soil cements to solid ground,' antiently stood the monastery so famous, in a much narrower space, all round which, except where the town stands, it is so moory that you may run a pole into the ground to the depth of 30ft., and nothing is to be seen on every side but beds of rushes, and near the church a grove of alders. It is, notwithstanding, full of inhabitants, who keep their cattle at a good distance from the town, and go to milk them in little boats, called skerries, which will hold but two persons; but their chief profit arises from the catching of fish and wild fowl, which they do in such quantities that in the month of August they drive 3,000 ducks into one net, and call their pools their fields. No corn grows within five miles of them. Higher up that same river lies Spalding, surrounded on all sides with rivulets and canals, an handsomer town than one

Camden.

would expect in this tract among stagnated waters. From hence to Deeping, a town ten miles off, the meaning of which is *deep meadow*, for the plain below it, extending many miles, is the deepest of all this fenny country, and the receptacle of many waters; and, which is very extraordinary, much below the bed of the river Glen, which runs by from the west, confined within its own banks."

<small>PETITION TO QUEEN ELIZABETH.</small>

<small>Dugdale.</small>

In the reign of Queen Elizabeth a petition was presented to the Queen by the inhabitants of Deeping and the other towns having right of common in the fens, *viz.*, Deeping, Spalding, Pinchbeck, Thurlby, Bourne and Crowland, setting out the lost condition of these fens, owing to the decay of the banks of the Welland and the Glen and the condition of the sewers and watercourses, and that by properly draining the same these fens might be greatly improved; and praying the Queen to direct a Commission of Sewers to make enquiry and undertake such works as they should deem necessary for their recovery, and recommending a Mr. Thos. Lovell as the Undertaker, he being " a man skilful in like works, wherein he had been beyond the seas much used and employed, as one fit and much desired by the inhabitants, to undertake the draining of the said fens."

<small>LOVELL'S SCHEME OF RECLAMATION. 1603.</small>

In compliance with the prayers of the memorialists, a Commission of Sewers was issued, which sat at Bourne, and also at Market Deeping. The Court directed that a sum of £12,000 should be levied upon the inhabitants of certain towns in Holland and Kesteven, and on the Commoners in the fens. This tax not being paid, the Commissioners " well tendering the great profit that would arise to all persons concerned, and to the commonwealth in general if the said lands were drained, they therefore granted to Thomas Lovell a concession of the right to drain these fens, on condition that the same should be done solely at his own expense, within a period of five years. As recompense, he was to have a third part of the reclaimed land, but only on condition that he should maintain the works in a state of efficiency, and perfect the drainage of the fens so that they should be firm and pasturable, both in summer and winter. Lovell at once commenced operations and expended the whole of his fortune, about £12,000. A third part of the fens containing 10,036 acres was allotted to him, and also, by order of the Court of Sewers, 5,000 acres additional as a further recompense. This arrangement was subsequently confirmed by an Act obtained in the reign of James I. Owing however to the 'unreasonableness of the times and riotous letts and disturbances of lewd people casting down his banks,' and otherwise destroying his works, the fen again returned to its original condition.

A Petition presented to the Court of Sewers stated that both Spalding and Pinchbeck were at that time in a miserable plight, three parts of the latter place being ' depopulate and forsaken ' through the state of the outfall of the Glen, which Lovell had undertaken to improve and make 6ft. deep and 40ft. wide, from the beginning of Surfleet.

Subsequently Deeping Fen, South Holland and the other low lands in this district were included in a great scheme for draining all the fens lying in the counties of Huntingdon, Cambridge, the Isle of Ely, Norfolk and Lincoln. Sir William Ayloff, Anthony Thomas, with other Adventurers, made an offer to King James I, to drain all the fens lying in these counties, and in return were to be allowed to hold all the land belonging to the King, whether drowned by salt or fresh water, at a rent of fourpence an acre above all rents then paid, and to have two-thirds of the lands belonging to private owners which were liable to be drowned all the year, and half of those which lay drowned half the year. The Undertakers signified that as far as the Lincolnshire Fens were concerned they intended to commence their works by opening the Outfall of the Nene and the Welland, and to make these rivers navigable to Wisbech and Spalding. These proposals meeting with the King's approval, he recommended them to the Court of Sewers, in order that they might aid the Undertakers in expediting such contracts as they should make. At a Sessions of Sewers, held at Peterborough, the approbation of the Court was given, and at a subsequent Court, held at Huntingdon, it was decreed that in order to expedite the work, and towards opening the ancient outfalls of the Nene and Welland, and draining the lands, every acre should be taxed twenty shillings, to be paid to the Undertakers when the works of draining were done, or in default the Commissioners would award such quantities of land as they thought fit. The tax not being paid, at a Court of Sewers, held at Spalding, it was decreed that the Undertakers should have " half the common lands in Deeping Fen, Spalding Fen and Pinchbeck South Fen ; Goggushland ; also two-thirds of the marsh called Bellesmore in Spalding and Weston, two-thirds of the marsh called Turpitts in Weston, one-fourth of the marsh ground called East Fen in Moulton Marsh ; half of Holbech and Whaplode Marsh or Fen ; and two-thirds of Sutton Fen, on the south side of the South Ea."

Difficulties arose in carrying out this arrangement and the decree fell through. Subsequently the Commissioners of Sewers decreed that they had no power to take away any man's lands without his assent, and that their power only extended to the rating of the land for the work done ; that if the Undertakers would agree to go on with the works, on condition that they should have a moiety of the clear profit which they should bring to each owner by their works, they would give all lawful aid in carrying out the bargain, but that if the Undertakers were not willing to consent to this, then the Commissioners would do the work themselves according to the antient course and legal power of their Commission. To these terms the Undertakers agreed, 'but whether it was the great disturbance about that time, or what else, no further progress was made.'

1629. In 1629 a decree was made by the Court of Sewers, levying a tax of six shillings an acre on "all the marsh, fenny, waste and surrounded grounds in order to do this general draining, notwithstanding which decree, no part of the said tax was paid, nor any prosecution of the work." At another Sessions of Sewers held at Lynn an offer made by Sir C. Vermuiden was accepted to carry out the work, but "the country being not satisfied to deal with Sir Cornelius, in regard that he was an alien, they intimated their dislike to the Commissioners." Finally the works for reclaiming Deeping Fen appear to have been carried out separately from those in the Bedford Level, and "divers gentlemen became Adventurers for the exsiccation thereof." Amongst these was Sir Philibert Vernatti, a Dutchman, from whom the Vernatt's Drain and Sluice received its name. In 1632 a decree of the Court of Sewers was confirmed, for conferring on the Earl of Bedford, Sir William Russell, Sir Robert Bevill and others, the concession for draining Deeping Fen, South Fen and Crowland. The works carried out by them in Deeping Fen included the widening and deepening of the Welland from Waldram Hall (near St. James Deeping) to Spalding and thence to the Outfall; the cutting of the Slaker Drain (the Counter Drain) about 20ft. in breadth, to ease the River Glen. This drain continued from Dovehirne, along the course of the Star Fen Graft and joined the Vernatt's. Hill's Drain branched off from North Drove Drain, and passed through Spalding Common to the Welland below Lock's Mill, where was 'a great sluice.' The Vernatt's Drain was cut from Pode Hole to the Welland, which it joined about 1½ miles below Spalding, or 3 miles above its present Outfall; the South Drove Drain was carried from Cranmore Common to the Welland near Cowbit. The Adventurers also improved Exeter Drain (the Wheat Mere Drain) from Cowbit tunnel to the sea, below Spalding. A large sluice was erected on the Welland near Lock's Mill. Numerous partition dykes were also made. The North and South Droves were then more than a quarter of a mile wide, with large drains on both sides of the droves.

The accompanying illustration taken from Blaeu's map of the *Regiones Inundatæ*, dated 1645, will show the condition of the fen at this time.

DEEPING FEN
FROM
REGIONES INUNDATÆ
BLAEW 1645.
Scale of Miles

In 1637 the fens were declared drained; two years later, however the Commissioners of the Bedford Level, sitting at Wisbech, decreed that, although the lands in Deeping Fen were much improved, yet that they were still subject to inundation in winter, and a tax of 30/- an acre was ordered to be levied and to be expended in completing the drainage.

In a pamphlet written by Andrewes Burrell in 1642, it is stated that the Earl of Bedford had expended £23,000 in draining Deeping Fen. In commenting on the scheme recommended by Vermuiden for diverting the Glen and the Welland to the Nene, so that the three rivers should have one common outfall to the sea, Burrell says "the most considerable danger is the condition of the stuff whereof the banks of the new river must be made. In regard that the greatest part of the Level is a light moor, which hath no solidity in it; for being dry, it is so spongy that it will both burn and swim,

1637.

1639.

A Burrell. 1642.

and is so hollow that a bank, which is this year large and firm to the eye, in four or five years will shrink to less than half the proportions which it had at the first making."

Dugdale.

Dugdale says that by the works above enumerated the land was so well drained that in summer the whole fen yielded great quantities of grass and hay, and would have been made winter ground in a short time, but that the country people, taking advantage of the confusion throughout the whole kingdom, which ensued soon after the convention of the long Parliament, possessed themselves thereof; so that the banks and sewers being neglected by the Adventurers, it became again overflowed.

BROTHERHOUSE BANK. 1650.

In 1650 the Commissioners of the Bedford Level in carrying out the works for the drainage of that district, in order to protect the North Level from the waters of the Welland, constructed a bank, extending from Peakirk to Crowland, and thence to Brotherhouse, where it unites with the Holland Bank. This bank was made 70ft. broad at the bottom and 8ft. high, and a road is maintained on its top forming a communication between Peakirk and Spalding.

FIRST DEEPING FEN ACT. 16 and 17 Chas. ii. 1664.

In the reign of Charles II, an Act of Parliament was passed, which, after reciting the above facts and repealing the grant made to Lovell, enacted that the Earl of Manchester, the Earl of Devonshire, Lord Barkley, Anchatill Gray and Henry Gray should be declared to be the Undertakers for draining the fen, then computed as containing 10,000 acres, in trust for such persons and intents as are mentioned in the Act. They were to accomplish the draining in seven years, so that they should be 'firm and depasturable for cattle at all times of the year,' except as to two or three hundred acres, or thereabouts, in the said fen called Deeping Fen and Goggushland and forty acres in Thurlby Fen and Bourne South Fen, which were to be left for 'lakes and sykes for the receipt of waters within the same.' They were for ever to maintain the works and the banks environing the fens and the bank on the east side of the Welland from Brotherhouse to Spalding High Bridge; also the bank on the north side of the Glen from Gutherham Cote to Dovehirne; also to keep the rivers Glen and Welland maintained with sufficient diking, roding, scouring and banking; the Welland from the Outgang at the east end of East Deeping unto the Outfall into the sea, and to preserve and maintain the navigation thereof free of toll; they were to make and maintain all necessary bridges not exceeding 12ft. in width, over all drains whereby passage may be had into the fens. To prevent the banks being injured by cattle and horses, it was provided that no person should at any time between Michaelmas and the first of May drive any horses, cattle or sheep upon any of the banks without paying certain tolls, and owners of horse boats were not to land any horsemen or horses and cattle upon the said banks, between the same times, except at Waldram Hall, Baston, Spoute, Dovehirne, Cloote, or Crowland, without a license; no swine were to be allowed to be put on the fens between the banks and the ditches, nor on any other part of the fens, without being ringed, under a penalty of twopence for each hog. Any inhabitants that might hereafter be upon any part of the third part allotted to the Trustees, or upon the Five Thousand Acres, and unable to maintain themselves, were to be provided for by the Adventurers and not allowed to be chargeable to any of the parishes; no water was to be taken out of the Glen or Welland, or any of the drains, without leave of the Trustees.

The Trustees were to have one-third of the fens, amounting to 10,036 acres, this being afterwards known as 'the taxable lands,' and the Five Thousand Acres, originally allotted to Lovell, in recompence for the money already expended, and in consideration of the work to be done in 'inning and draining the said fen.' This area was afterwards known as 'the Free Lands.' The Trustees were to enclose the lands granted to them. If the reclamation was not completed within the seven years, or if the Trustees afterwards failed to maintain the works, so that the fen was 'good and depasturable ground for cattle at all times in the year,' the lands were to pass over to the Court of Sewers, who were to apply the rents in preserving the lands adjoining from being surrounded and drowned. The Trustees were to pay £100 to the Court of Sewers, towards the repair and maintenance of the South Dozens and Hawthorne Banks. The Owners for the time being of a share of not less than 250 acres of the 10,036 acres were authorised to hold meetings for the better government and orderly management of the work of draining the fens. Three Adventurers were to have power to act under the Common Seal, and to make bye laws, and tax the Owners by an equal acre tax for the purpose of carrying on the work. In default of payment of the tax levied, the Adventurers were to have power to sell the land taxed. A Commission was appointed to determine the boundaries of the land to be inclosed.

"TAXABLE LANDS."

"FREE LANDS."

This Act was amended five years later and the time for completion was extended for a further period of three years, as, owing to 'the unseasonableness of the weather and other unavoidable accidents,' the works had not been completed. It was also enacted that the Adventurers should hold a public meeting annually at Spalding, on the Thursday next after the second Sunday in April, at which the acre tax was to be levied for payment on the 10th of October following. In default of payment a penalty not exceeding a third part of the tax was to be imposed. If the tax and penalty were not paid before the April following, the Adventurers could make an order at the annual meeting for the sequestration and sale of so much of the land as would satisfy the tax and penalty.

22 Car. ii, 1671.

TIME FOR ANNUAL MEETING.
11 Geo. ii, c. 39, 1738.

The time for holding the annual meeting was altered by a subsequent Act, by which two meetings were directed to be held on the Thursdays next after Midsummer and Michaelmas days. The time for laying the rates was altered by an Act, passed in the reign of George III, by which they were directed to be paid in two instalments, due respectively on the 22nd of May and the 11th of November.

In consequence of the wet seasons and the imperfect condition of the drainage, many Owners of the taxable lands were unable to pay the rates, and, being in arrear, nearly half the lands were sequestrated by the Trustees under the powers of the Act of 1664. In 1729 these lands were sold, for £4,000, to Capt. Perry, an Engineer who had been engaged on embanking works on the Thames. The proceeds were to be laid out on works in the fen.

CAPT. PERRY. 1729.

CONDITION OF THE FEN IN 1738.
11 Geo. ii, c. 39

The amending Act of 1738 recites that the lands granted to the Adventurers "had long since been fenced and inclosed, and were drained and kept drained for some years, yet that notwithstanding all the endeavours that had been used to preserve and keep the said fens drained, the same have for several years last past been, and now are, so overflowed with waters, through the defects of their Outfalls to the sea and other causes, that little or no profit can be made of them to the great loss and damage of the Owners, as well of the said free lands as of taxable lands, and to the impoverishment of the Commoners, having right of Common in the rest of the fens, being about 15,000 acres, and for which causes about 4,000 acres of the taxable lands had become forfeited for non-payment of the draining taxes charged thereon; and may be sold by the said Adventurers, or any three of them, so qualified as aforesaid; and that the said fens could never be made profitable, unless some new methods were taken to recover the same, which, according to a scheme and estimate made thereof by skilful and able engineers, would cost about £15,000; and that it had been enacted that the Court of Sewers could seize and appropriate all the rents of the Adventurers' lands unless they were kept properly drained." In order to prevent this loss an agreement had been come to with the Owners of the 5,000 acres of free lands, by which they undertook to raise one-third of the £15,000 required, by an acre tax of 20/-; £6,000 was to be found by a similar rate on the 6,000 acres of taxable lands, and when this sum was expended, then the remaining 4,000 acres, which had become forfeited for non-payment of the drainage taxes, were to be sold by the Adventurers, or so much thereof as was necessary to make up the £15,000, and the money applied to the perfecting of the draining of the level and its future preservation.

BOURNE FEN AND THURLBY PASTURES.

Bourne Fen and Thurlby Pastures, containing 336 acres, part of the 'Free Lands,' were exempted from payment of this tax, on the ground that they had been embanked and kept drained at the sole charge of the Owner, Sir John Heathcote.

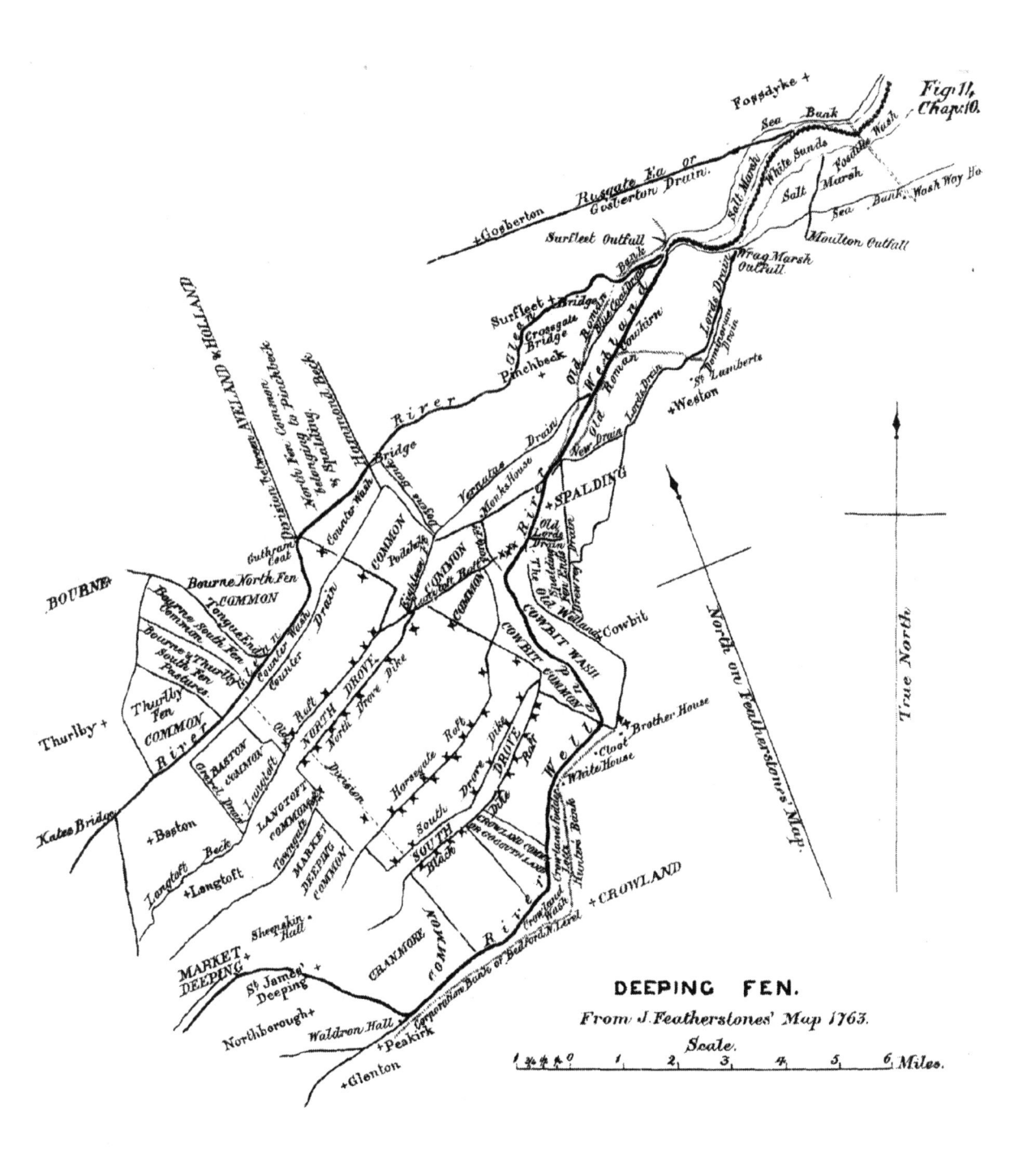

DEEPING FEN.
From J. Featherstones' Map 1763.

Fig. 14, Chap. 10.

Two large scoop wheels, worked by windmills, known then as 'Dutch Engines' were erected in 1741, at one end of the main drain, for lifting the water off the fen into the Vernatt's Drain. The wheels were 16ft. in diameter, with 13in. scoops. An Archimedean screw was at first worked by one of the larger mills, but was subsequently abandoned.

The total length of the rivers and drains in this district is given on a map, published by Jos. Featherstone, in 1763, as 99½ miles; and of the banks, 66¾ miles. On the same map are shown 50 windmills for lifting the water into the main drains.

In 1774, a third Act was passed for amending the previous Acts. The Preamble of this Act recites that such part of the River Welland as lies within the town of Spalding and between Hawthorn bank and the Outfall, had become very much contracted and that unless the Adventurers were empowered to cleanse the river, the fens and low grounds could not be effectually drained and improved.

They were authorised, and afterwards erected a sluice at the end of the Vernatt's Drain, 110ft. on the south side of the Outfall of the Glen, having a clear water-way of 30ft.; and a new sluice near the existing Podehole Sluice, the water-way of which was to be 3ft. less than that of the sea sluice; and to continue by a new cut the Vernatt's Drain, which then joined the Welland about 1½ miles below Spalding, down to the intended Outfall sluice at the Reservoir, having a bottom width of 20ft.; also to make and continue the drain called Langtoft Roft, 30ft. wide; North Drove Dike, 20ft. wide; Black Dike Roft, 30ft.; South Drove Dike, 20ft.; the 18ft. Drain, 40ft. wide; the bottom of all these drains to be level with the floor of the Pode Hole Sluice. The powers given by the Act of Charles, to the Commissioners of Sewers, to shut down the Sluice at Pode Hole, and to stop the Vernatt's Drain for two months in every year, in order to drain the lands in Pinchbeck and Spalding, were to cease when the new works were completed, and they were not to be allowed to stop the sluice for more than 28 days in a year, nor for more than three days together, within the space of 14 days. The powers of the Court of Sewers relating to the Vernatt's Drain and the sluices at Pode Hole were repealed by the *Welland Act of 1794* and also by the *Deeping Fen Act of 1801*. The Commissioners were also authorised to rebuild Surfleet Bridge, over the Glen, and also to enlarge Cross Gate Bridge to a width of 30ft. Gravel Drain was to be scoured to Swine's Meadow and a dam made at the south end, to convey the water into the Counter Wash; the south bank of the Counter Drain was to be repaired and enlarged and widened, and the drain from the end of Gravel Drain to Pode Hole, to be deepened for the purpose of conveying the upland waters along Vernatt's Drain to the sea.

TUNNELS.

Any Owners who had tunnels through Deeping Bank, Barston Bank, the Counter Bank, and Gravel Drain Bank, were, before the 30th of September in every year, to stop up the same 'with dove-tail or other piles' and keep them stopped till the first of the following May.

WELLAND ACT,
34 Geo. iii, c. 102,
1794.

In 1794, an Act was passed for improving the Welland and for the better drainage of the fen-land, through the same. By this Act the management of the river was entrusted to a Commission, consisting of the Owners of land paying taxes, and Representatives of Spalding, Boston, and Stamford. A new cut was to be made for the Welland from the Reservoir to Wyberton Roads and the tide excluded by a sluice with a navigable lock. The details of this Act will be found more fully described in the chapter on the Welland. It marks the time when the Welland was placed under a separate Commission. The contemplated works were only partially carried out, the new Cut terminating at Fossdyke Bridge and the construction of the sluices being abandoned. There was a clause in the Act for compelling the Adventurers of Deeping Fen to improve the Vernatt's Drain and providing that when it was enlarged it should be supported by the Adventurers, as also the South Dozens Bank; and that the powers given to the Court of Sewers, under the Act of 14 Geo. iii, as to closing the sluice doors for 28 days, and their jurisdiction over the Pode Hole Sluice and Vernatt's Drain should cease. This matter was also subsequently dealt with in the Deeping Fen Act.

VERNATT'S DRAIN.

CONDITION OF THE FEN IN 1798.

Stone, in his review of the survey of the Agriculture of Lincolnshire, remarks, with respect to the condition of Deeping Fen, at this time: "The drainage of Deeping Fen is chiefly effected by three wind engines, above Spalding, that lift the Deeping Fen water into the Welland, the bed of which is higher than the land to be drained, assisted by a side cut called the West Load, which falls into the Welland just below Spalding, and which district, in violent floods, in a calm when the engines cannot work, is reduced to a most deplorable condition, more especially when the banks of the Welland give way, or overflow, as happened in 1798."

Stone's Survey of Lincolnshire.

A. Young's Survey of Lincolnshire.

Arthur Young, in his survey of Lincolnshire, which was published at the end of the last century, speaking of Deeping Fen, says: "Twenty years ago the land sold for about three pounds an acre; some was then let at seven and eight shillings an acre; and a great deal was in such a state that nobody would rent it. Now it is in general worth twenty shillings an acre, and sells at twenty pounds. Ten thousand acres of it are taxable under Commissioners, and pay up to twenty shillings, but as low as two shillings; the average is about four shillings, including poor rate, and all tithes free."

At the beginning of the present century a joint report was obtained from Messrs. W. Jessop, J. Rennie, G. Maxwell and E.

Hare, as to the means to be adopted to improve the drainage of these fens. This report was submitted to a Meeting of the Proprietors of lands in the fen, held at Spalding, on the 26th September, 1800. They recommended that the Cut, authorised by the Welland Act, from Shepherd's Hole through the Salt Marshes of Surfleet and Algarkirk, as far as Fossdyke, should be proceeded with. The other works recommended were mainly those which were afterwards carried out by the General Commissioners appointed under the Act of 1801.

They further recommended that a New Drain should be made to relieve the Glen from Baston to Pinchbeck Bars ; and that proper engines should be erected at Pode Hole to lift the water into the Vernatt's. A supplemental report was appended, signed by W. Jessop and John Rennie, stating that they considered the erection of engines at Pode Hole as absolutely necessary for relieving the internal main drains, and advised the use of steam for this purpose, on the ground that although wind engines could be made of better construction than those hitherto in use, yet in calm weather such engines were frequently useless when most needed.

In 1801, application was made to Parliament, and an Act obtained, for draining, dividing and allotting the tract of land now generally known as Deeping Fen, the whole of which, with the exception of the Adventurers' lands, was Common. The following is the area of land dealt with by the Act.

	ACRES.
Market Deeping Common, Deeping St. James Common, Langtoft Common, Baston Common, Cowbit Common and Heath, Spalding Common, Pinchbeck South Fen	13,500
Pinchbeck North Fen	3,500
Droves and Waste Lands	800
Crowland Common, otherwise Goggushland, Commonable by occupants in Crowland only	1,200
Deeping Fen taxable and free lands under the control of the Adventurers. (The powers of the Commissioners only extended to the draining and not the allotting of this land). Fen lands in Bourne and Thurlby on the north of the Glen, and inclosed lands in Spalding and Pinchbeck lying between the Glen and the Welland	15,000
	34,000

George Maxwell of Fletton, Edward Hare of Castor, John Cragg of Threekingham and William Golding of Donington were appointed General Commissioners for executing the works of Drainage, and for dividing and allotting the Commons into Parochial or other parts and shares. The separate share of each parish was first to be determined. The Commissioners were to be allowed two-and-a-half guineas a day each for their services and travelling expenses.

The Commissioners were directed by the Act, before making any Allotment, to set out 120ft. of land next the banks of the rivers, for the purpose of selling such land to the Adventurers. They were to set out such carriage roads as they deemed necessary, of the width of 40ft.; and it was forbidden to erect any trees near the fences of these roads, at a less distance than 50 yards apart. The boundary between Holland and Kesteven along the North and South Droves, which had long been a subject of dispute, was to be settled by the Commissioners, and their decision was to be final and binding. As the rate to be levied on Crowland Common and the Washes and other lands under the Welland Act of 1794, had not been raised and paid, the Commissioners were to sell so much of the Common land as would raise a sum sufficient to pay the arrears of the tax, and hand the proceeds over to the Welland Commissioners. They were also directed to sell so much of Pinchbeck North Fen and other lands, as would raise a sum sufficient to discharge all taxes due to the Black Sluice Commissioners in respect of the North Fen. Sufficient of the Common land was also to be sold to defray the expenses of the Drainage Works, and of dividing and allotting the Commons.

NEW WORKS.

As soon as the Welland Commissioners had completed the new Cut for the Welland to Fossdyke, the Adventurers were at their own cost to enlarge and deepen the Vernatt's Drain, from Shotbolt's Bridge to Pode Hole, so as to give it a 30ft. bottom, and to erect carriage bridges over the drain, having a clear water-way of 30ft, and other bridges in place of those then existing, with clear waterways of 30ft.; also to widen and deepen Blue Gowt Drain, from its outfall in the Glen to its termination near the Turnpike Road, and continue it by a new drain to the Dozens Bank, having a 10ft. bottom at the lower end and 6ft. at the upper; also to erect a sluice of 14ft. water-way at its junction with the Glen; they were also to make a new drain, branching from the Blue Gowt Drain to the Vernatt's Drain, and so much further on the south side as might be found expedient, with a culvert under the Vernatt's, 3ft. in diameter, for the purpose of draining the lands in Spalding and Pinchbeck, lying between the Westlode Drain and the Glen, so as to discharge their water into the Glen.

The Proprietors of this District were also empowered, when the height of the water in the Vernatt's Drain prevented the water running into the Blue Gowt Drain, or from being discharged into the Glen, to erect an engine for discharging the water into the Glen. This part of the Act was repealed by the *Act* 41 *George III*, when a separate Act was obtained for the Blue Gowt District, an account of which will be found in Chapter IV.

The Adventurers were also to deepen the Welland from Spalding Lock upwards and to strengthen the north bank of the river. After the Adventurers had completed these works, they were to be maintained by the Dykereeves of Spalding and Pinchbeck, except Vernatt's Drain ; and the right of shutting down the doors at Pode Hole for twenty eight days was to cease. Vernatt's Drain and Podehole Sluice were to vest in the Adventurers. In the event of a breach in the banks of the Glen or Welland, the Commissioners of Sewers were to have the power to shut the sluice doors at Pode Hole and keep them shut 'until the breach or *gool* shall be stopped and made secure.' If, at the end of two years, it appeared to the Commissioners that the mills and engines erected by the Adventurers would be found useful for drainage, they were to pay the Adventurers for them; but if it was found that they were not wanted, the Adventurers were to be allowed to take them down and sell the materials. *VERNATT'S AND PODE HOLE SLUICES.* *DRAINAGE ENGINES.*

The following works were to be carried out by the Commissioners. A main drain, commencing at Pode Hole and extending to the Rampart Drain, and proceeding along that drain to the east end of the Commons at South Drove, and along this drove to its west end, and continuing thence to the Cross Drain, with a branch communicating with Crowland Common at its north end. This main drain was to be 24ft. at the bottom at the lower end. A main drain commencing at Pode Hole and continuing along the 18ft. Drain to the west end of the North Drove, and joining the Cross Drain. The width of the bottom at the lower end to be 24ft. A new drain across the Commons, having an 18ft. bottom, commencing at the north bank of the Welland, and extending to the south bank of the Counter Drain. The Counter Drain to be enlarged from Pode Hole to the Tunnel under the Glen from Thurlby Pastures; as also Hill's Drain for the use of the land in Deeping Fen. Bridges were to be erected over these drains as might be found necessary. King Street Drain was to be deepened. A Catchwater Drain was to be made near the Western boundary of the Commons, and the Glen was to be deepened and enlarged from the Reservoir to Kate's Bridge. These Works were to be done at the expense of the Owners of taxable and free lands in Deeping Fen, and the Owners of the Commons, lying between the Welland and the Glen. The money was to be raised by an equal acre rate. *NEW DRAINS.* *Fig. 12.*

The Commissioners were also to have a gauge stone erected near Pode Hole Sluice, with marks on it 7ft. 8in. above the level of the floor of that sluice, and similar stones erected by the side of the main drains, at intervals of a mile, up to the Cross Drain, and having a second mark, denoting the height of 1in. per mile, for every mile up the drains. The engines draining the fen were to have their wheels 'with the wallowers' thereof so constructed as to prevent their discharging water into the drains when the water rose above the higher of the two marks, *FLOOD GAUGES.*

The right to drain Bourne South Fen and Thurlby Fen Pastures, by the culvert under the Glen, was confirmed.

GLEN BANKS. For the preservation of the banks of the River Glen the General Commissioners in their Award were to nominate Trustees or Officers to have charge of such banks, with power to levy rates for the purpose. By the Act of 1823 the Trustees of the interior Districts were directed to pay the Glen Trustees such sums as should be rated on them for the repair of these banks.

WELLAND TRUST.
DEEPING FEN TRUST CREATED. After the works were completed and the Award made, a permanent Trust was created, consisting of 11 trustees, 4 elected by the Owners of 100 acres of the taxable lands in Deeping Fen; 2 by the Owners of 100 acres of the free lands; and 5 by the Owners of 100 acres of the allotted lands lying between the Welland and the Glen. An additional vote was given to every Owner for every 300 acres owned above the 100 acres. These Commissioners were to be elected every three years, and all the general works of drainage, &c., were to vest in and be maintained by them. They were to have the usual powers of appointing Officers and levying taxes not exceeding one shilling an acre, unless the approval of the Owners of the land were obtained for a larger sum. The taxes were to be laid at a meeting held at Spalding or Market Deeping, on the day after the last Thursday in April in every year. This was altered, by the Act of 1823, to the second Wednesday in April. The Trustees were to be allowed their reasonable expenses for attending such meetings.

DRAINAGE DISTRICTS. The Commissioners were to set out the lands divided into parochial allotments, into Districts. Trustees were to be elected by each separate District for the management of the internal drainage, and for this purpose were authorised to lay rates, not exceeding two shillings an acre in one year. Six Districts were thus set out and the maximum tax was increased by the subsequent Act of 1823 to five shillings. By the Act of 1856 the powers relating to these Districts, except the Fourth, were repealed and their powers transferred to the General Trustees. An account of the Fourth District is given in Chapter IV.

The Trustees were empowered to let the herbage of the banks and forelands of the main drains, to be grazed with sheep only. The Award of the General Commissioners was to be enrolled and copies deposited in the parish churches of Spalding and Market Deeping, copies to be supplied to persons requiring the same at the rate of twopence for every 72 words. The right to inspect was to be obtained on payment of one shilling.

CONDITION OF THE FEN IN 1815. The works executed under the direction of these Commissioners did not effect a permanent improvement. The recommendation of Mr. Rennie, in his report of 1800, as to the erection of steam engines at Pode Hole was not carried out, and in a report made by Mr.

Thomas Pear in 1815, it was stated that the drainage was in a very unsatisfactory condition, the water often standing 6ft. on the sill of the old Vernatt's Sluice, which was the outlet for the drainage of Deeping Fen, including an area of 30,000 acres which were then drained by means of 50 wind engines. The distance of the outfall at Pode Hole from low water in the estuary was about 17 miles, and the distance from the lowest land in the fen, 20 miles. The fall from the surface of the lowest lands to low water was about 15ft. The outlet of the Vernatt's Drain, which conveyed the water from Pode Hole to the Welland was over-ridden by the water coming down that river, owing to the defective condition of the channel below Fossdyke Bridge. To remedy this he advised a new Cut two miles in length across the embanked lands and salt marshes to a point near Holbeach Middle Sluice; also that a lock or sluice should be erected in the Welland, a little above the Reservoir, for the purpose of keeping up a navigable head of water in dry seasons, to be so contrived as to admit the free influx of the tides, and at the same time to be clear for the outflowing of the land water. He estimated the cost of the proposed works at £50,000. The recommendations contained in this report were not entertained. *[PEAR'S REPORT. 1815.]*

In the year 1818, Mr. John Rennie made a further report to the Proprietors of lands in Deeping Fen, on the improvement of the Outfall of the Vernatt's Drain. The result of his survey of the district was that he found the whole of Deeping Fen 'almost in a lost state.' At that time the sluice at Pode Hole, where the Vernatt's Drain commences, had three openings of 10ft. each, giving a water way of 30ft. The Vernatt's Sluice, the Outlet of the drain, had two openings with the same width of water way. *[J. Rennie. 1818]*

Mr. Rennie approved the scheme already proposed for making a new Cut from Fossdyke to the Witham, but as a modification of that plan, he proposed that a new Cut should be made from the Vernatt's Sluice, to take the Deeping Fen waters only, passing under the Glen by an aqueduct, and running along the north bank of the Welland to Fossdyke; then along the inclosed lands for half a mile, across the sea bank, and along the open marshes to the Witham at Hobhole, with a sluice at the end. The length of this channel would be 8¼ miles, the total distance from the Cross Drove Drain in Deeping Fen, to the Outfall, being 23¾ miles, and ordinary low water mark at that time, standing at 3ft. 3in. on Hobhole sill; which was 17ft. below the surface of the land in the fen, allowing the water to stand 2ft. under the surface of the land, and giving a fall throughout the whole length of the new channel of 6in. per mile. This Cut would also take the waters discharging from the lands draining by the Gosberton, Five Towns and Kirton Outfalls, amounting together to 18,000 acres. The estimated cost of this work was £123,650. *[PROPOSED CUT TO HOBHOLE.]*

STEAM DRAINAGE.
T. Pear.

Mr. Rennie's plan not being adopted, a report was obtained from Mr. Thomas Pear, who, failing other plans, recommended the application of steam power for the drainage of the fen. This recommendation was endorsed by Mr. Bevan, who, in a report dated March 1st, 1823, advised the erection of two engines at Pode Hole, and the deepening of the drains.

Bevan. 1823.

4 Geo. iv., c. 76. 1823.

Being thus advised, the Deeping Fen Trustees obtained an Act giving them further powers of carrying out works, and levying additional taxes. The Preamble of this Act recites that the Works of Drainage carried out under the Act of 1801, had been found insufficient, and that for the purpose of facilitating the discharge of the waters, it was necessary that engines worked by steam should be erected. The Trustees were therefore authorised to erect at Pode Hole one or more good and substantial engines to be worked by steam, and to deepen and improve the drains. A Civil Engineer was to be appointed to superintend the works, and he was authorised by the Act, with the consent and approbation of the Trustees, to contract with any persons for the execution of the works, and was to be paid at the rate of five guineas a day for his services and expenses.

PODE HOLE ENGINES.

To meet the cost of the works the Trustees were authorised to levy a rate of fifteen shillings an acre, and, with the consent of Owners of three-fifths of the land, a further tax of five shillings.

Under the powers of this Act, two beam engines of 80 and 60 horse-power, driving scoop wheels, were erected at Podehole in 1824. The average immersion of the scoops of these wheels was 2ft. 6in. and the head against which they worked was 6ft. The total quantity of land drained by these engines is 32,000 acres. Since their original construction the scoop wheels have been considerably altered and improved; under the direction of Mr. Alfred Harrison, the Superintendant of Deeping Fen, the engines have also been improved. A full description of these engines and scoop wheels will be found in Chapter XIII, on the Drainage System. The result from these scoop wheels was not altogether satisfactory, and Mr. W. S. Mylne, C.E., was called in to report on their working. In a report dated July 16th, 1830, he stated his opinion that the drains were not capable of bringing the water down fast enough to feed the wheels, and that it would have been better if the two engines had not been erected in one place. He advised the lowering of the wheels, and the deepening and enlarging of the interior drains.

Mylne. 1830

ANCIENT CANOE 1839.

In carrying out works of improvement in this fen, about this time there was discovered, at about 3ft. below the surface, a Canoe constructed of oak, hollowed out of a single tree, and 46ft. in length, its stem was 3ft. wide and stern 5ft. 8in., and it was 4ft. deep. There were eight ribs across the bottom inside, and a keel ran along it on the outside. It was estimated that the log from which it was excavated must have contained between 600 and 700 cubic feet.

In 1846 the lands in Deeping Fen were made into an ecclesiastical parish, under the name of Deeping St. Nicholas, and a church built and endowed at the sole cost of Messrs. Stevenson of Stamford. In 1856 this was made, except as to the part in Crowland, also a civil parish under the powers of an Act, with provision for the maintenance of the poor, who hitherto had been provided for by the Adventurers of the free and taxable lands. For the purposes of the maintenance of the highways the parish was divided into the north, middle, east and south townships, each maintaining separately its own highways.

DEEPING ST. NICHOLAS PARISH. 1846.

19 and 20 Vict., c. 65.

Difficulties frequently occuring in the efficient management of the drainage of Deeping Fen, owing to the powers possessed by the Adventurers and the Trustees of the interior Districts, in addition to those of the General Trustees, an Act was obtained in 1856 for the purpose of consolidating these different Trusts and for other purposes. This Act recites that the area of land lying between the Welland and the Glen, subject to taxation, was 27,469 acres, of which 10,030 acres belong to the Adventurers who were exclusively charged with the maintenance of certain works described in the Acts of 1665, 1774 and 1801, for the purposes of which they had power to levy taxes. It was therefore enacted that these Adventurers of taxable lands should be charged in perpetuity with an annual rate of eighteenpence per acre, payable to the General Works Trustees, and their liability to maintain works and levy taxes was to cease, and all works and lands belonging thereto were for the future to vest in the General Works Trustees. Power was given to the General Works Trustees to rebuild the sluice at the end of the Vernatt's Drain, which had been destroyed a few years previously and to erect temporary sluices; to enlarge the Vernatt's Drain; to maintain and improve the Glen, and to contribute out of their funds to any works deemed necessary, jointly by themselves and the Glen Trustees. A tax of one shilling an acre was to be levied for enlarging the Vernatt's Drain. The Adventurers had to pay £3.648/13/4 towards the expenses of constructing the new outfall sluice, and the Trustees were to tax the Adventurers' lands two shillings an acre annually and the other lands a rate of one shilling an acre. These taxes were not to continue for a longer period than five years, unless by the consent of the majority of the Owners. The lands in the first, second, third and fifth Districts were to be liable to an annual tax of one shilling an acre for maintaining the interior drainage works; and the District Trustees' powers were to cease and vest in the General Trustees. The power to levy taxes imposed by previous Acts was confirmed. The Adventurers having been exonerated from the maintenance of the

CONSOLIDATING ACT. 19 and 20 Vict., c. 65. 1856.

north bank of the Glen, from Gutherham Cote to Dovehirne, in consideration of an annual payment of £18, this was to be continued by the General Commissioners; who were also to pay, to the Officers having direction of the Glen Banks, such sums as the Adventurers' lands were rated at. Persons were forbidden to keep rabbits or geese on the banks or forelands.

<small>VERNATT'S SLUICE. 1857.</small>

The Vernatt's Sluice was destroyed in 1842, the water having forced its way under the foundations. It was replaced in 1857, at a cost of £11,000 by a new structure, under the direction of Mr. William Lewin. This Sluice has three openings of 11ft. each, its sill being placed lower than the old one and level with the bed of the Welland (0.80ft. below *Ordnance datum*). The foundation stone was laid by Sir John Trollope. Low water now stands from 6ft. to 7ft. on the sill. The total area, including high land which drains through the sluice, is about 40,000 acres.

The income and expenditure of the Deeping Fen General Works of Drainage was about as follows (1880-3):—

TAXES AND RECEIPTS.

General Works Tax.

	a.	r.	p.		£	s.	d.
The Adventurers' Tax...	10063	3	13	at 1/6	754	15	11
Deeping St. Nicholas ...	15412	2	0	at 3/-	2311	18	6
„ Wash Land	605	3	11	at 6d.	15	2	11
First District	988	3	1	at 2/-	98	18	0
Second „	1221	0	23	at 2/-	122	3	0
Third „	1383	0	6	at 3/-	207	9	10
Fourth „	1423	2	16	at 6d.	35	11	10
Fifth „	2407	1	30	at 2/-	240	15	0
Sixth „	2658	1	8	at 3/-	398	14	10
„ above Gravel Drain	295	2	18	at 6d.	7	7	10
Crowland Common ...	1064	2	34	at 3/-	159	15	3
Monk's House Farm ...	220	0	9	at 3/-	33	0	0
Duck Hall District	231	2	18	at 3/-	34	15	0
					4420	7	11
Rents					797	10	6
					5217	18	5

PAYMENTS.

	£	s.	d.
Cost of working engines at Pode Hole ...	1066	0	0
Roding and cleaning the Counter, Vernatt's and other Drains...	640	0	0
River Glen and Banks	340	0	0
River Welland...	580	0	0
Management and Sundries	1567	0	0
	£4193	0	0

During the previous ten years, in addition to the ordinary working expenses, there has been paid out of income the cost of the New Glen Sluice, amounting to £3,000, and of the alteration of the Pode Hole engines £5,000; and making good breaches in the Glen Bank £1,500. The cost of the works of the five interior Districts is about covered by the rents received for the herbage of the banks, &c.

There is no outstanding loan.

The cost of working the engines at Pode Hole varies considerably according to the season, from about £700 to £1,700.

BOURNE SOUTH FEN. This Fen lies on the west side of the River Glen; and is bounded on the north by Bourne Eau; on the south by Bourne and Thurlby Pastures; and on the west by the Car Dyke. It contains 850 acres. It was first reclaimed by Thomas Lovell for the Adventurers of Deeping Fen, and drained by a culvert under the Glen, which is maintained by the successors of the then Owner, John Heathcote. This land was exempted from taxation to Deeping Fen by the Act of 1738. 11 Geo. ii, c. 39. 1738.

By an Act passed in the reign of George III a clause was inserted to the effect that if the Deeping Fen Trust lowered the bed of the Glen, they should first lower the culvert which carried the water from Bourne South Fen, and Thurlby Fen Pastures, and the right to drain thereby was confirmed. 41 Geo. iii, c. 128.

By another Act passed in the same reign, for allotting and draining the Fen Lands and Commons in Bourne, which included this Fen, power was given to Sir Gilbert Heathcote to take soil for the repair of the South Fen Bank, to the extent of 60ft. from the bank, beyond the six score feet originally appropriated for that purpose. 6 Geo. iii, c. 5.

By this Act this District was reputed then to contain 870 acres, and was allotted by the Commissioners for the purpose of a Cow Pasture, to be used by the Owners of houses and toftsteads in Dyke and Cawthorpe.

Experience having shown that this cow pasture did not answer the purpose intended, being incapable in its then state of supporting the cattle depastured on it and being frequently overflowed with water, an Act was obtained for inclosing it. John Parker of Edenham, Thomas Hogard of Spalding, and Edward Hare of Castor, were appointed Commissioners for dividing, allotting and draining the fen. 12 Geo. iii. 1772.

Four acres of the fen were allotted for getting materials for the repair of the roads in Bourne; and the remainder was divided amongst the Owners of Commonable houses and toftsteads in the parishes of Bourne, Dyke and Cawthorpe. The Commissioners were directed to set out such roads as they considered necessary, and also a road to the old inclosures of Sir Gilbert Heathcote, called the South Fen Pastures; and to make drains and erect engines for taking the water off the land.

HERBAGE OF THE ROADS.

The herbage on the four acres set apart for the roads, and also on that for the repair of the South Fen bank, was vested in the Surveyor of Interior Drainage, the rents to be applied in maintaining the works, power being reserved to the Vestry at the annual meeting held at Bourne, on the Monday after the 5th of April, "to give leases to such industrious inhabitants, not renting or occupying lands or tenements to the amount of £8 per annum, to keep and depasture upon any of the roads and ways within the parish such number of oxen, cows and calves as the majority of the said inhabitants shall think most proper, but no other species of cattle whatever."

DRAINS.

If the Owners or Occupiers neglect to scour out their drains after 14 days' notice, given by the Surveyor of Interior Drainage, the work is to be done by the Surveyor, and the expenses recovered from the defaulter.

PRING WATER

The Commissioners were directed, as far as possible, to make an equal distribution of the water issuing from the spring in the South Fen amongst the several allotments.

IMBANKING AND DRAINING.

In the Award directions were given as to the imbanking and draining, and orders made as to the raising of money to pay the Surveyor and defray the annual expenses. The Award was to be enrolled with the Clerk of the Peace of Kesteven, copies being supplied at the rate of twopence per 100 words.

WORKS TO VEST IN BLACK SLUICE TRUST.

The works, after the Award was made, were to vest in the Black Sluice Commissioners, appointed under the Acts, 5th and 10th George III, and the duty of maintaining the drainage was then to devolve on that Trust.

TAXES.

The Commissioners were empowered to levy a tax, not exceeding a shilling an acre, for the maintenance of the works, recoverable by distress on the goods and chattels found on the lands charged with the taxes in arrear.

SOUTH FEN PASTURES.

The right of Sir Gilbert Heathcote to drain the South Fen Pastures and Thurlby Fen Pastures in the same manner as they were then drained, and of the Earl of Exter to take water from the Glen for his two Decoys in the precincts of Bourne and in Bourne Fen Pastures were reserved.

CONDITION OF THE DRAINAGE. 1871.

Up to about 1871 this land was imperfectly drained, partly by gravitation by the drains made by the Commissioners under the powers of the Act of 1772, and partly by scoop wheels worked by horses situated in different parts of the fen.

DRAINAGE DISTRICT. 34 and 35 Vict. 1871.

In 1871 an order was obtained under the Land Drainage Act, 1861, constituting this a separate Drainage District, which was confirmed by Parliament. Under this order a Board was formed with power to lay rates and carry out works for the drainage of the District.

A centrifugal pump, driven by an 8 H.P. portable engine, was erected at the lower end of the fen and the water lifted over a dam into the main drain, which carried it away through the culvert under the Glen into the Counter Drain, and so by the Vernatt's to the Welland.

An Injunction in Chancery was applied for by the Deeping Fen Trustees to prevent the use of this pump, on the ground that the lifting the water by steam power was an excess of the right which this land had to send its water to the Deeping Fen Drainage System. The Action was not proceeded with and the Board was allowed to continue the use of the engine.

Rates and Expenditure.

From the annual Taxation Return for 1892-3 the amount raised from taxes in this district was £177; maintenance of works cost £103, salaries and management £14, interest £46, repayment of loan £30; total £193. The amount of loan then outstanding was £930.

THURLBY FEN. Contains about 1500 acres. The first drainage of this fen was effected by one of the Adventurers who reclaimed Deeping Fen. A main drain was cut which carried the water of this and Bourne South Fen by a sunken culvert under the Glen into the Counter Drain and so by the Vernatt's to the Welland.

By the *Deeping Fen Act of* 1738 these lands, then computed to contain 336 acres, being part of the 'Free Lands' which had been awarded to the Adventurers for their recompense, were exempted from any payment of the taxes then imposed, on the ground that they had been embanked and preserved at the sole charge of the Owner, Sir John Heathcote.

11 Geo. iii., c. 39 1738.

By the Act of 1801 these lands were not included in the area of land subject to the Deeping Fen taxes, and the right to drain by the culvert under the Glen was confirmed.

41 Geo. iii, c. 128. 1801.

By an Act passed in 1802 the Common Fen, stated to contain 1,000 acres, was, with other common lands, inclosed. John Burcham, John Trumper and Edward Hare were the Commissioners appointed to divide and allot the land.

42 Geo. iii. 1802.

CHAPTER XI.

The Estuary of the Rivers Witham and Welland.

THE Estuary of the Witham and the Welland, known as 'Boston Deeps,' constitutes the northern portion of 'the Wash,' that large indent or bay, lying between the counties of Lincoln and Norfolk which covers about 300 square miles. The southern portion, or Lynn Well, receives the water from the the rivers Nene and Ouse.

The theory as to the original formation of this Estuary is dealt with in the chapter on the Geology of the Fenland.

The general features and outline of this Estuary and the principal sand banks have continued in their present condition for a period long anterior to the erection of the Roman Banks, about 1700 years ago. The only alteration which has taken place since that time, so far as can be ascertained, is due to the accretion along the shores of the alluvial matter brought down by the four rivers, and the inclosure of some of the accreted marshes.

During the last three centuries over 63,600 acres have been inclosed. The growth of these marshes on the north and west side has been at the rate of about half-a-mile in width since the inclosures made by the Romans; at the head of the bay, where the four rivers discharge, the growth has been much more rapid, the banks made by the Romans being now four miles inland. On the east, or Norfolk side, there has been very little accretion, the inclosures which have been made being due principally to the direction of the channel of the Ouse, and the reclamation of the former bed of the river.

Boston Deeps is divided from Lynn Well by a long ridge of sand, which rises from 8 to 10ft. above low water. Through this sand bank are several channels and swashways.

The channel runs from the North Sea, in a line parallel with the coast, for about 15 miles, past Skegness, Wainfleet, Friskney, Wrangle, Leake, Leverton, Benington, Butterwick, Freiston and Fishtoft. The depth of this channel, at low water of spring tides, decreases from about 6 fathoms to 2 fathoms at the upper end. At the lower end there is a bar, consisting of three narrow ridges of sand with a depth of only 12ft. on them, at low water of spring tides.

The width of the channel alters in nearly the same proportion, being about 1½ miles wide in the lower part, decreasing to about a quarter of a mile at the upper end. At the bar the width between the sand banks is only about a quarter of a mile.

In Lynn Well the bed of the Estuary, in places, is as much as 23 fathoms below the surface of low water.

FREEMAN'S CHANNEL.

The principal connection between Boston Deeps and Lynn Well is by Freeman's Channel, which lies between the Ants and Roger Sands. This is a straight channel, 2½ miles long, with a depth of 2¾ fathoms at Lynn Well end, 5 to 7 fathoms in the middle, and 2 fathoms over the bar at the Boston Deeps end. It was buoyed out for navigation in 1890, and, being well lighted, is of very great service to steamers and fishing trawlers and to all vessels which are unable to cross the bar at the lower end of Boston Deeps, owing to the tide being low.

MACCARONI CHANNEL.

Another buoyed channel, a little below Clayhole, termed the 'Maccaroni,' and the 'Gat' also goes to Lynn Well. The depth of water in the Maccaroni is from about half a fathom to two fathoms. In the Gat it increases to five fathoms. This channel, being shallow and tortuous at the upper end, is very seldom used. It has been gradually shoaling for some years, but more rapidly since the opening of the New Cut.

SOUTH CHANNEL.

At the beginning of the present century the navigable course from the Witham to Boston Deeps was by a channel, having an easy curve across the southern end of the Herring and Black Buoy Sands, turning in a north easterly direction and entering Boston Deeps at the western end of the Toft Sand. This was then known as the 'Maccaroni' channel and the northern half of it is still known by the same name. The course to the Gat channel branched off across the northern end of the present Hook Hill Sand. The River Welland joined this channel by a curved course, about half-a-mile to the south of its present direction. When the training works of the Welland were carried out, about 1838, the direction of the current was altered and driven more northerly, and, impinging on the water of the Witham deprived of a large portion of its tidal volume by the stoppage of the tide at the Grand Sluice, succeeded in diverting the principal portion of the ebb through the channel known as 'the Clays,' into Clay-hole. This being found a shorter course for the vessels and a more fixed channel, owing to its being clay, the Harbour Authorities encouraged the ebb and flood to keep this course by removing some hummocks of clay, which dried at low water in Spring tides. Previous to the construction of the new Outfall this had become the buoyed channel. The old channel known as 'the South Channel,' which had previously been the regular course for vessels navigating Boston Deeps, is still open and part of the water of the Welland occasionally finds its way by it to

CLAYS CHANNEL.

FORMER CONDITION OF THE NAVIGABLE CHANNELS.

the Gat, the principal Outfall for this river being through the Clays.

The channels of these two rivers used constantly to be changing their positions, varying as the sands were affected by the winds, the tides or the land freshets. The current thus exhausted its strength in forcing a way through these shifting sands and the water was spread over a wide surface, instead of being concentrated in a single channel of uniform width, the consequence being that the power, which should have been employed in deepening and scouring, was lost and absorbed in constantly shifting the sands. The better to illustrate this, it may be mentioned that an ordinary tide took three hours to reach Hobhole Sluice after it was flood in Clayhole, a distance by the then winding course of four and a half miles; but as soon as it reached the confined channel of the Witham, its speed increased and it reached the Grand Sluice, the distance being about the same, in less than one hour. The difference of level between Hobhole and Clayhole, in the year 1799, was 3ft. 3ins., in a course of four miles, or nine and one-third inches per mile. In 1822 the course had lengthened to five and a half miles, and the water was so much held up by the filling of the river with sand that the fall had increased to 5ft. 2in. The rate of inclination in the surface of the water from Hobhole to Clayhole, previous to the improvement of the channel, had become 8ft., or at the rate of twenty-one and one-third inches per mile.

TIDAL CURRENTS. The flood tide enters the Wash off Burnham Flats and takes a S.S.W. direction, the current running up Lynn Deeps at from 4 to 5 knots at springs, and 2½ knots at neaps. At half-flood the tide strikes the head of the bay and divides, one current running N.E. along the Norfolk coast, and the other S.W., the tide thus running in opposite directions at the same time, causing what is known as 'tide and half-tide.' At the head of the Estuary, at three-quarter flood, the set of the tides divides off the Gat, one current drawing S.W., towards the set-way of the Witham and Welland, and the other S.E. towards the Nene and Ouse. The flood and ebb current in the centre of the Wash, flowing at the rate of 2½ to 3 knots, together make a complete circle in the course of twelve hours. The flood tide makes into Boston Deeps very soon after it has commenced to flow in Lynn Well. At half-flood, when the sands are covered, there is a set of tide outwards, along the main from Leverton towards Gibraltar Point and Wainfleet Haven until high water, when it meets the flood over Wainfleet sands. There is a strong W.N.W. set through all the lows in the Long Sand on the S.E. side of Boston Deeps until first-quarter flood. After first-quarter flood the main tide sets straight up the Deeps, but there is a slight set out of Lynn Well when the Long Sand is covered. The ebb sets in the reverse direction to the flood.

It is high water, full and change, at six o'clock in the Deeps. *THE TIDES.* Spring tides rise 22ft. in Clayhole above mean low water of Springs, and at Neaps, 14ft. 6in., the range of the latter being 9ft. 2in. The tide flows about 5½ hours in Clayhole, and at Spring tides, about 3½ hours at Boston. The tides are greatly influenced by the wind. A strong north-west wind will generally raise a spring tide 2ft., and a south-west one depress it to the same extent, and other tides in proportion, the tide generally being raised or lowered as many inches, higher or lower, as the tide affected should rise in feet, according to the tide table. The highest tide ever recorded rose 4ft. 11in. above the level of an ordinary Spring tide. The particulars of the high tides which have occurred, and of the effect of the wind on the tides, will be found in the Appendix. The lowest tides of the year generally occur in June, *Appendix 5.* and as this is the time when the sea birds are rearing their young on the grass marshes, these tides are known locally as 'Bird Tides.'

When sailing ships were more in use, Boston Deeps was *BOSTON DEEPS A HARBOUR OF REFUGE.* frequently used as a harbour of refuge by the Colliers and other vessels navigating the North Sea, in stress of weather, especially during north east gales. It is stated by old inhabitants residing near the coast, that they have seen from 300 to 400 ships lying within a space of three miles, between Freiston and Wrangle. Boston Deeps was then considered one of the safest anchorages on the east coast, during north-east gales.

In the year 1751, Nathaniel Kinderley brought forward a scheme *RECLAMATION SCHEMES.* for the improvement of the Great Fen Rivers discharging into the Estuary. Adverting to the fact that the Outfall waters of the Nene, the Ouse, the Witham, and the Welland, the four rivers which empty into the estuary, were seriously impeded by the shifting sands which were being continually washed about by the tides, he says, "But what do we propose to do with these pernicious sands? Do we think to remove them? No, certainly, that would be quite an impracticable scheme; but though we can't remove them, we may certainly desert them, and if we don't we may be assured that the sea in time will desert us." He therefore proposed to bring the Nene *Kinderley. State of the Navigation &c., 1751.* into the Ouse by a new Cut through marsh land, these rivers when united to be carried to the sea under Wooton and Wolverton through the Marshes, and to discharge themselves into the deeps by Snettisham. The Welland was to be taken by a new channel inland from about Fossdyke, in the direction of Wyberton, to the Witham, near Skirbeck Quarter, and the two rivers united were to continue in a straight course through the country to some convenient place over against Wrangle or Friskney. The result of this he considered would be the entire silting up of the estuary and the gaining of 100,000 acres, the whole of which would become good land in the course of 50 years. 'A new habitable country, 15 miles long and from 8 to 10 in breadth.' Across this new formed country he proposed that a road should be made, connecting Lynn and Boston. The cost was estimated at £150,000. The waters were thus to he carried in confined channels by the nearest route, direct into deep water. The inadequancy of the estimate for this gigantic scheme will be realised by a reference to the fact that the improvement of the Witham Outfall alone has cost more than this amount.

<small>RECLAMATION OF THE WASH.</small>

<small>Sir J. Rennie. 1839.</small>

In the year 1837, a meeting of Landowners, and others interested in the drainage of lands which had their outfalls into the Wash, was held in London, the principal object being the improvement of the River Ouse. As a result of this conference, Sir John Rennie was directed to make a survey and report as to the best means of effecting the improvement. Accordingly he commenced his survey in the following year, but it was not completed till the summer of 1839.

Sir John Rennie suggested that one general scheme for the improvement of the whole of the Estuary was far preferable to partial measures; he therefore recommended that the channels of the four rivers should be confined by fascine work, and be led to one common outlet, and that the land should be embanked as it accreted. Referring to the two rivers which are more particularly dealt with here, he remarked that the Welland and Witham Outfalls, particularly the former, were then in a very defective state, and he suggested that they might be improved by either carrying them across the Clays into Clayhole, or by the Maccaroni or South Channel, to join the Nene and Ouse; the advantage of the former plan being that the distance to deep water would be considerably shorter, and in consequence it would be sooner effected; and that custom had hitherto pointed out Boston Deeps as the natural entrance or roadstead both for the Witham and the Welland. On the other hand, looking forward to one general grand plan, and the prospect of maintaining the general Outfall open, he thought that there could be little doubt that the greater the body or mass of fresh and tidal water that could be brought into one channel, the greater the certainty of its being able to maintain itself open. In order to effect this enlarged view of the subject, the junction of the Witham and Welland, the Nene and the Ouse, into one common outfall, in the centre of the great Wash, appeared the best and most certain plan; and he thought that if the Witham and the Welland were to be carried separately into Clayhole Channel, the Nene into Lynn Well, and the Ouse along the Norfolk shore, there would be a far greater quantity of embankments to make, the channels, by being separate, would not be able to maintain themselves open so well; the land gained would be divided into several separate islands, which would render it more difficult of access, and consequently of less value; whilst the expense of acquiring it would be greater; and lastly, the boundaries of the counties of Lincoln and Norfolk would be disturbed.

The quantity of land that he considered would be gained by the union of the four rivers in one common Outfall was 150,000 acres. This he estimated as being worth, in a few years, £40 per acre, or a total of £6,000,000, which, after deducting £12 per acre for the expense of obtaining the greater portion and £15 per acre for that portion lying nearest to the open ocean, together amounting to the sum of £2,000,000, left a clear gain of £4,000,000. This Report was presented to a meeting held in London in July, 1839, of which Lord George Bentinck was chairman; and it was then resolved, after adopting Sir John Rennie's report, and expressing the desirability of carrying on the work, "that the execution of the same must necessarily exceed the means of private individuals, and ought therefore to receive grave consideration and the eventual support of Her Majesty's Government, as a purely national object." And further, that although it appeared that great improvements would be made in the various rivers and drainage of land, "the Promoters of the undertaking do not feel it necessary to call either upon the Landowners or the parties interested in the navigation for any contribution in the shape of tax or tonnage duty, but will rest satisfied with the reimbursement of their expenses by the acquisition of the land they expect to reclaim from the sea." It being found impossible to raise the funds, no attempt was made to carry out the scheme.

The next attempt to improve the Outfall of the Witham and Welland and their Navigation, was by a company, called the 'Lincolnshire Estuary Company,' who obtained an Act of Parliament in 1851, 'for reclaiming from the sea certain lands abutting on the coast of Lincolnshire, within the parts of Holland.' The capital was £600,000, to be raised by 24,000 shares of £25 each, and power was given to reclaim and embank the marsh lands adjacent to the rivers Witham, Welland, and Nene. The navigation and drainage of the Witham and Welland were to be improved by new Cuts and Outfalls, but the company was not to have any power or control in the management of the Outfall. The exact line of the new banks, which it was proposed to construct, was, *first*, from a point near the sea bank at the lower end of the Nene Outfall, in Long Sutton, and along the western bank of the Nene to Clayhole, and thence in a south western direction up the Welland to Fossdyke Bridge; *second*, commencing at the northern end of Fossdyke Bridge, to continue down the Welland to the west side of Clayhole, and then curving in a western direction and continuing to the Channel of the Witham, opposite Hobhole; *third*, commencing at Hobhole Sluice, and continuing in a south-easterly direction for one-and-a-half miles, and then curving in an easterly direction to the west side of Clayhole, and continuing along the channel for eight miles, and

LINCOLNSHIRE ESTUARY COMPANY.
14 and 15 Vict., c. 136. 1851.

joining the old sea bank in the parish of Wrangle. The quantity to be enclosed was 30,000 acres. The Owners of the marshes adjoining the lands to be vested in the Company were to contribute towards the expense of making the banks, and the sum agreed on, between the principal Proprietors and the Company, was £8 15s. per acre of marsh land. Like its predecessor, this scheme was only born to die. So many obstacles presented themselves, from the scarcity of money at the time the scheme was brought out, and the difficulty of determining the rights and boundaries of the Frontagers, and the small assistance that was offered by those most to be benefited, that the Company preferred to lose all their preliminary expenses rather than proceed with the work. The time allowed by the Act for the completion of the work expired in 1858. The question as to the practicability of the Scheme, and its chance of commercial success, if carried out, is dealt with in the Chapter on the Geology of the Fenland.

<small>Geology. Chap. 16.</small>

<small>FREISTON SHORE RECLAMATION. 42 and 43 Vict., 1879.</small>
In 1879, a Company was incorporated and obtained an Act giving them power to reclaim the marsh lands in the parishes of Freiston, Butterwick and Benington, and to make an embankment commencing at the sea bank, in the parish of Fishtoft, extending seawards to the 'Tidal Gauge,' and terminating at the bank at the boundary between the parishes of Benington and Leverton. The Crown was to be paid £4,500 for the rights in the shore below high water mark. No works were carried out under this Act and its powers expired in 1889.

<small>RECLAIMED LAND. Chapters 3 & 4.</small>
The Works of Reclamation which have been carried out have been dealt with in the Chapters on North and South Holland.

CHAPTER XII.

THE PORT AND HARBOUR OF BOSTON AND THE WITHAM OUTFALL.

THE Port of Boston consists of all that portion of the Wash and the river Witham over which the Corporation of Boston hold control, under a Charter granted by Queen Elizabeth in 1573.

The Preamble of the Charter recites that "there has been an ancient Port in the Borough of Boston, in the County of Lincoln, for a long time past, serving many countries with provisions of victuals and divers other merchandise which has been very profitable to us and our most serene progenitors, Kings of England, for the increase and augmentation of the revenues of the Crown of England, by reason of the great profits of the said Port, called Customs, which are now greatly decreased and are likely to decrease more and more, by reason of the great decay of trade and merchandise of late happening there. And whereas our ships and those of all other persons, sailing on the coasts of our County of Lincoln, either northward or southward, have great refuge for preserving and defending both men and ships, against any sudden storms on the said coasts, in certain places adjoining to our said Port of Boston, commonly called the Norman Deeps, which said places called Norman Deeps lie so hidden and hard to be known, and are so very dangerous that many people passing that way have been shipwrecked and lost." To prevent further ruin and decay of the Port it was desirable that the Mayor and Burgesses of Boston should be better able to make and support a sufficient number of sea marks and for that purpose the "Borough and Port of the same, and also all and all manner of places and parts and water courses, and the streams of the washes near and in the parts of Holland, extending to the Haven or place called Wainfleet Haven, and to a certain other place called Pulley Head, and to another place or sand called the Knock, and to another place called the Dog's Head in the Pot, and to the uttermost limits of the flowing and ebbing of the waters aforesaid and every of them, and adjoining to the sea, and floods and streams, of the borders and confines of our county of Norfolk," and all places within the precincts, compass and liberties

THE PORT OF BOSTON.

Charter of Elizabeth. 1573.

of the said Borough and of the Port, as well on the land as on the waters, were for ever exempted "from any control and office of Admiral and Admiralty of England." An Admiralty Court was established at Boston for the trial of all maritime and other suits and all matters touching the office of Admiralty, and power give to levy fines and appropriate profits arising out of the Court. The Corporation was also to have control over all fishermen and their nets; and to have the anchorage, ballasting, lastage and liberty of ballasting and taking lastage, together with the profits therefrom, of all ships within the Port. In order to provide funds for maintaining the beacons and sea marks, the Corporation were empowered to levy, of all ships which should enter or leave the Port, and of the Fishermen the following dues, "of every ship or any other marine vessel, of every Scotchman four shillings, and of every other foreigner five shillings; of every other ship or marine vessel laden with wool and sailed out of the Port three shilling and fourpence; and of every ship of this our realm of England twenty-pence; and of every vessel laden with coals, three bushels of coals; and of every keel or lighter coming from Hull or Lynn, or any other coasts or counties of of our kingdom of England, eight-pence; and for every ship moored within the Deeps aforesaid and not unladen in the said Haven, twelve-pence for anchorage; and of all and singular the said Fishermen such sum of money as shall seem reasonable to the said Mayor and Burgesses in the Court aforesaid." The goods and chattels of felons, fugitives, outlaws and suicides, and all wrecks of the sea, "flotsam or things floating in the sea, jetsam or things cast out of any vessel into the sea, lagan, or goods fastened to a buoy, treasure found or to be found, deodands and derelict goods" &c.; also "all manner of royal fish, that is to say sturgeons, whales, porpoises, dolphins, riggs and grampusses, and all other fishes whatsoever having in them any great fatness or thickness,......antiently belonging to us by right or custom," coming within the "Borough, Port, Roads, Deeps, Streams, Washes and Liberties and within every place where the said streams ebb or flow, and precincts of the same," were granted to the Mayor and Burgesses of Boston.

CONDITION OF THE PORT IN 1594.

In a petition presented to the Queen, Boston is described as an ancient Sea Port, serving the neighbouring country with victuals and merchandise, and as being profitable in Customs; but that it was decaying; that the port was the only safe harbour on the Lincolnshire Coast, and yet was dangerous for want of sea marks in Boston Deeps, which the town was willing to erect and maintain, if allowed an import on all ships repairing to the said Deeps, but, as the town was impoverished by decay of trade and great inundations, they begged a license to export 10,000 quarters of grain in six years, paying the usual customs; also to hold lands in mortmain, of the value of £100 yearly, towards the charge of the sea mark also for freedom from Admiralty Jurisdiction, as enjoyed at Yarmouth and Goole.

It is difficult now to trace exactly the boundaries set out in this Charter. By the ' Norman,' probably a corruption for ' Northern,' Deeps is meant the area now known as Boston Deeps. The name Pulley Head cannot be localised, but, from information obtained from old Pilots, it would appear that the southern end of the Gat Sand used to be known as the Pulleye Heads. 'The Dog's Head in the Pot' is now known as the Dog's Head Sand. The boundary, in the Charter, follows the line of high water from Boston along the river to Fishtoft, and thence along the coast to Skegness, thence eastwards to the lower end of the Outer Knock, and Dog's Head Sands, and along the boundary of the Counties of Lincoln and Norfolk to the west side of the River Nene up to the line of high water at the sea bank, and following along the coasts of Gedney, Holbeach, Fossdyke, Kirton, Frampton and the west side of the Witham to Boston.

BOUNDARIES OF THE PORT.

Fig. 9.

This, practically, is the limit of the Port over which the Corporation exercise jurisdiction at the present time, and in which they are responsible for the maintenance of the buoys and the sea marks.

For Custom House purposes the limit is described as extending from Trusthorpe Tunnel to Sutton Corner, or Lutton Leam. The proceeds of all wreck found within this limit are paid over to the Corporation by the Custom House Authorities.

CUSTOMS' BOUNDARY.

The limits over which the Corporation had jurisdiction for the control of the Oyster and Mussel Fishery, under the order made in 1870, is described as extending along the line of high water, from the point where Dawesmere Creek intersects the sea bank in the parish of Gedney, to the west bank of the River Witham opposite Hobhole Sluice, thence to Hobhole Sluice along the line of high water, to the Coastguard Station at Skegness; thence eastward to the Outer Knock Buoy at the lower end of the Outer Knock Sand; thence to the lower end of the Dog's Head Sand and along the Long Sand to the Roger Buoy at the Roger Point at the south-west end of the Roger Sand; thence to the Gat Buoy at the south end of the Gat Sand; thence south-westerly along the north-west side of the Wisbech Channel to Bachelor's Beacon; and thence along the northern side of Dawesmere Creek to the point of starting.

MUSSEL FISHERY BOUNDARY.

The powers relating to the Admiralty Court and other matters were taken from the Corporation by subsequent legislation; and those relating to the navigation extended, and the dues altered by Acts of Parliament, obtained by the Corporation.

The positions of the buoys and beacons as first placed under the charter were as follows: The first, nearest to Boston, at Westward Hurn; the second, at South Beacon; the third, at Scalp Hurn; the fourth, between Scalp Hurn and Elbow Beacon; the fifth, the Elbow Beacon, at Stone Hawe; the sixth, South Clay Beacon;

BUOYS AND BEACONS IN 1580.

the seventh, the North Clay; the eighth, midway between the North and High Hurn; the ninth at High Hurn; the tenth on the Main between Boston and Benington; the eleventh and last, on the Long Sand. These beacons were fixed for the first time in the year 1580, and a survey of them was made by the Mayor, Aldermen and sundry Mariners.

PILOT TRUST.
16 Geo. iii. c. 23, 1775.
32 Geo. iii. c. 79, 1790.

In the years 1775 and 1790, two Acts were obtained for the better regulation and government of the Pilots conducting ships into and out of the Port of Boston. The Preamble of the first Act recites that for upwards of 200 years the Corporation had exercised Admiralty jurisdiction in the Port, and had erected Buoys and Beacons, but that owing to the continual shifting of the sands, the entrance to the Port had become very dangerous without the assistance of a skilful Pilot, and that many vessels had been lost, owing to the ignorance of the persons who had taken upon them to conduct them into and out of the Port, and that therefore it was desirable that rules should be enacted for the establishment of a system of Pilotage, and also for improving the existing accomodation for the navigation. A Commission was therefore appointed, consisting of 'the Mayor, Recorder, Deputy Recorder, Aldermen, Town Clerk, and Common Council of the Borough,' together with 45 Mariners and Merchants, who were to hold an annual meeting on the first Monday in the month of February, for settling the accounts of their Treasurer, Collector and other Officers. Upon a vacancy occurring the Commissioners were to appoint a successor, the same being either a Merchant, Owner or Commander of a vessel trading to the Port, or an inhabitant of the Borough.

The Commissioners are empowered to grant licenses to persons found to be duly qualified after examination to become Pilots, and no person is to be allowed to exercise the duties of a Pilot without such license, under a penalty not exceeding three pounds. The limits over which dues may be taken for pilotage extend only to High Horn Buoy and the Toft, and the rates were fixed according to the draught of the vessel. A provision was made for a charge not exceeding three guineas for a pilot conducting a ship from the Knock Buoy, or beyond, up to High Horn, at the desire of the Owner or Master. The Commissioners were also empowered to fix mooring posts, and bridges over the creeks on the marshes for the convenience of towing or haling vessels. The Commissioners were empowered to receive a penny a ton from every ship entering the Port, for the purpose of defraying the costs of their expenses. The second Act gives power to appoint a Harbour Master for the regulation of the shipping within the Port; and also to remove any shoals within the Harbour, to improve the channel of the river, and to make regulations for the better order and safety of the ships frequenting the Port.

In 1793 a scheme was brought forward for diverting the river Welland from its ancient course to Spalding set-way, to join the Witham near Wyberton. Captain Huddart was requested by Sir Joseph Banks to report as to whether this diversion would injure the navigation to Boston. Referring to the Scalp Reach, he says, "As those flat sands accumulate and grow higher they will be subject to raise the bed of the river, which will have a bad effect upon the navigation to Boston; for by decreasing the fall the river will be too languid to clear away the silt, and in course of time, by imperceptible degrees, the navigation will be lost to the Scalp, the channel will be subject to vary, sometimes better and at other times worse, but upon the whole it is my opinion the sands will continue to increase." Having treated on the then state of the Outfall, he gives his opinion decidedly that the navigation of Boston would not be rendered worse by the intended cut for the Welland to Wyberton, at a point nearly opposite Hobhole, as the joint effect to scour a channel would be greater with the two rivers united than with the Witham alone, and he further recommended that, if this were carried out, the water of the Witham should be diverted from its then course, to the South of the Herring and Black Buoy Sands to the Clayhole Channel; or otherwise that a cut should be made across the Scalp, by the Milk-house, in a straight line extending in a south-easterly direction from the intended junction to Clayhole, (the preference being decidedly given to the latter plan), and that the united waters of the Witham and the Welland should be conveyed by this cut to the Estuary.

This is the origin of the numerous schemes which were subsequently brought forward for '*cutting through the Clays*,' but with this merit belonging to it, which none of its successors had, that the Welland was to be united with the Witham at a point considerably higher up than their present course, and the two rivers were to flow through the new Cut; and so the waters of the united streams would be available for keeping the channel open.

In the year 1800 Mr. John Rennie was directed by the Corporation to report his opinion on the best mode of improving Boston Haven. He found that the channel was so crooked and wide in places, 'that unless art was judiciously applied to assist nature in her operations, no material improvement could be expected to arise.' He attributed the condition of the river partly to the Grand Sluice which had been erected above Boston, remarking, "If the Grand Sluice were entirely taken away, and the tide suffered to flow up the river, it is evident it must move with a greater velocity through the Harbour of Boston to fill the space above; and providing there is a sufficient quantity of fresh water and fall to drive back the tide, &c. during the ebb, it is equally evident the constant action of this great body of water passing through the harbour, would grind the channel deeper; but should the contrary prove to be the fact, Boston Harbour, instead of being made deeper, would become more shallow, and the drainage of the country above would become proportionately worse." He found that the width of the channel at low water varied from 82ft. near the church to 306ft. opposite Maud Foster; 429ft. at Wyberton Roads and 330ft. at Hobhole, increasing in places to 1,500ft. at high water; that the channel above Hobhole meandered through extensive shifting sands and became even worse below West Marsh Point, because the extent of flat shifting sands between high and low water was there very great, while the fall was small. The water coming from the Witham and the Welland shifted its course so frequently, as the freshet or tides prevailed, that the channel one day was in a different place to that which it occupied on the previous day. Mr. Rennie suggested two plans for improving the river. The one by making a straight Cut from Skirbeck church to Clayhole; and the other by straightening and contracting the present channel between Skirbeck church and Hobhole, and making thence a new Cut nearly in the direction laid down by Capt. Huddart. The expense of the first plan was estimated at £139,700, and of the second £113,700. He further added: "The improvements I have stated are confined to the channel below Skirbeck church; but when this is done, I think it will be found advantageous to make some improvements above; perhaps even to construct wet docks in some suitable situation. This, however, will be an after consideration, but ought nevertheless to be kept in view; and if some mode could be devised of establishing an accumulating fund for the purpose of repairing and improving the harbour, these different matters might be resumed as the wants of the trade should require."

On the strength of this Report, and in order to revise and increase the dues to which they were entitled under the Charter of Elizabeth, the Corporation obtained an Act of Parliament which repealed the old tolls, and in their place granted certain wharfage dues (according to a schedule) on all goods landed or shipped from any wharf or quay between the Grand Sluice and Maud Foster, the tonnage dues on all vessels entering the Port being fixed at sixpence for British and ninepence for foreign vessels. A lastage duty of one penny per quarter on wheat, and one half-penny on other grain was also imposed on all corn whatsoever, put on board or landed out of any ship within the limits of the port.

<small>52 Geo. iii, c. 105. 1812.</small>

On the security of these dues the Corporation were authorised to raise a sum of £20,000 to build new quays and wharves, and to improve the river by widening, deepening and contracting the same between the Grand Sluice and Maud Foster. The new wall built along the eastern side of the river, from the south end of the Pack House, or Custom House, Quay to the Bridge, and thence to the

<small>THE QUAYS.</small>

Fish-market, and the large warehouse, called the 'London warehouse,' were part of the improvements effected. About this time, also, a considerable improvement was made by straightening the upper part of the river by a new channel cut from the Grand Sluice to the Iron Bridge, the cost of which was £3,550, the work being contracted for by Messrs. Williamson and Woodward.

Notwithstanding the works carried out under this Act, the navigation continued to be very much impeded by the state of the river below Maud Foster Sluice. Several efforts had been made to induce the Drainage Commissioners to join with the Corporation in straightening and improving this portion of the river. Mr. Rennie had advised them to contribute liberally towards the cost of the work, and reported that a considerable saving could be effected in the drainage of the East and West Fens by bringing the whole of the waters to Maud Foster, into the channel, instead of making a new Cut, where the Hobhole Drain now is; but that to enable this to be done the river must first be improved.

CONDITION OF THE RIVER IN 1800.

The Harbour Commissioners were prepared to contribute one-half the cost of the work; and at a meeting held at Boston, December 9th, 1800, at which were present several Merchants, Shipowners and Traders, it was "resolved that to promote the improvement of Boston Haven there shall be levied on all vessels entering inward and clearing outward at the port of Boston a duty of fourpence per ton; which duty there is reason to believe will be equal to the interest of about one half the capital sum which the said improvement will require, according to the estimate of Mr. Rennie." The Drainage Commissioners declining to join with the Corporation, on the ground that their scheme did not go far enough, inasmuch as it did not include the improvement of the Outfall below Hobhole, the river was allowed to remain, for several years, in its imperfect condition.

In 1822, Sir John Rennie, by direction of a general meeting of all the Trusts interested in the drainage and navigation, made an examination of the river; and a chart and survey, accompanied by levels and soundings, was prepared by Mr. Giles. In this report, full particulars are given of the then state of the river and its Outfall, the causes of the impediments to the navigation and drainage, and the remedies necessary to be applied for their removal. Sir J. Rennie recommended that the river, from the Black Sluice to Maud Foster, should be confined by jetties, and that from Maud Foster a straight Cut should be made to Hobhole, adapting the old river course, where available, by training it by fascine work. This Cut was to have a bottom of 80ft. at its commencement, increasing 25ft. in width for every mile, and to be excavated to a depth at Maud Foster of 4ft. below Hobhole sill, and increasing to 5ft. at Hobhole. The estimated cost was £117,190. He further recommended a

SIR J. RENNIE'S SCHEME.

Report. 1822.

CLAYS CUT

continuation of this Cut in the same proportion to Clayhole, and following nearly the same direction, as recommended by Captain Huddart and Mr. Rennie.

The form of the Cut varied from that shown on Capt. Huddart's plan, being curved instead of straight and bending round the corner where the Milk House Farm stands, the site of the house being about the centre of the New Cut, and then across the salt marshes and sands to Clayhole. The estimated cost of this part of the scheme was £118,467, the estimate for the complete plan being £235,658. The advantages to arise from this outlay were, that the course of the river would be shortened one-third, and an increased declination of nearly 12in. per mile thereby effected between the Black Sluice and Hobhole. In his report he views other plans which have suggested themselves, but gives this the preference, as being economical and interfering less with existing works, and states that "if at any future time a dock should be required, a cut for the river could be made across to St. John's Sluice, and the old circuitous channel, converted into a spacious basin of 30 acres, with proper locks," &c. This would have involved the removal of the Black Sluice a quarter of a mile below Maud Foster, the cost of which would be £120,000. As to the question of the necessity of carrying out the whole of the works at once, he further remarked. "The scheme, however, may with propriety terminate at Hobhole, and if found insufficient, it may be continued to Clayhole at any future period; by that time I hope that the parties connected with the River Welland, animated by a like just regard for their own interest as the parties connected with the Witham, will come forward and join them in completing this useful and important enterprise by carrying the united waters of the two rivers into Clayhole."

THE SCALP.

Referring to the channels below Hobhole he describes the Scalp as a solid and compact bank, composed of sand, gravel and clay, averaging from 10ft. to 13ft. above Hobhole Sill. Owing to this high bank, the tide from Boston Deeps could not get into the Witham Channel until about two-thirds of the flood had made, and then its force became comparatively deficient as regards the Witham by the great indraught into Fossdyke Wash. The ebb current coming down the Witham, being met at right angles by the Welland, was diverted from its course to a south-easterly direction, the waters dividing themselves into the Clayhole and a channel running south of the Herring Sand to the Maccaroni, until the last quarter ebb, after which they were confined wholly to the latter and proceeded westerly to Boston Deeps, part of the water however passing off by the Hook Hill Bar to Lynn Well. These channels are described as being so uncertain as never to continue in the same course for more than a few days together, the Outfall of the Welland occasionally altering as much as half-a-mile. Communication between the

THE EXISTING CHANNELS.

Fig. 9.

Witham and Clayhole at that time was principally maintained by the Maccaroni or South Channel (that is the channel running south of the Black Buoy Sand) which, although circuitous, had been tolerably certain for 40 years previous to the date of the Report. There was also a channel by the 'Elbow' across the Clays, which however was only suited for vessels of light draught. The flood tide at that time ran about 4 hours at the Scalp, having first made up the South Channel until about one-third flood, when it was met by that coming through Clayhole across the Elbow. The velocity of the current was from 3 to $3\frac{1}{3}$ miles an hour. He considered the Clayhole Channel as a more preferable course from the Witham to Boston Deeps, than by the South Channel and through the Maccaroni and Gat Channels to Lynn Well. He found that vessels bound for Boston invariably preferred passing the Bar at the Knock, where was never known to be less than $1\frac{1}{2}$ fathoms, and, at that time 2 fathoms, at low water of spring tides, and proceeding by the Deeps to Boston Haven, as once arrived in the Deeps they were secure as it were in a large river, protected from all winds, in a good anchorage and plenty of depth of water; whereas by running up Lynn Well they were exposed to many dangers from the immense tracts of shifting sands, the great variety of currents setting up to Lynn, Wisbech, Spalding and Boston, and from the Hook Hill or Boston Toft Bar, where there was seldom above 2ft. at low water, and sometimes it was even dry.

In the following year Sir John Rennie was again called in, and at the same time Mr. Telford was also consulted. Mr. Telford, in a report dated March 22nd, 1823, addressed to the several Trusts interested in the drainage and navigation, prefaces his remarks by saying that "the state of the haven is so apparent that it is quite superfluous to enter upon any detailed description of it." He traces the existing defects to the following causes: first, and chiefly, to the obstruction caused by the Grand Sluice in preventing the tidal waters from flowing further up than the town of Boston; secondly, to carrying the drainage water of the fen lands on the eastern side of the river down towards Hobhole; thirdly, to suffering the river to form a crooked and wide channel by cutting away the marsh land, and to its consequently becoming encumbered with mud and sand banks.

TELFORD'S REPORT. 1853.

By removing the first, and, in his view, the chief cause of the evil, namely, the Grand Sluice, and admitting the tidal water to flow up the river, a natural power would be made to operate upon the whole Channel to the Outfall; which would not only restore the Harbour of Boston, but maintain a deep Channel for the whole drainage of the adjacent districts. To admit of this being done with safety, he advised that all that would be necessary would be that the banks above the Sluice should previously be made sufficiently high above the level of the highest tides, which, he was informed, could be done at a moderate expense. To remedy the third cause he proposed a new Cut from the Black Sluice across Bell's Reach to Hobhole, the expense of which he estimated at £106,846, and stated that he proposed "this scheme with more confidence, because if the outfall even after this new channel has been made should fall into decay, still a new channel may then be extended from Hobhole to Clayhole." He concluded his report with the words, "I consider the above only a portion of the general improvement which may be executed for the drainage and navigation."

With reference to a proposal which had been made to drain some of the lands discharging their waters by the Black Sluice by other means than into the river Witham, he gave it as his opinion that such a diversion by diminishing the power of the Witham to keep its channel open, would tend to its silting up, check the flux and reflux of the tide and lead to the decay of the Outfall and upper part of the bay.

Sir John Rennie's report bears the same date. He refers to his former one, and confirms the opinion therein expressed; he gives his sanction to the plan proposed by Mr. Telford, provided that Maud Foster Sluice is removed, involving a further expense, beyond Mr. Telford's estimate, of £18,564. He entirely concurs in Mr. Telford's remarks about the Grand Sluice, and concludes by "anxiously impressing upon all parties interested the necessity of making and maintaining a perfect Outfall, without which all interior works would be useless.

IMPROVEMENTS IN THE CHANNEL. 7 and 8 Geo. iv., c. 79. 1827.

In 1827 an Act was obtained, by which the limits over which the Corporation could make quays, wharves and jetties was extended from Maud Foster to Hobhole, and they were empowered to borrow a further sum of £20,000, and to carry out the works recommended by their Engineer. These consisted of the straightening of the river by means of a new Cut, 800 yards in length, through Burton's Marsh, thus cutting off the great bend at Wyberton Roads, and shortening the distance to deep water one mile and a half.

WYBERTON ROADS CUT. 1833.

The contract for this work was undertaken by Messrs. Joliffe and Banks for the sum of £24,000, and finally completed in the year 1833, at a total cost for land and works of £27,262.

BEASLEY'S CUT. 1841.

The remainder of Sir John Rennie's plan, embracing the straightening of the river from Skirbeck Church to join this new Cut, was not commenced till the year 1841, when Capt. Beasley undertook to train the channel, which was continually shifting between these two points, by fascine work, and to excavate, where necessary, so as to make the river as nearly straight as possible. This work he successfully accomplished at a cost (including land) of £11,627. In the following year Mr. Beasley completed a fascine barrier on the west side of the river, from nearly opposite Maud Foster Sluice to the end of Slippery Gowt Marsh, the length of the same being about one mile, at a cost of £2,775; and the water being thus confined in one channel, the land on either side gradually accreted, till it became level with the top of the fascine work, and rose to such a height as only to be covered with water at the top of spring tides. The land gained by these two new channels was embanked, about twenty-five years after the training works were completed, by Mr. Black and the Corporation.

Another considerable piece of training was the diversion of the waters from their circular course round Blue Anchor Bight Marsh to a straight line, by the fascine work carried out by the late Mr. Robt. Reynolds, who was then the Surveyor to the Trust, and the same result has followed on the inside of this work, as already mentioned as taking place higher up the river. This marsh was embanked in 1866.

The ancient course of the Witham was exceedingly circuitous, and, in fact, the present channel is almost entirely artificial. The only part of the course which has retained its original direction is that between Boston Church and the outfall of the Old Hammond Beck, at the commencement of Skirbeck Quarter. Previous to the erection of the Grand Sluice, and the subsequent new Cuts and training works, the channel made a long curve to the west, about a quarter of a mile above the site of the Grand Sluice; it then doubled back to the church, continuing nearly along its present course to Skirbeck Quarter, where, on the east side, was a large marsh, now covered by the Bath Gardens. Through this marsh, it was confined by a new bank on the east side, and below the Black Sluice, by fascine work on both sides; below this, the channel doubled round a projecting point, which was removed in making the entrance to the dock, and then went close under Skirbeck Church, thence bending westerly for a short distance, then returned and came close to the bank on the Fishtoft road. It then turned in a westerly direction, for about a quarter of a mile, along the bank to where the old Slippery Gowt still passes through the Roman Bank, and then bent easterly for nearly half a mile, up to the road in Fishtoft leading to the Scalp, this part being known as Blue Anchor Bight; from here it again turned westerly for about three quarters of a mile to Wyberton Roads, and after running for about a quarter of a mile in a south-easterly direction, turned sharply eastward to Hobhole, whence it continued in a southerly direction along the high bank known as the Scalp, bending again, when it left this, to the east, and after joining the Welland, about half a mile to the east of its present position, the two rivers continued in a north-easterly direction at the back of the Herring Sand through the Maccaroni Channel into Boston Deeps. The length of the channel, from Boston Bridge to Clayhole, by this winding course, was 13½ miles, as compared with 9 miles to the

ANCIENT COURSE OF THE RIVER.

same point by the present more direct course. The width of the water between the banks at high water was, a little below Skirbeck Church, nearly half a mile. The ancient course of the river may be traced by the Roman Banks, which are still maintained.

Vessels of too large a draught to get up the river, or when waiting for the tide, used to lie at the Scalp, and frequently delivered their cargoes there.

COST OF IMPROVEMENTS.

The amount expended by the Corporation in straightening and improving the channel of the river has been as follows:—

	£	s.	d.
1825.—Cutting new channel for the river from the Grand Sluice to the Iron Bridge...	3550	0	0
1828 to 1833.—Cutting a new channel through Burton's Marsh, diverting the old channel	27262	0	0
1841.—Cutting a channel through Corporation Marsh, and making a fascine barrier on the eastern side of the river, from Maud Foster to Corporation Point	11627	0	0
1842.—Fascine barrier on the west side of the river, from Rush Point to the south end of Slippery Gowt Marsh	2775	0	0
1823 to 1859.—Sundry small contracts for the extension of fascine work	7555	0	0
Expenditure (to 1868) in repairing and heightening the fascine work, and general maintenance of the river	5250	0	0
	£58019	0	0

This sum is in addition to the amount spent in building quays, &c., on both sides of the river, and in straightening and improving the channel by the inclosure of a marsh on the east side, opposite the Black Sluice. The amount spent on these works between 1825 and 1840 was £33,354.

POWERS TO IMPROVE THE OUTFALL.
4 and 5 Will. iv, c. 87, 1834.

TRANSFER OF DUES TO THE WELLAND.
5 Vict., c. 4. 1842

In 1834 an Act was obtained giving the Corporation power to execute works for improving the Witham from the Grand Sluice, and the Welland from Fossdyke to Clayhole. This Act was repealed by an Act obtained by the Welland Commissioners, by which in consideration of their paying to the Corporation of Boston £5,000, being part of a debt due to the Exchequer Loan Commissioners, on the security of the tolls and dues, and also undertaking to pay one-third of the annual expenses incurred by the Corporation, in maintaining the buoys, beacons and sea-marks, the Corporation gave up the dues on vessels navigating the Welland. Also under the powers of this Act, and another obtained by the Corporation in the same session, the Corporation was authorised to execute works between the Grand Sluice and the confluence of the Witham and the Welland, by training, leading and directing the

5 Vict., Sess. 2, c. 60. 1842.

water of the Witham in a confined channel to the sea, and conjointly with the Trustees of the Welland, to execute works for the improvement of the Outfall of the two rivers, from the point of their confluence to Clayhole. For the purpose of carrying out this work the Corporation were authorised to borrow £20,000.

After the opening of the Great Northern Railway in 1848, the shipping trading to the Port fell off more than one-half, or from 94,000 tons to about 40,000 tons. Subsequently there was a revival and the tonnage again increased. Before the construction of the railway a considerable trade was carried on by means of the Witham and other navigable canals with the interior of the country. The river was the only means of conveyance for the export of the corn brought to Boston from the large agricultural district by which it is surrounded, and for the import of coal and produce, for consumption by the inhabitants of the fens, which were brought by sea to Boston and carried thence by boat and barge up the canals and drains to the Fens. On the opening of the railway a fresh means of communication was provided, and a considerable amount of traffic diverted to it from the river. A very large trade in inland coal was also carried on by the Witham, the quantity which passed down through the Grand Sluice gradually increasing since the beginning of this century from about 12,000 chaldrons, to upwards of 30,000 in 1830. The duty being taken off sea coal in this year caused the amount to diminish to about 13,000 chaldrons. From the opening of the railway in 1848 a steady decrease again took place, and the quantity passing down the Witham became very small.

<small>TONNAGE OF VESSELS. 1848.</small>

Several schemes have been promulgated from time to time for providing the Port of Boston with better accommodation for its shipping. The most noticeable was a plan brought out by Mr. Staniland in the year 1845, at the time the Great Northern Railway was in progress. The Company was organised under the name of The Boston Dock Company, with a capital of £200,000, its professed object being the 'further improvement of the Haven and Outfall, and the construction of wet docks.' The scheme was very strongly supported, the Mayor of Boston and two-thirds of the Corporation being on the Provisional Committee, also seven Magistrates of the Borough, and several Commissioners of the Witham and Black Sluice, and a long array of Landowners and Merchants. The prospectus stated that "The Port of Boston has for ages been the natural point of access to the ocean for a very extensive and exceedingly fertile tract of country. In early ages Boston ranked amongst the principal seaports of the Island; in late years, however, partly owing to neglect and partly to other causes, the Outfall has become bad and the navigation difficult." This state of affairs the Company proposed to remedy by their scheme, and they considered the time a particularly opportune one, as the construction of the various

<small>BOSTON DOCK COMPANY. 1845.</small>

railways then in progress would bring the Port into connection with the whole of the Midland Counties. This scheme, so promising in appearance, proceeded no further than the formation of the Company. The scarcity of money at the time, and other difficulties, caused the promoters to abandon it.

<small>IMPROVEMENT OF THE OUTFALL.</small>

The season of 1860, having been unusually wet, caused a great quantity of the low lands to be flooded, considerably injuring the crops throughout the Fens. The attention of the parties interested was once more aroused to the defective state of the Outfall, and the necessity of taking active steps for its improvement. The Proprietors of lands in the East Fen being the greatest sufferers, the Witham Commissioners directed their Engineer, Mr. W. Lewin, to make a report on the state of the Outfalls of the rivers Witham and Welland. Mr. Lewin reported that he found the Outfalls of both rivers deteriorated to such an extent that when there was 7ft. 10in. of water on the sill of Hobhole sluice, there was not more than 9in. at low water, over the shifting sands at Spalding setway. The sands at the lower end of the rivers Witham and Welland, were being continually shifted during land floods, forming meandering streams, alternately to the eastward and westward, but never of sufficient capacity or area, to allow the proper utterance of the flood waters. He considered that if the channel of the Witham had been confined below Hobhole Sluice, and that of the Welland, from the fascine work already put in, to Clayhole, these accumulations of sand would not have taken place. After referring to the plans which had been suggested for improving the Outfall, either by dredging and confining the channel, between Hobhole and Clayhole by fascine work and for training the river Welland; or by taking the Witham water by a direct Cut from Hobhole to Clayhole, as already strongly recommended by Mr. Rennie, Mr. Cubitt and Sir John Rennie; he expressed his opinion in favour of the latter course. He advised that the bottom of the Cut should be laid out, 4ft. below the Sill of Hobhole Sluice; with an average width of 130ft. and length of 1¾ miles. The cost he estimated at £60,622. The benefit to be gained would be a depression of the water in floods at Hobhole Sluice, of 5ft., and from 2ft. to 3ft. at the Grand Sluice and the Black Sluice. He also advised the deepening and improvement of the river above the Grand Sluice. Mr. Lewin considered that if the works be recommended were carried out, in addition to the new Outfall, "all the engine power (used for pumping) would become useless in the several fens along-side the river Witham from Boston to Lincoln."

<small>C. Frow. 1861.</small>

In the year 1861, Mr. Charles Frow, of Holbeach, addressed letters to the public press, and subsequently in a communication made to the Boston Harbour Trustees, dated May 1864, called attention to the South Channel, as the proper Outfall for the waters of the Witham and Welland, and he proposed that the two rivers should be trained by fascine work across the numerous beds of sand into Lynn Well, in preference to the diversion of the waters across the Scalp by the proposed Cut to Clayhole, and also pointed out what he considered the defects of the latter scheme.

In the same year Sir John Hawkshaw was requested by the Witham Drainage Commissioners to advise, chiefly as to the improvements of the drainage of the Fourth District, but also as to a scheme that would be of more general improvement. In dealing with the general scheme, Sir John Hawkshaw, gave it as his opinion that the project which had been recommended so frequently and for so long a period of time, *viz.*, of forming a new Cut to Clayhole, was the best general plan, as it would not only assist the drainage of the Fourth District, but would also improve the Outfall of all the great drains which empty themselves into the Witham, and that it would benefit the navigation to and from the Port of Boston; but the construction of this new channel for the Witham into Clayhole would involve the necessity of extending the Welland to a junction with it at the same point. The report further continued, "In estimating the cost of the work I see no reason at present for departing from the dimensions that have been fixed by previous investigation and enquiry. They seem from such enquiry as I have been able to bestow upon them to have been judiciously determined and they appear on former occasions to have received the sanction of the Representatives of the different interests concerned. I have therefore assumed that the bottom of the Cut opposite to Hobhole Sluice will be 3ft. below the sill of that sluice, and that the width of bottom at that point will be 100ft.; the bottom to have a regular fall of 1ft. per mile from its commencement to its termination at Clayhole, the slopes of the sides of the Cut to be $4\frac{1}{2}$ft. horizontal to 1ft. perpendicular, to a height of 20ft. above the sill of Hobhole Sluice; the foreland to be 70ft. in width. The extension of the River Welland should start at the end of the fascine work now completed, and should fall uniformly to its junction with the Witham at Clayhole. I estimate the cost of the work as under:—The Boston Outfall, £80,000; The Welland Outfall, £20,000; Parliamentary and Engineering, say £15,000; Total, £115,000. It has been estimated by Engineers who have preceded me that the extension to Clayhole would depress the low water flood level about 3ft. at Hobhole. It is possible that this will be the result. I am of opinion that a depression of that level to the extent of 2ft. can very safely be reckoned upon as a minimum at all the before-mentioned sluices. Were the depression of the flood level not to exceed that dimension, it would effect a general improvement of all the Districts drained through those sluices; but as regards the navigation of Boston I am of opinion that a still greater amount of benefit would be derived, inasmuch as the low water of the river in dry weather would be depressed to a greater extent than the low water of the river in time of floods, and the channel would be scoured to an equivalent depth: while it is mainly on the depression of the low water level in the time of floods that drainage depends, the navigation will have the advantage of the former. This plan would also improve the navigation of, and the drainage into, the River Welland.......From all that I have read and thought on the subject it seems probable that the sands in the upper part of the estuary are steadily though slowly accumulating and encroaching on the sea. The evil effects of this can be counteracted only by training and straightening the rivers that empty themselves into the estuary, and by pushing them forward as the sea retires. The extension of the channels of the main Outfall is therefore a step in the right direction, and would be a permanent step as far as it goes. Should the Landowners generally not join you in the more comprehensive and general measure, I see nothing for it but to advise you to expend your money on the minor and internal scheme; but looking to the future, such a step would have to be regretted. Funds that otherwise might have helped to carry out the general measure will be lost to it when the time shall arrive when all who are interested in keeping open the Outfall, upon which so large a tract of rich land and so much valuable property have been made to depend, will be driven to act vigorously to secure its existence."

With regard to the scheme which had been advocated of carrying the channels of the Witham and Welland across the sands, and making a junction at the Maccaroni or South Channel, he considered that the estimate given by Mr. Frow had been greatly underrated, and all the enquiries he had made led him to the conclusion that Clayhole was the best point for the Outfall.

At a meeting of the General Commissioners of Drainage for the river Witham, resolutions were passed adopting the principles laid down in Sir John Hawkshaw's report, and the Fourth District agreed to contribute towards a general scheme such a sum, estimated at one shilling per acre, as it would cost them to carry out the alternative scheme for the internal improvement of their own District, provided the other Trusts would at once join them in carrying out the Outfall works proposed by Sir John Hawkshaw. Very strenuous efforts were made to induce all the interested parties to join in one general scheme, and a large meeting was held at the Guildhall, Boston, of Representatives from the several Drainage Trusts and the Boston Harbour Commissioners; but while the necessity of an improved Outfall, and the desirability of at once attempting the necessary works for ensuring it, was freely admitted, there seemed to be insuperable difficulties in reconciling the interests of the several Trusts, and the rate at which they should contribute towards the expense, and nothing was finally determined.

Forseeing this difficulty, and relying on the very strong feeling existing at the time in favour of an improved drainage and navigation, a Bill was promoted by persons interested in the navigation and drainage, and the necessary Parliamentary notices were given for the Session of 1861, but the matter was postponed till the following year, when an amended Bill was drawn up, intituled 'a Bill to authorize the making of new Outfalls 'for the rivers Witham and Welland, for improving the drainage by those rivers, and for other purposes.' The object of the Promoters, and the scope of the Bill, cannot be better explained than by the following quotation from a circular issued at the time.

IMPROVEMENT BILL. 1862.

" The necessity for improving the drainage of the districts bordering on the rivers Witham and Welland has been demonstrated for years past, and the evil effects of procrastination are experienced in the great and serious losses occasioned to the Agriculturists on every visitation of those heavy rains which periodically fall in this locality. Throughout the country great efforts are now being made to secure practical measures for perfecting on an extensive scale an improved system of Outfall drainage. With this object the Middle Level, the Nene, and the Hatfield Chase Drainage Districts are all seeking enlarged Parliamentary powers. The abundance and cheapness of capital, coupled with an increased disposition on the part of capitalists to advance large sums at a moderate rate of interest, on the security of drainage rates, particularly marks the present as the proper time for making strenuous efforts to utilize the resources and capabilities of the Districts and to turn to useful purposes the practical experience and suggestions of those whose valuable time has been directed to an improved measure of drainage. With this view it appears desirable to prescribe and carry out a drainage scheme adapted to the requirements of the district, with such useful modification as may be suggested, and so defined as to insure the greatest amount of benefit consistent with the least possible expense. This is proposed to be done by a Bill to be submitted to Parliament in the ensuing Session, embracing powers for carrying out a plan similar to the general plan suggested by Mr. Hawkshaw, with such alterations as may be deemed expedient, and for reclaiming about 15,000 acres of marsh lands by cutting through the Clays on Boston Scalp and conveying the Witham and Welland waters direct to the sea, thus shortening the distance three and a half miles, increasing the fall about six feet, and giving to the fens and uplands of Lincolnshire a most perfect and complete drainage. The entire cost of the works, including every expense, is estimated at £100,000. This charge is intended to be met by a rate, or assessment, upon the Commissioners and Trusts, in the proportions following, or as near thereto as may seem just and equitable : the Fourth District of Drainage by the river Witham, 62,276 acres, at 11½d. per acre, £3,000; the First, Second, Third, Fifth, and Sixth Districts, 65,381 acres, at 2d. per acre, £500; the Welland, 34,416 acres, at 4d. per acre, £500; the Black Sluice, 46,215 acres, at 3d. per acre £500; the Harbour of Boston on the dues of the port, £500; total £5,000. The above charge is to remain for thirty years, when if the reclaimed land is in a condition to sell, and the Commissioners effect a sale at a price reasonably estimated at £20 per acre, the sum produced from that source would, on the whole 15,000 acres, be very considerable. (The Harbour Commissioners of Boston have lately sold reclaimed land of the same character after 30 years accretion at £30 per acre.) It is proposed to appropriate the sum produced as follows: first, in payment of the monies borrowed; secondly, dividing the residue into three parts, two thereof to be handed over to the contributing Commissioners, and the other to be divided between the Harbour Trustees of Boston and the Trustees of the Welland. Should Parliament require provision to be made for a sinking fund, this can be done on the basis of repaying the borrowed monies in a period of thirty-five or forty years, but this would be unnecessary in the case of the reclaimed lands being realised as suggested. The Act is intended to be carried out by Commissioners to be appointed as follows: by the Witham District, 14; Black Sluice, 2; Welland, 2; Boston Harbour, 2; total 20. The Fourth District Commissioners of the river Witham having called in the services of Mr. Hawkshaw, whose very able and explanatory Report, with certain suggestions, they have adopted, it has been considered desirable to follow up as far as practicable the recommendations therein contained, and for that purpose to ask the co-operation of the landed proprietors and others interested in the drainage, and to seek for such aid and information as may enable the parties interested to perfect a measure calculated to carry out this great and necessary work, which has never for so many years past been attempted, and the want of which annually entails such grievous losses on the district."

The Promoters of this measure, after spending a considerable sum of money in preparing the necessary Parliamentary notices, and paying the other expenses incidental to obtaining an Act of Parliament, finding that they were not likely to receive that support from the Landowners and others who would derive the benefit of their exertions, were obliged to withdraw their Bill.

PIER AT CLAY-HOLE.

After this, several of the Merchants, Shipowners, and Traders of Boston, despairing of any improvement being ever effected in the river, and suffering from the continual lightening of the ships of their cargoes by barges, in order to enable them to reach the town, conceived the idea of carrying a railway from the Great Northern

Railway, in Skirbeck Quarter, to Clayhole, opposite Freiston Shore, and there constructing a pier and breakwater, by the side of which vessels of large size might lie afloat at all states of the tide. The Bill for obtaining the necessary powers for this, having passed through the preliminary stages in the House of Commons, was withdrawn, owing to its not being adequately supported.

The dry summer of 1864, having silted up the river to such an extent that its bed was raised from 10ft. to 11ft. at the town; and great inconvenience and loss being experienced by those engaged in the trade of the Port, at a Quarterly Meeting of the Harbour Commissioners, held on the 27th of October, 1864, a memorial was presented, "signed by the bankers, merchants, tradesmen, and ship-owners of Boston, requesting that the Trust would immediately take steps to improve the Outfall and state of the Haven," and in accordance with the prayer of the memorial, the Commissioners resolved that Sir John Hawkshaw should be consulted and requested to frame a report upon the state of the Haven, and to recommend the best means for its improvement.

HAWKSHAW'S REPORT. 1864.

Sir John Hawkshaw made his report on the 23rd of December following, in which he stated that the condition of the Haven on his examination was worse than he had before seen it; "that outside the doors of the Grand Sluice there was an accumulation of mud and sand 10ft. to 11ft. in height above the sill; the water in the drain then standing about 7ft. 6in. above the sill, so that the mud outside was about 3ft. higher than the surface of the water inside, and that the condition of the river at the other sluices was equally bad in proportion." This being the state of the Haven, he recommended that "there are two works which, if both were executed, would effect the greatest amount of improvement in Boston Harbour, *viz.*, first, to cut a new channel from Hobhole to Clayhole; second, to remove the Grand Sluice and allow the tide to ebb and flow in the Upper Witham."

Sir John Hawkshaw's observations with regard to the first part of this plan have already been given. With reference to the second, he remarked, "The removal of the Grand Sluice would still further improve the Harbour by allowing a large quantity of water to flow into the channel, the reflux of which would increase the scouring power. This measure would require the sanction of the Commissioners for Drainage by the River Witham, and of the Great Northern Railway Company, and the raising and strengthening of the banks above the Sluice. It is not improbable that due consideration and enquiry, which would, however, require time, might lead these bodies to see nothing incompatible with their interests in that measure." Beyond obtaining this report, no further action was at this time taken in the matter.

In the autumn of 1866, the attention of those interested in the Outfall was once more aroused by the Fourth District Commissioners, despairing of any general measure being carried out, taking active steps to adopt the alternative plan, recommended by Sir John Hawkshaw, for the erection of pumping engines to lift the water off the low lands in the East Fen. A strenuous effort was made to prevent, if possible, the diversion of funds to this purpose, which, otherwise, might be available for Outfall Works.

OUTFALL TRAINING SCHEME.

State of the Outfall of the Witham. Wheeler. 1867

There being no prospect of carrying out the large scheme which had been brought forward, owing to the difficulty of raising the capital, a modified plan was suggested by the Author of this work, which was described in a pamphlet, published in 1867, in which statistics were given in an Appendix, as to the silting up of the bed of the river at different times, owing to the effect of the Grand Sluice. It was pointed out, that the scouring action of the freshets, being dependent on the rain that falls, occurs only at certain periods and cannot be augmented; whereas the action of the tides is regular and constant, and their tendency is to increase the back water, by means of which the sea channels are kept open. The question of the necessity of raising the banks of the river above the Grand Sluice, if the tide were allowed to run up above it, was dealt with; and to meet this, the plan, suggested by Mr. Chapman, of regulating the tidal doors, so that while, during all ordinary seasons, these would remain open for the free passage of the tides, they would be closed against such tides as might rise high enough to be dangerous to the banks; or on occasions when heavy freshets were running down the river. For the improvement of the Outfall, it was suggested that this could be best obtained by continuing the training walls below Hobhole, and thus straightening and confining the channel of the river along its natural course; and that, if this trained channel were also deepened by dredging, low water mark could be depressed as low as by the scheme of cutting through the Clays, and as deep a navigable channel be obtained at one-fifth of the cost.

This subject was dealt with more fully in a Report made to the Harbour Commissioners by the Author, dated October 11th, 1870.

Wheeler's Report. 1870.

In this report it is admitted that the cutting a of new channel through the Clays would provide the shortest and most direct course to deep water, but that, as the expense of carrying it out appeared to stand forth as a bar to all improvement, the Commissioners were advised to carry out the less costly plan of training and dredging the river along its natural course to the junction of the Welland. It was pointed out in this report that by training and fixing the channel, the tidal and fresh water would be confined to one course, and the shifting sands at the mouth of the river be fixed and prevented from impeding the course of the water and shoaling the channel. By dredging out the clay in the trained channel, and in Clayhole, a better Outfall would be provided for the drainage water, and the fall in the surface of the water would be reduced, and consequently the level depressed at Hobhole and the other sluices, and at the same time a deeper channel would be secured for the navigation.

The estimated cost of thus improving the Outfall was £17,350, or, with the purchase of the Crown rights over the land which was capable of being reclaimed, between the channel and the shore, £21,000.

This work could have been carried out under the powers of the Act of 1842, and would have had the advantage of uniting the Witham and the Welland in one course.

<small>5 and 6 Vict., c. 60.</small>

The report was approved by the Harbour Commissioners, and also by Mr. James Abernethy, C.E., who had been instructed to report on its feasibility and on the advantage to be derived from the plan. Subsequently, in evidence given before a Committee of the House of Lords, the latter gave it his thorough sanction and support.

The Harbour Commissioners, however, considered that the surplus income at their disposal did not warrant their carrying out the scheme without the assistance of the Drainage Trusts.

When the matter of the Outfall was again revived, this scheme was dealt with in a Report made by the River Committee, in which it was stated that, on investigation, it was found that the Trust had expended, since 1825, a sum of £61,000 in the improvement of the river, towards which nothing had been contributed by the Drainage Authorities, although they depended on the river for the discharge of the water from the Witham and the large main drains. That, failing to obtain the necessary funds for carrying out the larger scheme for cutting an entirely new outfall, they considered it desirable to proceed with the scheme submitted in the report of their Engineer, Mr. Wheeler, provided the Witham and Black Sluice Drainage Trusts would be willing to join with them and contribute annually a share of the expense, until the work was completed. The Drainage Trusts, however, declined to give any assistance.

<small>Meeting of Harbour Trust. May 1, 1876.</small>

In 1878, Mr. J. E. Williams, who had been appointed Surveyor to the Witham Commissioners, made a Report on the condition of the drainage of his district, and more especially as to the Outfall. He advised that the loop of the river below the town of Boston, should be cut off, by the construction of a new straight channel, commencing at the ferry, in South End, and entering the river again near Maud Foster, and suggesting that the portion thus cut off might be made into a dock—as suggested by Sir J. Rennie in 1822—by constructing gates above the outfall of the Black Sluice. He expressed the opinion that the most effectual remedy for the defective condition of the Outfall was the proposed cutting through

<small>WILLIAMS' REPORT. 1878.</small>

the Clays, but that, failing the carrying out of this, he considered that the object desired could be effected by the alternative scheme which had been suggested, for training the natural channel, below Hobhole, to the junction of the Witham with the Welland. He pointed out that by this course the effect of the combined scour of the two rivers would be highly beneficial to the common Outfall. He showed that, by an expenditure of £28,500, the level of the low water could be depressed sufficiently to give an inclination in the bed of the river, from a point 1ft. below the sill of the Grand Sluice to low water of spring tides in the Estuary, of 1ft. per mile, and that a line drawn from these points would clear the sills of Maud Foster and Hobhole Sluices. He also proposed the removal of the Grand Sluice to Chapel Hill.

WITHAM OUTFALL ACT. 1879.

Appendix 5.

A series of nine wet years extending from 1875 to 1883, causing continuous and serious floods, with heavy losses, and in many cases ruin, to the agricultural interest, at last brought about a general conviction as to the imperative necessity of the Drainage Interests taking steps to obtain an improved Outfall for their main drains. Mainly through the influence and exertions of Mr. Thomas Garfit, M.P., a joint meeting of committees appointed respectively by the Commissioners of the Witham Drainage, the Black Sluice Drainage and the Boston Harbour, was held in Boston, on the 29th August, 1879, to consider the improvement of the river Witham below the Grand Sluice. At this meeting the two schemes for improving the Outfall, the one by cutting a new channel through the Clays, and the other by training and dredging the natural channel of the river, were submitted by Mr. Banks Stanhope, the chairman, and it was unanimously resolved to adopt the scheme for cutting through the Clays. The basis of calculation adopted for raising the money for the proposed work, estimated at £100,000, was that all lands comprised in the six Witham Drainage Districts and the Black Sluice District should contribute a uniform Acre Tax. The contribution of the Harbour Trust was fixed at £10,000, and they were to give up to the new Trust any right they possessed as to land that might be reclaimed. The cost of improving the river between Hobhole and the Grand Sluice was to be apportioned amongst the Trusts deriving benefit from each portion of the river. Steps were directed to be taken for preparing a Bill in the next session of Parliament, the Witham Commissioners, as the largest contributing Trust, undertaking the immediate charge of the Bill, and guaranteeing the expenses. A representative Committee of the Trusts interested was appointed to settle the drafting of the Bill, and the care of it through Parliament.

J. KINGSTON'S REPORT ON THE OUTFALL SCHEME. 1879.

Before the Outfall Bill came before Parliament, the Welland Outfall Trustees instructed their Surveyor, Mr. John Kingston, to report as to the effect likely to be produced on the Welland, by the diversion of the Witham by the new Cut. In his report, dated September 12th, 1879, after reviewing the opinion of all the Engineers who had reported on the subject, he advised that the gain to the Witham Drainage, by cutting through the Clays, would not give such an advantage over that by training and dredging the natural channel as would be equivalent to the £70,000 difference of cost; that the divergence of the Outfall of the Witham, by the former scheme, to a greater distance from the Welland Outfall, would have a prejudicial effect on both rivers; and that the cutting through the Clays, would have but little better effect on the depression of low water flood line in the Witham, than the less costly scheme. The Welland Trustees therefore determined to oppose the Bill.

The *Witham Outfall Bill* came before a Committee of the House of Lords in the session of 1880. The petition of the Welland Outfall Trustees against the Bill stated that the diversion of the water of the Witham, by the proposed new Cut, would diminish the scour, through what was then the common Outfall, so as to cause the shifting sands of the Wash to accumulate at the mouth of the Welland, to the injury of the drainage and navigation of that river. After hearing evidence on both sides, the Engineers called in support of the Bill being Sir John Hawkshaw, Mr. J. E. Williams, Mr. W. H. Wheeler and Mr. Lancaster, and for the Welland Trustees, Sir John Coode and Mr. J. Kingston, the Committee passed the Bill, subject to a clause that if, within 20 years after the completion and opening of the new Cut, the Welland Outfall Trustees should give notice that they intended to form an improved channel from the then point of confluence of the two rivers to the termination of the proposed new Cut, the Witham Outfall Board should pay half the cost of making such new channel and of maintaining it when made. [RIVER WITHAM OUTFALL ACT. 43 and 44 Vict., c. 153. 1880]

A second Act was subsequently obtained, extending the time for the completion of the works. [48 and 49 Vict., c. 155. 1885.]

Under this Outfall Act, the Witham Outfall Board were empowered to make a new Cut for the Outfall of the river, commencing a little below Hobhole Sluice and terminating at Clayhole; to dredge and deepen the channel from the commencement of the new Cut to the Grand Sluice; and subsequently to maintain the new Cut, and the fascine walls of the old channel, which were transferred from the Harbour Trust to the New Board. Provision was made for the extension of the Welland Outfall, as already mentioned. The control of the river and of the foreshores and unenclosed lands seaward of the Grand Sluice was vested in the Board. All rights were reserved to the Corporation, and also their powers under the Harbour Acts, in relation to the channel, and of making or erecting sea walls, jetties, wharves, lights, beacons, hauling paths and moorings. The Board were authorised to make bye-laws for preventing the discharge of sewage or refuse into the river, or the damaging of the banks ; and for preventing the netting and snaring of fish. The Board was to consist of seven Members chosen by the Witham Commissioners; five, by the Black Sluice Commissioners; the Mayor of Boston, and two members chosen by the Corporation. The Board were authorised to raise £161,000, apportioned as follows, The Witham General Commissioners, £37,000 ; the Fourth District, £49,000 ; the Black Sluice, £65,000 ; and the Corporation of Boston, £10,000.

CONSTRUCTION OF THE NEW CUT. 1880-84.

The contract for making the new Cut was let to Mr. Thomas Monk, for the sum of £96,052. The works were commenced in December, 1880, and the Cut was opened for seafaring vessels in April, 1884. The length of the new Cut is $2\frac{1}{4}$ miles, and there is a saving of distance over the old course of $1\frac{1}{2}$ miles. The bottom, at the upper end, is three feet below the sill of Hobhole Sluice, or 11.20 feet below *Ordnance datum*, and inclines at the rate of one foot per mile. The bottom was set out 100ft. wide at Hobhole, increasing to 130ft. at the lower end; the slopes are $4\frac{1}{2}$ to 1, a foreshore being left, making the total width, at high water in the centre of the Cut, 400ft. The depth of water at high water of ordinary Spring tides is $27\frac{1}{2}$ft., and at Neap tides, $20\frac{1}{2}$ft. at the lower end, decreasing one foot per mile up to Boston. The excavation amounted to two million cubic yards. The embankment closing the old channel is half-a-mile in length. It is 15ft. wide at the top, and has slopes of 5 to 1, its maximum height being 35ft. ; and its top, 8ft. above ordinary spring tides.

COST.

The total cost of the works was as follows—

Works A.

	£	s.	d.
Work in forming the New Cut and closing the old course of the river and deepening and training the river to Hobhole	107,668	4	4
Land and Compensation	19,358	11	0
Parliamentary, Engineering, Legal and other expenses	12,237	0	1
	£139,263	15	5

Works B.

	£	s.	d.
Dredging, deepening and training the river from Hobhole to the Black Sluice, (Portion by Outfall Board) ...	4,887	13	0
Engineering and Legal charges	216	10	8
	£5,104	3	8

Works C.

	£	s.	d.
Dredging, deepening and training the river from the Black Sluice to the Grand Sluice	9,775	15	4
Engineering, Legal and other charges	902	11	5
Land and Compensation	1,931	15	0

making a total of £155,978 0s. 10d.   £12,610 1 9

Following the opening of the Cut, the river was deepened by dredging from Hobhole to Boston, the work being done partially by the Outfall Board and completed by the Harbour Commissioners, so as to give a depth of 25ft. up to the Dock at ordinary Spring Tides.

EFFECT OF THE NEW CUT.

The available depth in the navigable channel has been increased 8ft. and the depression acquired at low water at the Sea Sluices, is as follows:—

	ft.	ins.
Hobhole Sluice	5	6
Maud Foster Sluice	4	3
Black Sluice	4	0
Grand Sluice	4	0

The water on the Black Sluice has run down within 9ins. of the sill at low water and at the Grand Sluice it has run out 3ft. below the Level of the old sill.

Although since the work was completed there have been some exceptionally dry seasons and consequently the water passing down the river has been below its normal quantity, there has been scarcely any accumulation of sand and silt in the channel, which, under similar conditions had, before the improvement of the Outfall, amounted to as much as 11½ft. above the bed of the channel at its upper end.

MAINTENANCE OF WORKS.

The accounts for works of construction were closed in 1886. Since that time up to March, 1894, there has been expended out of revenue in maintenance for the lower division (*Works A*) £8,083 13s. 3d. in works, and £3,361 15s. 8d. on management, &c., making an average annual cost for the 8½ years since completion, of £951 for works and £407 on management; on the division between Hobhole and the Black Sluice (*Works B*) the amount spent during the 8½ years has been £1,073 10s. 2d. on works and £851 12s. 0d. on management; and on the division between the Black Sluice and Grand Sluice (*Works C*) £956 10s. 6d. on works, and £71 6s. 1d. on management. Since 1889 nothing has been expended in maintaining the middle section of the river (*Works B*).

BOSTON DOCK

Very shortly after the Outfall Act was obtained and the prospect of a good navigable channel rendered the construction of a dock at Boston feasible, a Memorial was presented to the Corporation, signed by all the principal bankers, merchants and tradesmen in the town, asking them to take the necessary steps for securing to the

Port floating accommodation for ships. After a careful consideration of the matter instructions were given to their Engineer, Mr. W. H. Wheeler, to report as to the best site for the construction of a dock, and as to the cost.

<small>Wheeler's Report. Nov., 1880.</small>

Two schemes were submitted for consideration—the one, by making a new Cut from South End to Maud Foster Sluice, and converting the loop of the river between South End and the Black Sluice into a dock; and the other, for making the dock on the site known as the Dock Pasture, which had been suggested by Mr. Rennie for the purpose, 80 years previously. The only advantage in favour of the first plan was that which it would afford to the Outfall of the drainage of the Witham, but as the Commissioners, on being approached, declined to contribute towards the cost, and the Black Sluice Commissioners expressed their intention of strongly opposing the scheme, if proceeded with, it was given up.

At a meeting of the Corporation, held on the 10th of November, 1880, it was unanimously decided to apply to Parliament for powers to construct a dock on the present site, with an entrance near Maud Foster Sluice. The Bill was opposed in Committee by the Promoters of a scheme for making, what was termed, an "Ocean Dock." This Ocean Dock was to be constructed with an entrance into the lower end of the New Cut near Clayhole. The two Bills were taken together, and after hearing evidence on both sides, the Ocean Dock Scheme was thrown out. The Act for the Boston Dock received the Royal Assent on the 18th July, 1881.

<small>BOSTON DOCK ACT. 44 and 45 Vict. c. 112, 1881.</small>

By this Act, the Corporation of Boston were empowered to construct a dock, and to connect the same with the Great Northern Railway in Skirbeck Quarter, and, for this purpose, to borrow an amount not exceeding £180,000. The amount raised was to be repaid within a period of 70 years from the passing of the Act. If the revenue from the Harbour and Dock in any year is not sufficient to meet the interest and sinking fund, the deficiency has to be made good by a Borough Rate, levied on that portion of the Borough, which, at the time of the passing of the Act, paid the Urban Sanitary Rates.

The works for the construction of the Dock were commenced in 1882, the first sod being cut on the 15th of June. The contract was taken by Mr. W. Rigby, for £80,200, and that for the Hydraulic Machinery by Messrs. Abbot and Co., for £10,215. The plans for the work were prepared by Mr. W. H. Wheeler, the Engineer to the Harbour Trust, and were carried out under his direction, Mr. James Abernethy being the consulting Engineer. The first ship entered the dock on December 15th, 1884. The Dock is 6¾ acres in extent, and 825ft. in length. The lock is 300ft. long and 50ft. wide and has 25ft. of water on the sill at Spring tides. The railway crosses the river Witham by a swing-bridge, 126ft. in length, which turns on a cylinder in the centre of the river and has two openings of 55ft. each, giving a clear waterway of 110ft. The dock was fitted with hydraulic coal hoist and cranes. In addition to sheds on the quay, two grain warehouses, capable of holding 45,000 quarters of grain, were subsequently built and provided with machinery for conveying the grain from the dock side, through tunnels placed under the quay, and elevating it to any of the floors. A fish pontoon and ice warehouses were also constructed.

The cost of the dock has been has follows :—

COST OF THE DOCK.

	£	s.	d.
Cost of obtaining the Act, Legal, Parliamentary and Engineering expenses	12,096	0	4
Land, including Legal and other expenses	11,571	5	0
Contract for the Dock	88,909	0	0
Contract for the Machinery	10,215	17	7
Fish Quay, Ice Warehouse, Sheds, Roads and Railway	11,990	2	4
Witham Outfall Board, dredging the river	1,335	0	0
Two Grain Warehouses and Machinery	21,892	12	9
Sheds and Extension of Fish Quay, Cranes and Sundries	2,159	2	9
	£160,169	0	9

Soon after the opening of the dock, a Company was formed for the purpose of developing the Fishing Trade. Shops and offices were erected at the Dock by the Company and a fish-quay and ice warehouse by the Corporation. A second Company was formed in 1890, who erected a factory for the supply of the ice required. More than thirty steam trawlers are employed, besides several belonging to private firms.

FISHING COMPANY.

A regular line of steamers runs between Boston and Hamburg.

TRADE.

The trade at the Dock has steadily developed, the chief imports being timber, pit-props for mining purposes, grain, linseed, iron ore, and granite for road repairs; the exports being coal and machinery.

In 1800 the tonnage of shipping at the Port of Boston, on which dues were paid was 52,698 tons; in 1810 it had risen to 86,256 tons, and in that year lastage was paid on 356,040 quarters of grain. From then till 1850 the annual tonnage varied from 73,000 to 56,000 tons. After that it gradually declined to about 40,000 tons, the export of grain amounting to 120,000 quarters. In 1881 the number of vessels which entered the Port, as given in the return of the Board of Trade, was 396, having a registered tonnage of 27,137 tons. For 1894 the returns were 605 vessels, having a tonnage of 124,696 tons. These returns do not include the fishing trawlers or smacks. The Exports and Imports at the dock were :—

	TONS.
1892	219,107
1893	220,882
1894	273,190

TONNAGE OF VESSELS.

Vessels of considerable tonnage can now navigate the river. The largest which has entered the dock was 325ft. long, 40½ft. beam. The largest vessel which has entered with a full cargo on board, was 276ft. long, 36¾ beam, 20ft. draught, having 13,120 quarters of barley, weighing 2,624 tons.

The bed of the river, as finished by the Outfall Board, being from two to three feet above the sill of the Dock, the Corporation expended about £1,300 in removing the higher places, and reduced the bed to within one foot of the sill. It was also contemplated to remove the projecting corner on the west side, but objections being raised to the proposed plan by the Outfall Board, the work was not proceeded with. Subsequently the Corporation further deepened the channel by dredging for over a width of 80ft. to a level of 2ft. below the Dock sill, giving a depth of 27ft. up to the Dock, at high water of spring tides.

RECLAMATION OF MARSH LAND.

Reference has already been made to the lands that were gained by the improvements which were made in the river, in the years 1833 and 1841. The largest tract, containing about three hundred acres, was sold by the Harbour Trustees to the late Mr. Black, in the year 1863, for the sum of £10,000, which enabled them to pay off the money then remaining due on mortgage, which had been borrowed to effect the improvements in the river. In 1864, two other marshes were reclaimed, containing together about 160 acres. These marshes were enclosed from the tidal water, under the direction of the Author, the contract being carried out by Mr. George Hackford, by two embankments, a mile and a half in length, the water from the parish of Wyberton and the adjoining land being discharged through a sluice, built for that purpose, in the Slippery Gowt Embankment. A house and farmstead have also been erected on each of the enclosures.

BUOYS, BEACONS AND LIGHTS.

The Corporation, in their capacity as Harbour Commissioners, maintain the buoys and beacons, from the Outer Knock and Dog's Head, at the entrance of Boston Deeps from the North Sea, off Skegness, and from the Outer Gat and Roger Buoys, at the entrance to Lynn Well, up to Boston. In all, there are 66 buoys, and the Toft, Gat and Freeman's Beacons, and the Tidal Guage Beacon on Freiston Main. A Pilot vessel is also moored off Freiston Main, on which a light is exhibited at night. Two light towers were erected on Benington Main in 1892. These towers show two white lights, leading directly through Freeman's Channel, the towers themselves forming conspicuous objects, the back tower being 50ft. high. A light-ship is also moored about the middle of the Channel. A light tower and two leading lights are placed at the entrance of the New Cut, and there are 23 other lights between that point and the town.

The Pilot Trust remains the same as originally constituted, the limits of the Boston Pilots' jurisdiction being High Horn Buoy and the Toft Beacon. Below this, the North Sea Pilots take charge of ships.

The principal anchorage is East Countryman's Berth at the lower end of Clayhole, where there is good holding ground in a safe roadstead, with 4½ fathoms at low water of spring tides.

The average income and expenditure of the Harbour Commissioners, for the three years 1882-4, previous to the opening of the dock, and for the three years 1893-5, has been as follows:—

HARBOUR INCOME AND EXPENDITURE.

Receipts.	1882-4 £	1893-5 £
Tonnage and Wharfage dues	962	2,093
Rents of Land and Buildings	242	255
Sundries	—	26
Welland Contribution	157	217
Pilot Trust ,,	50	414
	£1411	£3005

Expenditure.	£	£
Buoys and Beacons, Lights and Light Vessels	435	1,066
River, repair of banks, dredging &c.	62	434
Warehouses, Quays, and Buildings	186	239
Witham Outfall Precepts	44	141
Salaries	221	253
Interest	—	458
Sundries	484	126
	£1432	£2717

The expenses during the years 1882-4, were greater than usual at that time, owing to some heavy repairs which had to be done to the banks enclosing the farms. In addition to the ordinary expenditure during the years 1893-5, as given above, there was paid out of revenue £316 for the new light towers at Benington, and £463, the balance of cost in removing the wreck Ethel.

THE DOCK.—YEAR 1895.

Income.	£	s.	d.
Rates and dues on shipping	6003	16	0
Warehouse and other rents	1495	16	9
Sundry profits	1216	10	4
	£8716	3	1

Expenditure.	£	s.	d.
Wages, repairs &c.	2186	6	1
Rates, Taxes and Insurance	605	17	8
Establishment charges	159	5	9
Salaries	370	0	0
Dredging	565	14	0
Sundries	205	9	1
	4092	12	7

Interest on Capital and repayment of loan ...   6224 11 2

£10317 3 9

The excess of expenditure over income is provided from the Borough rates.

Boston Admiralty Seal.

CHAPTER XIII.

The Drainage System.

THE whole of the Fenland lies below the level of high tides, and therefore depends upon the banks which have been erected for its protection. The main drains, which discharge the surplus rainfall into the tidal rivers, are protected from the tides by sluices with self-acting doors, which automatically close when the tidal water reaches higher than that coming down them, and which open again directly the tidal water falls below that which has accumulated during tide time.

DESCRIPTION OF THE OUTFALL.

The River Witham has practically been converted into a main drain, and is not tidal above Boston. It is protected by the Grand Sluice, which has four openings, including the navigation lock, having each a pair of self-acting doors which open during floods, the total waterway being 71ft. The Black Sluice District discharges into Boston Haven, and is protected by a sluice having three openings of 20ft., each having a pair of doors, giving a total waterway of 60ft. The high land water brought from the catchwater drains of the East and West Fens, is discharged at Maud Foster Sluice, which has three sets of doors, having a total waterway of 40ft. The East and West Fens discharge at Hobhole, which has four openings, each with one pair of doors, having a waterway of 60ft. The Steeping River discharges into Wainfleet Haven, the Outfall Sluices having a waterway of 30ft. The tidal conditions of the River Welland have not been interfered with, and the tide has a free course up this river. The Vernatt's Drain, which takes the water from Deeping Fen, and the River Glen, into which the Blue Gowt Drain discharges, are both protected by sluices, the former having a waterway of 33ft., and the latter, two openings of 15ft. each. The South Holland Drain discharges into the tidal River Nene by a sluice having three openings, with a total waterway of 31ft. There are, in addition to these principal drains, several smaller drains and sewers, which discharge either into the tidal rivers, or into creeks on the coast, which, in like manner, are protected by sluices with self-acting doors.

OUTFALL SLUICES

These sluices are also provided with draw doors, or slackers, which are either kept down, or partially or wholly raised or lowered according to the quantity of water coming down the drains. The water in the drains is thus regulated, and not allowed to run down below a certain level, in order to provide for the navigation, or to maintain the water in the ditches at a sufficient depth for fencing purposes, or to keep the sock at the level desired for feeding the crops or for water supply.

WATER LEVEL IN THE DRAINS.

In summer, the loss by evaporation and absorption in the fen drains, is made up by 'live water,' or that obtained from the highland rivers and drains, which is let into the fens from sluices provided for the purpose.

The main drains in the peat districts are so regulated, that the water in the division and field drains shall always stand at a level of about 2 to 2½ft. below the surface.

GRAVITATION AND STEAM POWER.

There are two methods of drainage in operation, one by gravitation, where the land is sufficiently above low water in the sea, and the other, for the lower lands, from which the water is raised by steam power from the district drains, into the rivers or arterial drains, the former being protected by sluices at their Outfalls.

In no case in the fen districts, where a system of drainage has been carried out for the reclamation of the low land, has the attempt to obtain what is called a 'natural drainage'—that is, drainage by gravitation—been completely successful. Where this has been attempted, the higher land has been well drained, but the lower fens, which often lie at the greatest distance from the Outfall, are constantly subject to flooding, the Outfall from these drains being over-ridden by the water from the higher land. Main drains also, which, at the time when they were made, afforded a sufficient Outfall, afterwards became insufficient, owing to the depression of the surface of the land, due to the shrinkage of the peat. To meet this, the drains have been increased in size, and their Outfalls deepened. But for the peat land, in no case has this been sufficient, and it has been found necessary to lift the water out of the drains by mechanical agency. Such, for example, has been the case in the East Fen, which formerly drained by gravitation, but is now only kept free from flooding, in wet seasons, by the pumps at Lade Bank. In the Black Sluice District the main drain, 21 miles in length, was enlarged and deepened, and a complete system of internal drainage carried out, with the expectation that the fen land would, by this means, be effectually drained. One district after another has, however, resorted to pumping as the only means of giving complete relief in times of flood. On the River Witham, over 36,000 acres still have to resort to steam drainage, although a very large amount has been spent in widening and deepening the river and improving the outfall. The whole of Deeping Fen, and a large tract of land to the east of Spalding, covering an area of 37,600 acres, depends entirely on steam power for its drainage.

In fact, it may be said that approximately, while the alluvial part of the Fenland can be drained by gravitation, the fen portion requires to have the water lifted from it by by mechanical agency. The total area drained by steam power is given by Mr. Gibbs, as 124,600 acres, divided as follows :—

LAND DRAINED BY STEAM POWER.

Gibbs' Pumping Machinery in the Fenland. Min. Pro. I.C.E. Vol. 94.

	Scoop Wheels.	Centrifugal Pumps.
The Witham above the Grand Sluice	33100	4700
The East Fen	—	35000
The Black Sluice	6150	3700
The Welland and Deeping Fen	38950	—

In addition to this there are between 3,000 to 4,000 acres which, to some extent, are drained by wind mills.

By the improvement of the main drains and the outfalls, the lift of the water, and consequently the cost of pumping, may be considerably reduced, but, with land lying at a low level, from which an adequate fall cannot at all times be obtained, the interest on the first outlay for machinery, and subsequent expense in connection with the pumping, will, as a rule, be found less than the interest on the money expended in attempting to drain these lands by simple gravitation.

RELATIVE ADVANTAGE OF PUMPING AND GRAVITATION.

The question of raising water off fen land, as compared with drainage by gravitation, was very carefully considered by the Author, when reporting on a gravitation scheme proposed for the South Level of the Bedford Level, and the facts and figures obtained in that enquiry satisfied him that, under certain conditions, pumping may be an economical means of draining low land.

Report on the River Ouse. W. H. Wheeler, 1884.

The great improvements which have been made in the steam engines and water raising machines, together with the greater facilities for obtaining, and the lower price of, coal, have considerably reduced the cost of lifting water compared to what it was when many of the improvements for the drainage of the Fens were originally carried out.

The choice as between gravitation and steam power resolves itself into a question of cost. If the annual charge for interest and outlay for a gravitation scheme, with a proportionate sum for repayment of the principal, exceeds the average annual cost of a pumping installation, including the interest and outlay, then the steam power is decidedly preferable, not only as being more economical, but as rendering the district more thoroughly independent of outside circumstances. The annual cost of a gravitation scheme is constant, be the seasons wet or dry; whereas a pumping station adapts itself more readily to the varying work to be done.

An effective Outfall is, however, in any case a necessity. Where pumping is used, if the water in the main drain is held up above a certain height, there is increased pressure on the protecting banks and danger of their breaking, and where the bank are porous as is frequently the case, an increased quantity of water has to be raised, due to the soakage through the banks.

RAINFALL.

In providing for a system of drainage, whether by gravitation or steam power, the quantity of water which has to be discharged is one of the first questions for consideration. The average annual rainfall cannot be taken as a guide. The drainage system, to be effective, must be equal to carrying off the floods of wet years.

Appendix V.

The annual rainfall of the recent wet years in the Fenland may be taken as 32·39ins., of which 17·52ins. were due to the six winter months September to February, which gives an average daily amount of ·097ins. Taking the periods of excessive rain which occurred during the same time, extending over 6 to 30 successive days, the gratest average fall per day was 0·41ins. for 14 days in October, 1883 and November, 1885, the next highest being 0·29ins. for 6 days in February, 1883. The average mean rainfall during the 21 floods since 1852 was 0·26 for 17 days.

QUANTITY OF WATER TO BE DISCHARGED FROM THE LAND.

The quantity provided for by the old fen Engineers was that due to the water arising from a continuous rainfall of a quarter of an inch in 24 hours, making no deductions for soakage or evaporation. This calculation was adopted by Sir John Hawkshaw, when designing the pumping installation for the East Fen. From the statistics of rainfall given in the Appendix for wet seasons, it would appear that this may be taken as a reliable quantity.

Appendix V.

GRAVITATION.

The system adopted by the Roman Engineers for the drainage of the Fens was that of first cutting a drain skirting the high land, for the purpose of intercepting all the streams and brooks and discharging their water into the rivers, thus freeing the fen from all water, except the rainfall which fell on it. To clear this off, main drains were cut, discharging into the rivers and protected by sluices. Many of these drains, although enlarged and improved, remain in use at the present time.

CATCH WATER DRAINS.

This system of cutting off the highland water from the Fens, by catchwater water drains and discharging their contents at Outfalls, separate from those of the fen drains, was also recommended by Vermuiden, the Dutch Engineer, who was largely engaged in reclaiming lands in the Isle of Axholme, and in the Bedford Level, in the 17th century.

Discourse on Drainage. 1642.

In a 'Discourse touching the Draining of the Great Fens,' published in 1642, Vermuiden says, "There is in use a general rule of draining and gaining of drowned lands, by embanking all the rivers, and leading away the downfall by drains and sluices, but in the case of the Great Fens, such a course would not apply, for it would require a vast length of bank, in level and moorish ground, and far distant from the falls. The head drains would require in many cases to be carried through higher ground than the drowned lands." He therefore advised that the rivers should be carried on the highest grounds;

that the drains should be laid in the lowest grounds; that there should be receptacles for the waters to bed in, in times of extremity; and that the river water and the downfall be kept separate and brought to the Outfall severally.

Vermuiden's 'Discourse' and his schemes for the drainage of the Great Fens, were attacked by Andrews Burrell, Gent., in his "Exceptions against Sir Cornelius Vermuiden's discourse, for the draining of the Great Fennes, which he had presented to the King for his design, wherein His Majesty was misinformed and abused in regard that it wanteth all the essential parts of a designe; and the great and advantageous workes made by the late Earl of Bedford, slighted, and the whole adventure disparaged." In this pamphlet he states that the discourse is contrived "in a mystical way, with many impertinent objections and answers in it, of purpose to dazzle the King's apprehension of the worke." He calls in question the works which Vermuiden had already carried out and says that he had been told by Sir Philoberto Vernatti, who was deeply interested in the level, that the banks he had made in Yorkshire had cost £9 an acre; that he "had found the art of Sluice making so hard to attaine that he cannot learne it, myself having seen four sluices made by him, near the banks of Sutton Marsh which had cost £11,000. Every one of them sunk and lost; the last which was made for the King having cost £3,000." In another part of the pamphlet he goes on to say that "when Sir Cornelius Vermuiden found that the King was sufficiently encouraged to undertake the work, it was so plotted that Secretary Windebancks and others did persuade His Majesty, that there was not a man in His dominions, that knew how to drain the Fens, but Sir Cornelius only, in which passage the King was extremely abused. For being desirous to effect the work, by this plot His Majesty was inforced to approve of his senseless discourse (instead of a designe) and to intreat him to accept of a salary exceeding his deserts (namely, £1,000 a year). For in disposing of £23,500 he hath mis-spent at the least £1,600 of the money, and willfully wasted many hundreds of acres of land, skimming the top thereof, to make counterfeit banks, without giving the owners thereof any satisfaction for them."

Burrell's Exception to the Discourse. 1642.

The principle of catchwater drains was adopted by Mr. Rennie in the drainage of the East and West Fens. He also bore valuable testimony, and in this he was supported by other Engineers, to the skill and wisdom of the old Roman Engineers, by advising that the Catchwater Drain made by them, where it skirts the Black Sluice Level, should be opened out again, and the water from the several becks and streams which now pour their water into the Black Sluice drain should be kept away by this means from the fen drains; but his opinion was over-ruled, and the highland water now finds its way to the sea, along the same course as the fen water, and frequently over rides it.

NEGLECT OF THE OUTFALLS.

In laying out their different systems of drainage, the early Adventurers confined their schemes to their own particular districts and neglected the rivers and the main Outfalls. The consequence was that their main drains, having only an imperfect communication between the Outfall Sluices and low water in the Estuary, afforded a very partial relief to the lower lands. Had the lower part of the rivers been improved in the manner that has recently been effected in the Witham, and as has to a limited extent been done in the Welland, the drainage could have been executed at considerably less cost than has been expended on it, and would have been far more efficient.

The reason of the neglect of the Outfall was, no doubt, due to the fact that this would have required a combination of all the interested Adventurers and public bodies concerned in the drainage. The difficulty of accomplishing such an undertaking is illustrated by the fact that the Witham Outfall Improvement was only accomplished after repeated attempts to carry it out, and nearly 100 years after it was first proposed, during which time each Trust went on wasting money in attempts to improve its own separate district, in its own way.

The Washes.

Considerable controversy existed amongst the old Adventurers as to Vermuiden's proposal to leave 'washes,' or receptacles at the sides of the river channels for the flood water to bed in. This plan, however, was adopted both on the Nene, the Welland, and the Witham. On the Witham the wash land was afterwards enclosed, but on the Welland the washes still cover an area of 2,500 acres.

In order to obtain further advice as to the disputed question of the advantage of these washes, the Earl of Bedford, the Undertaker of the Great Bedford Level, called in another Dutch Engineer, Westerdyke, who condemned this plan, and contended that if the banks of the river were set out at a convenient distance, one from the other, and one fair cut made for the water to pass in, much money might be saved and the work be far better. He contended that experience showed that waters kept in a body pass swiftly and mend their channel, but, divided and dispersed, pass away very slowly and in time lose their channel. Dodson and Scotton, who were both employed under Vermuiden, agreed with Westerdyke, their opinions also being that 'washes encourage violent waves which *whinder* the banks to pieces.' Washes can only afford a very temporary alleviation of flooding. In times of flood, a few hours' rainfall suffices to fill the receptacle, and, once filled, it is of no further value. It is true that the washes grow valuable crops of grass in summer, but they are constantly liable to be flooded and the crops spoiled.

PUMPING.

Owing both to the defective condition of the Outfall, and also to the low level at which some of the Fenland lies, the practice of raising the water by mechanical agency was from a very early period resorted to. At first this was accomplished by windmills, working scoop wheels, which lifted the water from the fen drains into the rivers. The origin of the introduction of windmills, as applied to drainage, is said to have arisen from the necessity that the Engineers of the Bedford Level Commission found, from to time, of employing some mechanical means for emptying the drains when requiring to be cleaned out. For this purpose, in the first instance, large scoops, so constructed as to be handled by a number of men, were used; but in 1687, the Corporation of the Bedford Level provided mills, consisting of a wheel with floats, very similar to the old breast wheel, to which motion was given by horses. In the year 1699, a person of the name of Green erected one of these mills, at Slade, to drain his land; and in 1703 another was erected by Silas Tytus. Both these were considered nuisances and ordered to be pulled down. The Owners resorted for relief to a Court of Equity, but the termination of the suit was favourable to the Corporation. In 1693, a drainage mill was erected at Tydd St. Giles, at a cost of £450.

Although, from this, it would appear that these mills were opposed to popular opinion, they made such advancement that they soon took their place as absolute necessities in the economy of drainage. The Level had become so inundated by the choking up of the interior drains, the defective state of the rivers themselves, and the neglect to improve the Outfalls to the sea, that the Corporation found it impossible to resist the importunity of the country to resort to an artificial system of interior drainage. In the year 1726, an Act was obtained for the effectual drainage of Haddenham Fen, by the use of mills, and after this their use became general.

Wells' Bedford Level.

In 1729, Capt. Perry erected a number of windmills for working scoop-wheels for lifting the water out of Deeping Fen. Arthur Young gives the following description of a windmill, which he found in use on the estate of Mr. Chaplin, at Blankney, in his Survey of Lincolnshire, made in 1799. "The sails go 70 rounds, and it raises 60 tons of water every minute, when in full work. The bucket-wheels, which in the mills of Cambridgeshire are perpendicular, without the mill; this, which is called *dritch*, has in a sloping direction in an angle of about 40 degrees, and within the mill. It raises 4ft. Two men are necessary in winter, working night and day, at 10/6 a week, with coals for a fire; add the expense of repairs, grease, and all together will amount to £2 per cent. with £1,000, first cost. It drains 1900 acres."

Windmills were first superseded by steam in this country in 1820, when Mr. Rennie applied one of Watts' engines to the working of a scoop wheel for draining Bottisham Fen, near Ely. In 1824, steam was applied to the drainage of Deeping Fen, and afterwards became general. There are still a few windmills to be found in the Lincolnshire Fens.

SCOOP WHEELS.
The Scoop or Float Wheel has been in use for lifting water, from very ancient times. There is no doubt that the Romans made use of it for lifting water, but there is no record that it was so used in the drainage of the Fens. It was introduced into Holland for drainage purposes by W. Wheler, in 1649. The Scoop Wheel as now used, resembles a breast water wheel with reverse action. In its simplest form it consists of an axle, upon which are fastened discs, to which are attached radial arms, terminating in a rim, upon which are fastened arms with boards, called scoops, floats or paddles. The wheel revolves in a trough, connected with the drain on one side and the river or place of discharge on the other. The scoops beat, or lift the water from the lower to the upper side, the waterway on the river or outlet side being provided with a self-acting door which closes when the wheel stops. These wheels vary in size, up to 50ft. in diameter. The largest in this district are those at Podehole, for the drainage of Deeping Fen, which are 31ft. in diameter.

Scoop wheels have done exceedingly good service in the drainage of the Fens, when well constructed; and for situations where the height to which the water has to be raised is not great, and where there is not much variation in the lift, they are effective and useful machines. The slow speed at which they travel fitted them for being driven by windmills, or the slow speed beam engines by which they were succeeded. They are simple in construction and easily repaired by the aid of such mechanical skill as is readily obtainable in the fen districts. They are not liable to get out of order when laid by, or easily damaged by floating substances, brought to them in the water. To the minds of those living by the side of the rivers and drains of low flat countries and accustomed to the slow practices of an agricultural life, there is a sense of power and solidity about a massive beam engine, with its slowly revolving fly wheel and heavy beam, rising and falling, driving a ponderous water-wheel, lifting a large mass of water; in place of which the small parts of a centrifugal pump, with its rapid movements, seem but a poor substitute. Scoop wheels are, however, exceedingly cumbrous, the wheel weighing as much as, or more than, the total body of the water lifted at each revolution. The larger wheels, of say 30ft. in diameter, weigh from 30 to 40 tons, and therefore require very heavy foundations and expensive masonry for the wheel race. The slow speed engines used for driving these wheels are themselves as ponderous as the wheels, and also require heavy foundations and a large area of buildings. They were very extravagant with fuel, the steam generated being used at a pressure of from 4lbs. to 5lbs.

As generally constructed, scoop wheels are very wasteful of power, and badly adapted to meet the alterations in the level of the water due to the falling of the level on the inside, as the water is pumped out of the drains; or on the outside, due to the rise and fall of the tide; or of flood waters in non-tidal rivers. The machinery, however, is in many cases capable of improvement, and may be altered so as to lift a much larger volume of water and to use very much less coal. The details of these improvements are fully described and illustrated in the Author's book on 'The Drainage of Fens and Lowlands.' *

Archimedean screw pumps, which are frequently met with in the drainage of the Polders in Holland, were tried in Deeping Fen and abandoned, and have never been used for the permanent drainage of land in the Fens.

Wherever it has become necessary to replace the old, or to erect new, machinery for pumping, the centrifugal pump has superseded the scoop wheel. When these pumps are constructed with direct acting high pressure engines, they are very efficient and, being compact, occupy only a small space, saving cost both in foundations and buildings. The weight of the machinery is about one-twentieth of that of a scoop wheel.

The average difference of cost of the pumping stations erected in Holland during recent years is £20 per actual horse power in favour of the pumps.

The centrifugal pump readily adapts itself to the varying lift which must be encountered in most drainage stations and automatically adjusts the work thrown on the engine as the lift varies. Where proper precautions are taken no practical difficulty has arisen from weeds and other substances which find their way into the pump well.

Pumps were first introduced for the drainage of the Fens, after the Exhibition of 1851, where one was exhibited at work; and there are several instances where they have been running for upwards of 30 years without trouble, and doing their work efficiently and economically.

There are two kinds of centrifugal pumps used for draining land, the one known as the turbine pump, having a vertical shaft, and placed below the water, at the bottom of a well, made either of brick or iron. The pumps at Lade Bank are of this type. The other kind have horizontal shafts, and the pumps are generally placed above the surface of the water in the engine house, the suction pipe going down to the engine drain on the inner side, and the discharge pipe over the top of the bank into the river. When the pump is once charged, the pipes act as a syphon, the lift being then only equal to the difference of level of the inner and outer water. This arrangement saves all necessity for sluices and leaves the pump accessible at all times. A valve on the bottom of the discharge pipe prevents any back flow of the water when pumping ceases.

* *The Drainage of Fens and Lowlands*, by W. H. Wheeler, M. Instit. C.E., 1888. E. & F. N. Spon, London.

This form of pump has been generally adopted in Holland, and, when driven by direct action from the engine, occupies very little space and a small amount of foundation.

The smaller pumps in the Fenland are driven by portable engines, by belting.

MANAGEMENT OF DRAINAGE ENGINES.—Although the saving of coal, as between one type of engine and another, may not be of such consequence as in engines used for commercial purposes, yet the total consumption is a matter which ought to engage the most serious attention on the part of the Managers, as on this, principally, will depend the annual cost of the pumping station, and the amount of taxes required to meet the expenses. The fuel should bear a direct proportion to the amount of water lifted. If more than is necessary is used, it is due to the fault of either the engine-man, the engine, or the pump. The excess has to be paid for. As regards the first, the engine-man, too great caution cannot be exercised in selecting a steady, careful and economical man. The best men can only be secured by paying good and sufficient wages. A good engine-man may save his wages many times over by careful stoking, an incompetent man may not only run up the coal bill, but do irreparable damage to the machinery by ignorant management.

The men who have charge of some of the smaller pumping stations in the Fens, are only labourers, who are employed during the summer in cleaning out the drains, and in winter in driving the engine. These men have had no training as engine-men, and no mechanical knowledge to assist them in the management of machinery. As a rule, however, they are very intelligent, and, considering their antecedents, it is surprising how well they manage to keep the machinery running, often by night and day, for long periods.

COAL CONSUMPTION.

The difference of the consumption of coal, due to good and bad stoking, is strikingly shown by the trials of engine-men at the Agricultural shows. It may be assumed that the men who enter for these competitions consider themselves as superior to the ordinary men, or they would not enter for them. Selecting two of these competitions as samples, with an interval of ten years between, it will be seen that there was a marked improvement on the part of the men in the work done. Some portion of the quantity may be due to the difference in the engines, but this would not amount to much; and it is fair to presume that the Managers would take care that the engine provided for the trials should be a competent machine.

At the trials at the Lincolnshire Agricultural Show at Spalding, in 1872, with an 8 h.p. portable engine, fifteen competitors entered the list. The best used coal at the rate of 7·86 lb. per horse-power per hour, the worst 20·2 lb., the average of the whole being 11½ lb., there being a difference of 61 per cent. between the best and the worst.

At Gainsborough, in 1883, there were nineteen competitors. The best man ran the engine with a consumption of coal at the rate of 6·77 lb. per horse-power per hour. The worst used 8·95 lb. The average of the whole was 7·69. There was thus a difference of 2·18 lb. of coal per hour in the driving of this engine by picked men.

Taking the ordinary type of drivers of agricultural engines, it may safely be taken that there would be a difference of at least 10lb. of coal per horse-power per hour between good and bad stoking. With an engine running at 10 horse-power, this would amount to over a ton in twenty-four hours. Beyond this, would be further waste in oil, and damage to machinery by want of skill, or carelessness.

With regard to the quantity of coal consumed, the Dutch Engineers in their contracts generally stipulate that this shall not exceed 6.60lb. of coal per horse-power per hour of water actually raised. Allowing an efficiency of 55 for the machinery, this is equal to 3.63lbs. per I.H.P. Some of the best pumping engines for land drainage purposes in this country consume from 4lb. to 4½lb. of coal per indicated horse-power per hour, which is above the Dutch standard.

The cost of raising water by steam power varies with the price of coal, the efficiency of the machinery, the height the water has to be lifted, and the skill and care of the engine-man. From returns obtained by the Author from 11 pumping stations in the Bedford Level, draining 120,000 acres, he ascertained that the average cost for the 3 years, 1881-3, which were very wet, and during which several floods occured, was 16.25 pence, or 1.86 pence per acre per foot of lift, of which 1.47 pence was for coal. With the best managed engines the cost fell as low as a penny per acre per foot of lift. The lifts varied from 6ft. to 14ft., the cost of coal being about 16/- per ton, delivered. During the same period the cost of working the Deeping Fen engines and scoop wheels, at Podehole, was 10.58 pence per acre, of which 7.56 pence was for coal. Taking the average lift at 5ft., this gives 1.51 pence per acre per foot of lift. The average working expenses of the engines and pumps at Lade Bank, for draining the East Fen, during the same period, were 7.46 pence per acre. Taking the average lift at 4ft., this is equal to 1.86 pence per acre per foot of lift.

The following description of the scoop wheels at Pode Hole, and of the centrifugal pump at Lade Bank, is taken from the Author's book on Drainage already referred to, where will be found illustrations of this machinery.

The water from Deeping Fen is pumped into the Vernatt's Drain, which discharges into the tidal river Welland, about six and a half miles distant. The machinery was erected in 1824, and consisted of two scoop wheels, worked by two low pressure condensing beam engines, of 80 and 60 nominal horse power, respect-

COST OF PUMPING.

Report on the River Ouse. Wheeler. 1884.

Drainage of Fens by Gravitation and Steam Power. Wheeler. 1883

PODE HOLE PUMPING STATION.

ively, working at a maximum pressure of steam in the boiler of 4lb. This pressure has since been raised and other improvements made. The crank shaft from the engine passes through the wall of the engine house, and carries a pinion gearing into a spur wheel on the shaft of the scoop wheels. The ratio of the velocity of the engines to the wheels is 16 to 5, and 22 to 4½ respectively. The larger engine--called the Holland—has a steam jacketed cylinder, 44in. in diameter, with 8ft. stroke. The fly wheel is 24ft. in diameter. The smaller engine—called the Kesteven—has a steam jacketed cylinder, 45in. in diameter, and 6ft. 6in. stroke. The fly wheel is 24ft. in diameter, making 22 revolutions a minute. The framing of the scoop wheels is of cast iron. The larger wheel was originally 28ft. in diameter, and fitted with 40 scoops, but the diameter was increased, about 10 years ago, to 31ft. The scoops are 6ft. 6in. long —radially—by 5ft. wide, giving an area, when wholly immersed, of 32.5 square feet. The mean diameter is 24ft. 6in., the number of revolutions a minute, 5; giving a gross discharge, after deducting the space occupied by the scoops, of 11, 215 cubic feet per minute, or 313 tons. These wheels, as altered, are very accurately fitted in their places, and run very true, so that there is a clearance of barely half an inch between the floats and the masonry at the bottom and sides. The smaller wheel is 31ft. in diameter, with the same number of scoops, each being 5ft. 6in. long by 5ft. wide, giving an area of 27·5 square feet. The mean diameter is 25ft. 6in.; number of revolutions a minute, 4½; equal to a discharge, after deducting scoops, &c., of 8,959 cubic feet per minute, or 250 tons. The scoops dip from the radial line at an angle of 25°, being tangents to a circle 7ft. 6in. in diameter. This angle being found too small to give the best results, the end of each scoop, for a length of 18in., was altered so as to dip further back, 6in. The straight part of the scoops enters the water at average flood level at an angle of 29°, and leaves it at 36°. The average dip in floods is 5ft., and the average head 5ft., rising to 7ft. in extreme floods. Steam is supplied to the engines by five double-flued Lancashire boilers, having water pockets above the furnaces; they are 7ft. in diameter by 26ft. long. The total discharge of the two wheels is 563 tons per minute. This is equal to about the fourth of an inch of rain over the whole area of 32,000 acres, when the wheels are working to their full capacity for 24 hours a day.

The efficiency of these wheels has been greatly increased by alterations carried out a few years ago. On the inlet side a shuttle has been added, by which the amount of water coming to the wheel can be adjusted and the supply regulated to the quantity best adapted for keeping the wheel fully charged without its being drowned by it. This shuttle is of the same width as the wheel, and consists of a wooden door fixed across the inlet, close up to the wheel, and working on friction wheels in a frame placed in the masonry. The door is fixed close to the wheel, at an angle of 45 degrees to the bottom of the raceway. It is provided with a balance weight, hung by a chain, working over a pulley. The shuttle is lifted or lowered by a toothed rack, gearing into a spur wheel and pinion attached to a shaft, which is carried up into the inside of the building. The floor drops away from the bottom of the shuttle on the inlet side in a circular form, so as to give a larger space for the admission of the water, and allow it to come up and pass freely under the shuttle. The water passing under the shuttle does not catch the scoops until they come towards the bottom of the trough, and then impinges on them in the same direction in which they are travelling, and with a velocity due to the head of water at the back of the door, and thus aiding in the forward motion of the wheel. The scoops become fully charged as they assume a vertical position. The apparent increase in the lift from the lower level from which the water has to be raised is more than compensated by the avoidance of the mass of dead water which a wheel generally has to encounter on first entering the water, and by the wheel being just sufficiently fed with water, having a velocity and direction which assist in sending it round. A much greater quantity of water is thus raised with the same amount of steam than could be done if the shuttle were not there. With the surface of the water in the inlet drain, during floods, standing 6ft. 10in. above the bottom of the scoops, the shuttle is lifted sufficiently to allow 1ft. 3in. of water to pass under it, and this keeps the wheel well supplied. A moveable breast has also been fixed on the outlet side. It is made of iron plates, and works into a recess cut in the masonry of the breast, so that its face is flush with it. The plates are bent so as to have the same radius as the wheel; the upper part of the segmental plate is hinged at the top into another flat wooden platform, fixed to an iron frame, which, when down, lies in a recess in the floor of the outlet, and rises with the breast. To enable this platform to adjust itself to the space in which it has to lie, it is so formed that one end slides in and out of the iron frame. The lower end of the frame is hinged to the floor; thus, when the breast is raised the floor is also raised for some distance, forming an inclined plane from the top of the moveable breast to the floor of the outlet channel. The breast is raised or lowered, to adapt it to the height of the water in the outlet drain, by a segmental toothed rack, gearing into a spur-wheel attached to a windlass fixed on the wall of the raceway. By raising this breast to a sufficient height to allow of the free egress of the water over it, the back current at the bottom of the outlet, which always exists with the old arrrangement, is entirely avoided. These improvements to the wheel have been carried out under the direction of Mr. Alfred Harrison, the Superintendent of the Deeping Fen Drainage District.

During the five years, 1876-80, the average work of the two engines amounted to 219¼ days of twenty-four hours each for one engine, and the consumption of coal averaged 5 tons 9 cwt. per day. These engines were thoroughly overhauled by Messrs. Watt & Co., in 1883, and new boilers provided, the working pressure of the steam being raised to 20lb. on the inch. The coal consumption has been reduced to 3·28 tons per day, the amount of work done by the engines being at the same time very largely increased. It was reported that, owing to these improvements, 60 per cent. more water was raised with 42 per cent. less fuel. The annual saving was estimated at 450*l*. in wet seasons.

The average annual cost of this pumping station for the three years 1880-83, when the rainfall was considerably above the average, was 1,412*l*., of which 1,009*l*. was for coal, which cost about 15s. a ton. The average quantity consumed during the three years was 1,356 tons per year. Taking the area drained at 32,000 acres, this gives 23·61 acres for each ton of coal. The cost per acre is 10.58d., or taking coal only, 7·56d. Taking the average lift at 5ft., this gives 1·51d. per acre per foot of lift for coal only. The following is the time the engines worked during the above period :—

	80-H.P. Engine, hours.	60-H.P. Engine, hours.	Coal consumed, tons.	Rainfall, inches.
1880-81	5112	3912	2104	37·12
1881-82	2616	1680	718	26·12
1882-83	2664	3756	1317	32·87

Taking the latter period as a fair sample of a wet season, and allowing the average dip of the wheels, throughout the whole period the wheels were running, to be 2ft. 6in., and the head 4ft. 6in., the average work done, in water lifted, would be 83·63. H.P.; the average consumption of coal, 44²lb. per hour, equal to 5·28lb. of coal per hour per horse-power of water lifted and discharged.

LADE BANK PUMPS.—These pumps discharge into Hobhole Drain, about 9 miles above the Outfall sluice. The area of land which is pumped is 35,000 acres. The average lift is about 4ft., the extreme being 5ft.; and it was assumed by Sir John Hawkshaw that pumping power should be provided, equivalent to lifting a continuous rainfall of a ¼in. in 24 hours, over the whole district. The machinery consists of two pairs of high-pressure condensing vertical and direct-acting steam engines, of 240 aggregate nominal H.P., of the *A* frame type. Two massive *A* frame span over either side of the pump well, and carry the crank-shaft, on which is fitted a large mortice bevel fly-wheel. The cylinders, which are 30in. diameter by 30in. stroke, are placed outside of either *A* frame, being carried on a heavy base plate. Two small *A* frames, fixed on the cylinder covers, carry the parallel motion of a wrought iron grasshopper beam, one end of which is attached to the crosshead of the piston-rod, the other end being carried on a vibrating column,

From this beam the air-pump and feed-pump are worked. The slide valves are worked by means of eccentrics on the crank shaft, situate just inside the A frames. The bevel mortice fly-wheel gears directly into a pinion on the pump spindle, which is suspended from a bracket, spanning the engines, by means of an onion bolt bearing. By this arrangement, not only can the fan be readily withdrawn, but the bolt allows of any necessary adjustment in the level of the fan.

Steam is supplied by 6 Lancashire boilers, 23ft. by 6½ft., the furnaces being 5ft. long by 2½ft., the working pressure being 50lb. to the inch, and steam being cut off in the cylinder at quarter stroke. The base-plates of the engine are partly supported by the brickwork, and rest on and are bolted to the cast iron cylinder, which forms the lining of the pump well. There is one pump well to each pair of engines. The pumps are of the turbine type, the cases consisting of cast iron cylinders, 12ft. in diameter, 9ft. 6in. deep, open throughout their whole depth on the delivery side, and furnished with self-acting gates, 12ft. wide. In each well is a double-inlet Appold centrifugal pump. The fan is placed horizontally, and is 7ft. in diameter and 2ft. 4½in. wide, the mouth of the lower suction pipe being 3ft. 6in. above the floor of the well, and 4ft. 6in. below the surface of the water at the ordinary drainage level. The upper suction pipe curves over, the mouth being about 1ft. 6in. above the other. Each pair of engines and pumps works independently, and is capable of lifting 350 tons of water a minute, 5ft. high, being the largest amount in volume for one pump which had been raised at the time. The engines are placed in a brick building 34ft. by 46ft. and 18ft. high. The boiler house is 69ft. by 38ft. The chimney shaft is square, 90ft. high, and 4ft. 9in. inside, at the bottom. The foundations rest on a bed of Portland cement concrete. Across the main drain are two sluices, each 12ft. wide, having doors to shut against the water on the lower side, and a lock, 70ft. long by 12ft. wide, for the barges which navigate the main drain. The surface area of the main drains between the pumping station and the Outfall sluice is about 100 acres. The machinery, buildings, and lock were erected by Messrs. Eastons, Amos and Anderson, under the direction of Sir John Hawkshaw, and cost £17,000. The engines commenced working for the first time in Sept. 1867.

Taking the work done as 700 tons, lifted 4ft. 6in. high per minute, this gives £80·37 as the cost per H.P. of water lifted.

The following account of the working of these pumps, a few years after their erection, was given by Mr. E. Welsh, the Engineer to the Commissioners :—

	Years ending March 31st,	
	1871	1872
Weight of water discharged in tons	13,564,190	18,296,130
Average lift in inches	44·77	45·00

	Year ending March 31st, 1871	1872
Average revolutions made by engines per minute	36·02	38·20
Sum of hours worked by both pumps	794·25	980·5
Coal consumed during working hours in tons	328·00	397·25
Engine oil used, gallons	25·75	20·25
Tallow used, lbs.	181·00	135·00
Waste used, lbs.	135·00	85·00
Wages paid to first & second drivers yearly	£158 12 0	£158 12 0
Boy, yearly	15 12 0	18 14 0
Firemen, 2085½ hours at 3½d., and 2033 at 3½d.	30 8 0	29 13 0

Taking the above account of work done and coal consumed, the H.P. of water lifted for both engines is equal to 72·52 H.P. for 1871 and 79·17 for 1872, the coal used equal to 11·37lbs. per H.P. of water lifted for the former year, and 11·46lb. for the latter. This seems a very large consumption of coal for machinery of this class but the correctness of the result is borne out by the quantity used by the engines and pumps for the North Sea Canal in Holland, which are similar to these, and which are reported as using 11lb. per H.P. of water lifted.

In 1875 there occurred a heavy flood in this district. The total quantity of rain registered for October and November was 9·49in. To cope with this, both pumps were running continuously from November 14th to the 20th, after which one pump only was used. The two pumps were running 177 hours, and one pump for 562 hours, during which time 300 tons of coal were used.

In the flood of 1876-77 the engines were running from December 27th to January 11th; the highest lift being 5ft. 2in., the lowest 3ft. 3in., and the average during that period 4·20ft.

The cost of working the engines varies very considerably with the amount of rainfall. Thus in the two wet years of 1881-1883, when the amount of rain which fell between the 1st of September and the 31st of the following August was over 34in., in each year, the working charges of the Lade Bank Stations averaged £1,261, whereas in the three dry years, 1888-1890, when the average rainfall was only about 20in., the cost was £305. The average cost, taking wet and dry years, is about £674, which is equal to about £28 for every inch of rainfall, or, taking the quantity of land drained by the engines as 35,000 acres, about the fifth of a penny per inch of rainfall per acre.

RIGHT TO LIFT WATER INTO THE MAIN DRAINS. The right to lift the water from the interior drains into the main water ways by pumping, has been contested. When the Nocton Trustees superseded the windmills in their district, by steam power, the Witham Commissioners applied for an injunction to restrain them from doing this, on the ground that the steam engine would, by throwing an increased quantity of water into the river, damage the banks. The application was refused, Lord Brougham holding that the injury was problematical, and that it did not follow that the steam engine would be so used as to cause the injury which was apprehended.

Earl of Ripon v. Hobart.

The fen land in Bourne North Fen being very imperfectly drained, the landowners made arrangements for raising the water by steam power. This was opposed by the Black Sluice Commissioners, on the ground that the water thus sent into the main drain would have a tendency to over-ride the drains from the other Fens. After a protracted struggle the matter was settled by the Proprietors of the fen obtaining a special Act of Parliament in 1841, giving them power to use steam.

When the Bourne South Fen Commissioners erected an engine for pumping the water into the Counter Drain, the Deeping Fen Trustees applied for an injunction to stop this, but the action was not proceeded with.

CHAPTER XIV.

Agriculture.

ANCIENT AGRICULTURE.

SUCH parts of the Fenland as were inhabited by the Ancient Britons were tenanted by persons who pursued a pastoral life. The British name, *Cor Iceni* or *Coritani*, applied to this district of England was a compound of the two words, *Cor*, sheep, and *Iceni*, oxen, and designated the occupation of the inhabitants.

After the Fenland was protected from the inundation of the sea, by the embankments made during the Roman occupation, and the land secured by the Car Dyke and the Witham from the high land floods, it became practicable to grow crops of corn on the alluvial soils. The Romans had to send large quantities of food for the use of their troops and colonists in Germany and Gaul; and the corn grown on the rich soil of the Fenland, by their settlers here, was exported from Wainfleet, Boston and Spalding, for the colonists, as in more modern times corn has been exported from the settlements in the rich embanked lands of the Mississipi Valley, for use in this country.

SAXON SETTLEMENTS.

At the close of the Roman occupation the Saxons began to settle in the Fenland. Selecting a raised place, secure from winter floods, it was first surrounded by a mound or low bank, within which were built the dwellings for the chief and for his followers and servants. After a time other settlers attached themselves to this little colony, and built dwellings. Under the Saxon law, any man was at liberty to build himself a dwelling on his lord's land, and to hunt fowl and fish and provide for himself until such time as he could earn a 'bocland.' The land around this settlement afforded excellent grazing ground for sheep and cows. At night the cattle were brought up within the enclosure of the 'ton' and were made secure from thieves and other dangers; also when floods occured the stock were driven off the low land and folded on the higher pastures. This constant folding of the stock on the high ground may account, to some extent, for the richness of some of the pasture fields which are to be found scattered about the fenland.

ORIGIN OF COMMON RIGHTS.

All the pure fen and low lying land, which afforded pasture in summer, remained common land and was stocked by the settlers, who had taken up their residence on the surrounding high lands.

Hence the origin of the common rights of the numerous parishes which had to be dealt with at the time of the Enclosure.

A certain portion of the land near the homestead was tilled, and corn was grown both for use and barter. Early documents of the Anglo Saxons show that considerable quantities of wheat were raised for bread corn; and a very copious supply of cereals would be required for malting, large quanties of ale and beer being consumed by our Saxon forefathers. *CORN GROWING. Kemble's Saxons in England.*

The spread of Christianity in this country and the settlement of religious houses at Crowland in the eighth century, and subsequently at Bardney, Boston, Swineshead, Kirkstead, Kyme, and other places, led to a considerable development of agriculture in the Fens. The Monks were generally good farmers and took great pains to improve the value of the land round their monasteries. The large population of residents and visitors which had to be fed, daily, required the production of meat, corn and vegetables to supply their wants. *THE MONKS AS FARMERS.*

In the eleventh century, some of the Landowners in South Holland agreed to divide amongst them the Marshes, which were then common, so as to be able to till the land, and cut the grass for hay. The land thus broken up for tillage was found to be rich and fruitful. Abbot Egelric is stated to have so improved a portion of the marshes belonging to the monastery of Crowland, as to be able to plough and sow them with corn. "In dry years he tilled the Fens in four places, and for three or four years, had the increase of a hundred-fold of what seed so-ever he sowed," the Monastery being so enriched by these crops, that the whole country thereabout was supplied therewith. In William the Conqueror's reign, Richard de Rulos, Chamberlain to the King, 'being a man much given to good husbandry, such as tillage and breeding cattle,' took in a great part of the Common of Deeping Fen, and converted it into meadows and pasture. *EARLY ENCLOSURES. Ingulph.*

In the twelfth and thirteenth centuries, wool was the staple commodity of the country. Large quantities of sheep were kept, and a considerable amount of wool and sheep skins were exported in vessels sailing from the Wash to Flanders, in exchange for manufactured goods, which were brought back. The quantity of wool which was allowed to be exported, was limited by public enactment to 30,000 sacks for the whole kingdom, each parish being allotted a definite quantity. Thus the parish of Fishtoft was allowed to export 1st. 8¾lbs.; Butterwick, 1 sack, 6st. 2½lbs.; Benington, 2 sacks, 23st. 1lb.; Leverton, 7 sacks, 19st. 7lb., which was the largest of any parish in North Holland, except Boston. *WOOL. Thompson.*

Eight to twelve bushels of wheat per acre was reckoned a fair yield, in the reign of Edward I, and the farmer considered himself unable to pay his rent with a less yield than six bushels. Rent was then about 6d. per acre for arable land and double this for grass land, *AGRICULTURE IN THE 13TH AND 14TH CENTURIES.*

Thompson.

Some insight into the method of cultivation of those times may be gained from the account of an Inquisition taken by a Jury at Freiston, in 1343. as to certain lands belonging to William de Ros, containing about 200 acres. It was found that they were worth twelve-pence per acre; that 100 acres were sown with winter seeds; 30 acres with oats and 30 with beans and peas; 4 score acres were in fallow and unsown, every acre whereof was worth to let in pasture, because in severalty, twopence and not more, because it is often diverted by the plough; also 4 score acres of meadow, worth only twelvepence per acre, because the soil was dry and gravelly; also 30 acres of pasture, worth fourpence per acre annually, because between Michaelmas and Lady Day they were in common.

CONDITION AT THE END OF THE LAST CENTURY.

It is unnecessary further to follow the history of agriculture in olden times, as it would vary little from that generally pursued throughout the kingdom. The land free from floods, and such as could be drained by the natural drains of the country and the works carried out under the direction of the Commissioners of Sewers, was enclosed and cultivated in the same way as the rest of the country. The low lands and fens continued to be unenclosed Commons, up to the begining of the present century, when they were drained, enclosed and divided. They afforded a scanty subsistence to the Fenmen, a hardy, rough and uncultivated set of inhabitants, who gained their living by fishing, fowling and the raising of geese, and attending to stock sent by the surrouuding farmers to graze on the Fens in summer.

Cox, Magna Britannia. 1719.

Cox, in his description of Lincolnshire, speaking of the division of Holland, says, "The soil produces very little corn, but much grass, and is well stocked with fish and sea fowl. It is so soft that they work their horses unshod. There is a great want of fresh water in places, they having no other supply than rain water, preserved in pits, which, if deep, soon turn the water brackish, and, if shallow, grow presently dry. Here are also many quicksands, which, the shepherds find to their cost, have a notable faculty to suck in anything that comes upon them, their sheep being often devoured by them."

In a petition to King Charles I., respecting the condition of the East Fen, it was stated that the land, which before the draining was not worth fourpence an acre, had become so fertile that they had abundant crops of all sorts of corn and grain and seed for oil. In the middle of the 17th century, the price paid for 'hassocking,' *i.e.*, burning the hassocks and planting and sowing the reclaimed land with coleseed, was stated to be £1 per acre; that every acre of seed, wheat, barley or oats cost 8/-; reaping, threshing and carriage of coleseed, to be fit to put on the boats, £3 per last.

State Papers.

Some idea of the condition of the common fen land may be gathered from the fact that the value of the common rights, in the

East and West Fens, at the end of the last century, was put at only 2/10 per acre, and that land in the Witham Fens was let at the rate of 1/6 an acre; the best land in Deeping Fen, previous to its reclamation in 1779, was let for 7/- or 8/- an acre, and a great deal was in such a state that nobody would rent it. Some of the land was sold for £3 an acre.

The Fens were rendered less profitable than they otherwise would have been, owing to their being overstocked. Arthur Young remarks, " Some stock so largely as to injure themselves and oppress the common; others, in the line of jobbing, put in great quantities of stock to sell again, which are altogether injurious to the fair Commoner, who only stocks with what his farm produces." He gives instances of a cottager, whose rental was £5 per year, having 1,500 to 2,000 breeding geese in the fen: of another cottager, living at Brothertoft, who paid twenty shillings for his cottage and croft, his stock in Holland Fen being 400 sheep, 500 geese, 7 milch cows, 10 or 12 young horses, and 10 young beast. After the Inclosure, this same cottager rented 50 acres of the inclosed land at 25/- an acre, and ' he greatly preferred his new situation, not only for comfort, but for profit also.'

The difficulties of farming the uninclosed land may be realised from the fact that, in the Witham Fens near Chapel Hill, the sheep had frequently to be carried to their pastures in boats, and the cows swam from island to island. Large tracts of these fens were covered with thistles and water, four feet high. The sheep were constantly subject to the rot, 40,000 having perished from this disease, in the three fens, in one year. The cattle plague also made great devastation amongst the beast grazing on the fens. In 1746, this distemper broke out in the East and West Fens, and in a presentment made to the Grand Jury at Lincoln, it is recorded, " That the cattle then depasturing on the said fens were beginning to die very fast, and, no persons being appointed to bury them, they became a great nuisance." Inspectors were therefore appointed with authority to pay tenpence for every beast that was buried, the amount being raised by a special rate. The number of beast which died or were killed, between May, 1747 and January, 1748, in the Wapentake of Kirton, was 6,628, of which 2,784 were buried in the three fens, and only 2,346 remained alive. In the Wapentake of Skirbeck, 1,401 beast died, out of a total of 4,201.

In Holland Fen, the 'respe' was a fatal malady among the sheep fed on cole, the loss often amounting to 15 per cent. The cole was supposed to have a narcotic effect, which prevented the sheep from making water. The remedy was for the shepherd to go into the field at night and disturb them, and drive them along the roads in the day time. Sheep also suffered from sore noses, owing to the enormous number of thistles. These sore noses ran matter, which prevented the sheep from feeding, and ultimately killed them.

In addition to the plague of disease, and constant quarrels as to the stock, immense numbers of sheep and cattle were stolen, and frequent outrages were committed on cattle 'by laming, killing, cutting off tails, and wounding a variety of cattle, hogs, and sheep.'

THE FENMEN. So wild a country naturally reared up a people as wild as the fen, and many of the Fenmen were as destitute of all the comforts and amenities of civilised life as their isolated huts could make them. Their occupation consisted in dairying and haymaking, looking after the beast and sheep which grazed in the fen in summer; and in winter, gaining a living by fishing and fowling.

FEN STOCK. The sheep and cattle were large in limb, and covered with the coarsest and shaggiest covering that was able to preserve life. Those sent into the Fens from the high lands, for the summer grazing, were of a different class, being the progenitors of the Lincoln sheep and beast of the present day. Many Scotch beast were summered in the West Fen and then sent on to Norfolk to be fed on turnips. Great numbers of a small breed of hardy horses, called 'Wildmore Tits,' were bred in the Fens, and remained there all the winter. Many of these were lost from getting upon the frozen pools, when, their legs spreading outwards, they becamed 'screeved' or split, and thus perished.

A. Young.

AGRICULTURAL DEPRESSION. Even before the reclamation and drainage of the Fens, and the introduction of the improved system of agriculture, there appears to have been periodical times of depression, and agriculture in Lincolnshire was in as bad, or even a worse, condition than has recently befallen the county, in common with the rest of the country. In a letter preserved in the Record Office, written by Sir William Pelham of Brocklesby, in 1623, he says, " I am now heare with my sonn to settle some countrie affairs, and my own private, which were never soe burdensome unto mee as now, for manie insufficient tenants have given upp theyr farmes and scheep walks, soe as I am forced to take them into my owne hands, and borrow munnie uppon use to stocke them. . . Our cuntry was never in that wante that now itt is, and more of munnie than corn, for there are many thousands in thease parts who have soulde all they have, even to theyr bedd straw, and cann not gett worke to earne any munny. Dogg's flesh is a dainty disch, and found upon search in many houses; and also such horse flesch as hath laine long in a dike for hounds; and the other day one stole a scheepe who for meere hunger tore a legg out and did eatte it raw. All that is most certaine true, and yete the great time of scarcity not yett come."

1623.

Lincolnshire Notes & Queries.

In the following century the country was again suffering from bad times, due to wet seasons and low prices.

In 1735, a petition was presented to the Court of Sewers, from Landowners and holders of land in the parishes lying between Boston and Wainfleet, representing the great damage the petitioners were suffering from want of drainage; and the Court, having viewed the district, found it "in a grievous and deplorable condition, by reason of the violent and excessive inundation of fresh water, which in the late extroardinary wet season has descended upon them from the high country." In consequence, certain works were ordered to be done, and a tax laid to raise the necessary money; but, owing, "to the general poverty of the kingdom and universal want of trade, or reasonable profit for the sale of any commodities produced, and the particular distress in East Holland," it was found very difficult to collect the tax, and time was given for payment.

<small>Records of Boston Court of Sewers. 1735.</small>

Arthur Young, in his General View of the Agriculture of the County of Lincoln, drawn up for the Board of Agriculture, in 1799, has given a very full description of the condition and farming of the Fens previous to their enclosure, from which the following particulars are taken. He describes the Fenland thus. "Contiguous to the sea, in the southern part of Lincolnshire, there spreads a great extent of low land, much of which was once marsh and fen; but is now become, by the gradual exertions of above 150 years, one of the richest tracts in the kingdom; these great works are yet not finished, but, from the noble spirit which has animated this country, promise speedily to be effected. It is a region of fertility without beauty, in a climate not salubrious to the human constitution." He describes the country from Long Sutton to Freiston, with some variations of peat near Spalding, as one of the finest tracts he has seen: "a rich brown, dark loam of admirable texture. The land near Boston is a rich loam, upon clay first, to some depth; and then the silt, which is a porous sea sand, which has been deposited ages ago, becomes firm with rain, but is not fertile. Near the sea there is an infertile, very stiff blue clay upon the surface; grass almost always mown; the very richest pastures are a black mould, or mass of vegetable particles. The fen lands consist of a heavy deep sandy loam, which makes very rich breeding pastures for sheep, but not for feeding; another part of rich soapy blue clay, and another of black peat, consisting of decayed vegetables, and, when drained, is deemed by the inhabitants to be, of all others, proportioned to rent, the best for arable." With respect to the size and character of the holdings, he says that "a fifth part of South Holland is in small freeholds, and in the fen parishes half is so." In Holland, the largest farms ran from 100 to 400 acres, but many were very small. "In the Hundred of Skirbeck, property is very much divided and freeholds numerous, (very few farms exceeding a rental of £100 a year). In the parish of Freiston, containing about 3,000 acres, there is not one plot of more than 48 acres together, belonging to one person." Several farms he found

<small>CONDITION OF THE FENS PREVIOUS TO INCLOSURE. A. Young. 1799.</small>

occupied by the Wold farmers for the purpose of maintaining their stock. Of the farm buildings he says little, but remarks that large numbers of cottages had been built in the newly inclosed Fens, many of which were made of 'mud and straw' and thatched, and cost £30 each, or £40 a pair; brick and tile cottages cost £60 a pair; each cottage containing a room below and one above, with entrance through a small room used for washing, and a small dairy.

Speaking generally of this district he considered that the farming was carried out under great advantages, from the richness of the soil, which he reckoned amongst the first in the kingdom; from the freedom from tithes of the greater part of the land; and the low burden of poor rates, as compared with other counties.

The plough used in the Fenland, he considered "a most excellent tool; the mould board of a good sweep, the throat a segment of an ellipsis, and the form of the share, of great merit, well steeled and sharpened with files; the coulter a sharpened steel wheel." Two horses were used to draw this implement, and in this business many of the men were very clever, making their furrows as straight as a line.

COURSE OF CROPPING.

The method of cultivation pursued on the land in the newly inclosed Fens, was to pare and burn the surface, the ashes being spread over the land. The land was then cropped with oats and cole, till the first luxuriance of the soil was somewhat abated. When the land began to acquire consistence from mixing, by tillage, wheat was sown. In Holland Fen the course of cropping generally followed was 1, fallow for cole to be eaten by sheep; 2, oats; 3, beans; 4, wheat; 5, clover, mown once and then fed; or 1, oats; 2, wheat; 3, cole; 4, oats; 5, white clover for 3 years.

On the old arable land the course was cole, oats, wheat, clover. Fallowing was not uncommon and was called 'bobbing.' The land was ploughed over in the winter, cross ploughed in the spring, and harrowed and ploughed again in May or June, when the roots of weeds, &c., were collected together by a long-tined wooden harrow, and an instrument called a bob, and burnt, and the land afterwards sown with cole seed. A little barley was grown and also a few beans.

Clarke. R. A. Society's Journal.

About fifty years later Mr. Clarke gives the course of cultivation in the Peat Fens, as generally commencing with paring and burning, then coleseed; two crops of oats; seeds and rye grass, lasting 3 years; then the surface pared and burnt again for cole, followed by wheat; then seeds and wheat again. The drainage was entirely on the surface, the clay land being ploughed into eight-feet lands. He says that pastures of rye grass, if sown on the newly broken up peat lands, after being left 6 or 7 years, reverted to the natural fen grass, which then required to be again pared and burnt.

Many of the rich alluvial lands formerly became much impoverished by continual cropping, as many as ten corn crops having been taken in succession.

A great improvement has in recent years taken place in the farming of this district, the land on the whole being well cultivated, kept clean from weeds and highly manured. The ordinary system pursued is the 'five field'; two-fifths of the arable land being sown with white corn; one-fifth, clover seeds; one-fifth, fallow and sown with green crop; one-fifth, beans or peas, the wheat following either seeds, beans or peas. The course of cropping is, however, exceedingly various, owing to the many special crops that are grown, and the freedom allowed the tenants. *Clarke.*

The crops principally grown on the newly enclosed Fens were oats, rape and coleseed. The crops most generally cultivated in the Fenland at the present time, are wheat, potatoes and mustard; oats are largely grown, also peas and beans and, in a less degree, barley. A great deal of the land is also cultivated with special crops, as celery, woad, and vegetables for human food. The following description covers all the principal crops now, or formerly, grown in the Fenland. *CROPPING.*

Rape was cultivated in Deeping and Holland Fens, the seed being sown after paring and burning the old grass land. The crop was worth from £2 to £3 an acre for feeding sheep. An acre would carry 10 sheep for 10 weeks, and be worth sixpence per head per week. Sheep were frequently sent from the high country into the Fens to eat the rape. It was sometimes left for seed. Two acres of seed, in Holland Fen, soon after the enclosure, produced a last of seed, worth 50 guineas, and the price realised was seldom less than 30 guineas. *RAPE. A. Young. 1799.*

Coleseed was a staple crop for the newly broken up lands. As early as the middle of the 17th century, the Adventurers grew coleseed on their newly reclaimed land in the Bedford Level. It was sown between March and August, and grew from 3ft. to 4ft. high. A crop would carry 20 sheep to the acre for 20 weeks, the value being from 30/- to 60/- an acre, a very good crop fetching as much as 80/-. Sheep fattened on it with great rapidity. When allowed to stand for seed, the yield varied from 2½ to 4 or 5 quarters to the acre. The newly reclaimed land along the Witham yielded about 3 quarters. *COLE SEED.*

Both coleseed and rape were largely used for making soap and oil. In a petition sent to King Charles I, it is stated that since the draining of the Fens in the Bedford Level, they had abundant crops of all sorts of grain and 'seed for oyl.'

Oats were very largely grown on the newly enclosed fen land, generally following coleseed. In some cases they were taken for three years in succession, followed by cole and then oats again. The yield in Deeping Fen was from 8 to 10 quarters. In Holland Fen the crop is given as producing, at the end of the last century, 7 quarters; and along the Witham 8 to 9 quarters was an average *OATS.*

crop. Marat gives the average yield in East Holland as 6 quarters. The grain of the crops first grown was generally light, but improved as the land became more cultivated. The quantity of oats sent away from Boston, after the inclosure of the Fens, much exceeded that of all other grain. The quantity of corn shipped from Boston for the 5 years (1805 to 1809) was as follows:—

Marat's Lincolnshire

Wheat	3,983 quarters
Oats	25,5951 ,,
Barley	751 ,,
Beans and peas	1,363 ,,

In 1813 the wheat had increased to 60,591 qrs. and oats to 273,993 qrs.

WHEAT.

Wheat was not generally grown on the new lands, until after several crops of oats and cole. In Holland Fen, a great deal of the wheat grown was of inferior quality, owing to the luxuriance of the straw, the yield being about four quarters to the acre. On the newly broken up marsh lands the yield averaged about five quarters. The yield on the old arable land, in the Hundred of Skirbeck, is given as three-and-a-half quarters.

At the present time the Fenland is one of the largest wheat producing districts in England, the soil being admirably adapted for its cultivation, and the quality of the corn grown being very good. The average yield of a fairly good season may be taken as being about four-and-a-half quarters to the acre, on the good lands, but crops of seven and even eight quarters have been obtained. The average price of wheat, which varied from 55/9 to 44/4 between 1870-80, fell to 29/9 in 1889 and 26/4 in 1893. In 1894, the price of good fen wheat fell as low as 16/6 per quarter, which is the lowest price recorded during the present century. After the harvest of 1896, the price was about 23/- a quarter. In the Appendix will be found particulars as to the time of harvest, and other matters relating to this crop for the past 60 years.

Appendix V.

The average time, for the past 25 years, when the first new corn has been sold in Boston Market, which may be taken as about ten days from the commencement of harvest, is the 20th of August.

The best crops in the Fens, since 1841, were in 1844, 1847, 1849, 1851, 1852, 1854, 1855, 1857, 1863, 1864, 1868, 1870, 1874, 1885, 1887, and 1896, and the worst in 1845, 1850, 1855, 1859, 1860, 1861, 1869, 1872, and 1880.

BEANS.

Beans are grown on all the strong lands, intervening between the cereal crops. The yield may be taken as about five quarters to the acre, large crops, in good seasons, yielding six to seven quarters.

PEAS.

Blue peas are grown, following on oats and succeeded by wheat. The yield is from three to five quarters to the acre. The price, during recent years, has varied from 50/-, about 20 years ago, to 35/- in 1887, and, since then, from 60/-, to about 44/- at the present time.

The land requires to be in clean condition for the cultivation of this crop, otherwise it becomes smothered with the weeds.

Potatoes were largely cultivated at the begining of the present century about Spalding. Also at Tattershall, Coningsby and Brothertoft, the crop there being 480 bushels per acre, at 80lb. per bushel. The cost of raising the crop is given by Young as £9 8s. 8d. and the return £6 11s. 4d. The Potatoes were valued at 8d. per bushel, and used for feeding bullocks, and young cattle. One farmer at Spalding is reported as having grown 200 acres, for feeding bullocks, &c., but ' was ruined though the crops were very great.' At Freiston they were grown by Mr. Linton, but " though they were a valuable crop, yet the uncertainty of sale, and the extraordinary attention they demanded, induced him to give up the cultivation. At Leake and Wrangle there were some wastes which the cottagers took in, and on which they cultivated potatoes ; they had, however, no right, and being rather a lawless set, the practice was found productive of some evils." About Tattershall and Coningsby they were grown for human food. The cost of production is given as £9 19s. 6d., and the yield £12 13s. 4d. leaving a profit of £2 13s. 10d. per acre. The yield was put at 1,400 pecks and the price obtained, 2d. per peck, or 2/- a sack. The kind grown were ' Ox Nobles.' The best eating potatoes at that time are given by Young as Spotted Lemons, Old Rough Reds, Red Rose Kidneys, Early Reds, Early Manlys and Captain Harts. The return from these he estimated at 1,000 pecks of marketable potatoes per acre, worth threepence per peck.

POTATOES.

A. Young. 1799

Potatoes are still extensively grown in this district, and a large area of the best pasture land has been broken up for potato growing, the course of cropping being alternately potatoes and wheat. These lands have been generally purchased or occupied by small Owners and Occupiers and very high prices paid for them. Old pasture land let by auction for a term of five years, to break up, fetched as much rental as £10 to £12 per acre, a few years ago. In the neighbourhood of Wainfleet, the rent of some of the Toft land, which is admirably adapted for growing early potatoes, reached £5 per acre.

The sort then principally grown were Flukes, followed by Champions. These have since gone out of favour, and been succeeded by Early Roses, Magnum Bonums and Imperators. Other description grown in less quantities, are Beauties of Hebon, White Elephants, Schoolmaster, and for the early sort, Myatt's Prolifics ; Snowdrops, Sutton's Abundance, and Reading Giants are the favourites at the present time.

The early seed potatoes are generally placed in shallow wooden trays, about 2ft. 6in. long, 1ft 8in. wide and 2½in. deep, in February ; and kept in a warm outhouse, where they are allowed to sprout before being placed in the ground.

The yield varies according to the season. On good land the early crops produce from 6 to 10 tons per acre. The later crops yield from 7 to 10 tons and up to 13 or 14 under favourable conditions.

Report to Royal Commission on Agriculture. Wilson Fox. 1895. The method of cultivation for potatoes is generally as follows: the land is ploughed up in the autumn; in the spring it is harrowed and worked to a fine tilth. It is then ridged in 30in. ridges. From 10 to 15 loads of fold yard manure to the acre is spread in the furrows, and from 4 to 7 cwt. of superphosphate of lime is also sown over the land. The sets are put in the furrows by women at from 10 to 15in. apart, taking about seven sacks of seed potatoes to the acre. The ridges are then split with the plough. When the potatoes are taken up, if they are not sent off at once to market, they are deposited in long mounds or 'graves,' and covered over first with straw and then with earth of sufficient thickness to keep out the frost, tufts of straw being carried through the top of the grave for ventilation.

If wheat succeeds the potatoes, the seed is drilled in without any further working of the land.

WOAD. Woad. (*Isatis Tinctoria*). Derived from the Saxon, 'Wad,' the word now commonly used by fen men to describe this plant. There is no record as to the early cultivation of this plant in the Fens, but that it was cultivated in this country from very early times may be gathered from the following description given by Julius Cæsar:—"All the Britons die themselves with woad, which makes them a sky blue colour and thereby more terrible to their enemies." It was also used for giving its colour to the famous Lincoln green cloth. The use of woad as a dye has been superseded by indigo, and it is now chiefly used by woollen dyers for mixing with indigo to excite fermentation and to fix the colour. The first authentic description of its growth is given by Arthur Young, who says that at the end of the last century it was grown on an extensive scale by Mr. Cartwright, at Brothertoft.

A. Young. Being a tap-rooted plant, penetrating 8in. or 9in., it requires a deep soil, and can only be grown on new, rich land. The plant was found to thrive best on fresh grass land. Grass land was frequently hired for 3 or 4 years, with permission to break it up and grow woad. The rent paid was from £4 to £5 an acre. The seed was sown from March to May, in rows, 8in. or 9in. asunder, requiring 88 bushels of seed in husk. Old grass land required harrowing as many as 12 or 15 times to get all the clods and roots off. The crop required twice weeding. When the plant was about 8in high the leaves were gathered, two crops being obtained in a year, the weeding and plucking being done by men, women and children on their knees.

The leaves as gathered were taken to a mill to be crushed. These mills consisted of 3 wheels, about 7ft. in diameter on one side, and 6 on the other, and 3ft. wide, formed of wood with projecting iron bars on their circumference, 4in. apart. The path on which the wheels revolved was about 30ft. in diameter. It required 8 horses to drive the mill. The leaves, after being crushed in the mill, were made into balls, which were laid upon trays and placed under a shed, covered only at the top, and left to dry. In winter the dry balls were taken from the store, broken up, turned over several times and ground to powder by the same mills as previously used, spread on the floor, and after being moistened with water, allowed to ferment, the process being termed 'couching.' This fermenting process required considerable care in order to make the material 'beaver' well, a term descriptive of the fineness of the capillary filaments into which it draws out when broken between the finger and thumb. When the fermenting process was completed, the woad was cooled and brought to a proper condition for packing in casks, and sent to the manufacturers in Yorkshire and Lancashire. After being packed in the casks it can be kept for several years. The growing of woad is confined to very few districts. At the time of Young's inspection, the only places were at Brothertoft, 300 acres on Moulton Common on the inclosure, and at 3 other places, whose names are not given. Beyond this there were not 50 tons grown in the rest of the kingdom.

The crop requires the richest loam soil with a clay bottom, and is considered as exhaustive to the land, but this is partly compensated for by the thorough cleaning it gives. The yield is given by Mr. Clarke as from 2 to 3 tons to an acre. In bad seasons the yield falls to about half a ton. Where oats were grown after woad, very large crops were obtained, and the wheat that followed yielded 6 quarters to the acre.

Clarke's *Agriculture of Lincolnshire.* 1851.

The supply of woad is still almost entirely obtained from the Fen districts. The process of growing and manufacture is the same as that already described, except that the horses for driving the mill have been superseded by a steam engine. The quantity required being very limited, an arrangement is generally entered into by the growers not to have more than a certain number of acres under cultivation in any one year. The only growers of woad in England at the present time are Messrs. Nussey at Algarkirk, Mr. Graves of Skirbeck, Mr. Short of Wyberton and Mr. Howard at Parson Drove. Each of these grow about ten acres, but Mr. Graves in some seasons has had as much as fifty acres and has given as much as £10 an acre rent, and from £150 to £200 for the purchase of the best pasture land on which to grow it. The price has declined from £20 to £25 per ton, which it formerly made, to about £9 per ton.

Chickory was also formerly grown in the same districts as woad, the leaves being used for the stock, and the roots, which

CHICKORY.

were taken up about Michaelmas, being sent away for grinding and mixing with coffee.

HEMP AND FLAX. Hemp and flax have been cultivated in this county from very early times, spinning and weaving being practised by the Britons. It was much grown in the last century, in the neighbourhood of Swineshead. The cultivation of the crop was very similar to that of hemp, the process being to sow the seed in May, at the rate of 3 bushels to the acre. The crop was pulled up at old Lammas, and after being bound in sheaves was soaked in water or 'retted'; it was then laid on an eddish field where it remained for two or three weeks, then tied in bundles, taken to the barn, broken and swingled and sent to market. The value varied from 2/6 to 7/6 a stone, 5/- being about the average. An average crop was about 45 stones, and the cost of growing, including rent of land &c, was from £8 to £9. There used to be flax mills at Surfleet and in the East Fen. There was also a fair for hemp and flax at Spalding, held on the 27th April. Neither of these crops have been grown in the Fenland for several years.

PARSLEY. Parsley was also grown in Holland Fen. It was formerly cultivated as an artificial grass, mixed with white clover. It lasted three years and supported from 6 to 10 sheep to the acre. The quantity of seed was about 2lbs. of parsley, mixed with 14lbs. of white clover. The experience gained in the use of this plant led to the observation that "it seemed to merit more attention than it has received and would probably be found a valuable article upon any sheep farm." The practice of mixing parsley with grass seeds is still pursued to a limited extent.

A. Young.

CABBAGES. Cabbages were grown at the beginning of the present century, both in Holland Fen and at Freiston, and were used for feeding sheep and bullocks. As an example of their use it may be stated that Mr. Linton of Freiston, "in the winter of 1795, fed 8 bullocks with cabbages and a small quantity of hay, given in cribs in a well littered yard; they were, at putting to cabbages, worth £16 each, on the 16th December, and about the end of February were sold in Smithfield for £25 each. Their consumption of hay was not one third of their food. They ate three acres, which yielded £48."

A. Young.

Cabbages are still grown to a large extent, but principally for human food, and are sent away by railway to Sheffield, Manchester, Sunderland, Newcastle and other large towns in the midland and northern counties. The cost of carriage varies according to distance, from 10/- to 20/- per ton. A good crop yields from 18,000 to 20,000 scores of cabbages, or about 15 tons to the acre. They are sometimes sent loose in the trucks, but generally packed in crates, containing 8 dozen, weighing 1½ cwt. The price realised is about 6d. per dozen.

Cauliflowers and cauliflower broccoli are also now much cultivated, the former for autumn and the latter for spring use. Except where these crops follow potatoes, which the former generally do, the land is manured very highly. A good crop of these vegetables yields from 6,000 to 7,000 score per acre, equal in weight to about 12 tons. They are packed in crates, containing about 5 dozen and weighing 2 cwt., each crate.

Celery is another special crop that is grown by the smaller holders on the rich alluvial soils. The principal market for this crop is in the large towns in the midland and northern counties and in London. A fair crop yields 1,500 dozen heads to the acre, equal in weight to about 30 tons. A bundle containing 12 heads weighs about 42lbs., although, occasionally, picked heads will weigh as much as double this. The price realised a few years ago by the grower was eighteen-pence per dozen, a good crop realising at this price over £100 per acre. It has now fallen to sixpence per bundle. The celery is frequently planted in rows, 6ft. apart, with two rows of potatoes between, the plants being set 4in. apart. When potatoes and celery are thus planted together, as much as 50 tons of stable manure to the acre is placed on the land. If the celery is planted alone about half this quantity is used.

Mangolds are very extensively grown all over the Fenland. The best crops are obtained in the peat district in the East Fen and in Deeping Fen. They are frequently exported and sent away for the use of cow-keepers in the large towns. An ordinary crop of mangolds yields 20 tons to the acre, a good crop 40 tons, and even up to 60 tons have been grown. The price obtained varies from 14/- to 20/- per ton. Sugar beet has been tried in the East Fen, but it grew too coarse and its cultivation was given up. Mangolds are occasionally grown for seed, the method of treatment being the same as for turnips. In 1893 a crop from 26 acres realised £2,000, equal to £80 an acre.

Carrots are grown to a considerable extent on the peat and silty lands. An average crop yields about 15 tons to the acre, and crops of 20 tons are occasionally gathered. The price obtained is about 20/- a ton.

The supply of **mustard** comes almost entirely from the fen districts of England and from Holland. A mustard market is held at Wisbech during the months of October and November, which the agents of the principal manufacturers attend. A large portion of the cropping is however sold privately, the agents visiting the crops during their growth. Mustard is grown largely on the peat land in the East Fen, in Deeping Fen, and also on the alluvial lands. Two sorts are grown, the brown and the white. The former is considered to be of the better quality, produces most, and fetches the highest price, but it requires the best land. The white will stand bad weather better than the brown, does not shake out so readily, and will remain out until September, whereas the brown should be harvested a month earlier.

The growth of mustard was first commenced in the Bedford Level, about the begining of the present century, and gradually extended to Lincolnshire. Very high prices were then obtained for the produce of this crop. It is narrated that a waggon load of mustard taken to Wisbech market by a Lincolnshire farmer, and sold at the rate of 50/- a bushel, realized £500. Arthur Young makes no mention of the growth of this crop in Lincolnshire in his report (1799.)

Mustard is sown in March or April, following potatoes or wheat and is succeeded by wheat or oats, although this rotation is varied by the mustard following fallows. An average crop yields from 2½ to 4 quarters to the acre. Five quarters is sometimes obtained on new land highly manured.

The price has gradually declined from 20/- a bushel, which it fetched about 20 years ago, to 15/-, 10 years ago; 10/- in 1887, and about 12/- in recent years.

TURNIP SEED. Turnips are not very extensively grown for sheep feeding in the Fenland, but the crop is frequently allowed to stand for seed. The yield is from 3 to 4 quarters per acre, 4½ quarters being considered a very good crop. The price realized used to be about £1 1s. 0d. a bushel, but in 1894 it had fallen to about 12/- a bushel. The seed is sown in July. The turnips are taken up and re-planted in November, and the seed is ready for harvesting in July. The best method of planting is by dibbling the turnips in, at intervals of 18in. apart, a man and a boy doing about the third of an acre in a day. They are sometimes put in with a spade, and occasionally by merely planting in a furrow made by the plough and then covered in by splitting the ridge.

POPPIES. In the neighbourhood of Holbeach, where the soil is some of the most productive of any in the Fenland, poppies were formally frequently grown, the yield being from 20,000 to 30,000 large heads to the acre. The small heads were crushed for laudanum.

ONIONS. Onions have also been largely grown in South Holland. In suitable seasons the quality of the crop is very good, but in wet weather the onions grow coarse. The cost of growing this crop is very great, seed sometimes costing as much as 10/- per lb., 30lb. being required for sowing an acre. Weeding costs from £5 to £6. A good yield of pickling onions is about 7 to 8 tons, and of large onions 10 to 12 tons, an acre.

PEPPERMINT. Peppermint was at one time grown, the soil being well suited to produce bulk, but the quality was not so fine as that grown at Mitcham. Mr. Wilson Fox states that a farmer in the neighbourhood of Deeping St. James still grows a considerable acreage.

FRUIT.

The Fenland does not possess any special reputation for the growth of any particular kind of fruit. Formerly "there was one sort of pippin apple peculiar to Lincolnshire which grew at Kirton and thereabouts and from thence was called the Kirton Pippin, which is a most wholesome and delicious apple." *Cox, Magna Britannia.*

The cultivation of fruit trees and bush fruit has, however, within the last few years very largely increased amongst the small holders. The fruit is grown on the system of mixed cropping, the apple, pear or plum trees being planted in rows, one chain apart, the trees being about 7 yards apart in the rows, and having four gooseberry or three currant trees between them. The land between the rows is cultivated for vegetables, an occassional crop of oats or wheat being taken. Bush trees are used, as the drip from these does not interfere with the cropping as much as from the standards.

The apples principally grown are, Keswick Codling, Normanton Wonder, Blenheim Orange, King of the Pippins, Lord Grosvenor Warner's King, Ecklinville Seedling, and, for the newer sorts, Domino, and Bramley's Seedling. The average produce from trees after ten years growth may be take at about 15 pecks from each tree, 25 pecks being a large crop.

The rich alluvial land of the Fens suits the Bush fruits exceedingly well and occassionally very large crops are obtained, instances being given where black currants have yielded as much as £80 an acre. An average crop of these currants may be taken at 7lbs. for each tree, and of gooseberries, after about five years growth, 8lbs. The gooseberries principally grown are Crown Bob, Aston Red and Winham's Industry.

The cost of planting an acre of land in the way above described may be estimated at about £3, the number of standard trees required being 25, which cost eighteenpence each, and of bushes 150, costing 15/- per hundred.

Raspberries are the best paying crop of any of the small fruits, being sent away in large quantities for making preserves, to Rotherham, Hull, and other towns. The price realised is about £20 per ton. The canes cost 5/- per hundred, and are set in rows, 4½ft. apart and 3ft. in the rows. They are either tied to wire run on posts along the rows, or two canes arched over and tied together.

WEIGHT OF FRUIT.

The weight of a peck of fruit as fixed by the authorities in Boston Market is as follows: apples 10lbs.; cherries and currants 14lbs.; gooseberries 16lbs.; pears and plums 18lbs.

FLOWER BULBS.

Scattered about in different parts of the Fenland, especially in the neighbourhood of Spalding, Gosberton, Holbeach, Whaplode, Surfleet, Swineshead and Wyberton will be found small plots of snowdrop, crocus and other bulbs, which are grown for sale.

Snowdrops appear to flourish better in this neighbourhood than in Holland and command a better market than other bulbs. They are a crop well adapted for cultivation by the Cottager and yield a large return, a perch of snowdrops, three years after being set, yielding about 2,000 marketable bulbs, worth at the present time about 10/- a thousand. A few years ago an acre of land in the East Fen yielded 300,000 marketable bulbs, and nearly as many small ones for replanting, the former selling for £140. The bulbs are planted in October, in rows, 9in. to 12in. apart, and are spaced 3in. apart. They are taken up and sold in July, after being planted 3 years.

The crocus bulb does not meet with such a ready sale or command half the price of snowdrops, those from Holland being considered by the gardeners of better quality. They yield about 2,000 marketable bulbs to the perch.

During the last few years other bulbs, such as daffodils and Narcissus have also been grown, both for the bulbs and flowers, the latter being sent up to Covent Garden. In a garden at Pinchbeck the first year's growth of Narcissus yielded a profit of £5 an acre, the second year £15, and the third £20. They cost from £10 to £15 to plant.

Wilson Fox's Report to Commission on Agriculture. 1895.

Violets and other flowers are also grown for market. Mr. Fox mentions one case where an acre of violets was being grown, and another where a gardener, who was growing half an acre, lost £50, in 1894, from red spider.

PASTURE.

A. Young.

Arthur Young, in describing the grazing lands of the Fenland as 'the glory of Lincolnshire,' says, that "the soil is of rich loamy clay, some very stiff, but of uncommon fertility. Generally these lands in summer will carry a bullock to an acre and a half, besides 4 sheep to the acre, and 2 sheep an acre in winter. Some of the lands in Long Sutton that were once Common, will carry 5 or 6 sheep to the acre, and 4 bullocks on 10 acres. On the grass land in Deeping Fen, 5 sheep are kept on an acre from Lady Day to Michaelmas, and 1½ in winter....Near Boston, a field of 21 acres kept from Lady Day to Michaelmas 19 heavy beast and 100 sheep, and wintered 50 sheep; another field of 8 acres, 10 oxen and 40 sheep in summer and 30 sheep in winter....Forty acres at Algarkirk, 300 sheep, 16 fatting bullocks, 3 cows and 4 horses; and 3 sheep to the acre in winter....In the grazing lands at Swineshead a beast an acre of from 40 to 70 stones and 2 or 3 sheep, with 2 sheep to the acre in winter....At Gosberton, (marsh land,) 7 sheep to the acre and a bullock also; and 300 tod of wool have been clipped from 90 acres. In the parishes of Skirbeck, Fishtoft, Freiston, Butterwick, Benington, Leverton, Leake and Wrangle, about two-thirds were pasture, part mown, and one-third tillage....The best kind of pasture was stocked with shearling wethers bought at the spring markets at Boston, and by beasts, the medium lands by young beasts and hogs, and the poorer grass land mown. The best lands carried 3 sheep per acre, winter and summer, 10 acres carrying 10 beasts, weighing from 54 to 100 stones; the medium land winters about 5 sheep to 2 acres, with 4 per acre in summer, with a few cows and young beasts.... The hay crop was estimated at 35/- an acre, the eddish being eaten by cattle or lamb hogs." The measurement of some of these pasture lands was considerably above a statute acre, and contained about 4¾ roods.

Mr. Clarke, writing in 1847, describes the soil of the Fenland as being of a rich dark loam, of admirable texture, containing some of the richest grazing land in the kingdom.

Clarke's Agriculture of Lincolnshire. 1851.

The salt marshes outside the sea banks, at the present time, afford very useful sheep pasture, especially to stock brought from the high country. The herbage has frequently a scouring effect on sheep when first turned on, but this soon passes off, and the saline matter contained in the soil and herbage is considered beneficial to the feet of the sheep. The grazing on the marshes is in the best order after rain, which washes the grit off the grass left by the tides, and freshens the growth. The rental of these marshes varies from 6/- to 10/- an acre.

SALT MARSHES.

The land of the Fenland is very highly cultivated, the Occupiers having long since realized the fact that it is more economical to obtain a large crop off a small area of land than the same quantity off a larger area. Artificial manures have, therefore, been largely resorted to, to supplement that made by feeding in the yards.

MANURE

The use of oil cake, for feeding cattle and enriching the farm-yard manure, appears to have been in vogue since the last century, and very large quantities of linseed and cotton cake are now used throughout the Fenland. There is a large mill for crushing the seed at Boston, and there are mills at Lincoln. The rest of the supply required is obtained from Hull and other places. Crushed bones were very largely used at one time, but have been superseded by superphosphate of lime. Fish is frequently used as a manure, when it can be obtained. In winter, very large quantities of sprats are brought to Boston by the fishing boats, and sold for manure, at the rate of about 20/- per ton. Mussels have also been used, but the protective laws regulating the fishery now prevent the small mussels being carried off the beds for this purpose. Before the inclosure of the East Fen, large quantities of sticklebacks used to find their way into the pits, and were collected and sold for manure. The peat lands, after their first inclosure, were very considerably benefited by sinking trenches, at intervals of from 7 to 12 yards, three feet wide and two feet deep, digging up the clay and spreading it over the peat. This process cost from one shilling and eightpence to two shillings a chain.

Lime is seldom used as a manure. No doubt this is the result of experience as to its benefit, but it would appear as if it were a manure well adapted to neutralise the acid formed in the peat, and to warm and improve the mechanical texture of the clay soils.

CATTLE.

The cattle originally bred and fattened in the Lincolnshire marshes and fens were large boned and rather coarse animals, of a hardy nature. They fattened rapidly on the rich marsh land near Burgh and the sea coast, and on the pastures in the Fenland, weighing, when fat, about 70 to 80 stones.

In the beginning of the present century Mr. Cartwright of Brothertoft obtained a short-horned bull from Mr. Collins of Durham; others followed his example. By mixing the fine short-horn with the old Lincolnshire breed, great size with constitution and quality were united in such a degree as to retain the merit of each. The old Lincolnshire ox maintained his majestic porportions, without his clumsiness, and a large proportion of lean flesh was secured.

The beast which have been grazed during the summer are put into the crewyards about October. Those intended for the butcher during the winter, have turnips and hay, and 10lbs. of linseed cake per day; the store cattle getting 4lbs. The cattle are turned out of the yards into the pastures in May. The best grazing lands will carry a bullock and a sheep to the acre, and will make them ready for the butcher by the autumn, weighing about 60 stones of 14lbs. The best cattle shown at the Fat Stock Markets of Spalding and Boston in December, will weigh as much as 100 stones.

SHEEP.

Clarke.

The old Lincolnshire sheep are described as being ungainly animals, with carcasses long and thin, razor backs, legs thick and rough, bones large, pelts thick, and, though attaining great weight, were a long time arrriving at maturity. Their chief merit was their wool, which was from 10in. to 18in. long and weighed 8lb. to 16lb. per fleece. This heavy skin made the breed profitable to the fen graziers. Very large quantities of these sheep were sent from the high country to graze on the Fens in summer. In the Wildmore and West Fens and those parts where the grass grew, there would be as many as 5 sheep to the acre, besides horses, young cattle and geese. The Fens are said to have been perfectly white with sheep in dry seasons.

Clarke.

At the end of the last century an attempt was made to improve the old long-wool Lincoln sheep by a mixture with the fine Leicester, which, although more delicate in constitution, was of a finer character both as regards the quality of the wool and meat. This cross resulted in a sheep which came to maturity in one-fourth less time than the old Lincolnshire breed, and fetched more money, when sold fat, than that breed did. This breed is exceedingly well adapted for the rich pastures of the marshes and fens, as it fattens rapidly and yields heavy fleeces of wool. A wether kept till $2\frac{1}{2}$ years old will weigh 28lbs. per quarter and have yielded 2 clips of wool of from 20lbs. to 25lbs. It used not to be unusual for the fat sheep prepared for the Christmas markets to weigh from 50lbs. to 70lbs per quarter, but during recent years the practice of fattening sheep up to this extent has been abandoned. A cross between the Lincolnshire and South Down has come very much into favour during the last few years, the size of the joints and the quality of the meat being more useful to the butcher than those of the pure bred Lincoln.

Large numbers of sheep bred in the high country, bordering on the Fenland, are sold for grazing, at the fairs held in the spring at Lincoln, Boston and Spalding. The number penned at Lincoln and Boston fairs in former times has reached as high as 30,000. Owing to the improved means of communication the numbers have greatly fallen off, the quantity now shown at Lincoln being from 8,000 to 12,000, and at Boston from 6,000 to 8,000. A greater quantity than formerly are however brought to the weekly markets. *Wilson Fox's Report. 1895.*

At the beginning of the present century the average price for shearling wethers was from 36/- to 42/-, although at times they reached as high as 60/-. Hogs were worth in 1796 from 25/- to 30/-. The highest average prices obtained at Lincoln Fair for sheep since 1874 was 70/- a head in 1878, and the lowest 45/7, in 1893; the average for the 18 years being 57/6.

Breeding ewes are kept on all farms which have grass land, and great care is exercised in selecting rams of good quality. The fall of lambs is rather late, not taking place generally till March. In good seasons the ewes will average a lamb and a half each. *RAMS.*

Some of the most noted Ram breeders in the kingdom have lived in Lincolnshire, on the borders of the Fenland.

In 1796 a new Tup Society was established at Lincoln for the purpose of improving the breed by a union with the Leicesters. The Club consisted of 10 members originally. The rules provided that the Leicester breeders should show their rams two days previous to the letting day; that no rams should be let by members of the Society to a wether breeder in the County of Lincoln, under 30 guineas; that preference should be given in letting rams in Lincolnshire to the members of the Society; and in return that no ram in Lincolnshire should be taken to market, or let under 5 guineas, and no ewes were to be sold except to the Butchers. *A. Young.*

Nearly 100 years ago Mr. Skipwith of Alesby gave as much as 200 guineas for his rams. The average price for letting being from 5 to 50 guineas. In one year he realised from 1,000 to 1,200 guineas. *A. Young.*

Among the best known ram breeders of the present century, the following names may be mentioned: Mr. Kirkham of Biscathorpe, Mr. Clarke of Scopwick, Mr. Vessey of Halton, Mr. Mayfield of Dogdyke, Mr. Casswell of Pointon, Messrs. Dudding and Mr. Swain of Wrangle in the East Fen.

The rams are let by auction. Very high prices were reached when agriculture was flourishing, as much as £50 being given for the hire of a ram for one season, and £80 to £90 for the purchase of shearling rams, the average price of hire for a ram of good quality being from £10 to £15, and for purchase from £50 to £60.

WOOL.

The sheep bred and reared in the fens yield very heavy fleeces of good quality. Arthur Young, after a careful survey of the county made at the end of the last century, found that the general opinion amongst sheep owners was that the yield of wool was less from the new cross-bred Leicester sheep than from the old long-wool Lincolns, by ½lb. to 2lb. per fleece.

A. Young.

The price of Lincolnshire wool during the last century varied from about 27/- per tod of 28lbs., the highest price in 1792, to 11/- the lowest in 1782; the average for the 37 years between 1758 and 1794 being 17/- per tod, equal to 7·28d. per lb. At the time when wool was fetching 27/-. mutton was about 6d. per lb. The yield of wool from a flock of sheep was from 11½ to 12lbs. per fleece.

Bradford Observer Wool Tables. 1894.

During the present century the price of Lincoln Half Hog Wool has varied from 37⅜d. per lb. which it fetched in 1864, to 8¾d. in 1892; the average of 80 years, 1814-93, being 15¼d.; for the 10 years, 1864-73, 22·94d.; 1874-83, 15·09d., and for 1884-93, 10·07d.

Royal Commission on Agriculture. 1894

In the evidence given by Mr. Epton of Wainfleet before the Royal Commission on the depression of Agriculture in 1894, he stated that the average price he had realised for wool from 1860-76 was 44/6 per tod. Since 1876 it had averaged only 24/-. The average price for 34 years for full mouthed ewes had been 49/6 each, but in 1894 only 36/- each.

AUCTION STOCK SALES.

During the past few years a custom has grown up of selling the stock by auction, and stock sales are held weekly at Sleaford, Burgh, Wainfleet, Donington, Holbeach and Long Sutton.

PRICES.

The price of cattle has dropped considerably during recent years. The prices obtained at Lincoln fair, have been as follows:

Wilson Fox's Report. 1895.

	1882-83. £	1893-4. £
Yearlings	9 to 13½	6 to 8
Two-year olds	15 to 20	11 to 14½
Three-year	24 to 30	17¼ to 21½
Drapes	16 to 24½	11½ to 14½

BUTTER AND CHEESE.

Formerly very few cows were kept for the purpose of making butter and cheese, but owing to the increasing number of small holders, the quantity of butter sent to market has largely increased. Cheese is not made in any quantity, and little milk is exported to the large towns.

The butter is not considered of good quality, partly from a want of properly making up, but principally from the fact that the pastures on the east coast are not so well adapted for the purposes of dairying as those on the west. The instruction given under the direction of the Agricultural Society has had a beneficial effect, and the quality is reported to be better now than it was formerly.

Before the common fens were inclosed, a great many rough hardy horses were bred and reared, especially in Wildmore Fen. These horses were known by the name of Wildmore Tits.

HORSES.

The cart horses now generally in use in the Fenland are strong well made animals, and from the mares many of the large London dray horses are procured. Great encouragement has been given in recent years to the breeding of good horses by the foal fairs which are held annually at Boston, Donington, Holbeach and Long Sutton. Large prices are realised for good foals at these fairs, as much as £100 having been given for a colt foal, 4 to 5 months old. The average price for a sound foal is £20 to £25.

There is always a good show of entire horses at the markets in the spring.

A few nag horses are bred, but little attention is given to the breeding of hunters or blood horses.

The ordinary breed of pigs in the fen district is a large framed, long haired, lop eared, coarse animal. They feed well and will weigh when fattened as much as 60 stones. The usual weight is from 25 to 30 stones when twelve months old.

SWINE.

Berkshire pigs have been introduced in many farms, and these, crossed with the Lincolnshire, improve the quality of the meat, and produce an animal that fattens readily and produces joints of a smaller and more marketable size.

The district has suffered very much in recent years from swine fever, and it has been found necessary an several occasions to close all the pig markets.

Large quantities of poultry are kept. The kind most in use is a mixture of the Dorking and Cochin China, large ungainly birds, but which grow rapidly and sell well. Flocks of turkeys are also kept on some farms.

POULTRY.

The number of small holdings is conducive to the rearing of poultry, the sums realized by the sale of the eggs and birds, when ready for market, forming an important item in the income of the small holder. In many cases the wives clothe themselves and the children, and help to keep the house going by the poultry. On the large farms it is customary for the foreman's wife to rear poultry for the farm, receiving in exchange for her services a share of the produce, or a sum of 6d. for each chicken, the farmer finding all the food. Poultry farming on a large scale was tried at Woodhall, but was not found successful.

Wilson Fox's Report.

The Fens in their uninclosed state were well adapted for the rearing of geese, and very large flocks were kept. Some cottagers, whose rental did not exceed £5, are said to have kept as many as 1,500 breeding geese. Arthur Young gives the details of a flock

GEESE.

Survey of Lincolnshire. 1799.

kept by a man in the East Fen. His stock consisted of 160 geese, from these he reared from 500 to 700 birds in a year, an average brood being 8. The price realized was from 1/- to 2/- each, the feathers from pluckings making 1/8. The average produce he put at 2/6 for each bird, about half of which was spent in corn; leaving a net profit of about £40 a year. The labour in attendance was provided by the wife and children.

During the breeding season these birds were frequently kept in the cottages, and even in the bedrooms. The nests were made in wicker pens, placed in tiers, one above the other, in huts erected for the purpose. Twice in a day the Gooseherd or Gozzard, lifted the birds off the nests, attended them to water, and fed and replaced them. So skilled were these men in their occupation that they knew every bird and the nest to which it belonged.

The geese were plucked four, and sometimes five, times a year. The first plucking was at Lady Day for quills and feathers, and the other pluckings, for feathers only, between then and Michaelmas. The goslings were also plucked with the object of increasing their succeeding feathers. In cold seasons numbers of the birds perished after the early plucking.

In days when feather beds were more used than they are now, there was a great demand for these feathers, and a Lincolnshire 'goose-cote' feather bed was handed down as a family heir-loom. Lincolnshire feathers still retain their reputation, and two of the largest factories in England, for purifying and preparing goose feathers, are at Boston.

IMPLEMENTS.

The implements used in the Fenland do not vary sufficiently from those used in other parts of the country to require any special description. The fen farmer has always been ready to avail himself of the most improved form of implement, and the large number of makers of agricultural machinery and implements, who have their works at Lincoln, Grantham or Gainsborough, all in the County of Lincoln, adjacent to the Fenland, testify to the ready sale of machinery.

The first portable engine was made at Howden's Foundry, Boston; and Tuxford and Sons, of Boston, were for many years noted for supplying the best portable engine in the market. The portable engines and thrashing machines made by Clayton and Shuttleworth, of Lincoln, are known all over the world. In busy seasons this firm is reported to turn out more than an engine a day. Large numbers of thrashing machines and engines are exported to the Continent from Boston Dock.

The old fen plough was a very simple implement, the mould board was attached to the frame by a vertical share, and was shaped something like a shield; the coulter was a steel wheel with a sharp edge. The plough, used for fallowing the peat land, had a wooden pin to connect the heel tree with the plough stock, and directly the share caught a tree, the pin broke and let the team go on without breaking the plough.

Although a great many one-horse carts are in use, the farmers still use waggons of a very heavy and clumsy character. The wheels of all the carts and waggons, throughout the Fenland, are placed the same width apart. This practice arose at the time when the roads were allowed to have deep ruts in them, and the wheels were all made to the same gauge, so as 'to run in the ruts.' This practice has become so fixed in the minds of the carters, that, now, even on good level roads, all the carts follow in the same track, making it very difficult, in wet weather, for the roadmen to maintain a level surface.

Owing to the large number of small Occupiers, a great number of steam threshing machines are kept for hire, and are taken about from one farm to the other, by the horses of those requiring the machine. Jack Straws for raising the straw on to the stack now almost universally accompany the threshing machines. The price charged for wheat or beans is 1s. 0d. per quarter, and for oats 10d., the farmer providing coal and labour. THRASHING MACHINES.

Steam cultivating and ploughing has been largely practised in this district. Some of the largest farmers have machinery of their own, but the steam cultivating is generally done by hire, the cost for ploughing being 10s. 0d. and for cultivating 9s. 0d. per acre. It is the opinion of many agriculturists that land in some cases has been injured by steam cultivation, especially were the soil below the ordinary depth of cultivation has been brought to the surface. On strong lands in wet seasons there is a prejudice with some farmers in favour of the ridge and furrow system, because by this means the surface water is prevented from standing on the land and starving the corn, even when it has been under drained. Ridges and furrows cannot be used with steam ploughing. STEAM CULTIVATING MACHINERY.

Reaping machines are in very general use, but only a few self-binding reapers have as yet found their way on to the Fenland farms. The cost of this implement is too great to make it of service to the small holders. REAPING MACHINES.

The farm buildings are generally good, but do not differ in any essential particular from those found in other parts of the country. The stock or crew yards are not covered in, but are provided with open sheds. Mr. Wilson Fox, in his report, says that he found the buildings excellent, both as regards convenience and the state of repair, and that Lincolnshire compared very favourably with other counties in this respect. BUILDINGS.

Agriculture Commission. 1895.

The old fen cottages were built of 'stud and mud' and thatched with the reeds which grew in the meres, the 'studs' being the frame COTTAGES.

work of timber, which was filled in between with well punned clay, mixed with chopped straw. They were very low and frequently consisted of only one storey, with two rooms, and sometimes in addition a small room in the roof. They were very warm in winter. They cost about £30 to build. The rent of these cottages with a garden, was from 7d. to 1s. 2d. a week. Many of these cottages are still to be found throughout the Fens.

The modern cottages are generally good, well built, brick and tiled or slated structures, containing 2 living rooms and 3 bedrooms. A great number have been erected during the last half century, and, except in some of the remoter fens, the men have not far to go to their work. The cost of a double cottage with outbuildings is from £250 to £300. The rent of such cottages, with about a rood of land, is from 1s. 9d. to 2s. 3d. a week. The cottages built for the foremen on the larger farms have more accommodation, as frequently the labourers hired by the year are boarded with them.

LABOUR AND WAGES.

The rate of wages for agricultural labourers in the Fenland, has always ranged higher than in other parts of England, consequently the labourers, being well fed, are strong and healthy. They are as a rule intelligent, sober and hard working. The better class of work as thatching, hedging, and ditching, is frequently done by piece work by men occupying small holdings, who fill up their time by assisting the neighbouring farmers at harvest, and in doing work that requires skill. These small Occupiers are exceedingly thrifty and hard working and of very great service in the neighbourhood where they live. Horsemen, shepherds and labourers engaged by the year, if unmarried, are housed and fed by the farmer or boarded with the foreman, at from 8s. 0d. to 10s. 0d. a week for their board. They are called 'confined men.'

The confined men are hired by the year. The hiring takes place at the principal market towns in May, the married men being usually engaged in February and entering their new situations at May-day.

The single men and also the dairy maids and women servants were formerly hired for the year at May-day. The practice is, however, now gradually dying out, the hiring taking place through register offices, and the term of engagement being subject to one month's notice. The hiring used to take place in the open market place. At Boston and other towns a public hall is now engaged for the purpose by the authorities.

Women are not much employed on the land. In the last century they were reported to be better off in the Fenland than in any other part of the country. When working in the fields they then earned 6d. per day. A great deal of their time was also occupied in spinning flax. They now generally assist at harvest, and in planting and getting in the potatoes, also occasionally in weeding and gathering twitch. They are also employed amongst the woad. Their wages have varied from 9d. a day at the beginning of the century, to 1s. and 1s. 3d. at the present time.

In harvest time, the women and children are generally employed in gleaning in the corn fields, and collect about 6 bushels of wheat, and even up to 12 bushels.

Foremen's wives also add to their income by rearing poultry for the farmer, the food being found from the farm, and the woman being allowed so much a head for all she rears.

From an order of the Commissioners of Sewers made for the repair of the banks, in the reign of Edward III, (1324,) it appears that the rate of wages for labourers was about 2d. per day, the price of wheat being then under 1s. a bushel. This order was to the effect that each owner of land was to find a tumbril and man, not less than 18 years of age, or pay 4d. per day for the tumbril and 2d. for the man.

In the sixteenth century, labourers' wages were about 8d. per day. In the year 1500, in the contract made with May Hake for the erection of the sluice across the Witham, masons were paid 5s. a week.

In Elizabeth's reign, wages were from 6d. to 8d. per day. The rate fixed for the labourers employed in repairing Skirbeck Gowt was 8d. per day. The price of wheat was then about 4s. a bushel. In the reign of Charles II, the wages for this district were fixed, as was then customary, at Quarter Sessions, for a farm labourer at 6d. per day; a bailiff was to have £4 a year and his living; a hind £2 and his living; a dairy maid £2 a year and her living; ordinary women servants £1 10s. 0d.; hedgers and ditchers 10d. per day; common labourers 8d., finding their own food; carpenters and masons 1s. a day. Wheat at that time was about 36s. a quarter.

In the middle, and up to nearly the end of the seventeeth century, ordinary farm labourers were paid from 1s. to 1s. 2d. per day in summer, and 10d. in winter. In the Dykereeves' account of the Parish of Moulton, the wages of the men employed in cleaning out the sewers and similar work were 1s. a day in 1690, and 1s. 3d. in 1737. Later on, 1s. 6d. a day was paid. During the earlier period wheat averaged 45s., varying from 32s. to 60s. During the last 20 years of the eighteenth century the price of wheat increased to 50s., and afterwards to £5 and £6 a quarter. Wages in consequence increased to 10s. and 12s. a week. Foremen then had £16 16s. with their food and lodging; confined labourers, £14 14s.; dairymaids, £5 5s.; carpenters, 2s. 6d. to 2s. 8d. a day; masons and bricklayers, 3s. Meat was about 6d. per lb., butter 9d. to 1s. per lb., coal, 27s. to 30s. per ton.

From 1837-40 the average weekly rate of wages was 14s., wheat averaging 63s. 8d. a quarter. From 1840-60 the average was 12s. a week, and 10s. in winter, wheat averaging 53s. a quarter. The lowest price reached was in 1850-51, when the rate was 2s. a day, wheat being 40s. a quarter, and flour selling at 2s. a stone. In 1855-56, when wheat averaged 72s. 4d. a quarter and flour was sold at 3s. 2d. a stone, wages rose to 2s. 6d. a day. From 1867 to 1872 wages varied from 2s. 3d. to 2s. 6d. a day, wheat averaging 56s. a quarter. From 1873-78 the rate was 2s. 6d. to 2s. 9d., wheat averaging 51s. 4d. During part of this period, owing to an agitation got up by a labourer's union, as much as 3s. a day was paid for a short time. From 1879-86 the rate fell to 2s. and 2s. 3d., and during part of this time, in some places, only 1s. 8d. was paid, wheat averaging only 32s. a quarter. From 1889-95 the rate has been about 2s. a day, the better men getting 2s. 3d.

The following is the rate of wages paid at the May hirings at Boston, for single men:—

Wilson Fox's Report. 1895.

	1892. £	1893. £	1894. £
Head waggoners	18 to 21	18 to 20	18
Horsemen	12 to 15	12 to 14	12 to 14
Plough boys	6 to 13	6 to 12	6 to 12

Ordinary labourers, including piecework, earn from £30 to £40 a year. A man with a family can earn about £10 for the month's work at harvest time, or £6, if he has no family.

Confined and married horsemen, and shepherds hired by the year, and not boarded, earn from £43 to £48 a year. They have also many perquisites, such as free house and garden, potatoes, milk, &c.

Foremen get from 16s. to 20s. a week, with free house and garden, and frequently firing, milk and other perquisites, making their earnings worth about £52 a year.

Wheat has been exceptionally low in price during this period, falling to 16s. a quarter in 1894, and averaging about 20s. The price of food, clothing, and all requisites has also been very low, shop goods costing only about half what they did 25 years ago. A tradesman who has had considerable experience in a village shop states as his opinion, that 25 years ago, "the labouring classes did not live anything like as well as they do now. If they had to live as they used to, they would think they were not living at all."

Wilson Fox's Report.

The average cost of labour for cultivating an acre of wheat has only decreased about 9½ per cent., as compared between 1873 and 1894, whereas the price of wheat has fallen during the same period 64½ per cent.

Willson Fox's Report.

In a report made in 1894 it was stated that from 1860-74 labour cost 35s. an acre, the value of the produce being £8 5s. 0d. In 1894

Boston Chamber of Agriculture Report.

labour cost 30s., as against the value of the produce, £4 8s. 6d.

From enquiries made by the Commissioner as to whether the labour was as efficient as it used to be, the replies he received were to the effect that 90 employers out of 100 were of opinion that the men did less work, and that, owing to the scarcity of able men, farmers had been driven to use machinery more, which was found to be less economical than good labour. The conclusion he arrived at, however, generally, was that labour in Lincolnshire was of very good quality, and that the farmers concurred in saying that it compared favourably with other counties. Some farmers expressed the opinion that they would rather employ a Lincolnshire labourer at 2s. 6d. a day, than a Norfolk or Suffolk man at 1s. And at another meeting he was told that 'our men are very good, compared with other counties,' and that they had some of the best men in the world. He was further informed by a Contractor that the men he obtained from Lincolnshire were the best he ever came across. *Wilson Fox's Report. 1895.*

The tenure of land in the early days of the Fens, during the Saxon period, was so different to that which afterwards prevailed that it is not possible to define with any accuracy the services that were paid for its use either in money or kind. *RENT AND VALUE OF LAND.*

As some guide to its value, there is a record that 20 hides of land were leased at Sempringham, on which the following rents were reserved for the monastery: 2 oxen fit for slaughter, 2 measures of welsh ale and 600 loaves; for the Abbot's private estate 1 horse, 30 shillings of silver or half a pound, one night's pasture, 15 mittan of bright ale, 5 of welsh ale, and 15 sesters of mild ale. *Freeman's Saxons.*

In the beginning of the 13th century the rent of ordinary land in the Fenland was about 6d. per acre, and the better class of land about Frampton and Boston was rented at a shilling an acre. The value of a sheep was then about a shilling; an ox and a horse, 8s. each, wheat, 10d. a bushel. In the early part of the 14th century corn, was very scarce in the Fenland, owing to great floods, and wheat rose to 24s. a quarter, or about three times its ordinary value. In 1324 an abundant harvest reduced the price to 6s. 8d.

The value of the Fens before the attempts made to inclose them, in the middle of the 17th century, was estimated at about 4d. per acre. After the works were completed, as stated in a petition made to the House of Lords, the value of the land in the East Fen was increased to about 12s. an acre, and in the West and Wildmore Fens to 15s.

About a century later the uninclosed fen land in Deeping Fen was worth from 7s. to 8s. an acre, and some of it was in such a state that it could not be let. The value of the common rights on the East and West Fens was estimated at 2s. 10d. an acre. After the West Fen was inclosed, land let by auction realised 34s. an acre. In Holland Fen, soon after inclosure, the average annual value was put by Mr. Parkinson, one of the Inclosure Commission, at 23s. an acre over 22,000 acres, the previous value being about 3s. an acre.

Parkinson.

After the embankment of the peat land on the Witham the average rental of 21,407 acres was 13s., the old value of these lands averaging 2s. 3d. an acre.

Marat's Lincolnshire. 1814.

In 1814 the average rental of land is given by Marat as follows: in Brothertoft, Leverton and Freiston, 45s.; Butterwick, Frampton, Fossdyke, Whaplode and Moulton, 40s.; Swineshead, 30s. to 60s.; Fleet, 30s. to 40s.; Quadring, Surfleet, Leake and Benington, 35s.; Weston, 28s.

Clarke, Royal Ag. Soc. Journal. 1851.

In 1849 Mr. Clarke estimated the average value of the land in the Fenland at 40s. an acre.

The gross estimated rental, as taken from the poor rate assessment for the year 1878, for the three Unions of Boston, Spalding, and Holbeach, containing about 331,807 acres, averaged 40s. an acre. After this, land rose very considerably, but, owing to the continuous wet seasons and low prices, rents fell from 25 to 30 per cent., and, in some cases, are not half now what they were 15 years ago. In the evidence given before the Commission on the Depression in Agriculture, the average reduction in rent, in the neighbourhood of Wainfleet, was given at 30 per cent. Mr. Druce, who reported on the Fen District for the Royal Commission on Agriculture, in 1880, estimated the average value of good arable land, near Boston, at 50s. an acre, and in the East Holland Parishes, at 45s. This was for arable land of good quality and adapted for the growth of celery and potatoes.

As a test of value, the rents, at which some of the land belonging to Charities has been let, may be given. Thus, the land belonging to Porrell and Cowell's Charity, at Benington, containing about 50 acres of grass and arable land and four cottages, was let in 1818, at £142; in 1830, at £144; in 1850, £141; 1860, at £145; 1870, £153 10s.; 1880, £174; 1890, £179. The higher rent, obtained in 1890, was due to the land being let by auction. Conington's Charity, at Leake, containing about 43½ acres, half pasture and half arable, let in 1837 for £97; in 1857 the rental was £104; 1887, £112 10s.; 1877, £114; 1887, £119 12s. The Decoy Farm, in Leake, belonging to Hunston's Charity, let for £50 in 1655; in 1854, with the fen allotments and five acres which had been purchased, making together 397a. 2r. 28p. and a farmstead, the rental was £600. The rent was subsequently raised to £793. A farm in the East Fen, containing about 365 acres of peat soil, the site of which, at the beginning of the present century, was covered with water and reeds, was rented 50 years ago for 30s. an acre; from 1856 to 1876, the rent was 34s. 9d. an acre; from 1876 to 1886, the rent had increased to 60s. an acre; during the next three years it fell to about 40s., and in 1889 had fallen to the old rent of 30s.; and is now let at 25s. an acre. Pinchbeck's Charity Lands in Butterwick, Freiston and Leverton, containing 122a. 1r. 30p., let for £248 in 1837.

A farm in Bourne Fen, let in 1872 for £770, was re-let in 1886 for £250.

In 1893, the assessment in the Kirton Hundred for the Income Tax, under Schedule A, including villages and residences, was £2 3s. 9d. an acre, and in the Skirbeck Hundred, leaving out the parish of Boston, £3 0s. 2d. per acre.

From a report, made by the Boston Branch of the Chamber of Agriculture, in January, 1895, it is stated that rents varied in that district, from 15s. to 30s. an acre, the average being 24s. or 25s. Since 1880, there has been a reduction of from 30 to 50 per cent. A large farm of mixed soil, rented at £1,600 in 1880, was now let at £800. The letting value of land had fallen one-third for best lands, and more than one-half for heavy soils. As regards profits made by the tenants, in 1880 they averaged about £1 an acre, whereas, at the time of the report, there were no profits, except in exceptional cases. *Boston Chamber of Agriculture.*

Mr. Wilson Fox gives the rents as averaging, in the Wainfleet District, 30s. to 50s. for marsh land, 25s. to 45s. for fen land, and 60s. to 100s. for toft, or early potato land; near Boston, for the very best land in small holdings, 60s. to 100s.; farms of about 60 acres, 40s.; Spalding District, 30s. to 40s. Some heavy clay land was let as low as 5s. an acre. *Commission on Agriculture. 1895.*

There is a great demand for land suited for growing early potatoes, and from £4 to £5 an acre is given for this.

Taking an average, in the neighbourhood of Spalding, the reduction in rents on small farms, of from 20 to 70 acres of good land, is estimated to be from 30 to 50 per cent. during the past 20 years; on farms of 70 to 250 acres of good land, 30 per cent.; on farms of 250 acres and upwards, 30 to 40 per cent.; and where the land is bad, 70 per cent.; in the neighbourhood of Grantham, 50 per cent.; and round Sleaford, 33 per cent. on good land, and 60 per cent. on land of bad quality. *Wilson Fox's Report, 1896.*

The Lincolnshire Chamber of Agriculture put the reduction at from 25 to 40 per cent. for good land.

The following examples, taken from Mr. Wilson Fox's report, will show what the freehold value of land was when times were good, as compared to what it is now, in the depressed condition of Agriculture. An arable farm of 300 acres at Spalding, of fair quality, having mixed peat and clay soil, was purchased in 1876 for £19,000, or about £63 an acre; and in 1894 could not find a purchaser at £23 an acre. Another peat farm, in the same locality, of 100 acres, bought 18 years ago for £65 an acre, was sold in 1894 for £23 an acre. A farm of 461 acres, bought in 1885 for £65 an acre *FREEHOLD VALUE. Wilson Fox's Report. 1895.*

was sold in 1892 at the rate of £13 an acre. A farm of 110 acres of good alluvial soil, at Kirton, bought in 1870 for about £74 an acre, could not be sold for £40 an acre in 1891. A farm of 118 acres, in Blankney Dales, bought in 1877 at the rate of £65 an acre, was sold for half this in 1894; and a farm of 92 acres, at Whaplode Drove, the original price of which was about £85 an acre, could not be sold for £40 an acre.

CAUSES OF DEPRESSION.

The fall in the rental and freehold value of land is due to the unfavourable seasons and the low prices of produce. During the series of wet seasons, 1874-1882, the condition of the land became seriously affected, the pastures were deteriorated and the manure washed out of the arable land and there was no opportunity of properly cleaning it. This resulted in a decreased yield and in rot in the sheep. On farms where 10 quarters of oats were grown to the acre, the yield fell to 7, and where 7 or 8 quarters of barley were grown, only 5 or 6 could be harvested. Following on the bad seasons, began a decline in prices, which has since continued. Between 1874 and 1894 the average price of wheat has fallen 60 per cent.; of barley, 53 per cent.; and of oats, 50 per cent.; the average price of wheat for 1874-1884 being 44s. 9d.; for 1894, 19s. 2d.; barley for the same period fell from 35s. to 20s. and oats from 22s. 4d. to 14s. 6d. Wool also has steadily decreased, the average for 1873-1877 being 40s. 2d. a tod; 1883-1887, 21s. 3d. and 1893-1894, 21s. 4d., a decrease of 46 per cent. Cattle have fallen in price during the 12 years, 1882-1894, from 28½ to 34 per cent.

Mr. R. Roberts of Horncastle.

Fieldsend.

Wilson Fox.

RATES AND TAXES.

A. Young.

Arthur Young estimated the parochial rates, at the end of the last century, at 2s. in the £, calculated on the real rent. In the Hundred of Skirbeck he gives 'all sorts of charges' at 3s. 3d. in the £; poor rate only, 2s.

Taking an average of the rates spread over the three Unions of Boston, Spalding and Holbeach, for the year 1878, the amount averaged 2·73s. per acre for poor, sanitary, education and county rate, and 1·61s. for highways; together, 4s. 4d. per acre.

Wilson Fox's Report.

In 1888, the poor and highway rates in the £, in the Spalding Union, came to 25·3d.; in 1893 they were 30·9d.; in the Boston Union, 39·5d. and 39·90d., respectively; in the Holbeach Union 34·1d and 30·9d.

DRAINAGE RATES.

The drainage rates vary very considerably throughout the Fens. In the fens in the Witham district the general taxes vary from 1s. to 7s. 6d. an acre, to which have to be added those levied on the several separate enclosures or Districts, varying from 2s. to 12s. per acre.

In the Black Sluice level, the general taxes vary in the different Districts from 6d. to 1s. 6d., and in the interior Districts from 1s. to 2s. 6d. per acre. The whole of these districts pay the Outfall tax, which amounts to about 1s. 4d. an acre.

In Deeping Fen the general taxes vary from 6d. to 3s. an acre, in addition to the Welland tax of 3s. 2d. an acre.

In the districts under the Court of Sewers, the Dykereeve rates vary from 3d. to 6d. an acre for ordinary purposes, and, when special works have been carried out, reach as high as 2s. 6d.

TITHES.

The Fenland is free from tithes. This is owing to the allotments made in lieu of tithes at the time of the Inclosure of the Fens.

The Fens were originally commons in which every parish had rights. When the several Acts were obtained for dividing and allotting the fens, allotments were given to the Owners of both the great and small tithes, not only for their interests in the inclosed fens but also in lieu of those on the old lands. The income of the Rectors and Vicars is therefore now derived from the rents of these allotted lands.

TENURE.

The Fenland, owing to the circumstances by which it is surrounded, has always had a large number of Freeholders. In the early days the district was a sort of no man's land, and little notice was taken of a Fenman who built himself a mud hut and inclosed a small island. After the Norman Conquest, grants were made to the King's followers of this part of Lincolnshire, in common with the rest of the country, but it was only in the higher part of the Fens that the grantees ever had any real possession of the land granted them. The monasteries, by means of grants made to them from time to time, and by land reclaimed and gradually annexed, became possessed of a considerable tract. These lands were afterwards alienated and distributed. Thus, the Fenland has never been dominated by any large territorial Owners. The distribution of land was also increased by sales made by the Adventurers who reclaimed the Fens in the 17th century; and, subsequently, when the last reclamations were carried out, land was sold in small lots by the Commissioners, to pay for the expenses of inclosure. There are few attractions in the Fenlands to induce a Landowner to live in the district, and, consequently, there are scarcely any resident Owners. It may be said that, throughout the whole of the South Lincolnshire Fenland, there are not, at the present time, any large estates held by single Owners. The high price that land in this district made a few years ago, induced some of the larger Owners to sell the land they held, by auction, in small parcels, the lots frequently consisting of only a single field. This land was either purchased by the tenants or by farmers in the neighbourhood. Times being prosperous, there was also great inducement to invest savings in the purchase of land, and the competition for these small plots was very great.

Land accumulated by purchase during the life of a farmer almost invariably comes into the market again at his death. There is thus constant opportunity for men of small means to become the owners of the land they cultivate. During the prosperous times, between 1860 and 1875, a very large number of small freeholds were thus created, the area of the holdings varying from as little as five acres, up to ten or twenty. On these the purchasers built cottages costing from £150 to £200, and buildings for cows and poultry. At that time, any industrious foreman or labourer of good character, who had saved sufficient money to pay the deposit of 10 per cent. on the purchase money, could obtain the remainder from a lawyer, at 4 per cent. interest. On these small holdings, by dint of work as hard and fare as scanty as that of any colonist, the holder and his family obtained a living. The crops grown were principally wheat and potatoes, which then realised good prices. Cabbages, celery, and bush fruits were also grown, and by the profits from these crops and from butter and poultry, sufficient was made, not only to pay the way, but gradually to clear off the mortgage, or to buy additional land.

During the bad times, which occurred during the wet seasons of 1875-80, and owing to the low prices which have since prevailed, although a very great number of holders of larger farms failed and had to give up their holdings, these little Freeholders held on, and very few of them went under. One of the witnesses who gave evidence before the Small Holdings Committee came from Long Sutton. He was the owner of 7½ acres, which cost him £52/10/- an acre in 1855. He stated that he made a profit off this, although half was cropped with wheat from which he obtained an average of 48 bushels, which sold for only 30/- per quarter. The clear annual profit to the occupying owner was about £40 a year. The same witness stated that within a mile from his house there were 23 Occupiers, not one holding 50 acres. From this land 30 cows yielded 6,000lbs. of butter; 400 hens produced 16,000 eggs, and chickens to the value of £300. All these Occupiers, except two, had sprung up within the last 20 years.

The demand for these small holdings is certainly increasing, and considering the care and attention that is bestowed on the cultivation of the land, the most being made of everything, the quantity of poultry reared, and the large amount of labour employed, the increase of these holdings appears to be a national gain. The children of these small occupiers are sturdy and robust, well fed, well housed and well clothed; they are intelligent and, being brought up to careful and thrifty habits, these families form as fine a population as can be found anywhere in the world.

A. Young.

. The remarks made ninety years ago as to the inhabitants of the Isle of Axholme applies almost as forcibly to the Fenmen. "Almost every house you see is inhabited by a farmer, the proprietor of his farm, of some four or five, to twenty, forty or more acres, cultivated with all the minutiæ of care and anxiety by the hands of the family which are found abroad in some of the rich parts of France and Flanders. They are very poor respecting money, but very happy respecting their mode of existence. Contrivance, mutual assistance by barter and hire, enable them to manage their little farms, though they break all the rules of rural proportion. A man will keep a pair of horses, that has but 3 or 4 acres, by means of vast commons (the unenclosed fens), and working for hire. Their cultivated land being of uncommon fertilty, a farm of 20 acres supports a family very well, as they have generally speaking no fallows, but a endless succession of corn, potatoes, hemp, flax, beans, &c. They do nearly all the work themselves, and are passionately fond of buying a bit of land. Though I have said they are happy, yet I should note that it was remarked to me that these little Proprietors work like negroes, and do not live so well as the inhabitants of the poor house; but all is made amends for by possessing land."

The returns made to the Agricultural Department in 1886 of the Holdings in Great Britian, are grouped in counties, and give therefore no guide as to the number of acres held by each Occupier in the Fens, the circumstances of the rest of the county of Lincoln being entirely different from those of the Fenland.

Mr. Wilson Fox in his report, speaking of the small Freeholders and the effect which the bad seasons and the depression in prices has had on them, says, "They work marvellously hard and for far longer hours than the labourers, while many of them say that they are not in such a good pecuniary position as labourers, and that they do not live as well, seldom eating fresh meat. The sons and daughters of many of them are working simply for their food and clothes" The small men work like slaves; sometimes, in the summer, from 3 a.m. to 9 p.m. As to the size of holdings, some of the early potato men live on 3 acres. Near the towns and on soils suitable for vegetables and fruit, a man can live on a holding of from 5 to 10 acres; but where the ordinary course of farming is followed the least average on which a living can be made is from 30 to 50 acres. The following description of a small holder in the neighbourhood of Wainfleet may be taken as typical of many of the class. "He began life as a labourer and, having saved money out of his wages, he hired 6 acres of land at 66/- an acre. About twenty years ago he bought 12 acres at £106 an acre. He put up all the sheds, built a good stable and made all the fences, which are well kept. He grows early potatoes, bulbs of all sorts, tree and bush fruit, mustard, wheat, mangolds, flowers; also keeps pigs, poultry and bees. His land is kept as clean and neat as it is possible to be. He sells everything to buyers who come round, and only goes to market once a year. His profits for 1893 and 1894 were respectively £86 and £111, besides which bacon, poultry, eggs and vegetables were consumed in the house. The largest items of profit in 1894 were mustard £45; early potatoes £55; potatoes £32; bulbs £27; and pigs £20.

Wilson Fox's Report. 1895.

Druce's Report.

The following figures will give some idea of the number of small Occupiers in the Fenland. In the parish of Leake, containing nearly 10,000 acres, there are only seven Occupiers whose holdings in the parish exceed 100 acres. The total number of Occupiers in the parish is 390, giving an average holding of 25 acres each.

In Friskney, which contains 6,500 acres, there are 129 persons who own their own land. There are 94 persons who own and occupy plots of 20 acres and under, and only 35 who own and occupy farms of over 20 acres; there are 88 tenants of 20 acres and under, against 57 of farms above this size.

J. Russell Jackson.

In Moulton, containing 11,391 acres, there are 231 owners of land, of whom 208 do not own over 100 acres; and of these 181 do not own over 50 acres. Of the 231 Owners, 71 cultivate their own land. There are 169 Occupiers not exceeding 50 acres, of whom 59 occupy under 5 acres.

TENANCIES

Land in the Fenland, except in the case of that leased by public bodies, is as a rule let on yearly tenancies. Where leases are given, they generally run for 7 or 10 years. The covenants as to cropping are very easy and seldom enforced, and are only inserted in order to secure protection against bad tenants. A reasonable view is always taken by all parties of breaches of agreement as to selling off and the course of cropping. As a matter of practice the covenants as to cropping are put on one side and if a tenant farms fairly, he may do as he likes. Tenancies almost invariably run from Lady Day.

Commission on Agriculture. 1895.

The tenants as a rule consider that they have all the fixity of tenure they require and on the whole a very friendly relationship exists between all classes on the land.

TENANT RIGHT.

A sound system of tenant-right existed in Lincolnshire long previous to the passing of the *Agricultural Holdings Act*, and the farmers prefer to hold under this, as they consider it more fair. Both Mr. Druce and Mr. Wilson Fox in their reports bear testimony to the fact that the farmers in this district almost universally prefer to hold under the Custom of the Country than under the Act. It is the invariable practice, when tenants are entering or quitting farms, for each to appoint a valuer to settle the amount to be paid by the incoming or outgoing tenant. A general scale of allowances for tenant-right has been agreed to by the Lincolnshire Valuers' Association. Briefly these allowances are as follows:

Commission on Agriculture.

The tenant is allowed on quitting:

(*a*) Cost of all permanent buildings and other substantial repairs put up with the sanction of the landlord on a 20 years' principle, and 10 years when the tenant has only found labour.

(*b*) Under draining with pipes at proper depth, 10 years for labour only, 15 when tenant has found tiles. The accounts have to be presented at the audit following the completion of the work.

(c) Linseed, cotton or rape cake one-third; corn cake, malt or other manufactured feeding stuffs, a sixth, if consumed during the last year of tenancy; or one-sixth and one-twelfth for two years.

(d) Bones, if dry, used with green crops consumed on the farm, the whole cost, if used the last year, and half for the preceding year. If used on pasture, if dry, 10 years; dissolved 5 years.

(e) Artificial manures, used with green crops consumed on the farm on the last year of tenancy, the whole cost.

(f) The claim for bones and manure is not to exceed the average cost of the two preceding years.

(g) Lime, 7 years' allowance; claying, marling or chalking, 12 years.

(h) Grass seeds, the last year's bill and sowing, if not stocked after October 11.

(i) Dead fallows all labour, but not rents, rates or taxes, unless these were paid on entrance.

(j) Wheat and other seed, cost of seed and sowing.

The out-going tenant generally prepares and sows the land coming for wheat; he also ploughs the land coming for fallows, and prepares and sows the land coming for spring corn, being paid in each case for seed and labour. On fallows manure is allowed for, and the herbage, if the land was ploughed in October.

The valuations generally amount, under ordinary conditions, from 25s. to 40s. an acre. Say, a farm having one-sixth in pasture where a fair quantity of cake has been used, 35s. to 45s.

Allowances for cross cropping, and dilapidations are generally taken as only extending over the last year.

The charges for valuing tenant-right run from $3\frac{1}{2}$ per cent. on an inventory of £100 to $2\frac{1}{2}$ per cent. on £300, and on large farms about $1\frac{1}{2}$ per cent., exclusive of stamp.

ALLOTMENTS.

A. Young's *Survey of Lincolnshire.*

The system of small holdings has been in existence in the Fenland for more than a century. In 1799 the allotment system in the parish of Freiston is thus described, "Mr. Linton's grandfather, and father before him, continued Allotments of so much land to cottagers as will enable the labourer living in them to keep a cow, a pig and a very few sheep, chiefly raised from cade lambs, (the fens were unenclosed commons at that time), which Mr. Linton himself also continued and formed others...In general they have from 2 to 7 acres at the rent of the country, paying about 40/- for the cottage, exclusive of the value of the land ... Fencing and digging the garden, he does himself in mornings and evenings; all other attentions by his wife and family. He fattens the calf and sells to the butcher. He sells some butter, except when the lambs are rearing. Mr. Linton has not observed that having land in this manner has an effect in taking them from their work, whilst the system tends to bring up their families in habits of industry; and he scarcely knows an instance of families thus provided applying to the parish for assistance ; and he is well convinced that he loses nothing by this application of land .Wherever this system is found poor rates are low."

At Crowland, for over 50 years, there have been about 150 half-acre allotments and there are about 100 occupiers of from 2 to 7 acres.

Near Spalding, Lord Carrington has 177 holdings and allotments, under and including 5 acres. Those of an acre are let at 32s. and 33s., and those of a rood in the fen at 30s., the landlord paying all the rates, and allowing each tenant who pays his rent on the rent day, a bonus of 1s.

Mr. Charles Sharpe of Sleaford has about 120 acres of allotments, of an acre each, near Heckington and Hale. The system was commenced with half acre plots, about 10 or 12 years ago, but owing to the representation of the men, that $\frac{1}{2}$ an acre was an inconvenient size to work, the plots were increased to an acre. The number of plots has since been increased by the Benefit Societies, and the Rural Authority to 230, in addition to Mr. Sharpe's. The chief crops grown on these allotments are barley and potatoes; but enough vegetables are also grown for home consumption.

Under the recent Allotment Act, the Corporation of Boston has provided 33 acres of allotment ground in the neighbourhood of the town, which is let out in plots of about a rood each, at rentals varying from £4 10s. to £6, free of all taxes. The Holland County Council has also purchased land and provided allotments in the parishes of Skirbeck, Kirton and Brothertoft, Wigtoft and Chapel Hill, Holbeach Hurn, and St. Marks, Pinchbeck West and East, Gosberton, Moulton Eaugate, Whaplode and Whaplode Drove, the total area purchased being $184\frac{1}{2}$ acres. The takes vary from half an acre to one acre ; and the rent averages £2 16s. an acre.

SMALL HOLDINGS ACT.
Under the powers of the Small Holdings Act, the County Council has purchased $47\frac{1}{2}$ acres of land at Freiston, at £55 10s. an acre, and 88 acres at Spalding, at £42 11s. an acre, which is let out in plots of from 1 to 4 acres, at an average rent of about 44/- an acre. Altogether applications have been made to the Council for small holdings to the extent of 900 acres. The money for the purchase of this land was raised by a loan from the Public Works Loan Commissioners, repayable over 50 years, at $3\frac{1}{2}$ per cent. interest.

MARKETS AND FAIRS.
The Fenland is well provided with markets, especially in the southern part, a very great advantage to the small occupiers, for the disposal of their butter, eggs, fruit and other produce. In the northern part, Boston has a market on two days in the week for corn and general produce, and on one of these days for cattle, sheep and pigs. Lincoln, Sleaford, Spilsby and Horncastle, although not in the Fens, are sufficiently near to afford markets for the northern and western part of the district. At Sleaford, a weekly auction is held

for cattle, sheep and pigs, to which a great deal of stock is sent from the Fens. In the south-west, Bourne has a market, and Donington also, on Thursday; and in the south-east, there is a market at Crowland, for pigs on one day of the week, and for meat and vegetables on another day. Spalding has its market on Tuesday, Holbeach on Thursday, and Long Sutton on Friday, at which there is also a weekly auction sale for stock.

The principal fairs are, at Boston, in May for sheep and cattle; in August for fat stock; in September for mares and foals; in November for horses, and in December, the Christmas show of fat stock. At Spalding, at the end of April, in June, August, September and December. At Long Sutton, in May, for cattle and sheep, and in September for horses. At Donington, in May for cattle, September for beast, and October for cattle and horses. Holbeach, May and September for cattle, sheep and horses. A fair for the sale of cheese used to be held at Swineshead, in October; the fair still continues, but the sale of cheese has ceased.

The Lincolnshire Agricultural Society holds its meetings at Boston and Spalding, in rotation with the other towns in the county.

AGRICULTURAL SOCIETY.

The first Society was established in 1819, and was subsequently merged into the North Lincolnshire Society, and in 1868 extended to the whole county. In addition to the encouragement given by this Society, by its exhibition and prizes, to improvement in the quality of stock, and in bringing before the small Holders novelties in implements, it has endeavoured to practically educate the men in charge of machinery, by giving prizes for the management of steam engines and the economical consumption of coal. There is also an annual show of horses, cattle and poultry at Long Sutton by a Society established in 1836.

For several years a Society for the Encouragement of Good Ploughing, was held at Benington, at which prizes were given away; but this ceased to exist a few years ago.

CHAPTER XV.

WATERWAYS, ROADS, BRIDGES AND RAILWAYS.

MEANS OF TRANSPORT.

THE Fenland has from the earliest times been well provided with the means of transporting the produce from the land to market and of obtaining supplies for the use of the farm. The Romans not only caused good main roads to be made, leading from the coast to the interior, and traversing the district from north to south; but also provided navigable waterways which extended throughout the whole length of the Fenland. The three main rivers, the Witham, the Welland and the Glen, and also Wainfleet Haven, afforded a means of communication from the sea to the different parts of the district. In modern times, to the facilities of transport already existing have been added the railway system provided by the Great Northern, Great Eastern and Midland Companies.

WATERWAYS.

In North Holland and Lindsey the River Witham has from very early times been the chief waterway. As far as can be ascertained with any reasonable approach to historical accuracy, the Romans made this a navigable river, and connected it with the Trent by means of the Fossdyke, and with the sea by means of the tidal creek which extended to Dogdyke. For some time after their first settlement at Lincoln, the port to which their vessels made was in Wainfleet Haven. This involved several miles of land carriage, and to avoid this the Witham channel was opened out, if not of sufficient size to allow of the vessels which came across the sea to get up to Lincoln, yet so as to allow these to reach Dogdyke on the tide, and there to discharge into smaller boats which were adapted for the navigation above this point. By this course and also by the Fossdyke into the Trent, the large quantities of grain which were grown in the Fenland were exported for the use of the troops in Germany and Gaul. The Car Dyke on the west side of the Witham Fens was also used as a canal reaching from Lincoln to the Nene, and supplied a waterway for all the western side of the Fens from Boston to Bourne, while the centre of this district was supplied by the Hammond Beck, connected with which was the Risegate Eau, which also joined Bicker Haven.

In South Holland the Welland extended through the Fenland from the Wash (*Metaris Estuarium*) to Crowland, and the Glen afforded a waterway for the district between the Welland and the Car Dyke. The Westlode, another work of the Romans, also afforded an outlet for land lying south of Spalding. The Old Shire Drain was a natural water course running from Crowland to the coast, while other parts of the South Holland district were provided for by the tidal creeks now known as Lutton Leam, Fleet Haven, Lawyer's Creek and Holbeach River. From this it will be seen that during the Roman occupation the Fenland was well provided with means of transit by water. All these means of communication remained in existence up to the time of the reclamation of the Fens.

Previous to the reclamation there may also be added Kyme Eau, Billinghay Skerth, and Holland Dyke, the North Forty-Foot Drain, Mid-Fen Dyke, the Sibsey River and Hilldyke River which communicated with the Witham at Anton's Gowt. Several of the more important sewers, too, were available for small boats. In the orders made by Commissions of Sewers, frequent reference is made to the fact that sewers ought to be maintained of sufficient capacity for boats to pass along. Thus, in the 16th century, in an order directing that new bridges shall be built over the Risegate Eau in Quadring Fen and Bicker, it is directed that they shall be 'of such height that boats might pass under.' So also with regard to the bridges over the sewers in Kirton Fen, Frampton Fen, and at Lichfield End, it is directed that they shall be 12ft. wide and of sufficient height for boats.

When the works for the improvement of the Witham were carried out in the middle of the last century, and the Grand Sluice erected across the river, provision was made for its navigation by the construction of locks. Subsequently the navigation was handed over to a Company of Proprietors. Until the establishment of the Great Northern Railway, the Witham navigation with its branches, the Horncastle and Sleaford Canals, formed the most important means of transport for corn and coal in North Holland. The Witham was also extensively used as a means of locomotion, steam packet-boats running regularly between Lincoln and Boston, and taking passengers to and from the market towns. The large main drains were also provided with locks and in other ways made suitable for navigation. Hobhole and Maud Foster Drains, with several of their branches, were extensively used for the conveyance of coal, corn and road material to the farms in the East and West Fens; and the Black Sluice afforded a connection between Boston, Swineshead and Donington, and the villages adjacent to it. In the south, the Welland afforded navigation for coasting vessels up to Spalding, whence barges could get to Crowland, and by the Glen and Bourne Eau to Bourne, and also by the Vernatt's to Pode Hole, and by the canalised portion of the river to Stamford. After the construction of railways, the traffic on the rivers and drains fell off considerably. At the present time, the amount of produce, road material, manure and similar heavy traffic conveyed, is very limited. From those parts of the Fenland not provided with railway accommodation, packet boats drawn by horses, still bring passengers, with their baskets of butter and other produce, to market.

The history of these navigations has already been dealt with, to a certain extent, in the Chapters on the Witham, the Welland and Boston Harbour.

FOSSDYKE NAVIGATION.

This navigation was originally made by the Romans, but subsequently allowed to go to decay. It was opened out again by King Henry I, in 1121, 'for the purpose of bringing navigable vessels from the Trent to the city of Lincoln.' In the reign of Charles II, an Act was passed empowering any person to open the communication through the Fossdyke to Torksey. Under the powers of this Act, the channel was again cleaned out. In 1846 the Great Northern Railway Company leased the navigation from Mr. Ellison, who was then the owner of it, for 894 years, at a yearly rent of £9,570 5s. 3d. In 1879 the navigation became vested in the Joint Committee of the Great Northern and Great Eastern Railway Companies.

22 and 23 Car. ii.

1846.

42 and 43 Vict. 1879.

The length is 10 miles 60 chains. There is one lock at Torksey into the Trent, 80ft. long, 16½ft. wide, with 5ft. on the sill. The traffic in 1888 from the Board of Trade Returns amounted to 25,096 tons. The Revenue was £1,699, and the expenses of maintenance £1,010 leaving a net revenue of £689.

WITHAM NAVIGATION.

The early history of this navigation has been already given with that of the river. In 1846 it was leased to the Great Northern Railway Company for 999 years, at an annual rent of £10,545. Since the Railway Company became the owners, the traffic has very much fallen off. The chief articles of transport are manure, corn, gravel and coal. Boats carrying from 50 to 60 tons can navigate to and from the Trent, the Ouse and the Humber, and the canals connected with those rivers. The tolls between Boston and Lincoln or Torksey are 2/- per ton. For shorter distances, 1d. per mile. The rate for manure is less. The length of the navigation from Boston to Lincoln is 31 miles 60 chains. There are 3 sets of locks. The lock at the Grand Sluice is 59ft. long, 30ft. wide, with 10ft. of water; at Horsley Deeps, 84ft. long, 17ft. 6in. wide, with 6½ft. on the sill; at Stamp End, near Lincoln, 82ft. long, 17ft. 10in. wide, with 6½ft. on the sill. The rise at Horsley Deeps is 8ft. and at Stamp End, 5ft. Barges, 78ft. long, 14ft. 10in. beam, and 5ft. deep, can navigate from Boston to the Trent. The traffic is given in the Board of Trade Returns of 1888, as 20,567 tons; the revenue, as

£1,546; expenses of maintenance, £2,301; leaving a deficiency of £755.

HORNCASTLE NAVIGATION.

At the end of the last century, a canal was constructed from the Witham near Tattershall Ferry to the town of Tattershall, by John Gibson of Tattershall and John Dyson of Bawtry. An Act was obtained in 1792 for purchasing this canal for the sum of £840, and for enlarging and extending it along the course of the river Bane to Horncastle. The capital authorised to be raised was £25,000. The tolls were fixed at 2/- per ton for the whole distance and in proportion for portions of the same. The canal was 11 miles in length. There were to be 7 locks, and the excavation was not to exceed 5ft. below the surface of the land. If in any one year the revenue allowed of a dividend of more than 8 per cent., the tolls were to be reduced. This clause was repealed in the subsequent Act. In 1800 a second Act was obtained, giving power to raise a further sum of £20,000, and authorising a further maximum toll of 1/3 per ton. The canal was opened in 1802.

32 Geo. iii, c. 107. 1792.

39 and 40 Geo. iii. c. 109. 1800.

At the present time the canal is practically derelict, the locks are decayed and out of order, and it is no longer used for navigation.

KYME EAU AND THE SLEAFORD NAVIGATION.

This waterway is fed by a natural stream, which rises on Willoughby and Sudbrooke Heaths, and, flowing past Wilsford, is fed by a number of springs at Bully Wells a short distance west of Sleaford, whence, under the name of the river Slea, it flows past Haverholme Priory and Anwick, and thence, under the name of Kyme Eau, through the fens of Ewerby, Anwick and South Kyme, to the Witham at Chapel Hill. The lower part of this river appears to have been navigable from very early times.

In the 16th year of the reign of Edward III, the Earl of Angus exhibited a petition to the King, representing that "there was a certain water called the Ee of Kyme, betwixt Docdyke, on the east, and Brent Fen, on the south, which did run through the lands of the said Earl for the space of 6 miles in length; but was so obstructed and stopped, by reason of mud and filth, that ships laden with wine, wool and other merchandise could neither pass through the same in summer nor winter as they used to do, except it were scoured and cleansed, and the banks so raised, that the tops of them might appear to mariners passing that way, whensoever the marshes there should be overflowed," and he stated that he was willing to do the work at his own expense, provided the King would grant him certain dues on the merchandise passing in ships though the same. Reference is again made to this river in a Presentment made in the 50th year of the same reign, in which complaint is made of the dues enacted by the Earl on boats going from Boston to Kesteven by this navigation.

In 1794 an Act was obtained for making a canal from the Witham near Chapel Hill, along the course of the Kyme Eau and the river Slea, to Sleaford. This canal is about 13½ miles long. Two locks were constructed, one at Lower Kyme and the other at Flax Dyke in Ewerby. The capital authorised to be raised was £19,500. The dividend was limited to eight per cent. and the maximum tolls fixed at 2/- per ton.

<small>32 Geo. iii. c. 106. 1794.</small>

The amount of navigation along this canal having become very small the Company, in 1878, obtained power to abandon it. By the Act, power was obtained to close the canal for navigation and dissolve the Company, and to dispose of any property belonging to it. After the 1st of December, 1878, all rights in reference to the navigation, created by the first Act, ceased; the Landowners were to be compensated by the Company for any culverts, banks, or other works, constructed for the purposes of the canal or for the convenience of the Landowners, which it was necessary should be maintained after the navigation was closed, if a claim were sent in within six months after the notice of abandonment; the company were to fill up the locks at the Corn Mill, the site of Dyer's Mill and the Coggleford Mill to a level corresponding with the height of the adjacent banks; for the protection of the Haverholme Estate, through which the canal extended for five miles, the Anwick Lock, the Haverholme Lock and the Paper Mill Lock were to be placed in repair; and the navigation between these locks was to be vested in the owner of the Estate. Power is reserved to the Owner to substitute at any time for the upper gates of the three locks a pair of draw doors and to remove the lower gates; or he may fill up the lock pits; the right of using the towing path on the north bank of the navigation, between Haverholme Lock and Anwick Lock, is reserved to the owner of the Haverholme Estate, so long as he shall think fit to use it, and he is liable during such period to repair and make good any injury to the bank; the company were also bound to put Kyme Lower Lock, the first lock from the River Witham on the Kyme Eau, in repair, and this lock was vested in the Witham Commissioners, the cost of maintaining the lock to be repaid by the riparian proprietors on the stream above the lock, in the proportion in which the same is used by such Owners; the Commissioners may at any time, if they deem it desirable, remove the gates, and fill up the lock pit. The Company were to scour out the navigation and put any public banks or bridges in repair, before being relieved of their responsibility with respect to the same; the duty of scouring out and roding Kyme Eau and maintaining the banks was to revert to the parties who were liable before the canal Act was passed.

<small>41 Vict., c. 88. 1878.</small>

THE WELLAND (STAMFORD AND SPALDING) NAVIGATION.

In the reign of Queen Elizabeth, a petition of the Corporation of Stamford complained that "the pitiful sight of the ruins, decays

<small>1876.</small>

and remains as well of the ancient buildings of many parish churches, as of other large and strong houses and beautiful monuments, sometime erected and built within the said town ; that the same hath not only been environed and walled with a wall of good strength for that time, but also very populous and well inhabited by a number of wealthy and notable merchants, whose wealth and riches began, grew and increased, by reason of an ancient river, named the Welland, which passed from and through that town to the sea, and to the ports of Boston and Lynn and other low countries in Lincolnshire, Norfolk and Cambridgeshire, to the great enriching of the said counties, but that to have and enjoy again the benefit of the said river and to make the same navigable (as before time it hath been) is, by the judgement of wise and expert men, feasible and manifestly to be proved how it may be done, although the accomplishing thereof be chiefly hindered by the division of the ancient course thereof into divers streams for the erection of 6 or 7 water mills now standing between Stamford and Deeping, which mills not being of that account as to be preferred to the advantage which would follow the making the said river again navigable," they asked for power to be given to make a river or new cut for the passage of boats, ' bellingers,' lighters and other vessels. An Act of Parliament was passed, granting the powers asked for, which were further extended in the reign of King James.

At a General Session of Sewers, held at Stamford, in the reign of King James I, it was decreed that it should be lawful for the Corporation of Stamford to make a river, of such breadth and depth as they should think fit, for the passage of boats and barges, from the north side of the River Welland, from the east end of the town of Stamford and Hudd's Mill, across the river called Newstead River or the Wash, and thence through Affington, Tallington, West Deeping, Market Deeping, and past Market Deeping corn mill, to rejoin the ancient course of the river, and thence in the course before stated, unto the Outfall to the sea at Boston Deeps. The Corporation were enabled to make such locks, sluices and other works as were necessary for the navigation, the expense of which undertaking was then estimated at £2,000. The Commissioners of Sewers also ordained, as this work was undertaken at the expense of the Corporation and their friends, that the Aldermen and Burgesses, and their successors, should receive, for all boats passing through each lock, such a competent consideration as should be fit and convenient. This order was confirmed by King James I, who fixed the tonnage at the sum of 3d. ; and also granted to the Corporation the fishery of the new river.

The work of constructing the new river was undertaken by Daniel Wigmore, and the tolls arising from the navigation were leased to him by the Corporation of Stamford at a very nominal rent for 80 years, and afterwards the lease was renewed every 40 years, on payment of a fine of £100.

The length of the Cut from Hudd's Mill below Stamford to the lock, at East Deeping, was 9½ miles, and on this length 12 locks were erected, which were made of a capacity to receive vessels of 7ft. beam. Vessels of greater burden than 15 tons could not navigate the Cut. Before the construction of railways, the goods, consisting chiefly of coal and timber, were usually taken up to Stamford in gangs of four lighters, of from 7 to 14 tons burden. The voyage from the Scalp, at the mouth of the River Witham, where the ships lay to discharge their cargoes, through Spalding to Stamford was about 50 miles, and was performed in 3 or 4 days.

Report of T. Telford. 1810. In 1809, a Meeting of Landowners, Merchants and Traders, held at Stamford, directed Mr. Thomas Telford to report to them as to the best means of improving the inland communication between the neighbourhood of Stamford and the sea. In a report dated January 8th, 1810, Mr. Telford, after describing the more inland portion of the proposed canal from Oakham to Stamford, stated that it would be necessary to improve the navigation of the Welland to the second lock, a distance of three miles, but that, as it would have cost much more to render the old navigation perfect, he advised that a new canal should be made to near Kate's Bridge, and thence passing along the Car Dyke to Horbling, should there join 'that excellent drain,' the South Forty-Foot, by which means access would be obtained to the Witham at Boston. The South Forty-Foot was to be deepened two feet, and the lock at the Black Sluice enlarged. This scheme was never carried out.

Another scheme was submitted by Mr. Brown, by which the Welland was to be the means of communication between Stamford and the sea, the difficulty in this case being the condition of the Welland, which was reported to have been growing worse and worse for some years from neglect and mismanagement, in consequence of which the channel required deepening, and the locks and other works extensive repairs. It was contended, on behalf of the Promoters, that, as the Lessee had neglected to maintain the canal in proper order, the Corporation of Stamford ought to take it out of his hands.

The tolls, liberties and profits arising from the navigation were let by the Corporation from time to time to various lessees, but the traffic from the navigation decreased so much, after the opening of the railways, that the amount received from the tolls did not cover the working expenses. There being no probability of an increase, and the locks and other works having become ruinous through the neglect of the Lessees to perform the covenants entered into by them, *Abandonment of the Navigation. 1864.* in 1864, by agreement with the Corporation, the existing lease was surrendered and the navigation became disused. *1870.* In 1870 the Corporation, with the consent of the Treasury, sold their rights in the canal to the adjoining Landowners, and the channel in many places is now filled up.

BOURNE EAU.

This river runs between Bourne North and South Fens, from Bourne to the River Glen at Tongue End, a distance of 3¼ miles. It is fed by a strong spring, which rises on the west side of the town. This rivulet drives three mills before it reaches Bourne Eau.

There is no record existing as to when this natural stream was first embanked, but reference is made to it under the name of 'Bourne Ald Ea,' or 'Brunne Ea,' as far back as the 13th century, when an Order of Sewers was made that "Brunne Ea ought to be raised and scoured by the towne of Brunne to Goderam's Cote, on the north side, and on the south to Merehirne." In 1376 an order was made by a Commission of Sewers that Brunne Ald Ea ought to be repaired, raised and cleansed, and maintained by the town of Brunne and the Abbot of Brunne, from Brunne unto Goderam's Cote; and subsequently another order was made, to the effect that the banks ought to be enlarged to 12ft. thick, and made 2ft. higher.

1376.

By the Black Sluice Act of 1765 provision was made for the heightening and strengthening of the bank of Bourne Eau, by the Black Sluice Commissioners.

1765.

The bed of Bourne Eau is above the level of the adjacent fens, and the banks, being made of peat, are very porous, and a constant source of danger to the fen land. For the protection of the fens the Black Sluice Commissioners, who are liable for the maintenance of the north bank, have placed self-acting doors across the Eau at Tongue End, pointing towards the Glen, to prevent the flood water from that river backing up; and an overfall of 20ft. in length has been fixed in the bank, so that when the water rises to a height equal to 23ft. above the sill of the Black Sluice, or 14·30ft. above *Ordnance datum*, it flows over into the Wear Dyke, which is connected with the South Forty-Foot at Gutheram Cote.

In 1781 an Act was obtained for improving the navigation of the River called Bourne Eau, from the town of Bourne to its junction with the river Glen, at a place called Tongue End. The Preamble of this Act recites that the river had become choked with mud and the navigation nearly lost; that if it were scoured out and cleansed, and a staunch erected, it would be of great local advantage. The Act gave power to appoint Trustees to carry the works out. The Trustees were to be the Lord of the Manor of Bourne, and the Members for the time being; the owner of the old inclosure called Bourne South Fen and Thurlby Fen pastures, the Lord of the Manor of Bourne Abbots, and nine other persons appointed by these Trustees, together with all holders of £100 stock in the company. The tolls were limited to 2s. 6d. per ton of goods carried. The

NAVIGATION ACT.
21 Geo. ii, c. 22.
1781.

owner of Bourne South Fen and Thurlby Fen pastures, who was then liable for the maintenance of the South Bank, adjoining Bourne South Fen, was to be exonerated from future liability on payment to the Trustees of £60 a year, the bank in future to be maintained by the Trustees. The depth of water was to be 5ft., and the width 30ft.

STOPPAGE OF THE NAVIGATION. 1860.

The navigation ceased to be of any importance after the opening of the Railway to Spalding in 1860. In 1866 all navigation on the river ceased.

The particulars of a serious breach which occured in the North Bank, flooding the fens, has already been described.

ROADS.

Although previous to the Roman occupation there must have been means of communication between the different parts of the country, it is very doubtful whether any defined or constructed roads existed. Of the main roads made by the Romans there exist not only historical accounts, but traces of them remain to the present day. The direction of some of the branch roads rests more upon conjecture.

Galen.

The Romans commenced the construction of roads when Agricola was the Proprætor, and they were continued, and those that had been allowed to get out of order repaired, by Trajan. "Such as were rough and over-grown with thorns he cleared and ridded; and where rivers were not fordable he made bridges; if a way lay too much about he made it more direct and straight, and if the way was rugged he took care to smooth and level it."

ROMAN ROADS.

The main line passing through the Fenland was a loop of the great road leading from south to north, said to be a British road or track, called Ermyn Street, afterwards adopted by the Romans, (*Via Herminia*). It is now known as the High Dyke. This road, after crossing the river Nene, went by Lolham Bridges, a construction made by the Romans to carry the road over the fenny ground adjacent to the Welland, pursued a north easterly course across the Glen at Kate's Bridge, through Thurlby, Bourne, Cawthorpe, and Ancaster (*Causennæ*), thence passing about a quarter of a mile east of Sleaford, through Ruskington, Dorrington, Blankney and Metheringham, to Lincoln, where at the bottom of Canwick Hill it joined the Foss Road from Newark, and passing along the lower part of the City, ascended the hill and passing through Newport gate, finally joined the main road to the Humber. Another road stated to be of Roman origin is the one coming from the high country by Bolingbroke, Stickford, Sibsey, crossing the Witham by a ferry, the site of which was a little above the present ferry at St. John's Lane, then along the west side of the Haven and across the Hammond Beck, by another ferry, through Kirton to Gosberton, at the top end of Bicker Haven, and thence to Donington and by the Bridge End

Stukely.

Causeway through Horbling, to join the main road to Lincoln. From Gosberton another branch went eastward, through Surfleet and Pinchbeck to Spalding, and thence across the Welland and through Holbeach to Wisbech. Along part of this course, at Bridge End, remains of the foundations of the original road, consisting of stone and gravel have been found, and along the road through Lincoln distinct traces of the old Roman causeway have been discovered, from 8ft. to 9ft. below the level of High Street, buried by a mass of rubbish and earth. *Anderson's Guide to Lincoln.*

Another road which must undoubtedly have been in existence in the time of the Romans is the one from Wainfleet, passing through Irby, Steeping, Spilsby, Winceby, and Horncastle—which was a Roman station—and thence by Baumber, Wragby, Sudbrooke, Holme and Langworth, to Lincoln. This road formed the means of communication between the Port of Wainfleet and the camps at Horncastle and Lincoln, a branch going off also to another camp at Burgh.

The main road from Wainfleet, through all the villages in East Holland, to Boston; and the road from Heckington, through Swineshead and Wigtoft to join the Spalding road at Gosberton, if not made by the Romans, must both have existed from very early times. The Roman Bank, made by the Romans, afforded a road from the Welland at Cowbit to the Nene at Tydd St. Mary.

Later on, a road was made by the monks along the east side of the Welland, connecting Crowland and Spalding. This was afterwards superseded, and probably buried, by the Barrier Bank.

The road from Sutterton through Fossdyke, crossing the sands called the Welland Wash, and thence to Holbeach, has attracted some attention, as this is supposed to be the route taken by King John after his stay at Swineshead Abbey, when his luggage was lost in the sea. The crossing of the Wash was always a dangerous proceeding, and guides obtained a living by piloting passengers across the sands and marshes. In an old Map of Lincolnshire, by Ewan Brown, published in the middle of the last century, is given a perpetual tide table for Fossdyke and Cross Keys Washes. The first column contains the age and appearance of the moon, then follows the time at which it is 'full sea,' and then the time at which the Wash begins and ends, the interval between being that when it would be safe to pass over. There is no date attached to the map, but there is reason to fix the time of its publication about the year 1730. FOSSDYKE WASH.

A bridge was built across the Welland at Fossdyke in 1794, which will be described in a subsequent part of this Chapter.

There is very little information obtainable as to the condition of the roads previous to the reclamation of the Fens. Occasional references are to be found as to orders made on the Abbots and other owners of lands to repair certain roads, on the

NORDYKE CAUSEWAY.

ground that land had at one time been specially granted to them for this purpose Thus, with respect to the road leading from Spilsby to Boston, which was designated as "The King's Highway from Boston to the Humber," the part lying between Stickney and Sibsey was frequently flooded and always dangerous, especially near Nordyke Causeway, and when the floods were out it was unsafe for a horsemen to cross without a guide. In the 13th century a presentment was made before the Justices itinerant, that two men carrying a corpse from Stickney to Sibsey, to be buried in the Churchyard there, 'drowned' it on Nordyke Causeway; and that, in consequence of the neglect of the Abbot of Revesby to repair the road, divers persons were drowned every year; and the Sheriff was ordered to seize the goods of the monastery if the Abbot continued to neglect the repairs.

RAMPER.

This road, as also that leading from Wainfleet to Boston, and also other roads in the Fenland which are higher than the surrounding land, are frequently spoken of as 'the Ramper' probably from their having formerly acted as *ramparts* against the spread of the floods.

BROTHERHOUSE AND SPALDING ROAD.

In the eleventh century Abbot Egelric made a 'causey' or roadway, called Elrick Road, of faggots with gravel over them, from Deeping to Spalding, a distance of 12 miles, for the advantage of passengers, 'a most costly work but of extraordinary necessity.'

Dugdale. 1324.

In 1324 the Commissioners appointed by the King to view the banks in Holland presented this road, which is described as the common road betwixt Pichale and Brotherhouse and thence to the Clote and to Croyland, as having been damaged by trenches cut across it; and they ordered that from henceforth no trenches should be made to the hindrance of the King's Highway; and that where the trenches had been made bridges should be provided so that carts and ordinary droves could pass over.

HOLLAND CAUSEWAY. 1283.

In the reign of Henry III, the Jurors for the Wapentakes of 'Kirketone, Ellow, and Aveland,' chosen to enquire concerning a certain causey called Holand Causey, and of the bridge called Peccebrigge or Briggdyke (Bridge End Causeway), found that certain lands had been given to the Prior of St. Saviour's, at the head of the said causey, near the site of the Priory, for the repair and maintenance of this road from the head thereof to the Innome of Donington. Also, that the Canons of that Priory had obtained a Bull from the Pope to exhort the people of the country to contribute towards the repair of that causey, by means whereof they collected much money, with which, and the rents of the land, they used to repair the same, till 20 years last past, when they were hindered by a flood and could not do it, since when they had appropriated the money to other purposes. The Jury found that this causey ought to be repaired by the Prior of St. Saviour's and by the town of

Dugdale.

Donington, unto the head of the same towards Holland, in respect of their lands lying on each side of the ground called the Innome, given for that purpose; and as to the bridge, that this had been built by the Prior of Spalding, and had since been repaired by him, and that he took toll of persons passing over it; and they found that the Prior of Spalding was liable for the maintenance, and that the causey ought to be so broad that carts and carriages might meet thereon; and the bridge of Peccebrigge to be so made as that men riding on horseback might also meet thereon. In 1280 the Prior of Spalding was summoned and ordered to repair Peccebrigge.

Again in the reign of Edward I, at an Inquisition held at Gosberton, an order was made as to the repair of 'Holand Causey,' with the little bridges, by the Landowners in Donington, as to the east end, and by the Prior of St. Saviour's, as to the west end. [1293.]

In 1376, a Jury found that the Prior of Haverholme "ought to provide a boat at the Bothe near Wath Mouth, at its junction with Kyme Eau, to transport foot folks over the water, as well by night as by day, so often as any man should have occasion to pass that way, and that he had not done it, to the great damage of passengers travelling that way; also that the town of Great Hale, with the commons, ought to repair and maintain the Causey of Gerwick into Pingelhyrne, both for horse men and foot folk." [KYME EAU FERRY. 1376.]

On the inclosure of the Fens, the various Acts which were passed for the allotment of the lands belonging to each separate parish directed that the Commissioners should set out in their Awards both public and private roads, and also directed that a certain number of acres of land should be set apart for the repair of these roads. Thus, nearly all the parishes which had right of Common in Holland Fen were awarded the right to obtain material from a plot of land at Amber Hill, which contained gravel. When the Donington Turnpike Act was obtained, the Proprietors of these roads were also empowered to obtain material from this land. When the Act determined and the tolls were abolished, this land was sold, and the proceeds, with other assets, were divided amongst the parishes through which the turnpike road passed. [INCLOSURE ROADS.]

The public roads, in the newly inclosed lands, were directed by the Inclosure Acts to be of a width varying from 40ft. to 60ft., which accounts for the large grass margins which, at the present time, exist at the sides of many of the Fen roads. In some of the Awards it was ordered that these roads should become public highways, but in many, no provision appears to have been made for forming the roads or covering them with hard material, and, consequently, several of them soon became in a deplorable condition. Although, within the last few years, most of the roads have been metalled, some by the voluntary act of the parishioners, and others by order of the

Trustees, yet there are still several in existence that are only grass droves, or the centre of which has had only a covering of silt.

EAST AND WEST FEN ROADS.

The allotted roads, in the East, West and Wildmore Fens, were at first maintained and repaired by the several townships through which they passed, but, subsequently, disputes having arisen, some of the new parishes refused to maintain and repair them, and consequently the roads became utterly neglected and almost impassable. In winter time, the ruts were so deep that no light conveyance could safely pass over the roads, and it was not an uncommon occurrence for vehicles to become so embedded in the mud that the driver had to seek the assistance of some neighbnuring farmer to extricate his waggon with the aid of several horses. It was attempted, by an indictment against one of the parishes through which the roads passed, to compel the parishes to repair them. The case being carried to the Court of Queen's Bench, a decision was given in favour of the parish. Several influential owners and occupiers of land in the neighbourhood then met together and determined to put an end to this state of affairs, and in 1853, an Act was obtained 'for the better maintenance and repair of the highways in Wildmore and the East and West Fens,' by which it was enacted that the whole of the roads set out under the Inclosure Awards, as public ways, should be deemed highways, and be made subject to the same laws and regulations as govern the highways throughout the country.

16 and 17 Vict., c. 115. 1853.

BARRIER BANK.

The Barrier Bank Road, extending from Spalding to Cowbit, and thence along the Welland, through the Bedford Level, was the first turnpike road in the Fenland. It was constructed by the Adventurers of Deeping Fen, under an Act passed in the reign of Charles II. On the formation of the South Holland Drainage Trust, this road from Spalding to Cowbit was vested in the Trustees, and they were allowed to take the tolls.

16 & 17 Car. ii.

12 Geo. iii. 1772.

1 and 2 Vict. 1838.

In 1838 it was declared to be a Turnpike road, and leave was given to take tolls for 31 years. On the expiry of this term in 1869, the tolls ceased, and the road was taken charge of by the Surveyors of Highways of Spalding and Cowbit, and, on the passing of the *Highways Act of* 1878, became a main road.

1869.

BROTHERHOUSE AND CROWLAND ROAD.

The road from Brotherhouse Bar to Crowland was, until recently, subject to tolls payable to the owner of the estate. In 1892, the parish having obtained the abolition of the tolls by a payment to the owner of them, the road also became a main road under the charge of the County Council.

TURNPIKE ROADS.

The next Turnpike Trust which obtained Parliamentary powers was the one between Spalding and Tydd, which was formed in 1764; the next was the Spalding and Deeping, in 1820; the Boston and Donington, and the Spalding and Bourne, in 1822; and the

Spalding and Donington, the Swineshead and Holbeach, and the Boston and Spilsby, in 1826.

The following is a list of the Turnpike Roads, with their mileage and the date when their first Acts were obtained.

	Date of Act.	Length of road in the Holland Division.		
		M.	F.	C.
Boston and Alford road, as far as Cowbridge	1826	1	5	0
" " " to Hilldyke	"	2	2	2
The Donington road, from Boston through Kirton and Sutterton, to the eighth mile stone; and from Boston through Kirton Fen, Swineshead and Donington, up to the Hammond Beck; and from Kirton Holme to Langrick	1822	26	0	2
The Swineshead and Fossdyke road, passing through Hofleet and Sutterton	1826	12	6	3
The Spalding and Donington road, from Donington through Quadring, Gosberton, and Pinchbeck to Spalding, and from Gosberton on the Boston road to join the Donington Turnpike	1826	11	3	3
The Spalding and Tydd road, passing through Weston, Holbeach and Sutton St. Mary to Tydd and Sutton Bridge	1764	19	1	1
The Barrier Bank from Spalding through Cowbit to the Turnpike at Brotherhouse Bar	1665	6	0	0
The road from Brotherhouse Bar to Crowland and to the boundary of Northamptonshire	——	4	7	6
The Spalding and Market Deeping road from Spalding to the county boundary in the parish of Deeping St. Nicholas	1820	6	0	5
The Spalding and Bourne road, passing through Pode Hole and Dovehirne to the county boundary at Gutheram	1822	5	7	8
		96	2	0

MAIN ROADS. The above were all constituted Main Roads, under the *Highway Act of* 1878, except the road from Brotherhouse Bar to Crowland, together with other highways, making a total mileage of main roads in Holland, under that Act, of 117m. 4f. 1ch. In 1889, these main roads were transferred to the County Council, and in 1892 further main roads were adopted, making a total of 177m. of. 8ch.

HOLLAND FEN HIGHWAY BOARD.

The only Highway Board that was constituted in the Fenland was that for the management of the roads in Holland Fen. The Fen allotments in this district being situated a long way from the mother parishes made the management of the highways difficult. There were three principal roads which ran the whole length of the

Fen, from 7 to 8 miles in length, without any cross road at the northern end, thus making communication from one part of the Fen to another very inconvenient. The parish of North Forty-Foot Bank consisted of a narrow slip of land, about one chain wide and 6¼ miles long, on which a church and school, a brewery and 40 houses had been erected. The road, never having been metalled, was in a disgraceful state, and at times access to the houses on the bank was almost impossible. This land was extra parochial, and after it was formed into a parish, the rateable value was so small that it was not possible to raise the money necessary to put the road in proper repair, or to maintain it. Under these circumstances the Author was directed by the Court of Quarter Sessions for the parts of Holland, in 1878, to prepare a report on the condition of the roads and to advise as to a scheme for forming a Highway District. The Court adopted the scheme proposed in the Report, made the necessary order for the formation of the District, and a Highway Board, consisting of 13 members, was constituted. The District included the parishes and parish allotments in Holland Fen, with the exception of Boston West, Skirbeck Quarter, Wyberton, Frampton, Wigtoft and the land near Swineshead, west of the Skirth. The area of the District was 16,000 acres, and included the whole, or portions of, 16 parishes. The rateable value at the time of the formation was £14,585. The length of the roads placed under the management of the new Board was 42m. 3f. 9ch., of which 5m. 1f. 1ch. were main roads. The average cost of maintenance of these roads by the Highway Board for the three years 1885-1888, was £20 15s. This included the interest on the money borrowed for improvements. The Board, during its existence, metalled the North Forty-Foot Bank at a cost of £2,049; opened out a cross road at the north end of the district, from Cheetham Bridge to Reed's Point, a distance of 3f. 2ch.; and built a bridge over Claydyke, making a communication with the road to South Kyme; also a road 1m. 2f. 9ch. long to Langrick Ferry, at a cost of £230. A bridge was also erected over Clay Dyke, giving connection between Algarkirk and Sutterton Fen, south of Amber Hill, at a cost of £242. The total cost of these improvements was £2,367, for which £2,000 was borrowed, and the remainder paid out of the rates. The money borrowed is being repaid by annual instalments.

REPAIR OF ROADS.

The Highway Board was superseded when the District Council was formed, and took over the management of all the Highways.

The only material available in the Fenland itself for the construction and repair of roads is silt, and many of the highways have been formed by a covering of this material, dug from pits in the neighbourhood, or from ground allotted by the Commissioners for the purpose. A ton of silt was reckoned to cover 1 yard in a length of a road, 18in. thick, and 10ft. wide, the silt costing about 8d. to 10d.

per ton for digging and spreading. In some cases a road was formed by being 'turned over,' the top soil being being removed to a depth of 2ft. or 3ft. A pit was sunk in the middle of the road, 12ft. wide, till the silt was reached. This was dug out and placed on the surface, the top soil of the next length being thrown into the bottom of the pit, and this process continued until the whole road was covered with a layer of silt. The cost of thus silting a road, with a pit from 5ft. to 6ft deep, was 15/- per chain.

Sea shingle brought from the beach, on the opposite coast of Norfolk, has been largely used for covering and repairing the highways. This is delivered by barges at Boston or Fossdyke, or on the main for the parishes adjoining the coast, and costs about 4/- per ton.

Gravel obtained from land near Horncastle, in the neighbourhood of New York and from pits near the Witham, and also from Norfolk, used to be largely used, costing from 5/- to 6/- a ton. The quantity of gravel put on a road, which had not previously been metalled, was at the rate of 7 tons to a chain, 12ft. in width. For ordinary repairs one ton was considered sufficient for 1½ chains.

The use of granite for the repair of the roads in the Fenland was first introduced by the Author, about 25 years ago. At first its adoption was confined to the turnpike and urban roads. Its use gradually spread until now it is put on all the principal highways in this part of the county. The granite is obtained by railway from the quarries in Leicestershire, or by sea from Belgium, and costs from 8/- to 12/- per ton. On the principal highways, about 40 tons of granite per mile, a year, is considered sufficient for ordinary repairs.

Almost without exception, both the main roads and highways are without any proper foundation and have only a very thin coating of material, which makes it very difficult to maintain the surface level and in good order, especially in wet and frosty weather. The practice which also prevails in this part of the county, of making the width apart of the wheels of all the carts and waggons exactly to the same gauge, leads the carters to follow in the same track along the road, enhancing the difficulty of keeping the surface level and free from ruts.

Within this last few years, the County Council have greatly improved the main roads, by coating them thickly with granite or slag and rolling the material in with a steam road roller.

From a Report made to the Court of Quarter Sessions, by the Author in 1879, it appears that 32 parishes round Boston had 511 miles of road. The highway rates in the different parishes varied from 2/6 to 6d. in the £, the average being 1/5. The number of acres to each mile of road was 221. The average cost per mile was:— *COST OF MAINTENANCE.*

		£
Manual labour	...	6·05
Carting	...	2·55
Materials	...	15·45
Sundries	...	1·55
Management	...	1·45
		£27·05

This included the main roads.

From the Reports made annually to the Quarter Sessions, the average cost of the 117½ miles of main roads in the division of Holland, which is nearly conterminous with the Fenland, was for the six years, 1884-9, £41·65 per mile, (including the cost of the urban roads,) which was divided as follows :—

		£
Labour	...	12·12
Materials	...	26·06
Carting	...	3·12
Sundries	...	0·35
		41·65

In a Return made to the Holland County Council, of the mileage and cost of the roads, other than main roads, of the forty-four parishes in the division of Holland, the total mileage is given as 1116m. 7f. 1ch. The average cost, for the three years, 1886-7-8, was £18,165/13/6. and the average cost per mile £16·26.

From a Return prepared by Mr. H. Snaith, in 1895, for the Rural District Council of the Boston Union, comprising all the parishes in the Union, and covering an area of 78,015 acres, the mileage of roads is given as 375 miles. The cost was shown as varying from £36 to £12 a mile, the average of the whole being £20·6, exclusive of the main roads, which are given as costing, in 1888, £43·04 per mile. The mileage per £1,000 of rateable value is given as 3 miles 1 furlong.

The average cost of the main roads for the Division of Holland for the 6 years, 1884-89, when they were maintained by the parishes and received grants from the county rate, was £41·65 per mile. For the 3 years, 1889-92, when they were maintained by the County Council, the average cost, for 92 miles of rural main roads, was £5,182, or at the rate of £56·33 per mile. In 1892 the system of management was altered. A steam roller was purchased and the principal roads received a substantial coating of material, which was rolled down, and the roads were very greatly improved. Additional main roads were also created, making the total length of the rural main roads, 145m. 7f. 4ch., and of the urban roads, 39m. 7c. The average cost per mile for the 146 miles of rural main roads for the four years, 1892-6, including the purchase of the steam roller, was £11,158, or at the rate of £76·42 per mile. The grants to the urban main roads came to about £4,000 a year.

The total length of the highways, including main roads, in the Holland Division is about 1,294 miles. The area which these roads serve is 244,317 acres, giving an average of 189 acres to 1 mile of road. From Mr. Snaith's Return for the Boston Union, the area averages 178 acres to a mile of road.

MILEAGE OF ROADS.

Bridges and Ferries.

The bridges which span the rivers in the Fenland are all of comparatively modern construction, and have been erected in most cases as adjuncts to the drainage works. All the bridges which cross the drains belonging to the various Trusts are maintained by the Drainage Commissioners.

There does not appear to be any reliable record as to when a bridge was first erected across the Witham at Boston. Anciently the means of crossing the river was by a ferry, the site of which is supposed to have been a little above the present St. John's Ferry. There is mention of 'pontage' granted to the Earl of Richmond and others in the 14th century, for repairing a bridge at St. Botolph's across the river, between the lands of the Earl and those of William de Ros; and on subsequent occasions the bridge was described as being 'ruinous and broken up,' and a grant made for its repair.

BOSTON BRIDGE

In 1500 a sluice was built across the river, a few yards above the present iron bridge, for the purpose of stemming the tides. It consisted of a stone pier, 13ft. wide, in the middle of the river, and 43¾ft. long. To each side of this pier doors were hung, which closed against piers erected at the sides of the river. These piers were connected together at the top by wooden beams, which formed a roadway. The openings between the piers were respectively 44ft. and 21½ft. Although this structure failed to answer the purpose for which it was originally built, it continued as a bridge up to the beginning of the present century. Frequent notices are contained in the Corporation records as to sums spent in repairing it. Leland describes this as 'a bridge of wood over Lindis and a pile of stones in the middle of the river.' About 50 years after this bridge was built, it became in a ruinous and dangerous condition and finally in 1556 the superstructure fell down. A new bridge was built by the Corporation of Boston and opened in the following year. The old brick pier in the middle of the river was allowed to remain and made use for the new bridge. During its construction communication was kept up by a ferry, for the use of which the Corporation took toll.

BOSTON FERRY.

It was during this time that the right to this toll was tried in the Duchy Court of Lancaster. The action being brought by Nicholas Worlicke of Spalding, against Thomas Sowthen, the

Duchy of Lancaster. Pleadings. Ph. and Mary. vol. viii.

Mayor of Boston, and Richard Kelsage, for the detention of a mare, because the plaintiff had refused to pay the toll of one penny demanded for crossing the ferry. In the proceedings the river is described as part of the "Porte or Haven of salt water called Boston Haven, which issueth and hath his course through the towne of Boston to the mayne seas, there nigh adjoining, and is, and of long time hath been, a very dangerous and swift water and stream and would in short time, if it were not defended and kept by continual maintenance and repair of the banks and and piers there adjoining, surround and destroy not only the town, but also annoy and put in peril the whole country." It is further stated that, "for the convenience of the inhabitants living on the east and west side of the river, the Dukes of Richmond, who owned the manor of Boston, of their mean benevolence, only for the ease and relief of their servants, residents and inhabitants of Boston, did find, maintain and keep to their great charges and expenses, within the said manor, upon the soil and ground belonging to the same manor, one ferry or passage over the said port, and water, and certain watermen, boats and great bottoms or keals, called horse-boats and wayne boats, only for the conveyance and transporting over the said water and port of their tenants and inhabitants and their beasts, goods, chattles, wares and merchandise." For the use of the ferry and the boats were paid such sums of money, sometimes more and sometimes less, having regard to the labour and travail of the watermen; it was further pleaded that this ferry was not a public highway, but a passage on sufferance at the will of the Lord of the Manor; that any foreign persons, who, not being inhabitants of Boston, attempted to cross by this ferry were withstanded and resisted as trespassers; that at sundry times of the year, when the banks of the said haven had been impared and worn away by the rage of the water, the ferry was stopped until the banks were again repaired; and that about 50 years last past, the Aldermen and Brethren of the late Guild and Fraternity of our Lady, founded in the Parish Church of Boston, by the license of the then Duke of Richmond, Lord of the Manor, did build upon the soil belonging to the manor a bridge over the said haven; which bridge was always afterwards kept and used and occupied as a private way and passage, at the will of the Lord of the Manor, for the use of the inhabitants; that the yearly charges of the repair and maintenance amounted to £30; that subsequently to the building of this bridge the rights of the Lord of the Manor therein had been transferred to the Mayor and Burgesses of Boston; that by the extreme rage and influence of the seas the bridge about one year since, was suddenly 'braste and overthrown,' and that in consequence the ferry had again to be used, and that in the meantime, the Mayor and Burgesses did 'extend their uttermost power for, and towards the building and re-edifying' of the same, and "after long study and travail and good advise taken therein, did condescend and agree amongst themselves, to set on work a great number of masons, carpenters, wrights and other artificers, about the making and erection of the same bridge, and the said workmen and artificers being so set on work, at the only charges and expenses of the Mayor and Burgesses, a great number of well-disposed persons travelling into the Borough, perceiving the charge of the making of the said bridge to extend far above the ability and power of the said Mayor and Burgesses, did give and devise sums of money and other things necessary towards the making of the said bridge."

A grant of lands and houses in Boston was made to the Corporation by Philip and Mary, the Charter stating that this grant was "in consideration of the great charges and expenses, which the Mayor and Burgesses daily and continually sustain, in and about the reparation of the bridge and the port, and to the end that the said Mayor and Burgesses may be better enabled to support the charges and expenses of the repairs and maintenance of the said bridge and port."

This wooden bridge continued to be a constant source of expense. In 1626 the Chamberlain was ordered to repair it "but not to touch the sluice, because such repairs belong to the Landowners in Lindsey, Kesteven and Holland. In 1631, and again in 1741, the superstructure of the bridge was taken down and replaced, the ferry being again brought into use while the works were going on.

In 1642 this bridge is referred to, and it is stated that the doors of the sluice were not then in existence, and that the tide flowed above the town.

In 1807 the present bridge was erected, about 20 yards south of the old one. This bridge is one of the earliest examples of cast-iron as applied to bridge building, and was erected from the design of Mr. John Rennie, at a cost, including land and approaches, of £22,000. *BOSTON IRON BRIDGE. 1807.*

In the Preamble of the Act empowering the Corporation to erect this bridge, it is stated that 'the existing bridge over the Witham, was very ancient and out of repair, and was very narrow, inconvenient and dangerous for the passing of carriages and cattle.' The Act reserved the right of the Corporation to take the same tolls or pontage for the horses, cattle, carriages, waggons and carts passing over the new bridge, as they had immemorially demanded and taken. The toll over the bridge was abolished in 1830. The bridge is stated in the Act to be of one arch, with not less than 72ft. clear water-way, and 36ft. roadway. The actual width of water-way between the piers is 86ft. *42 Geo. iii. 1802.* *Thompson's Boston.*

The Grand Sluice at Boston has a roadway across it, connecting the two sides of the Witham. This structure is maintained by the

GRAND SLUICE BRIDGE.

Witham Commissioners. The roadway is repaired by the Town authorities.

FERRIES.

There are two ferries for foot passengers across the tidal portion of the river, one at the end of the Skirbeck Road and the other at the end of High Street, in Skirbeck Quarter. The men who own the boats pay an acknowledgement of 1s. a year to the Harbour Commissioners, who keep the steps and approaches in repair.

Until within the last few years the only means of passing across the Witham between Boston and Lincoln, except at Tattershall, where a bridge had been erected, was by ferry boats. The Act of 1762 authorised the Drainage Commissioners to construct a bridge between Anton's Gote and Boston, for the purpose of preserving communication between the severed parts of Holland Fen; but this work was not carried out.

The existing ferries are at Langrick, Dogdyke, Stixwould and Washingborough and, until the erection of the bridges, at Kirkstead and Bardney. The ferry boats are large enough to take a waggon and horses, and are moved backwards and forwards by a chain lying on the bed of the river and passing round a drum on the boat, motion being given by a windlass worked by the man in charge.

KIRKSTEAD BRIDGE.

In 1891, the Great Northern Railway Company constructed a swing-bridge across the river at Kirkstead, for the convenience of passengers and goods going to their station there, and this has superseded the ferry.

BARDNEY BRIDGE.

In 1893, a bridge was erected across the river at Bardney by the County Councils of Lindsey and Kesteven. The estimated cost of this bridge was £7,250, towards which the Great Northern Railway contributed £3,000. The bridge was built under the direction of Mr. Thropp, C.E., the County Surveyor of Lindsey, the Contractor for the abutments and approaches being Mr. S. Sherwin, and for the ironwork Messrs. Pitts and Matthews. The amount of the Contract of the former was £3,437, and of the latter £2,392. The rights of the ferry which was established in 1714, were bought up for £777, including the land for the approaches to the bridge. It is estimated that this bridge gives accomodation to an area of about 2,500 acres in Branston, Potterhanworth and Nocton Fens.

WELLAND BRIDGES.

The Welland has only two bridges across it, one at Spalding and the other at Fossdyke.

SPALDING BRIDGE.

A bridge at Spalding has existed for a very long period. It is stated that the Romans built a bridge here to carry their main road across the Welland.

1207.

In the reign of Richard I, in an order made as to disafforesting the marshes, they are described as extending to the 'great bridge of Spalding.' In a Commission sent by the king to make enquiry and to view the banks and sewers in Holland, it was presented 'that the great bridge, called Spalding brigge, was then broken and ought to be repaired at the charges of the whole town.' At the Survey of the Fens made by order of King James, the bridge over the Welland at Spalding is mentioned. In 1642, the bridge is described as being of great antiquity, and as 'twelve foote in the waterway and five foote deepe,' and 'the stone pillar or pier in the midst thereof which supported the two arches,' as having been 'lately removed by the drainers of Deeping Fen, when they widened the river.' In the *Deeping Fen Act of* 1651, the Adventurers are required forthwith to build 'the great bridge over Spalding River, commonly called the High Bridge, of lime and stone.' The present stone bridge was erected by the Trustees of Deeping Fen, in 1836.

There are two foot bridges across the river at Spalding; the Victoria Bridge, the present iron structure of which was built in 1868 to replace a former wooden one; and the Albert Bridge, below the High Bridge, erected in 1844, which took the place of an old chain bridge and was made to open for the navigation.

Fossdyke Bridge.

In the *Welland Improvement Act of* 1794, power was given to erect a bridge at Fossdyke, over the intended new Cut, and to "amend and render safe for passengers and cattle, at all times of the tide, the public way over the Wash, from the south bank in Moulton, to the north bank in Fossdyke." These powers were repealed by a subsequent Act, in which fresh powers were granted for building a bridge over the Welland. Under the powers of this Act the present opening bridge and the embankment across the open salt marsh and sands, about half-a-mile in length, were constructed by a Company. The original capital of the Company was £14,000, raised by shares of £100 each, the amount of capital being subsequently increased to £17,000. The bridge was built from the designs of Mr. John Rennie. The works were commenced in 1812, and finished in 1815. The bridge is described as having 'a very grand effect,' and that its appearance is 'extremely light, and the design reflects the highest credit on the taste and judgment of the Engineer.' It was built of oak, the roadway resting on a series of oak piles, driven into the bed of the river. These piles are about 18in. in diameter, and some of them 42ft. in length. The bridge has three openings of 30ft., two of 29ft., and three of 27ft., leaving a total waterway of 202ft. The central part of the bridge opens for the passage of vessels, the two leaves being raised vertically by means of a rack and pinion.

After the opening of the Great Northern Railway, the tolls diminished so much, as not to pay the cost of collection and repairs. The bridge consequently fell into decay and became dangerous. In 1868 it was closed against road traffic, and the drawbridge was left permanently open for the passage of vessels, a temporary arrangement for the passage of foot passengers being provided. In the following year the Proprietors applied at Lincoln Assizes, with the view of getting relieved of their responsibility, but did not succeed. In 1870 the bridge was made a County bridge by an Act of Parliament obtained for the purpose. The County repaired the bridge, and it was re-opened for traffic in 1871. The repairs cost £2,325. The tolls were let by auction, realizing about £180 a year, the Lessee undertaking the duty of opening and closing the bridge.

1870.

FOSSDYKE BRIDGE TRANSFER ACT.
33 and 34 Vict., c. 34. 1870.

The management of the Bridge passed from the County Justices to the Holland County Council, on its establishment in 1889, and in 1890 it was thrown open to the public free from toll.

GLEN BRIDGES.

There does not appear to be any record as to the date when, or by whom, the bridges over the Glen were first constructed. The *Deeping Fen Act of* 1664, directs that the Adventurers shall pull up any bridges over the rivers Glen and Welland, or over the Vernatt's, that hinder the passage of the water, and re-build and for ever after maintain the same, and that all ancient bridges over any of the rivers and drains shall be repaired and maintained by the Adventurers.

There are seven bridges over the river Glen : Kate's Bridge, at the extreme limit of the Fen country ; Dovehirne, or Pinchbeck Bars Bridge, which is maintained by the County ; the present iron bridge, a single span of 49ft. 4in., which was re-built at the expense of the County, under the direction of Mr. Kingston, Mr. Dixon of London being the Contractor. The rest are Boarden Bridge, an old wooden structure, about a quarter of a mile lower down ; Money Bridge, about a mile below Dovehirne ; Herring Bridge, 1½ miles further down, built in 1775 by the Deeping Fen Adventurers, and since maintained by that Trust ; and Cross Gate or New Bridge, ½ mile further, enlarged by the Adventurers of Deeping Fen, to a waterway of 30ft., under the Act of 1774. The latter bridges are not maintained by the County.

SURFLEET BRIDGE.
14 Geo. iii, c. 23.

Surfleet Bridge has been in existence from very ancient times. It is referred to in a Commission of Sewers, in the reign of Edward II, as 'Surflete Brigge.' By the *Deeping Fen Act of* 1774, the Adventurers were directed to replace the then existing bridge by another ' good and sufficient Bridge, of not less capacity and dimensions than Money Bridge.' The present iron bridge was erected at the expense of the County, under the direction of Mr. John Kingston, about 1844, Messrs. Handyside & Co., of Derby, being the Contractors. A sum of £3,000 was borrowed to cover the expense.

TYDD GOTE AND TRETTON BRIDGES.

Tydd Gote Bridge, over the Shire Drain, is maintained by the County, and Tretton Bridge, jointly with the County of the Isle of Ely. Crowland Bridge has been already described in Chapter X.

Eleven Towns Bridges.

The Bridges over the principal watercourses and drains in the eleven parishes of the Kirton Wapentake have from ancient times been known as the 'Eleven Towns Bridges.' From about the time of the formation of the Black Sluice Drainage Trust in 1765, up to 1892, when the Holland County Council was constituted, they were under the management of a separate body of Commissioners, consisting of one Representative from each of the parishes. The money required for maintaining the bridges was provided by a Precept directed to the several Highway Surveyors. The origin of this Commission is not known. A clause in the *Black Sluice Act of* 1765 gave the Drainage Commissioners power to authorise the inhabitants of the eleven parishes, having right of common in Holland Fen, to erect bridges over the new drain at the expense of such inhabitants, and this probably resulted in the formation of the Commission. [5 Geo. iii, c. 86.]

Before the formation of the Black Sluice Trust, these bridges were under the charge of the Court of Sewers, and they were repaired previous to 1744 by the Dikereeves, in accordance with the Redstone Gote Law. Subsequently they were repaired by the 'General Surveyor,' at the cost of the Eleven Towns, as appears by a Law of Sewers made in 1744. [Court of Sewers, June 16, 1744; also July 26 and Oct. 22, 1750.]

The Eleven Towns were defined in the reign of Henry III, when "a precept was directed to the Shirereeve touching the partition of Haut Huntre Fen, by the consent of those that had right therein, whereby the King gave special command that each town might have their due proportion thereof assigned to them." By the Law of Sewers of 1744, it was ordered that in future the works relating to certain drains should be *presented* by the General Surveyor of Sewers, together with the bridges over the same, namely, Swineshead High Bridge, Kirton Holme Bridge, Kirton Bridge, Frampton Bridge with a gate to the same, Wyberton Bridge, the Bridge into Dawson's Piece with two horse gates to the same, two bridges over the new Cut from the North Forty-Foot to the South Forty-Foot, the Forty-Foot bridges in the West Causeway, Hubbert's Bridge, Wyberton Bridge, and Litchfield Bridge over the South Forty-Foot. Three of these bridges are referred to in a Commission of Sewers, as far back as 1571, which directed "that one bridge over the sewer (Hammond Beck) in Kirton Fen, another at Frampton Fen, and another at Litchfield End, should be re-formed by the townships or persons who of right ought to do the same; and be of 12ft. in breadth, and of height sufficient for boats to pass under, upon pain of £3 6s. 8d. for every bridge unfinished at Michaelmas following." [Dugdale, Chap. xliii.] [Dugdale.]

In 1802, an indictment was preferred at the Quarter Sessions at Boston by certain inhabitants, against the Eleven Towns Commissioners, for not maintaining Hubbert's Bridge in a safe condition. This indictment was quashed, but was laid again, at a subsequent Sessions, against the parishes, certain inhabitants being selected for the purpose, and an order made for the repair of the bridge; the fine imposed being subsequently remitted.

After the formation of the County Council, objections were raised by some of the parishes to the payment of the call made by the Eleven Towns Commissioners, it being contended that these bridges ought to be repaired by that body. The Commissioners being advised that they had no power to enforce payment of the Precept, resigned in a body, and, no fresh Commissioners having been elected, the Trust has ceased to exist.

The following are the bridges which were maintained by the Commission, in addition to Hubbert's Bridge, which was taken over by the County: the two wooden 'White' foot bridges over the Redstone Gowt and the South Forty-Foot in Skirbeck Quarter; the main road brick bridges over the South Forty-Foot in Wyberton Fen and the 'High Bridge' at Swineshead; the main road brick bridge over the North Forty-Foot in Skirbeck Quarter Fen, known as the Cut Bridge; and the bridge at Brothertoft known as Toft Tunnel; the highway bridge over the North Forty-Foot, in Wyberton Fen, called Shuff Fen Bridge; the main road bridges over the New Hammond Beck in Wyberton Fen, at Kirton Holme and Swineshead; and the highway bridge, in Frampton Fen, known as Baker's Bridge; the highway bridge over the Old Hammond Beck, in Wyberton Fen, known as the Chain Bridge; one at Kirton Holme; and one in Frampton West 'under the road to Kirton; and the main road bridge at Kirton Holme.

The rate levied used to amount to about one penny per acre.

The eleven parishes which contributed and elected Commissioners, were Boston West, Brothertoft, Skirbeck Quarter, Frampton, Kirton, Sutterton, Algarkirk, Fosdyke, Wyberton, Wigtoft and Swineshead.

The *Black Sluice Act* refers to two bridges to be erected, one being described as being near Syke mouth. This does not appear ever to have been erected, the other was, no doubt, Hubbert's

HUBBERT'S BRIDGE.

Bridge, This was a wooden structure, carried on piles driven into the drain. This bridge, having becomg unsafe, was taken over by the County Justices for the Parts of Holland in 1888, and was replaced, at the expense of the County funds, by the present brick structure, having a single span of 56ft., which was erected from the designs of Mr. John Kingston, the County Surveyor, at a cost of £2,000.

RAILWAYS.

COMPANIES.

The Companies which own the railways in the Fenland are the Great Northern; the joint Committee of the Great Northern and

Great Eastern; and the joint Committee of the Great Northern and Midland. The Great Northern has a complete monoply of North Holland and the Witham Fens, by its loop line from Lincoln to Peterborough, the East Lincoln line from Grimsby to Boston, and the Grantham line through Holland Fen and Swineshead. In South Holland, radiating from Spalding, are the Great Northern and Great Eastern joint lines, running northward through Pinchbeck, Gosberton and Donington, and southward through Cowbit and Postland; the Great Northern, through Deeping Fen to Peakirk; and the Great Northern and Midland joint lines, through Deeping Fen to Bourne on the west, and eastward, through Moulton, Holbeach and Sutton St. Mary to Sutton Bridge and Lynn.

MILEAGE.
At the present time there are about 123 miles of railway, serving an area of 519 square miles, giving one mile of railway to about 2,700 acres of land. The greatest distance of any part from a railway station may be taken at about 6 miles.

TRAFFIC IN PRODUCE.
Owing to the large quantities of potatoes, roots and vegetables grown, the traffic from some of the stations is very heavy. The quantity of agricultural produce of all kinds sent from the three stations, Kirton, Algarkirk and Surfleet, in a year, is about 23,000 tons, of which Kirton despatches about 11,000 tons and the other two, 6,000 tons each. The area of land which these three stations serve may be taken at 32,500 acres, including grass land, of which there is a large area, roads, villages, &c. This gives 0·71 tons to an acre exported from the district.

RATE OF CARRIAGE.
The rate of carriage varies with the class of goods carried. For vegetables in truck loads it is 1½d. per ton per mile, making the cost to Sheffield, Manchester and other manufacturing towns to vary from 10s. to 20s. a ton.

STEAM TRAMWAY.
An effort was made in 1877 to establish a steam tramway by the side of the main road from Boston to Wainfleet, similar to that which runs from Wisbech to Upwell and Outwell. An Act was applied for, but owing to the prejudice which prevailed at the time as to the use of steam on highways, and the harassing restrictions imposed by the Board of Trade, the Promoters withdrew the Bill and the project was allowed to drop. The convenience of a steam tramway in carrying coal, road material, manure, oilcake and other goods, and in taking back produce from such a highly cultivated district, and to the inhabitants of the several villages through which it passed, would have been very great.

The district through which this tramway would have passed is 9 miles long, and the Promoters calculated that a section of country, 3 miles wide, would use the line, equal to an area of 17,280 acres. It was taken that about 12,000 acres of this was arable, and that the carriage of roots, corn and other produce outwards, and manure, coal, &c., inwards, would average a ton per acre over every acre, whether grass or arable, and that the average rate for goods would be 4s. per ton. It was intended to run the line at the side of the road so as not to interfere with the ordinary traffic. The standard gauge was to be used so that trucks would be brought off the railway without transferring their contents. The engine was to be covered in and similar in construction to those used on steam tramways in towns. There were to be stopping places at the villages and principal cross roads, and sidings into some of the larger farm yards. The scheme was promoted by some of the principal farmers of the district and traders of Boston, and it was warmly supported by Mr. W. Ingram, the Member for the Borough. The Solicitors engaged in promoting the Bill were Messrs. Staniland and Wigelsworth and the Engineers Mr. W. Shelford, M. Instit. C.E., of London, and the Author.

Fig: 15.

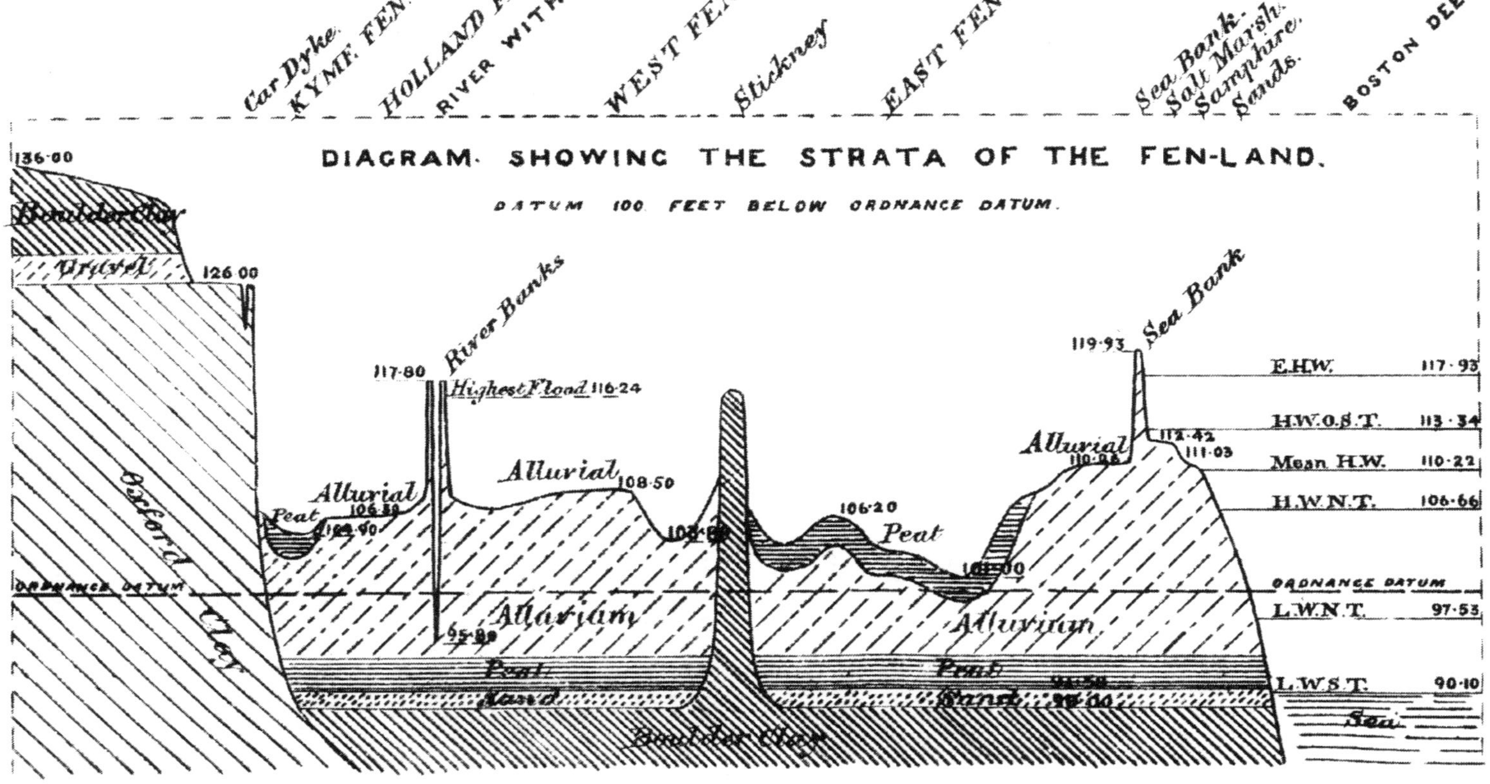
Car Dyke
KYME FEN
HOLLAND FEN
RIVER WITHAM
WEST FEN
Stickney
EAST FEN
Sea Bank
Salt Marsh
Samphire
Sands
BOSTON DEEPS
DIAGRAM SHOWING THE STRATA OF THE FEN-LAND.
DATUM 100 FEET BELOW ORDNANCE DATUM.
136·00
Boulder Clay
Gravel
126·00
Oxford Clay
ORDNANCE DATUM
Peat
Alluvial
117·80
River Banks
Highest Flood 116·24
Alluvial
108·50
Alluvium
95·80
Peat
Sand
Boulder Clay
106·20
Peat
101·00
Alluvium
Peat
Sand
119·93
Sea Bank
Alluvial
112·42
111·03
E.H.W. 117·93
H.W.O.S.T. 113·34
Mean H.W. 110·22
H.W.N.T. 106·66
ORDNANCE DATUM
L.W.N.T. 97·53
L.W.S.T. 90·10
Sea

CHAPTER XVI.

GEOLOGY AND WATER SUPPLY.

THE Geology of the Fenland has been so fully dealt with by Mr. Skertchley in the memoir of the Government survey that it is only necessary to describe generally the character of the strata of this district. *Skertchley's Memoir.*

The surface soil of about three fourths of the South Lincolnshire Fenland consists of alluvial deposit, the remaining fourth being peat. The total area is divided as follows:— *Peat and Alluvium.*

	Acres.
Alluvial soil	277,795
Peat	85,248
	363,043

The relative positions and levels of the different strata are shown on the diagram, Fig. 15. *Fig. 15.*

Scattered over the district are a few elevated spots, consisting of Glacial Drift, on which many of the villages are built. On the margin of the Fens are patches of gravel and sand, the remains of the beach of the ancient estuary. *Glacial Drift. Fig. 15.*

The base or substratum of nearly the whole of the Fenland consists of Oxford and Kimmeridge clay, the latter being a very dark coloured, tenacious substance, termed locally 'clunch clay,' and found chiefly to the east of a curved line, extending from Lincoln by Boston to March. The Oxford clay lies to the west of this line, and is a tenacious dark blue substance, sometimes turning brown on exposure to the air, and containing numerous Ammonites, some being of a large size, Belemnites and Septaria, or turtle stones, iron pyrites and Selenite are also found in this soil. The thickness of this formation probably exceeds 500ft. At Boston, a boring was made in search of water in 1828, the strata passed through being Fen beds, 24ft., Boulder clay, 166ft., Kimmeridge or Oxford clay, 382ft.; total depth, 572ft. At Fossdyke, a boring made in 1875 passed through Fen beds, sand and gravel, 78ft., sandy clay, 37ft., Boulder clay, 51½ft., Kimmeridge clay, 159ft., total, 326ft. The details of other borings made in this district will be found in the Appendix. *Substratum.*

Appendix.

BOULDER CLAY.

Overlying this clay, throughout a considerable area, is a deposit known as the 'Chalky Boulder clay.' This is an unstratified mass of lead coloured clay, interspersed with fragments of chalk and limestone and also with basalt, granite, sandstone and other formations quite foreign to this part of the country. Many of these pieces of rock are polished and scratched, or striated, in a manner peculiar to stones which have been subject to glacial action. The following specimens of rocks were found by the Author amongst the clay excavated for the New Outfall of the River Witham and for the Boston Dock : red granite with large quartz crystals, grey granite, volcanic ash, amygdaloid, felstone, felspar and quartz, porphyry, five different kinds of quartz rock, jasper, several different flints, ferruginous and argillaceous sandstones, mountain limestone, dark blue silicious limestone with quartz veins, silicious, argillaceous and carboniferous limestones, great oolite, iron ore, greensand, chalk; also Ammonites of large size, some having a diameter of more than a foot. In the excavation for deepening the upper Witham, some boulders of Lias limestone and sandstone were found, the largest of which was about 6ft. by 4ft. and 2ft. 6in. deep, containing about 57 cubic feet.

Many of the fragments of rock found in the Boulder clay must have travelled very long distances, some from the North of England and Scotland ; whilst some have been recognised as belonging to Norway; the rocks being thus pioneers of the Scandinavians who followed and settled here. The surface of the underlying strata, on which the Boulder clay rests, is very uneven, and gives evidence of valleys, river-beds and other depressions having been filled up by it. Large pot holes, filled with gravel and sand, are frequently met with, and in many places this Boulder clay rises up above the general level in the shape of mounds or hills, as at Sibsey, and at Beacon Hill near Sleaford.

The clay is exceedingly tough, tenacious and compact, giving the idea that it has been subjected to enormous pressure. Of all soils it is the most difficult to excavate. It is so hard that the power of the foot is utterly inadequate to drive the tool into it, and so unstratified that the pickaxe only loosens the small area with which it immediately comes in contact. It is composed chiefly of the *débris* of the Oxford and Kimmeridge clays of the neighbourhood, interspersed with fragments of chalk derived from the stratum of this material, with which, it is supposed, it was originally covered, before it was denuded by glacial action. If burnt, it forms exceedingly hard ballast, of a white or light yellow colour. It has been estimated that this deposit was formed upwards of 200,000 years ago, when all this country was buried beneath a thick crust of ice and snow and when large confluent glaciers came sliding down from the north, pushing before them and grinding up under their enormous weights, the rocks and soils over which they passed.

Geike's Great Ice Age

On the top of the Boulder clay is generally found a covering of sand, the thickness varying from 6in. to a foot. In places also are large holes, filled with the same material, which was probably deposited by the action of the water flowing from the melting glaciers. The quality and colour of this sand varies from fine, white silver sand to green, yellow, black and red, the latter being composed of large coarse grains and small pebbles.

As the climate became milder, the glaciers disappeared; great floods descended from the melting ice and scoured out valleys and water courses, leaving the surface of the country in much the same condition as it is now. With a milder temperature vegetation soon sprang up, and the Fenland became covered with trees, which, in the course of years, grew to a very large size.

After the lapse of a long interval, a mild, damp period must have followed, which was favourable to the rapid growth of vegetation and the formation of peat.

PEAT.

This peat consists of the remains of mosses, water grasses, reeds, flags, and other fresh water plants, common to ditches and ponds, the most abundant being the *Hypnum fluitans* and the *Arundo Phragmites*. In excavating in the peat, there is frequently met with a substance which appears to be a mixture of decayed vegetation, clay and compressed rushes. It is very tough, has an extremly fetid smell, and is locally known as 'Bear's muck.' As the peat increased, it gradually destroyed the trees, which fell and became embedded in it.

A substratum of peat extends throughout the whole of the Fenland, which is covered over with a thick deposit of alluvial matter, and on this, in some places, are beds of surface peat. The upper peat beads were formerly the sites of large meres or lakes. One of these now forms the district known as Deeping Fen. Another large mere extended on the western side of the Fenland, from Washingborough to Helpringham Eau on the west, and to Dogdyke on the east; in length this mere was about 17 miles, and in width 3 miles. A portion of the peat of this mere is now covered with alluvial deposit. The East Fen was the site of another large mere. A third mere began about Helpringham Fen and continued, with a gradually extending width, to Bourne and Deeping Fens, its length being 16 miles and its width from 1¼ to 4 miles.

Appendix vi.

The area of the surface of the upper peat is about 85,248 acres. It is the lowest land in the district, its level varying from 1ft. to 7ft. above *Ordnance datum*, or from 12½ft. to 6½ft. below high water of spring tides in the estuary, the average being about 6ft. above *Ordnance datum*.

Fig 15.

The peat land is remarkable for the absence of trees and hedges; and, being almost entirely arable, few sheep or cattle are to be seen feeding in the fields. The houses are few and scattered. In winter the appearance of the peat district, with its dark coloured soil and long straight drains is rather desolate and cheerless, but in summer the scene is entirely altered and the vast expanse of corn, when moved by the breeze, looks like a sea with golden waves.

The surface peat varies in thickness from 1ft. to 10ft. In Deeping Fen, now, it is not more than about 1ft. in thickness and about the same in the East Fen, although there may be small areas where the thickness is much greater than this. In the West and Wildmore Fens there is a large admixture of sand with the peat, making the soil 'moory' and very poor. In Thurlby Fen the peat varies from 3ft. to 5ft. From Bourne to Heckington it is seldom more than 3ft. and more frequently less than 1ft., and is here generally 'skirty' or mixed with silt and clay. Along the Witham it varies from 18in. to 2ft., thinning off to 6in. as it approaches Lincoln, although there are some places where it attains a thickness of from 6ft. to 8ft.

SHRINKAGE OF THE PEAT.

Where the peat is thin it is gradually disappearing, owing to the decomposition of the vegetable matter of which it consists, by exposure to the air, by cultivation, and by the shrinkage due to the draining away of the water with which it was formerly saturated. On some land nothing but peat was met with, when first brought into cultivation, but, after some years' working, the clay from the substratum was turned up and brought to the surface by the plough; which accounts for the general impression amongst the Fenmen, that the clay grows. Large trees are also encountered by the plough where formerly there was no obstruction.

In the East Fen, in the places where the peat was the thickest, it has shrunk since the reclamation from 6ft. to 2ft., or 4ft. in 80 years, being at the rate of rather more than ½in. in a year. No doubt the rate was much more rapid during the first few years. In other parts the shrinkage has been 2ft. in 60 years. In the Witham Fens, the surface has been lowered from 4ft. to 6ft. since 1743, owing to the improvement of the drainage, or at a mean rate of about 0·36in. a year.

In Deeping Fen the peat sank 24ins. in 25 years, or at a rate of 1in. a year.

Skertchley.

The same rate has been found to prevail in the peat in the Bedford Level. In Hilgay Fen it settled 52 inches in 26 years, or at the rate of 2in. a year. In Wood Fen, near Ely, 37in. in 20 years, or 1·9in. a year. In Whittlesea Mere the peat at first sank 3ft. 6in. in nine years, or at the rate of 4·66 in. a year, the rate spread over the subsequent 22 years was 92in., or 4·18in. a year; after this the shrinkage was only at the rate of 0.2in. a year. In Wilbraham Fen, inclosed in 1804, the peat sank 6ft. in 60 years, or at the rate of 1·20in. a year.

From borings and observations made by Mr. R. Atkinson of Outwell, along the districts bordering on the Nene and the Ouse, he arrived at the conclusion that the peat had settled over the whole level, from 5ft. to 8ft., from 1605, when the first reclamations were commenced, to 1852, when his observations were taken. This would give a mean annual shrinkage at the rate of ·24in. to ·38in. a year, spread over 247 years. Comparing the general level of the surface of the peat in the South Level of the Bedford Level, as given in Mr. Rennie's Report of 1809, with what it is at the present time an average subsidence of 4ft. 6in. is shown, being a mean depression of 0·68in. a year. *Report on Ouse. Wheeler.*

The trees found embedded in the peat consist of oak, birch, beech, fir, yews, alder, hazel and willow. Oaks are the most abundant. Some of these are of very large size, measuring as much 90ft. in length, and 16ft. in girth. The colour of the wood varies from a rich red brown to jet black. Much of it, when excavated from the lower peat, is soft and spongy when first exposed to the air, but hardens as it dries. After some time has elapsed, it becomes very hard and as black as ebony, and takes a beautiful natural polish. Many pieces taken out of the peat, during the excavations for the Boston Dock, at 20ft. below the surface, were made into articles of ornament, or furniture.* The bark of the beech found in the same stratum, was as white and silvery as if newly cut down. The same was the case with some found at Billinghay, the wood found here being principally oak, birch, alder and fir, the proportionate quantity being in the order given. In Digby Fen, in the upper peat, oak, elm, birch and hazel have been found, and the Author has picked up, from the newly excavated peat, hazel nuts with the shells quite perfect. In Thurlby Fen, Mr. Bettinson states that the timber found has been principally oak, yew and beech, lying from 3 to 4ft. below the surface. Near Sutton, Sir Joseph Banks found birch, fir and oak, and in the soft clay overlying the roots, were found perfect leaves of the common holly, also remains of the willow and *Arundo Phragmites*. TREES IN THE PEAT.

Mr. Skertchley states that he found the direction in which the trees lay was, almost invariably, N.E. and S.W. This being the direction of the prevailing winds and also the direction in which many existing trees in the Fenland incline at the present time. The trees have the appearance of having been broken and not cut. He supposes that this is due to the action of the peat, causing the trees to decay, as it gradually increased and buried the bottom of the stems, which thus becoming weakened, were blown over by the wind and became embedded in the peat where they fell.

* A paper knife made from this wood will be found in the library of the Gentlemen's Society at Spalding.

It has been estimated that the peat formation must be at least 7,000 years old, but it is probably much older than this.

From the level at which the peat now lies, with reference to the water in the Estuary, it is evident that, subsequent to its formation, a general depression of this part of the coast must have taken place. At its present level it would be constantly covered with salt water, and under these circumstances, neither the trees nor vegetation of which the peat is composed could have grown.

ALLUVIAL SOIL. The lower layer of peat subsequently became covered with alluvial matter.

The alluvium, or silt, covers an area of about 277,795 acres, and varies from a light silty soil to stiff clay. Its surface is from 8ft. to 12ft. above *Ordnance datum*, the average being about 10ft. or 3½ft. below the level of spring tides. On this soil is found some of the richest corn and pasture land in England. There is a fair sprinkling of trees, and the hedges in many places on the old pasture are of very vigorous growth, and, when allowed to grow unchecked, attain heights of from 10ft. to 15ft.

Fig. 15.

Appendix vi.

This alluvial soil varies from a mixture of argillaceous sand, called silt, to soft buttery clay of a blue or brown colour. On the richer lands the surface, for a depth of 1ft. or more, consists of a rich loam, containing a mixture of clay, silt and decayed vegetable matter. Such are the rich grazing lands lying between Boston, Kirton, Sutterton, Wigtoft, Fossdyke, and along a great part of East Holland, and in South Holland.

The marsh land between Holbeach and the coast, inclosed since the Roman Banks were made, is much of this character, but the pastures, being newer, are not so rich.

SILT LAND. The silt-lands, though easy to work, are not so productive as the richer loams. In some parts are large patches of poor and hungry soils, while in others, as the proportion of argillaceous matter increases, they become good land for market gardens, especially when there is, as frequently, a substratum of clay.

ACCRETION OF ALLUVIAL MATTER. The greatest deposit has taken place nearest the sea coast, and along the sides of the Outfalls of the tidal rivers. The depth at Boston is as much as 16ft. to 18ft. It thins off gradually from the coast and the rivers, to nothing where its joins the peat, or the gravel beaches of the high land. The action to which this is due may be seen in operation at the present time on the salt marshes, where on the margin of every creek, and for a short distance away, the ground is higher than over the rest of the marsh.

RATE OF ACCRETION. Some idea of the rate at which alluvial deposits have taken place in past ages may be gathered from what is now going on, and from the area of the land which has been recovered from the sea, during the last six centuries. The greatest accretion, naturally, has taken place at the head of the bay, off the coast of Holbeach.

Here successive enclosures have taken place, until the bank, made by the Romans for the protection of the land from the sea, is left from 3 to 4 miles inland. Allowing that these banks were made 1,500 or 1,600 years ago, it will be found that the rate of growth has been about 9ft. to 10ft. a year. Allowing the same rate of accretion in past ages, it would take 13,000 to 15,000 years for the formation of the alluvial deposits of the present Fenland.

The inclosures which have been made at different times vary considerably in level, the most inland being lower than those more recently inclosed. Thus, the average level of the land lying to the north of the Roman Bank in South Holland is 3ft. to 4ft. higher than that on the inside; and the modern inclosures along the east coast are about 4ft. higher than those on the inner side of the Roman Bank.

Appendix vi.

The following description of the growth of salt marshes on this coast, is extracted from a paper read by the Author before the Institution of Civil Engineers in 1876. "If not assisted by artificial means the process of accretion is stationary after a certain distance from the shore. The oldest salt marshes are about half to three quarters of a mile in depth, beyond which there is nothing but bare sands. Directly the marsh is inclosed by a bank, and the water shut off, the accretion at once becomes rapid, and, in the course of a few months, the sand is covered with warp, then a growth of sampire follows, succeeded by grass, and in a few years a marsh is formed outside the recent inclosure, which rapidly rises by the accession of warp, through which the grass grows, until, for a foot or more in depth, the soil is a mass of the finest warp, mixed with roots of grass and decayed vegetation. This process, repeated during several years, makes some of the most valuable and fertile soil in the country. The cause of the accretion not extending beyond a certain point is easily explained. The tidal water, carrying matter in suspension, spreads over the foreshore up to the banks, and for the short time when there is a period of quiet, the matter in suspension is deposited. The silicious particles of silt and sand, having the heaviest specific gravity, are deposited first, the warp or loamy particles being carried back with the ebbing current. Gradually, as the marsh rises, the silt is deposited before the water reaches the banks, the warp alone being carried to the upper part and there deposited. As samphire and grass respectively grow, this process is hastened, the vegetation holding the warp and filtering it from the water as it recedes. For the deposit of this light flocculent material, constituting the argillaceous portion of the suspended matter, a state of rest in the water is necessary, agitation keeping it in a state of suspension. After a certain breadth of marsh has been formed,—generally, on this coast, about one third of a mile,—the body of water flowing off the marsh on the recession of the tide becomes so great,

Fascine Work at the Outfall of Fen Rivers. Wheeler, Min. Pro. I.C.E. Vol. 46.

as to form a current sufficiently strong to carry with it both the silicious and argillaceous particles held in suspension. After a time, from the action of the forward and retrograde motion of the wavelets of the ebbing tide, a marked and broken line, or steep, from 1ft. to 2ft. in height, appears at the edge of the newly formed marsh, up to which the neap tides reach, and beyond which the marsh ceases to grow. The existing marsh is then covered by ordinary spring tides, but continues to rise slowly until at last it is only covered by the few spring tides, which rise above the average height.

"Warp begins to take place at 12ft. above low water. Mean low water in the estuary is 7·32ft. below the *Ordnance datum*. Samphire commences to grow when the surface is just covered at neap tides, or from 14ft. to 15ft. above low water, and disappears when the level of the soil is about 16ft. above low water, or 2ft. above an ordinary neap tide; the samphire being gradually replaced by grass.

"Newer and more recently formed salt marshes are about 18ft. above low water, and the old marshes 20½ft.

"The following are the approximate levels at which the process of accretion takes place, compared with the *Ordnance datum*.—

		Feet.	
Mean low water	... ...	7·32	below
Warp first deposited	... ...	5·50	above
Samphire	... ...	6·68	,,
Grass first appears	... ...	8·68	,,
New Marsh	... ...	10·68	,,
Old high Marsh	... ...	13·15	,,
Ordinary neap tides	... ...	6·69	,,
Ordinary spring tides	... ...	13·34	,,
Mean high water	... ...	10·21	,,

"The period of time, during which the process is maturing, varies according to the situation of the marsh and to the artificial means taken to assist the warping process. Silt foreshores, outside a newly-erected inclosure, become grass marsh in about ten years; but after this a period of from twenty to twenty five years ought to elapse before any inclosure takes place, during which time the marine vegetation and grass filter the finer particles of warp from the water, and the roots and decayed vegetation fill the soil with organic matter."

Kirton and Frampton Marsh, inclosed in 1870, was on an average about 45 chains deep. This marsh extends out from the Roman Bank and had therefore been growing ever since its construction.

GROWTH OF SALT MARSHES.

In 1837, when the training works of the Welland were commenced, a large area of the foreshore on the Moulton and Frampton shores was bare sand; in 1851 it was all grassed over, the Moulton marsh extending over 800 acres, and the Frampton over 300 acres. The latter was inclosed in 1864.

Moulton Marsh, when inclosed in 1875, was 35 chains deep and had been growing for 38 years.

Gedney Marsh, which had been growing since the last century, had an average width, when inclosed, of 35 chains.

SOURCE OF ALLUVIAL MATTER.

The alluvial matter of which the upper surface of these marshes is composed is derived from the warp brought down in suspension by the rivers which discharge into the head of the Wash, principally from that derived from the Witham and the Welland, partly also from that from the Nene, and in a less degree from that of the Ouse. The warp transported by these rivers in heavy floods is carried in suspension, for some distance beyond the mouth of the rivers, into the estuary, and oscillates backwards and forwards with the ebbing and flowing of the tides, until it is finally carried on to the marshes and deposited. The largest amount of accretion has taken place between the Nene and the Welland, a large amount between the Nene and the Ouse, a less quantity between the Welland and the Witham and along the Lincolnshire coast, and only a very small area on the Norfolk coast.

RECLAMATION SCHEMES.

Several schemes have been brought forward for reclaiming land in the Wash, and this idea is from time to time revived, with the view of providing work for the unemployed. In the first edition of this work the Author expressed an opinion favourable to such schemes. In doing so, he relied on the reports of Sir John Rennie and others, but the time that has since elapsed has given him the opportunity of more thoroughly investigating the subject, and he has been forced reluctantly to the conclusion that, beyond small and gradual reclamations, as the marshes grow up and become ripe for inclosure, no general attempt at reclamation on a large scale can be successful.

SOURCE OF ALLUVIUM.

With regard to the conditions favourable to accretion on which the promoters of the inclosure of land in the Wash relied, it was contended by Sir John Rennie that the Wash was gradually silting up, due to the deposit brought down by the rivers, but principally to material brought in by the tides. Mr. Skertchley, of the Geological Survey, endorsed this view, and stated that it is to the sea that is due 'the ceaseless supplies of sand and silt which daily encroach on the waters of the Wash,' and with regard to the proposed reclamation scheme, that ' by inclosing and warping this 150,000 acres, it would be entirely converted into good land in 50 years.'

Geological Memoir. 1877.

The fact, however, appears to have been lost sight of that any alluvium brought into the Wash from the sea must come from the north, as that is the direction from which the flood tides come. The coast lying north of the Wash is low, flat and sandy, and there are no cliffs from which a supply of alluvium could be derived south of the Humber, or for a distance of 50 miles. The velocity of the current, due to the flood tide, is not more than 2½ to 3 knots, and, as it only runs southward for 6 hours and the current is then reversed, it is obvious that any alluvial matter in suspension would not be carried a greater distance from the source of supply than 15 or 20 miles, when it would be carried again northwards, or settle on the bottom of the sea during slack water. The depth of water in the sea, along the coast north of the Wash, is from 7 to 8 fathoms, and, considering the enormous volume of tidal water due to such a depth, with which the comparatively small amount of alluvium derived from the erosion of the cliffs is mixed in suspension, it is impossible that any of it could ever find its way into the Wash. Repeated examinations of the water at the lower end of the Estuary, both on the flood and ebb tides, and of samples taken at various depths, show the water to be bright and clear, and free from all alluvial matter. The samples generally give on filtration a few grains of clear silica, derived from sand disturbed from the bottom by the action of the tides, but this sand simply oscillates backwards and forwards with the flood and ebb. Occasionally, after very heavy north-east gales and on-shore winds, when the surface of the coast is disturbed, the water is turbid, and at such times a small amount of *detritus* is no doubt carried into the Estuary; but to set against this is the material carried away to sea on the ebb during very heavy freshets. Within the Wash the erosion of the cliffs at Hunstanton affords a small supply, but the few acres washed away from this cliff would go a very little way towards raising the large area contemplated by the promoters of the reclamation scheme.

LAND FIT FOR INCLOSURE.

The sand forming the coasts of the Wash is utterly unfit for inclosure as it lacks the qualities necessary to sustain vegetation. Neither is the silty foreshore, if inclosed, adapted to grow either grass or corn. Where the accreted land has been inclosed, before it has risen to a certain height, although capable of growing marine grass, it has proved worthless for cultivation and has not been worth the cost of inclosure. Unless the accreted land consists of a sufficient depth of alluvial matter, incorporated with the accumulation of organic matter derived from the decay of the marine vegetation of a long period, it is poor and hungry; unless raised to a sufficient height above the tides, the salt does not get sufficiently washed out, but remains in too great excess to suit crops of corn or grass; when also the surface is too low, every high tide drives the underground salt water upwards to the roots of the crops and stunts their growth.

ALLUVIUM BROUGHT DOWN BY THE RIVERS.

As already pointed out, the only source from which a supply of alluvial matter, fit for warping up the Estuary, can be derived is that brought down in suspension by the five rivers—the Ouse, the Nene, the Welland, the Witham, and Steeping river. Alluvium brought down in times of flood by these rivers has been deposited in the Delta formed at their mouths, to a lesser extent along the coast on the west side, and to a very small extent on the east, or Norfolk, coast.

The area of land drained by these rivers is 3,724,800 acres (5,820 square miles). Of the rain which falls on this drainage basin, it was estimated by the Author that only 4½in. is, on an average, discharged by the rivers in floods, and this calculation was accepted by Mr. Skertchley in the Government Geological Memoir. The remainder is taken up by evaporation, absorption by the vegetation and soakage into the chalk and Oolite strata. A number of samples of water, taken by the Author from the Ouse, the Welland and the Witham, in different conditions of the rivers, gave an average result of 100 grains of alluvial matter and sand in suspension in a cubic foot of water. This would yield a total quantity of matter brought down in suspension of 385,560 tons annually. Owing to the small inclination in the bed of the rivers, and the low velocity of their currents, the quantity rolled along the bed of the channels is so small that it need not be taken into account. Allowing 1½ tons to a cubic yard when deposited, and supposing that it were all deposited on an area of one acre, to a depth of 5ft., this would make 32 acres in a year.

Allowing a period of 1,700 years to have elapsed since the Roman Banks were made, there would have accreted, according to this calculation, 54,400 acres, up to the present time. The depth of 5ft. is taken as giving the space between the average surface of the marshes which have been inclosed, and the level at which warp first begins to deposit on the sands, and samphire to grow, in accordance with the data given previously. If, however, the inclosures were made on any large scale, the depth to be accreted would be considerably more than this, the average level of the sands between low water and the shore being about 12ft. below the level of the salt marshes, and this would represent the average height to which these sands must be raised before they would be fit for inclosure.

AREA OF ACCRETED LAND.

The quantity of land actually reclaimed, outside the Roman Banks, is as follows:—

	Acres.
West Side or East Holland	6,336
Head of the Wash including South Holland, outside the Roman Bank	35,163
Bicker Haven and the Welland Marshes	10,464
Nene Marshes	9,536
Norfolk Coast, by Estuary Company	1,800
	63,299

This is equal to an average growth of 37·23 acres a year. The calculated quantity of deposit available, as given above, approximates sufficiently close to the quantity of marsh that has formed and that has actually been inclosed, or rendered fit for reclamation, since the Roman Banks were made, to show that the alluvial matter available for making land suitable for cultivation is limited. If the average height, that the 150,000 acres proposed to be reclaimed would require to be raised by accretion, be taken at 12ft., the quantity of material required would be 290,400,000 cubic yards, and, allowing the quantity brought down by the rivers to be as given above, it would require 11,102 years before the land was fit for inclosure.

NORFOLK ESTUARY INCLOSURES.

As a further proof of the impracticability of any such scheme, the results obtained by the Norfolk Estuary Company may be quoted.

On the east side of the Wash, the Norfolk Estuary Company obtained Parliamentary powers in 1846, to reclaim 30,000 acres of sands and marshes, submerged at high tides, lying at the mouth of the Ouse and the Nene. Accord to the Preamble of a Bill, promoted in 1876 for amending the previous Act, a sum of £325,000 had then been expended by the Company, in diverting the river Ouse, as part of their scheme of reclamation and in other works. Since then, further expenditure has been incurred, and up to the present time only about 1,800 acres have been reclaimed, of which about 1,000 acres is the property of the frontagers, and which was grass before the Company came into existence. There is at the present time, a small area nearly ready for inclosure, but the greater part of the remainder of the 30,000 acres, which it was proposed to reclaim, is still little more than bare sands.

LARGE SCHEMES OF INCLOSURE IMPRACTICABLE.

From this statement of facts, it is evident that the gigantic scheme of reclamation, as proposed by Sir John Rennie, is utterly impracticable, and, even if practicable, judging from the results which have been obtained from attempts to inclose lands in the Wash on a large scale, would be financially disastrous.

Tidal Rivers. Wheeler. 1893.

The subject of the transporting power of water, the quantity of material brought down by the rivers, and the action of the tides in moving solid matter, is fully dealt in Chapters IV, *On the transporting power of water*, and VI, *On the physical conditions of tidal rivers*, of the Author's book on Tidal Rivers.*

ANNUAL OUTWARD GROWTH OF THE MARSHES.

The following table will further illustrate the slow rate at which the accreted land, along the coasts of the Wash, has increased. It gives the average annual extension outwards from the Roman banks, since their construction, including the land reclaimed and that now nearly ready for inclosure.

	Feet	Miles
On the East Holland Coast	1·12	along a distance of 16
Along the Welland	2·00	,, ,, 4
In South Holland	13·00	,, ,, 11

Tidal Rivers, their Hydraulics, Improvement and Navigation, by W. H. Wheeler. M. Instit. C.E. *Longmans & Co., London and New York*, 1893.

	Feet.		Miles.
The Nene reclamation	5·50	,, ,,	7
On the Norfolk Coast	1·55	,, ,,	4

Water Supply.

Sources of Supply.

The water for use in the Fenland is derived almost entirely from rivers, drains, ponds or shallow wells.

Wells.

The wells seldom exceed from 12ft. to 15ft. in depth. If carried too low the water becomes impregnated with salt, or brackish, and unfit for use; the same remark applies to ponds; great care has therefore to be exercised in sinking these, as a slight extra depth may spoil the quality of the water.

The Sock.

In silty soils there is a continuous underground flow of water, which rises and falls throughout the whole district, coincidently with the rise and fall of the water in the rivers or main drains, due to floods or droughts. This variation in the level of the water is locally termed the 'sock' or 'soak.' The underground level of the water is also affected by the tides. At high tides the drainage and spring water flowing underground towards the estuary is driven back by the head of water in the sea, and the level of the water in the wells for a considerable distance inland is stated to vary with the condition of the tide. It is asserted by well sinkers that if shallow wells are sunk anywhere near the coast when the 'sock' is high, due to spring tides, the water in them will be permanently 'brack,' or so much impregnated with salt as to be unfit for use, but that if the sinking takes place during neap tides, fresh water will be secured. The Author has not had an opportunity of personally verifying these statements, but there is no doubt that at a certain distance below the surface the water contains sufficient salt in solution to make it unfit for use.

Deep Wells.

Attempts to obtain water by sinking deep wells have been only partially successful. At Boston, after boring to the depth of 572ft., the attempt was abandoned. At Fossdyke a boring to the depth of 326ft. was equally unsuccessful. In Deeping Fen a good supply was obtained at a depth of 200ft., and at Donington, at a depth of 286ft.

Mineral Springs.

On the east side of the Witham, on the margin of the Fenland, at Woodhall, a valuable spring of mineral water was discovered in 1828, by Mr. J. Parkinson, when sinking a shaft, with the hope of finding coal. The spring was discovered at a depth of 530ft. in the inferior Oolite. The water stands naturally at 50ft. from the surface. The proportion of iodine and bromine in this water is greater than in any other known spring, and it is very efficacious for all rheumatic complaints.

There is also a chalybeate spring at Monks' Abbey, near Lincoln, the water from which has a temperature of about 10 degrees more than that of the neighbouring wells, and another at Catley Abbey, the water from which is designated as 'natural seltzer water.'

URBAN SUPPLIES.

Bourne is supplied by very excellent water derived from springs which break out between the Oxford clay and the Oolite stone.

The town of Boston has an artificial water supply, derived from a reservoir at Miningsby, on the northern edge of the Fenland, about 12 miles from the town, at an elevation of 164ft. above it. This reservoir covers an area of 34 acres, and contains, when full, 75½ million gallons. The gathering ground extends nearly to the village of Asgarby and covers 3 square miles. The water is conveyed to the reservoir by a natural brook, the quantity flowing off the gathering ground during the winter months being sufficient to fill the reservoir.

Spalding was formerly supplied from a neighbouring watercourse, the water from which was derived from springs, 20 miles away, rising between the Oxford clay and the Oolite. The water is now derived from wells at Bourne, and brought in pipes for a distance of 10 miles. When boring for the supply, water impregnated with iron was met with, and at 12ft. below this, the main spring was tapped; at 100ft. the overflow was at the rate of 1,872,000 gallons a day.

ANALYSIS OF FEN WATER.

The following analysis of different Fen waters, is given in the Sixth Report of the Rivers' Pollution Commission, 1868.

RESULTS EXPRESSED IN PARTS PER 100,000.

	\multicolumn{7}{c}{DISSOLVED MATTERS.}	\multicolumn{3}{c}{HARDNESS.}
	Total solid impurity.	Organic Carbon	Organic Nitrogen.	Ammonia.	Nitrogen, as Nitrates and Nitrites.	Total combined Nitrogen.	Previous sewage or animal contamination.	Chlorine.	Temporary.	Permanent.	Total.
Boston, Miningsby.	19·88	·152	·033	—	—	·033	—	2·15	10·6	3·8	14·4
Spalding	28·48	·179	·043	—	—	·043	—	2·70	8·0	9·7	17·7
Pode Hole, Fen water.	110·40	1·327	·159	·080	—	·225	·340	12·75	25·2	42·1	67·3
Do. Rain do.	5·28	·142	·029	—	·031	·060	—	·90	—	3·8	3·8
Bourne, Well Head.	42·92	·104	·020	—	—	·020	—	3·10	23·4	11·8	35·2

The analysis of the Spalding water was taken in 1873, from the former source of supply. The water analysed at Pode Hole was from that pumped for the use of the hamlet, and may be taken as a favourable representation of the water supply of Deeping Fen. The Commissioners remarked that they considered it to be utterly unfit for domestic use; and that a sample of rain water, taken from the tank belonging to the Pode Hole engines, was very much purer, more palatable and more wholesome. The contents of this tank fairly represented the water which can be obtained in the Fens, wherever a clean roof, and a sufficiently capacious tank is provided.

The principal fen drains are replenished in summer by water admitted into them from the high land streams, which restores the loss by evaporation and absorption, and also affords a fresh supply for the cattle. The water thus introduced is termed 'living' water to distinguish it from the stagnant water in the drains. Thus, Deeping Fen is supplied with fresh water in summer time from the river Glen.

On the western margin of the Fenland, at Bourne, Horbling and Sleaford, very strong springs of water of excellent quality break out from the Oolite rocks, and feed the numerous Becks which discharge into the Black Sluice Drain, and also the River Slea which discharges into the Witham. There are also several small becks or streams, from the higher land between the Slea and Lincoln, which discharge into the drains of the fens along the Witham.

The Witham is replenished by several tributaries which afford a perennial supply of clear spring water to the river in summer time. The East and West Fens are supplied from the Steeping River and the Catchwater Drain.

Rain water is made use of for domestic purposes to a large extent, many of the houses and cottages being supplied with underground brick tanks for storing it. Considering the difficulty of obtaining a supply of pure water, however, this source is not made as much use of as it ought to be. The Author has brought this matter forward on several occasions in the *Stamford Mercury*, in the *Fenland Circular* for October, 1895, and also in a paper read at the request of the Lincolnshire Chamber of Agriculture at Lincoln, in 1879, from which the following is an extract:—

"On this side of the country, where the quantity of rain is small, there is yet a sufficient fall on every house in the course of the year, if properly husbanded, to yield a supply to the inmates. A cottage covers about 500 square feet of ground: the rain falling on the slated roof, supposing it to amount to 22in. a year, the average for Lincolnshire, would yield about 5,700 gallons, or a daily supply of $15\frac{1}{4}$ gallons. The tank to contain this must be so proportioned as to be large enough to take the winter supply, supplemented by thunderstorms and ordinary showers during the rest of the year. The roofs of the house and buildings on a farm of about 100 acres may be taken to cover about 4,500 square feet of ground, and would yield 51,384 gallons, equal to a daily supply of 140 gallons, sufficient for the requirements of the farm and homestead. As a guide, in providing tanks for rain water in the district, it may be taken that they should hold 2 gallons for every square foot of roof, where they are slated. Thatch and tiled roofs are more absorbent than slates, and soak up many a shower which would find its way into the tank from off slates. The loss on a tile roof has been proved to amount to as much as one inch of rain during the summer months, or 602 gallons on a cottage roof. Churches and schools afford a valuable source of supply for villages, which is almost entirely neglected. An ordinary village church covers about 7,000 square feet, and the schools 1,000 more. These together would yield over 90,000 gallons in the course of the year, equal to a daily supply of 250 gallons."

Stamford Mercury. Oct. 21, 1870. To this may be further added the following extract from a letter of the author in the *Stamford Mercury* of October 21st, 1870. "An examination of the rainfall during a dry summer shows that storage room should be provided for 76 days' supply, equal to about 22 hogsheads for a cottage. A tank to hold this quantity requires to be 6¼ft. in diameter and 6ft. deep below the dome. The cost of such a tank, made with two rims of brick-work in mortar and covered inside with cement, domed over and provided with a manhole and stone slab with iron lid, is about 7s. a hogshead, or £7 14s."

The average amount of rainfall is rather under-stated in the above calculation.

CHAPTER XVII.

Natural History, Physical Products, Climatology and Health.

Natural History.

IN the following Chapter it is not intended to enter into any technical or lengthened descriptions of the natural Flora or Fauna of the Fenland. These subjects have been treated with much detail in *The Fenland Past and Present*, in which is given a list of all the wild birds, fishes and plants, that either formerly existed, or still remain.

Fenland. Miller and Skertchley.

A history of the Fenland would however not be complete without some general account of its natural products.

A very complete collection of fen-birds, and of the water-fowl which are to be found in the estuary, has been placed in the museum at Wisbech, where are also many interesting fen relics, antiquities and specimens of Fenland geology.

Birds.

The Fens, in their natural condition, formed a congenial breeding ground for water-fowl of nearly every description, the taking and sale of which was the chief means of subsistence of the *Fen Slodger*.

Camden, whose description of England was written before the inclosure of the Fens, gives the following quaint account of the feathered tribes frequenting these parts. "At certain seasons of the year, not to mention fish, amazing flights of fowl are found all over this part of the country, not the common ones which are in great esteem in other places, such as teal, quails, woodcocks, pheasants, partridges, &c., but such as have no Latin names, the delicacies of the tables and the food of heroes, fit for the palates of the great—puittes, godwittes, knots, which I take to mean Canute's birds, for they are supposed to come hither from Denmark; dotterell, so called from their extravagant dotishness, which occasions these imitative birds to be caught by candle light; if the fowler only puts out his arm they put out a wing, and if his leg they do the same; in short, whatever the fowler does, the bird does the same, till the net is drawn over it."

Drayton's Polyolbion.

Drayton also thus describes this bird :—

> For as you creep or lower, or, lie, or stoop, or go;
> So marking you with care, the apish bird doth do;
> And acting everything doth never mark the net,
> Till he is in the snare which men for him have set.

Camden's Britannia.

Again Camden says, "The fen, called the West Fen is the place where the ruffs and reeves resort in greatest numbers; and many other sorts of water fowl, which do not require the shelter of reeds and rushes, migrate hither to breed; for this fen is bare, having been imperfectly drained by narrow canals, which intersect it for many miles. The multitude of starlings that roost in the reeds in the East Fen, in winter, break down many by perching on them .. The birds which inhabit the different fens are very numerous. Besides the common wild duck, wild geese, garganies, pochards, shovellers, and teals breed here. Pewits, gulls and black tern abound, and a few of the great terns or tickets are seen among them; the great crested grebes, called gaunts, are found in the East Fen, the lesser crested, the black and dusky and the little grebe, cootes, water hens, spotted water hens, water rails, ruffs, redshanks, lapwings or wipes, red-breasted godwits and whimbrels are inhabitants of these fens. The godwits breed near Washingborough. The whimbrels only appear for about a fortnight in May, near Spalding, and then quit the country. Opposite to Fosdyke Wash, during summer, are vast numbers of avosettas, called there yelpers, from their cry as they hover over the sportsman's head, like lapwings. Knots are taken in nets along the shores near Fosdyke in great numbers, during winter, but disappear in spring. The short-eared owl visits the neighbourhood of Washingborough with the woodcocks, and probably performs its migration with those birds, quitting the country at the same time. It does not perch on trees, but conceals itself in old long grass."

Drayton's Polyolbion.

Michael Drayton enumerates the following birds inhabiting the fens. The duck and mallard, the teal, the goosander, the widgeon, the golden eye, the smeath, the coote, the water hen, the water ouzel, the dab chick, the puffin, the wild swan, the ilke, the heron, the crane, the snipe, the bidcock, the redshank, the bittern and the wild goose. Among such as feed flying, the seamew, the sea pie, gull, curlew, cormorant and osprey.

Magna Britannia. Cox.

Cox, in his description of Lincolnshire, referring to the fen country, says, "The rivers, together with the adjoining sea, afford plenty of all sorts of fish and fowl, most of them common to other countries of the same situation, but some few peculiar, or particularly excellent. As to the fowl, this shire, as Dr. Fuller says, may be termed the aviary of England, for the wild fowl thereof being remarkable for their (1) plenty, which is so great that sometimes in the month of August, 3,000 mallards and other birds of that kind have been caught at one draught (as 'tis here said); (2)

variety, there being scarce names enough for the several kinds; (3) deliciousness, wild fowl being more dainty than some, because of their continual motion. But particularly, this shire affords two sorts of birds, most admirable meat, viz., knutes and dotterells. The knute is a delicious bird, brought here out of Denmark, at the charge and for the use of King Knut or Kanutus, when he was received King of England. As it has a royal name, so it is esteemed royal dainties, and no country almost hath them but this. . . . To these we may add, not only such as are of great value in other countries, as teal, quail, woodcocks, pheasants, partridges, &c., but such as are of so delicate and agreeable flesh, that the nicest palates always covet them, as puits and godwits."

In Percy's *Household Book* of 1512, the value of these birds is thus given: lapwings, knots and dotterells, 1d. each; sea gulls, plovers, woodcocks and redshanks, 1½d.; pigeons, terns and snipes, 3 for 1d.; stints, 6 for 1d.; ruffs, reeves and partridges, 2d. each; bitterns and curlews, 1½d. each.

As further showing the esteem in which the wild fowl of the Fens were held, there is an entry in the Lincoln Corporation Records of a present sent to the Lord Treasurer, consisting of '1 doz. godwits, 5 doz. knots, and 1 doz. pewitts.' Even as recently as the last century, knots used to be netted, fattened and sent in large numbers to the London market.

To these accounts may be added the beautiful, but imaginary, description of Charles Kingsley: "But grand enough it was . . . while dark green alders and pale green reeds stretched for miles round the broad lagoon, where the coot clanked, and the bittern boomed, and the sedge bird, not content with its own sweet song, mocked the notes of all the birds around; while high overhead hung, motionless, hawk upon hawk, buzzard beyond buzzard, kite beyond kite, as far as the eye could see. Far off upon the silver mere, would rise a puff of smoke from a punt, invisible from its flatness and its white paint. Then down the wind came the boom of the great stanchion gun, and after that sound, another sound, louder as it neared, a cry as of all the bells of Cambridge, and all the hounds of Cottesmore, and overhead rushed and whirled the skein of terrified wild fowl, screaming, piping, clacking, croaking, filling the air with the coarse rattle of their wings, while clear above all, sounded the wild whistle of the curlew, and the trumpet note of the great wild swan. They are all gone now." *C. Kinsley. Prose Idylls.*

The Fenmen long resisted the enclosure of the Fens, as being destructive of the birds and fishes, from the catching of which they obtained their living, the sympathising poet expressing their feelings in the following lines:—

> Come, brethren of the water,
> And let us all assemble,

> To treat this matter, which
> Doth make us quake and tremble;
> For we shall rue, if it be true,
> That fens be undertaken,
> And where we feed, in fen and reed,
> They'll feed both beef and bacon.

Of the many fen birds which have disappeared since the inclosure, one of the most beautiful was the bittern, with his frill of feathers. This bird used to be called the butter-bump, and his melancholy booming was heard for long distances over the Fens. The ruffs and reeves were also very beautiful birds, having a frill of feathers round the neck, hardly two birds being marked alike. Bustards were also to be found in the Fens, although they were more plentiful on the Wolds. These birds fed in large flocks; owing to their weight, some weighing as much as 14lb., they could not rise quickly, but had to run a short distance first. They were hunted by dogs trained for the purpose, which was said to give as much sport as coursing hares.

Snipe are occassionally met with. Barn and tree owls used to be very common along the coast, between Wainfleet and Freiston, and a few are now occasionally caught, and sent with other birds to Boston market.

Camden's Britannia. Herons were once very common. Camden says that in his time there was " a vast heronry at Cressy Hall. The herons resort hither in February to repair their nests, settle there in spring to breed, and quit the place during the winter. They are as numerous as rooks, and their nests so crowded together that Mr. Pennant counted 80 in one tree...They have been considerably reduced on account of the mischief which they do the land." There were heronries until recently at Cawood Hall, at the Wykes Farm, Donington, and also at Leverton.

Cranes were very common; there are a few still left in the neighbourhood of Bicker Fen, and they are occasionally to be seen on the marshes, and on the shore at the mouth of the Witham.

Rooks are very common, considering the scarcity of trees.

Thompson's Boston. In the reign of Henry VIII, the swans in the Witham were considered of sufficient importance to warrant an ordinance being passed by the Justices of the Peace for their preservation. A copy of this ordinance is given in Thompson's *Boston*.

DECOYS. Large numbers of decoys existed in the Fens for the capture of wild fowl; and from these the London markets were principally supplied. A decoy consisted of pools surrounded by trees and plantations, and branching off from them were small channels or ditches called 'pipes.' At the time of catching the birds, these pipes were covered with nets, which rested on hoops, and were terminated by a drawing net. Into these the wild fowl were enticed by various devices; but the usual mode was by means of a decoy duck, trained for the purpose. This bird was taught to obey the whistle of the decoy man, who tempted it to swim up to the trapping tunnel when he saw a number of wild fowl; these, following the tame one and being led into the channel, were then enclosed and ultimately taken by the net. These decoy birds would fly away to sea in the morning, where meeting and consorting with strange birds during the day-time, at night they would lead them away inland to the decoy ponds. Dogs were also kept, which by their sagacity and training were of the greatest assistance to the keeper, in drawing the birds into the nets. Of such importance were decoys deemed, that special Acts of the Legislature were passed for their regulation and protection. By an Act passed in Queen Anne's reign, the clauses of which were re-enacted in the 10th year of George II, it was made an offence against the law to take birds at unseasonable times, under a penalty of five shillings for every bird. The time allowed was from the end of October to February.

At the time of the original drainage of the Bedford Level, under the 'Lynn law,' the pools of the decoys, or 'meeres,' were specially excepted from the grants made to the Undertakers, and they were restricted from draining them. The wild fowl has since had to yield to the drainer, and the site of these inland lakes is now only indicated by their names—the 'meeres' having become dry land.

Friskney was noted for its decoys, and one of these was continued in use and worked until recently. Immense quantities of birds were caught in these decoys. In one season, a few winters previous to the inclosure of the East Fen, ten decoys, five of which were in Friskney, furnished 31,200 birds for the London market. It was not considered a good season unless the decoys yielded 5,000 birds. The birds usually taken in the decoy were the Mallard (*Anas boschas*), the Teal (*Anas craca*) and the Pochard (*Anas ferina*). {Oldfield's Wainfleet.}

Beside the decoys the open fens and marshes yielded large numbers of birds to the Fen Slodger and the 'Gunner.' At certain seasons the Fen Slodgers used to assemble in great numbers to have an annual drive of the young ducks, before they took wing. A large track of marsh was beaten and the birds driven into a net. Sometimes as many as 2,000 birds have thus been taken at one time. {THE FEN SLODGERS.}

The marshes on the coast are still the resort of large numbers of wild fowl, including geese, duck, widgeon, golden plover, curlews, godwits and redshanks. The knots, birds about the size of a small pigeon and delicious eating, come over from the northern latitudes in winter, in large flocks. The little dunlins, or stints, as they are more commonly called, flit along the shore and sometimes up the river in large flocks. {MARSH BIRDS.}

During the winter months, commencing about October, large nets, about 6ft. high and from 100yds. to 200yds. long, called 'flight nets,' are suspended between poles on the marshes and sands adjoining, the intervals between each line of net {FLIGHT NETS.}

sometimes being as little as 100yds. The nets are made of fine twine, with meshes 5in. square. Great numbers of birds get entangled in these nets at night. Rough nights and rough weather fill the nets the most. As soon as the tide ebbs, the fowler visits his nets and removes the birds, before the hooded crows or gulls have time to make a meal of them. The birds taken consist of curlews, knots, stints, widgeons, plovers and larks. They fetch from 6d. to 6s. a dozen, according to their size, the price obtained for some of the larger birds being 2s. each. Sometimes a flock of geese or ducks will fly through the nets and break them down.

The smaller birds are known as 'half-birds,' four of these being reckoned by the dealers who buy them as a couple.

GUNNERS.

Along the shores of the estuary and amongst the sandbanks are still to be found Fenmen or 'Gunners' who gain their living by shooting the duck, mallard and other wildfowl. For this purpose they use a small open boat or punt called a 'shout,' a word which has its origin from the same source as the modern Dutch word for a boat, *Schuyt*. These boats vary in size but may be taken generally as about 15ft. long, 3½ft. wide, and draw about 4in. of water. They are worked by a double bladed paddle, or, if going in close to the shore, by a pole or poy. A heavy duck gun, about 8ft. long, weighing from ¾ to 1½ cwt., is carried, resting on the stem. An average size gun fires ¾lb. of shot, requiring ⅜oz. of powder. A fortunate shot will occasionally bring down from 20 to 30 'whole birds' at a shot, at a distance of 80 to 100 yards.

GAME.
State Papers, Domestic. 1623.

Partridges appear to have been always abundant. In 1623, Sir Edward Peyton asked the King for a warrant to take 100 partridges annually in the Isle of Ely, Marshland and Holland 'where gentlemen cannot hawk,' on condition of 'planting them at his own charge in the champaign country about Isleham.' And again in 1628 there is a record of a warrant granted to Christopher Walton, to take partridges or any other fowl with nets, trammels, or any other engine, within the compass of Marshland and Lincoln, Holland, for the better storing of His Majesty's game near Royston and Newmarket.

Partridges are still abundant in the Fenland, and afford a considerable amount of sport over the cultivated land.

Owing to the absence of cover, there are no pheasants, and for the same reason there are no foxes.

HARES AND RABBITS.

RABBITS.

Rabbits are not very plentiful in the Fenland, but there are a great many scattered about. They are considered to be so dangerous to the sea banks that it is forbidden by the laws of the Court of Sewers to keep them anywhere near, and in an Act passed for their preservation, in the reign of George III, the sea banks of Lincolnshire were especially exempted from the provisions of the Act. Further particulars as to this subject are given in the first chapter.

Chap. i.

Hares at one time were very plentiful and gave good sport at the coursing meetings, which were frequently held. Cox, writing nearly 200 ago, says that the greyhounds " of this county are said to excel those of other countries as the first hunting hounds . . . and that the hares give the gentlemen a great deal of sport."

HARES.

FISH.

The inland fisheries in the Fens have had a recognised value from very early times. No less than 77 fisheries are mentioned in Domesday Book as paying rents in the Lincolnshire Fenland; the rents varying from 8d. and upwards a year. Rents were frequently paid in fish; thus a fishery at Bourne paid 2,500 eels a year. A farm at Pinchbeck paid 1,500 eels a year. Turner thus refers to the value of fisheries: " The Saxons eat various kinds of fish, but of this description of food the species that is most profusely noticed is the eel. They used eels as abundantly as swine. Two grants are mentioned, each yielding 1,000 eels, and by another 2,000 were received as an annual rent; 4,000 eels were an annual present from the monks of Ramsey to those of Peterboro'. We read of two places, purchased for £21, wherein 16,000 of these fish were caught every year; and in one charter 20 fishermen are stated to have furnished during the same period 60,000 eels to the monastery." In the dialogues composed by Elfric to instruct the Anglo-Saxon youths, when giving an account of the fisheries, the following are mentioned as forming the food of the people; eels, haddocks, skate, lampreys, and whatever swims in the river; and as the products of the sea, herrings, salmon, porpoises, sturgeons, oysters, crabs, mussels, cockles and such like.

ANCIENT FISHERIES.

History of the Anglo-Saxons.

Camden says that the Witham was famous for its pike, whence the old saying, ' Witham pike, England hath none the like.'

Oliver informs us that, owing to the abundance and quality of fish found in the fen rivers, the monks and holy men were led to choose situations near their banks for the erection of their religious houses. Right of fishery in the Witham was granted by William de Gaunt, in the year 1115, to the Abbey of Bardney; and in the year 1162 a fishery, near Dogdyke, was given to the monks of Kirkstead by William de Kyme. The Abbots of Bardney had 11 fisheries altogether, and the other monasteries, one or more each; besides the stew ponds attached to the houses. Thus it has been remarked, " The rivers abounding in excellent fish, supplied the Abbots' stew ponds plentifully; shell and sea fish were furnished by the fishermen of Boston; so that the Lents and fast days of the Abbeys had more the appearance of festivals than days of mortification, and every kind of fish in its season was placed on the well-stocked board."

Religious Houses on the Witham.

Oliver.

The town of Crowland used to pay £300 yearly to the Abbot of the Monastery for the liberty of fishing. Large quantities of inland fish were sent from Crowland and eight other places in the Fens to London by road.

From a journal kept by Sir Joseph Banks of his annual fishing parties held in the Witham, at the end of the last century, which generally lasted 4 days, we find that the quantity taken in some years amounted to over a ton in weight, the average for 9 years being about 1,600lbs. The largest fishes recorded as taken are a pike of 31lbs., carp 5¼lbs., burbot 3½lbs., perch 2lb., tench 2¼lbs., salmon 10lb.

Camden.

Both in the Witham and in the East and West Fens, immense shoals of sticklebacks used at intervals to make their appearance and came in such quantities that they were taken for manure. Attemps were also made to extract oil from them. The men employed in taking them could get 100 bushels a day, which realised a halfpenny a bushel.

FISHERY AT THE PRESENT TIME.

Since the inclosure of the Fens the rivers and drains have remained stocked with fish, and yield a large quantity of food, and also sport, to anglers who come in considerable numbers during the summer months from Sheffield and other towns, to fish in these waters, which are considered the best in England for the kind of fish they produce; consisting of pike, roach, perch, rudd, tench, bream and eels. A few trout are occasionally found in the upper part of the Witham, whence they have found their way from the Langworth, Bane or Slea rivers. Salmon, which at one time were to be found in the Witham, are never found now, the Grand Sluice being an obstacle to their ascending the river.

The pike are very large, an ordinary weight being from 10lbs. to 15 lbs., and occasionally reaching 25lbs.

Eels are very abundant, and frequently weigh from 4 to 5 lbs. They pass down the rivers and drains, on their way to sea in the autumn, in immense quantities, ascending to the fresh water streams again in the spring. At the time of the annual migration, as much as half a ton of eels has been taken at one time in nets, in the river immediately below the Grand Sluice. They are obtained in the drains by spearing or stanging, the fisherman using a flat bottomed boat, called a shout, for the purpose.

FISHERY BYE-LAWS.

The fishery in the Witham and Hobhole and Maud Foster and other drains adjacent thereto is free, but is regulated by Byelaws, made by the Witham Commissioners, under the power of their Acts, by which fishing by any other means than by rod and line, and all trailing or dragging for pike, is forbidden. The close season for fishing is fixed between the 15th March and 15th of June, during which all fishing is stopped.

In the Black Sluice District fishing is only permitted by license obtained from the Commissioners, for which a charge of 2/6 is made, and the fishing is subject to the same regulations as in the Witham.

The salt water fishery in Boston Deeps, extending along the coast of the Fenland, has from time immemorial been of great value. The Romans are reported to have sent oysters from *Metaris Estuarium* (Boston Deeps) to Rome. In 1613 a present of oysters and other fish was made by the Corporation of Boston to 'my Lord of Rutland.' In 1732 the Corporation directed that 'no person, not being a Freeman should take oysters upon the scalps or any fishery belonging to the Corporation without a license.' SALT WATER FISHERY.

In the Corporation records of 1777, it is stated that mussels were much sought after, as an article of trade, and the Marshall of the Admiralty used to receive between £3 and £4, for collecting the duties due to the Corporation, from mussel vessels coming into the port. MUSSEL FISHERY.

The mussel scalps have always been much in demand, for obtaining bait for the line fishery in the North, and at the beginning of the present century the mussels were carried by water to Bridlington, Scarborough and other northern ports. Frequently, 50 vessels would come in one season and carry away more than a 1,000 tons. After the opening of the Great Northern Railway, this trade was transferred to the Railway, and was further extended, the mussels being exported to Eyemouth, and other Scotch ports. They were also largely used as food in the manufacturing districts, as much as £50 a week being paid by one smack owner, for carriage to Leeds, Manchester, Birmingham, &c. The price was then a 1/- per bushel at Boston, realizing about 2/6 at their destination. About 50 sail of boats were then employed. In 1853, 100 tons a week were exported.

In 1863 the Royal Commissioners, appointed to report on the state of the Fisheries of the Kingdom, held a sitting at Boston, when evidence was produced before them, showing that owing to the want of supervision, and the reckless way in which the mussels had been taken—large quantities being sold for manure—the beds had been almost exhausted. Thompson's *Boston.*

Under the charter granted to the Corporation by Queen Elizabeth, control was given over the Fishery, but with the abolition of the Local Admiralty Court, by the operation of the Municipal Reform Act, the means of enforcing the penalties was lost. The powers of the Corporation therefore became useless.

In 1870 the Corporation obtained an order under the Sea Fisheries Act, giving them power to regulate the oyster and mussel Fishery in Boston Deeps. A Bailiff was appointed to see that the regulations were carried out. The mussel scalps were partially closed for a time, and became once more profitable. A few years after the order was obtained 4,500 tons of fish were obtained in one season, worth at Boston £1 per ton. The quantity sent away from Boston by railway, during the months of November and December OYSTER AND MUSSEL FISHERY. 33 Vict., c. 6, 1870.

amounted to 1,134 tons. Other scalps subsequently yielded at the same rate.

The mussels are principally taken during the winter months, but the season extends from the 1st of September to the end of May. During June, July and August, the beds are closed and fishing is prohibited. The mussels are collected on the beds by small hand rakes, and are packed in bags containing 2 bushels, weighing 2 cwt. When sent for bait they are not sorted or packed, but put loose into the railway trucks. Under the bye-laws of the Corporation it is not permitted to take mussels of a less length than 2in., or oysters of a less diameter than 2½in. The area of the beds on which mussels were found in Boston Deeps when the order was obtained was estimated at 3,400 acres. It is, however, considerably less at the present time.

As regards the yield, the mussels on the Old South Middle Bed, covering 240 acres, brooded in 1869. In the winter of 1871 4,500 tons were removed, giving 18¾ tons to the acre. The greater part of these were sent away for bait to the north of England and Scotland, and realised at Boston £1 a ton, the carriage amounting to nearly the same amount. The Gat Sand Bed, covering 158 acres, was covered with brood mussels in 1869 and in the winter of 1872 2,139 tons of mussels were taken, equal to 13½ tons to the acre. From 670 acres on the Tofts 4,000 tons were taken in 1876, equal to 6 tons to the acre. At this time 58 boats belonging to Boston, employing 115 men and boys, were engaged in this fishery. About the same number of Lynn fishermen were employed, many of whom came to the Boston Scalps. Owing to the falling off of the supply and the competition of fish sent from Holland, the trade is much less profitable, and the number of men employed is much less. The quantity of mussels sent from Boston by railway in 1893 was only 610 tons. The largest broods of mussels are obtained when the spring and early summer are warm. Strong north-east gales are very destructive, frequently causing the water to be so rough that the beds of young brood are broken up and destroyed. Considerable damage is done to the matured fish by a kind of star fish called 'five fingers,' which sucks out the fish from the inside of the shell; they are so abundant at times as to make it worth while for the fishermen to collect and sell them for manure. The mussels fatten most and are in best condition when there is a good run of fresh water coming down the rivers.

COCKLES.

The gathering of cockles off the sands in Boston Deeps gives employment to a great number of men and boys. The cockles were formerly sent away in their shells, but now the fish is removed from the shell, the process being aided by putting them in hot water. They are then sprinkled with salt, packed and sent by railway to the large towns. Nearly 100 men and boys were at one time employed in cockle gathering. The quantity of cockles landed at Boston during the last few years and their value was as follows:

	cwts.	£
1889	54,630	2,277
1890	46,420	2,667
1891	69,700	5,622
1892	70,790	4,964
1893	82,860	5,671
1894	69,210	4,562
1895	75,000	5,000

The above quantities are the weights of the cockles in their shells. When sent away by railway the fish only is sent, considerably reducing the weight.

PERIWINKLES. Periwinkles, or, as they are locally called, 'pinpaunches,' are also obtained in great quantities.

WHELKS. Whelks are found on the bed of the Deeps, and are taken by means of baskets, baited with flesh, lowered to the bottom of the water from the smacks. There are only one or two Boston boats engaged in this fishing, a greater number coming from Lynn. The quantity landed at Boston in 1895 was 400 cwts., of the value of £80; and from Lynn 8,000 cwt., of the value of £1,400.

OYSTERS. There were formerly some good beds of oysters in Boston Deeps, but these have disappeared. Oysters, are, however, still obtained at the lower end of Lynn Well. These oysters were of a very large size, the shells sometimes measuring as much as 5 inches in diameter. The flavour of the fish is very good, but not so delicate as the natives grown at Colchester. The quantity of oysters landed at Boston is very small, varying from 62,000 in 1885 and 1889, to 4,000 in 1895.

The quantity of shell fish landed at places along the north side of the Wash, other than Boston, was in 1895, as follows:—

	Crabs. Number.	Shrimps. Cwts.	Cockles.	Mussels.
Skegness	220,000	225	—	—
Wainfleet	—	500	—	—
Friskney	—	600	10,000	—
Wrangle	—	400	—	—
Leake	—	200	—	—
Leverton	—	300	—	—
Benington	—	80	—	—
Fossdyke and Kirton Skeldyke	—	160	860	2,000
Gedney Drove End	—	200	—	—
Sutton Bridge	—	110	—	370

H. Donnison, *Report on Eastern Sea Fisheries.* 1896.

SHRIMPS AND PRAWNS. Boston shrimps are noted for their good quality and these with prawns still constitute one of the chief sources of livelihood to the fishermen. They are taken nearly all the year round, the exception being during the frosts and cold weather of winter. The shrimp fishery may be said to extend over 9 months of the year. The smacks employed are about 5 to 6 tons in size and are worked by a man and a boy. They have a copper on board and boil the shrimps after they have done fishing, as they come up the river. The trawl net used, has a beam, 12ft. wide and 22ft. long, the meshes being ⅝in. Shrimps are also taken by men using a cart and horse along the shore, which drags the net along the water as the tide ebbs out. About twenty-eight carts and horses along the Lincolnshire coast are thus employed.

The quantity of shrimps and prawns sent from Boston during the last few years has been as follows:—

	Cwts.		£
1892	1423	of the value of	1423
1893	1577	,,	1396
1894	1111	,,	1017
1895	800	,,	800

The quantity of prawns and shrimps landed at Lynn, in 1894, was 6,494 cwts., of the value of £2,478.

SOLES. The soles caught in Boston Deeps are noted for their excellent quality. They are considered by the fishermen as a distinct species from those in the North Sea, being of less size and finer quality. They have become very scarce, and realize, to the fishermen, as much as 1/- per lb. The season for soles is considered to extend from May to November. The quantity of soles taken locally, and landed at Boston in 1894, was 93 cwt., of the value of £490.

HERRINGS. The herrings are also considered by the fishermen as belonging to Boston Deeps and different to those in the North Sea, which occasionally come into the Deeps in large shoals. They are smaller and finer than those caught off Yarmouth, seldom attaining a greater length than from 8in. to 9in. The herring nets have ⅞in. meshes. Large numbers of these fish are taken by nets spread on the main. These nets are each 20yds. long, and 5ft. high, and 12 of them are put in a row, making a length of 240ft. They have 13 knots to a foot. In one set of nets as many as 5,000 of these fish have been taken. The take varies generally from 200 to 2,000 fish.

SPRATS Sprats frequent the Deeps in winter shoals, and are taken in large quantities for manure, the price obtained being from 20/- to 25/- a ton.

The quantity and value of the sprats landed at Boston, during the last ten years, has been as follows:—

		Cwt.	£
1886	...	13,949	830
1887	...	11,972	692
1888	...	7,009	521
1889	...	4,781	350
1890	...	14,298	1,256
1891	...	22,561	1,827

	Cwt.	£
1892	4,855	504
1893	5,135	558
1894	4,662	412
1895	21,000	1,400

BUTTS & PLAICE. Butts, or, as they are called in other parts of the coast, flounders, are a small flat fish, from 6in. to 7in. long, which is plentifully found along the coast, and in the tidal portion of the rivers. When the tide is out these fish bury themselves in the silt and mud. They are caught in the rivers by spearing or 'pricking,' and, along the coasts, in the nets. They have a brown back and white belly. There is also another fish called a fluke, or 'in-shore' plaice, which is very like a butt, but has a blueish white belly, and is sometimes spotted. It is a different fish from the plaice caught in the open sea. Sandlings are also much like butts, but have a rough skin, more like a sole. A dab, or 'sal dab,' is a kind of plaice that is of very little value for food, being very watery when cooked. The spawn from the butts and 'in-shore' plaice is deposited in the silt foreshore, about April.

SMELTS. Smelts of fine quality are taken in the lower part of the river and in Boston dock.

QUANTITY OF FISH LANDED AT BOSTON. The following are the quantities and value of fish, not including sprats or shell fish, landed at Boston, and the value for the last ten years. This includes the fish caught in the North Sea, by the steam trawlers. The quantity landed at Lynn in 1894, was 1,429 cwt., of the value of £1,057.

	Cwt.	£
1886	28,086	14,462
1887	56,933	24,873
1888	59,476	28,165
1889	68,007	32,851
1890	77,189	43,382
1891	102,440	52,117
1892	129,896	68,867
1893	147,644	84,546
1894	138,245	82,509
1895	153,900	84,650

The total value of the wet fish landed at Boston and the various places on the north side of the Wash, in 1895, was £86,594. This was principally due to the fish caught in the North Sea by the steam trawlers, and delivered at Boston. The value of the shrimps and shell fish, almost the whole of which was caught in Boston Deeps, was £11,175. *H Donnison's Report. 1896.*

NETS. The fish in the Wash are caught in light trawl nets, about 12yds. long, having a beam 14ft. long. The meshes for soles are 1¼in. wide, from knot to knot. The herring nets have ⅞in. meshes and the shrimping nets ⅝in.

FISHING SMACKS. The smacks engaged in the fishery in Boston Deeps are generally half-decked, cutter rigged boats, from 5 to 10 tons, the crew consisting of one man and a boy, or two men. The boats engaged in the oyster and sprat fishing are wholly decked, reaching up to 20 and 30 tons. The fishermen engaged in these smacks have been truly described as "a hardy skilful race, whose seamanship is often beyond all praise, and whose knowledge of the intricate tides and currents is simply astonishing. Looking at the falling water on a sand bank, the smack master will say, 'I think, Sir, we can just run the tail of the sand, if the little 'un steers. We'll have to rush forward as she grazes, and cant her over, but we are just in time to save a mile or two,' and so you run, the sea hissing and seething as the boat dips; then comes a slight shock; all run forward, she dips her nose and rises with a shake. 'There, Sir, I know'd she do it,' is the quiet remark, and three minutes afterwards the spot shows dark above the foam."

On the sands off Wainfleet, and also on the Roger and Ant Sands there are large flocks of seals, which have had their habitation there for many generations. Many of these seals are white and of very large size. Porpoises also are found in the Deeps, and occasionally a whale has strayed up the channel and got stranded on the sands. Some years since, a whale was stranded on the coast, and its skeleton was for many years exhibited at 'the Skeleton of the Whale,' in Boston. A whale or grampus was also stranded in the river, nearly as far up as Skirbeck marsh; and recently a grampus, or bottle-nosed whale, was left by the tide in a creek, at Freiston Shore. It measured 16½ft. in length, 7ft. 2ins. in girth and was estimated to weigh 2½ tons.

VEGETABLE PRODUCTIONS.

The botany of the Fenland, has been fully dealt with, in an article by the late Mr. Marshall of Ely, in his *Fenland Past and Present*, where also will be found a list of the plants, with their botanical names. It will be unnecessary to deal in any detail with this subject. There are, however, a few vegetable products, which, whether growing naturally, or specially cultivated, are peculiar to the South Lincolnshire Fenland, which deserve a short description. The cultivation of woad, a crop solely grown in this district, is described in the chapter on Agriculture.

Mercury (*Chenopodium bonus Henricus*) is a vegetable resembling spinach, but is perennial and less watery. It is to be found in nearly all the farm and cottage gardens in the South Lincolnshire Fenland, and makes a very useful vegetable in the spring and early summer. A bed, once made, lasts a very long time without any other care than weeding, and occasionally manuring, and, being considered as tenant right, is paid for by an incoming tenant.

Although the growth of the marine plant called Samphire (*Salicornia herbacea*), is not confined to the Lincolnshire coast, it is perhaps made more use of in this neighbourhood than in other parts of the country, being largely gathered for making pickle. Samphire is the first vegetation which springs up on the foreshore, except a species of seaweed called 'cot.' It does not appear until the surface is raised about 14ft. above low water (6·68ft. above *Ordnance datum*), this being the level at which the alluvial matter, or 'warp,' first begins to desposit. When the surface attains to 16ft. above low water, the samphire gradually disappears, the ground then becoming covered with marine grass.

REEDS & SEDGE.

Reeds grew naturally in all the uninclosed fens, and before the introduction of tiles and slates, were used very generally for thatching house roofs. They are still occasionally used for this purpose. Camden says that a stack of reeds well harvested was worth from £200 to £300. Sedge (*Cladium Mariscus*) was also used for thatching. The sedge was tied in bundles, and carried from the fen, on a litter, made of two poles, to barges. The time and manner of cutting reeds and sedge was regulated by the Fen Code.

CRANBERRIES.

Cranberries grew to a considerable extent on the borders of the East Fen, before the common land was inclosed. The area of the Mossberry, or Cranberry, Fen, near Friskney, was estimated by Arthur Young at 300 acres. The soil in which these bushes grew was a deep peat moss. In favourable seasons as many as 4,000 pecks of the berries were collected, the average being about 2,000. The price paid to those who picked them was 5/- a peck.

Oldfield's *Wainfleet*.

TREES.

From the numerous remains of trees which are found buried at a considerable depth below the present surface of the Fenland, it is evident that in prehistoric times this must have been a well-wooded country. Below the peat, growing in the Boulder clay, from 15ft. to 18ft. under the surface, are to be found the remains of oak, alder, birch, yew and other trees, some of which are of very large size.

The richness of the land of the Fenland, and its value for cultivation is not conducive to the presence of woods, or even of trees in the fields. In the fen portion of Holland trees are conspicuous by their absence, but on the alluvial lands, in the hedgerows, and round the houses of some of the larger occupiers, especially in the neighbourhood of Wyberton, Algarkırk, Frampton, Sibsey, Pinchbeck, Spalding and Holbeach, very fine trees are to be found. The tree of the Fenland and the one which attains to a very large growth is the elm. Poplars are not so common as would be expected in a fen county. Sycamores are common, oaks, beeches, chestnuts, ashes and fir trees are only occasionally met with. The whitethorn hedges found by the side of the old pastures grow to a great height and size.

SALT.

Before the production of salt from rock salt, this was obtained by evaporating the salt water obtained from the sea, and large quantities of 'bay salt' were thus manufactured, on the coasts of the Fenland and on the margin of Bicker Haven, there being no less than 20 salt pans in that parish. The shallow pits by the side of the main road between Sutterton and Boston, are generally supposed to be the remains of salt pits, which were supplied with water from Bicker Haven.

In Domesday Book there is mention of over 100 salt pans as existing in the Fenland parishes, the value of a salt pan being from 8d. to 1s.

The method of procuring salt was by allowing the water brought up by the tides to run into shallow ponds, in the same manner as is still practised on the coast of Spain. The salt water was run through three pits. In the first it was allowed to remain until the mud and sand had settled, it was then allowed to flow into the second until it became brine, and was then run into the third pit where it remained exposed to the sun until the water was evaporated and the crystals of salt were formed. The salt was carried inland on horses, one of the roads from the coast being known as the *Salters' Road*.

Bullein. 1562. In an old book called 'The Bulwarke of defence against all sickness' it is stated that "much salt is made in England as of sand and salt water in pits, in Hollande, in Lincolnshire; and only by a marvellous humor of water at the witch far from the sea."

CLIMATOLOGY AND HEALTH.

The climate of the Fenland may be described as moderate, and not subject to any great extremes. Violent thunderstorms, equally with heavy falls of snow, are rare. When other parts of England are suffering from floods and tempests, the rivers in the Fenland are frequently only in their normal condition, the efficiency of the drainage arrangements having placed the discharge of the water under thorough control.

In the *Polyolbion*, written in the 17th century, South Lincolnshire is thus described:—

Drayton.
>Thus of her foggy fennes, to hear rude Holland prate;
>That with her fish and fowle, here keepth such a coyle,
>As her unwholesome ayre, and more unwholesome soyle.

In another work, written at a much later period, the writer says, "The air upon the east and south part of Lincolnshire is both thick and foggy, by reason of the fens and unsolute ground, but therewithal very moderate and pleasing, and the winds that are sent off her still working sea do disperse those vapours from all power of hurt."

THE ATMOSPHERE. Whether or not these descriptions were true at the time they were written, they do not apply now. The Fenland is particularly free from fogs, and the atmosphere is remarkable for its brightness and clearness. On a clear day, objects can be seen over the Fenland for very long distances, especially when the wind is from the north east. When the wind is from this quarter, that peculiar optical illusion, the mirage, is very apparent, Looking shorewards, when on a boat in Boston Deeps, the water will appear to extend far inland beyond the banks, and the trees and corn stacks seem to the observer as if standing in the water, and objects several miles distant, stand out with remarkable clearness. A complete delineation of the masts and rigging of vessels will also show distinctly in the water vertically beneath the hulls within range of the observer. MIRAGES.

The splendid sunrises and sunsets and magnificent cloudscapes, frequently to be witnessed, are acknowledged by all who know the Fenland to be unrivalled in any other part of England. At sunset the clouds frequently form a canopy of purple and gold, and give effects peculiar to this district, which are nowhere matched for beauty. A modern writer, who, though not an inhabitant, knew the Fenland well, has remarked, "A day's fog is rare. The air is beautifully clear and transparent. The inhabitants enjoy as sunny skies, as beautiful starlit nights, and as magnificent cloudscapes, as any people in England...and the sunsets are of surpassing grandeur."

It must, however, be admitted that this part of the country also has an unenviable notoriety for the keenness with which the north-east winds prevail during the spring, generally up to the beginning of May, but frequently lasting till June. The prevailing wind during the rest of the year comes from the south-west. WINDS

The rainfall is small, being about half that on the west coast. The average of the 60 years, 1830-89, is 23·49 inches. The greatest fall recorded in one year was 35·53 inches in 1880 and the least, 12·94 inches in 1887. The average number of days on which rain fell during the last 20 years is 160; the greatest number 214, in 1872; and the least 117, in 1887. The wettest period recorded was during the 9 years, 1875-83, when the average annual rainfall was 29·06 inches. From 1884-92 was a dry period, with an average of 20·23 inches. RAINFALL.

The mean temperature of the whole year is 48·70 degrees; for July, the warmest month, 62·80, and for January, the coldest, 36·50. The highest recorded temperature in the shade is 95, and the lowest, 4ft. from the ground, zero. TEMPERATURE.

Full statistics as to the barometer, temperature, wind, and rain as recorded at Boston, as also the effect of the weather on the wheat crop and the time of harvest, will be found in the Appendix. Appendix v.

HEALTH AND DISEASE.

The general effect of the climatic conditions on the health of the inhabitants may be described as decidedly favourable. The people who reside in the Fenland enjoy, as a rule, excellent health, and live to a good old age. It is not uncommon to meet with persons of more than four score years, of active habits and in full LENGTH OF LIFE.

possession of all their faculties. An examination of the tombstones in the churchyards, or of the Registers of deaths, will show that the number of inhabitants who have lived above the prescribed three score years and ten is very large, and that there are a few who have attained the century. From statistics which have been furnished me by Mr. W. Clegg, the former Medical Officer of Health for Boston and the Rural District round it, it appears that out of a total of 1,545 deaths in Boston, during the five years, 1889-93, 313 of the persons who died were over 70 years of age; 149 over 80; and 24 over 90; thus 38 per cent. of the whole number were over 70 years. In the Rural District, out of the total number of deaths in the five years, 564, or 32 per cent., were of persons over 70; of whom 313 were between 70 and 80; 214 between 80 and 90; and 37 over 90.

The atmosphere is neither enervating nor depressing, but, whether from the flatness of the land, or its peculiar climatic conditions, resembling that of Holland, there is a general feeling of contentment amongst the inhabitants, and an absence of that restlessness and love of change which is to be found in the more stimulating air of districts situated at a higher level.

AGUE.

There are no special diseases peculiar to the district. Formerly, the Fens were noted for the prevalence of rheumatism and ague, the latter disease is now unknown, and the former is no more prevalent than in other parts. The persons suffering from ague were attacked intermittently with severe shiverings, which shook the whole body and even the chair or bed on which the sufferer was resting, accompanied by intense pains in the limbs. At one time, they were burning hot, and at another equally cold, and fever and thirst ensued. The fits came on at varying intervals, the disease being distinguished as 'tertian' or 'quotidian,' the latter being the most prevalent form.

The prevalence of ague in the Fens, before they were reclaimed, was due to the malaria which arose from the sun acting on the decomposing vegetation, when alternately covered and uncovered by the water. Large areas of stagnant water alone do not produce malaria. This is evidenced by the condition of the Fens at the present time, which are intersected in all directions by large drains, the water in which is practically stagnant all the summer. The poisonous germs floating in the air, which caused the malaria from which ague arose, were developed from decaying vegetation, sometimes covered with water and at other times left dry and exposed to the sun. The peat itself was not productive of poisonous germs. At the present day the milder form now known as intermittent fever, which is occasionally met with, but in no greater degree than in other parts of the country, is more prevalent in dry than in wet seasons; as in the former the water is evaporated from the smaller drains and ditches, and becomes lowered in the larger ones, leaving exposed to the sun's rays decaying vegetation, which remains alive and healthy when covered with water. The quality of the water in the wells and cisterns is also more impure in dry than in wet seasons. Shortly after the Fens were inclosed and drained, ague was very prevalent owing to the exsicction of soil which hitherto had been covered with water, and to a greater surface being exposed by its being ploughed and broken up. As, however, this decaying organic matter disappeared in the process of cultivation, the miasmatic exhalations and poisonous germs gradually disappeared, and with their disappearance ague ceased to be a fen product.

USE OF OPIUM.

Quinine not being in general use in the last century, the remedy invariably resorted to was opium. The use of this drug once resorted to, it became a habit which was seldom abandoned, and this habit has continued to a large extent up to the present time, although the original cause of its use has long since departed. It is said that more opium used to be sold by the chemists, at the shops in the towns in the Fenland of Lincolnshire, Cambridge and Norfolk, as a stimulant used by the labouring classes, than in all the rest of England put together.

The quantity of this drug which a confirmed opium taker will consume is very large, averaging as much as a dram a day, and a labouring man or his wife will spend from a shilling to eighteen-pence a week in obtaining it. The habit, however, is now gradually dying out, not one-third of the quantity being sold now that used to be.

The opium is obtained from the juice of the poppy and is made up into a thick tenacious paste, a dram representing a piece about the size of a small walnut, and the quantity taken at one time being about the size of a pea.

The effect on the taker, however, is not that which has been described by persons who have formed their opinions from exaggerated reports of isolated cases. Its effect, both, on the taker and on those about him, is far less deleterious than excessive beer or dram drinking. The man or woman who takes opium is never riotous or disorderly, and gives no trouble to the police as an effect of its use. It tends however to make the taker silent and morose. The amount of work done is not less, nor is the life shorter than of those who do not take it, many of the confirmed opium takers living to 80 and 90 years of age. It is not pretended to defend its use, but it would seem that when the habit has once been contracted, the system requires its stimulating effect to be kept up to its normal working capacity.

APPENDIX I.

NAMES AND INDEX OF PLACES IN THE SOUTH LINCOLNSHIRE FENLAND, THEIR SITUATIONS, AREA, RATEABLE VALUE, DERIVATION AND OTHER PARTICULARS.

ABBREVIATIONS. *D. B.*, Domesday Book. *Dug.*, Dugdale's *Embanking and Draining* (Ed. 1772.) *A*, Area in Acres. *R. V.*, Rateable Value on Assessment for *Schedule A.* of the *Income Tax* as given in the County Council Memoranda for 1893-4. This relates only to land and buildings in the parishes, and does not include the valuation of Railway or other public undertakings. *A. S.*, Anglo-Saxon. *D.*, Danish. *S.*, Scandinavian.

The numbers after the names of places refer to the corresponding pages in the preceding chapters.

ABBOTESFORD. On the Glen, between Kate's Bridge and Gutheram Cote.

ABBEY HILLS. The site of an ancient monastery in the parish of Friskney, half a mile west of the church, to which it is connected by a causeway.

ABBOT'S PREMISES. In Wrangle parish.

ACRELAND CLOUGH. On the Three Towns' Drain, near Fishmore End, at the junction of the parishes of Wigtoft and Sutterton. 86.

ALDERLOUND. Near Crowland

ALGARKIRK. *Alderchurch*, Dug. *Algarekirk*, D.B. A village and parish, 7 miles S.S.W. from Boston. Contains 2,624 acres, R. V. £6,698 ; named from Algar, a Saxon King, who opposed the invasion of the Danes. In 1840 the allotment in Holland Fen was transferred to the new parish of Amber Hill. 86.

ALMOND'S FARM BRIDGE. Over South Holland Drain. 110.

ALVELODE. A drain near Surfleet. Dug.

AMBER HILL. A plot of land of 30 acres, allotted under the Holland Fen Inclosure Award, for the purpose of providing materials for repairs of the roads of several parishes having right of Common in Holland Fen. Under the Parish Awards, the Donington Turnpike Trustees were allowed to let this land, subject to the parish rights, but no buildings were to be erected thereon. This field was sold when the Turnpike Trust expired. Amber Hill was extra parochial. 91. 287.

AMBER HILL. A Fen Parish in Holland Fen, formed in 1880 by uniting the Fen Allotments of Algarkirk and Sutterton and the extra parochial place Amber Hill. It comprises 5,261 acres rated at £8,265. 289.

AMYTOFT. A raised piece of land with traces of a moat round it, in the parish of Holbeach. Remains of foundations of buildings and Roman urns and curiosities have been found here. (*Camden.*)

ANCARIG. Another name for Thorney. Dug.

ANCHOR CHURCH HILL, OR ANCHORITE. ¼ mile N.E. of Crowland Abbey. St. Guthlac built himself a cell on this land in 697. In 948 a chapel was built here by Abbot Turketul, the foundations of which were removed in 1866.

ANDERSON'S SLUICE. In South Holland. 101, 129, 130.

APPENDIX I.

ANDREW'S COMMON. In the parish of Swineshead.

ANWICK FEN. *Haniuuic, Amuinc* D. B. In the Fifth Witham District, between Billinghay Skirth and Kyme Eau, inclosed in 1791. 240.

ANGOT. A gutter or small drain in Quadring. 60.

ANTON'S GOTE. *Anthony's Gote or Gowt.* A sluice on the east side of the River Witham, about two miles above Boston. It has a lock for passing boats from the Witham to the West Fen Drains and Hobhole. The original sluice was used for draining the water from the East and West Fens into the Witham. A new sluice was built for this purpose about the time of Charles I, and this was superseded when the New Cut was made for the Witham. 145, 146, 148, 154, 161, 205, 217.

APENHOLT, otherwise WODE LODE. Near Crowland. Dug.

APPLE TREE NESS. On Kyme Eau, at the north corner of Ewerby Fen.

ARMTREE FEN. *Armtre.* A river passage or ferry, is mentioned in Domesday Book and is supposed to be the same place as Langrick. 206.

ARMTREE GOTE. On the Witham, below Dogdyke. 199.

ARMITAGE CAUSEY. In Wildmore Fen.

ASWICK GRANGE. A high piece of land with traces of a moat round it, near Whaplode Drove. Several Roman coins and urns have been dug up here.

ASEWICKLODE. A drain near Fleet Bridge.

ASWARDHURN WAPENTAKE. One of the divisions of the county, in which the Lindsey Level is situated. *Aswardetierne* D.B.; *Asewarhirne, Asewardthyrne,* Hundred Rolls.

ASAPH or ASPATH. The entrance to the Island of Crowland, Dug. Aspath Dike is on the Holland Boundary near the Welland.

ASENDIK. A Sewer emptying into the Welland and forming the ancient boundary of Crowland on the north.

ASGARBY FEN. In the Sixth Witham District and Ninepenny Black Sluice District, on the west side of Midfodder Drain, contains 76a. 1r. 0p.

ASLACKBY FEN. In the Black Sluice Level, contains 997a., enclosed, 1765. 275.

ASPERTON COMMON. In the parish of Wigtoft, allotted under the Enclosure Act of 1772. 90.

ASSENDYKE. *See* Austendyke.

ASWIKTOFT OR ASEWYGTOFT HIRNE. Near Crowland.

AUSINESGOTE. A sewer of Spalding.

AUSTENDYKE OR ASSENDYKE. A hamlet in Moulton Parish, 1½ miles south of the village.

AWSTROP FEN. In the Lindsey Level joining Ewerby Fen.

AUSTERBY. In the Parish of Bourne. Formerly a Manor-house of the Abbots of Bourne.

AX HEAD. A piece of Common Land, in the parish of Kirton, enclosed under the Act of 1772. 85.

BALBERDEBOTHE. In Swineshead. 247.

BAKER'S BRIDGE. Over the New Hammond Beck, in Frampton Fen. 82, 452.

BAKER'S SLUICE. In South Holland. 116, 126.

BANE, OR BAIN, RIVER. A tributary of the Witham, which joins it near Dogdyke. Has been canalised as far as Horncastle. The name, according to Mr. Streatfeild, is of Celtic origin. 135.

Appendix I.

BANOVALLUM. Horncastle. 5.

BARKESMERE. A watercourse running from the north end of Bicker Fen to Kyme Eau. (Holland Dyke).

BARDNEY. *Bardenai*, D.B. A village and parish on the east side of the Witham, 10 miles south of Lincoln. The word is of British origin with a Saxon termination, signifying Bard's Island. Dr. Oliver supposes that this was a place of sacred celebration of the Druids. An Abbey was founded here in the 7th century by the Saxons It was plundered and burnt by the Danes in 870. Restored by Gilbert de Gaunt, Earl of Lincoln, 200 years afterwards. The present church was erected in the 15th Century. The fen land is in the Third Witham District, and was enclosed by an Act passed in 1843. 196.

BARDNEY BECK. A tributary of the Witham. 155.

BARDYKE SLUICE. In Boston Haven. 150.

BARDNEY BRIDGE. 448.

BARGATE DRAIN. A name given to that part of Maud Foster Drain which runs through Skirbeck and Boston.

BARGATE DRAIN. Near Lincoln. 165.

BARKESMERE. In the Black Sluice Level. 245.

BARLINGS. *Berlings*, D.B. A village on the river Langworthy. Contains the ruins of an Abbey founded in 1154. The fen is in the Third Witham District. 192.

BARLING'S LOCK. 161, 162, 164, 173.

BARLING'S EAU. A tributary of the Witham. 155, 174.

BARLIEU BRIDGE. 110.

BARLODE. *Barloade*. A drain in the East Fen, running between the Catchwater and Hobhole. 199, 204, 225, 226.

BARRIER BANK. Between Spalding and Brotherhouse. 107, 440. *See also* Brotherhouse Bank.

BARTHORPE. In the parish of Swineshead, 2 miles N.N.W. of the village

BASTON EE. A sewer described in the time of Edward I. as running from Katesbridge to Escote, by Pynsebec and Escote to Surflete, and which ought to be repaired by the towns of Baston, Thurleby, Obstorpe, and Wywelstorpe. The only water course which answers to this description is the the River Glen.

BATEMANNEBRIGG. A bridge over the Westlode, near Spalding.

BAXTER'S SLUICE. In South Holland. 102, 103, 129, 130.

BAY HALL. An ancient brick mansion in the parish of Benington.

BEATS, Great and Little. Part of the bed of the old river Witham, 10 miles north of Boston, formerly extra parochial; added to the parish of Pelham's Lands in 1883.

BECHE. A sewer running through Gosberton, Pinchbeck and Surfleet and maintained by these parishes. It is described in the time of Edward III, as being 3ft. wide at the head, and 16ft. towards the sea, and as discharging into the river of Surfleet (the Glen). 59, 245, 247, 250, 254.

BELL'S REACH. In the Witham near Fishtoft. 352.

BELNEY, OR BELNIE, BRIDGE. Across the Risegate Eau in Gosberton. 91.

BELLWATER. The name of one of the pits or deeps in the East Fen. Now a drain running from near the Steeping River to Hobhole Drain, through the site of the pits.

BENDER SLOUGH DRAIN. 110.

APPENDIX I.

BENDIKE FIELD. A piece of Common Land in the parish of Kirton, inclosed under the Act of 1772. 85.

BENINGTON. *Beningtone, Benincton.* Derived from the name of the Danish Chief, *Bening.* A village on the Wainfleet Road, 5 miles N.E. of Boston. The parish contains 2,306 acres and is rated at £6,129. The fen allotment contains 502a. 3r. 31p. 73.

BENTON'S BRIDGE. Over the North Forty-Foot Drain between Wyberton Fen and Shuff Fen. 81, 452.

BERGEBI. *See* Ewerby.

BERHOLM POOLES. In Rippingale. 250.

BICKER. *Byker, Bikere, Bichere.* A village 9 miles S.W. of Boston. The parish contains 3,571 acres. R.V. £7,536. The fen allotments amount to 2,000 acres. According to Domesday Book there were formerly 20 salt pans in Bicker. 98.

BICKER EA. 60.

BICKER HAVEN. Described in the Hundred Rolls as *Aqua de Swin.* An estuary extending from the River Welland to Bicker. This was inclosed about the middle of the 17th century. The banks of the haven can still be traced. 93, 292.

BICKER OR BYKER, river of. A sewer running from Bicker Gauntlet through the village and formerly discharging into Bicker Haven. 25, 59, 96, 247.

BICKER BEAUMONT. A manor in Bicker.

BILLINGBOROUGH. *Billingeburg, Billingberg, Bolingburg.* Named after the Danish Chief, Billing. The parish contains 2,020 acres, including a tract of fen land in the Black Sluice district, lying between the Ouse Mer and Billingborough Lodes. The fen was inclosed in 1768. 274.

BILLINGBOROUGH LODE. A drain passing through the fen. 258.

BILLINGHAY. *Belingei.* Named after the Danish family Billing or Billingas. The village is situated on the Car Dyke, 10 miles N.E. of Sleaford. The parish contains 3,530 acres, including the fen and dales. 189, 190.

BILLINGHAY DALES. A tract of fen land on the west of the River Witham and south of Billinghay Skirth. 190.

BILLINGHAY SKIRTH OR SKIRT. A drain running from the Car Dyke, through Billinghay, to the Witham, which it joins near Tattershall Bridge. The west bank of this drain gave way during a flood in 1877 and flooded 2,390 acres of fen land, causing damage estimated at £20,000. 146, 154, 155, 165, 173, 191, 429.

BILLINGHAY SOUTH FEN. In the First Witham District, inclosed 1777. 189, 191.

BLACK ARKE. In South Holland. 103.

BLACK FLEET. Near Gutheram Cote.

BLACK DYKE ROFT. In Deeping Fen. 323.

BLACK DYKE. In the East Fen. 202, 213.

BLACK GOTE. A drain in the East Fen. 202, 205.

BLACK SLUICE DRAINAGE DISTRICT. 244. *See* South Forty-Foot. First Act obtained, 254.

BLACK SLUICE. The outlet of the main drain of the Black Sluice District. The first sluice was built by the Adventurers in the 17th century. 252. It was rebuilt under the Act of 1765. 256. The present sluice was erected under the Act of 1846 and has 3 openings of a total waterway of 60ft. 266, 268.

BLACK SYKE. A drain between Westhouse and Medlam in the West Fen. 204.

BLAKE KYRK. 246.

APPENDIX I.

BALBERDEBOCHE, OR BALDERDEBOTHE. North of Gibbet Hills and 3 miles N. W. of Swineshead. 247.

BLANKNEY FEN. On the west of the Witham in the First District, enclosed in 1787. The village of Blankney (*Blachene*) is 3 miles west of the fen. An establishment of Bards existed here in the time of the Druids. 187.

BLUE ANCHOR BIGHT AND MARSH. In Fishtoft, inclosed by the Boston Corporation. 71.

BLUE GOTE DRAIN, OR BLUE COAT. *Burley Gote*, Dug. A drain between the Welland and the Glen, running from Dozens Bank, in Pinchbeck, to the Glen, near its outfall in Surfleet. In the Act of 1664, described as Blewgate, in that of 1801 as Blue Goat, and in the Act of 1832, as Blue Gowt. 117, 326.

BOARDEN BRIDGE. Across the River Glen. 450.

BOATMERE CREEK. In South Holland. 101, 115.

BODINES BRIGGE. A bridge over the Holbeach Sewer.

BOLLERSGATE. A common sewer in the parish of Moulton.

BOLINGBROKE, NEW. *Bulinbroke, Bollinbroc.* In the West Fen, 9 miles north of Boston. It was founded in 1823 by John Parkinson, the lessee of the Crown lands. The church was erected in 1853, under the Fen Chapel Act, at a cost of £2,400. Formed into an ecclesiastical parish in 1858 from parts of the civil parishes of Carrington, Revesby and the West Fen. Contains 750 acres. The Tuesday market, which was established here in 1821, is obsolete, but a pleasure fair is still held on July 10th. The name is taken from the old parish of Bolingbroke, which was formerly a market town and had a castle. It is 4 miles west of Spilsby, and had allotments of 306 acres in Wildmore Fen. The name is derived from the Saxon *Bolingas*. Chapel erected by Inclosure Commissioners. 228.

BONDSISTAKE. *Bondstake.* Near Bicker. 60, 96.

BOSTON. Called Botolph's town, or Botulfstun, until about the 16th century, also the Port of St. Boutoul. The name is derived from St. Botulf, or Botolph, who founded a monastery here in 654. In 1204, King John granted a charter, and subsequent charters were granted by Henry VIII, confirmed by Edward VI, and by Philip and Mary. Queen Elizabeth granted a charter, conferring Admiralty jurisdiction on the port, and other privileges in connection with the navigation. The area of the parish was considerably diminished in 1880, by the transfer, under the Divided Parishes Act, of the outlying Fen Allotments in the East and West Fens, and also of the part known as Boston East, to other parishes. The parish now includes only the town area and the land in Boston West and that lying between the town and Frith Bank. The reduced area is 2,128 acres, of which the rateable value is £65,023. The area, formerly, including the allotments, was 4,678 acres. 68.

BOSTON. Port and Harbour. Charter granted, 343. Condition of, in 16th century, 344. Customs and Fishery Boundary, 345. Buoys and Beacons, 345.

BOSTON DEEPS. The northern side of the Wash. 336.

BOSTON BRIDGE. 447.

BOTHAMLEY'S SLUICE. In South Holland. 129, 130.

BOTHE. Near the Wathe mouth in Kyme Eau.

BOURNE. *Bourn, Burne, Brunne,* D.B. *Brune.* Name derived from the Anglo-Saxon *Burne*, a stream rising from a spring. A town on the west side of the Car Dyke, 9½ miles west of Spalding. The area of the parish is 9,352 acres, including the hamlets of Dyke and Cawthorpe and the fens, the area of which is about 5,000 acres, and was inclosed under an Act, 6 George III. An Act for the better drainage of the North Fen and Dyke Fen, containing 4,000 acres, was obtained in 1846, under the powers of which the pumping station was erected. Bourne South Fen, containing 900 acres, was created a Drainage District under the Land Drainage Act in 1871. The town of Bourne has held an important place in the history of the Fens. The castle of Brunn was held by Hereward the Saxon. An Abbey was

APPENDIX. I.

founded here in 1138. Robert of Brunne, or Robert Manning, is credited with being the 'patriarch of the new English,' or, the first great writer in modern classic English. He went to Cambridge in 1300 and wrote the poem *Handlyng Synne*. Leland in his *Itinerary* states that '*Bourne* is a bubbling stream, *Bourn* is a running stream.' On this ground it is claimed that the practice adopted in modern times of spelling the name without the final *e* is wrong, and further that it is desirable to retain the *e*, in order to distinguish this place from Bourn in Cambridgeshire, which has only a running stream. Bourne derives its name from the bubbling sources of Bourne Eau, in St. Peter's Pool, in Hereward's Castle Meadow.

BOURNE EAU *Burne Old Ee*. A stream running from Bourne to the Glen at Tongue End, converted into a navigation in 1781, but now disused for this purpose. Banks, 260, 267. Navigation, 435.

BOURNE SOUTH FEN. Separated from North Fen, 279. Right to drain under Glen, 328. District formed, 333.

BOURNE NORTH FEN. Farm allotted to Black Sluice, 268. Inclosed in 1776, 278. Divided from South Fen, 279. Erection of steam pumping engine, 263, 279. Breach of banks, 282. Rates and expenditure, 282. Exemption from taxation in Deeping Fen, 322.

BRANSTON FEN. On the west side of the river Witham in the First District. It was inclosed under an Act passed in 1765. The fen was divided by a new cut, called the South Delph, made for the river Witham in 1812. The severed portion on the east side of the river is called Branston Island. The village of Branston is situated about 3 miles from the fen. 170, 171, 173, 184, 185.

BRAND END. (Little Brand End Plot; Great Brand End Plot.) In Holland Fen, 1½ miles north-west of Swineshead Church, allotted to Swineshead under the Act of 1767. Brand End Plot contains 25 acres. Amalgamated with Swineshead, by order of Council, April 23, 1890. 88, 89, 90.

BRAND DYKE. A drain running through Hale Fen, made in 1633. 252.

BRANDSFORD BRIDGE. Over the Three Towns' Drain, under the main road.

BRAYFORD MERE. Near Lincoln. 136, 138, 159, 160, 168.

BRAYFORTH ROSE PLOT. In Sutterton Fen. Part of the land awarded to Sutterton parish, under the Holland Fen Inclosure Award.

BREACH EA. A common sewer in South Holland.

BRIDGE PIECE. An Allotment in Holland Fen to Frampton Parish. Formerly extra parochial. 82.

BRIDGE END, BRIG END OR HOLLAND CAUSEWAY. A hamlet in the fen of the parish of Horbling, on the east side of the Car Dyke, 1½ miles N.E. of the village. Here was formerly the Priory of Holland Bridge (*de Ponte Aslacki*) or St. Saviour's, founded by Godwin, Earl of Lincoln. 96, 248.

BRIGDYKE, THE CROSS OF. Near Neslam.

BRIGEFLEET. *Biggeslecter*. A sewer in Heckington. 246.

BROADGATE. *See* Gedney.

BROTHERHOUSE. On the road between Crowland and Spalding. An ancient cross of St. Guthlac, originally fixed to show the boundary of the Crowland Abbey lands, still remains here.

BROTHERHOUSE BANK. *See also* Barrier Bank, between Spalding and Peakirk. 297, 438, 440.

BROTHERTOFT. *Goosetoft*. Name derived from the Saxon word *Broder*. In Holland Fen, about 4 miles W.N.W. of Boston. Was formerly a township of Kirton parish, but has been formed into an Ecclesiastical Parish. Fossdyke Fen was added for civil purposes in 1880. The area is now 1,786 acres. R. V. £3,350. The inhabitants of this township formerly claimed unrestrained rights of pasturage, fowling and fishing in Holland Fen.

Appendix I.

BROADGATE. In the parish of Sutton St. Edmunds.

BRUNNE, RIVER OF. *Brunne Hee, Burne Alde Ee.* In Dugdale the Brunne Ee is described in the margin as 'now the Glene.'...'Which had its course through the midst of the town of Pinchebec.' The 'Ware' Dyke is described as extending along 'the river of Burne Ee to Goodramscote,' in a Commission of Sewers held at Helpringham in Queen Elizabeth's time. 246, 247.

BUCIFEN GOTE. Near Pinchbeck.

BUCKLEGATE. At the S.W. extremity of the parish of Kirton.

BUCKLEGATE FIELD. A piece of common land in the parish of Kirton, enclosed under the Act of 1772. 85.

BUCKNALL FEN. In the Third Witham District. 193.

BURLIEU BRIDGE. Over the South Holland Drain.

BULL DOG BANK AND SLUICE. The sea bank near Gedney. So named from the fact that the navvies, when engaged in making the bank, killed and buried a bull dog belonging to a bailiff, who was sent to arrest one of them.

BULLINGTON BECK. A tributary of the Witham. 155.

BUNKER'S HILL. A part of the parish of Thornton-le-Fen, in Wildmore Fen.

BURTON BRIGG. The King's Highway. Dug.

BURTON'S MARSH. New Cut for the Witham made through, 1827. 352.

BURTON MARSH. In Fishtoft. 71.

BURNE or BRUNE. *See* Bourne.

BURGH-IN-THE-MARSH. From A. S. *Burg*, meaning rising ground, and used for a camp. This was the site of an old Roman camp.

BURTOFT. A hamlet in the parish of Wigtoft.

BURTOFT COMMON. In Wigtoft. Allotted under the Act of 1773.

BUTTERWICK. *Botwyke, Butruic, Boterwick.* The name is derived from the Scandinavian *Botnegard* or *Butsecarlas*, a shipmaster, and *wick*, a haven. The village is about 4 miles east of Boston. The area of the parish is 1,416 acres, R. V. £4,307. In Domesday Book there is mention of two churches in Butterwick, one of these probably being Freiston, which at that time was a hamlet of Butterwick. 72.

BUTT'S MARSH. In Wrangle.

BYKER, RIVER OF. *See* Bicker.

BYRKHOLM. On the Witham.

CADENHAM TOFT. Mentioned by Dug.

CALSCROFT. On the Witham. 139.

CANDLEBY HILL. In Swineshead. Dug. 60.

CAPELODE. *See* Whaplode.

CAPEL BRIGGE. 103.

CAPRON BRIGG. A sluice ordered to be built here. Dug.

CARDYKE. *Carr*, a low place or fen. D. *Ker*, a marsh. The drain made by the Romans from Lincoln to the Nene, 10, 25. Proposal to open for drainage of Black Sluice Level, 263, 264. Part in Black Sluice Level deepened under the Act of 1846. 266.

CARR DYKE. 'A certain stream which was called the South Ee, and extended to Byker Fen.' Dug.

APPENDIX I.

CARRINGTON. In the West Fen, 8 miles north of Boston. From A.S. *Cerringas*(Kemble). Was formed into a township in 1812, (52, Geo. III). Area at that time 2,416 acres. The church was built by the Fen Chapel Trustees in 1816. In 1880 the fen portions of the parishes of Boston, Miningsby, and Asgarby, and detached portions of Revesby and Bolingbroke were added to this parish. The area including New Bolingbroke is 3,418 acres. R. V. £3,418. Township formed, 229, Chapel erected by Inclosure Commissioners. 228.

CASTLEDYKE DRAIN. In the West Fen. 225.

CATEBRIDGE WATER. The Glen.

CATLEY ABBEY. In the hamlet of Walcot, on the west side of the Witham. The Abbey was founded in the reign of Stephen. There is a spring of mineral water here. 467.

CATCH COLT CORNER OR CAT COVE. Near Whaplode Drove. The remains of a Roman Castellum, have been discovered here. *Camden*.

CATTLE HOLME, the Far and the First. Part of Holland Fen, allotted to the parish of Swineshead under the Act of 1767. 88, 89.

CAT WATER. In South Holland. 104.

CAUSTON HOUSE. A vacherie, or cow pasture, originally belonging to Kirkstead Abbey on the Witham.

CAWOOD HALL. In Gosberton Parish. There was a heronry here at one time, but the herons deserted the place, and went to the Wykes Farm in Donington.

CAWTHORPE FEN. Hamlet, in the parish of Bourne. 254, 255, 256.

CAYTHORPE CROSS. In the parish of Freiston, near the church.

CAXTON HOUSES. On the Witham. Kept up by the Abbot of Kirkstead.

CHAIN BRIDGE. On the Wyberton West End Road, over the Hammond Beck. Before inclosure this was the entrance to the fen. 452.

CHALLANS BRIDGE. In Gosberton. Dug. 61, 92.

CHAPEL GATE. Near Spalding. Dug.

CHAPEL HILL, OR CHAPEL HILL HURN. A hamlet on the west side of the Witham in Holland Fen, 5 miles above Langrick Ferry, alloted to Swineshead parish, under the Act of 1773. 88,287. Transferred to the Parish of Pelham's Lands, in 1883, 289. The name is derived from an ancient chapel now used as a farm house. The surface is from 2ft. to 3ft. above the adjacent land in Holland Fen. The area is about 1,000 acres. 88, 90, 148, 151, 154, 178.

CHEAL. A Hamlet in the parish of Gosberton.

CHERRY WILLINGHAM. The low land is in the Third Witham District. 192.

CHERRY CORNER. At the junction of Mill Drain and Stone Bridge Drain, in Sibsey Northlands. 77, 210.

CHILEBECHE, CHEYLBECHE, OR EARTHS LODE. In the Lindsey Level. The boundary between Holland and Kesteven.

CHELLEGOTE. Near Pinchbeck. Dug.

CHIME. *See* Kyme.

CHEPDIC. A sewer, running from 'Fletebrigge to Asewick Lode.' Dug.

CHIRCHETONE. *See* Kirton.

CHRISTHURN, OR GRISTHAM. One of the places mentioned in the boundary line between Kesteven and Holland.

CHURCH LEEDES. In the parish of Leake.

APPENDIX I.

CIBECY. *See* Sibsey.

CLAPPS. In Ewerby.

CLARK'S HILL. A hamlet in the parish of Gedney, 2 miles S.W. of the village.

CLAYS, THE. A high bank of clay, otherwise known as the Scalp, at the mouth of the Witham, 350. Huddart's scheme for cutting a new channel for the Witham, 340. Rennie, 348; Sir J. Rennie, 349; Lewin, 356; Hawkshaw, 357, 361; Wheeler, 361.

CLAYS CHANNEL. The course for the Witham and Welland, along the south side of the Clays. 357.

CLAYHOLE. The upper end of Boston Deeps, which, with East Countryman's Berth, is the roadstead for vessels. 171, 177, 337, 338. Proposed pier, 360.

CLAYDIKE. A drain in Holland Fen, made in 1633. 252. Deepened 1846. 266.

CLAY HILLS. Part of Holland Fen, awarded to Algarkirk Fen. 171, 177, 337, 338.

CLOOTE OR CLOTE. In Deeping Fen, on the south bank of the Welland, about 1 mile above Brotherhouse Bar. One of the authorised approaches to Deeping Fen, mentioned in the Act of Charles II. 103, 321.

CLOWS CROSS. On the Nene. 104.

COCKLE BRIDGE. In Holbeach Fen, where the rivers unite. 124.

COLDALE, OR COLDALEGOTE GOTE. Near Spalding, on the east side of the Welland.

COLD HARBOUR. In Wrangle.

COLEHOUSE. Near Bourne. 242, 250.

COLLINS' BRIDGE. Over Maud Foster Drain. 215.

COLDER BRIDGE. Over the Five Towns' Drain.

COLN DRAIN. In Bicker. 25.

CONEY GARTH OR KONING GARTH. In Butterwick.

CONINGER. Near Spalding. Dug.

CONINGSBY. *Cuninesbi, Coninghesbi.* (*Linc. Survey, Temp. Hen. I.*) From *Koning,* D. *King,* and *By,* a settlement. The fen in the Fourth Witham District. 197.

CONSNERGATE. In Weston. Dug.

COOKING GREEN. In Wrangle.

COPPING SYKE. From A. S. *Coppingas,* the name of a Chief, and *Syke,* a low place where water stands. 8 miles N.W. of Boston, formerly extra parochial, now parochialised. Contains 238 acres. R. V. £1,572. 148.

COPPLEDYKE. A manor in Freiston.

COUNT WADE BRIDGE. Over the Five Towns' Drain.

COUNTER DRAIN. In Deeping Fen. 120, 326.

COUNTER DRAIN WASHES. District, 120, 323.

COVENHAM GOTE. An ancient gutter, near Spalding. Dug.

COWBIT. *Cubbet, Cubyt.* From S. *Kyr,* a cow and *Beit,* pasturage; cow pasturage; or from, A. S. *Cubingas.* 3 miles south of Spalding on east side of the Welland. Cowbit Wash, on the west side of the village, is 4 miles long by 1 mile wide, and is the place where the Fen skating matches take place. Cowbit had anciently a Court of Swan Mark. In this parish, near Brotherhouse Toll Bar, is St. Guthlac's

APPENDIX I.

Cross, which formerly marked the boundary of the lands of Crowland Abbey. Has been erected 1,100 years. Contains 1,863 acres. R. V. £4,485. Washes, 310. Drainage Act, 34.

COWHIRNE, OR COWHURN. On the east side of the River Welland, about 3 miles below Spalding. There was a ferry here formerly, for the road leading from Weston and Moulton to Surfleet and Gosberton. A guide was established here, who charged sixpence for his services. In old parish records there is mention of a Sessions being held at Cowhurn.

COWBRIDGE. *Cubrigge*. At the junction of the Frith Bank and the West Fen Drain, 3 miles north of Boston. Mr. Besant says, "The name is derived from a small town in Glamorganshire, from which the Cromwell family came, a branch of which settled near Earlscroft, and the present Cow Bridge Drain runs past part of their estate. In the 13th Century a jury *presented* that the Earl of Lincoln had established a new Court at Cubrigge." 202.

CRABHOLE. The Outfall of the River Nene, where the training ends. 110.

CRAYLE EAU. The division sewer between Frampton and Kirton.

CRAGMERE. In Wrangle.

CRANMORE COMMON. On the south side of Deeping Fen, near St. James' Deeping.

CREASY PLOT. In Holland Fen, near Syke Mouth. Part awarded to Wigtoft and part to Swineshead, under the Act of 1767. 88.

CRESSY HALL. In the parish of Surfleet. The ancient seat of the Heron family. A heronry existed here until the birds were disturbed by the cutting down of the trees, and they then went to Cawood.

CROFT. 2 miles north of Wainfleet. Drains by the East Fen System. Land mostly rich marsh. 229.

CROSS DRAIN. In Deeping Fen. 327.

CROSS GATE. A hamlet in Crowland, half-a-mile north of the village. 103.

CROSS GATE BRIDGE. Over the Glen. 323, 450.

CROWLAND. D.B., *Croyland, Croulande. Gogisland,* Dug. 205. *Crulande,* Charter of Ethelbald. 10 miles south of Spalding. The place where St. Guthlac, the patron saint of the Fens, settled in 697. An Abbey was founded here by Ethelbald, King of Mercia, in 716. The present abbey was built in 1113. There is a stone triangular bridge in the village, originally built in 860, formed of 3 semi-arches. The 3 streams which formerly passed under this bridge are now covered over. In the original charter, the lands belonging to the Abbey comprehended the 'whole island of Crolande formed by the 4 waters of the Shepishee on the east, Nene on the west, Southee on the south, and Assendyke on the north.' The northern part of the fen was called Goggisland. The cell of St. Guthlac was situated on the site now known as Anchorite, or Anchor Church Hill, about ¼ mile N.E. of the Abbey. A chapel was subsequently built here by Abbot Turketul, the foundations of which were removed in 1866. Area 13,048 acres. R.V., £30,931, 15, 312. St. Guthlac, 312. Abbey, 313. Bridge, 313. Reclamation of fen, 313. Crowland Washes, 310. Crowland Bridge, 450.

CUCKHOLD'S HYRNE. On the north side of the old River Witham, above Langrick Ferry.

CUCKOO BRIDGE. A hamlet in Pinchbeck, 5 miles south of the village.

CUT BRIDGE. Over the North Forty Foot, on the Boston and Swineshead Road. 452.

DALES, THE. On the Witham. 183.

DALES HEAD DYKE. West of the Witham. 169.

DALES BANK. In South Holland. 102.

DALES GOTE. In the East Fen. 201.

DALPROON. *See* Dolproon.

APPENDIX I.

DAMPFORD TUNNEL AND ENGINE. On Kyme Eau, at the end of Clay Dyke. 148, 155, 210, 260.

DANEBOOTH. On the Witham. 111.

DAWSMERE. An outlying part of the parish of Gedney, 4½ miles N.E. of the village.

DAWSDYKE. In Moulton. 122.

DAWSMERE CREEK AND SLUICE. A sewer discharging through the sea bank, about 3 miles north-west of the Nene Outfall. 116, 126.

DEANCOTE HALL. Formerly *D'Eyncourt*. A manor in Kirton Parish.

DEDMAN'S LAKE. Alias *Oggot*. Near Crowland. Dug.

DEEPDALES. An ancient drain, running eastwards from Cherry Corner near Stickney to Valentine's Drain.

DEEPING FEN. *Depinge, Depyng*. From D. *Djupr*, a deep hollow, and *Ing*, a meadow. 31, 314. *see* Index.

DEEPING FEN WASHES DRAINAGE DISTRICT. 120.

DEEPING ST. NICHOLAS, OR LITTLEWORTH. In Deeping Fen. The village is 5 miles S.W. from Spalding. Formerly extra parochial, but formed into a civil parish in 1856 by the Act 19 & 20 Vict. c. 65. It had been formed into an ecclesiastical parish in 1846. A. 8,637 acres. R. V., £20,410. 331.

DEEPING ST. JAMES. A village on the borders of Deeping Fen, on the west side of the Welland. 325.

DEEPING WEST. A village 2 miles west of Market Deeping. At the inclosure of Deeping Fen in 1813, 360 acres of the fen, lying 5 miles E.N.E. of the village were added to the parish.

DELPH BANK. In Holland Fen. 102.

DEREHAM DRAIN. In South Holland. 101, 106.

DEYNBOOTH. Near Frampton. Dug. 60.

DIGBY FEN. About 1½ miles east of the village of Digby. Contains 1410 acres of land. In the Fifth Witham District. Formed into a Drainage District in 1861. 212

DIPPLE GOWT. The Outfall of the Bar Ditch into the Witham, on the east side, near the Grand Sluice. 67.

DISTRITHE. In Swineshead. 248.

DOG'S HEAD SAND. In the Charter, *Dog's Head in the Pot*. At the outer end of Boston Deeps. 343, 345.

DOGDYKE. *Docdyke Hurne, Doc-dic, Docedik, Dockedigg*. D. B., *Duvedic*, from D. *Dokk* and *Dyke*, a bank. An enclosed pool, or harbour, where boats can lie safely. Vessels going up to Lincoln used formerly to lie here, and there is a record in the Hundred Rolls of tolls being paid for vessels. It is a township, on the River Witham, in the parish of Billinghay. By a Local Government order, Dec. 24th, 1886, a detached portion of the township, containing 291 acres, was transferred to Amber Hill parish. A steam engine for draining the land was erected in 1841. A. 727 acres. 139, 141, 204.

DOLPROON or DOLPRUN. A village or cluster of houses in Long Sutton, which is recorded to have existed near the South Holland Sluice on the Nene, and which was washed away in a storm in 1236. 128.

DONINGTON. A. S. *Doningas, Dunnas-ton, Donynton, Dunington, Donnedyk*. D. B. *Duninctune*. 11 miles S.W. of Boston. The ings and low lands in the parish were formed into a district under the Land Drainage Act in 1884. A. 6,180 acres. A

APPENDIX I.

market was held here in ancient times, on Saturday, but the day has now been changed to Thursday. It has three fairs: Sept. 4th for beast, May 26th and Oct. 17th for horses, beast and sheep. 96.

DONINGTON NORTHORPE. A hamlet of Donington.

DOUBLE TWELVES DRAIN. Formerly ran from Swineshead to Gutherham Cote. 252.

DORMANDIKE. On the Witham.

DORRINGTON FEN. In the Fifth Witham District. 240.

DOUNCE CHIURNE. On the north side of the Glen, near Pinchbeck. Dug.

DOVEDALE CLOTE. Near Crowland, near the division between Whaplode and Moulton. Dug.

DRODYKE. In South Holland, mentioned in an Inquisition of the Court of Sewers held in 1571.

DOVEHIRNE. *Dovehurne*, Dug. *Hyrne*, an angle, or corner. On the Glen, where the main road crosses, near Pinchbeck Bars. 117, 250, 257, 321.

DOVEHIRNE BRIDGE. Over the Glen. 450.

DOWDYKE. Part of the parish of Sutterton, 1½ miles S.W. of the village. Dowdyke Hall, a manor in Swineshead.

DOWSDALE. In the parish of Whaplode, 2½ miles S.W. of Whaplode Drove.

DOWSBY FEN. An allotment to Dowsby parish, in the Black Sluice District. Inclosed in 1765. 275.

DOWSBY LODE. A drain in Dowsby Fen. 258. Deepened, 266.

DOZEN'S BANK. A bank on the north side of Deeping Fen, running from Hawthorne Bank, Spalding, past Pode Hole to the Glen, on which is now the main road to Bourne. 117, 321, 324, 326.

DRAINAGE MARSH, OR FEN. A small parish, formerly extra parochial, near the Roman Bank, on the west of the main road leading from Sutterton to Gosberton Formerly part of Bicker Haven. A., 45 acres. R. V., £100.

DRAYTON. D. B. *Draitone.* 'Soke of the Manor of Drayton, afterwards called Kirton.'

DRURY DYKE. A drain in the south of Billinghay Fen. 189.

DUNSBY FEN. An allotment to Dunsby parish, in the Black Sluice District, containing 1,183 acres. 247, 276.

DUNSDYKE. A beck running through the low grounds in the parish of Metheringham, and discharging into the Witham. 151, 155.

DUNSTON FEN. On the west side of the Witham, 8 miles from Lincoln. Inclosed in 1762. 186.

DYKE FEN. In the Black Sluice District, near Bourne. 250.

EARLE'S CROFT AND EARLE'S STOCK. Part of the parish of Sibsey, at Frith Bank, on the north side of Cowbridge Drain, now known as Sibsey Willows.

EARL'S HALL. A manor in Frampton.

EARL'S OR ERLIS FEN. Adjoining Wildmore Fen. A division was set out between the two fens, in 17 Edward III. 205.

EARTH LODE. Near Dowsby Fen. One of the places mentioned in the boundary between Holland and Kesteven.

EASTCOTE OR ESTCOTE. In Deeping Fen, on the west side of the River Glen, at Tongue End. Deeping Fen Act, Chas. II. Dug.

APPENDIX I.

EASTHORPE COMMON. In Wigtoft. Inclosed 1772. 90.

EASTER EVENING. A manor in Swineshead.

EAST HOLLAND TOWNS. The villages on the coast between Wainfleet and the Witham, namely Boston East, Skirbeck, Fishtoft, Freiston, Butterwick, Benington, Leverton and Leake. *See* East Fen Inclosure Act of 1801.

EAST FEN. On the N.E. of the Fenland. Formerly consisted of low undrained peat, and a number of pools or meres, covering 12,664 acres, over which all the adjoining parishes had rights of common. 31, 197. It was inclosed, divided and allotted about 1801. 197. The engines and pumps at Lade Bank, for draining the fen were erected in 1867. 235.

EAST FEN. In Moulton.

EAS. A sewer in the East Fen. 200.

EE DYKE. A bank extending from Pinchbeck by Eastcote to Dovehirne. Dug.

EE DYKE BRIDGE. Over a sewer in Dyke Fen. Dug.

EASTVILLE. Formerly an extra parochial allotment. 12 miles N. E. of Boston in the East Fen. Created a township in 1812. (52 Geo. iii., c. 144.) New Leake is included in this parish for ecclesiastical purposes. A. 2,657 acres. Township formed. 229.

EAU BRIDGE FIELD. Common land in Kirton. Enclosed 1772. 85.

EAU DYKE. In the parish of Friskney.

ECHINTUNE. *See* Heckington.

EDLINGTON FEN. In the Third Witham District. 193.

EDYKES. In Wyberton and Frampton. Dug. 60.

EEL POOL LANE. In Wrangle.

EIGHT HUNDREDS. *See* Holland Fen. 247.

ELBOW BUOY. Formerly the point of junction of the Witham and the Welland. 351.

ELLOE. D. B. *Elloho*. Hund. Rolls *Hellowe and Helloe, Ellowarp*. A hundred in South Holland. Includes Cowbit, Crowland, Deeping St. Nicholas, Fleet, Gedney, Gedney Hill, Holbeach, Lutton, Moulton, Pinchbeck, Spalding, Sutton St. Edmunds, Sutton St. James, Sutton St. Mary, Tydd St. Mary, Weston, Whaplode and Central Wingland. A. 142,683 acres. 105.

ELLOE STONE. The site of an old stone, between the parishes of Moulton and Whaplode, where the Great Court for the Hundred of Elloe was held. The stone was 3ft. in circumference, and 2ft. above ground. It has been moved from its original place. Stukeley says, " Between Moulton and Whaplode is a green lane. Northwards stands a little stone, called the Ellostone, whence the name of the Hundred is derived."

ELLWOOD ELMES. Near Quadring and Donington. Dug. 30, 92.

ENCLUSE. *Enclouse*. A sewer, near Boston, on the west side of the river, 3ft. wide, temp. 23 Edw. I. Dug. 246.

ENGINE. A hamlet in Crowland parish.

EWERBY FEN. An allotment to the parish, in the Black Sluice District.

EYTHORPE. On the Glen. 247.

FENBRIGG. A sewer in Haconby. Dug. 247.

FENDYKE. The drain which used to run from Firsby Clough to White Cross Bridge and thence to Wainfleet Haven. 199.

APPENDIX I.

FENDYKE BANK. The southern boundary of the East Fen, before its inclosure. Dug. 202.

FENNE. A hamlet in Fishtoft, now known as Willoughby Hills and Long Hedges. A part of this district was known as Chapel Green, on which the Ball House now stands, but where formerly the chapel of the hamlet stood. Fenne, or Rochford, Manor belonged to the Dean and Chapter of Westminster.

FEN ENDS AND LONG FEN. Formerly part of the parish of Boston, adjoining Willoughby Hills.

FEN SIDE DRAIN. In the East Fen. 225.

FENTHORPE. A hamlet of Leake.

FERRY CORNER PLOT. 5 miles N.W. from Boston, on the west of the Witham Formerly part of the old river and extra parochial; now a parish. A. 49 acres R. V. £205.

FERRERS' BRIDGE. In South Holland. Inquis. Court of Sewers, 1571.

FIFTEEN FOOT DRAIN. In the Black Sluice District. 260.

FILDWARD, OR PHILWORTH MERE. Near Frith Bank.

FINKLE STREET, from D. *Vinkel.* A corner or angle near Leake.

FISHTOFT. D. B., *Toft.* D. *Fisker,* O. Norse *Fiskr.* 2½ miles S. E. of Boston. In 1880 Boston East, 770 acres, was transferred to this parish, and the allotments in the West Fen, 526 acres, to Frithville. The hamlet of Fenne is in this parish. The church is dedicated to St. Guthlac, the Patron Saint of the Fens, and there is a statue of the saint in a niche over the west porch. There used to be an old tradition to the effect that so long as the whip, the emblem of the saint, remained in his hand the parish would not be infested with rats or mice. The hand and the whip have long since been broken away. A. 4,719 acres. R. V. £8,410. 70.

FISHTOFT GRAFT. The principal sewer in the parish. The lower part, from the village to the river, was formerly an open tidal creek. 25, 69, 70.

FISHTOFT GOTE. In Boston Haven, on the east side of the river, a short distance above Hobhole. This was formerly the Outfall of the Graft Sewer, but is now abandoned. 70, 217.

FISHMORE END. In the parish of Sutterton, 1 mile N. W. of the village.

FISH MEER. In the parish of Wrangle.

FISKERTON. A portion of the low land of this parish is in the Third District of the River Witham. 194.

FIVE BELLS BRIDGE. 93.

FIVE MILE HOUSE. A station on the S. E. side of the River Witham, in Washingborough Fen.

FIVE WILLOW WARTH. South of Heckington Fen. 260.

FIRSBY CLOUGH. 199.

FIVE TOWNS' DRAIN. A public sewer, draining the five parishes of Swineshead Wigtoft, Sutterton, Algarkirk and Fossdyke, and discharging into the River Welland. 25, 86.

FIVE THOUSAND ACRE DISTRICT. Part of the Fourth Witham District. 197. Report as to Drainage, and added to Fourth Witham District. 229. Steeping River Act, 237.

FLEET. D. B., *Fleot* and *Flec.* From *Fleot,* a salt water creek. A market was granted to Thomas de Multon, in Fleet, by King John, in 1205. This had ceased to be held before Leland's time. A. 6,560 acres. R. V. £16,510. 107, 127.

Appendix I.

FLEET HAVEN. A tidal creek, running across the foreshore up to the sea bank in the parish of Holbeach, where is a sluice. The creek extends through the inclosed lands to the N. E. corner of Fleet parish. At an Inquisition taken in the time of Edward I. reference is made to the right of 'wrecks of the sea from the said port of Flet, as far as Holbeche.' 26, 115, 127.

FLEET NOOK. In Algarkirk Fen. Part of the land awarded under the Holland Fen Inclosure Award.

FLEET HURN. 100.

FLOORS. In Leake.

FODDER DYKE. A drain in the East Fen, running from Stickney Bridge to Hobhole Drain.

FOLINGE WORTH. Little and Great. Mentioned in the boundary of Holland and Kesteven in 1501.

FONT BRIDGE. Over a public drain in Leake.

FORE FEN. In Wigtoft, lying W. of the Five Towns' Drain, and S. of the main road from Boston to Swineshead, allotted to the parish under the Holland Fen Award. 89.

FORE FEN REACHES. Allotted to the parish of Swineshead under the Holland Fen award, and inclosed in 1773. 89.

FORTY PENCE SAND. A fishery in the parish of Wrangle.

FORTY FOOT, SOUTH. The main drain in the Black Sluice District, extending from Gutheram Cote to Boston.

FORTY FOOT, NORTH. Also called Lodowick's Drain. A drain in Holland Fen, running parallel with the Witham, and extending from Chapel Hill to the South Forty Foot at Boston. Formerly emptied into Witham at Lodowick's or Trinity Gowt. It now empties into the Black Sluice at Cook's Lock. 144, 253.

FOSSDYKE. On the Welland, 6 miles N.W. of Holbeach. D.B., *Stith. Fosse* and *Fossdyke*, Dug. The allotment to this parish in Holland Fen was transferred to Brothertoft in 1880. The name is derived from the Latin *Fossa*, an embanked ditch, and the S. *Dyke*, which has the same meaning. A. 1,859 acres. R. V., £4,384. 85.

FOSSDYKE WASH. 437.

FOSSDYKE BRIDGE. The Roman Fossway crossed the Welland at this place. An Act was obtained for making the present bridge in 1811, and it was opened for traffic in 1815. It was taken over by the County in 1870, under the Act, 33 & 34 Vict., c. 34. In 1890 it was freed from toll by the County Council. 449.

FOSSDYKE. A canal extending from Lincoln to the Trent at Torksey. Originally made by the Romans. Now belongs to the Great Northern and Great Eastern Railways. 10, 138, 159, 430.

FOUR TOWNS' DRAIN. A sewer draining the parishes of Sutterton, Algarkirk and Fossdyke. 86, 87.

FOULFLETE. A creek in Holbeach. Dug.

FOULWARDSTAKING. Near Crowland. Dug.

FRAMPTON. D.B., *Franeton. Fraunkton*, Dug. From *Frem*, strange. The strangers' settlement. 3 miles south of Boston. A. 5,187 acres. R.V. £12,179. 82.

FRAMPTON TOWN DRAIN. The public sewer. 25, 260.

FRERE BARRE HURNE. Near Bourne. 250.

FREEMAN'S CHANNEL. A navigable way between Lynn and Boston Deeps. 337.

APPENDIX I.

FREISTON. D.B., *Fristune*. 3 miles S E. of Boston. The name probably derived from *Freyer*, the god of fertility. At the time of the Domesday Book, Freiston was only a hamlet of Butterwick. The fen allotment was transferred to the parish of West Fen in 1880. A. 4,250 acres. R.V. £10,876. 72.

FREISTON SHORE. A hamlet of Freiston, adjoining the coast.

FRIEST FIELD. A common in Bicker, inclosed under the Act, 6 Geo. III, 1766. 98.

FRITH BANK. D., *Frithiof*. A hamlet of Sibsey. The name given to a large tract of land of undefined area, forming the southern portion of the West and Wildmore Fens. Frith Bank was the higher portion of the Frith, containing 1,200 acres. It is in the parish of Sibsey. The land formerly belonged to Kirkstead Abbey. By an Act passed in 1216 (10 Henry III) the land was conveyed to the Earl of Chester and Lincoln, and it was ordered that it should be protected and inclosed with ditches, and that a raised road should be made. In 1322 it became the property of Edward II. In 1512 it was mentioned as a Royal Farm, and is described as 'the Fryth in Sibsey Manor and Wildmore Waste.' From 1784 Frith Bank and Earl's Croft was recognised as part of the parish of Sibsey. A., 1,204 acres.

FRITH BANK DRAIN. Extends from Cowbridge to the Witham at Anton's Gowt. 161.

FRITHS, THE. Part of Holland Fen, on the north side of the old Hammond Beck, about ¾ mile from Wyberton Chain Bridge. Formerly extra parochial, now a parish. A., 166 acres. R. V., £258.

FRITHVILLE. In West Fen. Made into a township in 1812, under 52 Geo. III., c. 8. A. then 2,717 acres. In 1880 a detached portion of this parish was transferred to Sibsey and outlying portions of Boston, Sibsey and Fishtoft were added to the parish. A., 3,856 acres. Township formed. 229.

FRISKNEY, OR FRISKNEY BULLINGTON. D.B., *Frischenei*. Holinshed, *Friscon*. On the East Coast, 14 miles N.E. of Boston. The fen land was inclosed and allotted under an Act in 1809, at which time also an inclosure was made outside the Roman Bank. Before the inclosure it was noted for its decoys, and for the large quantities of cranberries which were gathered off the uninclosed land. Several antiquities, both of British and Roman origin, have been discovered in the parish; also the remains of salt pans. Contains 6,867 acres. 76, 214.

FRIST. A hamlet in the parish of Bicker.

FROG HALL IN WILDMORE. A church erected here in 1816, out of the revenues of the Fen Chapel Trustees. Now in the parish of Wildmore.

FROGHALL. A hamlet in the parish of Deeping St. James.

FULNEY. A hamlet on the east side of Spalding.

FULNEY DROVE. In Spalding. 103.

FULNEY GOTE. A sewer near Spalding, 20ft. wide in the time of Edward II.

FYNSETT. Near Crowland.

GALNE, OR GALWE GOTE. A sewer in Pinchbeck, on the north side of the Westlode, 16ft. wide. Dug. 294.

GAMOCK STAKE. In the East Fen. 205.

GANNOCK STAKE. Near Medlam. Dug.

GARLAND'S SLUICE. In South Holland. 126.

GARNER DYKE. In Moulton. The bank running north of the fen.

GARNSGATE. About one mile west of Sutton St. Mary village.

GARWICK. *Gerwyck, Gerdwike, Gerwyke*. A hamlet in the parish of Heckington, 2¼ miles east of the village. Channel of Gerwyck. Dug. Causey of, 247, 248.

Appendix I.

Gat Channel and Sand. In Boston Deeps. From D. *Gata*, a thoroughfare, or passage from one place to another, thus the *Cattegat* in Denmark. The word is frequently in use along the shores of the North Sea.

Gauntlet. A hamlet in the parish of Bicker.

Gedney. D. B. *Gadenai*. *Geddenay, Gedeneye*. In South Holland, 3 miles east of Holbeach. The surface of the land, where the village stands, is higher than the surrounding land, and the termination of the name denotes that this was land surrounded by water. A market was granted by King John to Falco de Oyre in 1332, but is now abolished. A., 10,562 acres. R. V., £21,540, (including Gedney Dyke and Gedney Drove.) 126.

Gedney Broadgate. About 1 mile S. E. from the village.

Gedney Hill, or Fen End Chapelry. A township of Gedney and ecclesiastical parish, near the Old South Eau. 10 miles S. S. W. of the village. Contains 2,040 acres. R. V., £5,188.

Gedney Dyke. A hamlet in Gedney, 1½ miles N. E. of the village. 100.

Gedney Drove End. A hamlet of Gedney, near the coast. 5 miles N. E. of the village. Made, with Dawesmere, into a parish in 1855. A., 5,573 acres.

Gerwick. *See* Garwick.

Gibbet Bar. Toll bar, on the road from Spalding to Peakirk, belonging to the Bedford Level.

Gibbet Hills. Part of Holland Fen, about 3 miles N. W. of Swineshead Church, formerly extra parochial, now in Swineshead parish. This land was sold by the Commissioners to pay the expense of inclosure. A., 174 acres. R. V., £615. 90, 248.

Gibraltar Point. A tongue of land in the parish of Wainfleet All Saints. projecting out from the coast, and which affords shelter to Wainfleet Haven. 338.

Gilsyke. Near Langrick. A drain which formerly emptied into Bicker Haven. Dug, And afterwards through the gote at Langrick. 252, 253.

Gipsy Bridge. Part of the parish of Thornton-le-Fen.

Glen, River. Called also Brunne River, Catebridge Water and Brunne Ee. Runs through the Fenland from Kate's Bridge to the Welland. The name is derived from the British word *Glyn* or *Glean*, a valley. 247, 251. Banks, 260. The Black Sluice Commissioners were authorised to contribute towards a new sluice. 266. Length and drainage area, 292. New sluice erected 1879, 308. Report on, 309. Breaches in banks, 309. Taxes and expenditure, 310. Trustees appointed, 328. Payment for maintenance by Deeping Fen Trust, 332.

Gobbald Park. A tract of land lying west of Dyke Fen.

Gobion Bothe, or Goben Bothe, or Moleboth. Near Helpringham and Bicker, below Wragmere Stake. Mentioned in the boundary line of Kesteven and Holland. 248.

Goderam Cote. *See* Gutheram.

Goggisland, *Goukeslound, Gokesland*, **Marsh of.** Part of the lands belonging to the Monastery of Crowland. 313.

Good Dyke. A drain on the north of the East Fen, running from Bellwater to Wainfleet. 25, 199, 200, 201, 203, 208, 213. Enlarged, 226.

Goole Fen Dyke. In the East Fen.

Goosetoft. *See* Brothertoft.

Gosberton. D.B *Gozeberdecherea* also *Gosebetechirche*. Dug. *Gosberkyrk*. *Gosberchirche*. 6 miles north of Spalding. The original termination seems to

APPENDIX I.

imply that this was originally a British village, the later word, *ton*, denoting that it was afterwards taken possession of by the Saxons. A., 7,714 acres. R.V., £21,518. 59, 60, 90.

GOSBERTON CLOUGH. At the junction of the Risegate Eau with the Black Sluice 257, 260.

GOWT DRAIN, LITTLE AND GREAT. Near Lincoln. 165.

GOWT PLOT. In Holland Fen. Part of this was allotted to Fossdyke, under the Holland Fen Inclosure Act, and the remainder sold.

GRAFT DRAIN. *See* Fishtoft.

GRAND SLUICE. Across the River Witham in Boston. Erected 1766. It has 3 openings of 17ft. 2in. each, and a lock 30ft. wide. 151, 154, 156, 160, 166, 167, 171, 178, 179, 351.

GRAFT BULL HURN. A common in Bicker, inclosed in 1766.

GRAVES FIELD. Common land in Kirton, inclosed in 1772. 85.

GRAVEL DRAIN. In Deeping Fen. 323.

GREAT FEN. Part of Holland Fen, between the North and South Forty-Foot Drains It was awarded to Kirton, Frampton and Wyberton, under the Holland Fen Inclosure Award. 81, 82.

GREAT SLUICE. 'In the Witham, where the Hundreds of Kirton and Skirbeck divide.' Built by Alan de Croun. 26.

GREEN ROW. A common in Wigtoft, inclosed 1772. 90.

GREETWELL. In the Witham Third District. 192.

GRIDE BRIDGE. Over a public sewer in Leake, about ½ mile N.W. of the Church.

GRIST. A sewer near Moulton. Dug.

GRIST HURN, OR CHRISTHURN. Mentioned in the boundary of Holland and Kesteven.

GROYNES. Dug. Near Crowland. Mentioned in the Charter of Bertulph.

GRUBB HILL. Near Horsley Deeps, on the Witham. 161, 193.

GUANNOCK GATE. In the parish of Sutton St. Edmunds.

GUIDE HOUSE. In South Holland. 101, 121.

GUTHERAM COTE. Dug. *Goderamescote, Godramscote, Gotherhamscote*. A hamlet of Pinchbeck 4 miles S.W. of the village, on the river Glen, where Bourne North Fen engine is situated; named from *Guthrum*, a Danish Chief, who settled the treaty with King Alfred. 245, 246, 247, 249, 250, 257.

GUTHRUM. In Wrangle.

GYRWAS. The Fenland occupied by the *Gyrwys*, or Fenmen, in Saxon times.

HACONBY LODE. *Hachelode*. A common sewer from the marshes to the river of Surfleet. Dug. Deepened under the Act of 1846. 236.

HACONBY FEN. A tract of fen land in the Black Sluice Level, belonging to the parish of Haconby. Inclosed in 1773. 247, 277.

HAGGEBOTHE. 248.

HAGNABY. In the Fourth Witham District. 197.

HAGNABY BECK. In the East Fen. 199.

HAINNICK. *See* Anwick.

APPENDIX I.

HALE FEN. Two fens, lying in the Sixpenny District of the Black Sluice, on the west side of the Forty Foot. Great Hale Fen contains 1,926½ acres, and Little Hale Fen, 1,332¼ acres. Inclosed in 1700.

HALE CAUSEY. Near Sibsey.

HALE BRIDGE. 214.

HALL GATE. In the parish of Sutton St. Edmunds.

HALL HILLS. 1 mile north of Boston. East of the Witham. Formerly part of the bed of the old River Witham. For many years extra parochial, now a parish in Boston Union. A., 20 acres. R.V., £237.

HALLTOFT END, OR ULTRA END. Parish of Freiston. 1 mile west of church.

HALLSTOCK. Formerly common land in the parish of Kirton. Inclosed in 1772. 85.

HALMERGATE. On the east side of the Welland at Spalding. 103.

HALUNLEEN-DEE. One of the common sewers of the fen between Deeping and Spalding. Dug.

HAMMOND BECK. *Hammonde Bek, Hamund Bek, Holand Fen Dyke*. Dug. 204. From *Hamund*, a Danish chief, who fought the Saxon chief Algar, and *Beck*, a stream. Either a natural stream improved and straightened, or an artificial cut made by the Romans. It extends from Pinchbeck to Boston, 17 miles, and forms the drain for a large area of land on its east side. Is under the control of the Black Sluice Commissioners. It was at one time navigable for small boats. 10, 25, 58, 59, 67, 246. Enlarged, 257. Deepened 1846, 266.

HAMMOND BECK, THE NEW. Formerly called the Redstone Gowt or Adventurers' Drain. A drain, 3½ miles long, extending from Kirton Holme to the Black Sluice near Boston. Made in 1601. 251, 257.

HANDKERCHIEF HALL. On the Brotherhouse Bank, 2 miles south of Spalding.

HANENDI. *See* Potterhanworth.

HANDTOFT. Formerly a piece of common land in Kirton. Inclosed in 1772. 85.

HAPPELTRENESSE. *See* Apple Tree Ness.

HARINHOLT. Near Crowland. Dug.

HAREBY. The allotment in this parish, in the West Fen, transferred to West Fen parish, 1880.

HARESHEAD DRAIN. On the south side of the Witham, in Nocton Fen. 150, 151.

HARRISON'S FOUR ACRES. The site on which the Grand Sluice at Boston was erected. 151, 154.

HART'S GROUNDS. On the west side of the Witham, near Dogdyke, formerly part of the old river, and extra parochial. Now parochialised. A., 444 acres. R. V., £1,234.

HAUT HUNTRE FEN. *See* Holland Fen.

HAVEN BANK. On the east side of the Witham, formerly part of the old river Witham and extra parochial. Included in Wildmore parish in 1884. A., 66a. 0r. 37p.

HAWEWELL. A sewer in Dyke, Haconby and Dunsby Fens. Dug. 242.

HAWTHORNE. Near the Witham. Dug. 420.

HAWTHORNE BANK. A bank on the Welland, in the parish of Spalding, at the S. E. boundary of Deeping Fen, mentioned in the Act 16 and 17 Chas. II. 105, 106, 321

HECKINGTON FEN. In the Ninepenny District of the Black Sluice Level, containing 2,572½ acres. Inclosed in 1764. 284.

APPENDIX I.

HECKINGTON HEAD DRAIN, 258. Deepened 1846, 266.

HECKINGTON EAU. A stream emptying into the North Forty Foot. 155, 173.

HEIGHINGTON FEN. Near Lincoln. 184.

HEKENDALE WATHE AND HILLS. In Bicker. 61, 92, 250.

HELPRINGHAM FEN. In the Eighteenpenny Black Sluice District, contains 1,362 acres. Inclosed in 1773. 273.

HELPRINGHAM EAU. A brook running through the village to the Black Sluice Drain. Placed in Black Sluice District, 258. Deepened, 266.

HERRING BRIDGE. Over the Glen. 450.

HERGATE. Near Spalding. 103.

HERMITAGE. In the Fourth Witham District. 197.

HIGH DALES. In Gedney, 2 miles north of the South Ea Bank. A square, double moated, where ancient foundations have been discovered, and some Roman coins. (*Camden*)

HIGH FEN DYKES. In Holland Fen. 104.

HIGH FEN AND HIGH FEN BOTTOM. Part of Holland Fen, near Hubbert's Bridge. Awarded to Kirton and Sutterton parishes under the Inclosure Act.

HIGH HILLS. In Skirbeck. 69.

HIGH HORN BUOY OR HIGH HURN. The limit of the Boston Pilot jurisdiction. 345, 346.

HILL DYKE. A drain running from the S. W. corner of the East Fen, to the Frith Bank Drain. Formerly navigable for boats. *See* Sibsey River. 25, 77, 199, 202, 214.

HILL DYKE CAUSEWAY. 34.

HILL'S DRAIN. In Deeping Fen, near Spalding. 327.

HILL'S SLUICE. In South Holland. 104.

HILL SIX ACRES. In the parish of Algarkirk, containing extensive traces of foundations of old buildings.

HOBHOLE. The main drain of the East Fen, running from Toynton to the River Witham at Hobhole. First proposed for drainage of East Fen, 219. Sluice and drain constructed in 1801, 225, 256. Enlarged, 237.

HOCHELADE, HOTCHLODE. A common sewer, repaired by the town of Pinchbeck. 23 Edward I. Dug.

HODGE DYKE. In Ewerby Fen. 258. Deepened in 1846. 266.

HOFF. A water-course in the parish of Swineshead, formerly emptying into Bicker Haven.

HOFLET STOW. *Hof-fleet.* From *Fleot*, a tidal water creek. A hamlet in the parish of Wigtoft, 1 mile west of the village, on the margin of the old Bicker Haven.

HAGGESBOTHE. Near Heckington. Dug.

HOLBEACH. Charter of Witlaf, *Holebecke* and *Holbech*. D.B. *Holebech, Holben, Holeben* and *Holobech*. Dug. *Holbeche, Holbysche, Holeben*. Leland, *Old Beache, Old Bek*. Parish Registers, *Holbek, Holbecke, Holbyche, Holbeache, Holbeach*, 1641. From *Hohl*, hollow, and *Bech*, a stream. One of the largest parishes in England, being 15½ miles in length and containing 21,133 acres. R.V., £50,064. The parish was increased to nearly three times its original size by inclosures made from the sea

APPENDIX I.

outside the Roman Bank, the present inclosed land extending from 4 to 5 miles beyond the Roman Bank, 101, 124. The following have been made ecclesiastical parishes: the fen portion in the South Holland Drainage District, containing 6,182 acres, known as Holbeach St. John's, in 1867; Holbeach Hurn, on the northeast, near Fleet Haven, 3,250 acres, in 1870; Holbeach St. Mark's and St. Matthew's in the marsh on the north of the town, containing 9,240 acres, in 1869. The right to hold an annual fair on the eve of St. Michael was granted by Henry III to Thomas de Multon, and a weekly market on Thursday. 123.

HOLBEACH CLOUGH. A hamlet near where the Holbeach river, or sewer, crosses the Roman Bank, formerly the extent of the inclosed land. 100, 124.

HOLBEACH ST. JOHN'S. A hamlet, 4½ miles south of the town. Made into a parish in 1867.

HOLBEACH DROVE. A hamlet in the extreme south of the parish, in St. John's parish

HOLBEACH HURN. Near the Roman Bank where it enters Fleet. 100.

HOLBEACH RIVER AND CREEK. 26, 115.

HOLBEACH SLUICE. 115.

HOLEDALE. Near Wainfleet. Dug.

HOLLAND. The southern division of the County of Lincoln, comprising the Hundreds of Skirbeck, Kirton and Elloe, containing 244,317 acres. Assessed for the County Rate at £732,779, and for the Poor Rate in 1893, at £484,253. The name is derived from A.S. *Hohl*, hollow, or low, German *Holig*. Thus, hollow or low land. *See also* North Holland and South Holland.

HOLLAND CAUSEWAY, HOLAND, OR HOYLAND, BRIGGE OF. Dug. *Holand Causey. Holand Fen Dyke.* A causeway between Holland and Kesteven. 'The King's Highway.' *See also* Bridge End. 96, 246, 438.

HOLLAND DYKE. A drain lying between South Kyme Fen and Algarkirk Fen, the boundary of Holland and Kesteven. Called also Old Ea. 245.

HOLLAND FEN. *Eight Hundreds, Haut Huntre.* Dug. In an Inquisition in reign of Edward II described as *Mariscus Octo Hundredorum.* Formerly comprised parts of eleven parishes which had rights of common over the fen. It was inclosed in 1767. Contains 22,000 acres. The separate parishes have now been either formed into new parishes or amalgamated with others. 245. First reclamation, 251. Inclosure, 260. Ancient Drainage and Boundary, 285, 288. Inclosure Act, 1767, 284. Land sold, 287. Parish Allotments, 288. New Parishes, 289. Drainage, 290. Rates, 290. Highway Board, 441.

HOLLAND FEN. An ecclesiastical parish, formed in 1868, containing Algarkirk, Sutterton, Kirton and Fossdyke Fens. Subsequently Algarkirk and Sutterton Fens, with Amber Hill and the part of Dogdyke in the fen, were formed into the civil parish of Amber Hill, making 5,261 acres, in 1880. Kirton Fen, for civil purposes, remains a part of the mother parish. Fossdyke Fen, for civil purposes, became a portion of Brothertoft in 1881. Ferry Corner and Wyberton Fen adjacent, were added to Langriville in 1883. Pelham's Lands, including Chapel Hill, and the Beats Plots, having an area of 803 acres, was made a parish in 1883. The Mown Rakes, containing 100 acres, and Hall Hills, containing 20 acres, were parochialised in 1886 and added to Boston Union. Brand End Plot, 25 acres, Copping Syke, 233 acres, the Friths, 166 acres, North Forty Foot Bank, Ferry Corner Plot, Pepper Gowt Plot, 102 acres, are all separate parishes in Boston Union. Gibbet Hills was added to Swineshead in 1890.

HOLLAND EAST, AND EAST HOLLAND TOWNS. The villages along the coast from Wrangle to Boston.

HOLT HILLS. In Swineshead. On the west side of Swineshead Low Grounds, 2½ miles west of the village.

HORBLING FEN. In the Eighteenpenny Black Sluice District. Contains 1,344½ acres. Inclosed in 1764. 274.

Appendix I.

HORBLING DRAIN. Placed in the Black Sluice District, 258. Deepened, 266.

HORNCASTLE. The castle at the Hyrn, or Corner. The Roman *Bano Vallum*, or fort, on the Bane. This is a Roman station overlooking the Fens, and through which the road, from the Roman Port of Wainfleet to Lincoln, passed. Remains of the ancient Roman walls are in existence, and several Roman coins of the Emperor Vespasian and others have been found.

HORSLEY DEEPS. On the Witham. 161, 164.

HORSINGTON FEN. The Third Witham District. 193.

HORNCASTLE NAVIGATION. 160, 431.

HOWBRIDGE DRAIN. Runs through Wildmore Fen, from opposite Chapel Hill, to join the West Fen Drain at Stephenson's Bridge. 225.

HOWBRIDGE, OR HOWBRIGGS. In Wildmore Fen. Dug. 155, 204.

HOWELL FEN. In the Ninepenny Black Sluice District. Contains 290 acres.

HOWDYKE DRAIN. 72.

HUBBERT'S BRIDGE. The name is derived from *Hubba*, a Danish king, who invaded Lincolnshire, A.D. 865. It was formerly a wooden bridge over the South Forty-Foot Drain, being the road from the old parishes into the fen. The bridge was made a county bridge and replaced by the present structure in 1888. 82, 452.

HUNGATE. A hamlet of Leake.

HUNTINGFIELD HALL. A manor mentioned in the Bicker Fen Act, 1766.

HUNDLE HOUSE. Dug. In South Witham District. 197, 204.

HURDLE TREE BANK. A bank in Whaplode and Moulton, part of the boundary of the South Holland Drainage District. 105.

HURN FIELD. Common land in Kirton. Inclosed in 1772. 85.

HYNSBECK. Dug.

HYRN. Near Langrick. Dug.

IGERAM BRIGGE. A bridge near Moulton. Dug.

INKERSON FEN. In South Holland. 131.

INNOME. Near Donington. Dug.

IRELODE DRAIN. In Rippingale Fen. Dug. 250.

IVES CROSS. On the Roman Bank, half a mile west of the village of Sutton St. James.

IVORY. In Wrangle.

JAY'S BANK. In Fleet Fen. 102.

JIGGIN'S OR JENKEN'S BANK. In Holbeach Fen. 102.

JINGLE HIRNE. In Gedney, ¾ mile south of Raven's Clough.

JOBSON'S POUND. Formerly the boundary between Boston and Fishtoft, on the road leading to Wainfleet. Vestry Book of Boston, 1768.

JOCESACULAND. In Holbeach. Dug.

KATE'S BRIDGE. *Catebrigge*. Over the Glen, above Thurlby Fen. 450.

KETEL A monastic cell in the parish of Long Sutton, on the east side of the village near Little London

KENULPH'S STONE. *Kenulphston*. A boundary stone near Crowland.

APPENDIX I.

KELFIELD. Near Bicker Dug.

KING'S HILL. A mound in Wrangle, near Wrangle Bank. Supposed to have been put up by the Romans for a beacon station.

KING STREET DRAIN. In Deeping Fen. 327.

KIRTON. D. B. *Chirchetune. Chirchetone, Kirketon, Kyrkton.* From British *Circ,* a circle Supposed to have been of Druidical origin, this being a place where Druidical rites were performed. A village, 4 miles S. W. of Boston. Once a market town, the market being held on Saturday, near the Market-stead house, about ½ mile south of the village. Two fairs were also held here annually. The Earl of Exeter was formerly Lord Paramount of the Soke of Kirton, and had here a Session Hall, in which was held the Quarter Sessions, and the Great Goose Court, which had jurisdiction over the whole of the Kirton Wapentake; but it ceased to act after the inclosure of the Fens. In 1772 the Sessions were permanently removed. In 1771 an Act was obtained for establishing a Court of Requests, for the recovery of debts not exceeding 40s., within the Soke of Kirton. This was superseded by the County Court. From official returns made in the reign of Queen Elizabeth, Kirton was the third town of any size in the county, and at that time had only 143 fewer households than Boston, 231 less than Lincoln, 74 more than Spalding, 81 more than Holbeach, 96 more than Grantham, 54 more than Bourne, and 14 more than Stamford. Stukeley says that the place was famous for its apples, and the 'Kirton Pippin,' which grew in the parish, was described by an old writer as a 'most wholesome and delicious apple.' The fen and common land were inclosed under an Act passed in 1772 (12 Geo. III.) 83. In 1657 'the Sea Bank Estate' was purchased and vested in trust, for the maintenance of the banks in the parish. The estate now only contains 2a. 2r. 19p., the remainder having been used for the repair of the banks. In 1873 an inclosure of salt marsh, containing 676 acres, was added to the parish. The area of the parish is 8,966 acres. R.V., £21,775. 60, 83.

KIRTON HUNDRED. *Kirton Warp, or Wapentake.* Includes the parishes of Algarkirk, Bicker, Brothertoft, Donington, Fossdyke, Frampton, Gosberton, Hart's Grounds, Kirton, Quadring, Skirbeck Quarter, Sutterton, Swineshead, Surfleet, Wigtoft, Wyberton, Amber Hill, Great and Little Beats, Copping Syke, Drainage Marsh, Ferry Corner Plot, the Friths, Hall Hills, North Forty-Foot Bank, Pelham's Lands, Pepper Gowt Plot, Seven Acres, Shuff Fen, Simon Weir, South of the Witham. It contains an area of 70,422 acres, and an assessable value to the County Rate of £188,895. Part of the Borough of Boston is also in the Kirton Hundred. 57.

KIRTON TOWN'S DRAIN. The public sewer. 25, 83, 260.

KIRTON END. A hamlet, 1½ miles N. W. of the village.

KIRTON MERE, OR MEARE. A hamlet, 1 mile west of the village.

KIRTON HOLME. D., *Holm,* an island. A hamlet, 3½ miles N. W. of the village, adjoining the fen. The cattle from the fen used to be collected here to be marked once a year.

KIRTON INGS. Common land. Inclosed 1772. 85.

KIRTON SEA DYKE, OR SKELDYKE. 2 miles, S. E. of the village.

KIRKSTEAD. On the Witham. A Cistercian monastery was founded here by Hugh Brito, Lord of Tattershall. The fen is in the Third Witham District, 196.

KIRKSTEAD LOCK. On the Witham. 161, 162, 164.

KIRKSTEAD BRIDGE. Over the Witham. 448.

KNEDYKE. 'A common sewer of the whole fen, betwixt Deping and Spalding.' A sluice was ordered to be built here in the reign of Edw. II. Dug.

KNOCK. D., *Knok,* a mound. A sand at the lower end of Boston Deeps. 343.

KNOLL. Brit., *Cnol,* a hillock. A sand at the lower end of Boston Deeps.

APPENDIX I.

KYME. D.B., *Chime*. North and South Kyme Fens and Kyme Low Grounds. A large tract of fen land, lying between Billinghay Skerth and Kyme Eau, and extending up to the Car Dyke in the First and Fifth Witham Districts. 190, 241.

KYME SOUTH FEN. In the Sixth Witham District. 283.

KYME EAU, EE OF KYME, OR KYME EA. First mentioned in a Commission of Sewers, 15 Edward III, 1342. 'So obstructed that ships could not pass.' The Outfall of the River Slea into the Witham, near Chapel Hill, navigable in ancient times. Canalised in 1794, forming a waterway to Sleaford, 431. Power was obtained by an Act, passed in 1878, to abandon the navigation. 25, 154, 155, 247, 252, 429, 431.

KYME FERRY. 439.

KYME VACHERIE. A cow pasture, in North Kyme Fen, formerly attached to the monastery at Kyme.

KYME TOWER. The remains of a castle, situated in South Kyme, formerly belonging to the Umfraville family. The castle was pulled down about 1720.

LADE BANK DRAIN, AND ENGINES. In the East Fen. The drain discharges into Hobhole, and runs parallel with the bank. 226. There is a bridge over Hobhole Drain. The pumping engines for draining the East Fen are situated here, on the west side of Hobhole Drain, about 7 miles N.E. of Boston. 205, 226. Erected in 1867. 235.

LAFEN, LATHAM, LODE. A public sewer in the parishes of Surfleet and Gosberton 25, 94.

LAMPSON'S CLOUGH. On the Risegate Eau. 93.

LANGRICK. *Langrett*. Dug. *Langrake*. D.B. *Tric*. D. *Rekja*, a reach, literally, Long Reach. At one time the ferry, which crosses the river here was called Armtree. In the Fourth Witham District, 197. Township formed and chapel erected by the Inclosure Commissioners, 228.

LANGRICK GOTE. An ancient sluice, on the west side of the Witham, removed in the latter half of the 18th century. It was situated near the present railway station, and had 3 openings, giving a total waterway of 24ft. 142, 155. Controversy as to erection of sluice 1602. 249.

LANGRICK VILLE, OR LANGRIVILLE. Township formed in 1812, under an Act passed in 52 George III, 228. Area at that time 1,912 acres. 5 miles N. W. of Boston. It contains the hamlets of Copping Syke, Silt Pits and South of the Witham. Is included in the consolidated chapelry of Wildmore, formed in 1881. It consists of the southern portion of Wildmore Fen, which, at the inclosure, was allotted to the Earl of Stamford, in lieu of his manorial rights over Armtree and Wildmore Fens. The church was built under the Fen Inclosure Act, in 1829, 228. By a Local Government order, dated Dec. 24th, 1880, detached parts of Fishtoft, Coningsby, Kirkstead, Scrivelsby, Woodhall, Dalderby and Martin Fen allotments were transferred to Langrick Ville. 228.

LANGDYKE DRAIN. In Wildmore Fen. 199.

LANGTOFT ROFT. A drain in Deeping Fen. 323.

LANGWORTH DRAIN. In Wildmore Fen. 199.

LANGWATHE, OR LANGWORTH. On the Witham. In the Fourth District, 140, 197, 201.

LANGWORTH RIVER. Tributary of the Witham. 135.

LAPWATER HALL. In South Holland. 101.

LAUNDERSTHORPE HALL. In the parish of Fishtoft, on the road leading from the village to Hobhole Bank.

LAW FEN. Near Holland Dyke. Dug.

LAWRENCE BRIDGE. Over the Three Towns' Drain.

LEADEN HALL. In South Holland. 101.

LEAKE. A village 8 miles N. E. of Boston. D.B. *Leche*. Stukeley considers that the name denotes a watery or marshy place. Another derivation is from S. *Leekr*, a brook. A., 5,767 acres. R. V., £20,221. By an order of the Local Government Board, dated Dec. 24th, 1880, detached portions of Benington, Butterwick, Leverton, Revesby and Boston East Fen, were transferred to New Leake. Tradition says that at a place called 'The Floors' a light house once stood, outside the Roman Bank. 73.

LEAKE, NEW. A hamlet of Leake, 5 miles N. N. W. of the church. It is included in the ecclesiastical parish of Eastville.

LEEDS GATE. On the South Holland Drain, at the north end of Gedney Fen.

LE FLEGGE. Formerly Oggott, where was a broken cross of St. Guthlac, being one of the boundary marks between Kesteven and Holland.

LEVEBRIGGE. In 'Brunne, near the river of Brunne.' Dug. 202, 247.

LEVEL TOWNS. The villages on the north of the East Fen. 202.

LEVERTON. D. B. *Levertune, Lavintone*. In the parish records, about 1562, the name is written *Lenton* and *Levrton*. Stukeley derives the name from Leofric, Seneschal of Earl Algar. Another derivation is from the A. S. Chief *Læferingas*. A., 2,894 acres. R. V., £6,111. The allotment to this parish, in the West Fen, was transferred to the new parish of West Fen, by 24 Vict., c. 17. Also in 1881 a detached part of the parish was transferred to Leake. In 1801, 395 acres of marsh land was inclosed. In 1810 an Act was obtained for inclosing the commons. 73.

LEVERTON OUTGATE. A hamlet, about 1¼ mile east of Leverton church.

LUKE'S CORNER. Near Sibsey. 224.

LIMB OR LYMM. An old name for part of the Steeping River. 213, 230.

LINCOLN. An early British town, called *Lincoit*. Afterwards one of the principal Roman settlements and called *Lindum Colonia*. The name is from the British *Llyn*, a pool. (Brayford Mere.) Freeman states that at one time it was called *Caerlindcoit*, meaning the hill fort by the pool. After the Roman time the word was spelt *Lindisii* or *Lindisey*, the island of Lindis. *Lindecollinum, Lindecollina* (Bede) *Lindocollyne, Lincoll*. In old Norman charters, and in records kept by the Earls of Lincoln, it is described as *Nichol* and the County as *Nicholshire* (Marat.) Robert of Brunne, in his poem of 'Handlyng Synne' calls it *Linkolne*. It is rather remarkable that Christian missionaries came from Lindisfarne, in Northumberland, to convert the Saxons in Lindisey. 4, 5, 11.

LINDSEY, OR LYNDSEY, LEVEL. In the southern part of the Eighteenpenny District of the Black Sluice District. 31, 245. Parishes in, 273.

LINWOOD FEN. In the First Witham District. 187.

LITCHFIELD, OR LICHFIELD END. Near Kirton and Frampton. 61, 250.

LITCHFIELD BRIDGE. Formerly over the Hammond Beck, near the Redstone Gowt Drain. 250.

LITTLE HURN AND INGS. A plot of common land in Kirton. Inclosed in 1772. 85.

LITTLE LONDON. A hamlet in the parish of Long Sutton.

LOCK'S MILL. On the Welland, near Spalding. 311.

LODE DYKE. A bank near Crowland. Dug.

LODOWICK'S, OR LODOVICK'S, GOWT. The Outfall of the North Forty-Foot Drain, situated on the west side of the old channel of the Witham, about ¼ mile above Boston Church. It had a waterway of 15ft. Was also called Trinity Gowt. 144, 145, 147, 244, 253.

LONG DROVE. A sewer in Pinchbeck.

Appendix I.

Long Sutton. *See* Sutton.

Long Dyke Drain. In the West Fen. 225.

Lord's Drain. Runs from the east side of Spalding to the Welland near Wrag Marsh. 101, 106, 121.

Lost Bridge. In Pinchbeck. Dug.

Low Gate's End. In South Holland. 103.

Lunn's Bridge. A bridge over Hobhole Drain, between Fishtoft and the sluice.

Lurtlake. Near Crowland. Dug.

Lusdyke. An ancient drain in the East Fen, emptying into Wainfleet Haven. Part of Steeping River. 199, 200.

Lutton. *See* Sutton.

Lutton Corner. 101.

Lutton Gate. In Sutton St. Edmunds. 100.

Lutton Gote. The original Outfall of Lutton Leam. 130.

Lutton Leam. An ancient water course, or sewer, running from the north of Long Sutton to the Nene, the Outfall sluice being about half a mile below the lighthouse tower. 26, 101, 110, 127, 130.

Lutton Marshes. 101.

Lyme. A sewer in the north of the East Fen. 200.

Lyndsey Level. *See* Lindsey. 245.

Maccaroni. A channel between Boston and Lynn Deeps. 337, 351.

Mandyke Gate Bridge. Over the Five Towns' Drain.

Mantle Cerncroft, Great and Little. Common land in Kirton. Inclosed in 1772. 85.

Man War Ings. Remains of a Danish encampment in Swineshead.

Maple Bush. One of the boundaries of the Witham Bank, which had to be maintained by the Abbot of Kirkstead.

Mareham Fen. Allotment in Wildmore Fen. Added to the new parish of Wildmore in 1881. 197.

Marisbeck. A sewer in the Lindsey Level, near Pinchbeck. Dug.

Martin Fen. On the west side of the Witham, in the First District. Inclosed in 1789. 187.

Market Lands. In Wrangle.

Matehirne. On the south side of the Glen, near Pinchbeck. Dug.

Maud Foster Drain. First made in 1568, being a new Cut from Cow Bridge to Boston Haven. In the Verdict of Sewers of 1735, it is referred to as 'otherwise Moll Foster.' 202, 207, 209, 224.

Maud Foster Gote, or Sluice. 205, 206, 208, 209, 214, 217. New Sluice built, 1801. 224, 226.

Maumgate, or Mornsgate. Common land in Kirton. Enclosed 1772. 85.

Mariscus Octo Hundredorum. *See* Holland Fen.

APPENDIX I.

MAVIS ENDERBY. An allotment to this parish, in the West Fen, transferred to West Fen parish, 1880.

MEDLAM. A hamlet in the West Fen, formerly in the parish of Revesby, transferred to Carrington in 1880.

MEDLAM DRAIN. In the West Fen, running from the West Fen Drain at Mount Pleasant to Revesby. 225.

MEDEHAMSTEAD. Peterborough.

MEARS, OR MEERS. In Kirton, on the west side of Kirton Drain, 1½ miles N.W. of the village, formerly common land. Enclosed 1772. 85.

MENGARLAKE. Near Crowland.

MERE BOOTH. On the north side of the old River Witham, above Anton's Gowt.

MEREDYKE. On the Witham. 140.

MERLODE, OR OUSE MER LODE. A sewer running from the Hammond Beck to Risegate Eau, between the parishes of Quadring and Donington, and maintained by the former. 25, 60, 92. Placed in Black Sluice District, 258. Deepened in 1846, 266.

MEREWIN CORNER, *Merehirn*. Near Gutheram Cote. 246.

MERRYLANDS. In Sutterton Fen. 240.

METHERINGHAM FEN. Extends 6 miles east of the village to the Witham. In the Second Witham District. 186.

MID FODDER DYKE. In the Black Sluice Level. 266.

MID FEN DYKE. The ancient boundary between Holland and Kesteven from the Welland to the Witham. Dug. Now superseded by the South Forty Foot. 245, 254.

MIDDLE FEN. Part of Holland Fen, between the Hammond Beck and the South Forty Foot, allotted to Skirbeck Quarter under the Inclosure Act.

MIDDLEHAM. In the Fourth Witham District. 197.

MIDDLETON. A hamlet of Leake.

MIDVILLE. A parochial township in the East Fen, 10 miles north of Boston. Formed into a township in 1812 (52 Geo. III, c. 44). Contains 2,501 acres. In 1885, this was formed into a consolidated chapelry with Eastville, 228, which includes portions of Benington, Boston, Butterwick, Leake, Leverton, Revesby, Spilsby and West Keal. Township formed, 229. Chapel erected by Inclosure Commissioners, 228.

MILK HOUSE MARSH. In Fishtoft. The Witham Outfall cut through this. 71.

MEEKING HILL FIELD. Common land in Bicker. Inclosed 1766. 98.

MILL BANK. In South Holland. 102.

MILL DRAIN. In the East Fen, near Sibsey. 199, 211, 217.

MILLER'S STILE. On the old sea bank in Boston, at the boundary with Skirbeck Now absorbed in the dock.

MILL GREEN. A hamlet in Pinchbeck, 2 miles S.W. of the village.

MILTHORPE, OR MYLTHORPE. A hamlet in the parish of Asgarby, lying 2 miles east of the village. Entitled to send a member to the Black Sluice Trust. 254.

MOLL FOSTER. *See* Maud Foster.

MONEY BRIDGE. A hamlet in Pinchbeck and Bridge over the Glen, 1¾ miles west of the village. 450.

MONK'S HALL. A manor in Gosberton and Quadring.

APPENDIX I.

MONK'S GROUND. On the Witham. 147.

MOORE'S COTE, OR COOTE. On the west side of the River Glen, between Gutherham and Tongue End.

MOORHOUSE. Hamlet in West Fen, 3½ miles south of Revesby. Formerly the Dairy Farm of the Abbey of Revesby. In the Fourth Witham District. 197, 204.

MOREDYKE. A bank near Crowland, 'reaching from Shepee to Asendyke.'

MORTON FEN. Extends 4 miles east of the village of Morton on the east side of the Cardyke. In the Black Sluice District. 277.

MOULTON. A village, 5 miles east of Spalding, containing 11,391 acres. R.V., £22,792. D.B., *Multune*. Dug., *Multon*. The moot for the Wapentake of Elloe was held here in the time of the Saxons. There is a stone still existing which marked the place where the courts are supposed to have been held, called the 'Elloe Stone,' in a green lane, called Spalding Gate, which was formerly the main road from Spalding to King's Lynn. The portion of the parish lying south of the Austendyke Road, containing 3,800 acres, was made into a separate parish for ecclesiastical purposes by an order in council, dated May 17th, 1890. Several Roman coins were found in this parish, near Raven Bank, in 1721. About 2,237 acres of marsh land were enclosed in 1660, 1081 acres in 1793, and 400 acres in 1875, 101. A large area of common land was inclosed and divided in 1793. 121. *See also* Elloe Stone.

MOULTON AUSTENDYKE. A hamlet 1½ miles south of the village.

MOULTON EAUGATE. A hamlet in Moulton Fen, 5 miles south of the village.

MOULTON SEA'S END. A hamlet on the Roman Bank, 2¼ miles north of the village. 100.

MOULTON CHAPEL. A chapelry in the fen, 4 miles south of the village.

MOULTON RIVER, OR MERE DRAIN. 26, 121.

MOUNT PLEASANT. In the West Fen, formerly a hamlet of Boston, to which parish it was allotted on the Inclosure. Now in the parish of Frithville. Contains 3,856 acres. Chapel erected by Inclosure Commissioners. 223.

MOWN RAKES. In Holland Fen, allotted to Swineshead at the Inclosure. 1¼ miles N.W. of the station. Formerly extra parochial. Added to Swineshead by order in Council, April 23rd, 1890. Contains 100 acres. R.V., £194. 88, 90.

NARWEHEE. A drain running from 'Brunne to Godramscote.' Dug. (The Wear Dyke.) 247.

NESLAM FEN. In the Black Sluice District, 1¾ miles east of Sempringham.

NEVERALE. On the Witham.

NEVIL'S DAM. A bridge in Swineshead, over the Five Towns' Drain.

NEW BOLINGBROKE. A village in the West Fen, originally established by J. Parkinson. A market commenced in 1821 is obsolete. *See* Bolingbroke.

NEW BRIDGE. *See* Cross Gates.

NEW CUT. The Outfall for the Witham, constructed 1884. *See* Witham Outfall.

NEWBURY. On the River Glen, near Surfleet.

NEW EE. In Surfleet. 61.

NEW EE DYKE OR NEWDYKE. In Dyke Fen, running from Eedyke Bridge to Holland Fendyke. 257.

NEWDYKE. One of the boundary stations, between Holland and Kesteven.

NEW GOTE. A sluice on the east side of the old River Witham, for the drainage of the West and Wildmore Fens. 145, 199, 205, 208, 212.

APPENDIX I.

NEW NEW GOTE. A sluice on the east side of the old River Witham, for the drainage of the West and Wildmore Fens. 145, 199, 205, 208, 212.

NEWGATE. Near Spalding. 103.

NEWHAM DRAIN. In the West and Wildmore Fens, running from Anton's Gowt, past Moor Houses, nearly up to the Catchwater. 225.

NEWHOLME. In the Fourth Witham District. 197.

NEWLAND INCLOSURE. In Long Sutton. 128.

NEW YORK. A village in Wildmore Fen, 8 miles N.W. of Boston, in the parish of Wildmore.

NOCTON FEN. On the west side of the Witham, in the First District. Inclosed in 1831. Contains 2,315 acres. 184.

NOCTON DYKE. 151.

NOMAN'S LAND HIRNE. Near Crowland.

NOMAN'S FRIEND. In Wildmore Fen, south of Moor Houses. 218.

NORTHDYKE, OR NORDYKE CAUSEWAY AND BRIDGE. A part of the main road lying between Stickney and Sibsey. Before the inclosure of the Fens this road passed over a very swampy tract of land lying between the East and West Fens, which was frequently flooded. There were 4 arches under the road, for the escape of the water out of the East Fen. This causeway was originally maintained by the Abbot of Revesby. 34, 77, 208, 225, 438.

NORTH GRAFT. An ancient sewer near Haconby, belonging to this parish, Dunsby and Pinchbeck. Dug. 250.

NORTH DROVE DYKE. In Deeping Fen. 323.

NORTHOLME. Near Wainfleet Haven.

NORTH FORTY FOOT BANK. In Holland Fen. Formerly extra parochial, now a parish and village, consisting of a long strip of land running by the side of the drain. R.V., £215. 253, 442.

NORTH FORTY FOOT DRAIN. *See* Forty Foot.

NORTH HOLLAND. The northern part of the division of Holland, containing the Hundreds of Skirbeck and Kirton and the Boston Union. A., 101,634 acres. 57.

NORTHORPE. A hamlet in Donington Parish.

NORMAN DEEPS. Spelt *Normandeepe*, in a deed of the time of Elizabeth; also *Norman Depe*. The northern part of the Wash. From *Djupr*, O.N. for *deep*. 201, 343.

NUNHAM DRAIN. In the West and Wildmore Fens. 199, 207.

NUN'S BRIDGE. Over Hobhole Drain, about 1 mile above the sluice.

OBTHORPE. On the Glen. 247.

OGGOT, OR DEADMAN'S LAND. Near Crowland. Dug.

OLD EA, OR OLD HEE. One of the ancient boundaries of Kesteven and Holland. 'A ditch between the marsh of Holand and the marshes of Hekyngton and Kyme.' Dug.

OLD FEN DYKE. In Spalding. Dug.

ONSTHORPE, THE TOWN OF. Had to repair the sewer from Apple Tree Ness to Kyme. Dug.

ORBELINGE. Horbling.

OSGODYKE BANK. In Holland Fen. 102.

APPENDIX I.

OUSE MER LODE. *See* Mer Lode.

OUT WEARE BANK. In Leake. Dug.

PARTYE BRIDGE. Near Quadring. Dug. 60, 92.

PEAKHILL. A hamlet in the parish of Cowbit.

PEACHY. *Pechs*, or *Pekke Hall.* Near Scrane End, Freiston.

PECKEBRIGGE, OR BRIGGDYKE. A bridge built on the Holland Causeway by the Prior of Spalding, and directed to be sufficiently wide for horsemen to pass over. It was near the site of the present bridge over the Hammond Beck. 97, 103, 246.

PEDDER'S BRIDGE. Formerly across the Scire Beck, near where Bargate Bridge now stands. Displaced when the Maud Foster Drain was cut. 67, 69.

PELHAM'S LANDS. In Holland Fen, formerly extra parochial. Formed into a parish with Chapel Hill and the Beats Plot in 1833. A., 803 acres. R.V., £2,231· 90.

PENNY HILL. A hamlet in the parish of Holbeach, 1¼ miles north of the town.

PEPPER GOWT. An ancient Outfall for a natural creek, called Pepper Syke, draining Shuff Fen, on the west bank of the old River Witham, opposite New Gote. Taken up, 1767.

PEPPER GOWT PLOT, OR ROWLAND'S MARSH. Formerly extra parochial, now a parish 2½ miles north of Boston, on the west bank of the Witham. Formerly part of the bed of the old River Witham. A., 102 acres. R.V., £430.

PEPPER SYKE. *See* Pepper Gowt.

PESEHOLME GOTE. A sewer in Spalding. Dug. 103.

PESEHOLME HIRNE. In Spalding. Dug.

PETER'S POINT. On the west side of the Nene, near Sutton Bridge. 106.

PICHALE. At the South End of Spalding, near the commencement of the Barrier Bank. Dug. 103.

PINCHBECK. D. B., *Picebech.* Dug. *Pynsebek, Pynchebec.* The village is on the Glen, 2 miles north of Spalding. The parish is 12 miles long and 7 miles wide, and contains 13,710 acres. R. V., £30,892. There was formerly a Market Cross in Mill Green, called the Fish Cross, where fish and wild fowl were brought from the sea marshes and fens, to be sold. A cross also formerly stood near the Red Lion Inn. The stock were brought to this cross before being turned into the Common Fen, and marked. In October they were brought back to the cross and claimed by the owners, who then paid Hoven Dues. 120, 121, 246, 316.

PINCHBECK WEST. Formerly part of Pinchbeck, 4½ miles N. W. from Spalding. Was made into an ecclesiastical parish in 1815. It includes the Fen and Pinchbeck Bars, where the church is situated.

PINCHBECK NORTH FEN. In the Black Sluice District, north of the Glen. 121, 255.

PINCHBECK SOUTH FEN. In Deeping Fen, south of the Glen. 120.

PINCHBECK BARS. 2½ miles west of the village.

PINCHBECK BARS BRIDGE. Over the Glen at Dovehirne. 450.

PIPPIN HALL BRIDGE. Over Five Towns' Drain, in Swineshead South.

PHILWORTH, OR PHILWARD MERE. Near Frith Bank.

PINEGATE. Near Spalding. Dug.

PODE HOLE. A hamlet in Pinchbeck, 4 miles S. W. of the village. The name is derived from A. S. *Padde*, a toad. The engines and wheels for draining Deeping Fen are situated here. 323. Sluice vested in Adventurers, 327. Engine erected, 330. Description of, 383.

APPENDIX I.

POINTON LODE. A drain in Pointon Fen. 258.

POINTON FEN. In the Black Sluice District. Inclosed 1790. 275.

POSTLAND. A hamlet in Crowland.

POTTERHANWORTH FEN. In the First Witham Drainage District. 184.

POYNTON HALL. In Freiston, adjoining Butterwick.

PRINGLE. In North Kyme Fen. 241.

PRY CLOSES. In Digby Drainage District. 242.

PULVERGOTE. A sewer in Holbeach. Dug.

PULLEYE HEAD. The limit of the Port of Boston, at the outer end of the Gat Channel. 343, 345.

PURCEYNT. A marsh near Crowland. Dug.

PYNGEL HYRNE. On the Sleaford Road, in the parish of Swineshead. Dug.

QUADRING. D.B., *Quedhaveringe* and *Quadheureringe*. Dug., *Quadryng, Quadavering*. Derived from A. S. Chief *Cwædringas*. Village 8 miles N. W. of Spalding. A., 3,950 acres. R. V., £8,654. 90.

QUADRING EAUDYKE. A hamlet in Quadring, 1½ miles east of the village.

QUADRING EE. A sewer, 16ft. wide, maintained by Quadring. 23 Edw. I. 59.

QUAPELODE *See* Whaplode.

QUAPELODEDYKE. A bank near Crowland. Dug.

QUARLES. In the parish of Leake.

QUEEN'S GOTE. Otherwise Wainfleet Clough. 214. *See* Wainfleet.

QUEEN'S BANK. In South Holland. 121.

RAITHBY ALLOTMENT. In the West Fen. Transferred to the West Fen parish in 1881.

RAKES. The Common Rakes in Holland Fen, allotted partly to the parish of Swineshead under the Inclosure Act of 1767, and partly to Algarkirk. 88.

RAKES, THE MOWN. *See* Mown Rakes.

RAMPART DRAIN. In Deeping Fen. 327.

RATUN ROW. A roadway, on the west of the Welland, leading to Spalding. Dug. 103.

RAVEN BANK. Extends from the Welland, near Cowbit, in an easterly direction towards the Nene, and joins the Roman Bank at Tydd. Made by the Romans to inclose the higher land from the Fens south of this bank, which were at that time liable to flooding from the Nene and the Welland. 100, 121.

RAVEN'S CLOUGH. On the Raven Bank, 2½ miles south of the village of Fleet. Roman coins and a Roman urn have been found here.

RAYDYKE. In Wildmore Fen. Dug.

REACHES MARSH. Part of the old river Witham, 1½ miles N. W. of Langrick Ferry. In the parishes of Wyberton and Frampton. Inclosed under the Acts of 1784 and 1789. 81, 83.

RED COW DISTRICT. In Moulton. 121.

RED HOUSE BRIDGE. On the South Holland Drain, 5 miles from the Outfall. 112.

APPENDIX I.

REDSTONE GOWT. Was erected by order of the Court of Sewers in 1601, and a new Cut made to take the water from the Hammond Beck, which it joined at Litchfield Bridge. In 1677 it was reported to be in a ruinous condition, and was rebuilt at a cost of £1,200. It is now disused. 250, 258, 263.

REVESBY. The village is 12 miles north of Boston. The parish includes the hamlets of Medlam and Moor Houses in the West Fen. The allotment to this parish, in the West Fen, was transferred to Carrington in 1882, and the Sibsey allotment added to Revesby in 1881. Wydale, formerly belonging to this parish, was added to Leake in 1881. An Abbey for Cistercian Monks was founded here in 1142. The remains of a supposed British camp are to be found near the village. Sir Joseph Banks, the chief promoter of the inclosure of the East, West and Wildmore Fens, resided at Revesby.

RICHMOND TOWER. *See* Rochford.

RIGBOLT OR WRIGHTBOLT. A hamlet in the parish of Gosberton.

RIGBOLT CLOUGH. On the Beche, at the S. E. corner of Gosberton Fen. 250

RINGLE HURN. Formerly on the old Sea Bank, at the junction of the parishes of Boston and Skirbeck

RINGSTONE. In the parish of Rippingale. One of the places entitled to send a member to the Black Sluice Trust. 254.

RIPPINGALE FEN. In the Black Sluice District. Allotted to the parish in 1803. 276.

RIPPINGALE RUNNING DYKE. A stream which brings the high land water from beyond the village, and empties into the Forty-Foot. 250, 258. Deepened, 266, 276.

RISEGATE. A hamlet in the parish of Gosberton.

RISEGATE EAU. D. B., *Riche*. Dug.;*Risgate Ees*; *Risgate, Sewer of*; *Reesgate Ee*. An ancient stream coming from Gosberton and empying into Bicker Haven. Now the main sewer of the district, which runs along the old bed of the Haven, and discharges into the Welland, 1 mile above Fossdyke Bridge. 25, 61, 91, 247.

ROCHFORD TOWER. Near the supposed site of the ancient Richmond Tower, 1½ miles east of Boston.

ROOS HALL. A manor in the parish of Freiston.

ROTTEN ROW. In the parish of Benington and Freiston. From A. S. *Rotteren*, the mustering place.

ROWLAND'S MARSH. *See* Pepper Gowt Plot.

ROYALTY FARM. In Swineshead, 7½ miles from Boston, formally extra parochial, Parochialised in 1886, and added to Swineshead, by order in Council, April 23rd, 1890. A., 120 acres. R.V., £228. 90.

RUSHES, THE. Formerly Common Land in Swineshead. Enclosed under Act of 1773. 88.

RUSSIAN INGS. Formerly a piece of Common Land in Kirton, enclosed under Act of 1772. 85.

RUSKINGTON FEN. In the Fifth Witham District. 241.

SAINECOTE. In the Fourth Witham District. 197.

SALEM, OR SALE HAM. SALEM BRIDGE. Near Wainfleet. 213, 230, 237.

SALTEN EE. Formerly a tidal creek in Surfleet. Dug.

SALTENEY. In 1593 the precincts of Boston Deeps and the jurisdiction of the Mayor were described as extending to Salteney Gates. John of Brittany claimed to have all waifs and wrecks from Salteney to Wrangle by the sea shore.

SAND HILLS. In Algarkirk Fen.

Appendix I.

SANGOTE. Formerly a gote in Gosberton. Dug. 60.

SCALP, BOSTON. A high clay bank at the mouth of the Witham. 350.

SCATHERGRAFT. A sewer in Donington, 16ft. wide. in the time of Edward I. Dug. 96.

SCOBDYKE. In Pinchbeck. Dug.

SCOFT. Near Tydd. 102.

SCOTTEN DYKE. In the Black Sluice District, near Bourne. 258. Deepened under the Act of 1846. 266.

SCIRBECK. The ancient watercourse of Skirbeck, forming the boundary between this parish and Boston, now a sewer. Commences near Hall Hills and flows along Robin Hood's Walk, crosses Norfolk street to the Cowbridge Road, which it crosses near the Catholic Chapel, whence it went in a winding course nearly in the direction of the present Maud Foster Drain, which has now taken its place. Leaving this drain near Mount Bridge, it crossed the Skirbeck Road and entered the river near the site of the old Gallows Mill. The portion between Hall Hills and Maud Foster and between the Skirbeck Road and the Sailor's Houses is still used as a sewer. 25, 69.

SCHUST. Near Frampton. Dug. 60.

SCOTIA CREEK. Formerly the Outfall of the Graft Drain in Fishtoft into Boston Haven. The name is derived from the *Scotia* steamer, which at one time traded between Boston and London, making this her berth. 70.

SCRANE END, OR CRANE END. D, *Skrayne*, or *Skreyng*. A hamlet in the parish of Freiston, 1½ miles S.E. of village.

SCRUBB HILL. In the parish of Wildmore, near Dogdyke Station.

SCULL RIDGE. A.S., *Skola*, to be covered with water. A sand in Boston Deeps.

SEAS END. A hamlet in the parish of Moulton.

SEA LATHES. A district in Moulton, containing 1,200 acres, on which the great tithes were apportioned.

SEMPRINGHAM FEN. In the Black Sluice District, 3 miles east of the Abbey Church.

SHEPHERD'S HOLE. On the Welland, below Spalding. 325.

SHEDING FLETE. One of the places mentioned in the Inquisition to enquire into the boundaries of Holland and Kesteven.

SHEEPWASH GRANGE. On the Witham. 139.

SHEPHAYSTOW. Part of Whaplode, 1 mile south of Whaplode Drove.

SHEP'S EE. *Shepishee, Shepey*. A watercourse, which bounded Crowland on the east. Dug.

SHIRE DRAIN, OR OLD SOUTH HOLLAND DRAIN. Formerly a branch of the Welland, also called the South Ea. It forms the boundary of the County. 101, 104, 105, 297.

SHOFF. In Quadring Fen. 95.

SHOFT, RIVER OF. Near the boundary of the Counties of Lincoln and Cambridge. Dug 25.

SHORT FERRY. 7 miles east of Lincoln, at the junction of the Langworthy with the Witham.

SHOTBOLT'S BRIDGE. Carries the main road from Pinchbeck to Spalding over the Vernatt's Drain. 326.

SHOTTLES. Near Sibsey. Dug. And in Skirbeck Quarter. 79, 205.

Appendix I.

SHUFF FEN. In Holland Fen, on the north bank of the North Forty-Foot Drain, adjoining Brothertoft. Allotted by the Inclosure Act, 1794, to Wyberton. Formerly extra parochial, now added to Boston Union. A., 93 acres. R. V., £186. 81.

SHUFF, OR BENTON'S BRIDGE. Over the North Forty-Foot, in Shuff Fen. 452.

SHEARCROFTS. Inclosure in South Holland. 129, 130.

SIBSEY. D. B., *Sibolci*. Dug., *Sibolsey, Cibecey*. From A. S. *Sib*, a brother, and *Ey*, an island. The meaning being *Sib's*, or brother's, island. The village is 4½ miles north of Boston. The fen allotments in this parish, in the West Fen, were added to Frithville in 1881, and those in Skirbeck, with an outlying part of Frithville, added to the parish. The parish includes the hamlet of Frith Bank. 77.

SIBSEY RIVER. An ancient watercourse, running from Nordyke to Hilldyke, and thence to the Witham, now absorbed by Stone Bridge Drain. 25, 77, 199.

SIDECROFT COMMON. In the parish of Swineshead. Inclosed under the Act of 1767. 89.

SILVER PIT DRAIN. The drain which ran from the Silver Pit, one of the deeps in the East Fen. 199.

SILT PITS. A hamlet in Langrick Ville.

SIMON GOTE. In the East Fen. 202.

SIMON HOUSE. Near Lade Bank, in the East Fen. 226.

SIMON WEIR. 3 miles S. W. of Kirton church, formerly extra parochial, now a parish in the Boston Union. A., 2½ acres. R. V., £27.

SINCYL DYKE. A drain on the south of Lincoln. 156, 159, 161, 165, 167.

SIX HUNDREDS. A hamlet in the parish of Heckington, containing 615 acres. 4 miles east of the village. In the Sixth Witham District. 283.

SKATE'S CORNER. On the Nene. 129.

SKELDYKE. A hamlet in the parish of Kirton, 2 miles S. E. of the village. From *Skjel*, a division.

SKELDYKE FIELD. Common land in Kirton. Inclosed 1772. 85.

SKREYNG. A manor in Freiston, purchased in the time of Henry VII, for the endowment of the Abbey of Westminster.

SKIRBECK. D. B., *Schirebec*. Dug. *Skirbek, Skirbeche, Skyrbeck, Schirebeck*. Hollinshed *Skerbike*, from D. *Skjorbeck*, meaning dividing stream. *See also Scircbeck*. A., 2,479 acres. R. V., £18,285. The fen allotment of this parish in the West Fen was transferred to Sibsey parish in 1881. 69.

SKIRBECK HUNDRED. D. B., *Ulmerstig*. Includes the parishes of Boston, Butterwick, Benington, Fishtoft, Freiston, Leverton, Leake, Skirbeck, Wrangle, and contains 29,064 acres. 57, 65.

SKIRBECK GOTE. The Outfall of the Hammond Beck into Boston Haven, in Skirbeck Quarter. Dug. 176, 370, 204.

SKIRBECK QUARTER. A hamlet of Skirbeck, on the west side of Boston Haven, in the Kirton Hundred, containing 934 acres. R. V., £7,215. 78.

SKIRTH, OR SKERTH, DRAIN. In the Black Sluice Level. On the south-west side of Algarkirk Fen. 257, 266.

SKITISHIRNE. Near Peccebrigge. Dug.

SLEA RIVER. A tributary of the Witham. 135.

SLEAFORD CANAL. 160, 431.

APPENDIX I.

Smeeth Hall. In Holland Fen, at the north end of Kirton Fen. Allotted to the parishes of Kirton and Swineshead in 1767. 88.

Sond, or Soud. A sewer in Donington. Dug. 247.

South Channel. Once the course of the Witham, from the Scalp to Clayhole. 337.

South Ea, or Eau. A branch of the Welland, known as the Shire or Old South Holland Drain. 103, 105.

South Delph. A new Cut on the River Witham. 167, 170, 173, 185, 186.

South of Witham. A hamlet in the parish of Langrick Ville, formerly extra parochial, now a parish in the Boston Union. A., 19 acres. R. V., £249.

South Drove Dyke. In Deeping Fen. 323.

South Hee. A bank in Fleet. Dug.

South Forty-Foot Drain. The main drain, in the Black Sluice District, extending from Boston Haven to Gutherham Cote. This drain was first cut by the Adventurers who drained the Lindsey Level in the middle of the 17th century. 252. It was afterwards opened out and improved under the Black Sluice Act of 1765, 257. Again deepened and improved under the Act of 1846. 244, 266.

South Holland. The southern division of the parts of Holland, containing the Hundred of Elloe, and the Unions of Spalding and Holbeach. A., 142,683. 31, 98.

South Holland Drain, Old. *See* Shire Drain.

South Holland Drain, New. A drain, 14 miles long, extending from Peak Hill in Crowland, across the South Holland Fens, to the Nene, at Peter's Point, where it discharges through a sluice, about ¾ of a mile south of Sutton Bridge. Originally constructed under the South Holland Drainage Act of 1793. 107.

South Holland Drainage District. Embraces the fen portion of South Holland. 105.

South Holland Sluice. The Outfall of the New South Holland Drain, above described. The first sluice was erected in 1795. The existing sluice was erected in 1852, and has two openings of 8ft. each, and one of 15ft., making a total waterway of 31ft. 106, 112.

South Holland Embankment. The bank, inclosing a large area of marsh land, in South Holland. Constructed 1793. 114.

South Kyme Fen. *See* Kyme.

Southedic. A bank of Gedney and Fleet. Dug.

Southrey Fen. On the east side of the Witham, in the Bardney District and in the Third Witham District. 193.

Southrey Eau. 151, 155.

Spalding. A market town in South Holland, on the River Welland. D.B., *Spallinge*. Dug., *Spaldyng*, *Spaldeling*. King Ethelbald's Charter, *Spaeltelyng* and *Spaldelyng*. A.S., *Spaldingas*, a Saxon tribe. *Spalda* was one of the Saxon divisions of the county adjoining the Welland (*Saxons in England*). Spalding was in existence before the establishment of Crowland Abbey, the boundary in King Ethelbald's charter being described as extending *usque ad Ædificia Spaldeling*. A cell was founded here in 952, in connection with Crowland, by Thorold de Bokenhale. One of the principal Roman roads passed through Spalding across the Welland and it is said that the Romans built a bridge across the river. At an inspection of the Fens, made by order of King James in 1605, the bridge over the Welland is mentioned. The present bridge was erected by the Adventurers of Deeping Fen, in 1836. 449. A., 10,259 acres. R.V., £54,153. The ecclesiastical parish of St. John the Baptist was formed in 1874, and consists of part of Spalding and Pinchbeck; and of St. Paul, at Fulney, in 1877. 121, 316

APPENDIX I.

SPALDING COMMON. Inclosed under Act, 1801. 121, 325.

SPALDING NORTH FEN. On the east side of the Hammond Beck, and on the north of the Glen, about 1 mile west of Dovehirne. In the Black Sluice District. 254.

SPALDING SOUTH FEN. In Deeping Fen, between the Glen on the north and the Counter Drain on the south, and extends up to Dozens Bank. Contains 1,425 acres. 117.

SPITTLE LAKE. A road in Fleet. Dug.

SPITTAL HILL. On the east side of the parish of Freiston.

SPOUTE HIRNE. On the Glen Bank, in Thurlby Fen. Act of Charles II. 321.

SAINT SAVIOUR. *See* Bridge End.

STAINFIELD BECK. A tributary of the Witham. 155.

STAKER. A drain near Spalding.

STAKES GRAFT. A sewer in Donington.

STAMP END LOCK. On the Witham at Lincoln. 156, 159, 161, 164.

STAMFORD CANAL. 31, 432.

STAR FEN, OR TRUSS FEN. On the west side of the Cardyke in Heckington, one mile N.E. of the village.

STEEPING RIVER. Runs along the north of the East Fen and discharges into Wainfleet Haven. Length, 18 miles Drainage area, 101 square miles. 199, 213, 226 Enlarged, 229. Improvement Act, 237.

STELEGOTE, THE GUTTER OF. Near Spalding. Dug.

STEPHENSON'S BRIDGE. Over the West Fen Drain, at its junction with Newham Drain.

STEVENSON'S CROSS. In Sutterton.

STICKFORD. A parish on the borders of the East and West Fens, 8½ miles from Boston. Here was formerly a ford across the swamp or low land, lying between the East and West Fen, through which ran the main road.

STICKNEY. D B., *Stickenhai*. Dug., *Stickeney*. A village, 8½ miles north of Boston. 197.

STICKWITH GOWT. Outfall of Blue Gowt Drain. 118, 119.

STITH. *See* Fossdyke.

STIXWOULD FEN. On the east side of the Witham, in the Third Witham District. 193, 173.

STIXWOULD BECK. A tributary of the Witham. 151, 155.

STONEBRIDGE DRAIN. A highland drain in the West Fen, running from near Stickney to Cowbridge, formerly known as the Sibsey River. Deepened and straightened as part of the works done under the Act of 1801, for draining the East and West Fens 77, 199, 217.

STONE HALL. A manor in Frampton.

STRIP'S LANE BRIDGE. Over the Three Towns' Drain.

STUNG GLEANE. Mentioned on the Holland and Kesteven boundary line in 1501.

STRUGG'S HILL. In Sutterton, 1 mile north of the village. There is a bridge here on the main road, over the Three Towns' Drain.

SURFLEET. D₁ B., *Surfleet*. Dug., *Surflete, Surflet*. The village is on the Glen, 4 miles north of Spalding. The termination of the name, *fleet*, denotes that this was once on a tidal creek or stream. The marsh was inclosed in 1777. A., 3,926 acres. R. V.,

APPENDIX I.

£9,683. The bridge over the Glen was referred to by the Sewers' Commissioners, in 1320 as ' Surfleet Brigge.' Dug. And the Glen was described as ' The River of Surflete.' 60, 90, 246. Bridge re-built, 450.

SUTTON, LONG. Includes the four hamlets of Sutton St. Mary, Sutton St. Nicholas, otherwise Lutton, Sutton St. James, and Sutton St. Edmunds. Each of these is rated separately for poor and other purposes. 128.

SUTTON BRIDGE. An ecclesiastical parish, formed in 1874. Part of Sutton St. Mary. The bridge across the Nene was erected in 1831; the passage across the Wash previous to this, being by fording, or boats, across 2 miles of sands. The original oak bridge was replaced by the present swing bridge in 1850, and taken by the Railway Company in 1866. 129.

SUTTON ST. EDMUNDS. A hamlet in Long Sutton Fen. It is intersected by four straight droves or gates, called Lutton Gate, Hall Gate, Broad Gate, and Guanoc Gate. It extends 7 to 9 miles S. W. of Long Sutton, down to the border of Cambridgeshire. A., 5,468 acres. R. V., £11,026. 129, 131.

SUTTON ST. JAMES. A hamlet and village, 4½ miles S. W. of Long Sutton. A., 2,847 acres. R. V., £5,942.

SUTTON ST. MARY. The town of Long Sutton in this hamlet is 5 miles east of Holbeach. A., 9,322 acres. R. V., £32,027. 129.

SUTTON ST. NICHOLAS, OR LUTTON. Sometimes called Lutton Bourne. Name derived from the Lode or Leam which runs through the parish. A hamlet of Long Sutton. The village is 1½ miles north of Long Sutton A., 3,807 acres. R. V., £8,607. 129.

SUTTON MARSHES. In South Holland. 101, 129.

SUTTERTON. Dug., *Sotterton, Soutterby*. Not mentioned in Domesday Book. From S. *Sutter*, south; *Southerton*. The village is 6 miles south of Boston. A., 2,959 acres. R. V., £7,475. The allotment to this parish, in Holland Fen, transferred to the parish of Amber Hill in 1880. 60, 86.

SURWOOD HYRNE. On the old River Witham.

SWANELODE. A sewer in Donington, ordered to be 16ft. wide in the time of Edw. I. 96, 247.

SWANSTON. Near Donington.

SWATON. *Swaneton*. 'Inundation of the fens betwixt Swaneton and Donington.' Dug. 220. Swaton Fen is in the Black Sluice District.

SWATON EAU. A drain in Swaton Fen. 258. Deepened, 266.

SWINESHEAD. Not mentioned in Domesday Book. Dug., *Swynesheved, Swynehevd*. A.S., *Swinesheafod*. Temp. Chas. I., *Swineshed*. A name derived from *Swin* a channel, Dutch *Szin*, a creek. Bicker Haven was described in the Hundred Rolls as *Aqua de Swin*. Dugdale mentions the River of Swynesheved. The tides from Bicker Haven formerly came up to Swineshead by the Hoff Fleet or creek, and there was a haven formerly near the market place, crossed by a bridge, which was removed about 1796. A market of some importance was formerly held here, but was discontinued in the middle of the 17th century. A fair is still held on Oct. 2. In 1134 an abbey of Cistercian monks was founded on a spot about 1 mile east of the town, on the site of the Swineshead Abbey Farm. In 1216 King John, marching from Lynn, forded the Wash at Cross Keys and, being overtaken by the tide, lost all his baggage. Afterwards he crossed the Wash at Fossdyke and stayed at Swineshead Abbey, where he was taken ill and, moving on, died at Newark. About ¼ mile west of the village there are the remains of a supposed Danish encampment, known as the Man War Ings, forming a circle 60 yards in diameter. By an order in Council, dated April 23, 1890, the parochialised places of Gibbet Hills, Royalty Farm, Mown Rakes, Little Brand End Plot and Great Brand End Plot were amalgamated with this parish. The outlying portion of the parish in Holland Fen, at Chapel Hill, was added to Pelham's Lands parish in 1883. 60, 247. Drainage and Inclosure Act, 86. Land awarded under Holland Fen Act, 88. Alteration of parish, 90.

Appendix I.

SWINESHEAD HIGH BRIDGE. Over the South Forty-Foot. 452.

SWINESHEAD EE. 59.

SWINESHEAD DE LA MERE. A manor in Swineshead.

SWINESBOOTH. On the north side of the old River Witham, nearly opposite the junction of Kyme Eau.

SWYFLEET, OR SWYTHUT HYRNE. On the old River Witham. 140.

SWYNEMAN DAM. A sewer in Donington, ordered to be 16ft. wide in the time of Edw I. Dug. 96, 247.

SWYNECOTES. Near Mount Pleasant. 225.

SYMON GOTE. A drain in the East Fen, called in Dugdale 'an old drain.' 205.

SYKEMOUTH. In Holland Fen, between the Hammond Beck and the South Forty Foot, north of Kirton Holme. 88.

TAMWORTH GREEN. On the south of the parish of Butterwick.

TAMMOCKS. In Wrangle.

TATTERSHALL FEN. In the Third Witham District. 196.

TATTERSHALL BRIDGE. Across the Witham, about 1 mile above Dogdyke. 166.

TED WARTHAR. A fen near Crowland. Dug.

TERRY BOOTH. In Sutterton Fen, being part of the land allotted to Sutterton under the Holland Fen Inclosure Award.

THIEVES' CREEK OR THEVIS CRICK. A sewer in the East Fen. 200, 203.

THIMBLEBY FEN. In the Third Witha District. 193.

THORNDALE. Near Whaplode. Dug.

THORNTON LE FEN. In Wildmore Fen, 6 miles, N.W. of Boston. A township created in 1802 under an Act, 52 Geo. III, c. 144. Area at that time, 1,425 acres. A detached portion of Coningsby and Toynton St. Peter was added in 1880 and a detached part of Thornton transferred to Wildmore. The name was derived from the largest Proprietor in the neighbourhood at the time of the inclosure of the Fens. Township formed, 229.

THORPE DALES. In the East Fen. Dug.

THREE TOWNS' DRAIN. A public sewer, draining Swineshead South, Wigtoft and Sutterton, running from Acre Land Clough to Nevil Dam. 86, 87.

THURGATE. A gutter in Gosberton. Dug.

THURLBY FEN AND PASTURES. On the west side of the Glen. Drains by a culvert under the river into the Counter Drain. Exempted from taxation to Deeping Fen, 322. Right to drain under the Glen, 328. Inclosure Act, 335.

TILE HOUSE LOCK. On the Witham at Bardney. 151.

TILL RIVER. A tributary of the Witham. 161.

TIMBERLAND AND TIMBERLAND THORPE FENS. In the First Witham District. Inclosed 1785, 188.

TITTON HALL. A manor in Frampton.

TOFT. *See* Fishtoft. (Also used for Wigtoft.)

TOFT SAND, AND BUOY. In Boston Deeps. The Boston Pilots' limit. 346.

TOFT TUNNEL BRIDGE. Over North Forty-Foot, in Brothertoft. 452.

TOLLON, TOLLUM OR TOLHAN. On the river of Brunne. Dug. 246, 247.

Appendix I.

Toot Hill. In Skirbeck. There used to be a mound here which was used as a signal beacon hill. 'A Tote Hill is an eminence from which there is a good look out.' (*Taylor.*) A.S., *Toeten*, to blow a horn.

Tongue End. On the River Glen, at the junction of Bourne Eau. 257, 260.

Torksey Lock. At the junction of the Fossdyke with the Trent. 160, 161, 162.

Torre Booth, Sluice of. Near the Old Ea, mentioned on the boundaries of Holland and Kesteven in 1501.

Tottibridge. 60.

Tretton Bridge. 450.

Tric. *See* Langrick.

Trinity Gowt. *See* Lodowick's Gowt.

Trokenhouse. Near the boundary of Lincolnshire and Cambridgeshire. Dug.

Trundle Gowt. On the Boston East Sewer Drain, on the west side of Bargate Bridge, near where Peddar's Cross Bridge used to be. (*Appendix VIII, p.* 1.)

Truss Fen. *See* Star Fen.

Tupham Dyke. A stream emptying into the Witham. 151, 155.

Tupholm Fen. In the Third Witham District. 193.

Turpitts. In Weston. Dug.

Two Towns' Drain. A sewer draining Wigtoft and Sutterton. 87.

Twenty Foot Drain. In the Black Sluice. 266.

Tydd St. Mary. D. B., *Tite*. Dug., *Tyd* and *Tydd*. Hundred Rolls, *Tid*. Monument in Church, 14th century, *Tidde*. From D., *Tita*, small. A., 4,771 acres. R. V., £10,403. On the borders of the Counties of Lincoln, Norfolk, and the Isle of Ely. 3 miles from Sutton Bridge. 101, 132.

Tydd Gote. A hamlet of Tydd St. Mary. ½ mile S. E. from the church. The earliest recorded gote or sluice here was in 1293, the second in 1551, and the third and present sluice, called 'Hill's Sluice,' or Tyd Gote Bridge in 1632. 103, 133.

Tydd Bridge. 450.

Ulmerstig. *See* Skirbeck Hundred.

Vachery of Revesby. A cow pasture, called More House.

Vainona. *See* Wainfleet.

Valentine Dyke. An ancient drain, on the west side of the East Fen, near Stickney. Dug. 199, 205, 212.

Vernatt's Drain. The Outfall of the Deeping Fen drainage, running from Pode Hole to the Welland, at the Reservoir. The drain was first cut by the Adventurers in 1642, and joined the Welland 1½ miles below Spalding. 323, 324. It was extended to the Reservoir, when the works, under the Act of 1774, were carried out. Deepened in 1801, 326. Vested in Adventurers, 327. Water on sill, 329. Enlarged and new sluice erected 1867, 331, 332. The drain was named after Vernatti, one of the Dutch Adventurers, who found the money for carrying out the works promoted by Vermuiden, 318, 118, 301. Drain first cut, 313. Drainage engine erected, 1741, 312. Extended, 323. To be maintained by the Adventurers, and regulation as to water, 324, 327. Size of, in 1815, 329.

Vernatt's Sluice. Erected in 1857, in the place of the old sluice erected in 1774. 332. Has 3 openings, 11ft. each. First erected, 323.

Wainfleet. D. B., *Wemflet*. Dug., *Waynflete*. Holinshed, *Wenfleet*. Linc. Survey, 1101, *Weinflet*. From A. S., *Fleot* or *Fleet*, a tidal creek and *Wayn*, a

APPENDIX I.

marsh. This was a Roman station and landing place, called *Vainona*. Several Roman ruins and remains of pottery and pavement have been found from time to time. The town is in the parish of Wainfleet All Saints, and is generally known as High Wainfleet, to distinguish it from Low Wainfleet, or Wainfleet St. Mary. It is situated 2¼ miles from the coast, on the River Steeping, the sluice across which, below the the town, is called, Queen's Gowt, 214, and Wainfleet Clough. 5, 76.

WAINFLEET HAVEN. In the Port of Boston. 343 The Outfall of the Steeping River, which discharges at Gibraltar Point, 2¼ miles from Queen's Gowt. The Outfall of this river was at one time larger than it is now, having been 30ft. wide for a mile above the town of Wainfleet. At one time a large number of vessels used to trade to Wainfleet, the harbour being well sheltered by the protection of Gibraltar Point. It is now only occasionally frequented by small craft and barges. In 1886, the river was straightened and improved from Salem Bridge to the sea, a staunch erected at Croft Bank, and a new sea sluice by the side of the old one at Queen's Gowt. An Act was passed in 1818 for improving the drainage of the parish. 50 acres of common land were inclosed in 1870. 201, 213. Report on Drainage. 229. Grundy's scheme for improving drainage by, 213. New Sluice erected, 238.

WAINFLEET CLOUGH. 203, 214.

WAITHE COMMON. On the south side of Kyme Eau, 1½ miles west of South Kyme.

WALCOT FEN AND DALES. In the First Witham District. 190, 191.

WALCOT COMMON. In the Digby Drainage District. 242.

WALDRAM HALL. On the south side of the Welland, near Peakirk. Mentioned in the Deeping Fen Act of Chas. II. There was a ferry here for passengers going to and from Crowland. In 1330 the toll was fixed by the Abbot at one penny for inhabitants and double to strangers. A treble charge was allowed in stormy and tempestuous weather. 297, 321.

WANTON'S CLOUGH. In Tydd St. Mary. 132.

WARDYKE DRAIN. In the Five Thousand Acre District. 229.

WARGATE BRIDGE. Over the Risegate Eau, between Surfleet and Gosberton.

WASH, THE. The large bay on the East Coast, between Lincolnshire and Norfolk. Probably from O.N., *Oss*, an estuary or inlet of the sea. 336.

WASHINGBOROUGH FEN. On the west side of the Witham, in the First Witham District. 184.

WASHINGBOROUGH BECK. A tributary of the Witham. 155.

WATHE. Dug. *See* Waithe.

WEARDYKE, WARDICK AND WAREDYKE. 'Extending along Bourne Ea to Goderam Cote and Dovehirne.' Dug. 250.

WELLAND, RIVER. Dug., *Weland*. Also called *Wiland*. 'Wasch and Wiland shall drown all Holand.' 72¾ miles long and drains 707 square miles, including the Glen. Rises near Market Harborough, not far from the source of the Nene. For further particulars *see* Index.

WELLAND NAVIGATION AND STAMFORD CANAL. 432.

WEST BANKE. In Holland Fen, near Langrick. Dug.

WEST COOTE. On the west of the River Glen, near Thurlby.

WEST FEN. In the Fourth District of the Witham Commission. Drained and inclosed, 1801-18. 81, 197, 210, 222, 227. Commissioners for, 231.

WEST FEN. A parish, 9 miles north of Boston, formed in 1880, under the Act, 44 Vict. cap. 17. Consists of detached portions of, or Fen Allotments of Mavis Enderby, Hareby, Hundleby, West Keal, Raithby, Freiston and Leverton.

APPENDIX I.

WEST FEN DRAIN. In West Fen. 225.

WEST HOUSES. Near Sibsey, 3 miles N.W. of the village. In the Fourth Witham District. 197.

WEST LODE, OR WESTLOAD. An ancient sewer in Spalding, supposed to have been made by the Romans, for draining Deeping Fen. It ran from Podehole, by Dozens Bank and Hawthorn Bank, and along the west side of the town along the street which now bears this name, to the Welland. It is mentioned in the Deeping Fen Act, 16 & 17 Car. II, as being navigable, and was, until it was superseded, used by boats, bringing corn, &c. to Spalding. At one time there were locks in the Welland for running the water out of the river into the West Lode, so as to ease the washes. They were removed in 1815. The fishery in the West Lode was granted to the monastry of Spalding by Ivo Taillebois, and was a considerable source of profit. 25, 103, 106, 117, 118, 294, 298.

WEST MERE CREEK. 101.

WESTHORPE, OR WESTROP. A hamlet in Gosberton. 61, 92.

WESTON ST. MARY. A village, 3½ miles east of Spalding. D.B., *Westune*. Dug., *Weston* and *Westone*. The parish contains 5,391 acres. R.V., £12,043. 121.

WESTON HILLS. In the parish of Weston, 2¼ miles south of the village.

WEST VILLE. In the West Fen, 7¼ miles N.W. of Boston. Created a township in 1812, under the Act, 52 Geo. III, c. 144. A., 1,950½ acres. Township formed, 229.

WEYDIKE. In South Holland. 102.

WHAPLODE. D.B., *Copelade*. Dug., *Quaplode, Quappelode*. A village, 2 miles west of Holbeach. Parish contains, with Whaplode Drove, 10,224 acres. R.V., £24,135 102, 123.

WHAPLODE DROVE. A hamlet or Fen Chapelry attached to Whaplode, 7 miles south of the village.

WHAPLODE RIVER. Runs from Whaplode Drove to the Holbeach Outfall. 26, 124.

WHEAT MERE DRAIN. Extends from Cowbit to the Lord's Drain, near Weston. 106.

WHITE CROSS. In South Holland. Mentioned in an Inquisition of the Court of Sewers. 1571.

WHITE CROSS DRAIN. In the East Fen. 208, 230.

WHITE CROSS BRIDGE. In the East Fen. 199.

WHITE BRIDGES. Over the Forty-Foot and Redstone Gowt Drains. 452.

WICKHAM OR WYKEHAM. A hamlet in Spalding, 3 miles N.E. of the town.

WIKEDIC BRIDGE. In Whaplode. Dug.

WINSOVER. A hamlet in Spalding, 1 mile south of the town.

WIGTOFT. D.B., *Toft*. Dug. *Wyktoft, Wiketoft*. From Scan., *Vik*, a bay or creek. Formerly Bicker Haven came nearly up to the village. The parish contains 3,386. acres. R.V., £7,999. 60, 86.

WIGTOFT GOTE. 60.

WIGTOFT MARSH. Formerly part of Bicker Haven. Inclosed under Swineshead Inclosure Act, 1773.

WILDMORE FEN. In the Fourth Witham District. Inclosed. 197, 222, 228, 231.

WILLOWS, SIBSEY. Formerly part of the Revesby Abbey Estate, 2 miles S.S.W. of the village.

WILDMORE. A parish in Wildmore Fen, formed in 1880, comprising fen allotments in West Ashby, Bolingbroke, Coningsby, Haltham, Horncastle, Mareham-on-the-Hill,

APPENDIX I.

Moorby, Roughton, Thimbleby, Toynton All Saints, High and Low Toynton, Wilksby, Wood Enderby, Tattershall and Thornton-le-Fen. The ecclesiastical parish includes the civil parishes of Langriville, Thornton-le-Fen and detached parts of Coningsby, Mareham-le-Fen, Revesby and Tumby. Area 4,066 acres. 206.

WILGRIPE. A place on the coast, mentioned by Leland as being 4 miles from Skegness.

WILSON DYKE FIELD. A common in Bicker, inclosed 1766.

WINGFIELD CENTRAL. A new parish, of which 1,649 acres is in the Holland Division, having a R.V., of £3,326. Land inclosed in 1831, 1848 and 1869.

WINKHILL. A manor, 1 mile N.E. of Heckington.

WITHAM, RIVER. Dug., *Witham, Withom, Withome,* from *Wyeom,* a river plain, or O.N., *Wyme,* to linger. Another derivation is *Withe,* a willow, and *Ham,* a village. Leland, *Lindis.* Length 89 miles. Drainage area, 1,050 square miles. 134. For further particulars *see* Index.

WOLMERSLEY. The name of part of the parish of Wrangle.

WODELOPE. In Deeping Fen. Dug.

WODLOAD OR WODELAKE. The site of one of the crosses mentioned on the boundary between Kesteven and Holland, near Crowland. Also referred to as Wadload Grayns, or Cross in the Flags.

WRAG STAKE, OR BLACK STAKE. On the west side of the South Forty-Foot, near Gibbet Hills. Dug. 249.

WRAG, OR RAG, MARSH. East of the Welland, 1 mile south of Fossdyke. 101, 115, 121.

WRANGLE. D. B *Weranghe.* Dug., *Wrangel.* In the 15th century, *Wranghill.* A village, 9 miles N.E. of Boston. A., 6,233 acres. R. V., £12,267. It is stated that a tidal creek ran within a quarter of a mile of the Church, which boats could navigate. Stukeley, derives the name from *Hangel,* a reedy lake. Evidently a considerable fishing industry was at one time carried on here, from the names which are still extant, as Butts Marsh, Fish Meer, and Eel Pool Lane. A Market was held here in the 13th century, from which 'Market Lands' derives its name. Wrangle Common, formerly called 'The Meer,' containing 1,250 acres, was with other common lands inclosed in 1807. 74.

WRIGHTBOLT. *See* Rigbolt.

WYBERTON TOWN DRAIN. 260.

WYBERTON. D B., *Wibertune.* Dug., *Wyberton.* From Wibert, who had a settlement here, and was in 865 a Knight, or Seneschal, of King Algar. The village is 2 miles S. of Boston. A., 3,465 acres. R. V., £3,659. The remains of an old castle, with its moat, is to be found in a field, 1¼ miles east of the village. About 300 acres were added to the parish in 1864-6, by the inclosure of marsh land. An Allotment of 891¼ acres was awarded to this parish under the Holland Fen Inclosure Act, in 1794. The common lands were inclosed in 1789, under the Act, 29 Geo. III. 60, 80.

WYBERTON WEST END. 1 mile N. of the village.

WYBERTON CHAIN BRIDGE. Over the Hammond Beck, at Wyberton West, 80. This was formerly the entrance into the Fens. 451, 452.

WYDALE. On the main road, 1¾ miles south of Stickney. A farm, formerly in the parish of Revesby. Transferred to Leake in 1880. There was a bridge which the Abbot of Revesby had to maintain in consideration of the grant of this land. Referred to in Court of Sewers in the time of Chas. I, as Stickney Wydalls.

WYKES, DONINGTON. A manor. Formerly there was a heronry on the Wykes Farm. The birds migrated from here to Cressy Hall.

WYKES. A manor in the parish of Frampton. Also in Quadring.

WYKE. A sewer or gutter in Weston. Dug.

YEALE FEN. Between Heckington Fen and the Six Hundreds.

YOLEDALE, OR YOWL DYKE. 'A fossat,' on the old river Witham, at the junction of the Bane. 140.

APPENDIX II.

BOOKS RELATING TO THE HISTORY OF THE FENS OF SOUTH LINCOLNSHIRE.

THE FENS.

A discourse touching the drayning of the Great Fennes lying within the several Counties of Lincoln, Northampton, Huntingdon, Norfolk, Suffolk, Cambridge and the Isle of Ely, as it was presented to His Majesty by Sir Cornelius Vermuiden, Knight. London: published by Thomas Fawcett, dwelling in Grub street, neere the Lower Pumpe. *Vermuiden*, 1642.

Exceptions against Sir Cornelius Vermuiden's discourse for the draining of the Great Fennes, &c., which in January, 1638, he presented to the King for his Designe, wherein His Majesty was misinformed and abused, in regard it wanted all the essential parts of a Designe, and the great and advantageous works, made by the late Earl of Bedford, slighted; and the whole adventure disparaged. Published by Andrewes Burrell, Gent. Printed at London, by T. H., and to be sold by Robert Constable, at his shop in Westminster Hall. *A. Burrell*, 1642.

A Brief Relation discovering plainely the true causes why the great Level of the Fenns, in the several Counties of Norfolk, Lincoln, &c., being 307,000 acres of low lands, have been drowned and made unfruitful for many years past, and briefly how they must be drained and preserved from inundation in time to come, Humbly presented to the Honourable House of Commons, assembled in Parliament, by Andrewes Burrell, Gent. London, printed for Francis Constable. *A. Burrell*, 1642.

The Present state of the Navigation of the Towns of Lyn, Wisbeach and Spalding. *N. Kinderley*, 1721.

The Ancient and Present state of the Navigation of the Towns of Lyn, Wisbeach, Spalding and Boston. *N. Kinderley*, 1751.

The History of Imbanking and Draining of divers Fens and Marshes &c., &c. Second Edition, revised by C. N. Cole. (*₊*The first Edition was published at the request of Lord Gorges, the Surveyor General of the Bedford Level, in 1652.) *W. Dugdale*, 1772.

An Historical Account of the Great Level of the Fens, called the Bedford Level, and other Fens, Marshes and low lands. *W. Elstob*, 1793.

A True Report of certain wonderful Overflowings of Waters. 1607.

The Statute of Sewers. *Callis*, 1647.

A Letter on the proposed Change in the Outfall of the Welland, with observations on the river Witham and the Boston Harbour Act. 1814.

History of the Drainage of the Great Level of the Fens, with Constitutions and Laws of the Bedford Level Corporation, 2 vols. *S. Wells*, 1830.

Fens and Floods of Mid-Lincolnshire, with a description of the River Witham *J. S. Padley*, 1882.

History of Wisbech and the Fens. *Walker and Craddock*, 1849.

Fen Sketches, a Description of the Great Level of the Fens. *J. A. Clarke*, 1852.

Appendix II.

THE FENS—*Continued.*

An Account of Religious Houses on the Eastern Side of the Witham. *G. Oliver*, 1853

History of the Fens of South Lincolnshire. *W. H. Wheeler*, 1868. (Out of print.)

Reminiscences of Fen and Mere. *J. M. Heathcote*, 1876.

On an Ancient Canoe found Embedded in the Fen Peat, in the River Ouse. Paper read at the Cambridge Antiquarian Society. *W. Marshall*, 1878.

The Fens. A paper read at the Incorporated Law Society's Meeting at Cambridge. *W. Marshall*, 1879.

The Fens of South Lincolnshire. Their Early History and Reclamation. Linc. Arch. Society. *W. H. Wheeler.*

The Fenland, Past and Present. *Miller and Skertchley*, 1878.

Memoirs of the Geological Survey of the Fenland. *Skertchley*, 1877.

Rainfall, Water Supply and Drainage of Lincolnshire. Paper read at Lincoln, at the Meeting of the Chamber of Agriculture. *W. H. Wheeler*, 1879.

Report on the River Ouse, for the South Level Drainage Commissioners. *W. H. Wheeler*, 1884.

Pumping Machinery in the Fenland. Min. Pro. Institution Civil Engineers, vol. 94. *Gibbs*, 1887.

The Drainage of Fens and Low Lands by Gravitation and Steam Power. *Wheeler*, 1888.

AGRICULTURE.

General View of the Agriculture of the County of Lincoln. *A. Young*, 1799

A Review of A. Young's Agricultural Survey of Lincolnshire. *T. Stone*, 1800.

The Great Level of the Fens, including South Lincolnshire (Royal Agr. Soc. Journal). *J. A. Clarke*, 1847.

Farming of Lincolnshire. (Royal Agr. Soc. Journal.) *J. A. Clarke*, 1851.

Report to the Royal Commission on Agriculture in the County of Lincoln. *Wilson Fox*, 1895.

EARLY HISTORY.

Existing Remains of the Ancient Britons, within a Small District, lying between Lincoln and Sleaford. *G. Oliver*, 1846.

Ermine Street Old Roman Road (Lincs. Arch. Society.) *E. Trollope*, 1868.

The Danes in Lincolnshire. (Lincs. Arch. Soc.) *E. Trollope*, 1859.

Horncastle under the Romans (Linc. Arch. Socy.) *E. Trollope*, 1858.

Lincolnshire and the Danes. *G. S. Streatfeild*, 1884.

Translation of that part of Domesday Book relating to Lincolnshire and Rutlandshire. *C. G. Smith*, 1870.

HISTORY AND LITERATURE.

Magna Britannia. Part relating to Lincolnshire. *Cox*, 1778.

History of Lincoln. *No Author's name given*, 1810.

Appendix II.

HISTORY AND LITERATURE—Continued.

History of Lincolnshire. *Marat*, 1814.

Historical and Descriptive Sketches of Boston and of the Villages around, and of the towns and places in South Holland. 1813.

History, Gazetteer and Directory of Lincolnshire, (*₊*contains papers on Ancient History, Agriculture, Botany, Geology of the County, and the Drainage of the Fens.) *W. White*, 1893.

Directory of Lincolnshire, (*₊*contains a paper on the Geology of the County.) *Kelly*, 1889.

The Lincoln Pocket Guide. *C. H. J. Anderson*, 1881.

Handbook of Lincolnshire. *Murray*, 1890.

Handbook of the Fenland. *Miller*, 1889.

Provincial Words and Expressions Current in Lincolnshire. *J. E. Brogden*, 1866.

Bygone Lincolnshire. *W. Andrewes*, 1891.

Fenland Notes and Queries. Published quarterly, from April, 1889.

PARISH HISTORIES.

The History and Antiquities of Boston and the neighbouring Villages. *Pishey. Thompson*, 1856.

Chronicle of the Abbey of Crowland. Bohn's Edition, edited by Riley, 1854. *Ingulph.*

A Topographical and Historical account of Wainfleet and the Wapentake of Candleshoe. *Oldfield*, 1829.

Crowland Abbey: Historical Sketch. *Perry, no date.*

Visitors' Guide to Crowland. *No Author's name*, 1839.

Crowland, the Abbey, Bridge, and St. Guthlac. *E. M. Sanderson, no date.*

The Anglo-Saxon Version of the life of St. Guthlac, originally written in Latin by Felix of Crowland. *C. W. Goodwyn*, 1848.

Memorials of St Guthlac. *Birch*, 1881.

Topographical account of Tattershall, published by Weir and Son, Horncastle. *No Author's name*, 1813.

The Church of St. Mary, Whaplode. *W. E. Foster*, 1889.

All Saints' Church, Moulton. *W. E. Foster*, 1891.

A History of Spilsby. *H. C. Smith*, 1892.

Historical Notices of the Parish of Holbeach. *G. W. Macdonald*, 1890.

Holbeach Parish Register. *G. W. Macdonald*, 1892.

Kyme and its Tower, (Linc. Arch. Society). *C. Kirk*, 1881.

MISCELLANEOUS AND FICTION.

Boston in the Olden Time. Traditions of Lincolnshire. Tales and Legends illustrative of the History and Antiquities of Boston, by Roger Quaint. 1841.

The Camp of Refuge. A tale of the Conquest of the Isle of Ely. New Edition, edited by J. H. Miller. 1880.

Sketches of Lincolnshire. 1813.

Appendix II.

MISCELLANEOUS AND FICTION—*Continued*.

Tales and Rhymes in the Lindsey Folk Speech. *M. Peacock*, 1886.

Lincolnshire Tales. *M. Peacock*, 1889

Hereward the Wake. *C. Kingsley*.

A Desolate Shore. (*₊*A Tale of Freiston Shore.) *M. E. Shipley*, no date.

Dick o' the Fens. *G. Manville Fenn*, 1888.

RIVER WITHAM.

The present bad state of the River Witham, between the City of Lincoln and the Borough of Boston, humbly represented to the consideration of the Mayor and Aldermen of the said city, and to the Gentlemen of the adjacent towns, with proposals for restoring and preserving the navigation, and for the more effectual drainage of the Fens, Commons and Low Marshes. *James Scribo*, 1733. *₊*This report is printed *in extenso* in Mr. Padley's *Fens and Floods*.

Observations on the River Witham, from Boston to Lincoln. *N. Kinderley*, 1736.

A Scheme for Restoring and Making Perfect the Navigation of the River Witham, from Boston to Lincoln, and also for Draining the Low Lands and Fens contiguous thereto. *John Grundy, sen., John Grundy, jun.*, 1744.

Proposals for the more effectual Draining all the Levels contiguous to the River Witham, from the City of Lincoln to Chapple Hill, &c. *Daniel Coppin*, 1745.

Plan and proposition for improving the river Witham. *J. Grundy*, 1753.

Report upon the Scheme proposed by Mr. Grundy, for restoring the Drainage and Navigation through the River Witham, in pursuance of an order for referring the said scheme to the examination of Mr. Edwards. *Langley Edwards*, 1760.

Report concerning the ruinous condition of the River Witham, &c., &c., with a scheme for its improvement. *J. Grundy, Langley Edwards, J. Smeaton*, 1761.

Report of John Smeaton and John Grundy, Engineers, concerning the practicability of improving the Fossdyke Navigation, and draining the land laying thereupon, from a view and levels taken August, 1762. *J. Smeaton, J. Grundy*, 1762.

Report on the present state of the drainage of the low lands, on both sides of the River Witham, from the City of Lincoln through Boston to the sea. And also how far a complete Drainage is or can be performed by the powers given in the present Act of Parliament, together with my observations on the plan and estimate drawn by Mr. Creassy, for effecting the purposes of a General Drainage of this Extensive Country. Likewise such improvements and additions as, I apprehend, will be necessary for effecting all the purposes above mentioned. *John Smith*, 1776.

Report concerning a plan of improvement of the navigation of the River Fossdyke, and for improving the Drainage of the lands on each side of the said river. *J. Smeaton*, September 2nd, 1782.

Report upon the improvement of the Navigation of the Fossdyke, and for improving the drainage of the low lands on each side of the said river. *J. Smeaton*, Dec. 31st., 1782

Report on the Navigation of the Fosdyke. *W. Jessop*, 1792.

Facts and Remarks relative to the Witham and the Welland, their past and present state and means of Improving the channel of the Witham and the Port of Boston, with remarks on the Grand Sluice at Boston, and on Wainfleet Haven. *W. Chapman*, 1800.

Report on the Drainage of the River Witham. *J. Rennie*, 1802.

Report on the Drainage of the River Witham. *J. Rennie*, 1803.

Report on, and estimate of, the probable expense in executing the drainage and navigation of the river Witham from Boston to Lincoln. *A. Bower*, 1806.

APPENDIX II.

RIVER WITHAM—*Continued.*

Report as to the effect of the enlargement of the tunnel at the head of the Great Gowts Drain. *J. Rennie*, 1806.

Report on the improvement of the navigation of the Fossdyke and the Witham. *J. Rennie*, 1807.

Report to the Commissioners for Drainage and the Commissioners for Navigation by the river Witham. *J. Rennie*, 1807.

Report to the Proprietors of Lands in the First District of the Witham, as to Mr. Rennie's Scheme. *W. Chapman*, 1808.

Report to the Commissioners of the river Witham Drainage and Navigation. *J. Rennie*, 1811.

Report to the General Commissioners for the Drainage of the Witham (as to the effect of the proposed new works on the low lands as between Kirkstead and Chapel Hill.) *J. Rennie*, 1813.

Report to the Committee of the Proprietors of the river Witham (as to the progress and cost of the Improvement Works.) *J. Rennie*, 1816.

Report to the General Commissioners for the Drainage and Navigation by the river Witham (as to the Enlargement of the Grand Sluice.) *J. Rennie*, 1818.

Report concerning the Improvement of Boston Haven, addressed to the Mayor and Corporation of Boston, Commissioners of the River Witham, Commissioners of the Black Sluice. *J. Rennie, afterwards Sir J. Rennie*, 1822.

Report for the improvement of the drainage of the lands lying on the South Side of the River Witham. *Sir J. Rennie*, Aug. 9, 1830.

Ditto, ditto. *Sir J. Rennie*, Sep. 17, 1830.

Report to the Commissioners on Hobhole Jetty. *W. Cubitt*, 1853.

Report upon the Outfalls of the Rivers Witham and Welland, and Clay Hole, and the improvements of the River Witham above the Grand Sluice. *W. Lewin*, 1860.

Report upon the state of the Drainage of the River Witham above the Grand Sluice. *J. Hawkshaw*, 1862.

River Witham Drainage. Statement (as to Districts, Banks, Engines, &c.) *F. T. White*, 1864.

Description of the River Witham and its Estuary. Min. Pro. Instit. C.E., Vol. 28. *Wheeler*. 1868.

The Conservancy of Rivers in the Eastern Midland District of England. (*⁎*The Witham, The Welland, The Nene and The Ouse.) Min. Pro. Instit. C.E., Vol. 67, 1882

Remarks on the State of the Outfall of the River Witham, with Suggestions for its Improvement. *W. H. Wheeler*, 1867.

Reports to the Commissioners on the River Witham. *E. Welsh*, 1875, 1876, 1877.

Statement of the Surveyor as to the Accumulation of Silt on the Sea Side of the Grand Sluice. *E. Welsh*, 1874.

Report on the Witham Drainage. *J. Hawkshaw*, 1877.

Report on the Witham Drainage. *J. E. Williams*, 1878.

The Witham New Outfall Channel and Improvement Works. Min. Pro. Instit. C.E., Vol. 9. *J. E. Williams*, 1888.

APPENDIX II.

EAST FEN, &c.

Observations resulting from Surveys, Levels and Views made on the East Fen, the Low Grounds and Fens adjoining thereto belonging to the Soke of Bolingbroke, East Holland and the Level Towns, with report of the causes of their present drowned state and condition, also Schemes for the Drainage thereof, and Estimate of the expense of executing those schemes, by John Grundy of Spalding, Lincolnshire, Engineer. *J. Grundy*, Nov. 14, 1774.

A Scheme for Draining the East and West Fens and the low lands in the Soke of Bolingbroke by Boston Haven. (*⁎*There is no name or date to this, but it is supposed to be by *J. Robertson, circa* 1775.)

A Practicable Plan for the relief of the country at a moderate expense, and an estimate of the expense of deepening and widening the lots in Wainfleet Haven, and for repairing the Clough and rebuilding the Sluice. *J. Hudson*, 1775.

Report concerning the Drainage of Wildmore Fen, and of the East and West Fens. *J. Rennie*, April 7, 1800.

Second Report concerning the Drainage of Wildmore Fen, and of the East and West Fens. *J. Rennie*, Sept. 1, 1800.

Report and Estimate respecting the Drainage of the East, West and Wildmore Fens and the East Holland Towns. *W. Pocklington*, 1800.

Observations on the Improvement of Boston Haven, by William Chapman, (*⁎*principally relating to the West and Wildmore Fens). *W. Chapman*, 1800.

Ditto, Part II. 1801.

A letter on the Drainage of the East, West and Wildmore Fens. *T. Stone*, 1800.

A Remonstrance against the Postscript to the report of Mr. John Rennie, addressed to the Proprietors of the East Fen and of East Holland. *No Author's name*, 1800.

A Remonstrance against the Postscript to the Report of Mr. John Rennie, concerning the Drainage of the East, West and Wildmore Fens. *A Holland Watchman*, 1800.

A Letter to the Proprietors of Estates and Owners of Commons, Houses and Toftsteads having right of common in the East and West Fens. *J. Cope*, 1801.

A Letter to the Commoners on the Drainage Expenditure and Accounts relating to the East, West and Wildmore Fens. *A Commoner*, 1804.

Report on the state of the Works of Drainage of the East, West and Wildmore Fens. *J. Rennie*, 1805.

An Address to the Ninety Commoners having Rights in the East, West and Wildmore Fens, who signed an ineffectual requisition to Mr. Joseph Banks, Chairman, to call a general Meeting of Commoners in the Soke of Bolingbroke. *E. Walls*, 1807.

Statement as to the Drainage and Levels of the Fens north of Boston, and comparison with the Levels and Drainage of the Low Lands of South Holland and the Bedford Level, directed to the Governors, Bailiffs and Conservators of the Bedford Level Corporation. *A. Bower*, 1814.

Report to the proprietors and occupiers of Low Grounds in Wainfleet All Saints Thorpe Croft, Irby, Firsby, &c., draining through Wainfleet Haven. *W. Walker*, 1814.

Report on the drainage of the Low Grounds in the Parishes of Great Steeping, Thorpe, Wainfleet All Saints, Irby, Firsby, Bratoft and Croft into Hobhole Drain. *J. Rennie*, 1818.

Report—River Witham Drainage. (*⁎*On the Improvement of the Drainage of the Fourth District). *J. Hawkshaw*, 1861.

Remarks and Suggestions as to the Best Mode of Draining and Supplying Living Water to the Fourth District. *D. Martin*, 1867.

Appendix II.

EAST FEN, &c.—Continued.

Report on the application of Steam power to the draining of the Fourth District. *E. Welsh*, 1865.

Report on the Fourth District Drainage. *E. Welsh*, 1875.

Do. Do., 1876.

Do. Do., 1877.

River Witham Drainage. The Pumping Machinery and Works at Lade Bank, Min. Pro. Instit. C.E., Vol. 34. *E. Welsh*, 1872.

BLACK SLUICE LEVEL.

Report on the Drainage, with Scheme for its Improvement. *Langley Edwards*, 1764.

Report as to any Improvement that might be made in the Drainage of the Black Sluice by the removal of obstructions between the Haven and Wyberton Roads. *Jarvis, Golding, Have*, 1799.

Report on the Most Effectual Mode of Improving the Drainage of the Low Marsh and Fen Land lying between Boston Haven and Bourne. *J. Rennie*, 1815.

Report on the Black Sluice Drainage. *W. Lewin*, 1843.

Report on the Black Sluice Drainage. *Sir J. Rennie*, 1845.

Report on the Black Sluice Drainage. *W. Cubitt*, 1846.

RIVERS WELLAND AND GLEN, AND CROWLAND WASHES.

Report on the Drainage of Crowland and Cowbit Washes, with Estimate of expenses. *J. W. Hastings*, 1846.

Navigation of the River Welland. *B. Bevan*, 1810.

The History of the Navigation of the River Welland, from Stamford to the Sea (*⁎*An excerpt from Harod's History of Stamford). *S. Edwards*, 1810.

A Letter to the Subscribers to the Intended Stamford Junction Navigation. *W. Thompson*, 1810.

A Letter to the Rev. J. Monkhouse and Rev. Dr. Maurice Johnson, on the Wanton Misrepresentation contained in the resolutions passed at Deeping, on the 31st December, 1810, and at Spalding, on the 1st January, 1811. *An Inhabitant of Stamford*, 1811.

A Letter on the Projected change of The Outfall of the River Welland. *W. Chapman*, 1814.

On the Improvement of the Outfall of the River Welland. *T. Pear*, 1815.

Report to the Trustees of the Outfall of the River Welland, on the improvement thereof. *James Walker*, 1835.

Newboro' Fen and River Welland. *W. Cubitt*, 1837.

Report to the Secretary to the Commissioners for the Loan of Exchequer Bills in the Improvement of the Navigation of the River Welland. *James Walker*, 1837.

Report on the state of the river Welland Outfall Works. *J. Kingston*, 1866.

Report on the Outfalls of the Rivers Witham and Welland, and the projected Schemes of improvement therewith connected. *J. Kingston*, 1879.

River Glen; Report. *J. Kingston, A. Harrison*, 1883.

APPENDIX II.

DEEPING FEN.

Report on the Drainage of Deeping, Langtoft, Baston, Crowland, Cowbit, Spalding and Pinchbeck Commons. *Maxwell and Hare*, Feb. 24th, 1800.

Report on the drainage of Deeping Enclosed Fens and The Commons. *Jessop Rennie, Maxwell and Hare*, Aug., 1800.

Report on the Drainage of Deeping Fen. *T. Pear*, 1815.

Report on the Improvement of the Outfall of the Vernatt's Drain. *J. Rennie*, 1818.

Report on the Improvement of the Drainage of Deeping Fen and adjoining Commons, by Steam power. *T. Pear*, 1820.

Report on the Improvement of the Drainage of Deeping Fen by Steam power. *B. Bevan*, March 1st, 1823.

Report on the Steam Engine Drainage. *W. S. Mylne*, July 16th, 1830.

Deeping Fen; Adventurers' Joint Works. *W. Cubitt*, 1842.

SOUTH HOLLAND DRAINAGE.

Report on a Scheme for completely Draining South Holland. *J. Rennie*, 1813.

Report on the South Holland Drainage. *E. Millington*, 1848.

BOSTON HARBOUR.

Report on the Improvement of the Port and Harbour of Boston. *Hudart*, 1793.

Report on ditto, ditto. *J. Rennie*, 1793.

Report concerning the Improvement of Boston Haven. *J. Rennie*, 1800.

Report on the Improvement of Boston Haven. *Sir J. Rennie*, 1822.

Ditto, ditto. *Sir J. Rennie*, 1823.

Ditto, ditto. *T. Telford*, 1823.

Report upon the Outfalls of the Rivers Witham and Welland and Clay Hole, and the Improvement of the River Witham above the Grand Sluice. *W. Lewin*, 1860.

Report with reference to the Improvement of Boston Harbour and Outfall. *J. Hawkshaw*, 1864.

Report on the Scheme for improving the Outfall of the River Witham by Fascine Training Works. *W. H. Wheeler*, 1870.

SEA BANKS.

Report on the Sea Banks from Friskney to the River Glen, after the Great Tide of 1810, with an estimate of the cost of repairing the same. *J. Rennie*, Feb. 4th, 1812.

APPENDIX III.

Titles of Acts of Parliament relating to the Fenland.

RIVER WITHAM.

22 & 23 Car. ii, 1671.
    An Act for Improving the Navigation between the Town of Boston and the River of Trent.

2 Geo. iii, c. 32, 1762.
    An Act for Draining and Preserving certain Low Lands called the Fens lying on both sides of the River Witham in the County of Lincoln, and for Restoring and Maintaining the Navigation of the said River, from the High Bridge in the City of Lincoln, through the Borough of Boston to the Sea.

48 Geo. iii, 1808. (*Repealed*).
    An Act for Rendering more Effectual an Act of His present Majesty for draining certain low lands lying on both sides of the River Witham in the County of Lincoln and for restoring the Navigation of the said river from the High Bridge in the City of Lincoln to the Sea.

52 Geo. iii, c. 108, 1812.
    An Act for Rendering more Effectual an Act of His present Majesty, for Draining lands lying on both sides of the River Witham, in the County of Lincoln, and restoring the Navigation of the River, and for repealing another Act of His present Majesty, in relation to the said Drainage and Navigation.

10 Geo. iv, c. 123, 1829.
    An Act to Authorize the raising a further Sum of Money for completing the Drainage and Navigation by the River Witham and for amending the Act relating thereto.

28 & 29 Vict., c. 124, 1865.
    An Act for the further Improvement of the Drainage by the River Witham, in the County of Lincoln, and for amending the Acts relating thereto, and for other Purposes.

44 & 45 Vict., c. 90, 1881.
    An Act for further Improving the Drainage in the River Witham, in the County of Lincoln, and for amending the Acts relating thereto, and for other Purposes.

WITHAM OUTFALL.

43 and 45 Vict., c. 153, 1880.
    An Act to Authorise the Construction of a new Cut and other Works for improving the Outfall of the River Witham, in the County of Lincoln and the Constitution of a Joint Board, for effecting such Works and for other Purposes.

48 and 49 Vict., c. 155, 1885.
    An Act for extending the time for completing the works for improving the Outfall of the River Witham, in the County of Lincoln, authorised by the River Witham Outfall Improvement Act, 1880.

WITHAM DISTRICTS. *First District*.

37 Geo. iii, c. 77, 1791. *Dales Head Dyke*.
    An Act to Embank and Drain the open and unembanked lands and grounds lying between the Dales Head Dyke and the River

APPENDIX III.

WITHAM DISTRICTS. *First District.* (*Continued.*)

Witham, in the several townships or Hamlets and Parishes of Walcot, Timberland Thorpe, Timberland, Martin, Linwood and Blankney, all in the County of Lincoln.

7 and 8 Geo. iv., c. 49, 1827.
Washingborough.

An Act for Dividing, Inclosing and Exonerating from Tithes the Open and Common Fields, Meadows, Pastures, Fens, Ings and Waste Lands, in the parish of Washingborough, in the County of Lincoln and Township of Heighington in the same Parish ; and also for embanking, draining and improving certain lands within the same Parish and Township.

10 Geo. iv., c. 94, 1830.
Washingborough.

An Act for Amending and Enlarging the Act for Dividing, Enclosing &c., in the Parish of Washingborough, &c., &c.

14 Geo. iii, c. 51, 1774.
Potterhanworth.

An Act for Dividing and Inclosing the Open and Common Fields, Meadows, Pastures, Fens, Heath and Waste Lands within the Parish of Potterhanworth, in the County of Lincoln.

29 Geo. iii., c. 32, 1789.
Nocton, Potterhanworth and Branston.

An Act for Embanking and Draining certain Fens and low lands, in the Parishes of Nocton and Potterhanworth in the County of Lincoln ; and in the parish of Branston in the County and City of Lincoln.

2 and 3 Will. iv., c. 96, 1832.
Nocton and Potterhanworth.

An Act for Repealing Parts of and Amending and Enlarging the Powers of Other Parts of an Act, for Embanking and Draining certain Fens and Low Lands in the Parishes of Nocton and Potterhanworth in the County of Lincoln, and in the the Parish of Branston in the County of the City of Lincoln.

29 Geo. iii., c. 70, 1789
Dunston, Metheringham.

An Act for Dividing and Inclosing the open Common, Fen and Ings in the Parish of Dunston in the County of Lincoln, and for Draining and Improving certain parts thereof ; and also certain inclosed low lands in the said Parish and in the Parish of Metheringham in the said County.

27 Geo. iii, c. 66, 1783.
Martin, Blankney, Timberland.

An Act for Dividing and Inclosing the low lands and Common Fens within the Hamlet of Martin in the Parish of Timberland, and within the Parish of Blankney in the County of Lincoln, and for Draining and Preserving the low lands and Fens within the said Hamlet of Martin and Parish of Blankney.

2 and 3 Will. iv., c. 94, 1835.
Blankney Fen.

An Act for the more effectual Drainage of the lands in Blankney Fen, Blankney Dales, Linwood Fen, Linwood Dales, and Martin Fen and Martin Dales, in the County of Lincoln.

Geo. 5, iii, c. 74, 1765.
Branston Fen.

An Act for Dividing and Inclosing the Fen Grounds, Moors, Sheep Walks, Wood Ings, Sike Closes, Open and Common Fields, and other Commonable Lands and Grounds in the Parish of Branston in the County of the City of Lincoln.

25 Geo. iii, c. 14, 1761.
Timberland.

An Act for Draining and Preserving Certain Low Lands within the Parish of Timberland in the County of Lincoln.

2 and 3 Vict, c. 10, 1839.
Timberland Fen and Dales.

An Act for the more effectual Drainage of Certain Lands called the Fen and Dales of Timberland, and Timberland Thorpe in the Parish of Timberland in the County of Lincoln.

17 Geo. iii,. c 70, 1777.
Billinghay.

An Act for Dividing and Inclosing the Open Common Fields, Meadows, Dales and Common Fen within the Parish of Billinghay in the County of Lincoln, and for Draining and Preserving the said Dales and Common Fen, and also certain inclosed Low Lands thereto adjoining in the said Parish.

3 and 4 Vict., c. 90, 1840.
Billinghay Fen and Dales.
Walcot Fen and Dales.

An Act for the more effectual Drainage of Certain Lands called Billinghay Fen, Billinghay Dales and Walcot Fen, Walcot Dales and North Kyme East Fen and Ings, in the Parishes or Places of Billinghay, Walcot, Dogdike, Harts Grounds, Coningsby, Swineshead, North Kyme and South Kyme in the County of Lincoln.

Second District. (*see Black Sluice*).

APPENDIX III.

WITHAM DISTRICTS. *Third District.*

25 Vict., c. 149, 1861.
Greetwell.

An Act for the Better Drainage of the Greetwell District, in the County of Lincoln.

6 and 7 Vict., c. 76, 1843.
Bardney.

An Act for Draining, Embanking and Improving the Fen lands and low grounds within the Parishes, Hamlets, Townships or Places of Bardney, Southrow otherwise Southry, Tupholme, Bucknall, Horsington, Stixwould, Edlington and Thimbleby, in the County of Lincoln.

19 and 20 Vict., 1856.
Bardney Drainage.

An Act to Amend "An Act for Draining, Embanking and Improving the Fen lands and low grounds within the Parishes, Hamlets, Townships or Places of Bardney, Southrow otherwise Southry, Tupholme, Bucknall, Horsington, Stixwould, Edlington and Thimbleby, in the County of Lincoln," and to confer further Powers on the Commissioners under such Act and for other Purposes.

36 Geo. iii, 1796.
Tattershall.

An Act for Dividing and Inclosing the Open and Common fields, Marsh, Meadow and Moor grounds and other commonable and waste lands in the Parish of Tattershall and Townships of Tattershall Thorpe and Kirkby-super-Bain, in the County of Lincoln, and for more effectually Embanking and Draining the said Marsh and Meadow Grounds and certain other low lands and grounds in the said Parish of Tattershall and township of Tattershall Thorpe, abutting on the river Witham and river Bane in the said County of Lincoln.

Fourth District.

41 Geo. iii, c. 135, 1801.
East and West Fens Drainage.

An Act for the Better and more Effectually Draining certain tracts of land called Wildmore Fen, and the West and East Fens, in the County of Lincoln, and also the Low Lands and Grounds in the several Parishes, Townships and Places having right of Common on the said Fens, and other Low Lands and Grounds lying contiguous or adjoining thereto.

41 Geo. iii, c. 141, 1801.
Wildmore Fen.

An Act for Dividing and Allotting certain Fens called the East and West Fens, in the County of Lincoln.

41 Geo. iii, c. 142, 1801.
East and West Fens Allotments.

An Act for Dividing and Allotting a certain Fen called Wildmore Fen, in the County of Lincoln.

42 Geo. iii, c. 108, 1802.
Wildmore Fen.

An Act for altering, amending and rendering more effectual an Act passed in the last Session of Parliament, intituled An Act for Dividing and Allotting a certain Fen called Wildmore Fen; and for Dividing, Allotting in severalty and Inclosing the parochial or general Allotments set out or to be set out in pursuance of the said Act, for compensating for the Tythes of such allotments and for declaring and determining to what Parish or Parishes the several Allotments of the said Fen shall belong.

43 Geo. iii, c. 118, 1803.
Wildmore and East and West Fens.

An Act for amending an Act passed in the forty-first year of the Reign of His present Majesty, for more Effectually Draining certain Tracts of Land called Wildmore Fen, and the West and East Fens, in the County of Lincoln, and other Low Lands and Grounds lying continuous or adjoining thereto.

50 Geo. iii, c. 129.
East and West Fens.
1810.

An Act for amending and rendering more effectual an Act of His present Majesty, for Dividing and Allotting certain Fens called the East and West Fens in the County of Lincoln, and for dividing and inclosing the Parochial Allotment Lands and Grounds belonging to, and in certain parishes having rights of common on the said fens, and for declaring to what Parishes such allotments shall belong.

52 Geo. iii, c. 144, 1812.
Extra Parochial Place.
East, West and Wildmore Fen.

An Act for forming into Townships certain extra parochial lands in Wildmore Fen, and the West and East Fens, in the County of Lincoln.

58 Geo. iii, c. 60, 1818.
East Fen.
(Adding Lands in Steeping, Thorpe, Irby, &c.)

An Act for rendering more effectual several Acts of His present Majesty, for draining certain Low Lands on both sides of the River Witham, and in Wildmore Fen, and in the West and East Fens, and other Low Lands, adjoining or contiguous thereto, in the County of Lincoln.

APPENDIX III.

WITHAM DISTRICTS. *Fourth District.* (*Continued.*)

30 and 31 Vict., 1867.
Lade Bank Engines.

An Act to provide additional means for draining the Fourth District of the Witham Drainage in the County of Lincoln, and for other purposes relating to the Witham Drainage.

48 and 49 Vict., c. 98, 1885.
Steeping River.

An Act to provide further means for protecting and draining the Fourth District of the Witham Drainage, and other lands in the County of Lincoln, by improving Steeping River, and for other purposes relating to the Witham Drainage.

50 and 51 Vict., c. 104, 1887.
Hobhole Sluice.

An Act to authorise the General Commissioners for Drainage by the River Witham to widen and improve Hobhole Sluice, and to confer further Powers upon those Commissioners and upon the District Commissioners under the Witham Drainage Acts, and for other purposes.

Fifth District.

31 Geo. iii, c. 95, 1791.
Anwick and North Kyme.

An Act for Dividing and Inclosing the open Common fields, Meadow Ground, Half-year Land, Common Fens and Waste Lands in the Parish of Anwick, in the County of Lincoln, and for embanking and draining the said Common Fens, and certain enclosed low lands called the Praie Grounds in the township of North Kyme in the said County.

28 Geo. iii, c. 14, 1788.
North Kyme.

An Act for more effectually Draining and Preserving certain Fen Lands, and low grounds, in the manor of, or township of North Kyme in the County of Lincoln.

41 Geo. iii, 1801.
N. Kyme Amendment Act.

An Act to alter, amend and render more effectual an Act passed in the 28th year of the reign of His present Majesty, King George III, intituled an Act for more effectually draining and preserving certain Fen lands, and low grounds in the Manor of North Kyme in the County of Lincoln.

Ruskington.
1778.

An Act for Dividing and Inclosing the open Common Fields, Meadow Grounds, Common Fen, Cow Pasture and other Commonable Lands, in the parish of Ruskington, in the County of Lincoln.

2 and 3 Will. iv., c. 70, 1832.
Ruskington and Dorrington, N. Kyme.

An Act for Inclosing, Draining, and Embanking Lands, within the parishes of Ruskington and Dorrington, and the Township or Hamlet of North Kyme, in the parish of South Kyme, all in the County of Lincoln.

34 and 35 Vict., 9, 1871.
Digby Fen.

An Act to confirm certain Provisional Orders under "The Land Drainage Act, 1861."

BLACK SLUICE.

5 Geo. iii, c. 86, 1765.

An Act for Draining and Improving certain low Marsh and Fen lands lying between Boston Haven and Bourn in the Parts of Kesteven and Holland in the County of Lincoln.

10 Geo. iii, c. 41, 1770.

An Act for amending and rendering more effectual the Act 5 Geo. iii, c. 86.

9 and 10 Vict., c. 297, 1846.

An Act for better Draining and Improving certain low marsh and Fen lands lying between Boston Haven and Bourn in the County of Lincoln, and for further improving the Navigation through such lands.

12 and 13 Vict., c. 59, 1849.

An Act to alter and amend the provisions of the several Acts relating to the Black Sluice drainage, to extend the time by the Black Sluice Drainage Act, 1846, limited for the completion of the works, to authorise the levying and raising of further rates and monies, to alter existing rates and tolls and for other purposes.

Appendix III.

BLACK SLUICE. (*Continued.*)

43 and 44 Vict., 1880.	An Act for subjecting lands within the Black Sluice Level to further taxation for Outfall Improvements and for increasing the area of taxation, and for other purposes.
7 Geo. iii, 1767. *Holland Fen.*	An Act for dividing a certain Fen called the Haute Huntre, Eight Hundred or Holland Fen, and certain other Commonable places adjoining thereto in the Parts of Holland in the County of Lincoln.
10 Geo. iii, c. 40, 1770. *Holland Fen.*	An Act amending and rendering more effectual an Act made in the seventh year of His present Majesty's reign intituled, an Act for dividing a certain Fen called the Haute Huntre, Eight Hundred, or Holland Fen and certain other Commonable Places adjoining thereto, in the Parts of Holland, in the County of Lincoln.
16 and 17 Vict., c. 3, 1853. *The Witham Second District Act.*	An Act for amending the provisions with respect to the Commissioners of the Second District for Drainage by the River Witham, contained in the Witham Drainage Act of the second year of George III, Chapter thirty two, and for other purposes, and of which the short title is "The Witham Drainage Second District Act, 1853."
4 Geo. iii, c. 5, 1764. *Heckington.*	An Act for Dividing and Inclosing the open Common fields, Common Meadows and other Commonable lands in the parish of Heckington in the County of Lincoln.
19 Geo. iii, 1779. *Helpringham.*	An Act for Dividing and Inclosing the open Common fields, Meadow grounds, Common Fen, Cow pasture, and other commonable lands in the parish of Helpringham, in the County of Lincoln.
45 Geo. iii, 1805. *Swaton.*	An Act for Inclosing lands in the parish of Swaton, in the County of Lincoln.
4 Geo. iii, c. 2, 1764. *Horbling.*	An Act for Dividing and Inclosing the Open and Common Fields, Meadows and Common Fen in the parish of Horbling, in the County of Lincoln, and for draining and improving the said Fen.
8 Geo. iii, c. 15, 1768. *Billingborough.*	An Act for Dividing and Inclosing the Open and Common Fields, Meadows, and Common Fen, within the Parishes of Billingborough and Birthorpe, in the County of Lincoln, and for draining and improving the said Fen.
30 Geo. iii, 1790. *Pointon.*	An Act for Dividing and Inclosing the Common Cow Pasture and Common Fen, in the parish of Pointon in the County of Lincoln.
5 Geo. iii, c. 73, 1765. *Aslackby, Dowsby.*	An Act for Dividing and Inclosing a certain Common Fen, in the Parishes of Aslackby and Dowsby in the County of Lincoln; and draining and improving the said Fen; and also certain inclosed Low Grounds adjoining the said Fen.
43 Geo iii, 1803. *Rippingale.*	An Act for Dividing, Allotting and Inclosing the open Common Fields, Meadows, Fen Washes, and other Commonable Lands within the Parishes of Rippingale and Kirkby Underwood in the County of Lincoln.
13 Geo. iii, 1773. *Hackonby.*	An Act for Dividing and Inclosing the Open Common Fields, Meadow Grounds and Common Fen in the Parish of Hackonby in the County of Lincoln.
8 Geo. iii, c. 41, 1768. *Morton.*	An Act for Dividing and Inclosing the Open Common Fields, Meadows, Grounds, and Common Fen, in the Parish of Morton, in the County of Lincoln, and for draining and improving the said Fen.
55 and 56 Vict., c. 207, 1892.	An Act to confirm a Provisional order under the Land Drainage Act of 1861 relating to Morton Fen in the Parish of Morton in the County of Lincoln.

Appendix III.

BLACK SLUICE. (*Continued.*)

6 Geo. iii, 1766.
Bourne Fen.

An Act for Allotting, Dividing, Inclosing and Draining several open and Common fields, Meadows, Waste and Fen Grounds within the Manor and Parish of Bourn in the County of Lincoln.

4 and 5 Vict., c. 113, 1841.
Bourne North Fen.

An Act for the better draining of Lands in Bourn North Fen and Dyke Fen in the Manor and Parish of Bourn, in the County of Lincoln.

6 and 7 Vict., c. 37, 1843.
Bourne North Fen.

An Act for altering, amending and enlarging the powers and provisions of an Act passed in Her present Majesty's reign, for the better drainage of lands in Bourn North Fen and Dyke Fen in the Manor and Parish of Bourn, in the County of Lincoln.

Bourne South Fen Act (*See Deeping Fen*).

RIVER WELLAND.

13 Eliz., c. 1, 1570.

An Act for making the River of Welland in the County of Lincoln navigable.

34 Geo. iii, c. 102, 1794.

An Act for Improving the Outfall of the River Welland in the County of Lincoln, and for the better Drainage of the Fen Lands, low grounds and marshes, discharging their waters through the same into the sea; and for altering and improving the navigation of the said River Welland by means of a New Cut to commence below a certain place called the Reservoir, and to be carried from thence through the enclosed marshes and open salt marshes into Wyberton Roads, between the Port of Boston and a place called the Scalp and for disposing of the bare or white sands adjoining to the said river, and for building a bridge over the said cut.

5 Geo. iv., c. 96, 1824.

An Act for explaining, amending and rendering more effectual an Act for Improving the Outfall of the River Welland in the County of Lincoln.

1 Vict., c. 113, 1837.

An Act to increase the Tonnage Rates and Duties granted by an Act passed in the Fifth year of the reign of His late Majesty King George IV, for Improving the Outfall of the River Welland in the county of Lincoln, and to alter and enlarge the powers of the said Act.

5 and 6 Vict., c. 55, 1842.

An Act for transferring to the Trustees of the River Welland in the County of Lincoln certain Dues payable in respect of Vessels using the said River, Part of the Port and Harbour of Boston, and their Cargoes, for better effecting Improvements authorized by a former Act, and for amending several Acts relating to the same.

30 and 31 Vict., c. 195, 1867.

An Act for subjecting to further Taxation Lands Draining by the River Welland, and for increasing the Area of such Taxation.

SOUTH HOLLAND DRAINAGE.

33 Geo. iii, c. 109, 1793.

An Act for Draining, Preserving and Improving certain lands lying in the several Parishes of Spalding (including the Hamlets of Cowbit and Peakill), Weston, Moulton, Whaplode, Holbech, Fleet, Gedney, Sutton St. Mary and Sutton St. Nicholas, otherwise Lutton, all in South Holland in the County of Lincoln.

35 Geo. iii, c. 166, 1795.
Barrier Bank.

An Act to Enable the Commissioners and Trustees for executing an Act passed in the thirty-third year of the reign of His present Majesty, intituled an Act for Draining, Preserving and Improving certain lands lying in the several Parishes of Spalding (including the Hamlets of Cowbit and Peakill), Weston, Moulton, Whaplode, Holbeach, Fleet, Gedney, Sutton St. Mary and Sutton St. Nicholas, otherwise Lutton, all in South Holland in the County of Lincoln, to support and repair a certain bank extending from Spalding High Bridge to Brother House in the said County; and to amend and repair the bank thereupon; and for compounding

APPENDIX III. 7

SOUTH HOLLAND DRAINAGE. (*Continued.*)

with the Creditors under an Act passed in the twelfth year of His present Majesty's reign, for making and keeping in repair the said road.

57 Geo. iii, c. 69, 1817.

An Act for amending and rendering more effectual an Act of His present Majesty for Draining lands in South Holland; and for continuing and amending another Act of His present Majesty for maintaining and repairing a certain bank, and the Road thereon from Spalding High Bridge to Brother House, all in the County of Lincoln.

1 and 2 Vict., c. 78, 1838.

An Act for amending an Act of King George III, for Draining lands in South Holland, and for repairing and maintaining the Road from Spalding High Bridge to Brother House, all in the County of Lincoln.

14 and 15 Vict., 1851.

An Act to Enable the Trustees of the South Holland Drainage in the County of Lincoln to raise further monies.

SOUTH HOLLAND EMBANKMENT.

33 Geo. iii, 1793.

An Act for Embanking and Draining certain Salt Marshes and Low Lands within the Several Parishes of Spalding, Moulton, Whaplode, Holbech and Gedney, in the County of Lincoln; and for preventing the same Marshes and Lands from being overflowed by the sea; and for altering an Act passed in the thirty-first year of the reign of His present Majesty, intituled an Act for dividing and inclosing the Common Marshes, Droves, Waste Lands and Grounds in the Parish of Gedney and Hamlet thereof, called Gedney Fen, in the County of Lincoln.

52 Geo. iii. c. 17, 1812.

An Act for amending and rendering more effectual an Act of the thirty-third year of His present Majesty for embanking and draining certain Salt Marshes in the Parishes of Spalding, Moulton, Whaplode, Holbech and Gedney, in the County of Lincoln, and also for repealing so much of an Act of the thirth-fourth year of His present Majesty, as affects the Marshes and Sands on the outside of the Sea Bank, lately made by virtue of the first mentioned Act.

DEEPING FEN, BOURNE SOUTH FEN, THURLBY FEN AND COUNTER DRAIN WASHES.

16 and 17 Car. ii, c. 2, 1666.

An Act for Draining of the Fen called Deeping Fen, and other Fens therein mentioned.

22 Car. ii, c. 15, 1671.

An Act for Settling the Draining of the Fens in Lincolnshire called Deeping Fens.

11 Geo. ii, c. 39, 1738.

An Act to enable the Adventurers, Owners and Proprietors of the taxable lands, and the Owners and Proprietors of the Free Lands in Deeping Fens, and in other Fens in the County of Lincoln therein mentioned, to raise a competent sum of money for the effectual Draining and future Preservation of all the said Fens, according to their Agreement in that behalf, and to carry the said Agreement into Execution, and for other Purposes therein mentioned.

14 Geo. iii, c. 23, 1774.

An Act for amending and rendering more effectual Several Acts of Parliament of the 16th, 17th and 22nd years of King Charles II, and of the 11th year of His late Majesty, for draining and preserving certain lands called Deeping Fens in the County of Lincoln.

41 Geo. iii, c. 128, 1801.

An Act for Draining, Dividing and Inclosing Deeping, Langtoft, Baston, Spalding, Pinchbeck and Cowbit Commons, within the parts of Kesteven and Holland, in the County of Lincoln; and also for Draining Crowland Common or Goggusbland, certain Lands and Grounds in the Parishes of Bourn and Thurlby, ad-

APPENDIX III.

DEEPING FEN, BOURNE SOUTH FEN, THURLBY FEN, AND COUNTER DRAIN WASHES. (*Continued.*)

joining or lying contiguous to the North Bank of the River Glen and certain inclosed lands in Deeping Fen, and in the Parishes of Spalding and Pinchbeck adjoining to the said Commons, and lying between the Rivers Glen and Welland ; and also for rendering more effectual several Acts of Parliament heretofore passed for draining and preserving the several Lands, Grounds and Commons hereinbefore mentioned or certain parts thereof.

19 and 20 Vict., c. 65, 1856.

An Act to consolidate the Drainage Trusts in Deeping Fen, in the County of Lincoln, and for other purposes relating to the said Fen.

41 Geo. iii, 1801.
Crowland Common.

An Act for Draining, Dividing and Inclosing a Common called Crowland Common or Goggushland, and certain open half year Meadow, Commonable and Waste Grounds called The Washes and Fodder Lots, in, adjoining, or near to the Township of Crowland, in the County of Lincoln.

4 Geo. IV, c. 76, 1823.

An Act for explaining, amending and rendering more effectual an Act of His late Majesty, for draining certain Commons and Fens lying between the Rivers Glen and Welland, in the County of Lincoln and for increasing the Rates thereby authorized and imposing additional Rates for more effectually draining the said Lands.

10 and 11 Vict., c. 267, 1847.
Crowland Washes.

An Act for the better Drainage of lands called Crowland Washes and Fodder Lots, Cowbit Wash and Deeping Fen Wash, in the Several Parishes of Crowland, Spalding and Pinchbeck, the Hamlets of Cowbit and Peakhill and the Extra Parochial place or lands called Deeping Fen or Deeping Fen Welland Washes, all in the County of Lincoln.

12 Geo. iii, 1772.
Bourne Fen. South Fen.

An Act for Dividing, Inclosing and Draining a certain parcel of land called or known by the name of the Cow Pasture lying in the South Fen in the Parish of Bourn in the County of Lincoln ; and for amending and rendering more effectual an Act made in the sixth year of His present Majesty's reign, entitled An Act for Allotting, Dividing, Inclosing and Draining several open and Common Fields, Meadows, Waste and Fen Grounds within the manor and Parish of Bourn in the County of Lincoln.

34 and 35 Vict., 1871.
South Fen Drainage District.

An Act to confirm certain Provisional Orders under "The Land Drainage Act, 1861."

42 Geo. iii, 1802.
Thurlby.

An Act for, Dividing, Allotting and Inclosing the open Common fields, Meadows, Pastures, Fen Washes and other Commonable lands within the Parish of Thurlby in the County of Lincoln.

COUNTER DRAIN WASHES.

36 and 37 Vict., c. 24. 1873.

An Act to confirm a Provisional Order under the Land Drainage Act, 1861, relating to Deeping Fen.

PARISH ENCLOSURE AND RECLAMATION ACTS.

58 Geo. iii, 1817.
Skirbeck.

An Act for Inclosing lands in the Parish of Skirbeck in the County of Lincoln.

51 Geo. iii, c. 50, 1810.
Boston East.

An Act for Inclosing Lands in that Part of the Parish of Boston, in the County of Lincoln, called Boston East.

48 Geo. iii, 1808.
Freiston and Butterwick.

An Act for Embanking the Salt Marshes in the Parishes of Freiston and Butterwick, in the County of Lincoln, and for Inclosing the same and other lands within the said Parishes.

50 Geo. iii, c. 53, 1810.
Fishtoft.

An Act for Inclosing Lands in the Parish of Fishtoft, in the County of Lincoln.

APPENDIX III.

PARISH ENCLOSURE AND RECLAMATION ACTS.
(Continued.)

55 Geo. iii, c. 86, 1815. *Benington.*	An Act for Embanking and Inclosing Lands in the Parish of Benington in the County of Lincoln.
50 Geo. iii, c. 126, 1810 *Leverton.*	An Act for Inclosing Lands in the Parish of Leverton, in the County of Lincoln, and for providing for the repair of a certain sea bank within the said Parish.
50 Geo. iii, c. 127, 1810. *Leake.*	An Act for Inclosing Lands in the Parish of Leake in the County of Lincoln; and for providing for the repair of the new sea bank within the said Parish.
47 Geo. iii, c. 29, 1807. *Wrangle.*	An Act for Inclosing Lands in the Parish of Wrangle in the County of Lincoln.
49 Geo. iii, c. 120, 1809. *Friskney.*	An Act for Embanking, Inclosing and Draining Lands within the Parish of Friskney in the County of Lincoln.
53 Geo. iii, c. 201, 1813. *Wainfleet St. Mary.*	An Act for Embanking, Inclosing and Draining Lands in the Parish of Wainfleet Saint Mary's.
6 Geo. iv, c. 188, 1825. *Wainfleet.*	An Act to amend an Act of the fifty-third year of His late Majesty for Embanking, Inclosing and Draining Lands in the Parish of Wainfleet Saint Mary, in the County of Lincoln.
50 Geo. iii, c. 60, 1810. *Sibsey.*	An Act for Inclosing Lands in the Parish of Sibsey, in the County of Lincoln.
2 Geo. iii, 3. 110, 1771. *Boston West.*	An Act for Dividing and Inclosing the Common Fen belonging to Boston West in the County of Lincoln.
2 Geo. iii, c. 111, 1771. *Skirbeck Quarter.*	An Act for Dividing and Inclosing the Common Fen belonging to Skirbeck Quarter, in the Parish of Skirbeck, in the County of Lincoln.
29 Geo. iii, 1789. *Wyberton.*	An Act for Dividing, Allotting and Inclosing the several Parcels of Common Fen and other Commonable Lands and Waste Grounds within or belonging to the Parish of Wyberton, in the Parts of Holland, in the County of Lincoln.
24 Geo. iii, c. 26, 1784. *Frampton.*	An Act for Dividing and Inclosing the several Open Fields, Parcels of Common Fen and other Commonable Lands and Waste Grounds within the Parish of Frampton, in the Parts of Holland, in the County of Lincoln; and also certain Plots of Land called The Reaches, Marsh and Holmes's, in and near to the said Parish of Frampton.
12 Geo. iii, c. 111, 1772. *Kirton.*	An Act for Dividing and Inclosing the Common Fen and certain other Commonable Places and Open Fields within the Parish of Kirton, in the Parts of Holland, in the County of Lincoln.
12 Geo iii, c. 113, 1772. *Sutterton.*	An Act for Dividing and Inclosing the Common Fen, Common Marsh and other Commonable Places within the Parish of Sutterton in the County of Lincoln.
2 Geo. iii, c. 69, 1771. *Algarkirk.*	An Act for Dividing and Inclosing several Parcels of Fen Land within the Parish of Algarkirke *cum* Fosdyke, in the Parts of Holland, in the County of Lincoln.
12 Geo. iii, c. 112, 1772. *Wigtoft.*	An Act for Dividing and Inclosing the Common Fen, Open Fields and certain other Commonable Places belonging to and in the Parish of Wigtoft, in the County of Lincoln.
13 Geo. iii, c. 106, 1773. *Wigtoft Marsh and Swineshead.*	An Act for Dividing and Inclosing the several Parcels of Fen and other Commonable Lands within the Parish of Swineshead, in the County of Lincoln, and also a certain Plot of Land called Wigtoft Marsh, in and near to the said Parish of Swineshead.

APPENDIX III.

PARISH ENCLOSURE AND RECLAMATION ACTS.
(Continued).

6 Geo. iii, c. 82, 1766.
Bicker.

An Act for Dividing and Inclosing the Open and Common Fields, Meadows, Common Fen and other Commonable Places, in the Parish of Bicker, in the County of Lincoln, and for Draining and Improving the same.

7 Geo. iii, c. 62, 1767.
Donington.

An Act for Dividing and Inclosing several Open Fields, Meadows, Common Fens, and other Commonable Places within the Parish of Donington, in the County of Lincoln, and for Draining and Improving the same.

47 and 48 Vict., c. 41, 1884.
Donington.

An Act to confirm Certain Provisional Orders under the Land Drainage Act, 1861.

17 Geo. iii, c. 140, 1777.
Surfleet.

An Act for Dividing and Inclosing the Common Fen, Common Marsh, Common Fields and Waste Grounds in the Parish of Surfleet, in the County of Lincoln.

39 Geo. iii, c. 96, 1798.
Gosberton.

An Act for Dividing, Allotting and Inclosing the Common, Fen Droves and Waste Lands in the Parish of Gosberton, in the County of Lincoln.

15 Geo iii, c. 70, 1775.
Quadring.

An Act for Dividing and Inclosing the Common Fens, Common Meadows, Common Fields and Waste Grounds in the Parish of Quadring and in Quadring Hundred, in the County of Lincoln.

2 and 3 William iv, c. 95, 1832.
Spalding & Pinchbeck Common.

An Act for the better Drainage of Certain Lands in the Parishes of Spalding and Pinchbeck, in the County of Lincoln, the waters from which are discharged by the Blue Gowt Drain.

33 Geo. iii, c. 73, 1793.
Moulton Marsh.

An Act for Dividing and Inclosing the Commonable Salt Marshes, Droves, Commons, and Waste Lands within the Parish of Moulton, in the County of Lincoln.

36 and 37 Vic., c. 170, 1873.
Moulton Marsh.

An Act for the Reclamation of Open Salt Marshes in the Parish of Moulton and elsewhere in Lincolnshire.

52 and 53 Geo. iii, c. 163, 1812.
Holbeach and Whaplode.

An Act for Inclosing Lands in the Parishes of Holbeach and Whaplode, in the County of Lincoln.

4 and 5 William iv, c. 64, 1825.
Holbeach and Gedney.

An Act for Embanking, Draining, and otherwise Improving Lands in the Parishes of Holbeach and Gedney, in the County of Lincoln.

34 Geo. iii, c. 94, 1794.
Fleet and Amending South Holland Drainage.

An Act for Dividing, Allotting and Inclosing the Common Droves and Waste Lands, in the Parish of Fleet, in the County of Lincoln; and for Altering an Act of Parliament, passed in the thirty-third year of the reign of His present Majesty, "for Draining Preserving, and Improving Lands lying in the several Parishes of Spalding (including the Hamlets of Cowbit and Peakhill), Weston, Moulton, Whapload, Holbeach, Fleet, Gedney, Sutton St. Mary and Sutton St. Nicholas, otherwise Lutton, all in South Holland, in the County of Lincoln.

31 Geo. iii, c. 49, 1793.
Gedney.

An Act for Dividing and Inclosing the Common Marshes, Droves, Waste Lands and Grounds, in the Parish of Gedney and Hamlet thereof called Gedney Fen, in the County of Lincoln.

36 and 37 Vict., c. 213, 1873.
Gedney Enclosure.

An Act for Embanking, and for Dividing, Allotting and Inclosing Lands in the Parish of Gedney, in the County of Lincoln.

28 Geo., iii, 1788.
Long Sutton.

An Act for Dividing and Inclosing the Common Marsh, Common Fen, and other Waste Grounds in the Parish of Long Sutton, otherwise Sutton in Holland, in the County of Lincoln.

13 Geo. iii, c. 60, 1773.
Tydd St. Giles & Tydd St. Mary.

An Act for Draining and Preserving certain Lands and Grounds in the Parishes of Tydd St. Giles and Newton in the Isle of Ely, in the County of Cambridge, and in Tydd St. Mary, in the County of Lincoln.

APPENDIX III

PARISH ENCLOSURE AND RECLAMATION ACTS.
(Continued.)

48 Geo. iii, c. 23, 1808.
Tydd St. Giles and Tydd St. Mary (Amendment.)

An Act for Amending and Rendering more Effectual an Act passed in the thirteenth year of His present Majesty, for Draining and Preserving Certain Lands and Grounds, in the Parishes of Tyd St. Giles and Newton, in the Isle of Ely in the County of Cambridge, and in Tyd St. Mary's in the County of Lincoln, and for adding thereto certain other Lands in Tyd St. Mary's aforesaid, lying contiguous to the Land described in the said Act.

32 Geo. iii, c. 25, 1792.
Tydd St. Mary Enclosure.

An Act for Dividing and Inclosing the Common Marsh, and other waste grounds in the Parish of Tydd St. Mary in the County of Lincoln.

49 Geo. iii, c. 119, 1809.
Sutton St. Edmunds.

An Act for effecting the Draining and Improvement of the Lands and Grounds lying in the late Great Common of Sutton St. Edmunds, within the Parish of Sutton St. Mary, otherwise Long Sutton in the County of Lincoln; and for authorising the Drainage and Improvement of the Lands and Grounds lying in the late Little Common in Sutton St. Edmund's aforesaid.

46 Geo. iii, c. 73, 1806.
Market Deeping and Deeping St. James.

An Act for Inclosing Lands in the Parishes of Market Deeping and Deeping St. James in the County of Lincoln, and for Altering and Repealing an Act passed in the forty-first year of His present Majesty for Draining &c. Deeping, Langtoft, Baston, Spalding, &c. And for other purposes in the said Act mentioned, so far as the same relates to the division of the said Common.

ESTUARY RECLAMATION AND FISHERY.

14 and 15 Vict., c. 136, 1851.
Lincolnshire Estuary.

An Act for Reclaiming from the Sea Certain Lands abutting on the Coast of Lincolnshire, within the Parts of Holland.

42 and 43 Vict., c. 195, 1879.
Freiston Shore Reclamation.

An Act for Incorporating of the Freiston Shore Reclamation Company, and for Authorising them to Reclaim Certain Lands in the Estuary of the Wash, and for other purposes.

33 and 34 Vict., c. 6, 1870.
Mussel Fishery.

An Act to Confirm Certain Orders made by the Board of Trade under the Sea Fisheries Act, 1868, relating to Boston Deeps and Emsworth.

SEA BANKS.

5 Geo. iii, c. 14, 1765.
Fish in Ponds and Rabbits in Sea Banks.

An Act for the more effectual Preservation of Fish in Fish Ponds and other Waters; and Conies in Warrens; and for preventing the Damage done to Sea Banks, within the County of Lincoln, by the breeding conies therein.

24 and 25 Vict., c. 96, 1861.

This Act repealed by 7 & 8 Geo. IV., c. 27, but the clause relating to the Sea Banks re-enacted in the 24 and 25 Vict., c. 96.

COURT OF SEWERS.

6 Henry vi, c. 5, 1427.

Several Commissions of Sewers shall be granted. The form of the Commission.

23 Henry viii. c. 5, 1531.

The Bill of Sewers with a new proviso, &c.

7 Anne, c. 10, 1708.

An Act for rendering more effectual the Laws concerning Commissions of Sewers.

3 and 4 Will. iv. c. 22, 1833.

An Act to Amend the Laws relating to Sewers.

4 and 5 Vict., c. 45, 1841.

An Act to Amend an Act passed in the third and fourth years of the Reign of His late Majesty King William IV, entitled, An Act to Amend the Laws relating to Sewers.

12 and 13 Vict., c. 50, 1849.

An Act for further Amending the Laws relating to Sewers.

24 and 25 Vict. c. 133, 1861.

An Act to Amend the Law relating to the Drainage of Land for Agricultural Purposes.

APPENDIX III.

BOSTON HARBOUR AND PILOT ACTS.

52 Geo. iii, c. 105, 1812.
    An Act for Improving the Port and Harbour of Boston, in the County of Lincoln, and for fixing the Wharfage of Goods landed within the said Port and Harbour; and for better maintaining Buoys, Beacons, and Sea Marks belonging thereto.

7 and 8 Geo. iv, c. 79, 1827.
    An Act to Extend and Enlarge the powers of an Act passed in the fifty-second year of His late Majesty, for Improving the Port and Harbour of Boston, in the County of Lincoln.

4 and 5 Will. iv., c. 87, 1834.
    An Act to Extend the powers of several Acts now in force for Improving the Port and Harbour of Boston, in the County of Lincoln.

5 and 6 Vict., c. 60, 1842.
    An Act for Amending the several Acts relating to the Port and Harbour of Boston, in the County of Lincoln.

5 Vict., c. 55, 1842.
    An Act for transferring to the Trustees of the River Welland, in the County of Lincoln, certain dues payable in respect of Vessels using the said River, part of the Port and Harbour of Boston, and their Cargoes, for better effecting Improvements authorised by a former Act and for Amending several Acts relating to the same.

43 and 44 Vict., c., 153, 1880.
Witham Outfall Improvement.
    An Act to Authorise the Construction of a New Cut and other works for improving the Outfall of the River Witham in the County of Lincoln and the Constitution of a Joint Board for effecting such works and for other purposes.

48 and 49 Vict., c. 155, 1885.
(*Extension of Time.*)
    An Act for Extending the time for completing the Works for Improving the Outfall of the River Witham, in the County of Lincoln, authorised by the River Witham Outfall Improvement Act, 1880.

44 and 45 Vict., c. 112, 1881.
Boston Dock Act.
    An Act to Authorize the construction of a New Dock and other Works at Boston, in the County of Lincoln, and for conferring further powers on the Mayor, Aldermen and Burgesses of the Borough of Boston, in relation to the Port and Harbour of Boston.

16 Geo. iii, c. 23, 1775.
    An Act for the better Regulation and Government of the Pilots conducting Ships and Vessels into and out of the Port of Boston, in the County of Lincoln, and for affixing and setting down Mooring Posts upon the Banks or High Marshes, within or adjoining to the Haven and Harbour of the said Port; and for affixing and laying down Bridges over the Creeks upon the High Marshes, within or adjoining the said Haven or Harbour, and for preventing mischiefs by fire in the said Haven and Harbour.

32 Geo. iii, c. 79, 1790.
    An Act for Amending an Act of the sixteenth year of His present Majesty, relating to to the Haven and Harbour of Boston, in the County of Lincoln, and for regulating the mooring and removing of Ships and other Vessels, within the said Haven and Harbour, and for removing obstructions therein.

NAVIGATION, ROADS AND BRIDGES.

52 Geo. iii, c. 108, 1812.
River Witham Navigation.
    An Act for rendering more effectual an Act of Parliament of His Present Majesty for draining lands lying on both sides of the River Witham, in the County of Lincoln, and restoring the Navigation of the said river, and for repealing another Act of His present Majesty in relation to the said Drainage and Navigation.

7 Geo. iv., c. 2, 1827.
    An Act for enabling the Company of the Proprietors of the Witham Navigation to complete the Drainage and Navigation by the River Witham, and to raise a further sum of money for that purpose.

9 and 10 Vict., c. 71, 1846.
Transfer of Witham Navigation to Great Northern Railway.
    An Act for making a railway from London to York, with branches therefrom, providing for the Counties of Hertford,

APPENDIX III.

NAVIGATION, ROADS AND BRIDGES. (*Continued.*)

Bedford, Huntingdon, Northampton, Rutland, Nottingham and the three Divisions of the County of Lincoln, a railway communication with London and York, to be called "The Great Northern Railway."

32 Geo. iii, c. 106, 1792.
Sleaford Navigation.

An Act for making and maintaining a Navigation from Sleaford Castle Causeway, through the town of Sleaford, in the County of Lincoln, along the course of Sleaford Mill Stream and Kyme Eau, to the River Witham at or near Chappel Hill, in the same County, and for making necessary Cuts for better effecting the said Navigation.

41 Vict., c. 88, 1878.
Sleaford Canal (Abandonment.)

An Act to provide for the closing of the undertaking of the Company of Proprietors of the Navigation from Sleaford Castle Causeway to the River Witham, in the County of Lincoln, and for the dissolution of the Company, and for other purposes.

32 Geo. iii, c. 107, 1792.
Horncastle Navigation.

An Act for Enlarging and Improving the Canal called Tattershall Canal, from the River Witham to the Town of Tattershall, and extending the same into the River Bain, and for making the said River Bain navigable thence to or into the Town of Horncastle, all in the County of Lincoln; and also for amending and rendering complete the Navigable Communication between the said River Witham and the Fosdike Canal, through the High Bridge, in the City of Lincoln.

39 and 40 Geo. iii, c. 109, 1780.

An Act to enable the Horncastle Navigation to raise a further sum of money to complete the said Navigation, and for amending an Act passed in the 32nd year of the reign of His Majesty for making and maintaining the said Navigation.

13 Eliz. c. 1, 1570.
River Welland and Stamford Navigation.

An Act for making the River Welland in the County of Lincoln navigable.

21 Geo. iii, c. 22, 1781.
Bourne Eau.

An Act for Improving the Navigation of the River called Bourn Eau from the river of Bourn to its junction with the River Glen, at a place called Tongue End, in the County of Lincoln.

42 Geo. iii, c. 96, 1802.
Boston Bridge.

An Act to Empower the Mayor, Aldermen, and Common Councilmen of the Borough of Boston, in the County of Lincoln, to take down the bridge over the River Witham, in the said Borough, and to erect a bridge over some other part of the said River within the said Borough, and to open and make proper avenues, ways, and passages thereto; and to enlarge and improve the Goal and House of Correction within the said Borough, and to purchase, and take down several houses for the purpose aforesaid.

34 Geo. iii, c. 102, 1794.
(Welland Act.)
Fossdyke Bridge.

An Act for Improving the Outfall of the River Welland, in the County of Lincoln, and for the better Drainage of the Fen Lands, Low Grounds, and Marshes, discharging their waters through the same into the Sea; and for Altering and Improving the Navigation of the said River Welland, by means of a New Cut, to commence below a certain place called the Reservoir, and to be carried from thence through the Inclosed Marshes, and open Flat Marshes, into Wyberton Roads, between the Port of Boston and a place called the Scalp; and for disposing of the bare or white sands, adjoining to the said River; and for building a Bridge over the said Cut.

51 Geo. iii, c 71, 1811.
Fossdyke Bridge.

An Act for repealing so much of an Act of His present Majesty as relates to making a Public Way over Fosdyke Wash, in the County of Lincoln, and for granting further powers for building a Bridge over the said Wash.

33 and 34 Vict., c. 34, 1870
Making Fossdyke Bridge a County Bridge.

An Act to Vest Fosdyke Bridge and certain Property connected therewith in the Inhabitants of the Parts of Holland in Lincolnshire, as a County Bridge and County Property.

APPENDIX III.

NAVIGATION, ROADS AND BRIDGES. *(Continued.)*

16 and 17 Vict., c. 115, 853.
Wildmore and East and West Fens Highway Act.

An Act for the Better Maintenance and Repair of the Highways in Wildmore Fen, and the East and West Fens, in the County of Lincoln, and for other purposes.

16 and 17 Car. ii.
(Deeping Fen Act.) Barrier Bank Road.

An Act for Draining of the Fen called Deeping Fen and other Fens therein mentioned.

12 Geo. iii, 1772.
Barrier Bank Turnpike.
1795. 35 Geo. iii, c. 166.
1817. 57 Geo. iii, c. 69.
1838. 1 & 2 Vict., c. 78.

An Act for the Better Preservation of the Great Bank of the River Welland, from Spalding High Bridge through Cowbit, Peakhill, Crowland and Peakirk, and for making and keeping in repair a road thereon, and from thence to the Village of Glenton, in the Counties of Lincoln and Northampton.

4 Geo. iii, 1764.
Spalding and Tydd Turnpike.
1785. 25 Geo. iiii c. 123.
1806. 46 Geo. iii, c. 31.
1827. 8 Geo. iv, c. 56.

An Act for Repairing and Widening the Roads from the High Bridge in Spalding, to a certain place called Tydd Goat in the County of Lincoln; and from Sutton St. Mary's to Sutton Wash in the said County.

1 and 2 Geo. iv, c. 34, 1821.
Spalding and Deeping Turnpike.

An Act for Repairing and Maintaining the Roads leading from Spalding High Bridge, through Littleworth and by Frognall to James Deeping Stone Bridge, in the County of Lincoln, and thence to Maxey Outgang in the County of Norfolk, adjoining the high land there.

3 Geo. iv, c. 9, 1822.
Boston and Donington Turnpike.

An Act for Repairing and Amending the Roads from Donington High Bridge to Hale Drove, and to the Eighth Mile Stone in the Parish of Wigtoft, and to Langret Ferry in the County of Lincoln.

7 Geo iv, c. 85, 1826.
Spalding and Donington Turnpikes.

An Act for Widening the Roads from Spalding High Bridge to the Market Place in Donington, and from the Tenth Mile Stone in the Parish of Gosbertown to the Eighth Mile Stone in the Parish of Wigtoft, in the County of Lincoln.

7 Geo. iv, 1826.
Swineshead and Fossdyke Turnpike.

An Act for making into a Turnpike Road a road leading from the Cross Gates in the Parish of Swineshead to the Southern extremity of the Parish of Fosdyke, in the County of Lincoln, and Repairing and Maintaining the same.

5 Geo. iii, c. 96, 1765.
Alford and Boston Turnpike.

An Act for Repairing and Widening the Road from Alford to Boston, and from thence to Cowbridge in the County of Lincoln.

24 Geo. iii, c. 62, 1784.

An Act for enlarging the Term and Powers of an Act, made in the fifth year of His present Majesty, intituled an Act, &c.

46 Geo. iii., 1806

An Act to Continue the Term and Enlarge the Powers of two Acts passed in the fifth and twenty-fourth years of His present Majesty, for Repairing and Widening the Road from Alford to Boston, and from thence to Cowbridge in the County of Lincoln.

8 Geo. iv. 1827.

An Act for Repairing the Road from Alford to Boston, and from thence to Cowbridge, in the township of Frithville in the County of Lincoln.

3 Geo. iv, c. 66, 1822.
Spalding and Bourne.

An Act for more Effectually Improving the Roads leading from the East of Lincoln Heath, to the City of Peterborough, and several of the Roads therein mentioned in the Counties of Northampton and Lincoln, and for making a new Branch Road to communicate with the Roads from Bourn to Spalding in the said County of Lincoln.

APPENDIX IV.

Vocabulary of words used in the Lincolnshire Fens and in old documents relating thereto.

Acre. A Saxon acre was 40 perches of 20ft. in length by 40ft. in width, equal to about 14·69 Imperial acres.

Acre Silver. A method of taxation for works of drainage &c., under order of the Court of Sewers.

Addle. To earn by wages "She mun be a governess, lad, and addle her bread" (*Tennyson*.) A. S. *Adlean*.

Addled. Rotten. An egg that has lost its vitality.

Addle-pated. Stupid, thoughtless.

Adventurers and Undertakers. The name applied to the persons who originally undertook to drain the Fens. Thus, King James " was pleased to declare himself the sole Adventurer for the drainage of Deeping Fen." The word *Undertaker* had also the same meaning, both words being used sometimes in the same document. Sir Anthony Thomas was described as the Undertaker for the drainage of the East Fen. The word " Undertakers " is used in the statute, 20 Elizabeth.

Aeger or Bore. The first wave of the tide coming up a river. Probably derived from *Ægir* the name of the Norse ocean god, or from *Egor*, the Saxon word for ocean.

Agait. An expression for setting about doing something. "To get agait o' coughing."

An all. Also. "The Measter were there, an all."

Anew. Enough.

Awm. To loll about or move in a listless lazy way.

Ax'd out. Asked out. When the banns of marriage have been asked for the third time.

Ayse or Aise. To ease or lift. A man is said to aise the water out of a ditch which has been held up by a dam for the purpose of cleaning it out.

Badging. Marking the garments given to the poor by the Overseers. In the parish books of Moulton a charge appears from time to time for " badging the poor."

Banker or Navvy. A labourer who works at banks and drains.

Back End. The Autumn, from Danish *bagende*, back part.

Back an Edge. Completely, thoroughly. " He stuck by the lad, back an edge."

Band. String, from Danish *band*, cord.

Barm. Yeast.

Battle-twig. An earwig.

Appendix IV.

BANK. An artificial mound of earth, made of the same material as that of the ground on which it stands, thrown up on the sea coast, or on the sides of rivers, to prevent the water from overflowing the land. The jurisdiction over the banks on the sea coast and in the tidal rivers is with the Court of Sewers, but the freehold of the bank and the right of grazing, except in a few cases where they are vested in the parish, belong to the Frontager, who as a rule is liable for the repairs. The use of a bank as a highway is common to all. The height of the sea bank was fixed by the Court of Sewers at a level 20ft. above *Ordnance datum.*

BASHED. Knocked about, torn or broken.

BAULK OR BALKER. A large wooden beam, formerly the sill of a workman's shop, half in and half out of the street, which acted as a counter. Also, formerly used to denote the line of green sward which separated ploughed lands in common fields; in some places called a *Eynchet*. ICEL. *Balks*, a beam.

BEEL. To call out, from the old Norse *Belia*, to bellow.

BELLY WARK. The Colic.

BECK. A Stream of high-land water as distinguished from a fen drain, DAN. *Beck*.

BELKING. Lazy. "A great, idle, belking fellow."

BEREWICK. A manor within a manor; generally only a vill or hamlet, severed from and yet appendant to, a manor.

BEAR'S MUCK. A substance resembling peat, consisting of a mixture of decaying vegetable matter and clay, having a fetid smell, found in some parts of the Fens. Generally the decaying roots and stalks of the *Arundo Phragmites*, originally growing in the clay and afterwards covered with alluvial deposit.

BECHE. A boundary.

BIRD TIDES. The tides in the middle of the summer are generally lower than at any other time of the year and are called Bird Tides, because the sea birds are then hatching their young on the marshes.

BINGE. The stopping the leaks in a tub or other wooden vessel which have been caused by the wood shrinking, by filling it with water. Also applied to a man who has been drinking a great deal.

BEASTLINGS or BESLINGS. The first milk from a cow after calving. A. S. *Bystings*.

BENTS. Dry stalks of grass, left after sheep have been feeding in a field.

BLASH or BLATHER. Idle talk. "Folks talk o' draaning fen and sic like blather; can't be done." (*Dick o' the Fens.*)

BLAMED. A mild way of swearing. "I'm blamed if I do."

BLEB. A blister.

BLOW UP. A term applied to the bursting of the water through a sluice or bank.

BOBBING. A term formerly used for fallowing, from the use of the bob, an instrument for collecting the weeds loosened by the harrows.

BOTTLE. A bundle or bunch. A bundle of hay or straw is called a bottle.

BONE IDLE. Naturally and thoroughly idle.

BORN DAYS. The term of one's life. "I never 'eard the like in all my born days."

BOUT. "He's just had a bad bout." A bad time of illness.

BOON. A term applied to the repair of the roads by putting gravel or other materials on to them. The highway surveyor is sometimes called the Boonmaster.

Appendix IV.

BLARING. Bellowing or crying for food. "A great blaring fellow," i.e., noisy.

BLETHER. Noisy talk. Also applied to the lowing of a calf. ICEL., *Bladra*, to bleat.

BOYKIN. A small boy.

BOVATE OR OXGANG. The quantity of land that a pair of oxen could keep in husbandry. In Lincolnshire about 15 acres, but the quantity varied according to the condition of the land. 8 Bovates made one Carucate.

BROVAGE. The surplus herbage after the cattle of those who had common rights in the fens were served. Claimed by the Lord of the Manor.

BORDARS. The holder of a small plot of land with a cottage on it. From *Bord*, a cottage.

BRASH. Rubbish. Nonsense.

BRIGHT. The term applied to the appearance of fens when flooded and the surface first glistens with the water.

BUST. Burst. A term used for a breach in a sea bank. "The bank's busted."

BRUSSEN. To burst "He's like to brussen himself." A.S., *Borsten*.

BRUSTING SATURDAY. The Saturday before Shrove Tuesday, on which frying pan puddings are made.

BREEDLINGS. A term sometimes applied to the dwellers in the Fens.

BRANGLEMENT. Confusion. Dispute. NORSE, *Branga*, a tumult.

BUMBLES. Reeds used for making the seats of chairs.

BUSICKING. Birds dusting themselves.

BUG. Proud, fussy. DAN., *Bugue*, to bulge or distend.

BUTTY. A mate or companion. The term is generally used by the bankers or navvies.

BUTTERBUMP. The bittern, a bird once common in the fens, before they were enclosed. It made a loud booming noise. (*Botaurus Stellaris*).

BUZZARD CLOCK. A cockchafer. "And 'eard 'um a bummin' awaay, loike a buzzard clock over my 'ead." (*Tennyson*.)

CAFFLE. To cavil or prevaricate.

CAR. Term used in the North of Lincolnshire for low, swampy, unenclosed land. *Ker*, Norse for marsh.

CARUCATE, Carve, or Plough land, Hide. A measure of land, varying according to quality, equal to 8 oxgangs or about 120 acres. As much land as may be tilled and laboured with one plough and the beasts belonging to it in one year, including the pass land. *Caruca*, a plough. According to some authorities, as much as was sufficient for one family.

CALCIES, Calcey, Causey, Causeway. A word frequently used in the old Inquisitions of the Court of Sewers, to denote raised causeways through the fens. *Calcius*, a boot.

CASELTY or CAZZELTY MEAT. The flesh of a sheep or beast which has died by accident.

CAULK. Chalk.

CALL. To abuse. To call a person opprobrious names. "He called me shameful."

CARVE. *See* CARUCATE.

CAUVE, Cauf, Calve. To bulge out. Often applied to the slipping away of earth from a bank. "The dyke side all calved in across the silt hill."

Appendix IV.

CESS. Margin or foreland, the space between the foot of a bank and the channel.

CAUSEWAY. *See* CALCIES.

CAVING. *See* KAVING.

CHIT. A term applied to the sprouting of potatoes when prepared for ear'y planting.

CHITTER To talk in a foolish or useless way. "What are you chittering about like that."

CLETCH. A brood of chickens. ICEL., *Kleuja*, to hatch.

CLAG. Clatty. To make muddy as when dirt sticks to clothes. Roads are described as being very clatty after a frost.

CLAGS. Locks of dirty wool clipped from a sheep.

CLATTING. Fidgeting. "What are you clatting about now."

CLAM. To choke with thirst. Clam is also used to denote hunger, also to take hold, "he clammed hold of me." DAN., *Clamma*, to cling.

CLOOT. A door or dam for stopping the water from backing up a drain.

CLOUGH. Clow. A sluice with doors which, when open, allow the interior water to run out and when closed, prevent the river or sea water from entering the drain.

CLUNCH. A hard chalk, brought for the repair of the sea banks, from the Humber; a hard clay soil with chalk mixed with it; also applied to a reserved, morose man. "A clunch fellow."

CLUNG. Heavy, sticky.

COGGLES. Large round pebbles used for paving. DAN., *Kugle*, a ball.

COIL or COYLE. To make a noise or disturbance. "That with her fish and fowle her keepeth such a coyle; as her unwholesome ayre and more unwholesome soyle." (*Drayton's Polyobion*)

CONFINED LABOURER. A man hired by the year, who sleeps and is boarded in thet farmhouse, or with the foreman.

COOMB. A sack of oats, or 4 bushels. This term is seldom used in Lincolnshire bu commonly in Norfolk.

COTS. Refuse or clotted wool.

COT. A weed that grows very abundantly in the fen drains, resembling thick moss also the mossy weed which appears on the sea shore before the samphire begins to grow.

COTE. A settlement, or house, built in a meadow.

COB. A small, round corn stack.

COUNTER DRAIN. A drain running parallel with, or counter to, another drain.

CRADGE. A small temporary bank. Throwing up earth on the top of a bank to fill up the low places and raise it temporarily to prevent the water flowing over.

CREE. To boil gently over the fire. Creed wheat, grain made soft for making frumenty.

CREW or CREWYARD. A fold yard or enclosure, bedded with straw, where cattle are kept in winter. SCAND., *Kyo*, a pen or fold.

CROFT. Enclosed land on the borders of a stream.

CROOMING. Clearing away weeds and deposit from a sluice or waterway, a 'crooming pole' being used for the purpose.

APPENDIX IV.

CRIKE. A creek on a sea marsh.

CUSH COW. The dairy-maid's call to the cows.

DABCHICK. A moor hen. (*Padiceps Minor.*)

DACKER. To waver, slacken speed, or to weary of what one is doing.

DANEGELT. A land tax of 2s. on every Carucate of land, levied to raise money to defend the Country of East Anglia against the Danes.

DEEPS. The deep part of a mere or of the Estuary. NORSE, *Djupa*, the deep water off the shore.

DELPH. Saxon for a ditch, frequently applied to a drain running parallel with and at the foot of a bank.

DITHER. To shake with cold, or with the ague. ICEL., *Titra*, to shake.

DILLY CART. A closed cart for removing night soil.

DYLING. A low place in a field or furrow, where water stands in wet weather

DOTTERELL. *Eudromias Morinellus.* A little fool.

DOWK, OR DOUCK. To drench with water; also applied to a stooping gait, to droop. DAN.; *dukke*, to dive

DRAPE. A dry cow intended for fattening.

DRIFT ROAD. A wide road with grass sides, suitable for driving cattle.

DUNNAKIN. A privy.

DYKE. The ancient English term for a bank protecting land from the inundation of water from the sea, or a water course. In Holland banks are still call *Dijks*. Gradually the term came to be applied to the hollow made by digging out the soil to make the bank, and then generally to all small drains and ditches. In Dugdale the term is applied to both banks and drains. Thus, in an agreement made in the reign of Henry II., by the Monks of Crowland, concerning the repairs of 'certain banks' called 'Winter Dyke,' 'Quapelode Dyke,' &c. It is equivalent to the Latin word, *Fossa*, a combination of ditch and bank, and is derived from the Danish *Dige*.

DYKE-REEVE. An Officer appointed by the Court of Sewers, for every Parish in the Fens, to look after the banks, sewers, and water-courses, and collect the Sewers, or "Dyke-reeve" rate. The word *Reeve* means a bailiff or officer. Dugdale, quoting from Bertius, say, with reference to Holland, "To which end and that their defense walls may be better preserved, they do constitute peculiar magistrates whose charge and office is to look to them; whom they call Diickgraven, that by them both the inner and outer banks may upon all occasions be repaired and made good, in case of any break or weakening in them." In the laws of Romney Marsh, ordained in the reign of Edward I, the officer corresponding to the Dyke-Reeve was called a Bailiff. Probably *Dykereeve* first came into use after the Dutch Adventurers came into the Fens.

EDDISH. The crop of grass in a meadow after the hay is cut. Generally applies to the period from July to May.

ENOUGH. An expression used to convey the idea of food being sufficiently cooked. "These potatoes are not enough," the word *cooked* being omitted.

EA. The Saxon, for an island or land surrounded by water.

EAU. A drain, from the Scandinavian *Aa*, water. An old Fenman always pronounces the word *Ea*, which no doubt is correct.

FEMBLE. Probably Wool or Flax. There are entries in the Parish books of Moulton for money spent on the purchase of Femble for the use of poor, the price being 4/- a stone. The Overseers allowed 1d. per lb. for heckling this, and 6d. per lb. for spinning it.

FENNIFERS. Officers appointed to see that fish were not taken from certain meres and rivers in the Bedford Level, at improper seasons.

FASTEN PENNY. Money paid by an employer, on engaging a servant, to fasten the bargain. DAN., *Fæste Penge*, earnest money.

FAR-WELTERED. Applied to a sheep lying on its back, and unable to get up, or 'cast,' "Worse nor a far-weltered yow." (*Tennyson*).

FAT HEN. A Weed. (*Chenopodium Album*).

FEN TIGERS. Supposed to be derived from the Celtic *Tiak*, a plow man.

FEND. To provide. "To fend for oneself."

FEN. A tract of low, peaty land with pools of water, or meres, in which grow reeds on the lower part, and grass on the higher parts. The whole generally covered with water in the winter, except on a few high places or islands. The Fens were generally common land to the surrounding parishes and afforded pasturage for cattle and sheep in the summer. Mr. Miller gives the derivation of the word from the Saxon verb, *fynegan*, to become musty or decayed ; fen being being the past participle of the verb, and meaning decayed. This seems a reasonable derivation, as the peat of which the fen is composed, consists of decayed vegetation. W. Gilpin in 'Forest Scenery' written in the last century, says "the fen is a plashy inundation formed on a flat, without depth, without lineal boundary, of ambiguous texture—half water and half land, a sort of vegetable fluid."

FEN NIGHTINGALE. A Frog.

FEZZON. To fasten. Fezzon Stakes are used for fastening sedge or reed on the top of a bank.

FIT. Ready.

FITTES. The outmarsh or land lying between the sea bank and the sea. NORSE, *fit*, a marsh.

FISHGARTH. A contrivance for taking fish, or places fenced off in the sides of a river, frequently mentioned in old records of the Court of Sewers, as an obstruction in a sewer or water course.

FLASH. A sheet of shallow water.

FLEET. A tidal creek or bay ; thus, Wainfleet, Surfleet, Fleet Haven.

FLOOR OF EARTH. A measure of earth used in making banks or drains being 400 square feet one foot in depth, equal to about 15 cubic yards.

FLOOD. The first of the tide. DAN., *Flod*.

FLOOD OH ! An exclamation used on noticing the tide coming up a river.

FLOW. The time of high water ; thus, "the tide flowed at 4 o'clock."

FLOOD-FANGED. The condition of a sea bank in course of construction, when it is raised just above the level of the tide, so as to exclude the water from the land being enclosed.

FOOTY. Poor, mean, "a footy little thing." SAX., *Futtig*, mean, paltry.

FOAL FOOT. The weed, Colt's foot. (*Tussilago Farfara*.)

FOND. Foolish, half-witted. DAN., *Fante*, idiotic.

FORELAND. The space between the foot of an enbankment and the channel, also called a Cess.

FORE-END. The beginning of the week or of the year.

Appendix IV.

FRUMITY, Frumenty, Fermity. Creed wheat in milk, with raisins and spice in it, a favourite dish at sheep-shearing suppers.

FUMMARD. A polecat.

GAD. A measuring pole, generally 10ft. in length; an eel spear, also called a stang gad. SAX., *Gaed*, a goad.

GARTH. A yard or small enclosure near a homestead. A stack-yard (*Danish*)

GAULT OR GALT. Hard blue clay. *Gaulting* is covering the peat land with a layer of clay, cast out of pits dug in the clay substratum.

GAIN. Near. "This is the gainest road."

GAIN-HAND. Ready, close to hand, ICEL., *Gega*.

GALLOUS. Mischievous. "He's a gallous young rascal."

GALLY-BALK. The iron bar across a kitchen fire place, from which a pot is suspended.

GAT. GATE. A road or way; an opening or entrance, thus Bargate, Wormgate; also applied to channels leading from an estuary to a river or harbour; thus Boston Gat in the Wash; also used as an expression "what's the good o' going on i' that gate," DAN., *gada*, SCAN., *gata*.

GAUM. To stare vacantly, from old Norse *Gaumr*, heed or observation.

GAWK. A fool.

GELD OR GELT. A tax, propably land tax.

GEN. To give. "I gen him a clout o' the 'ead."

GEAR. Harness.

GIVE AWAY. To speak disparagingly of, or abuse, a person in his absence. "He gave him away shameful."

GORE. A weir. An expression frequently found in old records of the Court of Sewers as an obstruction in watercourses.

GOTE, GŌUT or GOWT. Occasionally mis-spelt Goat. The Saxon term for a sluice. Callis describes them as "engines erected with portcullises and doors of timber, stone or brick. Invented first in Low Germany. They let out the fresh water and also the sea when it overflows; they sometimes serve as bridges." SAX., *Geotan*, to pour out. SCAND., *Gata*. The word Gote was superseded by Gowt which, continued in use up to about the beginning of the present century, since which it has been superseded by Sluice.

GOOD AND ALL. "He has left the town for good and all." For ever.

GOOLE. A hole or breach in a river bank. Mentioned in Deeping Fen Act of Charles II, and in the South Holland Act, 35 George III.

GOZZARD. Goose-herd. The man who had charge of a flock of geese. In the *Stamford Mercury* of 1819, an account is given of an Inquest held on the body of John Crawford, "an eminent gozzard" of Frith Bank.

GRAFT OR GRAFF. A small sewer or drain generally a parish division. DAN., *Grav*, a ditch.

GRAVE. A heap or store of roots, such as potatoes or mangold wurzels, covered with earth to protect them from the frost.

GRIP. A shallow surface drain for carrying off the water.

APPENDIX IV.

GUTTER. A drain belonging to a private owner, as distinguished from a sewer, which is public. A term frequently used in records of the Court of Sewers.

GRUNDGOTE. A hole or 'gull' made by the water on breaching a bank (*Dugdale*).

GYRVII. The inhabitants of the fens; from *Gyr*, low swampy ground.

HALES. Handles of a plough or wheel-barrow.

HAFFS. Tufts of coarse grass. "That the river be roaded, hooked, haffed, scoured and cleaned." *Order of Court of Sewers*, 1616.

HAG. A boggy place. 'Peat moor hags.' Deep holes in ruts in a road-way. "It was such a rough, haggy road there was no getting along."

HALF BIRDS, the smaller kind of wild-fowl, four birds being reckoned by the dealers as a couple.

HAP. To cover up; thus a man is directed "to hap up a potato grave."

HAPPEN ON. To meet with, "I happened on him at market."

HASSOCKS. Tufts of coarse grass. The Gozzards used to get across the fen "by jumping from hassock to hassock." Owners of land in the Bedford Level were entitled to have their land "hassocked by the Scotch prisoners at six shillings an acre."

HARDS. Hard places in a river, generally a deposit of gravel.

HAR, OR HOAR. A sea mist. DANISH, *Har*.

HAWM. To lounge or idle about. From Old Norse *Hyma*, to waver as one who is sleepy.

HEBLING WEIRS. Weirs laid at low water, for the purpose of catching fish.

HECK. A kind of fishing net.

HEDER. A male sheep.

HERDELLS. Obstructions in a water course. *See* SLAMP.

HEPPEN. Handy.

HIDE. The allotment of land to a free household. *See* CARUCATE.

HINDER ENDS. The small corn, or tailings, left after dressing the grain.

HIGGLER. A man who does carting for hire.

HOLME. Land surrounded by water.

HODDING SPADE. A tool used by Dykers in the Fens, so shaped as to take up a large square of turf.

HOOKING. Cutting the weeds at the side of a drain.

HOLLER. "He beat me holler," that is, thoroughly.

HOGS OR HOGGETS. Young sheep which have not been shorn. Described as he or she hogs, or heders and sheders.

HOVEN. A fee paid for marking stock when they were turned into the commons.

HOVERS. The grass growing on and cut from the top of a ditch; 'dykings and hovers.'

HUG. To carry.

HUNDRED. A division of the County. In Saxon times the Country was divided into companies of hundred families under a chief.

APPENDIX IV.

HYRNE OR HURN. A nook or angle. A corner of land bounded by water courses. (*Saxon*). A corner of a parish, as Guyhirn, Holbeach Hurn.

INTAK. Land enclosed from the sea. DAN., *intag*.

INGS. Open meadows. ICEL. for outlying pasture.

JANNICK. Fair, just. DAN., *Janka*, level.

JACK STRAW. A machine for conveying straw as thrashed, on to the straw stack.

JIFFLING. Fidgetting.

JYST OR JOIST. To agist, or take cattle in to feed.

KAVING OR CAVING. Sorting the straw from the thrashed wheat with a kaving rake

KEB. To sob, or pant for breath.

KETLOCK. The weed charlock, or wild mustard. (*Sinapis Arvensis*.)

KEDEL. A dam or weir in a water course with a narrow opening for catching fish, a term frequently used as one of the obstructions ordered to be removed by the Commissioners of Sewers. Now sometimes called kelltes or kettle nets. The word kedel is still in use amongst the fishermen on the Essex coast.

KID. A faggot. DAN., *Skid*., firewood.

KID-WORK OR BUSH-WORK. Fascine work, made with thorn faggots used in the training of the fen rivers. The faggots are made 6ft. long and 3ft. in girth, all the thick ends of the branches being put the same way.

KIST. A chest, A.S.

KINDLING. Sticks for lighting the fire. ICEL., *Kynda*, to light a fire.

KNIGHT'S FEE. Five hides, generally about 600 acres.

KNOT. A sea bird formerly very common on the salt marshes, named after the Danish King, Canute, or Knut. Tradition says they were first imported specially for his eating. (*Tringa Canutus*.)

KYE. QUE. A heifer calf.

LAM. To beat or hit with a stick. OLD NORSE, *Lama*, to break or bruise.

LANDED UP. The filling up of a drain with weeds and warp, or a river with warp. "The drain is cleaned landed up."

LAPWING OR PEEWIT. (*Vanellus Cristatus*)

LAST. A measure of corn. 10 quarters, or 80 bushels, of wheat, 84 of oats.

LEAD. To carry in a cart. 'Leading the corn.'

LEEK. To drain by throwing the water out with a wooden shovel or leek-scoop.

LESK. The groin or flank of an animal.

LID. A coarse grass growing on the Wash lands, called also White Leed. (*Poa Aquatica*).

LIEF. As soon, or as willingly. "I'd as lief he were dead as go on that how."

LIG. To lie down. ICEL., *Liggja*. "And meä liggin' ere aloän." (*Tennyson*).

LODE. A fen drain. 'A cut of water.'

LIVING WATER. Fresh water running into the fens from the higher land. Running water, as distinguished from the water in the fen drains which is often stagnant for several months in the year.

LOPE. To leap. SWEDISH, *Löpa*.

LOPING POLE. A pole used for jumping over the fen dykes.

'LOWANCE. Allowance of beer to workmen.

LOUK. Coarse grass on sea banks or fen lands. NORSE, *Louker*.

LUGS. The ears.

LUNGING. Lounging, idle.

MANAGEMENT. A term sometimes used to express the good cultivation of land, especially by the application of manure.

MARAM GRASS. A coarse grass growing in the blown sand hills on the sea coast. (*Psamma Arenaria*). NORSE, *Mar Almr*, sea grass.

MARDIK. Sea drain; from OLD NORSE, *Mar* the sea.

MAWKIN or MAUKIN. A term of reproach. 'A great clumsy Maukin.'

MEALS or MEOLS. Sand hills on the coast, covered with grass and scrub. The Meals near Gibraltar Point are described in a report of 1773 as 'a light blowing sand.'

MEN WORK or MENE WORK. A duty incident on the holders of lands liable for the repairs of the banks or sewers, to find men or horses. In the reign of Edwd. II an order of the Commission of Sewers was made "that all persons should be obedient to all MeneWorks to be made in the repairs of the banks and sewers." "The bridges are to be repaired by the inhabitants by common men work." *Finding of Sewers Jury*, 1571

MERCURY. A vegetable resembling Spinach, and to be found in most gardens in the Fens. (*Chenopodium Bonus Henricus*).

MERE or MEER. A Fen Lake.

MIDDEN. A manure heap, where the house refuse is thrown. DAN., *Modding*.

MING. Land undivided, belonging to two or more different Owners, is said to be 'in ming,' or mixed.

MOILED. Overworked. "But e' tued an' 'e moiled 'issen dead." (*Tennyson*.)

MOOR. This term is often used in the Fens to denote peat; though moor is generally understood to mean sandy peat covered with heather.

MOULD WARPE. The Mole. In a petition respecting the fens in the 17th century, it states that they are so drowned that the Mould Warpe cannot live there.

MOW FENS. A portion of the fens specially set apart for mowing the grass for hay.

NOWT. Nothing. "He's addled nowt sin' the back end of last week."

NOBBUT. Nothing but.

NOWT O' SORT. Nothing of the kind.

ON END. Upright. Sitting up, as distinguished from lying in bed. 'She was setten up on end.'

ORDNANCE DATUM. The mean level of the Sea at Liverpool, as determined for the datum of the Ordnance Survey of the Kingdom.

OUTGANG. The road or drove going out from a village to the Fen.

OWERY. Damp, cold, generally applied to the weather. ICEL., *Or*, a drizzling rain.

OWT. Anything. "Have you got owt?"

OXGANG. *See* BOVATE.

PASH. "As rotton as pash." Quite decayed.

APPENDIX IV.

PADDLE. Cow Paddle. Grazing ground for Cows.

PADDLE. The Boards or Scoops of a Pumping Wheel; also the doors of a sluice which can be drawn up to let the water out of a drain.

PAG-RAG DAY. May 14th. The day when the Servants pack up their clothes, and leave their places. It used to be the custom for all servants in the Fens, to leave their places on this day. Probably derived from *pag*, to carry on the back.

The fourteenth of May
Is Pag-p. , day,
When you pag your rags away.

PEART. Lively, impudent.

PECK SKEP. A measure made of basket work, used for feeding horses.

PEWITT, or PYE-WIPE. The Lapwing (*Vanellus cristatus*). SWEDISH, *Wipa*. DAN., *Vibe*.

PERCH. 20ft. In old Saxon records, the Perch varied from 16ft. to 20ft. In the Book of Orders made in 1226 relating to Wildmore Marshes, it is described thus, "a certain way of the breadth of 16 Perches of 20ft."

PLOUGH LAND. *See* CARUCATE.

POKE. A sack or bag.

POY. A pole used in propelling a gunning boat or shout.

PULL-OVER. An inclined plane forming a roadway over a sea bank.

PURVE. The Stint.

PYES or PIES. A heap of potatoes or roots covered with earth and stored for winter use.

PYE WIPE. *See* PEWITT.

QUARANTENE. Forty perches of land

QUARTER. A term used to denote the taking of a fresh track on a road so as to avoid the ruts.

QUE or KYE. A heifer calf.

RADIKE. The Outfall Drain, protected by a bank, where a pumping wheel is fixed. From *Rad*, a wheel.

RAFF YARD. A yard where timber is stored for sale. SCAN., *Raff*, a roof.

RAVE. To rout out. A housekeeper is said to 'make a regular rave' at house cleaning time.

RAMMEL. Hard rubbish, such as broken bricks or stones from a fallen building. DAN., *Ramle*, to tumble down.

RAMPER. A road running on the high ground near the fen, raised above it, forming a rampart from the floods. Frequently now called 'the high road,' as distinguished from the 'the low road' which was impassable in floods.

REMBLE. To remove or change the place of any thing. "'A niver rembles the st öanes." (*Tennyson*). SCAN., *Ryma*; SWED., *Rimma*, to make room for.

REACH. A straight length of river after a bend. SCAN., *Rack*, to stretch out.

RIGHTLE. To put in order. ICEL., *Retta*, to put straight.

RIT. To set out the edge of a road or path, or line of a new drain with a spade or ritting knife.

ROADING or RODING. The cutting and clearing away of the weeds in a drain. It is necessary to do this two or three times a year. *See* Rook.

ROOK. "The Welland to be roaded, rooked, hooked, haffed, scowered and cleansed." *Order of Sewers*, 1616.

Roil. To stir up and make thick. "He's roiled my temper." Made me angry.

Rood or Rod. A measure or length equal to 20ft., the same as a perch. Grundy's *Report on the Witham* gives a rod as equal to 20ft.

Rowan Tree. The Mountain Ash.

Ruff (male), Reeve (female). *Machetes pugnax.* Fen birds with ruffs round their necks. Now nearly extinct in the Fens.

Rung of a Ladder. The steps, or staves.

Samphire. A salt water plant, which grows on alluvial deposits on the shores of the Estuary; used for making pickle, (*Salicornea herbacea*). A samphire marsh is that part of the shore where accretion is going on and samphire is the first vegetation which appears. It begins to grows when the surface is 8·60ft above *Ordnance datum.*

Sasse. A sluice with doors for keeping out the tide. This word is frequently used in the early proceedings of the Bedford Level.

Scalp, Scaup. A mud bank uncovered at low water, where shell fish are foun . Thus the beds where mussels are found in the Estuary are called Scalps.

Scar or Scare. To frighten. "What are you scarred on?"

Scran. Poor food. Scan., *Scran*, rubbish.

Screed. A narrow strip of land.

Screeved. A term used to describe an accident which occasionally happened to horses in the fens when, running over the ice in winter, their legs became parted and torn off at the joint.

Seam of Wheat. Eight bushels.

Selion. A narrow strip of land between two furrows.

Sedge. A coarse grass or rush, which grew abundantly on the unenclosed Fens, used for thatching. (*Cladium Mariscum*).

Sewer The ancient drains in the Fenland are termed Sewers. In *Tomlin's Law Dictionary*, published in 1820, a Sewer is described as a fresh water trench, or little river, encompassed with banks on both sides to carry the water into the sea, and thereby preserve the land from inundation. Callis gives the derivation from *Suere* (?) to issue, and the meaning as 'the diminutive of a river.'

Shut of. To get shut of, *i.e.*, to get rid of.

Shout. A small boat worked by a pole or paddle, used for shooting Wildfowl or for fishing, Scan., *Schugt*. The word owns its derivation to the same source as the Dutch word for a boat, *Schuyt*.

Shards. Coarse grass used for thatching.

Sheder. A female sheep.

Sib. Related. Companionable.

Sid. The fine mud which accumulates in the bottom of a drain.

Sike, *see* Syke.

Skep or Skiff. A wooden shovel used to bale water out of shallow pool. Dan., *Shuffe*, a shovel. A wicker basket holding a peck, used for feeding horses.

Skerry. A small boat used on the fen drains.

Skelp. To upset, or throw down a load, to tip up a cart. Norse.

Skuttle. A wicker basket without a handle. These are now generally made of iron.

APPENDIX IV.

SLUICE. A structure placed in a sea or river bank, for the purpose of letting out the fresh water, and excluding the tidal water. From *Ex*, out, and *Claudo*, to shut. The doors are sometimes so hung as to act automatically. The old Saxon word was *Gote*. In an Inquisition of the Court of Sewers held in the reign of Edwd. II, 1316, referring to the Sluice in the Witham, it is described as "Exclusam, sive catteractam," and in a subsequent document it is referred to as "Slusa, sive le pyle in alveo aquæ." DAN., *Sluse*; GERMAN, *Schleuse*; DUTCH, *Sluis*; FRENCH, *Ecluse*.

SLAKER. The draw door on the inside of a tidal sluice, used for regulating the height of the water in the drain.

SLAKE. "Ordered that no one should make any dams, wayes, gravels, wares, slamps, slakes, flakes, herdells, cradgings or other annoyances over the river." *Commission of Sewers*, 1616.

SLAREY. Sticky or dirty; thus, to slare a window when cleaning means to smear it; a slarey day, wet drizzly weather: spoken also of a man who is not to be depended on. To slare a person is to say things about them which are not true.

SLIPE. A narrow strip of land lying between two drains.

SLAPE. Slippery; also applied to people, as "he's a slape fellow," cunning. ICEL., *Sleipr*.

SLATTERY. Rainy, especially applied to showery weather.

SLECK. To put out, or damp down, a fire with water. To quench thirst. To put water to lime.

SMUICE. The run of a hare through a hedge.

SOCK DYKE. or Soak dyke, a ditch or drain running parallel with an embankment, for the purpose of taking any water that soaks through from the river or drain.

SOCK. The level at which the underground water stands in the peat or silt. This varies as the water in the Drain rises or falls, or in accordance with the wetness or dryness of the season. A.S.

SOD BANK. An expression used by Fishermen for the dark bank of clouds often seen on the water in the Estuary, during North-east winds, which owing also to the peculiar clearness of the atmosphere causes trees, stacks, or other objects on the land, to be reflected in the water, in a reverse position and magnified. The latter effect being generally described as a mirage.

SOKE. Land held under a tenure giving a right to hold a Court of Enquiry, the old English meaning of the word being 'enquiring into.' An estate described as soke of a manor, meant that the tenants had to go to that place to have their complaints heard.

SOULE OR SULE. A term used to set dogs on animals, to drive them away. "Sule 'em!"

SQUAD. Mud on a road.

STANG OR STANG GAD. A long pole with a spear at the end, used for spearing eels in the fen drains. OLD NORSE, *Stong*, a stake or pole.

STANG. STONG. A rood of land.

STARNEL. The Starling.

STINT. An allotment of work, or limit to the number of cattle to be turned on a common, or open fen. To give a short supply.

STINT OR STYNTE. A marsh bird (*Tringa minuta*).

STOOK. Several sheaves of corn, set up on end in the field to dry.

STOWER. A pole with an iron shoe, used for pushing barges through the water.

STUD. A post. A. S., *Studa*. The old fen cottages were built with a frame work of wood, filled in with clay mixed with chopped straw, the erection being called *mud and stud*.

APPENDIX IV.

STRIKE. Half a bushel.

STEER. Steep.

STAVER. The step of a ladder. The length being reckoned by the number of stavers.

SURROUNDED. Land covered with water, drowned or flooded. In 1607 a bill was promoted "for the draining of 6,000 acres of surrounded land at Waldersea," this being the first local Act for improving the Fens. In this case, three persons *Undertook* to drain certain lands in Waldersea, for which *Undertaking* the *Adventurers* agreed to receive two-thirds of the land drained.

SWATCH. A low place where water stands.

SWATCHWAY. A depression in the sands, where water stands sufficiently deep to allow small boats to pass through.

SYKE or SIKE. A place for water to lie in. "Lands in the East Fen, except the deeps, creeks and sykes." *Holland Watchman*, 1800. A drain. Thus, Gill Syke, Syke-mouth.

TAR MARLIN. Thin cord, soaked in tar, used for tying faggots and similar purposes.

TEEM. To pour out or empty. ICEL., *tema*, to empty.

TIT. Wildmore Tits, small horses bred in Wildmore Fen.

TON. Originally a fenced enclosure, afterwards used for a collection of houses. SAX., *Ton*. The Villages along the East Coast were called the "Holland Towns."

THARMS. The small entrails of a pig, used for making sausages.

THORPE. A village. DANISH.

THRONG. Busy. ICEL., *Pröngr*, crowded.

THRUF. Through.

TRAY. A Hurdle.

TOFTS. High places in the Fens, from the same origin as *Tuft*.

TOFTSTEAD. A plot of land in the unenclosed Fens, on which a building was erected carrying with it a right of common.

TOOT. Looking, peeping. Toot Hills, places of observation.

TOD. A measure of wool, 28lbs. ICEL.

TUMBREL. An open box on legs in a crew yard, in which fodder is placed for the cattle; a Cart. In old records of the Court of Sewers of the reign of Edward II, Owners of land were ordered to find a *Tumbril* for 'men work' for repair of the banks.

TUN. The openings of a sluice were formerly described as *tuns*.

TURF. Peat.

TEW OR TUE. To fuss about, "'E tued an' 'e moiled 'issen dead" (*Tennyson*.)

TWO SHEAR, THREE SHEAR. A sheep which has been shorn twice or three times.

UNGAIN. Ungainly, inconvenient, awkward.

UNHEPPEN. Not handy, clumsy.

UPHAND. To maintain or back up.

UNDERTAKERS. *See* Adventurers and "Surrounded."

Appendix IV.

Vacherie or **Vachary**. An allotment of land in the unenclosed fens, where cows could be grazed. Thus, in a settlement of the dispute between Ralph Rhodes and the Abbot of Kirkstead, *temp.* Henry III. Ralph is declared the owner of " the Vachary of Revesby, called Morehouse."

Virgate or **Yard Land**. The fourth part of a Carucate (about 30 acres.)

Wapentake. The Scandinavian term for a Hundred or division of the County, meaning Weapon-touch; land held under a Lord whose tenure was so recognized. Dan,, *Vaabentag.* Sax., *Weapen,* weapon, *tac* touch.

Wall. A sea bank. In old documents of the Court of Sewers latinised into *Wallia.* Callis describes *Wallia* as an artificial edifice made of materials brought to the place where it is erected, in distinction from a bank made of material found on the site. The ownership of a wall, he says, belongs to the person who built it, and he is bound to repair it. The word, however, is frequently applied to the sea banks.

Wall-eyed. Having eyes of two different colours, or looking different ways. Many of the sheep dogs in the fens are wall-eyed.

Warp. Alluvial deposit left by the tide. Icel., *Verpa,* to throw up.

Ware. To spend. Icel., *Vevja,* to invest.

Wash Land. Land left unenclosed by the side of a river 'for the floods to bed in.'

Whaup. The Curlew. (*Numenius Arquatus*).

Whemble. To turn over.

Wire Into. To proceed with great energy. "He wired into it like all that."

Wick. Lively. Swed., *Vig,* nimble.

Wrack or **Wreck**. Weeds and floating rubbish carried about by the tides and deposited on the banks.

Woad. (*Isatis Tinctoria*). From the Saxon *Wad,* a plant cultivated in the Fens and used by dyers for fixing the blue colour obtained from Indigo.

Wong. Low land.

Yelper. The Avocet. 'So called from their cry.' (Camden). (*Recurvirostra Avocetta*). Now extinct as a Fenland bird.

APPENDIX V.

OBSERVATIONS AND STATISTICS AS TO RAINFALL, FLOODS, TEMPERATURE, WIND, HARVEST AND TIDES AT BOSTON.

The following particulars as to the rainfall at Boston during the thirty-two years (1864 to 1895 inclusive), the mean temperature and extremes of heat and cold, and the number of days on which the winds blew from each quarter; also as to the time of harvest and the condition of the crops, with the temperature and rainfall; and as to the average and extreme flow of the tides, are from observations recorded by W. H. Wheeler, M. Inst. C.E.

RAINFALL.

The rainfall in the Fens is not much more than half that which falls on the west side of England.

The average fall at Boston for the sixty years has been as follows:

For the ten years	Inches.
1830-39	22·58
1840-49	24·58
1850-59	20·72
1860-69	23·43
1870-79	24·28
1880-89	24·77
Average of 60 years	23·49

The average number of days on which rain fell during the last twenty-six years was 160; the greatest number, 214 in 1872; the least, 117 in 1887.

Between 1875-83 the excess of rain over the average amounted to 44·15 inches. Between 1884-94 the deficiency was 44·14 inches.

Periods of Wet and Dry Weather.—Wet years are considered as those above, and dry years those below, the average of the 60 years, 23·49. Between 1828 and 1849 the only continued period of rainfall above or below the average was from 1832 to 1838, when the average was 20·80. From 1849 to 1864, a period of 16 years, the rainfall was every year, with the exception of 1860, deficient, the average being 20·96. In 1854 the fall was only 13·79, and in, 1864 14·94. Then follow, between 1865 and 1872, 8 years, when the rainfall was in excess, the average for the period being 25·64. Then followed two dry years, when the average was 19.21. After this came, from 1875 to 1883, 9 wet years, with an average of 29·06. This was the wettest period recorded, and during which the rainfall of any one year was the highest recorded, the quantity for 1880 being 35·53. After this from 1884 to 1895 came a period of 12 dry years, when the fall averaged 20·26, the year 1886 being slightly above the average.

Dry Seasons.—The longest continuous period of dry weather since 1826 was during the four years 1861-65, the average annual rainfall of these years being 18·39 inches. The longest period during the last twenty-four years absolutely without any rain was, in March and April of 1893. From the 4th to the 15th of March, a period of 12 days, no rain fell. A slight shower of ·06 then fell, but after this for 30 days, to the 15th of April no rain fell. On that day there was again a slight shower amounting to 0·13 of an inch, and no more rain fell till the end of the month, Thus for 53 days only 0·29 of an inch fell. The fall for the four months of March, April, May, and June, only amounted to 2·90 inches, a deficiency of 4·23 inches below the average. In June, 1887, no rain fell from the 2nd of the month until the 4th of the following month, a period of thirty one days. In 1868 the dry weather lasted over three months. Only 1¼ inch fell during the months of May, June, and July in that year, and there were twenty-two continuous days in June without any rain. The drought commenced at the end of April and lasted till the beginning of August, a period of over three months. In 1870 there were thirty-five days in May and June during which only the third of an inch fell, and twenty-six days without any rain. In May, 1884, there were eighteen days; in July, 1885, fifteen days; and in June, 1876, seventeen days without rain. In June, 1887, no rain fell from the 2nd of June till the 4th of July, one of the longest periods recorded absolutely without rain; the rainfall of every month from Jan. 1887 to Feb. 1888 inclusive, was below the average, the total quantity which fell during that time being 15.14 inches which is only half an inch more than half the average quantity for that period. Occasionally in winter during frosts long spells of dry weather occur. Thus in December, 1873, there were fifteen days without rain or snow; and in Jan., 1879, seventeen days.

The following Table gives the Rainfall for the six months March to August, of the dry seasons for the past 63 years.

Quantity of Rainfall, in inches, during Spring and Summer of dry years.—

Month.	Average.	1826	1834	1863	1864	1868	1870	1874	1887	1890	1893
March	1.44	1.19	0.36	0.83	1.79	1.68	1.10	0.70	1.17	1.40	0.34
April	1.86	1.01	0.64	1.30	1.51	2.41	0.69	0.46	0.85	0.50	0.15
May	1.87	0.44	0.81	0.71	1.54	0.43	0.65	0.85	1.60	2.04	1.22
June	2.14	0.21	1.36	1.75	1.20	0.45	1.57	0.72	0.18	1.40	1.19
July	2.52	2.35	3.84	0.60	0.30	0.37	0.98	1.86	1.11	1.60	3.65
August	2.36	0.49	1.39	2.75	0.51	3.43	1.48	1.97	0.96	1.15	1.35
Total	12.19	5.69	8.40	7.94	6.85	8.77	6.47	6.56	5.87	8.09	7.90
Total for the year	25.90	15.43	14.66	18.38	14.94	52.61	18.66	18.22	12.94	17.63	23.58

The smallest rainfall in any one year was 12.94 inches in 1887; the next, 13.79 in 1854; 14.94, in 1864; 14.66, in 1834; 15.43, in 1826; 17.17, in 1884; 15.68 in 1890.

In 1854 the deficiency was chiefly in the first four months of the year during which time only 2.37in. fell against an average, at that time, of 5.36in.

1890.—The deficiency commenced in the previous autumn and continued all through the winter of 1889-90. The deficiency at the end of February being 4.11in. At the end of August the deficiency had increased to 8.11in. The winter of 1890-91 showed a still further deficiency up to the end of February of 7.08 inches. making altogether since Sept. of 1889 15.19 inches. The scarcity of water was very much felt, all the ditches and sewers having been dry. The water in the reservoir at Miningsby fell to 3ft. 2in. on the gauge, the lowest since 1879. For three days the supply was supplemented by pumping from the Witham

In 1892-3 the deficiency commenced in November and lasted up till the end of June the quantity falling during that period of 8 months being 6.46in. below the average. July was above the average, but August and September were both deficient, making a total deficiency of 8.48in.

Wet Seasons.—The longest continuous period of wet weather since 1826 was during the years 1880-3, when the average annual rainfall for the three years was 31.59in. The Drainage of the Fens is principally affected by the rain which falls during the six months, September to February. The following tables give the rainfall for the six months, September to February, of the wet winters of the last 63 years.

Appendix V.

Quantity of Rainfall in inches during the Winters of Wet Years.—1826-86.

Month	Average 1867-86	1836-7	1841-2	1848-9	1852-3	1866-7	1868-9
September	2·83	2·38	3·43	4·61	4·32	3·55	2·29
October	2·63	2·73	2·97	5·33	2·41	1·73	3·35
November	2·25	3·46	2·11	1·02	4·32	2·15	1·39
December	2·42	1·22	1·67	1·33	1·45	2·03	5·87
January	1·85	3·26	2·40	1·51	1·41	3·67	2·79
February	1·76	1·47	1·48	0·22	1·61	1·36	1·82
Total	13·74	14·52	14·06	14·02	15·52	14·49	17·51
For the whole year	25·69	21·38	27·26	32·64	25·30	25·58	25·61

Month	1872-3	1875-6	1876-7	1880-1	1882-3	1883-4	1885-6
September	2·10	2·24	5·24	4·91	3·34	6·75	3·11
October	3·17	3·50	1·17	7·14	4·78	2·43	4·89
November	2·94	4·90	2·55	1·94	2·79	2·82	3·08
December	3·28	1·20	4·26	2·23	3·74	1·06	0·93
January	1·90	1·82	3·08	0·81	2·04	1·90	2·49
February	1·68	2·13	2·09	3·70	3·20	0·72	0·11
Total	15·07	15·79	18·39	20·73	19·89	15·68	14·61
For the whole year	32·69	25·55	31·05	35·53	39·82	31·76	23·42

Up to 1884 the wet seasons were more frequent and the quantity of rain greater than during the previous thirty years. The winter rainfall only exceeded 14in. on four occasions from 1826 to 1856, and since then there have been nine winters in which this quantity was exceeded. The mean falls for the six months of the wet periods being 14·53in. and 16·90in. respectively. The average fall for the 9 years 1875-83 was 19·06in. The greatest fall during this period was 20·73in. in 1880-81. Taking the average of the four wettest seasons, the total fall for the six months averages ·106in. per day. Taking the wettest periods and times of flood, the greatest quantity that has fallen gives a mean of 0·41in. spread over fourteen days in November, 1885, and also in October, 1883. In September, 1880, the mean was 0·40in. for twelve days, or 0·21in. for 23 days. In October of the same year the rainfall averaged 0·61in. for 14 days,

The mean daily fall of rain which caused the 21 floods in the Witham since 1852 was 0·26in. for 17 days.

The largest annual rainfall since 1826 was 35·53in. in 1880; the next being 32·69in. in 1872; 32·64in. in 1848; 31·76in. in 1883; 31·05in. in 1876; 30·82in. in 1882; 30·69in. in 1860. These are the only years since 1826 when as much as 30in. fell in one year.

The greatest fall in one month was 8·32in. in July, 1828; the next 7·14in. in October, 1880; and the next 6·75in. in September, 1883. The greatest fall in one day was 3·10in. in September, 1883; the next 2·79in. in October, 1880. After this the greatest was 1·43in. in June, 1876; and 1·19in. in July, 1867. In June, 1880, 0·89in. fell in three-quarters of an hour.

APPENDIX V.

The following Tables give the average monthly and yearly rainfall with the maximum and minimum falls for the twenty years ending 1894.

MEAN OF OBSERVATIONS OF RAINFALL AT BOSTON—1866 TO 1894.

(The extremes are continued to 1895.)

Month	Means of 20 years. 1867-86	Means of 20 years. 1875-94	Greatest Fall since 1826. Inches.	Year.	Least Fall since 1826. Inches.	Year.
January	1.85	1.45	3.67	1867	0.12	1826
February	1.76	1.67	4.54	1833	0.11	1886
March	1.44	1.29	3.23	1851	0.12	1839
April	1.86	1.64	4.36	1876	0.20	1825
May	1.87	1.82	5.41	1847	0.18	1848
June	2.14	2.07	4.58	1839	0.18	1887
July	2.52	2.73	8.02	1828	0.30	1864
August	2.36	2.25	5.48	1878	0.48	1826
September	2.83	2.39	6.75	1883	0.30	1854
October	2.63	2.74	7.14	1880	0.48	1888
November	2.25	2.41	4.90	1875	0.74	1849
December	2.42	1.70	5.87	1868	0.12	1848
The year	25.90	24.16	35.53	1828	12.94	1886

The figures for the years previous to 1851 are from records kept by Mr. Veal, at Boston.

YEARLY RAINFALL AT BOSTON.

Years	Inches.	Years	Inches.	Years	Inches.	Years	Inches.
1826	15.43	1844	21.64	1862	19.98	1880	35.53
1827	20.27	1845	24.29	1863	18.28	1881	28.25
1828	28.59	1846	23.40	1864	14.94	1882	30.82
1829	24.14	1847	23.92	1865	25.63	1883	31.76
1830	25.90	1848	32.64	1866	25.58	1884	16.17
1831	25.87	1849	24.03	1867	25.94	1885	23.42
1832	22.55	1850	20.11	1868	25.61	1886	25.25
1833	22.62	1851	22.46	1869	27.26	1887	12.94
1834	14.66	1852	25.30	1870	18.66	1888	20.99
1835	21.87	1853	21.40	1871	23.81	1889	22.60
1836	21.38	1854	13.79	1872	32.69	1890	15.68
1837	23.58	1855	21.57	1873	20.21	1891	22.93
1838	18.95	1856	19.49	1874	18.22	1892	22.12
1839	28.48	1857	23.17	1875	25.55	1893	18.32
1840	18.61	1858	19.00	1876	31.05	1894	21.20
1841	27.26	1859	20.96	1877	26.14	1895	21.56
1842	24.73	1860	30.69	1878	26.77		
1843	25.29	1861	20.38	1879	25.72		

APPENDIX V.

BASINS OF THE WITHAM AND WELLAND.
RAINFALL FOR TWELVE YEARS—1869-80.

	County	Height above Sea.	Maximum.	Minimum.	Average.
		Feet.	Inches.	Inches.	Inches.
Witham :—					
Wytham-on-the Hill	Lincolnshire	167	32·83	14·40	23·88
Grantham	Lincolnshire	179	35·59	16·94	25·53
Haydor	Lincolnshire		34·87	14·84	25·52
Boston	Lincolnshire	24	35·53	18·22	26·02
Stubton	Lincolnshire	.	36·49	18·76	26·51
Navenby	Lincolnshire		36·14	18·38	26·67
Miningsby	Lincolnshire		33·12	17·90	26·32
Branston	Lincolnshire	136	35·40	19·07	26·56
Market Rasen	Lincolnshire	111	30·19	17·76	25·37
Lincoln	Lincolnshire	26	32·15	16·29	24·31
Welland :—					
Stamford		116	34·59	16·37	25·15
Spalding		20	37·12	16·22	26·10
Market Harboro'	L'stershire		39·47	18·49	29·33
Ryhall	Rutland		36·61	16·46	26·49
Oakham	Rutland		40·34	22·56	28·65

FLOODS.

The following Table gives the principal floods which have occurred during the past 35 years, with the rainfall of the previous month.

Year.	Month.	Grand Sluice. At high water. FT. IN.	Grand Sluice. At low water. FT. IN.	Black Sluice. At high water. FT. IN.	Black Sluice. At low water. FT. IN.	
1852	November	14 6				Highest known flood to this date
1857	January	14 7		15 9	12 6	
1862	March	13 7		16 1	13 0	
1867	January	14 0	9 6	16 1½	13 9	
1869	January	14 0	11 6	16 0	14 3	River full of deposit. 11ft. deep against door of the Grand Sluice.
1872	April	13 10	9 6	16 0	12 5	
	November	13 10		15 0	11 9	River in good order
	December	13 3		16 0	12 6	River in good order
1875	November	15 6	10 5	16 7	13 9	
1877	January	15 11	11 0	16 9	12 7	River in good order
1878	November	13 9	12 4	15 9		
1880	July	11 9	8 9	14 3	12 0	
	September	14 5	10 0	16 3	12 6	
	October	15 0	10 8	17 1	13 0	
1882	October	15 2	10 0	16 4	11 11	
	December	14 0	9 10	15 11	12 4	
1883	February	15 1	11 11	16 7	12 6	
	October	14 1	10 6	16 7	12 6	New Outfall open
	November	13 9	9 6	16 1	12 0	
1885	October	13 3	8 0	12 9	9 7	
	November	13 4	8 6	14 3	11 0	
	December	13 10	8 4	16 0	11 0	
1886	May	13 7	9 3	15 7	11 7	
	December	13 10	8 4	16 0	11 0	
1887	January	12 9	8 3	15 10	11 5	
1889	March	10 6	7 6	15 2	11 3	
	May	11 6	6 0	15 0	9 9	
1891	December	13 5	7 3	13 6	10 2	

APPENDIX V.

PARTICULARS OF THE FLOODS THAT HAVE OCCURRED IN THE FENS SINCE 1850.

1852—November. This flood was caused by a heavy autumn rainfall of nearly double the average quantity. This was the highest flood known in the Witham, to this date. The Bank of Bourne Eau broke, and flooded Bourne North Fen.

1857—January. This flood was due entirely to heavy rains in January, the fall for that month being more than double the average. The rainfall from the previous September to the end of December was nearly 2in. below the average.

1862—March. The rainfall of the previous autumn and winter was below the average, but there was an excess of 1½in. in March, causing a heavy freshet.

1867—January. This flood was caused by heavy rains and snow at the end of December and the beginning of January. Nearly the whole of the East Fen was under water. The Steeping River was so full that the water ran over the banks. The rainfall of the previous autumn had not been heavy.

1868-9—December and January. This flood was due to a very heavy fall of rain in December, amounting to 5·87in. The excess over the average quantity for the three months of October, November and December was 4·32in. The Haven at this time was full of deposit, the bed being 11ft. above its ordinary level at the Grand Sluice, the doors of which were not opened until the 7th of December, and the doors of the Black Sluice until the end of the month. In the Witham the water rose as high as the line of railway in several places. On Sunday, the 3rd of January, the bank of the Stixwould Drain gave way and the water spread itself over an area of about 1,500 acres, submerging the land from 5ft. to 6ft. deep. This partly relieved the overcharged Witham, the water at the Grand Sluice at once dropping 8in. This flood lasted on and off till February, the water in the Black Sluice rising to 14ft. at high water on the 3rd of the month, and at the Grand Sluice to 13·9ft. In the East Fen the Lade Bank engines had to stop pumping as the water flowed back over the doors of the lock. A large tract of land in Holland Fen, and the other Fens, up to the Black Sluice, was under water.

1872—April. This flood was due to a heavy fall of rain in March, preceded by several snow showers, amounting together to about 1ft. in depth. On the 2nd of April, 1·10in. of rain fell. The rainfall of the previous three months was 2½in. above the average. Boston Haven was in good order, all the deposit having been scoured out by the rains of the previous winter. The water in the Witham rose to 13ft. 1in. on the gauge at Bardney, and nearly ran over the bank at Stixwould. The engines at Lade Bank had to cease pumping, owing to the height of the water in Hobhole. In the Glen the water rose to 10ft. 9in. on the gauge at Tongue End, being 2ft. higher than it had ever been known to do before, and the north bank broke near Tongue End, inundating Bourne South Fen. This breach led to a trial at Lincoln Assizes against the Black Sluice Commissioners, which resulted in a verdict in their favour.

1872—November. This flood was due to a comparatively small amount of rain falling on ground completely saturated by previous rains. The total rainfall from the beginning of the year was 9·36in. above the average, the quantity being in excess in every month but May. The excess for the three months previous was 2·45in. A large area of low lands in the Fens, including Digby Fen, was covered with water, as also the Wash Lands on the Welland. The Bane overflowed its banks.

1872—December. A heavy fall of snow and rain, amounting to 0·80in., together with the rain which had fallen previously, caused a heavy flood in the Witham. The spring tides at the time of the flood were very small, and as the doors of the Grand Sluice were not closed, freshets never ceased running during the time of high water, a circumstance which had rarely, if ever, happened before. At Lincoln the low part of the City was flooded. The valley of the Bane was all under water. The water rose to 14ft. 5in. at Bardney. The becks passing through Scopwick and Digby were fuller than ever before known. The Welland rose so high that the low-lying thoroughfares near the river were flooded, and a very large tract of land in the Welland valley was inundated. In the Glen the water rose to 9ft. 8in. on the gauge, or within 13in. of the flood of April, 1872. The water ran over the overfall into the South Forty-Foot, to a depth of 1ft.

1875—November. Previous to this flood the land was thoroughly saturated, the long drought of the spring having terminated at the end of June with a fall of 4·79in.

APPENDIX V.

in 30 days, causing a strong freshet down the river in July, a very unusual occurrence at that time of the year. The water rose to 10ft. 2in. on the sill of the Grand Sluice. A great deal of deposit had accumulated in the river, but these freshets washed it out of the upper part of the channel. The pumping engines in the fens up the Witham, and also at Lade Bank, were at work for some days. The washes of the Welland were flooded to a depth of 5ft., the water rising nearly as high as the top of Cowbit Bank. The loss of cropping was very great. In October, 3·34in. of rain fell in 15 days, or at the mean rate of 0·22in. per day. These freshets occurred during neap tides, and the doors at the Grand Sluice were not closed for a week. The highest the water reached was 11ft. 4in., falling at low water to 9ft. 4in., and at the Black Sluice to 15ft., falling to 14ft. 3in. at low water.

1875. The flood in November was the highest known in the Witham up to this time. The rainfall for the month was 4·90in., that for the previous month having been 3·25in. The water rose in the Witham to 13ft. 4in. on the gauge at Bardney. The bank of Digby Drain broke and flooded 1,000 acres of land in Digby and Walcot Fens, the water covering the land in places to a depth of 6ft. The Bane and its tributaries overflowed their banks. All the low part of Holland Fen was under water. At Hobhole Sluice the water rose during tide time to 12ft. 5in., falling at low water to 9ft. The pumps at Lade Bank had to cease working, as the water rose above the top of the doors. The water was only kept from overflowing the banks of the Glen at Surfleet by employing a number of men to raise cradges. The water rose to 11ft. on the gauge at Tongue End. Cowbit Wash was covered 6ft. deep, and the streets of Deeping St. James and Market Deeping rendered impassable. The Welland rose up to the centre of the London Road at Spalding.

1877—January. During the flood at the end of December and beginning of January the spring tides were very high, and the height of the water at the Grand Sluice exceeded that of 1875 by 5in., this being the greatest flood height ever recorded at the Grand Sluice or the Black Sluice, up to this time. The average height of the water for 11 days at the Black Sluice was 15ft. 3in., falling at low water to 12ft. The water rose higher at Lincoln than on any previous occasion since 1828. It was 14in. higher at Bargate Weir than in 1852. The water overflowed the banks of the Witham, the Fossdyke and the Sincil Dyke. All the lower part of Lincoln was inundated. At Bardney the water rose to 18ft. 9in. on the gauge. The river bank, between Five Mile House and Bardney, broke, also the Branston Bank. The north bank of Billinghay Skerth gave way and caused the submersion of from 2,000 to 3,000 acres of land to the depth in some places of 5ft., the inhabitants being driven out of their houses. At the Black Sluice the water rose 2in. higher than ever before recorded, and at Donington Bridge, 3in. higher. The water ran over the Overfall at Tongue End for more than a fortnight. In the Welland the water rose so high as to cause serious fears for the Barrier Bank and the Deeping High Bank. The washes were covered with water for a length of 16 miles, and in places 1 mile in width, the depth on the level being 7ft. Deeping St. James was inundated and the streets covered with water, making the fifteenth time in 17 months. In the Glen the water rose 14in. higher than ever known before, the height on the gauge at Tongue End being 11ft. 11in. It ran over the top of the banks on both sides, and breaches were caused in three places, one near Pinchbeck, the water flowing nearly up to the Church; the others on the north side between Tongue End and the Railway Bridge over the Counter Drain. The whole of Bourne North Fen and Dyke Fen were inundated, the water extending, more or less, to the fens of Haconby and Morton. The traffic on the Bourne and Spalding Railway was stopped for a considerable time. On the south side of the Glen the Counter Drain Wash Lands were inundated, and the water rose to the top of the bank, which was split and opened in several places. This flood was caused by very heavy rains in December, the quantity which fell during that month being 4¼in., 3in. falling on the last 14 days of the month, or at the mean rate of 0·22 per day. The rainfall in September had been very heavy, the excess from August having been nearly 5in.

1878—November. This flood was due to a fall of 3·47in. of rain and snow in 14 days, or at the mean rate of 0·20in. per day. There had been a very heavy rainfall in August, but that of September and October were not above the average. The Haven was in good order, and the tides neaps. The water rose at Lincoln to within a few inches of the flood of 1877, and inundated the low part of the City, and a large area of land in Washingborough, Heighington, Branston, and Bracebridge. The river bank at Potterhanworth and Barlings, broke. In the East Fen, the water rose above the lock doors at Lade Bank, and the pumps had to cease working. A breach occurred in the bank

APPENDIX V.

of Steeping river. The Black Sluice and Welland Districts did not suffer much from this flood.

1879—June. This flood was due to heavy rains in May and June, amounting to 7¼in. in the two months. The water at the Grand Sluice rose to 12ft. 4in., the highest summer level reached for 30 years, the next being in 1872, when it rose to 11ft. The Witham, the Welland and the Glen were all much swollen, and several hundreds of acres of land, in the valley of the Witham, were flooded. Cowbit Wash was covered with water, to the depth of from two to three feet, and continued so till the end of July.

1880—July. This was due to heavy rains in June and July, 9·65in. of rain falling in the two months, the total quantity averaging 0·16in. for 60 days. 1·55in. fell in one day, 0·48 having fallen on the previous day. The land was thoroughly saturated with water, which in many fields stood in pools in all the low places. No large extent of land was inundated along the Witham. On the Welland the flood was very heavy, and the lower part of Stamford was flooded from two to three feet deep. Market Deeping, Deeping St. James, Elton and Maxey were flooded. The wash lands on the Welland were again submerged.

1880—September. This flood occurred during spring tides. The Outfall of the Witham was in very good order. The land had been thoroughly saturated by the very heavy rains which had fallen during the summer. In the middle of September, 4¼in. fell in four days, a rate of fall not previously recorded in the Fenland. On the Witham, all the lower fens were flooded. At Dogdyke, the water flowed into the lower rooms of the houses. In the West Fen, at Carrington, a very large area of land was flooded, the water standing up to the bands of the sheaves. The water rose, at Hobhole, to 12ft. 10in. at tide time, falling to 8ft. 6in. at low water. This is the largest flood recorded at this sluice. The engines at Lade Bank had to cease working. In the Steeping River, the water rose so high as nearly to run over the banks, and for upwards of a mile in length it was within three inches of the top. In Stonebridge Drain the water rose from six to seven feet in one night. Several corn fields, near Frithville, were under water. At the Black Sluice, the average height of the water, for eight days, was 15ft. 2in., falling at low water to 11ft. 8in., a depression of 3ft. 6in. In the Welland valley, a large area of land was flooded, the water rising, at Crowland, above the bottom of the stacks. Round Spalding and Long Sutton, a larger area of land was flooded than was ever known before. Market Deeping was again flooded, and all the Welland washes submerged.

1880—October. This is the third heavy flood of this year, and was due to heavy rains falling on land thoroughly saturated, 2·74in. of rain falling in 24 hours, and 4·38 in four days. This was even a higher rate than that recorded in September, and the greatest fall ever recorded in the Fenland ; later in the month, 2·36in. fell in 3 days. The total for this month was 7·14 inches, at the mean rate of nearly a quarter of an inch a day for 30 days. A very large area of land, both above and below Lincoln, and all the lower parts of the city were flooded. The banks of Heighington and Dorrington Fens gave way, flooding over 1000 acres of land. The recorded height of the water was 18ft. on the gauge at Bardney. At Hobhole the water rose to 13ft. 2in., the highest recorded. The engines at Lade Bank were again stopped. In Steeping river the water was level with the banks, and was only prevented from flowing over by cradging. In the Black Sluice the water was 17ft. 1in., or at tide time higher than ever before, or since, recorded. For ten days the average height of the water inside the sluice at tide time was 16ft., falling to 11ft. 11in. at low water, showing a depression of 4ft. In the Glen the flood rose to 11ft. 9in. on the gauge at Tongue End, running over the overfall to a depth of 1ft. 10in., this being the highest flood recorded. A breach occurred in the banks on the Deeping Fen side, which was fortunately stopped before any damage was done. On the opposite side near Wooley's Mill the bank gave way and flooded over 3,000 acres in Bourne South Fen and the adjoining districts. The Bourne Railway was closed to traffic for 4 months. The water rose to 11ft. 9in. on the gauge at Tongue End, which is 2in. less than the great flood of 1877. Water ran over the Overfall into the Black Sluice, 1ft. 10in. deep, a greater depth than ever known before. In the Welland the water rose so high that it was necessary to cradge the roads in Spalding and along Deeping High Bank. At Crowland the water rose 6in. higher than in 1877, thousands of acres of land being submerged. All the wash land was submerged.

1882—October. This flood was due to heavy rains in September and October. The total for the two months being 8·12in. There were heavy floods in the Witham and a large area of land about Lincoln was under water. Barlings Eau Bank gave way,

The water at Bardney rose to 18·6ft. on the gauge. One opening of the Grand Sluice was closed owing to the works for the enlargement of the sluice. The average height of the water inside the Black Sluice at tide time was 14ft. 11in. for seven days, falling to 11ft. 5in. at low water, giving a depression of 3ft. 6in. The water in the Glen rose to 11ft. on the gauge at Tongue End. A breach occurred in the bank on the south side, near Wooley's Mill, and the washes were inundated. This caused a large quantity of water from the Glen to flow down through the Deeping Fen Main Drain to the Welland.

1882—December. Nearly 2in. of rain in 10 days, falling on ground thoroughly saturated by previous rain, caused very strong freshets in the Witham and the Black Sluice. The water ran continuously through the Grand Sluice for several days during the neap tides, the doors not being closed. In the Black Sluice the average height of the water for 5 days was 15ft. 3in., falling to 11ft. 11in. at low water.

1883—February. This was the third flood this winter, and was due to 1¾in. of rain falling in 6 days, the previous rainfall for the whole of this winter being much above the average. The Witham overflowed its banks above Lincoln and flooded a large area of land. The banks of the river were in great danger in several places, and gave way at Southrey. The water in the Grand Sluice dropped 2ft. immediately after the breach occurred. A large quantity of land in Holland Fen was under water.

1883—October. This flood was due to the heaviest fall of rain recorded, more than 5¼in. of rain falling in 14 days, and over 3in. in 1 day ; the mean for 14 days being 0·39in. The water in the Witham rose 11ft. in 24 hours. The maximum flood level at Bardney was 18ft. 8in. A large area of low land in the Witham was flooded, and hundreds of acres of corn ready for carrying were submerged in the fields. In the East Fen, the water in the Steeping River overtopped the banks and flowed into the fen, in some places to a depth of 12in. Breaches occurred in the banks of the river, and of the East Fen Catchwater. The water in Hobhole Drain flowed back over the doors in greater quantity than on previous floods.

1883—November. This, the third flood of this winter, was due to a fall of 1¾in of rain in 14 days, the greater part of which fell in 4 days. The land was so saturated with wet that a comparatively small rainfall filled the ditches, and caused the rivers and drains to rise to flood height. No serious inundations were caused by this flood.

1885—April. Owing to heavy rains in the upper part of the basin of the Welland, a strong freshet came down the river and flooded the Cowbit Wash. This was very unexpected, as the season had been very dry, and there was no rain of any weight in Lincolnshire.

1885—October. This flood was due to 4¾in. of rain falling in 26 days, of which 2in. fell in 4 days. The rainfall of the previous month had also been above the average. Owing to the improved condition of the Outfall of the Witham, by the opening of the New Cut through the Clays, this flood passed rapidly away without causing any inundation. In the Welland the river was full, nearly to the top of the banks, and all the wash lands were flooded.

1885—November. A strong freshet occured in the Witham again, in this month, due to excessive rains, 4¾in. falling in 14 days, or at the mean rate of 0·34in. per day. The mean of the fall, for 30 days, being 0·21 per day.

1886—December. A heavy rainfall in December, following on heavy rains in the previous month, caused the water to rise to flood height in the Witham and Black Sluice. The low lands in the Welland Valley were submerged, and Cowbit Wash was once more under water. Owing to the improvement in the Outfall, the depression of the ebb between high and low water, was greater than on any previous flood, the difference at the Grand Sluice being 5ft. 6in., and at the Black Sluice 5ft. ; the average depression of the latter having previously been about 3ft. 6in.

1887. A rainfall of 1·22in. in 16 days in January caused a steady freshet down the Witham, the water rising at tide time to 12ft. 9in., and falling, at low water, to 8ft. 3in. In the Black Sluice the water rose to 15ft. 10in., falling to 11ft. 5in. at low water.

1889. A fall of 1·13in. of snow and rain in 2 days in March, following a fall of 1·40in. in February, caused the water in the Witham, at Bardney, to rise to 18ft. 5in., on the gauge, or within 3in. of the highest known flood ; at the Grand Sluice it only rose to 10ft. 6in., falling to 7ft. 6in. at low water. At the Black Sluice the height was 15ft. 2in. and 11ft. 3in. This freshet was partly due to the ground being frozen when the rain fell. The bank broke on the east side of Branston Island, and the water flooded about 700 acres. The washes on the Welland were flooded. In May, there was a good freshet in the Witham, following on a rainfall of 1·32in. in 3 days. The water rose to 9ft. 9in. at tide time, falling to 5ft. 6in. at low water. At the end of May, after a rainfall of 1·30in. in 5 days, the water rose to 11ft. 6in., falling at low water to 6ft. At the Black Sluice it rose to 15ft., falling to 9ft. 9in.

1891. In December, a continuous rainfall of 2·52, spread over 10 days, caused the water in the Witham to rise to 13ft. 5in., falling at low water 7ft. 3in.

1895. In January a fall of rain and snow of 3·07in., extending over the whole month, caused the water to rise to 18ft. 2in. at Bardney, on the 21st; at the Grand Sluice to 14ft. 6in., falling to 8ft. 6in.; at the Black Sluice to 15ft. 6in., falling to 11ft. 7in. The valley of the Welland and the Washes were flooded; the flood at Stamford being the highest since 1880.

TEMPERATURE AND PRESSURE OF THE ATMOSPHERE.

The observations for temperature are taken from thermometers, placed *four feet* from the ground and shaded from the sun. The mean temperature is that recorded at 9 a.m. The mean temperature as recorded at Boston is about 0·6 degrees less than at Greenwich. The mean temperature of the *different quarters* of the year is as follows:

```
Spring—March, April, May ............................  47·0
Summer—June, July, August ..........................  61·3
Autumn—September, October, November ...............  49·0
Winter—December, January, February .................  37·6
```

The barometer from which the observations are recorded is fixed about 18ft. above the mean level of the sea. No correction is made for altitude or temperature. If allowance were made for these, the mean reading of the year would be about 29·81, that at Greenwich being 29·77. The highest pressure at Greenwich was 30·89 in 1825, and the lowest 27·89 in 1821. The highest at Boston was 30·96, in May 1873, and the lowest, 28·20, in January, 1872.

Temperature and Pressure. Mean of observations at Boston—1864 to 1885.

EXTREMES TO 1894.

Month.	Mean Degs.	Temperature.				Barometer.			
		Maximum.		Minimum.		Mean. Pressr.	Highest		Lowest	
		Deg.	Year.	Deg.	Year.		Pressr.	Year.	Pressr.	Year.
January	36·5	58	1866	2	1881	29·92	30·95	1882	28·20	1872
February	38·8	59	1868	0	1895	29·85	30·83	1873	28·77	1867
March	40·5	72	1893	18	1883	29·88	30·82	1867	28·54	1876
April	47·5	83	1893	22	1892	29·86	30·62	1883	28·80	1882
May	53·2	87	1892	27	1877 & 91	29·97	30·96	1873	29·18	1877
June	59·2	95	1893	35	1881 & 90	30·00	30·65	1867	29·27	1866
July	62·8	95	1886	41	1888 & 91	29·98	30·57	1864	29·06	1884
August	61·3	95	1893	38	1887	29·94	30·54	1874	29·05	1882
September	56·7	90	1891	30	1887	29·98	30·80	1873	29·04	1885
October	48·8	82	1886	24	1887	29·87	30·66	1877	28·75	1865
November	41·5	65	1880	13	1890	29·88	30·67	1868	28·50	1880
December	37·5	60	1866	0	1879	29·88	30·72	1865	28·50	1876
The year	48·7	95	1886	0	1879	29·91	30·95	1873	28·20	1872

High temperature.—July is the hottest month of the year, the mean temperature being 62·8. The hottest months of the last 28 years were July, 1886, and August, 1893. The following figures gives the occasions, since 1864, when the temperature in the shade has been 90 degrees or over.

APPENDIX V.

		Max. Temperature.	No. of days with Temperature over 88 degs.
1867	Aug.	93	8
1868	July	90	9
1872	,,	90	13
1873	,,	90	4
1874	,,	92	11
1876	,,	90	7
1881	,,	92	11
1885	,,	93	9
1886	,,	95	10
,,	Aug.	90	13
1887	,,	92	10
1889	June	90	5
,,	July	90	3
1892	June	92	6
,,	,,	95	4
1893	Aug	95	12
1895	Sept.	84	8

Low temperature.—January has the lowest mean temperature of any month in the year, the average of the last 23 years being 36·5. The coldest month during the same period was in January, 1881, when the average for the whole month was 27·8, the next being December 1879, with 29·8. In the winter of 1890-1891 the mean temperature of 42 days in December and January was 26·78. The lowest temperature was in December, 1879, when the thermometer fell to zero, and the next in January, 1881, when it registered only 2, giving 30 degrees of frost.

1870—December. Sharp frost from 23rd to the 13th of January, 1871. On the 1st of January there were 27 degrees of frost. For 13 days the temperature never rose at any time of the day more than two degrees above freezing point. Nearly three weeks' skating on the river and drains.

1874—December. Frost began on the 15th and lasted till the 2nd January, 1875. Lowest temperature on the 30th, when there were 24 degrees of frost. For eight days the minimum temperature averaged 19 degrees of frost. Boston Haven, the Witham, and all the drains frozen. Skating lasted about ten days.

1878—December. Frost began on the 6th and lasted for three weeks. The greatest amount of frost was 18 degrees on Christmas Day, the mean minimum temperature of five days showing 13 degrees of frost. The Witham was frozen from Boston to Lincoln, and the Haven was also frozen over.

1879.—December and January. Frost set in on the 30th November, and lasted till the 15th of January. For seven days there were 19 degress of frost at the coldest period of the day. On the 7th December the temperature was never, during any part of the day, above 18. Boston Haven, the Witham and all the drains were frozen.

1881.—January. One of the sharpest frosts known lasted from the 12th to the 26th. For a fortnight the mean temperature of the day was 11 degrees below freezing point. On the 15th there were 30 degrees of frost at night. For five days there were 23 degrees of frost at the coldest period of the day. Skating lasted a fortnight, the ice in the Witham being 6½ inches thick.

1890. A frost set in on the 15th of December and lasted without intermission for 38 days, to the 21st of January, 1891. The lowest temperature was on the 19th of January, when 22 degrees of frost were recorded, and 20 degrees on the 11th. The mean temperature of the day for this period was 26·78, the highest reached during the day being 40. The Witham was frozen over from Boston to Lincoln and skating was practicable for nearly six weeks.

1895. This frost was remarkable for the very low temperature registered on two occasions in February, when there was registered 32° of frost. The temperature throughout the day was higher than in 1881, the mean for 9 days being 19·8°, and the maximum temperature during the day on only two occasions being below freezing point. The first frost commenced on the 6th of January and lasted till the 13th, the lowest temperature being 13°. A second frost set in on the 22nd of January and lasted till the 6th of March, a period of 44 days. The temperature fell to zero on the 8th and 10th. The lowest temperature previously recorded in February was 11° in 1889, and 12° in 1892.

Temperature on the Surface and at an Elevation.—During the years 1882-6, observations were taken by Mr. E. C. Hackford for the Council of the Meteorological Society of the temperature at 4ft. from the ground, and also at 170ft. and 260ft. above the surface, by instruments placed in the tower of Boston Church. From the table prepared from these observations, it appears that the mean temperature at 4ft., in every month exceeds that at 170ft., the difference ranging from 3·1° in July to 0·03° in December. The mean minimum at 4ft. is generally colder than at 170ft., except in the winter months, when the latter is slightly colder than the former. At 9 a.m. the mean temperature in the churchyard was always in excess of that up the tower, the difference being greatest in summer. The mean temperature at 4ft. during the day was always in excess of that at 260ft., the difference during the summer months amounting to 4°. The general result showed that the diurnal range of temperature was much less at the top of the tower and on the belfry than at 4ft. from the ground. The tables and details of these observations are recorded in the Journal of the Meteorological Society for October 1887.

WIND.

In the following table only the four quarters of the compass are given. The wind seldom blows exactly from any one point, but is constantly varying during the day; the figures give the prevailing wind for each day. The prevailing wind of this district is from the south-west, from which quarter it blows for more than one third of the year. North-east wind prevails from March to June, the number of days during these months being divided equally between north-east and south-west. South-east winds are most frequent in January, February, and October; south-west in January, December, and September; north-west in March, June, July, August, November, and December.

The force of the wind is greatest in February and March, and least in June and July.

GALES.

1828. On the 18th of July, a whirlwind passed over Boston, in a north-easterly direction towards Wyberton Fen. The space affected by the advancing column was about forty yards in width. As it advanced it drew up from the earth manure lying in the fields, the water out of the South Forty-Foot, a curb, which was carried forty yards, a roller and other moveable substances. The corn in the fields which lay in the track was completely levelled to the ground, and other damage done.

1859—The heaviest gale in recent years was that known as the Royal Charter Gale on the 25th October, 1859.

1871.—February and March. Very heavy gales occured during these months, and much damage was done to the fishing boats in the Deeps.

1875.—March. A very heavy gale from N.W., and several houses damaged.

1876.—April. Heavy gale from N.E., and damage done to buildings.

1881.—July 30th. A whirlwind from S.W. in Boston. Buildings damaged, trees torn up by the roots, one house completely wrecked. The area over which the effect was felt was very small.

1881.—October 14th. The worst gale since the Royal Charter Gale, direction S.W. to N.W. Immense number of trees blown down, and several buildings damaged.

1883.—December. Heavy gales from N.W. to S.W. Many chimneys blown down in Boston, and buildings and stacks damaged.

1884.—December 18th. A very severe gale from S.W., accompanied with hail and lightning. Over a small area, not exceeding 1½ acre, and for the space of a few minutes, the force of the wind was so great as entirely to wreck two large glass houses in Boston. The roofs were carried across the garden, and trees and shrubs were torn up by the roots. Great damage done to buildings.

1891.—A very severe gale blew on the 25th of August, doing immense damage to the fruit crops. On October 13th there was a very severe gale all along the East Coast. A large tree in Boston churchyard was blown down and other damage done.

APPENDIX V.

1893. Very heavy gales blew from S.E. to N.W., for four days in November. There were more wrecks caused by these gales in the Wash than ever known before.

1894.—December. Very heavy gale from S.W., on 21st and 22nd. A grea number of trees blown down.

1895—March. The heaviest gale from S.W. known for many years. More damage done to houses and buildings than on any previous occasion. A large number of trees blown down.

WIND.—1854 to 1886.

Month.	N.E.—Days.	S.E.—Days.	S.W.—Days.	N.W.—Days.
January	4·0	5·5	16·1	5·4
February	4·6	5·9	12·4	5·2
March	9.0	4·5	9·6	7·9
April	10·4	5·0	8·8	5·8
May	10·0	4·0	10·4	6·6
June	8·2	4·2	9·1	8·5
July	5·6	4·7	12·7	8·0
August	6·0	4·3	12·8	7·9
September	5·3	4·6	13·7	6·4
October	6·7	5·6	12·4	6·3
November	4·7	3·8	13·6	7·9
December	4·4	4·3	14·6	7·7
Total days	78·4	56·4	146·2	83·6

SNOW AND FROST IN SPRING.

1872.—Snow from 21st to 25th March, lying on the ground 6in. deep.

1874.—March. Heavy snow storm, lasting four days. Thermometer 12 degrees below freezing point.

1876—April 13th and 14th (Good Friday). Very heavy snow storm for two days. Snow 12in. thick.

1878. March 24th and 25th. Heavy fall of snow, 8in. to 10in. deep.

1883.—March 4th to 20th. Very sharp frosts. 16 degrees of frost on the 7th. Haven frozen over. Several snow storms.

1891.—May 17th. A very sharp frost and fall of snow. 5 degrees of frost were recorded. The minimum temperature on the 17th was 68 degrees lower than the maximum of four days previous.

THUNDER AND HAIL STORMS.

1874—July 29th. Heavy thunderstorm and rain. 0·73in. fell in half-an-hour.

1876—July 22nd. Heavy thunderstorm and hail. Hail stones very large. More than 100 panes of glass broken in the Hotel at Freiston Shore.

1879—August. Very heavy thunderstorm.

1880—June 19th. Very severe thunderstorm and hail. Much damage done to the crops by the hail. Much glass broken in greenhouses. The hail stones stated to be as large as pigeon's eggs. Birds and chickens killed by the hail, and boughs broken off trees. On one farm in Wisbech 100 young fowls were killed by the hail stones. 0·89in. of rain fell in three quarters of an hour.

1887—July 31st. Very severe thunderstorm. Houses in Boston damaged by the lightning.

APPENDIX V.

THE HARVEST AND THE WEATHER.

The exceptional years during the last fifty-two years were as follows:—

EARLY HARVESTS. July to August 2nd		LATE HARVESTS. After August 21st	
Harvest commenced.	Harvest commenced.	Harvest commenced.	Harvest commenced.
1834 July 18	1863 July 29	1839 Aug. 22	1860 Sept. 12
1846 July 22	1865 Aug. 2	1845 Aug. 28	1879 Sept. 1
1848 Aug. 2	1868 July 20	1854 Aug. 22	1888 Sept. 1
1857 July 31	1870 Aug. 1	1855 Aug. 22	1889 Aug. 28
1858 July 29	1874 Aug. 2		
1859 Aug. 1	1884 Aug. 2		

The best crops since 1841 were in 1844, 1847, 1849, 1851, 1852, 1854, 1855, 1857, 1863, 1864, 1868, 1870, 1874, 1885, 1887.

The worst crops were in 1845, 1850, 1855, 1859, 1860, 1861, 1869, 1872, 1880, 1892.

The average time, from the first peeping of the wheat ears to the cutting, averages 60 days. The shortest time recorded being 50, and the longest 71. (This is between 1834 and 1873).

The following table is from observations recorded at Boston. Wheat, being the principal crop grown in the neighbourhood, has been selected as indicative of the general results of the harvests of the Fenland. The datum taken for fixing the harvest is the day on which new wheat, grown in the Fens, was first shown in Boston Market. This varies from the time of cutting according to the weather, but on an average it may be taken as ten days from the time when wheat cutting generally commences. The yield is much influenced by the weather in May, June, and July, the mean temperature and rainfall of these months are therefore given. From the table it will be seen that the earliest harvest was in 1868. This also was the earliest harvest since 1832. The season was also the driest and hottest. The latest harvest, and worst yield, was in 1879. The temperature of this season was very low and the weather very wet. The average time of the past 23 years for showing wheat was the 23rd August. From records kept from 1832 to 1864, on two different farms in the Fens, one being near Wisbech, it appears that the earliest harvest, except 1868, was 1834, when cutting began on the 18th of July; and the latest in 1845 and 1860, when it did not commence till the 28th of August. This would be equivalent to the 28th of July and the 7th of September in the above tables.

Year.	May, June, July. Mean temperature	Rainfall. Inches.	Wheat first shown in Boston mkt.	Remarks.
1858	—	4·73	Aug. 19	
1859	—	4·84	Aug. 29	
1860	—	9·29	Sep. 21	
1861	—	7·78	Aug. 23	
1862	—	6·26	Aug. 28	
1863	—	3·06	Aug. 18	
1864	60·4	3·04	Aug. 18	Good yield. Rainfall in spring below average. Dry July and August.
1865	62·7	9·26	Sep. 1	Harvest late. Yield fair. Cutting began the beginning of August. July and August very wet.
1866	59·4	8·27	Sep. 4	Weather wet from June to September. Yield bad. Cutting began about 13th August.
1867	58·3	8·31	Aug. 16	Bad yield. May and July wet.
1868	62·6	1·25	July 30	Very good quality and yield. Temperature above the average and summer very dry.
1869	57·2	6·27	Aug. 25	Very bad yield.
1870	60·2	3·14	Aug. 10	Very good yield. Spring rainfall below average. Very dry summer and temperature above average.
1871	56·2	8·46	Aug. 23	Yield of wheat below the average. Other crops good. Wet in April, June, and July.

APPENDIX V.

Year.	May, June, July. Mean temperature	Rainfall. Inches.	Wheat first shown in Boston mkt.	Remarks.
1872	58·9	7·18	Aug. 14	Yield very bad. Wet sowing time. Mild winter and cold spring. Wet in March, April, June, and July.
1873	57·1	6·78	Aug. 13	Yield below average.
1874	58·0	3·43	Aug. 12	Yield very good. Dry seed-time. Very dry spring.
1875	58·9	7·26	Aug. 21	Yield below the average. Quality not good. Very good seed-time. Temperature, July very low. Dry spring. Wet in June and July.
1876	57.5	5·77	Aug. 16	Yield below average. Long cold wet winter. Heavy rain in spring, followed by drought till August.
1877	57·0	5·40	Aug. 22	Yield below average. Quality bad. Fair sowing time. Cold and late spring. Cold and stormy at flowering.
1878	59·6	7·04	Aug. 17	Yield below average. Quality bad. Spring dry. May and August very wet.
1879	54·5	10·92	Sep. 6	Yield very bad and quality bad. Very low temperature and heavy rainfall in February, April, May, June, and July.
1880	56·5	10·48	Aug. 25	Yield light. Wet in April, June, and July.
1881	59·2	6·61	Aug. 24	Yield above the average, and quality very good. Spring dry. Heavy rains July and August.
1882	57·2	7·14	Aug. 16	Yield under average. Quality fair. Harvest delayed by wet.
1883	56·9	6·98	Aug. 22	Yield below average. Quality good.
1884	58·7	3·98	Aug. 13	Yield above the average. Quality good. Dry spring.
1885	57·0	4·46	Aug. 19	Yield above average and quality good. Dry spring. July very dry.
1886	53·5	7·01	Sep. 4	Yield rather below the average. Quality good. Crops damaged by cold late spring.
1887	60·3	2·89	Aug. 17	Yield above the average. Quality very good.
1888	56·9	6·82	Sep. 12	Yield and quality about the average.
1889	59·5	5·13	Aug. 28	Yield and quality below the average and the crops very much laid.
1890	58·8	5·04	Aug. 20	Yield a good average. Quality good.
1891	57·5	6·38	Sep. 9	Yield and quality good.
1892	58·8	6·08	Sep. 10	Yield and quality bad.
1893	61·99	6·06	Aug. 9	Yield fair. Quality very good. Remarkably dry Spring, and hot, dry weather during harvest.
1894	58·22	8·18	Aug. 29	Yield not up to the average. Quality damaged by wet weather during harvest. The price of wheat fell to 16/- a quarter, the lowest ever recorded.
1895	61·57	4·99	Aug. 21	Yield and quality good.
1896	61·94	3·26	Aug. 5	Yield good, averaging about 5 quarters to the acre. Quality good.
Average, 39 years.	61·10	6.62	Aug. 23	

APPENDIX V.

THE HIGH TIDES AT BOSTON.

Height of Tides.—The following is the mean height for a whole year of each set of tides at Boston above the sill of the Black Sluice (8·70ft. below *Ordnance datum*) which is 1ft. 2¼in. above L.W.S.T. in Clayhole.

Number of Tides		Feet
3 tides are above		22
3 ,, ,,		21
4 tides are above		20
3 ,, ,,		19
3 ,, ,,		18
5 ,, ,,		17
3 ,, ,,		16
4 ,, ,,		15

Total tides in a fortnight 28   Mean height of tide for year 19

The mean height of springs is 22ft. and of neaps, 15ft. 4in. above the sill of the Black Sluice, or average low water in Clayhole, and 24·9ft. above the sill of the dock.

The water ebbs out at Clayhole 7ft. 6in. lower at spring tides than at neaps. Owing to the fact that the water is still ebbing out at Clayhole when flood has set in along the channel at the lower part of the Deeps the water ebbs out about 6in. lower at Clayhole than off Wrangle.

The tides are generally influenced by the wind. A strong north-west wind, by driving the water out of the Atlantic and down the coast of England, raises the tidal wave in the German Ocean and consequently in Boston Deeps. A continuance of N.W. gales, by influencing succeeding tidal waves, still further increases this effect. If a sudden change to the east, after strong N.W. gales, occurs, at the time of flood in the Deeps, this action is still further increased. A S.W. wind retards the motion of the tidal current, and prevents the tides from rising to their full height; also by driving the water out of the Deeps, a S.W. wind causes the lowest ebbs. N.E. and S.E. winds affect the tides in the same way, only to a much less extent, the N.E. winds raising, and the S.E. winds depressing, the tidal rise. A brisk N.W. gale will generally raise, and the S.W. gales lower, a spring tide about 2ft., and the other tides in proportion, or as many inches higher as an ordinary tide would rise in feet.

About one-fourth of the tides in the year vary 6in., and more, from the predicted height owing to the wind. During the two years, 1892-93, there were 30 tides which varied 2ft.; 7 tides, 3ft.; 6 tides, 3½ft.; 3 tides, 4ft.; 2 tides, 4½ft.; 1 tide, 5ft., and 1 tide, 6ft. 3in.

In November, 1893, during a gale from S.E. to N.E., the morning tide of the 17th was 2ft. 3in. below the expected height, and that of the following morning 5ft. 1in. above, making a difference in the height of the two tides of 7ft. 4in. The morning tide of the 19th was 4ft. 2in. above the expected height.

In November, 1894, during a gale from the S W., the evening tide of the 13th was 1ft. 2in. below the expected height, and the morning tide of the 14th, 3ft. 5in. below.

In January, 1895, during a gale from the N.W., the evening tide was 1¼ hour before time, and 6ft. 3in. above the expected height, the tide next morning being 1ft. 8in. lower than the height given in the table, a difference in the two tides of 7ft. 11in.

In May, 1895 during a N.W. gale on the 15th, the tide rose 3ft. 9in. above the expected height.

The highest tide recorded as affecting Boston was on March 2, 1820. This was 4in. higher than the great tide of November, 1810, which, by overflowing the sea banks, did such immense damage in this district. A record of the latter tide is preserved by a mark cut on the tower of the Parish Church. The mark is 26ft. 7in. above the sill of the Black Sluice.

High Tides.—The following table gives all the tides above 25ft. on the sill of the Black Sluice, of which there is any record:

APPENDIX V.

	Feet	Inches		Feet	Inches
1791 Oct. 19	25	9	1808 Feb. 8	25	5
1793 Oct.	25	9	1874 March 20	25	1
1801 Oct. 19	26	1	1874 Oct. 26	25	3
1807 Nov. 30	26	4	1877 Jan. 20	25	9
1810 Nov. 10	26	7	1877 Oct. 8	25	6
1820 March 2	26	11	1882 Feb. 19	25	2
1836 Feb.	26	1	1882 Sep. 29	25	1
1850 Jan.	25	7	1882 Oct. 28	25	8
1853 Feb.	25	9	1883 March 11	26	3
1854 Feb.	25	11	1890 Sep. 30	25	9
1859 Feb.	25	1			

There is not much difference in the height of the tides at different periods of the year. The tides nearest to the equinoxes, March 21st and September 21st, are generally the highest, especially if new or full moon should be coincident with these. A continuation of spring equinoctial tides with north-west gales is sure to make very high tides. Taking a period of five years, the average of all the highest tides at Boston occurred in August and September, and the lowest in January and December, but the difference is only 1ft. 2in. The average highest spring tides were in March and September, and the lowest in June and December, the difference being 1ft. 9in. The average highest neaps occurred in June and July, and the lowest in March and January, the difference in height being 2ft. 1in.

Of the extreme high tides during the present century, out of twenty-two of which a record has been kept, 6 occurred in October, 7 in February, 3 in March, and 2 each in September, November and January.

APPENDIX VI.

TABLE OF LEVELS.

Datum taken as 100ft. below *Ordnance datum*, or the mean level of the sea at Liverpool.

Estuary.   Feet.

		Feet.
Low water.	Spring Tides..	90·10
,,	Neap Tides ..	97·53
High water	Mean ..	110·22
,,	Ordinary Spring Tides	113·34
,,	Tide of 1810..	117·93
,,	Neap Tides ..	106·66

Sea Banks. Boston Haven.

	Feet.
Height of top, as ordered by Court of Sewers	119·93
Boston Dock Sill	88·55

River Welland.

	Feet.
Gauge at Fossdyke Bridge..	100·00

River Witham.

	Feet.
Grand Sluice Sill	96·80
,, New Lock	93·80
Bardney Lock	95·80
Bargate Weir..	121·05
Witham Banks as raised under the Act of 1864..	117·80
Bed of River at Lincoln	95·80
Surface of the Land—Bardney to Boston—average	107·30
,, ,, lowest in Nocton Fen and Potterhanworth Fen	106·10
,, ,, Lincoln, at Brayford Mere	118·80
,, ,, Lincoln, at Stamp End	119·60
,, ,, Washingboro' Fens	109·80
,, ,, Branston and Nocton Fens	106·80
,, ,, Metheringham and Timberland	105·80
,, ,, Lands above Chapel Hill	106·80

East and West Fens

	Feet.
Hobhole Sluice Sill ..	91·70
Hobhole New Sill	88·70
Maud Foster Sluice Sill	95·30
Surface of Land in West Fen	103·80 / 108·50
Surface of Land in East Fen	93·80 / 105·30

Black Sluice District.

	Feet.
Black Sluice Sill	91·30
Bourne Eau Overfall	114·31
Surface of Fens between Helpringham and Rippingale	106·55 / 108·30
Bourne North Fen	105·60 / 108·80
Bourne South Fen	107·59 / 113·26

APPENDIX VI.

Court of Sewers' District.   Feet.
- Risegate Eau, new Outfall Sill in River Welland   99·23
- Five Towns Drain Sill   99·38
- Kirton Outfall Sluice Sill   104·80
- Holbeach Outfall Sluice Sill   102·75
- Moulton Outfall Sluice Sill   106·72
- Surface of Land, Skirbeck Hundred   } 108·00 / 110·00
- Surface of Land, Kirton Hundred   } 110·50 / 112·00
- Surface of Land, South Holland, North of Roman Bank   112·50
- Surface of Land, South Holland, South of Roman Bank   108·50

Deeping Fen.
- Vernatt's Drain, Sill of Welland Sluice   99·20
- Pode Hole Sluice Sill   102·50
- Height of water when engines have to stop pumping   112·36
- Glen Sluice Sill at Welland (1879)   99·75
- Surface of Land in Fen. Low Fen   104·80
-      Average   106·00
-      High Fen   108·40

ORDNANCE BENCH MARKS.

	Above the surface of the ground. Feet.	Feet.
Boston Church tower	2·78	119·74
Skirbeck ,,	2·42	116·93
Fishtoft ,,	4·16	122·29
Freiston ,,	—	118·46
Freiston, Marine Hotel	2·28	113·24
Butterwick Church tower	—	114·80
Benington ,,	—	115·52
Wrangle ,,	—	115·34
Friskney ,,	3·27	115·85
Wainfleet ,,	1·57	117·06
Skegness ,,	3·43	111·38
Sutterton ,,	2·72	116·28
Algarkirk ,,	2·82	115·83
Wigtoft ,,	2·45	116·26
Swineshead ,,	2·78	121·50
Swineshead Bridge	3·85	115·56
Fossdyke Church Tower	1·65	115·53
Baker's Bridge	1·42	114·58
Cut Bridge, mark below surface	2·50	115·57
Holbeach Church Tower	3·14	118·55
Fleet ,,	2·94	118·13
Gedney ,,	4·23	120·89
Sutton St. Mary ,,	2·23	116·34
Sutton Bridge ,,	2·16	116·73
Lincoln Minster—West Front	2·01	317·71

APPENDIX VII.

BORINGS.

BOSTON. IN THE MARKET PLACE FOR WATER, IN 1746.

	Below surface.
	ft. in.
Made soil, sand and gravel	11 0
Clay	5 0
Stones, rubble and chalk	3 0
Clay with small hard stones	173 0
Clay and silt	283 0
	475 0

FOR WELL AT BOSTON. MESSRS. TUXFORD & CO., 1828.

	Below surface.
	ft. in.
Made soil and silt	24 0
Hard earth and stones	12 0
Clay with stones	4 0
Clay with stones and shells	532 0
	572 0

BOSTON DOCK. W. H. WHEELER, C.E., 1881. ON THE MARSH AT SIDE OF THE RIVER.

	100ft. below *Ordnance datum.*
Surface of land	110·86
Soft blue clay	106·86
Soft brown clay	104·86
Blue clay	99·86
Clay with peat	95·86
Clay and shells	92·86
Sand and peat	91·86
Boulder clay	90·36

BORING NEAR THE HAVEN IN BOSTON.

Level of surface	110·50
Clay and shells	102·50
Soft brown clay	101·50
Peat with trees	88·50
Yellow sand	87·50
Boulder clay	82·50

The average depth of 10 borings gave the Boulder clay at 88·99, and of 4 borings, the peat at 91·55. During the excavations a layer of black clay with cockle shells was found at 98·86, and in one place at 85·30 a large quantity of Septaria, some 1ft. in diameter, embedded in black clay.

APPENDIX VII.

NEAR THE GRAND SLUICE, BOSTON, 1882.

Surface	110·80
Soft buttery clay	
Peat	89·80
Sand	88·80
Boulder clay	84·80
Boring continued in Boulder clay to	69·80

WITHAM OUTFALL. W. H. WHEELER, 1880.

CLAY HOLE, NEAR MOUTH OF NEW CUT.

Surface	106·50
Silt	
Brown clay	97·60
Blue clay	94·50
Peat	91·50
Sand	90·50
Boulder clay	90·00

UPPER END OF CUT.

Surface	109·72
Silt	
Soft sandy clay	103·72
Peat	96·72
Soft clay	95·72
Stiff clay	94·72
Red sand	93·22
Boulder clay	92·72

At another boring in Clay Hole, the boulder clay was at the level of 81·00, and the peat at 83·00.

LADE BANK. FOR EAST FEN DRAINAGE ENGINES, 1867.

	ft.	in.
Warp and clay	4	0
Peat	0	6
Soft blue clay	3	0
Peat	0	6
Hard clay with chalk stones (Boulder clay) bored to	30	0

SOUTHREY. (RIVER WITHAM), 1868.

	ft.	in.
Peat	1	0
Warp	10	6

Below this, hard blue clay with Ammonites, Belemnites and pieces of Selenite.

DONINGTON. BORING FOR WATER AT THE VICARAGE, 1887.

	ft.	in.
Top soil and silt	25	0
Gravel	0	6
Clay with chalk stones (Boulder clay ?)	154	6
Blue rock	4	0
Clay	4	0
Rock	11	0
Clay	13	0
Rock	16	0
Clay with fetid vegetable matter (Bear's muck)	35	0
	263	0

APPENDIX VII.

BOURNE. FOR SPALDING WATERWORKS, 1893. MESSRS. ISLER & CO.

	ft. in.	ft. in.
Fen beds—		
Surface soil	3 6	
Gravel	1 0	
Clay	3 0	
Rock and shells	2 0	
		9 6
Limestone		4 0
Great Oolite—		
Blue and shelly clay	16 6	
Hard blue rock	4 0	
Blue clay	2 0	
Limestone	11 0	
Very hard rock	1 0	
Green clay	7 0	
Blue rock	1 0	
Clay	9 0	
Rock with Chalybeate water	0 10	
Green and sandy clay	9 4	
Black clay and peat	0 6	
		76 0
Grey porous rock		1 6
Hard Oolite limestone (Lincolnshire Oolite)		56 6

At 65ft. 10in. a spring of Chalybeate water was met with. At a depth of 100ft. the yield of water was 1,300 gallons a minute, at 134ft. 3,473 gallons. The pipes were 13in. in diameter, and the pressue of the water 10lbs. on the square inch.

SKEGNESS FOR WATER.

	ft. in.
Surface soil	3 6
Loamy clay	2 0
Black-brown mud	27 0
Brown clay with stones	2 3
Gravel	1 3
Brown clay	8 6
Sand and gravel	6 6
Rock chalk with salt water	10 0
Rock chalk, dry	11 0
Dry red marl	20 0
Green sand	8 6
Loamy green sand	1 6
Light clay	6 6
Blue clay	8 6
Sand stone	13 6
	130 6

Bottom Clay. Yield of water through two pipes, 6in. in diameter, about 60 gallons a minute and overflow about 1ft. above the surface. The water rises from the lower portion of the upper Green sand.

WOODHALL, 1828.

	ft. in.
Gravel and Boulder clay	10 0
Kimmeridge and Oxford clay	350 0
Kelloway rocks, blue clay, combrash, &c.	140 0
Great Oolite	
Lincolnshire Oolite	380 0

Appendix VII.

Lincoln. Sewerage Works. Opposite St. Mary's Church.

	ft.	in.
Surface of road	0	9
Made soil	4	0
Concreted stones (supposed Roman road)	2	0
Mud and sand	6	0

Lincoln. Opposite Mr. Walker's Shop.

	ft.	in.
Surface of road		
Rough, stony made soil	3	0
Stones, laid inclining	0	6
Sandy clay	0	0
Silt	1	0
Soft muddy soil	2	6
Sand	17	0
Blue lias		

Lincoln. Near St. Botolph's Church.

	ft.	in.
Surface of road	1	3
Made soil	1	3
Concreted stones (Roman Road)	0	8
Rough made soil	1	3
Ashes, &c.	0	3
Peaty mud	0	9
Red sand	8	0
Blue lias clay		

Near the Midland Railway the stones forming the old Roman Road were met with, covered over with about 5ft. of made ground.

APPENDIX VIII.

Court of Sewers.

Sewers and Sea Banks

Abstract of the Verdict of the Jury of 1862.

The following is a list of the sewers and sea banks contained in the Verdict of the Jury of 1862. The position of the sewers and the names of the Owners fronting the same is given with much detail in the Verdict; and reference is also made to certain letters and numbers on the plans of the several parishes.

In the following list the description is made as short as possible, and only sufficient to indicate the general position of the several sewers.

The sea banks in all the parishes are directed to be maintained 2ft. above the level of the high water mark of the great tide of the 10th of November, 1810. This makes the top 6·59ft. above the level of high water of an ordinary spring tide, or 19·93 above *Ordnance datum*. After the great tide of 1810 the banks were raised and level stones placed at the foot of the bank in each parish, the height of the top of the bank being marked on them, and this height is also given in the Verdict.

Boston East.

Sewers maintained by the Dykereeves.

1. A brick sewer from the Frith Bank road, near the crossing of the East Lincolnshire Railway and running at the back of Witham Green and Norfolk Place, along the Sluice Lane to Maud Foster Drain. The diameter of the culvert is not given.

2. A brick sewer, 18in. in diameter, from the north side of Fowler's Row and joining the sewer in Sluice Lane.

3. A brick sewer (dimensions not given) from the 'Deal Yard Gateway,' near the back of the premises of the Wesleyan Chapel and running to the sewer in Sluice Lane. The part at the back of the Wesleyan Chapel premises has to be repaired by the Chapel Trustees.

4. A brick sewer, 2ft. in diameter, from the north end of Silver Street, under Bargate Green to Maud Foster Drain, on the south side of Bargate Bridge.

5. A brick sewer, 18in. in diameter, from the north side of Bargate, across the Green, to No. 4.

6. A brick sewer, 18in. in diameter, from the north-end of Corpus Christi Lane to No. 4.

7. A brick sewer, 18in in diameter, running from Trundle Gowt, at the north east end of Wide Bargate, to sewer No. 4.

There are 11 public tunnels which have to be maintained by the Dykereeves.

The Gowts under the charge of the Dykereeves are:—

Dipple Gowt	.. ..	4ft. 8in. waterway.
St. John's Gowt..	.. ..	4ft. 8in. ,,
Trundle Gowt ..	.. ..	3ft. 9in. ,,

Appendix VIII.

The sea bank was *presented* to be 2ft. above the stone, and as being divided into 45 sections, repairable by the Owners of various plots of land. As a great portion of the bank has been superseded by the dock works and as otherparts form public streets, the liability of these Owners is of little effect now.

The area of land in this parish liable to the Dykereeve rate is 526 acres.

Sewers maintained by Frontagers.

1. From tunnel in North Gowt Lane to Maud Foster Drain at Trundle Gowt, at the junction of Horncastle Road, with the north-west end of Bargate, passing along Hob Lane, Horncastle Road, High Hills, Robin Hood's Walk and Sluice Lane (Norfolk Street) At the upper end to be 7ft. at the top, 2ft. at the bottom and 4ft. deep; increasing to 9ft. top, 2ft. 6in. bottom, and 5ft. deep, the lower part being of brick work, the dimensions of which are not given.

2. The Bar Ditch, from St. John's Gowt to Dipple Gowt in the River Witham near the Grand Sluice, passing at the back of the Grammar School, the Town Hall and the Peacock Hotel, under the Corn Exchange and the Red Lion Hotel Yard, and crossing New Street, Red Lion Street and Chapel Street to Union Street, and thence to the river. Where this sewer crosses any public road, it is repairable by the Dykereeves. The whole of this sewer is now covered over, its minimum dimensions being 4ft. 4in.

3. A brick sewer, 18in. in diameter, from a grate near Tully's Court in Wormgate to Dipple Gowt.

4. A brick sewer, 18in. in diameter, from Wormgate, under Fountain Lane, to the Bar Ditch in New Street.

5. A brick sewer, 18in. in diameter, running from the Churchyard, at the south end of Wormgate, in a westerly direction to the Haven.

6. A brick sewer, 18in. in diameter, from the Churchyard, near the west end of the church, in a westerly direction to the Haven

7. A brick sewer, 18in. in diameter, in the Churchyard, from the north end of Church Street and running in a westerly direction to the Haven.

8. A brick sewer, 18in. in diameter, from the east side of Church Street and running to the Haven.

9. A brick sewer, 18in. in diameter, from the south-east side of the Market Place, running in an easterly direction to the Bar Ditch.

10. A brick sewer, 3ft. in diameter, from the north-east corner of Pump Square, passing down Main Ridge, Chapel Row and across the end of Caroline Court to Maud Foster Drain.

11. A sewer from the south-east corner of St. John's Churchyard to St. John's Lane, and thence at the back of the Union Workhouse and the Dock Grain Warehouse to Maud Foster. At the time of the Verdict this was an open sewer, but it has since been converted into a brick sewer.

SKIRBECK.

Sewers maintained by the Dykereeves.

1. From Green Lane (highway from Frith Bank Road to Maud Foster Drain) and to the Frith Bank Drain, 2ft. bottom and 4ft. deep.

2. From Felland's Gate, in the Cemetery Lane, to the Sewer in Green Lane, 1½ft. bottom, 3ft. 6in. deep.

3. From Burton Corner, running on the west side of the Main Road to the Junction Drain, bottom 2ft. to 3ft. wide, depth 4ft. to 5½ft.

4. From the south side of the Spilsby Road, near Toll Wise Lane, along the west side of that lane, 2ft. bottom, 4ft. deep.

5. From the west end of Freiston Low Road along the north side of that road to the sewer which crosses that road, 2ft. bottom, 4½ft. deep.

Appendix VIII.

6. From the road leading to Fishtoft to the lane at King's Hill Pit, 2ft. bottom, 4½ft. deep.

7. From the pits near the sea bank on the Fishtoft Road.

8. From Mount Bridge, along the Church Road to Maud Foster Drain, 2½ft. bottom, 4½ft. deep. The latter part of this sewer is repaired by the Frontagers.

There are 24 public tunnels which have to be repaired by the Dykereeves.

The clow near Petter's Cross Bridge (now Bargate Bridge) and the tunnel extending from Maud Foster Drain is to be maintained by the Dykereeves, except that portion of the tunnel which passes under private lands, and there by the Frontagers.

The following culverts are also to be maintained by the Dykereeves, that at Frith Bank Drain, 3ft. in diameter; at the Junction Drain, 3ft. in diameter; at Maud Foster Drain 15in., in diameter; and one on the east side of the Drain, 2½ft. in diameter.

The sea bank is to be mantained 5ft. above the level stone. From Miller's Stile at the junction with Boston Parish to Ringle Hurn in Fishtoft it is repairable by the Frontagers, except that part fronting the Churchyard, the piece called the Church Bank and the piece between the Corporation Marsh and Fishtoft, all of which were to be maintained by the Dykereeves.

The area of land in this Parish subject to the Dykereeve rate is 2,423 acres.

Sewers maintained by Frontagers.

1. From High Hills on the Frith Bank Road, near Robin Hood's Walk, running along the Frith Bank Road to its junction with the Green Lane leading to Maud Foster Drain, 2ft. bottom, 4ft. deep.

2. From Robin Hood's Walk to the sewer in Felland's Gote, in Cemetery Lane, 1¼ft. bottom, 3ft. 6in. deep.

3. From the Main Road from Boston to Spilsby to Maud Foster Drain, 1½ft. bottom, 4ft. 6in. deep.

4. From Hospital Lane to Maud Foster Drain, 2ft. bottom, 4ft. 6in. deep.

5. From the south side of the Spilsby Road, nearly opposite Hospital Lane, to Maud Foster at Bargate Bridge, 2ft. bottom, 4ft. 6in. deep. This sewer is now a brick culvert

6. From Piper's Pit, near the river bank, between Corporation Point and Toft Jetty, running east and then northwards to Cragg's Lane, along this lane, crossing the Fishtoft Road and East Field Lane, Toothill Lane, Freiston Low Road to the end of Toothill Lane, and thence in a westerly direction to Maud Foster Drain at Bargate Bridge. The first part to have 2ft. 6in. bottom, and be 4ft. 6in. deep, and the latter part 5ft. 6in. deep.

7. From the boundary of the Parish of Fishtoft, on the north side of the Highway leading from Skirbeck, and to the sewer No. 6 at Cock Pit Hill, 2ft. 6in. bottom, 4ft. 6in. deep.

8. From King's Hill Pit at the junction of Toothill Lane and East Field Lane, along the last named lane and Toll Field Lane and thence westerly to Maud Foster Drain at Bargate Bridge, 2½ft. bottom, 4½ft. deep.

9 From Toothill Lane to No. 7 Sewer, 2½ft. bottom, 4½ft. deep.

FISHTOFT.

Sewers maintained by the Dykereeves.

1. The Graft Drain, commencing at Short Field Lane, and ending at the Gowt, in the river bank at Scotia Creek, 3½ft. to 4ft. bottom, 5ft. to 7ft. deep.

2. From Kyme Tower Lane, running easterly and then southerly and easterly again, to the Graft Drain, 2ft. bottom, 5ft. deep.

APPENDIX VIII.

3. From the north side of the road leading from the church to England Gate near Burnt Mill Hill, to the Graft, 1ft. bottom, 3½ft. deep.

4. From the east side of the road, running from the church to the Hawthorn Tree in a south-easterly direction to the Graft. The first part of this sewer is to be maintained by the Frontagers, 2½ft. bottom, 5ft. deep.

5. From Lettice Lane, running to the Graft, 2½ft. bottom and 5ft. deep. Part of this sewer is to be maintained by the Frontagers.

6. From the tunnel through the road leading to Lunn's Bridge to the Graft, 1½ft. bottom, 4ft. deep.

7. From the south-east corner of the School Five Acres to a sewer, against lands belonging to the Heirs of Edward Brown, 2ft. bottom, 4½ft. deep. Part of this is maintained by the Frontagers.

8. From the tunnel through the road, leading from the church to Hobhole Bank, to the sewer near Launderthorpe Hall, 2ft. bottom, 4ft. deep. Part of this is maintained by the Frontagers.

9. From the west bank of Hobhole Drain against lands called the Thoroughfare, to the tunnel through the road in South Field, 1ft. bottom, 3½ft. deep.

10. From the south-west corner of the Thoroughfare, and to the Graft, 1½ft. bottom, 4ft. deep.

11.—From the tunnel through the road, leading from the sea bank to Hobhole Drain, to Mill Field, and ending at the sewer against lands of Edward Brown, 2ft. to 3ft. bottom, 5½ft. deep. Part of this sewer is to be maintained by the parish.

12. From the north-east corner of Graft Field, to a sewer at the 30 acre close of Edward Brown, in the Sea Grounds, 2½ft. bottom 4½ft. deep.

13. From the south-west corner of lands in the Gayst Field, to a sewer against the road leading to the Rosdyke, 1½ft. bottom, 4ft. deep.

14. From the tunnel through Mill Field Lane, to the sewer having the road leading to Mill Field on the east, 1½ft. bottom, 4ft. deep.

15. From the south-west corner of lands belonging to Creasey's Heirs, to a tunnel near lands belonging to the Corporation of Boston, 1½ft. bottom, 4ft. deep.

There are 36 tunnels and the clough of the Graft Drain to be maintained by the Dykereeves, the latter having a 4ft. waterway. This is now closed and the drainage diverted to Hobhole.

All the sea banks in the parish have to be maintained by the Dykereeves. The height of the top is required to be 7ft. 9in. above the level stone.

The area of land in this parish subject to the Dykereeve Rate is 2,150 acres.

Sewers maintained by Frontagers.

1. From the south bank of the Junction Drain to the Graft Drain, 2½ft. bottom 4½ft. deep.

2. From Hen Meat Lane, on the south side of the Wainfleet Road, to the Graft Drain, 2ft. bottom, 4ft. deep.

3. From the east side of the road leading from the church to the Hawthorn Tree and running in a north-easterly direction across the Wainfleet Road to the sewer from Kyme Tower Lane, 2½ft. bottom, 4½ft. deep.

4. From the road, leading from the church to England Gate, to the Graft, 1ft. bottom, 4ft. deep.

5. From the same road to the Graft, 2½ft. bottom, 4ft. deep.

6. From the south side of lands belonging to Nicholas North, to the Graft, 2ft. bottom, 4½ft. deep.

7. From the tunnel through the road leading from the church to Lunn's Bridge, and ending at a sewer against lands of Six Poor Widows' of Boston, 2ft. bottom, 5½ft. deep.

8. From the west bank of Hobhole Drain to the south-east end of lands belonging to Sleaford School, called Bendlam, to the Graft, 3ft. bottom, 4ft. deep.

9. From the tunnel, leading from the church to the sea bank, to the Graft, 2ft. bottom, 5½ft. deep.

10. From the west side of the Thoroughfare to the Graft, against the lands of the Six Poor Widows, 2ft. bottom, 4½ft. deep.

11. From the west bank of Hobhole near the sea bank, to the Gowt, 3ft. bottom 5½ft. deep.

12. From north-west corner of lands belonging to the Dean and Chapter of Westminster, to the culvert through the east bank of Hobhole Drain, 3½ft. bottom, 5½ft. deep.

13. From the sea bank to lands of the Heirs of Edward Brown, 2½ft. bottom, 4½ft. deep.

14. From the east end of Back Hurn to a sewer against lands in Freiston, 2½ft. bottom, 4ft. deep.

Sewers maintained by the Witham Commissioners.

1. A sewer at the south-west corner of lands belonging to S. H. Jebb, and ending at a sewer against lands in Mill Field, 18in bottom, 4½ft. deep.

2. A sewer commencing at the north-west corner of Creasey's Seven Acres, adjoining the east side of Hobhole Drain and ending at the culvert through the east bank of Hobhole Drain, 2ft. bottom, 5ft. deep.

FISHTOFT HUNDRED.

Sewers maintained by the Dykereeves.

1. From lands of John Williamson's heirs, to the south-west bank of the Junction Drain, against Willoughby Hills Road, 1½ft. bottom, 4½ft. deep.

2. From the east side of lands belonging to Burnett, to a sewer on the west side of Willoughby Hills Road, 1½ft. bottom, 4ft. deep.

3. From the south-west corner of lands belonging to the Dean and Chapter of Westminster, to a tunnel called Pis Gowt, 1½ft. bottom, 4½ft. deep.

4. From the tunnel through the west end of Ing Dike Bank, to the tunnel through the south bank of New Dyke Drain, 1ft. bottom, 3½ft. deep.

5. Dyke Drain, commencing at the tunnel, at the west corner of lands belonging to Bellamy's heirs, and ending at the drain on the west side of Hill Dyke Bank, 5ft. bottom, 6ft. deep.

There are eight tunnels which have to be maintained by the Dykereeves, including the New Dyke through the main road leading to Spilsby, with 3½ft. waterway.

The area of land in this Hundred which is subject to the Dykereeve rate is 951 acres.

FREISTON.

Sewers maintained by the Dykereeves.

1. The Graft, beginning at the side of the Old Gowt, through the Sea Bank, and ending at the east side of Hobhole, in Meerholm, 4ft. bottom, 5½ft. to 6½ft. deep.

2. The Graft, branching out of No. 1, and ending at the east bank of Hobhole Drain, 3½ft. bottom, and 7ft. deep.

3. From the road called Salter's Gate to Hobhole Drain, 2½ft. bottom, 5ft. deep. Part of this is maintained by the Frontagers.

Appendix VIII.

4. From the tunnel through Swine Stye Road to Hobhole Drain, 2ft. bottom and 4ft. deep.

5. From the north-west corner of lands of John Crust, on the south side of Salter's Gate to Hobhole Drain, 2ft. bottom, 4ft. deep.

6. From lands of Thomas Plant on the Wainfleet Road to a sewer on lands of Thorold, 1½ft. to 2ft. bottom, 4½ft. deep.

7. From the east bank of Hobhole Drain to the Graft, against the tunnel at Wyson Meer, 1½ft. to 2ft. bottom, 5ft. deep.

8. From Crane Hill to lands of John Hayes, 1ft. bottom, 3½ft. deep.

9. From lands belonging to Thomas Hopkins' Heirs, to the New Road at Crane Hill, 1ft. bottom, 3½ft. deep.

10. From Grove Field to the tunnel through the road at the south-end of the same field, 1½ft. bottom, 4ft. deep.

11. From a sewer in the parish of Butterwick South, near Tamworth Green, to the Graft, 2½ft. to 3ft. bottom, 5ft. deep. The first part of this sewer in maintainable by the Frontagers.

12. From Twenty Acres in North Honey Toft to the tunnel through the road near the Silver Pits and Scrane End Mill, 2½ft. bottom, 5ft. deep.

13. From the Occupation Road in West Field to a Sewer near the Graft, 1ft. bottom, 3½ft. deep.

14. From Rustick to the Graft, crossing the road leading from the Scrane End to a farm belonging to John Sharp, 2ft. bottom, 5ft. deep.

15. From the west-end of Green Dyke Bank to the Graft, 2ft. bottom, 5ft. deep.

16. From the tunnel through the road leading from Scrane End Mill, to the tunnel through the road leading to Barney Gate, 1ft. bottom, 3½ft. deep.

There are 42 public tunnels maintainable by the Dykereeves, and five culverts through Hobhole Bank.

The Verdict states that the sea bank extending from Fishtoft to Butterwick Hundred is to be maintained at the expense of the Owners whose names are given in the same, and that boundary posts shall be set down marking each lot, the proportion being 5½ft. of bank for every acre of land. Since this Verdict an order has been made by the Court of Sewers that the bank shall be repaired by the Dykereeves and the cost paid out of the rate. The top of the bank is to be 9ft. 11in. above the stone posts.

The area of land in this parish subject to the Dykereeve rate is 2,131 acres.

Sewers maintained by Frontagers.

1. From near the Castle Inn at Haltoft End to Hobhole Drain, 1½ft. bottom, 3½ft. deep.

2. From the tunnel in Fox Hole Lane, to the tunnel through the road, leading from Haltoft End to the church, 1½ft. bottom, 4½ft. deep.

3. From the tunnel through the road leading from Haltoft End to the church, and ending at the Graft, 2ft. to 2½ft. bottom, 3½ft. deep.

4. From the tunnel through the road leading from the church to Scrane End Mill, to the Graft in the Fleet, 3ft. bottom, 5ft. deep.

5. From the south-west corner of lands belonging to John Buffham, on the south side of the occupation road to the Graft, 1ft. bottom, 3½ft. deep.

6. From the south-east end of a ditch on lands of Col. Linton to the Graft, passing along the east side of a road leading from the church to the Scrane End, 2½ft. bottom 5ft. deep.

7. From a sewer in the parish of Butterwick, at a place called Lady Coats, to the tunnel through the road leading to the church at Scrane End Mill, 2½ft. bottom and 4½ft. deep.

8. From Mackling to the Graft, 2½ft. bottom, 4½ft. deep.

9. From Weddersdam to the Graft, 2½ft. bottom, 4½ft. deep

10. From the north-east corner of lands belonging to Sylvester Tylson, to the Graft, 18in. to 3ft. bottom, 5ft. deep.

11. From the south-east corner of the house pasture of Plummer's Hotel, to the site of the Old Gowt in the sea bank, 3ft. bottom, 4ft. deep.

12. From east side of Brown's Lane to the Graft, into Brampton Lane, 1½ft. bottom, 3½ft. deep.

BUTTERWICK NORTH.

Sewers maintained by the Dykereeves.

1. The Graft Drain, from a tunnel through the highway leading from Spittal Hill to the church, to the Ings Drain, 3ft. to 3½ft. bottom, 6½ft. deep.

Sewers maintained by Frontagers.

1. From a tunnel, under the Low Road from Boston to Wainfleet, to the Main Drain, 2½ft. bottom, 5ft. deep.

2. From the north-west corner of lands belonging to Jonathan Johnson, to the tunnel through the road leading to Butterwick Hills, 1ft. to 2½ft. bottom, 5ft. deep. Part of this sewer is maintainable by the Frontagers.

3. From Butterwick Hills Road to the Graft, 18in. to 2½ft. bottom, 5ft. deep.

Sewers maintained by Frontagers.

1. From the tunnel under the Low Road from Boston to Wainfleet, to the Main Drain, 2½ft. bottom, 5ft. deep.

2. From the road at Poison Hills to the Graft, 2½ft. bottom, 5ft. deep.

3. From the Ings Bank to the last sewer, 2½ft. bottom, 5ft. deep.

Nine tunnels are to be maintained by the Dykereeves in Butterwick North.

Area of land subject to Dykereeve Rate, 783 acres.

BUTTERWICK SOUTH.

Sewers maintained by the Dykereeves.

1. The Graft Drain, from the tunnel through the lane leading from the church to the sea, at the sea bank, to the tunnel through the road from Spittal Hill to the church, 3ft. bottom, 6ft. deep.

2. From Benington Doors to the Graft, 1ft. to 2ft. bottom, 4ft½. deep.

3. From the west corner of lands belonging to Rev. E. S. Brooks, to the tunnel through the low road from Boston to Wainfleet, 18in. bottom, 4ft. deep.

4. From a tunnel through the Rampart near the pound, to the Graft, 2½ft. to 3ft. bottom, 5ft. deep. Part of this sewer is maintainable by the Frontagers.

5. From the end of Cole Gate Road to the road leading from Freiston church to the Scrane End, 2½ft. to 3ft. bottom, 7ft. deep. Part of this is maintainable by the frontagers.

6. From the tunnel through Coney Garth Lane to the west end of Wolves' Acre, 2½ft. bottom, 4½ft. deep.

Appendix VIII.

7. From the north side of lands belonging to Benjamin West Smith to the Main Drain, 18in. bottom, 3½ft. deep.

8. From the south-west corner of lands belonging to the poor of Freiston to a sewer in Freiston, at Tamworth Green, 1½ft. to 2ft. bottom, 4ft. deep.

9. From the west side of Butterwick Holt to a tunnel through the road leading from Freiston church to Butterwick school, 1½ft. to 2½ft. bottom, 4ft. deep.

10. From the south-west corner of lands belonging to Thomas Parnham to the tunnel through the land leading from the church to the sea bank, 2½ft. bottom, 4½ft. deep.

11. From Butterwick Holt to the boundary between Freiston and Butterwick, 1½ft. bottom, 3½ft. deep.

12. From the south-east corner of lands belonging to Joseph Day, to the sewer on the north-west side of sea bank, 1½ft. to 2ft. bottom, 4½ft. deep.

13. From the south-east corner of Lady Coates to a sewer at the north-east corner of Lady Coates, 2ft. bottom, 4ft. deep.

Sewers maintained by Frontagers.

1. From the tunnel through the Overgote, at the north side of the *Anchor* Inn. to the parish of Benington, 3ft. bottom, 5ft. deep.

2. From Benington Doors to the Graft, 1½ft. bottom, 5ft. deep.

3. From a road leading from Spittal Hill to the church to the Graft, 2ft. bottom, 4ft. deep.

4. From the north-west corner of lands belonging to Stephen Hudson, to the tunnel through the Gorril Dale Road, 1½ft. bottom, 3½ft. deep.

5. From Gorril Dale to the sewer on the south side of Coney Garth Road, 1½ft. to 2ft. bottom, 3½ft. deep.

6. From the north-east corner of Polar to a sewer in Gorril Dale, 1½ft. bottom, 3½ft. deep.

7. From the north-west corner of lands of John Buffham, to the sewer at Far Side Dale, 1½ft. bottom, 3½ft. deep.

8. From the road at Swaybutt Hill to the north-west corner of lands of Thomas Mitchell, 1½ft. bottom, 3½ft. deep.

9. From Moss Dale to the sewer on the north-west side of the sea bank, 2ft. bottom, 5ft. deep.

10. From the tunnel through the south end of Hasty Gate to the tunnel through the road leading from the church to the sea, 1½ft. to 2ft. bottom, 4ft. deep.

11. From Colegate Road to the tunnel through Broadgate Road, 1½ft. bottom, 3½ft. deep.

12. From the road from Peachey Hall to the Tuns at the shore, to the sewer on the north-west side of the sea bank, 2½ft. wide, 4½ft. deep.

13. From Barney Gate Road to a sewer at Long New Dyke, 1½ft. bottom, 3½ft. deep.

14. From the road leading from Peachey Hall to the Tuns at the shore, to the sewer in the Furlongs, 1½ft. bottom, 4½ft. deep.

15. From the south-west of lands of Benjamin West Smith to the sewer in the parish of Freiston, 1½ft. to 2ft. bottom, 4ft. deep.

There are 36 Tunnels maintainable by the Dykereeves.

The sea bank is maintainable by the Dykereeves for Butterwick, North and South, and Butterwick Hundred, extending from the Blue Stone in the sea bank of Freiston,

APPENDIX VIII.

to the south-west end of the sea bank in Benington. The top to be 9ft. 1in. above the level stone.

The Dykereeves also have to repair the gowt through the sea bank in Butterwick Hundred, having a 3½ft. waterway, and the Outfall thereof to the sea.

The area of land subject to the Dykereeve Rate is 1480 acres.

BENINGTON.
Sewers maintained by the Dykereeves.

1. From Cockwook, near the Old Sea Bank, to the tunnel through the highway leading from the church to the Ings, 3ft. bottom, 5ft. deep.

2. From north corner of lands belonging to the Rector of Horbling to the tunnel through Sea Bank Lane, 2ft. bottom, 4ft. deep.

3. From the east side of Wrangle 20 Acre Close to the sewer adjoining the parish of Leverton, 1½ft. bottom, 5ft. deep.

4. From the highway leading from Black's House to the sea, ending at lands belonging to Daniel Waldegrave, 2ft. to 3ft. bottom, 5ft. deep.

5. From the north side of lands of Waldegrave in the Fourth District to the tunnel through Double Bank, 4ft. bottom, 6ft. deep.

6. From the tunnel at the water flash called the Gold, near the sea bank, to the tunnel through the Sea End Lane, 3ft. bottom, 4½ft. deep.

7. From the south-east corner of Mrs. Moscript's lands, to the tunnel through Sea End Lane, 1½ft. bottom, 4ft. deep.

8. From the south-east corner of lands belonging to Shelley Pennel, near the old sea bank, to the tunnel at Ings Bank, 3ft. to 4ft. bottom, 6½ft. deep.

9. From the sewer in the parish of Butterwick, to the tunnel through the road leading from the Sea End to the church, 1½ft to 2ft. bottom, 5½ft. deep. Part of this is maintained by the Frontagers.

10. From the north-west corner of lands of John Hodgson, to the tunnel through the low road from Boston to Wainfleet, 1ft. to 2½ft. bottom, 4ft. deep.

11. From Boston and Wainfleet high road, to Wainfleet low road, 2ft. bottom, 4ft. deep.

12. From the north-east corner of lands of William Needham, to the sewer near Second Pits, 1½ft. to 2½ft. bottom, 5ft. deep.

13. From the north-east corner of lands belonging to John Hodgson, to the tunnel through Wainfleet Low Road, 1½ft. bottom, 3½ft. deep.

14. From the north-west corner of lands of John Adlard, to the New Drain, running on the south side of the road from the Ings to the church, 1½ft. to 2ft. bottom, 4ft. deep.

15. From the tunnel through the road from the church to the Ings, to the tunnel through the Ings Lane, 3ft. bottom, 4½ft. deep.

There are 56 tunnels maintainable by the Dykereeves.

The sea bank, extending from Butterwick to Leverton, is maintained by the Dykereeves. The top is to be kept 6ft. above the level stone.

The area of land subject to the Dykereeve Rate is 1,603 acres.

Sewers maintained by Frontagers.

1. From the south-west corner of lands belonging to George White, and ending at the tunnel through the Sea End Lane, 2ft. bottom, 4½ft. deep.

2. From the south-west corner of Second Pits to Hyle's Croft Tunnel, 3ft. bottom, 5ft. deep.

APPENDIX VIII.

LEVERTON.

Sewers maintained by the Dykereeves.

1. From the south-east corner of lands of Thomas Tennant, near the sea bank, to the Ings Drain, 3½ft. to 4½ft. bottom, 5½ft. deep.

2. From the south to the north side of the Churchyard, 3½ft. bottom, 5ft. deep.

3. From the north-east corner of lands of Richard Cammack to the sewer against lands of Rev. C. Lindsay, 1½ft. bottom, 4½ft. deep.

4. From the Outgate Lane to the tunnel through Highgate Lane, 2½ft. bottom, 4½ft. deep.

5. From the north-east corner of lands of Lady Ann Hill to the tunnel in the Main Drain near Outgate Lane, 18in. bottom, 3½ft. to 4½ft. deep. Part of this sewer is maintained by the Frontagers.

6 From the tunnel through Lucky Gote Road to the tunnel in the Main Drain, near Highgate Lane, 2½ft. bottom, 4½ft. deep. Part of this sewer is maintained by the Frontagers.

7. From lands belonging to John Woodward to the tunnel through Sheep Gote Lane, 2½ft. bottom, 4ft. deep.

There are 46 public tunnels maintainable by the Dykereeves.

The sea bank from Benington to the Overgote, between the Parishes of Leake and Leverton, has to be maintained by the Dykereeves. The top to be 7ft. 5in. above the level stone.

The area of land subject to the Dykereeve Rate is 1,535 acres.

Sewers maintained by Frontagers.

1. From the Marsh Bank Road to the Main Drain, 3ft. bottom, 4½ft. deep.

2. From a tunnel through the road at Leverton Out End to a tunnel through the end of the same road, 2½ft. bottom, 4½ft. deep.

3. From a tunnel at the west end of Long Bank to a tunnel in the Main Drain, 2ft. bottom, 4½ft. deep.

4. From the north-east corner of lands of the Poor of Leverton to the Main Drain at Scurvy Neck, 2ft. to 3ft. bottom, 5ft. deep.

5. From land belonging to Wrangle's Heirs to the tunnel in the Main Drain in Highgate Lane, 2½ft. bottom, 4½ft. deep.

6. From the south-east corner of lands of Wrangle's Heirs, to the public sewer No. 6, 2½ft. bottom, 4ft. deep.

7. From the north corner of lands of Thomas Tennant, to the tunnel through the occupation road leading to Ewerby's Field, 2ft. bottom, 4ft. deep.

8. From lands of Joseph Winter Dawson, to Highgate Lane, 2½ft. bottom, 4½ft. deep.

9. From Towdyke to the Main Drain, 2½ft. bottom, 4½ft. deep.

10. From the tunnel through Sheep Gote Lane, to another tunnel through the same lane, 2¾ft. bottom, 4½ft. deep.

11. From one sewer to another sewer under the control of the Fourth District Commissioners, running on the south and west sides of Little Mere Bank, 2ft. bottom, 4½ft. deep.

12. From the lane leading from the Rampart, to Jenkin Lane, to the tunnel through the road leading to Little Mere Bank, 2¾ft. bottom, 4½ft. deep.

13. From the east corner of lands of Thomas Tennant, to the Main Drain, 1½ft. bottom, 3½ft. to 4½ft. deep.

Appendix VIII.

Leake.

Sewers maintained by the Dykereeves.

1. From Dickendale Tunnel to the Gride Bridge, 3ft. to 5ft. bottom, 5ft. to 7ft. deep.

2. From the tunnel through Pannier Lid Lane, to Font Bridge, 2ft. to 3ft. bottom, 5ft. deep.

3. From the Sea Dyke Road, to Snail's Horn Tunnel, 2ft. to 3ft. bottom, 5ft. to 6ft. deep.

4. From lands of William Atkinson, on the south side of the road from Boston to Wainfleet, to the Main Drain, 2½ft. to 3ft. bottom, 5ft. to 7ft. deep. Part of this is maintained by the Frontagers.

5. From the tunnel though Clovergate, to Pode Lane, 2½ft. bottom, 4ft. to 4½ft. deep. Part of this sewer is maintained by the Frontagers.

6. From the north-east corner of lands of William Walker, to the east side of lands of Mrs. Eno, running partly along the south side of the main road from Boston to Wainfleet, 2½ft. bottom, 6ft. deep.

7. From the north-west corner of and along lands of William Welsh, 2ft. bottom, 6ft. deep.

8. From the tunnel through the west end of Catharine Bridge Lane, to the said bridge, 2½ft. bottom, 4½ft. deep.

9. From the tunnel through Sea Field Lane, to Dickendale tunnel, 2ft. to 2½ft. bottom, 4ft. to 5ft. deep. Part of this sewer is maintained by the Frontagers.

10. From Edward Oldfield's garden corner, to south-east corner of lands of Thomas Hayward, 2ft. bottom, 4ft. deep.

11. From south-west corner of lands of Charles Brookes, to Dickendale Tunnel, 2ft. to 2½ft. bottom, 5ft. deep. Part of this Sewer is maintained by the Frontagers.

12. From the Sea Dyke, to the south-west corner of lands of William Evison, 2ft. bottom, 5ft. deep.

13. From the north-west corner of lands of the Quaker Society, to the sewer on the Sea Field, 1ft. bottom, 3½ft. to 5½ft. deep.

There are 63 tunnels maintainable by the Dykereeves.

The sea bank, extending from the Overgote between Benington and Leake, to the Overgote between Leake and Wrangle, is to be maintained by the Dykereeves, the top to be 6ft. 2in. above the level stone.

The Pullover across the sea bank between Leake and Wrangle is to be maintained jointly by the Dykereeves of the two parishes.

The area of land subject to the Dykereeve rate is 2,575 acres.

Sewers maintained by Frontagers.

1. From the south-west corner of lands, to the sewer in Celly Ground, 2ft. to 3ft. bottom, 6ft. deep.

2. From the north-east corner of Hodge Gowt Three Acres, on the south side of Wickening Lane, to Font Bridge, 3ft. bottom, 6ft. deep.

3. From the tunnel, through the road leading from the church to Fold Hill, to the main Drain, 2f½t. bottom, 4½ft. to 5ft. deep.

4. From the north-west corner of Saul's Common, to the tunnel through the north-west corner of Pode Lane, against Roggy Warth, 2½ft. bottom, 4½ft. deep.

5. From the north-east corner of lands of William Staniland, to the tunnel through the South End Lane, 1ft. to 2½ft. bottom, 3½ft. to 4½ft. deep.

6. From the south-west corner of lands of Rev J. Wayet, to the tunnel in Shaw's Lane, 2½ft bottom, 5ft. deep.

7. From the tunnel through Leake Field Lane, to Dickendale Sewer, 2½ft. bottom, 4½ft. deep.

8. From the tunnel through Sea Field Lane, on the north side of the occupation road, to the tunnel at the north-east end of the said lane, 2ft. bottom, 5ft. deep

WRANGLE.

Sewers maintained by the Dykereeves.

1. From the tunnel through the main road from Boston to Wainfleet, to the north-east corner of lands of Wilks and Powell, 3ft. bottom, 4ft. to 5ft. deep.

2. From lands of George Gilson to the boundary of the Fourth District, and running part of the way along the south side of the main road, from Boston to Wainfleet, 2½ft. to 3ft. bottom, 4½ft. to 5ft. deep. Part of this sewer is maintained by the Frontagers.

3. From the tunnel through Greeney Gote Lane, to the tunnel through Soulby Lane, 2½ft. bottom, 4½ft. deep.

4. From the north-west end of lands of Robt. Chapman, to the Wash Dyke Tunnel 2½ft. to 5ft. bottom, 4ft. to 6ft. deep. Part of this sewer is maintained by the Frontagers.

5. From the Market Road, near the White Horse Inn, to the tunnel through Hair Cap Lane, 2½ft. bottom, 4ft. deep. Part of this sewer is maintained by the Frontagers.

6. From the south-west of lands of the Corporation of Boston, to the south end of Thoroughfare Lane, 2ft. bottom, 3½ft. deep.

7. From Workhouse Lane, to Gowt Bank Tunnel, 2½ft. bottom, 4ft. deep.

8. From the tunnel through Low Lane, to the sewer under the jurisdiction of the Fourth District Commissioners, 3ft. bottom, 5ft. deep.

9. From the south-east corner of lands of William Cowham, on the south side of Low Lane, to a sewer belonging to the Fourth District, 3ft. bottom, 4ft. deep

10. From the Old Hawes Common, to the tunnel through the lane, 3ft. bottom, 4ft. deep.

11. From the north-west corner of lands of Charles Swain, to a tunnel through a lane against Old Hawes Common, 3ft. bottom, 4ft. deep.

There are 23 public tunnels which are maintained by the Dykereeves.

The sea bank from the Overgote between Leake and Wrangle to Friskney is ordered to be repaired by the Frontagers. The top to be 7ft. above the level stone.

Three gowts in the sea banks are to be maintained by the Owners of the land which they adjoin, each having a 3ft. waterway.

The Pullover is to be maintained jointly by the Dykereeves of Leake and Wrangle.

The area of land subject to the Dykereeve rate is 1,126 acres.

Sewer maintained by Frontagers.

1. From a tunnel through the Old Hawes Lane to the boundary of the Fourth District, 2½ft. bottom, 4½ft. deep.

FRISKNEY.

Sewers maintained by the Dykereeves.

1. From the Hiddikes to the sewer of the Fourth District, called Fodderdyke Drain, 2½ft. to 3½ft. bottom, 4ft. to 5ft. deep.

Appendix VIII.

2. From the tunnel at Suckling Gote, to the Hiddike Sewer, 3ft. bottom, 5ft. deep.

3. From the south-east corner of lands of Thomas Johnson, to south-east corner of lands of George Parker, 2½ft. bottom, 4ft. deep.

4. From the tunnel through the Lowgate Road, near the site of the old engine, to the tunnel through Hallgarth Hall Road into the Fourth District, 3ft. bottom, 5ft. deep.

5. From lands of Sir J. Lake to the Fourth District Sewer, 1½ft. to 3ft. bottom, 3½ft. to 4ft. deep.

6. From the south-west corner of lands of Mrs. Hinkley, to the tunnel through the Lowgate Road, 1½ft. bottom, 3½ft. deep.

There are 11 public tunnels which have to be maintained by the Dykereeves.

The sea bank between Wrangle and Wainfleet has to be repaired by the Frontagers, 42 in number. The top to be 7ft. 3in. above the level stone.

Four sea gowts and their Outfalls to the sea have to be maintained by the Frontagers, and the Engine Gowt by the Dykereeves, each having 3ft. waterway.

The area of land subject to the Dykereeve rate is 972 acres.

Sibsey.

Sewers maintained by the Dykereeves.

1. From the boundary of the Fourth District at Shottell's Farm, to the tunnel through the main road from Boston to Spilsby, 3ft. bottom, 5ft. deep.

2. From the south-east corner of Little Field belonging to William Saul, to the south-west corner of Cracrofts, 2½ft. to 4ft. bottom, 4½ft. to 7ft. deep. Part of this sewer is maintained by the Frontagers.

3. From the tunnel though Little Sport Lane, to the Wardale Drain, 2½ft. bottom, 4ft. deep. Part of this sewer is maintained by the Frontagers.

4. From the tunnel through Little Sport Lane, to the south-west corner of Tilley Willy, 1½ft. to 2½ft. bottom, 3½ft. to 4ft. deep. Part of this sewer is repaired by the Frontagers.

5. Wardyke Drain from the west end of Moors Bank, to the west corner of lands belonging to Mr. Drax, 4ft. to 5ft. bottom, 4ft. to 7ft. deep.

6. From the tunnel through Ostler Lane, near the Vicarage, to Wardyke Drain, 1½ft. to 3ft. bottom, 3½ft. to 4½ft. deep.

7. From the north-side of Potter's Close, to the tunnel through Ostler's Lane 3ft. bottom, 4½ft. deep.

8. From the north-east corner of lands belonging to Mells, to the south-east corner of lands of Philip Meredith, 1½ft. bottom, 3½ft. deep.

9. From the tunnel through Ostler's Lane, to the sewer adjoining the Moors, 2½ft. bottom, 4ft. deep. Part of this is maintained by the Frontagers.

10. From the tunnel through the main road from Boston to Spilsby, to the Chapel Sewer, 2ft. bottom, 4ft. deep.

11. From the south side of lands of Henry Butler Pacey, to the Wardyke Drain, 2½ft. to 3ft. bottom, 4½ft. deep. Part of this is maintained by the Frontagers.

12. From the north-east corner of Northlands Field, to a sewer in the Fourth District, 1½ft. to 2ft. bottom, 3½ft. to 4ft. deep. Part of this is maintained by the Frontagers.

13. From the north-west corner of lands in the Northland Field to the West Fen, 1½ft. bottom, 3½ft. deep.

14. From the south-west corner of lands of William Upton, to the tunne through Little Moors Road, 2½ft. bottom, 4ft. deep.

APPENDIX VIII.

15. From the north-west corner of old inclosed lands of Mr. Drax, adjoining the main road, and ending in the West Fen at Little Moors, 1½ft. to 2½ft. bottom, 3½ft. to 4ft. deep. Part of this is repaired by the Frontagers.

16. From the south-west corner of Mill Field adjoining Set Close, to the tunnel through Hale Lane, 1½ft. bottom, 4ft. deep. Part of this is maintained by the Frontagers.

17. From the south-west corner of lands of Henry Butler Pacey, to the tunnel through Hall Lane, 2½ft. bottom, 4ft. deep. Part of this is maintained by the Frontagers.

18. The Maze Sewer, from the south-west corner of lands belonging to Sills Heirs to the West Fen at Hale Gate, 2½ft. to 3ft. bottom, 4ft. to 4½ft. deep. Part of this is maintained by the Frontagers.

19. From the north-west corner of the Four Acre Close to the Maze Sewer, 1½ft. bottom, 4ft. deep.

20. From the west side of lands of Sills' Heirs, to the Maze Sewer, 1½ft. to 2ft. bottom, 4ft. deep.

There are 31 public tunnels which the Dykereeves have to maintain.

The area of land chargeable to the Dykereeve Rate in this parish is 1,868 acres.

Sewers maintained by Frontagers.

1. From the tunnel through the main road from Boston to Spilsby, to Wardike Drain, 2½ft. to 3ft. bottom, 4½ft. to 5ft. deep.

2. From the tunnel through Holland Balk Road, to the south-east corner of lands of Thomas Hubbert, on the west side of the main road from Boston to Spilsby, 2ft. bottom, 4ft. deep.

KIRTON WAPENTAKE.

BOSTON WEST.

The area of land subject to the Dykereeve Rate in this parish is not given. The rateable property includes houses and buildings.

The Dykereeves in this parish have to maintain a Petty Sewer, running from Pulvertoft Lane to the tunnel in the Haven, and the tunnel and door.

The sea bank, from the Grand Sluice to Skirbeck Quarter, has to be maintained by the owners of lands in the parish, which are described in the Verdict, and it was ordered that boundary posts should be set down at the south end of each length, the number of portions being 56. The top of the bank to be 9ft. 4in. above the top of the level stone in Skirbeck Quarter.

SKIRBECK QUARTER.

The area of land subject to the Dykereeve Rate in this parish, exclusive of the 45 acres which pay to Wyberton, is 563a. 3r. 8p.

The Sewers maintained by the Dykereeves are as follows:

1. From Butcher Lane, to the South Forty Foot, with 3ft. bottom.

2. From a tunnel under the lane leading out of the low road to Wyberton, at the back of Rowell Row, thence through a tunnel under the main road to Spalding, near a house belonging to John Wadsley, (now Oldman,) to the South Forty Foot. This sewer is tunneled over. The last part of this sewer is maintained by the Black Sluice Commissioners, 3ft. bottom.

There are 13 public tunnels which have to be maintained by the Dykereeves and a 'cloot' in a division ditch near the sea bank.

There are 45 acres of land in this hamlet called Loate's Plot, which drain into Wyberton Town Drain, and pay Dykereeve Rate to Wyberton, and so drain in accordance with a Law of Sewers, made October 22nd, 1754.

Appendix VIII.

The sea bank was *presented* as having to be maintained by the owners of certain lands, which are described in the Verdict, and it was ordered that boundary posts should be fixed at the end of each length, the number of such lengths being 17. The top of the bank is to be maintained 9ft. 4in. above the level stone.

Petty Sewers maintained by Frontagers.

Each to have 3ft. bottom and brick tunnels under the gateways.

1. The Gravel Cut from a tunnel under the main road to Spalding, running on the north-west side of the road across Gibbet Lane to the Town's Drain at the Gravel Cut now tunnelled over.

2. From the south-east corner of lands of Sheriff Potter, near the sea bank, to the Town's Drain.

3. A branch of the last sewer, commencing at the north-east corner of lands of Joseph Osborn, west of Middlecote Charity, to the sewer No 2.

4. From the west side of the lane leading to Wyberton to the west side of an occupation road leading to Wyberton, near lands of Laughton's Charity, and thence to the Town's Drain.

5. From the north-west end of a lane leading to a pasture belonging to Francis Robinson's Heirs, passing through a culvert under the Great Northern Railway, and so to the last mentioned sewer.

6. From the north-east corner of a pasture belonging to Henry Clarke's Trustees, to the Town's Drain.

Wyberton.

The public sewers, tunnels and cloots in the parish have to be maintained out of the Dykereeve Rates of the parish, and also from 45 acres of land in Skirbeck Quarter and 363 acres in Frampton, according to a law of sewers made in 1754.

The area of land in Wyberton, subject to Dykereeve Rate is 2,087a. 0r. 6p. The public sewer under the charge of the Dykereeves, called the Town's Drain, extends from the Hammond Beck, past the church, to Slippery Gowt.

The Dykereeves have to maintain a clow at Hammond Beck; a clow in a petty sewer near Slippery Gowt; a clow in the Town's Drain near Slippery Gowt; the clow called Slippery Gowt; eight bridges, viz., over the Town's Drain in Butcher's Lane, under Titton Lane, under the main road at the old milestone, at the Church Pit, near the Double Roofed House, at Well Slade, at Spring Pits, and at Older Pits, each 8ft. wide; and 36 public tunnels. 14 cloots or dams have to be maintained by the lands in Skirbeck Quarter and Frampton only. These are to be of sufficient height to prevent the waters in Frampton and Skirbeck Quarter from falling on the Parish of Wyberton and *vice versâ*. 20 cloots or dams are maintained by the whole district.

The Wear Bank, being part of the highway leading from the corner of the marsh, belonging to Richard Thorold, and a lane leading from the highway near Frampton Church to the Mill Field Lane, to be maintained of sufficient height and thickness to prevent any other lands in the Parish of Wyberton from draining by Wyberton Sea Gowt.

The Great Northern Railway Company have to maintain the following culverts under the railways.

The Town's Drain Culvert	Waterway	6ft.
A Petty Sewer near Tytton Hall	,,	4½ft.
A branch of the last Petty Sewer	,,	4½ft.
Between lands of John Pearson and John Robinson	,,	3½ft.
A Petty Sewer	,,	3ft.

The Owners of the land belonging to Doctor Doncaster's Heirs have to maintain the culvert in the branch of the Petty Sewer under the occupation land leading to this land, with a waterway of 4½ft.

The sea bank between Skirbeck Quarter and Frampton has to be maintained by the Dykereeves. The top to be 7ft. 5½in. above the level stone.

Appendix VIII.

Petty Sewers maintained by Frontagers.

1. Running between lands of Mrs. Susannah Claypon and John Hardwick Hallway to a tunnel under the Hammond Beck.

2. From lands of Mrs. Claypon to the Town's Drain.

3. From lands of Mrs. Claypon, running northward into the Town's Drain.

4. From the Hammond Beck Bank into the Town's Drain.

5. From Five House Lane to the Town's Drain.

6. From Five Houses to the Town's Drain.

7. From lands of Christopher Robinson and William Popple to the West End Road to the Town's Drain.

8. From the south side of West End Road to the Town's Drain.

9. From the main road to Spalding to the Town's Drain.

10. From a tunnel under the main road, running between lands of the Corporation of Boston, to the Town's Drain.

11. From a tunnel under the main road, near lands of the Corporation of Boston, along Titton Lane, to the Low Road from Boston to Wyberton, to the next mentioned sewer.

12. From lands of John Pearson, to the east side of the lane leading to Slippery Gowt, to the next mentioned sewer.

13. From the High Land Close in Slippery Gowt Lane to the Town's Drain.

14. From the division ditch between Skirbeck Quarter and Wyberton, near lands of the Baptist Chapel Trustees, adjoining the sea bank, to the Town's Drain.

15. From lands of Eardley Norton to the Town Sewer.

16. From the sea bank near lands of Thomas Elkington, to the Town's Drain.

17. From the road near the sea bank, near lands of Richard Thorold, to the sea bank.

18. The division ditch between Wyberton and Frampton, extending from the sea bank to a road leading from Wyberton Church to Frampton, to a lane leading to Frampton Church.

19. From the east side of Hurn Field, beginning at the division ditch, to Hurn Lane to the Town's Drain.

20. From the division ditch to the Town's Drain.

21. From the division ditch, across Alder Pit Lane and Rowdyke Lane, to the Town's Drain.

22. From the division ditch to the lane leading to Rowland Cross, to the Town's Drain.

23. From the division ditch to the road leading to Rowland Cross, to the Town's Drain.

24. From the division ditch, to Saunder Gate Road, and under the Causeway or Milestone Lane, to the Town's Drain.

25. From lands of James Grant and the Rev. Martin Sheath's Trustees, near Saunder Gate Road, under the railway, to the last mentioned sewer.

26. From the division ditch, near lands of John Short and William Ellis West, to join the last sewer at the Saunder Gate Road.

27. From the main road to Spalding, to join the last sewer at Saunder Gate Road·

APPENDIX VIII.

28. From lands of Martin Sheath's Trustees to the Town's Drain.

29. From a lane leading from the church to the Roads, and along the Low Road to the Town's Drain.

30. From the Low Road leading to Boston to the Town's Drain.

31. From a tunnel under Mill Hill Lane, under Well Slade Lane, to the Town's Drain.

Petty sewers in Frampton, maintained by Frontagers, the lands through which they run paying Dykereeve Rates to Wyberton, for draining by Wyberton Sea Gowt and the Hammond Beck.

1. From a tunnel under a lane leading from Mill Field Lane into the division ditch.

2. From a tunnel under Kyme Leys Lane to the division ditch.

3. From the last mentioned sewer to the division ditch.

4. From a tunnel under Kyme Leys Lane to the division ditch.

5. From the end of Eight Acre Gote Lane to the next mentioned sewer.

6. From a tunnel under Sea Bank Road to the division ditch.

FRAMPTON.

The sea bank in this parish has to be maintained by the Dykereeves, the top to be one inch above the level stone.

The Dykereeves have to maintain the Town's Drain, running from the Hammond Beck to the Sea Gowt, and its Outfall to the sea; also five clows through Hammond Beck Bank, namely :—

1. At the beginning of the Town's Drain.

2. The lands of John Mastin.

3. Near lands of Richard Thorold.

4. Near lands of Magdalen College, called the demesnes of Multon Hall.

5. Near the sea bank.

The gowt, called the Sea Gowt, through the sea bank.

Four bridges over the Town's Drain, namely :—

1. Under the Donington Road, near the Spot Field.

2. Under the main road to Spalding, near the Mill Field Road.

3. Under the land leading from Hunwell Common.

4. Under the Sandholm Road, called the Old Man.

Forty-four public tunnels.

Three cloots or dams, with 'horses' set thereon.

1. Near Walrus Lane.

2. Near the Crayle Eau.

3. Adjoining the Crayle Eau.

The Great Northern Railway Company have to maintain the following culverts under the railway.

1. For the Town's Drain .. .. .. with waterway 6ft.
2. For Petty Sewer .. .. ,, 2½ft.
3. For Petty Sewer, called Crayle Eau .. ,, 2½ft

Appendix VIII.

The following petty sewers have to be maintained by the Frontagers, each with 3ft. bottom, proper slopes and batters, and of sufficient depth to admit the free course of the water, with substantial tunnels through the gateways, with 2ft. waterway.

1. From the lands of Daniel Goose, running eastward on the south side of Hammond Beck Bank, to the Town's Drain.

2. From a tunnel under Cow Gate Road, near the pond, running east to the Town's Drain.

3. From lands of Daniel Goose, on the south side of Five Houses Warth Lane, eastward to the Town's Drain.

4. From the south-west corner of lands of James Watson, called the Holmes, to the Hammond Beck.

5. From a tunnel under Holmes Lane, running south to the Old Hammond Beck.

6. Crayle Eau, the division ditch between this parish and Kirton, from the south-east corner of Honey Holme Field, across the Donington Road, to Mill Hill, adjoining the main road to Spalding, to the sewer to the next mentioned sewer.

7. From the Crayle Eau, northwards to Multon Hall Lane, and again joining the Crayle Eau.

8. From a tunnel under Multon Hall Lane, eastward through clow No. 3, into Hammond Beck.

9. From a tunnel under Multon Hall Lane, past the west end of Cuthbert Lane, to the Hammond Beck.

10. From a tunnel under the Donington Road, running north-west to Multon Ings Lane, to the last mentioned sewer.

11. From Buck Hall to Multon Ings Lane, to the last mentioned sewer.

12. From Crayle Eau, under a lane leading to Self Green Hill to the Donington Road to the north side of Multon Ings lane to Cuthbert Lane to clow No. 2 in the Hammond Beck.

13. From lands of George Plumtree to Self Green Lane.

14. From Self Green Lane, along the south side of the Donington Road, to the last sewer.

15. From the sewer No. 13, near lands of John Burkitt, to Self Green Lane, to the Fleet and adjoining No. 13.

16. From a tunnel from the Fleet, along the east side of a lane to Cuthbert Lane, to the Donington Road, to the Town's Drain.

17. From a tunnel under the road leading to the west end, southerly along east side of Self Green Lane, under the Donington Road, to the next mentioned sewer.

18. From a tunnel under Self Green Lane, northwards, along the lane to the Donington Road, to the next mentioned sewer at the main road.

19. From Crayle Eau, in a circular course to the main road, and thence to Walladale Field into the Town's Drain.

20. From the main road to Spalding, northwards, along the division ditch between Frampton and Wyberton, to the Town's Drain.

21. Crayle Eau, from a dovecote on lands of Samuel Margerison across Horse Shoe Lane, to the next mentioned sewer.

22. From the end of the last sewer, opposite Mill Hill, along the east side of the main road, across Church Road, to the north end of Tanford Lane to the next mentioned sewer.

APPENDIX VIII.

23. From a tunnel under the Church Road, under the railway along the Tanford Lane, to join the last mentioned sewer.

24. From the main road to Spalding, across Tanford Lane, into the Town's Drain.

25. From the main road to Spalding, along the north side of Tanford Lane, to the Town's Drain.

26. From the Church Road to the Crayle Eau.

27. From a tunnel under Coupledyke Lane to the next mentioned sewer.

28. From the north-west corner of lands of Samuel Margerison, across and along Coupledyke Lane to the Town's Drain.

29. From lands of James Goose to the Parks Lane, to the last mentioned sewer.

30. From a tunnel leading to Sandholme, northerly to a lane leading to Kirton Skeldyke, to the last mentioned sewer.

31. From a tunnel under a lane leading to Sandholme to the next mentioned sewer.

32. From lands of Thomas Steed Watson to a sewer near the Town's Drain.

33. From a tunnel under Sandholme lane, northwards, to the last mentioned sewer.

34. From the division ditch, between Frampton and Wyberton, to the next mentioned sewer.

35. From the main road to Spalding, westerly to Mill Field Lane, and easterly to the Town's Drain.

36. From a close belonging to Daws to the last mentioned sewer.

37. From the south-west side of Mill Field Lane to the Town's Drain.

38. From a plantation belonging to Major Moore to the Town's Drain.

39. From the south side of Mill Field Lane, easterly, to the Town's Drain.

Lands estimated at 363 acres—but containing 562a. 0r. 4p., a schedule of which is given, lying between a road leading from the Old Sea Dyke Bank, to Frampton church south; the Sea Bank, east; and the division ditch or sewer between Frampton and Wyberton, on the north—issue their water into the division ditch, and drain by Wyberton Gowt, under a Law of Sewers passed in 1754.

The area of land in Frampton, subject to the Dykereeve Rate, exclusive of the above, is 3,084a. 0r. 26p.

KIRTON.

The area of land subject to the Dykereeve Rate in this parish is 4,836a. 1r. 17p.

The Sea Bank between Frampton and Algarkirk and Fossdyke has to be maintained by the Dykereeves. The top is to be 6ft. 11in. above the level stone.

The Town's Drain, extending from the Old Hammond Beck to the Sea Gowt, and to the Outfall into the Welland, has to be maintained by the Dykereeves.

The Dykereeves have also to maintain four gowts and clows, one at the Hammond Beck, with draw and folding doors; one near the Sea Bank, with a draw door; one sea gowt through the sea bank, with a draw door; and a gowt or clow through the sea bank.

11 bridges, one being at the clow at the Hammond Beck, nine over the Town's Drain, and one (a foot bridge) over the Town's Drain.

90 public tunnels.

1 petty sewer tunnel.

9 cloots or dams with 'horses' set thereon.

Appendix VIII.

The Great Northern Railway Company have to maintain the Culvert Bridge over Kirton Town's Drain, with 6ft. water way; the culvert belonging to the Petty Sewer with 3ft. waterway; and the culvert over the division ditch, with 3ft. waterway.

The following petty sewers are to be maintained with 3ft. bottoms with proper batters, and of sufficient depth to admit the free course of the water, with brick tunnels through the gateways, having 2ft. square waterway.

1. From Kirton Holme to a tunnel called Asher's Tunnel, and into the Old Hammond Beck.

2. From the last mentioned sewer at the Old Hammond Beck Bank to the Town's Drain.

3. From No. 1 sewer to the Town's Drain.

4. From a road leading along the east bank of the Town's Drain, to lands belonging to the Trustees of Kirton School.

5. From Little Mantle to the Old Hammond Beck Bank, and along it to the Asher Tunnel.

6. From Kirton Holme Road to Town's Drain.

7. From lands of Erastus Vessey, southwards, to No. 6.

8. From Simon Weir Bank, through a tunnel under Kirton Holme Road, to the Town's Drain.

9. From Simon Weir Bank to No. 10.

10. From a house belonging to William Dales, southerly, through a tunnel under he Kirton Holme Road, to the Town's Drain.

11. From Simon Weir Bank, under the Kirton Holme Road, to the Town's Drain

12. From Fore Fen Stow, along Swineshead Gate Road, along the west side of Kirton Holme Road, to the Town's Drain.

13. From a tunnel on the north side of Swineshead Gate Road, to No. 15 on the Kirton Holme Road.

14. From the north side of Swineshead Gate Road to No. 15.

15. From Lockster Hill, along the west side of Kirton Holme Road, to the tunne in lands of the parish of Kirton.

16. From lands of George Naylor, to the Town's Drain.

17. From a tunnel southerly, on the east side of Mantle Bank, to the Town's Drain.

18. From a boundary post in the Holmes Lane, along the west side of the lane, across Whitebread Lane, across the Donington Road, through the Fleet, across Kirton End Road, to the Town's Drain.

19. From the west side of Willington Road to No. 18.

20. From a tunnel under Willington Road to the Town's Drain.

21. From lands of John Pearson, across the Willington Road, to No. 20.

22. From a tunnel under Bungley Lane, across Willington Road, along Church Lane, to the Town's Drain.

23. From the west side of Willington Road to No. 22.

24. From a highway tunnel under Willington Road, near the church, along the west side of the road, to No. 23.

25. From the Marketstead Bridge to No. 24.

APPENDIX VIII.

26. From Simon Weir Bank, along the South side of the Donington Road, across the east end of Mornsgift Lane.

27. From a tunnel under the west end of Donington Road, near Simon Weir Bank, through a tunnel on the east side of Mornsgift Lane, across the Meers Lane, across the Drain Side Road to the Town's Drain.

28. From the south side of the Donington Road, along the north side of Mornsgift Lane, to No. 27.

29. From the south-east corner of lands of the Rev. Robert Wadegery, to Mornsgift Lane, and along the Lane to No. 28.

30. From the east side of the lands of the Rev. Robert Wadegery, across the Meers Lane, across the Drain Side Road, to the Town's Drain.

31. From No. 30 to the north-west side of the Meers Lane, to No. 33.

32. From the south side of Mornsgift Lane, to No. 31.

33. From a tunnel at the north-east end of Meers Lane, to No. 31.

34. From Coat House Barn near Simon Weir Bank, eastwards along the bank to Strip's Bridge.

35. From the south-west end of Russian Ings Lane, along the north-west side of the lane, to No 36.

36. From No. 34 at Simon Weir Bank, across Russian Ings Lane, across Engine Lane, to No. 37.

37. From No. 34 at Simon Weir Bank, across the Meers Road and the Drain Side Road, to the Town's Drain.

38. From a highway tunnel under a lane on the west side of the Meers Common along the south side of the road across the Common, to No. 37.

39. From a tunnel under the road on the east side of the Meers Common to No. 37.

40. From the parks, along the north side of a lane leading from the Meers to the Town's Drain, and across this lane to the Town's Drain.

41. From a tunnel under a road at the south-east corner of the Meers Common, across the Drain Side Road to the Town's Drain.

42. From lands of Samuel Richard Fydell across the turnpike across the Drain Side Road, to the Town's Drain near Lays Tunnel.

43. From the Horsegate, near Strip's Bridge, to the division ditch, and thence to the main road to Spalding, to No. 42.

44. From Coat Field, being the division ditch between Kirton and Sutterton, across the Great Northern Railway, across Hare's Lane, to No. 41.

45. From No. 44, through a culvert under the road, into the Town's Drain.

46. From lands of Mrs. Mawer, on the south side of the main road, across Cut Throat Lane, to the Town's Drain.

47. From the Fleet to No. 46.

48. From the north-east corner of lands of John Hodgson's Trustees to Cut Throat Lane, to the Town's Drain.

49. From the homestead belonging to John Short, along the east side of the Wash Road, to the Town's Drain.

50. From the east end of Bungle Lane, across the main road, to the east end of Toot Lane, across the railway and the Skeldyke road, to the Little and Great Hale Weirs, across the north end of Eleven Acres Lane, to the Town's Drain.

Appendix VIII.

Swineshead.

The area of land in this parish subject to the Dykereeve Rate is 1,880a. 3r. 10p.

The sea bank, next to and adjoining the parish of Sutterton, to Hoffleet Stow, has to be maintained by the Dykereeves of Swineshead and Wigtoft.

The following public sewers have to be maintained by the Dykereeves with 3ft. bottom, and proper slopes and batters. and of sufficient depth to admit the free course of the water. Brick tunnels under gateways to have 2ft. square waterway.

A sewer in the north part of Swineshead, in divers branches.

1. From the Old Eau, near the main road, to sewer No. 3, in the Mill Lane.

2. From the main road, opposite Coney Hills, running eastward along the north side of the Drayton Road, across Mill Lane, to the Abbey Lane, to No. 3.

3. From the Cross Roads, near the guide post, running northward to the east side of the Abbey Lane.

4. From the Fen Houses, across Fen Houses Lane, to the Donington Road, across the Abbey Lane and the Town's Lane, to No. 5.

5. From lands of Edward Fox, near the town, along the south side of the Town's Lane, to No. 6.

6. From the Plantation to No. 7.

7. From the Swineshead North End, to the sewer at Fore Fen.

8. A sewer in the south part of Swineshead, from the Drayton Road to No. 9.

9. From the Brick Clamp Pit, along the west side of Asperton Road.

10. From Ball Hall Lane, being the division between Wigtoft and Swineshead, to Asperton Road, across it and to Dale Lane. to No. 11.

11. From the south-west corner of lands belonging to the Swineshead Poor, to Elm Hole, at Asperton Lane, to No. 12.

12. From Boston Rigg Sewer to Guildford Drain.

13. From Guildford Drain, on the Donington Road, to No. 14.

14. From the north-west corner of Asperton Common, across the Bridle Road, to No. 15.

15. From the north-west corner of Asperton Common, running northward on the west of Wigtoft Drove, to No. 16.

16. From the north end of lands belonging to Joseph Cox, running westward along the south side of Timberland Lane to the north end of Langmore Lane, to Cocktoft, to Fishmore End Drove, to the division ditch between Swineshead and Wigtoft, to Fishmore Drove, to Black Jack House, to a tunnel under Fishmore End Drove, to the Four Towns' Drain.

There are 15 public tunnels which the Dykereeves have to maintain.

The Dykereeves of this parish, with those of Wigtoft and Sutterton, have to maintain the Three Towns' Drain, from Acreland Clough to Nevil Dam ; also a branch of the said sewer, from Strip's Lane Bridge, to Strugg's Hill ; and another branch from near the Church Lane, to Andrew's Common, where it joins the Five Towns' Drain

The Dykereeves of the three parishes jointly have to maintain Acreland Clough, and 20 bridges over the Three Towns' Drain.

The Dykereeves of this parish, with those of Wigtoft, Sutterton, Algarkirk and Fossdyke have jointly to maintain the Five Towns' Drain from the bridge at Strugg's Hill, under the main road, to Spalding, to Fossdyke Sea Gowt, and thence to the Outfall to the Welland also a branch of the said gowt, called the Fossdyke Sea Gowt ; laso 10 bridges over the Five Towns' Drain.

APPENDIX VIII.

WIGTOFT.

The area of Land in this Parish, subject to Dykereeve Rate is 2,259a. 3r. 22p.

The Sea Bank adjoining Sutterton to Hoffleet Stow has to be maintained by the Dykereeves of this parish and Swineshead.

The following public drains and sewers have to be maintained by the Dykereeves.

1. The East Drain on the east side of the parish, from the Four Towns' Drain. near Acreland Clough, to Cawdron Sluice into the Two Towns' Drain.

2. The West Drain on the west side of the parish, from Asperton Common to Cawdron Sluice, into the Two Towns' Drain.

3. The Cross Drain from High Crowden Toft on the west side of the Parish, across Hoffleet Lane, to the West Drain, then northward to the west end of Hagger's Lane, and along the lane across Asperton Road to Easthorpe Common, across Fishmore End Road, along the south side of Shettle Lane, to the East Drain.

The Dykereeves have to maintain :—

13 bridges over the above drains.

25 tunnels with 2ft. square waterways.

The Dykereeves of this parish, in common with those of Sutterton, have to maintain the Two Towns' Drain from Cawdron Sluice to the Three Towns' Drain, the Cawdron Sluice, and 5 bridges over this drain.

The Dykereeves of this parish in common with those of Swineshead and Sutterton have to maintain the Three Towns' Drain, from Acreland Clough to Nevil Dam, also a branch of this drain, from Strip's Lane Bridge to Strugg's Hill Bridge, and another branch from near Church Lane to Andrew Common, also Acreland Clough, Nevil Dam and 8 other bridges.

The Dykereeves of this parish in common with those in Sutterton, Algarkirk and Fossdyke have to maintain the Four Town Drains' from Fore Fen Stow to Acreland Clough, and 3 bridges over the same.

The Dykereeves of this parish, in common with those in Swineshead, Sutterton, Algarkirk and Fossdyke have to maintain the Five Towns' Drain from Strugg's Hill to Fossdyke Sea Gowt, and to the Outfall into the Welland ; also a branch from Nevil Dam ; also Fossdyke Sea Gowt, and 10 bridges over the drain.

The following petty sewers have to be maintained by the Frontagers, with 3ft. bottom, with proper slopes and batters, and of sufficient depth to admit the free course of the water, and brick tunnels under the gateways of 2ft. square waterway.

1. From the Half Acre belonging to Trinity College, along the east side of Marsh Bank, across Hopper Lane to the West Drain.

2. From Hoffleet Stow along the south side of the main road and across it to the West Drain.

3. From the north side of the main road to Asperton Road, and across it to the West Drain.

4. From a tunnel under Hoffleet Lane, running eastward of Bulham's, and thence into the Cross Drain.

5. From Town Field Half Acre to No. 4.

6. From Hoffleet to the west end of the Cross Drain.

7. From the north side of Hoffleet Lane to the west end of Asperton Fieldway and across Hoffleet Lane to the Cross Drain.

8. From Campley's to Asperton Fieldway, to Cross Acre, to the West Drain.

APPENDIX VIII.

9. From the road near Asperton Common at Jack Pit to Staggar's Lane, and to a tunnel under the lane.

10. From Asperton Road to the North Field Lane, to the East Drain, with four branches.

11. From the north end of Northfield Lane to No. 12, on the west side of Fishmore End Drove.

12. From the division ditch between Wigtoft and Swineshead, running southward along the west side of Fishmore End Drove, to the Town's Drain.

13. From Abraham Garth, running eastward on the south side of the Low Road to Sutterton, to Love Holme, to the East Drain at Brightman's Slade.

14. From lands of Lord Brownlow, on the south side of the main road, to the East Drain.

15. From the north end of Burtoft Lane eastward, along the main road to the East Drain.

16. From the Pooles, near the churchyard, to the Cross Drain.

17. From the Rigg, across Lowdyke Lane, across the Burtoft Road, to the East Drain.

18. From Golden Field, to the West Drain.

19. From No. 18, along the west side of the Burtoft Road, across the road into the East Drain.

20. From the west side of the Burtoft Road, across the road to the East Drain.

21. From No. 20, running southward to the West Drain.

22. From Singer House, across the Burtoft Lane, to the West Drain.

SUTTERTON.

The area of land in Sutterton subject to the Dykereeve rate is 2,701a. 2r. 39p.

The Dykereeves have to maintain the sea bank from Algarkirk and Fossdyke to Cutch Acre, adjoining Swineshead and Wigtoft ; 36 public tunnels ; a cloot or bank called the Driftway, adjoining the division ditch between Sutterton and Kirton, from the bank of the Four Towns' Drain, as far as the parish extends towards the sea.

The Two Towns' Drain, from Cawdron Sluice to the Three Towns' Drain, has to be maintained in common with Wigtoft ; also the Cawdron Sluice, and 5 bridges.

The Three Towns' Drain from Acreland Clough to Nevil Dam has to be maintained in common with Sutterton and Swineshead ; also a branch of the same from Strip's Lane Bridge to Strugg's Hill Bridge ; another branch to Andrew Common the Acreland Clough ; Nevil's Dam Bridge ; and 8 other bridges.

The Four Towns' Drain from Fore Fen Stow to Acreland Clough has to be maintained in common with Wigtoft, Algarkirk and Fossdyke, and the 3 bridges over it.

The Five Towns' Drain, from Strugg's Hill to Fossdyke Gowt, has to be maintained in common with Swineshead, Wigtoft, Algarkirk, Fossdyke and Swineshead ; also a branch of the same from Nevil Dam and the Gowt and Fossdyke Sea Gowt ; also 10 bridges over this sewer.

The Great Northern Railway Company have to maintain under their line,

1. A culvert under the Three Towns' Drain, with 6ft. waterway.

2. A culvert in the Two Towns' Drain, with a 5ft. waterway.

3. A culvert in a petty sewer, with a 3ft. waterway.

The following petty sewers have to be maintained by the Frontagers —

Appendix VIII.

1. From a tunnel under the main road, near lands of George Nussey, to the Three Towns' Drain.

2. From the north side of lands of the Rev. Basil Beridge, to the Three Towns' Drain.

3. From Catchway, across the main road, to the Three Towns' Drain, at Strugg's Hill Bridge.

4. From a tunnel under the Thirteen Acre Lane to the Five Towns' Drain.

5. From the Driftway, along the west side of the main road, across Cherry Holt Lane, into the Three Towns' Drain.

6. From Brandon Pit Four Acres, across Fishmore End Road, to the Three Towns' Drain.

7. From a tunnel under the Driftway, to the Three Towns' Drain.

8. From lands of Charles Wellman, along Rain Walls Road, to the Three Towns' Drain.

9. From lands of John Hanks, across Shettle Field Lane, to No. 8.

10. From lands of Brownlow Toller's Heirs, on the west side of the main road, across Mill Lane, to Asperton Road, to No. 11.

11. From a tunnel under the main road, leading to Wigtoft, along the north side of this road, across a road near the Five Houses and Rain Walls Road, to No. 12.

12. From the homestead belonging to George Kirkby, on the south side of Kirkstead Field Lane, across the west end of the lane, to the Three Towns' Drain.

13. From a road joining the Pools, across the Kirkstead Fields Lane, to the Three Towns' Drain.

14. From a tunnel under the main road to Wigtoft, to the Bell Meer runlet, to the Three Towns' Drain.

15. From a tunnel under a lane on the west side of the main road leading to Fossdyke, across the main road, to the Three Towns' Drain.

16. From a tunnel under a lane near the main road, leading to Samuel Pocklington's House, to the main road leading to Spalding, to White Cross Lane, to Wall Dike Field and Broad Lane, to the Two Towns' Drain.

17. From No. 16, across Broad Lane, along and across Stone Lane, to Waterbelly Lane, to the Two Towns' Drain.

18. From the Pidgeons, across Waterbelly Lane, to the Two Towns' Drain.

19. From Kit Cat Lane, along the Marsh Bank, across Waterbelly Lane, to the Two Towns' Drain.

20. From lands of Anthony Wilson, under the railway, across the Marsh Road, to No. 21.

21. From the Marsh Bank, to the Three Towns' Drain, near Nevil's Dam.

Algarkirk *cum* Fosdyke.

The area of land subject to Dykereeve Rate in Algarkirk is 2,436a. 0r. 6p., and in Fossdyke 1,161a. 3r. 16p.

The Sea Bank extending from Kirton to Sutterton banks has to be maintained by the Dykereeves. The top is to be kept 6ft. 6¼in. above the level stone.

There are 43 public tunnels which the Dykereeves have to maintain.

The Great Northern Railway Company have to maintain the following culverts under their railway.

Appendix VIII.

Over the Five Towns' Drain, 6½ft. waterway.

Over 5 petty sewers, each 3ft. diameter.

The Dykereeves of this parish, in common with those of Wigtoft and Sutterton, have to maintain the Four Towns' Drain, from Fore Fen Stow to Acreland Clough, and 3 bridges over the same.

The Dykereeeves of these parishes, in common with those in Swineshead, Wigtoft, and Sutterton, have to maintain the Five Towns' Drain, from Strugg's Hill to Fossdyke Sea Gowt, and the Outfall; also a branch of the same, from Nevil's Dam; and 10 bridges over the Five Towns' Drain.

The following Petty Sewers have to be maintained by the Frontagers, with 3ft. bottom, with proper slopes and batters, and of sufficient depth to admit the free course of the water, with brick tunnels through the gateways of 2ft. square waterway.

1. From a bridge under the lane near Strugg's Hill, southward, to the Five Towns' Drain.

2. From Catchway, near the main road to Strugg's Hill Lane, and across the lane and under the railway, across Calder Bridge Lane, to the Five Towns' Drain.

3. From the north-west corner of lands of Sir. Thos. Whichcote, across Bates Cross Lane and under the railway, to Strugg's Hill Lane and sewer No. 2.

4. From lands of John Cabourn's Heir, northward, near Strugg's Hill Lane, across Calder Bridge Lane, to the Five Towns' Drain.

5, From the east side of the road to Algarkirk Church, to Dunham House Green to the Three Towns' Drain.

6. From the church, under the railway, across a lane at Coln Pit to the Three Towns' Drain.

7. From the north-west corner of Sir Thos. Whichcote's Fifteen Acres, south wards to Mandergote Lane, to the Five Towns' Drain.

8. From the Church Lane, eastward, under the railway to Snart's lands, again passing under the railway, under a lane leading to Andrew Common to Cockthorpe Lane, and thence to the Three Towns' Drain.

9. From the south-west corner of Queenlands, eastward, to the Five Towns' Drain.

10. From a tunnel under a lane leading from the main road to Andrew Common, southward, across a lane near Count Wade Bridge to Grine Hedge Field, and the main road to Fossdyke, passing near Stevenson's Cross and Froglands to the Five Towns' Drain.

11. From the south of the main road leading to Fossdyke to the Five Towns' Drain.

12. From the Silt Pit on the south side of the main road, near Stevenson's Cross, eastward, to the Green Lane and Cockfield West, to the Five Towns' Drain.

13. From High House Ground to the Five Towns' Drain.

14. From Red Dyke Cross Pit, northward to Waste Green Lane, to the Five Towns' Drain.

15. From the south-west corner of the Lays, near Red Dyke Cross Pit, to Waste Green Lane, to No. 18.

16. From the division ditch between Algarkirk and Sutterton, at the Roman Bank to Garley Rigg, to the Five Towns' Drain.

17. From a Farm House of George Nussey & Co., across the road at Crabdam's Cross, to the Five Towns' Drain.

18. From the sea bank to the Outgate, across the lane leading to the sea bank, to the Five Towns' Drain.

APPENDIX VIII.

19. From Hodsman's Cross to the lane leading to the sea bank, thence to the Wash Road, across Puttock Gote Lane, across the main road from Fossdyke Church to the Bridge, to the Five Towns' Drain.

20. From Gull Choaks southward to the Inmarsh Lane, across Hilton Lane and the Wash Road, across Bailey Pit Lane and the main road to the bridge, to the Five Towns' Drain.

21. From the north-east corner of Thomas Eyre's Thirteen Acres, across the Wash Road to Stocks Hill, across Leapholme Lane to Pluckertoft to Easedyke near the Mill to Mandike Gote Cross, across the road leading to Fossdyke Church to No. 20.

22. From the north-west corner of Filder's Close to Camplin Gate Road, across the road leading to the church, to No. 21.

23. From the north-west corner of Oldham Field, across the Turnpike Road, to the Five Towns' Drain.

24. From the west side of Pluckertoft to the Mill Road, and thence to the Five Towns' Drain.

25. From the east end of Beridge's Two Acres to No. 26 at Dughills.

26. From the Wash Road to West Cross Gote Hill to a lane leading to Dughills, to the Five Towns' Drain.

27. From the west side of Martin Gote, to the Five Towns' Drain.

28. From a tunnel under Martingale Lane, to the Five Towns' Drain.

29. From a tunnel under Martingale Lane, to No. 28.

30. From a tunnel under the Wash Road, at Washingham Wheels, to the division ditch between Algarkirk and Kirton, to the Five Towns' Drain.

QUADRING.

The area of land in this parish, subject to the Dykereeve Rate is 1,631a. 0r. 13p. The area of lands in Gosberton, subject to the Dykereeve Rate in Quadring for defraying the expenses of draining by Merlode, reputed at 122 acres, is by measurement 305a. 0r. 35p., a schedule of which is given in the Verdict.

The following sewers have to be maintained by the Dykereeves out of the rates charged on lands in this parish, Quadring Hundred, and a portion of Gosberton.

The Merlode Drain, from Stang's Tunnel to the Risegate Eau at Lampson's Clough ;

Also a branch of the same, called the Coln Drain ;

And the following bridges over the Merlode; Crane Bridge, under the main road ; Bedford Bridge, near Quadring Eau ; the Chain Bridge, under the main road leading to Boston, with clow doors ; and Coln Bridge, over the Branch Drain, and under the main road to Donington ;

Also 39 public tunnels.

There is no mention in the Verdict as to the liability of this parish to a share in maintaining the Risegate Eau, but it is referred to in the Quadring Hundred Verdict.

The following petty sewers have to be maintained by the Frontagers, with 3ft. bottom, proper slopes and batters, and of sufficient depth to admit the free course of the water ; with brick tunnels, having 2ft. square waterway.

1. From Boston Hills to the Bedford Bridge Road, under Eaudike Road to the Merlode.

2. From Mallard Marsh, across White House Lane and Tundrum Road, to the Merlode.

APPENDIX VIII.

3. From the division ditch between Quadring and Donington to White House Lane and Crane Pit Lane, to No. 4.

4. From Crane Pit Lane to Littlewood Lane and Church Lane, across Tundrum Road, to the Merlode.

5. From the south-east corner of lands of Cowley's Charity, eastwardly, to Willow Toft, across Tundrum Road, to the Merlode.

6. From the road leading from the church to the main road, to the Merlode.

7. From a garden of the Rev. Edward Brown, to the Home Close, to Jockey Lane, across Tundrum Road, to the Merlode.

8. From Jockey Pasture, across Tundrum Road, to the Merlode.

9. From lands of John Kenning, across Watergate Lane and Tundrum Road, to the Merlode.

10. From Mill Lane northward, across Watergate Lane, and then dividing into two branches, both going to the Merlode.

11. From a tunnel in Alldyke Lane, southerly, to Alldyke Lode.

12. From the silt pit, at the north-west corner of Portable Field eastward, o No. 13.

13. Alldyke Lode, emptying into Coln Drain.

14. From the main road to Coln Drain.

15. From lands of Edward Brown to Coln Drain.

16. From the north-west corner of Dimstoft, across the Fen Drove to Stang's Lane and Scupholme, to Merlode.

17. From the division ditch between Quadring and Quadring Hundred, between Sandygate Lane to the Fen Drove, to Tundrum Road, to the Merlode.

18. From the Droll Footpath, across Tundrum Road, to the Merlode.

The following petty sewers are in Gosberton, but are under the charge of the Dyke-reeve of Quadring, and all drain into the Merlode.

19. From the south-east corner of Rush Lane, across Rush Marsh.

20. From the Donington main road, near Gosberton Church, to No. 21.

21. From the main road eastward, along Dowsby Lane.

22. From lands of Lord Saye and Sele.

QUADRING HUNDRED.

The area of land subject to Dykereeve Rate is 744a. 2r. 0p.

The Lands in this parish subject to Dykereeve Rate, in common with those in Quadring and a part of Gosberton, have to maintain the Merlode from Stang's Tunnel to the Risegate Eau at Lampson's Bridge, also the Coln Drain, the 4 bridges over these drains and 39 tunnels.

This Hundred has, jointly with Quadring, Gosberton and Surfleet, to maintain the Risegate Eau from Lampson's Bridge to the Sea Gowt and the Outfall into the Welland, with Lampson's Clough.

The following petty sewers have to be maintained by the Frontagers, with 3ft. bottoms, proper slopes and batters, and of sufficient depth to admit the free course of the water, and brick tunnels under the gateways, with 2ft. square waterway.

1. From Anderton Lane near the Bell Inn, to Quadring Eaudyke, across Kirk field Lane, near the north-west corner of Flaxtoft, to the Coln Drain.

APPENDIX VIII.

2. From the main road leading to Donington, northward, to Bowgate Lane, to Sandygate Lane.

3. From the north side of lands belonging to Samuel Everard, northward to Bowgate Lane, to No. 2.

4. From Westhorpe to No. 2.

5. From John Tindall's Four Acres to No. 2.

6. From the Westhorpe Road to No. 2.

7. From the west side of lands of Henry Fielding to No. 2.

8. From lands of the Poor of Billingborough to Sandygate Lane, to No. 2 at Bowgate Lane.

9. From the Westhorpe Road to Goose House Lane near the Fen Bank, across Coldhurn Lane, to No. 8.

10. From the division dyke between Quadring and Quadring Hundred to the north end of Coln Drain.

11. From a tunnel under Sandygate Lane to Coln Drain.

12. From a tunnel under Bowgate Lane, eastward, to Coln Drain.

13. From a tunnel under Bowgate Lane, northward, to Coln Drain.

GOSBERTON AND SURFLEET.

The area of land subject to the Dykereeve Rate in Gosberton is 8,878a. 2r. 0p., exclusive of 305a. 0r. 35p. which pays to Quadring for draining by the Merlode ; and in Surfleet 2,504 acres.

The sea banks, extending from Surfleet to Quadring Eaudike have to be maintained by the Dykereeves of Gosberton, and those from the River Glen at Surfleet Seas End to Gosberton Marsh Bank, by the Dykereeves of Surfleet.

The Dykereeves of Gosberton and Surfleet jointly have to maintain the following public sewers :

The Risegate Eau, from Hammond Beck Bank to Lampson's Bridge.

1. The Latham or Lafen Lode in divers branches, namely, one branch running from Beverley Lake, through Drummer Tunnel.

2. From the Old Beach Drain.

3. From Cheal Pan Bridge, through Creek's Tunnel.

4. From the Old Sea Dyke, near the Marsh Bank to Bird's Drove.

5. The Old Sea Dyke, near the old Beach Drain, at the Marsh Bank.

6. The Old Beach Drain, from the Old Sea Bank, to the Old Hammond Beck Bank.

7. From Newbury Tunnel, under Cheal Road, into the Old Beach Drain.

8. From the River Glen to the Old Beach Drain.

9. From Timin's Tunnel to the Old Beach Drain.

Numbers 7, 8, and 9 take water from the River Glen.

10. Double Dyke Sewer from Gosberton Church to No. 11.

11. Along the north-west side of Belshmire Road to Belshmire Bridge, to the Risegate Eau.

12. Reed Shoal Sewer, from lands of William Dodd, through a tunnel into Risegate Eau.

Appendix VIII.

Six Bridges over Risegate Eau, namely, Shopdike Bridge, Carter's Bridge, Drummer's Bridge, Wardyke Bridge, the Main Road Bridge; the clow at the west end of the Eau.

Seventeen bridges over Lafen Lode, namely, Baropies Drove Bridge, Cheal Road Bridge, Dockengate Road Bridge, Cheal Pan Bridge, Sweetland Hill Bridge under the road from the Eau to Sweetland Hill, Bird's Drove Bridge, High Regg Bridge, Tays Field Bridge, Calbeach Bridge, Newland's Bridge, Old Sea Dyke Bridge, Old Sewer Bridge, Belshmire Bridge, Marsh Bank Bridge over the Old Sea Dyke, Coney Garth Lane Bridge, Cowbelly Lane Bridge.

There are 68 public tunnels which the Dykereeves have to maintain.

The Great Northern Railway Company have to maintain the bridge over Risegate Eau, and the following brick culverts under their railway.

1. Lafen Lode .. .. with waterway of 3½ft
2. Old Sea Dyke .. .. ,, 4ft.
3. The old Beach Drain .. .. .. ,, 4ft.
4. Petty Sewer.. .. .. ,, 3ft.

Lord Saye and Sele and the other Frontagers have to maintain a brick culvert over Lafen Lode, with 4ft. waterway.

The Risegate Eau from Lampson's Bridge to the River Welland and the Sea Gowt and Outfall have to be maintained by lands paying Dykereeve Rates in Gosberton, Surfleet, Quadring and Quadring Hundred.

The following petty sewers have to be maintained by the Frontagers, with 3ft. bottom, proper slopes and batters, and of sufficient depth to admit the free course of the water, and with brick tunnels under the gateways, having 2ft. square waterways.

1. From the main road to Boston to High Bridge Lane, to the Reed Shoal Sewer.
2. From the main road to Spalding, near the Baptist Chapel, to the Risegate Eau.
3. From premises of Samuel Everard to the sewer on the east side of Church Road.
4. From Caywood Lane to Risegate Eau.
5. From the Church Road across the Caywood Lane to Risegate Eau.
6. The Old Lode to Beach Lane.
7. From No. 6 to the Risegate Eau.
8. From No. 6, along the west side of Mill Lane, to Risegate Eau.
9. From No. 6 to Risegate Eau.
10. From Beach Lane, part of the Old Lode, to Risegate Eau.
11. From Park Lane to No. 10.
12. From the south-east corner of lands of Edward Jackson to No 10.
13. From No. 10 to the Risegate Eau.
14. From the Hammond Beck Bank to the Risegate Eau.
15. From lands of William Saxton to Risegate Eau.
16. From the west end of Park Lane to No. 15.
17. From No. 16 to the Risegate Eau.
18. From Rigbolt, along the east side of the Hammond Beck Bank to Risegate Eau.
19. From Rigbolt Entry Way to Risegate Eau.
20. From lands of Lord Brownlow and Thomas Sandall to Risegate Eau.

APPENDIX VIII.

21. From the north end of the lane leading to lands of George Brown to Risegate Eau.

22. From the Old Beach Bank to the Fen Road, to the Risegate Eau.

23. From the Old Beach Bank to the Fen Road, to No. 22.

24. From No. 23 to Baropier Drove, to Lafen Lode.

25. From Stibard's Entry to Lafen Lode.

26. From a tunnel under Gosberton Cheal Road to Lafen Lode.

27. From lands of Benjamin Rose to Lafen Lode.

28. From the road leading from Cheal to Sweetland Hill, to No. 27.

29. From a tunnel under Clay Gote across Cheal Road, under Dockholme Lane, to Lafen Lode.

30. From lands of Benjamin Crosby to No. 29.

31. From the Five Acres belonging to the Vicar of Gosberton, along the south side of Claygate, and then under this land to Lafen Lode.

32. From lands of Joseph Langwith to Claygate and Lafen Lode.

33. From the Cheal Road to Newbury Drain.

34. From the Old Beach Drain to Lowgate Road, and Cheal Road to Lafen Lode

35. From a tunnel under Cheal Road to No. 34 at Sweetland Hill.

36. From Bloodsmore to Lafen Lode.

37. From the south side of Bird's Drove to Lafen Lode.

38. From Sweetland Hill Six Acres to Lafen Lode.

39. From Wargate Field Lane to Lafen Lode.

40. From No. 39 near lands of the Bourne Baptist Chapel under Wargate Field Lane to Risegate Eau.

41. From the corner of Wargate Field Lane to Lafen Lode.

42. From the Old Beach Drain, near Surfleet Mill, under Clubborn Lane, to Lafen Lode.

43. From lands of Theophilus Buckworth to the Old Beach Drain.

44. From the Old Beach Drain to the Old Beach Drain.

45. From lands of Surfleet Charity to a drain on the east side of Hungate Lane.

46. From the Old Beach Drain to Lafen Lode.

47. From the Old Beach Drain to Long Newland Drain.

48. From the Short Newlands to Lafen Lode.

49. From a tunnel under Belnie Lane to a tunnel under Cold Beach Road.

50. From the Old Sea Dyke, under Belnie Lane, to Lafen Lode.

51. From Miss Banks' Three Acres under Burnthouse Lane to a bridge, and under Old Sea Dyke Road to the Eleven Acres Lane, to Toynton's Tunnel and the Risegate Eau.

52. From the Brick Clamps to Risegate Eau.

53. From the Marsh Bank Road, under the Great Northern Railway, to Risegate Eau.

INDEX.

For Names of Places see Appendix I.

Abernethy, J. Improvement of the Witham Outfall, 235. 362.
Accretion. *See* Reclamation.
Adventurers, The. 31. Reclamation of land on the Witham, 143. East Fen, 205. Black Sluice, 252. Deeping Fen, 318.
Agriculture, 390, 392. Depression in farming before Reclamation of Fens, 394. In modern times and causes, 420. Societies, 427.
Ague in the Fenland, 488.
Algar, Earl, 18.
Allotments and Small Holdings, 425.
Alluvial Soil, Area of, 455. Formation, 460.
Alluvium. Rate of accretion, 460. Source of, 463.
Antiquities, Roman. 11.
Atmosphere of Fenland. 486.
Ayloff, Sir W. Undertaker for East Fen, 32. Deeping Fen, 317.
Banks, Sea. Preservation of, 39. Roman, 7, 100. Rabbits in, 39. Horses on, 39. Swine on, 40. Penalty for damaging, 40; in Black Sluice District, 259. Ownership and liability to repair, 49, 50. Care of by Court of Sewers, 49. In North Holland, 57, 62. Height of, fixed by Court of Sewers, 66. Assessment of parishes for extraordinary repairs, 79. In South Holland, 100. Raised, and level of, 66. Witham, liability as to maintenance of, 170. Of river Glen and Bourne Eau, 261, 282; report and breaches, 309. Barrier, 107. Breach of Bourne Fen, 282.
Banks, Sir Jos., 149. Drainage of East Fen, 216. Employed Capt. Huddart to report on Outfall of the Witham, 347.
Beasley, Capt. Introduction of fascine work into the Witham, 304. Introduction of fascine work into the Welland, 352.
Beans, 397.
Bedford, Earl of. Drainage of Deeping Fen, 318.
Bedford Level Act, 30.
Bevan, B. Reports on, Welland, 300; steam power in Deeping Fen, 330.
Bicker Haven, 291. *See also* Appendix.
Birds, 471. On Marshes, 475.
Bower, Anthony. Report on the Witham, 162. Report on the East Fen, 216.

Superintended works in the East Fen, 262.
Black Sluice. *See* Appendix 1. Drainage District, Boundary and Area, 244, 256. Disafforestation, 246. First attempt at Reclamation, 249. Holland Fen, 252. Condition in 18th century, 253, First Drainage Act obtained, 1765, 254. Boundary of the District set out in the Act, 256. Works carried out, 256. Navigation, 260. Action for damages for Breach of the Banks, 262. Rennie's Report on the Drainage, 263. Surreptitious Drainage and Mr. Kingsman Foster's Scheme 264. Lewin's Report, 264. Cubitt's Report on Drainage and System of Taxation, 265. Act of 1846, Works authorised, 266. New Sluice, 268. Sleaford Railway, 268. Improvement of the Witham Outfall, 269. Taxes, Expenditure and Loans, 270. Area of parishes liable to Taxation, 271.
Black Sluice Districts. Eighteenpenny, 273. Ninepenny, or Sixth Witham, 283. Sixpenny (Holland Fen) and Witham Second District, 284.
Blue Gowt Drain and District, 117.
Boston, the Great Sluice at, 26. Sewer in, 67. Bridge, 27. East Inclosure Act, 67. Transfer of Land to other Parishes, 68. West Inclosure Act, 68. Port, Harbour and Dock, 343. Bridge, 447. *See also* Appendix I.
Boulder Clay, 455.
Bourne South Fen, 312, 333. *See also* Appendix 1.
Bourne North Fen, 278. *See also* Appendix 1.
Bridges. In the Black Sluice District, 257. Triangular at Crowland, 313. Boston, 447. Grand Sluice, 448. Kirkstead and Bardney, 448. Spalding, 448. Fossdyke, 449. Glen, 450. Eleven Towns', 451.
Brocoli, 403.
Britons in the Fens, 4.
Buoys and Beacons in Boston Deeps, 345, 370.
Butter, 410.
Buildings on Fen Farms, 413.
Bulbs, growth of 405.
Cabbages, 402.
Canoe found in Witham. 167.
Canoe found in Deeping Fen, 330.
Carrots, 403.

INDEX.

Catchwater Drains, 376.
Cardyke, 10.
Cattle in Fens, 394, 408.
Cattle disease in Fens, 393.
Cauliflowers, 403.
Celery, 403.
Centrifugal Pumps for Draining, 381.
Chapman, W. Reports on, North Forty-Foot, 144, 154; Grand Sluice, 156, 157; Witham, 160, 163; Hobhole Drain, 221; Welland, 301.
Chapels erected in Fens, 228.
Cheese, 410.
Chickory, 397.
Christianity. Introduction of, in the Fenland, 14.
Churches in Norman times, 22.
Clarke, on Agriculture, 396. Value of land on the Witham, 182.
Clays, Scheme for cutting through, 347. *See also* Appendix 1.
Climatology, 471, 486.
Cockle Fishery, 480.
Coal used for Drainage Engines. 382.
Code, Fen, 36.
Cole, 397.
Common Rights in Fens, Origin of, 390. Value, 393.
Coode, Sir J. Witham Outfall, 365.
Coppin, D. Reports on Witham, 146, 14.
Corn grown by Saxons, 391.
Cottages, 413.
Cor.-Iceni, The tribe of, 4.
Counter Drain Washes District. *See* Deeping Fen Washes.
Court of Sewers. *See* Sewers.
Cranberries, 485.
Creasey, J. Report on the Witham, 158.
Cressy, W. Lutton Leam Sluice, 130.
Cropping in the Fens, 396, 397.
Crowland Abbey and Bridge. *See* Appendix 1.
Crowland Washes, 291.
Cubitt, Sir W. Reports on, Holbeach Outfall, 125; Black Sluice, 264; Welland, 304.
Cultivating Machinery, 413.
Danes in the Fenland, 13, 17.
Danish Names, 13.
Diseases, Cattle and Sheep, 393.
Deeping Fen Washes Drainage District, 120.
Deeping Fen, 31. Boundary, 312. Ancient condition, 314. Lovell's Scheme of Reclamation, 1603, 316. Ayloff's Scheme, 317. Taxable Lands, 321. Free Lands, 321. Condition of the Fens, 1738, 322. Erection of Scoop Wheels, 323. Act of 1774, 323. Condition in 1798, 324. Inclosure Act, 325. Flood Gauges in Drains, 327. Drainage Districts formed, 328. Pode Hole Engines erected, 330. Consolidation Act, 331. Taxes and Expenditure, 332.
Diseases Prevalent in the Fenland, 487.
Dock at Boston. Site for, by Sir J. Rennie, 1822, 350. Company formed 1845, 355. Williams' Scheme, 363. Wheeler's Scheme, 368. Dock Act, 368. Description of, 368. Tonnage of vessels, receipts, &c., 370.
Donington Drainage, 96. New Inclosures, 96. Inclosure Act, 97. Drainage District, 97. Rates, 98.
Drainage. Works of the Romans, 10. In 13th century, 25. Fen, 41. Engines, *see* Pumping. System of the Fenland, 373. Gravitation and Pumping 374. Area of Land Drained by Steam Power, 375. Water due to Rainfall, 376. Catchwater Drains, 376. Rates, 420.
Decoys, 474.
Dykereeves, 48.
East Fen. Boundary, 197. Parishes having Common Rights, 198. Condition previous to Reclamation, 198. First Attempt at Reclamation, 31, 204. Construction of Maud Foster Sluice and Drain, 208. Complaints about the Draining by the Fenmen, 211. Report on Drainage by J. Rennie, 217. Drainage by Wainfleet Haven, 219. Reclamation Act, 222. Drains, 225. Inclosure Act, 227. Condition of Drainage in 1861, 322. Lade Bank Engines Erected, 235. Taxes, Expenditure and Debt, 238. Interior Districts, Management and Taxes, 240.
Edmunds, Sir C. Report on Welland, 296.
Edwards, Langley. Report on Witham, 145, 149, 150, 156. Report on the Fourth District, 212. Report on the Black Sluice Drainage, 253.
Eleven Towns' Commission and Bridges, 257, 451.
Elstob, W. On Grand Sluice, 157.
Engines. Drainage. *See* Pumping.
Engineers engaged in Fens, 41.
Estuary of the Witham and Welland, 336.
Fairs in the Fenland, 427.
Fascine Training in the Welland, 304; in the Witham, 352.
Fen Code, 36.
Fen Marks, 37.
Fenland. Early History, 1. Boundary and Acreage, 1. Level, 1. Physical Condition, 2, 471. Features, 2. Condition in Roman times, 3. Saxon Settlements, 12. Introduction of Christianity, 14. Danish Invasion, 17. Norman Occupation, 19. Language, 21. Norman Churches, 22. Monasteries, 23. Condition of in 12th and 13th Centuries, 24. First Reclamation, 30. Condition previous to Reclamation 33, 41. Engineers engaged in, 41. Drainage System, 41, 373. Agriculture, 390. Geology, 455. Physical Products, Climatology and Health, 471.
Fenmen, description of 394.
Fen Slodgers, 35, 475.
Ferries, 445. At Boston, 446. In Witham, 448.
Fishery, 477. Ancient, 477. At present time,

478. Bye Laws, 478. Salt Water, 479. Mussel, 479. Cockle, 480. Periwinkle, 481. Whelks, 481. Oysters, 479, 481. Shrimps and Prawns, 481. Soles, 482. Herrings and Sprats, 482. Butts and Plaice, 483. Smelts, 483. Quantity of Fish landed at Boston, 483. Nets, 483. Boats, 483.

FitzWilliam, Earl. Construction of North Forty Foot Drain, 144, 253.

Flax, Cultivation of, 402.

Flower Bulbs, Cultivation of, 405.

Fourth Witham District, 197. Taxes, Expenditure and Debt, 238. Interior Districts, 240.

Fox, Wilson. Agriculture in Fens, 406.

Freiston Shore Reclamation Scheme, 342.

Fruit. Growth, 404. Weight, 405.

Frow, C. Scheme for Witham Outfall, 356, 358.

Fydell, Mr., 149, 150, 152.

Gale, Great of 1810, 49, 62.

Game in Fens, 476.

Garfit, Thomas. Improvement of Witham Outfall, 178.

Geese, 411.

Geology, 455.

Gedney. Inclosure of Marshes, 126. The Fen, 126. Rates, 127. Drainage, 127.

Glacial Drift, 455, 456.

Glen River, 291. *See also* Appendix I.

Gote, Gowt, 45.

Gosberton. Drainage, 90, 94. Fen, 94. Inclosure Act, 94.

Grand Sluice at Boston, erection of, 154, 156. Effect of upon the river, 157, 160, 164, 167. Deposit, 174. Proposed Enlargement, 166, Lowering of Sill, 172, Removal to Chapel Hill, 178. *See also* Appendix I.

Gravitation, Drainage by, 374.

Grundy. Reports on, the Witham, 122, 137, 142, 145, 146, 148, 149, 159; Drainage of Fourth District, 212, 213; Black Sluice, 254.

Great Eastern Railway, 453.

Great Northern Railway. Loop-line opened, 169. Witham Navigation transferred to, 169. Improvement of Navigation, 173, 453.

Gunners, 476.

Guthlac Saint, 14, 312, 314.

Guthrum, 18, 22.

Gyrwas, 12.

Hackford, G. Construction of Sea banks, 370.

Hake, May. Construction of Grand Sluice, 29, 141.

Hare. Report on, Welland, 300; Deeping Fen, 324.

Hares in Fenland, 476.

Hastings, J. W. Report on Cowbit Washes, 311.

Harrison, A. Reports on, Glen banks, 262, 309; Pode Hole Engines, 330.

Hawkshaw, Sir J. Reports on, Grand Sluice, 158; Witham, 171. Instructions by landowners to report on the Witham, 174. Scheme of improvement for Witham, 175. East Fen Drainage, 232. Witham Outfall, 357, 365.

Health of Inhabitants, 471, 486.

Hemp, Cultivation of, 402.

Hereward. 20.

Herring Fishery. 482.

Hobhole Drain and Sluice constructed, 225. *See also* Appendix I.

Holdings, Small, and Allotments, 426.

Holland Fen. First Reclamation Scheme, 251, 260. Boundary, 285. Inclosure Act. 285. Land sold, and price, 286.

Holland North. Boundary and Parishes, 57. Drainage and Sea Banks, 57.

Holland South. First Inclosure of Marshes, 31. Boundary, 100. Roman Banks, 100 Reclamation of Marshes, 100. The Fen 102.

Holland, South, Drainage District, 104.

Horncastle Canal, 160.

Horses, 411.

Huddart, Capt. Witham Outfall, 347.

Implements used in the Fens, 412.

Jessop, W. Report on, the Fossdyke, 160; Welland, 300; Deeping Fen, 324.

Killigrew, Sir W. Reclamation of land, on Witham, 143; East Fen, 204; Holland Fen, 252.

Kinderley, N. Report on Witham, 122, 145. Reclamation Scheme, 339.

Kingston, J. Report on, Glen Banks, 262; Welland, 305; Witham Outfall, 308, 364, 365; Glen, 309; Hubbert's Bridge, 452.

Kirton Hundred, 57, 61. Verdict of Jury as to area liable to rating by Court of Sewers, 65. *See also* Appendix I.

Land. Ownership of, 53. Rent and value, 417. Tenure, 421.

Labour and Wages. 414.

Lancaster, James. Witham Outfall, 365.

Language of Fenland, 21.

Leake. Drainage, 73. Inclosure, 73. Alteration of parish, 73.

Level of Surface of Fenland, 1.

Leverton. Drainage, 73. Inclosure Act, 74. Sea Banks, 74. Alteration of parish, 74. Taxes, 74.

Lewin, William, 113. Report on, Witham, 171; Black Sluice, 264; Vernatt's Sluice, 332; Witham Outfall, 356.

Leather, J. W., Bardney District Engineer, 194.

Life, length of, in Fenland, 487.

Lights in Boston Deeps and River, 370.

Linton, Mr. Farming at Freiston, 402. Allotments, 425.

Lindsey, Earl of. Reclamation of, Lindsey Level, 31, 251; Land on Witham, 143; East Fen, 204; Black Sluice, 257.

Lindsey Level. *See* Appendix I.

Lincolnshire Estuary Company, 341.

Lovell, Thos., 31. Deeping Fen, 295, 316. Bourne South Fen, 333.

Mangolds, 403.

Manure, 407.
Markets and Fairs, 426.
Marshes. Inclosure of in South Holland, 31, 100. Ownership of, 53. Salt, for grazing, 407. Growth of, 461, 466. Accretion. *See* Reclamation.
Marsh Birds, 475.
Martin, D. On drainage of East Fen, 233.
May Hake, 29.
Maxwell. Report on Welland, 300, 324.
Mercury, 474.
Millington, E. Reports on South Holland, 112, 123, 125, 129, 130, 131.
Mineral Springs, 467.
Mirages in Boston Deeps, 487.
Monk, Thomas, Contractor for Witham Outfall, 366.
Monks as farmers, 391.
Monasteries, 23. Value to Agriculture, 391. Fisheries, 477.
Moulton. Drainage, 121. Inclosure of Marshes, 121, 123. Division of Parish, 121. Sea Bank, 122. Inclosure Act, 122.
Mounds, Fen, 9.
Mussel Fishery, 479. Boundary in Boston Deeps, 345.
Mustard, 403.
Mylne, W.S. Report on Pumping Engines in Deeping Fen, 330.
Names of Places, origin of, 22.
Natural History, 471.
Navigation, Witham, Formation of, 154, 428, 430. Transfer to G.N.R. Company, 161 to 169. Black Sluice, 260. Fossdyke, 430. Horncastle, 431. Kyme Eau and Sleaford Canal, 431. Stamford Canal, 432. Bourne Eau, 435.
Nets. Flight, 476. Fish, 483.
Norfolk Estuary Reclamation, 466.
Norman Occupation, 19.
Oats, 397.
Onions, 404.
Opium, use of, 489.
Outfall of Witham. *See* Witham.
Outfalls for Drainage, 373, 378.
Outfall Sluices. *See* Sluices.
Oyster Fishery, 479.
Parsley, Cultivation of, 402.
Pastures, 406.
Peas, 397.
Peat, 455. Formation and area, 457. Shrinkage, 458.
Pear, T. Reports, 130. Black Sluice Drainage, 264. Welland, 301. Deeping Fen, 329. Steam Power for Deeping Fen, 330.
Peppermint, Cultivation of, 404.
Perry, Capt. Deeping Fen, 322.
Physical Condition of the Fenland, 2.
Pilot Trust, Boston, 346.
Pinchbeck and Spalding District, 117, 121.
Pinchbeck South Fen, 120.
Places, Origin of and Names, 22.
Pocklington, W. Report on East Fen, 220.
Port of Boston, 343.
Porpoises, 484.

Pode Hole Pumping Engines, erection of, 333. Description of, 383.
Potatoes, 399.
Poultry, 411.
Poppies, 404.
Products of the Fenland, 471.
Pumping Engines. Blue Gowt District, 191, 120. Washingborough, 184. Branston, 185. Metheringham, 187. Blankney, 187. Timberland, 188. Billinghay Dales, 190. Billinghay North Fen, 191. On the Witham, 168, 169. Greetwell, 193. Bardney, 196. Tattershall, 197. Erected at Lade Bank, 235; description of Engines, 386. Ruskington and Donington Fen, 242. Size of Scoop Wheels allowed by the Act in the Black Sluice, 258. Bourne Fen and Black Sluice, 263. Rippingale, 276. Dunsby, 276. Haconby, 277. Bourne North Fen, 279, 280. South Kyme, 283. Pode Hole, Deeping Fen, 323, 330, 383. Bourne South Fen, 333. Relative Merits of Pumping and Gravitation, 374. Introduction of, into the Fenland, 378. Wind Engine at Blankney, 389. Steam first used, 379. Scoop Wheels, 380. Centrifugal Pumps, 381. Management of Engines, 382. Coal consumption, 382. Cost of pumping, 383. right to lift water by steam power, 388.
Railways, 453. Traffic on, and rate of carriage, 453.
Rainfall, 376, 487. *See also* Appendix V.
Rates on Land, 420.
Rabbits in Sea Banks, 39. In Fenland, 476.
Rams, 409.
Rape, Cultivation of, 397.
Reaping Machines, 413.
Reclamation of the Fens. First attempt, 30.
Reclamation of the Marshes, 53, 336. Ownership of Land left by the tide, 53. In Estuary, 336. Kinderley's Scheme, 339. Lincolnshire Estuary Scheme, 340. Freiston Shore Scheme, 342. Feasibility of, in Estuary, 463. Norfolk Estuary, 466. Area of Accreted Land, 465. Growth of Marshes, 466.
Reeds and Sedge, 485.
Rent and Value of Land, 417.
Red Stone Gowt Law, 58, 251.
Rennie, J. Reports on, Sea Banks, 64; South Holland, 110; Grand Sluice, 157; Witham, 160, 161; Navigation 162, 166; Grand Sluice Enlargement, 167; East Fen, 217, 223; Wainfleet Haven, 329; Black Sluice, 262; Welland, 300; Deeping Fen, 324, 329; Boston Haven and Witham Outfall, 347; Catchwater Sytem, 377; Steam Pumping, 379.
Rennie, Sir J. Reports on the Outfall of the Witham, 168, 169, 349, 352. Reclamation Scheme, 340. Black Sluice, 264.
Reynolds, Robert. Fascine Work in the

Witham. 353.
Rigby, W., Contractor for Boston Dock, 368.
Roads, 436. Roman, 436. Inclosure, 439. Turnpike, 440. Main, 441. Highway Board, 441. Repair, 442. Cost of Maintenance, 443. Mileage, 445.
Romans in the Fens, 4, 6. Banks, 7, 100. Drainage Works, 10. Antiquities, 4, 11. Roads, 136.
Romney Marsh, laws of, 45.
Salt, manufacture of, 485.
Samphire, 484.
Saxons in the Fenland, 12.
Saxon names and places, 13.
Saxon settlements in the Fens, 390.
Sedge, 485.
Scoop wheels, 380.
Scribo, J., Report on the Witham, 144.
Sea banks. *See* Banks.
Seals, 484.
Sewers, meaning of, 44. Commissioners, 29, 44. Court of, origin of, 43. Bill of, 44. Present constitution and power of Court, 47. Riding Juries, 48. Property liable to be rated, 48. Liabilities of, 49. Power to execute works, 55. Formation of new courts, 56. Lincolnshire courts, 56. Verdict of Boston Court, 61 and Appendix VIII. Hundred of Elloe Court, 105. Rates in South Holland, 105.
Sheep in Fens, 394, 408.
Silt land, 460.
Shrimp Fishery, 481.
Skertchley, Mr. Course of Witham, 138. Reclamation of Wash, 463. Geology of Fens, 455.
Slodgers, 35, 394.
Sleaford Railway, 268.
Skirbeck Hundred, 57, 61. *See also* Appendix I. Verdict of Jury as to area liable to rating for sewers, 65. *See also* Appendix VIII.
Sleaford Canal, 160.
Sluice, the Great, at Boston, 26, 29.
Sluice, May Hake's, 141.
Sluices. Outfall for drainage of Fenland, 373.
Smith, J. Report on Witham, 158.
Smeaton, J. Report on, Witham, 150; Lincoln Drainage, 159; East Fen, 212.
Sock or Soakage, 467.
Sole Fishery, 482.
South Holland, *see* Holland.
South Holland Drainage District, 104, 105. Drainage Act, 106. Works carried out, 106. Formation of Trust, 107. Trustees, 111. Taxes, 111. Borrowing Powers, 111. Herbage of Banks, 111. Admission of Adjacent Lands, 111. New Outfall Sluice, 112. Taxes and Expenditure, 113.
South Holland Embankment, 100. Act, 102, 114. Trustees, 116.
South Forty Foot. *See* Black Sluice.
Spalding and Pinchbeck Drainage District, 117.
Sprat Fishery, 482.

Stanhope, Mr. Banks, 178, 364.
Storms and Tides, 38. *See also* Appendix V.
Storm of 1810, 49, 62.
Stukeley, Dr., 7. Course of Witham, 138.
Swine in Fenland, 411.
Taxes on Land, 420.
Temperature of Fenland, 487. *See also* Appendix V.
Tenant Right, 424.
Tenancies, 424.
Tenure of Land, 421.
Telford, T. Reports on, the Grand Sluice, 158; Witham Outfall, 351; Sleaford Canal, 434.
Thrashing Machines, 413.
Thomas, Sir Anthony. Concession in the East Fen, 205.
Tides, High, 38. *See also* Appendix V. 1810, 38, 62. Tidal currents in Boston Deeps, 338, 339.
Tidal Lands, Ownership of, 53.
Tithes on Land, 420.
Tons, Saxon, 13.
Townships formed in East and West Fens 228.
Tramway, Steam, Proposed, 453.
Trees in Peat, 459. In Fens, 485.
Trollope, Sir John. Vernatt's Sluice, 332.
Turnip Seed, 404.
Tydd St. Mary. Inclosure of Marshes, The Commons, Inclosure Act, Drainage Acts, 132. Tydd Gote, 133.
Turnpike Roads, 440.
Vermuiden, Sir C. On the Glen and Welland, 296. Offer to Drain Deeping Fen, 318. Catchwater Drain System, 376.
Vernatti, Sir P. Adventurer for draining Deeping Fen, 318.
Vegetable productions, 484.
Villages, Saxon names of, 100.
Wages of Labourers, 415.
Walker, J. Report on the Welland, 402.
Washes, System of. 310, 378.
Washes. Cowbit and Crowland, 310.
Washes. Deeping Fen Drainage District, 120.
Waterways, 428.
Water. Supply, 467. Wells, 467. Mineral, 467. Analysis of Fen, 468. Urban Supplies, 468. Rain, 469. Living, 469.
Welland River. Drainage area and length, 291. Ancient course, 292. Ancient condition, 295. Deeping Fen Act, 298. Welland Act, 1794, 298. Proposal to carry to Hobhole, 301. Welland Trust, 1824, 301. Walker's Report, 1835. Fascine training, 304. Dues transferred from Boston, 305. Outfall Act, 306. Land liable to taxation, 307. Taxes and Expenditure, 309. *See also* Appendix I.
Wells, 467.
Welsh, E. Report on, the Witham, 173; the East Fen, 232.
Wheat, 397.
Wheels for Drainage. *See* Scoop Wheels.
Wheeler, W. H. Reports on, Holbeach

Sewers, 125. Grand Sluice, 158. Outfall Scheme, 177, 362, 365. Pumping Scheme, East Fen, 234. Fascine Training, 304. Boston Dock, 368. Reclamation Banks, 370. Roads, 442. Tramway 454. Water Supply, 469.

Williams, J. E. Reports on the Witham, 177; Grand Sluice, 179; Steeping River, 237; Witham Outfall, 363, 365.

Wind Engines, 379.

Wind Engines, Deeping Fen, 301, 323.

Winds, prevailing, 487. *See also* Appendix V.

Witham. In the time of the Romans, 10. Course of, 134. Length and Drainage Area, 135. Origin of name 135. Ancient course, 136. Alteration by Romans, 136. Limit of tide, 137. Sincyl Dyke, 137. Outfall, 138. Ancient Navigation, 139. Early condition of, 140. May Hake's Sluice, 142. Reclamation of Fens on, 143. Improvement of Navigation, 143. Drainage Act, 152. Districts, 153. Commission, 153. Works carried out for the improvement of the river under the Act of 1761, 154. Erection of the Grand Sluice, 154. Anton's Gowt, 154. Navigation Trust, 155. Condition of river, 1802, 161. Water going down Fossdyke, 162. Navigation Act, 164. Tolls, 166. Dimensions of river, 1830, 167. Taxable area, 168. Condition of the Outfall, 1822, 168. Pumping Engines, 168, 169. Navigation transferred to Great Northern Railway, 169. Maintenance of banks, 170. Condition, 1860, 171. Improvement Act, 1865, 172. Floods, 173. Sir John Hawkshaw's Scheme of Improvement, 175. Mr. Williams' Scheme, 178. Proposed removal of Grand Sluice to Chapel Hill, 178. Improvement of Outfall, meeting of Trusts, 178. Outfall Act, 1880, 179. Act for improving the river above the Grand Sluice, 179. Taxes, Expenditure and Debts, 180. Navigation, 430.

Witham Districts. First, 182. Second, 191, 244. Third, 191. Fourth, 197. Fifth, 240. Sixth, 243, 244, 283.

Witham Outfall. Ancient Course, 353. Huddart's Scheme for Improving, 347. Rennie's Scheme, 348. Sir J. Rennie, 349. Telford, 351. Improvement Act, 352. Cut through Burton's Marsh, 352. Expenditure on Works, 354. Transfer of Welland Dues, 354. Tonnage of Vessels entering the Port, 1848, 355. Dock Company, 355. Lewin's Scheme of Improvement, 356. Hawkshaw, 357, 361. Proposed Act of 1862, 359. Proposed Railway and Pier at Clayhole, 360. Wheeler's Scheme, 362. Williams', 363. Outfall Act, 364, 365. Kingston's Report, 364. Construction of the New Cut, 366. Deepening of the River, 367. Maintenance of the Works, 367. Boston Dock, 367. Reclamation of Marsh Land, 370. Buoys, Beacons and Lights, 371. Income and Expenditure, 371.

Woad, 397.

Wool Exported from the Fenland, 391. Yield and Prices, 410.

Young, Arthur. Agriculture in Fenland 393. Land on the Witham, 182. Drainage Mill at Blankney, 187.

BOSTON:
PRINTED AND BOUND BY J. M. NEWCOMB.
1896.